Lecture Notes in Artificial Intelligence 2424

Subseries of Lecture Notes in Computer Science
Edited by J. G. Carbonell and J. Siekmann

Lecture Notes in Computer Science
Edited by G. Goos, J. Hartmanis, and J. van Leeuwen

T0140098

Springer
Berlin
Heidelberg
New York
Barcelona
Hong Kong
London
Milan
Paris
Tokyo

Sergio Flesca   Sergio Greco
Nicola Leone   Giovambattista Ianni (Eds.)

Logics in Artificial Intelligence

8th European Conference, JELIA 2002
Cosenza, Italy, September 23-26, 2002
Proceedings

 Springer

Series Editors

Jaime G. Carbonell, Carnegie Mellon University, Pittsburgh, PA, USA
Jörg Siekmann, University of Saarland, Saarbrücken, Germany

Volume Editors

Sergio Flesca
Sergio Greco
University of Calabria, DEIS
P.te P. Bucci, Cubo 41C
87036 Rende (CS), Italy
E-mail: {flesca, greco}@deis.unical.it

Giovambattista Ianni
Nicola Leone
University of Calabria, Department of Mathematics
P.te P. Bucci, Cubo 30B
87036 Rende (CS), Italy
E-mail: {leone, ianni}@mat.unical.it

Cataloging-in-Publication Data applied for

Die Deutsche Bibliothek - CIP-Einheitsaufnahme

Logics in artificial intelligence : European conference ; proceedings /
JELIA 2002, Cosenza, Italy, September 23 -26, 2002. Sergio Flesca ...
(ed.). - Berlin ; Heidelberg ; New York ; Barcelona ; Hong Kong ;
London ; Milan ; Paris ; Tokyo : Springer, 2002
    (Lecture notes in computer science ; 2424 : Lecture notes in artificial
    intelligence)
    ISBN 3-540-44190-5

CR Subject Classification (1998): I.2, F.4.1, D.1.6

ISSN 0302-9743
ISBN 3-540-44190-5 Springer-Verlag Berlin Heidelberg New York

Springer-Verlag Berlin Heidelberg New York,
a member of BertelsmannSpringer Science+Business Media GmbH

http://www.springer.de

© Springer-Verlag Berlin Heidelberg 2002
Printed in Germany

Typesetting: Camera-ready by author, data conversion by Olgun Computergrafik
Printed on acid-free paper   SPIN: 10873845   06/3142   5 4 3 2 1 0

Preface

The European Conference on Logics in AI provides a major biennial forum for the discussion of logic-oriented approaches to artificial intelligence. Following previous workshops held in France (1988), The Netherlands (1990), Germany (1992), England (1994), Portugal (1996), Germany (1998), and Spain (2000) the eighth conference was in Cosenza, Italy, September 23–26, 2002. The international level and the overall technical quality of this event is now well established. As a consequence, the Program Committee wished to explicitly mark JELIA 2002 as a milestone by promoting the event from a "Workshop" to a "Conference".

The aim was to bring together active researchers interested in all aspects concerning the use of logics in artificial intelligence to discuss current research, results, problems, and applications of both theoretical and practical nature. JELIA strived to foster links and facilitate cross-fertilization of ideas among researchers from various disciplines, among researchers from academia, industry, and government, and between theoreticians and practitioners.

The technical program of JELIA 2002 comprised three invited talks that were given by Georg Gottlob, Michael Gelfond, and Moshe Y. Vardi and 41 refereed contributions selected by the Program Committee amongst more than 100 submitted papers. As a part of the technical program, the conference featured a special session consisting of 11 system presentations. Finally, the program included three tutorials by V.S. Subrahamanian, Dino Pedreschi and Fosca Giannotti, and Gerald Pfeifer. Technical papers presented at the conference dealt with the following topics: abduction, active and deductive systems, applications of logic-based systems, automated reasoning, belief revision and updates, common-sense reasoning, computational complexity in AI, constraint satisfaction, description logics, hybrid reasoning systems, inductive reasoning and data mining, knowledge representation, logic based AI systems, logic based expert systems, logic based planning and diagnosis, logic databases, logic programming, logics and expressiveness, logics in machine learning, model checking, multi-agent systems, nonmonotonic reasoning, ontologies, semantic web, theorem proving, and uncertain and probabilistic reasoning.

We would like to thank all authors who submitted papers and all conference participants. We are grateful to the members of the program committee and the external referees for their thorough efforts in reviewing submitted contributions with expertise and patience. A special thanks is due to the University of Calabria Organizing Committee which made this event possible.

September 2002

Sergio Flesca
Sergio Greco
Nicola Leone
Giovambattista Ianni

Organization

JELIA 2002 was organized by the Department of Mathematics and by the Department of Electronics, Computer Science, and Systems of Università della Calabria (Italy).

Executive Committee

Program Committee Co-chairs:

Sergio Greco   (University of Calabria, Italy)
Nicola Leone   (University of Calabria, Italy)

Organizing Committee Co-chairs:

Sergio Flesca   (University of Calabria, Italy)
Giovambattista Ianni   (University of Calabria, Italy)

System Session Co-chairs:

Gerald Pfeifer   (Vienna University of Technology, Austria)
Mirek Truszczynski   (University of Kentucky at Lexington, USA)

Program Committee

Rachel Ben-Eliyahu	(Ben-Gurion University, Israel)
Gerhard Brewka	(University of Leipzig, Germany)
Jürgen Dix	(University of Manchester, UK)
Wolfgang Faber	(Vienna University of Technology, Austria)
Luis Fariñas del Cerro	(University of Toulouse, France)
Katsumi Inoue	(Kobe University, Japan)
Antonis Kakas	(University of Cyprus)
Fausto Giunchiglia	(University of Trento, Italy)
Vladimir Lifschitz	(University of Texas at Austin, USA)
Fangzhen Lin	(The Hong Kong University of Science and Technology, China)
John-Jules Meyer	(University of Utrecht, The Netherlands)
Ilkka Niemelä	(Helsinki University of Technology, Finland)
Manuel Ojeda-Aciego	(University of Malaga, Spain)
David Pearce	(European Commission, Belgium)
Luís Moniz Pereira	(Universidade Nova de Lisboa, Portugal)
Francesco Scarcello	(University of Calabria, Italy)
Torsten Schaub	(University of Potsdam, Germany)
Miroslaw Truszczynski	(University of Kentucky at Lexington, USA)
Andrei Voronkov	(University of Manchester, UK)
Mary-Anne Williams	(University of Newcastle, Australia)

External Referees

José Alferes
Stefano Basta
Philippe Besnard
Blai Bonet
Richard Booth
Alfredo Burrieza
Marco Cadoli
Carlos Chesnevar
Samir Chopra
Pablo Cordero
Stefania Costantini
Carlos Damásio
Alexander Dekhtyar
Pierangelo Dell'Acqua
Carmel Domshlak
Mark E. Stickel
Thomas Eiter
Manuel Enciso
Esra Erdem
Solomon Eyal Shimony
Michael Fink
Sergio Flesca
Gianluigi Folino
Enrico Franconi
Christian G. Fermüller
Alfredo Garro
O. Gasquet

Gianluigi Greco
Paul Harrenstein
Ian Horrocks
Ulrich Hustadt
Giovambattista Ianni
Koji Iwanuma
Tommi Junttila
Reinhard Kahle
Michael Kaminski
Makoto Kikuchi
Miyuki Koshimura
Daniel Le Berre
Thomas Linke
Lengning Liu
Thomas Lukasiewicz
Thomas Lukasiewicz
Felip Manyà
Victor Marek
Elio Masciari
Cristinel Mateis
Jesús Medina
Abhaya Nayak
Pascal Nicolas
Maurice Pagnucco
Luigi Palopoli
Simona Perri
Gerald Pfeifer

Inna Pivkina
Axel Polleres
Luigi Pontieri
Paulo Quaresma
Carlos Rossi
Chiaki Sakama
Ken Satoh
Renate Schmidt
Yasuyuki Shirai
Frieder Stolzenburg
Tommi Syrjanen
Andrea Tagarelli
Giorgio Terracina
Sergio Tessaris
Satoshi Tojo
Hans Tompits
Domenico Ursino
Agustín Valverde
Peter Vojtáš
Toshiko Wakaki
Kewen Wang
Emil Weydert,
Frank Wolter
Stefan Woltran
Dongmo Zhang

Organizing Committee

Francesco Calimeri
Tina Dell'Armi
Filippo Furfaro
Stefania Galizia
Gianluigi Greco

Giuseppe Ielpa
Giuseppe Manco
Elio Masciari
Simona Perri
Luigi Pontieri

Andrea Pugliese
Andrea Tagarelli
Giorgio Terracina
Ester Zumpano

External Referees

Organizing Committee

Table of Contents

Multi-agent Systems

Evolution and Changes

Description Logic and Semantic Web

Complexity Issues

Satisfiability

Paraconsistent Reasoning

Actions and Causation

Logics for Agents

Semantics

Optimization Issues in Answer Set Semantics

System Session

Invited Talks

Invited Talks

Tutorials

A Logic Programming Language
for Multi-agent Systems*

Stefania Costantini and Arianna Tocchio

Università degli Studi di L'Aquila
Dipartimento di Informatica
Via Vetoio, Loc. Coppito, I-67010 L'Aquila - Italy
{stefcost,tocchio}@di.univaq.it

Abstract. This paper presents a new logic programming language for modelling Agents and Multi-Agent systems in computational logic. The basic objective of the specification of this new language has been the identification and the formalization of what we consider to be the basic patterns for reactivity, proactivity, internal "thinking", and "memory". The formalization models these concepts by introducing different kinds of events, with a suitable treatment. We introduce a novel approach to the language semantics, called the evolutionary semantics.

1 Introduction

This paper presents a new logic programming language for modelling Agents and Multi-Agent systems in computational logic. Traditional logic programming has proved over time to be a good knowledge representation language for rational agents. Logical agents may possibly interact with an external environment by means of a suitably defined observe–think–act cycle. Significant attempts have been made in the last decade to integrate rationality with reactivity and proactivity in logic programming (see for instance [3], [20], [19], [13], [14] and [9] for a discussion). In [10] we have called logic programming augmented with reactive and proactive features "Active Logic Programming".

DALI is an Active Logic Programming language, designed for executable specification of logical agents, without committing to any specific agent architecture. DALI allows the programmer to define one or more agents, interacting among themselves, with an external environment, or with a user.

The basic objective of the specification of this new language has been the identification and the formalization of what we consider to be the basic patterns for reactivity, proactivity, internal "thinking", and "memory". The formalization models these concepts by introducing different kinds of events, with a suitable

* Research funded by MIUR 40% project *Aggregate- and number-reasoning for computing: from decision algorithms to constraint programming with multisets, sets, and maps*. Many thanks to Stefano Gentile, who has joined the DALI project, has cooperated to the implementation of DALI, has designed the language web site, and has helped and supported the authors in many ways.

S. Flesca et al. (Eds.): JELIA 2002, LNAI 2424, pp. 1–13, 2002.
© Springer-Verlag Berlin Heidelberg 2002

treatment. We introduce in particular the classes of external, present, past and internal events (Sections 3–5). Events are represented by special atoms, and are managed by special rules. A limited treatment of time is provided: events are time-stamped, so as internal events are considered at specified intervals and past events are kept or "forgotten" according to suitable conditions.

An important aim in the definition of DALI has been that of introducing in a declarative fashion all the essential features, keeping the language as close as possible to the syntax and semantics of the plain Horn–clause language. DALI inference engine is based on an extended resolution (Section 6).

We have devised a novel approach to the language semantics, called the *evolutionary semantics* (Section 7) In this approach, the semantics of a given DALI program P is defined in terms of a modified program P_s, where reactive and proactive rules are reinterpreted in terms of standard Horn Clause rules. The agent reception of an event is formalized as a program transformation step. The evolutionary semantics consists of a sequence of logic programs, resulting from this subsequent transformations, together with the sequence of the Least Herbrand Model of these programs. Therefore, this makes it possible to reason about the "state"of an agent, without introducing explicitly such a notion, and to reason about the conclusions reached and the actions performed at a certain stage.

The semantic approach we propose in this paper is orthogonal, rather than competing, to the approach of *Updating Logic Programs* (ULP for short) [2] [12] [1]. The common underlying assumption is that of representing state evolution as program evolution. In ULP, program evolution is explicit (and can even be controlled by means of the special-purpose meta-language LUPS) and has the objective of incorporating knowledge changes. In DALI, program evolution is implicit (the program code does not actually change) and is determined by the events. Then, the two approaches do not collide, and might be profitably combined. This is also true for the EPI language [15], which is an extension of LUPS that takes into account external events. There are interesting relationships and similarities between the EPI semantics and the DALI evolutionary semantics, that might lead in the future to a useful integration.

The DALI language was first presented in [10]. Since then, the treatment of events has been extended and refined, the declarative semantics has been properly defined (after a first sketch given in the aforementioned paper), and the language has been implemented. What is completely new in this paper is: (i) the treatment of time, and of the relations among different classes of events; (ii) the approach to belief revision through internal events; (iii) the evolutionary semantics.

A prototype implementation of the DALI language has been developed in Sicstus Prolog by the authors of this paper at the University of L'Aquila. The implementation, together with a set of examples, is available at the URL http://gentile.dm.univaq.it/dali/dali.htm.

2 Syntactic Features of DALI

A DALI program is syntactically very close to a traditional Horn-clause program. In particular, a Prolog program is a special case of a DALI program. Specific syntactic features have been introduced to cope with the agent-oriented capabilities of the language.

DALI agents cope with events, that are represented as special atoms, called *event atoms*. In order to emphasize event atoms, the corresponding predicates are indicated by a particular postfix.

Let us consider an event incoming into the agent from its "external world", like for instance *alarm_clock_rings*. ¿From the agent's perspective, this event can be seen in different ways.

Initially, the agent has perceived the event, but she still have not reacted to it. She can however reason about the event (for instance thinking that it is a nuisance to be waked up so early). In this situation, the event is called *present event*, and is written *alarm_clock_ringsN*, postfix N standing for "now".

Later on, the agent decides to react to this event (for instance in order to switch the alarm off) At this stage, the event is called *external event*, and written *alarm_clock_ringsE*, postfix E standing for "external".

After reaction, the agent is able to remember the event. An event that has happened in the past will be called *past event*, and written *alarm_clock_ringsP*, postfix P standing for "past".

A special feature of DALI is the concept of *internal event*. An internal event is a conclusion reached by the agent, to which the agent may want to react, in the sense of triggering further inference. For instance, *food_is_finished* may be such a conclusion, since the agent may want to react and go to buy other food. Whenever a conclusion is intended to trigger a proactive behavior, it will be called *internal event*, and written *food_is_finishedI*, postfix I standing for "internal". The agent is able to remember internal events as well, and then they will become past events.

Some atoms denote *actions* that the agent performs in order to achieve an effect on its environment. To point out actions, each *action atom* like for instance *buy_food* will be written *buy_foodA*, postfix A standing for "action". If the agent wants to remember to have previously performed this action, it will be kept in the form *buy_foodPA*, postfix PA standing for "past action".

All rules are in the form of Horn clauses, but *reactive rules* that have an event in their head are syntactically emphasized. If the head of a rule is an event, then the body of the rule represents the agent's reaction to the event: i.e., the event "determines" the reaction. In order to make it visually evident, the connective ":-" is replaced by ":>", where ":>" reads "determines".

Notice that the conceptual distinction between the different kinds of events and the introduction of reactive rules are fundamental features of the DALI language. Instead, the above-mentioned syntactic notation is syntactic sugar, and therefore it just suits the particular taste of the authors of the paper.

3   External and Present Events, and Actions: Reactivity

The rule below is an example of a *reactive rule* in DALI, modelling a waiter in a cafeteria shop, when a customer approaches.

   customer_entersE :> *say_good_morningA, offer_helpA.*

Predicate *customer_entersE* denotes an *external event*, i.e. something that happens in the "external world" in which the agent is situated.

To make it recognizable that rules with an external event in the conclusion are reactive rules, the token ":-" has been replaced by ":>". In the declarative semantics however, as discussed in Section 7 this rule is treated as a plain Horn clause. The subgoals in the body are in this case actions (discussed below), recognizable by the postfix A. The body of a reactive rule can consist of any mixture of actions and other subgoals, since a reaction to an event can involve rational activity. Formally, we associate to agent Ag a set of distinct predicates

$$PE_{Ag} = \{pE_1, \ldots, pE_s\}, \quad s \geq 0$$

representing external events, to which the agent is able to respond. An atom of the form $pE_j(Args)$ is called an *event atom*. The set of all the event atoms, which is a subset of the Herbrand Universe, is called E_{Ag}.

Events are recorded in a set $EV \subseteq E_{Ag}$. As soon as an event happens, it is inserted into EV, that represents the "input channel" of the agent. In the declarative semantics, EV is represented by a list, indicating the order in which the agent *consumes* the events. An event is consumed whenever the corresponding reactive rule is activated, in the usual resolution style: when the event atom is unified with the head of a reactive rule with mgu θ, $Body\theta$ is added to the current goal, and the event atom is removed from EV. For each event atom $pE_j(Args)$, Ag may possibly provide **only one** rule of the form:

$$pE_j(Fargs) :> R_{j,1}, \ldots, R_{j,q}. \qquad q \geq 1$$

where $pE_j(Args)$ and $pE_j(FArgs)$ are unifiable.

In the implementation, events are time-stamped, and the order in which they are "consumed "corresponds to the arrival order. The time-stamp can be useful for introducing into the language some (limited) possibility of reasoning about time. It is for instance possible to write the following rule:

   customer_entersE : T :> *lunchtime(T), offer_appetizersA.*

It is also possible to have a conjunction of events in the head of a reactive rule, like in the following example.

   rainE, windE :> *close_windowA.*

In order to trigger the reactive rule, all the events in the head must happen within a certain amount of time. The length of the interval can be set by a directive, and is checked on the time stamps.

An important feature of DALI is that each event atom in EV is also available to the agent as a *present event* (indicated with postfix N, for "Now") and can occur as a subgoal in the body of rules.

The introduction of present events establishes a distinction between *reasoning* about events and *reacting* to events. In the following example, the bell at the door is ringing, and the reaction is that of going to open the door. Before the reaction however, the event is perceived as a present event, allowing the agent to draw the conclusion that a visitor has arrived.

> visitor_arrived :- bell_ringsN.

> bell_ringsE :> open_doorA.

Notice that the action subgoals previously seen in the above examples do not occur in the head of any rule. In DALI, these *action atoms* represent actions without preconditions, and always succeed. If however the action cannot properly affect the environment, the interpreter might generate a "failure event", to be managed by a suitable rule. For actions with preconditions, action atoms are defined by *action rules*. In the example below, the agent emits an order for a product P of which she needs a supply. The order can be done either by phone or by fax, in the latter case if a fax machine is available.

> need_supplyE(P) :> emit_oder(P).

> emit_oder(P) :- phone_orderA.

> emit_oder(P) :- fax_orderA.

> fax_orderA :- fax_machine_available.

Action subgoals always succeed also for actions with preconditions, since the implementation automatically adds a rule of the form: *ActionA:- emit_error_message* so as to cope with potential failures.

External events and actions are used also for expressing communication acts. An external event can be a message from another agent, and, symmetrically, an action can consist in sending a message. In fact, current techniques for developing the semantics of Agent Communication Languages trace their origin in speech act theory (see [27] and the references therein), and in the interpretation of speech acts as rational actions [6] [7].

We do not commit to any particular agent communication language, but we attach to each event atom the indication of the agent that has originated the event For events like *rainsE* there will be the default indication *environment*. Then, an event atom can be more precisely seen as a triple:

> Sender : Event_Atom : Timestamp

The *Sender* and *Timestamp* fields can be omitted whenever not needed.

4 Past Events: Memory

A DALI agent keeps track of the events that have happened in the past, and of the actions that she has performed. As soon as an event is removed from EV (and then the corresponding reactive rule is triggered), and whenever an action subgoal succeeds (and then the action is performed), the corresponding atom is recorded in the agent database. Past events are indicated by the postfix PE, and past actions by the postfix PA.

Past events are recorded in the form: *Sender : Event_Atom : Timestamp* and past actions in the form: *Action_Atom : Timestamp*. The following rule for instance says that Susan is arriving, since we know her to have left home.

> is_arriving(susan) :- left_homePE(susan).

The following example illustrates how to exploit past actions. In particular, the action of opening (resp. closing) a window can be performed only if the window is closed (resp. open). The window is closed if the agent remembers to have closed it previously. The window is open if the agent remembers to have opened it previously.

> sunny_weatherE :> open_the_windowA.
>
> rainy_weatherE :> close_the_windowA.
>
> open_the_windowA :- window_is_closed.
>
> window_is_closed :- close_the_windowPA.
>
> close_the_windowA :- window_is_open.
>
> window_is_open :- open_the_windowPA.

It is important that an agent is able to remember, but it is also important to be able to forget. In fact, an agent cannot keep track of *every* event and action for an unlimited period of time. Moreover, sometimes subsequent events/actions can make former ones no more valid. In the previous example, the agent will remember to have opened the window. However, as soon as she closes the window this record becomes no longer valid and should be removed: the agent in this case is interested to remember only the last action of the sequence. In the implementation, past events and actions are kept for a certain default amount of time, that can be modified by the user through a suitable directive. Also, the user can express the conditions exemplified below:

> keep shop_openPE until 19:30.

The information that the shop is open expires at closing time, and at that time it will be removed. Alternatively, one can specify the terminating condition. As soon as the condition is fulfilled (i.e. the corresponding subgoal is proved) the event is removed.

> keep shop_openPE until shop_closed.
>
> keep open_the_windowPA until close_the_windowA.

In particular cases, an event should never be dropped from the knowledge base, as specified below:

> keep born(daniele)PE : 27/Aug/1993 forever.

5   Internal Events: Proactivity

A DALI agent is now able to cope with external events, and to reason about the past and the present. We want now to equip the agent with a sort of "consciousness", so as to determine an independent proactive behavior. The language does not commit to a fixed infrastructure: rather, it provides a mechanism that a user can program according to the application at hand.

The mechanism is that of the *internal events*. To the best of our knowledge, this mechanism is an absolute novelty in the context of agent languages. Any subgoal occurring in the head of a rule can play the role of an internal event, provided that it also occurs in the head of a reactive rule, with postfix I. Consider the following example, where the agent goes to buy food as soon as it is finished. The conclusion $finished(Food)$ is interpreted as an event. The internal event is treated exactly like the external ones, i.e. can trigger a reactive rule.

$$finished(Food) \ :\text{-} \ eaten(Food).$$

$$finishedI(Food) :> go\_to\_buyA\,(Food, Where).$$

$$go\_to\_buyA\,(Food, bakery) \ :\text{-} \ bread\_or\_biscuit(Food).$$

$$go\_to\_buyA\,(Food, grocery\_shop) \ :\text{-} \ dairy(Food).$$

Goals corresponding to internal events are automatically attempted from time to time, so as to trigger the reaction as soon as they succeed. The implementation provides a default timing, and also gives the possibility of explicitly stating the timing by means of directives.
The format of this directive is:

$$try \ \ Goal \ \ [Time\_Interval] \ \ [Frequency] \ \ [until\,Condition]$$

Below in an example of a goal that should be tried often.

$$too\_high(Temperature) \ :\text{-} \ threshold(Th), \ Temperature > Th.$$

$$too\_high(Temperature)I :> start\_emergencyA, \ alert\_operatorA.$$

Like external events, internal events are recorded as past events, and are kept according to user indication. Internal events can be also used for triggering belief revision activities, so as to take past events into consideration, and decide whether to take them, cancel them, or incorporate them as knowledge of the agent. A declarative approach to belief revision based on meta-knowledge about the information, that in our opinion might be well integrated in DALI is that of [4], [5]. However, presently we do not commit to any specific belief revision strategy. We are planning to provide a distinguished predicate *incorporate* that might be either explicitly invoked, or, optionally, treated as an internal event. The user should be in charge of providing a suitable definition for this predicate, according to her own favorite approach to belief revision. When attempted, *incorporate* might return lists of facts or rules to be either added or removed by the DALI interpreter.

6   Procedural Semantics

Procedural semantics of DALI consists of an extension to SLD–resolution. DALI resolution is described in detail in [10]. Its basic features are summarized below.

We assume to associate the following sets to the goal which is being processed by a DALI interpreter: (i) the set $EV \subseteq E_{Ag}$ of the external events that are available to the agent (stimuli to which the agent can possibly respond); (ii) the set $IV \subseteq I_{Ag}$ of subgoals corresponding to internal events which have been proved up to now (internal stimuli to which the agent can possibly respond); (iii) the set $PV \subseteq EP_{Ag}$ of past events (both internal and external); (iv) the set EVT of goals corresponding to internal events, to be tried from time to time.

A goal in DALI is a *disjunction* $G^1; G^2; \ldots; G^n$ of *component goals*. Every G^k is a goal as usually defined in the Horn–clause language, i.e. a conjunction. The meaning is that the computation fails only if all disjuncts fail.

The procedural behavior of a DALI agent consists of the interleaving of the following steps. (i) Trying to answer a user's query like in plain Horn–clause language. (ii) Responding to either external or internal events. This means, the interpreter picks up either an external event from EV or an internal event form IV, and adds this event G^{ev} as a new query, i.e. as a new disjunct in the present goal. Thus, goal $G^1; G^2; \ldots; G^n$ becomes $G^1; G^2; \ldots; G^n; G^{ev}$, and G^{ev} is inserted into PV. (iii) Trying to prove a goal corresponding to an internal event. the interpreter picks up an atom from EVT, and adds this atom G^{evt} as a new query, i.e. as a new disjunct in the present goal. Thus, goal $G^1; G^2; \ldots; G^n$ becomes $G^1; G^2; \ldots; G^n; G^{evt}$.

The interleaving among these activities is specified in the basic cycle of the interpreter. As mentioned before, the user can influence the behavior of the interpreter by means of suitable directives included in an initialization file.

7   Evolutionary Semantics

We define the semantics of a given DALI program P starting from the standard declarative semantics (Least Herbrand Model[1]) of a modified program P_s, obtained from P by means of syntactic transformations that specify how the different classes of events are coped with. P_s is the basis for the evolutionary semantics, that describes how the agent is affected by actual arrival of events.

For coping with external events, we have to specify that a reactive rule is allowed to be applied only if the corresponding event has happened. We assume that, as soon as an event has happened, it is recorded as a unit clause (this assumption will be formally assessed later). Then, we reach our aim by adding, for each event atom $p(Args)E$, the event atom itself in the body of its own reactive rule. The meaning is that this rule can be applied by the immediate-consequence operator only if $p(Args)E$ is available as a fact. Precisely, we transform each reactive rule for external events:

$\qquad p(Args)E\ :> \ R_1, \ldots, R_q.$

into the standard rule:

$\qquad p(Args)E\ :- \ p(Args)E, R_1, \ldots, R_q.$

Similarly, we have to specify that the reactive rule corresponding to an internal event $q(Args)I$ is allowed to be applied only if the subgoal $q(Args)$ has been proved. To this aim, we transform each reactive rule for internal events:

$\qquad q(Args)I\ :> \ R_1, \ldots, R_q.$

into the standard rule:

$\qquad q(Args)I\ :- \ q(Args), R_1, \ldots, R_q.$

Now, we have to declaratively model actions, without or with an action rule. Procedurally, an action A is performed by the agent as soon as A is executed as a subgoal in a rule of the form

$\qquad B\ :- \ D_1, \ldots, D_h, A_1, \ldots, A_k. \quad h \geq 1, k \geq 1$

where the A_i's are actions and $A \in \{A_1, \ldots, A_k\}$. Declaratively, whenever the conditions $D_1, \ldots, D_h$ of the above rule are true, the action atoms should become true as well (given their preconditions, if any), so as the rule can be applied by

---

[1] The Least Herbrand Model is obtained as usual for the Horn-Clause language, i.e., by means of the immediate-consequence operator, iterated bottom-up.

the immediate-consequence operator. To this aim, for every action atom A, with action rule

$$A \text{ :- } C_1, \ldots, C_s. \quad s \geq 1$$

we modify this rule into:

$$A \text{ :- } D_1, \ldots, D_h, C_1, \ldots, C_s.$$

If A has no defining clause, we instead add clause:

$$A \text{ :- } D_1, \ldots, D_h.$$

We need to specify the agent *evolution* according to the events that happen. We propose here an approach where the program P_s is actually affected by the events, by means of subsequent syntactic transformations. The declarative semantics of agent program P at a certain stage then coincides with the declarative semantics of the version of P_s at that stage.

Initially, many of the rules of P_s are not applicable, since no external and present events are available, and no past events are recorded. Later on, as soon as external events arrive, the reactive behavior of the agent is put at work, according to the order in which the events are received.

In order to obtain the *evolutionary* declarative semantics of P, as a first step we explicitly associate to P_s the list of the events that we assume to have arrived up to a certain point, in the order in which they are supposed to have been received. We let $P_0 = \langle P_s, [] \rangle$ to indicate that initially no event has happened.

Later on, we have $P_n = \langle Prog_n, Event\_list_n \rangle$, where $Event\_list_n$ is the list of the n events that have happened, and $Prog_n$ is the current program, that has been obtained from P_s step by step by means of a *transition function* Σ. In particular, Σ specifies that, at the n-th step, the current external event E_n (the first one in the event list) is added to the program as a fact. E_n is also added as a present event. Instead, the previous event E_{n-1} is removed as an external and present event, and is added as a past event.

Precisely, the *program snapshot* at step n is $P_n = \Sigma(P_{n-1}, E_n)$ where

Definition 1. *The* transition function Σ *is defined as follows.*
$$\Sigma(P_{n-1}, E_n) = \langle \Sigma_P(P_{n-1}, E_n), [E_n | Event\_list_{n-1}] \rangle$$
where
$$\Sigma_P(P_0, E_1) = \Sigma_P(\langle P_s, [] \rangle, E_1) = P_s \cup E_1 \cup E_{1N}$$
$$\Sigma_P(\langle Prog_{n-1}, [E_{n-1} | T] \rangle, E_n) =$$
$$\{\{Prog_{n-1} \cup E_n \cup E_{nN} \cup E_{n-1PE}\} \setminus E_{n-1N}\} \setminus E_{n-1}$$

It is easy to extend Σ_P so as to remove the past events that have expired according to the conditions specified in *keep* directives.

Definition 2. *Let* P_s *be a DALI program, and* $L = [E_n, \ldots, E_1]$ *be a list of events. Let* $P_0 = \langle P_s, [] \rangle$ *and* $P_i = \Sigma(P_{i-1}, E_i)$ *(we say that event* E_i *determines the transition from* P_{i-1} *to* P_i*). The list* $\mathcal{P}(P_s, L) = [P_0, \ldots, P_n]$ *is the* program evolution *of* P_s *with respect to* L.

Notice that $P_i = \langle Prog_i, [E_i, \ldots, E_1] \rangle$, where $Prog_i$ is the program as it has been transformed after the ith application of Σ.

Definition 3. *Let P_s be a DALI program, L be a list of events, and PL be the program evolution of P_s with respect to L. Let M_i be the Least Herbrand Model of $Prog_i$. Then, the sequence $\mathcal{M}(P_s, L) = [M_0, \ldots, M_n]$ is the* model evolution *of P_s with respect to L, and M_i the* instant model *at step i.*

The evolutionary semantics of an agent represents the history of the events received by the agents, and of the effect they have produced on it, without introducing a concept of a "state".

Definition 4. *Let P_s be a DALI program, L be a list of events. The* evolutionary semantics $\mathcal{E}_{P_s}$ *of P_s with respect to L is the couple $\langle \mathcal{P}(P_s, L), \mathcal{M}(P_s, L) \rangle$.*

It is easy to see that, given event list $[E_n, \ldots, E_1]$, DALI resolution simulates standard SLD-Resolution on $Prog_n$.

Theorem 1. *Let P_s be a DALI program, $L = [E_n, \ldots, E_1]$ be a list of events and P_n be the program snapshot at step n. DALI resolution is correct and complete with respect of P_n.*

The evolutionary semantics allows standard model checking techniques to be employed for verifying several interesting properties. By reasoning on the program evolution, it is possible for instance to know whether a certain event will be at a certain stage in the memory of the agent. By reasoning on the model evolution, it will be possible for instance to know whether a certain action A has been performed at stage k, which means that A belongs to M_k.

The evolutionary semantics can be extended to DALI multi-agent programs, by considering the evolutionary semantics of all agents involved. A requirement is that the sequence of incoming events for each agent must be somehow specified.

8   Related Work and Concluding Remarks

The main objective in the design of DALI has been that of understanding whether modelling agents in logic programming was possible, and to which extent. We wanted this new language to be as simple and easy to understand as the Horn clause language: therefore, both syntax and semantics are very close to the Horn clause language, and so is the procedural semantics. Experiments in practical applications will tell to which extent such a simple language can be satisfactory. Clearly, in order to develop real–world examples, DALI can be equipped with an agent communication language, and with primitives for coordination and cooperation among agents. Moreover, past experience of the authors in the field of meta-logic programming has suggested to use a meta-programming approach for coping with important aspects such as the ontology problem, and management of incomplete information. For lack of space we cannot further comment on these aspects here: a preliminary discussion can be found in [9]. However, the examples that the reader will find on the DALI web page show that nice multi-agent applications can be obtained with the simple features of DALI.

Presently, DALI does not includes specific features for planning. Our view is that the planning features should constitute a separate module that an agent can invoke on specific goal(s), so as to obtain possible plans and choose among them. In this direction, we mean to integrate an Answer Set Solver ([21] and references therein) into the implementation.

DALI is meant to be a logic general-purpose programming language like Prolog, aimed at programming agents. DALI does not commit to any specific agent architecture, and also, as mentioned above, does not commit to any planning formalism. Then, DALI does not directly compare (at least for the moment) with approaches that combine logic and imperative features, and that are mainly aimed at planning. Two important such approaches are ConGolog [11], which is a multi-agent Prolog-like language with imperative features based on situation calculus, and 3APL [18], [17], which is rule-based, planning-oriented, and has no concept of event. Also, a comparison with very extensive approaches for Multi-Agent-Systems like IMPACT [26] is premature, since IMPACT is not just a language, but proposes a complex agent architecture.

A purely logic language for agents is METATEM [16] [22], where different agents are logic programs which are executed asinchronously, and communicate via message-passing. METATEM has a concept of time, and what happened in the past determines what the agent will do in the future. Differently from DALI, METATEM agents are purely reactive, and there are no different classes of events.

In the BDI (Belief-Desire-Intention) approach [25] [24], agents are systems that are situated in a changing environment, receive perceptual input, and take actions to affect their environment, based on their internal mental state. Implementations of BDI agents are being used successfully in real application domains. An experiment that we want to make is to use DALI as an implementation language for the BDI approach. This experiment follows the example of AgentSpeak(L) [23], a purely reactive logic language with external events and actions, meant to (indirectly) model BDI features in a simple way. The internal state of an AgentSpeak agent constitutes its beliefs, the goals its desires, and plans for achieving goals its intentions. External events are interpreted as goals, which are pursued in some order (according to a selection function) by means of plans (selected by another special function). A plan can include new goals that, when encountered during the execution of the plan, become the highest in priority, i.e. the first ones that will be attempted. These goals are called internal events. However, apart from the name, DALI internal events are aimed at triggering proactive behavior, while AgentSpeak internal events are aimed at refining plans.

In conclusion, we claim that some of the features of DALI are really novel in the field: in particular, the different classes of events (especially the internal and present events), their interaction, the interleaving of different activities, and the use of past events and past actions.

References

1. J. J. Alferes, P. Dell'Acqua, E. Lamma, J. A. Leite, L. M. Pereira, and F. Riguzzi. A logic based approach to multi-agent systems. *ALP Newsletter*, 14(3), August 2001.

2. J. J. Alferes, J. A. Leite, L. M. Pereira, H. Przymusinska, and T. Przymusinski. Dynamic updates of non-monotonic knowledge bases. *J. Logic Programming*, 45(1):43–70, September/October 2000.

3. J. Barklund, K. Boberg, P. Dell'Acqua, and M. Veanes. Meta-programming with theory systems. In K.R. Apt and F. Turini, editors, *Meta-Logics and Logic Programming*, pages 195–224. The MIT Press, Cambridge, Mass., 1995.

4. G. Brewka. Declarative representation of revision strategies. In C. Baral and M. Truszczynski, editors, *NMR'2000, Proc. Of the 8th Intl. Workshop on Non-Monotonic Reasoning*, 2000.

5. G. Brewka and T Eiter. Prioritizing default logic. In *Festschrift 60th Anniversary of W. Bibel*. Kluwer Academic Publishers, 2000.

6. P. R. Cohen and H. J. Levesque. Rational interaction as the basis for communication. In P. R. Cohen, J. Morgan, and M. E. Pollack, editors, *Intentions in Communication*, pages 221–256. MIT Press, 1990.

7. P. R. Cohen and H. J. Levesque. Communicative actions for artificial agents. In V. Lesser, editor, *Proc. 1st Intl. Conf. on Multi-agent Systems*, AAAI Press, pages 65–72. MIT Press, 1995.

8. S. Costantini. Meta-reasoning: a survey. In A. Kakas and F. Sadri, editors, *Computational Logic: From Logic Programming into the Future: Special volume in honour of Bob Kowalski (in print)*. Springer-Verlag, Berlin. invited paper.

9. S. Costantini. Meta-reasoning: a survey. In *Computational Logic: From Logic Programming into the Future –Special volume in honour of Bob Kowalski(to appear)*. Springer-Verlag. invited paper.

10. S. Costantini. Towards active logic programming. In A. Brogi and P. Hill, editors, *Proc. of 2nd International Workshop on Component-based Software Development in Computational Logic (COCL'99)*, PLI'99, Paris, France, September 1999. http://www.di.unipi.it/ brogi/ ResearchActivity/COCL99/ proceedings/index.html.

11. G. De Giacomo, Y. Lespérance, and Levesque. H. J. Congolog, a concurrent programming language based on the situation calculus. *Artificial Intelligence*, (121):109–169, 2000.

12. P. Dell'Acqua and L. M. Pereira. Updating agents. In *Procs. of the ICLP'99 Workshop on Multi-Agent Systems in Logic (MASL'99)*, Las Cruces, New Mexico, 1999.

13. P. Dell'Acqua, F. Sadri, and F. Toni. Combining introspection and communication with rationality and reactivity in agents. In J. Dix, F.L. Del Cerro, and U. Furbach, editors, *Logics in Artificial Intelligence*, LNCS 1489, Berlin, 1998. Springer-Verlag.

14. P. Dell'Acqua, F. Sadri, and F. Toni. Communicating agents. In *Proc. International Workshop on Multi-Agent Systems in Logic Programming, in conjunction with ICLP'99*, Las Cruces, New Mexico, 1999.

15. T. Eiter, M. Fink, G. Sabbatini, and H. Tompits. A framework for declarative update specifications in logic programs. In Bernhard Nebel, editor, *Proc. 17th Intl. Joint Conf. on Artificial Intelligence, IJCAI 2001*, Seattle, Washington, USA, 2001. Morgan Kaufmann. ISBN 1-55860-777-3.

16. M. Fisher. A survey of concurrent METATEM – the language and its applications. In *Proceedings of First International Conference on Temporal Logic (ICTL)*, LNCS 827, Berlin, 1994. Springer Verlag.

17. K. Hindriks, F. de Boer, W. van der Hoek, and J. J. Meyer. A formal architecture for the 3apl programming language. In *Proceedings of the First International Conference of B and Z Users*, Berlin, 2000. Springer Verlag.

18. K. V. Hindriks, F. de Boer, W. van der Hoek, and J.-J.Ch. Meyer. Agent programming in 3apl. *Autonomous Agents and Multi-Agent Systems*, 2(4):357–401, 1999.

19. R. A. Kowalski and F. Sadri. From logic programming to multi-agent systems. In *Annals of Mathematics and Artificial Intelligence*. (to appear).

20. R. A. Kowalski and F. Sadri. Towards a unified agent architecture that combines rationality with reactivity. In *Proc. International Workshop on Logic in Databases*, LNCS 1154, Berlin, 1996. Springer-Verlag.

21. V. Lifschitz. Answer set planning. In D. De Schreye, editor, *Proc. of ICLP '99 Conference*, pages 23–37, Cambridge, Ma, 1999. MIT Press. Invited talk.

22. M. Mulder, J. Treur, and M. Fisher. Agent modelling in concurrent METATEM and DESIRE. In *Intelligent Agents IV*, LNAI, Berlin, 1998. Springer Verlag.

23. A. S. Rao. AgentSpeak(L): BDI Agents speak out in a logical computable language. In W. Van De Velde and J. W. Perram, editors, *Agents Breaking Away: Proceedings of the Seventh European Workshop on Modelling Autonomous Agents in a Multi-Agent World*, LNAI, pages 42–55, Berlin, 1996. Springer Verlag.

24. A. S. Rao and M. Georgeff. BDI Agents: from theory to practice. In *Proceedings of the First International Conference on Multi-Agent Systems (ICMAS-95)*, pages 312–319, San Francisco, CA, June 1995.

25. A. S. Rao and M. P. Georgeff. Modeling rational agents within a BDI-architecture. In R. Fikes and E. Sandewall, editors, *Proceedings of Knowledge Representation and Reasoning (KR&R-91)*, pages 473–484. Morgan Kaufmann Publishers: San Mateo, CA, April 1991.

26. V.S. Subrahmanian, Piero Bonatti, Jürgen Dix, Thomas Eiter, Sarit Kraus, Fatma Özcan, and Robert Ross. *Heterogenous Active Agents*. MIT-Press, 2000. 580 pages.

27. M. Wooldridge. Semantic issues in the verification of agent communication languages. *Autonomous Agents and Multi-Agent Systems*, 3(1):9–32, 2000.

A Proof-System for the Safe Execution of Tasks in Multi-agent Systems

A. Ciampolini[1], E. Lamma[2], P. Mello[1], and P. Torroni[1]

[1] DEIS, Università di Bologna
Viale Risorgimento 2, 40136 Bologna, Italy
{aciampolini,pmello,ptorroni}@deis.unibo.it
[2] Dip. di Ingegneria, Università di Ferrara,
Via Saragat 2, 44100 Ferrara, Italy
elamma@ing.unife.it

Abstract. In this work, we propose an operational semantics based on a proof system for the consistent execution of tasks in a constrained multi-agent setting. The tasks represent services, and are associated with abstract specifications that express conditions on such services. The constraints, contained in the body of the agents, may include – but are not limited to – policies on provided services, and limitations about the use and allocation of bounded resources. The contribution of this work is two-fold. Firstly, a formalism and an operational semantics is introduced, to express the way agents can coordinate their requests of services, and to verify that they do not collide with each other's conditions. Then, we prove the soundness and completeness of such operational semantics to be used to verify the correct execution of tasks.

1 Introduction

Multi-agent systems are generally conceived as societies of entities that are *sociable* and *autonomous*, and exhibit both a *reactive* and a *pro-active* behaviour, in that they should act in anticipation of future goals, while coping with the (generally unpredictable) changes of a dynamic environment. While on the one hand the agent metaphor is appealing and challenging, because of its ability to reflect current computing reality and complex organizations, on the other hand, if we want to actually implement such complex entities, we must tackle all aspects of this scenario.

According to [1], 'there are two major drawbacks associated with the very essence of an agent-based approach: (1) the patterns and the outcomes of the interaction are inherently unpredictable; and (2) predicting the behaviour of the overall system based on its constituent components is extremely difficult (sometimes impossible) because of the strong possibility of emerging behaviour.'

This could be a drawback in many cases. In fact, the need for making agents 'predictable', and – for most applications – as deterministic as possible, is indeed in contrast with the concept itself of autonomy. Nonetheless, it is reasonable to believe that societies (of agents) can only exist as long as the individuals' autonomy does not represent a threat for the other individuals, and for the society

S. Flesca et al. (Eds.): JELIA 2002, LNAI 2424, pp. 14–26, 2002.

in general. Therefore, the important counterpart of autonomy is represented by private constraints and public laws, that can make the agents, if not predictable, at least not colliding with each other needs and constraints.

In this paper, we tackle the problem of ensuring that the execution of tasks in a constrained multi-agents setting is consistent with respect to its constraints. We call *safe* this kind of execution. In the paper, the tasks represent services, and are associated with abstract specifications that express conditions on such services. The constraints, contained in the body of the agents, may include – but are not limited to – policies on provided services, and limitations about the use and allocation of bounded resources. The agent model presented in the paper is abstracted from our previous work on abductive logic agent [2,3], and it is generalized in the paper.

We start by introducing a formalism and an operational semantics, to express the way agents can coordinate the requests of services, and to verify that they do not collide with each other's conditions, in dynamic, possibly adaptive systems. To this purpose, we introduce some operators, that could be mapped, in a concrete implementation, into part of a library of the language(s) used to encode the agents in the system. The operators provided by such library could be used to specify the need to obtain different services form diverse sources, in a *coordinated* fashion. For example, let A_0, A_1, and A_2 be agents in the system, and s_1 and s_2 services, respectively provided by A_1 and A_2. It could be the case that A_0 needs both s_1 from A_1 and s_2 from A_2, but in a coordinated way, that is, if either of the two cannot be provided, the other becomes useless. Moreover, we can imagine that due to system policy regulations, the two services require conflicting authorizations (e.g., there is a policy stating that an agent cannot be provided both service s_1 and s_2). A_0, as a client, could be unaware of any system policies. Therefore, if we want the system to comply with such constraints, we should give the agents an infrastructure to check the requests against any possible integrity threat that could arise from the execution of their tasks.

In this work, we propose a dynamic mechanism to ensure the system consistency, assuming that not all the hypotheses on the external world are necessarily known a priori by the system programmer(s). In particular we propose a protocol that is able to guarantee that a request or set of requests is allowed only if at execution time there is no constraint in the system that is violated.

Once a formalism is defined, we give such formalism an operational semantics, in the form of inference rules, in a sequent-style notation. Inference rules can be used as an abstract specification of an algorithm, that guarantees the correct execution of multiple, possibly conflicting, tasks. In this work we prove that, if the abstract machine underlying the agent code implements such operational semantics, all requests involving integrity constraints are allowed only if no constraint in the system is violated. In doing that, each agent performs a consistency check only within its own (private) set of constraints (as for instance, in an abductive logic programming setting). That is, we ensure the consistency of the constraints in the whole system, without each agent needing to disclose its constraints to other agents.

The paper is structured as follows. In Section 2 we introduce the formalism used to express the way agents can coordinate the requests of services. In Section 3 we give such formalism an operational semantics, and define a proof system to check the consistency of service requests in a constrained multi-agent system. In Section 4 we present the soundness and completeness results of the system with respect with the safe execution of tasks. A brief discussion follows.

2 Formalism

In this section, we introduce the formalism expressing the way agents can coordinate the requests of services, while verifying that they do not collide with each other's conditions. In doing this, we draw inspiration from a logic language for constrained cooperative problem solving, LAILA [2], which is tailored to the particular setting of logic agents provided with hypothetical (abductive) reasoning capabilities [3]. Here, we abstract away from the specific reasoning capabilities and internal knowledge representation of the agents. We generalize the language to cope with service requirements and constraints in general. The only assumption that we make is that it is possible to describe the problem in question, in terms of constraints and conditions on the services, possibly expressed in the form of logic predicates.

Before we proceed with the syntax, we define what we intend by agent and by agent system.

Definition 1 (*Agent*) An agent is a triple $< P, S, IC >$, representing a program P written in a language that allows the definition of *functions*, a set S of such functions called *services*, and a set IC of *integrity constraints*.

The services $s \in S$ are annotated with pairs $< s, \delta >$, that represent the agent's denotation, as defined below. We do not make assumptions on the syntax of the agent programs, services, and ICs, although we assume that the agents are provided with a mechanism, that we call 'local consistency check', that is able to determine if the constraints are violated. In the examples of this paper we use a syntax for the ICs and a semantics for the (local) consistency check that is derived from the abductive logic programming literature [4] (see *footnote* 1 in Section 3).

Definition 2 (*Agent denotation*) Let A be an agent, s a service and δ a set of conditions. We call *denotation of agent A* ($Den(A)$) the following set:

$Den(A) \overset{def}{=} \{< s, \delta >: s$ is locally provided by A under the conditions δ and $\delta \cup IC_{\{A\}} \nvDash \bot\}$ (where $\bot$ stands for false).

We assume that $Den(A)$ is sound and complete with respect to the notion of local computation.

Definition 3 (*Agent system*) An *agent system* is represented as a finite set of atoms, each one standing of an agent of the system.

2.1   Syntax

We give the syntax of the operators in BNF. Let $\mathcal{V}$ be the vocabulary of the language used to write the agents' program P. We add to its vocabulary the set $\{\ \&\ ,\ ;\ ,\ >\ ,\downarrow\}$ of operators, where:
- $\downarrow$ is the *local execution* operator;
- $>$ is the *communication* operator;
- $\&$ is the *collaborative* coordination operator;
- $;$ is the *competitive* coordination operator.

Such operators are part of *expressions*, possibly enclosed in the agent programs, where the *local execution* operator has a maximum priority, followed by the *communication* operator; the *competitive* coordination operator has the minimum priority. As far as associativity, they are all left-associative. An expression is defined as follows:

$$\begin{aligned}
Expression & \quad ::= Formula\ ;\ Expression \mid Formula \\
Formula & \quad ::= SingleFormula\ \&\ Formula \mid \\
& \qquad SingleFormula \\
SingleFormula & \quad ::= Agent > SingleFormula \mid \\
& \qquad \downarrow Service \\
Agent & \quad ::= \mathbf{A_0} \mid \mathbf{A_1} \mid\ \dots\ \mid \mathbf{A_n}
\end{aligned}$$

We label the agents by $\mathbf{A_0}\ \dots\ \mathbf{A_n}$. *Service*, as introduces in Definition 1, is a function call in the language that embeds the communication, competitive and collaborative coordination operators; we will often label such services s_0, s_1, etc. Services are associated with *conditions*. Conditions are grouped into sets that in the operational semantics are usually labelled δ, δ', δ_1, etc. The communication operator can also be used to issue requests to 'local' services involving some local constraints, as it is shown by the following example.

Example 1.   Let the following expression be enclosed in an agent program, say A_0:

$$\text{A0} > \downarrow \text{s1}\ ;\ \text{A1} > \downarrow \text{s2}$$

It means that A_0 must either perform a local service, s_1, *or* ask agent A_1 for service s_2. Should both service be available, possibly under different conditions, the system will select non-deterministically only one of them.

Let us consider, now, the following expression, also embodied in agent A_0's program, representing a collaborative request composed of two different subrequests, whose conditions must be coherent with one another:

$$\text{A1} > \downarrow \text{s3}\ \&\ \text{A2} > \downarrow \text{s4}$$

Agent A_0 asks agent A_1 for the service s_3 and A_2 to for the service s_4; after both A_1 and A_2 reply to A_0 by giving each a set of conditions for the requested service, the result is obtained by merging such sets of conditions in a unique consistent set, with respect to the bunch of agents (A_0, A_1, and A_2) dynamically considered along the computation. Such set could be bigger than the union of the parts, due to additional constraints that are fired in the cross checking phase. $\square$

3   Operational Semantics

We have so far described the operators' syntax. In this section, we give them an operational semantics, in the form of inference rules of a proof system. Such a system can be used as an abstract specification of an algorithm that guarantees the correct execution of multiple, possibly conflicting, tasks. The inference rules could be implemented to extend the operating system or virtual machine that supports the execution of agents.

For the sake of simplicity, the rules we define refer to the case of propositional expressions, not including variables, but they can be easily generalized. In the following, $\mathcal{U}$ is the universe of agents, and $A_0, \ldots, A_n$ denote agents in the system, i.e., $\{A_0, \ldots, A_n\} \subset \mathcal{U}$. The entailment symbol adopted is $\vdash_\delta^B$, whose superscript denotes the bunch B of agents involved in the computation, and whose subscript the set of conditions δ, both of which are output parameters of the derivation process. Given $A \vdash_\delta^B F$, F is the *formula* to prove (a *formula* is in general an expression), and A is the agent asking for its derivation. The agent's code embodies both the integrity constraints IC and the program P of Definition 1: for the sake of simplicity, and with abuse of notation, we will write the name of the agent instead of its code. Therefore, $A \vdash_\delta^B F$ means that the formula F is proven within A's code, producing as an output a set of hypotheses δ and a bunch B. Finally, we will adopt the following notation for the consistency derivation:

$$B \overset{cons}{\vdash}_\delta \Delta$$

where Δ is a set of conditions on a (set of) service(s), $\overset{cons}{\vdash}$ denotes the "consistency check" of the conjunction of all atoms in Δ, with respect to the integrity constraints of all agents in bunch B; in particular, let $S \subseteq \{0, \ldots, n\}$. Given a bunch of agents $B \subseteq \{A_i | i \in S\}$, let IC_i denote the set of integrity constraints of agent A_i. The declarative semantics of $B \overset{cons}{\vdash}_\delta \Delta$ is defined as follows:

$$\begin{cases} \delta \cup IC_B \not\models \bot \\ \Delta \subseteq \delta \end{cases}$$

where $IC_B = \bigcup_{A_j \in B} IC_j$. That is, δ satisfies[1] all the integrity constraints of agents in B. In Section 4, Lemma 1 formally proves the equivalence between the operational notion of consistency in a bunch, and this declarative counterpart. We achieve in that a separation among the agents knowledge bases, ensuring the absence of conflicts between δ and each of their integrity constraints. Moreover, we would like to notice that, while in describing the declarative semantics we refer – for the sake of simplicity – to the union of the agents' integrity constraints, the actual implementation of the system does not require at all that the agents share

---

[1] There are several notions of constraint satisfaction. The one adopted in this work refers to a formalization of integrity constraints used in abductive logic programming of the kind: $\bot \leftarrow body$, where *body* is a set of conditions. $\delta \cup IC \not\models \bot$ means that $\forall ic \in IC, body(ic) \not\subseteq \delta$, i.e., δ does not make $body(ic)$ true. We also rely on the hypothesis, from now on, that $\forall x \in ic, \forall ic \in IC$, x is a *condition*.

any knowledge in that respect (see the consistency check operational semantics further on for details). Knowledge bases and therefore integrity constraints are kept separate, as we would expect in a multi-agent setting.

We also define a concept of 'local consistency', and adopt the following notation: $A \overset{l-cons}{\leadsto}_\delta \Delta$, where Δ is a set of conditions. By 'local consistency' we mean that Δ is consistent with agent A's integrity constraints, IC, returning a (possibly enlarged) set of conditions δ:

$$\begin{cases} \delta \cup IC \nvdash \bot \\ \Delta \subseteq \delta \end{cases}$$

Beside understanding the role that integrity constraints play to ensure the correct behaviour of a system, as briefly exemplified above, it is also important to understand the consequences that it brings to extend the concept of consistency to the multi-agent case. The main point is that while the union of two given sets of hypotheses (conditions) could be enough to ensure the consistency of two separate sets of integrity constraints, it may become insufficient if we want to ensure the consistency of the union of the integrity constraints, as it is shown by the following example.

Example 2.   Let us consider two different sets of constraints, $IC_1 = \{\leftarrow a, c\}$ and $IC_2 = \{\leftarrow b, not\ c\}$, a, b and c being possible conditions on a service. If we check the consistency of the set of hypotheses $\{a, b\}$ against either of IC_1 and IC_2 separately, we obtain no inconsistency. In fact, as a result of such a check we could obtain (assuming for instance that we are adopting a proof-procedure such as that defined in [5]) two separate sets of conditions: $\{a, b, not\ c\}$ and $\{a, b, c\}$. But, if we join the constraints in a unique set $IC_3 = IC_1 \cup IC_2$, it is understood that $\{a, b\}$ cannot be the case, since we would have both c and its negation in the (enlarged) set of hypotheses that includes a and b. Therefore, it is not enough to check $\{a, b\}$ against, say, IC_1, and then $\{a, b\}$ again against the other constraint IC_2, but we need instead a different mechanism to verify the consistency of an enlarged set of hypotheses $\{a, b, not\ c\}$ resulting from the first check, against the other constraint IC_2, thus detecting the inconsistency. $\square$

For this reason, in a distributed setting such as that of multi-agents, the individuals must communicate to each other the possible sources of inconsistency, like it was c in Example 2. The sets of conditions may therefore grow bigger while the consistency check is made, and the enlarged set of conditions checked for consistency again by all the involved agents, until fixpoint is reached.

Let us describe now the operational behavior of the system, by giving, in a sequent-style notation, the inference rules of the operators. The *communication* operator is used to request a service to an agent, which could possibly be the requester itself.

Definition 4 (*Communication formula*)

$$\frac{Y \vdash^B_{\delta_1} F \ \wedge \ B \cup X \overset{cons}{\vdash}_\delta \delta_1}{X \vdash^{B \cup X}_\delta Y > F}$$

where X and Y may either be two distinct agents, or the same one, $X, Y \in \{A_0, ..., A_n\}$. F is a *single formula* that contains properly combined service requests. If F is simply a local execution such as $\downarrow s$, X asks Y to locally perform the service s. In general, however, F may include several nested communication formulas, involving several agents possibly enclosing some private integrity constraints. Therefore, the communication formula $Y > F$ used by X to ask Y to perform the services F requires a consistency check within the bunch composed by X and by those agents that participated in F. Clearly, this bunch will at least include X and Y. This makes the communication operator more than just a simple call to another agent's knowledge base and reasoning module: the answer possibly returned back from Y to X is put in the form of a set of conditions, δ_1, and needs to be agreed upon and possibly modified (enlarged) by the whole bunch of agents, through a consistency step.

There could be the case that an agent requires a service that can be performed in several ways, but it does not really matter which one is selected for execution. This is why we introduce the *competitive* operator, that introduces a degree of non-determinism, since in the expression f ; F there is no precedence relationship between the two operands, f and F.

Definition 5 (*Competitive formula*)

$$\frac{A \vdash^B_\delta f}{A \vdash^B_\delta f; F}$$

$$\frac{A \vdash^B_\delta F}{A \vdash^B_\delta f; F}$$

where A is an agent, $A \in \{A_0, ..., A_n\}$, f is a *formula*, F is an *expression* and B is a bunch of agents, $B \subseteq \{A_0, ..., A_n\}$. The competitive formula results in a non-deterministic choice of one inference rule between the two listed above.

The third operator that we define is the *collaborative* coordination operator. It is used to indicate that two services are both required, and must be consistent with each other. From the inference rule below, we see that the collaborative coordination requires a consistency step involving all agents that contribute to provide the service.

Definition 6 (*Collaborative formula*)

$$\frac{A \vdash^{B'}_{\delta'} f \quad \wedge \quad A \vdash^{B''}_{\delta''} F \quad \wedge \quad B' \cup B'' \overset{cons}{\vdash_\delta} \delta' \cup \delta''}{A \vdash^{B' \cup B''}_\delta f\&F}$$

where A is an agent, $A \in \{A_0, ..., A_n\}$, f is a *formula*, F is an *expression* and B, B' and B'' are three possibly distinct bunches of agents, $B, B', B'' \subseteq \{A_0, ..., A_n\}$.

Finally, we describe the semantics of the consistency check through the following inference rules:

Definition 7 (*Consistency check*)

$$\frac{\forall A_i \in B \ A_i \overset{l-cons}{\leadsto}_{\delta_i} \delta \ \wedge \ \delta \subset \bigcup_{A_j \in B} \delta_j \ \wedge \ B \overset{cons}{\vdash}_{\delta'} \bigcup_{A_i \in B} \delta_i}{\begin{array}{c} B \overset{cons}{\vdash}_{\delta'} \delta \\ \forall A_i \in B \quad A_i \overset{l-cons}{\leadsto}_{\delta} \delta \end{array}}$$
$$B \overset{cons}{\vdash}_{\delta} \delta$$

where A_i, A_j are agents, $A_i, A_j \in \{A_0, ..., A_n\}$, h is a literal, G is an *expression* and B is a bunch of agents, $B \subseteq \{A_0, ..., A_n\}$.

Therefore, the consistency check of δ is first performed individually by every single agent via an abductive derivation, which could result in an enlargement of δ (in particular, this happens if exists a δ_i such that $\delta \subset \delta_i$). In case no agent raises new hypotheses, i.e., for all $A_i \in B$, $\delta \equiv \delta_i$, then $\delta \subset \bigcup_{A_j \in B} \delta_j$ is not true any more, fixpoint is reached, and the consistency check terminates; otherwise the union of the δ_i has to be checked again within the bunch.

Definition 8 (*Local computation formula*)

$$\frac{local\_computation(A, s, \delta') \ \wedge \ A \overset{l-cons}{\leadsto}_{\delta} \delta'}{A \vdash_{\delta}^{\{A\}} \ \downarrow s}$$

where A is an agent, $A \in \{A_0, ..., A_n\}$, s is a service, and $\{A\}$ is the bunch composed by the only agent A. *local_computation* is a relation evaluated by agent A, that returns the conditions δ' associated with a certain service s, that A is asked to execute. δ' must be checked for consistency with the other constraints of A, which could result in an enlargement of δ' leading to a $\delta \supseteq \delta'$. The local computation formula, characterized by the $\downarrow$ operator, is intended not as an actual execution of a service, but rather as a preliminary step that anticipates the execution of a service.

Finally, we can introduce the definition of a successful top-down derivation.

Definition 9 (*Successful top-down derivation*) Let A be an agent and F an expression that possibly describes the request for a service. A *successful top-down derivation* for F in A, which returns a set of conditions δ and the bunch of agents B dynamically involved in the service, can be traced in terms of a (finite) tree such that:

- The root node is labeled by $A \vdash_{\delta}^{B} F$;
- The internal nodes are derived by using, backwards, the inference rules defined above;
- All the leaves are labeled by the empty formula, or represent a successful local computation.

For instance, we have seen how a collaborative formula $A \vdash_{\delta}^{B} f \ \& \ F$ develops into three branches (sub-trees), one for proving f, another one for F and a last one for the consistency check. Similarly, the communication formula produces two sub-trees, while the down reflection and the competitive formulas produce only one branch, and so on.

4   Soundness and Completeness

In this section, we prove the soundness and completeness properties of the proof system, which guarantees the safe execution of tasks. To this purpose, we start by introducing two basic properties we rely upon, Properties 1 and 2, and concerning the soundness and completeness of local consistency derivations. We assume that they hold for all the local consistency computations[2].

Property 1 (*Soundness of the local consistency derivation*) Given an agent A_i and a set of conditions δ,

$$A_i \overset{l-cons}{\leadsto}_{\delta_i} \delta \Rightarrow \delta_i \cup IC_i \nvDash \bot$$

where IC_i represents the integrity A_i's constraints.

This means that, if there exists a local consistency derivation for δ in A_i that returns a set of conditions δ_i, then δ_i is consistent with the integrity constraints IC_i of A_i itself.

Property 2 (*Completeness of the local consistency derivation*) Given an agent A_i and a set of conditions δ,

$$\forall \delta : \delta \cup IC_i \nvDash \bot \Rightarrow \exists \delta_i : A_i \overset{l-cons}{\leadsto}_{\delta_i} \delta \wedge \delta_i \supseteq \delta$$

where IC_i represents the integrity A_i's constraints.

This means that, if a set of conditions δ is consistent with the integrity constraints of an agent A_i, then there exists a local consistency computation for δ in A_i itself, which possibly adds some new conditions to δ, returning $\delta_i \supseteq \delta$. For instance, the proof-procedure of [5] is such that an initial set δ of conditions (abducible predicates) gets enlarged to falsify all the bodies of constraints that contain some predicates that are also contained in δ (see Example 2).

In the following, we prove two lemmas about the soundness and completeness of the consistency check in a bunch of agents of Definition 7, that we will use to prove Theorem 1 and 2 below.

Lemma 1 (*Soundness of the consistency check*) Given a bunch of agents B and a set of conditions δ,

$$B \overset{cons}{\vdash}_{\delta'} \delta \Rightarrow \delta' \cup IC_B \nvDash \bot \wedge \delta' \supseteq \delta$$

where IC_B represents the union of the ICs of all the agents in B.

Proof The proof is given by separately proving the two conjuncts in the right hand side of the implication. In particular, we prove inductively that $\delta' \supseteq \delta$. If $B \overset{cons}{\vdash}_{\delta'} \delta$ is 1-length computation, then by the second inference rule in Def. 7, $\delta' = \delta$. If $B \overset{cons}{\vdash}_{\delta'} \delta$ is n-length, we assume the lemma holds for n-1. Then, by the

---

[2] Although our system does not rely upon a logic system, there exist in literature some proof procedures that implement a local consistency derivation, such as [5,6], some of which are proved correct and complete.

first inference rule in Def. 7, $\delta' \supseteq \bigcup_{A_i \in B} \delta_i$. Since $\delta \subset \bigcup_{A_i \in B} \delta_i$, then follows: $\delta' \supset \delta$.

We prove inductively that $\delta' \cup IC_B \nvDash \bot$. For one-length computation, $B \overset{cons}{\vdash}_\delta \delta$ is equivalent to $\forall A_i \in B\ A_i \overset{l-cons}{\leadsto}_\delta \delta$ by the second inference rule in Def. 7. By the soundness of the local consistency derivation (Prop. 1) follows that $\forall A_i \in B, \delta \cup IC_i \nvDash \bot$. For an n-length computation, $B \overset{cons}{\vdash}_{\delta'} \delta$ by the first inference rule of Def. 7 is equivalent to $\forall A_i \in B, A_i \overset{l-cons}{\leadsto}_{\delta_i} \delta \wedge \delta \subset \bigcup_{A_j \in B} \delta_j \wedge B \overset{cons}{\vdash}_{\delta'} \bigcup_{A_i \in B} \delta_i$. By the inductive hypothesis, $B \overset{cons}{\vdash}_{\delta'} \bigcup_{A_i \in B} \delta_i$ implies $\delta' \cup IC_B \nvDash \bot$. ∎

It is worth stressing that, when proving $B \overset{cons}{\vdash}_\delta \delta \equiv \forall A_i \in B\ A_i \overset{l-cons}{\leadsto}_\delta \delta$, we refer to the case in which the local consistency derivation does not affect δ. In particular, with respect to Example 2, if we use [5], which indeed affects δ, neither $\{a, b, c\}$ is consistent with IC_1 nor $\{a, b, not\ c\}$ is consistent with IC_2, and of course both are inconsistent with $\{IC_1, IC_2\}$. If we use a weaker notion of consistency, instead, $\{a, b\}$ could be consistent with both IC_1, IC_2 and $\{IC_1, IC_2\}$.

Lemma 2 (*Completeness of the consistency check*) Given a bunch of agents B,

$$\forall \delta' : \delta' \cup IC_B \nvDash \bot \Rightarrow \exists \delta \supseteq \delta' : B \overset{cons}{\vdash}_\delta \delta'$$

Proof $\delta' \cup IC_B \nvDash \bot$ implies $\forall ic \in IC_B : \delta' \cup ic \nvDash \bot$. This implies, by Prop. 2, that $\forall A_i \in B\ \forall ic_i \in IC_i \exists \delta_i : A_i \overset{l-cons}{\leadsto}_{\delta_i} \delta' \wedge \delta_i \supseteq \delta'$. By induction on the length of the computation, for a 1-length computation, by the second inference rule of Def. 7, the statement is trivially proven. For an n-length computation, by the first inference rule of Def. 7, and by the inductive hypothesis the statement is proven as well. ∎

In the following, we state the soundness theorem for our proof system. The theorem states that, for any successful top-down derivation, under the assumption of soundness of the local consistency derivations (Prop. 1), the computed conditions satisfy all the integrity constraints of the bunch of agents dynamically involved in the service in question. This implements in a sense the introduced notion of *safe execution*.

Theorem 1 (*Soundness*) Let A be an agent and F an expression that possibly describes the request for a service. If there exists a *successful top-down derivation* for F in A, which returns a set of conditions δ and a bunch of agents B, then the computed set δ is consistent with the integrity constraints of bunch B. Formally:

$$A \vdash^B_\delta F \Rightarrow \delta \cup IC_B \nvDash \bot$$

Proof The proof is given by induction on the length of the derivation. For a 1-length derivation, F has the form $\downarrow s$, where s is a service. By Def. 8, $A \vdash^{\{A\}}_\delta \downarrow s$, which implies that there exists in A a local computation for s returning δ' and $A \stackrel{l-cons}{\leadsto}_\delta \delta'$. By Prop. 1, it follows that $\delta \cup IC_{\{A\}} \not\models \bot$.

For any n-length computation, we consider several cases:

(i) F is in the form $Y > f$. Then, $A \vdash_\delta^{B \cup \{A\}} f$ by Def. 4 implies $Y \vdash_\delta^B f$ and $B \cup \{A\} \stackrel{cons}{\vdash}_\delta \delta'$. By the inductive hypothesis, $\delta' \cup IC_B \not\models \bot$, and by Lemma 1, $\delta \cup IC_{B \cup \{A\}} \not\models \bot$ and $\delta \supseteq \delta'$. Then, it follows that $\delta' \cup IC_{B \cup \{A\}} \not\models \bot$.

(ii) When F is in the form $f; F'$, the statement is trivially proven.

(iii) F is in the form $f \& F'$. Then, $A \vdash_\delta^{B' \cup B''}$ by Def. 6 implies $A \vdash_{\delta'}^{B'} f \wedge A \vdash_{\delta''}^{B''} F' \wedge B' \cup B'' \stackrel{cons}{\vdash}_\delta \delta' \cup \delta''$. The first two conjuncts imply, by the inductive hypothesis, $\delta' \cup IC_{B'} \not\models \bot \wedge \delta'' \cup IC_{B''} \not\models \bot$. The third conjunct implies, by Lemma 1, $\delta \cup IC_{B' \cup B''} \not\models \bot \wedge \delta \supseteq \delta' \cup \delta''$ ∎

In the rest of the section, we also state a completeness theorem for a subset of the possible expressions occurring in a top-level request. The completeness theorem ensures that, if a set of conditions δ can be found, satisfying the integrity constraints of a bunch of agents, and it belongs to the meaning of some agent, as defined below, then there exists an expression F and a successful top-down derivation for F in A leading to the bunch B of agents, and to conditions δ.

Theorem 2 (*Completeness*) Let B be a bunch of n agents, s a service and δ a set of conditions.

$\forall B = \{A_1, \ldots, A_n\}, \forall < s, \delta > \in Den(A_i), A_i \in B : \delta \cup IC_B \not\models \bot \Rightarrow \exists F, A \in B : A \vdash_{\hat{\delta}}^B F \wedge \hat{\delta} \supseteq \delta$ where F is an expression occurring in a top-level request.

Proof The proof is given in the case of a communication formula F expressed in the form: $F = A_{1i} > A_{2i} > \ldots > A_{ki} > A_i > \downarrow s$, where $k \geq n - 2$, and $\{A_{ji} : j = i..k\} \cup \{A\} \cup \{A_i\} = B$.

By Def. 2, being $< s, \delta > \in Den(A_i)$, it follows that (i)$local\_computation(A_i, s, \delta) \wedge \delta \cup IC_{A_i} \not\models \bot$. By Prop. 2, it follows that (ii) $\exists \delta \supseteq \delta'$ such that $A \stackrel{l-cons}{\leadsto}_{\delta'} \delta$. Therefore, by Def. 8, (i), and (ii), it follows that (iii) $A_i \vdash_{\delta'}^{\{A_i\}} \downarrow s, \delta' \supseteq \delta$.

Now, being $\delta \cup IC_B \not\models \bot$, by Lemma 2 it follows that $B \stackrel{cons}{\vdash}_{\delta''} \delta, \delta'' \supseteq \delta$. Now, by Lemma 1, $\delta'' \cup IC_B \not\models \bot$, and, again by Lemma 2, $B \stackrel{cons}{\vdash}_{\tilde{\delta}} \delta''$. From Def. 7 it is possible to prove that $\delta' \subseteq \delta''$. Therefore, $\{A_i\} \cup \{A_{ki}\} \stackrel{cons}{\vdash}_{\delta'''} \delta'$. From this, Def. 4 and (iii), it follows that $\{A_i, A_{ki}\} \stackrel{cons}{\vdash}_{\delta'''} A_i > \downarrow s$, and $\delta''' \supseteq \delta'$. Now, by iteratively applying Def. 4, we can prove that $\exists \hat{\delta} : A \vdash_{\hat{\delta}}^B A_{1i} > A_{2i} > \ldots > A_{ki} > A_i > \downarrow s \wedge \hat{\delta} \supseteq \delta$ ∎

In a similar way it is possible to give the proofs referring to other kinds of formula.

5   Conclusion

In this work, we tackled the problem of 'safe' task execution in multi-agent systems. The tasks are services that agents can request / provide, to other agents.

The feasibility of such services may be constrained by "policies", i.e., integrity constraints embodied in the agents themselves. We defined a formalism to express the combination of service requests, and an operational semantics as a proof system that can be used to extend an operating system or virtual machine supporting the agents' execution, to ensure a safe task execution. We presented two results, with respect to the semantics. The first one is a soundness result, which implements the notion of safe execution, ensuring that no constraint is violated by a service request which is possibly composed of several services, asked to several agents. In other words, if the operational semantics allows the execution of a certain service, then it is safe to execute it. The second one is a completeness result, which states that if such service could be safely executed, then its execution is allowed by the operational semantics. This result has been proven for a particular service composition pattern, but it is possible to extend the proof for other more general patterns.

In related work, a considerable effort has been dedicated towards characterizing agents as logical systems, providing several operational semantics to the logical specifications of agent programming languages [7,8,9]. Nevertheless, to the best of our knowledge, our work is among the few ones that give a sound and complete semantics to a formalism that allows to express the agents' execution, in a way that is independent of the notion of consistency adopted and that at the same time ensures that the system's constraints are not violated. In that, this paper represents a progress from our previous work, which presumes a system of logic based agents and is tailored to the case of abductively reasoning agents.

In the future, we intend to study and formalise the relationship between composition operators of knowledge bases and programs of different agents, and their corresponding operational coununterpart, given as proof systems for the multi-agent case. We also intend to provide a concrete implementation of the operators here introduced, and write a library that extends a virtual machine.

Acknowledgements

We would like to thank the anonymous referees for their precious comments. This work was supported by the SOCS project, funded by the CEC, contract IST-2001-32530.

References

1. Jennings, N.R.: On agent-based software engineering. Artificial Intelligence **117** (2000) 277–296
2. Ciampolini, A., Lamma, E., Mello, P., Torroni, P.: LAILA: A language for coordinating abductive reasoning among logic agents. Computer Languages **27** (2002)
3. Ciampolini, A., Lamma, E., Mello, P., Toni, F., Torroni, P.: Co-operation and competition in *ALIAS*: a logic framework for agents that negotiate. In: Computational Logic and Multi-Agency. Special Issue of the Annals of Mathematics and Artificial Intelligence, Baltzer Science Pub. (to appear)

4. Kakas, A.C., Kowalski, R.A., Toni, F.: The role of abduction in logic programming. Handbook of Logic in AI and Logic Programming **5** (1998) 235–324
5. Kakas, A.C., Mancarella, P.: Generalized stable models: a semantics for abduction. In: Proc. 9th ECAI, Pitman Pub. (1990)
6. Fung, T.H., Kowalski, R.A.: The IFF proof procedure for abductive logic programming. Journal of Logic Programming (1997)
7. Lesprance, Y., Levesque, H.J., Lin, F., Marcu, D., Reiter, R., Scherl, R.B.: Foundations of a logical approach to agent programming. In: Intelligent Agents II – Proc. ATAL'95. LNCS, Springer-Verlag (1996)
8. Rao, A.S.: AgentSpeak(L): BDI agents speak out in a logical computable language. In: Agents Breaking Away, Proc. MAAMAW'97. LNCS 1038, Springer (1996) 42–55
9. Hindriks, K., Boer, F.D., van der Hoek, W., Meyer, J.J.: Formal semantics for an abstract agent programming language. In: Intelligent Agents IV, Proc. ATAL'97. LNCS 1365, Springer-Verlag (1998) 215–229

An Argumentation Framework
for Merging Conflicting Knowledge Bases

Leila Amgoud[1] and Simon Parsons[2]

[1] IRIT, 118 route de Narbonne, 31062
Toulouse Cedex, France
amgoud@irit.fr
[2] Department of Computer Science
University of Liverpool, Chadwick Building
Liverpool L69 7ZF, United Kingdom
s.d.parsons@csc.liv.ac.uk

Abstract. The problem of merging multiple sources of information is central in many information processing areas such as databases integrating problems, multiple criteria decision making, etc. Recently several approaches have been proposed to merge classical propositional bases. These approaches are in general semantically defined. They use priorities, generally based on Dalal's distance for merging classical conflicting bases and return a new classical base as a result. In this paper, we present an argumentation framework for solving conflicts which could be applied to conflicts arising between agents in a multi-agent system. We suppose that each agent is represented by a consistent knowledge base and that the different agents are conflicting. We show that by selecting an appropriate preference relation between arguments, that framework can be used for merging conflicting bases and recovers the results of the different approaches proposed for merging bases [8, 12, 14, 13, 16, 17].

1 Introduction

In many areas such as cooperative information systems, multi-databases, multi-agents reasoning systems, GroupWare, distributed expert systems, information comes from multiple sources. In these areas, information from different sources is often contradictory. For example, in a distributed medical expert system, different experts often disagree on the diagnoses of patients' diseases. In a multi-database system two component databases may record the same data item but give it different values because of incomplete updates, system error, or differences in underlying semantics. Some researchers claim that, on an abstract level, the above problem can be subsumed under the general problem of merging multiple bases that may contradict each other. Several different approaches have been proposed for that purpose [8, 12, 14, 13, 16, 17]. Starting from different bases (Σ_1, $\cdots$, Σ_n) which are conflicting, these works return a unique consistent base. However, in the case of multi-agent reasoning systems where each agent is supposed to have its own knowledge base, merging their bases looks debatable, since the goal of retaining all available information is quite legitimate in that case. As a

S. Flesca et al. (Eds.): JELIA 2002, LNAI 2424, pp. 27–37, 2002.
© Springer-Verlag Berlin Heidelberg 2002

result, other authors have considered reasoning with such bases without merging them. Argumentation is one of the most promising approaches developed for that purpose.

Argumentation is based on the construction of arguments and counter-arguments (defeaters) and the selection of the most acceptable of these arguments (see [7, 15] for a survey of the different argumentation frameworks).

Inspired by the work presented in [1], we present a preference-based argumentation framework for reasoning with conflicting knowledge bases where each base could be part of a separate agent. This framework uses preference relations between arguments in order to determine the acceptable ones. We show that by selecting an appropriate preference relation between arguments, the preference-based argumentation framework can be used to merging conflicting bases in the sense that it recovers the results of fusion operators defined in [8,12,14,13,16,17]. Thus this approach could be used by an agent, engaged in the kind of dialogue we have described in [2] as a means of handling conflicts between different agents' views of the world. This paper is organized as follows: section 2 introduces the preference-based argumentation framework developed. In section 3 we show that the new framework recovers the results of other approaches to fusion namely those proposed in [14, 13]. Section 4 is devoted to some concluding remarks and perspectives.

2   Basic Definitions

Let us consider a propositional language $\mathcal{L}$ over a finite alphabet $\mathcal{P}$ of atoms. Ω denotes the set of all the interpretations. Logical equivalence is denoted by $\equiv$ and classical conjunction and disjunction are respectively denoted by $\wedge$, $\vee$. $\vdash$ denotes classical inference. If ϕ is a formula of $\mathcal{L}$, then $[\phi]$ denotes the set of all models of ϕ. A literal is an atom or a negation of an atom. Σ_i represents a classical propositional base. Let $E = \{\Sigma_1, \cdots, \Sigma_n\}$ ($n \geq 1$) be a multi-set of n consistent propositional bases. We denote by Σ the set $\Sigma_1 \cup \cdots \cup \Sigma_n$ for short ($\Sigma = \Sigma_1 \cup \cdots \cup \Sigma_n$). Note that Σ may be inconsistent.

Definition 1. *An argumentation framework (AF) is a triplet $\langle \mathcal{A}(\Sigma), Undercut, Pref \rangle$. $\mathcal{A}(\Sigma)$ is the set of all the arguments constructed from Σ, Undercut is a binary relation representing defeat relationship between arguments. Pref is a (partial or complete) preordering on $\mathcal{A}(\Sigma) \times \mathcal{A}(\Sigma)$. $>>^{Pref}$ denotes the strict ordering associated with Pref.*

There are several definitions of *argument* and *defeat* among arguments. For our purpose, we will use the definitions proposed in [11].

Definition 2. *An argument of $\mathcal{A}(\Sigma)$ is a pair (H, h), where h is a formula of the language $\mathcal{L}$ and H a subset of Σ satisfying:*

1. *H is consistent*
2. *$H \vdash h$*
3. *H is minimal (no strict subset of H satisfies 1 and 2).*

H is called the support *and h the* conclusion *of the argument.*

Definition 3. *Let (H, h) and (H', h') be two arguments of $\mathcal{A}(\Sigma)$. (H, h) under-cuts (H', h') iff for some $k \in H'$, $h \equiv \neg k$. An argument is undercut if there exists at least one argument against one element of its support.*

Different preference relations between arguments may be defined. These preference relations are induced by a preference relation defined on the supports of arguments. The preference relation on the supports may be itself defined from a (total or partial) preordering on the knowledge base. So, for two arguments (H, h), (H', h'), (H, h) is preferred to (H', h') (denoted by $(H, h) >>^{Pref}$ (H', h')) iff H is preferred to H' w.r.t $Pref$.

In the next section, we will show some examples of the origin of a preordering on the base.

An example of a preference relation is the one based on the elitism principle (ELI-preference [5]). Let $\geq$ be a total preordering on a knowledge base $\mathcal{K}$ and $>$ be the associated strict ordering. In that case, the knowledge base $\mathcal{K}$ is supposed to be stratified into $(\mathcal{K}_1, \cdots, \mathcal{K}_n)$ such that $\mathcal{K}_1$ is the set of $\geq$-maximal elements in $\mathcal{K}$ and $\mathcal{K}_{i+1}$ the set of $\geq$-maximal elements in $\mathcal{K} \setminus (\mathcal{K}_1 \cup \cdots \cup \mathcal{K}_i)$.

Let H and H' be two subbases of $\mathcal{K}$. H is *preferred* to H' according to ELI-preference iff $\forall k \in H \setminus H'$, $\exists k' \in H' \setminus H$ such that $k > k'$.

Let (H, h), (H', h') be two arguments of $\mathcal{A}(\Sigma)$. $(H, h) >>^{ELI} (H', h')$ iff H is preferred to H according to ELI-preference.

Example 1. $\mathcal{K} = \mathcal{K}_1 \cup \mathcal{K}_2 \cup \mathcal{K}_3$ such that $\mathcal{K}_1 = \{a, \neg a\}$, $\mathcal{K}_2 = \{a \rightarrow b\}$, $\mathcal{K}_3 = \{\neg b\}$ and $a, \neg a \rangle a \rightarrow b \rangle \neg b$. $(\{a, a \rightarrow b\}, b) >>^{ELI} (\{\neg b\}, \neg b)$.

Using the defeat and the preference relations between arguments, the notion of *acceptable arguments* among the elements of $\mathcal{A}(\Sigma)$ can be defined. Inspired by the work of Dung [10], several definitions of the notion of acceptability have been proposed in [1] and the acceptable arguments are gathered in a so-called *extension*. For our purpose, we are interested by the extension satisfying a stability and the following coherence requirements:

Definition 4. *A set $S \subseteq \mathcal{A}(\Sigma)$ of arguments is* conflict-free *iff there doesn't exist A, $B \in S$ such that A undercuts B and not($B >>^{Pref} A$).*

Definition 5. *Let $\langle \mathcal{A}(\Sigma), Undercut, Pref \rangle$ be an AF. A* conflict-free *set of arguments S is a* stable extension *iff S is a fixed point of a* function *$\mathcal{G}$ defined as:*
$\mathcal{G} : 2^{\mathcal{A}} \times 2^{\mathcal{A}}$
$S \rightarrow \mathcal{G}(S) = \{A \in \mathcal{A}(\Sigma) \mid$ there does not exist $B \in S$ such that B undercuts A and not $(A >>^{Pref} B)\}$

Given a set of arguments $\mathcal{A}(\Sigma)$, a set $\Pi = \{S_1, \cdots, S_n\}$ of stable extensions can be found. These extensions represent the different sets of *acceptable arguments*. They include all the arguments defending themselves against any undercutting argument and those defended. These notions of defense have been defined in [1] as follows:

An argument A is *defended* by a set S of arguments (or S *defends* A) iff $\forall$ $B \in \mathcal{A}(\Sigma)$, if B undercuts A and not$(A >>^{Pref} B)$ then $\exists C \in S$ such that C undercuts B and not$(B >>^{Pref} C)$.

If B undercuts A and $A >>^{Pref} B$ then we say that A *defends itself* against B.

$\mathcal{C}_{Pref}$ denotes the set of all the arguments defending themselves against their defeaters.

All the proofs of the results presented in this paper can be found in [3].

Let $T \subseteq \mathcal{A}(\Sigma)$, $\mathcal{F}(T) = \{A \in \mathcal{A}(\Sigma) \mid A$ is defended by $T\}$.

Property 1. Let $\langle \mathcal{A}(\Sigma), Undercut, Pref \rangle$ be an AF. For any stable extension $S_i \in \Pi$, the following inclusion holds:

$$\underline{S} = \mathcal{C}_{Pref} \cup [\bigcup \mathcal{F}^{i \geq 1}(\mathcal{C}_{Pref})] \subseteq S_i.$$

This means that each stable extension contains the arguments which are not undercut, the arguments which can defend themselves against the undercutting arguments, and also the arguments defended by that extension.

Property 2. Let $\Sigma \neq \emptyset$ and $\langle \mathcal{A}(\Sigma), Undercut, Pref \rangle$ be an AF. The set Π is not empty $(\Pi \neq \emptyset)$. This means that each argumentation framework has at least one stable extension.

Property 3. Let $\langle \mathcal{A}(\Sigma), Undercut, Pref \rangle$ be an AF.

$$\underline{S} = \bigcap S_i, i = 1, n.$$

This means that each argument which is in one extension and not in another does not defend itself and it is not defended.

Acceptable arguments are defined in order to define the acceptable conclusions of an inconsistent knowledge base. So from the notion of acceptability, we define the following consequence relations.

Definition 6. Let $\langle \mathcal{A}(\Sigma), Undercut, Pref \rangle$ be an AF. Let ϕ be a formula of the language $\mathcal{L}$.

1. ϕ is a plausible consequence of Σ iff there exists $H \in \Sigma$ such that $(H, \phi) \in \mathcal{A}(\Sigma)$.
2. ϕ is a probable consequence of Σ iff there exists a stable extension S_i and $\exists (H, \phi) \in \mathcal{A}(\Sigma)$ such that $(H, \phi) \in S_i$.
3. ϕ is a certain consequence of Σ iff $\exists (H, \phi) \in \mathcal{A}(\Sigma)$ such that $(H, \phi) \in \underline{S}$.

The terms *plausible, probable* and *certain* are taken from [11].

Let's denote by $\mathcal{C}_{pl}, \mathcal{C}_{pr}, \mathcal{C}_{ce}$ respectively, the set of all plausible consequences, all probable consequences and all certain consequences. The following inclusions hold.

Property 4. Let $\langle \mathcal{A}(\Sigma), Undercut, Pref \rangle$ be an AF.
$\mathcal{C}_{ce} \subseteq \mathcal{C}_{pr} \subseteq \mathcal{C}_{pl}$.

Note that when the different bases are not conflicting, the relation Undercut is empty. Formally:

Property 5. Let Σ be a consistent base and $\langle \mathcal{A}(\Sigma), Undercut, Pref \rangle$ be an AF.

- Undercut = $\emptyset$
- There exists a unique stable extension $\underline{S} = \mathcal{A}(\Sigma)$ = the set of arguments which are not undercut.
- $\mathcal{C}_{ce} = \mathcal{C}_{pr} = \mathcal{C}_{pl} = Th(\Sigma)$ ($Th(\Sigma)$ denotes the deductive closure of Σ)

Example 2. *Let's consider three bases* $\Sigma_1 = \{a\}$, $\Sigma_2 = \{a \rightarrow b\}$, $\Sigma_3 = \{\neg b\}$. *We suppose that* Σ_1 *is more reliable than* Σ_2 *and* Σ_2 *is more reliable than* Σ_3. *Then* $a > a \rightarrow b > \neg b$. *In the framework* $\langle \mathcal{A}(\Sigma), Undercut, ELI \rangle$, *the set* $\mathcal{A}(\Sigma)$ *is* $\{A, B, C, D, F\}$ *such that:* $A = (\{a\}, a)$, $B = (\{a \rightarrow b\}, a \rightarrow b)$, $C = (\{\neg b\}, \neg b)$, $D = (\{a, a \rightarrow b\}, b)$, $E = (\{\neg b, a \rightarrow b\}, \neg a)$ *and* $F = (\{a, \neg b\}, \neg(a \rightarrow b))$.

According to ELI-preference, $A >>^{ELI} E$, $D >>^{ELI} C, E, F$ *and* $B >>^{ELI} F$. *A, B and D are preferred to their defeaters, so A, B, D* $\in \underline{S}$. *In this example, there is a unique stable extension which is* $\underline{S}$.

3   Connection with Works on Merging Conflicting Bases

Recently, several approaches have been proposed to merge classical propositional bases. These approaches can be divided into two categories: those approaches in which (*explicit or implicit*) priorities are used, and those in which priorities are not used. These approaches define a merging operator Λ which is a function associating to a set $E = \{\Sigma_1, \cdots, \Sigma_n\}$ a consistent classical propositional base, denoted by $\Lambda(E)$.

Let B be a subset of $\mathcal{A}(\Sigma)$, $Supp(B)$ is a function which returns the union of the supports of all the elements of B.

Let T be subset of Σ, $Arg(T)$ is a function which returns the arguments having their support in T.

Case 1. Non use of priorities

There are two straightforward ways for defining $\Lambda(E)$ depending on whether the bases are conflicting or not, namely:

- **Classical conjunctive merging:** $\Lambda(E) = \wedge \Sigma_i$, i = 1, n. In this case, $\Lambda(E) = \Sigma$.
- **Classical disjunctive merging:** $\Lambda(E) = \vee \Sigma_i$, i = 1, n.
  If we have two bases $\Sigma_1 = \{a\}$ and $\Sigma_2 = \{\neg a\}$, the result of merging is $\Lambda(E) = \{a \vee \neg a\}$ a tautology, which does support neither a nor $\neg a$.
  Let's see what is the result provided by the argumentation framework. We consider then the base $\Sigma = \{a, \neg a\}$. $\mathcal{A}(\Sigma) = \{(\{a\}, a), (\{\neg a\}, \neg a)\}$. Since no preferences are used in this approach, the preference relation between arguments Pref is empty. Two stable extensions are computed: $S_1 = \{(\{a\}, a)\}$ and $S_2 = \{(\{\neg a\}, \neg a)\}$. Consequently, a and $\neg a$ are two probable consequences of the base Σ.

Other approaches, developed in [16], consist of computing the maximal (for set inclusion) consistent subsets of the union of the knowledge bases and then take as the result the intersection of the deductive closure of these subsets.

The result of that merging operator is captured by our argumentation framework. Since no preferences exist, the relation Pref is empty (Pref $= \emptyset$). In this particular case, the set $\underline{S}$ contains the arguments which are not undercut. Let's denote by $T = \{T_1, \cdots, T_n\}$ the set of maximal consistent subsets of Σ. In that case, the following result has been proved in [6].

Proposition 1. *Let* $\langle \mathcal{A}(\Sigma), Undercut, Pref = \emptyset \rangle$ *be an AF.* $\Pi = \{S_1, \cdots, S_n\}$ *is the set of the corresponding stable extensions.*

- $\forall S_i \in \Pi,\ Supp(S_i) \in T$.
- $\forall T_i \in T,\ Arg(T_i) \in \Pi$.
- $\forall S_i \in \Pi,\ Supp(S_i)$ *is consistent.*

As a direct consequence of this result we have:

Proposition 2. *Let* $\langle \mathcal{A}(\Sigma), Undercut, Pref \rangle$ *be an AF.*

$$\Lambda(E) = \mathcal{C}_{ce}.$$

In other words, the result of merging the knowledge-bases is the set of certain consequences. The above results show that the approach developed in [16] is captured by our preference-based argumentation framework.

Example 3. *Let's extend the above example to three bases* $\Sigma_1 = \{a\}$, $\Sigma_2 = \{\neg a\}$, $\Sigma_3 = \{a\}$.

There are two maximal (for set-inclusion) subsets of $\Sigma_1 \cup \Sigma_2 \cup \Sigma_3$: $T_1 = \{a\}$ *and* $T_2 = \{\neg a\}$. *The result of merging these three bases is the empty set since the intersection between* T_1 *and* T_2 *is empty. In the argumentation framework, a and* $\neg a$ *are two probable consequences, but there are no certain consequences.*

Case 2. Use of priorities

Two kinds of approach which use priorities can be distinguished depending on whether they use implicit or explicit priorities. In [8] for example, the different bases are supposed weighted, the base having a higher weight is more reliable than the others. In presence of such weights, the maximal consistent subsets are computed by taking as many sentences as possible from the knowledge bases of higher weights (or priorities). In this case, the result $\Lambda(E)$ is also captured by the argumentation framework presented in section 2, provided that we choose an appropriate preference relation between arguments and strengthen the definition of *conflict-free*.

The most appropriate relation is the one based on certainty level and defined in [4] in a possibilistic context. In that case, a knowledge base E is supposed to be stratified in $E_1, \cdots, E_n$ such that the beliefs in E_i have the same certainty level and are more certain than the elements in E_j where $i < j$. (This notion of *certainty* corresponds to the degree of belief that an agent has in given propositions, and can be combined with a notion of its belief in other agents when that proposition is from another agent's knowledge base).

For our purpose, we suppose that $\Sigma = \Sigma'_1 \cup \cdots \cup \Sigma'_k$ such that Σ'_i is the union of the bases having the same weight. Σ'_1 is the union of the bases having the highest weight and Σ'_k is the union of the bases having the smallest weight.

Definition 7. *The weight of a non-empty subset H of Σ is the highest number of a layer (i.e. the lower layer) met by H, so:*

$$weight(H) = max\{j \mid 1 \leq j \leq k \text{ and } H_j \neq \emptyset\},$$

where H_j denotes $H \cap \Sigma'_j$.

Definition 8. *Let H, H' be two subsets of Σ. H is preferred to H' (denoted H $Pref_1 H'$) iff weight(H) < weight(H').*
    Consequently, (H, h) is preferred to (H', h'), (denoted $(H, h) >>^{Pref_1}$ (H', h')), iff $H Pref_1 H'$.

The new definition of conflict-free is the following one:

Definition 9. *A set $S \subseteq \mathcal{A}(\Sigma)$ of arguments is conflict-free iff there does not exist $A, B \in S$ such that A undercuts B.*

Let's denote by $T = \{T_1, \cdots, T_n\}$ the set of maximal consistent subsets of Σ. As in the case without preferences, these subsets can be computed from the stable extensions of the framework $\langle \mathcal{A}(\Sigma), Undercut, Pref_1 \rangle$.

Proposition 3. *Let $\langle \mathcal{A}(\Sigma), Undercut, Pref_1 \rangle$ be an AF. $\Pi = \{S_1, \cdots, S_n\}$ is the set of the corresponding stable extensions.*

- $\forall S_i \in \Pi, Supp(S_i) \in T$.
- $\forall T_i \in T, Arg(T_i) \in \Pi$.
- $\forall S_i \in \Pi, Supp(S_i)$ is consistent.

Proposition 4. *Let $\langle \mathcal{A}(\Sigma), Undercut, Pref_1 \rangle$ be an AF. $\Lambda(E) = \mathcal{C}_{ce}$.*

Propositions 3 and 4 show that the approach developed in [8] is captured by our preference-based argumentation framework as well.

Some recent approaches are proposed for merging conflicting knowledge bases using implicit priorities. These priorities are extracted from the different interpretations. The three basic steps followed in [12, 14, 13, 17] for the semantic of a merging operator Λ are:

1. Rank-order the set of interpretations Ω w.r.t each propositional base Σ_i by computing a local distance, denoted $d(\omega, \Sigma_i)$, between ω and each Σ_i.
   The local distance is based on Dalal's distance [9]. The distance between an interpretation ω and a propositional base Σ_i is the number of atoms on which this interpretation differs from some model of the propositional base. Formally, $d(\omega, \Sigma_i) = min \, dist(\omega, \omega')$, $\omega' \in [\Sigma_i]$ where $dist(\omega, \omega')$ is the number of atoms whose valuations differ in the two interpretations.

2. Rank-order the set of interpretations Ω w.r.t all the propositional bases. This leads to the overall distance denoted $d(\omega, E)$. This later, computed from local distances $d(\omega, \Sigma_i)$, defines an ordering relation between the interpretations defined as follows: $\omega \leq \omega'$ iff $d(\omega, E) \leq d(\omega', E)$.
3. $\Lambda(E)$ is defined by being such that its models are minimal with respect to $\leq$, namely: $[\Lambda(E)] = min(\Omega, \leq)$.

Example 4. *Let's consider the three following bases* $\Sigma_1 = \{a\}$, $\Sigma_2 = \{\neg a\}$, $\Sigma_3 = \{a\}$. *There exist two interpretations* $\omega_0 = \{a\}$ *and* $\omega_1 = \{\neg a\}$.

- $d(\omega_0, \Sigma_1) = d(\omega_0, \Sigma_3) = 0, d(\omega_0, \Sigma_2) = 1$
- $d(\omega_1, \Sigma_1) = d(\omega_1, \Sigma_3) = 1, d(\omega_1, \Sigma_2) = 0$

Once $d(\omega, \Sigma_i)$ is defined for each knowledge base Σ_i, several methods have been proposed in order to aggregate the local distances $d(w, \Sigma_i)$ according to whether the bases have the same weight or not. In particular the following operators have been proposed respectively in [14] and [13]:

$d(\omega, E) = \sum_{i=1}^{n} d(\omega, \Sigma_i)$ and
$d(\omega, E) = \sum_{i=1}^{n} d(\omega, \Sigma_i) \times \alpha_i$

where α_i is the weight associated with the base Σ_i. We denote by Λ_1 the first operator and by Λ_2 the second one.

Example 5. *Let's consider the three following bases* $\Sigma_1 = \{a\}$, $\Sigma_2 = \{\neg a\}$, $\Sigma_3 = \{a\}$. *According to the first operator* Λ_1, $d(\omega_0, E) = 1$ *and* $d(\omega_1, E) = 2$. *Then the generated base has* ω_0 *as an interpretation.*

Let's suppose now that Σ_2 *is more reliable than the two others and it has a weight 3.* Σ_1, Σ_3 *have weight 1. Using the operator* Λ_2, $d(\omega_0, E) = d(\omega_0, \Sigma_1) \times 1 + d(\omega_0, \Sigma_2) \times 3 + d(\omega_0, \Sigma_3) \times 1 = 3$ *and* $d(\omega_1, E) = 2$. *Then the generated base has* ω_1 *as an interpretation.*

To capture the results of these two merging operators, we consider the new definition of conflict-free (given in definition 8) and we define two new preference relations between arguments $Pref_2$ and $Pref_3$. These relations are based on Dalal's distance. The basic idea is to associate to the support of each argument a *weight*. This last corresponds to the minimal distance between the support and the different bases. The distance between a support H and a base Σ_i is computed as follows:

$$\text{dist}(H, \Sigma_i) = min \ \text{dist}(\omega, \omega'), \ \omega \in [H] \ \text{and} \ \omega \in [\Sigma_i].$$

Example 6. $\Sigma_1 = \{a\}$, $\Sigma_2 = \{a \rightarrow b\}$, $\Sigma_3 = \{\neg b\}$ *are three bases.* $H = \{a, a \rightarrow b\}$, $H' = \{\neg b\}$ *are two subsets of* Σ. $dist(H, \Sigma_1) = dist(H, \Sigma_2) = 0$, $dist(H, \Sigma_3) = 1$, $dist(H', \Sigma_1) = 0$, $dist(H', \Sigma_2) = 0$, $dist(H', \Sigma_3) = 0$.

To capture the results of the merging operator Λ_1, the weight of a support is defined as follows:

Definition 10. *Let H be a subset of Σ.*
$Weight(H) = \sum_{i=1}^{n} dist(H, \Sigma_i)$.

Pursuing definition 7, a subset H of Σ is preferred to another subset H' (denoted $HPref_2H'$) iff $weight(H) < weight(H')$. Consequently, (H, h) is preferred to (H', h'), (denoted $(H, h) >>^{Pref_2} (H', h')$), iff $HPref_2H'$.

Example 7. $H = \{a, a \rightarrow b\}$, $H' = \{\neg b\}$ *are two subsets of Σ. $Weight(H) = 1$ and $weight(H') = 0$, then H' is preferred to H. Consequently, $(\{\neg b\}, \neg b) >>^{Pref_2} (\{a, a \rightarrow b\}, b)$.*

Proposition 5. *Let $S_1, \cdots, S_n$ be the stable extensions of the framework $\langle \mathcal{A}(\Sigma), Undercut, Pref_2 \rangle$.*

- *S is not necessarily included in each S_i.*
- *$\forall S_i$, $Supp(S_i)$ is consistent.*
- *$[Supp(S_1)], \cdots, [Supp(S_n)]$ are the models obtained by the merging operator Λ_1.*

Example 8. $\Sigma_1 = \{a\}$, $\Sigma_2 = \{a \rightarrow b\}$, $\Sigma_3 = \{\neg b\}$. $\mathcal{P} = \{a, b\}$, *so the possible models are:* $\omega_0 = \{a, b\}$, $\omega_1 = \{a, \neg b\}$, $\omega_2 = \{\neg a, b\}$ *and* $\omega_3 = \{\neg a, \neg b\}$.
$d(\omega_0, E) = d(\omega_1, E) = d(\omega_3, E) = 1$ *and* $d(\omega_2, E) = 2$, *then the result of merging is the three models* ω_0, ω_1, ω_3.
Let's consider now the framework $\langle \mathcal{A}(\Sigma), Undercut, Pref_2 \rangle$ where:
$\mathcal{A}(\Sigma) = \{A = (\{a\}, a), B = (\{a \rightarrow b\}, a \rightarrow b), C = (\{\neg b\}, \neg b), D = (\{a, a \rightarrow b\}, b), E = (\{\neg b, a \rightarrow b\}, \neg a), F = (\{a, \neg b\}, \neg(a \rightarrow b))\}$.
$Undercut = \{(D, C), (D, E), (D, F), (E, D), (E, A), (E, F), (F, E), (F, D), (F, B)\}$.
$weight(\{a\}) = weight(\{a \rightarrow b\}) = weight(\{\neg b\}) = 0$ *and* $weight(\{a, a \rightarrow b\}) = weight(\{\neg b, a \rightarrow b\}) = weight(\{a, \neg b\}) = 1$.
Three stable extensions can be computed: $S_1 = \{B, C, E\}$, $S_2 = \{A, B, D\}$, $S_3 = \{A, C, F\}$. $[Supp(S_1)] = [\{\neg b, a \rightarrow b\}] = \{\neg a, \neg b\} = \omega_3$, $[Supp(S_2)] = [\{a, a \rightarrow b\}] = \{a, b\} = \omega_0$, $[Supp(S_3)] = [\{a, \neg b\}] = \{a, \neg b\} = \omega_1$.

To capture the results of the merging operator Λ_2, we suppose that each base Σ_i is equipped with a weight (priority) α_i. The definition of a support weight is:

Definition 11. *Let H be a subset of Σ. $Weight(H) = \sum_{i=1}^{n} dist(H, \Sigma_i) \times \alpha_i$.*

This new definition of weight leads to a new preference relation denoted by $Pref_3$.

Proposition 6. *Let $S_1, \cdots, S_n$ be the stable extensions of the framework $\langle \mathcal{A}(\Sigma), Undercut, Pref_3 \rangle$.*

1. *$\forall S_i$, $Supp(S_i)$ is consistent.*
2. *$[Supp(S_1)], \cdots, [Supp(S_n)]$ are the models obtained by the merging operator Λ_2.*

Propositions 5 and 6 show that the approach developed in [12, 14, 13, 17] is captured by our preference-based argumentation framework too.

Overall, then, we can conclude that the approach outlined in this paper can capture a wide range of different approaches to merging information from inconsistent knowledge-bases.

4   Conclusions and Future Work

The work reported here concerns reasoning with conflicting knowledge-bases, that is knowledge bases which are mutually inconsistent in a classical sense. Our first main contribution is to propose a preference-based argumentation framework which resolves the conflicts. This approach is different from the ones existing in the literature. The existing approaches consist of first merging the various knowledge bases to obtain a unique one and then draw conslusions from the new base. In contrast, our approach allows arguments to be built from separate knowledge bases, and the arguments to then be merged. This method of obatining conclusions is much more practical in the context of multi-agent systems. The second contribution of this paper is to show that the preference-based argumentation framework we introduce is general enough to capture the results of some of the merging operators which have been developed. To cover the works proposed in [14] and [13], we have proposed two new preference relations between the arguments, relations which are based on Dalal's distance. Thus we can obtain all the advantages of the approaches for merging conflicting information, we can draw the same conclusions, but without having to actually construct the merged knowledge base. An extension of this work would be the study of the properties of the new preference relations. Another immediate extension would be to consider several inconsistent knowledge bases instead of consistent ones, thus we can develop a distributed argumentation framework. This looks likely to be very useful in multi-agent systems where each agent is supposed to have its own (consistent / inconsistent) knowledge base.

References

1. L. Amgoud and C. Cayrol. A reasoning model based on the production of acceptable arguments. In *Annals of Mathematics and Artificial Intelligence*, To appear in 2002.
2. L. Amgoud, N. Maudet, and S. Parsons. Modelling dialogues using argumentation. In *Proceedings of the International Conference on Multi-Agent Systems, ICMAS*, Boston, MA, 2000.
3. L. Amgoud and S. Parsons. An argumentation framework for reasoning with conflicting bases. In *Technical Report, Department of Electronic Engineering, Queen Mary and Westfield College*, 2000.
4. S. Benferhat, D. Dubois, and H. Prade. Argumentative inference in uncertain and inconsistent knowledge bases. In *Proceedings of the 9th Conference on Uncertainty in Artificial Intelligence*, pages 411–419, 1993.

5. C. Cayrol, V. Royer, and C. Saurel. Management of preferences in assumption-based reasoning. In *Lecture Notes in Computer Science (B. Bouchon-Meunier, L. Valverde, R.Y. Yager Eds.)*, 13-22, 1993.
6. C. Cayrol. On the relation between argumentation and non-monotonic coherence-based entailment. In *Proceedings of the 14th International Joint Conference on Artificial Intelligence*, pages 1443–1448, 1995.
7. C. I. Chesnevar, A. Maguitman, and R. P. Loui. Logical models of arguments. *ACM Computing Surveys*, 32(4):337–383, 2000.
8. L. Cholvy. A general framework for reasoning about contradictory information and some of its applications. In *Proceedings of the ECAI workshop*.
9. M. Dalal. Investigations into a theory of knowledge base revision: preliminary report. In *Proceedings of AAAI'88*, pages 475–479, 1988.
10. P. M. Dung. *On the acceptability of arguments and its fundamental role in non-monotonic reasoning, logic programming and n-person games*, volume 77.
11. M. Elvang-Goransson and A. Hunter. Argumentative logics: Reasoning with classically inconsistent information. In *Data and Knowledge Engineering*, volume 16.
12. S. Konieczny and R. Pino Perez. On the logic of merging. In *Proceedings of KR'98*, pages 488–498, 1998.
13. J. Lin and A. O. Mendelzon. *Merging databases under constraints*, volume 7.
14. J. Lin. *Integration of weighted knowledge bases*, volume 83.
15. H. Prakken and G. Vreeswijk. Logics for defeasible argumentation. *D. Gabbay (ed.), Handbook of Philosophical Logic, 2nd edition. Kluwer Academic Publishers, to appear*, 4, 2001.
16. N. Rescher and R. Manor. *On inference from inconsistent premises*, volume 1.
17. P. Z. Revescz. On the semantics of arbitration. international journal of algebra and computation. In *International journal of Algebra and Computation*, volume 7.

Multi-agent Logics of Dynamic Belief and Knowledge*

Renate A. Schmidt[1,2] and Dmitry Tishkovsky[1]

[1] Department of Computer Science, University of Manchester
{schmidt,dmitry}@cs.man.ac.uk
[2] Max-Planck-Institut für Informatik, Saarbrücken, Germany
schmidt@mpi-sb.mpg.de

Abstract. This paper proposes a family of logics for reasoning about the dynamic activities and informational attitudes, i.e. the beliefs and knowledge, of agents. The logics are based on a new formalisations and semantics of the test operator of propositional dynamic logic and a representation of actions which distinguishes abstract actions from concrete actions. The new test operator, called informational test, can be used to formalise the beliefs and knowledge of particular agents as dynamic modalities. This approach is consistent with the formalisation of the agents' beliefs and knowledge as *K(D)45* and *S5* modalities. Properties concerning the preservation of informativeness, truthfulness and belief are proved for a derivative of the informational test operator. It is shown that common belief and common knowledge can be expressed in these logics. As a consequence, these logics are more expressive than propositional dynamic logic with an extra modality for belief or knowledge. However, the logics are still decidable and in 2EXPTIME. Versions of the considered logics express natural additional properties of beliefs or knowledge and interaction of beliefs or knowledge with actions. A simulation of *PDL* is constructed in one of these extensions.

1 Introduction

It is accepted that multi-agent systems are important to many areas in computer science, starting from specifying and verifying multi-threading systems and multi-processor computers to modelling populations of robots which have animal or human-like behaviour (more applications of multi-agent systems can be found in e.g. [23]). In order to reason about agents appropriate mathematical tools must be developed. Logical methods are widely used for studying and formalising multi-agent systems. Modal logics, in particular, are often used for this purpose and offer a number of advantages [20,21]. In the landscape of agent systems among the more well-known agent formalisms with a modal flavour are the seminal combination of dynamic logic and epistemic logic by [16], the *BDI* model [17,18], the *KARO* framework [15,21], and temporal logics of knowledge

---

* We thank C. Dixon, M Fisher and U. Hustadt for valuable discussions. This research is supported by EPSRC Research Grants GR/M88761 and GR/R92035.

S. Flesca et al. (Eds.): JELIA 2002, LNAI 2424, pp. 38–50, 2002.

and belief [3,6,7]. Examples of more recent work is the proposal of a modal logic framework of belief and change in [12], and an epistemic dynamic logic in [10].

This paper is an investigation of actions and the informational attitudes, i.e. beliefs and knowledge, of agents. For reasoning about actions, a single agent framework is usually considered and then multiple copies of the framework are taken to formalise a multi-agent system. It is accepted that this approach has limitations and is generally not sufficient. For example, the approach does not allow the formalisation of the statement that 'if Michael does something then his brother Jerry does the same'. The key in this example is the implicit quantifier over the action 'does something'. It is easy to see that 'does something' and 'does the same' both stand for the same action. In a single agent framework the actions an agent can perform are fixed and, hence, disjoint copies of this framework will give us an independent set of actions for the different agents. This is not natural, because, for instance, both Michael and Jerry are able to eat, to sleep, etc. The action expressed by the verb 'to eat' is a general action which belongs to both agents Michael and Jerry. In the logic proposed in this paper the aim is to eliminate this independence. This is done by distinguishing between abstract and concrete actions. In our example, the verb 'to eat' is considered an abstract action, while 'Michael eats' is a concrete action.

Another idea proposed in this paper is an action of making the implicit informational attitudes (belief or knowledge) of an agent explicit, that is, we introduce an action of confirming belief or knowledge. The action of confirming belief (or knowledge) is modelled by a modified test operator, called *informational test*. The informational test operator was introduced in [19] as replacement for the standard test operator of propositional dynamic logic (*PDL*). Thus instead of having the rather strong capability of confirming all true properties in the current world, agents only have the capability of confirming formulae in their belief or knowledge states. It is not normal that agents have full awareness of the environment in which they operate, because usually, some parts of the environment are hidden from an agent. For example, due to some defect or an obstacle an agent may not be able to test whether a door is open or closed. However, if the agent's sensor has successfully tested the door, the agent's belief or knowledge state will be updated and now the agent can bring her belief/knowledge to the fore with the informational test operator. There are also logical reasons for not admitting the standard test operator of *PDL*. In [19] it was shown that the test operator interacts negatively with the epistemic *S5* modality in the axiomatic product of *PDL* and *S5*. In particular, the interaction of the dynamic modalities and the epistemic modality the commuting axioms of no learning and perfect recall (these axioms will be defined below) has the unwanted effect of eliminating the epistemic operator.

The structure of the paper is as follows. In Section 2 we define a logic, called *BDL*, as a basic semantical formalism. In particular, we define the language and a formal semantics. A finite axiomatisation of *BDL* is given in Section 3 and we describe a family of important extensions of *BDL* for which we prove the completeness, the small model property and decidability. We also construct a simulation of *PDL* in one of the extensions of *BDL*. In Section 4 we consider some useful properties of the informational test operator which it has in contrast to the standard test operator of *PDL*. Section 5 discusses the contributions of the paper and contains some remarks about further directions of research.

2   Language, Semantics and Expressiveness

Before we define the language and formal semantics we discuss from an informal point of view what we want to express in the language and which properties of real examples of multi-agent systems must be incorporated in the semantics.

First of all, we assume that a typical agent is active and intelligent. An example of an agent is a user of the Internet. Such a user is usually very active (at least, during her Internet session) and her requests are reasonable. (We do not speak about the IQ level or professional skills of an agent and determine her intelligence by her ability to make some logical reasoning and decisions.) Second, we work under the thesis that agents interact with each other, acting in some common environment. If there is no interaction between the agents then, obviously, a multi-agent system can be reduced to a single agent system. Continuing our example, all users of the web can interact with each other via protocols such as PPP, FTP, HTTP, SMTP, etc. Also, the common environment changes due to the agents' activities. The state of the web is changed simply by a file transfer using FTP and because of the quantity of such, or other, information transfers being done by large numbers of generally unpredictable users the web is changing unpredictably every fraction of a second. This requires the formal semantics to be a semantics of *states* and it must take account of the unpredictability of the agents behaviour, i.e. it must reflect a kind of *non-determinism* in the system.

As agents are active, they can perform some basic or *atomic actions* allowed in the system. For example, our Internet user can upload and download documents. Of course, these actions can be disassembled into more primitive actions like the instructions of a transfer protocol but we are not interested in such detail and will reason about actions *in general* in some abstract way.

Further, an agent has intelligence and is allowed to combine simple actions into complex ones, for example the action 'download a file from a site and then send it to an address' is the composition of two obvious actions. The actions which are allowed to be performed by *any* agent will be called *abstract actions*. We already know that they can be atomic or complex.

An abstract action is just a name for a real, *concrete action* which an agent can perform. Any concrete action is always associated with some agent because different agents can perform an (abstract) action in different ways. For example, one of the users of the web might use a standard web-browser to download a file, while another user might use telnet and her knowledge of a transfer protocol to get access to the same file. But from an abstract point of view users do the same action, only in different ways.

We want the agent herself to choose how to perform an action. This again is motivation for *non-deterministic* actions or alternative path execution. Nondeterminism actually means that we do not have complete information about the system behaviour or it is difficult to obtain or store such information. The web example is a case in point. Indeed, we cannot know a priori which user will connect to a server and what kind of requests she will make.

Another property which we aim to preserve is that concrete actions even if they are associated with different agents can be composed in complex blocks. This property is very helpful for describing the joint work of some group of agents, i.e. teamwork. For example, we want to be able to express the (concrete) action: 'agent 1 designs a database and then agent 2 implements the database'.

Finally, because agents are intelligent in some sense, they must have some *knowledge* or, at least, *beliefs* about the world. One can think about an agent's beliefs (knowledge) as some set of formulae in which the agent believes (or which the agent knows). Because agents act and 'learn' during their activity there must be some kind of interdependence between beliefs (knowledge) and actions. The paper introduces and investigates the idea that obtaining information about the agent's beliefs or knowledge is nothing other than a certain action inside the agent's mind. The agent's beliefs and knowledge are incorporated through a dynamic operator, called *informational test*. This operator confirms the belief (knowledge) of an agent as opposed to confirming the properties of the actual state as the classical test operator does in *PDL*.

The Language of BDL. The language of *BDL* has four disjoint sorts: the sort Ag for agents, the sort AA for abstract actions, the sort CA for concrete actions, and the sort For for formulae. Abstract actions can be atomic or complex. Concrete actions are abstract actions associated with some concrete agent. They can also be composed to form complex concrete actions, and the semantics of these actions must incorporate the non-deterministic nature of agents. As usual, formulae describe the properties of multi-agent systems.

The language $\mathcal{L}$ of the logic *BDL* is defined over a countable set Var $= \{p, q, r, \ldots\}$ of propositional variables, a countable set AtAA $= \{a, b, c, \ldots\}$ of *abstract atomic action* variables, and a countable set Ag $= \{i, j, k, \ldots\}$ of agent variables. The logical connectives include the classical connectives, $\rightarrow$ and $\bot$, the *informational test* operator ?, the standard *PDL* connectives on action formulae, $\cup$, ;, and $*$, and the dynamic modal operator $[\_]$ (box). Abstract actions, concrete actions and formulae are defined by simultaneous induction so that AA, CA and For are the smallest sets that satisfy the following conditions.

- AtAA $\subseteq$ AA, Var $\cup \{\bot\} \subseteq$ For.
- If $\phi \in$ For and $\alpha, \beta \in$ AA then $\phi?, \alpha^*, \alpha \cup \beta, \alpha;\beta \in$ AA.
- If $\alpha \in$ AA and $i \in$ Ag then $\alpha_i \in$ CA.
- If $\alpha, \beta \in$ CA then $\alpha^*, \alpha \cup \beta, \alpha;\beta \in$ CA.
- If $\phi, \psi \in$ For and $\alpha \in$ CA then $\phi \rightarrow \psi, [\alpha]\phi \in$ For.

The following are assumed to be defined formula connectives: $\neg, \top, \vee, \wedge, \leftrightarrow$. As usual $\langle \_ \rangle$ is the dual of $[\_]$, defined by $\langle \alpha \rangle \phi \leftrightarrow \neg[\alpha]\neg\phi$. We define the *belief* operator $\mathbf{B}_i$ as the modal operator $[(\top?)_i]$. The formula $\mathbf{B}_i p$ is read as 'agent i believes p'.

By a *logic* we understand any subset of the set For closed under the inference rules of modus ponens, generalisation and the substitution rule.

(Modus ponens) $\qquad\qquad\qquad\qquad\qquad \phi, \phi \to \psi \vdash \psi$

(Generalisation) $\qquad\qquad\qquad\qquad\qquad\quad \phi \vdash [\alpha]\phi$

(Here $\phi, \psi \in$ For and $\alpha \in$ CA.) If a formula belongs to a logic then the substitution rule specifies that all substitution instances belong to the logic. The substitution rule allows the uniform substitution of formulae for propositional variables, abstract actions for atomic abstract actions and agent variables for agent variables in the following sense.

Definition 1. *Assume x denotes an agent variable, a propositional variable, or an atomic abstract action in any formula ϕ. Let s denote any agent variable, respectively any formula or abstract action. A formula ψ is a* substitution instance *of ϕ under the substitution of s for x, written $\psi = \phi\{s/x\}$, if all occurrences of the variable x in ϕ are replaced by the term s in ψ.*

Definition 2. *Let a be an atomic abstract action. Suppose a does not occur in any complex abstract actions in the formula ϕ, and $a_{i_1}, \ldots, a_{i_n}$ are all the occurrences of a in ϕ. Suppose the agent variables $i_1, \ldots, i_n$ do not occur anywhere else in ϕ except in $a_{i_1}, \ldots, a_{i_n}$. Let j be a distinguished agent variable in a concrete action α. A formula ψ is a* substitution instance *of ϕ under the substitution α for a_j, written $\psi = \phi\{\alpha/a_j\}$, if all occurrences of $a_{i_1}, \ldots, a_{i_n}$ of the term a in ϕ are respectively replaced by the occurrences of $\alpha\{i_1/j\}, \ldots, \alpha\{i_n/j\}$ in ψ.*

Examples of legal substitutions for an atomic action variable are:

$$([a_i]\mathbf{B}_i p \to \mathbf{B}_i[a_i]p)\{(b;c)/a\} = [(b;c)_i]\mathbf{B}_i p \to \mathbf{B}_i[(b;c)_i]p$$
$$([(a_i)^*]p \to [a_i][(a_i)^*]p)\{(b_j;c_k)/a_j\} = [(b_i;c_k)^*]p \to [b_i;c_k][(b_i;c_k)^*]p$$

In the first example, an abstract action is substituted for an atomic abstract action. The second example shows, we can substitute for a_j if occurrences of a_i do not bind any other actions via agent i. The following is illegal, because a_i is bounded through i with $\mathbf{B}_i$.

$$([a_i]\mathbf{B}_i p \to \mathbf{B}_i[a_i]p)\{(b_j;c_k)/a_j\} = [b_i;c_k]\mathbf{B}_i p \to \mathbf{B}_i[b_i;c_k]p$$

Remark 1. According to the substitution rule each formula of the logic is true independently from the values of propositional variables, atomic actions and agents. This means, the substitution rule permits reasoning about *the most general* properties of agent systems in a uniform way. More specifically, any formula of a logic is true if and only if the universal closure of the formula over all propositional variables, abstract atomic actions and agents is true in the logic.

For any two sets of formulae Γ and Δ, $\Gamma \oplus \Delta$ denotes the least logic which contains both Γ and Δ.

By definition, the logic *BDL* is the set of formulae valid in all *BDL* models, which are defined next.

Semantics. A *BDL model* is a tuple $M = \langle S, Q, R, \models \rangle$ of a non-empty set S of states, a mapping Q which associates with each concrete action α a binary relation $Q(\alpha)$, a mapping R from the set of agents into the set of transitive and Euclidean relations over S, and $\models$ is the truth relation. Any model must satisfy the following ten conditions. The usual conditions on Q for any *concrete* actions α and β:

(M1) $Q(\alpha \cup \beta) = Q(\alpha) \cup Q(\beta)$
(M2) $Q(\alpha; \beta) = Q(\alpha) \circ Q(\beta)$
(M3) $Q((\alpha)^*) = (Q(\alpha))^*$

Here $\circ$ denotes relational composition and $*$ is the reflexive transitive closure operator. The conditions which link the concrete actions with abstract actions, for any *abstract* actions α, β and agent i:

(M4) $Q((\alpha \cup \beta)_i) = Q(\alpha_i \cup \beta_i)$
(M5) $Q((\alpha; \beta)_i) = Q(\alpha_i; \beta_i)$
(M6) $Q((\alpha^*)_i) = Q((\alpha_i)^*)$

The standard conditions on the truth relation must be true, where s denotes any state, ϕ and ψ are arbitrary formulae and α is any *concrete* action:

(M7) $M, s \not\models \bot$
(M8) $M, s \models \phi \to \psi \iff M, s \models \phi \Rightarrow M, s \models \psi$
(M9) $M, s \models [\alpha]\phi \iff \forall t\, ((s, t) \in Q(\alpha) \Rightarrow M, t \models \phi)$

And the semantics of the informational test operator is given by:

(M10) $Q((\phi?)_i) = \{(s, t) \in R_i \mid \forall u\, ((t, u) \in R_i \Rightarrow M, u \models \phi)\}$.

(In this paper, we write R_i instead of $R(i)$.) Intuitively $p?$ is an action which can be successfully accomplished only if agent has p as one of her *beliefs* in the current state. Thus, $p?$ is the action of confirming the agent's own beliefs. This is in contrast to the interpretation of the classical test operator in *PDL*. The classical test operator gives the agent the (rather strong) capability of confirming the universal truth of any formulae, rather than just confirming own beliefs.

A formula ϕ is said to be *valid* in a state s of a model M if $M, s \models \phi$, and ϕ is *valid* in M if it is valid in all states of the model.

Informally, a model is a set of states of some multi-agent system. Each state is characterised by the set of properties of the multi-agent system which hold in the state and is represented by a set of formulae. The truth relation of a model assigns such a set of properties to any state. Each action is interpreted as a set of transitions between the states, roughly speaking, a set of arrows which connect the states. Every arrow describes one possible way of executing the action. Thus, any Kripke model is a multi-agent system represented on some level of abstraction. Of course, one can propose other levels of abstraction and detailisations of multi-agent systems, and each of them will have it's own notion of a model, for instance, interpreted systems [7], Aumann structures [3], hypercubes [14], general Kripke models and algebras [24].

What Is the Expressiveness of the Logic Just Defined? Trivially, *PDL* without the (classical) test operator is a sublogic of *BDL*. Consequently, it is possible to reason about simple programs inside *BDL*. To give us the capability to reason about any programs a minimal reinforcement is used in the next section (Theorem 5).

It is possible to show that *BDL* is more expressive than formalisms given by the combination of multiple copies of *PDL* with belief operators. For example, in such logics the notion of common belief cannot be expressed. In *BDL* common belief can be defined as follows. Let I be a finite set of agents, i.e. $I = \{i_0, \ldots, i_m\} \subseteq \mathrm{Ag}$. The operator 'every agent in I believes that $\ldots$', denoted by $\mathbf{E}_I$, is defined by the formula $\mathbf{E}_I p \leftrightarrow [(\top?)_{i_0} \cup \cdots \cup (\top?)_{i_m}]p$. The operator $\mathbf{C}_I$ of common belief among the agents in I can then be defined by: $\mathbf{C}_I p \leftrightarrow [((\top?)_{i_0} \cup \cdots \cup (\top?)_{i_m})^*]\mathbf{E}_I p$. That is, common belief is actually the transitive closure of everyone believes.

3 Axiomatisation, Decidability and Complexity

A Hilbert-style axiomatisation of *BDL* is given by the following set of axioms and the previously defined inference rules of modus ponens, generalisation and substitution.

(A1) Axioms of classical propositional logic
(A2) *PDL*-like axioms for test-free actions:
    (A2.1) $[a_i](p \rightarrow q) \rightarrow ([a_i]p \rightarrow [a_i]q)$
    (A2.2) $[a_i \cup b_j]p \leftrightarrow [a_i]p \wedge [b_j]p$
    (A2.3) $[a_i;b_j]p \leftrightarrow [a_i][b_j]p$
    (A2.4) $[(a_i)^*]p \rightarrow p \wedge [a_i]p$
    (A2.5) $[(a_i)^*]p \rightarrow [a_i][(a_i)^*]p$
    (A2.6) $p \wedge [(a_i)^*](p \rightarrow [a_i]p) \rightarrow [(a_i)^*]p$
(A3) *K45* axioms for the belief operators:
    (A3.1) $\mathbf{B}_i p \rightarrow \mathbf{B}_i \mathbf{B}_i p$
    (A3.2) $\neg \mathbf{B}_i p \rightarrow \mathbf{B}_i \neg \mathbf{B}_i p$
(A4) Axioms of correspondence between abstract and concrete actions:
    (A4.1) $[(a \cup b)_i]p \leftrightarrow [a_i \cup b_i]p$
    (A4.2) $[(a;b)_i]p \leftrightarrow [a_i;b_i]p$
    (A4.3) $[(a^*)_i]p \leftrightarrow [(a_i)^*]p$
(A5) An axiom for the informational test operator:
    (A5.1) $[(p?)_i]q \leftrightarrow \mathbf{B}_i(\mathbf{B}_i p \rightarrow q)$

Remark 2. Because the substitution rule is one of the inference rules it follows in this axiomatic system that, for example, $[(\alpha)^*]\phi \rightarrow \phi \wedge [\alpha]\phi$ is true for all concrete actions α and any formula ϕ, i.e. it is the generalisation the axiom (A2.4). Similarly, for all other axioms.

It is easy to check that the proposed axiomatic system is sound with respect to all *BDL* models. The proof of completeness is omitted due to lack of space.

Theorem 1 (Completeness). *The above axiomatic system is complete with respect to the class of all BDL models.*

Useful Extensions of BDL. In some examples of the multi-agent systems, the agents have more intelligence than we have put into *BDL*. Fagin, Halpern and Moses [3] give numerous examples of reasonable extra properties of the agents' beliefs. We consider here two important properties.

Very often a property is required that the agent's beliefs adequately reflect the properties of the system, that is, the agent's beliefs actually become knowledge in this case. In order to accommodate this extra intelligence of agents we need to add the following axiom to *BDL*:

$$(T) \qquad\qquad\qquad\qquad \mathbf{B}_i p \rightarrow p.$$

Then $\mathbf{B}_i$ is an *S5* modality and represents the knowledge operator.

Another natural requirement is the consistency of the agents' beliefs. For instance, local copies of the database from a server must be consistent. This property can be formulated by an additional axiom for *BDL* [3].

$$(D) \qquad\qquad\qquad\qquad \mathbf{B}_i p \rightarrow \neg \mathbf{B}_i \neg p.$$

In modelling intelligent agents a key concern is the connection between informational attitudes and action. The most well-known and natural connection between informational attitudes and action are the properties of no learning and prefect recall (see e.g. [10,20]). No learning is commonly formulated by the axiom schema

$$(NL) \qquad\qquad\qquad [a_i]\mathbf{B}_i p \rightarrow \mathbf{B}_i[a_i]p,$$

where $\mathbf{B}_i$ normally represents an epistemic operator. The axiom schema says that agent i knows the result of her action in advance; in other words, there is no learning. Perfect recall, also called accordance, is commonly formulated by the axiom schema

$$(PR) \qquad\qquad\qquad \mathbf{B}_i[a_i]p \rightarrow [a_i]\mathbf{B}_i p.$$

It expresses the persistence of the agent's knowledge (sometimes belief) after the execution of an action.

Note 1. It should be noted that the axiom schema *PR* together with *D* has a counterintuitive meaning when p in *PR* is substituted with falsum [9]. In this case the reading of *PR* is: 'If the agent believes she cannot perform an action then she cannot perform this action at all'. This shows that *PR* combined with *D* in *BDL* is quite a strong logic. However, weaker versions of *PR* can be considered to avoid this unwanted property [9].

We consider the following properties on models.

(eq) $\forall i\, R_i$ is an equivalence relation

(br) $\forall i \forall s \exists t\, (s,t) \in R_i$

(com^l) $\forall i \forall \alpha\, (R_i \circ Q(\alpha_i) \subseteq Q(\alpha_i) \circ R_i)$

(com^r) $\forall i \forall \alpha\, (Q(\alpha_i) \circ R_i \subseteq R_i \circ Q(\alpha_i))$

Main Results. The main results in this paper are the following. The proofs use well-known methods of modal and dynamic logic [7,3,5,4], but require non-trivial modifications due to the presence of the new informational test operator.

Theorem 2 (Completeness). *Let L be an extension of BDL by any combination of the axioms T, D, NL, and PR. Then L is complete with respect to the class of all models restricted by the corresponding combinations of the properties (eq), (br), (com^r), and (com^l).*

Theorem 3 (Small Model Theorem). *Let ϕ be an arbitrary formula. Suppose n is the number of symbols in ϕ, and m is the number of different agents associated with some test actions in ϕ. If ϕ is satisfiable in a model with (or without) the properties from the list (eq), (br), (com^r), and (com^l), then ϕ is satisfiable in a (finite) model satisfying the same properties but which has no more than $2^n \cdot (2^{2^n})^m$ states.*

Theorem 4 (Decidability and Complexity). *The satisfiability problem in all extensions of BDL by all possible combinations of axioms T, D, NL, and PR, and in BDL itself, is EXPTIME-hard and decidable in 2EXPTIME.*

Note 2. If we do not consider NL and PR then it is possible to prove the above theorems even without the requirement that the relations R_i are transitive and Euclidean. In other words, the theorems are still true for the logic without axioms (A3). More precisely, let ϕ is an axiom which (i) contains $\mathbf{B}_i$ as the only modal operators, and (ii) has a corresponding first-order frame property P for the relations R_i and P is persistent under the least filtration. Then the axiomatic system, which consists of the axioms (A1), (A2), (A4), (A5) and ϕ as an extra axiom, is (sound and) complete with respect to the class of models with the property P, has the small model property and is decidable in the sense of Theorems 3 and 4.

The axiom schemas NL and PR should be used with care, since decidability is easily lost. If the condition on actions in Definition 2 that binds actions to the same agent is omitted, then schemas of the form $\mathbf{B}_i\mathbf{B}_jp \to \mathbf{B}_j\mathbf{B}_ip$ are valid. As a consequence, the logic has the axiomatic product of several copies of S5 embedded in it. It then follows from results in [13] that the logic with T, NL and PR becomes undecidable if there are more than two agents.

Now we define a simulation of (full-test) *PDL* in $BDL \oplus T$. This proves that despite the absence of the standard test operator it is possible to reason about while programs in the logic *BDL*. Select an agent, agent i say, and define a mapping σ from formulae of *PDL* to For by the following.

$$
\begin{array}{lll}
\sigma p = \mathbf{B}_ip & \sigma\bot = \bot & \sigma a = a_i \\
\sigma(\psi?) = ((\sigma\psi)?)_i & \sigma(\alpha \cup \beta) = \sigma\alpha \cup \sigma\beta & \sigma(\alpha;\beta) = \sigma\alpha;\sigma\beta \\
\sigma(\alpha^*) = (\sigma\alpha)^* & \sigma(\phi \to \psi) = \mathbf{B}_i(\sigma\phi \to \sigma\psi) & \sigma([\alpha]\psi) = \mathbf{B}_i[\sigma\alpha]\sigma\psi
\end{array}
$$

The following theorem shows that the translation σ preserves truth of formulae in both directions.

Theorem 5. *For any PDL-formula ϕ, $\phi \in PDL$ iff $\sigma\phi \in BDL \oplus T$.*

4 Properties of Informational Test

In this section we show the informational test operator has properties which are generally regarded as good [22].

One of the most important features of a test operation is the fact that it confirms the agent's beliefs. For example, a student has been preparing for an examination and done this thoroughly. But she is not certain yet whether she is prepared really well. As a good student she tests herself on some mock examination exercises. Does this testing add something to her belief? The answer is no, because her beliefs were formed during her preparation. She already believed that she has prepared well and the action of the pre-examination just confirms her beliefs. Thus, the action of examination (testing) can be regarded as making the agent's implicit beliefs explicit. In this respect, we prove that the action of confirming a formula together with the action of confirming the negation of the formula can provide belief (knowledge) for an agent, i.e. following [22], this combined action is an *informative* action. Like [11] we call any action of confirming a formula and its negation an *alternative test*.

Another desirable feature of alternative test is the fact that the truth or falsity of the formula that is tested should not be affected by the actual act of testing, i.e. the outcome of the alternative test should correspond to the state in which the test is performed. This characteristic of alternative tests is called *truthfulness* [22]. In our example, it means that if the student is prepared well and knows a lot about the subject of the examination then she remains well-prepared after the examination.

We also consider the property of *minimal change* for alternative test [22]. This property states that an alternative test must not add or remove formulae from the belief set of an agent which are not relevant to the action of testing. It means that, if the student believed before the examination on a topic of mathematics that Sydney is a city in Australia then after the examination she believes that Sydney is still a city in Australia.

Definition 3. *(i) An abstract action α is informative with respect to a formula ϕ in a logic L, if the formula $[\alpha_i](\mathbf{B}_i\phi \vee \mathbf{B}_i\neg\phi)$ belongs to L. (ii) An action α is strongly informative with respect to ϕ in L, if α is informative with respect to ϕ in L and the formula $\langle\alpha_i\rangle(\mathbf{B}_i\phi \vee \mathbf{B}_i\neg\phi)$ belongs to L.*

Definition 4. *(i) An abstract action α is truthful with respect to a formula ϕ in a logic L, if the formula $(\phi \rightarrow [\alpha_i]\phi) \wedge (\neg\phi \rightarrow [\alpha_i]\neg\phi)$ belongs to L. (ii) An action α is strongly truthful with respect to ϕ in L, if α is truthful with respect to ϕ in L and the formula $(\phi \rightarrow \langle\alpha_i\rangle\phi) \wedge (\neg\phi \rightarrow \langle\alpha_i\rangle\neg\phi)$ belongs to L.*

Definition 5. *An abstract action α preserves beliefs in logic L, if the formula $\mathbf{B}_i\phi \rightarrow [\alpha_i]\mathbf{B}_i\phi$ belongs to L for any formula ϕ.*

Proposition 1. *(i)* $[(p?)_i]\mathbf{B}_i p, [(p? \cup \neg p?)_i](\mathbf{B}_i p \vee \mathbf{B}_i \neg p) \in BDL$. *(ii) For any formula* ϕ, $\langle (p? \cup \neg p?)_i \rangle \phi \notin BDL$. *(iii)* $p \rightarrow [(p? \cup \neg p?)_i]p \in BDL \oplus T$.

Theorem 6. *(i) The action* $p? \cup \neg p?$ *is informative with respect to* p *but not strongly informative with respect to any formula in BDL. (ii) The action* $p? \cup \neg p?$ *is truthful but not strongly truthful with respect to* p *in the logic BDL* $\oplus$ *T of knowledge. (iii) The action* $p? \cup \neg p?$ *preserves beliefs in BDL.*

5 Conclusion

The paper proposed a multi-agent logic *BDL* and extensions for reasoning about the actions agents can perform and their informational attitudes. In this paper we focused on belief given by *K45* or *KD45* modalities and knowledge given by *S5* modalities. *BDL* logics provide an abstract way of reasoning about multi-agent systems and provide a basis for the reasoning about multi-agent systems. Many other agent logics which pretend to be real multi-agent logics (for reasoning about actions and beliefs or knowledge) can be represented as extensions of *BDL*. Some axiomatic extensions frequently considered were studied in this paper and results of soundness, completeness, decidability and the finite model property were proved. It turned out that Sahlqvist correspondence [1] does not completely work for *BDL* but nevertheless we could prove the expected model properties for the axioms of permutability of the informational modalities and action modalities (perfect recall and no learning). These extensions of *BDL* are therefore closely related to the products of logics [5]. It was shown in [5] that, usually, results on decidability is hard to obtain for the products and some advanced techniques must be developed for each particular instance. Nevertheless, the decidability for such extensions of *BDL* was shown in this paper. For further work, it would be interesting to find in the framework of *BDL* an appropriate axiomatisation of logics of interpreted systems, hypercubes and full systems as it was done in [14] for reasoning about knowledge and also investigate the decidability of these logics.

The language of the logic *BDL* is very expressive. It is more expressive than *PDL*, and *BDL* $\oplus$ *T* is more expressive than known logics of common knowledge. It is therefore surprising that the complexity of the logic does not increase too much. The expressiveness is mainly achieved by introducing dynamics into agent beliefs which is incorporated via the new informational test operator. It was proved that this operator has many advantages in comparison to the usual test operator of *PDL*. The distinction between abstract and concrete actions is also crucial. This property makes it possible to reason about groups of agents rather than just about single agents, i.e. is suitable to express cooperation between agents and teamwork [2]. In this respect, some operators on the set of agents, for instance, an operator of grouping of agents and a pipeline operator (i.e. an operator which forms a sequence of agents), can also be added to represent some kinds of cooperation inside groups of agents. It seems that such operators will not considerably increase the expressivity of the language but can represent some properties of multi-agent systems in more compact notation (very similar to what quantifiers do in quantified Boolean logic with respect to Boolean logic). The decidability of such extended logic needs careful further investigation. Another way to enhance the logic is to add quantifiers over agents. This could lead to undecidability, though it may be hard to prove (the decidability or undecidability of this logic).

References

1. P. Blackburn, M. de Rijke, and Y. Venema. *Modal Logic*. Cambridge Univ. Press, 2001.
2. P. R. Cohen and H. J. Levesque. Teamwork. *Noûs*, 25(4):487–512, 1991.
3. R. Fagin, J. Y. Halpern, Y. Moses, and M. Y. Vardi. *Reasoning about knowledge*. MIT Press, 1995.
4. M. J. Fischer and R. E. Ladner. Propositional dynamic logic of regular programs. *J. Comput. Syst. Sci.*, 18(2):194–211, 1979.
5. D. Gabbay and V. Shehtman. Products of modal logics, part 1. *Logic J. IGPL*, 6(1):73–146, 1998.
6. J. Y. Halpern and Y. Moses. A guide to completeness and complexity for modal logics of knowledge and belief. *Artificial Intelligence*, 54:319–379, 1992.
7. J. Y. Halpern and M. Y. Vardi. The complexity of reasoning about knowledge and time. I Lower bounds. *J. Computer and System Sci.*, 38:195–237, 1989.
8. D. Harel, D. Kozen, and J. Tiuryn. *Dynamic Logic*. MIT Press, 2000.
9. A. Herzig, 2002. Personal communication.
10. A. Herzig, J. Lang, D. Longin, and T. Polacsek. A logic for planning under partial observability. In *Proc. AAAI'2000*, pp. 768–773. AAAI Press/MIT Press, 2000.
11. A. Herzig, J. Lang, and T. Polacsek. A modal logic for epistemic tests. In *Proc. ECAI'2000*, Berlin, 2000. IOS Press.
12. A. Herzig and D. Longin. Belief dynamics in cooperative dialogues. *J. Semantics*, 17(2), 2000.
13. M. Kracht. Highway to the danger zone. *J. Logic Computat.*, 5(1):93–109, 1995.
14. A. R. Lomiscio, R. van der Meyden, and M. Ryan. Knowledge in multi-agent systems: Initial configurations and broadcast. *ACM Trans. Computational Logic*, 1(2):247–284, 2000.
15. J.-J. C. Meyer, W. van der Hoek, and B. van Linder. A logical approach to the dynamics of commitments. *Artificial Intelligence*, 113(1–2):1–40, 1999.
16. R. C. Moore. A formal theory of knowledge and action. In J. R. Hobbs and R. C. Moore, editors, *Formal Theories of the Commonsense World*. Ablex, 1985.
17. A. S. Rao. Decision procedures for propositional linear-time belief-desire-intention logics. In *Proc. ATAL'95*, vol. 1037 of *LNAI*, pp. 102–118. Springer, 1996.
18. A. S. Rao and M. P. Georgeff. Modeling rational agents within a BDI-architecture. In *Proc. KR'91*, pp. 473–484. Morgan Kaufmann, 1991.
19. R. A. Schmidt and D. Tishkovsky. On Axiomatic Products of PDL and S5: Substitution, Tests and Knowledge. *Bull. the Section of Logic*, 31(1):27–36, 2002.
20. W. van der Hoek. Logical foundations of agent-based computing. In *Multi-Agent Systems and Applications*, vol. 2086 of *LNAI*, pp. 50–73. Springer, 2001.
21. B. van Linder, W. van der Hoek, and J.-J. C. Meyer. Formalizing abilities and opportunities of agents. *Fundamenta Informaticae*, 34(1, 2):53–101, 1998.
22. B. van Linder, W. van der Hoek, and J.-J.Ch. Meyer. Tests as epistemic updates. In *Proc. ECAI'94*, pp. 331–335. John Wiley & Sons, 1994.
23. M. Wooldridge. Agent-based computing. *Interoperable Comm. Networks*, 1(1):71–97, 1998.
24. M. Zakharyaschev, F. Wolter, and A. Chagrov. *Advanced Modal Logic*. Kluwer, 1998.

Evolving Logic Programs

José Júlio Alferes[1], Antonio Brogi[2],
João Alexandre Leite[1], and Luís Moniz Pereira[1]

[1] CENTRIA, Universidade Nova de Lisboa, Portugal
[2] Dipartimento di Informatica, Università di Pisa, Italy

Abstract. Logic programming has often been considered less than adequate for modelling the dynamics of knowledge changing over time. In this paper we describe a simple though quite powerful approach to modelling the updates of knowledge bases expressed by generalized logic programs, by means of a new language, hereby christened EVOLP (after *EVOl*ving *Logic Programs*). The approach was first sparked by a critical analysis of previous efforts and results in this direction [1,2,7,11], and aims to provide a simpler, and at once more general, formulation of logic program updating, which runs closer to traditional logic programming (LP) doctrine. From the syntactical point of view, evolving programs are just generalized logic programs (i.e. normal LPs plus default negation also in rule heads), extended with (possibly nested) assertions, whether in heads or bodies of rules. From the semantics viewpoint, a model-theoretic characterization is offered of the possible evolutions of such programs. These evolutions arise both from self (or internal) updating, and from external updating too, originating in the environment. This formulation sets evolving programs on a firm basis in which to express, implement, and reason about dynamic knowledge bases, and opens up a number of interesting research topics that we brush on.

1 Introduction

Until recently, LP has often been considered less than adequate for modelling the dynamics of knowledge changing over time. To overcome this limitation, languages like LUPS [2] and EPI [7] have been defined. For this purpose, LUPS provides several types of update commands: **assert**, **retract**, **always**, **cancel**, **assert event**, **retract event** and **always event**, all of which having a rule as argument. Such commands can be made conditional on the current state, the conditions being preceded by the keyword **when**. An example of a LUPS command is: **always** $L \leftarrow L_1, \ldots, L_k$ **when** $L_{k+1}, \ldots, L_m$, meaning that, from the moment it is given onwards, whenever all of $L_{k+1}, \ldots, L_m$ are true, the knowledge base should be updated with the rule $L \leftarrow L_1, \ldots, L_k$. A declarative, as well as a procedural semantics for sequences of sets of commands is defined in [2], where its application to several areas is illustrated. EPI [7] proposes two additional main features, both achieved by extensions of LUPS commands: to allow for the specification of commands whose execution depends on the concurrent execution of other commands; and to allow for external events to condition the evolution of the knowledge base.

S. Flesca et al. (Eds.): JELIA 2002, LNAI 2424, pp. 50–62, 2002.

Both these languages, a bit against the spirit of LP (which, in pure programs, has no keywords), are too verbose. Their verbosity makes them complex, difficult to use, and to prove program properties. Moreover, each keyword encodes a high-level behaviour for the addition of rules. And this constitutes a problem in case one wants to describe a different, unforeseen, high-level behaviour. For instance, one may want: to make the addition of a command dependent upon conditions that may span more than one state; to model changes to update commands themselves; etc. None of these high-level behaviours are achievable by LUPS or EPI commands. Of course, one could further extend these languages. Not only would this make them more and more complex, but also some yet unforeseen but desirable commands would certainly be still missing. We took the opposite approach: instead of extending these languages with new commands, we analyzed what is basic in them, what they offer that is new compared to classical LP, and then minimally add constructs to LP to account for the new capabilities of evolution and updating. The resulting language, EVOLP, provides a simpler, and at once more general, formulation of logic program updating, which runs closer to traditional LP doctrine.

EVOLP generalizes LP to allow specification of a program's own evolution, in a single unified way, by permitting rules to indicate assertive conclusions in the form of program rules. Such assertions, whenever they belong to a model of the program P, can be employed to generate an updated version of P. This process can then be iterated on the basis of the new program. When the program semantics affords several program models, branching evolution will occur and several evolution sequences are possible. Branching can be used to specify incomplete information about a situation. The ability of EVOLP to nest rule assertions within assertions allows rule updates to be themselves updated down the line, conditional on each evolution strand. The ability to include assertive literals in rule bodies allows for looking ahead on program changes and acting on that knowledge before the changes take place.

The ensuing notion of self evolving programs is more basic than the subsequent elaboration of general evolving programs, those that also permit, besides internal or self updates, for updates arising from the outside. So first we define a language of programs able to express changes to its very programs, and study how programs may evolve by themselves. Only afterwards do we analyze and define extensions that cater for the interference from external updates.

The proposed formulation sets EVOLP on a firm formal basis in which to express, implement, and reason about dynamic knowledge bases, and opens up a number of interesting research topics that we brush on. As a consequence of the richness of the new paradigm, our emphasis in this paper will be much more on the appealingness of its foundational precepts and scaffolding, than on exploring specific properties, as these require constraining the general core setting with distinctive further options. Accordingly, in the next two sections we formally define the syntax and semantics of EVOLP. Then we present examples of usage. We end with a section on discussion, brief comparisons with related work, open issues, and themes of future work.

2 Self-evolving Logic Programs

What is required to let logic programs evolve by themselves? To start with, one needs some form of negation in heads of rules, so as to let older rules to be supervened by more recent ones updating them, and thus admit non-monotonicity of rules. Second, one needs a means to state that, under some conditions, some new rule or other is to be added to the program.

Accordingly, for the syntax of EVOLP we simply adopt that of generalized LPs augmented with the reserved predicate $assert/1$, whether as the rule head or in its body, whose sole argument is itself a full-blown rule, so that arbitrary nesting becomes possible. Formally:

Definition 1. *Let $\mathcal{L}$ be any propositional language (not containing the predicate $assert/1$). The extended language $\mathcal{L}_{assert}$ is defined inductively as follows:*

1. *All propositional atoms in $\mathcal{L}$ are propositional atoms in $\mathcal{L}_{assert}$.*
2. *If each of $L_0, \ldots, L_n$ is a literal in $\mathcal{L}_{assert}$ (i.e. a propositional atom A or its default negation not A), then $L_0 \leftarrow L_1, \ldots, L_n$ is a generalized logic program rule over $\mathcal{L}_{assert}$.*
3. *If R is a rule over $\mathcal{L}_{assert}$ then $assert(R)$ is a propositional atom of $\mathcal{L}_{assert}$.*
4. *Nothing else is a propositional atom in $\mathcal{L}_{assert}$.*

An *evolving logic program over a language $\mathcal{L}$ is a (possibly infinite) set of generalized logic program rules over $\mathcal{L}_{assert}$.*

We decided not to include an explicit retract construct in the basic language. Indeed, as we have default negation available also in rule heads, retraction of rules can be encoded in EVOLP. This encoding is, however, left out of this paper.

Self-evolving programs can update their own rules and exhibit a dynamic, non-monotonic behaviour. Their meaning is given by a set of *evolution stable models*, each of which is a sequence of interpretations or states. The basic idea is that each evolution stable model describes some possible self-evolution of one initial program after a given number n of evolution steps. Each self-evolution is represented by a sequence of programs, each program corresponding to a state.

The sequences of programs are treated as in Dynamic Logic Programs (DLP) [1], where the most recent rules are put in force, and the previous rules are valid (by inertia) as far as possible, i.e. they are kept for as long as they do not conflict with more recent ones. In DLP, default negation is treated as in stable models of normal [8] and generalized programs [12]. Formally, a *dynamic logic program* is a sequence $P_1 \oplus \ldots \oplus P_n$ (also denoted $\bigoplus \mathcal{P}$, where $\mathcal{P}$ is a set of generalized logic programs indexed by $1, \ldots, n$), and its semantic is determined by[1]:

Definition 2. *Let $\bigoplus \{P_i : i \in S\}$ be a dynamic logic program over language $\mathcal{L}$, let $s \in S$, and let M be a set of propositional atoms of $\mathcal{L}$. Then:*

$$Default_s(M) = \{not\ A \leftarrow .\ |\ \nexists A \leftarrow Body \in P_i (1 \leq i \leq s) : M \models Body\}$$
$$Reject_s(M) = \{L_0 \leftarrow Body \in P_i\ |\ \exists\ not\ L_0 \leftarrow Body' \in P_j, i < j \leq s \land$$
$$M \models Body'\}$$

---

[1] For more details, the reader is referred to [1].

*where A is an atom, not L_0 denotes the complement w.r.t. default negation of
the literal L_0, and both Body and Body' are conjunctions of literals.*

Definition 3. *Let $\mathcal{P} = \bigoplus\{P_i : i \in S\}$ be a dynamic logic program over language
$\mathcal{L}$. A set M of propositional atoms of $\mathcal{L}$ is a stable model of $\mathcal{P}$ at state $s \in S$ iff:*

$$M' = least\left(\left[\bigcup_{i \leq s} P_i - Reject_s(M)\right] \cup Defaults_s(M)\right)$$

*where $M' = M \cup \{not\_A \mid A \notin M\}$, and least(.) denotes the least model of the
definite program obtained from the argument program by replacing every default
negated literal not A by a new atom not_A.*

The primordial intuitions for the construction of the program sequences are
as follows: regarding head asserts, whenever the atom *assert(Rule)* belongs to
an interpretation in a sequence, i.e. belongs to a model according to the stable
model semantics (SM) of the current program, then *Rule* must belong to the
program in the next state; asserts in bodies are treated as any other predicate
literals. Before presenting the definitions that formalize these intuitions, let us
show an illustrative example. Consider the self-evolving program *P*:

$$a \leftarrow . \quad assert(b \leftarrow a) \leftarrow not\,c. \quad assert(not\,a \leftarrow) \leftarrow b. \quad c \leftarrow assert(not\,a \leftarrow).$$

The (only) stable model of *P* is $I = \{a, assert(b \leftarrow a)\}$ and it conveys the
information that program *P* is ready to evolve into a new program $P \oplus P_2$ by
adding rule $(b \leftarrow a)$ at the next step, i.e. in P_2. In the only stable model I_2 of
the new program $P \oplus P_2$, atom *b* is true as well as atom *assert(not a $\leftarrow$)* and
also *c*, meaning that $P \oplus P_2$ is ready to evolve into a new program $P \oplus P_2 \oplus P_3$
by adding rule *(not a $\leftarrow$)* at the next step, i.e. in P_3. Now, the (negative) fact in
P_3 conflicts with the fact in *P*, and so this older fact is rejected. The rule added
in P_2 remains valid, but is no longer useful to conclude *b*, since *a* is no longer
valid. Thus, *assert(not a $\leftarrow$)* as well as *c* are also no longer true. In the only
stable model of the last sequence both *a*, *b* and *c* are false.

Definition 4. *An evolution interpretation of length n of an evolving program
P over $\mathcal{L}$ is a finite sequence $\mathcal{I} = \langle I_1, I_2, \ldots, I_n \rangle$ of sets of propositional atoms
of $\mathcal{L}_{assert}$. The evolution trace associated with an evolution interpretation $\mathcal{I}$ is
the sequence of programs $\langle P_1, P_2, \ldots, P_n \rangle$ where:*

$$P_1 = P, \text{ and } P_i = \{R \mid assert(R) \in I_{i-1}\}, \text{ for each } 2 \leq i \leq n.$$

Definition 5. *Let $M = \langle I_1, I_2, \ldots, I_n \rangle$ be an evolution interpretation of an
evolving logic program P, and let $\langle P_1, P_2, \ldots, P_n \rangle$ be its evolution trace. M is
an Evolution Stable Model of P iff for every i $(1 \leq i \leq n)$, I_i is a stable model
at i of the DLP: $P_1 \oplus P_2 \oplus \ldots \oplus P_i$.*

Being stable models based, it is clear that a self-evolving program may have
various evolution models of a given length, as well as no evolution stable models at all. We say that a self-evolving program is inconsistent when it has no

evolution stable models of any length, and that it is inconsistent after n-steps if it has at least one stable model after $n - 1$ steps and has no stable models thereafter. Note that if a program has no stable models after n steps then, for every $m \geq n$ it has no stable model after m steps. It is also important to observe that the set of all evolution stable models of a program, up to any length n, can be constructed incrementally by means of an operator $\mathcal{T}_P$.

Definition 6. *Let P be an evolving program. The operator $\mathcal{T}_P$ on sets of evolution interpretations is defined by:*

$$\mathcal{T}_P(\mathcal{I}) = \{\langle I_1, \ldots, I_i, I_{i+1} \rangle \mid \langle I_1, \ldots, I_i \rangle \in \mathcal{I} \wedge$$
$$\wedge \; I_{i+1} \; \text{is a stable model of} \; P_1 \oplus \ldots \oplus P_i \oplus P_{i+1} \; \text{at state} \; i + 1 \}$$
where $P_1 = P$ and, for $1 < j \leq i + 1$, $P_j = \{R \mid assert(R) \in I_{j-1}\}$.

Theorem 1. *Given an evolving program P, build the sequence of sets of evolution interpretations: $\mathcal{I}_1 = \{\langle I \rangle \mid I \; \text{is a stable model of} \; P\}$, and $\mathcal{I}_{i+1} = \mathcal{T}_P(\mathcal{I}_i)$. M is an evolution stable model of length n iff M belongs to $\mathcal{I}_n$.*

Each evolution stable model represents one possible evolution of the program, after a given number of steps. However, they do not directly determine a truth relation. What is true (resp. false) after a given number of evolution steps? This is an important question, when one wants to study the behaviour of a self-evolving program. Here, one will be interested in knowing what is guaranteed to be true (or false) after n steps of evolution, and what is unknown (or uncertain). In the example above a is guaranteed true after 1 and 2 steps and false after n steps, for any $n \geq 3$; b and c are true after 2 steps and false after n steps for any $n \neq 2$.

Definition 7. *Let P be an evolving program over the language $\mathcal{L}$. We say that a set of propositional atoms M over $\mathcal{L}_{assert}$ is a stable model of P after n steps iff there exist $I_1, \ldots, I_{n-1}$ such that $\langle I_1, \ldots, I_{n-1}, M \rangle$ is an evolution stable model of P. We say that propositional atom A of $\mathcal{L}$ is: true after n steps iff all stable models of P after n steps contain A; false after n steps iff no stable model of P after n steps contains A; unknown after n steps otherwise (iff some stable models of P after n steps contain A, and some do not).*

3   Evolving Logic Programs

With this alone, evolving programs are autistic: there is no way one can control or influence their evolution after initialization. To allow for control and influence from the outside, full-fledged evolving programs consider, besides the self-evolution of a program, that new rules may arrive from an outside environment. This influence from the outside may be, at each moment, of various kinds. Notably: observation of facts (or rules) that are perceived at some state; assertion orders directly imposing the assertion of new rules on the evolving program. Both can be represent as EVOLP rules: the former by rules without the assert predicate, and the latter by rules with it. Consequently, we shall represent outside influence as a sequence of EVOLP rules:

Definition 8. *Let P be an evolving program over the language $\mathcal{L}$. An event sequence over P is a sequence of evolving programs over $\mathcal{L}$.*

The rules coming from the outside, be they observations or assertion orders, are to be understood as events given at a state, that are not to persist by inertia. I.e. if R belongs to some set S_i of an event sequence, this means that R was perceived or given after $i - 1$ evolution steps of the program and that this perception is not to be assumed by inertia from then onward. With this understanding of event sequence, it is easy to define the evolution stable model of an evolving program influenced by a sequence of events. Basically, a sequence of interpretations is a stable model of a program given a sequence of events, if each I_i in the sequence is a stable model at state i of the trace plus the events added at state i.

Definition 9. *An evolution interpretation $\langle I_1, I_2, \ldots, I_n \rangle$, with evolution trace $\langle P_1, P_2, \ldots, P_n \rangle$, is an evolution stable model of P given $\langle E_1, E_2, \ldots, E_k \rangle$ iff for every i ($1 \leq i \leq n$), I_i is a stable model at state i of $P_1 \oplus P_2 \ldots \oplus (P_i \cup E_i)$.*

Notice that the rules coming from the outside indeed do not persist by inertia. At any given step i, the rules from E_i are added and the (possibly various) I_i obtained. This determines the programs P_{i+1} of the trace, which are then added to E_{i+1} to determine the models I_{i+1}.

Clearly this definition generalizes the one of self evolving programs (if all the sets of events in a sequence are empty, this definition collapses to Definition 5).

The definition assumes the whole sequence of events given a priori. In fact this need not be so because the events at any given step n only influence the models in the evolution interpretation from n onward.

Proposition 1. *Let $M = \langle I_1, \ldots, I_n \rangle$ be an evolution stable model of P given an event sequence $\langle E_1, \ldots, E_n \rangle$. Then, for any $m > n$ and any sets of events $E_{n+1}, \ldots, E_m$, M is also an evolution stable model of P given an event sequence $\langle E_1, \ldots, E_n, E_{n+1}, \ldots, E_m \rangle$.*

In fact, the evolution stable models of a program given a sequence of events can also be constructed incrementally by means of an operator $\mathcal{T}_P^{ev}$.

Theorem 2. *Let P be an evolving program, and let $\mathcal{I}$ be a set of evolution interpretations of P given the event sequence $\langle E_1, \ldots, E_i \rangle$. The operator $\mathcal{T}_P^{ev}$ is, where $P_1 = P$ and, for $1 < j \leq i + 1$, $P_j = \{R \mid assert(R) \in I_{j-1}\}$:*

$$\mathcal{T}_P^{ev}(\mathcal{I}, E_{i+1}) = \{\ \langle I_1, \ldots, I_i, I_{i+1} \rangle \mid \langle I_1, \ldots, I_i \rangle \in \mathcal{I} \wedge$$
$$\wedge\ I_{i+1} \text{ is a stable model of } P_1 \oplus \ldots \oplus P_i \oplus (P_{i+1} \cup E_{i+1})\}$$

Consider the sequence: $\mathcal{I}_1 = \{\langle I \rangle \mid I \text{ is a stable model of } P \cup E_1\}$, and $\mathcal{I}_{i+1} = \mathcal{T}_P^{ev}(\mathcal{I}_i, E_{i+1})$. M is an evolution stable model of length n given the event sequence $\langle E_1, \ldots, E_n \rangle$ iff M belongs to $\mathcal{I}_n$.

A notion of truth after a number of steps given an event sequence can be defined similarly to that provided for self-evolving programs:

Definition 10. *Let P be an evolving program over the language $\mathcal{L}$. We say that a set of propositional atoms M over $\mathcal{L}_{assert}$ is a stable model of P after n steps given the sequence of events SE iff there exist $I_1, \ldots, I_{n-1}$ such that $\langle I_1, \ldots, I_{n-1}, M \rangle$ is an evolution stable model of P given SE. We say that propositional atom A of $\mathcal{L}$ is:* true after n steps given SE *iff all stable models after n steps contain A;* false after n steps given SE *iff no stable model after n steps contains A;* unknown after n steps given SE *otherwise.*

4   Examples of Usage

Having formally presented EVOLP, we next show examples of usage. For lack of space, we do not elaborate on how EVOLP actually provides the results shown.

EVOLP was developed as a language capable of undergoing changes in a knowledge base, both by self-evolution as well as imposed from the outside. One immediate application area is that of modelling systems (or agents) that evolve over time and are influenced and/or controlled by the environment.

Example 1. Consider an agent in charge of controlling a lift that receives from outside signals of the form $push(N)$, when somebody pushes the button for going to floor N, or $floor$, when the lift reaches a new floor. Upon receipt of a $push(N)$ signal, the lift records that a request for going to floor N is pending. This can easily be modelled by the rule: $assert(request(F)) \leftarrow push(F)$.[2] Mark the difference between this rule and the rule $request(F) \leftarrow push(F)$. When the button F is pushed, with the latter rule $request(F)$ is true only at that moment, while with the former $request(F)$ is asserted to the evolving program so that it remains inertially true (until its truth is possibly deleted afterwards).

Based on the pending requests at each moment, the agent must prefer where to go. This could be modelled in the evolving program by the rules:

$going(F) \leftarrow request(F), not\ unpref(F).$ $better(F1, F2) \leftarrow at(F),$
$unpref(F) \leftarrow request(F2), better(F2, F).$ $\mid F1 - F \mid < \mid F2 - F \mid.$

Predicate $at/1$ stores, at each moment, the number of the floor where the lift is. Thus, if a $floor$ signal is received, depending on where the lift is going, $at(F)$ must be incremented/decremented i.e., in EVOLP:

$$assert(at(F + 1)) \leftarrow floor, at(F), going(G),\ G > F.$$
$$assert(not\ at(F)) \leftarrow floor, at(F), going(G),\ G > F.$$
$$assert(at(F - 1)) \leftarrow floor, at(F), going(G),\ G < F.$$
$$assert(not\ at(F)) \leftarrow floor, at(F), going(G),\ G < F.$$

When the lift reaches the floor to which it was going, it must open the door. After that, it must remove the pending request for going to that floor:

$open(F) \leftarrow going(F), at(F).$ $assert(not\ request(F)) \leftarrow going(F), at(F).$

Note that there is no need to remove the facts $going(F)$: by removing the $request(F)$, $going(F)$ will no longer be concluded for that F. To illustrate the

---

[2] In the examples, rules with variables simply stand for all their ground instances.

behaviour of this evolving program, consider that initially the lift is at the 5th floor (i.e. $at(5)$ also belongs to the program), and that the agent receives the sequence $\langle\{push(10), push(2)\}, \{floor\}, \{push(3)\}, \{floor\}\rangle$. This program with this event sequence has, for every n, a single stable model after n steps which, the reader can check, gives the desired results modelling the intuitive behaviour of the lift. Apart from the (auxiliary) predicates to determine the preferred request, for the first 6 steps the stable models are (with the obvious abbreviations):

1 $step$: $\{at(5), push(10), push(2), as(req(10)), as(req(2))\}$
2 $steps$: $\{at(5), req(10), req(2), going(2), floor, as(at(4)), as(not\,at(5))\}$
3 $steps$: $\{at(4), req(10), req(2), going(2), push(3), as(req(3)))\}$
4 $steps$: $\{at(4), req(10), req(2), req(3), going(3), floor, as(at(3)), as(not\,at(4))\}$
5 $steps$: $\{at(3), req(10), req(2), req(3), going(3), open, as(not\,req(3))\}$
6 $steps$: $\{at(3), req(10), req(2), going(2)\}$

The first rule above specifies the effect of the action of pushing a button. Actions specify changes to an evolving knowledge base, and so they can be represented by EVOLP rules specifying those changes. In general, an action, $action$, with preconditions $preconds$ and effect $effect$ can be represented by: $assert(effect) \leftarrow preconds, action$. Moreover, unlike existing languages for describing actions or updates, EVOLP allows for changes in the rules that specify action effects. Suppose the lift becomes old and sometimes the buttons get stuck and don't work. The knowledge base can be updated accordingly by sending to it an event: $assert(not\,assert(request(F)) \leftarrow stuck(F))$. The effect of this event rule is that, from the moment it is given onward, $request(L)$ is only asserted if there is a $push(F)$ action and $stuck(L)$ is false at the moment the push occurs.

Another interesting aspect which, unlike existing languages, is easy to deal with in EVOLP, is that of incomplete knowledge of the outside environment. Suppose that, in the sequence of events above, instead of the last event the system receives a signal that may (or may not) be a $floor$ signal. This can easily be coded by replacing the corresponding fact $floor$ by the two rules:

$$floor \leftarrow not\,na\_signal. \qquad\qquad na\_signal \leftarrow not\,floor.$$

With this, after 4 steps (and from then onwards), there are 2 evolution stable models: one corresponding to the evolution in case the floor signal is considered; the other, in case it isn't. The truth relation can here be used to determine what is certain despite the undefinedness of the events received. E.g. after 5 steps, it is true that the lift is going to the 3rd floor, has requests for floors 2, 3 and 10, it is unknown whether the lift is at floor 3 or 4 (though it is false that the lift is at any other floor), and unknown whether the door is open.

This example does not exploit the full power of EVOLP. In particular the assertions made are of simple facts only. For illustrating how an assertion of a rule can be used, consider the following example from legal reasoning:

Example 2. Whenever some law is proposed, and before it is made valid it must first be voted by parliament $(v\,(.))$ and then approved by the president $(a\,(.))$.

Further consider a scenario where a law stating that abortions are punishable with jail is proposed (r_1). This can be added to an evolving program as an event:

$$assert\left(assert\left(assert\left(jail\left(X\right)\leftarrow abort\left(X\right)\right)\leftarrow a\left(r_1\right)\right)\leftarrow v\left(r_1\right)\right)$$

Subsequently, after the events $v\left(r_1\right)$ and $a\left(r_1\right)$ are observed, the rule $jail\left(X\right)\leftarrow abort\left(X\right)$ is in force and anyone who performs an abortion goes to jail. For example, if the knowledge base contains $abort\left(mary\right)$, then it also entails $jail\left(mary\right)$. Now suppose that a law stating that abortions are not punishable with jail if there is life danger for the pregnant is proposed (r_2). This rule can be added as:

$$assert\left(assert\left(assert\left(not\,jail\left(X\right)\leftarrow abort\left(X\right),danger\left(X\right)\right)\leftarrow a\left(r_2\right)\right)\leftarrow v\left(r_2\right)\right)$$

After $v\left(r_2\right)$ and $a\left(r_2\right)$ are observed, rule $not\,jail\left(X\right)\leftarrow abort\left(X\right),danger\left(X\right)$ is in force, and anyone who performs an abortion and is in danger would not go to jail. If the knowledge base also contains, e.g., the facts $abort\left(lisa\right)$ and $danger\left(lisa\right)$ then it would not entail $jail\left(lisa\right)$. Note that before the events $v\left(r_2\right)$ and $a\left(r_2\right)$ are observed Lisa would go to jail, and even after those events, Mary still goes to jail because $danger\left(mary\right)$ is not true.

Lack of space prevents us from showing here more examples from other potential application areas of EVOLP. Instead of doing so, we end this section by schematically showing how to code in EVOLP some high level behavioural changes to knowledge bases. Starting with a simple one, which happens to correspond to the behaviour of a LUPS **always** command, suppose we want to state that whenever some conditions $Cond$ are met then rule $Rule$ is to be asserted. This can be coded by $assert(Rule)\leftarrow Cond$. If such a behaviour is to be included not from the beginning of the program evolution, but rather only after some time, instead of adding that rule in the evolving program one can send, at the appropriate time, an outside event $assert(assert(Rule)\leftarrow Cond)$.

One may also want the rule to be in force after some other condition is met, e.g. if $Cond_1$ then add a rule imposing that whenever $Cond_2$ then $Rule$ is asserted. This is not possible to code directly in LUPS, but is easy in EVOLP, due to availability of nested asserts: $assert(assert(Rule)\leftarrow Cond_2)\leftarrow Cond_1$.

In EVOLP the rules coming from the outside are time point events, i.e. do not persist by inertia, and rules in the evolving program are subject to inertia. But one may want to specify, as part of the self evolution of the program, a non inertial rule. For example: "whenever $Cond$ is met add $L\leftarrow Body$ in the next state as a time point event, i.e. add it in the next state and then remove it from subsequent states (unless in the following states something else adds the rule again)". The coding of such a rule in EVOLP is not that direct. First one may make the rule $L\leftarrow Body$ conditional on the truth of say $event(L\leftarrow Body)$, and add both the rule and a fact for $event(L\leftarrow Body)$ whenever $Cond$ is met:

$$assert(event(L\leftarrow Body))\leftarrow Cond.$$
$$assert((L\leftarrow Body,event(L\leftarrow Body)))\leftarrow Cond.$$

Now, if at any state, for some rule R, $event(R)$ is true then we must make it false at the next state. But only unless the rule is not going being added as an event, for some other reason, at that next state, i.e. unless $assert(event(R))$ is not itself true. And this can be coded in EVOLP by:

$$assert(not\,event(R)) \leftarrow event(R), not\,assert(event(R))$$

This rule illustrates one usage of *assert* in rule bodies. It is needed here to state that some rule is to be asserted unless some other rule is not going to be asserted. It is easy to think of examples where such constructs are needed. E.g. in chain updates to databases where one might want to state that if something is going to be asserted, then something else must be asserted, etc. This kind of chain updates, difficult to model in LUPS, are easy to model in EVOLP.

5   Concluding Remarks

We have presented the foundational framework of evolving logic programs, to express and reason about dynamic knowledge bases. Somewhat related approaches can be found in the literature, and some words on comparison are in order.

Stemming from the very initial motivation for setting forth this framework, it is mandatory that we begin with comments on the relation with LUPS [2] and EPI [7]. Even though their semantics are based on a notion of stable models, where a sequence of programs can have several stable models, the conditions of the LUPS and EPI commands are evaluated against a single valuation based on the union (in [2]) or intersection (in [11,7]) of all stable models. As a result, each state transition, unlike for EVOLP, produces a single program i.e., the evolution does not involve branching. This prevents a direct embedding of LUPS and EPI in EVOLP, but it is possible to informally assume a modified version of these languages where the conditions would be evaluated at each individual stable model, for the sake of comparison. Conversely, EVOLP could be easily modified in the opposite way so as to not have branching, by evaluating the rules bodies at the union (or intersection) of the stable models to construct the next program in the sequence. With this caveat, we are ready to state that LUPS and EPI commands are all specifiable within the language of EVOLP. In the previous section, we have already shown how to specify in EVOLP a couple of LUPS commands. This alone is a major achievement inasmuch one of our motivations was to simplify the rather complex extant languages of updates. But EVOLP endorses more than LUPS or EPI, e.g.: by employing arbitrary nesting of assertions, one can for example specify updates whose conditions span more than one state, e.g. assertions that depend on a sequence of events as in Example 2; since persistent commands in LUPS and in EPI can be encoded as plain rules in EVOLP, they can be the subject of updates by other rules, as illustrated in Example 1. Finally, unlike in LUPS and EPI, where update commands and object level rules are written in different languages, by unifying states and state transitions in the same language and semantics, EVOLP constitutes a simple framework not just to understand and write specifications in, but to study the general properties of updates as well .

A logic-based modelling of simple updates is described in [5], where a deductive database approach to planning is presented. In [5], STRIPS-like plans are modelled by means of $Datalog_{1s}$ programs [6] which have a stable model semantics amenable to efficient implementation. Updates are used to model state changes determined by executing planning actions. This approach shares with ours the choice of the stable model semantics to provide a logical characterization of updates. However, [5] models only updates of positive literals, while our approach accounts for (possibly nested) updates of arbitrary rules. Moreover, while [5] syntactically hacks program evolution inside programs by using stage arguments, EVOLP models program evolution at the semantics level, without adding arguments to predicates.

Action languages [9] and Event Calculus [10] have been proposed to describe and reason about the effects of actions and events. Intuitively, while such frameworks and EVOLP are both concerned with modelling changes, the former focus on the notions of causality, fluents and events, while EVOLP focusses its features on the declarative evolution of a general knowledge base.

Transaction Logic (TL) [3] is also a LP language for updates. TL is concerned with finding, given a goal, the appropriate transactions (or updates) to an underlying knowledge base in order to satisfy the goal. Contrary to EVOLP, the rules that specify changes are separate from the knowledge base itself, making it impossible to change them dynamically. Moreover the whole process in TL is query driven. On the contrary, in EVOLP goals are not needed to start an update process: an EVOLP knowledge base evolves by itself. Also, we have no notion of finding updates to satisfy a goal: the updates are given, and EVOLP is concerned with determining the meaning of the KB after those given updates. Determining such updates amount to a form of abduction over EVOLP programs, driven by goals or integrity constraints. Similar arguments apply when comparing EVOLP to Prolog asserts, though in this case there is the additional argument of there not being a clear semantics (with attending problems when asserts are subject to backtracking).

Space limitations prevent us discussing quite a number of other interesting issues and directions for further work. Nevertheless, we briefly touch upon some of them here.

A *transformational definition* of the semantics of EVOLP programs has already been defined. Informally, the idea is to label program literals with a state argument so the truth of L^n denotes the truth of literal L after n evolution steps. The interest of the transformational definition is two-fold. On the one hand, it provides an alternative characterization of the semantics of EVOLP programs in terms of the standard semantics of generalized programs. On the other hand, it is the basis on which we have developed a query-based implementation of the EVOLP language (available from http://centria.fct.unl.pt/~jja/updates/).

The proffered semantics models *consistent* evolutions of programs. Indeed, according to the definition of evolution stable model, a program is considered to be inconsistent after n evolution steps if it has at least one evolution stable model of length $(n-1)$ but no evolution stable model of length n. An important direction for future work is to extend the basic semantics to allow programs to continue their computations even if they reach some inconsistency. Different forms of dealing with contradiction can be considered ranging from naive removal of directly contradicting rules, to paraconsistency, to forms of belief revision.

A very interesting perspective to explore is the use of the EVOLP language to specify evolving *agents* that interact with the external environment. While the semantics of evolving programs accounts for rules and updates that may arise in the external environment, we have not addressed here the issues concerning the overall software architecture of an evolving agent. For instance, the agent architecture will be in charge of suitably filtering perceptions and requests that arrive from the outside, as well as of mastering the asynchronicity between the agent and the external environment. Another important aspect to be explored concerns the "acting" abilities of agents. These may be naturally expressed by means of outgoing updates (directed towards other agents or the external environment). Yet another direction discerns between sets of controlled and of uncontrolled events in the environment.

Finally, the availability of a description of the possible behaviours of evolving programs is a firm ground for performing static *program analysis* before putting agents to work with the environment. It is of interest to develop resource-bounded analyses, quantitative and qualitative, of evolving programs along the lines of [4] so as to statically determine both their possible and invariant beliefs.

Acknowledgements

This work was partially supported by a bilateral project ICCTI-CNR, and by project FLUX (POSI/40958/SRI/2001).

References

1. J. J. Alferes, J. A. Leite, L. M. Pereira, H. Przymusinska, and T. Przymusinski. Dynamic updates of non-monotonic knowledge bases. *Journal of Logic Programming*, 45(1-3):43–70, 2000.
2. J. J. Alferes, L. M. Pereira, H. Przymusinska, and T. Przymusinski. LUPS : A language for updating logic programs. *Artificial Intelligence*, 138(1-2), 2002. A short version appeared in M. Gelfond et al., LPNMR-99, LNAI 1730, Springer.
3. A. Bonner and M. Kifer. Transaction logic programming. In David S. Warren, editor, *ICLP-93*, pages 257–279. The MIT Press, 1993.
4. A. Brogi. Probabilistic behaviours of reactive agents. *Electronic Notes in Theoretical Computer Science*, 48, 2001.
5. A. Brogi, V.S. Subrahmanian, and C. Zaniolo. The logic of totally and partially ordered plans: A deductive database approach. *Annals of Mathematics and Artificial Intelligence*, 19((1,2)):27–58, 1997.
6. J. Chomicki. Polynomial-time computable queries in temporal deductive databases. In *PODS'90*, 1990.
7. T. Eiter, M. Fink, G. Sabbatini, and H Tompits. A framework for declarative update specifications in logic programs. In *IJCAI'01*, pages 649–654. Morgan-Kaufmann, 2001.
8. M. Gelfond and V. Lifschitz. The stable semantics for logic programs. In R. Kowalski and K. Bowen, editors, *ICLP'88*, pages 1070–1080. MIT Press, 1988.
9. M. Gelfond and V. Lifschitz. Action languages. *Linkoping Electronic Articles in Computer and Information Science*, 3(16), 1998.
10. R. Kowalski and M. Sergot. A logic-based calculus of events. *New Generation Computing*, 4:67–95, 1986.
11. J. A. Leite. A modified semantics for LUPS. In P. Brazdil and A. Jorge, editors, *EPIA-01*, volume 2258 of *LNAI*, pages 261–275. Springer, 2001.
12. V. Lifschitz and T. Woo. Answer sets in general non-monotonic reasoning (preliminary report). In B. Nebel, C. Rich, and W. Swartout, editors, *KR'92*. Morgan-Kaufmann, 1992.

A Compilation of Updates plus Preferences*

José Júlio Alferes[1], Pierangelo Dell'Acqua[1,2], and Luís Moniz Pereira[1]

[1] Centro de Inteligência Artificial - CENTRIA
Departamento de Informática, Faculdade de Ciências e Tecnologia
Universidade Nova de Lisboa, 2829-516 Caparica, Portugal
{jja,lmp}@di.fct.unl.pt
[2] Department of Science and Technology - ITN
Linköping University, 601 74 Norrköping, Sweden
pier@itn.liu.se

Abstract. We show how to compile programs formalizing update plus preference reasoning into standard generalized logic programs and show the correctness of the transformation.

1 Introduction

Update reasoning and *preference reasoning* are two pervasive forms of reasoning. Update reasoning is used to model dynamically evolving worlds. Given a piece of knowledge describing the world, and given a change in the world, the problem is how to modify the knowledge to cope with that change. The key issue is how to accommodate, in the represented knowledge, any changes in the world. In this setting it may well happen that change in the world contradicts previous knowledge, i.e. the union of the previous knowledge with the representation of the new knowledge has no model. It is up to updates to remove from the prior knowledge representation a piece that changed, and to replace it by the new one.

The addition of mechanisms for handling preferences in Logic Programming has proven essential in several different application areas, such as legal reasoning [14], data cleaning [8], and intelligent agents for e-commerce [11]. In general, preference information is used along with incomplete knowledge. In such a setting, due to the incompleteness of the knowledge, several models may be possible. Preference reasoning acts by choosing among those possible models. A classical example is the birds-fly problem where the incomplete knowledge contains the rules that "birds normally fly" (1) and "penguins normally don't fly" (2). Given an individual which is both a penguin and a bird, two models are possible: one model obtained by using the first rule, and the other obtained by using the second rule. Preference information among the rules can then be used to choose one model. Cf. [5,6] for additional motivation, comparisons, applications, and references.

---

* This work was partially supported by POCTI project 40958 "FLUX - FleXible Logical Updates". The second author acknowledges a Research Grant by the *Stiftelsen Lars Hiertas Minne*.

S. Flesca et al. (Eds.): JELIA 2002, LNAI 2424, pp. 62–74, 2002.

Alferes and Pereira [3] proposed an approach that combines these two separate forms of reasoning in the context of Logic Programming (for an overview see [4]). They showed how they complement each other, in that preferences select among pre-existing models, and updates actually create new models. Moreover, preferences may be enacted on the results of updates, and updates may be pressed into service for the purpose of changing preferences. Brewka and Eiter's preferred stable models [7] are generalized in [3], for the ground case, to take into account the language of generalized logic programs and to allow for updating the priority information.

Consider the following example, where rules as well as preferences change over time. It requires a combination of preferences and updates, including the updating of preferences themselves. This example could form the basis of an e-commerce application where, depending on the user's preferences, a number of alternative choices could be offered. Such an application would require that the knowledge base rules as well as the user's preferences change over time. An example would be a pay-TV company that wants to target its marketing by maintaining user's profiles in order to inform its users about their favourite programs.

Example. (TV-program) Suppose a scenario where a user, say Stefano, watches programs about football, tennis or news. (1) In the initial situation, being a typical Italian, Stefano prefers both football and tennis to news, and in case of international competitions he prefers tennis to football. In this situation, Stefano has two alternative TV programmes equally preferable: football and tennis. (2) Next, suppose that a US-open tennis competition takes place. Now, Stefano's favourite programme is tennis. (3) Finally, suppose that Stefano's preferences change and he becomes interested in international news. Then, in case of breaking news he will prefer news over both football and tennis.

In this paper we show how to compile programs formalizing update plus preference reasoning into standard generalized logic programs. Lack of space prevents us from showing here the correctness of the transformation, though it can be found in [1]. The proposed transformation has the advantage of being modular: it is a combination of a transformation for update reasoning and a transformation for preference reasoning. Moreover, we have implemented this transformation and tested on several examples.

2   Logic Programming Framework

We consider propositional Horn theories. In particular, we represent default negation *not A* as standard propositional variable (atom). Suppose that $\mathcal{K}$ is an arbitrary set of propositional variables whose names do not begin with a "not". By the propositional language $\mathcal{L}_\mathcal{K}$ generated by $\mathcal{K}$ we mean the language whose set of propositional variables consists of $\{A, not\, A : A \in \mathcal{K}\}$. Atoms $A \in \mathcal{K}$ are called *objective atoms* while the atoms *not A* are called *default atoms*. From the definition it follows that the two sets are disjoint. Objective and default atoms are generically called *literals*.

Definition 1 (Generalized Logic Program). *A generalized logic program in the language $\mathcal{L}_\mathcal{K}$ is a finite or infinite set of ground generalized rules:*

$$L_0 \leftarrow L_1, \ldots, L_n \quad (n \geq 0)$$

where each L_i is a literal over $\mathcal{L}_\mathcal{K}$.

By *head*(r) we mean L_0, by *body*(r) the set of literals $\{L_1, \ldots, L_n\}$, by *body*$^+(r)$ the set of all objective atoms in *body*(r), and by *body*$^-(r)$ the set of all default atoms in *body*(r). We refer to *body*$^+(r)$ as the prerequisites of r. Whenever a literal L is of the form *not A*, *not L* stands for the objective atom A.

The semantics of generalized logic programs [12,13] is defined as a generalization of the stable model semantics [10]. Here we use the definition that appeared in [2] (proven there equivalent to [12,13]).

Definition 2 (Default Assumptions). *Let M be an interpretation of P. Then:*

$$Default(P, M) = \{not\, A \mid \nexists r \in P : head(r) = A \text{ and } M \models body(r)\}.$$

Definition 3 (Stable Models of Generalized Programs). *Let P be a generalized logic program and M an interpretation of P. M is a (regular) stable model of P iff $M = least(P \cup Default(P, M))$.*

To express preference information in logic programs, we introduce the notion of priority rule and prioritized logic program. Let $N = \{n_{r_1}, \ldots, n_{r_k}\}$ be a name set containing a unique name for every generalized rule in the language $\mathcal{L}_\mathcal{K}$. Given a rule r, we write n_r to indicate the constant in N that names r. Let $<$ be a binary predicate symbol[1] whose set of constants is N. $n_r < n_u$ means that rule r is preferred to rule u. Denote by $\bar{\mathcal{K}}$ the following superset of the set $\mathcal{K}$ of propositional variables:

$$\bar{\mathcal{K}} = \mathcal{K} \cup \{n_r < n_u : \{n_r, n_u\} \subseteq N\}.$$

Definition 4 (Priority Rule). *A priority rule over the language $\mathcal{L}_{\bar{\mathcal{K}}}$ is a generalized rule of the form:*

$$Z \leftarrow L_1, \ldots, L_n \quad (n \geq 0)$$

where Z is a literal of the form $n_r < n_u$ or its default complement, not $n_r < n_u$, and each L_i is a literal over $\mathcal{L}_{\bar{\mathcal{K}}}$.

Note that the set of constants of $<$ does not include $<$ itself (that is, $< \notin N$), and that $<$ can only occur in the head and (possibly) in the body of priority rules.

Definition 5 (Prioritized Logic Program). *Let P be a generalized logic program over the language $\mathcal{L}_\mathcal{K}$ and R a set of priority rules over the language $\mathcal{L}_{\bar{\mathcal{K}}}$. Then (P, R) is a prioritized logic program.*

The generalized rules in P formalize the domain knowledge while the priority rules in R express preferences among the rules in P.

---

[1] In order to establish the preferred stable models (cf. Def. 14), we require the relation induced by $<$ to be a well-founded, strict partial ordering on program rules.

3   Dynamic Prioritized Programs

In this section we recall the approach of Dynamic Logic Programming [2] that can be used to model the evolution of prioritized logic programs through sequences of updates (including the update of priority rules).

In Dynamic Logic Programming, sequences of generalized programs $P_1 \oplus \cdots \oplus P_s$ are given. Intuitively a sequence may be viewed as the result of, starting with program P_1, updating it with program P_2, ..., and updating it with program P_s. In such a view, dynamic logic programs are to be used in knowledge bases that evolve. New rules (coming from new, or newly acquired, knowledge) can be added at the end of the sequence, bothering not whether they conflict with previous knowledge. The role of Dynamic Logic Programming is to ensure that these newly added rules are in force, and that previous rules are still valid (by inertia) as far as possible, i.e. they are kept for as long as they do not conflict with newly added ones. In the remaining, let $S = \{1, \ldots, s, \ldots\}$ be a set of natural numbers. We call the elements $i \in S$ states.

Definition 6 (Dynamic Logic Program). *Let S be a set of states. A dynamic logic program $\bigoplus\{P_i : i \in S\}$ is a set of a generalized logic programs P_i indexed by the states i in S.*

The semantics of dynamic logic programs is defined according to the rationale above. Given a model M of the program P_s, start by removing all the rules from previous programs whose head is the complement of some later rule with true body in M (i.e. by removing all rules which conflict with more recent ones). All other persist through by inertia. Then, as for the stable models of a single generalized program, add facts *not A* for all atoms A which have no rule at all with true body in M, and compute the least model. If M is a fixpoint of this construction, M is a stable model of the sequence up to P_s.

Definition 7 (Rejected Rules). *Let $s \in S$ be a state. Let $P = \bigoplus\{P_i : i \in S\}$ be a dynamic logic program over the language $\mathcal{L}_K$ and M an interpretation over $\mathcal{L}_K$. Then:*

$Reject(s, M, P) =$
$\quad \{r \in P_i \mid \exists r' \in P_j, head(r) = not\, head(r'), i < j \leq s \text{ and } M \models body(r')\}.$

To allow for querying a dynamic program at any state s, the definition of stable model is parameterized by the state.

Definition 8 (Stable Models of a DLP at State s). *Let $s \in S$ be a state. Let $P = \bigoplus\{P_i : i \in S\}$ be a dynamic logic program over the language $\mathcal{L}_K$ and M an interpretation over $\mathcal{L}_K$. M is a stable model of P at state s iff:*

$$M = least([\mathcal{P} - Reject(s, M, P)] \cup Default(\mathcal{P}, M))$$

where $\mathcal{P} = \bigcup_{i \leq s} P_i$.

To allow the updating the priority rules, the notion of dynamic prioritized programs has been introduced into Dynamic Logic Programming. Instead of a sequence of programs representing knowledge, the idea is to use a sequence of pairs:

of programs representing knowledge, and of programs describing the priority relation among rules of the knowledge representation. In general, an update of the priority rules may depend on some other predicate. To permit this generality, priority rules are allowed to refer to predicates defined in the programs that represent knowledge.

Definition 9 (Dynamic Prioritized Program). *Let S be a set of states. Let $P = \{P_i : i \in S\}$ be a dynamic logic program over the language $\mathcal{L}_{\mathcal{K}}$. Let $R = \{R_i : i \in S\}$ a dynamic logic program, where each R_i is a set of priority rules over the language $\mathcal{L}_{\bar{\mathcal{K}}}$. Then, $\bigoplus\{(P_i, R_i) : i \in S\}$ is a dynamic prioritized program over the language $\mathcal{L}_{\bar{\mathcal{K}}}$.*

The next example illustrates the use of dynamic prioritized programs.

Example 1. The TV-program example presented in the Introduction can be formalized via a dynamic prioritized program $\bigoplus\{(P_i, R_i) : i \in S\}$ with $S = \{1, 2, 3\}$. We abbreviate football by f, tennis by t, news by n, breaking news by bn and US-open by us. We use n_i to name a rule r_i.

$$P_1 = \left\{ \begin{array}{ll} f \leftarrow not\ t, not\ n & (r_1) \\ t \leftarrow not\ f, not\ n & (r_2) \\ n \leftarrow not\ f, not\ t & (r_3) \end{array} \right\} \quad R_1 = \left\{ \begin{array}{l} n_1 < n_3 \\ n_2 < n_3 \\ n_2 < n_1 \leftarrow us \\ x < y \leftarrow x < z, z < y \end{array} \right\}$$

$$P_2 = \{\ us \quad (r_4)\ \} \qquad R_2 = \{\}$$

$$P_3 = \{\ bn \quad (r_5)\ \} \qquad R_3 = \left\{ \begin{array}{l} not\ (n_1 < n_3) \leftarrow bn \\ not\ (n_2 < n_3) \leftarrow bn \\ n_3 < n_1 \leftarrow bn \\ n_3 < n_2 \leftarrow bn \end{array} \right\}$$

The stable models of a dynamic prioritized program P are defined in terms of the stable models of the dynamic logic program obtained by the union of all the P_is and R_is in P. Consequently, the preference information expressed by the priority rules in the R_is is not taken into account here.

Definition 10 (Stable Models of a DPP at State s). *Let $s \in S$ be a state. Let $P = \bigoplus\{(P_i, R_i) : i \in S\}$ be a dynamic prioritized program over the language $\mathcal{L}_{\bar{\mathcal{K}}}$ and M an interpretation over $\mathcal{L}_{\bar{\mathcal{K}}}$. M is a stable model of P at state s iff M is a stable model of the dynamic logic program $\bigoplus\{P_i \cup R_i : i \in S\}$ at state s.*

Example 2. Let P be the dynamic prioritized program of Example 1. At state 2, P has three stable models:

$$M_{21} = \{f\} \cup X \quad M_{22} = \{t\} \cup X \quad M_{23} = \{n\} \cup X$$

where $X = \{us, n_1 < n_3, n_2 < n_3, n_2 < n_1\}$. At state 3, the stable models are:

$$M_{31} = \{f\} \cup Y \quad M_{32} = \{t\} \cup Y \quad M_{33} = \{n\} \cup Y$$

where $Y = \{bn, us, n_2 < n_1, n_3 < n_1, n_3 < n_2\}$.

4   Compiling Dynamic Programs

A transformational semantics for dynamic logic programs is presented in [2]. According to it, a sequence of generalized logic programs is translated into a single generalized program whose stable models are in one-to-one correspondence with the stable models of the dynamic logic program. In this section we adapt that transformation to cope with priority rules, and we add new generalized rules to make explicit which rules in the program are rejected. These modifications make the transformation suitable to be extended further to incorporate preference information (cf. Section 6).

By $\widehat{\mathcal{K}}$ we denote the following superset of the set $\bar{\bar{\mathcal{K}}}$ of propositional variables:

$$\widehat{\mathcal{K}} = \bar{\bar{\mathcal{K}}} \cup \{A^-, A_i, A_i^-, A_{F_i}, A_{F_i}^- : A \in \bar{\bar{\mathcal{K}}}, i \in S \cup \{0\}\} \cup \{\text{reject}(n_r) : n_r \in N\}.$$

Definition 11. *Let s be a state. Let $P = \bigoplus\{(P_i, R_i) : i \in S\}$ be a dynamic prioritized program over the language $\mathcal{L}_{\bar{\bar{\mathcal{K}}}}$. Then $DLP(s, P)$ is the normal logic program over the language $\mathcal{L}_{\widehat{\mathcal{K}}}$ consisting of the following rules.*

(RP) Rewritten Program Rules:

$$A_{F_i} \leftarrow A_1, \ldots, A_n, A_{n+1}^-, \ldots, A_m^- \tag{1}$$

or

$$A_{F_i}^- \leftarrow A_1, \ldots, A_n, A_{n+1}^-, \ldots, A_m^- \tag{2}$$

for any rule:

$$A \leftarrow A_1, \ldots, A_n, \text{not } A_{n+1}, \ldots, \text{not } A_m$$

respectively, for any rule:

$$\text{not } A \leftarrow A_1, \ldots, A_n, \text{not } A_{n+1}, \ldots, \text{not } A_m$$

in the program $F_i = P_i \cup R_i$, where $i \in S$. The rewritten rules are obtained from the original ones by replacing atoms A (resp. not A) occurring in their heads by the atoms A_{F_i} (resp. $A_{F_i}^-$) and by replacing default atoms not A_i in their bodies by A_i^-.

(UR) Update Rules:

$$A_i \leftarrow A_{F_i} \tag{3}$$
$$A_i^- \leftarrow A_{F_i}^- \tag{4}$$

for all objective atoms $A \in \bar{\bar{\mathcal{K}}}$ and all $i \in S$. The update rules state that an atom A must be true (resp. false) in the state $i \in S$ if it is true (resp. false) in the updating program F_i.

(IR) Inheritance Rules:

$$A_i \leftarrow A_{i-1}, not\ A_{\overline{F}_i} \tag{5}$$

$$A_i^- \leftarrow A_{i-1}^-, not\ A_{F_i} \tag{6}$$

for all objective atoms $A \in \overline{\overline{\mathcal{K}}}$ and all $i \in S$. The inheritance rules say that an atom A is true (resp. false) in a state $i \in S$ if it is true (resp. false) in the previous state $i - 1$ and it is not forced to be false (resp. true) by the updating program F_i.

(DR) Default Rules:

$$A_0^- \tag{7}$$

for all objective atoms $A \in \overline{\overline{\mathcal{K}}}$. Default rules describe the initial state 0 by making all objective atoms initially false.

(RE) Rejection Rules:

$$\text{reject}(n_r) \leftarrow A_{\overline{F}_t}^- \tag{8}$$

or

$$\text{reject}(n_r) \leftarrow A_{F_t} \tag{9}$$

for any rule:

$$A \leftarrow A_1, \ldots, A_n, not\ A_{n+1}, \ldots, not\ A_m$$

respectively, for any rule:

$$not\ A \leftarrow A_1, \ldots, A_n, not\ A_{n+1}, \ldots, not\ A_m$$

r in the program $F_i = P_i \cup R_i$, and for all $t \in S$ such that $i < t \le s$. Rejection rules state that a rule r in the program F_i will be rejected if it is forced to be false (resp. true) by a subsequent updating program F_t.

(CS$_s$) Current State Rules:

$$A \leftarrow A_s \tag{10}$$

$$A^- \leftarrow A_s^- \tag{11}$$

$$false \leftarrow A, A^- \tag{12}$$

for all objective atoms $A \in \overline{\overline{\mathcal{K}}}$. Current state rules specify the current state s in which the dynamic prioritized program is being evaluated and determine the values of the atoms A, A^- and not A.

The next theorem proves the correctness of the $DLP(s, P)$ transformation. The proof of this and the next results can be found in [1].

Theorem 1 (Soundness and Completeness). *Let $s \in S$ be a state. Let $P = \bigoplus\{(P_i, R_i) : i \in S\}$ be a dynamic prioritized program over the language $\mathcal{L}_{\overline{\mathcal{K}}}$. The (regular) stable models of $DLP(s, P)$, restricted to $\mathcal{L}_{\overline{\mathcal{K}}}$, coincide with the stable models of P at state s.*

The following proposition shows that an atom reject(n_r) belongs to a stable model M of $DLP(s, P)$ iff the rule r is effectively rejected by the model.

Proposition 1. *Let $s \in S$ be a state. Let $P = \bigoplus\{(P_i, R_i) : i \in S\}$ be a dynamic prioritized program over the language $\mathcal{L}_{\bar{\mathcal{K}}}$. Let M be a (regular) stable model of $DLP(s, P)$ and $J = M \cap \mathcal{L}_{\bar{\mathcal{K}}}$. Then reject($n_r$) $\in M$ iff $r \in Reject(s, J, Q)$, where $Q = \bigoplus\{P_i \cup R_i : i \in S\}$.*

5 Preferred Stable Models

We recapitulate the notion of preferred stable model presented in [3]. Intuitively, the priority information specified by the R_is in a dynamic prioritized program P is used to prefer among the stable models of P. This is achieved by first deleting (from P) all the rejected rules according to updates and then by deleting all the rules that are unpreferred according to preference information. The set of unpreferred rules contains (1) the rules defeated by the head of some more preferred rule, (2) the rules that attack a more preferred rule, and (3) the unsupported rules.

Definition 12 (Unsupported Rules). *Let P be a set of generalized rules over the language $\mathcal{L}_{\bar{\mathcal{K}}}$ and M an interpretation over $\mathcal{L}_{\bar{\mathcal{K}}}$. Then:*

$$Unsup(P, M) = \{r \in P : M \models head(r) \text{ and } M \not\models body^-(r)\}.$$

Definition 13 (Unpreferred Generalized Rule). *Let P be a set of generalized rules over the language $\mathcal{L}_{\bar{\mathcal{K}}}$ and M an interpretation over $\mathcal{L}_{\bar{\mathcal{K}}}$. Unpref($P, M$) is a set of unpreferred generalized rules of P and M iff:*

$$Unpref(P, M) = least(Unsup(P, M) \cup \mathcal{X})$$

where:

$$\mathcal{X} = \{r \in P \mid \exists r' \in (P - Unpref(P, M)) \text{ such that:}$$
$$M \models r' < r, \ M \models body^+(r') \text{ and}$$
$$[\ not \ head(r') \in body^-(r) \text{ or}$$
$$(not \ head(r) \in body^-(r'), \ M \models body(r)) \ ] \ \}.$$

Note that it is not possible to express preferences among the rules for predicate $<$. Therefore, no rule r for $<$ in P can be unpreferred, that is, $r \notin Unpref(P, M)$, for any set P of generalized rules and any interpretation M of P.

Definition 14 (Preferred Stable Models at State s). *Let $s \in S$ be a state. Let $P = \bigoplus\{(P_i, R_i) : i \in S\}$ be a dynamic prioritized program and M a stable model of P at state s. Then M is a preferred stable model of P at state s iff:*

- *$\forall r : (r < r) \notin M$*

- *$\forall r_1, r_2, r_3 : \ if \ (r_1 < r_2) \in M$ and $(r_2 < r_3) \in M$ then $(r_1 < r_3) \in M$*

- *$M = least([\ \mathcal{X}_s - Unpref(\mathcal{X}_s, M)\ ] \cup Default(\mathcal{PR}, M))$*

where $\mathcal{PR} = \bigcup_{i \leq s}(P_i \cup R_i)$, $Q = \bigoplus\{P_i \cup R_i : i \in S\}$, $\mathcal{X}_s = \mathcal{PR} - Reject(s, M, Q)$.

Notice that the definition above requires M to be a stable model of P in order for M to be a preferred stable model of P. This reflects the requirement that preference information is intended to select among alternative stable models of P. In general, there may exist several preferred stable models. If the priority relation induced by the priority rules is a total order over the generalized rules in P, then P will admit at most one preferred stable model.

Def. 12 of unsupported rules differs from the original one [3] in that we do not require the positive part of the body of r to be true in the model for r to be unsupported. Though this new definition may increase the number of unsupported rules, the preferred stable models are not affected. In fact, any extra rule r' in the new definition does not contribute to a model (since its body is false) nor can it be used to unprefer a less priority rule r (cf. Def. 13 where for r to be unpreferred by r', it is required that $M \models body^+(r')$).

Example 3. Let P be the dynamic prioritized program of Example 1. At state 2, P has a unique preferred stable model $M_{22} = \{t, us, n_1 < n_3, n_2 < n_3, n_2 < n_1\}$. At state 3, the preferred stable model of P is $M_{33} = \{n, bn, us, n_2 < n_1, n_3 < n_1, n_3 < n_2\}$.

6   Compiling Dynamic Prioritized Programs

In this section, we show how the Updates Plus Preferences approach [3] for dynamic prioritized programs can be encoded within standard stable model semantics. The encoding consists essentially of two parts: the encoding $DLP(s, P)$ for updating generalized and priority rules, and the new encoding $\tau(r)$ for taking into consideration preference information. The encoding $\tau(r)$ is based on the encoding developed in [9] for preferences alone. This encoding relies on several predicates that enable us to detect when a rule r has been applied ap(n_r), blocked bl(n_r), unsupported ko(n_r), and a predicate ok(n_r) that enables application of rules. If r is OK, then r can be applied or found to be inapplicable, that is, r is blocked. ok(n_r) relies on an auxiliary predicate ry(n_r, n_u). The idea of the translation is to control the order of rule application with respect to the priority information. This is achieved in the following way. If a rule r is preferable to a rule u (i.e., $n_r < n_u$), then ok(n_u) holds if r is OK and either r has been applied (i.e., ap(n_r)) or found to be inapplicable (i.e., bl(n_r)). Basically, the translation delays the consideration of less preferred rules until the applicability question has been settled for higher ranked rules. If there exists a rule in the program that cannot be proved OK, then the model does not respect the preference information and therefore it is not preferred.

In order to combine the $\tau(r)$ encoding with the $DLP(s, P)$ encoding, we have adapted the encoding in [9] to take into account the language $\mathcal{L}_{\widehat{\mathcal{K}}}$ of $DLP(s, P)$. Thus, we have substituted each default atom *not A* in a rule r with A^-. As in the updating phase rules can be rejected, and therefore cannot be used within the preferring phase, we need to consider them not in $\tau(r)$. This is achieved via the predicate reject(n_r). For the head of a rule r to be true, we further require that r is not rejected. Moreover, a rule is only enabled to be applicable if each more preferred rule has been applied, has been blocked or has been rejected. The integrity constraint in $\tau(r)$ rules out unpreferred models. A model is unpreferred if there exists a rule that is not rejected in the updating phase and cannot be proved OK.

By $\overline{\mathcal{K}}$ we denote the following superset of the set $\mathcal{K}$ of propositional variables:

$$\overline{\mathcal{K}} = \widehat{\mathcal{K}} \cup \{\tilde{A}, \tilde{A}^- : A \in \mathcal{K}\} \cup \{\mathrm{ko}(n_r), \mathrm{ap}(n_r), \mathrm{bl}(n_r), \mathrm{ry}(n_r, n_u) : \{n_r, n_u\} \subseteq N\}.$$

Given a rule r, we write $\tilde{r}$ to indicate the rule obtained from r by replacing each objective atom A occurring in r with $\tilde{A}$ and each default atom $not\,A$ with $not\,\tilde{A}$. For instance, if r is the rule $not\,A \leftarrow A_1, \ldots, A_n, not\,A_{n+1}, \ldots, not\,A_m$, then $\tilde{r}$ is $not\,\tilde{A} \leftarrow \tilde{A}_1, \ldots, \tilde{A}_n, not\,\tilde{A}_{n+1}, \ldots, not\,\tilde{A}_m$.

Let $\lceil . \rceil$ be a function from literals to objective atoms, where $\lceil A \rceil = A$ for every objective atom A and $\lceil not\,A \rceil = A^-$ for every default atom $not\,A$. We abbreviate $\lceil L_1 \rceil, \ldots, \lceil L_n \rceil$ by $\lceil L_1, \ldots, L_n \rceil$.

Definition 15. *Let $s \in S$ be a state. Let $P = \bigoplus\{(P_i, R_i) : i \in S\}$ be a dynamic prioritized program over the language $\mathcal{L}_{\overline{\mathcal{K}}}$. Let $\mathcal{P} = \bigcup_{i \leq s} P_i$. Suppose $\mathcal{P} = \{r_1, \ldots, r_k\}$. Then $\Gamma(s, P)$ is the following generalized logic program over the language $\mathcal{L}_{\overline{\mathcal{K}}}$:*

$$\Gamma(s, P) = DLP(s, P) \cup \bigcup_{r \in \mathcal{P}} \tau(r) \cup DA \cup SPO.$$

$\tau(r)$ **Rules:** *consists of the following collection of rules, for $A \in body^+(r)$, $not\,B \in body^-(r)$ and any rule $u \in \mathcal{P}$:*

$$\lceil head(\tilde{r}) \rceil \leftarrow \mathrm{ap}(n_r), not\,\mathrm{reject}(n_r)$$
$$\mathrm{ap}(n_r) \leftarrow \mathrm{ok}(n_r), \lceil body(r) \rceil, \lceil body^-(\tilde{r}) \rceil$$
$$\mathrm{bl}(n_r) \leftarrow \mathrm{ok}(n_r), A^-, \tilde{A}^-$$
$$\mathrm{bl}(n_r) \leftarrow \mathrm{ok}(n_r), B, \tilde{B}$$

$$\mathrm{ok}(n_r) \leftarrow \mathrm{ry}(n_r, n_{r_1}), \ldots, \mathrm{ry}(n_r, n_{r_k})$$
$$\mathrm{ry}(n_r, n_u) \leftarrow not\,(n_u < n_r)$$
$$\mathrm{ry}(n_r, n_u) \leftarrow (n_u < n_r), \mathrm{ap}(n_u)$$
$$\mathrm{ry}(n_r, n_u) \leftarrow (n_u < n_r), \mathrm{bl}(n_u)$$
$$\mathrm{ry}(n_r, n_u) \leftarrow \mathrm{ko}(n_u)$$
$$\mathrm{ry}(n_r, n_u) \leftarrow \mathrm{reject}(n_u)$$

$$false \leftarrow not\,\mathrm{ok}(n_r), not\,\mathrm{reject}(n_r)$$

$$\mathrm{ko}(n_r) \leftarrow \lceil head(r) \rceil, B$$

(DA) Default Atom Rules:

$$\tilde{A}^- \leftarrow not\,\tilde{A} \tag{13}$$

for all objective atoms $A \in \mathcal{K}$.

(SPO) Strict Partial Order Constraints:

$$false \leftarrow n_{r_1} < n_{r_1} \tag{14}$$

$$false \leftarrow n_{r_1} < n_{r_2}, n_{r_2} < n_{r_3}, (n_{r_1} < n_{r_3})^- \tag{15}$$

for every generalized rule $\{r_1, r_2, r_3\} \subseteq \mathcal{P}$.

The next result proves the correctness of the $\Gamma(s, P)$ transformation.

Theorem 2 (Soundness and Completeness). Let $s \in S$ be a state. Let P be a dynamic prioritized program over the language $\mathcal{L}_{\bar{\mathcal{K}}}$. An interpretation M of P is a (regular) stable model of $\Gamma(s, P)$ iff M, restricted to $\mathcal{L}_{\bar{\mathcal{K}}}$, is a preferred stable model of P at state s.

Next we summarize the technical properties of the $\tau(r)$ translation.

Proposition 2. Let $s \in S$ be a state. Let $P = \bigoplus \{(P_i, R_i) : i \in S\}$ be a dynamic prioritized program over the language $\mathcal{L}_{\bar{\mathcal{K}}}$ and M a (regular) stable model of $\Gamma(s, P)$. Let $\mathcal{P} = \bigcup_{i \leq s} P_i$. Then the following properties hold:

1. $\forall r \in \mathcal{P}$ if $reject(n_r) \notin M$, then $ok(n_r) \in M$.
2. $\forall r \in \mathcal{P}$ if $reject(n_r) \notin M$, then $[\ ap(n_r) \in M$ iff $bl(n_r) \notin M\ ]$.
3. $\forall r \in \mathcal{P}\ ko(n_r) \in M$ iff $r \in Unsup(\mathcal{P}, M)$.
4. $\forall r \in \mathcal{P}$ if $reject(n_r) \notin M$, then $[\ ko(n_r)$ implies $bl(n_r)\ ]$

7   Conclusions and Future Work

The technical motivation for our work consisted in obtaining a correct compilation into normal programs of logic programs subjected to updates and preferences combined under a stable models semantics. The transformation, achieved by a preprocessor, can be submitted to a stable models implementation to obtain the solutions, and we have done that too[2]. We started from three previous results, under a stable models semantics: (1) a semantical characterization of general logic programs updates plus preferences combined, including the updating of preferences [3] (2) a transformation into normal programs (and its implementation) of sequences of general logic program updates [2] (3) a transformation into normal programs of logic programs with preferences [9]. We then took (1) and extended (2) on the basis of a generalization of (3).

Importantly, the preference part of our transformation is modular or incremental with respect to the update part of the transformation, in the sense that successive updates only require incremental additions to the preference part of the transformation. Moreover, the size of the transformed program $\Gamma(s, P)$ in the worst case is quadratic on the size of the original dynamic prioritized program P. Ongoing work addresses the issue of garbage collection in DLP programs and

---

[2] An implementation of updates plus reference reasoning is available at:
http://centria.fct.unl.pt/~jja/updates.

extensions thereof. Namely, one wants to know under what conditions update rules can be ignored or permanently deleted, or how the transformed program may be compacted without loss of information for a class of queries. Related to this is the topic of making the most of tabling techniques to avoid repeated recomputations via the inertial rule.

The applications motivation of this technical work stems from some important application areas: e-commerce rule updating and preferring, including the updating of preferences; abductive reasoning with updatable preferences on the abducibles; updatable preferring among actions in planning; dynamically reconfigurable web-sites which adapt to updatable user profiles; reasoning under nonmonotonic uncertainty, where a solution must be sought and preferred among changing options.

Future work, apart from exploring some of the above mentioned application areas (e.g., the web-site one in project FLUX), will involve theoretical and technical solutions towards combining preferences and updates within the purview of well-founded semantics, namely by preferring among its partial stable models.

References

1. J. J. Alferes, P. Dell'Acqua, and L. M. Pereira. A compilation of updates plus preferences. Technical report, LiTH-ITN-R-2002-7, Dept. of Science and Technology, Linköping University, Sweden, 2002. Available at: http://www.itn.liu.se/english/research/.
2. J. J. Alferes, J. A. Leite, L. M. Pereira, H. Przymusinska, and T. C. Przymusinski. Dynamic updates of non-monotonic knowledge bases. *The J. of Logic Programming*, 45(1-3):43–70, 2000.
3. J. J. Alferes and L. M. Pereira. Updates plus preferences. In M. O. Aciego, I. P. de Guzman, G. Brewka, and L. M. Pereira (eds.) *Logics in AI, Procs. JELIA'00*, LNAI 1919, pp. 345–360, Berlin, 2000. Springer.
4. J. J. Alferes and L. M. Pereira. Logic Programming Updating - a guided approach - Essays in honour of Robert Kowalski. In A. Kakas and F. Sadri (eds.) *Computational Logic: From Logic Programming into the Future*. Springer, 2002. To appear. Available at: http://centria.di.fct.unl.pt/~lmp/.
5. G. Brewka. Well-founded semantics for extended logic programs with dynamic preferences. *Journal of Artificial Intelligence Research*, 4, 1996.
6. G. Brewka and T. Eiter. Preferred answer sets for extended logic programs. *Artificial Intelligence*, 109, 1999.
7. G. Brewka and T. Eiter. Preferred answer sets for extended logic programs. *Artificial Intelligence*, 109:297–356, 1999.
8. B. Cui and T. Swift. Preference logic grammars: Fixed-point semantics and application to data standardization. *Artificial Intelligence*, 2002. To appear.
9. J. Delgrande, T. Schaub, and H. Tompits. A compilation of Brewka and Eiter's approach to prioritization. In M. O. Aciego, I. P. de Guzman, G. Brewka, and L. M. Pereira (eds.), *Logics in AI, Procs. JELIA'00*, LNAI 1919, pp. 376–390, 2000.
10. M. Gelfond and V. Lifschitz. The stable model semantics for logic programming. In R. A. Kowalski and K. Bowen (eds.) *Proceedings of the Fifth International Conference on Logic Programming*, pp. 1070–1080, 1988. The MIT Press.
11. B. Grosof. Courteous logic programs: Prioritized conflict handling for rules. Research Report RC 20836, IBM, 1997.
12. K. Inoue and C. Sakama. Negation as failure in the head. *Journal of Logic Programming*, 35:39–78, 1998.
13. V. Lifschitz and T. Woo. Answer sets in general non-monotonic reasoning (preliminary report). In B. Nebel, C. Rich, and W. Swartout (eds.) *KR'92*. Morgan-Kaufmann, 1992.
14. H. Prakken. *Logical Tools for Modelling Legal Argument: A Study of Defeasible Reasoning in Law*, volume 32 of *Law and Philosophy Library*. Kluwer academic publishers, 1997.

Towards Service Description Logics

Piero A. Bonatti

Dip. di Tecnologie dell'Informazione, Università di Milano
bonatti@dti.unimi.it

Abstract. Semantic service description and matchmaking are needed in embedded and disappearing computing, cooperative multiagent systems, and the semantic web. Standard program semantics formalizations are not suited to modeling service semantics, because they are generic w.r.t. the data manipulated by programs, and because computation details are often irrelevant to the aforementioned applications of service descriptions. An ontology-based approach seems more appropriate. However, current ontology specification languages do not have primitives for service description. In this paper, we identify some useful service description constructs and study their impact on the decidability of reasoning with description logics.

Keywords: Description Logics, Semantic Web

1 Introduction

New application scenarios are posing challenging interoperability requirements on heterogeneous software and hardware components. They are designed, deployed and maintained independently, and may be dynamically added to, and removed from a common "environment" that may range from a single virtual machine or a local network to the World Wide Web.

The functionalities supported within the common environment arise from the interplay of different components. Therefore, new components may have to find partners to accomplish their task (or to offer their services), and existing components may have to find new partners as other components are removed or replaced. The scenario can be further complicated by assuming component cooperation to be occasional and demand driven.

Clearly, similar scenarios require a means to describe, index, retrieve and compare services, flexibly enough to accomodate dynamic service creation and deletion, as well as approximate matchmaking of service requests and offers. It is widely agreed that such generality and flexibility can only be achieved by describing service *semantics*, in some way. In the framework of the WWW, this is just a particular instantiation of the *semantic web*'s philosophy[1]. Semantic service descriptions may help both human users and software agents to locate and use web resources including the services behind web page forms.

---

[1] See the W3C pages at www.w3.org/2001/sw/

S. Flesca et al. (Eds.): JELIA 2002, LNAI 2424, pp. 74–85, 2002.

Now the question is: What kind of semantic description is needed for these purposes? The standard formalizations of program semantics seem not suited to service description, first of all because they are *generic* with respect to the data manipulated by the program. For example, a single piece of code that searches a table for a key value and returns the information associated to the key, may be used both to find an employee's salary given the employee's name, and to retrieve a credit card's expiration date given the card number. The intended applications of service descriptions need to distinguish these two cases, but standard program semantics cannot, because they are not sensitive to what the table contents encode.

Second, service descriptions should not (necessarily) describe computations. The focus should be on *what* is computed rather than *how*. Computation details can be profitably abstracted away in many cases, and service descriptions may turn out to be simpler to write and understand than typical program specifications. For example, a satisfactory service description may simply state that "given an address, the service returns a map of the 10000 square meters area around it".

A knowledge-based approach seems more appropriate to service description. Ontologies (as understood in computer science) are currently the most promising approach to content-based resource description. Informally, they are reference collections of symbols with an intended meaning. As such, ontologies are able to capture the differences behind isomorphic data structures and computations. Moreover, the knowledge representation languages currently adopted for expressing (the machine-understandable part of) ontologies have the right level of abstraction to describe what services do, as opposed to how they do it (e.g., the input and output of the above map service description could easily be encoded in a description logic).

A similar view can be found in [8], where a sophisticated matchmaking architecture is illustrated. However, in that paper service descriptions and the underlying ontology are not fully integrated. Service semantics is described by means of Horn clauses, and reasoning is based on clause subsumption (an incomplete inference method). The symbols occurring in Horn clauses are related to a reference ontology, but the potentialities of this link are not fully exploited. A tighter integration of service descriptions and ontologies is desirable. Service descriptions could become *part* of the ontology, and service semantics and matchmaking could perhaps be modelled more accurately through the rich operators and inferences of description logics.

Currently, description logics do not directly support service descriptions. Suitable constructs should be identified, and their impact on complexity and decidability should be investigated. In this paper, we move the first steps along this direction of research.

One of the main contributions is a *service description logic* $SDL(X)$, parametric with respect to an underlying concept description logic X. $SDL(X)$ is designed to capture service semantics and support semantic matchmaking with no reference to the underlying computation. From a technical standpoint, we are adding analogues of set abstraction and (simplified) joins to a simple description logic with n-ary relations.

It will be shown that reasoning with unrestricted service descriptions (similar to the usual TBoxes) is undecidable. Fortunately, under suitable restrictions (compatible with the intended applications of $\mathcal{SDL}(\mathcal{X})$), matchmaking is decidable, and service descriptions can be embedded into a concept description logic. It should be pointed out that service semantics—which this paper is focussed on—is only one aspect of service description. Other important issues such as service usage, cost, quality, etc., lie beyond the scope of this paper. Moreover, some important semantic aspects, such as side effects, are not covered by this work. For the sake of simplicity, we start by modeling *functional* services only.

The next section recalls some of the basic notions about description logics. Section 3 lays down a minimalistic list of desiderata for an ontology-based service description logic. $\mathcal{SDL}(\mathcal{X})$ is introduced in Section 4. Some undecidability results are proved in Section 5. Then, in Section 6 we will show how to reduce service matchmaking to decidable concept subsumption under suitable hypotheses. A brief discussion will conclude the paper. Most proofs will be omitted due to space limitations.

2   Preliminaries on Description Logics

The language of description logics is based on a vocabulary of atomic concepts and atomic roles. Let A range over atomic concepts and R range over atomic roles. The syntax of the description logic $\mathcal{ALC}$ is defined by the following grammar.

$$C, D \rightarrow A \mid C \sqcap D \mid C \sqcup D \mid \neg C \mid \exists R.C \mid \forall R.C \mid \top \mid \bot.$$

The semantics is based on interpretations of the form $\mathcal{I} = \langle \Delta^{\mathcal{I}}, \cdot^{\mathcal{I}} \rangle$ where $\Delta^{\mathcal{I}}$ is a set of *individuals* and $\cdot^{\mathcal{I}}$ is an interpretation function satisfying the following constraints.

$$
\begin{array}{ll}
A^{\mathcal{I}} \subseteq \Delta^{\mathcal{I}} & (C \sqcap D)^{\mathcal{I}} = C^{\mathcal{I}} \cap D^{\mathcal{I}} \\
R^{\mathcal{I}} \subseteq \Delta^{\mathcal{I}} \times \Delta^{\mathcal{I}} & (C \sqcup D)^{\mathcal{I}} = C^{\mathcal{I}} \cup D^{\mathcal{I}} \\
\top^{\mathcal{I}} = \Delta^{\mathcal{I}} & (\exists R.C)^{\mathcal{I}} = \{x \mid \exists y.[(x,y) \in R^{\mathcal{I}} \wedge y \in C^{\mathcal{I}}]\} \\
\bot^{\mathcal{I}} = \emptyset & (\forall R.C)^{\mathcal{I}} = \{x \mid \forall y.[(x,y) \in R^{\mathcal{I}} \rightarrow y \in C^{\mathcal{I}}]\} \\
(\neg C)^{\mathcal{I}} = \Delta^{\mathcal{I}} \setminus C^{\mathcal{I}}.
\end{array}
$$

An *assertion* of the form $C \sqsubseteq D$ is satisfied by $\mathcal{I}$ iff $C^{\mathcal{I}} \subseteq D^{\mathcal{I}}$. C *subsumes* D iff all interpretations $\mathcal{I}$ satisfy $C \sqsubseteq D$.

$\mathcal{ALC}$ can be extended with several useful constructs, some of which are recalled in the following. *Inverse roles* are denoted by R^- (where R is an atomic role). Their semantics is $(R^-)^{\mathcal{I}} = \{(x,y) \mid (y,x) \in R^{\mathcal{I}}\}$. Inverse roles may occur wherever atomic roles are allowed. *Features* are roles whose interpretations are restricted to partial functions. *Nominals* are distinguished atomic concepts that are interpreted as singletons in every interpretation (i.e., nominals represent individuals). *Fixpoints* are recursive concept definitions $\mu X.C$, where X is a *concept variable* that can be used in C as an atomic concept. An occurrence of X in C is *free* if it does not occur within the scope of μ. The semantics is $(\mu X.C)^{\mathcal{I}} = \bigcap \{ S \mid C^{\mathcal{I}}_{[X/S]} \subseteq S \}$, where $C^{\mathcal{I}}_{[X/S]}$ denotes the value of C in $\mathcal{I}$ when all the free occurrences of X in C are evaluated to S.

By convention, the name of a description logic contains an $\mathcal{I}$ if inverse roles are supported, an $\mathcal{O}$ if nominals are supported, and a μ if fixpoints are supported. For example, $\mathcal{ALCIO}$ denotes the extension of $\mathcal{ALC}$ with inverse roles and nominals. For more details, the reader is referred to [2,1,4,5].

3 Desiderata for a Service Description Logic

The issue informally investigated in this section is: Given a domain ontology $\mathcal{O}$ expressed with a description logic $\mathcal{X}$, and given a set of services $\mathcal{S}_1, \ldots, \mathcal{S}_n$ whose inputs and outputs can be described in terms of $\mathcal{O}$, identify some basic helpful constructs that could be added to $\mathcal{X}$ to describe the semantics of $\mathcal{S}_1, \ldots, \mathcal{S}_n$ and their mutual relationships.

Let us start with the simplest possible services (w.r.t. $\mathcal{O}$). Since ontologies define concepts and roles (or *attributes*), in the simplest case a service may just compute the extension of a concept, or some attribute of a given individual. So we get the first requirement for a service description logic (SDL, for short).

R1 For each concept C and role R in $\mathcal{O}$, a SDL should provide some expressions $C_{\to}$ and $R_{\to}$ to denote the corresponding services.

More generally, $\mathcal{S}$ may compute some attributes of concept instances identified by means of other attributes. Recall the map example. Suppose $\mathcal{O}$ defines a notion of *place*, whose attributes include an *address* and a *map*. Then the service returns the *map* attribute of the place whose *address* is given as input. In turn, the address can be a structured object, with attributes *state*, *city*, *street* and *number*, and the service may take these values as input. So, in general, the SDL should define services that map attribute chains (or *paths*) onto other attribute chains.

R2 For all concepts C in $\mathcal{O}$, a SDL should support some expression of the form $\{ p_1, \ldots, p_n \to q_1, \ldots, q_n \mid C \}$, to denote the mapping from the values of paths $p_1, \ldots, p_n$ onto the values of paths $q_1, \ldots, q_n$, for all the instances of C. We call such expressions *service abstractions*.

The map service could then be expressed by an expression similar to

$$\{ \, address.state, \ldots, \, address.number \to map \mid place \, \} \, .$$

A given component may happen to need a service $\mathcal{S}$ not available in the current environment. In that case, $\mathcal{S}$ may be replaced by another service $\mathcal{S}'$ whose semantics is related to the semantics of $\mathcal{S}$. $\mathcal{S}$ and $\mathcal{S}'$ need not necessarily be equivalent. For example, a service $\mathcal{S}'$ that computes at least the same input/output mappings as $\mathcal{S}$ may be just as good as (or even better than) $\mathcal{S}$

(consider a map service covering more countries than S). We call such replacement *service strengthening*. On the contrary, if S is a web search engine, we may be willing to replace it with a "sharper" search engine, i.e., one that returns no more documents than S. In that case S' should compute no more input/output mappings than S. We call such replacement *service weakening*.

R3 The SDL inferences should be able to test both service strengthening and service weakening.

Sometimes, S and its replacement S' are only required to be comparable on a restricted domain. For example, the map service might cover only addresses in Europe, but this may be enough if we are planning a travel to France. Technically, we need to check whether S' is a strengthening of the *restriction* of S to French addresses. Analogous considerations hold for service range. A component may ask for a service that strengthens the restriction of S to French maps.

R4 The SDL should feature domain and range restrictions.

Even if S is not immediately available, an equivalent service can be obtained by composing simpler services. For example, the map service can be reconstructed from a service S' mapping addresses onto latitude and longitude, plus a service S'' mapping latitude and longitude onto a map of the place.

R5 The SDL should model service composition (in a functional sense).

Of course this may require a flexible way of connecting outputs to inputs. For instance, a single output may have to be fed into multiple inputs, while other values may have to be ignored. This can be obtained as follows.

R6 The SDL should provide means for restructuring inputs and outputs—say—by replicating them, changing their order (if any), and ignoring them.

Services often operate on data sources that do not cover the whole extension of a concept or relation. Together, different services may extend the coverage. So, another useful form of composition is *service union*, corresponding to the set-theoretic union of the mappings. To see what this can be useful for, consider a portal that provides users with a unified view of two map services, one for Europe and one for the US, hiding the details of the composition.

R7 The SDL should support a form of service union.

The above constructs are simple and minimal, but they are powerful enough to capture a number of typical web services, including library catalogues, wheather reports, express mail delivery status, comparison shopping, bank information, financial and insurance information services, etc. In some applications, it is even possible to model services with side effects, such as reservations (provided that the temporal sequence in which reservations are produced is irrelevant).

4   The Parametric Service Description Logic $\mathcal{SDL}(\mathcal{X})$

The service description logic $\mathcal{SDL}(\mathcal{X})$ is defined by the grammar below. In the following, metavariables C, D, E (possibly with subscripts or superscripts) range over the concept expressions of the description logic $\mathcal{X}$, and R ranges over $\mathcal{X}$'s role expressions. Letters i and n (possibly with subscripts) denote integers. Letters F and G range over *service expressions*. Metavariable p and q range over *paths*, i.e., sequences of role names separated by dots, e.g., $R_1.R_2.\cdots.R_l$.

$$F, G \rightarrow \{\, p_1, \ldots, p_k \rightarrow q_1, \ldots, q_m \mid C \,\} \mid C_\rightarrow \mid R_\rightarrow \mid F \circ_i G \mid F[i_1, \ldots, i_m] \mid$$
$$\mid F(i_1, \ldots, i_k/n) \mid F \sqcup G \mid F \Downarrow (C_1 * \ldots * C_k \rightarrow D_1 * \ldots * D_m) \mid F^* \mid \mathrm{Id}.$$

Some constructs can be immediately identified with those introduced in the previous section. The others are service union $(F \sqcup G)$ and

- functional composition $(F \circ_i G)$, where the output of G is fed into the i-th input of F,
- the output-restructuring operator $F[i_1, \ldots, i_m]$ transforming the i_j-th output of F into the j-th output of the modified service,
- the input-restructuring operator $F(i_1, \ldots, i_k/n)$, that makes the new service accept n inputs and connects the i_j-th one to the j-th input of F,
- the operator $F \Downarrow (C_1 * \ldots * C_k \rightarrow D_1 * \ldots * D_m)$, for restricting F's domain and range to the given concepts.

Finally, we add two constructs that are not part of the minimal list of Section 3, but may be helpful for service description: transitive closure (F^*) and identity (Id). Even if $\mathcal{SDL}(\mathcal{X})$ is not supposed to model computations, some form of service iteration like F^* can be useful (e.g., to obtain ancestors from parents, or the indirect owners of a given company).

Each service expression F is associated to an *arity*, that is a pair of integers $(in(F), out(F))$ corresponding to the number of input and output values of the service. For example, if $F = \{\, p_1, \ldots, p_k \rightarrow q_1, \ldots, q_m \mid C \,\}$, then $in(F) = k$ and $out(F) = m$. The arity of $R_\rightarrow$ is $(1, 1)$. The restructuring operators may change their argument's arity to $out(F[i_1, \ldots, i_m]) = m$ and $in(F(i_1, \ldots, i_k/n)) = n$. *Well-typed* service expressions satisfy obvious constraints on their subexpressions' arity. In $F \sqcup G$, F and G should have the same arity. In $F \circ_i G$, $1 \leq i \leq in(F)$ and $out(G) = 1$. In F^*, the arity of F should be $(1, 1)$, and so forth.

The semantics of $\mathcal{SDL}(\mathcal{X})$ extends the semantics of $\mathcal{X}$ by mapping each well-typed service expression onto a set of tuples of the form $\langle x_1, \ldots, x_k, \langle y_1, \ldots, y_m \rangle \rangle$, where the x_is are the inputs of the service and the y_js are its outputs. Such tuples will be denoted by $x \mapsto y$. We do *not* assume that x uniquely determines y. The underlying intuition is that for each given input vector x, the service returns the set of all the associated y (this facilitates modelling query-like services, such as search engines and those mentioned in Section 3)[2].

---

[2] In other frameworks, similar non-functional mappings can be used to model nondeterministic services.

Let $\mathcal{I} = \langle \Delta^{\mathcal{I}}, \cdot^{\mathcal{I}} \rangle$ be an interpretation of $\mathcal{X}$. The interpretation function is extended to well-typed service expressions as shown by Figure 1. We abbreviate sequences of terms $t_1, \ldots, t_n$ using vector notation $\boldsymbol{t}$. In most cases, n is obvious from the context. For all paths $p = R_1.R_2.\cdots.R_l$, we denote by $p^{\mathcal{I}}$ the set of pairs $\langle d_1, d_{l+1} \rangle \in \Delta^I \times \Delta^I$ such that $\langle d_i, d_{i+1} \rangle \in R_i$ $(1 \leq i \leq l)$.

$$\{p \to q \mid C\}^{\mathcal{I}} = \left\{ \boldsymbol{d} \mapsto \boldsymbol{d'} \mid \exists e \in C^{\mathcal{I}}. \bigwedge_i \langle e, d_i \rangle \in p_i^{\mathcal{I}} \wedge \bigwedge_j \langle e, d'_j \rangle \in q_j^{\mathcal{I}} \right\}$$

$$C_{\to}^{\mathcal{I}} = \left\{ \mapsto d \mid d \in C^{\mathcal{I}} \right\}$$

$$R_{\to}^{\mathcal{I}} = \left\{ d_1 \mapsto d_2 \mid \langle d_1, d_2 \rangle \in R^{\mathcal{I}} \right\}$$

$$(F \sqcup G)^{\mathcal{I}} = F^{\mathcal{I}} \cup G^{\mathcal{I}}$$

$$(F \circ_i G)^{\mathcal{I}} = \left\{ d_1, \ldots, d_{i-1}, \boldsymbol{d'}, \boldsymbol{d''} \mapsto e \mid \boldsymbol{d'} \mapsto d_i \in G^{\mathcal{I}} \wedge \right.$$
$$\left. \wedge \, d_1, \ldots, d_{i-1}, d_i, \boldsymbol{d''} \mapsto e \in F^{\mathcal{I}} \right\}$$

$$F[i_1, \ldots, i_m]^{\mathcal{I}} = \left\{ \boldsymbol{d} \mapsto d'_{i_1}, \ldots, d'_{i_m} \mid \boldsymbol{d} \mapsto d'_1, \ldots, d'_n \in F^{\mathcal{I}} \right\}$$

$$F(i_1, \ldots, i_k/n)^{\mathcal{I}} = \left\{ d_1, \ldots, d_n \mapsto \boldsymbol{d'} \mid d_{i_1}, \ldots, d_{i_k} \mapsto \boldsymbol{d'} \in F^{\mathcal{I}} \right\}$$

$$F \Downarrow (C_1 * \ldots * C_k \to C_{k+1} * \ldots * C_m)^{\mathcal{I}} = \{ d_1, \ldots, d_k \mapsto d_{k+1}, \ldots, d_m \in F^{\mathcal{I}} \mid$$
$$d_i \in C_i \ (1 \leq i \leq m) \}$$

$$(F^*)^{\mathcal{I}} = \bigcup_{i \geq 0} (F^i)^{\mathcal{I}}, \text{ where } F^0 = \text{Id and } F^{i+1} = F \circ F^i$$

$$\text{Id}^{\mathcal{I}} = \left\{ d \mapsto d \mid d \in \Delta^{\mathcal{I}} \right\}$$

Fig. 1. $\mathcal{SDL}(\mathcal{X})$ semantics

An $\mathcal{SDL}(\mathcal{X})$ *TBox* is a set of *concept assertions* $C \sqsubseteq D$ and *service assertions* $F \sqsubseteq G$. Pairs of symmetric assertions such as $X \sqsubseteq Y$ and $Y \sqsubseteq X$ will be abbreviated by $X \equiv Y$. As usual, an interpretation $\mathcal{I}$ *satisfies* an assertion $X \sqsubseteq Y$ iff $X^{\mathcal{I}} \subseteq Y^{\mathcal{I}}$. If $\mathcal{I}$ satisfies all the assertions in a TBox $\mathcal{T}$, we say that $\mathcal{I}$ is a *model* of $\mathcal{T}$. If $\mathcal{T}$ has a model, we say that $\mathcal{T}$ is satisfiable. A TBox $\mathcal{T}$ *entails* an assertion $X \sqsubseteq Y$ —in symbols, $X \sqsubseteq_{\mathcal{T}} Y$ —if every model of $\mathcal{T}$ satisfies $X \sqsubseteq Y$. Notation $X \equiv_{\mathcal{T}} Y$ abbreviates the conjunction of $X \sqsubseteq_{\mathcal{T}} Y$ and $Y \sqsubseteq_{\mathcal{T}} X$.

Now, w.r.t. the definitions in $\mathcal{T}$, F is a *strengthening* of G (equivalently, G is a *weakening* of F), iff $G \sqsubseteq_{\mathcal{T}} F$, while F and G are *equivalent* if $G \sqsubseteq_{\mathcal{T}} F$ and $F \sqsubseteq_{\mathcal{T}} G$.

This is enough to cover all the forms of matchmaking outlined in Section 3. For example, service comparisons can be relativized to restricted domains $\boldsymbol{C}$ and range $\boldsymbol{D}$ with the restriction operator, as in $G \Downarrow (\boldsymbol{C} \to \boldsymbol{D}) \sqsubseteq_{\mathcal{T}} F \Downarrow (\boldsymbol{C} \to \boldsymbol{D})$. Service F can be strengthened by composing G and H if $F \sqsubseteq_{\mathcal{T}} G \circ_i H$, and so on.

Example 1. Suppose service `mapservice` $= \{\text{address} \to \text{map} \mid \text{ItalianPlaces}\}$ is needed, but only the following services are available:

$$\text{addr2coord} = \{\text{address} \to \text{coordinates} \mid \text{place}\}$$
$$\text{mapservice}_0 = \{\text{coordinates} \to \text{map} \mid \text{place}\}.$$

If the ontology $\mathcal{T}$ defines ItalianPlaces = place $\sqcap$ $\exists$address.$\exists$country.Italy and declares role coordinates$^-$ to be functional (i.e., coordinates is injective), then it can be verified that mapservice $\sqsubseteq_{\mathcal{T}}$ mapservice$_0$ $\circ_1$ addr2coord, that is, the desired service can be replaced by a suitable composition of the available services.   □

In the following sections we study the complexity of the entailment problem with respect to different classes of TBoxes.

5 Undecidability Results

First consider the most general class of $\mathcal{SDL}(\mathcal{X})$ TBoxes: those that may contain both concept assertions and service assertions. Unfortunately, under mild assumptions on the description logic $\mathcal{X}$, we can prove that reasoning with unrestricted TBoxes is undecidable.

We adopt a standard technique, and reduce *domino problems*—that are known to be undecidable—to reasoning with $\mathcal{SDL}(\mathcal{X})$ TBoxes. Domino problems are often represented as follows (for more details, see [3]).

Definition 1. *A domino system is a triple* $\mathcal{D} = (D, H, V)$, *where D is a finite set of* tile types *and $H, V \subseteq D^2$. A mapping τ from pairs of integers onto D is a* solution *of $\mathcal{D}$ if*

1. *if $\tau(x, y) = d$ and $\tau(x+1, y) = d'$ then $(d, d') \in H$, and*
2. *if $\tau(x, y) = d$ and $\tau(x, y+1) = d'$ then $(d, d') \in V$.*

Domino problems will be encoded into $\mathcal{SDL}(\mathcal{ALCI}_f)$. The description logic $\mathcal{ALCI}_f$ is a variant of $\mathcal{ALCI}$ where all roles are features. $\mathcal{ALCI}_f$ can be regarded as a common fragment of most description logics, including the DAML+OIL emerging standard[3]. Therefore, an undecidability result relative to $\mathcal{ALCI}_f$ well represents the difficulty of extending an existing ontology with service descriptions.

Domino problems can be encoded into $\mathcal{SDL}(\mathcal{ALCI}_f)$ in at least two ways. In both cases, a general TBox is built from the axioms in Figure 2 (where $C \Rightarrow D$ abbreviates $\neg C \sqcup D$), and the solution of the domino problem is reduced to TBox satisfiability as stated by the next lemma.

Lemma 1. *Consider the axioms in Figure 2, let $\mathcal{T}_1$ be the union of (1) and (3), and let $\mathcal{T}_2$ be the union of (2) and (3). The following statements are equivalent.*

1. *$\mathcal{T}_1$ is satisfiable.*
2. *$\mathcal{T}_2$ is satisfiable.*
3. *$\mathcal{D}$ has a solution τ.*

For the expert reader, we note that axioms (1) and (2) are two alternative ways of modelling the grid on which domino tiles are located, while (3) models the

---
[3] www.daml.org/2001/03/daml+oil-index

$$\{\, x.y \rightarrow y.x \mid \top \,\} \equiv \mathrm{Id} \tag{1}$$

$$\{\, x^- \rightarrow y \mid \top \,\} \equiv \{\, y^- \rightarrow x \mid \top \,\} \tag{2}$$

$$\top \sqsubseteq \left(\bigsqcup_{d \in D} D_d \right) \sqcap \prod_{d \in D} \prod_{d' \in D \setminus \{d\}} \neg (D_d \sqcap D_{d'}) \sqcap$$

$$\prod_{d \in D} \left(D_d \Rightarrow \exists x. \bigsqcup_{(d,d') \in H} D_{d'} \right) \sqcap \prod_{d \in D} \left(D_d \Rightarrow \exists y. \bigsqcup_{(d,d') \in V} D_{d'} \right) \tag{3}$$

Fig. 2. Axioms for a domino problem (D, H, V)

tiling. The functional roles x and y link adjacent grid nodes along the horizontal and vertical dimensions, respectively. Moreover, for each tile type d, a distinct concept name D_d is introduced. Axioms (1) and (2) both say that moving along the x axis and then along the y axis is equivalent to moving along the y axis first, and then along the x axis. Axiom (3) basically states that each individual in the interpretation is a tile (first term), that distinct tile types contain different tiles (rest of the first line), and that the tiling preserves the constraints specified by H and V (second line).

There exist tight relationships between this result and the undecidability of concept satisfiability in $\mathcal{ALCIF}$, proved in [4]. Here $\mathcal{F}$ stands for *feature agreement*, as $\mathcal{ALCIF}$ has constructs for forcing different paths to converge to the same individual. Note that both (1) and (2) force paths $x.y$ and $y.x$ to converge. Therefore, abstractions exhibit an expressive power similar to feature agreement.

Now we apply Lemma 1 to prove the undecidability of entailment.

Theorem 1. *The problem of deciding whether $F \sqsubseteq_{\mathcal{T}} G$, for given F, G and $\mathcal{T}$, is undecidable.*

Note that the axioms in Figure 2 use only a fragment of $\mathcal{SDL}(\mathcal{X})$. In $\mathcal{T}_1$ (cf. Lemma 1) no inverse roles are used, therefore $\mathcal{ALC}_f$ (the fragment of $\mathcal{ALCI}_f$ without inverse roles), extended with abstractions and Id is undecidable. Similarly, in $\mathcal{T}_2$, Id is not used, which means that $\mathcal{ALCI}_f$ plus abstractions is undecidable.

6   Decidability Results

Since reasoning with general TBoxes is undecidable, it is interesting to investigate entailment from $\mathcal{X}$-*TBoxes*, i.e., sets of concept assertions. This brings us back to the initial idea of deriving service specifications from the concepts and roles of an underlying ontology $\mathcal{O}$. Under a strict interpretation, this means that services and their mutual relationships must be defined only with $\mathcal{SDL}(\mathcal{X})$ operators and the axioms of $\mathcal{O}$—no service assertions are allowed. Fortunately, the examples mentioned so far can still be modelled in the restricted framework.

One positive consequence is that service descriptions cannot introduce new unexpected relationships between concepts and roles, i.e., a rudimentary form of modularity is enforced.

$\mathcal{SDL}(\mathcal{X})$ entailment from $\mathcal{X}$-TBoxes is often decidable. Decidability is established by reducing the entailment problem to TBox satisfiability in $\mathcal{ALCIO}_\mu$ (cf. Section 2).

Theorem 2. *In $\mathcal{ALCIO}_\mu$, TBox satisfiability and entailment are decidable in ExpTime.*

This theorem can be proved by extending in the obvious way the standard translations of description logics into propositional modal logics (eg., see [2]). In this case, the target modal logic is the *hybrid μ-calculus*, whose decidability and ExpTime completeness was proved recently [7].

Entailment of service assertions from $\mathcal{X}$-TBoxes can be reduced to concept satisfiability through the translation $\Psi_n^{C;D}(\cdot)$ illustrated in Figure 3. There, for all paths $p = R_1.\cdots.R_l$, we abbreviate $\exists R_1.\cdots.\exists R_l$ to $\exists p$.

The reduction between the two problems is obtained in three steps. First, service satisfiability is related to concept satisfiability.

$$\Psi_n^{C;D}(\{\boldsymbol{p} \to \boldsymbol{q} \mid E\}) = D_n \sqcap \exists q_n^-.\left[E \sqcap \left(\prod_i \exists p_i.C_i\right) \sqcap \left(\prod_{j \neq n} \exists q_j.D_j\right)\right]$$

$$\Psi_1^{;D}(C_\to) = C \sqcap D$$

$$\Psi_1^{C;D}(R_\to) = D \sqcap \exists R^-.C$$

$$\Psi_n^{C;D}(F \sqcup G) = \Psi_n^{C;D}(F) \sqcup \Psi_n^{C;D}(G)$$

$$\Psi_n^{C;D}(F \circ_i G) = \Psi_n^{C';D}(F),$$
$$\text{where } \boldsymbol{C}' = C_1, \ldots, C_{i-1}, \Psi_1^{C'';\top}(G), C_{i+in(G)}, \ldots C_{|C|}$$
$$\text{and } \boldsymbol{C}'' = C_i, \ldots, C_{i+in(G)-1}$$

$$\Psi_n^{C;D}(F[i_1, \ldots, i_m]) = \Psi_{i_n}^{C;D'}(F), \quad \text{where } D'_l = \begin{cases} D_j & \text{if } l = i_j \\ \top & \text{otherwise} \end{cases}$$

$$\Psi_n^{C;D}(F(i_1, \ldots, i_k/n)) = \Psi_n^{C';D}(F), \quad \text{where } \boldsymbol{C}' = C_{i_1}, \ldots, C_{i_k}$$

$$\Psi_n^{C;D}(F \Downarrow (E_1 * \ldots * E_k \to E_{k+1} * \ldots * E_m)) = \Psi_n^{C';D'}(F),$$
$$\text{where } C'_i = C_i \sqcap E_i \text{ and } D'_i = D_i \sqcap E_{i+k-1}$$

$$\Psi_1^{C;D}(F^*) = \Psi_1^{C;D}(\text{Id}) \sqcup \Psi_1^{C';D}(F)$$
$$\text{where } C' = \mu X.\left(\Psi_1^{C;\top}(\text{Id}) \sqcup \Psi_1^{X;\top}(F)\right)$$

$$\Psi_1^{C;D}(\text{Id}) = D \sqcap C$$

Fig. 3. Translation into concept expressions

Lemma 2. *Let F be a service expression in $\mathcal{SDL}(\mathcal{X})$ with arity (k,m) and let $1 \leq n \leq m$. Let $\mathcal{I}$ be an interpretation. Let $\boldsymbol{C}$ and $\boldsymbol{D}$ be two sequences of $\mathcal{X}$-concept expressions with k and m elements, respectively. Then the following statements are equivalent:*

1. *There exist two sequences of individuals $\boldsymbol{d} \in \boldsymbol{C}^{\mathcal{I}}$ and $\boldsymbol{d'} \in \boldsymbol{D}^{\mathcal{I}}$, such that $\boldsymbol{d} \mapsto \boldsymbol{d'} \in F^{\mathcal{I}}$.*
2. *There exists an individual d such that $d \in \Psi_n^{C;D}(F)^{\mathcal{I}}$.*

Next, $\mathcal{SDL}(\mathcal{X})$ entailment is reduced to TBox satisfiability by means of a form of skolemization based on fresh nominals.

Theorem 3. *Let $\mathcal{T}$ be an $\mathcal{X}$-TBox and F, G be $\mathcal{SDL}(\mathcal{X})$ service expressions with arity (k, m). Let $\boldsymbol{s}$ and $\boldsymbol{t}$ be two sequences of k and m distinct nominals (respectively), not occurring in F, G, $\mathcal{T}$. Then $F \sqsubseteq_{\mathcal{T}} G$ iff $\mathcal{T} \cup \{t_1 \sqsubseteq \Psi_1^{\boldsymbol{s};\boldsymbol{t}}(F), \Psi_1^{\boldsymbol{s};\boldsymbol{t}}(G) \sqsubseteq \bot\}$ is not satisfiable.*

Proof. (Sketch) $F \sqsubseteq_{\mathcal{T}} G$ is false iff there exists a model $\mathcal{I}_0$ of $\mathcal{T}$ such that $F^{\mathcal{I}_0} \setminus G^{\mathcal{I}_0} \neq \emptyset$. Since $\boldsymbol{s}$ and $\boldsymbol{t}$ do not occur in F, G, $\mathcal{T}$, their valuation in $\mathcal{I}_0$ can be changed without affecting the interpretation of F, G and $\mathcal{T}$. It follows that $F \sqsubseteq_{\mathcal{T}} G$ is false iff there exists a model $\mathcal{I}$ of $\mathcal{T}$ such that $\boldsymbol{s} \mapsto \boldsymbol{t} \in F^{\mathcal{I}} \setminus G^{\mathcal{I}}$ (for simplicity, we identify each nominal x with the unique member of $x^{\mathcal{I}}$). By Lemma 2, this condition is equivalent to $\exists d \in \Psi_1^{\boldsymbol{s};\boldsymbol{t}}(F)^{\mathcal{I}} \wedge \forall d.\ d \notin \Psi_1^{\boldsymbol{s};\boldsymbol{t}}(G)^{\mathcal{I}}$. Moreover, it can be verified by a straightforward structural induction on F that $d \in \Psi_n^{\boldsymbol{s};\boldsymbol{t}}(F)^{\mathcal{I}}$ implies $d \in t_n$. Then $F \sqsubseteq_{\mathcal{T}} G$ is false iff there exists a model $\mathcal{I}$ of $\mathcal{T}$ satisfying $t_1 \sqsubseteq \Psi_1^{\boldsymbol{s};\boldsymbol{t}}(F)$ and $\Psi_1^{\boldsymbol{s};\boldsymbol{t}}(G) \sqsubseteq \bot$. The theorem immediately follows. □

Now decidability follows immediately from theorems 2 and 3, and from the observation that the translation of service expressions needs only the operators of $\mathcal{ALCIO}_\mu$.

Corollary 1. *If $\mathcal{X}$ is an extension of $\mathcal{ALCIO}_\mu$ and TBox satisfiability is decidable in $\mathcal{X}$, then entailment from $\mathcal{X}$-TBoxes is decidable in $\mathcal{SDL}(\mathcal{X})$. In particular, entailment from $\mathcal{X}$-TBoxes in $\mathcal{SDL}(\mathcal{ALCIO}_\mu)$ is decidable.*

7   Discussion and Future Work

Summarizing, we have identified a minimal list of prerequisites that a service description logic should meet in order to model services of a functional nature. The (parametric) description logic $\mathcal{SDL}(\mathcal{X})$ has been defined to meet these requirements. The basic inferences related to service matching have been proved to be decidable under two conditions: (i) TBoxes should be limited to concept assertions, and (ii) the union of $\mathcal{X}$ and $\mathcal{ALCIO}_\mu$ should have a decidable satisfiability problem. The proof of decidability introduces a skolemization technique based on nominals. It is remarkable that the translation of Id does not require the identity role.

$\mathcal{SDL}(\mathcal{X})$ has some analogies with $\mathcal{DLR}_\mu$ [1]. Both logics model n-ary relations of some sort, but $\mathcal{SDL}(\mathcal{X})$ features the analogue of set abstractions and a simplified form of join ($\circ_i$), while $\mathcal{DLR}_\mu$ supports unrestricted fixpoints (that have been restricted to $(\cdot)^*$ in $\mathcal{SDL}(\mathcal{X})$). It is not hard to see—by analogy with the results for $\mathcal{SDL}(\mathcal{X})$—that if $\mathcal{DLR}_\mu$ were extended with set abstractions then its reasoning problems would become undecidable, as well. It remains to be seen whether abstractions and unrestricted fixpoints can be simultaneously supported without affecting decidability, at least under condition (i).

This is not the only interesting open problem. The complexity of $\mathcal{SDL}(\mathcal{X})$ for the major logics $\mathcal{X}$ has not yet been characterized. In particular, the complexity of the hybrid μ-calculus with counting is still unknown [7], and hence the same is true of the complexity of $\mathcal{SDL}(\mathcal{X})$ when $\mathcal{X}$ features number restrictions.

We believe that in $\mathcal{SDL}(\mathcal{X})$ the restriction to $\mathcal{X}$-TBoxes can be relaxed, as far as service specifications remain a conservative extension of the underlying ontology (e.g., by admitting acyclic service definitions).

Several interesting operators could be added to $\mathcal{SDL}(\mathcal{X})$, including conditionals, inverse services, and a parallel form of composition. Some interesting reasoning services have not been considered in this paper. Services with side-effects and the other aspects of service description (such as cost, quality etc.) are still unexplored. All these aspects will be dealt with in future work.

Moreover, for an experimental evaluation of our approach, we are developing in Prolog a prototype implementation of the *-free fragment of $\mathcal{SDL}(\mathcal{X})$, where $\mathcal{X}$ is $\mathcal{ALCIO}$ extended with functional and injective roles. We have implemented strengthening checks and are currently adding more reasoning functionalities.

References

1. D. Calvanese, G. De Giacomo, M. Lenzerini. Reasoning in expressive description logics with fixpoints based on automata on infinite trees. In *Proc. of IJCAI'99*, 1999.
2. G. De Giacomo. Decidability of class-based knowledge representation formalisms. PhD Thesis, Università di Roma "La Sapienza", 1995.
3. E. Grädel, M. Otto, E. Rosen. Undecidability results on two-variable logics. Archive for Mathematical Logic, 38:213-354, 1999.
4. C. Lutz. NExpTime-complete description logics with concrete domains. LTCS-Report 00-01, LuFG Theoretical Computer Science, RWTH Aachen, Germany, 2000.
5. C. Lutz, U. Sattler, F. Wolter. Description logics and the two-variable fragment. In *Proc. of DL'01*, 2001.
6. A. Omicini, F. Zambonelli, M. Klusch, R. Tolksdorf (eds). *Coordination of Internet Agents*, Springer, 2001.
7. U. Sattler, M.Y. Vardi. The hybrid μ-calculus. In *Proc. of IJCAR'01*, 2001.
8. K. Sycara, J. Lu, M. Klusch, S. Widoff. Matchmaking among heterogeneous agents on the internet. In *Proc. of the AAAI Spring Symposium on Intelligent Agents in Cyberspace*, Stanford, USA, 1999.

P-$\mathcal{SHOQ}$(D): A Probabilistic Extension of $\mathcal{SHOQ}$(D) for Probabilistic Ontologies in the Semantic Web

Rosalba Giugno[1] and Thomas Lukasiewicz[2,*]

[1] Dipartimento di Matematica e Informatica, Università degli Studi di Catania
Città Universitaria, Viale A. Doria 6, 95152 Catania, Italy
giugno@dmi.unict.it

[2] Dipartimento di Informatica e Sistemistica, Università di Roma "La Sapienza"
Via Salaria 113, 00198 Roma, Italy
lukasiewicz@dis.uniroma1.it

Abstract. Ontologies play a central role in the development of the semantic web, as they provide precise definitions of shared terms in web resources. One important web ontology language is DAML+OIL; it has a formal semantics and a reasoning support through a mapping to the expressive description logic $\mathcal{SHOQ}(\mathbf{D})$ with the addition of inverse roles. In this paper, we present a probabilistic extension of $\mathcal{SHOQ}(\mathbf{D})$, called P-$\mathcal{SHOQ}(\mathbf{D})$, to allow for dealing with probabilistic ontologies in the semantic web. The description logic P-$\mathcal{SHOQ}(\mathbf{D})$ is based on the notion of probabilistic lexicographic entailment from probabilistic default reasoning. It allows to express rich probabilistic knowledge about concepts and instances, as well as default knowledge about concepts. We also present sound and complete reasoning techniques for P-$\mathcal{SHOQ}(\mathbf{D})$, which are based on reductions to classical reasoning in $\mathcal{SHOQ}(\mathbf{D})$ and to linear programming, and which show in particular that reasoning in P-$\mathcal{SHOQ}(\mathbf{D})$ is decidable.

1 Introduction

The development of the *semantic web*, a vision for a future generation of the world wide web, aims at making web resources more easily accessible to automated processing by annotating web pages with machine-readable information on their content [2].

In the semantic web, ontologies are playing a central role as a source of shared and precisely defined terms that can be used in machine-readable semantic annotations of web pages. One important web ontology language is DAML+OIL [12,13], which was developed by merging DAML [10] and OIL [5]. A formal semantics and an automated reasoning support is provided to DAML+OIL through a mapping to the expressive description logic $\mathcal{SHOQ}(\mathbf{D})$ [16,25] with the addition of inverse roles.

In the recent decades, dealing with probabilistic uncertainty has started to play an important role in database systems and knowledge representation and reasoning formalisms. We expect expressing and handling probabilistic knowledge to also play an

---

* Alternate address: Institut für Informationssysteme, Technische Universität Wien, Favoritenstraße 9-11, 1040 Wien, Austria. E-mail: lukasiewicz@kr.tuwien.ac.at.

S. Flesca et al. (Eds.): JELIA 2002, LNAI 2424, pp. 86–97, 2002.
© Springer-Verlag Berlin Heidelberg 2002

important role in web ontology languages, which are essentially standardized languages for knowledge representation and reasoning, where significant research efforts are currently inspired by ideas from databases, such as supporting query languages and large instances [12,13]. In particular, probabilistic web ontology languages may act as standardized tools to provide automated global web access to existing local data and knowledge base systems containing probabilistic information. It is thus not surprising that the OIL group writes in [14] that "a further level of extension" of OIL "could include modeling primitives such as defaults and fuzzy / probabilistic definitions". However, to our knowledge, there are no such extensions of web ontology languages so far.

In this paper, we propose such an extension. The main contributions of this paper can be summarized as follows:

- We present a probabilistic extension of the description logic $\mathcal{SHOQ}(D)$, called P-$\mathcal{SHOQ}(\mathbf{D})$, which is based on the notion of probabilistic lexicographic entailment; this approach is motivated by recent advances to probabilistic default reasoning [22,23]. Note especially that probabilistic lexicographic entailment has very nice properties for the use in probabilistic reasoning with generic and assertional (i.e., Abox) probabilistic knowledge [22,23].
- P-$\mathcal{SHOQ}(\mathbf{D})$ allows to express default knowledge as a special case of generic probabilistic knowledge, where reasoning with such default knowledge is based on the sophisticated notion of lexicographic entailment by Lehmann [20].
- We present sound and complete techniques for probabilistic reasoning in the description logic P-$\mathcal{SHOQ}(\mathbf{D})$, which are based on reductions to classical reasoning in $\mathcal{SHOQ}(\mathbf{D})$ and to linear programming, and which show in particular that reasoning in P-$\mathcal{SHOQ}(\mathbf{D})$ is decidable. Note that due to the presence of individuals in P-$\mathcal{SHOQ}(\mathbf{D})$ (and also $\mathcal{SHOQ}(\mathbf{D})$), these techniques are technically more involved than the ones for probabilistic default reasoning in [22,23].

There are several related approaches to probabilistic description logics in the literature [9,18,19], which can be classified according to the supported forms of probabilistic knowledge and the underlying probabilistic reasoning formalism. Heinsohn [9] presents a probabilistic extension of the description logic $\mathcal{ALC}$, which allows to represent generic probabilistic knowledge about concepts and roles, and which is essentially based on probabilistic reasoning in probabilistic logics, similar to [24,1,6,21]. The work [9], however, does not allow for assertional knowledge about concept and role instances. Also Jaeger [18] gives a probabilistic extension of the description logic $\mathcal{ALC}$, which allows for generic (resp., assertional) probabilistic knowledge about concepts and roles (resp., concept instances), but does not support probabilistic knowledge about role instances (but he mentions a possible extension in this direction). The uncertain reasoning formalism in [18] is essentially based on probabilistic reasoning in probabilistic logics, as the one in [9], but coupled with cross-entropy minimization to combine generic probabilistic knowledge with assertional probabilistic knowledge. The work by Koller et al. [19] gives a probabilistic generalization of the CLASSIC description logic. Like Heinsohn's work [9], it allows for generic probabilistic knowledge about concepts and roles, but does not support assertional knowledge about concept and role instances. However, differently from [9], it is based on inference in Bayesian networks as underlying probabilistic reasoning formalism. Note that approaches to fuzzy description logics [29,28,26,27] are less closely related, as fuzzy uncertainty deals with vagueness, rather than ambiguity and imprecision.

The probabilistic description logic in this paper differs from [9,18,19] in several ways. First, it is a probabilistic extension of the expressive description logic $\mathcal{SHOQ}(\mathbf{D})$, which provides a formal semantics and reasoning support for DAML+OIL (without inverse roles). Second, it allows to represent both generic probabilistic knowledge about concepts and roles, and also assertional probabilistic knowledge about concept and role instances, Third, it is based on probabilistic lexicographic entailment from probabilistic default reasoning [22,23] as underlying probabilistic reasoning formalism.

Note that detailed proofs of all results and further technical results are given in the extended paper [7].

2 Motivating Example

To illustrate the possible use of probabilistic ontologies in the semantic web, consider some medical knowledge about patients. It is advantageous to share such knowledge between hospitals or medical centers [11], for example, to follow up patients, to track medical history, and for case studies research. Furthermore, in medical knowledge, we often have to deal with probabilistic uncertainty.

For example, consider patient records related to cardiological illnesses. The patients may be classified according to their gender, as the probability that a man has a cardiological illness or a pacemaker is different from the corresponding probability associated with a woman. We may have the *default knowledge* that cardiological illnesses typically cause high blood pressure, but that pacemaker patients typically do not suffer from high blood pressure. We may have the *probabilistic knowledge* that the symptoms of a pacemaker patient are abnormal heart beat (arrhythmia) with a probability in $[.98, 1]$, chest pain with a probability in $[.9, 1]$, and breathing difficulties with a probability in $[.6, 1]$.

In the description logic $\mathcal{SHOQ}(\mathbf{D})$, we distinguish between *concrete datatypes*, *individuals*, *concepts* (i.e., sets of individuals), and *roles* (i.e., binary relations on concepts, or between concepts and datatypes). For example, we may have concepts for patients, pacemaker patients, heart patients, female patients, male patients, symptoms, health insurances, and illness statuses. As individuals, we may have the heart patient John, the symptoms arrhythmia, chest pain, and breathing difficulties, and the illness statuses advanced and final. Moreover, we may use roles to relate patients with their health insurances and with the status of their illnesses.

In P-$\mathcal{SHOQ}(\mathbf{D})$, we can express the following forms of probabilistic knowledge:

- The probabilistic knowledge that an instance of a concept is also an instance of another concept. E.g., the probability that a pacemaker patient is a man is in $[.4, 1]$.
- The probabilistic knowledge that an arbitrary instance of a concept is related to a given individual by a given role. E.g., the probability that a heart patient has a private insurance is in $[.9, 1]$.
- The probabilistic knowledge that an individual is an instance of a concept. E.g., the probability that difficulty breathing is a symptom of a pacemaker patient is in $[.6, 1]$, while the probability that chest pain is such a symptom is in $[.9, 1]$.
- The probabilistic knowledge that an individual is related to another individual by a role. E.g., the probability that the status of John's illness is final is in $[.2, .8]$.

3 $\mathcal{SHOQ}(D)$

In this section, we briefly recall the description logic $\mathcal{SHOQ}(D)$ from [16].

3.1 Syntax

We assume a set $\mathbf{D}$ of *concrete datatypes*. Every datatype $d \in \mathbf{D}$ is assigned a *domain* $\mathrm{dom}(d)$. We use $\mathrm{dom}(\mathbf{D})$ to denote the union of the domains $\mathrm{dom}(d)$ of all datatypes $d \in \mathbf{D}$. Let $\mathbf{C}$, $\mathbf{R}_A$, $\mathbf{R}_D$, and $\mathbf{I}$ be nonempty finite disjoint sets of *atomic concepts*, *abstract roles*, *concrete roles*, and *individuals*, respectively.

Concepts are inductively defined as follows. Every atomic concept from $\mathbf{C}$ is a concept. If o is an individual from $\mathbf{I}$, then $\{o\}$ is a concept. If C and D are concepts, then also $(C \sqcap D)$, $(C \sqcup D)$, and $\neg C$ (called *conjunction*, *disjunction*, and *negation*, respectively). If C is a concept, R is an abstract role from $\mathbf{R}_A$, and n is a nonnegative integer, then $\exists R.C$, $\forall R.C$, $\geq nR.C$, and $\leq nR.C$ are concepts (called *exists, value, atleast,* and *atmost restriction*, respectively). If T is a concrete role from $\mathbf{R}_D$, and d is a concrete datatype from $\mathbf{D}$, then $\exists T.d$ and $\forall T.d$ are concepts (called *datatype exists* and *value*, respectively). We write $\top$ (resp., $\bot$) to abbreviate $C \sqcup \neg C$ (resp., $C \sqcap \neg C$), and we eliminate parentheses as usual.

A *concept inclusion axiom* is an expression of the form $C \sqsubseteq D$, where C and D are concepts. A *role inclusion axiom* is an expression of the kind $R \sqsubseteq S$, where either $R, S \in \mathbf{R}_A$ or $R, S \in \mathbf{R}_D$. A *transitivity axiom* has the form $\mathrm{Trans}(R)$, where $R \in \mathbf{R}_A$. A *terminological axiom* is either a concept inclusion axiom, a role inclusion axiom, or a transitivity axiom. A *terminology* $\mathcal{T}$ is a finite set of terminological axioms. A role R is called *simple* w.r.t. $\mathcal{T}$ iff for each role S, it holds that $S \sqsubseteq^* R$ implies $\mathrm{Trans}(S) \notin \mathcal{T}$, where $\sqsubseteq^*$ is the transitive and reflexive closure of $\sqsubseteq$ on $\mathcal{T}$.

It is important to point out that the above terminologies are expressive enough to also express knowledge about instances of concepts and abstract roles: The knowledge that the individual o is an instance of the concept C can be expressed by the concept inclusion axiom $\{o\} \sqsubseteq C$; the knowledge that the pair of individuals (o_1, o_2) is an instance of the abstract role R can be expressed by the concept inclusion axiom $\{o_1\} \sqsubseteq \exists R.\{o_2\}$. We thus use $o \in C$ (resp., $(o_1, o_2) \in R$) to abbreviate $\{o\} \sqsubseteq C$ (resp., $\{o_1\} \sqsubseteq \exists R.\{o_2\}$). Note also that attributes (that is, functional roles) of concepts can be expressed as follows. To say that the concept D has the attribute A with the possible values $v_1, \ldots, v_k$, we can write $D \sqsubseteq \geq 1A.C \sqcap \leq 1A.C \sqcap \forall A.C$, where A is an abstract role from $\mathbf{R}_A$, and C is an atomic concept from $\mathbf{C}$ that is defined by $C \sqsubseteq \{v_1\} \sqcup \cdots \sqcup \{v_k\}$ and $\{v_1\} \sqcup \cdots \sqcup \{v_k\} \sqsubseteq C$, where $v_1, \ldots, v_k$ are individuals from $\mathbf{I}$.

3.2 Semantics

An *interpretation* $\mathcal{I} = (\Delta, I)$ w.r.t. $\mathbf{D}$ consists of a nonempty *(abstract) domain* Δ and a mapping I that assigns to each atomic concept from $\mathbf{C}$ a subset of Δ, to each $\{o\}$ with $o \in \mathbf{I}$ a singleton subset of Δ, to each abstract role from $\mathbf{R}_A$ a subset of $\Delta \times \Delta$, and to each concrete role from $\mathbf{R}_D$ a subset of $\Delta \times \mathrm{dom}(\mathbf{D})$. The interpretation I is extended by induction to all concepts as follows (where $\#S$ denotes the cardinality of a set S):

- $I(C \sqcap D) = I(C) \cap I(D)$, $I(C \sqcup D) = I(C) \cup I(D)$, and $I(\neg C) = \Delta \setminus I(C)$,
- $I(\exists R.C) = \{x \in \Delta \mid \exists y \colon (x, y) \in I(R) \wedge y \in I(C)\}$,
- $I(\forall R.C) = \{x \in \Delta \mid \forall y \colon (x, y) \in I(R) \rightarrow y \in I(C)\}$,
- $I(\geq nR.C) = \{x \in \Delta \mid \#(\{y \mid (x, y) \in I(R)\} \cap I(C)) \geq n\}$,
- $I(\leq nR.C) = \{x \in \Delta \mid \#(\{y \mid (x, y) \in I(R)\} \cap I(C)) \leq n\}$,
- $I(\exists T.d) = \{x \in \Delta \mid \exists y \colon (x, y) \in I(T) \wedge y \in \mathrm{dom}(d)\}$,
- $I(\forall T.d) = \{x \in \Delta \mid \forall y \colon (x, y) \in I(T) \rightarrow y \in \mathrm{dom}(d)\}$.

The *satisfaction* of a terminological axiom F in $\mathcal{I}$, denoted $\mathcal{I} \models F$, is defined by: (i) $\mathcal{I} \models C \sqsubseteq D$ iff $I(C) \subseteq I(D)$, (ii) $\mathcal{I} \models R \sqsubseteq S$ iff $I(R) \subseteq I(S)$, and (iii) $\mathcal{I} \models \mathrm{Trans}(R)$ iff $I(R)$ is transitive. The interpretation $\mathcal{I}$ *satisfies* the axiom F, or $\mathcal{I}$ is a *model* of F, iff $\mathcal{I} \models F$. It *satisfies* a terminology $\mathcal{T}$, or $\mathcal{I}$ is a *model* of $\mathcal{T}$, denoted $\mathcal{I} \models \mathcal{T}$, iff $\mathcal{I} \models F$ for all $F \in \mathcal{T}$. We say $\mathcal{T}$ is *satisfiable* iff $\mathcal{T}$ has a model. A terminological axiom F is a *logical consequence* of $\mathcal{T}$, denoted $\mathcal{T} \models F$, iff every model of $\mathcal{T}$ is also a model of F.

3.3   Reasoning Tasks

The following are some important reasoning tasks related to terminologies $\mathcal{T}$:

Terminology-Satisfiability: Given $\mathcal{T}$, decide whether $\mathcal{T}$ is satisfiable.
Concept-Satisfiability: Given $\mathcal{T}$ and a concept C, decide whether $\mathcal{T} \not\models C \sqsubseteq \bot$.
Concept-Subsumption: Given $\mathcal{T}$ and concepts C, D, decide whether $\mathcal{T} \models C \sqsubseteq D$.
Concept-Membership: Given $\mathcal{T}$, $o \in \mathbf{I}$, and a concept C, decide whether $\mathcal{T} \models o \in C$.
Role-Membership: Given $\mathcal{T}$, $o_1, o_2 \in \mathbf{I}$, and $R \in \mathbf{R}_A$, decide if $\mathcal{T} \models (o_1, o_2) \in R$.

Obviously, Concept-Membership and Role-Membership are special cases of Concept-Subsumption. Furthermore, Terminology-Satisfiability is a special case of Concept-Satisfiability, as $\mathcal{T}$ is satisfiable iff $\mathcal{T} \not\models \top \sqsubseteq \bot$. Finally, Concept-Satisfiability and Concept-Subsumption can be reduced to each other, as $\mathcal{T} \models C \sqcap \neg D \sqsubseteq \bot$ iff $\mathcal{T} \models C \sqsubseteq D$. These last two problems are decidable in $\mathcal{SHOQ}(\mathbf{D})$, if all atmost and atleast restrictions in $\mathcal{T}$ are restricted to simple abstract roles w.r.t. $\mathcal{T}$ [16].

4   P-$\mathcal{SHOQ}$(D)

In this section, we present the description logic P-$\mathcal{SHOQ}(\mathbf{D})$, which is a probabilistic extension of $\mathcal{SHOQ}(\mathbf{D})$. We first define the syntax of P-$\mathcal{SHOQ}(\mathbf{D})$, where we use conditional constraints [21] to express probabilistic knowledge in addition to the terminological axioms of $\mathcal{SHOQ}(\mathbf{D})$. We then define the semantics of P-$\mathcal{SHOQ}(\mathbf{D})$, which is based on lexicographic entailment from probabilistic default reasoning; see especially [22,23] for background, intuitions, and further examples. We finally summarize some important reasoning problems in P-$\mathcal{SHOQ}(\mathbf{D})$.

4.1   Syntax

We now define the notion of a probabilistic terminology. It is based on the language of conditional constraints [21], which encode interval restrictions for conditional probabilities over concepts. Every probabilistic terminology consists of a generic part, which expresses generic classical and probabilistic knowledge about concepts, and an assertional part, which represents classical and probabilistic knowledge about a set of individuals. In the sequel, we partition the set of individuals $\mathbf{I}$ into the set of *classical individuals* $\mathbf{I}_C$ and the set of *probabilistic individuals* $\mathbf{I}_P$. Intuitively, probabilistic individuals are those individuals in $\mathbf{I}$ for which we explicitly store some classical and probabilistic knowledge in a probabilistic terminology.

A *conditional constraint* is an expression of the form $(D|C)[l, u]$ with concepts C, D, and real numbers $l, u \in [0, 1]$. A concept (resp., concept inclusion axiom, conditional constraint) is *generic* iff no probabilistic individual $o \in \mathbf{I}_P$ occurs in it. A concept inclusion axiom (resp., conditional constraint) is *assertional* for a probabilistic individual $o \in \mathbf{I}_P$ iff it is of the form $\{o\} \sqsubseteq D$ (resp., $(D|\{o\})[l, u]$), where D is generic. A *generic probabilistic terminology* (resp., an *assertional probabilistic terminology* for a probabilistic individual $o \in \mathbf{I}_P$) $\mathcal{P} = (\mathcal{T}, \mathcal{D})$ consists of a classical terminology $\mathcal{T}$ and a finite set of conditional constraints $\mathcal{D}$ such that every concept inclusion axiom in $\mathcal{T}$ and every conditional constraint in $\mathcal{D}$ is generic (resp., assertional for o). A *probabilistic terminology* $\mathcal{P} = (\mathcal{P}_g, (\mathcal{P}_o)_{o \in \mathbf{I}_P})$ with respect to $\mathbf{I}_P$ consists of a generic probabilistic terminology $\mathcal{P}_g$ and an assertional probabilistic terminology $\mathcal{P}_o$ for every $o \in \mathbf{I}_P$.

The different kinds of probabilistic knowledge that can be represented through conditional constraints in P-$\mathcal{SHOQ}(\mathbf{D})$ are briefly illustrated as follows:

- The probabilistic knowledge that "an instance of the concept C is also an instance of the concept D with a probability in $[l, u]$" can be expressed by $(D|C)[l, u]$.
- The probabilistic knowledge that "an arbitrary instance of the concept C is related to a given individual $o \in \mathbf{I}_C$ by a given role $R \in \mathbf{R}_A$ with a probability in $[l, u]$" can be expressed by $(\exists R.\{o\}|C)[l, u]$.
- The probabilistic knowledge that "the individual $o \in \mathbf{I}_P$ is an instance of the concept D with a probability in $[l, u]$" can be expressed by $(D|\{o\})[l, u]$.
- The probabilistic knowledge that "the individual $o \in \mathbf{I}_P$ is related to the individual $o' \in \mathbf{I}_C$ by the role $R \in \mathbf{R}_A$ with a probability in $[l, u]$" can be expressed by $(\exists R.\{o'\}|\{o\})[l, u]$.

4.2 Semantics

We now define the semantics of P-$\mathcal{SHOQ}(\mathbf{D})$. We first generalize classical interpretations to probabilistic interpretations by adding a probability distribution over the abstract domain. We then define the satisfaction of terminological axioms and conditional constraints in probabilistic interpretations. We finally define the notions of consistency and entailment for probabilistic terminologies, which are based on the notions of consistency and lexicographic entailment in probabilistic default reasoning [22,23].

A *probabilistic interpretation* $Pr = (\mathcal{I}, \mu)$ w.r.t. the set of concrete datatypes $\mathbf{D}$ consists of a classical interpretation $\mathcal{I} = (\Delta, I)$ w.r.t. $\mathbf{D}$ and a probability function μ on Δ (that is, a mapping $\mu \colon \Delta \to [0, 1]$ such that all $\mu(o)$ with $o \in \Delta$ sum up to 1).

We now define the probability of a concept and the satisfaction of terminological axioms and conditional constraints in probabilistic interpretations as follows. The *probability* of a concept C in a probabilistic interpretation $Pr = (\mathcal{I}, \mu)$ with $\mathcal{I} = (\Delta, I)$, denoted $Pr(C)$, is the sum of all $\mu(o)$ such that $o \in I(C)$. For concepts C and D with $Pr(C) > 0$, we use the expression $Pr(D|C)$ to abbreviate $Pr(C \sqcap D) / Pr(C)$. We say

Pr *satisfies* a conditional constraint $(D|C)[l, u]$, or Pr is a *model* of $(D|C)[l, u]$, denoted $Pr \models (D|C)[l, u]$, iff $Pr(D|C) \in [l, u]$. We say Pr *satisfies* a terminological axiom F, or Pr is a *model* of F, denoted $Pr \models F$, iff $\mathcal{I} \models F$. We say Pr *satisfies* a set of terminological axioms and conditional constraints $\mathcal{F}$, or Pr is a *model* of $\mathcal{F}$, denoted $Pr \models \mathcal{F}$, iff $Pr \models F$ for all $F \in \mathcal{F}$. We say $\mathcal{F}$ is *satisfiable* iff a model of $\mathcal{F}$ exists.

We next define the notion of consistency for probabilistic terminologies and generic probabilistic terminologies. We first give some preparative definitions.

A probabilistic interpretation Pr *verifies* a conditional constraint $(D|C)[l, u]$ iff $Pr(C) = 1$ and $Pr \models (D|C)[l, u]$. We say Pr *falsifies* $(D|C)[l, u]$ iff $Pr(C) = 1$ and $Pr \not\models (D|C)[l, u]$. A set of conditional constraints $\mathcal{D}$ *tolerates* a conditional constraint F under a terminology $\mathcal{T}$ iff $\mathcal{T} \cup \mathcal{D}$ has a model that verifies F.

A generic probabilistic terminology $\mathcal{P}_g = (\mathcal{T}_g, \mathcal{D}_g)$ is *consistent* iff there exists an ordered partition $(\mathcal{D}_0, \ldots, \mathcal{D}_k)$ of $\mathcal{D}_g$ such that each $\mathcal{D}_i$ with $i \in \{0, \ldots, k\}$ is the set of all $F \in \mathcal{D}_g \setminus (\mathcal{D}_0 \cup \cdots \cup \mathcal{D}_{i-1})$ that are tolerated under $\mathcal{T}_g$ by $\mathcal{D}_g \setminus (\mathcal{D}_0 \cup \cdots \cup \mathcal{D}_{i-1})$. We call this ordered partition of $\mathcal{D}_g$ the *z-partition* of $\mathcal{P}_g$. A probabilistic terminology $\mathcal{P} = (\mathcal{P}_g, (\mathcal{P}_o)_{o \in \mathbf{I}_P})$, where $\mathcal{P}_g = (\mathcal{T}_g, \mathcal{D}_g)$ and $\mathcal{P}_o = (\mathcal{T}_o, \mathcal{D}_o)$ for all $o \in \mathbf{I}_P$, is *generically consistent* (or *g-consistent*) iff $\mathcal{P}_g$ is consistent. We say $\mathcal{P}$ is *consistent* iff $\mathcal{P}$ is g-consistent and $\mathcal{T}_g \cup \mathcal{T}_o \cup \mathcal{D}_o \cup \{(\{o\}|\top)[1, 1]\}$ is satisfiable for all $o \in \mathbf{I}_P$.

We finally define the notion of lexicographic entailment for probabilistic terminologies. In the rest of this subsection, let $\mathcal{P} = (\mathcal{P}_g, (\mathcal{P}_o)_{o \in \mathbf{I}_P})$, where $\mathcal{P}_g = (\mathcal{T}_g, \mathcal{D}_g)$ and $\mathcal{P}_o = (\mathcal{T}_o, \mathcal{D}_o)$ for all $o \in \mathbf{I}_P$, be a consistent probabilistic terminology.

We use the *z-partition* $(\mathcal{D}_0, \ldots, \mathcal{D}_k)$ of $\mathcal{P}_g$ to define a lexicographic preference relation on probabilistic interpretations as follows. For probabilistic interpretations Pr and Pr', we say Pr is *lexicographically preferable* (or *lex-preferable*) to Pr' iff some $i \in \{0, \ldots, k\}$ exists such that $\#(\{F \in \mathcal{D}_i \mid Pr \models F\}) > \#(\{F \in \mathcal{D}_i \mid Pr' \models F\})$ and $\#(\{F \in \mathcal{D}_j \mid Pr \models F\}) = \#(\{F \in \mathcal{D}_j \mid Pr' \models F\})$ for all $i < j \leq k$. A model Pr of a set of terminological axioms and conditional constraints $\mathcal{F}$ is a *lexicographically minimal model* (or *lex-minimal model*) of $\mathcal{F}$ iff no model of $\mathcal{F}$ is *lex*-preferable to Pr.

We now define the notion of lexicographic entailment for conditional constraints from sets of terminological axioms and conditional constraints under generic probabilistic terminologies as follows. A conditional constraint $(D|C)[l, u]$ is a *lexicographic consequence* (or *lex-consequence*) of a set of terminological axioms and conditional constraints $\mathcal{F}$ under $\mathcal{P}_g$, denoted $\mathcal{F} \mathrel{||\!\!\sim}^{lex} (D|C)[l, u]$ under $\mathcal{P}_g$, iff $Pr(D) \in [l, u]$ for every *lex*-minimal model Pr of $\mathcal{F} \cup \{(C|\top)[1, 1]\}$. We say $(D|C)[l, u]$ is a *tight lexicographic consequence* (or *tight lex-consequence*) of $\mathcal{F}$ under $\mathcal{P}_g$, denoted $\mathcal{F} \mathrel{||\!\!\sim}^{lex}_{tight} (D|C)[l, u]$ under $\mathcal{P}_g$, iff l (resp., u) is the infimum (resp., supremum) of $Pr(D)$ subject to all *lex*-minimal models Pr of $\mathcal{F} \cup \{(C|\top)[1, 1]\}$. Note that we define $[l, u] = [1, 0]$ (where $[1, 0]$ represents the empty interval), when no such model Pr exists.

We are now ready to define which generic (resp., assertional) conditional constraints follow under lexicographic entailment from a probabilistic terminology. A generic conditional constraint F is a *lex-consequence* of $\mathcal{P}$, denoted $\mathcal{P} \mathrel{||\!\!\sim}^{lex} F$, iff $\emptyset \mathrel{||\!\!\sim}^{lex} F$ under $\mathcal{P}_g$. We say F is a *tight lex-consequence* of $\mathcal{P}$, denoted $\mathcal{P} \mathrel{||\!\!\sim}^{lex}_{tight} F$, iff $\emptyset \mathrel{||\!\!\sim}^{lex}_{tight} F$ under $\mathcal{P}_g$. An assertional conditional constraint F for $o \in \mathbf{I}_P$ is a *lex-consequence* of $\mathcal{P}$, denoted $\mathcal{P} \mathrel{||\!\!\sim}^{lex} F$, iff $\mathcal{T}_o \cup \mathcal{D}_o \mathrel{||\!\!\sim}^{lex} F$ under $\mathcal{P}_g$. We say F is a *tight lex-consequence* of $\mathcal{P}$, denoted $\mathcal{P} \mathrel{||\!\!\sim}^{lex}_{tight} F$, iff $\mathcal{T}_o \cup \mathcal{D}_o \mathrel{||\!\!\sim}^{lex}_{tight} F$ under $\mathcal{P}_g$.

4.3 Reasoning Tasks

We now summarize some important reasoning tasks in P-$\mathcal{SHOQ}(\mathbf{D})$ related to probabilistic terminologies $\mathcal{P}$. The following tasks concern the *generic knowledge* in $\mathcal{P}$:

P-Terminology-G-Consistency: Given $\mathcal{P}$, decide whether $\mathcal{P}$ is g-consistent.
P-Concept-Satisfiability: Given a g-consistent $\mathcal{P}$ and a generic concept C, decide
  whether $\mathcal{P} \not\models (C|\top)[0,0]$.
P-Concept-Overlapping: Given a g-consistent $\mathcal{P}$ and two generic concepts C and D,
  compute $l, u \in [0,1]$ such that $\mathcal{P} \parallel\!\!\sim_{tight}^{lex} (D|C)[l,u]$.
P-Concept-Role-Overlapping: Given a g-consistent $\mathcal{P}$, a generic concept C, an individual $o \in \mathbf{I}_C$, and $R \in \mathbf{R}_A$, compute $l, u \in [0,1]$ with $\mathcal{P} \parallel\!\!\sim_{tight}^{lex} (\exists R.\{o\}|C)[l,u]$.

We next give some reasoning tasks that are related to instances of concepts and abstract roles, and thus also concern the *assertional knowledge* in $\mathcal{P}$:

P-Terminology-Consistency: Given a g-consistent $\mathcal{P}$, decide whether $\mathcal{P}$ is consistent.
P-Concept-Membership: Given a consistent $\mathcal{P}$, an individual $o \in \mathbf{I}_P$, and a generic
  concept D, compute $l, u \in [0,1]$ such that $\mathcal{P} \parallel\!\!\sim_{tight}^{lex} (D|\{o\})[l,u]$.
P-Role-Membership: Given a consistent $\mathcal{P}$, individuals $o' \in \mathbf{I}_C$ and $o \in \mathbf{I}_P$, and an
  abstract role $R \in \mathbf{R}_A$, compute $l, u \in [0,1]$ such that $\mathcal{P} \parallel\!\!\sim_{tight}^{lex} (\exists R.\{o'\}|\{o\})[l,u]$.

In the sequel, **GCON** abbreviates P-Terminology-G-Consistency. Clearly, P-Terminology-Consistency is reducible to the problem of deciding whether a finite set of terminological axioms and conditional constraints is satisfiable, which we call **SAT**. It is then easy to see that P-Concept-Satisfiability is reducible to Concept-Satisfiability. Finally, P-Concept-Overlapping, P-Concept-Role-Overlapping, P-Concept-Membership, and P-Role-Membership can be reduced to computing tight *lex*-entailed intervals from finite sets of terminological axioms and conditional constraints under generic probabilistic terminologies, which we call **TLEXC**. Techniques for solving **SAT** and **GCON** are described in Section 6; a similar technique for solving **TLEXC** is given in [7].

5 Examples

In this section, we give some examples. Our first example illustrates the inheritance of default knowledge along subconcept relationships.

Example 5.1. The strict knowledge "all pacemaker patients (pp) are heart patients (hp)" and the default knowledge "generally, heart patients have high blood pressure (hb)" can be represented by the generic probabilistic terminology $\mathcal{P}_g = (\{\text{pp} \sqsubseteq \text{hp}\}, \{(\exists\text{hb}.\{\text{yes}\} \mid \text{hp})[1,1]\})$, where hb is a binary attribute.

It is then easy to see that $\emptyset \parallel\!\!\sim_{tight}^{lex} (\exists\text{hb}.\{\text{yes}\} \mid \text{hp})[1,1]$ and $\emptyset \parallel\!\!\sim_{tight}^{lex} (\exists\text{hb}.\{\text{yes}\} \mid \text{pp})[1,1]$ under $\mathcal{P}_g$. That is, under lexicographic entailment we conclude "generally, heart patients have high blood pressure" and "generally, pacemaker patients have high blood pressure". That is, the property of having high blood pressure is inherited from the concept of all heart patients down to the subconcept of all pacemaker patients. □

The next example shows that default knowledge attached to more specific concepts overrides default knowledge inherited from less specific superconcepts.

Example 5.2. The strict knowledge "all pacemaker patients (pp) are heart patients (hp)" and the default knowledge "generally, heart patients have high blood pressure (hb)" and "generally, pacemaker patients do not have high blood pressure" can be expressed by $\mathcal{P}_g = (\{pp \sqsubseteq hp\}, \{(\exists hb.\{yes\} \mid hp)[1, 1], (\exists hb.\{no\} \mid pp)[1, 1]\})$.

It is then easy to see that $\emptyset \hspace{2pt} \Vdash^{lex}_{tight} (\exists hb.\{yes\} \mid hp)[1, 1]$ and $\emptyset \hspace{2pt} \Vdash^{lex}_{tight} (\exists hb.\{no\} \mid pp)[1, 1]$ under $\mathcal{P}_g$. That is, under lexicographic entailment we conclude "generally, pacemaker patients do not have high blood pressure" and "generally, heart patients have high blood pressure". That is, even though the property of having high blood pressure is inherited from the concept of all heart patients down to the subconcept of all pacemaker patients, it is overridden by the property of not having high blood pressure of the more specific concept of all pacemaker patients. □

The following example illustrates probabilistic properties of concepts and the probabilistic membership of individuals to concepts.

Example 5.3. Consider the strict knowledge "all pacemaker patients (pp) are heart patients (hp)" and the generic probabilistic knowledge "a heart patient has a private insurance (hi) with a probability of at least 0.9". Consider also the assertional probabilistic knowledge "John is a pacemaker patient with a probability of at least 0.8". This knowledge can be represented by the probabilistic terminology $\mathcal{P} = (\mathcal{P}_g, (\mathcal{P}_{John}))$, where $\mathcal{P}_g = (\{pp \sqsubseteq hp\}, \{(\exists hi.\{yes\} \mid hp)[.9, 1]\})$ and $\mathcal{P}_{John} = (\emptyset, \{(pp \mid \{John\})[.8, 1]\})$.

Then, $\mathcal{P} \hspace{2pt} \Vdash^{lex}_{tight} (\exists hi.\{yes\} \mid \{John\})[.72, 1]$. That is, under lexicographic entailment, "John has a private insurance with a probability of at least 0.72". □

6   Probabilistic Reasoning in P-$\mathcal{SHOQ}$(D)

We now present techniques for solving the problems **SAT** and **GCON**. A similar technique for solving **TLEXC** is given in [7]. These techniques are based on reductions to classical reasoning in $\mathcal{SHOQ}$(D) and to linear programming. They show in particular that probabilistic reasoning in P-$\mathcal{SHOQ}$(D) is decidable.

6.1   Preliminaries

Roughly, the key idea behind developing algorithms for **SAT** and **GCON** is to eliminate the classical interpretation $\mathcal{I}$ in a probabilistic interpretation $Pr = (\mathcal{I}, \mu)$. This is done by using probability functions on sets $R \in \mathrm{Max}(\mathcal{R}_{\mathcal{T}}(\mathcal{F}))$ of pairwise disjoint and exhaustive concepts instead of probability functions on the abstract domain.

We start by defining the set $\mathcal{R}_{\mathcal{T}}(\mathcal{F})$ of pairwise disjoint and exhaustive concepts for a classical terminology $\mathcal{T}$ and a set of conditional constraints $\mathcal{F} = \{F_1, \ldots, F_n\}$. Let $\mathcal{R}_{\mathcal{T}}(\mathcal{F})$ be the set of all mappings r that assign to each $F_i = (D_i | C_i)[l_i, u_i] \in \mathcal{F}$ a member of $\{D_i \sqcap C_i, \neg D_i \sqcap C_i, \neg C_i\}$, such that $\mathcal{T} \not\models r(F_1) \sqcap \cdots \sqcap r(F_n) \sqsubseteq \bot$. For such mappings r, we use $\sqcap r$ to abbreviate $r(F_1) \sqcap \cdots \sqcap r(F_n)$. For such mappings r and concepts C, we use $r \models C$ to abbreviate $\emptyset \models \sqcap r \sqsubseteq C$.

We next define the set $\mathrm{Max}(\mathcal{R}_{\mathcal{T}}(\mathcal{F}))$ of subsets of $\mathcal{R}_{\mathcal{T}}(\mathcal{F})$ such that the models Pr of $\mathcal{T}$ correspond to the probability functions on all $R \in \mathrm{Max}(\mathcal{R}_{\mathcal{T}}(\mathcal{F}))$. We denote by $\mathcal{R}_{\mathcal{T}}(\mathcal{F})$ the set of all $R \subseteq \mathcal{R}_{\mathcal{T}}(\mathcal{F})$ such that $\mathcal{T} \cup \{\{o_r\} \sqsubseteq \sqcap r \mid r \in R\}$ is satisfiable,

$$\sum_{r \in R,\, r \models \neg D \sqcap C} -l\, y_r + \sum_{r \in R,\, r \models D \sqcap C} (1 - l)\, y_r \ \geq \ 0 \quad \text{(for all } (D|C)[l, u] \in \mathcal{F},\ l > 0)$$

$$\sum_{r \in R,\, r \models \neg D \sqcap C} u\, y_r + \sum_{r \in R,\, r \models D \sqcap C} (u - 1)\, y_r \ \geq \ 0 \quad \text{(for all } (D|C)[l, u] \in \mathcal{F},\ u < 1)$$

$$\sum_{r \in R} y_r \ = \ 1 \tag{1}$$

$$y_r \ \geq \ 0 \quad \text{(for all } r \in R)$$

Fig. 1. System of linear constraints for Theorem 6.1

where o_r is a new individual in $\mathbf{I}$ for every $r \in R_{\mathcal{T}}(\mathcal{F})$; we then denote by $\mathrm{Max}(R_{\mathcal{T}}(\mathcal{F}))$ the set of all maximal elements in $R_{\mathcal{T}}(\mathcal{F})$ w.r.t. set inclusion.

Observe that $\mathrm{Max}(R_{\mathcal{T}}(\mathcal{F}))$ can be computed by classical reasoning in $\mathcal{SHOQ}(\mathbf{D})$. It is also important to point out that, due to the concepts $\{o\}$ with individuals $o \in \mathbf{I}$ (also called *nominals*) in P-$\mathcal{SHOQ}(\mathbf{D})$ (and also $\mathcal{SHOQ}(\mathbf{D})$), it is in general not sufficient to define probability functions only on the set $R_{\mathcal{T}}(\mathcal{F})$.

6.2 Satisfiability

The following theorem shows that **SAT** can be reduced to deciding whether a system of linear constraints over a set of variables that corresponds to some $R \in \mathrm{Max}(R_{\mathcal{T}}(\mathcal{F}))$ is solvable. As $\mathrm{Max}(R_{\mathcal{T}}(\mathcal{F}))$ can be computed by classical reasoning in $\mathcal{SHOQ}(\mathbf{D})$, this shows that **SAT** can be reduced to classical reasoning in $\mathcal{SHOQ}(\mathbf{D})$ and to deciding whether a system of linear constraints is solvable.

Theorem 6.1. *Let $\mathcal{T}$ be a classical terminology, and let $\mathcal{F}$ be a finite set of conditional constraints. Then, $\mathcal{T} \cup \mathcal{F}$ is satisfiable iff the system of linear constraints (1) in Fig. 1 over the variables y_r $(r \in R)$ is solvable for some $R \in \mathrm{Max}(R_{\mathcal{T}}(\mathcal{F}))$.*

6.3 G-Consistency

The problem **GCON** can be reduced to **SAT**, as Algorithm z-partition in Fig. 2 shows, which decides whether a generic probabilistic terminology $\mathcal{P}_g$ is consistent. If this is the case, then z-partition returns the z-partition of $\mathcal{P}_g$, otherwise *nil*. In Step 5 of z-partition, a number of instances of **SAT** must be solved. Note that Algorithm z-partition is essentially a reformulation of an algorithm for deciding ε-consistency in default reasoning from conditional knowledge bases by Goldszmidt and Pearl [8].

7 Summary and Outlook

The main motivation behind this work was to develop a probabilistic extension of DAML+OIL for representing and reasoning with probabilistic ontologies in the semantic web. To this end, we worked out a probabilistic extension of $\mathcal{SHOQ}(\mathbf{D})$, which is the description logic that provides a formal semantics and a reasoning support for DAML+OIL (without inverse roles). The resulting new probabilistic description logic

---

Algorithm z-partition

Input: Generic probabilistic terminology $P_g = (T_g, D_g)$ with $D_g \neq \emptyset$.
Output: z-partition of P_g, if P_g is consistent, otherwise *nil*.

1. $\mathcal{H} := D_g$;
2. $i := -1$;
3. **repeat**
4. $i := i + 1$
5. $\mathcal{D}[i] := \{C \in \mathcal{H} \mid C$ is tolerated under T_g by $\mathcal{H}\}$;
6. $\mathcal{H} := \mathcal{H} \setminus \mathcal{D}[i]$
7. **until** $\mathcal{H} = \emptyset$ **or** $\mathcal{D}[i] = \emptyset$;
8. **if** $\mathcal{H} = \emptyset$ **then return** $(\mathcal{D}[0], \ldots, \mathcal{D}[i])$
9.   **else return** *nil*.

Fig. 2. Algorithm z-partition

P-$\mathcal{SHOQ}(\mathbf{D})$ is based on the notion of probabilistic lexicographic entailment from probabilistic default reasoning. It allows to express rich probabilistic knowledge about concepts and instances, as well as default knowledge about concepts. We also presented sound and complete reasoning techniques for P-$\mathcal{SHOQ}(\mathbf{D})$, which show in particular that reasoning in P-$\mathcal{SHOQ}(\mathbf{D})$ is decidable.

An interesting topic of future research is to analyze the computational complexity of probabilistic reasoning in P-$\mathcal{SHOQ}(\mathbf{D})$. Another issue for further work is to define a probabilistic extension of $\mathcal{SHOQ}(\mathbf{D_n})$ [25], which is a recent generalization of $\mathcal{SHOQ}(\mathbf{D})$ that also supports n-ary datatype predicates as well as datatype number restrictions. In particular, such an extension may also allow for expressing probabilistic knowledge about how instances of concepts are related to datatype values by roles. Finally, it would also be very interesting to allow for complex types and to develop more complex probabilistic query languages (e.g., similar to [3,4]).

Acknowledgments

This work was partially supported by a Marie Curie Individual Fellowship of the European Community (Disclaimer: The authors are solely responsible for information communicated and the European Commission is not responsible for any views or results expressed) and the Austrian Science Fund Project N Z29-INF. We are grateful to the referees for their useful comments, which helped to improve this paper.

References

1. S. Amarger, D. Dubois, and H. Prade. Constraint propagation with imprecise conditional probabilities. In *Proceedings UAI-91*, pages 26–34, 1991.
2. T. Berners-Lee. *Weaving the Web*. Harper, San Francisco, 1999.
3. T. Eiter, J. J. Lu, T. Lukasiewicz, and V. S. Subrahmanian. Probabilistic object bases. *ACM Transactions on Database Systems*, 26(3):264–312, 2001.
4. T. Eiter, T. Lukasiewicz, and M. Walter. A data model and algebra for probabilistic complex values. *Ann. Math. Artif. Intell.*, 33(2-4):205–252, 2001.

5. D. Fensel, F. van Harmelen, I. Horrocks, D. L. McGuiness, and P. F. Patel-Schneider. OIL: An ontology infrastructure for the semantic web. *IEEE Intelligent Systems*, 16(2):38–45, 2001.

6. A. M. Frisch and P. Haddawy. Anytime deduction for probabilistic logic. *Artif. Intell.*, 69:93–122, 1994.

7. R. Giugno and T. Lukasiewicz. P-$\mathcal{SHOQ}(\mathbf{D})$: A probabilistic extension of $\mathcal{SHOQ}(\mathbf{D})$ for probabilistic ontologies in the semantic web. Technical Report INFSYS RR-1843-02-06, Institut für Informationssysteme, Technische Universität Wien, April 2002.

8. M. Goldszmidt and J. Pearl. On the consistency of defeasible databases. *Artif. Intell.*, 52(2):121–149, 1991.

9. J. Heinsohn. Probabilistic description logics. In *Proceedings UAI-94*, pages 311–318, 1994.

10. J. Hendler and D. L. McGuiness. The DARPA agent markup language. *IEEE Intelligent Systems*, 15(6):67–73, 2000.

11. Health level seven, 1997. www.hl7.org.

12. I. Horrocks. DAML+OIL: A description logic for the semantic web. *IEEE Bulletin of the Technical Committee on Data Engineering*, 25(1):4–9, 2002.

13. I. Horrocks. DAML+OIL: A reason-able web ontology language. In *Proceedings EDBT-02*, volume 2287 of *LNCS*, pages 2–13. Springer, 2002.

14. I. Horrocks, D. Fensel, J. Broekstra, S. Decker, M. Erdmann, C. Goble, F. van Harmelen, M. Klein, S. Staab, R. Studer, and E. Motta. OIL: The ontology inference layer. Technical Report IR-479, Vrije Universiteit Amsterdam, 2000.

15. I. Horrocks, P. F. Patel-Schneider, and F. van Harmelen. Reviewing the design of DAML+OIL: An ontology language for the semantic web. In *Proceedings AAAI-02*, 2002. To appear.

16. I. Horrocks and U. Sattler. Ontology reasoning in the $\mathcal{SHOQ}(\mathbf{D})$ description logic. In *Proceedings IJCAI-01*, pages 199–204, 2001.

17. I. Horrocks, U. Sattler, and S. Tobies. Practical reasoning for expressive description logics. In *Proceedings LPAR-99*, volume 1705 of *LNCS*, pages 161–180. Springer, 1999.

18. M. Jaeger. Probabilistic reasoning in terminological logics. In *Proceedings KR-94*, pages 305–316, 1994.

19. D. Koller, A. Levy, and A. Pfeffer. P-CLASSIC: A tractable probabilistic description logic. In *Proceedings AAAI-97*, pages 390–397, 1997.

20. D. Lehmann. Another perspective on default reasoning. *Ann. Math. Artif. Intell.*, 15(1):61–82, 1995.

21. T. Lukasiewicz. Probabilistic deduction with conditional constraints over basic events. *J. Artif. Intell. Res.*, 10:199–241, 1999.

22. T. Lukasiewicz. Probabilistic logic programming under inheritance with overriding. In *Proceedings UAI-01*, pages 329–336, 2001.

23. T. Lukasiewicz. Probabilistic default reasoning with conditional constraints. *Ann. Math. Artif. Intell.*, 34(1–3):35–88, 2002.

24. N. J. Nilsson. Probabilistic logic. *Artif. Intell.*, 28:71–88, 1986.

25. J. Z. Pan and I. Horrocks. Semantic web ontology reasoning in the $\mathcal{SHOQ}(\mathbf{D_n})$ description logic. In *Proceedings DL-02*, 2002.

26. U. Straccia. A fuzzy description logic. In *Proceedings AAAI-98*, pages 594–599, 1998.

27. U. Straccia. Reasoning within fuzzy description logics. *J. Artif. Intell. Res.*, 14:137–166, 2001.

28. C. B. Tresp and R. Molitor. A description logic for vague knowledge. In *Proceedings ECAI-98*, pages 361–365, 1998.

29. J. Yen. Generalizing term subsumption languages to fuzzy logic. In *Proceedings IJCAI-91*, pages 472–477, 1991.

A Temporal Description Logic
for Reasoning over Conceptual Schemas and Queries

Alessandro Artale[1], Enrico Franconi[2], Frank Wolter[3], and Michael Zakharyaschev[4]

[1] Dept. of Computation, UMIST, Manchester, UK
artale@co.umist.ac.uk
[2] Faculty of Computer Science, Free Univ. of Bolzano, Italy
franconi@inf.unibz.it
[3] Inst. für Informatik, Univ. of Leipzig, D
wolter@informatik.uni-leipzig.de
[4] Dept. of Computer Science, Kings College, London, UK
mz@dcs.kcl.ac.uk

Abstract. This paper introduces a new logical formalism, intended for temporal conceptual modelling, as a natural combination of the well-known description logic $\mathcal{DLR}$ and point-based linear temporal logic with *Since* and *Until*. We define a query language (where queries are non-recursive Datalog programs and atoms are complex $\mathcal{DLR}_{\mathcal{US}}$ expressions) and investigate the problem of checking query containment under the constraints defined by $\mathcal{DLR}_{\mathcal{US}}$ conceptual schemas—i.e., $\mathcal{DLR}_{\mathcal{US}}$ knowledge bases—as well as the problems of schema satisfiability and logical implication.

1 Introduction

Temporal information systems are information systems that store historical information, i.e., past, present, and potential future data. Many formalisations have been proposed for temporal information systems which are based on first-order temporal logic [14]. Although these formalisations can be very useful for characterising semantical problems arising in temporalised ontologies and in temporal databases, like conceptual modelling or querying, usually they are computationally unfeasible for performing deduction tasks (for example, logical implication in the first-order temporal logic of the flow of time $\langle \mathbb{Z}, < \rangle$ or $\langle \mathbb{N}, < \rangle$ is not even recursively enumerable). Note that we are interested in deduction rather than model checking. An obvious solution to this problem would be to look for well-behaved fragments of first-order temporal logic (see e.g. [14] and references therein); however this way has not been successful—the only promising approach we know of is the recent paper [19]. Another idea is to deviate from the first-order paradigm and start from computationally more friendly languages such as description logics which have been used in the area of non-temporal information management to characterise in a uniform framework both conceptual modelling and queries [9,6,7].

The *temporal description logic* $\mathcal{DLR}_{\mathcal{US}}$ we devise in this paper is based on the expressive and decidable description logic $\mathcal{DLR}$ which allows the logical reconstruction and the extension of representational tools such as object-oriented and semantic data models, frame-based and web ontology languages [10,11]. In this setting, an interesting

S. Flesca et al. (Eds.): JELIA 2002, LNAI 2424, pp. 98–110, 2002.

feature of $\mathcal{DLR}$ is the ability to completely *define* classes and relations as $\mathcal{DLR}$ views over other classes and relations of the conceptual schema. Moreover, $\mathcal{DLR}$ formulas can express a large class of integrity constraints that are typical in databases, for instance, existence dependencies, exclusion dependencies, typed inclusion dependencies without projection of relations, unary inclusion dependencies, full key dependencies [9]. Logical implication in $\mathcal{DLR}$ is EXPTIME-complete [9]; practical correct and complete algorithms exist, used in conceptual modelling applications [20,16].

$\mathcal{DLR}$ is not only a very powerful language for conceptual modelling. The problem of view-based query processing under $\mathcal{DLR}$ constraints has also been studied [9]. View-based query answering requires to answer a query over a virtual database (constrained by a $\mathcal{DLR}$ theory playing the role of the conceptual schema and of the integrity constraints) for which the only information comes from a set of materialised views over the same database; this problem with non-recursive Datalog queries and views is a co-NP-complete problem (in data complexity) under the closed world assumption. Checking query containment of non-recursive Datalog queries under $\mathcal{DLR}$ constraints is decidable in 2EXPTIME [9].

Given all these nice features of $\mathcal{DLR}$, it is natural to try to extend it with a temporal dimension, to understand the expressive power of the resulting hybrid with respect to the needs of temporal conceptual modelling and view based query processing, and to investigate its computational properties. This paper reports the results of such an attempt. We construct $\mathcal{DLR}_{\mathcal{US}}$ as an organic combination of $\mathcal{DLR}$ and the propositional linear temporal logic with *Since* and *Until* (which usually serves as the temporal component in the first-order approach) by allowing applications of temporal operators to all syntactical terms of $\mathcal{DLR}$: classes, relations, and formulas. We then investigate computational properties of reasoning with $\mathcal{DLR}_{\mathcal{US}}$ by analysing schema, class, and relation satisfiability, logical implication, and query containment for non-recursive Datalog queries under $\mathcal{DLR}_{\mathcal{US}}$ constraints.

The full $\mathcal{DLR}_{\mathcal{US}}$ turns out to be undecidable. The main reason for this is the possibility to postulate that a binary relation does not vary in time—a very small fragment of $\mathcal{DLR}_{\mathcal{US}}$ (say, $\mathcal{DLR}$ augmented with a single time invariant binary relation) can encode the undecidable tiling problem (cf. [26,19]). The fragment $\mathcal{DLR}_{\mathcal{US}}^{-}$ of $\mathcal{DLR}_{\mathcal{US}}$ deprived of the ability to talk about temporal persistence of n-ary relations, for $n \geq 2$, is still very expressive, as is illustrated by examples in this paper, but its computational behaviour is much better. We obtain the following non-trivial novel complexity results: (1) reasoning in $\mathcal{DLR}_{\mathcal{US}}^{-}$ with atomic formulas is EXPTIME-complete, (2) satisfiability and logical implication of arbitrary $\mathcal{DLR}_{\mathcal{US}}^{-}$ formulas is EXPSPACE-complete, and (3) the problem of checking query containment of non-recursive Datalog queries under $\mathcal{DLR}_{\mathcal{US}}^{-}$ constraints is decidable in 2EXPTIME with an EXPSPACE lower bound.

The results obtained in this paper are novel for several reasons. Previous approaches to temporal description logics considered much weaker languages having only binary relations (i.e., roles), without the cardinality constructs, without the inverse construct (which $\mathcal{DLR}_{\mathcal{US}}$ implicitly is able to express by considering only binary relations), and without ever considering the ability to express queries [21,25,28,23]. In this paper for the first time an upper bound for the complexity of reasoning in a temporal description logic with both future and past operators is proved, leading to a tight EXPSPACE-completeness result which automatically holds for the weaker basic temporal description logic $\mathcal{ALC}^-_{\mathcal{US}}$ as well. In this paper for the first time non trivial decidability and complexity results are presented for the problem of temporal query containment under complex constraints. For a survey of the previous various approaches to temporal description logics see [4].

2   The Temporal Description Logic

In this paper, we adopt the classical *snapshot* representation of abstract temporal databases (see e.g. [14]). The flow of time $\mathcal{T} = \langle \mathcal{T}_p, < \rangle$, where $\mathcal{T}_p$ is a set of time points (or chronons) and $<$ a binary precedence relation on $\mathcal{T}_p$, is assumed to be isomorphic to $\langle \mathbb{Z}, < \rangle$. Thus, a temporal database can be regarded as a mapping from time points in $\mathcal{T}$ to standard relational databases, with the same interpretation of constants and the same domains along time.

As a language for expressing temporal conceptual schemas we use the combination of the propositional temporal logic with *Since* and *Until* and the (non-temporal) description logic $\mathcal{DLR}$ [9]. The resulting $\mathcal{DLR}_{\mathcal{US}}$ *temporal description logic* can be regarded as a rather expressive fragment of the first-order temporal logic $L^{\{\text{since, until}\}}$; cf. [14,19] and Section 3 below; note that $\mathcal{DLR}$ itself is neither in the guarded fragment of FOL nor in the two variable variables fragment of FOL with counting quantifiers.

The basic syntactical types of $\mathcal{DLR}_{\mathcal{US}}$ are *entities* (i.e., unary predicates, also known as *concepts* or *classes*) and n-ary *relations* of arity ≥ 2. Starting from a set of *atomic entities* (denoted by *EN*), a set of *atomic relations* (denoted by *RN*), and a set of *role symbols* (denoted by U) we define inductively (complex) entity and relation expressions as is shown in the upper part of Fig. 1, where the binary constructs $(\sqcap, \sqcup, \mathcal{U}, \mathcal{S})$ are applied to relations of the same arity, i, j, k, n are natural numbers, $i \leq n$, and j does not exceed the arity of R.

The non-temporal fragment of $\mathcal{DLR}_{\mathcal{US}}$ coincides with $\mathcal{DLR}$. For both entity and relation expressions all the Boolean constructs are available. The selection expression $U_i/n : E$ denotes an n-ary relation whose argument named U_i ($i \leq n$) is of type E; if it is clear from the context, we omit n and write $(U_i : E)$. The projection expression $\exists^{\leq k}[U_j]R$ is a generalisation with cardinalities of the projection operator over the argument named U_j of the relation R; the plain classical projection is $\exists^{\geq 1}[U_j]R$. It is also possible to use the pure argument position version of the model by replacing role symbols U_i with the corresponding position numbers i.

The language of $\mathcal{DLR}_{\mathcal{US}}$ is interpreted in *temporal models* over $\mathcal{T}$, which are triples of the form $\mathcal{I} \doteq \langle \mathcal{T}, \Delta^{\mathcal{I}}, \cdot^{\mathcal{I}(t)} \rangle$, where $\Delta^{\mathcal{I}}$ is non-empty set of objects (the *domain* of $\mathcal{I}$) and $\cdot^{\mathcal{I}(t)}$ an *interpretation function* such that, for every $t \in \mathcal{T}$, every entity E, and every n-ary relation R, we have $E^{\mathcal{I}(t)} \subseteq \Delta^{\mathcal{I}}$ and $R^{\mathcal{I}(t)} \subseteq (\Delta^{\mathcal{I}})^n$. The semantics of entity and relation expressions is defined in the lower part of Fig. 1, where $(u, v) = \{w \in \mathcal{T} \mid u < w < v\}$ and the operators $\square^+$ (always in the future) and $\square^-$ (always in the past) are the duals of $\diamondsuit^+$ (some time in the future) and $\diamondsuit^-$ (some time in the past), respectively, i.e., $\square^+ E \equiv \neg\diamondsuit^+\neg E$ and $\square^- E \equiv \neg\diamondsuit^-\neg E$, for both entities and relations. For entities, the temporal operators $\diamondsuit^+$, $\oplus$ (at the next moment), and their past counterparts can be defined via $\mathcal{U}$ and $\mathcal{S}$: $\diamondsuit^+ E \equiv \top \mathcal{U} E$, $\oplus E \equiv \bot \mathcal{U} E$, etc. However, this is not possible for relations of arity > 1, since $\top_n$—the top n-ary relation—can be interpreted

$$R \rightarrow \top_n \mid RN \mid \neg R \mid R_1 \sqcap R_2 \mid R_1 \sqcup R_2 \mid U_i/n : E \mid$$
$$\Diamond^+ R \mid \Diamond^- R \mid \square^+ R \mid \square^- R \mid \oplus R \mid \ominus R \mid R_1 \, \mathcal{U} \, R_2 \mid R_1 \, \mathcal{S} \, R_2$$

$$E \rightarrow \top \mid EN \mid \neg E \mid E_1 \sqcap E_2 \mid E_1 \sqcup E_2 \mid \exists^{\leq k}[U_j]R \mid$$
$$\Diamond^+ E \mid \Diamond^- E \mid \square^+ E \mid \square^- E \mid \oplus E \mid \ominus E \mid E_1 \, \mathcal{U} \, E_2 \mid E_1 \, \mathcal{S} \, E_2$$

$$(\top_n)^{\mathcal{I}(t)} \subseteq (\Delta^{\mathcal{I}})^n$$
$$RN^{\mathcal{I}(t)} \subseteq (\top_n)^{\mathcal{I}(t)}$$
$$(\neg R)^{\mathcal{I}(t)} = (\top_n)^{\mathcal{I}(t)} \setminus R^{\mathcal{I}(t)}$$
$$(R_1 \sqcap R_2)^{\mathcal{I}(t)} = R_1^{\mathcal{I}(t)} \cap R_2^{\mathcal{I}(t)}$$
$$(U_i/n : E)^{\mathcal{I}(t)} = \{\, \langle d_1, \ldots, d_n \rangle \in (\top_n)^{\mathcal{I}(t)} \mid d_i \in E^{\mathcal{I}(t)} \}$$
$$(R_1 \, \mathcal{U} \, R_2)^{\mathcal{I}(t)} = \{\, \langle d_1, \ldots, d_n \rangle \in (\top_n)^{\mathcal{I}(t)} \mid$$
$$\exists v > t.(\langle d_1, \ldots, d_n \rangle \in R_2^{\mathcal{I}(v)} \wedge \forall w \in (t,v). \langle d_1, \ldots, d_n \rangle \in R_1^{\mathcal{I}(w)}) \}$$
$$(R_1 \, \mathcal{S} \, R_2)^{\mathcal{I}(t)} = \{\, \langle d_1, \ldots, d_n \rangle \in (\top_n)^{\mathcal{I}(t)} \mid$$
$$\exists v < t.(\langle d_1, \ldots, d_n \rangle \in R_2^{\mathcal{I}(v)} \wedge \forall w \in (v,t). \langle d_1, \ldots, d_n \rangle \in R_1^{\mathcal{I}(w)}) \}$$
$$(\Diamond^+ R)^{\mathcal{I}(t)} = \{\, \langle d_1, \ldots, d_n \rangle \in (\top_n)^{\mathcal{I}(t)} \mid \exists v > t. \langle d_1, \ldots, d_n \rangle \in R^{\mathcal{I}(v)} \}$$
$$(\oplus R)^{\mathcal{I}(t)} = \{\, \langle d_1, \ldots, d_n \rangle \in (\top_n)^{\mathcal{I}(t)} \mid \langle d_1, \ldots, d_n \rangle \in R^{\mathcal{I}(t+1)} \}$$
$$(\Diamond^- R)^{\mathcal{I}(t)} = \{\, \langle d_1, \ldots, d_n \rangle \in (\top_n)^{\mathcal{I}(t)} \mid \exists v < t. \langle d_1, \ldots, d_n \rangle \in R^{\mathcal{I}(v)} \}$$
$$(\ominus R)^{\mathcal{I}(t)} = \{\, \langle d_1, \ldots, d_n \rangle \in (\top_n)^{\mathcal{I}(t)} \mid \langle d_1, \ldots, d_n \rangle \in R^{\mathcal{I}(t-1)} \}$$

$$\top^{\mathcal{I}(t)} = \Delta^{\mathcal{I}}$$
$$EN^{\mathcal{I}(t)} \subseteq \top^{\mathcal{I}(t)}$$
$$(\neg E)^{\mathcal{I}(t)} = \top^{\mathcal{I}(t)} \setminus E^{\mathcal{I}(t)}$$
$$(E_1 \sqcap E_2)^{\mathcal{I}(t)} = E_1^{\mathcal{I}(t)} \cap E_2^{\mathcal{I}(t)}$$
$$(\exists^{\leq k}[U_j]R)^{\mathcal{I}(t)} = \{\, d \in \top^{\mathcal{I}(t)} \mid \sharp\{\langle d_1, \ldots, d_n \rangle \in R^{\mathcal{I}(t)} \mid d_j = d\} \lessgtr k \}$$
$$(E_1 \, \mathcal{U} \, E_2)^{\mathcal{I}(t)} = \{\, d \in \top^{\mathcal{I}(t)} \mid \exists v > t.(d \in E_2^{\mathcal{I}(v)} \wedge \forall w \in (t,v).d \in E_1^{\mathcal{I}(w)}) \}$$
$$(E_1 \, \mathcal{S} \, E_2)^{\mathcal{I}(t)} = \{\, d \in \top^{\mathcal{I}(t)} \mid \exists v < t.(d \in E_2^{\mathcal{I}(v)} \wedge \forall w \in (v,t).d \in E_1^{\mathcal{I}(w)}) \}$$

Fig. 1. Syntax and semantics of $\mathcal{DLR}_{\mathcal{US}}$.

by different subsets of the n-ary cross product $\top \times \cdots \times \top$ at different time points; the reason for this is the ability of $\mathcal{DLR}$ to talk only about difference between relations rather than of the complement of a relation. Then, we may have $\langle d_1, d_2 \rangle \in (\Diamond^+ R)^{\mathcal{I}(t)}$ because $\langle d_1, d_2 \rangle \in R^{\mathcal{I}(t+2)}$, but $\langle d_1, d_2 \rangle \notin (\top_2)^{\mathcal{I}(t+1)}$. The operators $\Diamond^*$ (at some moment) and its dual $\square^*$ (at all moments) can be defined for both entities and relations as $\Diamond^* E \equiv E \sqcup \Diamond^+ E \sqcup \Diamond^- E$ and $\square^* E \equiv E \sqcap \square^+ E \sqcap \square^- E$, respectively.

A *temporal conceptual database schema* (or a *knowledge base*) is a finite set Σ of $\mathcal{DLR}_{\mathcal{US}}$-formulas. Atomic formulas are formulas of the form $E_1 \sqsubseteq E_2$ and $R_1 \sqsubseteq R_2$, with R_1 and R_2 being relations of the same arity. If φ and ψ are $\mathcal{DLR}_{\mathcal{US}}$-formulas, then so are $\neg \varphi, \varphi \wedge \psi, \varphi \mathcal{U} \psi, \varphi \mathcal{S} \psi$. $E_1 \doteq E_2$ is used as an abbreviation for $(E_1 \sqsubseteq E_2) \wedge (E_2 \sqsubseteq E_1)$, for both entities and relations. The global atomic formula $E_1 \sqsubseteq^* E_2$ is used as an abbreviation for $\square^*(E_1 \sqsubseteq E_2)$, for both entities and relations. Temporal conceptual database schemas specify the constraints for temporal databases.

Given a formula φ, an interpretation $\mathcal{I}$, and a time point $t \in \mathcal{T}$, the truth-relation $\mathcal{I}, t \models \varphi$ (φ holds in $\mathcal{I}$ at moment t) is defined inductively as follows:

$\mathcal{I}, t \models E_1 \sqsubseteq E_2$ iff $E_1^{\mathcal{I}(t)} \subseteq E_2^{\mathcal{I}(t)}$ $\mathcal{I}, t \models \varphi \mathcal{U} \psi$ iff $\exists v > t.(\mathcal{I}, v \models \psi \wedge$
$$\forall w \in (t, v).\mathcal{I}, w \models \varphi)$$
$\mathcal{I}, t \models R_1 \sqsubseteq R_2$ iff $R_1^{\mathcal{I}(t)} \subseteq R_2^{\mathcal{I}(t)}$ $\mathcal{I}, t \models \varphi \mathcal{S} \psi$ iff $\exists v < t.(\mathcal{I}, v \models \psi \wedge$
$$\forall w \in (v, t).\mathcal{I}, w \models \varphi)$$
$\mathcal{I}, t \models \neg \varphi$ iff $\mathcal{I}, t \not\models \varphi$
$\mathcal{I}, t \models \varphi \wedge \psi$ iff $\mathcal{I}, t \models \varphi$ and $\mathcal{I}, t \models \psi$

A formula φ is called *satisfiable* if there is a temporal model $\mathcal{I}$ such that $\mathcal{I}, t \models \varphi$, for some time point t. A conceptual schema Σ is *satisfiable* if the conjunction $\bigwedge \Sigma$ of all formulas in Σ is satisfiable (we write $\mathcal{I}, t \models \Sigma$ instead of $\mathcal{I}, t \models \bigwedge \Sigma$); in this case $\mathcal{I}$ is called a *model* of Σ. We say that Σ is *globally satisfiable* if there is $\mathcal{I}$ such that $\mathcal{I}, t \models \Sigma$ for every t ($\mathcal{I} \models \Sigma$, in symbols). An entity E (or relation R) is *satisfiable* if there is $\mathcal{I}$ such that $E^{\mathcal{I}(t)} \neq \emptyset$ (respectively, $R^{\mathcal{I}(t)} \neq \emptyset$), for some time point t. Finally, we say that Σ (*globally*) *implies* φ and write $\Sigma \models \varphi$ if we have $\mathcal{I} \models \varphi$ whenever $\mathcal{I} \models \Sigma$.

Note that an entity E is satisfiable iff $\neg(E \sqsubseteq \bot)$ is satisfiable. An n-ary relation R is satisfiable iff $\neg(\exists^{\geq 1}[i]R \sqsubseteq \bot)$ is satisfiable for some $i \leq n$. A conceptual schema Σ is globally satisfiable iff $\Box^*(\bigwedge \Sigma)$ is satisfiable. And $\Sigma \models \varphi$ iff $\Box^*(\bigwedge \Sigma) \wedge \neg\varphi$ is not satisfiable. Thus, all reasoning tasks connected with the notions introduced above reduce to satisfiability of formulas.

2.1   Temporal Queries

In this Section we extend $\mathcal{DLR}_{\mathcal{US}}$ with a temporal query language, and we define the problem of evaluating a temporal query under $\mathcal{DLR}_{\mathcal{US}}$ constraints and the problem of temporal query containment under constraints (see, e.g., [14,12,1] for a survey and a discussion about temporal queries). A *non-recursive Datalog query* (i.e., a disjunction of conjunctive queries or SPJ-queries) over a $\mathcal{DLR}_{\mathcal{US}}$ schema Σ is an expression of the form

$$Q(\vec{x}) :- \bigvee_j Q_j(\vec{x}, \vec{y_j}, \vec{c_j}), \quad \text{where} \quad Q_j(\vec{x}, \vec{y_j}, \vec{c_j}) \equiv \bigwedge_i P_j^i(\vec{x}_j^i, \vec{y}_j^i, \vec{c}_j^i),$$

P_j^i are $\mathcal{DLR}_{\mathcal{US}}$ entity or relation expressions possibly occurring in Σ, $\vec{x}_j^i$, $\vec{y}_j^i$, and $\vec{c}_j^i$ are sequences of distinguished variables, existential variables, and constants, respectively, the number of which is in agreement with the arity of P_j^i. The variables $\vec{x}$ in the head are the union of all the distinguished variables in each Q_j; the existential variables are used to make coreferences in the query, and constants are fixed values. Q is a n-ary relation (not appearing in Σ) whose arity is the number of variables in $\vec{x}$.

It is to be noted that we allow entities and relations in the query to occur in the conceptual schema Σ. This approach is similar to that of [9], where atoms in a query can be constrained by means of schema formulas. Furthermore, query expressions do not directly manipulate explicit temporal attributes, but time is implicit in each query expression. Indeed, the temporal dimension is handled by means of the temporal modal operators in $\mathcal{DLR}_{\mathcal{US}}$. In this perspective, the query language is in strict relation with the First-Order Temporal Logic with *since* and *until*, $L^{\{\text{since, until}\}}$, used in [14] for querying temporal databases.

The semantics of queries is based on the snapshot representation of a temporal database, and defined as follows. Given a temporal schema Σ, let $\mathcal{I}$ be a temporal model, and t be a time point in $\mathcal{T}$ such that $\mathcal{I}$ satisfies Σ at t, i.e., $\mathcal{I}, t \models \Sigma$. The snapshot interpretation

$$\mathcal{I}(t) = \langle \Delta^{\mathcal{I}}, \{E^{\mathcal{I}(t)} \mid E \in EN\}, \{R^{\mathcal{I}(t)} \mid R \in RN\}\rangle$$

can be regarded as a usual first-order structure (i.e., a snapshot, non-temporal, database at time t conforming in a sense to the conceptual schema), and so the whole $\mathcal{I}$ as a first-order temporal model (with constant domain $\Delta^{\mathcal{I}}$ in which some values of the query constants are specified). The *evaluation* of a query $\mathcal{Q}$ of arity n, under the constraints Σ, in the model $\mathcal{I}$ that satisfies Σ at moment t, and the *answer* to the query $\mathcal{Q}$, are respectively the sets:

$$\mathsf{eval}(\mathcal{Q}, \mathcal{I}(t)) = \{\overrightarrow{o} \in (\Delta^{\mathcal{I}})^n \mid \mathcal{I}, t \models \bigvee_j \exists \overrightarrow{y_j}.\mathcal{Q}_j(\overrightarrow{o}, \overrightarrow{y_j}, \overrightarrow{c_j})\}$$
$$\mathsf{ans}(\mathcal{Q}, \mathcal{I}) = \{\langle t, \overrightarrow{o}\rangle \in \mathcal{T} \times (\Delta^{\mathcal{I}})^n \mid \overrightarrow{o} \in \mathsf{eval}(\mathcal{Q}, \mathcal{I}(t))\}$$

We obtain a so called *sequenced semantics* for queries, which is based on the view of a database as a time-indexed collection of snapshots. The query language is also *snapshot-reducible* in the sense that non-temporal queries—i.e., queries without any temporal connective—are still valid queries, and are interpreted using the sequenced semantics. Our language allows also for *upward compatible* queries. Intuitively, a non-temporal query is upward compatible if the answer set on a temporal database is the same as the answer set on an associated non-temporal database. This is a temporal *slice* of the temporal database at the current time: $\mathsf{eval}(\mathcal{Q}, \mathcal{I}(\mathsf{now}))$.

Given two queries (of the same arity) $\mathcal{Q}_1$ and $\mathcal{Q}_2$ over Σ, we say that $\mathcal{Q}_1$ is *contained* in $\mathcal{Q}_2$ under the constraints Σ, and write $\Sigma \models \mathcal{Q}_1 \subseteq \mathcal{Q}_2$, if, for every temporal model $\mathcal{I}$ of Σ we have $\mathsf{ans}(\mathcal{Q}_1, \mathcal{I}) \subseteq \mathsf{ans}(\mathcal{Q}_2, \mathcal{I})$. The *query satisfiability problem*—given a query $\mathcal{Q}$ over a schema Σ, to determine whether there are $\mathcal{I}$ and t such that $\mathcal{I}, t \models \Sigma$, and $\mathsf{eval}(\mathcal{Q}, \mathcal{I}(t)) \neq \emptyset$—is reducible to query containment: $\mathcal{Q}$ is satisfiable iff $\Sigma \not\models \mathcal{Q}(\overrightarrow{x}) \subseteq P(\overrightarrow{x}) \wedge \neg P(\overrightarrow{x})$, where P is a $\mathcal{DLR}_{\mathcal{US}}$-relation of the same arity as $\mathcal{Q}$.

2.2   Examples

As an example, let us consider the following conceptual schema Σ:

```
Works-for ⊑* emp/2 : Employee ⊓ act/2 : Project
Manages ⊑* man/2 : TopManager ⊓ prj/2 : Project
Employee ⊑* ∃⁼¹[from]PaySlipNumber ⊓ ∃⁼¹[from](PaySlipNumber ⊓ to/2 : Integer) ⊓
           ∃⁼¹[from]Salary ⊓ ∃⁼¹[from](Salary ⊓ to/2 : Integer)
⊤ ⊑* ∃≤¹[to](PaySlipNumber ⊓ from/2 : Employee)
Manager⊑* Employee ⊓ (AreaManager ⊔ TopManager)
AreaManager ⊑* Manager ⊓ ¬TopManager
TopManager ⊑* Manager ⊓ ∃⁼¹[man]Manages
Project ⊑* ∃≥¹[act]Works-for ⊓ ∃⁼¹[prj]Manages
Employee ⊓ ¬(∃≥¹[emp]Works-for) ⊑* Manager
Manager⊑* ¬(∃≥¹[emp]Works-for) ⊓ (Qualified S (Employee ⊓ ¬Manager))
```

The theory introduces Works-for as a binary relation between employees and projects, and Manages as a binary relation between managers and projects. Employees have exactly one pay slip number and one salary each, which are represented as binary relations

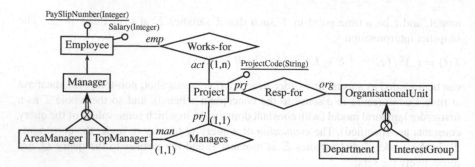

Fig. 2. The example EER diagram.

(with `from` and `to` roles) with an integer domain; moreover, a pay slip number uniquely identifies an employee (it acts as a key). It is stated that managers are employees, and are partitioned into area managers and top managers. Top Managers participate exactly once in the relation `Manages`, i.e., every top manager manages exactly one project. Projects participate at least once to the relation `Works-for` and exactly once in the relation `Manages`. Finally, employees not working for a project are exactly the managers, and managers should be qualified, i.e., should have passed a period of being employees. The meaning of the above conceptual schema (with the exception of the last two formulas) is illustrated by the left part of the diagram in Fig. 2.

The conceptual schema Σ globally logically implies that, for every project, there is at least one employee who is not a manager, and that a top manager worked in a project before managing some (possibly different) project:

$$\Sigma \models \mathtt{Project} \sqsubseteq^* \exists^{\geq 1}[\mathtt{act}](\mathtt{Works\text{-}for} \sqcap \mathtt{emp} : \neg\mathtt{Manager})$$
$$\Sigma \models \mathtt{TopManager} \sqsubseteq^* \Diamond^- \exists^{\geq 1}[\mathtt{emp}](\mathtt{Works\text{-}for} \sqcap \mathtt{act} : \mathtt{Project})$$

Note also that if we add to Σ the formula

$$\mathtt{Employee} \sqsubseteq^* \exists^{\geq 1}[\mathtt{emp}]\mathtt{Works\text{-}for}$$

saying that every employee should work for at least one project, then all the entities and the relations mentioned in the conceptual schema are interpreted as the empty set in every model of Σ, i.e., they are not satisfiable relative to Σ.

The expressivity of the query language can be understood with the following examples, taken from [14]:

"*Find all people who have worked for only one project*"
$\mathcal{Q}(\mathtt{x}) :\text{-}(\exists^{=1}[\mathtt{emp}](\Diamond^*\mathtt{Works\text{-}for}))(\mathtt{x})$
"*Find all managers whose terminal project has code* prj342"
$\mathcal{Q}(\mathtt{x}) :\text{-}\mathtt{Manager}(\mathtt{x}) \wedge \mathtt{Manages}(\mathtt{x}, \mathtt{prj342}) \wedge (\square^+\neg\mathtt{Manages})(\mathtt{x}, \mathtt{y})$
"*Find all project-hoppers—people who never spent more than two consecutive years in a project*"
$\mathcal{Q}(\mathtt{x}) :\text{-}(\square^*\neg\exists^{\geq 1}[\mathtt{emp}](\mathtt{Works\text{-}for} \sqcap \oplus \mathtt{Works\text{-}for} \sqcap \oplus \oplus \mathtt{Works\text{-}for}))(\mathtt{x})$

"Find all people who did not work between two projects"
$Q(x) :- (\Diamond^- \exists^{\geq 1} [\text{emp}] \text{Works-for})(x) \wedge$
    $(\neg \exists^{\geq 1} [\text{emp}] \text{Works-for})(x) \wedge (\Diamond^+ \exists^{\geq 1} [\text{emp}] \text{Works-for})(x)$

We now consider an example of query containment under constraints, where the constraints are expressed by the above schema Σ. Consider the following queries:

$Q_1(x, y) :- \neg \text{AreaManager}(x) \wedge \text{Manages}(x, z) \wedge \text{Project}(z) \wedge$
    $\text{Resp-for}(y, z) \wedge \text{Department}(y)$
$Q_2(x, y) :- (\Diamond^- \exists^{\geq 1} [\text{emp}] \text{Works-for})(x) \wedge \text{Manages}(x, z) \wedge$
    $\text{Resp-for}(y, z) \wedge \neg \text{InterestGroup}(y)$

It is not hard to see that Q_1 is contained in Q_2 under the constraints in Σ, i.e., $\Sigma \models Q_1 \subseteq Q_2$.

3 Decidability and Complexity

In this section, we present and briefly discuss our main results on the computational behaviour of $\mathcal{DLR}_{\mathcal{US}}$ and its fragments over the flow of time $\langle \mathbb{Z}, < \rangle$.

Unfortunately, full $\mathcal{DLR}_{\mathcal{US}}$, even restricted to *atomic* formulas, turns out to be undecidable. One can actually show that the undecidable tiling problem reduces to satisfiability of atomic formulas in $\mathcal{DLR}_{\mathcal{US}}$.

Theorem 1. *The global satisfiability problem for $\mathcal{DLR}_{\mathcal{US}}$ conceptual schemas containing only atomic formulas is undecidable.*

It follows, in particular, that (a) the problem of satisfiability of complex $\mathcal{DLR}_{\mathcal{US}}$ formulas is undecidable, and (b) the problem of global logical implication in $\mathcal{DLR}_{\mathcal{US}}$—even involving only atomic formulas—is undecidable as well. The main technical reason for undecidability is the possibility to 'temporalise' binary relations, cf. [26]. The fragment $\mathcal{DLR}_{\mathcal{US}}^-$, in which the temporal operators can be applied only to entities and formulas (but not to n-ary relations, with $n \geq 2$), exhibits a much better computational behaviour. The following theorem presents the complexity results we have obtained for schema and query reasoning in $\mathcal{DLR}_{\mathcal{US}}^-$:

Theorem 2. *Let the flow of time be $\langle \mathbb{Z}, < \rangle$. Then*
    (1) *the problem of logical implication in $\mathcal{DLR}_{\mathcal{US}}^-$ involving only atomic formulas is EXPTIME-complete;*
    (2) *the formula satisfiability problem (and so the problem of logical implication) in $\mathcal{DLR}_{\mathcal{US}}^-$ is EXPSPACE-complete;*
    (3) *the query-containment problem for non-recursive Datalog queries under $\mathcal{DLR}_{\mathcal{US}}^-$-constraints is decidable in 2EXPTIME and is EXPSPACE-hard.*

The main ideas of the proof are as follows:
    (1) EXPTIME-hardness follows from the EXPTIME-hardness of $\mathcal{DLR}$. An EXPTIME-algorithm is obtained by means of a polynomial reduction from $\mathcal{DLR}_{\mathcal{US}}^-$ to the logic $\mathcal{DLR}_{reg}$, where logical implication is known to be decidable in EXPTIME [9]. The reduction extends the one proposed in [21].

(2)The EXPSPACE-hardness of the formula satisfiability problem is proved in [17], even for the sublanguage $\mathcal{ALC}_\square$ of $\mathcal{DLR}_{\mathcal{US}}^-$, by reducing to it the n-CORRIDOR tiling problem [24]. But the most interesting and original result presented in this paper is the EXPSPACE upper bound. We briefly sketch the main new contribution. First, we take the road proposed in [25,27,28] and show that the satisfiability problem can be equivalently formulated as a problem about the existence of certain *quasimodels*. Roughly, the idea behind the notion of a quasimodel is to represent 'the state' of the (in general, infinite) domain of a temporal model at each moment of time by finitely many 'types' of the domain objects at this moment. A set T is a *quasistate candidate* for φ if it is a set of concept types (i.e., a subset of all the subconcepts in φ which is Boolean saturated). Not all quasistate candidates can represent proper states. Denote by $c(t)$ the type which results from t when all concepts starting with a temporal operator are replaced by new atomic concepts. Thus, $c(t)$ abstracts from the temporal content of T. We say that the quasistate candidate T is a *quasistate* for φ if the following (non-temporal) $\mathcal{DLR}$-formula α_T

$$\left(\bigsqcup_{t \in T} c(t) \doteq \top \right) \wedge \bigwedge_{t \in T} \neg (c(t) \doteq \bot)$$

is satisfiable. A *quasimodel* for φ is a sequence of quasistates for φ satisfying some additional conditions. It was proved in [28] that given an oracle deciding whether a given quasistate candidate is a quasistate, the question whether a quasimodel for φ exists can be decided in EXPSPACE. Hence, the main new ingredient providing us with an EXPSPACE procedure deciding the existence of quasimodels for φ is the following:

Lemma 1. *Given a $\mathcal{DLR}_{\mathcal{US}}^-$-formula φ, it is decidable in EXPSPACE whether a quasistate candidate for φ is a quasistate.*

Since α_T is exponential in the size of φ, this lemma does not follow from known results and, in fact, a number of new ideas are required to prove it.

(3) The query containment problem can be reduced to satisfiability in quasimodels and the query-containment problem for (non-temporal) $\mathcal{DLR}$. Since we proved in (2) that the satisfiability problem is EXPSPACE-complete, while for $\mathcal{DLR}$ the problem was shown to be decidable in 2EXPTIME time in [9] we can conclude that also in $\mathcal{DLR}_{\mathcal{US}}^-$ the query containment problem is in 2EXPTIME.

4   Conceptual Modelling

In this section we briefly show how the temporal description logic $\mathcal{DLR}_{\mathcal{US}}$ can provide a formal semantic characterisation of the most important temporal conceptual modelling constructs (for the valid time representation). We refer mostly to the temporal extended entity-relationship data model, for which a detailed literature exists [18,22].

The extended entity-relationship (EER) model—i.e., the standard entity-relationship data model, enriched with IsA links, disjoint and covering constraints, and full cardinality constraints—may be viewed as a temporalised EER model which assigns to every construct a temporal interpretation but provides no explicit temporal constructs. Gregersen and Jensen [18] call this approach *implicit*, because the temporal dimension is hidden in the interpretation structure so that entities and relationships are always time-dependent.

The non-temporal fragment of $\mathcal{DLR_{US}}$, i.e., $\mathcal{DLR}$, is enough to capture the EER model with implicit time. For the non-temporal EER model, such an encoding, introduced by [10,11], establishes a precise correspondence between legal database states of the EER diagram and models of the derived $\mathcal{DLR}$ theory. That this encoding is correct for the EER model with implicit time was shown in [2,3], where $\mathcal{DLR}$ was interpreted by a temporal semantics. The example knowledge base in Section 2.2 (without the last two formulas) shows the exact encoding for the left-hand part of the temporally implicit EER diagram in Fig.2. This encoding could support the design of a temporal conceptual schema by exploiting the reasoning in $\mathcal{DLR_{US}}$: it becomes possible to verify the conceptual specification, infer implicit facts and stricter constraints, and manifest any inconsistencies. Note that the same ideas presented here would apply to non-temporal UML class diagrams (encoded in $\mathcal{DLR}$ in [8]) and DAML+OIL ontologies.

We now introduce the basic temporal constructs that can be added on top of a temporally implicit model leading to a full fledged temporal conceptual model.

Temporal Entities and Relations. Both entity and relation instances in a temporal setting have an existence time associated to them. $\mathcal{DLR_{US}}$-formulas can enforce either that entities (relations) cannot last forever—we call them *temporary entities* (*temporary relations*), or that their extension never changes in time—we call them *snapshot entities* (*snapshot relations*). Temporary entities and relations are captured by the following $\mathcal{DLR_{US}}$-formulas:

$$ E \sqsubseteq^* (\Diamond^+ \neg E) \sqcup (\Diamond^- \neg E) \qquad R \sqsubseteq^* (\Diamond^+ \neg R) \sqcup (\Diamond^- \neg R) $$

saying that there must be a past or a future time point where the entity (relation) does not hold. In other words, instances of temporary entities (relations) always have a limited lifetime. On the other hand, snapshot entities and relations are captured by the following $\mathcal{DLR_{US}}$-formulas:

$$ E \sqsubseteq^* (\Box^+ E) \sqcap (\Box^- E) \qquad R \sqsubseteq^* (\Box^+ R) \sqcap (\Box^- R) $$

saying that whenever the entity (relation) is true it is necessarily true in every past and every future time point, i.e, they never change along time. Snapshot entities and relations are used to capture the semantics of legacy non-temporal schemas when included in a temporal model, thus enforcing the upward compatibility. In our example (Fig. 2), Employee, Department, Resp-For could be constrained by snapshot $\mathcal{DLR_{US}}$ formulas, while Manager, Work-For by temporary formulas.

Temporal Attributes. At different points in time, an entity may have different values for the same attribute. Attributes can be forced either to remain unchanged in time (*snapshot* attribute), or to necessarily change (*temporary* attribute) with the following $\mathcal{DLR_{US}}$-formulas, respectively:

$$ E \sqsubseteq^* \exists^{\geq 1}[\texttt{from}]\Box^* R_A \qquad E \sqsubseteq^* \exists^{=1}[\texttt{From}](R_A \sqcap (\Diamond^+ \neg R_A \sqcup \Diamond^- \neg R_A)) $$

When considering the interaction between the temporal behaviour of an attribute and that of the owner entity, it is consistent in $\mathcal{DLR_{US}}$ to have both snapshot attributes of a temporary entity and temporary attributes of a snapshot entity. In the former case, the $\mathcal{DLR_{US}}$ semantics says that during the lifespan of an entity the value of a snapshot attribute never changes. In the latter one, the meaning is that each instance always belongs to the snapshot entity but the value of the temporary attribute will change during its existence. In our running example, where `Employee` is a snapshot entity, `Salary` is modelled as a temporary attribute, while `Names`, `PaySlipNumber` are modelled as snapshot attributes. In particular, `PaySlipNumber` plays the role of a full fledged temporal key (see the formula for `PaySlipNumber` in Sect. 2.2).

Temporal Cardinalities. Cardinality constraints limit the participation of entities in relationships. In a temporal setting, we can distinguish between *snapshot participation constraints* (true at each point in time) and *lifespan participation constraints* (evaluated during the entire existence of the entity). While the standard $\mathcal{DLR}_{\mathcal{US}}$ cardinality construct captures snapshot participation constraints, the lifespan participation constraints are defined by the following $\mathcal{DLR}_{\mathcal{US}}$-formula:

$$E \sqsubseteq^* \exists^{\leq n}[i] \Diamond^* R$$

i.e., over its lifespan, an instance of the entity E must participate as the ith argument in at least n (at most n, or precisely n) tuples of the relation R. Obviously, since for snapshot relations the set of instances does not change in time, there is no difference between snapshot and lifespan participation constraints with respect to snapshot relations. In our example, we could say for example that managers should manage at most 5 different projects in their entire existence as managers, while still being constrained in managing exactly one project at a time.

Dynamic Entities. In the temporal conceptual modelling literature, two notions of dynamic transitions between a entities (also called object migrations) are considered [22]: *dynamic evolution*, when an object ceases to be an instance of a source entity, and *dynamic extension*, when an object continues to belong to the source. Let E_s be the source entity and E_t be the target one; the two cases are captured by the following formulas, respectively:

$$E_s \sqsubseteq^* \Diamond^+(E_t \sqcap \neg E_s) \qquad E_s \sqsubseteq^* \Diamond^+ E_t$$

An interesting consequence of dynamic evolution is that the source is necessarily a temporary entity.

$\mathcal{DLR}_{\mathcal{US}}$ is also able to capture *safety* and *liveness* constraints. A *safety* constraint intuitively says that "*nothing bad ever happens*" and can be captured by the formula $\Box^* \neg (E \sqsubseteq \bot)$. On the other hand, *liveness* constraints saying that "*something good will happen*" can be expressed by existential temporal formulas: $\Diamond^* \neg (E \sqsubseteq \bot)$.

Schema Evolution. We consider here a simplified case of conceptual schema evolution [15], which can be called a *monotonic* approach. This allows only for changes in the schema such that the resulting conceptual schema is compatible with the previous *global* constraints.

Let Γ and ϕ_p be atomic formulas, or possibly a Boolean combination of atomic formulas, which introduce, respectively, a new schema portion and a condition to be checked. The formula $\Box^*(\neg \phi_p \vee \Box^+ \Gamma)$ states that as soon as the property ϕ_p becomes true for the data, the conceptual schema will include the additional Γ constraint. A simple example is:

$\phi_p \equiv (\texttt{InterestGroup} \sqsubseteq \bot)$

$\Gamma \equiv (\exists^{\geq 1}[\texttt{amount}](\texttt{Salary} \sqcap \texttt{payee}/2 : \texttt{TopManager}) \sqsubseteq \texttt{LowAmount})$

meaning that as soon as the organisation does not include interest groups anymore, the salary of top managers should be in the "low amount" class.

Note that the $\mathcal{DLR}_{\mathcal{US}}^{-}$ with only atomic formulas (i.e., the EXPTIME-complete fragment of $\mathcal{DLR}_{\mathcal{US}}$) is enough to capture most of the modelling constructs discussed in this Section—in fact, in the case of (global) logical implication for atomic formulas, there is no difference between $\sqsubseteq$ and $\sqsubseteq^*$—with the exception of (a) schema evolution constraints, (b) safety and liveness conditions, (c) snapshot relations and attributes, and (d) temporal cardinalities. Full $\mathcal{DLR}_{\mathcal{US}}^{-}$ (i.e., the EXPSPACE-complete fragment of $\mathcal{DLR}_{\mathcal{US}}$) is able to express (a) and (b) as well. However, (c) and (d) require temporalised relations which, by Theorem 1, lead to undecidability.

5 Conclusion

This work introduces the temporal description logic $\mathcal{DLR}_{\mathcal{US}}$ and illustrates its expressive power. A temporal query language was defined and the problem of query containment under the constraints defined by a $\mathcal{DLR}_{\mathcal{US}}$ conceptual schema is investigated.

Tight complexity results were proved. In particular, reasoning in the full logic $\mathcal{DLR}_{\mathcal{US}}$ was shown to be undecidable, while decidability was obtained using a still expressive fragment, $\mathcal{DLR}_{\mathcal{US}}^{-}$. We have also shown that the problem of checking query containment of non-recursive Datalog queries under constraints with arbitrary $\mathcal{DLR}_{\mathcal{US}}^{-}$ formulas is decidable in 2EXPTIME with an EXPSPACE lower bound. This result is the first decidability result we are aware of on containment of temporal conjunctive queries under expressive constraints.

This work has been partially funded by the EPSRC grants GR/R45369/01, GR/R04348/01, GR/R09428/01. The second author wishes to thank the University of Manchester, where most of the work presented in this paper was carried out.

References

1. S. Abiteboul, L. Herr, and J. Van den Bussche. Temporal versus first-order logic to query temporal databases. In *Proc. of the 15th ACM SIGACT SIGMOD SIGART Sym. on Principles of Database Systems (PODS'96)*, pages 49–57, 1996.
2. A. Artale and E. Franconi. Reasoning with enhanced temporal entity-relationship models. In *Proc. of the International Workshop on Spatio-Temporal Data Models and Languages*. IEEE Computer Society Press, August 1999.
3. A. Artale and E. Franconi. Temporal ER modeling with description logics. In *Proc. of the International Conference on Conceptual Modeling (ER'99)*. Springer-Verlag, November 1999.
4. A. Artale and E. Franconi. A survey of temporal extensions of description logics. *Annals of Mathematics and Artificial Intelligence*, 30(1-4), 2001.
5. F. Baader, D. Calvanese, D. McGuinness, D. Nardi, and P. F. Patel-Schneider, editors. *Description Logic Handbook: Theory, Implementation and Applications*. Cambridge University Press, 2002.
6. A. Borgida and R. J. Brachman. Conceptual modelling with description logics. In Baader et al. [5].

7. A. Borgida, M. Lenzerini, and R. Rosati. Description logics for databases. In Baader et al. [5].

8. A. Calì D. Calvanese, G. De Giacomo, and M. Lenzerini. A formal framework for reasoning on UML class diagrams. In *Proc. of the 13th Int. Sym. on Methodologies for Intelligent Systems (ISMIS 2002)*, 2002.

9. D. Calvanese, G. De Giacomo, and M. Lenzerini. On the decidability of query containment under constraints. In *Proc. of the 17th ACM SIGACT SIGMOD SIGART Sym. on Principles of Database Systems (PODS'98)*, pages 149–158, 1998.

10. D. Calvanese, M. Lenzerini, and D. Nardi. Description logics for conceptual data modeling. In Chomicki and Saake [13].

11. D. Calvanese, M. Lenzerini, and D. Nardi. Unifying class-based representation formalisms. *J. of Artificial Intelligence Research*, 11:199–240, 1999.

12. J. Chomicki. Temporal query languages: a survey. In *Proc. of the 1st International Conference on Temporal Logic (ICTL'94)*, pages 506–534, 1994.

13. J. Chomicki and G. Saake, editors. *Logics for Databases and Information Systems*. Kluwer, 1998.

14. J. Chomicki and D. Toman. Temporal logic in information systems. In Chomicki and Saake [13], chapter 1.

15. E. Franconi, F. Grandi, and F. Mandreoli. A semantic approach for schema evolution and versioning in object-oriented databases. In *Proc. of the 1st International Conf. on Computational Logic (CL'2000), DOOD stream*. Springer-Verlag, July 2000.

16. E. Franconi and G. Ng. The ICOM tool for intelligent conceptual modelling. In *Proc. of the 7th International Workshop on Knowledge Representation meets Databases (KRDB'2000)*, 2000.

17. D. Gabbay, A.Kurucz, F. Wolter, and M. Zakharyaschev. *Many-dimensional modal logics: theory and applications*. Studies in Logic. Elsevier, 2002. To appear.

18. H Gregersen and J. S. Jensen. Temporal Entity-Relationship models - a survey. *IEEE Transactions on Knowledge and Data Engineering*, 11(3):464–497, 1999.

19. I. Hodkinson, F. Wolter, and M. Zakharyaschev. Decidable fragments of first-order temporal logics. *Annals of Pure and Applied Logic*, 106:85–134, 2000.

20. M. Jarke, C. Quix, D. Calvanese, M. Lenzerini, E. Franconi, S. Ligoudistiano, P. Vassiliadis, and Y. Vassiliou. Concept based design of data warehouses: The DWQ demonstrators. In *2000 ACM SIGMOD Intl. Conference on Management of Data*, 2000.

21. K. Schild. Combining terminological logics with tense logic. In *Proceedings of the 6th Portuguese Conference on Artificial Intelligence, EPIA'93*, October 1993.

22. S. Spaccapietra, C. Parent, and E. Zimanyi. Modeling time from a conceptual perspective. In *Int. Conf. on Information and Knowledge Management (CIKM98)*, 1998.

23. H. Sturm and F. Wolter. A tableau calculus for temporal description logic: the expanding domain case. *Journal of Logic and Computation*, 2002. To appear.

24. P. van Emde Boas. The convenience of tiling. Technical Report CT-96-01, ILLC—Univ. of Amsterdam, 1996.

25. F. Wolter and M. Zakharyaschev. Satisfiability problem in description logics with modal operators. In *Proc. of the 6th International Conference on Principles of Knowledge Representation and Reasoning (KR'98)*, pages 512–523, Trento, Italy, June 1998.

26. F. Wolter and M. Zakharyaschev. Modal description logics: Modalizing roles. *Fundamenta Informaticae*, 39(4):411–438, 1999.

27. F. Wolter and M. Zakharyaschev. Multi-dimensional description logics. In *Proc. of IJCAI'99*, pages 104–109, 1999.

28. F. Wolter and M. Zakharyaschev. Temporalizing description logics. In D. Gabbay and M. de Rijke, editors, *Frontiers of Combining Systems*, pages 379–401. Studies Press-Wiley, 1999.

Polynomial-Length Planning Spans the Polynomial Hierarchy

Hudson Turner

University of Minnesota, Duluth
hudson@d.umn.edu

Abstract. This paper presents a family of results on the computational complexity of planning: classical, conformant, and conditional with full or partial observability. Attention is restricted to plans of polynomially-bounded length. For conditional planning, restriction to plans of polynomial size is also considered. For this analysis, a planning domain is described by a transition relation encoded in classical propositional logic. Given the widespread use of satisfiability-based planning methods, this is a rather natural choice. Moreover, this allows us to develop a unified representation—in second-order propositional logic—of the range of planning problems considered. By describing a wide range of results within a single framework, the paper sheds new light on how planning complexity is affected by common assumptions such as nonconcurrency, determinism and polynomial-time decidability of executability of actions.

1 Introduction

This paper presents a family of results on the computational complexity of planning problems in which a plan of polynomially-bounded length is sought. A planning problem traditionally consists of three elements: a description of the planning domain (specifying how actions can affect the state of the world), a description of the initial state of the world, and a description of the goal. A solution to a planning problem is a *valid* plan—one whose execution is guaranteed to achieve the goal, and whose executability is also guaranteed. In investigating the computational complexity of planning, it is convenient to focus on the associated decision problem: Does a valid plan exist?

In classical planning, the initial state is completely specified, the action domain is deterministic, and a plan is a finite sequence of actions to be performed. These assumptions can be relaxed to obtain larger classes of planning problems. For instance, in conformant planning, one no longer assumes that the initial state is completely specified, and actions are allowed to have nondeterministic effects, but a plan is still a sequence of actions. Another class of planning problems is obtained by allowing conditional plans, in which the execution of a plan at each step may depend on the previous execution history. In characterizing this dependence, we may assume that the current state is fully observable or only partially observable during plan execution. The paper considers the complexity of each of these classes of planning problems.

S. Flesca et al. (Eds.): JELIA 2002, LNAI 2424, pp. 111–124, 2002.
© Springer-Verlag Berlin Heidelberg 2002

This is not a new line of research; among the papers with results on planning complexity published in the last decade are [3,1,6,10,11,4,8,14,2,5]. The work presented here is unusual in employing a single framework to study the complexity of such a wide range of polynomial-length planning problems.

In fact, one contribution of the paper is a unified representation—in second-order propositional logic—of the decision problems associated with classical, conformant and conditional planning (with full or partial observability). In many cases, membership of a planning problem in a given complexity class can be determined by the form of its QBF representation. Moreover, several of the hardness results are especially easy to obtain in this setting.

The analysis employs a simple, general action representation framework in which a planning domain is described by a transition relation encoded in classical propositional logic. This is technically convenient, given our interest in QBF representations, and also sensible in light of the widespread use of satisfiability methods in automated planning, which depends on the fact that such descriptions can be obtained by polynomial-time translation from many other action description languages. Thus, the results obtained here have wide applicability.

Moreover, this action representation framework allows for such complications as nondeterminism and concurrent execution of actions, which makes it convenient to consider the incremental effect of imposing common planning assumptions such as determinism and nonconcurrency. Consequently, our analysis sheds new light on the role such assumptions play in determining the complexity of each of the families of planning problems considered.

Many accounts of planning are based on action representations with another significant (but less often remarked on) property: the executability of actions in a state can be determined in polynomial time. This assumption does not hold for the action representation framework used here. Let us consider very briefly why it can be convenient to abandon it. In general, this assumption will not hold for action representations that allow for *implied* action preconditions. For example, a domain description may describe the fact that two blocks cannot occupy the same position, and from this general fact many action preconditions may follow. For instance, it can be inferred that block B_1 cannot be moved to the location of block B_2 (unless block B_2 is moved somewhere else). It also follows that blocks B_1 and B_2 cannot be moved concurrently to the same location.

A number of results reported here are similar to (although distinct from) results in [10,14,2,5]. In each case this will be noted when the result is encountered in the text. (A more comprehensive survey of planning complexity results is beyond the scope of this paper.) Due to space restrictions, proofs are omitted.

2   Preliminaries

2.1   Action Representation Framework

Begin with a set A of action symbols and a disjoint set F of fluent symbols. Let $state(F)$ be a formula in which the only nonlogical symbols are elements of F. The formula $state(F)$ encodes the set of states that correspond to its models.

Let $act(F, A, F')$ be a formula with nonlogical symbols taken from $F \cup A \cup F'$, where F' is obtained from F by priming each element of F. (Assume F' is disjoint from $F \cup A$. From now on similar disjointness assumptions will be left unstated.) Let $state(F')$ be the formula obtained from $state(F)$ by substituting for each occurrence of each fluent symbol its primed counterpart. (Throughout, this sort of notation will be used to generate formulas by substitution.) Of course each model of $state(F')$ also corresponds to a state in the obvious way. Finally, the formula

$$state(F) \wedge act(F, A, F') \wedge state(F') \tag{1}$$

encodes the set of transitions that correspond to its models: that is, each model of (1) encodes the transition such that (*i*) the start state corresponds to the interpretation of the symbols in F, (*ii*) the set of actions (concurrently) executed corresponds to the interpretation of the symbols in A, and (*iii*) the end state corresponds to the interpretation of the symbols in F'. We abbreviate (1) as

$$tr(F, A, F') .$$

This domain representation framework accomodates nondeterminism, concurrent actions and dynamic worlds. We do not address in this paper how such action representations are to be obtained. There are many possibilities. For instance, domain descriptions in STRIPS-based languages are easily translated (in polynomial time) into domain descriptions in the format used in this paper. Such descriptions can also be obtained from more expressive action languages, such as the high-level action language $\mathcal{C}$ [7], for which "definite" descriptions yield such classical propositional theories in polynomial time by the syntactic process of "literal completion" introduced in [12].

2.2 Planning Framework

In the remainder of the paper, we use this action representation framework to investigate the computational complexity of several classes of planning problems. That is, we consider the complexity of the associated decision problem—existence of a valid plan. The input size parameter for these complexity results is (any reasonable measure of) the size of (1) plus the size of the formulas $init(F)$ and $goal(F)$ describing, respectively, the initial state and the goal. (As before, we assume that the nonlogical symbols in these formulas are taken from F.) Henceforth, we will find it convenient to assume that $init(F) \models state(F)$. We will focus on plans whose length is bounded by a polynomial in the input size.

2.3 The Polynomial Hierarchy and PSPACE

For our purposes, it is convenient to characterize complexity classes in terms of second-order propositional logic. (See, for instance, [13].) Consider quantified boolean formulas (QBFs) of the form

$$Q_1 x_1 \, Q_2 x_2 \, \cdots \, Q_k x_k \, \Phi(x_1, x_2, \ldots, x_k) \tag{2}$$

where (i) each of $x_1, x_2, \ldots, x_k$ stands for a tuple of propositional variables, (ii) each of $Q_1, Q_2, \ldots, Q_k$ stands for a quantifier, with each Q_{i+1} different from Q_i, and (iii) $\Phi(x_1, x_2, \ldots, x_k)$ is a formula without quantifiers and without nonlogical constants, whose variables are taken from $x_1, x_2, \ldots, x_k$. For a formula of this kind, the corresponding decision problem is this: Is it satisfiable? Equivalently, we can ask if it is logically valid, or, since no nonlogical constants occur in it, we may simply ask if it is true. For natural number k, complexity class Σ_k^P corresponds to the family of formulas of form (2) with $Q_1 = \exists$, and complexity class Π_k^P corresponds to the family of such formulas with $Q_1 = \forall$. That is, for each of these families of QBFs, the decision problem is complete for the corresponding complexity class. Some important special cases are $\Sigma_1^P = \mathbf{NP}$, $\Pi_1^P = \mathbf{coNP}$, and $\Sigma_0^P = \Pi_0^P = \mathbf{P}$. Finally, the complexity class $\mathbf{PSPACE}$ corresponds to the decision problem for the family of all QBFs of form (2).

2.4 Some Common Assumptions in Planning

The following QBFs describe some common assumptions in planning.

$$\exists f \ (init(f) \wedge \forall f' \ (init(f') \supset f = f')) \tag{3}$$

$$\forall f \ \forall a \ \forall f' \ \forall f'' \ (tr(f, a, f') \wedge tr(f, a, f'') \supset f' = f'') \tag{4}$$

$$\forall f \ \forall a \ \exists f' \ (state(f) \supset tr(f, a, f')) \tag{5}$$

The assumption that the initial state is completely described (i.e. unique) is expressed by (3) where f (respectively f') is a tuple of distinct propositional variables corresponding to the propositional constants in F (respectively F'), and $f = f'$ is shorthand for the conjunction of formulas $p \equiv p'$ for each pair of similar variables $p \in f$ and $p' \in f'$. (From now on we'll employ such notation without remarking on it.) An action domain is deterministic iff (4) is true. So determining that an action domain is deterministic is a problem in $\mathbf{coNP}$. Moreover, it is $\mathbf{coNP}$-hard. Actions are always executable iff (5) is true. So determining that actions are always executable belongs to Π_2^P. Again, hardness is easily shown.

In many accounts of planning, it is unusual for actions to be always executable. Nonetheless, action description languages used for planning often have a similarly useful property: there are polynomial-time algorithms not only for obtaining formulas $state(F)$ and $act(F, A, F')$, but also for obtaining a classical propositional formula $executable(F, A)$ (in which only atoms from $F \cup A$ occur) that is logically equivalent to $state(F) \supset \exists f' \ tr(F, A, f')$. Such action description languages make it easy to determine whether actions are executable in a state. In fact, we note (without going into details) that in such cases there is a p-time transformation that yields a description for which actions are always executable and yet the valid plans (for all classes of planning problems considered here) are exactly the same. (Moreover, this can be done without introducing additional concurrency or nondeterminism.) Thus, for instance, a planning problem posed using a STRIPS-based action representation language can be translated in polynomial time into our planning framework, with the additional guarantee that actions will be always executable in the resulting domain description.

We say that the executability of actions is polynomial-time computable iff, for every interpretation I of $F \cup A$ that satisfies $state(F)$, deciding whether $I \models \exists f' \, tr(F, A, f')$ can be done in polynomial time. In our framework it is in general not the case that the executability of actions in a state can be determined in polynomial time (assuming $\mathbf{P} \neq \mathbf{NP}$); one easily verifies that the problem of determining that given actions are executable in a given state is $\mathbf{NP}$-complete.

3   Classical Planning

For us, classical planning is essentially what is widely known as satisfiability planning [9]. In satisfiability planning, an action domain is (also) described by a finite theory of classical propositional logic. Typically, the language will include action atoms (representing the proposition that a certain action occurs at a certain time) and fluent atoms (representing the proposition that a certain fluent holds at a certain time). Assume that action atoms have the form α_t, where α is an action symbol and subscript t is a natural number—the "time stamp" of α_t. Similarly, assume that fluent atoms have the form φ_t, with φ a fluent symbol and t a time stamp. A plan of length k is obtained by finding a model of

$$init(F_0) \wedge \bigwedge_{t=0}^{k-1} tr(F_t, A_t, F_{t+1}) \wedge goal(F_k)$$

where each F_i (respectively A_i) is the set of fluent atoms (respectively action atoms) obtained by adding time stamp i to each fluent symbol (respectively action symbol). The plan is the sequence of (possibly concurrent) action occurrences corresponding to the interpretation of the action atoms. In order to guarantee that this plan is valid—that is, always executable and sure to achieve the goal under all possible executions—the initial state must be completely described, and the domain must be deterministic. If these assumptions are indeed satisfied, the existence of a valid plan is expressed by the QBF

$$\exists f_0 \, \overbrace{\exists a_0} \, \exists f_1 \, \cdots \, \overbrace{\exists a_{k-1}} \, \exists f_k \, \left(init(f_0) \wedge \bigwedge_{t=0}^{k-1} tr(f_t, a_t, f_{t+1}) \wedge goal(f_k) \right) \quad (6)$$

where each f_i (respectively a_i) is a tuple of distinct propositional variables corresponding to the propositional constants in F_i (respectively A_i). This shows once again what is widely known: classical planning, for plans of polynomially-bounded length, belongs to $\mathbf{NP}$.

Theorem 1. *Classical planning for plans of length 1 is $\mathbf{NP}$-hard, even if actions are always executable. Classical planning is $\mathbf{NP}$-complete for plans of polynomially-bounded length.*

Recall though that, in the current framework, classical planning includes the possibility of concurrent actions and dynamic worlds. Moreover, it may not be possible to determine in polynomial time whether given actions are executable in a given state. These complications do not push the problem beyond $\mathbf{NP}$.

4 Conformant Planning

In conformant planning, a plan is still a sequence of actions, but the action domain may be nondeterministic, and the initial state may be incompletely specified. As usual, a plan is valid if it is guaranteed to be executable, and every possible execution achieves the goal. The key issues can be illustrated by considering plans of length 1. There is at least one possible initial state:

$$\exists f_0 \ init(f_0). \tag{7}$$

There is an unconditional one-step plan that is executable starting from any of the possible initial states:

$$\exists a_0 \ \forall f_0 \ (init(f_0) \supset \exists f_1 \ tr(f_0, a_0, f_1)). \tag{8}$$

There is an unconditional one-step plan that achieves the goal in every possible execution starting from any of the possible initial states:

$$\exists a_0 \ \forall f_0 \ (init(f_0) \supset \forall f_1 \ (tr(f_0, a_0, f_1) \supset goal(f_1))).$$

So to say that there is a valid one-step unconditional plan—one that is both executable (starting in any possible initial state) and sufficient to achieve the goal (when executed starting in any possible initial state)—we can write

$$\exists a_0 \ \forall f_0 \ (init(f_0) \supset \exists f_1 \ tr(f_0, a_0, f_1) \land \ \forall f_1 \ (tr(f_0, a_0, f_1) \supset goal(f_1))). \tag{9}$$

Consequently, the decision problem for one-step unconditional planning is expressed by the conjunction of (7) and (9). We can put (9) in prenex form as follows: $\exists a_0 \ \forall f_0 \ \forall f_1 \ \exists f'_1 \ (init(f_0) \supset tr(f_0, a_0, f'_1) \land (tr(f_0, a_0, f_1) \supset goal(f_1)))$. Hence, the decision problem for one-step conformant planning belongs to the complexity class Σ_3^P. Hardness is easily shown.

As a step toward the general formulation, consider plans of length 2. We need not alter the formula (7) expressing the existence of at least one possible initial state. To say that there is an unconditional plan whose first step is executable in any possible initial state, we can (again) write (8). To say that there is an unconditional plan such that the second step is executable in any state reached after executing the first step in any possible initial state, we can write

$$\exists a_0 \ \exists a_1 \ \forall f_0 \ \forall f_1 (init(f_0) \land tr(f_0, a_0, f_1) \supset \exists f_2 \ tr(f_1, a_1, f_2)). \tag{10}$$

To say that there is an unconditional two-step plan whose execution is sufficient to achieve the goal (starting in any possible initial state), we can write

$$\exists a_0 \ \exists a_1 \ \forall f_0 \ \forall f_1 \ \forall f_2 \ (init(f_0) \land tr(f_0, a_0, f_1) \land tr(f_1, a_1, f_2) \supset goal(f_2)). \tag{11}$$

Combining (8), (10) and (11) appropriately in prenex form, we can obtain

$$\exists a_0 \ \exists a_1 \ \forall f_0 \ \forall f_1 \ \forall f_2 \ \exists f'_1 \ \exists f'_2 \ ((init(f_0) \supset tr(f_0, a_0, f'_1))$$
$$\land \ (init(f_0) \land tr(f_0, a_0, f_1) \supset tr(f_1, a_1, f'_2))$$
$$\land \ (init(f_0) \land tr(f_0, a_0, f_1) \land tr(f_1, a_1, f_2) \supset goal(f_2))).$$

The general form is similar. For conformant planning for plans of length k, take the conjunction of (7) and

$$\exists a_0 \cdots \exists a_{k-1} \; \forall f_0 \cdots \forall f_k \; \exists f_1' \cdots \exists f_k'$$
$$\left(\bigwedge_{t=0}^{k-1} \left(init(f_0) \wedge \bigwedge_{u=0}^{t-1} tr(f_u, a_u, f_{u+1}) \supset tr(f_t, a_t, f_{t+1}') \right) \right. \tag{12}$$
$$\left. \wedge \left(init(f_0) \wedge \bigwedge_{t=0}^{k-1} tr(f_t, a_t, f_{t+1}) \supset goal(f_k) \right) \right).$$

Theorem 2. *Conformant planning for plans of length 1 is Σ_3^P-hard. Conformant planning is Σ_3^P-complete for plans of polynomially-bounded length.*

In a comment following their formally stated complexity results, Eiter *et al.* [5] mention a similar Σ_3^P-completeness result for conformant planning, but their result is restricted to plans of a fixed length. They employ an expressive high-level action description language whose salient feature in this context is that determining the executability of given actions in a given state is **NP**-complete.

If we assume that actions are always executable, we can eliminate the check for plan executability from (12), which can then be reduced to

$$\exists a_0 \cdots \exists a_{k-1} \; \forall f_0 \cdots \forall f_k \; \left(init(f_0) \wedge \bigwedge_{t=0}^{k-1} tr(f_t, a_t, f_{t+1}) \supset goal(f_k) \right).$$

So the complexity of conformant planning falls to Σ_2^P if actions are always executable. We can then show hardness for plans of length 1 even if we assume determinism. On the other hand, we can show membership even if the executability of given actions in a given state is only polynomial-time decidable.

Theorem 3. *Conformant planning for plans of length 1 is Σ_2^P-hard for deterministic planning domains in which actions are always executable. Conformant planning is Σ_2^P-complete for plans of polynomially-bounded length, if the executability of actions is polynomial-time computable.*

A similar result (Theorem 2) in [2] is obtained using an action representation language that guarantees determinism and nonconcurrency, and makes it easy to determine whether actions are executable in a state (as discussed in Section 2.4). Our analysis suggests that only the last property is crucial for placing the problem within Σ_2^P. On the other hand, as mentioned previously, [5] employs a relatively expressive action description language, and a related Σ_2^P result reported there (Theorem 3) is also obtained by directly imposing polynomial-time decidability of executability of given actions in a given state. The latter result again assumes that plan length is fixed (not just polynomially-bounded).

5 Conditional Planning

Conditional planning is an extension of conformant planning in which the actions to be performed in executing a plan may depend on the previous execution history. For the analysis in this section, we assume that each step in the execution of a conditional plan may depend arbitrarily on the previous execution history. Thus, in a rather general sense, we address here the fundamental question of existence of a valid conditional plan.

As with conformant planning, it is convenient to begin by considering plans of length 1. Of course the existence of at least one possible initial state is again expressed by (7). To say that there is a one-step conditional plan that is executable in any possible initial state, we can write

$$\forall f_0 \ (init(f_0) \supset \exists a_0 \ \exists f_1 \ tr(f_0, a_0, f_1)). \tag{13}$$

To say that there is a one-step conditional plan that is sufficient to achieve the goal if executed starting in any possible initial state, we can write

$$\forall f_0 \ (init(f_0) \supset \exists a_0 \ \forall f_1 \ (tr(f_0, a_0, f_1) \supset goal(f_1))).$$

Consequently, a formula for the decision problem corresponding to one-step conditional planning is the conjunction of (7) and

$$\forall f_0 \ \exists a_0 \ \exists f_1' \ \forall f_1 (init(f_0) \supset tr(f_0, a_0, f_1') \wedge (tr(f_0, a_0, f_1) \supset goal(f_1))).$$

As a step toward obtaining the general form, let's consider conditional plans of length 2. We need not alter the formula (7) expressing the existence of at least one possible initial state. To say that there is a conditional plan whose first step is executable in any possible initial state, we (again) write (13). To say that there is a conditional plan such that the second step is executable in any state reached after executing the first step in any possible initial state, we write

$$\forall f_0 \ (init(f_0) \supset \exists a_0 \ \forall f_1 \ (tr(f_0, a_0, f_1) \supset \exists a_1 \ \exists f_2 \ tr(f_1, a_1, f_2))).$$

To say that there is a two-step conditional plan whose execution is sufficient to achieve the goal (starting in any possible initial state), we can write

$$\forall f_0 \ (init(f_0) \supset \exists a_0 \ \forall f_1 \ (tr(f_0, a_0, f_1) \supset \exists a_1 \ \forall f_2 \ (tr(f_1, a_1, f_2) \supset goal(f_2)))).$$

Combining (13) and these last two formulas in prenex form, we can obtain

$$\forall f_0 \ \exists a_0 \ \forall f_1 \ \exists a_1 \ \exists f_1' \ \exists f_2' \ \forall f_2 \ ((init(f_0) \supset tr(f_0, a_0, f_1'))$$
$$\wedge \ (init(f_0) \wedge tr(f_0, a_0, f_1) \supset tr(f_1, a_1, f_2'))$$
$$\wedge \ (init(f_0) \wedge tr(f_0, a_0, f_1) \wedge tr(f_1, a_1, f_2) \supset goal(f_2))).$$

Written in this form, it is clear that the "choice" of actions to be performed at time 0 depends only on the values of fluents at time 0. Similarly, the choice of actions to be performed at time 1 depends only on the values of fluents at time 0, the actions performed at time 0, and the values of fluents at time 1.

Here's the general form. For conditional planning for plans of length k, take the conjunction of (7) and the following.

$$\overbrace{\forall f_0 \ \exists a_0} \ \cdots \ \overbrace{\forall f_{k-1} \ \exists a_{k-1}} \ \exists f_1' \cdots \exists f_k' \ \forall f_k$$
$$\left(\bigwedge_{t=0}^{k-1} \left(init(f_0) \wedge \bigwedge_{u=0}^{t-1} tr(f_u, a_u, f_{u+1}) \supset tr(f_t, a_t, f_{t+1}') \right) \right. \tag{14}$$
$$\left. \wedge \left(init(f_0) \wedge \bigwedge_{t=0}^{k-1} tr(f_t, a_t, f_{t+1}) \supset goal(f_k) \right) \right)$$

If actions are always executable, (14) can be simplified:

$$\forall f_0 \; \overbrace{\exists a_0 \, \forall f_1} \; \cdots \; \overbrace{\exists a_{k-1} \, \forall f_k} \; \left(init(f_0) \wedge \bigwedge_{t=0}^{k-1} tr(f_t, a_t, f_{t+1}) \supset goal(f_k) \right).$$

Theorem 4. *Conditional planning for plans of length k is Π_{2k+1}^P-hard, even if actions are always executable. Conditional planning for plans of length k ($k > 0$) is Π_{2k+1}^P-complete. Conditional planning is* **PSPACE**-*complete for plans of polynomially-bounded length.*

A related **PSPACE**-completeness result is due to Littman [10] (Theorem 2). Although concerned with probabilistic planning, his proof construction for hardness uses just nondeterminism. Littman's result does not imply the **PSPACE** membership result in Theorem 4; in his approach actions are always executable.

If the action domain is deterministic, (14) can be equivalently replaced with

$$\forall f_0 \; \overbrace{\exists a_0 \, \exists f_1} \; \cdots \; \overbrace{\exists a_{k-1} \, \exists f_k} \; \left(init(f_0) \supset \bigwedge_{t=0}^{k-1} tr(f_t, a_t, f_{t+1}) \wedge goal(f_k) \right)$$

which reduces the complexity to Π_2^P! One can show hardness in this case even if actions are assumed to be always executable.

Theorem 5. *Conditional planning for plans of length 1 is Π_2^P-hard for deterministic planning domains, even if actions are always executable. Conditional planning is Π_2^P-complete for deterministic planning domains for plans of polynomially-bounded length.*

A related hardness result is obtained by Rintanen [14] (Theorem 2), using a deterministic action language, without concurrency, for which it is easy to determine executability of actions in a state[1]. A similar completeness result appears in [2] (Theorem 8), restricted, as mentioned previously, to deterministic action domains for which it is easy to determine executability of actions in a state. Our analysis suggests that the key is determinism.

6   Conditional Planning with Partial Observability

Despite the fact that Baral *et al.* in [2] consider only deterministic action domains, their Theorem 4 identifies a variant of polynomial-length conditional planning that is **PSPACE**-hard. This is because their action description language incorporates a rudimentary account of sensing actions, which allows them to model planning domains in which knowledge of the current state during plan

---

[1] The definition of planning used in Rintanen's theorem appears to subsume classical propositional STRIPS planning, and the theorem does not restrict consideration to bounded-length plans. Hence, it seems that **PSPACE**-hardness could have been derived immediately based on Bylander's well-known result [3]. On the other hand, Rintanen's proof construction utilizes only plans of polynomially-bounded length.

execution is incomplete because the current state is only partially observable. Such planning domains can be modeled in our setting by partitioning the set F of fluent symbols into two sets, F^O and F^N, intuitively corresponding to observable and nonobservable fluents, respectively.

Let's start again with plans of length 1. As usual, the existence of at least one possible initial state is expressed by (7). The existence of a conditional one-step plan that can be executed in any possible initial state is expressed by

$$\forall f_0^O \; \exists a_0 \; \forall f_0^N \; (init(f_0) \supset \exists f_1 \; tr(f_0, a_0, f_1)).$$

Notice that the choice of actions to be performed at time 0 depends only on the values of *observable* fluents at time 0. The existence of a conditional one-step plan sufficient to achieve the goal (when executed starting in any possible initial state) is expressed by

$$\forall f_0^O \; \exists a_0 \; \forall f_0^N \; (init(f_0) \supset \forall f_1 \; (tr(f_0, a_0, f_1) \supset goal(f_1))).$$

Again, the choice of actions to be performed at time 0 depends only on the values of observable fluents at time 0. As we did previously for simpler forms of planning, we combine formulas expressing executability and sufficiency, obtaining

$$\forall f_0^O \; \exists a_0 \; \forall f_0^N \; \forall f_1 \; \exists f_1' \; (init(f_0) \supset tr(f_0, a_0, f_1') \land (tr(f_0, a_0, f_1) \supset goal(f_1))),$$

which, conjoined with (7), expresses the decision problem for one-step conditional planning with partial observability.

To extend this to two-step conditional planning, we need to express the existence of a two-step conditional plan such that the second step is executable in any state reached by executing the first step in any possible initial state. In doing so, we must capture the fact that (i) the choice of actions to be performed at time 0 depends only on the observable fluents at time 0, and (ii) the choice of actions to be performed at time 1 depends only on the observable fluents at time 0, the actions performed at time 0, and the observable fluents at time 1.

$$\forall f_0^O \; \exists a_0 \; \forall f_1^O \; \exists a_1 \; \forall f_0^N \; \forall f_1^N \; (init(f_0) \land tr(f_0, a_0, f_1) \supset \exists f_2 \; tr(f_1, a_2, f_2))$$

We similarly need to express that there exists such a plan that is sufficient to achieve the goal when executed starting in any possible initial state.

$$\forall f_0^O \; \exists a_0 \; \forall f_1^O \; \exists a_1 \; \forall f_0^N \; \forall f_1^N \; (init(f_0) \land tr(f_0, a_0, f_1)$$
$$\supset \forall f_2 \; (tr(f_1, a_2, f_2) \supset goal(f_2)))$$

These observations suggest that two-step conditional planning with partial observability can be expressed by the conjunction of (7) and

$$\forall f_0^O \; \exists a_0 \; \forall f_1^O \; \exists a_1 \; \forall f_0^N \; \forall f_1^N \; \forall f_2 \; \exists f_1' \; \exists f_2' \; ((init(f_0) \supset tr(f_0, a_0, f_1'))$$
$$\land \; (init(f_0) \land tr(f_0, a_0, f_1) \supset tr(f_1, a_1, f_2'))$$
$$\land \; (init(f_0) \land tr(f_0, a_0, f_1) \land tr(f_1, a_1, f_2) \supset goal(f_2))).$$

Here's the general form. For conditional planning with partial observability for plans of length k, take the conjunction of (7) and the following.

$$\overbrace{\forall f_0^O \, \exists a_0}^{} \cdots \overbrace{\forall f_{k-1}^O \, \exists a_{k-1}}^{} \forall f_0^N \cdots \forall f_{k-1}^N \, \forall f_k \, \exists f_1' \cdots \exists f_k'$$
$$\left(\bigwedge_{t=0}^{k-1} \left(init(f_0) \wedge \bigwedge_{u=0}^{t-1} tr(f_u, a_u, f_{u+1}) \supset tr(f_t, a_t, f_{t+1}') \right) \right. \quad (15)$$
$$\left. \wedge \left(init(f_0) \wedge \bigwedge_{t=0}^{k-1} tr(f_t, a_t, f_{t+1}) \supset goal(f_k) \right) \right)$$

Theorem 6. *Conditional planning with partial observability for plans of length k $(k > 0)$ is Π_{2k+2}^P-complete. Conditional planning with partial observability is* **PSPACE**-*complete for plans of polynomially-bounded length.*

If actions are always executable, take the conjunction of (7) and the following.

$$\overbrace{\forall f_0^O \, \exists a_0}^{} \cdots \overbrace{\forall f_{k-1}^O \, \exists a_{k-1}}^{} \forall f_0^N \cdots \forall f_{k-1}^N \, \forall f_k$$
$$\left(init(f_0) \wedge \bigwedge_{t=0}^{k-1} tr(f_t, a_t, f_{t+1}) \supset goal(f_k) \right)$$

So the problem falls to Π_{2k+1}^P. We can show hardness even with determinism.

Theorem 7. *For deterministic planning domains with actions always executable, conditional planning with partial observability is Π_{2k+1}^P-hard for plans of length k, and so* **PSPACE**-*hard for plans of polynomially-bounded length. Conditional planning with partial observability for plans of length k $(k > 0)$ is Π_{2k+1}^P-complete, if the executability of actions is polynomial-time computable.*

7 Effect of No Concurrent Actions, Fixed Plan Length

Eliminating concurrency has little effect on hardness. The previous theorems establish hardness results for plans of fixed length, but the proof constructions rely on concurrency. Corresponding hardness results for nonconcurrent domains can be established by allowing instead plans of length $|A|$ (recall that A is the set of action symbols), so plan length can be linearly-bounded in the size of input. (In each case, there is a corresponding proof construction in which actions previously performed concurrently are performed sequentially instead.)

We have noted that the complexity results from [5] most closely related to those of this paper employ an assumption of fixed plan length (rather than polynomially-bounded plan length). It may be interesting to consider the effect of assuming both nonconcurrency and fixed plan length.

For classical and conformant planning, a fixed plan length guarantees that the number of possible plans with no concurrent actions is polynomially-bounded: there are $(|A| + 1)^k$ nonconcurrent plans of length k. Consequently, the existential quantifiers over actions in formula (6) for classical planning and formula (12) for conformant planning can be eliminated in polynomial time.

It is not clear that this possibility reduces the complexity of classical planning. Roughly speaking, after quantifiers over actions are eliminated from (6), we are left with a disjunction of a polynomially many "unambiguous sat" problems (which ask: Is a propositional theory with at most one model satisfiable?). This problem is thought to be beyond **P** without being **NP**-hard [13].

On the other hand, when plan length is fixed the complexity of conformant planning drops for nonconcurrent domains.

Theorem 8. *For nonconcurrent domains:*

(*i*)   *Conformant planning for plans of length 1 is Π_2^P-hard.*
(*ii*) *Conformant planning for plans of fixed length is Π_2^P-complete.*
(*iii*) *For deterministic planning domains in which actions are always executable, conformant planning for plans of length 1 is D^P-hard[2].*
(*iv*) *For deterministic planning domains in which the executability of actions is polynomial-time computable, conformant planning for plans of fixed length is D^P-complete.*

Parts (*ii*) and (*iv*) of Theorem 8 are very similar to results in [5] (Theorem 4 and subsequent remarks).

What about the effect of fixed plan length on the complexity of conditional planning without concurrency? It is clear that we do not obtain a polynomial bound on the number of possible plans. In fact, we do not even obtain a polynomial bound on the space needed to represent a conditional plan, since a conditional plan is essentially a function that maps the observable portion of a partial plan execution to the next action to be performed.

8   Conditional Planning with Polynomially-Bounded Plan Representations

Since even a fixed plan length and an assumption of nonconcurrency does not yield a polynomial bound on the size of conditional plans, we may wish to consider imposing such a bound directly. In fact this possibility is crucial to the computational approach to conditional planning described by Rintanen [14]. As mentioned previously, Rintanen's paper includes a proof of Π_2^P-hardness for conditional planning. But his main concern is with computational approaches based on problem encodings that directly restrict the size of possible plans to be considered. More precisely, he introduces several different planning problem encodings (in second-order propositional logic), each requiring only polynomial time to construct (given a domain description in his action representation language). Rintanen claims for such computational approaches a complexity of Σ_2^P. Notice though that we can understand conformant planning as perhaps the simplest possible manifestation of such an approach, and *it* is Σ_3^P-hard. It appears

---

[2] The complexity class D^P consists of problems that can be solved in polynomial-time given the answer to one **NP** problem and one **coNP** problem.

that Rintanen's informal argument depends on an implicit assumption that executability of actions in a state is polynomial-time computable.

Rintanen's approach resembles that of Littman *et al.* [11] in the setting of probabilistic planning (with the implicit assumption that actions are always executable). They consider several plan encodings of polynomially-bounded size and obtain complexity results intuitively related to the Σ_2^P result for propositional conditional planning (but instead of $\Sigma_2^P = \mathbf{NP^{NP}}$ the complexity is $\mathbf{NP^{PP}}$, which is still within **PSPACE**, but contains all of the polynomial hierarchy).

It appears that such results are necessarily fragmentary—that is, each depends on a particular choice of (polynomial-size) plan representation—because, unlike the case of k-length conditional plans, for instance, the set of k-size conditional plans apparently cannot be defined independent of a choice of plan representation. Presumably, not just any polynomial-size plan representation will do. In particular, one expects a plan representation that guarantees that the plan function—mapping partial execution histories to next actions—is computable. In fact, it seems reasonable to choose a representation guaranteed to allow polynomial-time computation of the plan function (as it seems Littman *et al.* and Rintanen do in all cases).

As with conformant planning, it appears that, for suitable choices of plan representation, the problem of existence of a valid conditional plan of polynomially-bounded size will fall in complexity class Σ_3^P, and will drop from Σ_3^P to Σ_2^P if the executability of actions is polynomial-time computable.

Acknowledgements

Thanks to Chitta Baral, Vladimir Lifschitz, Jussi Rintanen and a few of the (rather many) anonymous referees for helpful comments on various drafts. This work partially supported by NSF Career Grant #0091773.

References

1. Christer Bäckström and Bernhard Nebel. Complexity results for SAS+ planning. *Computational Intelligence*, 11(4):625–655, 1995.
2. Chitta Baral, Vladik Kreinovich, and Raul Trejo. Computational complexity of planning and approximate planning in presence of incompleteness. *Artificial Intelligence*, 122(1–2):241–267, 2000.
3. Tom Bylander. The computational complexity of propostional STRIPS planning. *Artificial Intelligence*, 69(1–2):165–204, 1994.
4. Giuseppe De Giacomo and Moshe Vardi. Automata-theoretic approach to planning for temporally extended goals. In *Proc. of 5th European Conf. on Planning*, 1999.
5. Thomas Eiter, Wolfgang Faber, Nicola Leone, Gerald Pfeifer, and Axel Polleres. Planning under incomplete information. In *Proc. Computational Logic 2000*, 2000.
6. Kutluhan Erol, Dana S. Nau, and V.S. Subrahmanian. Complexity, decidability and undecidability results for domain-independent planning. *Artificial Intelligence*, 76(1–1):75–88, 1995.

7. Enrico Giunchiglia and Vladimir Lifschitz. An action language based on causal explanation: Preliminary report. In *Proc. AAAI-98*, pages 623–630, 1998.
8. Patrik Haslum and Peter Jonsson. Some results on the complexity of planning with incomplete information. In *Proc. of 5th European Conf. on Planning*, 1999.
9. Henry Kautz and Bart Selman. Planning as satisfiability. In *Proc. of the 10th European Conf. on Artificial Intelligence*, pages 359–379, 1992.
10. Michael Littman. Probabilistic propositional planning: representations and complexity. In *Proc. of AAAI-97*, pages 748–754, 1997.
11. Michael Littman, Judy Goldsmith, and Martin Mundhenk. The computational complexity of probabilistic planning. *Journal of Artificial Intelligence Research*, 9:1–36, 1998.
12. Norman McCain and Hudson Turner. Causal theories of action and change. In *Proc. of AAAI-97*, pages 460–465, 1997.
13. Christos Papadimitriou. *Computational Complexity*. Addison Wesley, 1994.
14. Jussi Rintanen. Constructing conditional plans by a theorem prover. *Journal of Artificial Intelligence Research*, 10:323–352, 1999.

Complexity of Multi-agent Systems Behavior*

Michael Dekhtyar[1], Alexander Dikovsky[2], and Mars Valiev[3]

[1] Dept. of CS, Tver State Univ. 3 Zheljabova str. Tver, Russia, 170013
Michael.Dekhtyar@tversu.ru
[2] IRIN, Université de Nantes. 2
rue de la Houssinière BP 92208 F 44322 Nantes cedex 3 France
Alexandre.Dikovsky@irin.univ-nantes.fr
[3] Keldysh Inst. for Appl. Math. Moscow, Russia, 125047
valiev@spp.keldysh.ru

Abstract. The complexity of multi-agent systems behavior properties
is studied. The behavior properties are formulated using first order temporal logic languages and are checked relative to the state transition
diagram induced by the multi-agent system. Various tight complexity
bounds of the behavior properties are established under natural structural and semantic restrictions on agent programs and actions. There are
some interesting cases, where the check problem is decidable in deterministic or nondeterministic polynomial time.

Keywords: Intelligent agent, Logic program, Multi-Agent System, Temporal logics, Model checking, Complexity.

1 Introduction

The aim of this paper is to study the verification complexity of behavior properties of intelligent agents systems. Although the intelligent agents are inten-
sively investigated for at least twenty years, the research in this specific field
(see [12,6,7,20,13,22] and related publications [2,11,8,4]) is yet rather scarce.

The terms 'Intelligent Agent' and 'Multi-Agent System' (MA-system) refer
to a new and generic metaphor of an artificial intelligence based computing technology. The range of IA applications extends from operating system interfaces,
processing of satellite imaging data and WEB navigation to air traffic control,
business process management and electronic commerce. This is the reason why
there is no unified reading of the terms. We address the reader to the book [20]
and several publications [23,14,15,17,18] discussing their different readings and
definitions. However, the intuitive appeal of the term 'Intelligent Agent' is quite
clear:

- an IA is *autonomous*, i.e. it can function by itself in predetermined envi-
ronments;

---

* This work was sponsored by the Russian Fundamental Studies Foundation (Grants
01-01-00278, 00-01-00254 and 02-01-00652).

S. Flesca et al. (Eds.): JELIA 2002, LNAI 2424, pp. 125–136, 2002.

- it is *reactive,* i.e. it is capable of perceiving and responding to the stimuli of other agents or of its medium;
- it is *intelligent,* i.e. its actions are determined by a certain logic and estimation of its environment;
- and it is *goal oriented,* i.e. even if its functioning is continuous, it is oriented on reaching states with some predetermined properties.

Concrete realizations of these properties determine particular agent architectures. Agent's intelligence capacity can vary from finite state control structures or IF-THEN rules to logic programs, non monotone belief based systems or deontic logics (see [20] for a discussion and references).

Basically, the MA-systems we consider in this paper conform to the so called IMPACT architecture introduced and described in detail in the book [20]. This architecture is very elaborated. It includes rather expressive specification means and control structures, e.g. adaptive action bases, logic programs articulating decision policies, constraints, beliefs based meta-reasoning about other agents, uncertainty reasoning, reasoning about time, communication management, security related structures, interfacing, and some other facilities. Such abundance of expressive means makes this architecture well adapted for practical applications. At the same time, it complicates the theoretical investigation of agents' formal properties. The IMPACT architecture agents' semantics is described in terms of transitions between the agents' states and is shown in [20] to be untractable in general. In order to arrive at a polynomial time computable transition semantics, the authors of [20] impose very complex limitations on the agents features. As a result, the definition of such "polynomial" agents becomes bulky.

In this paper, we come up with another and rather simply formulated limitations leading to a polynomial time semantics. We focus on the agent features concerning actions, decision policies and communication. In particular, we do not consider features related to the legacy code, security, metaknowledge structures, temporal and uncertainty reasoning and some others. Moreover, we simplify the internal agent's data structure to be a relational database (in IMPACT a more general structure is allowed), and consider conventional logic programs as a means of an agent action policy definition (IMPACT agent programs include deontic modalities "permitted action", "forbidden action", "action to be performed", etc.). Even after these simplifications, the MA-system architecture remains very rich. So we study the behavior properties under various more or less restrictive constraints on MA-system's parameters and semantics.

We distinguish deterministic and nondeterministic semantics of MA-systems. Their behavior properties are expressed as the properties of trajectories (paths) in the state transition diagrams they induce: a single path in the deterministic case and multiple paths in the nondeterministic case. This allows the use of classical temporal logics: *PLTL, CTL, CTL** [9], μ-calculus [16] and their variants as behavior properties description languages. The *"MA-BEHAVIOR"* problem we consider in this paper, consists in verifying that a temporal logic formula Φ holds on the tree of trajectories of a given MA-system. So it is a model checking type problem. Model checking on abstract transition diagrams has been extensively studied since the early 80ies (see [3,19,21,9,10,5]). There is however, a substantial difference between the classical problem statement and that of this paper. Traditionally, the complexity results are established for explicitly presented transition diagrams or else for some of their fixed representations (by a finite automata, by OBDD). We establish the complexity bounds with respect to MA-systems whose operational semantics is presented in the form of transition systems. The novelty of this approach is that the problem complexity is determined by various structural and semantical constraints on MA-systems. MA-systems constitute a compact representation of the corresponding transition system. For example, even for a ground (i.e. variable-free) MA-system A, the transition system $T(A)$ describing its trajectories may have the size exponential in $|A|$, because it can occur that it has $O(2^{|A|})$ states. So sometimes, our lower bounds are more pessimistic as compared with the classical ones for the same classes of logics. As it concerns the upper bounds, either they are more informative and precise (in the case of polynomial time and space complexity), or they are simply translated from the corresponding classical results taking into consideration the size and the number of MA-system states. This being so, we nevertheless establish interesting classes of MA-systems, in which the MA-BEHAVIOR problem turns out to be decidable in deterministic or nondeterministic polynomial time. And this is due to a new possibility of formulating natural constraints in terms of structural parameters of MA-systems.

The paper is organized as follows. In section 2, the architecture of MA-systems is defined and illustrated. In section 3, the temporal logics we use are briefly discussed. In section 4, all results of the paper are presented in the form of a table and briefly commented.

2   Agent and MA-System Architecture

We start by presenting our simplified version of the IMPACT architecture.

2.1   Architecture and Semantics

A *multi-agent system (MA-system)* $\mathcal{A}$ is a finite set $\{a_1, ..., a_n\}$ of *intelligent agents* sharing the same signature. An intelligent agent a, as it shows up in this paper, has its *internal data base (DB)* I_a, which is a finite set of ground atoms. It communicates with the other agents in the system through its message box $MsgBox_a$. The messages that the agents exchange are also ground atoms. The internal DB and the current message box contents make up the agent's current *local state* $IM_a = (I_a, MsgBox_a)$. The set of local states $\{IM_a \mid a \in \mathcal{A}\}$ makes up the *state* of the MA-system.

Each agent is capable of performing a number of parameterized actions constituting its action base AB_a. An action can be seen as an update of the agent's internal DB (defined by a finite list ADD_a of insertions and a finite list DEL_a of deletions of facts) accompanied by a finite list $SEND_a$ of messages to load into the message boxes of recipient agents. Each action α is specified by an *action*

atom p_α playing the role of a pattern for the action application. p_α can have variables in common with the action updates and the action messages in the three lists. For example, in the action
$$\alpha = (check\_rel(X, Y),$$
$$ADD([table1(X, 1), table2(X, Y)]),$$
$$DEL([table1(a_1, Y)]),$$
$$SEND([(a_1, fax(X, Y, a))]))$$
$p_\alpha = check\_rel(X, Y)$.

Given a set GA of ground admissible action atoms (defined by the semantics below), each action $\alpha \in AB_a$ uniquely defines the set of admissible ground unifiers σ such that $p_\alpha \sigma \in GA$. As a result, GA uniquely determines the change in the local state $IM_a = (I_a, MsgBox_a)$ resulting from matching actions in AB_a with GA. Namely, the new internal DB $EFF_a(GA, I_a)$ is the result of:

(i) deleting from I_a all instances $\beta\sigma$ of atoms $\beta \in DEL_\alpha$, $\alpha \in AB_a$, such that $p_\alpha \sigma \in GA$,

(ii) and then adding to I_a all instances $\delta\sigma$ of atoms $\delta \in ADD_\alpha$, $\alpha \in AB_a$, such that $p_\alpha \sigma \in GA$.

For example, suppose that matching of the action α above against the current set GA of ground admissible actions defines two admissible unifiers: $\{X \mapsto 0.5, Y \mapsto 3\}$ and $\{X \mapsto 1, Y \mapsto 0\}$. Then the impact of α is that the atoms $table1(a_1, 3), table1(a_1, 0)$ will be deleted from I_a and then the atoms $table1(0.5, 1), table2(0.5, 3), table1(1, 1), table2(1, 0)$ will be added to it.

The parallel effect on message boxes consists in creating for each agent $b \neq a$ the set of messages from a to b, i.e. the set $EFF_a(GA, MsgBox_b)$ of all message instances $\mu\sigma$, where $\mu \in SEND_\alpha$ is addressed to b and $p_\alpha \sigma \in GA$.

In our example, the messages $fax(0.5, 3, a), fax(1, 0, a)$ will be sent to the agent a_1.

An action α is *expanding* if DEL_α is empty. Agent a is *expanding* if it has only expanding actions.

The policy of behavior of an agent a in its current local state IM_a is determined using its *program* P_a. The intension of P_a in a given local state serves to determine the set of admissible actions GA_a, which itself serves to change this local state through the actions in AB_a as we have explained above.

P_a is a logic program with the clauses of the form $H \leftarrow L_1, ..., L_n$, where $n \geq 0$, the head $H = \alpha(t_1, ..., t_l)$ is the pattern action atom of an action in AB_a, the literals L_i in its body are either action literals, or (extensional) internal DB literals, or atoms of the form $Received(Source\_agent, Message)$, or their negations $\neg Received(Source\_agent, Message)$, or else built-in predicate calls $q(\bar{t})$[1].

An agent's program is *positive* if there are no negations in its clauses. An agent with positive program is also called *positive*.

---

[1] We adopt a domain closure assumption fixing some finite set of constants **C** denoting the domain objects and considering a set **Π** of polynomial time computable built-in predicates and operations (e.g., the standard arithmetical operations over numbers).

We suppose that the program clauses are *safe* in the sense that all variables in the head H occur *positively* in the body $L_1, ..., L_n$, and that the program $P_a^{state} = P_a \cup \{p \leftarrow \mid p \in I_a\} \cup \{Received(Agent\_source, Message) \leftarrow \mid (Agent\_source, Message) \in MsgBox_a\}$ is *stratified* [1].

We consider different agent's one-step semantics and respectively different intentional admissible action sets GA_a. All these semantics are defined through the standard minimal model program semantics $Sem(P_a)(I_a, MsgBox_a)$ of P_a in the given local state. $Sem(P_a)(I_a, MsgBox_a)$ is the set M_a^{act} of ground *action atoms* in the minimal model M_a^{state} of P_a^{state}. As it is well known [1], this model is unique for the stratified logic programs and is computed by a polynomial time fixpoint computation procedure from the *groundization* $gr(P_a^{state})$ of the program P_a^{state} [2].

In other words, the semantics of P_a in the given local state is the set of ground actions implied by the program P_a^{state} and available for execution in the agent's current local state.

The agent's one-step semantics should choose (or guess) the set $GA_a \subseteq M_a^{act}$ of intended admissible actions in the set of all available actions M_a^{act}. So it is defined by an operator $Act_a(M)$ applied to a given set of available actions $M = M_a^{act}$. It is natural to suppose that a greater set of available actions leads to a greater set of chosen actions. Therefore, we assume the monotonicity of this operator: $Act_a(M) \subseteq Act_a(M')$ for $M \subseteq M'$. We distinguish *deterministic* and *nondeterministic* one-step semantics.

Deterministic one-step semantics is a function in the class $STEP^D = \{Act : 2^M \rightarrow 2^M \mid Act(M)$ is computable in polynomial time$\}$. For instance, the *total deterministic* semantics defined by $Act^{td}(M) = M$ belongs to this class. This semantics selects the whole M. We can also imagine other types of deterministic one-step semantics, e.g. priority driven deterministic semantics which presumes some partial order $\prec$ on ground actions and is defined by $Act^{\prec d}(M) = \{m \in M \mid \neg \exists m' \in M (m' \prec m)\}$. *Deterministic agents* are those having a deterministic one-step semantics in $STEP^D$.

Nondeterministic one-step semantics is a relation Act in the class $STEP^N = \{Act \subseteq 2^M \times 2^M \mid Act$ is recognizable in polynomial time$\}$. The simplest non-deterministic one-step semantics in this class is the *unit choice* one-step semantics defined by $Act^{un}(M) = \{\{p\} \mid p \in M\}$. It guesses some available action in M. Another example is the *spontaneous* one-step semantics defined by $Act^{sn}(M) = \{M' \mid M' \subseteq M\}$. It guesses any subset of available actions in M. *Nondeterministic agents* are those having a nondeterministic one-step semantics in $STEP^N$.

A particular one-step semantics operator Act_a being chosen, it uniquely defines the new local state of a in the way described above.

---

[2] I.e. from the set of all ground instances of clauses in P_a^{state}. It should be noted that the size of $gr(P_a^{state})$ can be exponential with respect to the size of P_a^{state}. We remind that the domain closure assumption we have adopted includes the requirement of polynomial time calculability of the built-in predicates. So the polynomial time complexity of the fixed point computation is preserved.

The *one step semantics* of the MA-system $\mathcal{A}$ induces a one step transition relation $\Rightarrow_\mathcal{A}$ on the set $\mathcal{S}_\mathcal{A}$ of global states of the form $S = < (I_{a_1}, MsgBox_{a_1}), \ldots, (I_{a_n}, MsgBox_{a_n}) >$. The transition $S \Rightarrow_\mathcal{A} S'$ starts by calculating the sets of available actions $M_i^{act} = Sem(P_{a_i})(I_{a_i}, MsgBox_{a_i})$ for all agents $a_i \in \mathcal{A}$. Next, each agent's one-step semantics Act_{a_i} implemented by a deterministic or nondeterministic operator creates *admissible action sets* $GA_{a_i} = Act_{a_i}(M_i^{act})$. The message boxes of all agents in $\mathcal{A}$ are emptied thereafter (so the messages in S are forgotten). Then each agent's internal DB state I_{a_i} is replaced by $EFF_{a_i}(GA_{a_i}, I_{a_i})$ and the message box of each agent a_i is initiated by $\bigcup_{j \neq i} EFF_{a_j}(GA_{a_j}, MsgBox_{a_i})$.

We see that the presented architecture covers the MA-systems of distributed autonomous parallel interacting agents. There are many applications ideally matching this framework, in particular the distributed intelligent programs interacting in local networks. On the other hand, this architecture does not fit asynchronous interactions in the Internet. The nondeterministic semantics we propose are only partially covering such kind of interactions. To find an appropriate concept of the asynchronous MA-system and its verification is an important problem which is out of the scope of this paper.

2.2   Classes of MA-Systems

We distinguish two main classes of MA-systems: deterministic and nondeterministic. A MA-system $\mathcal{A}$ is *deterministic* if all its agents are deterministic, otherwise it is *nondeterministic*.

In both classes of MA-systems, we consider the following subclasses induced by natural constraints imposed on agents' components. A MA-system $\mathcal{A} = \{a_1, ..., a_n\}$ is

- *ground* if each program P_{a_i} is ground[3];
- *k-dimensional* if the arities of the action atoms and of the message atoms are bounded by k (*dimension-bounded*, if *k-dimensional* for some k). In fact, this property fixes the maximal number of parameters involved in the actions and in the messages of $\mathcal{A}$;
- *expanding* if all its agents are *expanding*;
- *positive* if all its agents are *positive*;
- *m-agent* if $n \leq m$.
- *r-signal* if there are at most r different ground message atoms (*signals*).

The following simple proposition characterizes the complexity of the MA-system's one step semantics under these restrictions.

Proposition 1

(1) For each deterministic MA-system $\mathcal{A}$, the transition function $S \Rightarrow_\mathcal{A} S'$ is computable in polynomial time with respect to $|S| + |\mathcal{A}| + |S'|$ if $\mathcal{A}$ is ground or dimension bounded, and is computable in deterministic exponential time [4] in the general nonground case.

---

[3]   I.e., all its clauses are ground.

[4]   In fact, polynomial time with respect to the groundization size.

(2) For each nondeterministic MA-system $\mathcal{A}$, the transition relation $S \Rightarrow_{\mathcal{A}} S'$ is recognizable in nondeterministic polynomial time with respect to $|S| + |\mathcal{A}| + |S'|$ if $\mathcal{A}$ is ground or dimension bounded, and is recognizable in nondeterministic exponential time in the general nonground case.

2.3   MA-System Behavior

We define the behavior of MA-systems started in an initial global state with empty message boxes. For a MA-system $\mathcal{A}$, its behavior in some initial global state $S^0 = <(I_{a_1}^0, MsgBox_{a_1}^0), ..., (I_{a_n}^0, MsgBox_{a_n}^0)>$, where $MsgBox_{a_i}^0 = \emptyset$, $1 \leq i \leq n$, can be seen as the set $\mathcal{T} = \mathcal{T}_{\mathcal{A}}(S_0)$ of infinite trajectories (i.e. sequences of global states) of the form:
$$\tau = (S^0 \Rightarrow_{\mathcal{A}} S^1 \Rightarrow_{\mathcal{A}} ...S^t \Rightarrow_{\mathcal{A}} S^{t+1} \Rightarrow_{\mathcal{A}} ...).$$
For a deterministic MA-system $\mathcal{A}$, $\mathcal{T}$ consists of a single trajectory starting in S^0. If $\mathcal{A}$ is nondeterministic, then $\mathcal{T}$ is an infinite tree of trajectories with the root node S^0. The nodes of $\mathcal{T}$ are the global states $S \in \mathcal{S}_{\mathcal{A}}$ accessible from S^0 by the reflexive-transitive closure of $\Rightarrow_{\mathcal{A}}$. If S is a node of $\mathcal{T}$, then the states in $Next_{\mathcal{A}}(S)$ are its immediate successors in $\mathcal{T}$. An infinite branch of $\mathcal{T}$ starting in some state is a *trajectory* in $\mathcal{T}$.

We give (without implementation details) two examples of MA-systems. The first system is deterministic.

Example 1 *"Resource-allocation"*
A resource allocation system $\mathcal{RA}$ consists of a manager-agent m distributing among four user-agents u_1, u_2, u_3, u_4 an expendable resource on orders. The user-agents restart their orders periodically and they have different strategies of ordering the resource:
1) u_1 is the first to order a resource; then it repeats its order on receipt of the resource;
2) u_2 orders the next moment after u_1 has ordered;
3) u_3 orders the next moment after u_1 has received the resource from m;
4) u_4 orders every time.
The manager m maintains the list of orders and fulfills the first order on the list, one order at a time. Only one order of each user-agent can be held in the list. So if m receives an order from some user before the previous order of this user has been fulfilled, then the new order is discarded.

We see that the five agents are autonomous in the sense that any of them can function continuously with or without stimuli of the other agents. Meanwhile, these stimuli are necessary in order that the user-agents achieve their goals - to receive the resource. The agents should communicate through messages, which let know that an order has been placed or fulfilled. The intelligence of the four user-agents is rather primitive: just conditional actions. Meanwhile, the agent m must be quite smart in order to control correctly the incoming orders and the states of the queue. This queue and the inventory of messages make up the architecture of the MA-system $\mathcal{RA}$.

The second example presents a nondeterministic MA-system.

Example 2 *"A laboratory Recruiting Committee (RC)"*
The RC consists of six deterministic agents: agents-members $m_i, 0 \leq i \leq 4$ $(m_0$ being the laboratory director), and agent-secretary s, and one spontaneous nondeterministic agent c simulating at each recruitment cycle the submission of a number of candidatures $cand(C, Profile, Merits, Grants)$. C stands for the candidate's identification. $Profile$ stands for one of the activity profiles: lp (logic programming), ai (artificial intelligence), cl (computational linguistics) and mm (multimedia). An integer $Merits$ evaluates the candidate's scientific merits. An integer $Grants$ represents the sum of the grants the candidate has obtained. The only action of c is to introduce the set of all possible candidatures. Due to a spontaneous choice, a particular set of candidatures submitted for the new recruitment cycle is created. Besides the candidatures, the information about the staff member selected in the preceding recruitment is also available: $selected(C, Profile)$.
The secretary s controls the vote through messages. Before the vote, the members may speak out on the candidates (through messages). Then they vote by sending their secrete vote messages to the secretary: the selected candidate or the abstention. On receiving all members' votes, the secretary updates the information on the selected staff member according to the score and deletes the nonselected candidatures.

The RC members have different vote tactics but all of them abstain when their criteria do not ensure the uniqueness of choice:
m_0 votes according to the following profile preferences: $lp > ai > mm > cl$, selects a candidate with the best grants sum and announces his choice to all RC members;
m_1 always votes for the candidate of m_0;
m_2 selects a candidate with a profile different from that chosen by m_0 and having the best grants sum;
m_3 votes for the candidate with the best scientific merits whose profile is different from that of the last recruited candidate;
m_4 votes with the majority, if any; if there is no majority, then m_4 chooses the "antiboss" party candidate.

3   Verification of Behavior Properties

The crucial point about the examples above is that the behavior of the MA-systems $\mathcal{RA}$ and $\mathcal{RC}$ should verify some properties, e.g. the behavior of $\mathcal{RA}$ in example 1 should be *fair* in the sense that each user-agent is repeatedly served by m (i.e. served sometimes in the future after its order has been fulfilled). This property should be verified with respect to all runs of $\mathcal{RA}$.

We represent the MA-systems as transition systems on global states. In these terms, a run of a deterministic MA-system corresponds to a trajectory through states, each two adjacent states in the trajectory being related by a transition. As for nondeterministic MA-systems, a run of such a system corresponds to a trajectory in the tree of trajectories with the same condition on the adjacent states.

This makes the logics of linear or branching time a convenient tool of behavior specification and analysis. In particular, linear time logics are well suited for the deterministic MA-system behavior description, whereas the branching time logics and more expressive μ-calculus are more adapted to the nondeterministic MA-system behavior properties.

The *"MA-BEHAVIOR"* problem we consider in this paper, applies to deterministic MA-systems as well as to nondeterministic ones. Given such a system $\mathcal{A}$, an initial global state S_0 and a formula Φ expressing a property of trajectories, the MA-BEHAVIOR problem $\mathcal{A}, S_0, \Phi$ has a positive solution if Φ holds on the tree $\mathcal{T}_{\mathcal{A}}(S_0)$ of trajectories of $\mathcal{A}$ starting in S_0 (denoted $\mathcal{T}_{\mathcal{A}}(S_0), S_0 \models \Phi$). We see that it is a kind of the model checking problem, though applied to MA-systems in the role of transition diagram specification.

In order to specify the behavior properties of the deterministic MA-systems, we use the *propositional linear temporal logic* (PLTL) and its first order extension FLTL [9] with the standard linear time operators $\mathbf{X}$ ("nexttime"), $\mathbf{U}$ ("until"), $\mathbf{V}$ ("unless"), $\mathbf{G}$ ("always"), and $\mathbf{F}$ ("sometimes"). For nondeterministic MA-systems, we use simple subsets of classical branching time logics: $\forall$LTL and $\exists$LTL consisting respectively of the formulas of the form $\mathbf{E}(\phi), \mathbf{A}(\phi)$, where ϕ is in $FLTL$ [5], first order extension of the μ-calculus [16,10] (FO-μ) and its alternation depth bounded subsets (FO-$\mu_l, l \geq 1$).

For example, the MA-system $\mathcal{RA}$ above being deterministic, its fairness is expressed by the following simple LTL formula: $\bigwedge\limits_{i=1}^{4} \mathbf{G}\,\mathbf{F}\;receives_{u_i}$ (for each of the four user-agents u_i and at any time point, it is true that it will receive the resource in the future). As for the MA-system $\mathcal{RC}$ in example 2, we prove elsewhere that its behavior may have anomalies, e.g. the worst candidate may be selected under certain conditions.

4 Main Results

The main results of the paper are summarized in the table below[6].

The first four columns in this table categorize the classes of the MA-systems we consider. In the column **Type** the deterministic and nondeterministic MA-systems are distinguished. The columns **Gr** and **Exp** serve to distinguish between ground/non-ground and expanding/non-expanding systems. In the column **Parameters**, several architectural parameters are used to impose constraints leading to low complexity classes. In particular, N denotes the size of the system, m is the number of agents, k is the maximal arity of the action and message atoms (in the propositional case $k = 0$), r is the number of signals (i.e. of messages). The fifth column **Logic** serves to indicate the particular temporal logic used as a property formulation language. The sixth column presents the results obtained in the paper and the seventh column contains the references to

---

[5] The path quantifiers $\mathbf{A}$ and $\mathbf{E}$ mean respectively "for all trajectories" and "for some trajectory".

[6] The results are formulated without proofs due to space limitations.

these results. Each row of the sixth column indicates the complexity class of the problem identified by the corresponding rows of the first five columns.

Type	Gr	Exp	Parameters	Logic	Complexity	Nmb
Deter-ministic	Yes	Yes	positive	PLTL	P	d1
			$m^2 * r = O(\log N)$	PLTL	P	d2
			fixed $m \geq 2$	PLTL	PSPACE	d3
			fixed $r \geq 1$	PLTL	PSPACE	d4
		No		FLTL	PSPACE	d5
	No	Yes	positive, fixed k	PLTL	P	d6
			positive	PLTL	EXPTIME	d7
		No	fixed k	FLTL	PSPACE	d8
				FLTL	EXPSPACE	d9
Non-deter-ministic	Yes	Yes	$m^2 * r = O(\log N)$	$\exists$ LTL	NP	n1
				$\forall$ LTL	co-NP	n2
			fixed $m \geq 2$	FO-μ_1	EXPTIME	n3
			fixed $r \geq 1$	FO-μ_1	EXPTIME	n4
		No		FO-μ_l, fixed l	EXPTIME	n5
				FO-μ	in NEXPTIME ∩ co-NEXPTIME	n6
	No	Yes	fixed $r \geq 1$	$\exists$ LTL	NEXPTIME	n7
				$\forall$ LTL	co-NEXPTIME	n8
			positive	$\exists$ LTL	EXPSPACE-hard	n9
		No	fixed k	FO-μ	EXPTIME	n10
				FO-μ_l, fixed l	EXPEXPTIME	n11
				FO-μ	in NEXPEXPTIME ∩ co-NEXPEXPTIME	n12

In all rows except n6, n9 and n12, we mean that the corresponding problem is complete in the indicated complexity class. In the rows n6 and n12 only upper complexity bounds are indicated, whereas in the row n9, only lower bound is stated.

It is not surprising that in the general case the MA-BEHAVIOR problem is very complex: EXPSPACE-complete for the deterministic systems (d9), and EXPEXPTIME-complete for nondeterministic systems (n11). However, it turns out to be tractable for the deterministic systems under some restrictions reasonable for practical applications. Namely, it is polynomial time decidable under strong monotonicity conditions (d1, d6), or else under the condition that the system is expanding with the additional structural restriction $m^2 * r = O(\log N)$ (d2). The theorems (d3, d4, d7) show that removing any of these constraints leads to intractability. In fact, the theorem (d7) holds even for 0-signal 1-agent systems. The origin of the restriction $m^2 * r = O(\log N)$ is that the trajectory of a deterministic system $\mathcal{A}$ is periodic with some pre-period q and period p, and that under this restriction, $q + p \leq mN2^{rm^2} \leq cmN^2$ for some constant c, when $\mathcal{A}$ is ground and expanding. In particular, the theorems (d3, d4) show that ground expanding MA-systems cannot be simulated in polynomial time by single ground expanding agents (facts simulating messages should be updated), so the distribution really plays a role.

As for the nondeterministic systems, it would be difficult to hope that the behavior verification problem were polynomial time decidable. It seems likely that the theorems (n1,n2) stating (co-) nondeterministic polynomial time complexity of the problem in the case of nondeterministic MA-systems give the best results one might expect in this case. As in deterministic case, the theorems (n3,n4,n5) show that elimination of any of the constraints on r, m or on the deletions leads to exponential time complexity. In fact, in all these cases a more exact lower bound of the form $O(c^{n/\log n})$ can be obtained. It should be noted that all upper bounds concerning FO-μ, FO-μ_1, FO-μ_l are simple generalizations of the well known result in [10] on model checking complexity for the propositional μ-calculus.

5   Conclusion

The agent and MA-system architectures published within the past few years are dissimilar and diversified because they represent various application domains of this new software technology. Our study concerns one such specific architecture which covers the systems of distributed autonomous parallel interacting agents. On the other hand, this architecture does not fit exactly the asynchronous distributed algorithms frame. The nondeterministic semantics we propose are only partially covering such kind of interactions. To find an appropriate concept of the asynchronous MA-system and its verification is an important problem, which is out of the scope of this paper.

This paper illustrates the way in which penetrating in much detail in a complex MA-system architecture permits in some cases to better understand the behavior properties and in this way, to obtain more deep results. Considered from this point of view, this paper creates a perspective of applying similar analysis to other MA-system architectures in order to find interesting subclasses of MA-systems with efficiently checked behavior properties.

References

1. Apt, K. R., Logic Programming. In: J. van Leeuwen (Ed.) *Handbook of Theoretical Computer Science. Volume B. Formal Models and Semantics, Chapter 10*, Elsevier Science Publishers B.V. 1990, 493-574.
2. Bylander, T., The computational Complexity of Propositional STRIPS Planning, *Artificial Intelligence*, 69:165–204, 1994.
3. Clarke, E. M., Emerson, E. A. Design and synthesis of synchronization skeletons using branching time temporal logic. In: *Proc.of Workshop on Logics of Programs, Lecture Notes in Computer Science*, N. 181, 1981, 52-71.
4. Calvanese, D., De Giacomo, G., and Vardi, M.Y., Reasoning about actions and planning in LTL action theories, *Proc. of the 8th Int. Conf. on the Principles of Knowledge Representation and Reasoning (KR'02)*, 593-602, 2002.

5. Clarke, E. M., Grumberg, O. and Peled, D., *Model Checking,* MIT Press, 2000.
6. Dekhtyar, M., Dikovsky, A.,   On Homeostatic Behavior of Dynamic Deductive Data Bases. In: *Proc. 2nd Int. A.P.Ershov Memorial Conference "Perspective of Systems Informatics", Lect. Notes in CS,* N. 1181, 1996, 420-432.
7. Dekhtyar, M., Dikovsky, A., and Valiev, M., Applying temporal logic to analysis of behavior of cooperating logic programs. *Lect. Notes in CS,* N. 1755, 2000, 228-234.
8. Eiter, T., Fink,M., Sabbatini, G., and Tompits, H., "Reasoning about Evolving Nonmonotonic Knowledge Bases", *Proc. of LPAR01 ,* 2001.
9. Emerson, E. A. Temporal and modal logic. In: J. van Leeuwen (Ed.), *"Handbook of Theor. Comput. Sci.",* Elsevier Sci. Publishers, 1990.
10. Emerson, E. A. Model checking and the mu-calculus. In: N. Immerman, P. H. Kolaitis (Eds.), "Descriptive Complexity and Finite Models". *Proc. of a DIMACS Workshop,* 1996, 185-214.
11. Erol, K., Nau, D.S., and Subrahmanian, V.S., Complexity, Decidability and Undecidability Results for Domain-Independent Planning, *Artificial Intelligence Journal,* 76(1-2):75-88, 1995.
12. Fagin, R., Halpern, J.Y., Moses, Y. and Vardi, M., *Reasoning about Knowledge,* 1995, MIT Press.
13. Fisher, M., Wooldridge, M., Specifying and Verifying Distributed Intelligent Systems. In: M. Filgueiras and L. Damas (Eds.) *Progress in Artificial Intelligence – Sixth Portuguese Conf. on Artificial Intelligence. LNAI,* N. 727, 1993, pp.13-28, Springer-Verlag: Berlin, Germany.
14. Jennings, N., Sycara, K. and Wooldridge, M. A roadmap of agent research and development *Autonomous Agents and Multi-Agent Systems,* 1998, 1(1):7-38.
15. Müller, J. P., Architectures and applications of intelligent agents: A survey. *The Knowledge Engineering Review,* 1998, 13(4):353-380.
16. Kozen, D., Results on the Propositional μ-calculus. *Theoretical Computer Science,* 1983, v. 27, pp. 333–354.
17. Petrie, C., What is an agent? In: J.P. Müller, M. J. Wooldridge, and N. R. Jennings (Eds.) *Intelligent Agents III – Proc. of the Third Intern. Workshop on Agent Theories, Architectures, and Languages, Lecture Notes in Artificial Intelligence,* N. 1193, 41-43. Springer-Verlag.
18. Reiter, R. *Knowledge in Action: Logical Foundations for Specifying and Implementing Dynamical Systems.* MIT Press, 2001.
19. Sistla, A. P., Clarke, E. M., The complexity of propositional linear temporal logic. J.ACM, 32(3), 1985, 733-749.
20. Subrahmanian, V. S., Bonatti, P., Dix, J., et al., *Heterogeneous Agent Systems,* MIT Press, 2000.
21. Vardi, M., Wolper, P., An automata-theoretic approach to automatic program verification. In: *Proc. of the IEEE Symposium on Logic in Computer Science,* 1986, 332-344.
22. Wooldridge, M., The Computational Complexity of Agent Design Problem. In: E. Durfee, (Ed.) *Proc. of the Fourth Intern. Conf. on Multi-Agent Systems (ICMAS 2000),* IEEE Press, 2000.
23. Wooldridge, M., Jennings N. Intelligent agents: Theory and practice. *The Knowledge Engineering Review,* 1995, 10(2).

Complexity and Algorithms for the Matching of Bag and Set Terms

Gianluigi Greco and Ester Zumpano

DEIS
Università della Calabria
87030 Rende, Italy
{ggreco,zumpano}@si.deis.unical.it

Abstract. Bounded bag and set terms are complex terms in which every element can be a constant or a variable. These types of complex terms have been introduced in several logic languages, such as LDL, Coral and Godel, in order to increase their expressive power, and they have been recently used to define logic languages for database integration. The paper addresses the problem of computing the set of matchers of two bag (or set) terms, by providing a general complexity analysis and a closed formula for determining the number of matchers for tractable cases. An algorithm for the general problem and optimal algorithms for tractable cases are also provided.

1 Introduction

Bounded bag and set terms are terms of the form $\{e_1, \ldots, e_n\}$, where e_i is either a constant or a variable. These terms have been introduced in several logic languages in order to increase their expressive powers [2,5,10,21] and have been also used in logic languages for database integration [9]. The introduction of bag and set terms increases exponentially the expressivity and the computational complexity of languages; for instance, the unification of set terms may give an exponential number of unifiers. The unification problem differs from first-order unification in that it must take into account *commutativity* (i.e. the order of elements is immaterial) and (only for set terms) *idempotency* (i.e. two elements in a set term may refer to the same object) [6,22].

Matching is a simpler form of unification where one of the two terms is variable-free and it is the only form of unification used in the bottom-up resolution (i.e. fixpoint computation) of logic programs, that is the computation strategy favored by most of the database and AI systems implementing extensions of Datalog. Moreover, while for standard terms there is a unique maximal general unifier (modulo renaming of variables), for bag and set terms the number of maximal general unifiers and matchers can be exponential. For example, the two set terms $S = \{X_1, ..., X_n\}$ and $T = \{a_1, ..., a_n\}$, where $X_1, ..., X_n$ are distinct variables and $a_1, ..., a_n$ are distinct constants, have $n!$ matchers.

Therefore, an efficient matching algorithm plays a significant role in the construction of deductive systems. Actually, as matching is obviously simpler than

S. Flesca et al. (Eds.): JELIA 2002, LNAI 2424, pp. 137–148, 2002.
© Springer-Verlag Berlin Heidelberg 2002

general unification, the exclusive usage of matching is one of the reasons for which the bottom-up approach is preferred to the top-down strategy in many deductive systems.

The problems of bag and set terms unification and matching have been deeply investigated in the past; in particular, previous works addressed the case of unbounded terms, i.e. terms that may be constructed by means of *function* symbols too. In this case some of the functions may be *associative, commutative* and *idempotent*, giving rise to different variants of the matching problem [6,12,17,14,22,3]. An excellent review of significant results in this area has been provided by Siekmann [22] (see also [14]); various complexity results have been presented by Kapur and Narendran in [12]. In particular they prove that both unification and matching of terms with commutative and idempotent function are NP-hard; therefore the (unbounded) Set Term Unification (and Matching) Problem is NP-hard. Moreover, some algorithms have been proposed in the literature for unification with associativity and commutativity [17] as well as with associativity, commutativity and idempotency [18]; such algorithms cannot be extended to deal with commutativity only and with commutativity and idempotency.

In this paper we extend previous works, by addressing some issues related to the computation of the matchers of two (bounded) bag terms. In particular, we investigate the matching problem in the simpler case where each element in the bags is either a variable or a constant. We show that, also in this case, the problem of checking whether two bags admit a matcher remains intractable (NP-complete). This is a surprising result as the analogous problem considering set terms is NP-complete for general set terms [12], but becomes trivial when we consider simple sets (i.e. sets consisting of variables and constants) [1]. Therefore, we consider special cases and show that if one of the two bags only contains distinct elements the problem becomes tractable; for this case we provide a closed formula computing the number of matchers which is also used for defining optimal algorithms.

Our investigation extends the result of [12], in which it was proved the NP-completeness for the general case of unbounded terms and the result of [1] considering the matching of bounded simple set terms. The interest of our research lies in the fact that unbounded set and bag terms are the ones typically used in current deductive database and in nonmonotonic reasoning based systems.

The rest of the paper is organized as follows. In Section 2, we present basic (mainly, syntactic) definitions on standard logic programming and on its extension with bags and sets, and we formalize the problem of bag (set) term matching. In Section 3 we analyze the complexity of bag and set term matching and determine formulas for computing the number of matchers. On the basis of this analysis it is straightforward to devise a bag (set) term matching algorithm, presented in Section 4.

2   Basic Definitions

A *(simple) term* can be either a variable or a constant. A *substitution* is a finite set of pairs $\theta = \{X_1/t_1, ..., X_n/t_n\}$ where $X_1, ..., X_n$ are distinct variables and $t_1, ..., t_n$ are terms. Let $\theta = \{X_1/t_1, ..., X_n/t_n\}$ be a substitution and T be a term, then $T\theta$ is the term obtained from T by simultaneously replacing each occurrence of X_i in T by t_i $(1 \leq i \leq n)$. Substitutions can be composed. Given two substitutions $\theta = \{X_1/t_1, ..., X_n/t_n\}$ and $\sigma = \{Y_1/s_1, ..., Y_m/s_m\}$ their *composition*, $\theta\sigma$, is obtained from the set $\{X_1/t_1\sigma, ..., X_n/t_n\sigma, Y_1/s_1, ..., Y_m/s_m\}$ by deleting the pairs $X_i/t_i\sigma$ for which $X_i = t_i\sigma$ as well as the pairs Y_i/s_i for which $Y_i \in \{X_1, ..., X_n\}$. Given two substitutions σ and θ, θ is *more general* than σ, if there exists a substitution γ such that $\sigma = \theta\gamma$. Moreover if both σ is more general than θ and θ is more general than σ then they are *equivalent* or each other *variant*.

Let S be a finite set of terms. A substitution θ is a *unifier* for S if $S\theta$ is a singleton. We say that a set of terms S *unify* if there exists a unifier θ for S. A unifier θ for S is called a *most general unifier (mgu)* for S if, for each unifier σ of S, θ is more general than σ. The mgu is unique modulo renaming of variables, thus all *mgus* are equivalent. If S contains only two terms and one of them is ground, a unifier θ for S is called *matcher*; obviously, there exists at most one matcher and, therefore, at most one *mgu*. If the matcher exists then we say that the two terms *match*.

Bags and Sets. A bounded *bag term* S is of the form $\{s_1, ..., s_n\}$, where s_j $(1 \leq j \leq n)$ is a constant or a variable and the sequence in which the elements are listed is immaterial. Moreover, a bounded bag term $\{s_1, ..., s_n\}$ is called bounded *set term* if the number of occurrences of every s_j, for $1 \leq j \leq n$, is immaterial. Thus, the three sets $\{a, b\}$, $\{b, a\}$ and $\{b, a, b\}$ coincide, while the two bags $\{a, b\}$ and $\{b, a, b\}$ are different.

We point out that the enumeration of the elements of a set term can be given either directly or by specifying the conditions for collecting their elements *(grouping variables)*. Grouping variables may occur in the head of clauses with the following format

$r: \quad p(x_1, ..., x_h, <y_1>, ..., <y_k>, \ll y_{k+1}\gg, ..., \ll y_m \gg) \leftarrow B_1, ..., B_n$

where $B_1, ..., B_n$ are the goals of the rules, p is the head predicate symbol with arity $h + m$, y_i for $1 \leq i \leq m$ is a grouping variable, and $x_1, ..., x_h$ are the other arguments (terms or other grouping variables). To the grouping variable $\ll Y \gg$ (resp. $<Y>$) will be assigned the bag (resp. set) $\{Y\theta \mid \theta$ is a substitution for r such that $B_1\theta, ..., B_n\theta$ are true$\}$. A grouping variable is similar to the construct *GROUP BY* of SQL.

Example 1. Consider the database D consisting of the following facts: q(a, 2, x), q(a, 3, y), q(b, 4, x), q(b, 7, y), q(b, 4, z) and the program P consisting of the rule: p(X, $\ll$Y$\gg$) $\leftarrow$ q(X, Y, Z). The program P_D has only one minimal model: $M = D \cup \{p(a, \{2, 3\}), p(b, \{4, 7, 4\})\}$. Moreover, by replacing the bag constructor with the set constructor we get the rule p(X, $<$Y$>$) $\leftarrow$ q(X, Y, Z). The new program has $M = D \cup \{p(a, \{2, 3\}), p(b, \{4, 7\})\}$ as the only minimal model. $\square$

Generally, programs with bag and set term constructors are required to be stratified. Given a (positive) program[1] P, $G_P = \langle N, E \rangle$ is the dependency graph associated with P and defined as follows: (i) N is the set of predicate symbols in P, (ii) for each rule $A \leftarrow B_1, ..., B_n$ in P with $A = p(t_1, ..., t_h, < y_1 >, ..., < y_k >, \ll y_{k+1} \gg, ..., \ll y_m \gg)$ and for each body atom B_i with predicate symbol q there is an arc from q to p; moreover, the arc is marked with $*$ if B_i contains as argument a (grouping) variable y_i for some $i \in [1..m]$. The program P is (grouping) stratified if G_P does not contain cycles with arcs marked with $*$. As an extension of traditional logic language, built-in aggregate functions, such as $min, max, count, sum$ and avg applied to sets and bags, have also been considered. Thus, an aggregate term is of the form $f(S)$ where S is a grouping variable and $f \in \{min, max, count, sum, avg\}$ is an aggregate function.

2.1 Unification of Set and Bag Terms

Dealing with bag and set terms allows us to consider different notions of equality. Given two complex terms S and T, that can be either bags or sets, we say that $S =_c T$ if S is a permutation of T, where the subscript c stands for "commutativity". Furthermore, $S =_{ic} T$ if every element in S occurs in T and conversely, where the subscript ic stands for "idempotency and commutativity". Let us now extend unification and matching of bounded set and bag terms.

Definition 1. *Let S and T be two bag (resp. set) terms. A substitution θ for $\{S, T\}$ is a* unifier *if $S\theta =_c T\theta$ (resp. $S\theta =_{ic} T)\theta$; moreover, θ is a maximal general unifier (mgu) if a unifier σ does not exist such that σ is more general then θ. Finally, if either S or T is ground then any unifier is called a* matcher. $\square$

Note that in the case of set terms we use the idempotency and commutativity notion of equality, while in the case of bag terms we are only interested in the commutativity.

Furthermore, we observe that it is no longer true that a *mgu* is unique modulo renaming of variables, thus not all *mgus* are equivalent; for this reason, here *mgu* should stand for maximal general unifier instead of most general unifier.

Definition 2. *Let S and T be two bag (resp. set) terms. A set B of mgu for $\{S, T\}$ is a* complete set *(or* base*) of mgus if both no two mgus in B are equivalent and for each mgu θ, there exists a (not necessarily distinct) mgu in B that is equivalent to θ.* $\square$

Thus, the set of all *mgus* can be partitioned into equivalence classes using the equivalence relation for substitutions; the set obtained by collecting one representative for each class is a base of *mgus*. Two bases are equal modulo renaming of variables. In the case of matching, the base of *mgus* is unique although it is not necessarily a singleton.

---

[1] For the sake of simplicity we only consider positive programs, but it is also possible to consider programs with stratified negation [2].

3   The Bag Term Matching Problem

For the following, assuming S to be a bag, we denote with $var(S)$ and $ground(S)$ the sets of variables and constants occurring in S, respectively, and with $Set(S)$ $= \{x|x \in S\}$ the set of distinct elements occurring in S. Given a term t we denote with $occurs(t, S)$ the number of the occurrences of t in S. Finally, we denote with $|S|$ the number of elements of S by considering duplicates, and with $\|S\|$ the number of distinct elements, i.e. $\|S\| = |Set(S)|$. Observe that a set S is a special case of a bag where each term occurs once (i.e. $S = Set(S)$ or $|S|=\|S\|$). We can state the bag term matching problem as follows.

INPUT. We are given two bag terms, S and T of the form:

$$S = \{X_1, ..., X_{h_1}, a_1, ..., a_{h_2}\} = \mathbf{X} \cup \mathbf{a} \tag{1}$$
$$T = \{b_1, ..., b_{h_3}, c_1, ..., c_{h_4}\} = \mathbf{b} \cup \mathbf{c}$$

where $\mathbf{X} = \{X_1, ..., X_{h_1}\}$ is a bag containing only variables, while $\mathbf{a} = \{a_1, ..., a_{h_2}\}$, $\mathbf{b} = \{b_1, ..., b_{h_3}\}$ and $\mathbf{c} = \{c_1, ..., c_{h_4}\}$ are bags containing only constants such that (i) $|\mathbf{b} \cup \mathbf{c}| \geq 1$, (ii) $Set(\mathbf{a}) = Set(\mathbf{c})$ and (iii) $\mathbf{b} \cap \mathbf{c} = \emptyset$. Thus T is ground, but not empty, S contains at least one variable, $\mathbf{a}$ and $\mathbf{c}$ denote bags of constants appearing in both S and T and $\mathbf{b}$ denotes the bag of constants only appearing in T.

BAG TERM MATCHING PROBLEM. Find all matchers θ of $\{S, T\}$, i.e. all substitutions θ for the variables in $\mathbf{X}$ such that $S\theta = T$.
We first present a necessary condition for a successful matching of two bag terms.

Proposition 1. *Let $S = \mathbf{X} \cup \mathbf{a}$ and $T = \mathbf{b} \cup \mathbf{c}$ be two bag terms of the form (1). Then, S and T match only if*

1. $\forall t \in ground(S), occurs(t, S) \leq occurs(t, T)$;
2. $|S| = |T|$;
3. $|var(S)| \geq \|T - S\|$.

Proof. It is obvious that if Condition 1 or Condition 2 does not hold the two bags cannot match (with respect to the equality operator $=_c$). Suppose now that Condition 3 does not hold, then after the matching of the first $|var(S)|$ constants, the remaining $\|T - S\| - |var(S)|$ constants cannot be matched with any variable.   □

Proposition 1 provides necessary conditions for matching which can be easily checked. Thus, in the following we assume that the two bags S and T satisfy the conditions of Proposition 1. However, in the general case, the problem of checking if two bags admit a matcher is hard. This is shown in the following theorem.

Theorem 1. *Let S and T be two bag terms satisfying conditions of Prop. 1. Then, the problem of deciding if there exists a matcher θ of $\{S, T\}$ is NP-complete.*

Proof. Assuming that the two bag terms have already passed the test stated in Proposition 1, the bag term matching problem is the problem of finding all matchers θ of $\{\mathcal{S}, \mathcal{T}\}$, with $\mathcal{S} = \mathbf{X}$ being a bag containing only variables, and $\mathcal{T} = \mathbf{b} \cup (\mathbf{c} - \mathbf{a})$ being a bag containing only constants.

Assuming $Set(\mathcal{S}) = \{X_1, ..., X_s\}$ and $Set(\mathcal{T}) = \{d_1, ..., d_t\}$, the problem can be thought of as the one of finding a partition of the variables in $\mathcal{S}$ into $\|\mathcal{T}\| = t$ disjoint sets $V_1, \ldots, V_t$ such that for each V_i it is the case that

$$\sum_{X \in V_i} occurs(X, \mathcal{S}) \geq occurs(d_i, \mathcal{T}) \tag{2}$$

- (membership): we can guess nondeterministically a partition and verify in polynomial time that Condition 2 holds;

- (completeness): reduction from **PARTITION**.
  We recall that given a set A and a weight for each element $a \in A$, say $w(a)$, the problem of deciding if there exists a subset $A' \subset A$ such that $\sum_{a \in A'} w(a) = \sum_{a \in A-A'} w(a)$ is NP-complete. Without any loss of generality we can assume that $\sum_{a \in A} w(a)$ is an even number [7]. Given such a set A, we construct the bag $\mathcal{S}$ with $|A|$ distinct variables $X_1, ..., X_{|A|}$ such that every X_i is associated with a_i, for $i \in [1..|A|]$; clearly, each X_i occurs $w(a_i)$ times in $\mathcal{S}$. The bag $\mathcal{T}$ has only two different constants, say d_1 and d_2, each one occurring a number of times such that $occurs(d_1, \mathcal{T}) = occurs(d_2, \mathcal{T}) = \frac{1}{2}\sum_{a \in A} w(a)$. By construction, if the answer to **PARTITION** is yes, then the variables in $\mathcal{S}$ corresponding to the ones in A' can be matched with d_1, while all the other variables can be matched with d_2. The same argument holds for the converse. $\square$

We recall that for set terms, the problem of deciding the existence of a matcher is hard in the general case (sets containing terms with function symbols), but is trivial (constant time) for bounded simple sets (sets whose elements are either variables or constants)[1].

For bag terms, the problem is hard for general bags and remains hard for bounded simple bags. In order to develop a technique for finding a matching of two bags, we can think to formulate the problem in terms of a linear equations system; moreover, without loss of generality (as seen in the proof of the preceding theorem), we can deal with two bags $\mathcal{S} = \mathbf{X}$ containing only variables, and $\mathcal{T} = \mathbf{b} \cup (\mathbf{c} - \mathbf{a})$ containing only constants.

Let $Set(\mathbf{X}) = \{X_1, \ldots, X_n\}$, $Set(\mathcal{T}) = \{d_1, \ldots, d_m\}$, $k_i = occurs(X_i, \mathbf{X})$ for each $i \in [1..n]$ and $h_j = occurs(d_j, \mathcal{T})$ for each $j \in [1..m]$, then the bag matching problem consists in finding all the solutions of the following system:

$$\begin{cases} \sum_{i=1}^{n} k_i X_i^j = h_j \quad \forall j \in [1..m] \\ \\ \sum_{j=1}^{m} X_i^j = 1 \quad \forall i \in [1..n] \\ \\ X_i^j \in \{0, 1\} \end{cases}$$

where X_i^j denotes the matching of the variable X_i to the constant d_j. The problem of deciding whether S and T match is equivalent to the problem of deciding whether the above integer programming problem admits a solution.

Moreover, this formulation can be very useful for applying well known techniques for speeding up the computation, or for considering simple heuristics reducing the search space, as suggested by the following example.

Example 2. Consider two bags $S = \{X_1, X_1, X_2, X_2, X_3\}$ and $T = \{a, a, a, b, b\}$; the problem can be formulated as:

$$
\begin{cases}
2X_1^1 + 2X_2^1 + X_3^1 = 3 \\
2X_1^2 + 2X_2^2 + X_3^2 = 2 \\
X_1^1 + X_1^2 = 1 \\
X_2^1 + X_2^2 = 1 \\
X_3^1 + X_3^2 = 1 \\
X_i^j \in \{0, 1\}
\end{cases}
\qquad \square
$$

If the number of occurrences of a variable, say X_i, coincides with the occurrences of a constant, say d_j, we can apply an easy heuristic by assigning d_j to X_i; without loss of generality, the resulting problem is that of finding a matcher of the bags S' and T', derived from S and T by deleting all occurrences of $\mathbf{X}_i$ and $\mathbf{d}_j$, respectively.

In terms of equations system, the new set of equations is obtained by deleting the j-th equation in the second group and the variables X_i in all equations (because we have fixed $X_i^j = 1$ and, consequently, $X_i^k = 0$ for all $k \neq j$.

Considering the above example, by unifying X_2 with b, we fix $X_2^2 = 1$ and $X_2^1 = 0$; the derived problem consists in the matching of the two bags $\{X_1, X_1, X_3\}$ and $\{a, a, a\}$ that admits a trivial solution.

As the general problem is hard, we consider some interesting tractable cases where at least one of the two terms is required to have distinct elements. We'll show that these cases are not only tractable, but it is possible to find a closed formula calculating the number of matchers and an optimal algorithm computing the set of all matchers.

3.1   Distinct Variables: $Set(\mathbf{X}) = \mathbf{X}$

Assuming $S = \mathbf{X} \cup \mathbf{a}$ to be a bag with distinct variables (i.e. $\mathbf{X}$ is a set) and T to be a bag, we can explicitly derive the number of distinct matchers.

Proposition 2. *Let $S = \mathbf{X} \cup \mathbf{a}$ and $T = \mathbf{b} \cup \mathbf{c}$ be two bag terms satisfying conditions of Prop. 1, such that $\mathbf{X}$ contains distinct variables, i.e. $Set(\mathbf{X}) = \mathbf{X}$. Then*

1. *A matcher for S and T exists;*
2. *The number of matchers for S and T is equal to*

$$
matchers(\|\mathbf{d}\|, |\mathbf{X}|) = \prod_{i=1}^{\|\mathbf{d}\|} \binom{|\mathbf{X}| - \sum_{j=0}^{i-1} occurs(d_j, \mathbf{d})}{occurs(d_i, \mathbf{d})}
$$

where $\mathbf{d} = \mathbf{b} \cup (\mathbf{c} - \mathbf{a})$, $Set(\mathbf{d}) = \{d_1, \ldots, d_{\|\mathbf{d}\|}\}$ and $occurs(d_0, \mathbf{d}) = 0$.

Proof.

1. By Proposition 1, $|var(\mathcal{S})| \geq \|\mathcal{T} - \mathcal{S}\|$ is a necessary condition. We have to show that this condition is also sufficient. We can eliminate from both sets the constants in $\mathbf{a}$ and consider the matching of the two sets $\mathbf{X}$ and $\mathbf{d} = \mathbf{b} \cup (\mathbf{c} - \mathbf{a})$ where $|var(\mathbf{X})| \geq |\mathbf{d}|$ and $|\mathbf{X}| = |\mathbf{d}|$. Since the variables in $\mathbf{X}$ are distinct, it follows that $|var(\mathbf{X})| = |\mathbf{d}|$ and we can trivially assign each distinct variable to a different element of $\mathbf{d}$.

2. The number of matchers for $\mathcal{S}$ and $\mathcal{T}$ can be computed by considering the two sets $\mathbf{X}$ and $\mathbf{d} = \mathbf{b} \cup (\mathbf{c} - \mathbf{a})$ and is equal to the number of possible $\mathbf{d}$-idempotent substitution for the variables in $\mathbf{X}$. Let's consider the process of assigning each constant to a set of variables. A first constant, say d_1 can be assigned to $occurs(d_1, \mathbf{d})$ distinct variables with all permutations allowed; for assigning the second one, say d_2, we can refer to a set of $|\mathbf{X}| - occurs(d_1, \mathbf{d})$ variables using the same idea. The process continues till the assignment of the last constant, say $\mathbf{d}_h$, for which the set of variables to be matched with is consequently fixed. □

Example 3. Consider two bags $\mathcal{S} = \{X_1, X_2, X_3, a, a\}$ and $\mathcal{T} = \{b, b, a, a, a\}$. There are $\binom{3}{2} \times \binom{3-2}{1} = 3$ matchers for $\mathcal{S}$ and $\mathcal{T}$: $\theta_1 = \{X_1/b, X_2/b, X_3/a\}$, $\theta_2 = \{X_1/b, X_2/a, X_3/b\}$ and $\theta_3 = \{X_1/a, X_2/b, X_3/b\}$. □

3.2   Distinct Constants: $Set(\mathcal{T} - \mathcal{S}) = \mathcal{T} - \mathcal{S}$

In this case we consider two bags $\mathcal{S} = \mathbf{X} \cup \mathbf{a}$ and $\mathcal{T} = \mathbf{b} \cup \mathbf{c}$ where the constants in $\mathcal{T} - \mathcal{S}$ are distinct. We show that the problem can be reduced to the set term matching problem.

Proposition 3. *Let* $\mathcal{S} = \mathbf{X} \cup \mathbf{a}$ *and* $\mathcal{T} = \mathbf{b} \cup \mathbf{c}$ *be two bag terms satisfying conditions of Prop. 1, such that* $\mathcal{T} - \mathcal{S}$ *contains distinct constants, i.e.* $Set(\mathcal{T} - \mathcal{S}) = \mathcal{T} - \mathcal{S}$. *Then, a matcher for* $\mathcal{S}$ *and* $\mathcal{T}$ *exists if and only if* $\|\mathbf{X}\| = |\mathbf{b} \cup (\mathbf{c} - \mathbf{a})|$.

Proof. We can eliminate from both sets the constants in $\mathbf{a}$ and consider the matching of the two sets $\mathbf{X}$ and $\mathbf{d} = \mathbf{b} \cup (\mathbf{c} - \mathbf{a})$ where $\|\mathbf{d}\| = |\mathbf{d}|$.

If part. If $\mathbf{X}$ contains a number of distinct variables equal to the number of distinct elements in $\mathcal{T} - \mathcal{S}$, the two bags admit a matcher.

Only-if part. As a consequence of Proposition 1, we have $|var(\mathbf{X})| \geq |\mathbf{d}|$ and $|\mathbf{X}| = |\mathbf{d}|$. Moreover, $|\mathbf{d}| \leq |var(\mathbf{X})| = \|\mathbf{X}\| \leq |\mathbf{X}| = |\mathbf{d}|$; it follows $\|\mathbf{X}\| = |\mathbf{d}|$. □

Thus, the problem of finding a matcher of $\mathcal{S}$ and $\mathcal{T}$, being $\mathcal{T} - \mathcal{S}$ a set, admits a solution only if $\mathcal{S}$ is a set too. This is the traditional problem of matching of two set terms, that has been investigated in [1].

Fact 1 *[1] Let* $\mathcal{S} = \mathbf{X} \cup \mathbf{c}$ *and* $\mathcal{T} = \mathbf{b} \cup \mathbf{c}$ *be two set terms. Then, the number of matchers for* $\mathcal{S}$ *and* $\mathcal{T}$ *is equal to*

$$ss\_matches(|\mathbf{b}|, |\mathbf{c}|, |\mathbf{X}|) = \sum_{i=0}^{|\mathbf{b}|} (-1)^i \binom{|\mathbf{b}|}{i} (|\mathbf{b}| + |\mathbf{c}| - i)^{|\mathbf{X}|}$$

□

```
function First_Matcher(S, T : array of integer): array of integer;
var n : integer = ||S||;  m : integer = ||T||;
    R : array[1..n] of integer;  i : integer;

    function MatchR(R:array of integer; i: integer ):array of integer;
    var newAssign: array[1..n] of terms;
        begin
            if (i ≤ n) then begin
                while nextAssign(R, i, newAssign) do begin
                    R := MatchR(R ∪ newAssign, i + 1);
                    if Free(R) = 0 then return R;
                end
            end
            return R
        end MatchR;

begin
    for i := 1 to n do R[i] := 0;
    return MatchR(R, 1);
end First_Matcher;


Algorithm Bag_Matching;
Input: S, T : array of integer;
Output: {"yes", "no"};
begin
    if (Free(First_Matcher(S, T))=0  then output no
                                      else output yes
end Bag_Matching
```

Fig. 1. Bug Term Matching Algorithm

Corollary 1. *Let $S = \mathbf{X} \cup \mathbf{a}$ and $T = \mathbf{b} \cup \mathbf{c}$ be two bag terms satisfying conditions of Prop. 1, such that $T - S$ contains distinct constants, i.e. $Set(T - S) = T - S$. Then, the number of matchers for S and T is $|\mathbf{d}|!$ where $\mathbf{d} = \mathbf{b} \cup (\mathbf{c} - \mathbf{a})$.*

Proof. Derived from Fact 1, by assuming $|\mathbf{b}| = |\mathbf{d}|$ and $|\mathbf{c}| = 0$.   □

Example 4. Consider the bags $S = \{X_1, X_2, X_3, a, a\}$ and $T = \{b, c, a, a, a\}$. By deleting the shared constants, we obtain the two bags $S' = \{X_1, X_2, X_3\}$ and $T' = \{b, c, a\}$ which admits 3! matchers.   □

4   Computing Matchers

In order to make our results effective, we present an algorithm, called *Bag_Matching*, that given two bags checks the existence of a matcher. The *Input* of the algorithm consists of two arrays S and T containing the number of occurrences of the elements in the two input bags. Withous loss of generality,

---

procedure *BagSet_Matching*(**X**, **b**, **c** : *array of term*): list of matcher;
var $m = |\mathbf{b}|$; $n = |\mathbf{c}|$; $p = \|\mathbf{X}\| - |\mathbf{b}|$;
     θ : array $[1..(m+p)]$ of integer; $all\theta$: list of integer;
     L : list of integer   i : integer;

   procedure *assign*(*i* : *integer*);
   var k, q : *integer*;
   begin
       if $i > m + p$ **then** *insert*($all\theta, \theta$)
       else begin
           if $m + p - i + 1 > cardlist(L)$ **then begin**
               $k := 1$; $q := m + n$;
           end
           else begin
               $k := first(L)$; $q := m$;
           end
           while $k \leq q$ **do begin**
               $\theta[i] := k$;
               if $k \leq m$ **then begin**
                   $L[k] = L[k] + 1$; **if** $L[k] = 1$ **then** *remove*(L, k);
               end;
               assign($i + 1$);
               if $k \leq m$ **then begin**
                   $L[k] = L[k] - 1$; **if** $L[k] = 0$ **then** *add*(L, k);
               end;
               if $q = m + n$ **then** $k := k + 1$
               else $k := next(L, k)$
           end
       end
   end *assign*;

   begin
       $all\theta := <>$;
       for $i := 1$ **to** m **do** $L[i] := 0$;
       assign(1)
       return($all\theta$)
   end *BagSet_Matching*;

Fig. 2. Bug Term Matching Algorithm

we assume that the shared elements have been deleted, i.e. the two input bags are $\mathcal{S} = \mathbf{X}$ and $\mathcal{T} = \mathbf{b} \cup (\mathbf{c} - \mathbf{a})$. The output of the algorithm is *"yes"* or *"no"*.

The algorithm, reported in Fig. 1, is simply based on the backtracking technique. The function *First_Matcher* receives two arrays of integers and outputs a matcher (if one exists) in the form of an array of integers with cardinality $\|\mathcal{S}\|$. This array is such that each of its indexes represents a variable and the corresponding value represents the index of the constant to which the variable is assigned.

The function *nextAssign* chooses the variables to be assigned to each constant; the choice is made randomly, but it is possible to apply some greedy technique such as those used in fitting algorithms. The function *Free* returns the number of free constant, i.e the number of constants which have not been used in the current substitution.

Proposition 4. *The algorithm Bag Term Matching determines the existence of a matcher of S and T in time $O(2^{\|S\|})$.*

Proof (Sketch). In the worst case it needs to generate all the partitions.   □

As a specialization we can consider the problem of computing the matchers in the case where S contains distinct variables, for which we proved a necessary and sufficient condition to establish if a matcher exists (see Proposition 2). The algorithm is reported in Fig. 2 and is similar to the one solving the set term matching problem, as no substantial difference arises by considering variables occurring more than once.

Proposition 5. *The algorithm of Fig. 2 computes the first matcher in time $O(\|S\|)$ and hence it is an optimal algorithm.*

Proof (Sketch). The first matcher is obtained after the assignments of $(\|S\|)$ variables and each assignment is made in constant time; the optimality follows from the fact that the lower bound complexity is given by the size of the matcher equal to $\|S\|$.   □

5   Conclusions

In this paper we have analyzed bag term matching, showing its intrinsic difficulty. For some important subcases we have provided necessary and sufficient conditions for the existence of a matcher testable in polynomial time. Finally, we have proposed an algorithm for finding an optimal solution for the problem. Some questions are still open; for instance further research should be devoted in investigating a pseudo-polynomial time algorithm for finding a matcher of two bags, and in considering variants of the matching problem, like finding substitutions which guarantee bags containment.

References

1. N. Arni, S. Greco and D. Saccà, Matching of Bounded Set Terms in the Logic Language LDL++, *J. of Logic Programming* 27(1): 73-87, 1996.
2. C. Beeri, S. Naqvi, O. Shmueli and S. Tsur, Set Constructors in a Logic Database Language, *J. of Logic Programming*, Vol. 10, No 3 & 4, 1991.
3. E. Dantsin and A. Voronkov, A Nondeterministic Polynomial-Time Unification Algorithm for Bags, Sets and Trees. *Proc. Int. Conf. Foundations of Software Science and Computation Structures*, 180-196, 1999.
4. G. Dowek, Higher-order unification and matching, A. Robinson and A. Voronkov (eds.), *Handbook of Automated Reasoning*, pp. 1009-106, Elsevier, 2001.

5. A. Dovier, E. G. Omodeo, E. Pontelli and G. F. Rossi, { log }: A Logic Programming Language with Finite Sets, *Proc. Int. Conf. on Logic Programming*, 111-124, 1991.
6. F. Fages, Associative-Commutative Unification, *8th Int. Conf. on Automated Deduction*, pp. 416-430, 1986.
7. M.R. Garey and D.S. Johnson, *Computers and Intractability - A Guide to the Theory of NP-Completeness*, Freeman, San Francisco, 1979.
8. S. Greco, Optimal Unification of Bounded Set Terms, *Int. Conf. on Information and Knowledge Management*, pp. 326-336, 1996.
9. G. Greco, S. Greco and E. Zumpano, A logical Framework for the Integration of Databases. *Proc. Int. Symp. on Methodologies for Intelligent Sistems*, 2002.
10. N. Immerman, S. Patnaik and D. Stemple, The Expressiveness of a Family of Finite Set Languages, *Proc. PODS Conf.*, 37-52, 1991.
11. B. Jayaraman, Implementation of Subset-Equational Programs, *Journal of Logic Programming*, Vol. 12, 299-324, 1992.
12. D. Kapur and P. Narendran, NP-completeness of the Set Unification and Matching problems, *Proc. Int. Conf. on Automated Deduction*, 489-495, 1986.
13. D. Kapur and P. Narendran, Double-Exponential Complexity of Computing a Complete Set of AC-Unifiers, *Proc. LICS Conf.*, 11–21, 1992.
14. K. Knight, Unification: A Multidisciplinary Survey, *ACM Comp. Surveys*, Vol. 21(1), pp. 93-124, 1989.
15. G. M. Kuper, Logic Programming with Sets, *Journal of Computer and System Science*, No. 41(1), pp. 44-64, 1990.
16. W. Ledermann and S. Vajda, *Handbook of Applicable Mathematics*, Vol. 5(B), 1985.
17. C. Lincoln and J. Christian, Adventures in Associative-Commutative Unification, *Proc. 9th International Conference on Automated Deduction*, pp. 358-367, 1988.
18. M. Livesey and J.H. Siekmann, Unification of A+C-Terms (Bags) and A+C+I-Terms (Sets), *Tech. Report, 5/67, Facultat fur Informatik, Univ. Karlruhe*, 1976.
19. C. Mateis, Unification of Simple Set Terms, Master Thesis (in Italian), 1996.
20. M. S. Paterson, Linear Unification, *Journal of Computer and System Science*, No. 16, pp. 158-167, 1978.
21. O. Shmueli, S. Tsur and C. Zaniolo, Compilation of Set Terms in the Logic Data Language (LDL), *J. of Logic Programming*, Vol. 12(1) & 2, 89-119, 1992.
22. J. Siekmann, Unification Theory, *J. of Symbolic Computation*, No. 7, 207-274, 1989.
23. F. Stolzenburg, An Algorithm for General Set Unification and Its Complexity, *Journal of Automated Reasoning*, 22(1), pp. 45-63, 1999.
24. J.K. Ullman, *Principles of Database and Knowledge-Base Systems*, Vol. 1, Computer Science Press, Rockville, Md., 1988.
25. R. M. Verma and I. V. Ramakrishnan, Tight Complexity Bounds for Term Matching Problems, *Information and Computation*, No. 101(1), 33–69, 1992.
26. C. Zaniolo, N. Arni, K. Ong, Negation and Aggregates in Recursive Rules: the LDL++ Approach. *DOOD Conf.*, pp. 204-221, 1993.

Non-commutativity and
Expressive Deductive Logic Databases

S. Krajči[1,*], R. Lencses[1,*], J. Medina[2,**], M. Ojeda-Aciego[2,**],
A. Valverde[2,**], and P. Vojtáš[1,*]

[1] Institute of Informatics. P.J. Šafárik University. Slovakia
[2] Dept. Matemática Aplicada. Universidad de Málaga. Spain

Abstract. The procedural semantics of multi-adjoint logic programming is used for providing a model-theoretic semantics for a data model. A translation method for deductive logic databases is presented for obtaining a relational algebra with classical projection and enriched parametric join operator with aggregations. The use of non-commutative conjunctors allows for a model of different degrees of granulation and precision, whereas expressiveness is achieved by using multiple-valued connectives.

1 Introduction and Motivating Examples

The handling of imprecision in databases is a topic which is getting growing attention, for knowledge-base systems must typically deal with the intrinsic imprecision of the data, vagueness and imperfection in knowledge, in particular, in the form of incompleteness, inconsistency, and uncertainty.

Several frameworks for manipulating data and knowledge have been proposed. Our approach here is a lattice-valued logic programming and/or Datalog paradigm, which permits the articulation of vague concepts and, moreover, has the property that the truth of an argument can diminish as the number of inferences in it increases.

Multi-adjoint logic programming was introduced in [8] as a refinement of both initial work in [13] and residuated logic programming [2]. It allows for very general connectives in the body of the rules, and sufficient conditions for the continuity of its semantics are known.

Such an approach is interesting for applications: for instance, in [10] a system is presented where connectives are learnt from different users' examples and, thus, one can imagine a scenario in which knowledge is described by a many-valued logic program where connectives have many-valued truth functions representing conjunctions, disjunctors or, more generally, aggregation operators (arithmetic mean, weighted sum, etc.) where different implications could be needed for different purposes, and different aggregators are defined for different users, depending on their preferences.

It is important to recall that many different "and" and "or" operations have been proposed for use in fuzzy logic. It is therefore important to select the operations which

---

* Partially supported by Slovak grants VEGA 1/7557/20.
** Partially supported by Spanish DGI project BFM2000-1054-C02-02.

S. Flesca et al. (Eds.): JELIA 2002, LNAI 2424, pp. 149–160, 2002.

are the best for each particular application. Several papers discuss the optimal choice of "and" and "or" operations for fuzzy control, when the main criterion is to get the stablest control. In reasoning application, however, it is more appropriate to select operations which are the best in reflecting human reasoning, i.e., operations which are "the most logical".

In fuzzy logic there is a well developed theory of t-norms, t-co-norms and residual implications. In the rest of this section we will show some interesting non-standard connectives to motivate the consideration of a more general class of connectives in fuzzy logic. The motivation is the following:

When evaluating the relevance of answers to a given query it is common to use some subjective interpretation of human preferences in a granulated way. This is, fuzzy truth-values usually describe steps in the degree of perception (numerous advocations of this phenomenon have been pointed out by Zadeh). This is connected to the well-known fact that people can only distinguish finitely many degrees of quality (closeness, cheapness, ...) or quantity in control. Thus, in practice, although we use the product t-norm $\&_p(x, y) = x \cdot y$, we are actually working with a piece-wise constant approximation of it. In this generality, it is possible to work with approximations of t-norms and/or conjunctions learnt from data by a neural net like, for instance, those in [10].

For instance, assume that we are looking for a hotel which is close to downtown, with reasonable price and being a new building. Classical fuzzy approaches would assign a user "his" interpretation of "close", "reasonable" and "new". In practice, we recognize finitely many degrees of being close, reasonable, new, so the fuzzy sets have a stepwise shape. Actually, we are working on intervals of granulation and/or indistinguishability. It is just a matter of representation that the outcome is done by means of intervals. This motivates our lattice-valued approach, namely, the set of truth-values will be considered to be a lattice. It is easy to get examples in which the lattice can be:

- Generated by a partition of the real unit interval $[0, 1]$.
- All subintervals of $[0, 1]$.
- All the probability distributions on $[0, 1]$.

Regarding the use of non-standard connectives, just consider that a variable represented by x can be observed with m different values, then surely we should be working with a regular partition of $[0, 1]$ of m pieces. This means that a given value x should be fitted to this 'observation' scale as the least upper bound with the form k/m (analytically, this corresponds to $(\lceil m \cdot x \rceil)/m$ where $\lceil \_ \rceil$ is the ceiling function). A similar consideration can be applied to both, variable y and the resulting conjunction; furthermore, it might be possible that each variable has a different granularity.

Formally, assume in x-axis we have a partition into n pieces, in y-axis into m pieces and in z-axis into k pieces. Then the approximation of the product conjunction looks like

Definition 1. *Denote* $(z)_p = \dfrac{\lceil p \cdot z \rceil}{p}$ *and define, for naturals* $n, m, k > 0$

$$C_{n,m}^k(x, y) = \left((x)_n \cdot (y)_m \right)_k$$

Example 1. Connectives $C_{n,m}^k(x, y)$ need be neither associative nor commutative:

1. For instance $C_{10,10}^{10}$, denoted simply as C, is not associative.

$$C(0.7, C(0.7, 0.3)) = C(0.7, (0.21)_{10}) = C(0.7, 0.3) = (0.21)_{10} = 0.3$$
$$C(C(0.7, 0.7), 0.3) = C((0.49)_{10}, 0.3) = C(0.5, 0.3) = (0.15)_{10} = 0.2$$

2. $C_{10,5}^4(x, y)$ is not commutative.

$$C_{10,5}^4(0.82, 0.79) = ((0.82)_{10} \cdot (0.79)_5)_4 = (0.9 \cdot 0.8)_4 = (0.72)_4 = 0.75$$
$$C_{10,5}^4(0.79, 0.82) = ((0.79)_{10} \cdot (0.82)_5)_4 = (0.8 \cdot 1)_4 = 1$$

As previously stated, to model precision and granularity, it is reasonable to work with partitions of $[0, 1]$. In fact, in this case, the set of truth values is a finite linearly ordered set. In practical applications it happens that we change the perspective and work with finer and/or coarser partition. This is a special case studied in domain theory [1], in which one of the most fundamental questions is about the representation of a real number: a common approach to this problem is to identify each real number r with a collection of intervals whose intersection is $\{r\}$. In such a representation a smaller interval gives more information about a number than a bigger interval. So an interval I carries more information than an interval J, which we represent by writing $J \leq I$, provided that $I \subseteq J$.

Consider now the following interval extension of the connectives $C_{n,m}^k$.

Definition 2. *For naturals* $n, m, k > 0$ *and* $a \leq n, b \leq m$ *we define*

$$K_{n,m}^k \left(\left\langle \frac{a-1}{n}, \frac{a}{n} \right\rangle, \left\langle \frac{b-1}{m}, \frac{b}{m} \right\rangle \right) = \left\langle (a \cdot b)_k - \frac{1}{k}, (a \cdot b)_k \right\rangle$$

Several authors propose to model precision, uncertainty of our knowledge with the set of truth values being all closed subintervals of the real interval $[0, 1]$. In some papers the set of truth values is the set of pairs of closed intervals: the first one modelling our belief, confidence, or probability estimation, and the second modelling our doubts or disbelief on the content of information.

Our intuitive model will consider the lattice L of all closed subintervals of the interval $[0, 1]$, the ordering being the "truth" ordering, see [2,3,4,7]

$$\langle a, b \rangle \leq \langle c, d \rangle \qquad \text{iff} \qquad a \leq c \quad \text{and} \quad b \leq d$$

This is a complete lattice with $\perp = \langle 0, 0 \rangle$ and $\top = \langle 1, 1 \rangle$. The references cited above generally use t-norms as operations acting on endpoints of intervals. We would like to extend the set of connectives to arbitrary approximations of t-norms. The computations in the probabilistic and lattice valued fuzzy logic are the same, the only difference is handling and/or ignorance of probabilistic constraints.

Example 2. Another example justifying the use of (lattices of) intervals as truth-values, together with possibly some source of inconsistency problems comes, for instance, when considering the results of polls.

Some days before the polling day for the recent elections in Hungary, the following vote expectancy data was published:

- Between 35–45% of voters will favour party 1.
- Between 45–55% of voters will favour party 2.
- Between 5–10% of voters will favour party 3.
- Between 5–10% of voters will favour party 4.

The outcome of the election was the following: $P1$: 42%, $P2$: 41%, $P3$: 6%, $P4$: 4%; in which the results for two parties were outside the predicted interval.

Problems with probabilistic restrictions should be seen as a sign of possible inconsistencies, just note that if the predictions were correct for all parties with values taken at the right end of the interval of probability, then we would have a total 120% of votes(!). Furthermore, these measurements usually generate inconsistencies, because the questioned group could not be representing the whole population and/or people do not answer their real interests.

In our approach, the computation will be processed by lattice valued truth-functions. Instead of working with probabilistic constraints as cuts we could add a new degree with a measure of violation of probabilistic constraints. In this example, the degree of inconsistency could be, for instance, $\frac{2}{\pi} \arctan(0.2)$ because of the sum of upper bounds of estimations was 120%.

2   Biresiduated Multi-adjoint Logic Programming

We would like to build our semantics of deductive logic databases on a lattice valued logic with non-commutative conjunctions and based on residuation. There exists already the algebraic notion of biresiduated lattices [12], which seems to be a natural candidate for our model.

The preliminary concepts required to formally define the syntax of biresiduated multi-adjoint logic programs are built on those of the 'monoresiduated' multi-adjoint case [9]; to make this paper as self-contained as possible, the necessary definitions are included below.

Definition 3. *Let $\langle L, \preceq \rangle$ be a complete lattice. A biresiduated multi-adjoint lattice $\mathcal{L}$ is a tuple $(L, \preceq, \swarrow^1, \nwarrow_1, \&_1, \ldots, \swarrow^n, \nwarrow_n, \&_n)$ satisfying the following items:*

1. *$\langle L, \preceq \rangle$ is bounded, i.e. it has bottom and top elements;*
2. *$\top \&_i \vartheta = \vartheta \&_i \top = \vartheta$ for all $\vartheta \in L$ for $i = 1, \ldots, n$;*
3. *$(\swarrow^i, \nwarrow_i, \&_i)$ satisfies the following properties, for all $i = 1, \ldots, n$:*
   (a) *Operation $\&_i$ is increasing in both arguments,*
   (b) *Operations $\swarrow^i, \nwarrow_i$ are increasing in the first argument and decreasing in the second argument,*
   (c) *For any $x, y, z \in P$, we have that*
   $$x \preceq y \swarrow^i z \text{ if and only if } x \&_i z \preceq y \qquad x \preceq y \nwarrow_i z \text{ if and only if } z \&_i x \preceq y$$

The existence of multiple pairs satisfying property 3 above justifies the term *multi-adjoint*. The biresiduated structure comes from the fact that, for each $\&_i$ (called *adjoint conjunctor*) there are two 'sided' *adjoint implications* denoted $\swarrow^i$ and $\nwarrow_i$.

We will be working with two languages: the first one, $\mathfrak{F}$, to define the syntax of our programs, and the second one, $\mathfrak{L}$, to host the manipulation of the truth-values of the formulas in the programs. To avoid possible name-clashes, we will denote the interpretation of an operator symbol ω under $\mathfrak{L}$ as $\dot{\omega}$ (a dot on the operator), whereas ω itself will denote its interpretation under $\mathfrak{F}$.

In the sequel, we will omit the adjectives biresiduated and multi-adjoint if no confusion could arise. Furthermore, we will use the symbol $\leftarrow_i$ to denote either $\swarrow^i$ or $\nwarrow_i$, whenever the 'side' of the implication is not relevant to the case.

In the next definition we will consider a language $\mathfrak{F}$ which may contain some additional connectives, especially several aggregations, disjunctors and some additional conjunctors.

Definition 4. *A biresiduated multi-adjoint logic program (in short a program) on a language $\mathfrak{F}$ with values in a lattice $\mathfrak{L}$ is a set $\mathbb{P}$ of rules of the form $\langle A \swarrow^i B, \vartheta \rangle$ or $\langle A \nwarrow_i B, \vartheta \rangle$ such that:*

1. *The head of the rule, A, is a propositional symbol;*
2. *The body formula, B, is a formula of $\mathfrak{F}$ built from propositional symbols $B_1, \ldots, B_n$ ($n \geq 0$) and monotone operators (and no implications);*
3. *The confidence factor ϑ is an element (a truth-value) of L.*

As usual, facts are rules with body $\top$, and a query (or goal) is a propositional symbol intended as a question $?A$ prompting the system.

An *interpretation* is a mapping $I: \Pi \to L$. Note that each of these interpretations can be uniquely extended to the whole set of formulas, $\hat{I}: \mathfrak{F} \to L$. The set of all interpretations of the formulas defined by $\mathfrak{F}$ in is denoted $\mathcal{I}_\mathfrak{L}$.

The ordering $\preceq$ of the truth-values L can be easily extended to $\mathcal{I}_\mathfrak{L}$, which also inherits the structure of complete lattice. The minimum element of the lattice $\mathcal{I}_\mathfrak{L}$, which assigns $\perp$ to any propositional symbol, will be denoted $\triangle$.

A weighted rule of a biresiduated multi-adjoint logic program is satisfied whenever its truth-value is greater or equal than the confidence factor:

Definition 5.

1. *An interpretation $I \in \mathcal{I}_\mathfrak{L}$ satisfies $\langle A \swarrow^i B, \vartheta \rangle$ if and only if $\vartheta \mathbin{\dot{\&}}_i \hat{I}(B) \preceq \hat{I}(A)$.*
2. *An interpretation $I \in \mathcal{I}_\mathfrak{L}$ satisfies $\langle A \nwarrow_i B, \vartheta \rangle$ if and only if $\hat{I}(B) \mathbin{\dot{\&}}_i \vartheta \preceq \hat{I}(A)$.*
3. *An interpretation $I \in \mathcal{I}_\mathfrak{L}$ is a model of a program $\mathbb{P}$ iff all weighted rules in $\mathbb{P}$ are satisfied by I.*
4. *An element $\lambda \in L$ is a correct answer for a query $?A$ and a program $\mathbb{P}$ if for any interpretation $I \in \mathcal{I}_\mathfrak{L}$ which is a model of $\mathbb{P}$ we have $\lambda \preceq I(A)$.*

The immediate consequences operator, given by van Emden and Kowalski, can be easily generalized to the framework of biresiduated multi-adjoint logic programs. This operator will serve as our database query evaluation operator.

Definition 6. *Let $\mathbb{P}$ be a program, the immediate consequences operator $T_\mathbb{P}$ maps interpretations to interpretations, and for an interpretation I and propositional variable A is defined by*

$$T_\mathbb{P}(I)(A) = \sup\left\{ \{\vartheta \mathbin{\dot{\&}}_i \hat{I}(B) \mid \langle A \swarrow^i B, \vartheta \rangle \in \mathbb{P}\} \cup \{\hat{I}(B) \mathbin{\dot{\&}}_i \vartheta \mid \langle A \nwarrow_i B, \vartheta \rangle \in \mathbb{P}\} \right\}$$

The semantics of a biresiduated multi-adjoint logic program is characterised by the post-fixpoints of $T_{\mathbb{P}}$; that is, an interpretation I of $\mathcal{I}_{\mathcal{L}}$ is a model of a program $\mathbb{P}$ iff $T_{\mathbb{P}}(I) \sqsubseteq I$.

Our operator is a generalization of that in [7] (although they work with pairs of intervals). Their operator is continuous because they consider only connectives generated by Lukasiewicz, product and Gödel connectives acting on the endpoint of intervals. In general, when working with aggregations and constant approximations this is not always the case. We will justify this claim by using the example below, modified from [5]. A detailed description of this is out of the scope of this paper. More details on relations between annotated and fuzzy programs are in [6].

Example 3. Consider the following program in the language of lattice-valued generalized annotated programs with restricted semantics :

$$p: \langle 0, 0 \rangle \leftarrow \qquad p: \left\langle 0, \frac{1 + 2y}{4} \right\rangle \leftarrow p: \langle 0, y \rangle \qquad q: \left\langle 0, \frac{1}{2} \right\rangle \leftarrow p: \left\langle 0, \frac{1}{2} \right\rangle$$

The $T_{\mathbb{P}}$ operator iterates as follows:

$$T_{\mathbb{P}}^{1}(p) = \left\langle 0, \frac{1}{4} \right\rangle \ , \ T_{\mathbb{P}}^{2}(p) = \left\langle 0, \frac{3}{8} \right\rangle, \ldots, T_{\mathbb{P}}^{n}(p) = \left\langle 0, \frac{2^{n-1} - 1}{2^{n}} \right\rangle, \ldots$$

$$\ldots, T_{\mathbb{P}}^{\omega}(p) = \left\langle 0, \frac{1}{2} \right\rangle, T_{\mathbb{P}}^{\omega+1}(p) = \left\langle 0, \frac{1}{2} \right\rangle$$

$$T_{\mathbb{P}}^{1}(q) = \langle 0, 0 \rangle = T_{\mathbb{P}}^{2}(q) = T_{\mathbb{P}}^{3}(q) = \cdots = T_{\mathbb{P}}^{\omega}(q), T_{\mathbb{P}}^{\omega+1}(q) = \left\langle 0, \frac{1}{2} \right\rangle$$

so the operator is not continuous. Indeed, there is an upward directed set of interpretations of L for which $T_{\mathbb{P}}(\bigvee X) \not\leq \bigvee \{T_{\mathbb{P}}(I) \mid I \in X\}$. Namely, take $X = \{I_n \mid n \in \omega\}$ where $I_n: \{p, q\} \to L$ is defined as

$$I_n(p) = \left\langle 0, \frac{2^{n-1} - 1}{2^{n}} \right\rangle \qquad I_n(q) = \langle 0, 0 \rangle$$

then we have

$$\bigvee X(p) = \left\langle 0, \frac{1}{2} \right\rangle \quad T_{\mathbb{P}}(\bigvee X)(p) = \left\langle 0, \frac{1}{2} \right\rangle = \bigvee \{T_{\mathbb{P}}(I_n)(p) \mid n \in \omega\} = \left\langle 0, \frac{1}{2} \right\rangle$$

$$\bigvee X(q) = \langle 0, 0 \rangle \quad T_{\mathbb{P}}(\bigvee X)(q) = \left\langle 0, \frac{1}{2} \right\rangle \not\leq \bigvee \{T_{\mathbb{P}}(I_n)(q) \mid n \in \omega\} = \langle 0, 0 \rangle$$

The program of this example can be translated to

$$(p \leftarrow @_1(p), \top) \qquad (q \leftarrow @_2(p), \top)$$

where the truth-function $\dot{@}_i: L \to L$ are defined as

$$\dot{@}_1(\langle x, y \rangle) = \left\langle 0, \frac{1 + 2y}{4} \right\rangle \qquad \dot{@}_2(\langle x, y \rangle) = \begin{cases} \langle 0, \frac{1}{2} \rangle & \text{if } \langle x, y \rangle \geq \langle 0, \frac{1}{2} \rangle \\ \langle 0, 0 \rangle & \text{if } \langle x, y \rangle \not\geq \langle 0, \frac{1}{2} \rangle \end{cases}$$

The jump operator $\dot{@}_2$ is not lattice continuous: simply consider the following upward directed set

$$A \subset L \qquad A = \left\{ \left\langle 0, \frac{2^{n-1}-1}{2^n} \right\rangle \mid n \in \omega \right\}$$

Note that $\bigvee A = \langle 0, \frac{1}{2} \rangle$, therefore $\dot{@}_2(\bigvee A) = \langle 0, \frac{1}{2} \rangle$. Now, for every element of A, $\dot{@}_2(\langle 0, \frac{2^{n-1}-1}{2^n} \rangle) = \langle 0, 0 \rangle$, therefore

$$\dot{@}_2\left(\bigvee A\right) = \left\langle 0, \frac{1}{2} \right\rangle \nleq \bigvee \left\{ \dot{@}_2\left(\left\langle 0, \frac{2^{n-1}-1}{2^n} \right\rangle\right) \mid n \in \omega \right\} = \bigvee \{\bot\} = \bot$$

A possible solution to this, as proposed in [6], can be obtained by replacing constant annotations by annotation terms as functions, in order to work with lattice continuous connectives in the body.

Procedural Semantics: It can be shown that the $T_\mathbb{P}$ operator is continuous under very general hypotheses (the proof in [8] can be easily generalised to this framework), therefore the least model can be reached in at most countably many iterations. Now, it is worth to define a procedural semantics which allows us to actually construct the answer to a query against a given program.

Our computational model will work in an extended language in which we allow to use jointly propositional symbols and elements of the lattice as basic formulas (these 'mixed' formulas will be called *extended formulas*). Given a query, by using the rules below, we will provide a lower bound of the value of A under any model of the program. Intuitively, the computation proceeds by, somehow, substituting propositional symbols by lower bounds of their truth-value until, eventually, an extended formula with no propositional symbol is obtained, which will be interpreted in the lattice to get the computed answer.

Given a program $\mathbb{P}$, we define the following admissible rules for transforming any extended formula.

Definition 7. Admissible rules *are defined as follows:*

R1a Substitute an atom A in an extended formula by $(\vartheta \&_i B)$ whenever there exists a rule $\langle A \swarrow^i B, \vartheta \rangle$ in $\mathbb{P}$.

R1b Substitute an atom A in an extended formula by $(B \&_i \vartheta)$ whenever there exists a rule $\langle A \nwarrow_i B, \vartheta \rangle$ in $\mathbb{P}$.

R2 Substitute an atom A in an extended formula by $\bot$.

R3 Substitute an atom A in an extended formula by ϑ whenever there exists a fact $\langle A \swarrow^i \top, \vartheta \rangle$ or $\langle A \nwarrow_i \top, \vartheta \rangle$ in $\mathbb{P}$.

Note that if an extended formula turns out to have no propositional symbols, then it can be directly interpreted in the computation as an element in $\mathfrak{L}$, rather than like a formula. This justifies the following definition of *computed answer*.

Definition 8. Let $\mathbb{P}$ be a program in a language interpreted on a lattice $\mathcal{L}$ and let $?A$ be a goal. An element $\lambda \in L$ is said to be a computed answer if there is a sequence $G_0, \ldots, G_{n+1}$ such that

1. $G_0 = A$ and $G_{n+1} = @(r_1, \ldots, r_m)$ where[1] $r_i \in L$ for all $i = 1, \ldots m$, and $\lambda = \dot{@}(r_1, \ldots, r_m)$.
2. Every G_i, for $i = 1, \ldots, n$, is an extended formula.
3. Every G_{i+1} is inferred from G_i by exactly one of the admissible rules.

Note that our procedural semantics, instead of being refutation-based (this is not possible, since negation is not allowed in our approach), is oriented to obtaining a bound of the optimal correct answer of the query.

Greatest Answers and Reductants: The definition of correct answer is not entirely satisfactory in that $\perp$ is always a correct answer. Actually, we should be interested in the greatest confidence factor we can assume on the query, consistently with the information in the program, instead of in the set of its lower bounds.

By proving that models are post-fixpoint of $T_\mathbb{P}$, together with the Knaster-Tarski theorem, it is possible to obtain the following result:

Theorem 1. *Given a complete lattice L, a program $\mathbb{P}$ and a propositional symbol A, we have that $T_\mathbb{P}^\omega(\triangle)(A)$ is the greatest correct answer.*

Regarding the computation of the greatest correct answer, it might well be the case that for some lattices, our procedural semantics cannot compute the greatest correct answer. We can cope with this problem by generalizing the concept of reductant [5]; any rule $\langle A \leftarrow_{j_i} \mathcal{D}_i, \vartheta_i \rangle$ contributes with a value such as either $\vartheta_i \mathrel{\dot\&}_i b_i$ or $b_i \mathrel{\dot\&}_i \vartheta_i$ in the calculation of the lower bound for the truth-value of A, and we would like to have the possibility of reaching the supremum of all the contributions, in the computational model, in a single step.

Definition 9. *Let $\mathbb{P}$ be a program; assume that the set of rules in $\mathbb{P}$ with head A can be written as $\langle A \swarrow^{i_j} \mathcal{B}_j, \vartheta_j \rangle$ for $j = 1, \ldots, n$, and $\langle A \nwarrow_{k_l} \mathcal{C}_l, \theta_l \rangle$ for $l = 1, \ldots, m$, and contains at least a proper rule; a reductant for A is any rule*

$$\langle A \swarrow @(\mathcal{B}_1, \ldots, \mathcal{B}_n, \mathcal{C}_1, \ldots, \mathcal{C}_m), \top \rangle$$

where $\swarrow$ is any implication symbol and the operator $@$ is defined as

$$\dot{@}(b_1, \ldots, b_n, c_1, \ldots, c_m) = \sup\{\vartheta_1 \&_{i_1} b_1, \ldots, \vartheta_n \&_{i_n} b_n, c_1 \&_{k_1} \theta_1, \ldots, c_m \&_{k_m} \theta_m\}$$

If there were just facts with head A, but no proper rule, then the expression above does not give a well-formed formula. In this case, the reductant is defined to be a fact which aggregates all the knowledge about A, that is,

$$\langle A \swarrow \top, \sup\{\vartheta_1, \ldots, \vartheta_n\} \rangle$$

As a consequence of the definition, and the boundary conditions in the definition of biresiduated multi-adjoint lattice, the choice of the implication to represent the corresponding reductant is irrelevant for the computational model. Therefore, in the following,

---

[1] Here the r_i represent all the variables occurring in the G_{n+1}. Therefore we are abusing the notation, for $@$ represents the composition, as functions in the lattice, of all the operators inserted by rules R1a and R1b.

we will assume that our language has a distinguished implication to be selected in the construction of reductants, leading to the so-called *canonical reductants*.

It is possible to consider only programs which contain all its reductants, since its addition to the program does not modify the set of models.

Completeness Results: The two quasi-completeness theorems given in [9] can be extended to this more general framework as follows:

Theorem 2. *For every correct answer* $\lambda \in L$ *for a program* $\mathbb{P}$ *and a query* $?A$, *there exists a chain of elements* λ_n *such that* $\lambda \preceq \sup \lambda_n$, *such that for arbitrary* n_0 *there exists a computed answer* δ *such that* $\lambda_{n_0} \preceq \delta$.

A more standard statement of the quasi-completeness result can be obtained under the assumption of the following property:

Definition 10. *A lattice* L *is said to satisfy the* supremum property *if for all directed set* $X \subset L$ *and for all* ε *we have that if* $\varepsilon < \sup X$ *then there exists* $\delta \in X$ *such that* $\varepsilon < \delta \leq \sup X$.

Theorem 3 below states that any correct answer can be approximated up to any lower bound.

Theorem 3. *Assume* L *has the supremum property, then for every correct answer* $\lambda \in L$ *for a program* $\mathbb{P}$ *and a query* $?A$, *and arbitrary* $\varepsilon \prec \lambda$ *there exists a computed answer* δ *such that* $\varepsilon \prec \delta$.

3   A Non-commutative Expressive Deductive Data Model

In this section a relational algebra is defined for the semantics above. More expressiveness is obtained because it is built on a richer set of connectives. Furthermore, as its fixpoint semantics is built on a continuous operator, the computed answer to queries is reached in at most countably many steps and, thus, no transfinite computation phenomena appears here. Moreover, our semantics is replacing the constraint resolution semantics of [5] by a more effective one calculating the best possible answer. The underlying idea is to generalize the fuzzy relational algebra from [11] to the lattice-case and give a simplified presentation. The definitions of operations do not change substantially; what changes is the continuity problem for lattices.

The semantics of rules (without negation) is given by expressing them in a positive fuzzy relational algebra (as an extension of the classical positive relational algebra) which consists of selection, natural join, classical projection and union. The new lattice-valued relations are described as classical relations with one additional attribute, TV, for the truth value. The following notation will be used: $\mathcal{R}$ will denote the set of records, R will denote relations, and r will denote predicates.

Selection. Expressions in selections are allowed to use TV. The result of such a selection, e.g. $\sigma_{TV \geq t}(r)$, consists of those tuples from $\mathcal{R}$ which have the value of the truth value attribute at least t. This is the only extension of classical selection.

Join. The operation of a natural join is defined in our relational algebra wrt to crisp equality and an aggregation operator which tells us how to calculate the truth value degree of a tuple in the join. Assume we have relations $R_1, ..., R_n$ which evaluate predicates $r_1, ..., r_n$. Moreover, assume that the first k-attributes in each R_i are the same and $(b_1, ..., b_k, b_{k+1}^i, ..., b_{m_i}^i, \beta^i) \in R_i$ then

$$(b_1, ..., b_k, b_{k+1}^1, ..., b_{m_1}^1, ..., b_{k+1}^n, ..., b_{m_n}^n, \dot{@}(\beta^1, ..., \beta^n))$$

is in the relation $\bowtie_@ (R_1, ..., R_n)$, that is the truth value attributes in our join do not behave as in classical join, they disappear, forwarding the respective truth values to the new aggregated truth value. This way it is possible to obtain the following

Theorem 4. *The operation* $\bowtie_@ (R_1, ..., R_n)$ *is a sound and complete (wrt the satisfaction of fuzzy logic) evaluation of* $@(r_1, ..., r_n)$ *provided* $R_1, ..., R_n$ *are evaluations of* $r_1, ..., r_n$.

Projection. In [6] we have presented several transformations of generalised annotated programs and fuzzy logic programs (see also Example 3). Motivated by this, observe that a multi-adjoint rule

$$\langle H \leftarrow_i @(\mathcal{B}_1, ..., \mathcal{B}_n), \vartheta \rangle$$

is semantically equivalent to

$$\langle H \leftarrow \vartheta \,\&_i\, @(\mathcal{B}_1, ..., \mathcal{B}_n), \top \rangle$$

where $\&_i$ is the residuated conjunctor of the implication $\leftarrow_i$, and $\leftarrow$ is a fixed implication, having residuated conjunctor $\&$ satisfying $\top \,\&\, b = b$.

Note that

$$y \,\&_i\, \dot{@}(x_1, ..., x_n) = \dot{@}'(y, x_1, ..., x_n)$$

is also an aggregation in our lattice.

So all Datalog programs can be translated to programs with all rules having truth value $\top$ and using only one fixed implication with property above. All the richness of our multiadjoint biresidual programs with truth values of rules is now hidden in a richer set of aggregations used to evaluate bodies of rules, and this enables us to work with the classical projection.

Having the evaluation R of the whole body of the rectified rule we use the classical projection to get the evaluation of the (IDB) predicate $H(X_1, ..., X_h)$, So for $(b_1, ..., b_m, \beta) \in R$ the projection consists of tuples

$$(b_1, ..., b_h, \beta) \in \Pi_{X_1, ..., X_h}(R)$$

assuming the variables selected were at the beginning of the enumeration of the tuple.

Here is a substantial difference with some models of probabilistic databases which calculate the truth value of projection as a measure of a union of events (events being all records in R which equal on attributes $X_1, ..., X_h$).

Union. For the case in which there are more rules with the same predicate in the head we have to guarantee that different witnesses to the same conclusion are not lost. In the case of different rules, it means that these witnesses are aggregating together with the lattice join operator. This is determined by our semantics saying the graded statement is true in an interpretation if its truth value is bigger than or equal than the grade given in the syntactical part. Hence they unify wrt the union which calculates the truth value as a lattice join (recall the need of reductants here). Assume $R_1, \ldots, R_n$ are relations with same attributes and $(b_1, \ldots, b_k, \beta_i) \in R_i$ then

$$(b_1, \ldots, b_k, \bigvee\{\beta_1, \ldots, \beta_n\}) \in \bigcup_{i=1}^{n} R_i.$$

Theorem 5. *The operation*

$$\bigcup_{j=1}^{k} \Pi_{X_1, \ldots, X_h} \left(\sigma_{X_h = a_h^j} \left(\cdots \sigma_{X_1 = a_1^j} \left(\bowtie_@ (R_1^j, \ldots, R_{n_j}^j) \right) \cdots \right) \right)$$

is a sound and complete evaluation of the $H(X_1, \ldots, X_h)$ (wrt the satisfaction of our logic) wrt all rules with head H ranging from $j = 1$ to k

$$\langle H(X_1, \ldots, X_h) \longleftarrow X_1 = a_1^j \wedge \ldots \wedge X_h = a_h^j \wedge @(B_1^j, \ldots, B_{n_j}^j), \top \rangle$$

provided $R_1^j, \ldots, R_{n_j}^j$ were evaluations of $B_1^j, \ldots, B_{n_j}^j$.

Now the expressive power of our lattice valued relational algebra is given by the $T_\mathbb{P}$ operator and its fixpoint. The iteration of $T_\mathbb{P}$ is used to prove that the expressive power of lattice Datalog is the same as that of the relational algebra.

So if our declarative and procedural semantics is sound and complete for ground queries, it will be also for queries with free variables. The proof is exactly the same as in the crisp case, namely it suffices for every unbound variable we can extend our language by a new constant which will be evaluated by infimum of all truth values ranging through this variable. This is again a model of our fuzzy theory and the result holds. So our systems allows recursion and the relational algebra calculates it correctly.

Theorem 6. *Every query over the knowledge base represented by a lattice Datalog program (possibly with recursion, without negation) can be evaluated up to any arbitrary accuracy, by iterating described operations of lattice relational algebra.*

Every correct answer to a query is obtained by finite iteration of the $T_\mathbb{P}$ operator with any prescribed precision. This operator evaluates relations in interpretation in a same way as our relational algebra does.

4   Conclusions and Future Work

Our motivation comes from the usage to model some subjective interpretation of human preferences in a granulated way, e.g. by truth value set consisting of intervals. When restricting multi-valued connectives to intervals we observe they need not be neither associative nor commutative. To cover all these phenomena, a general framework of multi-adjoint lattice valued logic programming which allows rather general set of connectives in the bodies (including non-commutative ones) has been introduced.

A procedural semantics for this framework of multi-adjoint biresiduated logic programs has been presented and a quasi-completeness theorem proved. The generality of the framework allows for better expressiveness, as well as a means for handling imprecision in databases. The computational model, especially the corresponding generalization to our lattice-valued case of the $T_{\mathbb{P}}$ operator, is used to construct a positive relational algebra.

In the final section we proved that the expressive power of our relational algebra is the same as that of our Datalog programs (up to some approximation of the best answer and possible iterations).

References

1. K. Ciesielski, R. Flagg, and R. Kopperman. Polish spaces, computable approximations, and bitopological spaces. *Topology and applications*, 119(3):241–256, 2002.
2. C.V. Damásio and L. Moniz Pereira. Monotonic and residuated logic programs. In *Symbolic and Quantitative Approaches to Reasoning with Uncertainty, ECSQARU'01*, pages 748–759. Lect. Notes in Artificial Intelligence, 2143, 2001.
3. A. Dekhtyar and V. S. Subrahmanian. Hybrid probabilistic programs. *J. of Logic Programming*, 43:187–250, 2000.
4. T. Eiter, T. Lukasiewicz, and M. Walter. A data model and algebra for probabilistic complex values. *Annals of Mathematics and Artificial Intelligence*, 33(2–4):205–252, 2001.
5. M. Kifer and V. S. Subrahmanian. Theory of generalized annotated logic programming and its applications. *J. of Logic Programming*, 12:335–367, 1992.
6. S. Krajči, R. Lencses, and P. Vojtáš. A comparison of fuzzy and annotated logic programming. *Fuzzy Sets and Systems*, 2002. Submitted.
7. L.V.S. Lakshmanan and F. Sadri. On a theory of probabilistic deductive databases. *Theory and Practice of Logic Programming*, 1(1):5–42, 2001.
8. J. Medina, M. Ojeda-Aciego, and P. Vojtáš. Multi-adjoint logic programming with continuous semantics. In *Logic Programming and Non-Monotonic Reasoning, LPNMR'01*, pages 351–364. Lect. Notes in Artificial Intelligence 2173, 2001.
9. J. Medina, M. Ojeda-Aciego, and P. Vojtáš. A procedural semantics for multi-adjoint logic programming. In *Progress in Artificial Intelligence, EPIA'01*, pages 290–297. Lect. Notes in Artificial Intelligence 2258, 2001.
10. E. Naito, J. Ozawa, I. Hayashi, and N. Wakami. A proposal of a fuzzy connective with learning function. In P. Bosc and J. Kaczprzyk, editors, *Fuzziness Database Management Systems*, pages 345–364. Physica Verlag, 1995.
11. J. Pokorný and P. Vojtáš. A data model for flexible querying. In *Advances in Databases and Information Systems, ADBIS'01*, pages 280–293. Lect. Notes in Computer Science 2151, 2001.
12. C.J. van Alten. Representable biresiduated lattices. *J. Algebra*, 247:672–691, 2002.
13. P. Vojtáš and L. Paulík. Soundness and completeness of non-classical extended SLD-resolution. In *Extensions of Logic Programming, ELP'96*, pages 289–301. Lect. Notes in Comp. Sci. 1050, 1996.

Using Institutions for the Study of Qualitative and Quantitative Conditional Logics

Christoph Beierle and Gabriele Kern-Isberner

Praktische Informatik VIII - Wissensbasierte Systeme
Fachbereich Informatik, FernUniversität Hagen, D-58084 Hagen, Germany

Abstract. It is well known that conditionals need a non-classical environment to be evaluated. In this paper, we present a formalization of conditional logic in the framework of institutions. In regarding both qualitative and probabilistic conditional logic as abstract logical systems, we investigate how they can be related to one another, on the one hand, and to the institution of propositional logic, on the other hand. In spite of substantial differences between these three logics, we find surprisingly clear formal relationships between them.

1 Introduction

In [6], Goguen and Burstall introduced institutions as a general framework for logical systems. An institution formalizes the informal notion of a logical system, including syntax, semantics, and the relation of satisfaction between them. The latter poses the major requirement for an institution: that the satisfaction relation is consistent under the change of notation. Institutions have also been used as a basis for specification and development languages, see e.g. [2,13,7].

While the examples for institutions in [6] and [7] are based on classical logic, in [1] it is shown that also probabilistic logic can be formalized as an institution. In this paper, we will apply the theory of institutions to conditionals, investigating how the logics of qualitative and probabilistic conditionals fit into that framework. As default rules, conditionals have played a major role in defeasible reasoning (see, e.g., [9]), and assigning probabilities to them opens up a whole universe of possibilities to quantify the (un)certainty of information. It is well-known that conditionals are substantially different from classical logical entities [5]. Nevertheless, we will show that their logic can be formalized as an institution, and thus be compared to classical logical institutions, e.g. that of propositional logic. In detail, we will define an institution of conditional logic, using the semantics of plausibility preorders going back to the works of Lewis [10] and Stalnaker [14], as well as an institution of probabilistic conditionals, using the usual semantics of conditional probabilities.

Now that the logic of conditionals has been given an abstract formal frame, we can also study its relationships to other logics, also being viewed as institutions.

The research reported here was partially supported by the DFG – Deutsche Forschungsgemeinschaft within the CONDOR-project under grant BE 1700/5-1.

S. Flesca et al. (Eds.): JELIA 2002, LNAI 2424, pp. 161–172, 2002.

To do so, the formal tool of *institution morphisms* [6,7] can be used. This will tell us precisely the possibilities how we can interpret e.g. probabilistic conditionals as qualitative conditionals, or in a propositional setting, and vice versa. We will prove that indeed, the institutions of propositional logic, conditional logic and probabilistic conditional logic can be related intuitively, but we will also find that there is essentially exactly one such connection between each pair of these logics. In particular, we will necessarily arrive at a three-valued interpretation of probabilistic conditionals in the propositional framework, reminding us of the three-valued semantics of conditionals [5].

In Sec. 2, we formalize conditional logic as an institution. In Sec. 3, we investigate in detail the relationships between the institutions of conditional logic and of propositional, probabilistic, and probabilistic conditional logic. Section 4 contains some conclusions and points out further work.

2 Institutions and the Logic of Conditionals

After recalling the definition of an institution and fixing some basic notation, we first present propositional logic in the institution framework. We then formalize in three steps probabilistic propositional logic, the logic of probabilistic conditionals, and the logic of (qualitative) conditionals as institutions.

2.1 Preliminaries: Basic Definitions and Notations

If C is a category, $|C|$ denotes the objects of C and $/C/$ its morphisms; for both objects $c \in |C|$ and morphisms $\varphi \in /C/$, we also write just $c \in C$ and $\varphi \in C$, respectively. C^{op} is the opposite category of C, with the direction of all morphisms reversed. The composition of two functors $F : C \to C'$ and $G : C' \to C''$ is denoted by $G \circ F$ (first apply F, then G). For functors $F, G : C \to C'$, a *natural transformation* η from F to G, denoted by $\eta : F \implies G$, assigns to each object $c \in |C|$ a morphism $\eta_c : F(C) \to G(C) \in /C'/$ such that for every morphism $\varphi : c \to d \in /C/$ we have $\eta_d \circ F(\varphi) = G(\varphi) \circ \eta_c$. $\mathcal{SET}$ and $\mathcal{CAT}$ denote the categories of sets and of categories, respectively. (For more information about categories, see e.g. [8] or [11].) The central institution definition is the following:

Definition 1. [6] *An institution is a quadruple Inst* $= \langle Sig, Mod, Sen, \models \rangle$ *with a category Sig of signatures as objects, a functor Mod* : $Sig \to \mathcal{CAT}^{op}$ *yielding the category of Σ-models for each signature Σ, a functor Sen* : $Sig \to \mathcal{SET}$ *yielding the sentences over a signature, and a $|Sig|$-indexed relation $\models_\Sigma \subseteq |Mod(\Sigma)| \times Sen(\Sigma)$ such that for each signature morphism $\varphi : \Sigma \to \Sigma' \in /Sig/$, for each $m' \in |Mod(\Sigma')|$, and for each $f \in Sen(\Sigma)$ the following satisfaction condition holds:* $m' \models_{\Sigma'} Sen(\varphi)(f)$ *iff* $Mod(\varphi)(m') \models_\Sigma f.$

For sets F, G of Σ-sentences and a Σ-model m we write $m \models_\Sigma F$ iff $m \models_\Sigma f$ for all $f \in F$. The satisfaction relation is lifted to semantical entailment $\models_\Sigma$ between sentences by defining $F \models_\Sigma G$ iff for all Σ-models m with $m \models_\Sigma F$ we have $m \models_\Sigma G$. $F^\bullet = \{f \in Sen(\Sigma) \mid F \models_\Sigma f\}$ is called the *closure* of F, and F

is *closed* if $F = F^\bullet$. The closure operator fulfils the *closure lemma* $\varphi(F^\bullet) \subseteq \varphi(F)^\bullet$ and various other nice properties like $\varphi(F^\bullet)^\bullet = \varphi(F)^\bullet$ or $(F^\bullet \cup G)^\bullet = (F \cup G)^\bullet$. A consequence of the closure lemma is that entailment is preserved under change of notation carried out by a signature morphism, i.e. $F \models_\Sigma G$ implies $\varphi(F) \models_{\varphi(\Sigma)} \varphi(G)$ (but not vice versa).

2.2   The Institution of Propositional Logic

In all circumstances, propositional logic seems to be the most basic logic. The components of its institution $Inst_\mathcal{B} = \langle Sig_\mathcal{B}, Mod_\mathcal{B}, Sen_\mathcal{B}, \models_\mathcal{B} \rangle$ will be defined in the following.

Signatures: $Sig_\mathcal{B}$ is the category of propositional signatures. A propositional signature $\Sigma \in |Sig_\mathcal{B}|$ is a (finite) set of propositional variables, $\Sigma = \{a_1, a_2, \ldots\}$. A propositional signature morphism $\varphi : \Sigma \to \Sigma' \in /Sig_\mathcal{B}/$ is a function mapping propositional variables to propositional variables.

Models: For each signature $\Sigma \in Sig_\mathcal{B}$, $Mod_\mathcal{B}(\Sigma)$ contains the set of all propositional interpretations for Σ, i.e. $|Mod_\mathcal{B}(\Sigma)| = \{I \mid I : \Sigma \to Bool\}$ where $Bool = \{true, false\}$. Due to its simple structure, the only morphisms in $Mod_\mathcal{B}(\Sigma)$ are the identity morphisms. For each signature morphism $\varphi : \Sigma \to \Sigma' \in Sig_\mathcal{B}$, we define the morphism (i.e. the functor in $\mathcal{CAT}^{op}$) $Mod_\mathcal{B}(\varphi) : Mod_\mathcal{B}(\Sigma') \to Mod_\mathcal{B}(\Sigma)$ by $(Mod_\mathcal{B}(\varphi)(I'))(a_i) := I'(\varphi(a_i))$ where $I' \in Mod_\mathcal{B}(\Sigma')$ and $a_i \in \Sigma$.

Sentences: For each signature $\Sigma \in Sig_\mathcal{B}$, the set $Sen_\mathcal{B}(\Sigma)$ contains the usual propositional formulas constructed from the propositional variables in Σ and the logical connectives $\wedge$ (and), $\vee$ (or), and $\neg$ (not). Additionally, the classical (material) implication $A \Rightarrow B$ is used as a syntactic variant for $\neg A \vee B$. The symbols $\top$ and $\bot$ denote a tautology (like $a \vee \neg a$) and a contradiction (like $a \wedge \neg a$), respectively.

For each signature morphism $\varphi : \Sigma \to \Sigma' \in Sig_\mathcal{B}$, the function $Sen_\mathcal{B}(\varphi) : Sen_\mathcal{B}(\Sigma) \to Sen_\mathcal{B}(\Sigma')$ is defined by straightforward inductive extension on the structure of the formulas; e.g., $Sen_\mathcal{B}(\varphi)(a_i) = \varphi(a_i)$ and $Sen_\mathcal{B}(\varphi)(A \wedge B) = Sen_\mathcal{B}(\varphi)(A) \wedge Sen_\mathcal{B}(\varphi)(B)$. In the following, we will abbreviate $Sen_\mathcal{B}(\varphi)(A)$ by just writing $\varphi(A)$. In order to simplify notations, we will often replace conjunction by juxtaposition and indicate negation of a formula by barring it, i.e. $AB = A \wedge B$ and $\overline{A} = \neg A$. An *atomic formula* is a formula consisting of just a propositional variable, a *literal* is a positive or a negated atomic formula, an *elementary conjunction* is a conjunction of literals, and a *complete conjunction* is an elementary conjunction where all atomic formulas appear once, either in positive or in negated form. Ω_Σ denotes the set of all complete conjunctions over a signature Σ; if Σ is clear from the context, we may drop the index Σ. Note that there is an obvious bijection between $|Mod_\mathcal{B}(\Sigma)|$ and Ω_Σ, associating with $I \in |Mod_\mathcal{B}(\Sigma)|$ the complete conjunction $\omega_I \in \Omega_\Sigma$ in which an atomic formula $a_i \in \Sigma$ occurs in positive form iff $I(a_i) = true$.

Satisfaction relation: For any $\Sigma \in |Sig_\mathcal{B}|$, the satisfaction relation $\models_{\mathcal{B},\Sigma} \subseteq |Mod_\mathcal{B}(\Sigma)| \times Sen_\mathcal{B}(\Sigma)$ is defined as expected for propositional logic, e.g.

$I \models_{\mathcal{B},\Sigma} a_i$ iff $I(a_i) = true$ and $I \models_{\mathcal{B},\Sigma} A \wedge B$ iff $I \models_{\mathcal{B},\Sigma} A$ and $I \models_{\mathcal{B},\Sigma} B$ for $a_i \in \Sigma$ and $A, B \in Sen_{\mathcal{B}}(\Sigma)$.

Proposition 1. $Inst_{\mathcal{B}} = \langle\, Sig_{\mathcal{B}}, \, Mod_{\mathcal{B}}, \, Sen_{\mathcal{B}}, \, \models_{\mathcal{B}} \,\rangle$ *is an institution.*

Example 1. Let $\Sigma = \{s, t, u\}$ and $\Sigma' = \{a, b, c\}$ be two propositional signatures with the atomic propositions s – *being a scholar*, t – *being not married*, u – *being single* and a – *being a student*, b – *being young*, c – *being unmarried*. Let I' be the Σ'-model with $I'(a) = true$, $I'(b) = true$, $I'(c) = false$. Let $\varphi : \Sigma \rightarrow \Sigma' \in Sig_{\mathcal{B}}$ be the signature morphism with $\varphi(s) = a$, $\varphi(t) = c$, $\varphi(u) = c$. The functor $Mod_{\mathcal{B}}(\varphi)$ takes I' to the Σ-model $I := Mod_{\mathcal{B}}(\varphi)(I')$, yielding $I(s) = I'(a) = true$, $I(t) = I'(c) = false$, $I(u) = I'(c) = false$.

2.3 The Institution of Probabilistic Propositional Logic

Based on $Inst_{\mathcal{B}}$, we can now define the institution of probabilistic propositional logic $Inst_{\mathcal{P}} = \langle\, Sig_{\mathcal{P}}, \, Mod_{\mathcal{P}}, \, Sen_{\mathcal{P}}, \, \models_{\mathcal{P}} \,\rangle$. We will first give a very short introduction to probabilistics as far as it is needed here.

Let $\Sigma \in |Sig_{\mathcal{B}}|$ be a propositional signature. A *probability distribution* (or *probability function*) *over* Σ is a function $P : Sen_{\mathcal{B}}(\Sigma) \rightarrow [0, 1]$ such that $P(\top) = 1$, $P(\bot) = 0$, and $P(A \vee B) = P(A) + P(B)$ for any formulas $A, B \in Sen_{\mathcal{B}}(\Sigma)$ with $AB = \bot$. Each probability distribution P is determined uniquely by its values on the complete conjunctions $\omega \in \Omega_{\Sigma}$, since $P(A) = \sum\limits_{\omega \in \Omega_{\Sigma}, \omega \models_{\mathcal{B},\Sigma} A} P(\omega)$.
For two propositional formulas $A, B \in Sen_{\mathcal{B}}(\Sigma)$ with $P(A) > 0$, the *conditional probability of B given A*, denoted by $P(B|A)$, is $\dfrac{P(AB)}{P(A)}$. Any subset $\Sigma_1 \subseteq \Sigma$ gives rise to a distribution $P_{\Sigma_1} : Sen_{\mathcal{B}}(\Sigma_1) \rightarrow [0, 1]$ by virtue of defining $P_{\Sigma_1}(\omega_1) = \sum\limits_{\omega \in \Omega_{\Sigma}, \omega \models_{\mathcal{B},\Sigma} \omega_1} P(\omega)$ for all $\omega_1 \in \Omega_{\Sigma_1}$; P_{Σ_1} is called the *marginal distribution of P on* Σ_1.

Signatures: $Sig_{\mathcal{P}}$ is identical to the category of propositional signatures, i.e. $Sig_{\mathcal{P}} = Sig_{\mathcal{B}}$.

Models: For each signature Σ, the objects of $Mod_{\mathcal{P}}(\Sigma)$ are probability distributions over the propositional variables, i.e.

$$|Mod_{\mathcal{P}}(\Sigma)| = \{P \mid P \text{ is a probability distribution over } \Sigma\}$$

As for $Mod_{\mathcal{B}}(\Sigma)$, we assume in this paper that the only morphisms in $Mod_{\mathcal{P}}(\Sigma)$ are the identity morphisms.

For each signature morphism $\varphi : \Sigma \rightarrow \Sigma'$, we define a functor $Mod_{\mathcal{P}}(\varphi) : Mod_{\mathcal{P}}(\Sigma') \rightarrow Mod_{\mathcal{P}}(\Sigma)$ by mapping each distribution P' over Σ' to a distribution $Mod_{\mathcal{P}}(\varphi)(P')$ over Σ. $Mod_{\mathcal{P}}(\varphi)(P')$ is defined by giving its value for all complete conjunctions over Σ:

$$(Mod_{\mathcal{P}}(\varphi)(P'))(\omega) := P'(\varphi(\omega)) = \sum\limits_{\omega' \models_{\mathcal{B},\Sigma'} \varphi(\omega)} P'(\omega')$$

where ω and ω' are complete conjunctions over Σ and Σ', respectively.

Sentences: For each signature Σ, the set $Sen_P(\Sigma)$ contains *probabilistic facts* of the form $A[x]$ where $A \in Sen_B(\Sigma)$ is a propositional formula from $Inst_B$. $x \in [0,1]$ is a probability value indicating the degree of certainty for the occurrence of A.

For each signature morphism $\varphi : \Sigma \to \Sigma'$, the extension $Sen_P(\varphi) : Sen_P(\Sigma) \to Sen_P(\Sigma')$ is defined by $Sen_P(\varphi)(A[x]) = \varphi(A)[x]$.

Satisfaction relation: The satisfaction relation $\models_{P,\Sigma} \subseteq |Mod_P(\Sigma)| \times Sen_P(\Sigma)$ is defined, for any $\Sigma \in |Sig_P|$, by

$$P \models_{P,\Sigma} A[x] \quad \text{iff} \quad P(A) = x$$

Note that, since $P(\overline{A}) = 1 - P(A)$ for each formula $A \in Sen_B(\Sigma)$, it holds that $P \models_{P,\Sigma} A[x]$ iff $P \models_{P,\Sigma} \overline{A}[1-x]$.

Proposition 2. $Inst_P = \langle Sig_P, Mod_P, Sen_P, \models_P \rangle$ *is an institution.*

2.4   The Institution of Probabilistic Conditional Logic

We now use $Inst_P$ to define the institution of probabilistic conditionals $Inst_C = \langle Sig_C, Mod_C, Sen_C, \models_C \rangle$.

Signatures: Sig_C is identical to the category of propositional signatures, i.e. $Sig_C = Sig_P = Sig_B$.

Models: The models for probabilistic conditional logic are again probability distributions over the propositional variables. Therefore, the model functor can be taken directly from probabilistic propositional logic, giving us $Mod_C = Mod_P$.

Sentences: For each signature Σ, the set $Sen_C(\Sigma)$ contains *probabilistic conditionals* (sometimes also called *probabilistic rules*) of the form $(B|A)[x]$ where $A, B \in Sen_B(\Sigma)$ are propositional formulas from $Inst_B$. $x \in [0,1]$ is a probability value indicating the degree of certainty for the occurrence of B under the condition A. – Note that the sentences from $Inst_P$ are included implicitly since a probabilistic fact of the form $B[x]$ can easily be expressed as a conditional $(B|\top)[x]$ with a tautology as trivial antecedent.

For each signature morphism $\varphi : \Sigma \to \Sigma'$, the extension $Sen_C(\varphi) : Sen_C(\Sigma) \to Sen_C(\Sigma')$ is defined by straightforward inductive extension on the structure of the formulas: $Sen_C(\varphi)((B|A)[x]) = (\varphi(B)|\varphi(A))[x]$.

Satisfaction relation: The satisfaction relation $\models_{C,\Sigma} \subseteq |Mod_C(\Sigma)| \times Sen_C(\Sigma)$ is defined, for any $\Sigma \in |Sig_C|$, by

$$P \models_{C,\Sigma} (B|A)[x] \quad \text{iff} \quad P(A) > 0 \text{ and } P(B \mid A) = \frac{P(AB)}{P(A)} = x$$

Note that for probabilistic facts we have $P \models_{C,\Sigma} (B|\top)[x]$ iff $P(B) = x$ from the definition of the satisfaction relation since $P(\top) = 1$. Thus, $P \models_{P,\Sigma} B[x]$ iff $P \models_{C,\Sigma} (B|\top)[x]$.

Proposition 3. $Inst_C = \langle Sig_C, Mod_C, Sen_C, \models_C \rangle$ *is an institution.*

2.5   The Institution of Conditional Logic

The institution of conditional logic is $Inst_{\mathcal{K}} = \langle Sig_{\mathcal{K}}, Mod_{\mathcal{K}}, Sen_{\mathcal{K}}, \models_{\mathcal{K}} \rangle$ with:

Signatures: $Sig_{\mathcal{K}}$ is again identical to the category of propositional signatures, i.e. $Sig_{\mathcal{K}} = Sig_{\mathcal{C}} = Sig_{\mathcal{P}} = Sig_{\mathcal{B}}$.

Models: Various types of models have been proposed to interpret conditionals adequately within a formal system (cf. e.g. [12]). Many of them are based on considering possible worlds which can be thought of as being represented by classical logical interpretations $|Mod_{\mathcal{B}}(\Sigma)|$, or complete conjunctions $\omega \in \Omega$ (as defined in Sec. 2.2), respectively. One of the most prominent approaches is the *system-of-spheres* model of Lewis [10] which makes use of a notion of similarity between possible worlds. This idea of comparing worlds and evaluating conditionals with respect to the "nearest" or "best" worlds (which are somehow selected) is common to very many approaches in conditional logics. So, in order to base our conditional logic on quite a general semantics, we take the models to be total preorders over classical propositional interpretations, i.e.

$$|Mod_{\mathcal{K}}(\Sigma)| = \{R \mid R \text{ is a total preorder on } |Mod_{\mathcal{B}}(\Sigma)|\}$$

where a total preorder R is a reflexive and transitive relation such that for any two elements I_1, I_2, we have $(I_1, I_2) \in R$ or $(I_2, I_1) \in R$ (possibly both).

By identifying $Mod_{\mathcal{B}}(\Sigma)$ with the set of possible worlds Ω, we will consider the models $R \in Mod_{\mathcal{K}}(\Sigma)$ to be total preorders on Ω, ordering the possible worlds according to their *plausibility*. By convention, the least worlds are the most plausible worlds. We will also use the infix notation $\omega_1 \preceq_R \omega_2$ instead of $(\omega_1, \omega_2) \in R$. As usual, we introduce the $\prec_R$-relation by saying that $\omega_1 \prec_R \omega_2$ iff $\omega_1 \preceq_R \omega_2$ and not $\omega_2 \preceq_R \omega_1$. Furthermore, $\omega_1 \approx_R \omega_2$ means that both $\omega_1 \preceq_R \omega_2$ and $\omega_2 \preceq_R \omega_1$ hold.

Each $R \in Mod_{\mathcal{K}}(\Sigma)$ induces a partitioning $\Omega_0, \Omega_1, \ldots$ of Ω, such that all worlds in the same partitioning subset are considered equally plausible ($\omega_1 \approx_R \omega_2$ for $\omega_1, \omega_2 \in \Omega_j$), and whenever $\omega_1 \in \Omega_i$ and $\omega_2 \in \Omega_k$ with $i < k$, then $\omega_1 \prec_R \omega_2$. Let $Min(R)$ denote the set of R-minimal worlds in Ω, i.e.

$$Min(R) = \Omega_0 = \{\omega_0 \in \Omega \mid \omega_0 \preceq_R \omega \text{ for all } \omega \in \Omega\}$$

Each $R \in Mod_{\mathcal{K}}(\Sigma)$ induces a total preorder on $Sen_{\mathcal{B}}(\Sigma)$ by setting

$$A \preceq_R B \quad \text{iff} \quad \text{for all } \omega_2 \in \Omega \text{ with } \omega_2 \models_{\mathcal{B},\Sigma} B$$
$$\text{there exists } \omega_1 \in \Omega \text{ with } \omega_1 \models_{\mathcal{B},\Sigma} A \text{ such that } \omega_1 \preceq_R \omega_2$$

So, A is considered to be at least as plausible as B (with respect to R) iff the most plausible worlds satisfying A are at least as plausible as any world satisfying B. In particular, if $B \models_{\mathcal{B},\Sigma} A$, then $A \preceq_R B$ for each $R \in Mod_{\mathcal{K}}(\Sigma)$, since $\omega \models_{\mathcal{B},\Sigma} B$ implies $\omega \models_{\mathcal{B},\Sigma} A$. Again, $A \prec_R B$ means both $A \preceq_R B$ and not $B \preceq_R A$. Note that $A \prec_R \bot$ for all $A \not\equiv \bot$.

As before, we only consider the identity morphisms in $Mod_{\mathcal{K}}(\Sigma)$ for this paper.

For each signature morphism $\varphi : \Sigma \to \Sigma'$, we define a functor $Mod_K(\varphi) :$ $Mod_K(\Sigma') \to Mod_K(\Sigma)$ by mapping a (total) preorder R' over $Mod_B(\Sigma')$ to a (total) preorder $Mod_K(\varphi)(R')$ over $Mod_B(\Sigma)$ in the following way:

$$\omega_1 \preceq_{Mod_K(\varphi)(R')} \omega_2 \quad \text{iff} \quad \varphi(\omega_1) \preceq_{R'} \varphi(\omega_2) \tag{1}$$

Note that on the left hand side of (1) the complete conjunctions ω_1 and ω_2 are viewed as models in $Mod_B(\Sigma)$, whereas on the right hand side they are sentences in $Sen_B(\Sigma)$.

It is straightforward to check that $Mod_K(\varphi)(R')$ is a total preorder (the corresponding properties are all directly inherited by R'), so indeed $Mod_K(\varphi)(R') \in Mod_K(\Sigma)$. The connection between R' and $Mod_K(\varphi)(R')$ defined by (1) can also be shown to hold for propositional sentences instead of worlds:

Lemma 1. *Let $A, B \in Sen_B(\Sigma)$. Then $A \preceq_{Mod_K(\varphi)(R')} B$ iff $\varphi(A) \preceq_{R'} \varphi(B)$.*

Corollary 1. *Let $A, B \in Sen_B(\Sigma)$. Then $A \prec_{Mod_K(\varphi)(R')} B$ iff $\varphi(A) \prec_{R'} \varphi(B)$.*

Sentences: For each signature Σ, the set $Sen_K(\Sigma)$ contains (propositional) *conditionals* of the form $(B|A)$ where $A, B \in Sen_B(\Sigma)$ are propositional formulas from $Inst_B$. For $\varphi : \Sigma \to \Sigma'$, the extension $Sen_K(\varphi)$ is defined as usual by $Sen_K(\varphi)((B|A)) = (\varphi(B)|\varphi(A))$.

Satisfaction relation: The satisfaction relation $\models_{K,\Sigma} \subseteq |Mod_K(\Sigma)| \times Sen_K(\Sigma)$ is defined, for any $\Sigma \in |Sig_K|$, by

$$R \models_{K,\Sigma} (B|A) \quad \text{iff} \quad AB \prec_R A\overline{B}$$

Therefore, a conditional $(B|A)$ is satisfied (or accepted) by the plausibility preorder R iff its confirmation AB is more plausible than its refutation $A\overline{B}$.

Proposition 4. *$Inst_K = \langle Sig_K, Mod_K, Sen_K, \models_K \rangle$ is an institution.*

Example 2. We continue our student-example in this qualitative conditional environment, so let Σ, Σ', φ be as defined in Example 1. Let R' be the following total preorder on Ω':

$$R' : \quad \overline{abc} \prec_{R'} abc \approx_{R'} \overline{a}bc \prec_{R'} ab\overline{c} \approx_{R'} a\overline{b}c \approx_{R'} a\overline{b}\overline{c} \approx_{R'} \overline{a}b\overline{c} \approx_{R'} \overline{a}\overline{b}c$$

Now, for instance $R' \models_{K,\Sigma'} (a|\top)$ since $\top\overline{a} \equiv \overline{a}$, $\top\overline{\overline{a}} \equiv a$, and $\overline{a} \prec_{R'} a$. Thus, under R', it is more plausible to be not a student than to be a student. Furthermore, $R' \models_{K,\Sigma'} (c|a)$ – *students* are supposed to be *unmarried* since under R', ac is more plausible than $a\overline{c}$.

Under $Mod_K(\varphi)$, R' is mapped onto $R = Mod_K(\varphi)(R')$ where R is the following total preorder on Ω:

$$R : \quad \overline{s}t\overline{u} \prec_R \overline{s}tu \approx_R stu \prec_R s\overline{t}\overline{u} \prec_R st\overline{u} \approx_R s\overline{t}u \approx_R \overline{s}t\overline{u} \approx_R \overline{s}\overline{t}u$$

As expected, the conditionals $(t|s)$ and $(u|s)$, both corresponding to $(c|a)$ in $Sen_K(\Sigma')$ under φ, are satisfied by R – here, *scholars* are supposed to be both *not married* and *single*.

3   Relating Conditional Logic to Other Logics

Having stepwise developed conditional logic, we now turn to study its interrelationships to the other logics. For instance, there is an obvious translation of sentences mapping A to $(A|\top)$ and mapping $(A|B)$ to $(A|B)[1]$. Furthermore, there is a similar obvious transformation of a propositional interpretation I to a conditional logic model viewing I to be more plausible than any other interpretation, which in turn are considered to be all equally plausible. What happens to satisfaction and entailment when using such translations? In order to make these questions more precise, we use the notion of institution morphisms introduced in [6] (see also [7]).

An institution morphism Φ expresses a relation between two institutions $Inst$ und $Inst'$ such that the satisfaction condition of $Inst$ may be computed by the satisfaction condition of $Inst'$ if we translate it according to Φ. The translation is done by relating every $Inst$-signature Σ to an $Inst'$-signature Σ', each Σ'-sentence to a Σ-sentence, and each Σ-model to a Σ'-model.

Definition 2. [6] *Let* $Inst = \langle Sig, Mod, Sen, \models \rangle$ *and* $Inst' = \langle Sig', Mod', Sen', \models' \rangle$ *be two institutions. An* institution morphism Φ *from* $Inst$ *to* $Inst'$ *is a triple* $\langle \phi, \alpha, \beta \rangle$ *with a functor* $\phi : Sig \to Sig'$, *a natural transformation* $\alpha : Sen' \circ \phi \implies Sen$, *and a natural transformation* $\beta : Mod \implies Mod' \circ \phi$ *such that for each* $\Sigma \in |Sig|$, *for each* $m \in |Mod(\Sigma)|$, *and for each* $f' \in Sen'(\phi(\Sigma))$ *the following* satisfaction condition (for institution morphisms) *holds:* $m \models_\Sigma \alpha_\Sigma(f')$ *iff* $\beta_\Sigma(m) \models'_{\phi(\Sigma)} f'$.

Since $Inst_B$, $Inst_P$, $Inst_C$, and $Inst_K$ all have the same category Sig_B of signatures, a natural choice for the signature translation component ϕ in any morphism between these institutions is the identity id_{Sig_B} which we will use in the following.

3.1   Relating Propositional and Conditional Logic

The sentences of $Inst_B$ and $Inst_K$ can be related in an intuitive way by sending a propositional formula A to the conditional $(A|\top)$ having the trivial antecedent $\top$. It is easy to check that this translation yields a natural transformations

$$\alpha_{B/K} : Sen_B \implies Sen_K \qquad \alpha_{B/K,\Sigma}(A) = (A|\top)$$

Similarly, there is also an intuitive way of mapping a propositional model I to a conditional logic model (which we will denote by R_I). This model R_I views I to be more plausible than any other world, and all other worlds are looked upon as equally plausible. With ω_I denoting the unique complete conjunction with $I \models_{B,\Sigma} \omega_I$, the preorder R_I thus partitions Ω into the two sets $\{\omega_I\}$ and $\Omega \setminus \{\omega_I\}$. Therfore, $\omega_I \prec_{R_I} \omega$ for all $\omega \neq \omega_I$. Formally, R_I is defined by

$$\omega_1 \preceq_{R_I} \omega_2 \quad \text{iff} \quad I \models_{B,\Sigma} \omega_1 \text{ or } (I \not\models_{B,\Sigma} \omega_1 \text{ and } I \not\models_{B,\Sigma} \omega_2)$$

It is straightforward to check that this yields a natural transfromation

$$\beta_{B/K} : Mod_B \implies Mod_K \qquad \beta_{B/K,\Sigma}(I) = R_I$$

Having identified obvious standard translations for sentences and models from $Inst_B$ to $Inst_K$, the next question is how to use them in relations between these two institutions. As intuitive as the sentence translation $\alpha_{B/K}$ appears, the next proposition shows that it can not be used to define an institution morphism from $Inst_K$ to $Inst_B$:

Proposition 5. *There is no β such that $\langle id_{Sig_B}, \alpha_{B/K}, \beta \rangle : Inst_K \longrightarrow Inst_B$ is an institution morphism.*

When going in the other direction from $Inst_B$ to $Inst_K$ using the model translation $\beta_{B/K} : Mod_B \Longrightarrow Mod_K$, we must map conditionals to propositional formulas. A possible choice is to map $(B|A)$ to the formula AB confirming the conditional, thereby yielding the natural transformation

$$\alpha_{K/B} : Sen_K \Longrightarrow Sen_B \quad \text{with} \quad \alpha_{K/B,\Sigma}((B|A)) = AB$$

The next proposition shows that $\beta_{B/K}$ gives rise to exactly one institution morphism from $Inst_B$ to $Inst_K$, namely the one using $\alpha_{K/B}$ for sentence translation:

Proposition 6. $\langle id_{Sig_B}, \alpha, \beta_{B/K} \rangle : Inst_B \longrightarrow Inst_K$ *is an institution morphism iff $\alpha = \alpha_{K/B}$.*

3.2 Relating Conditional and Probabilistic Conditional Logic

It is quite straightforward to relate the sentences of $Inst_K$ and $Inst_C$ by sending a conditional to a probabilistic conditional with trivial probability 1, yielding the natural transformation

$$\alpha_{K/C} : Sen_K \Longrightarrow Sen_C \quad \text{with} \quad \alpha_{K/C,\Sigma}((B|A)) = (B|A)[1]$$

Relating the models of $Inst_K$ and $Inst_C$, however, is far less obvious. Many different ways can be devised to map preorders and probability distributions to one another. As a minimal requirement, we would certainly expect the preorder to be compatible with the ordering induced by the probabilities. As a first approach, we define a mapping sending a probability distribution P to a conditional logic model R_P. Under R_P, all complete conjunctions with a positive probability are considered most plausible, and all complete conjunctions with zero probability are taken as less (yet equally) plausible. Thus, R_P partitions Ω into two sets, namely $Min(R_P) = \{\omega \in \Omega \mid P(\omega) > 0\}$ and $\{\omega \in \Omega \mid P(\omega) = 0\}$. Formally, R_P is defined by

$$\omega_1 \preceq_{R_P} \omega_2 \quad \text{iff} \quad P(\omega_2) = 0 \text{ or } (P(\omega_1) > 0 \text{ and } P(\omega_2) > 0)$$

and it is easy to check that this yields a natural transformation

$$\beta_{C/K} : Mod_C \Longrightarrow Mod_K \quad \text{with} \quad \beta_{C/K,\Sigma}(P) = R_P$$

The next proposition shows that this indeed gives rise to an institution morphism from $Inst_C$ to $Inst_K$ which involves $\alpha_{K/C}$.

Proposition 7. $\langle id_{Sig_B}, \alpha_{K/C}, \beta_{C/K} \rangle : Inst_C \longrightarrow Inst_K$ *is an institution morphism.*

What other possibilities are there to generate a preorder from a probability distribution so that the intuitive sentence translation $\alpha_{\mathcal{K}/\mathcal{C}}$ yields an institution morphism? Although the preordering concept would allow a rather fine-grained hierarchy of plausibilities, it is surprising to see that the somewhat simplistic two-level approach of R_P is the *only* possibility to augment $\alpha_{\mathcal{K}/\mathcal{C}}$ towards an institution morphism.

Proposition 8. *If* $\langle id_{Sig_{\mathcal{B}}}, \alpha_{\mathcal{K}/\mathcal{C}}, \beta \rangle : Inst_{\mathcal{C}} \longrightarrow Inst_{\mathcal{K}}$ *is an institution morphism then* $\beta = \beta_{\mathcal{C}/\mathcal{K}}$.

Going in the other direction, i.e. from $Inst_{\mathcal{K}}$ to $Inst_{\mathcal{C}}$, we have to transform probabilistic conditionals into qualitative conditionals by a natural transformation $\alpha : Sen_{\mathcal{C}} \Longrightarrow Sen_{\mathcal{K}}$. We might anticipate problems in handling properly non-trivial probabilities, but we would certainly expect that $\alpha_{\Sigma}((B|A)[1]) = (B|A)$. The next proposition, however, shows even this to be impossible.

Proposition 9. *There is no institution morphism* $\langle id_{Sig_{\mathcal{B}}}, \alpha, \beta \rangle : Inst_{\mathcal{K}} \longrightarrow Inst_{\mathcal{C}}$ *such that* $\alpha_{\Sigma}((B|A)[1]) = (B|A)$ *for all signatures* Σ.

3.3   Relating Propositional and Probabilistic Conditional Logic

What is the situation between propositional logic $Inst_{\mathcal{B}}$ and probabilistic conditional logic $Inst_{\mathcal{C}}$? Here, the obvious standard translations are

$$\alpha_{\mathcal{B}/\mathcal{C}} : Sen_{\mathcal{B}} \Longrightarrow Sen_{\mathcal{C}} \qquad \alpha_{\mathcal{B}/\mathcal{C},\Sigma}(A) = (A|\top)[1]$$

$$\beta_{\mathcal{B}/\mathcal{C}} : Mod_{\mathcal{B}} \Longrightarrow Mod_{\mathcal{C}} \qquad \beta_{\mathcal{B}/\mathcal{C},\Sigma}(I) = P_I \qquad P_I(\omega) = \begin{cases} 1 & \text{if } I(\omega) = true \\ 0 & \text{otherwise} \end{cases}$$

In [1] it is shown that no institution morphism using the sentence translation $\alpha_{\mathcal{B}/\mathcal{C}}$ exists. When going from propositional logic to probabilistic conditional logic using the model translation $\beta_{\mathcal{B}/\mathcal{C}}$, we have to map probabilistic conditionals to propositional sentences. However, possibly a little surpising at first sight, all probabilistic conditionals with probabilities other than 0 and 1 must be viewed as contradictory propositions.

Proposition 10. *If* $\langle id_{Sig_{\mathcal{B}}}, \alpha, \beta_{\mathcal{B}/\mathcal{C}} \rangle : Inst_{\mathcal{B}} \longrightarrow Inst_{\mathcal{C}}$ *is an institution morphism, then for any* $\Sigma \in Sig_{\mathcal{B}}$, α_{Σ} *maps every sentence* $(B|A)[x]$ *with* $x \neq 0$ *and* $x \neq 1$ *to* $\bot$.

The only choices left for the translation of probabilistic conditionals is thus the translation of conditionals with the trivial probabilities 1 and 0. Although $(B|A)[1]$ represents a conditional *if A then B with probability 1*, we can not map it to the classical (material) implication $A \Rightarrow B$ (see [1]). By taking the antecedent as a context into account, we map $(B|A)[1]$ to $A \wedge (A \Rightarrow B)$, or equivalently, to AB. $(B|A)[0]$ is mapped to $\neg(A \Rightarrow B)$, or equivalently, to $A\overline{B}$, since $A \wedge \neg(A \Rightarrow B) = \neg(A \Rightarrow B)$. This yields the natural tranformation

$$\alpha_{\mathcal{C}/\mathcal{B}} : Sen_{\mathcal{C}} \Longrightarrow Sen_{\mathcal{B}} \qquad \text{with} \qquad \alpha_{\mathcal{C}/\mathcal{B},\Sigma}((B|A)[x]) = \begin{cases} AB & \text{if } x = 1 \\ A\overline{B} & \text{if } x = 0 \\ \bot & \text{otherwise} \end{cases}$$

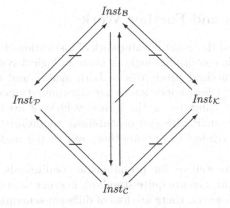

Morphism	Sentence translation		Model translation
$Inst_B \longrightarrow Inst_P$	$A[x]$	$\mapsto \begin{cases} A & \text{if } x = 1 \\ \overline{A} & \text{if } x = 0 \\ \bot & \text{otherwise} \end{cases}$	$I \mapsto P_I$
$Inst_C \longrightarrow Inst_P$	$A[x]$	$\mapsto (A|\top)[x]$	$P \mapsto P$
$Inst_B \longrightarrow Inst_C$	$(B|A)[x]$	$\mapsto \begin{cases} AB & \text{if } x = 1 \\ A\overline{B} & \text{if } x = 0 \\ \bot & \text{otherwise} \end{cases}$	$I \mapsto P_I$
$Inst_B \longrightarrow Inst_K$	$(B|A)$	$\mapsto AB$	$I \mapsto R_I$
$Inst_C \longrightarrow Inst_K$	$(B|A)$	$\mapsto (B|A)[1]$	$P \mapsto R_P$

Fig. 1. Institution morphisms between $Inst_B$, $Inst_P$, $Inst_C$, and $Inst_K$

Proposition 11. $\langle id_{Sig_B}, \alpha_{C/B}, \beta_{B/C} \rangle : Inst_B \longrightarrow Inst_C$ *is an institution morphism.*

Note that $\alpha_{C/B,\Sigma}$ reflects the three-valued semantics of conditionals, identifying the verifying part AB and the falsifying part $A\overline{B}$ as most important components of conditional information (cf. [4,3]).

Figure 1 summarizes our findings with respect to institution morphisms between the four institutions, where the relationships involving $Inst_P$ are investigated in [1]. Using the intuitive standard translations, we have (essentially) exactly one institution morphism between any pair of the four institutions connected by arrows in Figure 1, but none going in the respective opposite direction. Moreover, the diagram is a commuting one; for instance, $\alpha_{K/B}$ is the (vertical) composition of the standard sentence translations $\alpha_{K/C}$ and $\alpha_{C/B}$, sending $(B|A)$ first to $(B|A)[1]$ and then to AB. Correspondingly, $\beta_{B/K}$ is the composition of the standard model translations $\beta_{B/P}$ and $\beta_{C/K}$, sending I first to P_I and then to R_I.

4   Conclusions and Further Work

In this paper, we used the general framework of institutions to formalize qualitative and probabilistic conditional logic as abstract logical systems. This allowed us to study the structural properties of both syntax and semantics of these logics, telling us, e.g., how conditionals are interpreted under change of notation. Moreover, in making use of the formal vehicle of institution morphisms, we investigated how qualitative and probabilistic conditionals and their respective models can be related to one another, and to the underlying two-valued propositional logic.

For qualitative as well as for probabilistic conditionals, the semantics we based our considerations on are quite standard, in order to make our results most widely applicable. However, there are lots of different semantics for conditionals, and it is an interesting question whether other semantics can yield different relationships between the involved logics. This is a topic of our ongoing research.

References

1. C. Beierle and G. Kern-Isberner. Looking at probabilistic conditionals from an institutional point of view. In *Proceedings of the Workshop Conditionals, Information, and Inference*. Hagen, 2002.
2. R. Burstall and J. Goguen. The semantics of Clear, a specification language. In *Proceedings of the 1979 Copenhagen Winterschool on Abstract Software Specification*, volume 86 of *LNCS*, pages 292–332, Berlin, 1980. Springer-Verlag.
3. P. Calabrese. Deduction and inference using conditional logic and probability. In I. Goodman, M. Gupta, H. Nguyen, and G. Rogers, editors, *Conditional Logic in Expert Systems*, pages 71–100. Elsevier, North Holland, 1991.
4. B. DeFinetti. *Theory of Probability*, volume 1,2. John Wiley and Sons, New York, 1974.
5. D. Dubois and H. Prade. Conditioning, non-monotonic logic and non-standard uncertainty models. In I. Goodman, M. Gupta, H. Nguyen, and G. Rogers, editors, *Conditional Logic in Expert Systems*, pages 115–158. Elsevier, North Holland, 1991.
6. J. Goguen and R. Burstall. Institutions: Abstract model theory for specification and programming. *Journal of the ACM*, 39(1):95–146, January 1992.
7. J. A. Goguen and G. Rosu. Institution morphisms. In D. Sannella, editor, *Festschrift for Rod Burstall*. 2002. (to appear).
8. H. Herrlich and G. E. Strecker. *Category theory*. Allyn and Bacon, Boston, 1973.
9. G. Kern-Isberner. *Conditionals in nonmonotonic reasoning and belief revision*. Springer, Lecture Notes in Artificial Intelligence LNAI 2087, 2001.
10. D. Lewis. *Counterfactuals*. Harvard University Press, Cambridge, Mass., 1973.
11. S. Mac Lane. *Categories for the Working Mathematician*. Springer-Verlag, New York, 1972.
12. D. Nute. *Topics in Conditional Logic*. D. Reidel Publishing Company, Dordrecht, Holland, 1980.
13. D. Sannella and A. Tarlecki. Essential comcepts for algebraic specification and program development. *Formal Aspects of Computing*, 9:229–269, 1997.
14. R. Stalnaker. A theory of conditionals. In N. Rescher, editor, *Studies in Logical Theory*. American Philosphical Quarterly Monograph Series, No. 2, Blackwell, Oxford, 1968.

Theoretical and Empirical Aspects of a Planner in a Multi-agent Environment

Jürgen Dix[1], Hector Munoz-Avila[2], Dana Nau[3], and Lingling Zhang[3]

[1] The University of Manchester
Dept. of CS, Oxford Road
Manchester M13 9PL, UK
dix@cs.man.ac.uk

[2] University of Lehigh
Dept. of CS, 19 Memorial Drive West
Bethlehem, PA 18015, USA
munoz@cse.lehigh.edu

[3] University of Maryland
Dept. of CS, A.V. Williams Building
College Park, MD 20752, USA
{nau,lzhang}@cs.umd.edu

Abstract. We give the theoretical foundations and empirical evaluation of a planning agent, ashop, performing *HTN* planning in a multi-agent environment. ashop is based on *ASHOP*, an agentised version of the original *SHOP HTN* planning algorithm, and is integrated in the *IM-PACT* multi-agent environment. We ran several experiments involving accessing various distributed, heterogeneous information sources, based on simplified versions of noncombatant evacuation operations, NEO's. As a result, we noticed that in such realistic settings the time spent on communication (including network time) is orders of magnitude higher than the actual inference process. This has important consequences for optimisations of such planners. Our main results are: (1) using NEO's as new, more realistic benchmarks for planners acting in an agent environment, and (2) a memoization mechanism implemented on top of shop, which improves the overall performance considerably.

Keywords: planning, multi agent systems

1 Introduction

Planning a course of actions is difficult, especially for large military organisations (e.g., the U.S. Navy) that have their available assets distributed world-wide. Formulating a plan in this context requires accessing remote, heterogeneous information sources. For example, when planning for a *Noncombatant evacuation operation*, denoted by NEO, military commanders must access several information sources including: assets available in the zone of operations, intelligence assessment about potential hostiles, weather conditions and so forth.

ASHOP is an *HTN* planning algorithm for planning in a multi-agent environment. *ASHOP* can interact with external information sources,

S. Flesca et al. (Eds.): JELIA 2002, LNAI 2424, pp. 173–185, 2002.
© Springer-Verlag Berlin Heidelberg 2002

frequently heterogeneous and not necessarily centralised, via the *IM-PACT* multi-agent environment. The *IMPACT* project (see [1,2] and |http://www.cs.umd.edu/projects/impact/—) aims at developing a powerful and flexible, yet easy to handle framework for the interoperability of distributed heterogeneous sources of information.

In previous work we described the definition of the *ASHOP* planning algorithm, an agentised version of *SHOP* that runs in the *IMPACT* environment and formulated the conditions needed for *ASHOP* to be sound and complete [3].

In this paper we will focus on the actual implementation of *ASHOP* following the principles stated in our previous work and experiments we did on a transportation domain for NEO operations. Our analysis of the initial runs of *ASHOP* revealed that most of the running time was spent on communication between the *IMPACT* agents and accessing the information sources. Compared to that, the actual inferencing time in *ASHOP* was very small. Furthermore, we observed that frequently the same *IMPACT* query was performed several times. To solve this problem we implemented a memoization mechanism to avoid repeating the same *IMPACT* queries. As we will show, the key for this mechanism to work is that the *ASHOP* algorithm performs a planning technique called ordered task decomposition. As a result, *ASHOP* maintains partial information about the state of the world. Experiments performed show that the memoization mechanism results in a significant reduction of the running time in *ASHOP*. This reduction depends on the overall network time spent to access the information sources: the higher this network time, the higher is the gain obtained by our memoization technique.

This paper is organised as follows. The next section describes the Noncombatant evacuation operations (NEO's) planning domain, which partly motivated our approach. In Section 3 we introduce *IMPACT*, define *ASHOP* and the results establishing the soundness and completeness of *ASHOP*. Section 4 describes the actual implementation of *ASHOP*. Section 5 describes the memoization mechanism and its dependence on the Ordered Task Decomposition planning technique. In Section 6 we describe several experiments with *ASHOP* for logistics NEO problems. Finally, we discuss related work in Section 7 and conclude with Section 8.

2   Planning Noncombatant Evacuation Operations

Noncombatant evacuation operations (NEO's) are conducted to assist the U.S.A. Department of State (*DOS*) with evacuating noncombatants, nonessential military personnel, selected host-nation citizens, and third country nationals whose lives are in danger from locations in a host foreign nation to an appropriate safe haven. They usually involve the swift insertion of a force, temporary occupation of an objective (e.g., an embassy), and a planned withdrawal after mission completion.

The decision making process for a NEO is conducted at three increasingly-specific levels: *strategic*, *operational* and *tactical*. The strategic level involves

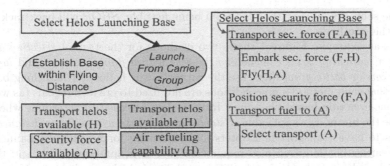

Fig. 1. NEO transportation example.

global and political considerations such as whether to perform the NEO. The operational level involves considerations such as determining the size and composition of its execution force. The tactical level is the concrete level, which assigns specific resources to specific tasks. Thus, this domain is particularly suitable for a hierarchical (*HTN*) planning approach.

JTF commanders plan NEO's by gathering information from multiple sources. For example, in preparation for *Operation Eastern Exit* (Mogadishu, Somalia, 1991), commanders accessed Intelligence Satellite Photographs from NIMA (National Imagery and Mapping Agency), intelligence assessment information from the *CIA*, the Emergency Action Plan (*EAP*) from the US Embassy in Mogadishu, among others [4]. Any automated system planning in this domain must be able to access these multiple distributed information sources.

3 Planning with Remote, Heterogeneous Information

In this section we review results obtained in [3]. After giving a brief overview on *SHOP* and *IMPACT* in Subsection 3.1, we state the main results of [3] in Subsection 3.2.

3.1 SHOP and IMPACT

Rather than giving a detailed description of the kind of *HTN* planning used by *SHOP* ([5]), we consider the following example.

In order to do planning in a given planning domain, *SHOP* needs to be given knowledge about that domain. *SHOP*'s knowledge base contains *operators* and *methods*. Each operator is a description of what needs to be done to accomplish some primitive task, and each method is a prescription for how to decompose some complex task into a totally ordered sequence of subtasks, along with various restrictions that must be satisfied in order for the method to be applicable.

Given the next task to accomplish, *SHOP* chooses an applicable method, instantiates it to decompose the task into subtasks, and then chooses and instantiates other methods to decompose the subtasks even further. If the constraints on the subtasks prevent the plan from being feasible, *SHOP* will backtrack and try other methods.

As an example, Figure 1 shows two methods for the task of *selecting a helicopter launching base*: *establishing the base within flying distance*, and *launch from carrier battle group* (i.e., use the carrier as the helicopter launching base). Note that each method's preconditions are not used to create subgoals (as would be done in action-based planning). Rather, they are used to determine whether or not the method is applicable. *Establishing the base within flying distance* requires to have transport helicopters and a security force available. Launching from carrier battle group also requires to have helicopters available and those helicopters have to have air refuelling capability (which wasn't necessary in the first method because the helicopters are within flying distance).

If the method *establishing base within flying distance method* is selected, the select helicopter launching base is decomposed into three subtasks: transport security force (F) using the helicopters (H) to the selected launching base (A), position the security force in the base, and transport the fuel to the base. Some of these tasks, such as transporting the security force, can be further decomposed. Others such as *position security force* cannot. The former are called *compound* tasks, the latter *primitive* tasks.

IMPACT. To get a bird's eye view, here are the most important features:

Actions: Each *IMPACT* agent has certain *actions* available. Agents act in their environment according to their *agent program* and a well defined *semantics* determining which of the actions the agent should execute.

Legacy Code: *IMPACT* Agents are built on top of arbitrary software code.

Agentisation: A methodology for transforming legacy code into an *agent* has been developed.

For example, in many applications a `math` agent is needed. This agent is able to do mathematical calculations shipped to it by other agents. For example it can determine the time it takes for a particular vehicle to get from one location to another. Another example is a `monitoring` agent, that keeps track of distances between two given points and the authorised range or capacity of certain vehicles. This information can be stored in several databases.

The Code Call Machinery. To perform logical reasoning on top of third party data structures (which are part of the agent's state) and code, the agent must have a language within which it can reason about the agent state. We therefore introduce the concept of a *code call atom*, which is the basic syntactic object used to access multiple heterogeneous data sources.

A code call (cc) executes an *API* function and returns as output a set of objects of the appropriate output type. Going back to our agent introduced above, `monitoring` may be able to execute the cc `monitoring`: *distance* (`locFrom, locTo`). The `math` agent may want to execute the following code call: `math`: *computeTime*(`cargoPlane, locFrom, locTo`).

What we really need to know is if the result of evaluating such code calls is contained in a certain set or not. To do this, we introduce code call atoms. These are *logical atoms* that are layered on top of code calls. They are defined through the following inductive definition.

Definition 1 (Code Call Atoms (in(X, cc))). *If* cc *is a code call, and* X *is either a variable symbol, or an object of the output type of* cc*, then* **in**(X, cc) *and* **not_in**(X, cc) *are code call atoms.* **not_in**(X, cc) *succeeds if* X *is **not** in the set of objects returned by the code call cc.*

Code call atoms, when evaluated, return boolean values, and thus may be thought of as special types of logical atoms. Intuitively, a code call atom of the form **in**(X, cc) succeeds if X can be set to a pointer to one of the objects in the set of objects returned by executing the code call.

As an example, the following code call atom tells us that the particular plane "$f22$" is available as a cargo plane at *ISB1*: **in**($f22$, transportAuthority: *cargoPlane*(ISB1))

Often, the results of evaluating code calls give us back certain values that we can compare. Based on such comparisons, certain actions might be fired or not. To this end, we need to define *code call conditions*. Intuitively, a code call condition is a conjunction of code call atoms, equalities, and inequalities. Equalities, and inequalities can be seen as additional syntax that "links" together variables occurring in the atomic code calls.

Definition 2 (Code Call Conditions (ccc)).
1. Every code call atom is a code call condition.
2. If s, t *are either variables or objects, then* s = t *is a code call condition.*
3. If s, t *are either integer/real valued objects, or are variables over the integers/reals, then* $s < t, s > t, s \geq t, s \leq t$ *are code call conditions.*
4. If χ_1, χ_2 *are code call conditions, then* $\chi_1 \& \chi_2$ *is a code call condition.*

A code call condition satisfying any of the first three criteria above is an atomic *code call condition.*

3.2 IMPACTING SHOP

A comparison between *IMPACT*'s actions and *SHOP*'s methods shows that *IMPACT* actions correspond to fully instantiated methods, i.e. no subtasks. While *SHOP*'s methods and operators are based on *STRIPS*, the first step is to modify the atoms in *SHOP*'s preconditions and effects, so that *SHOP*'s preconditions will be evaluated by *IMPACT*'s code call mechanism and the effects will change the state of the *IMPACT* agents. This is a fundamental change in the representation of *SHOP*. In particular, it requires replacing *SHOP*'s methods and operators with *agentised* methods and operators. These are defined as follows.

Definition 3 (Agentised Meth.: (AgentMeth $h \chi t$)). *An* agentized *method is an expression* **(AgentMeth** $h \chi t$*) where* h *(the method's head) is a compound task,* χ *(the method's* preconditions*) is a code call condition and* t *is a totally ordered list of subtasks, called the* task list.

```
procedure ASHOP(t, 𝒟)
  1. if t = nil then return nil
  2. t := the first task in t; R := the remaining tasks
  3. if t is primitive and a simple plan for t exists then
  4.    q := simplePlan(t)
  5.    return concatenate(q, ASHOP(R, 𝒟))
  6. else if t is non-prim. ∧ there is a reduction of t then
  7.    nondeterministically choose a reduction:
        Nondeterministically choose an agentised method,
        (AgentMeth h χ t), with μ the most general
        unifier of h and t and substitution θ s.t.
        χμθ is ground and holds in IMPACT's state 𝒪.
  8.    return ASHOP(concatenate(tμθ, R), 𝒟)
  9. else return FAIL
 10. end if
end ASHOP

procedure simplePlan(t)
 11. nondeterministically choose agent. operator
     Op = (AgentOp h χ_add χ_del) with ν the most
     general unifier of h and t s.t. h is ground
 12. monitoring : apply(Opν)
 13. return Opν
end ASHOP
```

Fig. 2. ASHOP, the agentised version of SHOP.

The primary difference between definition of an agentised method and the definition of a method in SHOP is as follows. In SHOP, preconditions were logical atoms, and SHOP would infer these preconditions from its current state of the world using Horn-clause inference. In contrast, the preconditions in an agentised method are IMPACT's code call conditions rather than logical atoms, and ASHOP (the agentised version of SHOP defined in the next section) does not use Horn-clause inference to establish these preconditions but instead simply invokes those code calls, which are calls to other agents (which may be Horn-clause theorem provers or may instead be something entirely different).

Definition 4 (Agentised Op.: (AgentOp $h \chi_{add} \chi_{del}$) **).** *An agentised operator is an expression* **(AgentOp** $h \chi_{add} \chi_{del}$), *where h is a primitive task and* χ_{add} *and* χ_{del} *are lists of code calls (called the* add- *and* delete-lists*). The set of variables in the tasks in* χ_{add} *and* χ_{del} *is a subset of the set of variables in h.*

The Algorithm

The ASHOP algorithm is now an easy adaptation of the original SHOP algorithm. Unlike SHOP (which would apply an operator by directly inserting and deleting atoms from an internally-maintained state of the world), *ASHOP* needs to reason about how the code calls in an operator will affect the states of other agents. One might think the simplest way to do this would be simply to tell these agents to execute the code calls and then observe the results, but this would not work correctly. Once the planning process has ended successfully, *ASHOP* will return a plan whose operators can be applied to modify the states of the other *IMPACT* agents—but *ASHOP* should not change the states of those agents during its planning process because this would prevent *ASHOP* from backtracking and trying other operators.

Thus in Step 12, *SHOP* does not issue code calls to the other agents directly, but instead communicates them to a `monitoring` agent. The `monitoring` agent keeps track of all operators that are supposed to be applied, without actually modifying the states of the other *IMPACT* agents. When *ASHOP* queries for a code call $cc = S:f(d_1, \ldots, d_n)$ in χ to evaluate a method's precondition (Step 7), the monitoring agent examines if cc has been affected by the intended modifications of the operators and, if so, it evaluates cc. If cc is not affected by application of operations, *IMPACT* evaluates cc (i.e., by accessing S). The list of operators maintained by the monitoring agent is reset whenever a planning process begins. The *apply* function applies the operators and creates copies of the state of the world. Depending on the underlying software code, these changes might be easily revertible or not. In the latter case, the monitoring agent has to keep track of the old state of the world.

3.3   Finite Evaluability of ccc's and Completeness of ASHOP

We have introduced syntactic conditions, similar to *safety* (and consequently called *strong safety*) in classical databases, to ensure evaluability and termination of ccc's (see [6,2]).

Theorem 1 (Soundness, Completeness). *Let $\mathcal{O}$ be a state and $\mathcal{D}$ be a collection of agentized methods and operators. If all the preconditions in the agentized methods and add- and delete-lists in the agentized operators are strongly safe wrt. the respective variables in the heads, then ASHOP is correct and complete.*

4   ASHOP: Implementation

Each cycle in the *ASHOP* algorithm consists of three phases (see lines 3 and 7 of Figure 2):

1. *Selection Phase*: Selecting a candidate agentized method or operator to reduce a task.
2. *Evaluation Phase*: Evaluating the applicability of the chosen agentized method or operator.
3. *Reduction Phase*: Performing the agentized method or operator.

To accomplish these phases we have implemented 3 *IMPACT* agents which perform pieces of these phases:

ashop: This is the agent that all *IMPACT* agents communicate with for generating a plan. It receives as input a problem and outputs a solution plan. The *ASHOP* agent also performs the Selection Phase and the evaluation phase for the situation in which an operator is chosen. The operator is then sent to the Monitor Agent, to perform a *virtual execution* of it. If the selection of a method is made, the *ASHOP* agent sends a message to the Preconditions Agent with the code-call condition of the selected method.

preconditions: Receives a code-call condition and evaluates each code-call by sending it to the Monitoring Agent.

monitoring: The monitor agent has two functions: firstly, it receives an operator and performs a virtual execution of it. Secondly, it receives code-calls and evaluates them. We explain both of these operations in detail below as they are closely inter-related.

One of the main issues we are confronted with during the implementation is how to cope with the *execution* of agentized operators. In classical AI planning, where the state is centralised, executing an operator is a matter of simply making the changes to the state indicated by the operator and keeping track of those changes in an stack; if backtracking occurs, the stack is used to restore to the previous state.

This approach is not working in a multi-agent environment, where the state is distributed among several information sources. Firstly, remote information sources might not be able to backtrack to a previous state. Secondly, even if backtracking was possible, performing such an operation may be costly. Thirdly, executing an operation may make resources unavailable temporarily for other agents and if backtracking takes place, these resources could have been used. For example, an operator may reserve a *recon* plane but a later operator trying to provide flight escort to the *recon* plane might not succeed. In this case the original *recon* plane should not have been reserved in the first place.

The Monitoring Agent overcomes these problems by keeping track of each operator execution without accessing the corresponding information sources to request an execution of the operation. For this reason we refer to this as a *virtual operator execution*. Since **monitoring** keeps track of the changes in the states of the remote information sources, the **preconditions** sends the code-calls to the **monitoring**. **monitoring** makes the code-call to the corresponding information source and then checks if the answer is affected by the previously virtually executed operators before sending its answer to the **preconditions**.

ASHOP is documented in [7] and available under the GNU licence.

5   Memoization in ASHOP

While our implementation ensures that the produced plans are consistent, the resulting running time was large compared to the inferencing time (we will describe the experiments later). Our experiments show that the bulk of the planning time has been spent in accessing the remote information sources. Further analysis revealed that the same code-calls were repeatedly being executed during the planning process. Our solution was to implement a cache mechanism to avoid repeated evaluations of the same code call in *IMPACT*.

Again this issue marked a difference from classical AI planning approaches. In *SHOP*, for example, we use a hash table to quickly check the validity of a condition in the current state. Other planning systems use more sophisticated data structures to reduce the time for evaluating a condition in the current state. For example, *TLPlan*, the winner of the 2000 AI planning competition, uses a bit map that allows checking conditions in almost constant time [8].

Obviously none of these techniques would be useful here since the information sources are remote and *ASHOP* has no control over how data is stored there and how it is updated. However, implementing a memoization mechanism turned out to be adequate for *ASHOP* for two reasons: Firstly, *ASHOP* performs *Ordered Task Decomposition*. Secondly, all access to the information sources is canalised through `monitoring`.

The fact that access to the information sources is canalised through `monitoring` makes this agent the natural place for maintaining the updated partial state of the world. As a result, we modified `monitoring`:

- When it receives a code-call from `preconditions`, the `monitoring` will first check if the code-call can be answered based on previous code-calls and the modifications indicated by the virtually executed operators. Only if it is not possible to answer this code call, the remote information source is accessed via the *IMPACT* code-call evaluation mechanism.
- After, receiving the answer from *IMPACT* for the evaluation of the code-call, `monitoring` records this answer.

In the example of the *recon* plane, after the first operator reserving the *recon* plane is virtually executed, `monitoring` knows that there are no more *recon* planes available. Thus, as it receives the code-call enquiring about the availability of *recon* planes it will answer that this code-call cannot be satisfied without having to access the corresponding remote information source via *IMPACT*. As will be shown next, these changes resulted in a reduction of the running time.

6   Empirical Evaluation

The test domain is a simple transportation planning for a NEO [9]. Its plans involve performing a rescue mission where troops are grouped and transported between an initial location (the assembly point) and the NEO site (where the evacuees are located). After the troops arrived at the NEO site, evacuees are re-located to a safe haven.

Planning involves selecting possible pre-defined routes, consisting of four or more segments each. The planner must also choose a transportation mode for each segment. In addition, other conditions were determined during planning such as whether communication exists with *State Department personnel* and the type of evacuee registration process. *ASHOP*'s knowledge base included six agentized operators and 22 agentized methods. There were four *IMPACT* information sources available:

- **Transport Authority**: Maintains information about the transportation assets available at different locations.
- **Weather Authority**: Maintains information about the weather conditions at the different locations.
- **Airport Authority**: Maintains information about availability and conditions of airports at different locations.
- **Math Agent**: `math` evaluates arithmetic expressions. typical evaluations include the subtract a certain number of assets use for an operation and update time delays.

The top level task for each problem in this experiment was the following: to perform a troop insertion and evacuees extraction plan. This top level task is decomposed into several subtasks, one for each segment in the route that the troops must cover (these segments are pre-determined as part of the problem description). Within each segment, *ASHOP* must plan for the means of transportation (planes, helicopters, vehicles etc.) to be used and select a route for that segment. The selection of the means of transportation depends on their availability for that segment, the weather conditions, and, in the case of airplanes, on the availability and conditions of airports. The selection of the route depends on the transportation vehicle used and may lead to backtracking. For example, the choice of ground transportation assets needs to be revised if no roads are available or they are blocked, or too risky to take.

Our test domain is a simplification of the actual conditions that occur in practice. Primarily, in practice many more information sources are available and as such the resulting plans will be more complicated. However, for the purpose of the experiment, it is sufficient to observe the effects of the memoization technique with fewer information sources available.

We ran our experiments on 30 problems of increasing size. The first five problems had four segments passing over five locations (including a particular location known as the Intermediate Staging Base *ISB*), the next five problems had five segments passing over six locations (two *ISB*'s), and so forth until the Problems 26–30 which had nine segments passing over 10 locations (five *ISB*'s).

We ran `shop` in two modes: with and without the memoization mechanism and measured for each mode two variables: *inferencing time* and *total time*. The inferencing time includes the time spent in the three agents implementing the *ASHOP* algorithm. Thus, the difference between the total time and the running time indicates the sum of the communication time needed by *IMPACT* to access the remote information sources and of the time needed by the information sources to compute the answers to the queries.

Figure 3 shows the results of the experiments. Not surprisingly the inferencing times with and without memoization are almost identical. More interesting is the fact that the inferencing time is only a fraction of the overall running time. In addition, the use of the memoization mechanism results in a decrease in the running time of more than 30%.

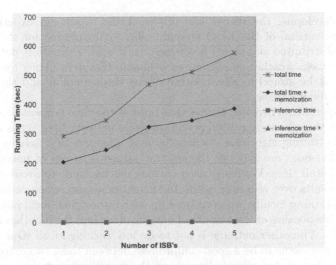

Fig. 3. Results of the experiments.

7   Related Work

Most AI planning systems are unable to evaluate numeric conditions at all. A few can evaluate numeric conditions using attached procedures (e.g., *SIPE* [10], *O-Plan* [11], *TLPlan* [12] and *SHOP* [5]), but the lack of a formal semantics for these attached procedures makes it more difficult to guarantee soundness and completeness. Integer Programming (IP) models appear to have excellent potential as a uniform formalism for reasoning about complex numeric and symbolic constraints during planning, and some work is already being done on the use of IP for reasoning about resources [13,14,15]. However, that work is still work in progress, and a number of fundamental problems still remain to be solved.

Approaches for planning with external information sources typically have in common that the information extracted from the external information sources is introduced in the planning system through built-in predicates [16,17,18,19]. For example, a modified version of *UCPOP* uses *information gathering goals* to extract information from the external information sources [18]. The information gathering goals are used as preconditions of the operators. The primary difficulty with this approach is that since it is not clear what the semantic of the built-in predicates is, this makes it difficult to guarantee soundness and completeness.

8   Conclusion

The original motivation of our work was to make *HTN* planning available in a multi-agent environment. This is beneficial for both, planners (they gain access to distributed and heterogenous information sources for free and can ship various tasks to other agents) as well as agent systems (which usually do not have available planning components that are highly sophisticated and efficient).

After developing the theory and implementing it, we ran experiments on a simplified version of the NEO domain, where data needed for the planning process is distributed and highly heterogenous. In such a situation, data changes dynamically, eg. weather conditions or available resources. Thus the available data can not be stored locally, because of the sheer amount and the dynamic changes in the database.

Our experiments revealed clearly that most of the time is spent on communication with the information sources and therefore network time. Thus improving the actual planning algorithm (as done by most planners that assume all info is there locally) does not pay off: the amount gained is orders of magnitude less than the overall time. We really need caching mechanisms, to avoid computing the same results over and over again. In the extreme case, when caching is just storing everything locally, we would end up with our original local planner. This is not feasible because of the amount of data involved and the fact that it changes dynamically. The other extreme is not to do any caching at all. Our memoization technique seems to be a good compromise between these two extremes. The decrease in time we are getting depends on the overall network time spent to access the information sources: the higher this network time, the higher is the gain obtained by our memoization technique. Consequently our experiments showed an overall gain ranging from 20%-40%.

References

1. Eiter, T., Subrahmanian, V., Pick, G.: Heterogeneous Active Agents, I: Semantics. Artificial Intelligence **108** (1999) 179–255
2. Subrahmanian, V., Bonatti, P., Dix, J., Eiter, T., Kraus, S., Özcan, F., Ross, R.: Heterogenous Active Agents. MIT Press (2000)
3. Dix, J., Munoz-Avila, H., Nau, D., Zhang, L.: IMPACTing SHOP: Putting an AI planner into a
   Multi-Agent Environment. Annals of Mathematics and AI (2002), to appear.
4. Siegel, A.: Eastern Exit: The noncombatant evacuation operation (NEO) from Mogadishu, Somalia, in January 1991 (TR CRM 91-221). Arlington, VA: Center for Naval Analyses (1991)
5. Nau, D., Cao, Y., Lotem, A., Muñoz-Avila, H.: Shop: Simple hierarchical ordered planner. In: Proceedings of IJCAI-99. (1999)
6. Eiter, T., Subrahmanian, V., Rogers, T.J.: Heterogeneous Active Agents, III: Polynomially Implementable Agents. Artificial Intelligence **117** (2000) 107–167
7. Zhang, L.: Documentation for ASHOP 1.0. Technical Report CSC-TR 2102, University of Maryland (2002) Master Thesis.
8. Bacchus, F.: The AIPS'00 Planning Competition. AI Magazine **22** (2001)
9. Munoz-Avila, H., Aha, D., Nau, D., Weber, R., Breslow, L., Yaman, F.: Sin: Integrating case-based reasoning with task decomposition. In: Proceedings of IJCAI-01. (2001)
10. Wilkins, D.: Practical planning - extending the classical AI planning paradigm. Morgan Kaufmann (1988)
11. Currie, K., Tate, A.: O-plan: the open planning architecture. Artificial Intelligence **52(1)** (1991)

12. Bacchus, F., Kabanza, F.: Using Temporal Logics to Express Search Control Knowledge for Planning. Artificial Intelligence **116** (2000) 123–191
13. Köhler, J.: Planning under Resource Constraints. In: Proceedings of the 13th European Conference on Artificial Intelligence. (1998) 489–493
14. Kautz, H., Walser, J.P.: State-space Planning by Integer Optimization. In: Proceedings of the 17th National Conference of the American Association for Artificial Intelligence. (1999) 526–533
15. Wolfman, S.A., Weld, D.S.: The LPSAT Engine and its Application to Resource Planning. In: Proceedings of the 15th International Joint Conference on Artificial Intelligence. (1999) 310–317
16. Etzioni, O., Weld, D., Draper, D., Lesh, N., Williamson, M.: An approach to planning with incomplete information. In: Proceedings of KR-92. (1992)
17. Golden, K., Etzioni, O., Weld, D.: Omnipotence without omniscience: efficient sensor management for planning. In: Proceedings of AAAI-94. (1994)
18. Knoblock, C.: Building a planner for information gathering: a report from the trenches. In: Proceedings of AIPS-96. (1996)
19. Friedman, M., Weld, D.: Efficiently executing information-gathering plans. In: Proceedings of IJCAI-97. (1997)

A   Agent Programs and Semantics

To make the paper self contained, we review here the very heart of the definition of an agent: its *agent program*. Such a program consists of rules of the form:

$$\mathsf{Op}\alpha(t_1, \ldots, t_m) \leftarrow \mathsf{Op}_1\beta_1(\ldots), \ldots, \mathsf{Op}_n\beta_n(\ldots),$$
$$ccc_1, \ldots, ccc_r,$$

where $\alpha, \beta_1, \ldots \beta_n$ are *actions*, $\mathsf{Op}_1, \ldots, \mathsf{Op}_n$ describe the status of the action (*obliged, forbidden, waived, doable*) and ccc_i are code call conditions to be evaluated in the actual state.

Thus, Op_i are operators that take actions as arguments. They describe the status of the arguments they take. Here are some examples of actions: (1) to load some cargo from a certain location, (2) to fly a plane from a certain location to another location, (3) to unload some cargo from a certain location. The action status atom **F** *load* (resp. **Do** *fly*) means that the action *load* is forbidden (resp. *fly* should be done). Actions themselves are terms, only with an operator in front of them they become atoms.

In *IMPACT*, actions are very much like STRIPS operators: they have preconditions and add- and delete-lists. The difference to STRIPS is that these preconditions and lists consist of *arbitrary code call conditions*, not just of logical atoms.

The agent program together with the chosen semantics SEM and the state of the agent determines the set of all status atoms. However, the doable actions among them might be conflicting and therefore we have to use a prespecified concurrency notion to finally determine which actions can be concurrently executed. The agent then executes these actions and changes its state.

Answer Set Planning under Action Costs*

Thomas Eiter[1], Wolfgang Faber[1], Nicola Leone[2], Gerald Pfeifer[1], and Axel Polleres[1]

[1] Institut für Informationssysteme, TU Wien, A-1040 Wien, Austria
{eiter,faber,polleres}@kr.tuwien.ac.at
pfeifer@dbai.tuwien.ac.at
[2] Department of Mathematics, University of Calabria, I-87030 Rende (CS), Italy
leone@unical.it

Abstract. We present $\mathcal{K}^c$, which extends the declarative planning language $\mathcal{K}$ by action costs and optimal plans that minimize overall action costs (cheapest plans). As shown, this novel language allows for expressing some nontrivial planning tasks in an elegant way. Furthermore, it flexibly allows for representing planning problems under other optimality criteria as well, such as computing "fastest" plans (with the least number of steps), and refinement combinations of cheap and fast plans. Our experience is encouraging and supports the claim that answer set planning may be a valuable approach to advanced planning systems in which intricate planning tasks can be naturally specified and effectively solved.

1 Introduction

Recently, several declarative planning languages and formalisms have been introduced, which allow for an intuitive encoding of complex planning problems including ramifications, incomplete information, non-deterministic action effects, or parallel actions [13,18,17,19,12,4,5,6]. While these formalisms are designed to generate any plans that establish the planning goals, in practice we are usually interested in particular plans that are optimal with respect to an objective function which measures the quality (or cost) of a plan. Often, this is just the number of time steps to achieve the goal, and many systems are tailored to compute shortest plans (e.g. CMBP [4] and GPT [2] compute shortest sequential plans, while Graphplan [1] computes shortest parallel plans).

However, there are other important objective functions to consider. If executing an action (such as traveling from Vienna to Lamezia Terme) causes some cost, then we may desire a plan which minimizes the overall cost of the actions in that plan. In answer set planning [18], where plans are represented by answer sets of a logic program, this kind of problem has not been addressed so far, to the best of our knowledge.

In this paper, we address this issue and present an extension of the planning language $\mathcal{K}$ [5,6], where one can associate actions with costs. The main contributions are:

- We define syntax and semantics of a modular extension to $\mathcal{K}$. Costs are associated to an action by a designated where-clause describing a cost value.
- Action costs may be dynamic, as they potentially depend on the current stage of the plan when an action is considered for execution. Dynamic action costs have natural applications, such as variants of the well-known Traveling Salesperson example.

---

* This work was supported by FWF (Austrian Science Funds) under the projects P14781 and Z29-INF

S. Flesca et al. (Eds.): JELIA 2002, LNAI 2424, pp. 186–197, 2002.

- We sketch how planning with costs can be implemented by mapping it to answer set programming, as realized in a system prototype that we have developed. The prototype, ready for experiments, is available at http://www.dlvsystem.com/K/.
- Finally, we show that our language is capable of easily modeling optimal planning under various criteria: computing (1) "cheapest" plans (which minimize overall action costs); (2) "fastest" plans (with the least number of steps); and combinations of these, viz. (3) fastest plans among the cheapest, and (4) cheapest plans among the fastest. To our knowledge, task (3) has not been addressed in other works so far.

The extension of $\mathcal{K}$ by action costs provides a flexible tool for representing different problems. Moreover, by $\mathcal{K}$'s nature, we get the possibility to easily combine dealing with incomplete knowledge and plan quality, which is completely novel.

Our experience is encouraging and gives further evidence that answer set planning, based on powerful logic programming engines, allows for the development of advanced declarative planning systems in which intricate planning tasks can be naturally specified and decently solved.

For space reasons, we provide proofs and more material in an extended paper [8].

2   Review of Language $\mathcal{K}$

In this section, we give a brief informal overview of the language $\mathcal{K}$. We assume that the reader is familiar with action languages and the notions of actions, fluents, goals, and plans and refer to [6] for further details. For illustration, we shall use the following running example, for which a $\mathcal{K}$ encoding is shown in Figure 1.

Bridge crossing. Four men want to cross a river at night. It is bridged by a plank bridge, which can only hold up to two persons at a time. The men have a lamp, which must be used in crossing, as it is pitch-dark and some planks are missing. The lamp must be brought back; no tricks (like throwing the lamp or halfway crosses) are allowed.   □

A state in $\mathcal{K}$ is characterized by the truth values of fluents, describing relevant properties in the universe of discourse. A fluent may be true, false, or unknown in a state; formally, a state is any consistent set s of (possibly negated) legal fluent instances. Note that in world-state planning, each fluent is either true or false in a state (this can be easily emulated in $\mathcal{K}$).

An action is only applicable if some precondition holds in the current state, and its execution may cause a modification of truth values of some fluents.

Background Knowledge. Static knowledge which is invariant over time is specified as a disjunction-free Datalog program which we require to have a total well-founded model (and therefore a unique answer set)[1].

In our example, the background knowledge is simply

```
person(joe).  person(jack).  person(will).  person(ave).
```

---

[1] The well-founded model can be calculated in polynomial time and if it is total it corresponds to the unique answer set.

(1)	actions :	cross2(X, Y) requires person(X), person(Y), X != Y.
(2)		cross(X) requires person(X).
(3)		takeLamp(X) requires person(X).
(4)	fluents :	across(X) requires person(X).
(5)		diffSides(X, Y) requires person(X), person(Y).
(6)		hasLamp(X) requires person(X).
(7)	initially :	caused -across(X). hasLamp(joe).
(8)	always :	executable cross2(X, Y) if hasLamp(X).
(9)		executable cross2(X, Y) if hasLamp(Y).
(10)		nonexecutable cross2(X, Y) if diffSides(X, Y).
(11)		executable cross(X) if hasLamp(X).
(12)		executable takeLamp(X).
(13)		nonexecutable takeLamp(X) if hasLamp(Y), diffSides(X, Y).
(14)		caused across(X) after cross2(X, Y), -across(X).
(15)		caused across(Y) after cross2(X, Y), -across(Y).
(16)		caused -across(X) after cross2(X, Y), across(X).
(17)		caused -across(Y) after cross2(X, Y), across(Y).
(18)		caused across(X) after cross(X), -across(X).
(19)		caused -across(X) after cross(X), across(X).
(20)		caused hasLamp(X) after takeLamp(X).
(21)		caused -hasLamp(X) after takeLamp(Y), X != Y, hasLamp(X).
(22)		caused diffSides(X, Y) if across(X), -across(Y).
(23)		caused diffSides(X, Y) if -across(X), across(Y).
(24)		inertial across(X).
(25)		inertial -across(X).
(26)		inertial hasLamp(X).
(27)	noConcurrency.	
(28)	goal :	across(joe), across(jack), across(will), across(ave)? (i)

Fig. 1. $\mathcal{K}$ encoding of the Bridge Crossing problem

Type Declarations. The ranges of the arguments of fluents and actions must be specified. For instance, line (1) in Figure 1 specifies the arguments of action cross2, where two persons cross the bridge together, while line (4) specifies a fluent describing the fact that a specific person is on the other side of the river. The literals after "requires" in a declaration are from Π or built-in predicates. DLV$^{\mathcal{K}}$ [7], our implementation of $\mathcal{K}$, currently supports built-in predicates "a < b", "a <= b", and "a != b" with the obvious meaning for strings and numbers, predicates "a = b + c", "a = b * c" for integer arithmetics, and "#int(X)" which enumerates all integers (up to a limit set by the user).

Causation Rules. Causation rules ("rules" for brevity) are syntactically similar to rules of the language $\mathcal{C}$ [13,18,17] and are of the basic form "caused f if B after A."

Informally, this reads: if B holds in the current state and A held in the previous state, then f is known to be true in the current state as well. Both the if and after parts are optional. A rule is called *static* if its after part is empty, and *dynamic* otherwise.

Rules are used to express effects of actions or ramifications. E.g., the rules (18) and (19) describe the effects of a single person crossing the bridge in either direction.

Initial State Constraints. Rules can apply to all states or only to the initial state (which may not be unique). This is expressed by the keywords "always :" and "initially :" preceding sequences of rules. For example, line (7) enforces the fluent across to be false in the initial state for all X satisfying the fluent declaration, i.e., for all persons.

Executability of Actions. This is expressed in $\mathcal{K}$ explicitly, as in lines (8) and (9) which state that two persons can jointly cross the bridge if one of them has a lamp. The same action may have multiple executability statements. Dually, "nonexecutable A if B." prohibits the execution of action A if condition B is satisfied. For example, line (13) says that two persons cannot cross the bridge together if they are on different sides of the bridge. In case of conflicts, nonexecutable A overrides executable A.

Parallel Actions. $\mathcal{K}$ permits simultaneous execution of actions. If, as on line (27), "noConcurrency." is specified, then at most one action at a time can be executed.

Default and Strong Negation. $\mathcal{K}$ supports strong negation (written as "-") where knowledge about a fluent f may be incomplete, i.e., in any given state neither f nor -f needs to hold. In addition, weak negation ("not"), interpreted like default negation in answer set semantics [11], is permitted in rule bodies. This allows for natural modeling of inertia, default properties, and dealing with incomplete knowledge in general.

Macros. $\mathcal{K}$ provides a number of macros as syntactic sugar. For example, the inertial statement in line (24) informally states that across(X) holds in the current state if across(X) held at the previous state unless -across(X) is explicitly known to hold. This macro expands to "caused across(X) if not -across(X) after across(X)."

Moreover, we can "totalize" the knowledge of a fluent by declaring "total f." which is a shortcut for a pair of rules "caused f if not -f." and "caused -f if not f." with the intuitive meaning that unless a truth value for f can be derived, the cases where f resp. -f are true will both be considered.

Planning Domains and Problems. In $\mathcal{K}$, a *planning domain* $PD = \langle \Pi, \langle D, R \rangle \rangle$ has a background knowledge Π, action and fluent declarations D, and rules and executability conditions R; a *planning problem* $\mathcal{P} = \langle PD, q \rangle$ has a planning domain PD and a *query*

$$q = g_1, \ldots, g_m, \text{not } g_{m+1}, \ldots, \text{not } g_n ? \ (i)$$

where $g_1, \ldots, g_n$ are ground fluents and $i \geq 0$ is the plan length (see line (28)). An *(optimistic) plan* for $\mathcal{P}$ is a sequence $P = \langle A_1, \ldots, A_l \rangle$ of action instances with a supporting *trajectory* $T = \langle \langle s_0, A_1, s_1 \rangle, \langle s_1, A_2, s_2 \rangle, \ldots, \langle s_{l-1}, A_l, s_l \rangle \rangle$ to the goal, i.e., starting at a legal initial state s_0, the actions in A_1, A_2 etc. are executable and lead to legal successor states s_1, s_2 etc. such that all literals in q are true in s_l.

If, as stated in Figure 1, joe initially carries the lamp, our problem has simple five-step plans where joe always carries the lamp and brings all others across; e.g.,

$P = \langle$ {cross2(joe,jack)}, {cross(joe)}, {cross2(joe,will)},
    {cross(joe)}, {cross2(joe,ave)} $\rangle$

3 Actions with Costs

Using $\mathcal{K}$ and $\text{DLV}^{\mathcal{K}}$, it is possible to express and solve involved planning tasks. However, $\mathcal{K}$ and $\text{DLV}^{\mathcal{K}}$ offer no means for finding optimal plans with respect to any criteria. In particular, this applies to action costs, which are needed for the following elaboration of the bridge crossing example that is well-known as a brain-teasing riddle.

Quick bridge crossing. The four guys need different times to cross the bridge, namely 1, 2, 5, and 10 minutes, respectively. Walking in two implies moving at the slower rate. Is it possible to get all of them across within 17 minutes?   □

On first thought, this is not feasible, since the seemingly optimal plan where joe, who is the fastest, keeps the lamp and leads all the others across takes 19 minutes. Surprisingly, as we will see, there *is* a better solution.

In order to allow for an elegant and convenient encoding of such optimization problems, we extend $\mathcal{K}$ to the language $\mathcal{K}^c$ where we can assign costs to actions.

3.1 Syntax of $\mathcal{K}^c$

Let σ^{act} denote the set of action names, and $\mathcal{L}_{typ}$ the set of literals over predicates defined in the background knowledge including built-in predicates. Furthermore, let σ^{var} denote the set of variable symbols. $\mathcal{K}^c$ merely extends action declarations in $\mathcal{K}$ to express action costs as follows.

Definition 1. *An action declaration d in $\mathcal{K}^c$ is of the form:*

$$p(X_1, \ldots, X_n) \text{ requires } t_1, \ldots, t_m \text{ costs } C \text{ where } c_1, \ldots, c_k. \tag{1}$$

where (1) $p \in \sigma^{act}$ has arity $n \geq 0$, (2) $X_1, \ldots, X_n \in \sigma^{var}$, (3) $t_1, \ldots, t_m, c_1, \ldots, c_k$ are from $\mathcal{L}_{typ}$ such that every X_i occurs in $t_1, \ldots, t_m$[2], (4) C is either an integer constant, a variable from the set of all variables occurring in $t_1, \ldots, t_m, c_1, \ldots, c_k$ (denoted by $\sigma^{var}(d)$), or the distinguished variable time, *and (5) $\sigma^{var}(d) \subseteq \sigma^{var} \cup \{$time$\}$, and* time *does not occur in $t_1, \ldots t_m$.*

If $m = 0$, the keyword 'requires' is omitted; if $k = 0$, the keyword 'where' is omitted and 'costs C' is optional. Planning domains and problems are defined as in $\mathcal{K}$.

Examples will be given in Section 3.3.

3.2 Semantics of $\mathcal{K}^c$

Semantically, $\mathcal{K}^c$ extends $\mathcal{K}$ by the cost values of actions at points in time. In any plan $P = \langle A_1, \ldots, A_l \rangle$, at step $1 \leq i \leq l$, i.e. at time i, the actions in A_i are executed.

We recall that a ground action $p(x_1, \ldots, x_n)$ is a *legal action instance* of an action declaration d w.r.t. a $\mathcal{K}$ planning domain $PD = \langle \Pi, \langle D, R \rangle \rangle$, if a ground substitution θ for $\sigma^{var}(d)$ exists such that $X_i\theta = x_i$, for $1 \leq i \leq n$ and $\{t_1\theta, \ldots, t_m\theta\} \subseteq M$, where M is the unique answer set of the background knowledge Π. Any such θ is called a *witness substitution* for $p(x_1, \ldots, x_n)$. Action costs are now formalized as follows.

---

[2] Informally, this means that all parameters of an action must be "typed" in the requires part.

Definition 2. *Let* $a = p(x_1, \ldots, x_n)$ *be a legal action instance with declaration* d *of the form (1), let* $i \geq 1$ *be a time point, and let* θ *be a witnessing substitution for* a *with* $\texttt{time}\,\theta = i$. *Then*

$$cost_{i,\theta}(p(x_1, \ldots, x_n)) = \begin{cases} 0, & \text{if the } \texttt{costs} \text{ part of } d \text{ is empty;} \\ val(C\theta), & \text{if } \{c_1\theta, \ldots, c_k\theta\} \subseteq M; \\ undefined, & otherwise. \end{cases}$$

By involving the variable $\texttt{time}$ it is possible to define time-dependent action costs. This can be used for complex variants of Traveling Salesperson, where the optimal tour does not only depend on the route taken, but also when a certain connection is used (e.g., imagine the traffic jams on some roads during the weekend, which could increase the cost of a connection). We do not elaborate on this application here due to space restrictions, see [8] or http://www.dlvsystem.com/K/.

Using $cost_{i,\theta}$, we introduce well-defined legal action instances and action costs:

Definition 3. *A legal action instance* $a = p(x_1, \ldots, x_n)$ *is* well-defined *iff for any time point* $i \geq 1$, *it holds that (i) there is some witness substitution* θ *for* a *such that* $cost_{i,\theta}(a)$ *is an integer* ≥ 0, *and (ii)* $cost_{i,\theta}(a) = cost_{i,\theta'}(a)$ *holds for any two witness substitutions* θ, θ' *with defined costs. For any well-defined* a, *its unique cost at time point* $i \geq 1$ *is given by* $cost_i(a) = cost_{i,\theta}(a)$ *where* θ *is as in (i).*

In this definition, condition (i) ensures that some cost value exists, which is an integer number, and condition (ii) ensures that this value is well-defined, i.e., different witness substitutions θ and θ' for a can not evaluate the $\texttt{cost}$ part to different integer cost values. In our framework, the semantics of a $\mathcal{K}^c$ planning domain $PD = \langle \Pi, \langle D, R \rangle \rangle$ is only well-defined, if all legal instances of action declarations in PD are well-defined. This will be fulfilled if, for instance, the variables $X_1, \ldots, X_n$ in (1) in database terms functionally determine the values of the other variables except $\texttt{time}$, i.e., any tuple of values $(x_1, \ldots x_n)$ for $X_1, \ldots, X_n$ has a unique extension to a tuple of values for all variables in d except $\texttt{time}$. In the rest of this paper, we assume well-definedness of $\mathcal{K}^c$ unless stated otherwise. Violations of well-definedness can be easily detected by introducing designated fluents and rules, see [8] for details. Using $cost_i$, we now define costs of plans.

Definition 4. *Let* $\mathcal{P}$ *be a planning problem. Then, for any plan* $P = \langle A_1, \ldots, A_l \rangle$ *for* $\mathcal{P}$, *its cost is defined as* $cost_{\mathcal{P}}(P) = \sum_{i=1}^{l} \left(\sum_{a \in A_i} cost_i(a) \right)$. *A plan* P *is optimal for* $\mathcal{P}$ *and fixed plan length* i, *if it has least cost among all plans of length* i, *i.e.,* $cost_{\mathcal{P}}(P) \leq cost_{\mathcal{P}}(P')$ *for each plan* P' *of length* i *for* $\mathcal{P}$. *The cost of* $\mathcal{P}$ *w.r.t. plan length* i *is the cost of an optimal plan for* $\mathcal{P}$ *and* i.

Usually one only can estimate some *upper bound* of the plan length, but does not know the exact length of an optimal plan. Although we have only defined optimality for a fixed plan length i, we will see in Section 4.1 that by appropriate encodings this can extended to optimality for plans with length *at most* i.

3.3   An Optimal Solution for Crossing the Bridge

To model the different times the four guys need to cross the bridge, we extend the background knowledge, where '$\texttt{max}$' determines which of two persons is faster:

```
speed(joe, 1). speed(jack, 2). speed(will, 5). speed(ave, 10).
max(A, B, A) :- speed(_, A), speed(_, B), A >= B.
max(A, B, B) :- speed(_, A), speed(_, B), B > A.
```

Next, we add costs to the action declarations for cross and cross2 (leaving takeLamp unchanged, as the time to hand over the lamp is negligible).

```
cross(X)    requires person(X) costs SX where speed(X, SX).
cross2(X, Y) requires person(X), person(Y), X < Y costs Smax
             where speed(X, SX), speed(Y, SY), max(SX, SY, Smax).
```

As easily seen, the cost of the 5-step plan considered in Section 2 is 19. However, when we also consider longer plans, we can find the following 7-step plan P with cost 17:

$$P = \langle \; \{cross2(joe, jack)\}, \; \{cross(joe)\}, \; \{takeLamp(will)\}, \; \{cross2(will, ave)\}$$
$$\{takeLamp(jack)\}, \; \{cross(jack)\}, \; \{cross2(joe, jack)\} \; \rangle$$

P has least cost over all trajectories of any length establishing the goal and thus constitutes an optimal solution of our problem for fixed plan length $i \geq 7$.

3.4 "Crossing the Bridge" under Incomplete Knowledge

$\mathcal{K}$ is well-suited to model problems which involve qualitative uncertainty such as incomplete initial states or non-deterministic action effects. The extension of $\mathcal{K}$ to $\mathcal{K}^c$ to include costs gracefully applies to so called secure (conformant) plans as well, which must reach the goal under all circumstances [5].

For example, assume we only know that some of the desperate guys has a lamp. If they now ask for a plan to safely cross the bridge, we need a (fast) secure plan that works under all possible initial situations. In $\mathcal{K}^c$, this can be easily modeled by replacing "initially : hasLamp(joe)." by the following, where the first statement says that each guy might have a lamp, and the second that at least one guy has one.

```
initially : total hasLamp(X).
            caused false if -hasLamp(joe), -hasLamp(jack),
                            -hasLamp(will), -hasLamp(ave).
```

Clearly, the optimal solution still takes at least 17 minutes, since the original case (where only joe has a lamp) is one of the possible initial situations. However, an optimal secure plan now takes at least 8 steps, since we must assure in the first step that either joe or jack has the lamp. One such a plan with cost 17 is

$$P = \langle \; \{takeLamp(joe)\}, \; \{cross2(joe, jack)\}, \; \{cross(joe)\}, \; \{takeLamp(will)\}$$
$$\{cross2(will, ave)\}, \; \{takeLamp(jack)\}, \; \{cross(jack)\}, \; \{cross2(joe, jack)\} \; \rangle$$

4 Applications

4.1 Cost Efficient versus Time Efficient Plans

In this section, we show how our approach can be used to minimize plan length together with the costs of a plan under parallel actions. In [15,16] various criteria for optimization are proposed for parallel action domains, such as minimizing the total number of actions, or the number of time steps. We will concentrate on the following generalizations of these optimization criteria with arbitrary action costs. Finding

(α) plans with minimal costs (cheapest plans) for a given number of steps,
(β) plans with minimal time steps (shortest plans),
(γ) shortest among the cheapest plans, and
(δ) cheapest among the shortest plans.

Fig. 2. A simple Blocks World instance

(α.) Cheapest plans for given plan length. As a guiding example, we refer to the blocks world problem in Figure 2, where we want to find the minimal number of moves (possibly in parallel) to achieve the goal state. As background knowledge Π_{bw}, we use:

```
block(1). ... block(6). location(table). location(B) :- block(B).
```

and the following $\mathcal{K}^c$ program:

```
fluents :    on(B,L) requires block(B), location(L).
             blocked(B) requires block(B).
             moved(B) requires block(B).
actions :    move(B,L) requires block(B), location(L) costs 1.
always :     executable move(B,L) if B!=L.
             nonexecutable move(B,L) if blocked(B).
             nonexecutable move(B,L) if blocked(L).
             nonexecutable move(B,L) if move(B1,L), B!=B1, block(L).
             nonexecutable move(B,L) if move(B,L1), L!=L1.
             nonexecutable move(B,B1) if move(B1,L).

             caused on(B,L) after move(B,L).
             caused blocked(B) if on(_,B).
             caused moved(B) after move(B,_).
             caused on(B,L) if not moved(B) after on(B,L).
initially :  on(1,2). on(2,table). on(3,4). on(4,table). on(5,6). on(6,table).
goal :       on(1,3), on(3,table), on(2,4), on(4,table), on(6,5), on(5,table) ? (i)
```

Each move is penalized with cost 1, minimizing the total number of moves. The instance has a two-step parallel solution which involves six moves:

$P = \langle$ {move(1,table),move(3,table),move(5,table)},
       {move(1,3),move(2,4),move(6,5)} $\rangle$

However, there is a sequential plan with only five moves:

$P = \langle$ {move(3,table)}, {move(1,3)}, {move(2,4)}, {move(5,table)}, {move(6,5)} $\rangle$

This plan can be parallelized to have 3 steps, but not to have 2 steps. For any length ≥ 3, we obtain optimal plans involving 5 actions. Consequently, the minimal number of steps for a maximally parallelized plan with a minimal number of actions is 3.

(β) Shortest Plan. For optimization *(β)* we assume that no action costs are specified in the original problem, and minimizing time steps is our sole target. We will show a general preprocessing method for $\mathcal{K}^c$ planning problems which, given an upper bound i of time steps, guarantees plans with a minimal number of steps. Many typical applications have an inherent upper bound for the plan length. In blocks world for a configuration with n Blocks, any goal configuration can be reached within at most $2n - s_i - s_g$ steps, where s_i and s_g represent the numbers of stacks in the initial and goal states[3]. Therefore, 6 is an upper bound for the plan length of our simple instance.

First, we add a new distinct fluent gr and a new distinct action finish to our domain and extend the always section of the program replacing the original goal:

```
fluents : gr.
actions : finish costs time.
always :  executable finish if g₁, ..., gₘ, not gₘ₊₁, ..., not gₙ, not gr.
          caused gr after finish.
          caused gr after gr.
goal :    gr ? (i)
```

where $g_1, \ldots, g_m$, not $g_{m+1}, \ldots$, not g_n are the original goal literals. Intuitively, finish represents a final action, which always has to be executed to finish the plan. The later it occurs, the more expensive is the plan. The fluent gr has the meaning "goal reached".

Furthermore, we want the action finish to occur exclusively and any occurrence of any other actions should be blocked as soon as the goal has been reached. Therefore, for any action A we add not gr to the if part of any executability condition for A and add a rule: nonexecutable A if finish.

Finally, to avoid any inconsistencies from static or dynamic effects, as soon as the goal has been reached, we add not gr to the if part of any causation rule of the original program except nonexecutable rules[4].

If now $P' = \langle A_1, \ldots, A_j, A_{j+1}, \ldots, A_l \rangle$ is an optimal cost plan for the modified $\mathcal{K}^c$ planning problem $\mathcal{P}min$ for plan length l where $A_j = \{\text{finish}\}$, then $P'' = \langle A_1, \ldots, A_{j-1} \rangle$ is a minimal length plan for the original planning problem and all $A_{j+1} = \ldots = A_l = \emptyset$. Using this method, we obtain all 2-step parallel plans for our blocks world example.

Note that this approach for minimizing plan length is only efficient, if we know an upper bound close to the optimum. Searching for a minimum length plan by simply iteratively increasing the plan length could be more efficient when no such bound is known, as the search space might explode with a weak upper bound.

(γ) and (δ). In the last section, no costs were specified in the original program. If we want to find the *shortest among the cheapest plans* with arbitrary action costs, we have to set the costs of all actions higher than the highest possible cost value of action finish. Obviously, the highest cost for finish is the plan length i. Thus, we simply modify all action declarations by multiplying the original costs C with factor i:

---

[3] We can trivially solve any blocks world problem sequentially by first unstacking all blocks ($n - s_i$ steps) and then building up the goal configuration ($n - s_g$ steps).

[4] There is no need to rewrite nonexecutable rules because the respective actions are already "switched off" by rewriting of the executability conditions.

```
            A requires B costs C₁ where C₁ = i * C,  D.
```

This lets all other action costs take priority over the cost of finish and we can compute plans satisfying criterion (γ). Applying this rewriting to our blocks world example, a possible plan for length $i = 7$ is

$P = \langle$ {move(3, table)}, {move(1, 3), move(5, table)},
            {move(2, 4), move(6, 5)}, {finish}, $\emptyset$, $\emptyset$, $\emptyset$ $\rangle$

As mentioned above, 6 is an upper bound for the plan length, but plan length $i = 7$ is needed for the final finish action. Analogously, in order to compute the cheapest among the shortest plans, the cost function of finish has to be adapted, such that the costs of finish take priority over all other actions costs. To this end, we set these costs high enough, by multiplying them with a factor higher than the sum of all costs of all legal action instances, i.e. the costs of all actions executed in parallel in i steps. We thus can compute solutions for optimization criterion (δ).

In our example, there are 36 possible moves; theoretically, we would have to set the costs of action finish to time $* 36 * i$. Though, at most 6 blocks can be moved in parallel, and it is sufficient to set the costs of finish to time $* 6 * i =$ time $* 42$. Accordingly, the action declarations are modified as follows:

```
    actions :   move(B, L) requires block(B), location(L) costs 1.
                finish costs C where C = time * 42.
```

An optimal plan for the modified program for plan length (at most) 7 which in fact amounts to a two-step plan, is:

$P = \langle$ {move(1, table), move(3, table), move(5, table)},
            {move(1, 3), move(2, 4), move(6, 5)}, {finish}, $\emptyset$, $\emptyset$, $\emptyset$, $\emptyset$ $\rangle$

5 Implementation

We briefly describe how planning under action costs can be implemented using a translation to answer set programming. We will define an extension $lp^w(\mathcal{P})$ of the logic program $lp(\mathcal{P})$ as defined in [7], such that its optimal answer sets (i.e., those minimizing weak constraint violation, see [10,3]) correspond to the optimal cost plans for a planning problem $\mathcal{P}$.

We recall that in $lp(\mathcal{P})$ fluent and action literals are extended by an additional time parameter, and executability conditions as well as causation rules are modularly translated into corresponding program rules and constraints; disjunction is used for guessing at each point in time the actions which should be executed in the plan.

The translation $lp^w(\mathcal{P})$ for $\mathcal{K}^c$ problem $\mathcal{P}$ includes all rules of $lp(\mathcal{P}')$ from [7] for the $\mathcal{K}$ problem $\mathcal{P}'$ which results from $\mathcal{P}$ by omitting all cost parts of action declarations. In addition, for any action declaration d of the form (1) with nonempty costs part, the following two statements are included (let $\overline{X} = X_1, \ldots, X_n$):

$$cost_p(\overline{X}, T, C) :\text{-} p(\overline{X}, T), t_1, \ldots, t_m, c_1, \ldots, c_k, U = T + 1. \qquad (2)$$

$$:\sim cost_p(\overline{X}, T, C). \ [C :] \qquad (3)$$

In statement (2), T and U are new variables and each occurrence of time is replaced by U. Statement (3) is a *weak constraint*. Intuitively, a weak constraint denotes a property which should preferably hold, and statement (3) associates a cost C to the weak constraint, which can be interpreted as a penalty to be considered if the weak constraint is not satisfied. An optimal answer set is an answer set for which the sum of the penalties of violated weak constraints is minimal (We refer to [10,3] for details). For example, the cross action defined in Section 3.3 is translated to:

cost$_{\text{cross}}$(X, T, SX) :- cross(X, T), person(X), speed(X, SX), U = T + 1.

:$\sim$ cost$_{\text{cross}}$(X, T, SX). [SX :]

As shown in [7], the answer sets of $lp(\mathcal{P})$ correspond to trajectories of optimistic plans for $\mathcal{P}$. We have similar results for plans with action costs.

Theorem 1 (answer set correspondence). *Let* $\mathcal{P} = \langle PD, q \rangle$ *be a (well-defined)* $\mathcal{K}^c$ *planning problem. Then, for each optimistic plan* $P = \langle A_1, \ldots, A_l \rangle$ *of* $\mathcal{P}$ *and supporting trajectory* $T = \langle \langle s_0, A_1, s_1 \rangle, \ldots, \langle s_{l-1}, A_l, s_l \rangle \rangle$ *of* P, *there exists an answer set* S *of* $lp^w(\mathcal{P})$ *representing this trajectory such that the sum of weights of violated weak constraints equals* $cost_{\mathcal{P}}(P)$, *and vice-versa.*

Corollary 1 (optimal answer set correspondence). *For any well-defined* $\mathcal{K}^c$ *planning problem* $\mathcal{P}$, *the (trajectories* $T = \langle \langle s_0, A_1, s_1 \rangle, \ldots, \langle s_{l-1}, A_l, s_l \rangle \rangle$ *of) optimal plans* P *for* $\mathcal{P}$ *correspond to the optimal answer sets* S *of* $lp^w(\mathcal{P})$.

Using these results, we have implemented an experimental prototype for planning in $\mathcal{K}^c$, which can be downloaded from http://www.dlvsystem.com/K/. Further documentation on techniques and usage of the prototype is available there and in [7]. For a more detailed discussion of the translation and the prototype we refer to [8].

6 Related Work and Conclusion

We have presented an extension of the language $\mathcal{K}$ which allows for the formulation of various optimality criteria of desired plans by means of variable action costs, and we sketched a translation to answer set programming with weak constraints. In fact, our implementation also supports computing admissible plans, i.e., plans the costs of which stay within a given limit (see [8]).

In the last years, it has been widely recognized that plan length alone is only one criterion to be optimized in planning. Several attempts have been made to extend heuristic search planners to allow for special heuristics respecting action costs, e.g. [9,14].

A powerful approach is given in [20], where planning with resources is described as a structural constraint satisfaction problem (SCSP). The problem is solved by local search combined with global control. However, [20] promotes the inclusion of domain-dependent knowledge; the general problem has an unlimited search space, and no declarative high-level language is provided. Among other related approaches, [15] generalizes the "Planning as Satisfiability" approach to use integer optimization techniques for encoding optimal planning under resource production/consumption. In [16] an extension of the action language $\mathcal{C}$ is mentioned which allows for an intuitive encoding of resources and costs, but optimization is not considered in that framework.

A crucial difference between resource-based approaches and ours is that the former build on fluent values, while our approach hinges on action costs. This is a somewhat different view of the quality of a plan. We plan to generalize our framework such that dynamic fluent values may contribute to action costs. Further possible extensions include negative action costs, which are useful for modeling producer/consumer relations among actions and resources, and different priorities (cost levels) to increase the flexibility and allow for optimizing different criteria at once. Another aspect to be explored is the computational complexity of $\mathcal{K}^c$, complementing the results in [6].

References

1. A. L. Blum and M. L. Furst. Fast planning through planning graph analysis. *Artificial Intelligence*, 90:281–300, 1997.
2. B. Bonet and H. Geffner. Planning with incomplete information as heuristic search in belief space. In *Proc. AIPS'00*, pp. 52–61, 2000.
3. F. Buccafurri, N. Leone, and P. Rullo. Enhancing disjunctive datalog by constraints. *IEEE TKDE*, 12(5):845–860, 2000.
4. A. Cimatti and M. Roveri. Conformant planning via symbolic model checking. *Journal of Artificial Intelligence Research*, 13:305–338, 2000.
5. T. Eiter, W. Faber, N. Leone, G. Pfeifer, and A. Polleres. Planning under incomplete knowledge. In: *Proc. CL-2000*, pp. 807–821, LNCS 1861, Springer, 2000.
6. T. Eiter, W. Faber, N. Leone, G. Pfeifer, and A. Polleres. A logic programming approach to knowledge-state planning: Semantics and complexity. Technical Report INFSYS RR-1843-01-11, Inst. f. Informationssysteme, TU Wien, December 2001.
7. T. Eiter, W. Faber, N. Leone, G. Pfeifer, and A. Polleres. A logic programming approach to knowledge-state planning, II: The DLV$^\mathcal{K}$ system. Technical Report INFSYS RR-1843-01-12, Inst. f. Informationssysteme, TU Wien, December 2001.
8. T. Eiter, W. Faber, N. Leone, G. Pfeifer, and A. Polleres. Answer set planning under action costs. Manuscript, 2002.
9. E. Ephrati, M. E. Pollack, and M. Mihlstein. A cost-directed planner: Preliminary report. In *Proc. AAAI-96*, pp. 1223–1228. AAAI Press, 1996.
10. W. Faber. Disjunctive Datalog with Strong and Weak Constraints: Representational and Computational Issues. Master's thesis, Inst. f. Informationssysteme, TU Wien, 1998.
11. M. Gelfond and V. Lifschitz. Classical negation in logic programs and disjunctive databases. *New Generation Computing*, 9:365–385, 1991.
12. E. Giunchiglia. Planning as satisfiability with expressive action languages: Concurrency, constraints and nondeterminism. In *Proc. KR 2000*, pp. 657–666. Morgan Kaufmann, 2000.
13. E. Giunchiglia and V. Lifschitz. An action language based on causal explanation: Preliminary report. In *Proc. AAAI '98*, pp. 623–630, AAAI Press, 1998.
14. P. Haslum and H. Geffner. Admissible heuristics for optimal planning. *AIPS'00*, pp. 140–149. AAAI Press, 2000.
15. H. Kautz and J. P. Walser. State-space planning by integer optimization. In *AAAI'99*, pp. 526–533. AAAI Press, 1999.
16. J. Lee and V. Lifschitz. Additive fluents. In *Proc. AAAI 2001 Spring Symposium on Answer Set Programming*, pp. 116–123, AAAI Press, 2001.
17. V. Lifschitz and H. Turner. Representing transition systems by logic programs. *LPNMR'99*, pp. 92–106.
18. V. Lifschitz. Answer set planning. *ICLP'99*, pp. 23–37. MIT Press, 1999.
19. N. McCain and H. Turner. Satisfiability planning with causal theories. *KR'98*, pp. 212–223. Morgan Kaufmann, 1998.
20. A. Nareyek. Beyond the plan-length criterion. In *Local Search for Planning and Scheduling, ECAI 2000 Workshop*, LNCS 2148, pp. 55–78. Springer, 2001.

On Fibring Semantics for BDI Logics

Guido Governatori[1], Vineet Padmanabhan[2], and Abdul Sattar[2]

[1] School of Information Technology & Electrical Engineering
The University of Queensland, Queensland, Australia
guido@itee.uq.edu.au
[2] Knowledge Representation & Reasoning Unit (KRRU)
School of Information Technology
Griffith University, GoldCoast Campus, Queensland, Australia
{vineet,sattar}@cit.gu.edu.au

Abstract. This study examines BDI logics in the context of Gabbay's *fibring* semantics. We show that *dovetailing* (a special form of fibring) can be adopted as a semantic methodology to combine BDI logics. We develop a set of interaction axioms that can capture static as well as dynamic aspects of the mental states in BDI systems, using Catach's *incestual* schema $G^{a,b,c,d}$. Further we exemplify the constraints required on fibring function to capture the semantics of interactions among modalities. The advantages of having a fibred approach is discussed in the final section.

1 Introduction

BDI based Agent-systems [1,7,4] have been well studied in the AI literature. The design of these systems hinges on mental attitudes like *beliefs* (B), *desires* (D) (or *goals* (G)) and *intentions* (I). The formalization of these three mental attitudes and their interactions have been captured to a great extend using Multi-Modal Logics (e.g., [14,17,3]). Moreover, some additional operators like *Capability, Opportunity, Obligation* [12,13,16] and several action constructs [18] have been introduced to improve the expressive power of the logics involved.

Much of the research in BDI is focused on improving the expressive power of the language with single operators and identifying formal properties of each of them. However, the general methodology for combining the different logics involved has been mainly neglected. For instance, any BDI system modelling rational agents consists of a combined system of logics of knowledge, belief, time and modal logic of actions. Each of these combined systems was presented and motivated by a different author for different reasons and different applications. We believe that investigating a general methodology for combining the component logics involved in BDI-like systems is an important research issue. This would result in a better understanding of the formal groundings of complex rational agent architectures and enable the designer to elegantly and easily incorporate new features of rational agency within her framework. Moreover the proposed general methodology should permit a modular treatment of the

S. Flesca et al. (Eds.): JELIA 2002, LNAI 2424, pp. 198–210, 2002.

modal components, whereby, each component is analysed and developed on its own, with the most appropriate methodology for it, and is then reused in the combination. Furthermore each module has its own features but the framework remains unchanged among the combined systems. Finally the combined system should offer preservation of some important logical properties of its elements.

In this study we investigate one such method, viz. *fibring* [6], and use it to reconstruct the logical account of BDI in terms of *dovetailing* (a special case of fibring) together with the multi-modal semantics of Catach [2]. In doing so we identify a set of interaction axioms for BDI, based on the incestual schema $G^{a,b,c,d}$, which covers many of the existing BDI axioms and also make possible the generation of a large class of new ones. Further we identify conditions under which completeness transfers from the component logics (L_1 and L_2) to their *fibred/dovetailed* composition ($L_{1,2}^F/L_{1,2}^D$), with the help of canonical model structures. We also show completeness preservation in the case of interaction axiom of the form $\Box_1\alpha \Rightarrow \Box_2\alpha$ ($L_{1,2}^{F,D} \oplus \Box_1\alpha \Rightarrow \Box_2\alpha$). Our study differs from that of other combining techniques like *fusion* in terms of the interaction axiom. For instance, normal bimodal and polymodal logics without any interaction axioms are well-studied as *fusions* of normal monomodal logics in [19]. Property transfer for such logics has been dealt with in [8]. For a slightly different account on fusions of logics one can refer [11]. Moreover *fusions* of normal modal logics without interaction axioms is the same as *dovetailing*. But difficulty arises with the extra interaction axiom. Then we need a more general concept like *fibring*. Our study starts with the assumption that the combination of two complete logics need not be complete when we add interaction axioms [9]. We want to identify conditions under which completeness can be preserved when we include interaction axioms like above.

2   BDI & Multi-modal Logics

The main advantage of using Multi-Modal Logics in BDI is their ability to express complex modalities, that can capture the inter-relationships existing among the different mental attitudes. This can be achieved by either composing modal operators of different types, or by using formal operations over modalities.

For instance the idea that an agent's goal is always supported by its belief is captured by the following BDI axioms:

$$\mathrm{GOAL}^{KD}(\alpha) \Rightarrow \mathrm{BEL}^{KD45}(\alpha) \tag{1}$$

$$\mathrm{GOAL}^{KD}(\alpha) \Rightarrow \mathrm{BEL}^{KD45}(\mathrm{GOAL}^{KD}(\alpha)) \tag{2}$$

The axiom systems for each of the mental operators is written as a superscript and the justification for such a preference is given in [14]. For a further account of the different axiom systems and the semantics for BDI logics refer to [14]; accordingly the semantic conditions for (1) and (2) are:

$$\text{if } (w_x, w_y) \in \mathrm{BEL} \text{ then } (w_x, w_y) \in \mathrm{GOAL} \tag{3}$$

$$\text{if } (w_x, w_y) \in \mathrm{BEL} \text{ and } (w_y, w_z) \in \mathrm{GOAL} \text{ then } (w_x, w_z) \in \mathrm{GOAL} \tag{4}$$

Condition (3) captures inclusion (containment) of a binary relation for beliefs in the relation for goals, whereas (4) captures the combined transitivity on two binary relations R_1 and R_2. The above mentioned axioms and conditions together with a range of additional axioms and constructs characterizes a typical BDI system. The properties of soundness, completeness etc are defined via canonical Kripke structures and for a further account see [15]

The point here is that the axiom systems for GOAL and BEL is a combination of other axiom systems and hence they are different. They can be considered as two different languages L_1 and L_2 with $\Box_1$ (BEL) and $\Box_2$ (GOAL) built up from the respective sets A_1 and A_2 of atoms and supported by the logics $KD45$ and KD. Hence we are dealing with two different systems S_1 and S_2 characterized, respectively, by the class of Kripke models $\mathcal{K}_1$ and $\mathcal{K}_2$ and this fact should be taken into consideration while defining semantic conditions for interaction axioms like those given above. For instance, we know how to evaluate $\Box_1\alpha$ (BEL(α)) in $\mathcal{K}_1$ ($KD45$) and $\Box_2\alpha$ (GOAL(α)) in $\mathcal{K}_2$ (KD). We need a method for evaluating $\Box_1$ (resp. $\Box_2$) with respect to $\mathcal{K}_2$ (resp. $\mathcal{K}_1$).

The problem in its general form is how to construct a multi-modal logic containing several unary modalities, each coming with its own system of specific axioms. The fibring technique introduced in the next section allows one to combine systems through their semantics. The fibring function can evaluate (give a yes/no) answer with respect to a modality in S_2, being in S_1 and vice versa. Each time we have to evaluate a formula α of the form $\Box_2\beta$ in a world in a model of $\mathcal{K}_1$ we associate, via the fibring function $\mathbf{F}$, to the world a model in $\mathcal{K}_2$ where we calculate the truth value of the formula. Formally

$$w \models_{m\in\mathcal{K}_1} \Box_2\beta \text{ iff } \mathbf{F}_2(w) \models_{m'\in\mathcal{K}_2} \Box_2\beta$$

α holds in w iff it holds in the model associated to w through the fibring function $\mathbf{F}$. Moreover α could be a mixed wff consisting of operators from L_1 and L_2 (for instance α can be $\Diamond_1\Box_2 q$). This is possible because the axiom systems of BEL and GOAL itself are combined systems. Then we have to say that the wff α belongs to the language $L_{(1,2)}$. The existing BDI semantics fails to give adequate explanation for such formulas. The problem becomes even more complex when we allow the system to vary in time. Then we have to combine the BDI system with a suitable temporal logic. The fibring/dovetailing technique provides a general methodology for such combinations as shown in the next section.

It is also important to note that since each mental operator (BEL, GOAL) itself is a combination of different axiom systems, the underlying multi-modal language (L_{BDI}) should be such that we should be able to develop each single operator on its own within its own semantics so that in the later stage the operators and models can be glued together through fibring/dovetailing to form a comprehensive system. The multi-modal language should also be able to express multiple concepts like rational agents, actions, plans etc. The problem with the existing BDI-Language is that each time we want to incorporate a new concept we have to redefine the system and come up with characterization results. For instance, if we want to capture the notion of actions, plans, programs etc. in

BDI, we need to come up with specific axiom systems for each of them and then show that they are characterized within the system. What we need is a set of interaction axioms that can generate a range of multi-modal systems for which there is a general characterization theorem so that we could avoid the need for showing it each time a new system is considered. To this end we adopt the class of interaction axioms $G^{a,b,c,d}$ of Catach [2] that can account for a range of multi-modal systems.

3   Fibring of Modal Logics

In this section we present a general semantic methodology, called fibring, for combining modal (BDI) logics and a variant of it called dovetailing. Two theorems stating relationships between dovetailing and BDI logics and dovetailing and fibring are shown. It is shown that the existing BDI logic is a dovetailed system.

The Fibring methodology allows one to combine systems through their semantics. The method helps in combining arbitrary logical systems in a uniform way and gives a new insight on possible worlds semantics [6,5]. Its idea is essentially to replace the notion of a possible world as a *unit* by another Kripke structure. For instance, if we consider the earlier example of a mixed formula, $\alpha = \Diamond_1 \Box_2 q$, the way the fibring function works can be shown as follows. α can be considered as a formula of L_1 (as the outer connective is $\Diamond_1$). From the point of view of language L_1 this formula has the form $\Diamond_1 p$, where $p = \Box_2 q$ is atomic since L_1 does not recognize $\Box_2$. The satisfaction condition for $\Diamond_1 p$ can be given considering a model $\mathbf{m}^1 = (S^1, R^1, a^1, h^1)$ such that $a^1 \models \Diamond_1 p$ (where S^1 is the set of possible worlds, $a^1 \in S$ is the actual world and $R \subseteq S \times S$ is the accessibility relation, h is the assignment function, a binary function, giving a value $h(t,p) \in \{0,1\}$ for any $t \in S$ and atomic p). For this to hold there should be some $t \in S^1$ such that $a^1 R^1 t$, and we have $t \models_1 p$, i.e., $t \models_1 \Box_2 q$. Since $\Box_2$ is not in the language of L_1 the normal evaluation is not possible. The basic idea of fibring is to associate with each $t \in S^1$, a model $\mathbf{m}_t^2 = (S_t^2, R_t^2, a_t^2, h_t^2)$ of L_2 and by evaluating $\Box_2 q$ in the associated model, thus we have

$$ t \models_1 \Box_2 q \text{ iff } a_t^2 \models_2 \Box_2 q. $$

If we take $\mathbf{F}^1$ to be the fibring function associating the model $\mathbf{m}_2^t$ with t then $F^1(t) = \mathbf{m}_2^t$ and the semantics for the language $\mathcal{L}_{(1,2)}$ has a model of the form $(S^1, R^1, a^1, h^1, \mathbf{F}^1)$.

Fibring two Semantics. Let I be a set of labels representing intentional states, and $L_i, i \in I$ be modal logics whose respective modalities are $\Box_i, i \in I$.

Definition 1 *[6] A fibred model is a structure* $(W, S, R, \mathbf{a}, h, \tau, \mathbf{F})$ *where*

- *W is a set of possible worlds;*
- *S is a function giving for each w a set of possible worlds, $S^w \subseteq W$;*

- R is a function giving for each w, a relation $R^w \subseteq S^w \times S^w$;
- $\mathbf{a}$ is a function giving the actual world $\mathbf{a}^w$ of the model labelled by w;
- h is an assignment function $h^w(q) \subseteq S^w$, for each atomic q;
- τ is the semantical identifying function $\tau : W \to I$. $\tau(w) = i$ means that the model $(S^w, R^w, \mathbf{a}^w, h^w)$ is a model in $\mathcal{K}_i$, we use W_i to denote the set of worlds of type i;
- $\mathbf{F}$, is the set of fibring functions $\mathcal{F} : I \times W \mapsto W$. A fibring function $\mathcal{F}$ is a function giving for each i and each $w \in W$ another point (actual world) in W as follows:

$$\mathcal{F}_i(w) = \begin{cases} w & \text{if } w \in S^{\mathbf{m}} \text{ and } \mathbf{m} \in \mathcal{K}_i \\ a \text{ value in } W_i, & \text{otherwise} \end{cases}$$

such that if $x \neq y$ then $\mathcal{F}_i(x) \neq \mathcal{F}_i(y)$.

Satisfaction is defined as follows with the usual truth tables for boolean connectives:

$$t \models p \text{ iff } h(t,p) = 1, \text{ where } p \text{ is an atom}$$
$$t \models \Box_i A \text{ iff } \begin{cases} t \in \mathbf{m} \text{ and } \mathbf{m} \in \mathcal{K}_i \text{ and } \forall s(tRs \to s \models A), \text{or} \\ t \in \mathbf{m}, \text{ and } \mathbf{m} \notin \mathcal{K}_i \text{ and } \forall \mathcal{F} \in \mathbf{F}, \mathcal{F}_i(t) \models \Box_i A. \end{cases}$$

We say the model satisfies A iff $w_0 \models A$.

A fibred model for L_I^F can be generated from fibring the semantics for the modal logics $L_i, i \in I$. The detailed construction runs as follows: Let $\mathcal{K}_i$ be a class of models $\{\mathbf{m}_1^i, \mathbf{m}_2^i, \ldots\}$ for which L_i is complete. Each model $\mathbf{m}_n^i$ has the form (S, R, a, h). The actual world a plays a role in the semantic evaluation in the model, in so far as satisfaction in the model is defined as satisfaction at a. We can assume that the models satisfy the condition $S = \{x \mid \exists n \, a \, R^n x\}$. This assumption does not affect satisfaction in models because points not accessible from a by any power R^n of R do not affect truth values at a. Moreover we assume that all sets of possible worlds in any $\mathcal{K}_i$ are all pairwise disjoint, and that there are infinitely many isomorphic (but disjoint) copies of each model in $\mathcal{K}_i$. We use the notation $\mathbf{m}$ for a model and present it as $\mathbf{m} = (S^{\mathbf{m}}, R^{\mathbf{m}}, a^{\mathbf{m}}, h^{\mathbf{m}})$ and write $\mathbf{m} \in \mathcal{K}_i$, when the model $\mathbf{m}$ is in the semantics $\mathcal{K}_i$. Thus our assumption boils down to $\mathbf{m} \neq \mathbf{n} \Rightarrow S^{\mathbf{m}} \cap S^{\mathbf{n}} = \varnothing$. In fact a model can be identified by its actual world, i.e., $\mathbf{m} = \mathbf{n}$ iff $a^{\mathbf{m}} = a^{\mathbf{n}}$. Then the fibred semantics can be given as follows:

- $W = \bigcup_{\mathbf{m} \in \cup_i \mathcal{K}_i} S^{\mathbf{m}}$;
- $R = \bigcup_{\mathbf{m} \in \cup_i \mathcal{K}_i} R^{\mathbf{m}}$;
- $h(w, q) = h^{\mathbf{m}}(w, q)$, for the unique $\mathbf{m}$ such that $w \in S^{\mathbf{m}}$;
- $a^w = a^m$ for the unique m such that $w \in S^{\mathbf{m}}$.

Dovetailing. Dovetailing is a special case of fibring in the sense that the dovetailed model must agree with the current world on the values of atoms. For instance, in the previous section we saw that the functions $\mathcal{F}$ can be viewed as functions giving for each $t \in S^1 \cup S^2$, an element $\mathcal{F}(t) \in S^1 \cup S^2$ such that if $t \in S^i$ then $\mathcal{F}(t) \in S^j, i \neq j$. If L_1 and L_2 share the same set of atoms Q then we can compare the values $h(t, q)$ and $h(\mathcal{F}(t), q)$ for an atom q which need not be identical. If we require from the fibring functions that for each $t \in S^i, \mathcal{F}_j(t) \in S^j$ and each $q \in Q$ we want

$$h(t, q) = h(\mathcal{F}_i(t), q).$$

Then this fibring case is referred to as *dovetailing*. This means that the actual world of the model fibred at t, $\mathcal{F}_i(t)$, can be identified with t. The set of fibring functions **F** is no longer needed, since we identified t with $\mathcal{F}_i(t)$, for every fibring function $\mathcal{F}$.

Definition 2 *[6] Let L_i be modal logics, with $\mathcal{K}_i$ the class of models for L_i. Let L_I^D (the dovetailing combination of $L_i, i \in I$) be defined semantically through the class of all (dovetailed) models of the form (W, R, a, h), where W is a set of worlds, $a \in W$, h is an assignment and for each $i \in I, R(i) \subseteq W \times W$. We require that for each i, $(W, R(i), a, h)$ is a model in $\mathcal{K}_i$. It is further required that all $t \in W$ be such that there exist $n_1, \ldots, n_k$ and $i_1, \ldots, i_k$ such that $aR^{n_1}(i_1) \circ R^{n_2}(i_2) \cdots \circ R^{n_k}(i_k)t$ holds. The satisfaction condition $w \models A$, is defined by induction as*

- $w \models q$ if $w \in h(q)$ for q atomic;
- $w \models \Box_i A$ if for all $y \in W$, such that $wR(i)y$ we have $y \models A$;
- $\models A$ iff for all models and actual worlds $a \models A$.

Two theorems are given below, the proof of which can be found in [6].

Theorem 1 (Dovetailing and Normal Modal Logic). *Assume L_i, $i \in I$ all are extensions of K formulated using traditional Hilbert axioms and the rule of necessitation, then L_I^D can be axiomatized by taking the union of the axioms and the rules of necessitation for each modality $\Box_i$ of each L_i*

Theorem 2 (Fibring = Dovetailing). *If L_i, $i \in I$ admit necessitation and satisfy the disjunction property, then $L_I^F = L_I^D$.*

It is immediate to see that BDI logic without interaction axioms is nothing else but normal multi-modal logics —combinations of normal modal logics (e.g., the basic BDI logic proposed in [14] is the combination of a $KD45$ modality for BEL, KD for GOAL and KD for INT)— hence, according to Theorem 1, dovetailing provides a general methodology for generating BDI-like systems.

4   Semantics for Mental States

In the previous section we have seen how to provide a general semantics for BDI logics without interaction of modalities. However, mental states are very often connected to each other, for example the interaction axioms like (1) and (2); thus what is needed is a methodology to capture them. In this section we use Catach approach [2] to extend dovetailing in order to develop a general semantics that covers both the basic modalities and their interactions. Briefly Catach's approach runs as follows:

Let I be a set of atomic labels; complex labels can be built from atomic ones using the neutral element "λ", the sequential operator ";", and the union operator "$\cup$". If i is an atomic label and α a well-formed formula, then the expression $[i]\alpha$ corresponds to the modal formula $\Box_i\alpha$, and $\langle i \rangle \alpha$ to $\Diamond_i\alpha$. Furthermore we assume that $[\lambda] = \langle \lambda \rangle$. The transformation of complex labels into modalities is governed by the following rules:

$$[\lambda]\alpha \Leftrightarrow \alpha; \qquad [a;b]\alpha \Leftrightarrow [a][b]\alpha; \qquad [a \cup b]\alpha \Leftrightarrow [a]\alpha \wedge [b]\alpha.$$

According to the above conditions we can identify, for example, the formula $\Box_1\Box_2 A \wedge \Box_3 A \wedge A$ with the expression $[(1;2) \cup 3 \cup \lambda]$.

Let us consider now the expression $\langle a \rangle [b]\alpha \Rightarrow [c]\langle d \rangle \alpha$, known as the a, b, c, d-incestuality axiom (we will use $G^{a,b,c,d}$ to refer to it). It can be used to generate, among others, the well know D, T, B, 4 and 5 axioms of modal logic. For example, when $a = b = \lambda$ and $c = d = 1$ we obtain the symmetry axiom B for $\Box_i$.

It is then immediate to see that the above axiom schema covers many existing systems of multi-modal logic, including the BDI system and make the generation of a large class of new ones possible.

Example 1. Let α be a formula and BEL, GOAL, INT, CAP, OPP and RES be the modal operators for the mental constructs; then the following are instances of $G^{a,b,c,d}$.

C1 GOAL(α) $\Rightarrow$ BEL(α)   (Inclusion)
C2 INT(α) $\Rightarrow$ {GOAL(α) $\Rightarrow$ BEL(α)}   (Relative Inclusion)
C3 RES(e) $\Leftrightarrow$ CAP(e) $\wedge$ OPP(e)   (Union)

The axioms C2 and C3 are possible additions to the existing BDI axioms. The above axioms (as well as others) can be used to represent various concepts such as rational agents, programs, actions etc. For instance C2 captures the fact that an agent's intention to achieve α is supported by having a goal towards α and this goal is based on its belief of α. The existing BDI framework lacks such axioms.

As far as dovetailed models are concerned it is possible to define a mapping ρ between labels and the accessibility relations of dovetailed models.

Definition 3 *Let a and b be labels, i an atomic label, and $(W, R(i), a, h)$ a dovetailed model. Then*

$$\rho(i) = R(i); \qquad \rho(\lambda) = \Delta; \qquad \rho(a;b) = \rho(a)|\rho(b); \qquad \rho(a \cup b) = \rho(a) \cup \rho(b);$$

where the operators $\cup$ (union) and $|$ (composition) are defined for binary relations, and Δ is the diagonal relation over W

Definition 4 *Let a, b, c, and d be labels. A dovetailed model* $D = (W, R(i), a, h)$ *enjoys the* a, b, c, d*-incestuality property iff the following condition holds for D.*

$$\rho(a)^{-1}|\rho(c) \subseteq \rho(b)|\rho(d)^{-1}.$$

The incestuality condition can be reformulated as follows:

> If $(w, w') \in \rho(a)$ and $(w, w'') \in \rho(c)$ then there exists w''' such that $(w', w''') \in \rho(b)$ and $(w'', w''') \in \rho(d)$.

Theorem 3. *[2] Let $\boldsymbol{L}_{BDI}$ be a normal multi-modal system built from a finite set of axioms $\boldsymbol{G}^{a,b,c,d}$. Then $\boldsymbol{L}_{BDI}$ is determined by the class of dovetailed models satisfying the a,b,c,d-incestuality properties.*

Catach originally proved the above theorem for what he calls multi-frames. Trivially multi-frames correspond to dovetailed models. In particular this result provides the characterization of a wide class of interaction axioms such as the relationships among mental attitudes of rational agents in terms of dovetailing.

5   Conditions on the Fibring Function

Section 3 establishes how BDI-like systems (without interaction axioms) can be reconstructed using dovetailing and section 4 introduces a general axiom schema through which we can generate a range of BDI-like interaction axioms. In this section we demonstrate with the help of an example what conditions would be required on the fibring functions in order to cope with the a, b, c, d-incestuality schema. As noted earlier we assume that the combination of two complete logics need not be complete when we include interaction axioms. We want to identify conditions under which completeness can be preserved. But before identifying the specific conditions on the fibring functions we need to introduce certain notions and constructions related to completeness preservation in terms of canonical models and canonical logics.

In the canonical model construction a *world* is a maximal consistent sets of wff. Thus for any normal propositional modal system S, its canonical model $\langle W, R, V \rangle$ is defined as follows:

- $W = \{w: w$ is a maximal S-consistent set of wff $\}$;
- For any pair of worlds w and any $w' \in W$, wRw' iff $\{\alpha : \Box\alpha \in w\} \subseteq w'$;
- For any variable p and any $w \in W$, $V(p, w) = 1$ iff $p \in w$.

But in the case of a fibred model the above construction needs to be modified accordingly as follows: Let $L_i, i \in I$ be monomodal normal logic with languages $\mathcal{L}_i$. Let M_L be the set of all L-maximal consistent sets of formula. Given a set S of formulas, $L^{\Box_i}(S) = \{A : \Box_i A \in S\}$ and $L^{\mathcal{L}_i}(S) = \{A : A = \Box_i B$ or $A = \Diamond_i B, A \in S\}$. The canonical model for L_I^F, C_I^F is the structure $\langle W, S, R, \mathbf{F}, a, \tau, h \rangle$, where

- $W = M_L \times I$.
- S is a function $W \mapsto \wp W$ such that $S^w = \{(x, i) \in W : \tau(w) = i\}$. In other words the set of worlds of the same type as w.

- $R^w \subseteq S^w \times S^w$ such that xR^wy iff $L^{\Box\tau(w)}(x) \subseteq y$.
- **F** is the set of functions $\mathcal{F}: I \times W \mapsto W$ (fibring functions) such that

$$\mathcal{F}_i, (x, j) = \begin{cases} (x, j) & i = j \\ (x, i) & x = a^w \\ (y, i) & \text{otherwise} \end{cases}$$

where $L^{\mathcal{L}_i(x)} \subseteq y$, and if $x \neq y$, then $\mathcal{F}_i(x) \neq \mathcal{F}_j(y)$.
- $a^w = w$.
- $\tau(x, i) = i$
- $h(p, w) = 1$ iff $p \in w$, for p atomic.

Lemma 1. *For every formula α and every world w in the canonical model*

$$h(w, \alpha) = 1 \text{ iff } \alpha \in w.$$

Proof. The proof is by induction on the complexity of α. The only difference with the proof of the monomodal case is when $\alpha = \Box_i\beta$ and $\tau(w) \neq i$. If $h(w, \Box_i\beta) = 1$, then for every $\mathcal{F} \in \mathbf{F}$ $h(\mathcal{F}_i(w), \Box_i\beta) = 1$, and we can apply the standard construction for modalities and we obtain that $\Box_i\beta \in \mathcal{F}_i(w)$. Let us now suppose that $\Box_i\beta$ is not in w. Since w is maximal $\neg\Box_i\beta \in w$; thus $\Diamond_i\neg\beta \in w$. $L^{\mathcal{L}_i} \subseteq \mathcal{F}_i(w)$, hence $\Diamond_i\neg\beta \in \mathcal{F}_i(w)$, from which we derive a contradiction. Thus $\Box_i\beta \in w$. The other direction is similar.

As an immediate consequence of the Lemma we have the following theorem.

Theorem 4. $L_I^F \vdash \alpha$ *iff* $C_I^F \models \alpha$.

Definition 5 *Let F_L be the frame of the canonical model for L. L is canonical iff for every valuation V, (F_L, V) is a model for L.*

Clearly the above definition is equivalent to the usual condition for a modal logic to be canonical (i.e., that the frame of the canonical model is a frame for L). However the fibring construction inherits the valuation functions from the underlying models, and we can obtain different logics imposing conditions on the fibring functions based on the assignments of the variables. The fibred frame for $\mathcal{L}_{1,2}$ is obtained in the same way as the fibred model, replacing the occurrences of models with frames.

Lemma 2. *Let $M_I^F = (W, S, R, \mathbf{F}, a, \tau, h)$ be the canonical model for L_I^F. Then for each $w \in W$ (S^w, R^w, h^w) is the canonical model for $\tau(w)$.*

Proof. By inspection on the construction of the canonical model for L_I^F.

From the above Lemma we obtain:

Theorem 5. *Let $L_i, i \in I$ be canonical monomodal logics. Then L_I^F is canonical.*

For instance the inclusion axiom $\Box_1 A \Rightarrow \Box_2 A$ is characterized by the dovetailed models where $R_2 \subseteq R_1$. However, such a constraint would be meaningless for fibred models where each modality has its own set of possible worlds. So, what is the corresponding condition on fibred models? A fibring function is defined as

$$\mathcal{F} : I \times W \rightarrow W$$

where I is the set of modalities involved and W is a set of possible worlds. It is worth noting that given a world we can identify the model it belongs to, and that there is a bijection M between the actual worlds and their models. So to deal with the inclusion axiom the following constraint must be satisfied:

$$\forall w \in W \forall \mathcal{F} \in \mathbf{F} : M(\mathcal{F}_2(w)) \sqsubseteq_N M(\mathcal{F}_1(w)) \tag{5}$$

where $\sqsubseteq_N$ is the inclusion morphism thus defined:

Definition 6 *Let* $\mathbf{m}_1$ *and* $\mathbf{m}_2$ *be two models. Then* $\mathbf{m}_2 \sqsubseteq_N \mathbf{m}_1$ *iff there is a morphism* $\mathbf{w} : W_2 \mapsto W_1$, *such that*

- *for each atom* p, $h_2(w, p) = h_1(\mathbf{w}(w), p)$;
- *if* $x R_2 y$ *then* $\mathbf{w}(x) R_1 \mathbf{w}(y)$.

The constraint on the fibring functions to support the *inclusion axiom*, is in alliance with the incestuality axiom $G^{a,b,c,d}$ as stated in the previous section, that is, $R_2 = \rho(c)$ and $R_1 = \rho(b)$. The incestuality axiom can be characterised by giving appropriate conditions that identify the (fibred) models $\mathbf{m}_1$ and $\mathbf{m}_2$ involved in the inclusion morphism.

It is now possible to provide a characterization of the fibring/dovetailing of normal modal logics L_1 and L_2 with inclusion axiom (i.e., $\Box_1 \alpha \Rightarrow \Box_2 \alpha$).

Theorem 6. *Let* L_1 *and* L_2 *be two canonical normal modal logics and let* $L_{1,2}$ *be the logics obtained by fibring/dovetailing* L_1 *and* L_2. *Then* $L_{1,2} \oplus \Box_1 \alpha \Rightarrow \Box_2 \alpha$ *is characterized by the class of fibred/dovetailed models satisfying (5).*

Proof. For the proof we have to note that, thanks to the fact that L_1 and L_2 are canonical, for any pair of world w and v, the sets of maximal consistent associated with them are the same, i.e., $S^w = S^v$, they are the set of all the maximal consistent sets. Thus no matter of the fibring function we chose, we have that the structure of the the models obtained from $\mathcal{F}_1$ and $\mathcal{F}_2$ are the same. Therefore we can use the identity over M_L as the morphism $\mathbf{w}$ in the inclusion morphism. Let $\mathbf{m}_1 = \mathcal{F}_1(w)$ and $\mathbf{m}_2 = \mathcal{F}_2(w)$. Clearly for every world v and every atom p, $h^2(v, p) = h^1(\mathbf{w}(v), p)$. Since $\Box_1 A \Rightarrow \Box_2 A$ is an axiom, then $\forall w \in W$, $\Box_1 A \Rightarrow \Box_2 A \in w$. This implies $L^{\Box_1}(w) \subseteq L^{\Box_2}(w)$. Hence if $w R^2 y$, then $L^{\Box_2}(w) \subseteq y$. Since the morphism $\mathbf{w}$ is the identity over M_L, we have that $L^{\Box_1}(\mathbf{w}(w)) \subseteq L^{\Box_2}(\mathbf{w}(w)) \subseteq \mathbf{w}(y)$. Therefore $\mathbf{w}(w) R^1 \mathbf{w}(y)$.

It is well known that normal modal operators have certain properties that are occasionally considered undesirable for the common sense notions that they are intended to formalise. For instance the property of *Logical Omniscience* though could hold for the beliefs of an agent is certainly undesirable for the knowledge part. For example to say that an agent knows all the logical consequences of its knowledge $(\Box\varphi \wedge \Box(\varphi \Rightarrow \psi)) \Rightarrow \Box\psi$ is to live in an idealized world. The fibring methodology can be used to combine single modal logics that are not normal. However, in general, simple adjustments are required to deal with classes of non-normal modal logics. In what follows we show the modifications required for quasi-normal modal logics (i.e. modal logics containing K and closed under RM $\vdash \alpha \Rightarrow \beta / \vdash \Box\alpha \Rightarrow \Box\beta$). The first thing we have to consider is that the structure of models appropriate for such a class is (W, N, R, a, h) where W and a are as usual, $N \subseteq W$ (representing the set of normal worlds), $R \subseteq N \times W$, and we have the following two additional clauses on the valuation function h:

$$\text{if } w \notin N, h(w, \Box\alpha) = 0; \qquad \text{if } w \notin N, h(w, \Diamond\alpha) = 1.$$

Fibred, dovetailed, and canonical models can be obtained accordingly with the appropriate trivial modifications (cf. [10])[1]. We are now ready to give the completeness theorem for the fibring of monotonic modal logics.

Theorem 7. *Let $L_i, i \in I$ be quasi-normal modal logics classes of structures $\mathcal{K}_i$ and set of theorems T_i. Let T_I^F be the following set of wffs of L_I^F.*

1. *$T_i \subseteq T_I^F$, for every $i \in I$;*
2. *If $A(x_m) \in T_i$ then $A(x_m/\Box_j\alpha_j) \in T_I^F$, for any $\Box_i\alpha_m, i \in I$;*
3. **Monotonic Modal Fibring Rule:** *If $\Box_i$ is the modality of L_i and $\Box_j$ that of L_j, where i, j are arbitrary, with $i \neq j$.*

$$\frac{\bigwedge_{k=1}^{n} \Box_i A_k \Rightarrow \bigvee_{k=1}^{m} \Box_i B_k \in T_I^F}{\Box_j^n \bigwedge_{k=1}^{n} \Box_i A_k \Rightarrow \Box_j^n \bigvee_{k=1}^{m} \Box_i B_k \in T_I^F} \text{for all } n;$$

4. *T_I^F is the smallest set closed under 1, 2, 3, modus ponens and substitution.*

Then T_I^F is the set of all wffs of L_I^F valid in all the fibred monotonic structures of L_I^F.

Proof. The proof is a trivial modification of that of Theorem 3.10 of [6].

Intuitively the meaning of the Monotonic Modal Fibring Rule has to do with the substitutions of formulas of one language into a formula of the other language. If the substituted formulas are proof theoretically related we want to propagate this relation to the other language. Moreover there are formal similarities between the Monotonic Fibred Rule and RM. Consider an implication of the form $A \Rightarrow B$ where A and B are built from atoms of the form $\Box_i C$. There our special RM says that if $\vdash A \Rightarrow B$ then we can derive $\vdash \Box_j A \Rightarrow \Box_j B$ for any modality $\Box_j$ other than $\Box_i$.

A similar theorem can be proved for the dovetailing of quasi-normal modal logics with the appropriate modifications on the Dovetail Modal Rule given by Gabbay [6].

At this stage we have to revise our definition of inclusion morphism.

---

[1] For normal modal logics $N = W$, thus any normal modal logic is also quasi-normal.

Definition 7 *Let m_1 and m_2 be two quasi-normal models. $m_1 \sqsubseteq_M m_2$ iff*

1. $m_1 \sqsubseteq_N m_2$; and
2. if $w \notin N_1$ then $\mathbf{w}(w) \notin N_2$.

Theorem 8. *Let L_1 and L_2 be the logic obtained by the canonical quasi-normal modal logic fibring/dovetailing of L_1 and L_2. Then $L_{1,2}^M \oplus \square_1 \alpha \Rightarrow \square_2 \alpha$ is characterized by the class of fibred/dovetailed models satisfying*

$$\forall w \in W \forall \mathcal{F} \in \mathbf{F} : M(\mathcal{F}_2(w)) \sqsubseteq_M M(\mathcal{F}_1(w)).$$

Proof. The proof is analogous to that of Theorem 6.

The main consequence of the above theorem is that it shows how to extend the full power of fibring to non-normal modal logics with interaction axioms, including combinations of a range of modalities required to model complex BDI systems.

Corollary 1. *Let L_1 and L_2 be the logic obtained by the canonical {quasi-} normal modal logic fibring/dovetailing of L_1 and L_2. Then $L_{1,2}^M \oplus \square_1 \alpha \Rightarrow \square_2 \alpha$ is canonical.*

6 Discussion

We have investigated the relationships between BDI logics and Gabbay's fibring semantics. In particular we have shown how to reconstruct the logical account of BDI in terms of dovetailing and Catach's approach. Roughly fibring (dovetailing) examines and develops each single operator on its own, within its own semantics, and then the operators and models are glued together to form a comprehensive system.

The proposed methodology provides a general framework for BDI in so far as it is not restricted to particular operators and, at the same time, it offers easy tools to study properties (e.g., soundness, completeness, ...) of the resulting systems. Transfer results, even if limited to very small cases of interaction axioms, would be of extreme importance to BDI theorists as this will help shift their attention from the single case analysis to the general problem of combination of mental states. The problem of interaction axioms between logic fragments in a combined logic might become more central among the BDI theorists. Moreover the proposed approach is not restricted to normal modal operators —the use of non-normal epistemic operators is one of the common strategies to (partially) obviate the problem of logical omniscience.

As we have seen dovetailing is a particular form of fibring, and the latter offers a more fine grained analysis of the concepts at hand. In other words we can say that fibring is more selective than dovetailing. Indeed, there are formulas which are valid under dovetailing but false under some interpretations using fibring; thus some unwanted consequences could be discarded by fibring. Remember that the condition for dovetailing states that sources and targets of the fibring functions agree on the evaluation of atoms. However, this is not required for fibring, so, we can say that fibring can be thought of as a change of perspective in passing from a model (modal operator) to another model (modal operator). This has some important consequences: for example, the interpretation of a piece of evidence may depend on the mental state used to look at it.

References

1. M.E. Bratman, D.J. Israel, and M.E Pollack. Plans and resource-bounded practical reasoning. *Computational Intelligence*, 4:349–355, 1988.
2. L. Catach. Normal multimodal logics. In *In Proc. National Conference on AI(AAAI-88)*, pages 491–495, 1988.
3. P. R. Cohen and H. J. Levesque. Intention is choice with commitment. *Artificial Intelligence*, 42(3), 1990.
4. K. Fischer and Muller J. P. & Pischel M. A pragmatic BDI architecture. In *Intelligent Agents II, LNAI-1037*, volume 1037, pages 203–218. Springer-Verlag, 1996.
5. D. M. Gabbay and G. Governatori. Dealing with label dependent deontic modalities. In *Norms, Logics And Information Systems*. IOS Press, Amsterdam, 1999.
6. D. M. Gabbay. *Fibring Logics*. Oxford University Press, Oxford, 1998.
7. M. Georgeff and F. Ingrand. Decision making in an embedded reasoning system. In *In proc. of the International Joint Conference on Artificial Intelligence- IJCAI*, pages 972–978, 1989.
8. M. Kracht and F. Wolter. Properties of independently axiomatizable bimodal logics. *The Journal of Symbolic Logic*, 56(4):1469–1485, 1991.
9. M. Kracht. *Tools and Techniques for Modal Logics*. Elsevier, 1999.
10. E.J. Lemmon. Algebraic semantics for modal logic II. *Journal of Symbolic Logic*, 31:191–218, June 1966.
11. Franz Baader & Carsten Lutz, Holger Sturn, and Frank Wolter. Fusions of description logics and abstract description systems. *Journal of Artificial Intelligence Research*, 16:1–58, 2002.
12. Lin Padgham and Patrick Lambrix. Agent capabilities: Extending bdi theory. In *Proccedings of AAAI-2000, Austin, Texas, USA*, pages 68–73. AAAI/MIT Press, 2000.
13. Vineet Padmanabhan, Guido Governatori, and Abdul Sattar. Actions made explicit in BDI. In *AI 2001: Advances in Artificial Intelligence*, LNAI-2256. Springer Verlag, 2001.
14. A.S. Rao and Georgeff M.P. Modelling rational agents within a bdi-architecture. In *Principles of Knowledge Representation and Reasoning (KR'91)*. Morgan Kaufmann, 1991.
15. A. S. Rao. Decision procedures for propositional linear-time belief- desire-intention logics. In *Intelligent Agents Volume II, LNAI-1037*, pages 33–48. Springer-Verlag, 1996.
16. Y. Shoham. Agent oriented programming. *Artificial Intelligence*, 60:51–92, 1993.
17. Munindar P. Singh. Semantical considerations on intention dynamics for bdi agents. *Journal of Experimental and Theoretical Artificial Intelligence*, 1998.
18. B. Van Linder. *Modal Logic for Rational Agents*. PhD thesis, Department of Computer Science, Utrecht University, 19th June 1996.
19. Frank Wolter. Fusions of modal logics revisited. In *Advances in Modal Logic*, volume 1. CSLI Lecture notes 87, 1997.

A Modal Formulation of McCain
and Turner's Theory of Causal Reasoning

Graham White

Department of Computer Science
Queen Mary
University of London
London E1 4NS, UK
graham@dcs.qmul.ac.uk
http://www.dcs.qmul.ac.uk/~graham

Abstract. McCain and Turner [6] have an interesting theory of causal reasoning. We give a modal treatment of McCain and Turner's theory of causal reasoning: we thereby formulate theories equivalent to their original model-theoretic treatment, while preserving its good properties (in particular, its independence of vocabulary).

1   The Original Procedure

McCain and Turner [6] use a new connective, which we will write ▷; this is to be distinguished from material implication, for which we will write →.[1] McCain and Turner intend $\phi \triangleright \psi$ to mean "necessarily, if ϕ then the fact that ψ is caused" [6, p. 460]; Lifschitz expresses this as "$[\psi]$ has a cause if $[\phi]$ is true, or ... $[\phi]$ provides a 'causal explanation' for $[\psi]$" [4, p. 451].

McCain and Turner now define their semantics as follows. We suppose, first that we are given an underlying propositional language, which we will call $\mathfrak{L}$, and (possibly) a theory in $\mathfrak{L}$, which we will call S. Let $\mathfrak{M}$ be the set of models of S. The McCain-Turner semantics was defined for a purely propositional language; for the moment, we will restrict ourselves to such languages.

1. A *causal law* is a formula of the form $\phi \triangleright \psi$, where ϕ and ψ are formulae of $\mathfrak{L}$.
2. A *causal theory* is a set of causal laws.
note that we have two different sorts of theory here; the background theory, S, and the causal theory, $\mathbb{T}$. Although it is possible to encode the background theory in the causal theory (see [5, p. 537]), it is conceptually simpler if we keep the two types of theories separate.

---

[1] McCain and Turner write their connective ⇒, and use ⊃ for strict implication; Lifschitz writes ← for the (converse of the) McCain-Turner connective and, again, ⊃ for material implication. We find it less confusing to use a symbol for the McCain-Turner connective which has never been used for material implication; we will be using a certain amount of set-theoretical notation, so that ⊃ is not really an option for material implication.

S. Flesca et al. (Eds.): JELIA 2002, LNAI 2424, pp. 211–222, 2002.

3. Suppose that we are given a causal theory: call it $\mathbb{T}$. Let M be a model of S. Define

$$\mathbb{T}^M \overset{\text{def}}{=} \{\psi| \text{ for some } \phi \in \mathcal{L}, \phi \triangleright \psi \text{ and } M \vDash \phi\} \qquad (1)$$

4. Now we say that M is *causally explained* (according to $\mathbb{T}$) if it is the only model of $\mathbb{T}^M$.
5. Finally, we say that $\phi \in \mathcal{L}$ is a *consequence* of a causal theory $\mathbb{T}$ if ϕ is true in every $\mathbb{T}$-causally explained model of S.

1.1   Extensionality

We should note an important property of this formalism: that it is independent of the *language* used. Suppose that we have another language $\mathcal{L}'$, together with an interpretation $\alpha : \mathcal{L} \to \mathcal{L}'$ of $\mathcal{L}$ in $\mathcal{L}'$. We can now translate both our background theory, S, and our causal theory $\mathbb{T}$, into $\mathcal{L}'$: a proposition ϑ of S is mapped to $\alpha(\vartheta)$, whereas an element $\phi \triangleright \psi$ of $\mathbb{T}$ is mapped to $\alpha(\phi) \triangleright \alpha(\psi)$. We thus obtain new theories S' and $\mathbb{T}'$ in the new language. α also induces a mapping, α^*, from models of $\mathcal{L}'$ to models of $\mathcal{L}$, with the property that, for any ϕ in $\mathcal{L}$ and any model M' of $\mathcal{L}'$,

$$M' \vDash \alpha(\phi) \iff \alpha^*(M') \vDash \phi$$

(see, for example, the treatment in [3]).

We can now show

Proposition 1. *If α^* is a bijection of models, then ϕ is a consequence of a causal theory $\mathbb{T}$ iff $\alpha(\phi)$ is a consequence of the causal theory $\alpha(\mathbb{T})$ (relative, of course, to background theories S and $\alpha(S)$).*

Proof. The proof is elementary: notice first that, for any model M' of S',

$$\begin{aligned}
M'^{\alpha(\mathbb{T})} &= \{\psi'|\phi' \triangleright \psi' \in \alpha(\mathbb{T}), M' \vDash \phi'\} \\
&= \{\alpha(\psi)|\alpha(\phi) \triangleright \alpha(\psi) \in \alpha(\mathbb{T}), M' \vDash \alpha(\phi)\} \\
&= \{\alpha(\psi)|\phi \triangleright \psi \in \mathbb{T}, \alpha^*(M') \vDash \phi\} \\
&= \alpha(\alpha^*(M)^{\mathbb{T}})
\end{aligned}$$

Consequently,

$\quad M'$ is causally explained according to $\alpha(\mathbb{T})$
$\iff M'$ is the only model of $M'^{\alpha(\mathbb{T})}$
$\iff M'$ is the only model of $\alpha(\alpha^*(M')^{\mathbb{T}})$
$\iff \alpha^*(M')$ is the only model of $\alpha^*(M')^{\mathbb{T}}$
$\iff \alpha^*(M')$ is causally explained according to $\mathbb{T}$.

And now we have the result:

$\quad \phi$ is a consequence of $\mathbb{T}$
$\iff$ for all models M of S, if M is causally explained according to $\mathbb{T}$,
    then $M \vDash \phi$

⇔ for all models M' of S', if $\alpha^*(M')$ is causally explained according to $\mathbb{T}$,
   then $\alpha^*(M') \vDash \phi$
⇔ for all models M' of S',
   if M' is causally explained according to $\alpha(\mathbb{T})$, then $\alpha^*(M') \vDash \phi$
⇔ for all models M' of S', if M' is causally explained according to $\alpha(\mathbb{T})$,
   then $M' \vDash \alpha(\phi)$
⇔ $\alpha(\phi)$ is a consequence of $\alpha(\mathbb{T})$.

This may seem trivial, but it is a property not shared by treatments of causality based on circumscription; see [11]. This property is – as I argue in [11] – important both philosophically and practically: philosophically, language-independence is desirable for a well-motivated semantics, whereas practically it means that we only have to be concerned about the correctness of our descriptions, rather than having, in addition, to fret about whether we have found the magical language that makes our circumscriptions work.

2   Reformulations

2.1   Reformulation 1: Model Theory

First a definition:

Definition 1. *A causal theory $\mathbb{T}$ defines a relation $\mathbf{R}_\mathbb{T}$ on models by*

$$M \, \mathbf{R}_\mathbb{T} \, M' \Leftrightarrow \text{for every } \phi \triangleright \psi \in \mathbb{T} \tag{2}$$
$$\text{if } M \vDash \phi, \text{ then } M' \vDash \psi$$

We then have:

Lemma 1. *For any $\chi \in \mathfrak{L}$,*

$$\mathbb{T}^M \vdash \chi \Leftrightarrow M' \vDash \chi \text{ for all } M' \text{ with } M \, \mathbf{R}_\mathbb{T} \, M' \tag{3}$$

Proof. Note first that, for any model M',

$$M' \vDash \mathbb{T}^M \Leftrightarrow \text{for all } \phi \triangleright \psi \in \mathbb{T}. \, M \vDash \phi \Rightarrow M' \vDash \psi,$$

so we have

$$\mathbb{T}^M \vdash \chi \Leftrightarrow M' \vDash \chi \text{ for all } M' \vDash \mathbb{T}^M$$
$$\Leftrightarrow \text{for all } M' \, (\text{for all } \phi \triangleright \psi \in \mathbb{T} \, M \vDash \phi \Rightarrow M' \vDash \psi)$$
$$\Rightarrow M' \vDash \chi$$
$$\Leftrightarrow \text{for all } M'. M \, \mathbf{R}_\mathbb{T} \, M' \Rightarrow M' \vDash \chi$$

So we have

Corollary 1. *For any model M, M is causally explained according to $\mathbb{T}$ iff*

$$\{M\} = \{M' | M \, \mathbf{R}_\mathbb{T} \, M'\}$$

2.2   Reformulation 2: Modal Models

We can now reformulate McCain and Turner's theory in modal terms. Turner [9] has a similar reformulation: however, his work is solely model-theoretic, and he must use predicate completion in order to prove results. We will give a proof theory for our modal logic, which will be considerably more general than Turner's formulation.

Definition 2. *Given, as above, a language $\mathfrak{L}$, a theory S, and a causal theory $\mathbb{T}$, define a Kripke model K as follows:*

the language *is $\mathfrak{L}_\square$, generated by $\mathfrak{L}$ together with the usual modal operators $\square$ and $\Diamond$.*

the frame *consists of the set of models $\mathfrak{M}$ of S, together with the accessibility relation $\mathbf{R}_\mathbb{T}$.*

the forcing relation *is given by the usual $\vDash$ relation between elements of $\mathfrak{M}$ and propositions of $\mathfrak{L}$, extended to modal formulae in the usual way. If we wish to be pedantic (but we rarely will), we could call the new forcing relation $\vDash_\square$.*

We could refer to this Kripke model as $K_{S,\mathbb{T}}$

Notice that we have:

Proposition 2. *For each causal law $P \triangleright Q$, the modal sentence*

$$P \to \square Q \tag{4}$$

is valid at each world of K.

Proof. This follows directly from the definition of $\mathbf{R}_\mathbb{T}$.

Then we have:

Proposition 3. *For $M \in \mathfrak{M}$, M is causally explained by $\mathbb{T}$ iff, as a world of the Kripke model,*

$$M \vDash (\square P \to P) \wedge (\Diamond P \to \square P) \tag{5}$$

for any proposition P.

Proof. This is a standard modal reformulation of the condition $M = \{M' | M \ \mathbf{R}_\mathbb{T} \ M'\}$; see, for example, [10].

This result is pretty rather than useful: it refers to a particular Kripke model, and models are hard to present in any effective sense. However, if we had a modal *theory* whose canonical model was $K_{S,\mathbb{T}}$, then we could reformulate the above model in terms of provability in a theory; this would, in principle, be much more amenable to computation (although whether this was useful in practice would depend a great deal on the tractability of proof search in the theory involved).

So how do we make $K_{S,\mathbb{T}}$ into the canonical model of a theory? Although the propositions (4) will certainly figure in this theory, we need more; although

Table 1. Basic modal axioms

Axioms: the axioms of first order predicate calculus, together with

$$\Box P \to \Box(P \to Q) \to \Box Q \quad \text{any } P, Q \tag{6}$$

$$P \quad (P \in \mathsf{S}) \tag{7}$$

$$P \to \Box Q \quad (P \triangleright Q \in \mathbb{T}) \tag{8}$$

Rules of Inference: modus ponens and necessitation.

---

these propositions do a good job of telling when necessities should be true, they do not tell us when they should be false.

One way of looking at the requirement is this. Let our new theory be called $\mathsf{S}_{\mathbb{T}}^{\Box}$; we want the set of worlds of our canonical model to be the set of models of our original, non-modal theory S. Now, given a modal theory, the set of worlds of its canonical model is simply the set of its models when it is considered as a non-modal language, with modal formulae being regarded as new atoms. So this means that the models of $\mathsf{S}_{\mathbb{T}}^{\Box}$ must be in bijection with the models of S; i.e. that $\mathsf{S}_{\mathbb{T}}^{\Box}$ must be a definitional extension of S. So, for every modal proposition $\Box X$, we must have a valid equivalence

$$\mathsf{S}_{\mathbb{T}}^{\Box} \vdash \Box X \leftrightarrow P$$

where P is a proposition in $\mathfrak{L}$.

2.3   Reformulation 3: Minimal Modalities

Consider the axiom system given in Table 1; call the corresponding entailment relation $\vdash_{bm1}$. There will, in general, be numerous modal operators $\Box$ satisfying this axiom system: consider the minimal such. To be precise:

Definition 3. *Given theories S and $\mathbb{T}$ as above, define $\Box_{min}$ to be the operator satisfying the basic modal axioms such that, given any modal operator Φ which satisfies those axioms, we have*

$$\Box_{min}P \vdash \Phi P \tag{9}$$

for all propositions P.

We have not, of course, shown that such an operator exists. However, we can actually write down $\Box_{min}$.

Theorem 1. *Suppose S and $\mathbb{T}$ are a pair of theories as above. Let $A \in \mathfrak{L}$: then*

$$\Box_{min}A \quad \cong \bigvee_{Q_1,\ldots,Q_n \vdash_{bml} A} P_1 \wedge \ldots \wedge P_n \tag{10}$$

where the sum is taken over all finite sets of instantiations of heads of causal rules which entail A (that is, for all i, $P_i \triangleright Q_i \in \mathbb{T}$).

Proof. We need to show first that the right hand side (call it $\Psi(A)$) is a modal operator, and secondly that it is minimal.

We show first that Ψ satisfies necessitation: that is, that, if we have $\vdash_{\text{bm }1} A$, we have $\vdash_S \Psi(A)$. If we have $\vdash_{\text{bm }1} A$, then the empty set of heads satisfies the conditions of the disjunction. The corresponding disjunct is the empty conjunction of bodies, i.e. $\top$. Consequently we have $\vdash_{\text{bm }1} \Psi(A)$.

Next we have to show that Ψ satisfies the K axiom (i.e. (6)). It suffices to assume $\Psi(A) \wedge \Psi(A \to B)$ and prove $\Psi(B)$: using the distributive law, the assumption is a disjunction of terms like

$$P_1 \wedge \ldots \wedge P_m \wedge P_{m+1} \wedge \ldots \wedge P_n,$$

where we have both $Q_1, \ldots, Q_m \vdash A$ and $Q_{m+1}, \ldots, Q_n \vdash A \to B$. However, the conditions imply that $Q_1, \ldots, Q_n \vdash B$, and so every disjunct of the antecedent is a disjunct of the consequent.

Next we have to show that, if $P \triangleright Q$, then $\vdash_{\text{bm }1} P \to \Psi(Q)$. However, one of the disjuncts of $\Psi(Q)$ is then P (corresponding to the entailment $Q \vdash_{\text{bm }1} Q$) and so $\Psi(\cdot)$ is a modal operator.

To show that Ψ is minimal, suppose that Φ is some other modal operator satisfying the conditions. We have to prove that, for all A, $\Psi(A) \vdash_{\text{bm }1} \Phi(A)$. It suffices to prove that, given one of the disjuncts of $\Psi(A)$, we can conclude $\Phi(A)$. So, we have

$$Q_1, \ldots, Q_n \vdash A \tag{11}$$

and we must conclude that

$$P_1, \ldots, P_n \vdash \Phi(A) \tag{12}$$

Now, by (11) and the fact that Φ is a modal operator, we have

$$\Phi(Q_1), \ldots, \Phi(Q_n) \vdash \Phi(A); \tag{13}$$

because $\Phi(\cdot)$ satisfies (8) we have

$$P_i \vdash_{\text{bm }1} \Phi(Q_i) \text{ for all } i, \tag{14}$$

and hence, by *modus ponens*, we have the conclusion.

Remark 1. Costello and Patterson [2] have a system in which they can universally quantify over modalities: this is a little like our system.

Remark 2. We define $\Psi(\cdot)$ as a disjunction: as Costello and Patterson explain, disjunctions do not, in general, behave like necessities (or, in their case, conjunctions do not behave like possibilities). What saves us here is the combinatorics of the indexing sets: to be precise, the fact that, if the disjuncts of $\Psi(A)$ are indexed by sets of heads $\{P_1, \ldots, P_m\}$, and if the disjuncts of $\Psi(B)$ are indexed by $\{P'_1, \ldots, P'_n\}$, then the disjuncts of $\Psi(A \wedge B)$ are indexed by the pairwise unions of the respective indices.

Definition 4. *Let us augment the basic modal axioms by adding to them the following "axiom schema":*

$$\Box A \vdash \bigvee_{Q_1,\ldots,Q_n \vdash_{bml} A} P_1 \wedge \ldots \wedge P_n$$

with the usual conditions on the P_i and Q_i. Call the resulting theory minimal modal logic, *and call the corresponding inference relation* $\vdash_{mml}$.

Remark 3. On the face of it, this may only be an "axiom schema" in a rather loose sense: the relation $Q_1, \ldots, Q_n \vdash_{bml} A$ will not, in general, be very tractable (and may not even be decidable), and the letter A in the indexed sum does not *prima facie* play the role of a propositional variable in an axiom schema (although one could give a type-theoretic version of this definition in which it would).

However, we will show – in Section 4 – that these rough definitions can be given a well-behaved proof theory, and that this will, in turn, mean that our "axiom schema" can be made honest.

Remark 4. This axiom scheme is, in some respects, similar to the literal completion procedure of Turner's [9, p. 93]. However, it is far more general than Turner's formulation: the latter only applies to rules with literal heads, whereas our axioms apply to modal axioms corresponding to any causal rules at all.

Lemma 2. $\mathfrak{L}_\Box$ *(with entailment given by $\vdash_{mml}$) is a conservative extension of $\mathfrak{L}$ (with entailment given by the theory S).*

Proof. We have maps:

$$i : \mathfrak{L} \to \mathfrak{L}_\Box$$
$$\psi : \mathfrak{L}_\Box \to \mathfrak{L}$$

where i is the inclusion and ψ is given by recursively replacing a modal expression $\Box X$ by $\Psi(\psi(X))$, where Ψ is the right hand side of (10). Both i and ψ respect the entailment relations given by $\vdash_{mml}$ and S: for i this is clear, because minimal modal logic extends S, whereas for ψ we use the proof of Theorem 1, where we showed that all of the axioms defining $\vdash_{mml}$ were mapped to tautologies of S.

We should also note that $\psi \circ i$ is the identity, whereas $i \circ \Psi$ maps propositions to $\vdash_{mml}$-equivalent propositions (we have enforced this by means of the axioms).

Now suppose that we have two propositions in $\mathfrak{L}$, A and B, and we have $i(A) \vdash_{mml} i(B)$. We then have $S \vdash \psi \circ i(A) \to \psi \circ i(B)$; but $\psi \circ i(A)$ is just A, and $\psi \circ i(B)$ is just B. So A entailed B all along.

Theorem 2. *The canonical model of minimal modal logic is exactly the Kripke model $K_{S,T}$ of Section 2.2; that is, minimal modal logic is exactly the theory $S_T^\Box$ of that section.*

Proof. By the above theorem and lemma, the models of S are exactly the same as the maximal consistent subsets of $\mathfrak{L}_\square$, i.e. the worlds of the canonical model. So the canonical model of minimal modal logic differs from $K_{S,\mathbb{T}}$ in, at most, the accessibility relation.

Consider the accessibility relation (call it R') given by the minimal modal logic. We have, for models M and M' of S,

$$MR'M' \Leftrightarrow \text{ for all } A$$
$$M \vDash \square A \Rightarrow M' \vDash A$$
$$\Leftrightarrow \text{if there are } P_1, \ldots, P_n$$
$$M \vDash P_i \text{ for all } i$$
$$\text{then } M' \vDash Q_i \text{ for all } i$$
$$\Rightarrow M' \vDash \mathbb{T}^M$$

(with the usual relations between the P_i and the Q_i, i.e. $P_i \rhd Q_i$ for all i, and where $\mathbb{T}^M$ is defined in Section1). But we defined the relation of $K_{S,\mathbb{T}}$ precisely in terms of the relation $\mathbb{T}^M$: so we have

$$R' \subseteq \mathbf{R}_\mathbb{T}$$

But R' is defined to be the accessibility relation on the canonical model of the minimal modal logic: and a little work with the definitions gives

$$\mathbf{R}_\mathbb{T} \subseteq R'$$

So the two relations coincide: that is, $K_{S,\mathbb{T}}$ is the canonical model of our minimal modal logic.

Consequently, we have attained our goal: we have produced a logic whose canonical model is $K_{S,\mathbb{T}}$.

3   Examples

We give here a few examples of the above theories in action.

Example 1. Consider a language with a single propositional atom, A, and causal rules $A \rhd A$ and $\neg A \rhd \neg A$. We find that $\vdash_{mm1} A \leftrightarrow \square A$, and $\vdash_{mm1} \neg A \leftrightarrow \square \neg A$: inductively, for all propositions P we have $\vdash_{mm1} P \leftrightarrow \square P$. Consequently, every model satisfies

$$M \vDash (\square P \to P) \wedge (\lozenge P \to \square P)$$

and thus every model is causally explained.

Example 2. Consider a language with two propositional atoms, A and B, and causal rules $A \rhd A$ and $\neg A \rhd \neg A$. We find the same results for A as above, but, since there are no heads of causal rules which entail B, we have

$$\vdash_{mm1} \square B \leftrightarrow \bot;$$

consequently, there are no models in which (5) is satisfied.

This example can clearly be generalised to similar results in any situation in which we can apply the Craig Interpolation Theorem [8, pp. 90ff.] to $\vdash_{bm1}$.

4   Cut Elimination

In this section we shall prove cut elimination (in a suitable sequent calculus) for $\vdash_{mm\, 1}$; the proof will be somewhat abbreviated, but fuller proofs for related systems can be found in [7].

First we give, in table 2, a sequent calculus formulation of our system: Note that we have used the multicut rule (which is derivable from the usual cut rule): this form of the rule is necessary in order to be able to prove cut elimenation in the presence of weakening (see [8, p 82]). It is easy to show that, if we define $\Diamond$ in terms of $\Box$, it is equivalent to the previous formulation. To be precise, we have

Proposition 4. *Given two theories S and $\mathbb{T}$ as above, let $S_{\mathbb{T}}^{\Box}$ be the modal theory defined in Section 2.2 (and identified in terms of minimal modalities in Theorem 2). Suppose that $\vdash_{seq}^{\mathbb{T}}$ be the entailment relation given by the rules in table 2, where the causal rules come from $\mathbb{T}$: then we have, for any (modal or nonmodal) proposition P,*

$$S_{\mathbb{T}}^{\Box} \vdash P \quad \Leftrightarrow \quad S \vdash_{seq}^{\mathbb{T}} P$$

So we can equally well work in terms of this sequent calculus: it will yield the same results.

We now have

Theorem 3. *Any sequent calculus proof can be transformed into a proof without any applications of the cut rule.*

Proof. For the sake of brevity, we give only the most interesting case: this is when we have a cut of $\Box R$ against $\Box L$, and where the cutformulae are principal on both sides. We have:

$$\cfrac{\cfrac{\begin{array}{c}\Pi\\\vdots\end{array}}{\cfrac{\Gamma \vdash P_1 \wedge \ldots P_k, (\Box X)^m \Delta}{\Gamma \vdash (\Box X)^{m+1}, \Delta}\,\Box R} \quad \cfrac{\left\{ \cfrac{\begin{array}{c}\Pi_i\\\vdots\end{array}}{\Gamma' P_{i_1}, \ldots, P_{i_{k_i}}, (\Box X)^n \vdash \Delta'} \right\}}{\Gamma', (\Box X)^{n+1} \vdash \Delta'}}{\Gamma, \Gamma' \vdash \Delta, \Delta'}\,\text{cut}$$

We also suppose that $m, n > 1$; other cases are similar but simpler. The set $P_1, \ldots, P_k$ on the left must correspond to one of the sets $P_{i_1}, \ldots, P_{i_{k_i}}$ on the right: so we obtain proofs as follows:

$$\cfrac{\cfrac{\begin{array}{c}\Pi\\\vdots\end{array}}{\Gamma \vdash P_1 \wedge \ldots P_k, (\Box X)^m \Delta} \quad \cfrac{\left\{ \cfrac{\begin{array}{c}\Pi_i\\\vdots\end{array}}{\Gamma' P_{i_1}, \ldots, P_{i_{k_i}}, (\Box X)^n \vdash \Delta'} \right\}}{\Gamma', (\Box X)^{n+1} \vdash \Delta'}}{\Gamma, \Gamma' \vdash P_1 \wedge \ldots \wedge P_k, \Delta, \Delta'}\,\text{multicut}$$

Table 2. Sequent Calculus Rules

$$\frac{}{A \vdash A}\,\text{Ax} \qquad\qquad \frac{}{\bot \vdash}\,L\bot$$

$$\frac{\Gamma \vdash \Delta}{\Gamma, A \vdash \Delta}\,LW \qquad\qquad \frac{\Gamma \vdash \Delta}{\Gamma \vdash A, \Delta}\,RW$$

$$\frac{\Gamma, A, A \vdash \Delta}{\Gamma, A \vdash \Delta}\,LC \qquad\qquad \frac{\Gamma \vdash A, A, \Delta}{\Gamma \vdash A, \Delta}\,RC$$

$$\frac{\Gamma, A \vdash \Delta}{\Gamma, A \wedge B \vdash \Delta}\,L\wedge_1 \frac{\Gamma, B \vdash \Delta}{\Gamma, A \wedge B \vdash \Delta}\,L\wedge_2 \qquad \frac{\Gamma \vdash A, \Delta \quad \Gamma \vdash B, \Delta}{\Gamma \vdash A \wedge B, \Delta}\,R\wedge$$

$$\frac{\Gamma, A \vdash \Delta \quad \Gamma, B \vdash \Delta}{\Gamma, A \vee B \vdash \Delta}\,\vee L \qquad \frac{\Gamma \vdash A, \Delta}{\Gamma \vdash A \vee B, \Delta}\,\vee R_1 \frac{\Gamma \vdash A, \Delta}{\Gamma \vdash A \vee B, \Delta}\,\vee R_2$$

$$\frac{\Gamma \vdash A, \Delta \quad \Gamma, B \vdash \Delta}{\Gamma, A \to B \vdash \Delta}\,\to L \qquad \frac{\Gamma, A \vdash B, \Delta}{\Gamma \vdash A \to B, \Delta}\,\to R$$

$$\frac{\Gamma, A[x/t] \vdash \Delta}{\Gamma, \forall x A \vdash \Delta}\,\forall L \qquad \frac{\Gamma \vdash A[x/y], \Delta}{\Gamma \vdash \forall x A, \Delta}\,\forall R^a$$

$$\frac{\Gamma, A[x/y] \vdash \Delta}{\Gamma, \exists x A \vdash \Delta}\,\exists L^b \qquad \frac{\Gamma \vdash A[x/t], \Delta}{\Gamma \vdash \exists x A, \Delta}\,\exists R$$

$$\frac{\Gamma \vdash P_1 \wedge \ldots \wedge P_n, \Delta \quad Q_1, \ldots, Q_n \vdash X}{\Gamma \vdash \Box X, \Delta}\,\Box R^c$$

$$\frac{\{\Gamma, P_{i_1}, \ldots, P_{i_k} \vdash A, \Delta, \quad Q_{i_1}, \ldots, Q_{i_k} \vdash X\}_{i=1,\ldots,n}}{\Box \Gamma, \Box X \vdash \Box A, \Diamond \Delta}\,\Box L^d$$

$$\frac{\Gamma \vdash X^m, \Delta \quad \Gamma', X^n \vdash \Delta'}{\Gamma, \Gamma' \vdash \Delta, \Delta'}\,\text{multicut}^e$$

[a] y not free in Γ or Δ, and either $y = x$ or y not free in A
[b] y not free in Γ or Δ, and either $y = x$ or y not free in A
[c] where, for all i, $P_i \triangleright Q_i$
[d] where, for each i, we have $P_{i_1} \triangleright Q_{i_1}, \ldots P_{i_k} \triangleright Q_{i_k}$, and where the $\{P_{i_j}\}$ and $\{Q_{i_j}\}$, for $i = 1, \ldots n$, are the only such sets of Ps and Qs that there are.
[e] where X^n stands for n occurrences of X; $m, n > 0$

Now the cut has been moved up on the left, and the cutformula is the same: so we may inductively apply cut elimination to this proof, and obtain a cutfree proof (call it $\mathcal{P}_0$) of its result.

The next proof we obtain is

$$
\cfrac{\cfrac{\Pi \\ \vdots \\ \Gamma \vdash P_1 \wedge \ldots \wedge P_n, (\Box X)^m, \Delta}{\Gamma \vdash (\Box X)^{m+1}, \Delta} \qquad \cfrac{\Pi_{i_0} \\ \vdots \\ \Gamma', P_1, \ldots, P_k, (\Box X)^n \vdash \Delta}{}}{\Gamma, \Gamma', P_1, \ldots, P_k \vdash \Delta, \Delta'} \text{ multicut}
$$

for a suitable i_0; again we have moved the cut up so we can, inductively, obtain a cut free proof (call this $\mathcal{P}_1$) of its result.

Finally we put these proofs together: we get

$$
\cfrac{\cfrac{\mathcal{P}_0 \\ \vdots \\ \Gamma, \Gamma' \vdash P_1 \wedge \ldots P_k, \Delta, \Delta'} \qquad \cfrac{\cfrac{\mathcal{P}_1 \\ \vdots \\ \Gamma, \Gamma', P_1, \ldots, P_k \vdash \Delta, \Delta'}{\Gamma, \Gamma', P_1 \wedge \ldots \wedge P_k \vdash \Delta, \Delta'} \wedge R}{}}{\cfrac{(\Gamma)^2, (\Gamma')^2 \vdash (\Delta)^2, (\Delta')^2}{\Gamma, \Gamma' \vdash \Delta, \Delta'} \, LC, RC} \text{ multicut}
$$

This cut has not been moved upwards, but the cutformula has been changed from $\Box X$ to $P_1 \wedge \ldots \wedge P_k$; although the logical complexity may have increased, the modal depth will (because of our restriction on the form of the causal rules) have decreased. So we can apply our induction.

4.1 Applications of Cut Elimination

The main application of cut elimination is this: we have a proof search procedure that is, in favourable cases, tractable. We should recall what we are searching for: we are looking for propositions X that satisfy

$$
\mathsf{S}, \{\Box P \to P, \neg \Box \neg P \to P\}_{\text{all } P} \vdash^{\mathrm{T}}_{\text{seq}} X
$$

What formulae can occur in proofs of such a sequent? Well, we find formulae in the proof tree by the following processes:

1. we pass from formulae to subformulae as we go up the proof tree, and
2. if we apply either of the modal rules, we take a formula which already occurs, find a head (or heads) of a causal rule Q such that $Q \vdash X$, and then insert the corresponding body P into the tree.

The first process is quite tractable: the second can fail to be tractable in general, but, in practical cases, can be handled quite well. In many concrete cases – see, for example, the examples in [9, pp. 110ff] – heads and bodies of relation symbols have the same relation symbols, and only differ in the values of their arguments.

Let us compare our results with those given by predicate completion: in our case, we can deal with causal rules of the form $P \triangleright Q$, where P and Q are *any* non-modal propositions. Predicate completion, although it ends up with proof searches which look very much the same, is restricted to causal laws where the heads are atoms.

References

1. Anthony G. Cohn, Lenhard Schubert, and Stuart C. Shapiro, editors. *Principles of Knowledge Representation and Reasoning: Proceedings of the Sixth International Conference (KR98).* Morgan Kaufmann, 1998. Trento, Italy, June 1998.
2. Tom Costello and Anna Patterson. Quantifiers and operations on modalities and contexts. In Cohn et al. [1], pages 270–281. Trento, Italy, June 1998.
3. J. Lambek and P.J. Scott. *Introduction to Higher order Categorical Logic.* Number 7 in Cambridge Studies in Advanced Mathematics. Cambridge University Press, 1986.
4. Vladimir Lifschitz. On the logic of causal explanation. *Artificial Intelligence*, 96:451–465, 1997.
5. Vladimir Lifschitz. Situation calculus and causal logic. In Cohn et al. [l], pages 536–546. Trento, Italy, June 1998.
6. Norman McCain and Hudson Turner. Causal theories of action and change. In *Proceedings of AAAI97*, pages 460–465, Providence, RI, 1997. AAAI.
7. Peter Schroeder-Heister. Cut-elimination in logics with definitional reflection. In D. Pearce and H. Wansing, editors, *Nonclassical Logics and Information Processing*, volume 619 of *Lecture Notes in Artificial Intelligence*, pages 146–171, Berlin, etc., 1992. Springer-Verlag. International Workshop, Berlin 1990.
8. A.S. Troelstra and H. Schwichtenberg. *Basic Proof Theory.* Number 43 in Cambridge Tracts in Theoretical Computer Science. Cambridge University Press, Cambridge, 1996.
9. Hudson Turner. A theory of universal causation. *Artificial Intelligence*, 113:87–123, 1999.
10. Johan van Benthem. Correspondence theory. In D. Gabbay and F. Guenther, editors, *Handbook of Philosophical Logic II*, volume 165 of *Synthese Library*, pages 167–247. Reidel, Dordrecht, 1984.
11. G. Graham White. Intentionality and circumscription. In Salem Benferhat and Enrico Giunchiglia, editors, *Proceedings of the 9th International Conference on Non-Monotonic Reasoning (NMR2002)*, pages 372–379, 2002. Toulouse, April 2002.

Second-Order Quantifier Elimination
in Modal Contexts*

Andrzej Szalas

The College of Economics and Computer Science, Olsztyn, Poland and
Department of Computer Science, University of Linköping, Sweden
andsz@ida.liu.se
http://www.ida.liu.se/~andsz/

Abstract. Second-order quantifier elimination in the context of classical
logic emerged as a powerful technique in many applications, including
the correspondence theory, relational databases, deductive and knowledge databases, knowledge representation, commonsense reasoning and
approximate reasoning.

In the current paper we generalize the result of [19] by allowing modal
operators. This allows us to provide a unifying framework for many applications, that require the use of intensional concepts. Examples of applications of the technique in AI are also provided.

1 Introduction

Second-order quantifier elimination in the context of classical logic emerged as
a powerful technique in many applications, including the correspondence theory [10,18,19,20,21,22,23,24], relational databases [7,8,12], deductive and knowledge databases [2,3], knowledge representation, commonsense reasoning and approximate reasoning [4,5,6,9,14,15]. All of the quoted results are based on elimination of predicate variables from formulas of the classical second-order logic.
On the other hand, many natural language phenomena have their natural counterparts in modal logics. It is then desirable to provide tools dealing directly
with modal logics, rather than with their translations into the classical logic.

In the current paper we generalize the result of [19] by allowing modal operators. This allows us to provide a unifying framework for many applications,
including:

- automated modal theorem proving
- modal deductive databases
- modal theory approximation
- modal abduction
- commonsense reasoning involving intensional concepts.

---

* Supported in part by the WITAS project grant under the Wallenberg Foundation,
  Sweden, KBN grant 8 T11C 009 19 and The College of Economics and Computer
  Science.

S. Flesca et al. (Eds.): JELIA 2002, LNAI 2424, pp. 223–232, 2002.
© Springer-Verlag Berlin Heidelberg 2002

The paper is organized as follows. In section 2 we introduce the notions used in the rest of the paper. In section 3 the main result is proved. Section 4 contains examples of applications of the main theorem, including most of the areas mentioned above. Finally, Section 5 contains conclusions and directions for further research and indicates the possibilities to extend results of the current paper.

2   Preliminaries

2.1   Notational Conventions

Modalities are denoted by $\Box$ and $\Diamond$, where as usual, $\Box\alpha \equiv \neg\Diamond\neg\alpha$. We use symbol $\triangle$ to denote $\Box$ or $\Diamond$.

By $\triangle^i\alpha$ we understand $\underbrace{\triangle\ldots\triangle}_{i\ \text{times}}\alpha$. By writing $\alpha(\triangle^i\beta)$ we shall indicate that all occurrences of β in α are of the form $\triangle^i\beta$ and that $\triangle^i\beta$ does not occur within a scope of a modal operator. In particular, notation $\alpha(p)$ is used when p does not appear in α within a scope of a modality.

By $\alpha(\bar{x})[\bar{x}/\bar{t}]$ we mean formula α applied to the tuple of terms $\bar{t}$.

Expression $\varepsilon\lfloor\delta := \eta\rfloor$ stands for the expression obtained from expression ε by substituting all occurrences of expression δ by expression η. Formula $\alpha\lfloor P(\bar{x}):=\beta(\bar{x})\rfloor$ stands for the formula obtained from α by substituting any occurrence of $P(\bar{a})$ in α by $\beta(\bar{x})[\bar{x}/\bar{a}]$. For example $(P(a) \vee P(b))\lfloor P(x) := Q(x)\rfloor$ stands for $(Q(x)[x/a] \vee Q(x)[x/b])$, i.e., for $(Q(a) \vee Q(b))$.

In what follows by $\mu P(\bar{x}).\alpha(P)$ we shall mean the least fixpoint of formula α, i.e., formula $\beta(\bar{x})$ such that $\beta \equiv \alpha\lfloor P(\bar{x}) := \beta(\bar{x})\rfloor$ and for any formula γ for which $\gamma \equiv \alpha\lfloor P(\bar{x}) := \gamma(\bar{x})\rfloor$ we have that $\beta \to \gamma$. By $\nu P(\bar{x}).\alpha(P)$ we shall mean the greatest fixpoint of formula α, i.e., formula $\beta(\bar{x})$ such that $\beta \equiv \alpha\lfloor P(\bar{x}) := \beta(\bar{x})\rfloor$ and for any formula γ for which $\gamma \equiv \alpha\lfloor P(\bar{x}) := \gamma(\bar{x})\rfloor$ we have that $\gamma \to \beta$. In the rest of the paper we shall always deal with formulas for which such fixpoints exist.

2.2   Modal Logics

In this paper we consider *normal modal logics*, i.e., extensions of logic K. Propositional modal logic K is defined as the least modal logic containing all tautologies of the classical propositional calculus, axiom

$$(K)\ \Box(\alpha \to \beta) \to (\Box\alpha \to \Box\beta)$$

and closed under rules:

$$(MP)\ \alpha,\ \alpha \to \beta \vdash \beta \quad \text{and} \quad (G)\ \alpha \vdash \Box\alpha$$

In the first-order case, we extend any propositional modal logic, say S, along the lines of the system Q1S (cf., e.g., [11]) that assumes the classical predicate calculus and axioms of the propositional logic S, rules $(MP), (G)$ together with the Barcan formula

(BF) $\forall \bar{x}.\Box\alpha(\bar{x}) \rightarrow \Box\forall\bar{x}.\alpha(\bar{x})$

and rules:

(RT) $t = t' \vdash \Box t = t'$ and $t \neq t' \vdash \Box t \neq t'$.

It is important to note, that Q1K (thus also any quantified normal modal logic) entails the converse of the Barcan formula (see, e.g., [11]):

(CBF) $\Box\forall\bar{x}.\alpha(\bar{x}) \rightarrow \forall\bar{x}.\Box\alpha(\bar{x})$.

We say that α *is positive* w.r.t. expression ε iff all occurrences of ε in α are within the scope of an even number of negations and α *is negative* w.r.t. expression ε iff all occurrences of ε in α are within the scope of an odd number of negations.

In the current paper we mainly concentrate on K, but some discussions refer to KD and S4 as well, where KD is obtained from K by adding axiom:

(D) $\Box\alpha \rightarrow \Diamond\alpha$

and S4 is obtained from K by adding axioms:

(T) $\Box\alpha \rightarrow \alpha$ and (4) $\Box\alpha \rightarrow \Box\Box\alpha$.

3   The Main Result

In this section we assume that the considered modal logics are Q1K (in the first-order case) and K (in the propositional case).

Theorem 3.1. *Let i be any natural number. Assume that $\alpha(P)$ is a classical first-order formula positive w.r.t. P and $\beta(\triangle^i P)$ is a modal first-order formula positive w.r.t. $\triangle^i P$. Then:*

$$\exists P.[\forall\bar{x}.(\Box^i(P(\bar{x}) \rightarrow \alpha(P(\bar{t}))) \wedge \beta(\triangle^i P(\bar{s}))] \equiv \qquad (1)$$
$$\beta\lfloor P(\bar{x}) := \nu P(\bar{x}).\,[\alpha(P(\bar{t}))]\rfloor.$$

If α does not contain P, then the righthand side of equivalence (1) reduces to $\beta\lfloor P(\bar{x}) := \alpha(\bar{x})\rfloor$.

Proof. Let us first prove the equivalence (1) in the case when $\triangle$ represents $\Box$.
Assume first that

$$\exists P.[\forall\bar{x}.(\Box^i(P(\bar{x}) \rightarrow \alpha(P(\bar{t}))) \wedge \beta(\Box^i P(\bar{s}))]$$

holds. By (BF) we have that $\Box^i\forall\bar{x}.(P(\bar{x}) \rightarrow \alpha(P(\bar{t}))$ holds, i.e., also

$$\Box^i\forall\bar{x}.(P(\bar{x}) \rightarrow \nu P(\bar{x}).\,[\alpha(P(\bar{t}))]).$$

We now apply (CBF) and (K) and obtain $\forall \bar{x}.(\Box^i P(\bar{x}) \to \Box^i \nu P(\bar{x}). [\alpha(P(\bar{t}))])$. By assumption, β is positive w.r.t. $\Box^i P$, thus also monotone w.r.t. $\Box^i P$. We then conclude that $\beta \lfloor P(\bar{x}) := \nu P(\bar{x}). [\alpha(P(\bar{t}))] \rfloor$ holds.

Let us now prove the converse implication. Assume that

$$\beta \lfloor P(\bar{x}) := \nu P(\bar{x}). [\alpha(P(\bar{t}))] \rfloor$$

holds. We shall define P satisfying $[\forall \bar{x}.(\Box^i(P(\bar{x}) \to \alpha(P(\bar{t}))) \land \beta(\Box^i P(\bar{s}))]$ and thus show that it indeed exists. Set $P(\bar{x})$ to be a relation such that

$$\Box^i(\forall \bar{x}. P(\bar{x}) \equiv \nu P(\bar{x}). [\alpha(P(\bar{t}))]).$$

By (CBF) and (K) we also have that $\forall \bar{x}.(\Box^i P(\bar{x}) \equiv \Box^i \nu P(\bar{x}). [\alpha(P(\bar{t}))])$. Formula $\beta(\Box^i P(\bar{s}))$ is then obviously satisfied. Consider $\forall \bar{x}.(\Box^i(P(\bar{x}) \to \alpha(P(\bar{t})))$. This formula is satisfied, as P is defined to be a fixpoint of $\alpha(P)$ exactly in the modal context $\Box^i$.

This proves the result for $\triangle$ representing $\Box$.

The proof of equivalence (1) with $\triangle$ representing $\Diamond$ is similar, but one additionally applies the following theorem of K:

$$\Box^i(p \to \alpha) \to (\Diamond^i p \to \Diamond^i \alpha). \qquad \blacksquare$$

The following fact follows directly from Theorem 3.1.

Corollary 3.2. *Let i be any natural number. Assume that $\alpha(p)$ is a classical propositional formula positive w.r.t. p and $\beta(\triangle^i p)$ is a modal propositional formula positive w.r.t. $\triangle^i p$. Then:*

$$\exists p.[\Box^i(p \to \alpha(p)) \land \beta(\triangle^i p)] \equiv \beta \lfloor p := \nu p.\alpha(p) \rfloor \qquad (2)$$

If α does not contain p, then the righthand sides of equivalence (2) reduces to $\beta \lfloor p := \alpha \rfloor$. $\blacksquare$

Note also that fixpoint formulas appearing in the above corollary easily reduce to the classical propositional formulas[1].

Observe also that the following dual forms of Theorem 3.1 and Corollary 3.2 hold.

Theorem 3.3. *Let i be any natural number. Assume that $\alpha(P)$ is a classical first-order formula positive w.r.t. P and $\beta(\triangle^i \neg P)$ is a modal first-order formula positive w.r.t. $\triangle^i \neg P$. Then:*

$$\exists P.[\forall \bar{x}.(\Box^i(\alpha(P(\bar{t})) \to P(\bar{x})) \land \beta(\triangle^i \neg P(\bar{s}))] \equiv \qquad (3)$$
$$\beta \lfloor P(\bar{x}) := \mu P(\bar{x}). [\alpha(P(\bar{t}))] \rfloor).$$

If α does not contain P, then the righthand side of equivalence (3) reduces to $\beta \lfloor P(\bar{x}) := \alpha(\bar{x}) \rfloor$. $\blacksquare$

---

[1] In the first iteration towards the fixpoint, one replaces p in α with True. In the next conjunct, p in α is replaced by this result. The fixpoint, a propositional formula, is always reached in a few iterations.

Corollary 3.4. *Let i be any natural number. Assume that $\alpha(p)$ is a classical propositional formula positive w.r.t. p and $\beta(\triangle^i\neg p)$ is a modal propositional formula positive w.r.t. $\triangle^i\neg p$. Then:*

$$\exists p.[\square^i(\alpha(p) \to p) \wedge \beta(\triangle^i\neg p)] \equiv \beta\lfloor p := \mu p.\alpha(p)\rfloor \tag{4}$$

If α does not contain p, then the righthand sides of equivalence (4) reduces to $\beta\lfloor p := \alpha\rfloor$. ∎

Observe that Theorems 3.1 and 3.3 subsume the results of [19]. In order to see this, it suffices to fix $i = 0$ and consider β's without modalities.

4 Applications

For the sake of simplicity we shall deal with propositional modal logics only. We believe, however, that the examples sufficiently illustrate the ideas.

4.1 Automated Modal Theorem Proving

The idea here depends on a simple observation that a formula $\alpha(\bar{p})$ is a tautology iff formula $\forall \bar{p}.\alpha(\bar{p})$ is a tautology, too. Now elimination of second-order quantifiers results in a formula that does not contain variables of $\bar{p}$, thus is substantially simplified.

Let us start with the second-order formulation of axiom (D), i.e.,

$$\forall p.(\square p \to \lozenge p).$$

After negating the axiom one obtains $\exists p.[\square p \wedge \square\neg p]$, i.e. $\exists p.[\square(\mathsf{True} \to p) \wedge \square\neg p]$. An application of Corollary 3.2 results in an equivalent formula $\square\neg\mathsf{True}$, thus (D) is equivalent to $\neg\square\neg\mathsf{True}$, i.e., to $\lozenge\mathsf{True}$.

Consider now another propositional modal formula:

$$[\square(p \to q) \wedge \square\neg q] \to \lozenge\neg p \tag{5}$$

In order to prove it, we consider formula (5) with p and q quantified universally:

$$\forall q.\forall p.[\square(p \to q) \wedge \square\neg q] \to \lozenge\neg p \tag{6}$$

In order to apply Corollary 3.2 we first negate (6):

$$\exists q.\exists p.\square(p \to q) \wedge \square\neg q \wedge \square p$$

After application of Corollary 3.2 we obtain the following equivalent formula:

$$\exists q.[\square\neg q \wedge \square q],$$

i.e., $\exists q.[\square(q \to \mathsf{False}) \wedge \square q]$, thus the application of Corollary 3.2 results in $\square\mathsf{False}$, i.e., formula (6) is equivalent to $\neg\square\mathsf{False}$, i.e., to $\lozenge\mathsf{True}$. Thus formula (5) is valid iff formula $\lozenge\mathsf{True}$ is valid.

Now the reasoning is substantially simplified. The formula $\lozenge\mathsf{True}$ is not a theorem of K (but one can easily note that it is a theorem, e.g., of any extension of KD - see the first example of this section).

As another nice example[2] consider formula

$$(\Diamond p \wedge \Diamond q) \rightarrow \Diamond(p \wedge q). \tag{7}$$

The same property can be expressed equivalently without using variable q, thus in a simpler form. To see this note that formula (7) is equivalent to:

$$\forall q.[(\Diamond p \wedge \Diamond q) \rightarrow \Diamond(p \wedge q)]. \tag{8}$$

We first negate the formula and obtain $\exists q.[(\Diamond p \wedge \Diamond q) \wedge \Box(\neg p \vee \neg q)]$, i.e.,

$$\exists q.[\Box(q \rightarrow \neg p) \wedge (\Diamond p \wedge \Diamond q)]. \tag{9}$$

An application of Corollary 3.2 to (9) results in $\Diamond p \wedge \Diamond \neg p$, thus formula (7) is equivalent to $\neg(\Diamond p \wedge \Diamond \neg p)$, i.e., to $\Diamond p \rightarrow \Box p$.

4.2   Modal Deductive Databases

Here the idea is again simple. In order to check whether a query α follows from a database D, one has to check whether $\forall \bar{p}.[\bigwedge D \rightarrow \alpha]$, where $\bar{p}$ consists of all Boolean variables appearing in α and $\bigwedge D$ denotes the conjunction of all formulas in D. According to the reduction to absurdity paradigm, usually applied in the context of deductive databases, one negates the implication and tries to show a contradiction. Negated implication is of the form $\exists \bar{p}.[\bigwedge D \wedge \neg \alpha]$. Therefore we propose here to apply the method based on second-order quantifier elimination.

Consider an exemplary deontic database, where $\Box \alpha$ stands for "α is obligatory" and $\Diamond \alpha$ stands for "α is allowed". Assume the database represents a statute of a company and contains, among others, the following simple rules, where s stands for a "serious violation of a rule", f stands for a "failure" and w stands for a "warning":

$$\Box(s \rightarrow f) \tag{10}$$
$$\Box(f \rightarrow w).$$

Assume that the database contains also fact $\Diamond s$ and no other rules or facts involve w or f [3]. Our query is $\Diamond w$. We are then interested to check whether the conjunction of rules (10) and fact $\Diamond s$ implies the query, i.e., whether

$$\forall w.[(\Box(s \rightarrow f) \wedge \Box(f \rightarrow w) \wedge \Diamond s) \rightarrow \Diamond w]. \tag{11}$$

In order to apply Corollary 3.4 we first negate the conjunction and obtain:

$$\exists w.[\Box(s \rightarrow f) \wedge \Box(f \rightarrow w) \wedge \Diamond s \wedge \Box \neg w].$$

After applying Corollary 3.4 we obtain:

$$\Box(s \rightarrow f) \wedge \Diamond s \wedge \Box \neg f,$$

---

[2] Suggested by a referee.
[3] If other rules or facts in the database would involve w or f, the second-order quantification in (11) and (12) would have to bind those rules and facts, too.

which, taking into account the contents of the database, reduces to $\Box \neg f$. Thus (11) is equivalent to $\neg \Box \neg f$, i.e., to $\Diamond f$. We still do not know whether $\Diamond f$ holds, thus ask whether it follows from the database. The suitable query is formulated as

$$\forall f.[(\Box(s \to f) \wedge \Box(f \to w) \wedge \Diamond s) \to \Diamond f]. \tag{12}$$

After similar calculations as before we obtain what the query is equivalent to $\neg \Box (s \to w) \vee \Diamond s$, which is True, as $\Diamond s$ is a fact contained in the database. Thus also the answer to the initial query is True, as expected.

4.3   Modal Theory Approximation

The concept of approximating more complex theories by simpler theories has been studied, e.g., in [1,9,13,16], mainly in the context of approximating arbitrary propositional theories by propositional Horn clauses. The concept of approximate theories is also discussed in [17]. It can easily be observed that strongest necessary and weakest sufficient conditions, as proposed in [16], provide us with approximations of theories expressed in a richer language by theories expressed in a simpler language.

The approach to compute strongest necessary and weakest sufficient conditions, developed in [9], is based on the use of second-order quantifier elimination techniques. According to [9], the weakest sufficient condition $\mathsf{WSC}(\alpha; Th; P)$ and the strongest necessary condition $\mathsf{SNC}(\alpha; Th; P)$ of a formula α on the set of relation symbols[4] P under theory Th in the propositional case is characterized as follows.

Lemma 4.1. *For any formula α, any set of propositions P and theory Th:*

1. *the strongest necessary condition $\mathsf{SNC}(\alpha; Th; P)$ is defined by $\exists \bar{q}.[Th \wedge \alpha]$,*
2. *the weakest sufficient condition $\mathsf{WSC}(\alpha; Th; P)$ is defined by $\forall \bar{q}.[Th \to \alpha]$,*

where $\bar{q}$ consists of all propositions appearing in Th and α but not in P.   ∎

Assume we have the following theory, where $\Box$ stands for "usually", $\Diamond$ stands for "sometimes", w stands for "being accompanied by a wife", c for "going to a cinema", t for "going to a theater" and p for "going to a pub". Assume that the situation is described by the following theory T:

$$\Box(w \to (t \vee c)) \wedge \Box(\neg w \to p) \wedge \Box(p \to (\neg t \wedge \neg c)). \tag{13}$$

Suppose one wants to describe the concept $\Box \neg p$ in terms of w only, perhaps occurring within a scope of modal operators. Thus the appropriate approximations of theory (13) w.r.t. $\Box \neg p$ are given by $\mathsf{SNC}(\Box \neg p; T; \{w\})$ and $\mathsf{WSC}(\Box \neg p; T; \{w\})$. According to Lemma 4.1, we have the following second-order characterizations of those conditions:

$$\mathsf{SNC}(\Box \neg p; T; \{w\}) \equiv \exists p.\exists t.\exists c.[T \wedge \Box \neg p] \tag{14}$$

$$\mathsf{WSC}(\Box \neg p; T; \{w\}) \equiv \forall p.\forall t.\forall c.[T \to \Box \neg p]. \tag{15}$$

---

[4] It is assumed that the conditions are to be expressed in the language not containing symbols other than those included in the set.

Consider (14). In order to eliminate quantifier $\exists c$ we transform the righthand side of equivalence (14) into the following equivalent form:

$$\exists p.\exists t.\exists c.\Box((w \wedge \neg t) \to c) \wedge \Box(\neg w \to p) \wedge \Box(p \to (\neg t \wedge \neg c)) \wedge \Box\neg p.$$

The application of Corollary 3.4 results in:

$$\exists p.\exists t.\Box(\neg w \to p) \wedge \Box(p \to (\neg t \wedge \neg(w \wedge \neg t))) \wedge \Box\neg p.$$

which is equivalent to $\exists p.\exists t.\Box(\neg w \to p) \wedge \Box(p \to (\neg t \wedge \neg w)) \wedge \Box\neg p$, i.e., by simple calculations, to $\exists p.\exists t.\Box(\neg w \to p) \wedge \Box(t \to \neg p) \wedge \Box(p \to \neg w) \wedge \Box\neg p$, We now apply Corollary 3.2 again and obtain $\exists p.\Box(\neg w \to p) \wedge \Box(p \to \neg w) \wedge \Box\neg p$, equivalent to $\exists p.\Box(\neg w \to p) \wedge \Box\neg p$. Now the application of Corollary 3.4 results in $\Box w$, which is the required strongest necessary condition.

The calculation of the weakest sufficient condition is quite similar, as after negating the righthand side of the equivalence (15) and eliminating second-order quantifiers we obtain $\Diamond\neg w$. The negation of this formula, i.e., $\Box w$ is then the required weakest sufficient condition, which happens to be the same as the strongest necessary condition.

4.4   Modal Abduction

As observed in [16], the weakest sufficient condition corresponds to the weakest abduction. Thus the methodology sketched in section 4.3 can be applied to modal abduction, too.

In order to illustrate the idea, consider the theory of section 4.3 and $\Box\neg p$ as the desired conclusion. Assume that one wants to check what is the weakest condition which:

- together with theory T given by conjunction (13) guarantees that the conclusion holds
- is expressed in terms of the target language, containing only proposition w.

According to [9,16], the condition is expressed by $\mathsf{WSC}(\Box\neg p; T; \{w\})$. The suitable condition is then $\Box w$, as calculated in section 4.3.

5   Conclusions

In the current paper we presented techniques that allow one to eliminate second-order quantifiers from second-order modal formulas. The techniques are purely syntactical and independent of any particular underlying semantics of modal logics, thus can easily be implemented.

The results of this paper can be applied in many areas, in particular in AI. Observe, however, that we mainly concentrated on modal logic K and its first-order extension Q1K. These logics are the simplest normal modal logics, but also provide one with a minimal set of logical equivalences that allow one to transform formulas into one of the forms required in Theorems 3.1, 3.3 and Corollaries 3.2, 3.4. Stronger modal logics provide additional axioms that make the elimination possible in more cases. Consider, for example, any extension of

S4. Due to axioms (4) and (T) one has that $\Box p \equiv \Box\Box p$ and $\Diamond p \equiv \Diamond\Diamond p$. By applying those equivalences one can equalize the modal contexts of conjuncts appearing within the equivalences in Theorems 3.1, 3.3 and Corollaries 3.2, 3.4. Also other modal reduction principles could serve the purpose. Thus a promising area of research is to develop analogous theorems for modal logics other than K, Q1K or (extensions of) S4. One could also develop algorithms for transforming formulas into the forms required in Theorems 3.1, 3.3 and Corollaries 3.2, 3.4 by extending the DLS/DLS* algorithm of [5,6]. It should be emphasized that such algorithms have to be developed and specialized for particular modal logics. It would also be interesting to investigate multi-modal contexts.

Because of the lack of space, applications were illustrated only via simple examples. We think that extending applications along the lines of [9] is very promising, as the approach allows one not only to compute strongest necessary and weakest sufficient conditions, but also to apply those in approximate reasoning, abductive reasoning, communicating agents, etc.

Another promising area of research can be based on adopting circumscription to the modal context. In fact, circumscription is a second-order formalism, but does not allow the use intensional notions. On the other hand, commonsense reasoning scenarios often have to reflect the intensional nature of many natural language connectives. Thus a possibility to use modal logics within this context seems fruitful.

Yet another direction of research depends on allowing more complex modal contexts in equivalences given in Theorems 3.1, 3.3 and Corollaries 3.2, 3.4. In particular, it is promising to deal with fixpoint formulas involving modal operators. In fact, for many modal logics this is not a difficult task and can result in interesting techniques.

References

1. M. Cadoli. *Tractable Reasoning in Artificial Intelligence*, volume 941 of *LNAI*. Springer-Verlag, Berlin Heidelberg, 1995.
2. P. Doherty, J. Kachniarz, and A. Szałas. Meta-queries on deductive databases. *Fundamenta Informaticae*, 40(1):17–30, 1999.
3. P. Doherty, J. Kachniarz, and A. Szałas. Using contextually closed queries for local closed-world reasoning in rough knowledge databases. In L. Polkowski and A. Skowron, editors, *Rough-Neuro Computing: Techniques for Computing with Words*, pages 217–248. Springer-Verlag, 2002.
4. P. Doherty, W. Łukaszewicz, A. Skowron, and A. Szałas. Combining rough and crisp knowledge in deductive databases. In L. Polkowski and A. Skowron, editors, *Rough-Neuro Computing: Techniques for Computing with Words*, pages 185–216. Springer-Verlag, 2002.
5. P. Doherty, W. Łukaszewicz, and A. Szałas. Computing circumscription revisited. *Journal of Automated Reasoning*, 18(3):297–336, 1997.
6. P. Doherty, W. Łukaszewicz, and A. Szałas. General domain circumscription and its effective reductions. *Fundamenta Informaticae*, 36(1):23–55, 1998.
7. P. Doherty, W. Łukaszewicz, and A. Szałas. Declarative PTIME queries for relational databases using quantifier elimination. *Journal of Logic and Computation*, 9(5):739–761, 1999.

8. P. Doherty, W. Łukaszewicz, and A. Szałas. Efficient reasoning using the local closed-world assumption. In A. Cerri and D. Dochev, editors, *Proc. 9th Int. Conference AIMSA 2000*, volume 1904 of *LNAI*, pages 49–58. Springer-Verlag, 2000.

9. P. Doherty, W. Łukaszewicz, and A. Szałas. Computing strongest necessary and weakest sufficient conditions of first-order formulas. *International Joint Conference on AI (IJCAI'2001)*, pages 145 – 151, 2001.

10. D. M. Gabbay and H. J. Ohlbach. Quantifier elimination in second-order predicate logic. In B. Nebel, C. Rich, and W. Swartout, editors, *Principles of Knowledge representation and reasoning, KR 92*, pages 425–435. Morgan Kauffman, 1992.

11. J.W. Garson. Quantification in modal logic. In D. Gabbay and F. Guenthner, editors, *Handbook of Philosophical Logic*, volume 2, pages 249–307. D. Reidel Pub. Co., 1984.

12. J. Kachniarz and A. Szałas. On a static approach to verification of integrity constraints in relational databases. In E. Orłowska and A. Szałas, editors, *Relational Methods for Computer Science Applications*, pages 97–109. Springer Physica-Verlag, 2001.

13. H. Kautz and B. Selman. Knowledge compilation and theory approximation. *Journal of the ACM*, 43(2):193–224, 1996.

14. V. Lifschitz. Computing circumscription. In *Proc. 9th IJCAI*, pages 229–235, Palo Alto, CA, 1985. Morgan Kaufmann.

15. V. Lifschitz. Circumscription. In D. M. Gabbay, C. J. Hogger, and J. A. Robinson, editors, *Handbook of Artificial Intelligence and Logic Programming*, volume 3, pages 297–352. Oxford University Press, 1991.

16. F. Lin. On strongest necessary and weakest sufficient conditions. In A.G. Cohn, F. Giunchiglia, and B. Selman, editors, *Proc. 7th International Conf. on Principles of Knowledge Representation and Reasoning, KR2000*, pages 167–175, San Francisco, Ca., 2000. Morgan Kaufmann Pub., Inc.

17. J. McCarthy. Approximate objects and approximate theories. In A.G. Cohn, F. Giunchiglia, and B. Selman, editors, *Proc. 7th International Conf. on Principles of Knowledge Representation and Reasoning, KR2000*, pages 519–526, San Francisco, Ca., 2000. Morgan Kaufmann Pub., Inc.

18. A. Nonnengart, H.J. Ohlbach, and A. Szałas. Elimination of predicate quantifiers. In H.J. Ohlbach and U. Reyle, editors, *Logic, Language and Reasoning. Essays in Honor of Dov Gabbay, Part I*, pages 159–181. Kluwer, 1999.

19. A. Nonnengart and A. Szałas. A fixpoint approach to second-order quantifier elimination with applications to correspondence theory. In E. Orłowska, editor, *Logic at Work: Essays Dedicated to the Memory of Helena Rasiowa*, volume 24 of *Studies in Fuzziness and Soft Computing*, pages 307–328. Springer Physica-Verlag, 1998.

20. H. Simmons. The monotonous elimination of predicate variables. *Journal of Logic and Computation*, 4:23–68, 1994. (special issue).

21. A. Szałas. On the correspondence between modal and classical logic: An automated approach. *Journal of Logic and Computation*, 3:605–620, 1993.

22. A. Szałas. On an automated translation of modal proof rules into formulas of the classical logic. *Journal of Applied Non-Classical Logics*, 4:119–127, 1994.

23. J. van Benthem. *Modal Logic and Classical Logic*. Bibliopolis, Naples, 1983.

24. J. van Benthem. Correspondence theory. In D. Gabbay and F. Guenthner, editors, *Handbook of Philosophical Logic*, volume 2, pages 167–247. D. Reidel Pub. Co., 1984.

Interpolation Theorems
for Nonmonotonic Reasoning Systems

Eyal Amir

Computer Science Division
University of California at Berkeley
Berkeley, CA 94720-1776, USA
eyal@cs.berkeley.edu

Abstract. *Craig's interpolation theorem* [3] is an important theorem known for
propositional logic and first-order logic. It says that if a logical formula β logically
follows from a formula α, then there is a formula γ, including only symbols that
appear in both α, β, such that β logically follows from γ and γ logically follows
from α. Such theorems are important and useful for understanding those logics
in which they hold as well as for speeding up reasoning with theories in those
logics. In this paper we present interpolation theorems in this spirit for three non-
monotonic systems: circumscription, default logic and logic programs with the
stable models semantics (a.k.a. answer set semantics). These results give us better
understanding of those logics, especially in contrast to their nonmonotonic charac-
teristics. They suggest that some *monotonicity* principle holds despite the failure
of classic monotonicity for these logics. Also, they sometimes allow us to use
methods for the decomposition of reasoning for these systems, possibly increasing their applicability and tractability. Finally, they allow us to build structured
representations that use those logics.

1 Introduction

Craig's interpolation theorem [3] is an important theorem known for propositional logic
and first-order logic (FOL). It says that if α, β are two logical formulae and $\alpha \vdash \beta$, then
there is a formula $\gamma \in \mathcal{L}(\alpha) \cap \mathcal{L}(\beta)$ such that $\alpha \vdash \gamma$ and $\gamma \vdash \beta$ ("$\vdash$" is the classical
logical deduction relation; $\mathcal{L}(\alpha)$ is the language of α (the set of formulae built with
the nonlogical symbols of α, $L(\alpha)$)). Such interpolation theorems allow us to break
inference into pieces associated with sublanguages of the language of that theory [2,21],
for those formal systems in which they hold. In AI, these properties have been used to
speed up inference for constraint satisfaction systems (CSPs), propositional logic and
FOL (e.g., [6,4,21,7,2,5]) and to build structured representations [4,1]

In this paper we present interpolation theorems for three nonmonotonic systems: *circumscription* [19], *default logic* [23] and *logic programs* with the Answer Set semantics
[12,10]. In the nonmonotonic setup there are several interpolation theorems for each system, with different conditions for applicability and different form of interpolation. This
stands in contrast to classical logic, where Craig's interpolation theorem always holds.
Our theorems allow us to use methods for the decomposition of reasoning (a-la [2,21])
under some circumstances for these systems, possibly increasing their applicability and

S. Flesca et al. (Eds.): JELIA 2002, LNAI 2424, pp. 233–244, 2002.
© Springer-Verlag Berlin Heidelberg 2002

tractability for structured theories. We list the main theorems that we show in this paper below, omitting some of their conditions for simplicity.

For circumscription we show that, under some conditions, $Circ[\alpha; P; Q] \models \beta$ iff there is some set of formulae $\gamma \subseteq \mathcal{L}(\alpha) \cap \mathcal{L}(\beta)$ such that $\alpha \models \gamma$ and $Circ[\gamma; P; Q] \models \beta$. For example, to answer $Circ[BlockW; block; L(BlockW)] \models on(A, B)$, we can compute this formula $\gamma \in \mathcal{L}(\{block, on, A, B\})$ from $BlockW$ *without applying circumscription*, and then solve $Circ[\gamma; block; L(BlockW)] \models on(A, B)$ (where γ may be significantly smaller than $BlockW$).

For default logic, letting $\alpha \hspace{1pt}\vdash\hspace{-6pt}\sim_D \beta$ mean that every extension of $\langle \alpha, D \rangle$ entails β (*cautious entailment*), we show that, under some conditions, if $\alpha \hspace{1pt}\vdash\hspace{-6pt}\sim_D \beta$, then there is a formula $\gamma \in \mathcal{L}(\alpha \cup D) \cap \mathcal{L}(\beta)$ such that $\alpha \hspace{1pt}\vdash\hspace{-6pt}\sim_D \gamma$ and $\gamma \hspace{1pt}\vdash\hspace{-6pt}\sim_D \beta$. For logic programs we show that if P_1, P_2 are two logic programs and $\varphi \in \mathcal{L}(P_2)$ such that $P_1 \cup P_2 \hspace{1pt}\vdash\hspace{-6pt}\sim^b \varphi$, then there is $\gamma \in \mathcal{L}(P_1) \cap \mathcal{L}(P_2)$ such that $P_1 \hspace{1pt}\vdash\hspace{-6pt}\sim^b \gamma$ and $P_2 \cup \gamma \hspace{1pt}\vdash\hspace{-6pt}\sim^b \varphi$ (here $\hspace{1pt}\vdash\hspace{-6pt}\sim^b$ is the *brave* entailment for logic programs).

This paper focuses on the form of the interpolation theorems that hold for those nonmonotonic logics. We do not address the possible application of these results to the problem of automated reasoning with those logics. Nonetheless, we mention that direct application of those results is possible along the lines already explored for propositional logic and FOL in [2,21].

No interpolation theorems were shown for nonmonotonic reasoning systems before this paper. Nonetheless, some of our theorems for default logic and logic programs are close to the *splitting theorems* of [17,26], which have already been used to decompose reasoning for those logics. The main difference between our theorems and those splitting theorems is that the latter change some of the defaults/rules involved to provide the corresponding entailment. Also, they do not talk about an interpolant γ, but rather discuss combining extensions.

Since its debut, the nonmonotonic reasoning line of work has expanded and several textbooks now exist that give a fair view of nonmonotonic reasoning and its uses (e.g., [8]). The reader is referred to those books for background and further details. *[Most proofs are shortened or omitted for lack of space. They are available from the author.]*

2   Logical Preliminaries

In this paper, we use the notion of *logical theory* for every set of axioms in FOL or propositional logic, regardless of whether the set of axioms is deductively closed or not. We use $L(\mathcal{A})$ to denote the signature of $\mathcal{A}$, i.e., the set of non-logical symbols. $\mathcal{L}(\mathcal{A})$ denotes the language of $\mathcal{A}$, i.e., the set of formulae built with $L(\mathcal{A})$. $Cn(\mathcal{A})$ is the set of logical consequences of $\mathcal{A}$ (i.e., those formulae that are valid consequences of $\mathcal{A}$ in FOL). For a first-order structure, M, in L, we write $U(M)$ for the universe of elements of M. For every symbol, s, in L, we write s^M for the interpretation of s in M.

Theorem 1 ([3]). *Let α, β be sentences such that $\alpha \vdash \beta$. Then there is a formula γ involving only nonlogical symbols common to both α and β, such that $\alpha \vdash \gamma$ and $\gamma \vdash \beta$.*

3   Circumscription

3.1   McCarthy's Circumscription: Overview

McCarthy's circumscription [19,20] is a nonmonotonic reasoning system in which inference from a set of axioms, A, is performed by minimizing the extent of some predicate symbols $\vec{P}$, while allowing some other nonlogical symbols, $\vec{Z}$ to vary.

Formally, McCarthy's circumscription formula

$$Circ[A(P, Z); P; Z] = A(P, Z) \wedge \forall p, z \, (A(p, z) \Rightarrow \neg(p < P)) \qquad (1)$$

says that in the theory A, with parameter relations and function vectors (sequence of symbols) P, Z, P is a minimal element such that $A(P, Z)$ is still consistent, when we are allowed to vary Z in order to allow P to become smaller.

Take for example the following simple theory: $T = block(B_1) \wedge block(B_2)$. Then, the circumscription of $block$ in T, varying nothing, is

$$Circ[T; block;] = T \wedge \forall p \, [T_{[block/p]} \Rightarrow \neg(p < block)].$$

Roughly, this means that $block$ is a minimal predicate satisfying T. Computing circumscription is discussed in length in [16] and others, and we do not expand on it here. Using known techniques we can conclude

$$Circ[T; block;] \equiv \forall x \, (block(x) \Leftrightarrow (x = B_1 \vee x = B_2))$$

This means that there are no other blocks in the world other than those mentioned in the original theory T.

We give the preferential semantics for circumscription that was given by [15,20,9] in the following definition.

Definition 1 ([15]). *For any two models M and N of a theory T we write $M \leq_{P,Z} N$ if the models M, N differ only in how they interpret predicates from P and Z and if the extension of every predicate from P in M is a subset of its extension in N. We write $M <_{P,Z} N$ if for at least one predicate in P the extension in M is a strict subset of its extension in N.*

A model M of T is $\leq_{P,Z}$-minimal if there is no model N of T such that $N <_{P,Z} M$.

Theorem 2 ([15]: Circumscript. Semantics). *Let T be a finite set of sentences. A structure M is a model of $Circ[T; P; Z]$ iff M is a $\leq_{P,Z}$-minimal model of T.*

This theorem allows us to extend the definition of circumscription to set of infinite number of sentences. In those cases, $Circ[T; P; Z]$ is defined as the set of sentences that hold in all the $\leq_{P,Z}$-minimal models of T. Theorem 2 implies that this extended definition is equivalent to the syntactic characterization of the original definition (equation (1)) if T is a finite set of sentences. In the rest of this paper, we refer to this extended definition of circumscription, if T is an infinite set of FOL sentences (we will note those cases when we encounter them).

Circumscription satisfied Left Logical Equivalence (LLE): $T \equiv T'$ implies that $Circ[T; P; Z] \equiv Circ[T'; P; Z]$. It also satisfies Right Weakening: $Circ[T; P; Z] \models \varphi$ and $\varphi \Rightarrow \psi$ implies that $Circ[T; P; Z] \models \psi$).

3.2   Model Theory

Definition 2. *Let M, N be L-structures, for FOL signature L and language $\mathcal{L}$. We say that N is an* elementary extension *of M (or M is an* elementary substructure *of N), written $M \preceq N$, if $U(M) \subseteq U(N)$ and for every $\varphi(\overrightarrow{x}) \in \mathcal{L}$ and vector of elements $\overrightarrow{a}$ of $U(M)$, $M \models \varphi(\overrightarrow{a})$ iff $N \models \varphi(\overrightarrow{a})$.*

For FOL signatures $L \subseteq L^+$, and for N an L^+-structure, we say that $N \upharpoonright L$ is the *reduct* of N to L, the L-structure with the same universe of elements as N, and the same interpretation as N for those symbols from L^+ that are in L (there is no interpretation for symbols not in L). For A theory T in a language of L^+, let $Cn^L(T)$ be the set of all consequences of T in the language of L.

3.3   Interpolation in Circumscription

In this section we present two interpolation theorems for circumscription. Those theorems hold for both FOL and propositional logic. Roughly speaking, the first (Theorem 4) says that if α nonmonotonically entails β (here this means $Circ[\alpha; P; Q] \models \beta$), then there is $\gamma \subseteq \mathcal{L}(\alpha) \cap \mathcal{L}(\beta \cup P)$ such that α classically entails γ ($\alpha \models \gamma$) and γ nonmonotonically entails β ($Circ[\gamma; P; Q] \models \beta$). In the FOL case this γ can be an infinite set of sentences, and we use the extended definition of Circumscription for infinite sets of axioms for this statement.

The second theorem (Theorem 7) is similar to the first, with two main differences. First, it requires that $L(\alpha) \subseteq (P \cup Q)$. Second, it guarantees that γ as above (and some other restrictions) exists iff α nonmonotonically entails β. This is in contrast to the first theorem that guarantees only that *if* part. The actual technical details are more fine than those rough statements, so the reader should refer to the actual theorem statements.

In addition to these two theorems, we present another theorem that addresses the case of reasoning from the union of theories (Theorem 6). Before we state and prove those theorems, we prove several useful lemmas.

Our first lemma says that if we are given two theories T_1, T_2, and we know the set of sentences that follow from T_2 in the intersection of their languages, then every model of this set of sentences together with T_1 can be extended to a model of $T_1 \cup T_2$.

Lemma 1. *Let T_1, T_2 be two theories, with signatures in L_1, L_2, respectively. Let γ be a set of sentences logically equivalent to $Cn^{L_1 \cap L_2}(T_2)$. For every L_1-structure, $\mathcal{M}$, that satisfies $T_1 \cup \gamma$ there is a $(L_1 \cup L_2)$-structure, $\widehat{\mathcal{M}}$, that is a model of $T_1 \cup T_2$ such that $\mathcal{M} \preceq \widehat{\mathcal{M}} \upharpoonright L_1$.*

Our second lemma says that every $<_{P,Q}$-minimal model of T that is also a model of T' is a $<_{P,Q}$-minimal model of $T \cup T'$.

Lemma 2. *Let T be a theory and P, Q vectors of nonlogical symbols (P includes only predicate symbols). If $\mathcal{M} \models Circ[T; P; Q]$ and $\mathcal{M} \models T \cup T'$, then $\mathcal{M} \models Circ[T \cup T'; P; Q]$.*

The following theorem is central to the rest of our results in this section. It says that when we circumscribe P, Q in $T_1 \cup T_2$ we can replace T_2 by its consequences in $\mathcal{L}(T_1)$, for some purposes and under some assumptions.

Theorem 3. *For T_1, T_2 theories and P, Q vectors of symbols from $L(T_1) \cup L(T_2)$ such that $P \subseteq L(T_1)$, let γ be a set of sentences logically equivalent to $Cn^{L(T_1) \cap L(T_2)}(T_2)$. Then, for all $\varphi \in \mathcal{L}(T_1)$, if $Circ[T_1 \cup T_2; P; Q] \models \varphi$, then $Circ[T_1 \cup \gamma; P; Q] \models \varphi$.*

PROOF   We show that for every model of $Circ[T_1 \cup \gamma; P; Q]$ there is a model of $Circ[T_1 \cup T_2; P; Q]$ whose reduct to $L(T_1)$ is an elementary extension of the reduct of the first model to $L(T_1)$.

Let $\mathcal{M}$ be a $L(T_1 \cup T_2)$-structure that is a model of $Circ[T_1 \cup \gamma; P; Q]$. Then, $\mathcal{M} \models T_1 \cup \gamma$. From Lemma 1 we know that there is a $(L_1 \cup L_2)$-structure, $\widehat{\mathcal{M}}$, that is a model of T_2 such that $\mathcal{M} \restriction L(T_1) \preceq \widehat{\mathcal{M}} \restriction L(T_1)$.

Thus, $\widehat{\mathcal{M}}$ is a $\leq_{P,Q}$-minimal model of $T_1 \cup \gamma$. To see this, assume otherwise. Then, there is a model $\mathcal{M}'$ for the signature $L(T_1 \cup T_2)$ such that $\mathcal{M}' <_{P,Q} \widehat{\mathcal{M}}$ and $\mathcal{M}' \models T_1 \cup \gamma$. Take $\mathcal{M}''$ such that the interpretation of all the symbols in $L(T_1)$ is exactly the same as that of $\mathcal{M}'$ and such that the interpretation of all symbols in $L(T_2) \setminus L(T_1)$ is exactly the same as that of $\mathcal{M}$. Then, $\mathcal{M}'' \models T_1 \cup \gamma$ because $T_1 \cup \gamma \subseteq \mathcal{L}(T_1)$. Also, $\mathcal{M}'' <_{P,Q'} \mathcal{M}$, for $Q' = Q \cap L(T_1)$ because $P \subseteq L(T_1)$ and $\mathcal{M}, \widehat{\mathcal{M}}$ agree on the interpretation of symbols in $L(T_1)$ ($\mathcal{M} \restriction L(T_1) \preceq \widehat{\mathcal{M}} \restriction L(T_1)$). Thus, $\mathcal{M}'' <_{P,Q} \mathcal{M}$, since $\mathcal{M}'', \mathcal{M}$ agree on all the interpretation of all symbols in $L(T_2) \setminus L(T_1)$. This contradicts $\mathcal{M} \models Circ[T_1 \cup \gamma; P; Q]$, so $\widehat{\mathcal{M}}$ is a $\leq_{P,Q}$-minimal model of $T_1 \cup \gamma$.

Thus, $\widehat{\mathcal{M}} \models Circ[T_1 \cup \gamma; P; Q]$, and $\widehat{\mathcal{M}} \models T_1 \cup T_2$. From Lemma 2 we get that $\widehat{\mathcal{M}} \models Circ[T_1 \cup T_2; P; Q]$. Now, let $\varphi \in \mathcal{L}(T_1)$ such that $Circ[T_1 \cup T_2; P; Q] \models \varphi$. Then every model of $Circ[T_1 \cup T_2; P; Q]$ satisfies φ. Let $\mathcal{M}$ be a model of $Circ[T_1 \cup \gamma; P; Q]$ in the language $\mathcal{L}(T_1 \cup T_2)$. Then there is $\widehat{\mathcal{M}}$ as above, i.e., $\widehat{\mathcal{M}} \models Circ[T_1 \cup T_2; P; Q]$ and $\mathcal{M} \restriction L(T_1) \preceq \widehat{\mathcal{M}} \restriction L(T_1)$. Thus, $\widehat{\mathcal{M}} \models \varphi$. Since $\mathcal{M} \restriction L(T_1) \preceq \widehat{\mathcal{M}} \restriction L(T_1)$, $\mathcal{M} \models \varphi$. Thus every model of $Circ[T_1 \cup \gamma; P; Q]$ is a model of φ.   ∎

Theorem 4 (Interpolation for Circumscription 1). *Let T be a theory, P, Q vectors of symbols, and φ a formula. If $Circ[T; P; Q] \models \varphi$, then there is $\gamma \subseteq \mathcal{L}(T) \cap \mathcal{L}(\varphi \cup P)$ such that*

$$T \models \gamma \quad and \quad Circ[\gamma; P; Q] \models \varphi.$$

Furthermore, this holds for every γ that is logically equivalent to the consequences of T in $L(T) \cap L(\varphi \cup P)$.

PROOF   We use Theorem 3 to find this γ. For T, φ as in the statement of the theorem we define T_1, T_2 as follows. We choose T_1 such that $\varphi \in \mathcal{L}(T_1)$ and $P \subseteq L(T_1)$: Let $T_1 = \{\varphi \vee \neg\varphi\} \cup \tau_1$ for τ_1 a set of tautologies such that $L(\tau_1) = P$. We choose T_2 such that it includes T and has a rich enough vocabulary so that $P, Q \subseteq L(T_1) \cup L(T_2)$. Let $T_2 = T \cup \tau_2$, for τ_2 a set of tautologies such that $L(\tau_2) = Q \setminus L(T_1)$. Let $L_1 = L(T_1)$, $L_2 = L(T_2)$.

Theorem 3 guarantees that if $P \subseteq L_1$ then γ from that theorem satisfies $Circ[T_1 \cup T_2; P; Q] \models \psi \Rightarrow Circ[T_1 \cup \gamma; P; Q] \models \psi$ for every $\psi \in \mathcal{L}(T_1)$. This implies that for every $\psi \in \mathcal{L}(\{\varphi\} \cup \tau_1)$, $Circ[T; P; Q] \models \psi \Rightarrow Circ[\gamma; P; Q] \models \psi$. In particular, $Circ[\gamma; P; Q] \models \varphi$, and this γ satisfies our current theorem.   ∎

Example 1. For example, if $\alpha = block(A) \land block(B) \land \forall b \, (clear(b) \Leftrightarrow (block(b) \land \forall x \neg on(x, b)))$, $\beta = clear(A)$, $P = on$, $Q = clear$, then one possible interpolant is $\gamma = clear(A) \Leftrightarrow \forall x \neg on(x, A)$ because $\alpha \models \gamma$ and $Circ[\gamma; P; Q] \models \beta$ (because $Circ[clear(A) \Leftrightarrow \forall x \neg on(x, A); on; clear] \equiv \forall x, b \neg(x, b) \land clear(A))$.

This theorem does not hold if we require $\gamma \subseteq \mathcal{L}(T) \cap \mathcal{L}(\varphi)$ instead of $\gamma \subseteq \mathcal{L}(T) \cap \mathcal{L}(\varphi \cup P)$. For example, take $\varphi = Q$, $T = \{\neg P \Rightarrow Q\}$, where P, Q are propositional symbols. $Circ[T; P; Q] \models \varphi$. However, every logical consequence of T in $L(\varphi)$ is a tautology. Thus, if the theorem was correct with our changed requirement, γ would be equivalent to $\emptyset$ and $Circ[\gamma; P; Q] \not\models \varphi$.

Theorem 5. *Let T_1, T_2 be two theories, P, Q two vectors of symbols from $L(T_1) \cup L(T_2)$ such that $P \subseteq L(T_1)$ and $P \cup Q \supseteq L(T_2)$. Let γ be a set of sentences logically equivalent to $Cn^{L(T_1) \cap L(T_2)}(T_2)$. Then, for all $\varphi \in \mathcal{L}(T_1)$, if $Circ[T_1 \cup \gamma; P; Q] \models \varphi$, then $Circ[T_1 \cup T_2; P; Q] \models \varphi$.*

From Theorem 3 and Theorem 5 we get the following theorem.

Theorem 6 (Interpolation Between Theories). *Let T_1, T_2 be two theories, P, Q vectors of symbols in $L(T_1) \cup L(T_2)$ such that $P \subseteq L(T_1)$ and $P \cup Q \supset L(T_2)$. Let γ be a set of sentences logically equivalent to $Cn^{L(T_1) \cap L(T_2)}(T_2)$. Then, for every $\varphi \in \mathcal{L}(T_1)$,*

$$Circ[T_1 \cup \gamma; P; Q] \models \varphi \iff Circ[T_1 \cup T_2; P; Q] \models \varphi$$

Theorem 7 (Interpolation for Circumscription 2). *Let T be a theory, P, Q vectors of symbols such that $(P \cup Q) \supseteq L(T)$. Let L_2 be a set of nonlogical symbols. Then, there is $\gamma \in \mathcal{L}(T) \cap \mathcal{L}(L_2 \cup P)$ such that $T \models \gamma$ and for all $\varphi \in \mathcal{L}(L_2)$,*

$$Circ[T; P; Q] \models \varphi \iff Circ[\gamma; P; Q] \models \varphi.$$

Furthermore, this γ can be logically equivalent to the consequences of T in $L(T) \cap (L_2 \cup P)$.

PROOF   Let T_1 be a set of tautologies such that $L(T_1) = L_2 \cup P$. Also, let $T_2 = T \cup \tau_2$, for τ_2 a set of tautologies such that $L(\tau_2) = Q \setminus L(T_1)$. Let $L_1 = L(T_1)$, $L_2 = L(T_2)$. Theorem 6 guarantees that γ from that theorem satisfies $Circ[\gamma; P; Q] \models \psi \iff Circ[T; P; Q] \models \psi$ for every $\psi \in \mathcal{L}_1 = L_2 \cup P$.   ■

Example 2. If α, β and P are taken as in Example 1, and $Q = \{clear, block, A, B\}$, then one interpolant for Theorem 7 is $\gamma = clear(A) \Leftrightarrow \forall x \neg on(x, A)$.

The theorems we presented are for parallel circumscription, where we minimize all the minimized predicates in parallel without priorities. The case of prioritized circumscription is outside the scope of this paper.

4   Default Logic

In this section we present interpolation theorems for *propositional* default logic. We also assume that the signature of our propositional default theories is finite (this also implies that our theories are finite).

4.1 Reiter's Default Logic: Overview

In Reiter's default logic [23] one has a set of facts W (in either propositional or FOL) and a set of defaults D (in a corresponding language). Defaults in D are of the form $\frac{\alpha:\beta_1,...,\beta_n}{\delta}$ with the intuition that if α is proved, and $\beta_1, ..., \beta_n$ are consistent (throughout the proof), then δ is proved. α is called the *prerequisite*, $pre(d) = \{\alpha\}$; $\beta_1, ..., \beta_n$ are the *justifications*, $just(d) = \{\beta_1, ..., \beta_n\}$ and δ is the *consequent*, $cons(d) = \{\delta\}$. We use similar notation for sets of defaults (e.g., $cons(D) = \bigcup_{d \in D} cons(d)$).

Definition 3. *An extension of $\langle W, D \rangle$ is a set of sentences E that satisfies W, follows the defaults in D, and is minimal. More formally, E is an extension if it is minimal (as a set) such that $\Gamma(E) = E$, where we define $\Gamma(S_0)$ to be S, a minimal set of sentences such that*

1. $W \subseteq S$; $S = Cn(S)$.
2. *For all $\frac{\alpha:\beta_1,...,\beta_n}{\delta} \in D$ if $\alpha \in S$ and $\forall i \ \neg\beta_i \notin S_0$, then $\delta \in S$.*

The following theorem provides an equivalent definition that was shown in [18,24] and others. A set of defaults, $\mathbb{D}$ is grounded in a set of formulae W iff for all $d \in \mathbb{D}$, $pre(d) \in Cn_{Mon(\mathbb{D})}(W)$, where $Mon(\mathbb{D}) = \{ \frac{pre(d)}{cons(d)} \mid d \in \mathbb{D}\}$.

Theorem 8 (Extensions in Terms of Generating Defaults). *A set of formulae E is an extension of a default theory $\langle W, D \rangle$ iff $E = Cn(W \cup \{cons(d) \mid d \in D'\})$ for a minimal set of defaults $D' \subseteq D$ such that*

1. *D' is grounded in W and*
2. *for every $d \in D$, $d \in D'$ if and only if $pre(d) \in Cn(W \cup cons(D'))$ and every $\psi \in just(d)$ satisfies $\neg\psi \notin Cn(W \cup cons(D'))$.*

Every minimal set of defaults $D' \subseteq D$ as mentioned in this theorem is said to be a set of *generating defaults*.

Normal defaults are defaults of the form $\frac{\alpha:\beta}{\beta}$. These defaults are interesting because they are fairly intuitive in nature (if we proved α then β is proved unless previously proved inconsistent). A default theory is *normal*, if all of its defaults are normal.

We define $W \mathrel{\vdash\!\!\sim}_D \varphi$ as cautious entailment sanctioned by the defaults in D, i.e., φ follows from every extension of $\langle W, D \rangle$. We define $W \mathrel{\vdash\!\!\sim}_D^b \varphi$ as brave entailment sanctioned by the defaults in D, i.e., φ follows from at least one extension of $\langle W, D \rangle$.

4.2 Interpolation in Default Logic

In this section we present several flavors of interpolation theorems, most of which are stated for cautious entailment.

Theorem 9 (Interpolation for Cautious DL 1). *Let $T = \langle W, D \rangle$ be a propositional default theory and φ a propositional formula. If $W \mathrel{\vdash\!\!\sim}_D \varphi$, then there are γ_1, γ_2 such that $\gamma_1 \in \mathcal{L}(W) \cap \mathcal{L}(D \cup \{\varphi\})$, $\gamma_2 \in \mathcal{L}(W \cup D) \cap \mathcal{L}(\varphi)$ and all the following hold:*

$$W \models \gamma_1 \quad \gamma_1 \mathrel{\vdash\!\!\sim}_D \gamma_2 \quad \gamma_2 \models \varphi \quad W \mathrel{\vdash\!\!\sim}_D \gamma_2 \quad \gamma_1 \mathrel{\vdash\!\!\sim}_D \varphi$$

PROOF   Let γ_1 be the set of consequences of W in $\mathcal{L}(D \cup \{\varphi\}) \cap \mathcal{L}(W)$. Let $\mathbb{E}$ be the set of extensions of $\langle W, D \rangle$ and $\mathbb{E}'$ the set of extensions of $\langle \gamma_1, D \rangle$. We show that every extension $E' \in \mathbb{E}'$ has an extension $E \in \mathbb{E}$ such that $Cn(E' \cup W) = Cn(E)$. This will show that γ_1 is as needed.

Take $E' \in \mathbb{E}'$ and define $E_0 = Cn(E' \cup W)$. We assume that $L(E') \subseteq L(\mathbb{D})$ because otherwise we can take a logically equivalent extension whose sentences are in $\mathcal{L}(\mathbb{D})$. We show that E_0 satisfies the conditions for extensions of $\langle W, D \rangle$ (Definition 3). The first condition holds by definition of E_0. The second condition holds because every default that is consistent with E_0 is also consistent with E' and vice versa.

For the first direction (every default that is consistent with E_0 is also consistent with E'), let $\frac{\alpha : \beta_1, ..., \beta_n}{\delta} \in D$ be such that $\alpha \in E_0$. We show that $\alpha \in E'$. By definition, $\alpha \in \mathcal{L}(D)$. $\alpha \in E_0$ implies that $E' \cup W \models \alpha$ because $Cn(E' \cup W) = E_0$. Using the deduction theorem for propositional logic we get $W \models E' \Rightarrow \alpha$ (taking E' here to be a finite set of sentences that is logically equivalent to E' in $\mathcal{L}(\mathbb{D})$ (there is such a finite set because we assume that $L(\mathbb{D})$ is finite)). Using Craig's interpolation theorem for propositional logic, there is $\gamma \in \mathcal{L}(W) \cap \mathcal{L}(E' \Rightarrow \alpha)$ such that $W \models \gamma$ and $\gamma \models E' \Rightarrow \alpha$. However, this means that $\gamma_1 \models \gamma$, by the way we chose γ_1. Thus $\gamma_1 \models E' \Rightarrow \alpha$. Since $E' \subseteq \gamma_1$ we get that $E' \models \alpha$. Since $E' = Cn(E')$ we get that $\alpha \in E'$. The case is similar for δ: if $\delta \in E_0$ then $\delta \in E'$ by the same argument as given above for $\alpha \in E_0 \Rightarrow \alpha \in E'$. Finally, if $\forall i \ \neg \beta_i \notin E_0$ then $\forall i \ \neg \beta_i \notin E'$ because $E' \subseteq E_0$. The opposite direction (every default that is consistent with E' is also consistent with E_0) is similar to the first one.

Thus, E_0 satisfies those two conditions. However, it is possible that E_0 is not a minimal such set of formulae. If so, Theorem 8 implies that there is a strict subset of the generating defaults of E_0 that generate a different extension. However, we can apply this new set of defaults to generate an extension that is smaller than E', contradicting the fact that E' is an extension of $\langle \gamma_1, D \rangle$.

Now, if φ logically follows in all the extensions of $\langle W, D \rangle$ then it must also follow from every extension of $\langle \gamma_1, D \rangle$ together with W. Let $\Lambda = E_1 \vee ... \vee E_n$, for $E_1, ..., E_n$ the (finite) set of (logically non-equivalent) extensions of $\langle W, D \rangle$ (we have a finite set of those because $L(W) \cup L(D)$ is finite). Then, $\Lambda \models \varphi$. Take $\gamma_2 \in \mathcal{L}(\Lambda) \cap \mathcal{L}(\varphi)$ such that $\Lambda \models \gamma_2$ and $\gamma_2 \models \varphi$, as guaranteed by Craig's interpolation theorem (Theorem 1). These γ_1, γ_2 are those promised by the current theorem: $W \models \gamma_1$, $\gamma_2 \models \varphi$, $W \vdash_D \gamma_2$, $\gamma_1 \vdash_D \gamma_2$ and $\gamma_1 \vdash_D \varphi$.   ■

Theorem 10 (Interpolation for Cautious DL 2). *Let $T = \langle W, D \rangle$ be a propositional default theory and φ a propositional formula. If $W \vdash_D \varphi$, then there are $\gamma_1, \gamma_2 \in \mathcal{L}(W) \cap \mathcal{L}(D)$, and all the following hold:*

$$W \models \gamma_1 \quad \gamma_1 \vdash_D \gamma_2 \quad \{\gamma_2\} \cup W \models \varphi \quad W \vdash_D \gamma_2$$

Example 3. If $\alpha = wet \wedge (wet \Rightarrow mud)$, $\beta = (rain \Rightarrow clouds) \Rightarrow clouds$, $D = \{\frac{mud:rain}{rain}\}$, then one possible pair of interpolants is $\gamma_1 = mud$, $\gamma_2 = rain$.

For another example, if the only objects are A, B, and $\alpha = block(A) \wedge block(B) \wedge \forall b \ (clear(b) \Leftrightarrow (block(b) \wedge \forall x \neg on(x, b)))$, $\beta = clear(A)$ and $D = \{\frac{:\neg on(a,b)}{\neg on(a,b)}\}$, then one possible pair of interpolants is $\gamma_1 = TRUE$, $\gamma_2 = \neg on(B, A) \wedge \neg on(A, A)$. To see that γ_1, γ_2 satisfy Theorem 10 notice that $\langle \alpha, D \rangle$ has one extension: $E = \{block(A),$ $block(B), \neg on(A, B), \neg on(B, A), \neg on(A, A), \neg on(B, B), clear(A), clear(B)\}$.

Corollary 1. *Let* $\langle W, D \rangle$ *be a default theory and* φ *a formula. If* $W \hspace{1pt}\vdash_D \varphi$, *then there is a set of formulae,* $\gamma \in \mathcal{L}(W \cup D) \cap \mathcal{L}(\varphi)$ *such that* $W \hspace{1pt}\vdash_D \gamma$ *and* $\gamma \hspace{1pt}\vdash_D \varphi$.

We do not get stronger interpolation theorems for prerequisite-free normal default theories. [14] provided a modular translation of normal default theories with no prerequisites into circumscription, but Theorem 4 does not lead to better results. In particular, the counter example that we presented after Theorem 4 can be massaged to apply here too.

Theorem 11 (Interpolation Between Default Extensions). *Let* $\langle W_1, D_1 \rangle, \langle W_2, D_2 \rangle$ *be default theories such that* $L(cons(D_2)) \cap L(pre(D_1) \cup just(D_1) \cup W_1) = \emptyset$. *Let* φ *be a formula such that* $\varphi \in \mathcal{L}(W_2 \cup D_2)$. *If there is an extension* E *of* $\langle W_1 \cup W_2, D_1 \cup D_2 \rangle$ *in which* φ *holds, then there is a formula* $\gamma \in \mathcal{L}(W_1 \cup D_1) \cap \mathcal{L}(W_2 \cup D_2)$, *an extension* E_1 *of* $\langle W_1, D_1 \rangle$ *such that* $Cn(E_1) \cap \mathcal{L}(W_2 \cup D_2) = \gamma$, *and an extension* E_2 *of* $\langle W_2 \cup \{\gamma\}, D_2 \rangle$ *such that* $E_2 \models \varphi$.

It is interesting to notice that the reverse direction of this theorem does not hold. For example, if we have two extensions E_1, E_2 as in the theorem statement, it is possible that E_1 uses a default with justification β, but $W_2 \models \neg\beta$. Strengthening the condition of the theorem, i.e., demanding that $L(W_2 \cup cons(D_2)) \cap L(pre(D_1) \cup just(D_1) \cup W_1) = \emptyset$, is not sufficient either. For example, if D_1 includes two defaults $d_1 = \frac{:}{a \Rightarrow \neg\beta}$, and $d_2 = \frac{:\beta}{\varphi}$, $W_1 = \emptyset$, D_2 includes no defaults and $W_2 = \{a\}$ then there is no extension of $\langle W_1 \cup W_2, D_1 \cup D_2 \rangle$ that implies φ, for $\varphi = \{c\}$.

Further strengthening the conditions of the theorem gives the following:

Theorem 12 (Reverse Direction of Theorem 11). *Let* $\langle W_1, D_1 \rangle, \langle W_2, D_2 \rangle$ *be default theories such that* $L(W_2 \cup cons(D_2)) \cap L(D_1 \cup W_1) = \emptyset$. *Let* φ *be a formula such that* $\varphi \in \mathcal{L}(W_2 \cup D_2)$. *There is an extension* E *of* $\langle W_1 \cup W_2, D_1 \cup D_2 \rangle$ *in which* φ *holds only if there is a formula* $\gamma \in \mathcal{L}(W_1 \cup D_1) \cap \mathcal{L}(W_2 \cup D_2)$, *an extension* E_1 *of* $\langle W_1, D_1 \rangle$ *such that* $Cn(E_1) \cap \mathcal{L}(W_2 \cup D_2) = \gamma$, *and an extension* E_2 *of* $\langle W_2 \cup \{\gamma\}, D_2 \rangle$ *such that* $E_2 \models \varphi$.

Corollary 2 (Interpolation for Brave DL). *Let* $\langle W_1, D_1 \rangle, \langle W_2, D_2 \rangle$ *be default theories such that* $L(cons(D_2)) \cap L(pre(D_1) \cup just(D_1) \cup W_1) = \emptyset$. *Let* φ *be a formula such that* $\varphi \in \mathcal{L}(W_2 \cup D_2)$. *If* $W_1 \cup W_2 \hspace{1pt}\vdash^b_{D_1 \cup D_2} \varphi$, *then there is a formula,* $\gamma \in \mathcal{L}(W_1 \cup D_1) \cap \mathcal{L}(W_2 \cup D_2)$, *such that* $W_1 \hspace{1pt}\vdash^b_{D_1} \gamma$ *and* $W_2 \cup \{\gamma\} \hspace{1pt}\vdash^b_{D_2} \varphi$.

Finally, Corollary 2 and Theorem 11 are similar to the *splitting theorem* of [26], which is provided for default theories with $W = \emptyset$ (there is a modular translation that converts every default theory to one with $W = \emptyset$). A *splitting set* for a set of defaults D is a subset A of $L(D)$ such that $pre(D), just(D), cons(D) \subseteq \mathcal{L}(A) \cup \mathcal{L}(L(D) \setminus A)$ and $\forall d \in D$ $(cons(d) \notin \mathcal{L}(L(D) \setminus A) \Rightarrow L(d) \subseteq A)$. Let $B = L(D) \setminus A$. The base of D relative to A is $b_A(D) = \{d \in D \mid L(d) \subseteq A\}$. For a set of sentences $X \subseteq \mathcal{L}(A)$, we define $e_A(D, X)$ to be

$$\left\{ \frac{\bigwedge(\{a_i\}_{i \le n} \cap \mathcal{L}(B)) : \{b_i\}_{i \le m} \cap \mathcal{L}(B)}{c} \;\middle|\; \begin{array}{l} \frac{\bigwedge_{i=1}^{n} a_i : b_1, \ldots, b_m}{c} \in D \setminus b_A(D), \\ \forall i \le n (a_i \in \mathcal{L}(A) \Rightarrow a_i \in Cn^A(X)), \\ \forall i \le m (\neg b_i \notin Cn^A(X)) \end{array} \right\}$$

Theorem 13 ([26]). *Let A be a splitting set for a default theory D over $\mathcal{L}(U)$. A set E of formulae is a consistent extension of D iff $E = Cn^{L(D)}(X \cup Y)$, for some consistent extension X of $b_a(D)$ over $\mathcal{L}(A)$ and Y a consistent extension of $e_A(D, X)$ over $\mathcal{L}(L(D) \setminus A)$.*

Roughly speaking, this theorem finds an extension X of the *base* ($b_A(D)$) and converts $D \setminus b_A(D)$ using this X into a theory $e_A(D, X)$. Then, an extension Y for $e_A(D, X)$ completes the extension for D if $X \cup Y$ is consistent. In contrast, our theorem does not change $D \setminus b_A(D)$, but it is somewhat weaker, in that it only provides a necessary condition for $D \mathrel{\vdash\!\!\!\sim}^b \varphi$. (however, notice that this *weaker* form is typical for interpolation theorems).

5 Logic Programs

In this section we provide interpolation theorems for logic programs with the stable models semantics. We use the fact the logic programs are a special case of default logic, and the results are straightforward. An *extended disjunctive logic program* [10,11,12,22] is a set of *rules*. Each rule, r, is written as an expression of the form

$$L_1 | \ldots | L_l \leftarrow A_1, \ldots, A_n, not\, B_1, \ldots, not\, B_m$$

where $L_1, \ldots, L_l, A_1, \ldots, A_n, B_1, \ldots, B_m$ are literals, that is, atomic formulae or their (classic) negations, $L_1, \ldots, L_l$ are the *head literals*, $head(r)$, $A_1, \ldots, A_n$ are the *positive subgoals*, $pos(r)$, and $B_1, \ldots, B_m$ are the *negated subgoals*, $neg(r)$.

[25] showed that disjunctive logic programs (no classic negation) with the stable model semantics can be translated to prerequisite-free default theories as follows:

1. For a rule $A_1 | \ldots | A_l \leftarrow B_1, \ldots, B_m, not\, C_1, \ldots, not\, C_n$ in P, we get the default

$$\frac{: \neg C_1, \ldots, \neg C_n}{B_1 \wedge \ldots \wedge B_m \Rightarrow A_1 \vee \ldots \vee A_l}$$

2. For each atom A appearing in P, we get the default $\frac{: \neg A}{\neg A}$

Each stable model of P is the set of atoms in some extension of D_P, and the set of atoms in an extension of D_P is a stable model of P (notice that, in general, an extension of D_P can include sentences that are not atoms and are not subsumed by atoms in that extension). [25] provide a similar translation to extended disjunctive logic programs by first translating those into disjunctive logic programs (a literal $\neg A$ is translated to a new symbol, A'), showing that a similar property holds for this class of programs.

We define $P \mathrel{\vdash\!\!\!\sim} \varphi$ as cautious entailment sanctioned from the logic program P, i.e., φ follows from stable model of P. We define $P \mathrel{\vdash\!\!\!\sim}^b \varphi$ as brave entailment sanctioned from the logic program P, i.e., φ follows from at least one stable model of P.

From the translation above we get the following interpolation theorems.

Theorem 14 (Interpolation for Stable Models (Cautious)). *Let P be a logic program and let φ be a formula such that $P \mathrel{\vert\!\!\sim} \varphi$. Then, there is a formula $\gamma \in \mathcal{L}(P) \cap \mathcal{L}(\varphi)$ such that $P \mathrel{\vert\!\!\sim} \gamma$ and $\gamma \models \varphi$.*

PROOF   Follows if γ_2 in Theorem 9 corresponding to our needed γ.   ∎

Theorem 15 (Interpolation for Stable Models (Brave)). *Let P_1, P_2 be logic programs such that $head(P_2) \cap body(P_1) = \emptyset$. Let $\varphi \in \mathcal{L}(P_2)$ be a formula such that $P_1 \cup P_2 \mathrel{\vert\!\!\sim^b} \varphi$. Then, there is a formula $\gamma \in \mathcal{L}(P_1) \cap \mathcal{L}(P_2)$ such that $P_1 \mathrel{\vert\!\!\sim^b} \gamma$ and $\gamma \cup P_2 \mathrel{\vert\!\!\sim^b} \varphi$.*

PROOF   Follows from the reduction to default logic and Corollary 2.   ∎

The last theorem is similar to the *splitting theorem* of [17]. This theorem finds an answer set X of the *bottom* (P_1) and converts P_2 using this X into a program P_2'. Then, an answer set Y for P_2' completes the answer set for $P_1 \cup P_2$ if $X \cup Y$ is consistent. In contrast, our theorem does not change P_2, but it is somewhat weaker, in that it does only provides a necessary condition for $P_1 \cup P_2 \mathrel{\vert\!\!\sim^b} \varphi$ (this is the typical form of an interpolation theorem).

6 Summary

We presented interpolation theorems that are applicable to the nonmonotonic systems of circumscription, default logic and Answer Set Programming (a.k.a. Stable Models Semantics). These results are somewhat surprising and revealing in that they show particular structure for the nonmonotonic entailments associated with the different systems. They promise to help in reasoning with larger systems that are based on these nonmonotonic systems.

Several questions remain open. First, γ promised by our theorems is not always finite (in the FOL case). This is in contrast to classical FOL, where the interpolant is always of finite length. What conditions guarantee that it is finite in our setup? We conjecture that this will require the partial order involved in the circumscription to be *smooth*. Second, are there better interpolation theorems for the prioritized case of those systems? Also, what is the shape of the interpolation theorems specific for prerequisite-free semi-normal defaults? Further, our results for default logic and logic programs are propositional. How do they extend to the FOL case?

Finally, the theorems for default logic and Logic Programming promise that $\alpha \mathrel{\vert\!\!\sim_D} \beta$ implies the existence of γ such that $\alpha \mathrel{\vert\!\!\sim_D} \gamma$ and $\gamma \mathrel{\vert\!\!\sim_D} \beta$. However, we do not know that the other direction holds, i.e., that the existence of γ such that $\alpha \mathrel{\vert\!\!\sim_D} \gamma$ and $\gamma \mathrel{\vert\!\!\sim_D} \beta$ implies that $\alpha \mathrel{\vert\!\!\sim_D} \beta$. Can we do better than Theorem 12 for different cases?

Acknowledgments

I wish to thank Esra Erdem, Vladimir Lifschitz and Leora Morgenstern for reading and commenting on different drafts of this manuscript. This research was supported by DARPA grant N66001-00-C-8018 (RKF program).

References

1. E. Amir. (De)composition of situation calculus theories. In *Proc. AAAI '00*, pages 456463. AAAI Press/MIT Press, 2000.
2. E. Amir and S. McIlraith. Paritition-based logical reasoning. In *Proc. KR '2000*, pages 389–400,2000.
3. W. Craig. Linear reasoning. a new form of the Herbrand-Gentzen theorem. *J. of Symbolic Logic*, 22:250–268, 1957.
4. A. Darwiche. Model-based diagnosis using structured system descriptions. *Journal of AI Research*, 8: 165–222, 1998.
5. R. Dechter. Bucket elimination: A unifying framework for reasoning. *Artificial Intelligence*, 113(1–2):41–85, 1999.
6. R. Dechter and J. Pearl. Tree Clustering Schemes for Constraint Processing. In *Proc. AAAI '88*, 1988.
7. R. Dechter and 1. Rish. Directional resolution: The Davis-Putnam procedure, revisited. In *Proc. KR '94*, pages 134–145. Morgan Kaufmann, 1994.
8. J. D.M. Gabbay, C.J.Hogger, editor. *Handbook of Logic in Artzjicial Intelligence and Logic Programming, Vol. 3: Nonmonotonic Reasoning and Uncertain Reasoning*. Oxford, 1993.
9. D. Etherington. *Reasoning with incomplete Information*. PhD thesis, University of British Columbia, 1986.
10. M. Gelfond and V. Lifschitz. The stable model semantics for logic programming. In *5th International Conference on Logic Programming*, pages 1070–1080, 1988.
11. M. Gelfond and V. Lifschitz. Logic Program with Classical Negation. In D. H. D. Warren and P. Szeredi, editors, *7th Int. Conf. on Logic Programming*, pages 579–597. MIT, 1990.
12. M. Gelfond and V. Lifschitz. Classical Negation in Logic Programs and Disjunctive Databases. *New Generation Computing*, 9, 199 1.
13. W. Hodges. *A shorter model theory*. Cambridge U. Press, 1997.
14. T. Imielinski. Results on translating defaults to circumscription. *Artificial Intelligence*, 32(1): 13 1–146, Apr. 1987.
15. V. Lifschitz. Computing circumscription. In *Proc. of IJCAI-85*, pages 121–127, 1985.
16. V Lifschitz. Circumscription. In D. Gabbay, C.J.Hogger, and J.A.Robinson, editors, *H.B. of Logic in Artificial Intelligence and Logic Programming*, Vol. 3. Oxford U. Press, 1993.
17. V. Lifschitz and H. Turner. Splitting a logic program. In *Proc. 11th Int'l Conf. on Logic Programming*, pages 23–37. MIT Press, 1994.
18. V. M. Marek and M. Truszczynski. *Nonmonotonic Logics; Context-Dependent Reasoning*. Springer Verlag, Berlin-Heidelberg-New York, 1 st edition, 1993.
19. J. McCarthy. Circumscription-A Form of Non-Monotonic Reasoning. *Artificial Inteligence*, 13:27–39, 1980.
20. J. McCarthy. Applications of Circumscription to Formalizing Common Sense Knowledge. *Artificial Intelligence*, 28:89–116, 1986. 2 1. S. McIlraith and E. Amir. Theorem proving with structured theories. In IJCAI '01, pages 624–631,2001.
21. S. McIlraith and E. Amir. Theorem proving with structured theories. In *IJCAI '01*, pages 624–631,2001.
22. T. Przymusinski. Stable semantics for disjunctive programs. *New Generation Computing*, 9:401–424, 1991.
23. R. Reiter. A logic for default reasoning. *Artificial Intelligence*, 13 (1–2):81–132, 1980.
24. V. Risch and C. Schwind. Tableau-based characterization and theorem proving for default logic. *Journal of Automated Reasoning*, 13:223–242, 1994.
25. C. Sakama and K. Inoue. Relating disjunctive logic programs to default theories. In *LP-NMR '93*, pages 266–282, 1993.
26. H. Turner. Splitting a default theory. In *Proc. AAAI '96*, pages 645–65 1, 1996.

Minimal Answer Computation and SOL[*]

Koji Iwanuma[1] and Katsumi Inoue[2]

[1] Yamanashi University, 4-3-11 Takeda, Kofu-shi 400-8511, Japan
iwanuma@iw.media.yamanashi.ac.jp
[2] Kobe University, Rokkodai-cho, Nada-ku, Kobe 657-8501, Japan
inoue@eedept.kobe-u.ac.jp

Abstract. In this paper, we study minimal and/or conditional answer computing and its related problems. At first, we study some features of minimal answers, and show a non-finiteness property of minimal answers with no function symbols. Next, we show that SOL, which is a model-elimination-like calculus extended with *Skip* operation, is complete for computing not only correct answers, but also minimal answers. Unfortunately, SOL sometimes produces non-minimal answers. Thus, we next investigate another computational problem of minimal answers. We show undecidability theorems for several membership problems of the minimal answer set, which implies the impossibility of perfectly eliminating non-minimal answers. Finally, we address an extended computation problem, called conditional answer computing. SOL is also complete for computing minimal conditional answers.

1 Introduction

Answer computation is important for various kinds of practical applications such as question-answering, error diagnosis, program synthesis, and so on [14]. The answer literal method, proposed by [6], is quite well known as a practical method for mechanically computing correct answers. Baumgartner et al. [1] exhaustively discussed the answer computation problem within the family of Restart Model Elimination (RME) tableaux, and proved that RME is complete for computing answers. They also showed that *Ancestry* Restart Model Elimination is complete for deriving *definite* answers. However, they also showed that the RME family is unfortunately incomplete for finding *minimal* answers. Minker's group [16] developed SLI resolution and studied its completeness of answer computation for positive disjunctive logic programs, which are clause sets consisting of non-negative clauses. However, they did not address minimal answer computing. The minimal answer computation problem has remained an *open problem*.

Answer computation should be regarded as an instance of consequence-finding problems in general. Consequence-finding plays an important role in various sorts of problems, such as nonmonotonic reasoning, abduction, knowledge compilation (see [10,3] for details), and inductive logic programming [19,11].

[*] This research was supported partly by Grant-in-Aid from The Ministry of Education, Science and Culture of Japan.

S. Flesca et al. (Eds.): JELIA 2002, LNAI 2424, pp. 245–258, 2002.

Skipping Ordered Linear resolution (SOL) was proposed by Inoue [10], which is a complete calculus for finding logical consequences of a first-order clausal theory. SOL-resolution can be viewed as either an extension of Loveland's model-elimination-like calculus [17] with *Skip* operation, or a generalization of Siegel's propositional production algorithm [20] into first-order logic. Compared with other procedures, SOL-resolution allows focusing on generating only interesting clauses, called *characteristic clauses*, rather than all minimal logical consequences. SOL-resolution is one of the most advanced calculi for the consequence-finding problem.

In this paper, we address a minimal and/or conditional answer computation problem and its related problems. First, we investigate some interesting properties of minimal answers, and show that there is a disjunctive first-order clausal theory which has *no function symbols*, but involves infinitely many minimal answers. Secondly, we show SOL-resolution is a complete calculus for deriving not only correct answers, but also *minimal answers*, with the answer literal method. SOL, however, may produce non-minimal answers as well. Thus, we thirdly investigate the elimination problem of non-minimal answers. We show the undecidability of membership problems of minimal answer sets, by proving that the first-order satisfiability problem can be reduced to the minimal answer membership problems. This undecidability immediately causes the impossibility of perfect elimination of non-minimal answers in principle. Moreover, the proof given here reveals that *no* algorithms can generate all and only minimal answers and subsequently terminate, even for disjunctive theories involving only finitely many minimal answers.

Finally, we address an extended computation problem, called *conditional answer computation* [2,4,5]. Conditional answer computing involves various interesting computational issues [9] such as "lazy evaluation" in the area of programming languages, "derived integrity constraints" in database theory, "resource limited computation", "abstracted answer" etc. Conditional answer computing is applicable to planning [7], program diagnosis/synthesis, intensional/conditional query answering in deductive/relational databases [9], abduction [2,10] and incomplete information reasoning, especially circumscriptive answers [8] etc. In this paper, we study the minimal condition answer computation. Demolombe studied *definite* minimal hypotheses generation in [5], and moreover investigated in [4] some strategies for computing minimal conditional *definite* answers in a deductive database context, i.e., a first-order clausal theory *without* function symbols. We show here SOL is also complete for deriving minimal conditional *disjunctive* answers for arbitrary first-order clausal theories, which possibly contain function symbols.

This paper is organized as follows: in Section 2, we define correct and minimal answers, and discuss some fundamental properties for minimal answers. In Section 3, we introduce characteristic clauses, and study a relationship with minimal answer computation. Section 4 is devoted to SOL resolution. In Section 5, we show the completeness of SOL for computing minimal answers. In

Section 6, we investigate some undecidability results with respect to minimal answers. Section 7 is for conditional answer computation.

2   Correct Answers and Minimal Answers

We define the first-order language as usual [17]. In this paper, according to [1,15], we define a *clause* as a multiset of literals, written as a disjunction $L_1 \vee \ldots \vee L_n$. The empty clause is denoted by $\square$. When $\Sigma = \{E_1, \ldots, E_n\}$ is a multiset of first-order expressions and θ is a substitution, the expression $\Sigma\theta$ exactly represents the multiset $\{E_1\theta, \ldots, E_n\theta\}$. Notice that merging or factoring of formulas never occurs in the application of θ to Σ, because we consider here a multiset of expressions. Thus, for example, given $C = p(X, a) \vee p(a, Y)$ and $\theta = \{X \leftarrow a, Y \leftarrow a\}$, $C\theta$ is the clause $p(a, a) \vee p(a, a)$, but not $p(a, a)$. Now we define *query* and *correct answer*, according to [1].

Definition 1 (Query). A *query* is a clause of the form $\leftarrow L_1 \wedge \cdots \wedge L_n$ where each L_i is a literal. We often abbreviate a query as $\leftarrow Q(X)$, where Q stands for for the conjunction of literals and X is an n-tuple of variables appearing in Q.

In [1], a query is defined as a formula $\leftarrow L_1 \wedge \cdots \wedge L_n$ where each conjunct L_i is restricted to an *atom*. Thus, the query considered here becomes a slight generalization of [1]. For a clausal theory, Herbrand's theorem implies the following important proposition:

Proposition 1 (Herbrand theorem for answer computation [14]). *Suppose Σ is a set of clauses and $\leftarrow Q(X)$ is a query. If $\Sigma \models \exists Q(X)$, then for some k, there is a tuple of substitutions $\theta_1, \cdots, \theta_k$ such that $\Sigma \models \forall(Q(X)\theta_1 \vee \cdots \vee Q(X)\theta_k)$.*

Definition 2 (Correct answer, definite answer). Let Σ be a set of clauses, $\leftarrow Q(X)$ be a query and $\theta_1, \ldots, \theta_n$ be substitutions for variables X. The disjunction $Q(X)\theta_1 \vee \cdots \vee Q(X)\theta_n$ is called an *answer* for $\leftarrow Q(X)$. An answer $Q(X)\theta_1 \vee \cdots \vee Q(X)\theta_n$ is a *correct answer* of Σ if $\Sigma \models \forall(Q(X)\theta_1 \vee \cdots \vee Q(X)\theta_n)$. A *definite* answer is an answer which consists of a single conjunction of literals; otherwise it is called a *disjunctive* answer.

Next, we define a *minimal* answer. *Subsumption* plays an important role to define a minimal answer. The inclusion relation $\subseteq_{ms}$ over multisets is defined as usual.

Definition 3 (Subsumption). Let Σ and Γ be multisets of first-order formulas. Σ *subsumes* Γ if there is a substitution θ such that $\Sigma\theta \subseteq_{ms} \Gamma$. We say, Σ *properly subsumes* Γ if Σ subsumes Γ but Γ does not subsume Σ.

For example, the clause $p(X, a) \vee p(a, Y)$ properly subsumes $p(a, a) \vee p(a, a)$ with $\theta = \{X \leftarrow a, Y \leftarrow a\}$, but does not subsume $p(a, a)$.

Definition 4 (Minimal answer). A correct answer $Q(X)\theta_1 \vee \cdots \vee Q(X)\theta_n$ of Σ is said to be *minimal* if there is no correct answer $Q(X)\sigma_1 \vee \cdots \vee Q(X)\sigma_m$ of Σ such that $Q(X)\sigma_1 \vee \ldots \vee Q(X)\sigma_m$ properly subsumes $Q(X)\theta_1 \vee \ldots \vee Q(X)\theta_n$.

Minimal answer was not defined explicitly in [1]. Therefore, this definition is original due to this paper. A minimal answer gives us the most concise and general *expression*, and thus, is the most desirable representation of a computable answer. In the sequel, we investigate a deductive mechanism for computing minimal answers.

Example 1 (Example 14 in [1]). Let Σ be the set of clauses $\{p(X) \vee \neg q(X) \vee \neg q(X),\ q(a) \vee q(b)\}$, and $\leftarrow p(X)$ be a query. The minimal answer is clearly $p(a) \vee p(b)$, whereas $p(a) \vee p(b) \vee p(b)$ is also a correct but non-minimal answer. The latter is obviously redundant, which will be discussed later in Section 5.

Remark 1. The definition of subsumption is a critical issue for defining minimal answers. For example, Inoue [10] pointed out that, in the traditional framework where a clause is identified with an ordinary set of literals, the length of clauses plays a substantially important role for defining minimal answers. Let us define, for clauses C and D as ordinary sets, C *weakly set-subsumes* D iff $C\theta \subseteq D$ for a substitution θ. Moreover C *strongly set-subsumes* D iff C weakly set-subsumes D and C has no more literals than D^1. If we adopt the weak set-subsumption as an ordering criterion, then we have to treat infinite descending sequences of correct answers in some cases, where each answer in the infinite sequence is subsumed by a successor. In such a case, a minimal answer fails to exist, though infinitely many correct answers are ordered within a partial ordering. See the next example for more details.

Example 2. Let us consider the clause set $\Sigma = \{p(X,Y) \vee p(Y,Z) \vee \neg p(X,Z),\ p(W,W)\}$, and the query $\leftarrow p(U_1,U_2)$. We can enumerate infinitely many correct answers of Σ as follows:

$$A_1 :\ p(W,W)$$
$$A_2 :\ p(W,Y_0) \vee p(Y_0,W)$$
$$A_3 :\ p(W,Y_1) \vee p(Y_1,Y_0) \vee p(Y_0,W)$$
$$A_4 :\ p(W,Y_2) \vee p(Y_2,Y_1) \vee p(Y_1,Y_0) \vee p(Y_0,W)$$
$$\vdots$$

Notice that, in the above sequence, each A_i is weakly set-subsumed by the successor A_{2i}. For example, for $\theta = \{Y_2 \leftarrow Y_0,\ Y_1 \leftarrow W\}$, $A_4\theta$ is the set $\{p(W,Y_0), p(Y_0,W)\}$ which is identical with A_2. Therefore, A_2 is not the minimal answer of Σ if we adopt the weak set-subsumption as a criterion. This means that the weak set-subsumption is *not* appropriate for an answer ordering criterion. On the contrary, the strong set-subsumption criterion allows each A_i in the above to be minimal in Σ. Notice that the answer ordering criterion in this paper, i.e., the subsumption given in Definition 3, also causes each A_i to be minimal.

Example 2 reveals another important feature of minimal answers, because Σ in Example 2 contains no occurrences of function symbols. If we replace all occurrences of p in Σ of Example 2 with $\neg q$, then we obtain the set of clauses $\Sigma' = \{\neg q(X,Y) \vee \neg q(Y,Z) \vee q(X,Z),\ \neg q(W,W)\}$ [2] and the query $\leftarrow \neg q(U_1, U_2)$. Notice that Σ' is a Horn theory, and Σ' also has infinitely many minimal *negative* disjunctive answers $\neg q(W, Y_i) \vee \neg q(Y_i, Y_{i-1}) \vee \cdots \vee \neg q(Y_0, W)$. As is well known, any *definite* theory without function symbols has only finitely many minimal definite answers, because the Herbrand universe is finite and every minimal answer takes the form of a positive unit clause. The above observation indicates that the finiteness property of answers does not hold for a *non-definite* theory.

Proposition 2 (Infinite minimal answers with no function symbols).
There is a non-definite clausal theory Σ such that Σ contains no constant nor function symbols, but has infinitely many minimal disjunctive answers.

The use of answer literals [6] is an well-known method for computing correct answers. Suppose a query $\leftarrow Q(X)$ represents $\leftarrow L_1(X) \wedge \cdots \wedge L_n(X)$. Then $\neg Q(X)$ denotes the disjunction $\neg L_1(X) \vee \cdots \vee \neg L_n(X)$.

Proposition 3 (Soundness and completeness of answer literals [14]).
Suppose Σ is a set of clauses and $\leftarrow Q(X)$ is a query where X is an n-tuple of variables. Let ANS be a new n-place predicate symbol, not appearing in Σ nor Q. Then

1. *Σ is satisfiable iff $\Sigma \cup \{\neg Q(X) \vee ANS(X)\}$ is satisfiable.*
2. *For any answer $Q(X)\theta_1 \vee \cdots \vee Q(X)\theta_n$ of $\leftarrow Q(X)$, the following are equivalent:*

   (a) $\Sigma \models \forall(Q(X)\theta_1 \vee \cdots \vee Q(X)\theta_n)$.
   (b) $\Sigma \cup \{\neg Q(X) \vee ANS(X)\} \models \forall(ANS(X)\theta_1 \vee \cdots \vee ANS(X)\theta_n)$.

Notice that Proposition 1 and 3 validate the use of answer literals from the *semantic* viewpoint. The answer literal method can reduce the minimal-answer finding problem to the problem of finding "minimal clauses" consisting of ANS literals. These "minimal clauses" can be characterized with *characteristic clauses*, which were proposed in the framework of the consequence-finding problem [10]. In the next section, we study some relationship between characteristic clauses and minimal answer computation.

---

[2] This axiom set Σ' was used in [18] in order to investigate whether *prime implicates* exist or not in the first-order case.

3   Characteristic Clauses and Minimal Answer Computation

Characteristic clauses are intended to present "interesting" clauses, and are constructed over a sub-vocabulary of the underlying language, which is called a *production field*. Let $\mathcal{R}$ be the set of all predicate symbols in the language. For $\mathbf{R} \subset \mathcal{R}$, we write $\mathbf{R}^+$ ($\mathbf{R}^-$) for denoting the positive (or respectively, negative) literals of predicates from $\mathbf{R}$ in the language. The set of all literals is expressed by $\mathcal{L}$ ($= \mathcal{R}^+ \cup \mathcal{R}^-$).

Definition 5 (Production field). A *production field* $\mathcal{P}$ is a pair $\langle \mathbf{L}, \mathit{Cond} \rangle$, where $\mathbf{L}$ is a subset of $\mathcal{L}$ and is closed under instantiation, and Cond is a certain condition to be satisfied. When Cond is not specified, $\mathcal{P}$ is just written as $\langle \mathbf{L} \rangle$. A clause C is said to *belong to* $\mathcal{P} = \langle \mathbf{L}, \mathit{Cond} \rangle$ if every literal in C belongs to $\mathbf{L}$ and C satisfies Cond. The set of theorems of a clause set Σ belonging to $\mathcal{P}$ is denoted by $Th_{\mathcal{P}}(\Sigma)$. A production field $\mathcal{P}$ is *stable* if, for any two clauses C and D such that C subsumes D, the clause D belongs to $\mathcal{P}$ only if C belongs to $\mathcal{P}$.

Stable production fields are substantially important in practice [10]. Throughout this paper, we assume production fields to be stable. For example, the production field $\langle \mathcal{L} \rangle$ is stable, and $Th_{\langle \mathcal{L} \rangle}(\Sigma)$ is the set of all theorems of Σ. The production field $\mathcal{P}_{ANS} = \langle \{ANS\}^+ \rangle$ is also stable, and $Th_{\mathcal{P}_{ANS}}(\Sigma)$ denotes the set of all clauses of the form $ANS(t_1) \vee \cdots \vee ANS(t_n)$ which are derivable from Σ. In the sequel, we shall use $\mathcal{P}_{ANS}$ without referring to the definition. A clause belonging to $\mathcal{P}_{ANS}$ is called an *ANS-clause*. For a set Σ of clauses, $\mu\Sigma$ denotes the set of clauses in Σ not properly subsumed by any clause in Σ.

Definition 6 (Characteristic clauses, new characteristic clauses). Let Σ be a set of clauses, and $\mathcal{P}$ be a production field. The set of *characteristic clauses of Σ with respect to $\mathcal{P}$*, denoted by $Carc(\Sigma, \mathcal{P})$, is $\mu Th_{\mathcal{P}}(\Sigma)$. The set of *new characteristic clauses of a formula F with respect to Σ and $\mathcal{P}$*, denoted by $NewCarc(\Sigma, F, \mathcal{P})$, is $\mu[Th_{\mathcal{P}}(\Sigma \cup \{F\}) - Th_{\langle \mathcal{L} \rangle}(\Sigma)]$.

Proposition 4 ([10]).

$$NewCarc(\Sigma, F, \mathcal{P}) = Carc(\Sigma \cup \{F\}, \mathcal{P}) - Carc(\Sigma, \mathcal{P}).$$

Notice that the empty clause $\square$ belongs to every stable production field $\mathcal{P}$. Hence $\Sigma \cup \{F\}$ is unsatisfiable and Σ is satisfiable if and only if $NewCarc(\Sigma, F, \mathcal{P}) = \{\square\}$. Thus, the computation of $NewCarc(\Sigma, F, \mathcal{P})$ is a generalization of the *refutation finding* problem.

Proposition 5. *Let Σ be a set of clauses, $\leftarrow Q(X)$ be a query, and ANS be a predicate symbol not appearing in Σ nor Q. Suppose F_{ANS} is the clause $\neg Q(X) \vee ANS(X)$. Then we have:*

1. For any answer $Q(X)\theta_1 \vee \cdots \vee Q(X)\theta_n$, the following are equivalent:

(a) $Q(X)\theta_1 \vee \cdots \vee Q(X)\theta_n$ *is a minimal correct answer of* Σ.

(b) $ANS(X)\theta_1 \vee \cdots \vee ANS(X)\theta_n$ *belongs to* $Carc(\Sigma \cup \{F_{ANS}\}, \mathcal{P}_{ANS})$.

2. *If* Σ *is satisfiable, then* $NewCarc(\Sigma, F_{ANS}, \mathcal{P}_{ANS}) = Carc(\Sigma \cup \{F_{ANS}\},$ $\mathcal{P}_{ANS})$.

Thus the minimal answer finding problem can be reduced to the one for computing new characteristic clauses.

4   Skipping Ordered Linear Resolution (SOL)

In this section, we recall Inoue's *SOL-resolution* [10][3], and show its soundness and completeness for consequence-finding. Inoue's original formulation is within the framework "ordered clause" and the strong set-subsumption criterion, thus we have to slightly modify the formulation of SOL within the framework "clause as a multiset of literals". The set-normalization is an adequate tool for such an adaptation. The *set-normal form* of a multiset Σ, denoted by $SN(\Sigma)$, is an ordinary set, not a multiset, which is obtained from Σ by merging all duplicated elements in Σ into a single element. For example, $SN(C)$ for $C = p(a) \vee p(b) \vee p(b)$ is the set $\{p(a), p(b)\}$. If no confusion arises, the set-normal form of a clause is denoted by a disjunction of literals as well, e.g., $SN(C) = p(a) \vee p(b)$.

An ordered clause $\overrightarrow{C}$ is a sequence of literals possibly containing *framed literals* which represent literals that have been resolved upon. From a clause C, an ordered clause $\overrightarrow{C}$ is obtained just by ordering the elements of C; conversely, from an ordered clause $\overrightarrow{C}$ a clause C is obtained by removing the framed literals and converting the remainder to the disjunction. We assume that literals are ordered from left to right in each ordered clause. A *structured clause* $\langle A, \overrightarrow{B} \rangle$ is a pair of a clause A and an ordered clause $\overrightarrow{B}$, whose clausal meaning is $A \cup B$.

Definition 7 (SOL-deduction). Given a set of clauses Σ, a clause C, a production field $\mathcal{P}$, an *SOL-deduction deriving a clause* S *from* $\Sigma + C$ *and* $\mathcal{P}$ consists of a sequence of structured clauses $D_0, D_1, \ldots, D_n$ such that:

1. $D_0 = \langle \Box, \overrightarrow{C} \rangle$.
2. $D_n = \langle S, \Box \rangle$.
3. For each $D_i = \langle A_i, \overrightarrow{B}_i \rangle$, $A_i \cup B_i$ is not a tautology.
4. For each $D_i = \langle A_i, \overrightarrow{B}_i \rangle$, B_i is not subsumed by any B_j with the empty substitution, where $D_j = \langle A_j, \overrightarrow{B}_j \rangle$ is a previous structured clause, $j < i$.
5. For each $D_i = \langle A_i, \overrightarrow{B}_i \rangle$, A_i belongs to $\mathcal{P}$.
6. $D_{i+1} = \langle A_{i+1}, \overrightarrow{B}_{i+1} \rangle$ is generated from $D_i = \langle A_i, \overrightarrow{B}_i \rangle$ according to the following steps:
   (a) let L be the *left-most* literal of $\overrightarrow{B}_i$. Then A_{i+1} and $\overrightarrow{R}_{i+1}$ are obtained by applying one of the rules:

---
[3] In [13], a variant of SOL-resolution was studied within the framework of *connection tableaux* [15] or *model elimination tableau* [1].

    i. **Skip**: if $SN(A_i \cup \{L\})$ belongs to $\mathcal{P}$, then $A_{i+1} = SN(A_i \cup \{L\})$ and $\overrightarrow{R}_{i+1}$ is the ordered clause obtained by removing L from $\overrightarrow{B}_i$.

    ii. **Resolve**: if there is a clause E_i from $\Sigma \cup \{C\}$ such that $\neg K \in E_i$ and L and K are unifiable with mgu θ, then $A_{i+1} = SN(A_i\theta)$ and $\overrightarrow{R}_{i+1}$ is an ordered clause obtained by concatenating $E_i\theta$ and $\overrightarrow{B}_i\theta$, framing $L\theta$, and removing $\neg K\theta$ (*extension*).

    iii. **Factoring**: A_i or $\overrightarrow{B}_i$ contains an unframed literal K such that L and K are unifiable with mgu θ, then $A_{i+1} = SN(A_i\theta)$ and $\overrightarrow{R}_{i+1}$ is obtained from $\overrightarrow{B}_i\theta$ by deleting $L\theta$. In particular, if mgu θ is the identity substitution, then this rule is called **Merge**.

    iv. **Reduction**: $\overrightarrow{B}_i$ contains a framed literal $\boxed{\neg K}$, and L and K are unifiable with mgu θ, then $A_{i+1} = SN(A_i\theta)$ and $\overrightarrow{R}_{i+1}$ is obtained from $\overrightarrow{B}_i\theta$ by deleting $L\theta$. If mgu θ is the identity substitution, then this rule is called *identical reduction*.

(b) $\overrightarrow{B}_{i+1}$ is obtained from $\overrightarrow{R}_{i+1}$ by deleting every framed literal not preceded by an unframed literal in the remainder (*truncation*).

Remark 2. In any SOL-deduction $\langle A_0, \overrightarrow{B}_0 \rangle, \dots \langle A_n, \overrightarrow{B}_n \rangle$, every A_i is essentially a set of literals, not a multiset, because of the set-normalizing function $SN(\_)$.

Theorem 1 (Soundness and completeness of SOL [10]).

1. *Soundness: if a clause S is derived by an SOL-deduction from $\Sigma + C$ and $\mathcal{P}$, thus S belongs to $Th_{\mathcal{P}}(\Sigma \cup \{C\})$.*
2. *Completeness: if a clause S does not belong to $Th_{\mathcal{P}}(\Sigma)$ but belongs to $Th_{\mathcal{P}}(\Sigma \cup \{C\})$, then there is an SOL-deduction deriving a clause T from $\Sigma + C$ and $\mathcal{P}$ such that T subsumes S.*

Corollary 1 (Completeness for new characteristic clauses). *If a clause S belongs to $NewCarc(\Sigma, C, \mathcal{P})$, then there is an SOL-deduction deriving S from $\Sigma + C$ and $\mathcal{P}$.*

5   Computing Minimal Answers in SOL

Theorem 1 and Proposition 3 immediately imply the following theorem.

Theorem 2 (Soundness and completeness for answer computation in SOL). *Let Σ be a clause set and $\leftarrow Q(X)$ be a query.*

1. *Soundness: if an ANS-clause $ANS(X)\theta_1 \vee \cdots \vee ANS(X)\theta_n$ is derived by an SOL-deduction from $\Sigma + (\neg Q(X) \vee ANS(X))$ and $\mathcal{P}_{ANS}$, then $Q(X)\theta_1 \vee \cdots \vee Q(X)\theta_n$ is a correct answer of Σ.*
2. *Completeness: If $Q(X)\theta_1 \vee \cdots \vee Q(X)\theta_n$ is a correct answer of Σ, then there is an SOL-deduction from $\Sigma + (\neg Q(X) \vee ANS(X))$ and $\mathcal{P}_{ANS}$ deriving an ANS-clause $ANS(X)\delta_1 \vee \cdots \vee ANS(X)\delta_k$ which subsumes $ANS(X)\theta_1 \vee \cdots \vee ANS(X)\theta_n$.*

Corollary 1 and Proposition 5 immediately imply the next corollary.

Corollary 2 (Completeness for minimal answer computation). *Suppose the same conditions as Theorem 2. If $Q(X)\theta_1 \vee \cdots \vee Q(X)\theta_n$ is a minimal correct answer for Σ, then there is an SOL-deduction from $\Sigma + (\neg Q(X) \vee ANS(X))$ and $\mathcal{P}_{ANS}$ deriving ANS-clause $ANS(X)\theta_1 \vee \cdots \vee ANS(X)\theta_n$.*

Remark 3. SOL sometimes derives non-minimal answers in general. Thus the soundness theorem does not hold for minimal answer computation in SOL. We will further discuss this issue in Section 6.

Example 3. Let us consider again the clause set Σ and the query $\leftarrow p(X)$ in Example 1, which corresponds with Example 14 in [1]. Recall Σ consists of

$$p(X) \vee \neg q(X) \vee \neg q(X), \tag{1}$$

$$q(a) \vee q(b), \tag{2}$$

Then, the minimal ANS-clause $ANS(a) \vee ANS(b)$ is derived by an SOL-deduction from $\Sigma + (\neg p(X) \vee ANS(X))$ and $\mathcal{P}_{ANS}$ as follows:

$\langle\ \square,$	$\neg p(X) \vee ANS(X)\ \rangle,$	given top clause (*)
$\langle\ \square,$	$\neg q(X) \vee \neg q(X) \vee \boxed{\neg p(X)} \vee ANS(X)\ \rangle,$	resolution with (1)
$\langle\ \square,$	$\neg q(X) \vee \boxed{\neg p(X)} \vee ANS(X)\ \rangle,$	Merge
$\langle\ \square,$	$q(b) \vee \boxed{\neg q(a)} \vee \boxed{\neg p(a)} \vee ANS(a)\ \rangle,$	resolution with (2)
$\langle\ \square,$	$p(b) \vee \neg q(b) \vee \boxed{q(b)} \vee \boxed{\neg q(a)} \vee \boxed{\neg p(a)} \vee ANS(a)\ \rangle,$	resolution with (1)
$\langle\ \square,$	$\underline{ANS(b)} \vee \boxed{p(b)} \vee \neg q(b) \vee \boxed{q(b)} \vee \boxed{\neg q(a)} \vee \boxed{\neg p(a)} \vee ANS(a)\ \rangle,$	resolution with (*)
$\langle\ ANS(b),$	$\boxed{p(b)} \vee \neg q(b) \vee \boxed{q(b)} \vee \boxed{\neg q(a)} \vee \boxed{\neg p(a)} \vee ANS(a)\ \rangle,$	skip
$\langle\ ANS(b),$	$\underline{\neg q(b)} \vee \boxed{q(b)} \vee \boxed{\neg q(a)} \vee \boxed{\neg p(a)} \vee ANS(a)\ \rangle,$	truncation
$\langle\ ANS(b),$	$\boxed{q(b)} \vee \boxed{\neg q(a)} \vee \boxed{\neg p(a)} \vee ANS(a)\ \rangle,$	identical reduction
$\langle\ ANS(b),$	$ANS(a)\ \rangle,$	truncation
$\langle\ ANS(b) \vee ANS(a),$	$\square\ \rangle,$	skip

Baumgartner et al. [1] showed that Restart Model Elimination (RME) is complete for answer computation, and also successfully gave a new calculus, called *Ancestry* Restart Model Elimination, which is complete for deriving *definite answers*. They, however, failed to give a calculus for computing all minimal answers. Baumgartner et al. [1] showed, for Example 1, that RME can construct exactly one connection tableau, from which only the non-minimal computed answer $p(a) \vee p(b) \vee p(b)$ can be extracted. On the contrary, SOL can derive the minimal answer $p(a) \vee p(b)$ as shown in Example 3.

Remark 4. In Example 1, the answer $p(a) \vee p(b)$ subsumes $p(a) \vee p(b) \vee p(b)$. Thus, the readers may think that the subsumption test performed after deduction is sufficient for producing all minimal answers. Unfortunately, this conjecture is not true, because the minimality test of a subsuming clause is undecidable. In Example 1, two unit clauses $p(a)$ and $p(b)$ are clauses which subsume both $p(a) \lor p(b)$ and $p(a) \lor p(b) \lor p(b)$. It is impossible in general to decide whether such a subsuming clause is a correct answer or not. We will show in the next section that the minimality check of a clause is highly undecidable.

Remark 5. The completeness of SOL reveals that a sort of factoring operation is necessary and sufficient for deriving minimal answers. Notice that the simplicity of the completeness proof presented here is due to SOL's excellent features, i.e., the completeness for computing new characteristic clauses. Indeed, if a underlying calculus involving a factoring operation is other than SOL, then proofs for the minimal-answer completeness of the calculus is not so easy. Although the necessity of the factoring operation might be predictable, the minimal-answer completeness has *not* yet been proved anywhere so far.

6   Undecidability of Eliminating Non-minimal Answers

SOL is complete for minimal answer computation. However, SOL produces non-minimal answers as well. It is highly desirable to restrict SOL-derivations to producing minimal answers only. In this section, we investigate some issues for eliminating non-minimal answers. Recall $NewCarc(\Sigma, \neg Q(X) \lor ANS(X), \mathcal{P}_{ANS})$ is identical with the minimal answer set if Σ is satisfiable (see Prop. 5).

Theorem 3 (Undecidability of minimal answer sets). *The following three membership problems are all undecidable, i.e., not even semi-decidable, in the sense that the satisfiability decision problem of first-order clausal theories can be reduced to each problem:*

1. *Given a satisfiable clausal clause set Σ, a clause Q and a production field $\mathcal{P}$, then decide whether Q is a member of $Carc(\Sigma, \mathcal{P})$, or not.*
2. *Given a clause set Σ and a clause F such that $\Sigma \cup \{F\}$ is satisfiable, a clause Q, and a production field $\mathcal{P}$, then decide whether Q is a member of $NewCarc(\Sigma, F, \mathcal{P})$, or not.*
3. *Given a satisfiable clause set Σ, a query $\leftarrow Q(X)$ and an ANS-clause $A = (ANS(X)\theta_1 \lor \cdots \lor ANS(X)\theta_n)$, then decide whether A is a member of $NewCarc(\Sigma, (\neg Q(X) \lor ANS(X)), \mathcal{P}_{ANS})$, or not.*

Proof. Due to the space limitation, we shall only outline the proof for the first problem. We first define *goal normal form*, denoted as $GN(\Sigma)$, of a clause set Σ as follows: let *Goal* be a unary predicate symbol not occurring in Σ, and # and @ be constant symbols not occurring in Σ. Then

$$GN(\Sigma) = \{L_1 \lor \cdots \lor L_n \mid L_1 \lor \cdots \lor L_n \text{ is a non-negative clause in } \Sigma\} \cup$$
$$\{Goal(\#) \lor L_1 \lor \cdots \lor L_n \mid L_1 \lor \cdots \lor L_n \text{ is a negative clause in } \Sigma\} \cup$$
$$\{Goal(\#) \lor Goal(@)\}.$$

Clearly $GN(\Sigma)$ must be satisfiable because $GN(\Sigma)$ has no negative clause. Moreover, Σ is satisfiable iff $GN(\Sigma) \cup \{\neg Goal(\#)\}$ is satisfiable. Thus, we can easily prove that Γ is satisfiable iff $Goal(\#) \vee Goal(@) \in Carc(GN(\Gamma), \langle\{Goal\}^+\rangle)$. $\qquad\square$

Remark 6. From Theorem 3, the set of pairs $\langle \Sigma_i, Ans_j \rangle$ such that Ans_j is a minimal answer of Σ_i is *not even recursively enumerable.* This fact immediately implies that there is no complete deductive system which derives only minimal answers of an arbitrarily given Σ.

Remark 7. The undecidability results given in Section 2.3 of [1] are essentially for $Carc(\Sigma, \langle\mathcal{L}\rangle)$, in our terminology, but there they did not impose the satisfiability constraint for Σ. The satisfiability condition as a problem setting is natural for ordinary answer computations.

Tamaki and Sato [23] investigated the search-incompleteness of a depth-first interpreter of logic programs, and gave a new excellent calculus OLDT-resolution, which is based on the tabulation technique. OLDT-resolution is guaranteed to terminate after enumerating all possible answers when a target logic program has only finitely many answers. We will show, on the contrary, it is impossible to construct such a terminating computation method for disjunctive programs possessing only finite answers.

Proposition 6 (Uncomputability of finitely many minimal answers).
Suppose D is the set of pairs $\langle \Sigma, \leftarrow Q(X) \rangle$ where Σ is a disjunctive clausal theory and $\leftarrow Q(X)$ is a query such that Σ has exactly one minimal answer for $\leftarrow Q(X)$. Then there is no algorithm $\mathcal{AL}$ such that, for any $\langle \Sigma, \leftarrow Q(X) \rangle \in D$, the algorithm $\mathcal{AL}$ first computes only the minimal answers for $\leftarrow Q(X)$ of Σ, and subsequently terminates.

Proof. Let us consider again $GN(\Gamma)$ in the proof for Theorem 3. For any clause set Γ, the theory $GN(\Gamma)$ always has exactly one minimal answer for $\leftarrow Goal(X)$, i.e., either of $Goal(\#) \vee Goal(@)$ and $Goal(\#)$. Hence, if there is an algorithm $\mathcal{AL}$ satisfying the above condition, then we can decide the satisfiability of arbitrary first-order clausal theory Γ. This is a contradiction. $\qquad\square$

Remark 8. The set D in Proposition 6 is the strictest class among the ones of program-query pairs involving finitely many minimal answers. Using the formula $GN(\Gamma)$, we can also prove the similar intractability of circumscriptions or positive disjunctive logic programs [16] with only finitely many minimal answers. Notice that $GN(\Gamma)$ is a positive disjunctive program.

Although complete elimination of non-minimal answers is impossible, some partial eliminations are available indeed. For example, *subsumption* is an well known pruning method [15]. Moreover, there are more cost-effective pruning methods [13] such as anti-lemma method with skipped literals [13], Merge and identical reduction [22], unit axiom matching [22], lemma matching and strong contraction [12], identical C-reduction [21], etc. These pruning rules can substantially reduce redundant derivations with rather small cost, and are quite important for practical application.

7   Computing Conditional Answers: A Problem Extension

In this section, we study an extended problem, called *conditional answer computation*, and show the completeness of SOL for this extended problem.

Definition 8 (Conditional answer). Let Σ be a set of clauses, $\mathcal{P}$ be a production field, $\leftarrow Q(X)$ be a query and $\theta_1, \ldots, \theta_n$ be substitutions for variables X. Suppose a clause $A_1 \vee \ldots \vee A_m$ belongs to $\mathcal{P}$. Then, the disjunction $(\bigvee_{i=1}^{m} A_i) \vee (\bigvee_{j=1}^{n} Q(X)\theta_j)$ is called a *conditional answer belonging to* $\mathcal{P}$, or simply called a *C-answer* for convenience.

As usual, a C-answer $(\bigvee_{i=1}^{m} A_i) \vee (\bigvee_{j=1}^{n} Q(X)\theta_j)$ is intended to represent the implication formula $\forall[(\bigwedge_{i=1}^{m} \neg A_i) \rightarrow (\bigvee_{j=1}^{n} Q(X)\theta_j)]$.

Imielinski [9] pointed out several useful features of conditional answers: for example, C-answer computing is an example of "lazy evaluation" which is familiar in the research field of programming languages, and can be helpful in "resource limited computation". Moreover, if the condition part of a C-answer of a query is evaluated yielding a set of final answers for the query, then the C-answer becomes "derived integrity constraints" in the view of the database.

Definition 9 (Minimal conditional answer). A C-answer $(\bigvee_{i=1}^{m} A_i) \vee (\bigvee_{j=1}^{n} Q(X)\theta_j)$ is said to be a *correct C-answer* of Σ if $\Sigma \models \forall[(\bigvee_{i=1}^{m} A_i) \vee (\bigvee_{j=1}^{n} Q(X)\theta_j)]$. A correct C-answer $(\bigvee_{i=1}^{m} A_i) \vee (\bigvee_{j=1}^{n} Q(X)\theta_j)$ of Σ belonging to $\mathcal{P}$ is *minimal* if there is no correct C-answer $(\bigvee_{i=1}^{k} B_i) \vee (\bigvee_{j=1}^{h} Q(X)\sigma_j)$ of Σ belonging to $\mathcal{P}$ such that $\{B_1, \ldots, B_k, Q(X)\sigma_1, \ldots, Q(X)\sigma_h\}$ properly subsumes $\{A_1, \ldots, A_m, Q(X)\theta_1, \ldots, Q(X)\theta_n\}$

Definition 10 (Conditional ANS-clause). Let ANS be a new predicate symbol. A *conditional ANS-clause*, or simply *C-ANS-clause*, is a clause of the form $(\bigvee_{i=1}^{m} A_i) \vee (\bigvee_{j=1}^{n} ANS(X)\theta_j)$.

Definition 11 (Condition vocabulary). Given a production field $\mathcal{P} = \langle \mathbf{L}, Cond \rangle$, the *condition vocabulary* $\mathcal{CV}_P$ based on $\mathcal{P}$ is the production field $\langle \mathbf{L} \cup \{ANS\}^+, Cond \rangle$.

In the sequel, we assume that, given a condition vocabulary $\mathcal{CV}_P = \langle \mathbf{L} \cup \{ANS\}^+, Cond \rangle$, the condition $Cond$ does not impose any restrictions for ANS-literals. Obviously, soundness and completeness theorem for conditional ANS-clause holds in a similar way to Proposition 3. Thus, with Theorem 1, the following theorem immediately holds.

Theorem 4 (Soundness and completeness for computing conditional answers in SOL). *Let Σ be a set of clauses, $\leftarrow Q(X)$ be a query and $\mathcal{P}$ be a production field.*

1. *Soundness: if a C-ANS-clause $(\bigvee_{i=1}^{m} A_i) \vee (\bigvee_{j=1}^{n} ANS(X)\theta_j)$ is derived by an SOL-deduction from $\Sigma + (\neg Q(X) \vee ANS(X))$ and $CV_\mathcal{P}$, then $(\bigvee_{i=1}^{m} A_i) \vee (\bigvee_{j=1}^{n} Q(X)\theta_j)$ is a correct answer of Σ.*

2. *Completeness: if $(\bigvee_{i=1}^{m} A_i) \vee (\bigvee_{j=1}^{n} Q(X)\theta_j)$ is a correct C-answer of Σ which belongs to $\mathcal{P}$. Then there is an SOL-deduction from $\Sigma + (\neg Q(X) \vee ANS(X))$ and $CV_\mathcal{P}$ deriving a C-ANS-clause $(\bigvee_{i=1}^{k} B_i) \vee (\bigvee_{j=1}^{h} ANS(X)\sigma_j)$ which subsumes the clause $(\bigvee_{i=1}^{m} A_i) \vee (\bigvee_{j=1}^{n} ANS(X)\theta_j)$*

Proof. The proof is almost identical with Theorem 2, so we shall omit it.   □

Corollary 3 (Completeness for computing minimal conditional answers). *Suppose the same conditions as Theorem 4. Let $(\bigvee_{i=1}^{m} A_i) \vee (\bigvee_{j=1}^{n} Q(X)\theta_j)$ be a minimal C-answer for Σ which belongs to $\mathcal{P}$. Then there is an SOL-deduction from $\Sigma + (\neg Q(X) \vee ANS(X))$ and $CV_\mathcal{P}$ deriving $(\bigvee_{i=1}^{m} A_i) \vee (\bigvee_{j=1}^{n} ANS(X)\theta_j)$.*

Demolombe [4] gave a complete calculi, called GASP, for deriving minimal conditional answers in the framework of database theory, i.e. a first-order clausal theory *without* function symbols. They also restrict queries to the simple form of $\leftarrow p(X)$; when a general formula $F(X)$ is given as a query, the formula $\forall(new(X) \leftrightarrow F(X))$ for a new predicate symbol new is added to a underlying theory Σ and the query is represented by $\leftarrow new(X)$. This technique can not exactly simulate the disjunctive answer computation, because a general formula $F(X)$ should be fixed before the derivation but the length n of the disjunctive answer $p(X)\theta_1 \vee \cdots \vee p(X)\theta_n$ can not be estimated in advance. Therefore, in [4] just minimal conditional *definite* answers are essentially computable. In this paper, we show SOL is a complete calculus for computing minimal conditional *disjunctive* answers for an arbitrary first-order clausal theory, which possibly contains function symbols.

References

1. P. Baumgartner, U. Furbach and F. Stolzenburg: Computing answers with model elimination, *Artificial Intelligence* **90** (1997) 135–176.
2. D. T. Burhans and S. C. Shapiro: Abduction and question answering, *Proc. of IJCAI-01 Workshop on Abductive Reasoning* (2001).
3. A. del Val: A new method for consequence finding and compilation in restricted languages, *Proc. of AAAI-99* (1999) 259-264.
4. R. Demolombe: A strategy for the computation of conditional answers, *Proc. of ECAI 92, LNAI*, **810** (1992) 134–138.
5. R. Demolombe and L. F. D. Cerro: An inference rule for hypothesis generation, *Proc. of IJCAI-91* (1991) 152–157.

6. C. Green: Theorem proving by resolution as a basis for question-answering systems, in: B. Meltzer and D. Michie (eds), *Machine Intelligence* **4** (1969) 183–205.
7. C. Green: Application of theorem proving to problem solving. *Proc. of IJCAI-69*, (1969) 219–239.
8. N. Helft, K. Inoue and D. Poole: Query answering in circumscription, *Proc. of IJCAI-91* (1991) 426–431.
9. T. Imielinski: Intelligent query answering in rule based systems, *J. Logic Programming* **4** (1987) 229–257.
10. K. Inoue: Linear resolution for consequence finding, *Artificial Intelligence* **56** (1992) 301-353.
11. K. Inoue: Induction, abduction, and consequence-finding, *Inductive Logic Programming: Proc. of the 11th ILP, LNAI* **2157** (2001) 65–79.
12. K. Iwanuma: Lemma matching for a PTTP-based top-down theorem prover, *Proc. of CADE-14, LNAI* **1249** (1997) 146-160.
13. K. Iwanuma, K. Inoue and K. Satoh: Completeness of pruning methods for consequence finding procedure SOL, *Proc. of FTP 2000* (2000) 89–100.
14. K. Kunen: The semantics of Answer Literals, *J. Automated Reasoning* **17** (1996) 83–95.
15. R. Letz: Clausal tableaux, in: W. Bibel, P. H. Schmitt, eds., *Automated Deduction. A basis for applications,* Vol.1, (Kluwer, 1998) 39-68.
16. J. Lobo, J. Minker and A. Rajasekar: *Foundations of Disjunctive Logic Programming* (MIT Press, 1992).
17. D. W. Loveland: *Automated Theorem Proving: A Logical Basis* (North-Holland, Amsterdam, 1978).
18. P. Marquis: Extending abduction from propositional to first-order logic, *Proc. of Inter. WS. on Fundamentals of Artificial Intelligent Research, LNAI* **535** (1991) 141–155.
19. S-H. Nienhuys-Cheng and R. de Wolf: *Foundations of Inductive Logic Programming, LNAI* **1228** (1997).
20. P. Siegel: Représentation et utilization de la connaissance en calcul propositionnel, Thèse d'État, Université d'Aix-Marseille II, Luminy, France, 1987 (in French).
21. R. E. Shostak: Refutation graphs, *Artificial Intelligence* **7** (1976) 51-64.
22. M. E. Stickel: A prolog technology theorem prover: Implementation by an extended prolog compiler, *J. Automated Reasoning* **4** (1988) 353-380.
23. H. Tamaki and T. Sato: OLD Resolution with tabulation, *Proc. the 4th ICLP,* (1986) 74–103.

Decidability of Interval Temporal Logics over Split-Frames via Granularity

Angelo Montanari, Guido Sciavicco, and Nicola Vitacolonna

University of Udine, via delle Scienze 206
33100 Udine (UD), Italy
{montana,sciavicc,vitacolo}@dimi.uniud.it

Abstract. Logics for time intervals provide a natural framework for representing and reasoning about timing properties in various areas of artificial intelligence and computer science. Unfortunately, most interval temporal logics proposed in the literature have been shown to be (highly) undecidable. Decidable fragments of these logics have been obtained by imposing severe restrictions on their expressive power.

In this paper, we propose a new interval temporal logic, called Split Logic, which is equipped with operators borrowed from other interval temporal logics, but is interpreted over specific interval structures based on a layered view of the temporal domain. We show that there exists a straightforward correspondence between Split Logic and the first-order fragments of the monadic theories of time granularity proposed in the literature. This connection allows us to transfer existing decidability results for such theories to Split Logic.

1 Introduction

Logics for time intervals provide a natural framework for dealing with timing properties in various fields of artificial intelligence and computer science [4,5,6,13]. As an example, in planning reasoning about time intervals rather than time points is far more natural and closer to common sense (a systematic account of the relationships between point-based and interval-based temporal logics can be found in [12]). Unfortunately, most interval temporal logics proposed in the literature, such as Moszkowski's Interval Temporal Logic (ITL) [5], Halpern and Shoham's Modal Logic of Time Intervals (HS) [6], Venema's CDT Logic [13], and Chaochen and Hansen's Neighborhood Logic (NL) [4], have been shown to be (highly) undecidable.

ITL is provided with the two modal operators $\bigcirc$ (*next*) and ; (*chop*). An ITL interval is a finite or infinite sequence of states. Given two formulae φ, ψ and an interval $\langle s_0 \ldots s_n \rangle$, $\bigcirc\varphi$ holds over $\langle s_0 \ldots s_n \rangle$ if and only if φ holds over $\langle s_1 \ldots s_n \rangle$, while $\varphi ; \psi$ holds over $\langle s_0 \ldots s_n \rangle$ if and only if there exists i, with $0 \leq i \leq n$, such that φ holds over $\langle s_0 \ldots s_i \rangle$ and ψ holds over $\langle s_i \ldots s_n \rangle$. The undecidability of Propositional ITL has been proved by a reduction from the problem of testing the emptiness of the intersection of two grammars in Greibach form [11]. HS features three basic operators $\langle A \rangle$ (after), $\langle B \rangle$ (begin), and $\langle E \rangle$ (end), together

S. Flesca et al. (Eds.): JELIA 2002, LNAI 2424, pp. 259–270, 2002.

with their duals $\langle \bar{A} \rangle$, $\langle \bar{B} \rangle$, and $\langle \bar{E} \rangle$. Given a formula φ and an interval $[a, b]$, $\langle A \rangle \varphi$ holds at $[a, b]$ if and only if φ holds at $[b, c]$, for some $c > b$, $\langle B \rangle \varphi$ holds at $[a, b]$ if and only if φ holds at $[a, c]$, for some $c < b$, and $\langle E \rangle \varphi$ holds at $[a, b]$ if and only if φ holds at $[c, b]$, for some $c > a$. A number of other operators, such as the future operator $\langle F \rangle$ and the (proper) subinterval operator $\langle D \rangle$, can be defined by means of the basic ones. As an example, the operator $\langle D \rangle$ such that $\langle D \rangle \varphi$ holds at a given interval $[a, b]$ if and only if φ holds at an internal subinterval $[c, d]$ of $[a, b]$ can be defined as $\langle B \rangle \langle E \rangle \varphi$ or, equivalently, $\langle E \rangle \langle B \rangle \varphi$. HS has been shown to be undecidable by coding the halting problem in it. CDT has three binary operators C, D, and T, which informally deal with the situations generated by adding an extra point in one of the three possible positions with respect to the two points delimiting an interval (before, in between, and after). Since HS is a subsystem of CDT, the undecidability of the latter easily follows. Finally, NL is a first-order interval logic with two expanding modalities $\Diamond_l$ and $\Diamond_r$ and a special symbol l which denotes the length of the current interval. Given a formula φ and an interval $[a, b]$, $\Diamond_l \varphi$ holds at $[a, b]$ if and only if φ holds at $[c, a]$, for some $c \leq a$, $\Diamond_r \varphi$ holds at $[a, b]$ if and only if φ holds at $[b, c]$, for some $c \geq b$, and the valuation of l over $[a, b]$ is $b - a$. Since HS can be easily embedded in NL, the undecidability of the latter immediately follows.

Decidable fragments of these logics have been obtained by imposing severe restrictions on their expressive power, e.g., [3,11]. As an example, Moszkowski [11] proves the decidability of the fragment of Propositional ITL with Quantification (over propositional variables) which results from the introduction of a *locality* constraint. Such a constraint states that each propositional variable is true over an interval if and only if it is true at its first state. This allows one to collapse all the intervals starting at the same state into the single interval consisting of the first state only. Decidability of ITL with locality can be easily proved by embedding it into Quantified Propositional Linear Temporal Logic.

In this paper, we propose a new interval temporal logic, called Split Logic (SL for short), which is equipped with operators borrowed from HS and CDT, but is interpreted over specific interval structures, called *split-frames*. The distinctive feature of a split-frame is that there is at most one way to chop an interval into two adjacent subintervals and, consequently, it does not possess "all" the intervals. We will prove the decidability of SL with respect to particular classes of split-frames which can be put in correspondence with the first-order fragments of the monadic theories of time granularity proposed in the literature. Furthermore, we will establish the completeness of SL with respect to the guarded fragment of these theories.

The paper is organized as follows. In Section 2 we introduce the relevant interval and granular temporal structures, while in Section 3 we describe the syntax and semantics of SL. In Section 4 we connect SL to first-order theories of time granularity, and then we establish some decidability results for SL. Furthermore, we state a completeness result for SL. In Section 5 we outline some decidable extensions of SL. Finally, in Section 6 we make some concluding remarks and discuss further research topics.

2   Temporal Structures

In the following, we separately introduce temporal structures for time intervals and time granularity. All the structures we will consider are *relational structures*, that is, tuples whose first component is a non-empty domain W and the remaining components are relations on W. We assume that every relational structure contains at least the equality relation.

2.1   Interval Structures

The aim of this section is to give a framework to represent and reason about intervals in general terms. Intervals can be either primitive entities or built up from points. If we take intervals as primitive objects, then there is a wide range of relations we can wrap around them. Following [12], we opt for two primitive relations on intervals, namely an *inclusion* relation $\sqsubset$, where $i \sqsubset j$ if and only i is a proper subinterval of j, and a *precedence* relation $\prec$, where $i \prec j$ if and only if i entirely precedes j.

Definition 1. *An* interval structure $\mathcal{I} = (I, \sqsubset, \prec)$ *is a relational structure in which $\sqsubset$ and $\prec$ are strict partial orderings on I, respectively called* inclusion *and* precedence, *and $\mathcal{I}$ enjoys the following properties:*

1. *for all $i, j \in I$, if $i \prec j$ then $k \prec j$ for all $k \sqsubset i$ and $i \prec k'$ for all $k' \sqsubset j$ (*monotonicity*);*
2. *for all $i, j, k \in I$ such that $i \prec j \prec k$ and for every $l \in I$ such that $i, k \sqsubset l$ we have $j \sqsubset l$ (*convexity*);*
3. *for all $i, j \in I$, if $i \not\sqsubseteq j$, then there is $k \sqsubseteq i$ such that for all $l \sqsubseteq k$ we have $l \not\sqsubseteq j$, where $i \sqsubseteq j$ stands for $i \sqsubset j$ or $i = j$ (*freedom*);*
4. *for all $i, j \in I$, if $i \not\prec j$ then there are $k \sqsubseteq i$ and $l \sqsubseteq j$ such that for all $m \sqsubseteq k$ and $n \sqsubseteq l$ we have $m \not\prec n$ (*star-freedom*).*

The elements of I are called intervals.

The property of *freedom* means that non-inclusion of i in j is "exemplified" by means of a subinterval of i "disjoint" from j. The property of *star-freedom* informs us about what happens when i does not precedes j: non-precedence is witnessed by two subintervals k of i and l of j, respectively, for which a sort of "strong non-precedence" holds, that is no subinterval of k precedes any subinterval of l.

An interval structure $\mathcal{I} = (I, \sqsubset, \prec)$ is *future* (resp., *past*) *unbounded* if for every $i \in I$ there exists $j \in I$ such that $i \prec j$ (resp., $j \prec i$). It is *unbounded* when it is both future and past unbounded. It is *linear* if for all $i, j \in I$ either $i \prec j$ or $j \prec i$ or $\exists k \, (k \sqsubseteq i \wedge k \sqsubseteq j)$. It is *atomic* when for every i there is a $j \sqsubseteq i$ such that no $k \sqsubset j$ exists. The interval j is called an *atom* or an *atomic interval*. $\mathcal{I}$ is *well founded* if for no k an infinite descending sequence $k \sqsupset i_1 \sqsupset i_2 \sqsupset \cdots$ exists. Every well-founded interval structure is atomic. $\mathcal{I}$ has *maximal intervals* if, for every $i \in I$, there is $j \in I$ such that $i \sqsubseteq j$ and there is no $k \in I$ such that $j \sqsubset k$. The interval j is called a *maximal interval*. Allen's relations can be first-order defined using $\sqsubset$ and $\prec$ [1]. In particular, i meets j if and only if $i \prec j \wedge \neg \exists k \, (i \prec k \prec j)$, i starts j if and only if $i \sqsubset j \wedge \neg \exists k \, (k \sqsubset j \wedge k \prec i) \wedge \exists k \, (k \sqsubset j \wedge i \prec k)$, and i ends j if and only if $i \sqsubset j \wedge \neg \exists k \, (k \sqsubset j \wedge i \prec k) \wedge \exists k \, (k \sqsubset j \wedge k \prec i)$. The *chopping relation* C is a ternary relation such that $C(i,j,k)$ if and only if i meets $j \wedge i$ starts $k \wedge j$ ends k. Note that $C(i,i,i)$ is never the case. An interval structure $(I, \sqsubset, \prec)$ is *dense* if for every $k \in I$ there exist $i, j \in I$ such that $C(i,j,k)$ holds. Finally, a function $f \colon I \to I'$ is an *isomorphism* between the interval structures $\mathcal{I} = (I, \sqsubset, \prec)$ and $\mathcal{I}' = (I', \sqsubset', \prec')$ if f is bijective, it respects precedence ($i \prec j$ if and only if $f(i) \prec' f(j)$) and it respects inclusion ($i \sqsubset j$ if and only if $f(i) \sqsubset' f(j)$).

If one opts for a point-based ontology, the basic structure is the *flow of time*.

Definition 2. *A* flow of time $(T, <)$ *is a strict partial ordering. The elements of T are called* points, *while the binary relation $<$ is called* precedence relation.

Definition 2 allows time to be finite, bounded or unbounded (in one or both directions), dense or discrete, linear or branching, continuous. Only circular flows of time are forbidden (this is of course an arbitrary choice, justified only by the fact that little attention has been put on such a notion of time so far).

Definition 3. *Given a flow of time $\mathcal{T} = (T, <)$, an* interval on $\mathcal{T}$ *is an ordered pair $\langle t, t' \rangle$, with $t < t'$. The points t, t' are called the* endpoints *of the interval. The set of all the intervals on $\mathcal{T}$ is denoted by* $\mathrm{INT}(T)$.

Intervals of Definition 3 can be easily mapped into "true" intervals (closed, half-open or open).

It is not difficult to show that, for every discrete or linear flow of time[1] $\mathcal{T} = (T, <)$, the structure $\mathcal{I}_{\mathcal{T}} = (\mathrm{INT}(T), \sqsubset, \prec)$ is an interval structure when $\sqsubset$ and $\prec$ are defined as follows: for all $\langle a, b \rangle, \langle c, d \rangle \in \mathrm{INT}(T)$, $\langle a, b \rangle \sqsubset \langle c, d \rangle$ if and only if $c \leq a$ and $b \leq d$ and $\langle a, b \rangle \neq \langle c, d \rangle$; $\langle a, b \rangle \prec \langle c, d \rangle$ if and only if $b \leq c$. Besides, $\mathcal{I}_{\mathcal{T}}$ is linear (resp., unbounded, well-founded, dense) if and only if $\mathcal{T}$ is linear (resp., unbounded, discrete, dense). $\mathcal{I}_{\mathcal{T}}$ is called the *induced interval structure* with respect to $\mathcal{T}$. Other interval structures can be generated starting from the same flow of time: they are obtained by taking a subset of the domain $\mathrm{INT}(T)$ that satisfies Definition 1. We do precisely this in Section 4.

2.2   Granular Structures

In the following we will establish a connection between interval structures and *layered structures*, in which a universe of domains replaces the single "flat" temporal domain. These domains are connected by *granular primitives* that relate

---

[1] Not every (non-linear) dense flow of time induces an interval structure—as we have defined it. The flow of time $(\mathbb{Q} \cup \{a, b\}, <)$, where $<$ extends the standard ordering of the rationals with $a < q$ and $b < q$ for all $q \in \mathbb{Q}$, is a counterexample. To obtain induced interval structures from every flow of time we should change Definition 3 by including pairs $\langle t, t \rangle$ and change $\prec$ by defining $\langle a, b \rangle \prec \langle c, d \rangle$ if and only if $b < c$. Since in this paper we are interested in the linear case, we prefer Definition 3 because density is preserved under the construction of the interval structure.

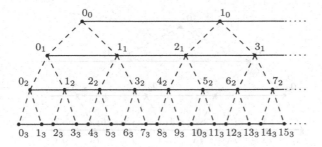

Fig. 1. A 2-refinable 4-layered structure.

points belonging to the same domain as well as points belonging to different domains. We do not give a formal definition of these structures, which can be found in [10]. However, the picture is as follows: the domain $\bigcup_i T^i$ of layered structures consists of (possibly infinitely) many copies T^i of $\mathbb{N}$, each one being a *layer* of the structure. If there is a fixed number n of layers, the structure is called *n-layered* (*n*-LS). Otherwise, the structure is called ω-*layered* and it can be *upward unbounded* (UULS), if there is a finest domain and an infinite sequence of coarser domains, or it can be *downward unbounded* (DULS), if there is a coarsest domain and an infinite sequence of finer ones. In every case, layers are totally ordered according to their degree of "coarseness" or "fineness" and each point in a layer is associated with k points in the immediately finer layer (*k-refinability*). This accounts for a view of these structures also as infinite sequences of (possibly infinite) complete k-ary trees. In the case of UULSs, there is only one infinite tree built up from leaves, which form its first layer (see Figure 2). In the case of *n*-LSs and DULSs, the infinite sequence of respectively finite and infinite trees is ordered according to the ordering of the roots, which form their first layer (Figure 1 shows an *n*-LS). The figures also show how layers are conventionally numbered (DULSs are numbered in the same way as *n*-LSs).

Decidability of monadic second-order theories of granular structures has been proved in [7,8]. In this paper we are interested in the first-order fragments of those theories, namely, $\mathrm{MFO}[<_1, <_2, \{\downarrow_i\}_{0 \le i < k}]$ interpreted over k-refinable *n*-LSs and DULSs, and $\mathrm{MFO}[<_2, \{\downarrow_i\}_{0 \le i < k}]$ interpreted over k-refinable UULSs. The symbols in the square brackets are (pre)interpreted as follows: for $0 \le i < k$, $\downarrow_i(x, y)$ is a binary relation (actually, it is a functional relation; so, we will often write $\downarrow_i(x) = y$ instead of $\downarrow_i(x, y)$) such that y is the i-th point in the refinement of x; $<_1$ is a strict partial order such that $x <_1 y$ when x is in a tree preceding the tree containing y; $x <_2 y$ holds when y is a descendant of x. For the sake of simplicity, in the next sections we will consider 2-refinable *n*-layered and ω-layered structures.

3   Sintax and Semantics of SL

The language of SL is based on a modal similarity type with four unary operators $\langle \mathsf{D} \rangle$, $\langle \bar{\mathsf{D}} \rangle$, $\langle \mathsf{P} \rangle$, and $\langle \bar{\mathsf{P}} \rangle$, and three binary operators C (called *chop*), D, and T.

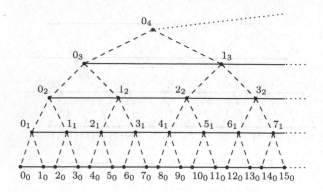

Fig. 2. A 2-refinable upward unbounded layered structure.

The former[2] are borrowed from HS, while the latter are the irreflexive variants of the operators of CDT [13]. The well-formed formulae of SL are given by the following grammar:

$$\varphi ::= Q \mid \varphi \wedge \varphi \mid \neg\varphi \mid \langle D \rangle \varphi \mid \langle \bar{D} \rangle \varphi \mid \langle P \rangle \varphi \mid \langle \bar{P} \rangle \varphi \mid \varphi C \varphi \mid \varphi D \varphi \mid \varphi T \varphi,$$

where Q ranges over a denumerable set of propositional letters AP. We also assume the existence of the two constants **true** and **false** as usual. For a unary modality $\langle X \rangle$, we denote with $[X]\varphi$ the formula $\neg \langle X \rangle \neg\varphi$.

The peculiar feature of the semantics of SL is that there is *at most one way* in which an interval can be chopped into two adjacent subintervals.

Definition 4. *An interval structure* $\mathcal{I} = (I, \sqsubset, \prec)$ *is a* split-frame *if, for every* $k \in I$, *there exists at most one couple of intervals* $i, j \in I$ *such that* $C(i, j, k)$ *holds, where* C *is the chopping relation on* $\mathcal{I}$. *A* split-interpretation *is a pair* (F, V) *where* $F = (I, \sqsubset, \prec)$ *is a split-frame and* $V : AP \to \mathcal{P}(I)$ *is a valuation function.*

It is worth remarking that, when chopping k into i and j, i and j are not constrained to have the same length.

Definition 5. *Let* $M = ((I, \sqsubset, \prec), V)$ *be a split-interpretation and let* $i, j, k \in I$. *The truth relation* $\Vdash$ *on* M *is inductively defined as follows:*

- $M, i \Vdash Q$ *if and only if* $i \in V(Q)$, *where* $Q \in AP$;
- $M, i \Vdash \neg\varphi$ *if and only if* $M, i \nVdash \varphi$;
- $M, i \Vdash \varphi \wedge \psi$ *if and only if* $M, i \Vdash \varphi$ *and* $M, i \Vdash \psi$;
- $M, i \Vdash \langle D \rangle \varphi$ *iff for some* j *we have* $j \sqsubset i$ *and* $M, j \Vdash \varphi$;
- $M, i \Vdash \langle \bar{D} \rangle \varphi$ *iff for some* j *we have* $i \sqsubset j$ *and* $M, j \Vdash \varphi$;
- $M, i \Vdash \langle P \rangle \varphi$ *iff for some* j *we have* $j \prec i$ *and* $M, j \Vdash \varphi$;

---

[2] $\langle P \rangle$ and $\langle \bar{P} \rangle$ are like $\langle \bar{F} \rangle$ and $\langle F \rangle$ in HS, respectively, while $\langle D \rangle$ and $\langle \bar{D} \rangle$ correspond to the "union" of $\langle D \rangle$, $\langle B \rangle$ and $\langle E \rangle$ and their duals, respectively (see [6]).

- $M, i \Vdash \langle \bar{\mathsf{P}} \rangle \, \varphi$ *iff for some* j *we have* $i \prec j$ *and* $M, j \Vdash \varphi$;
- $M, i \Vdash \varphi \, \mathsf{C} \, \psi$ *iff for some* j, k *we have* $C(j, k, i)$ *and* $M, j \Vdash \varphi$ *and* $M, k \Vdash \psi$;
- $M, i \Vdash \varphi \, \mathsf{T} \, \psi$ *iff for some* j, k *we have* $C(i, j, k)$ *and* $M, j \Vdash \varphi$ *and* $M, k \Vdash \psi$;
- $M, i \Vdash \varphi \, \mathsf{D} \, \psi$ *iff for some* j, k *we have* $C(j, i, k)$ *and* $M, j \Vdash \varphi$ *and* $M, k \Vdash \psi$.

Satisfiability and validity are defined in the standard way. Note that the semantics of C, D, and T is given by means of the chopping relation C, which is first-order definable using $\sqsubseteq$ and $\prec$ (cf. Section 2.1). It is also possible to introduce the modal constant π of CDT (which informally holds over all and only atomic intervals) as an abbreviation for the formula $\neg \langle \mathsf{D} \rangle \, \mathsf{true}$.

SL is expressive enough to capture useful timing properties. Conditions of the form "from now on, it will be true that any occurrence of **stop** is always preceded by an occurrence of **start**" (we found it in the context of the specification of a time-triggered protocol which allows a fixed number of stations to communicate via a shared bus) can be expressed as follows:

$$[\bar{\mathsf{P}}](\mathsf{stop} \rightarrow \langle \mathsf{P} \rangle \, \mathsf{start}). \tag{1}$$

As a second example, consider the following sentence: "During the run, the robot stopped to grasp the block", which can be expressed in SL as follows:

$$\langle \mathsf{P} \rangle (\mathsf{running} \wedge \langle \mathsf{D} \rangle (\neg \mathsf{running} \wedge \mathsf{taking\text{-}block})). \tag{2}$$

Note that in other logics, where the projection principle of homogeneity is assumed, this formula would evaluate to false.

As for the relationships between SL operators, we know that the operators of CDT can be used to define the ones of HS [13], provided that both logics are interpreted over induced interval structures including "all" the intervals. For instance, the subinterval relation can be apparently captured with two applications of the chop operator. On the contrary, if they are interpreted over split-frames, by chopping an interval one cannot get an arbitrary smaller subinterval, and hence one cannot go as deep in the inclusion chain as one would like. As a matter of fact, it is possible to define precedence and inclusion by using the binary operators only in a few cases. In particular, $\langle \mathsf{D} \rangle$ and $\langle \bar{\mathsf{D}} \rangle$ are definable when SL is interpreted on n-LSs (see Section 4); $\langle \mathsf{P} \rangle$ and $\langle \bar{\mathsf{P}} \rangle$ are definable over UULSs (see Section 4) provided that $\langle \mathsf{D} \rangle$ and $\langle \bar{\mathsf{D}} \rangle$ are added to the logic with C, D and T. In the remaining cases they are indeed primitive operators. A detailed analysis can be found in the full version of the paper [9].

4   Decidability Results for SL

Discrete Frames and n-LSs. We first consider linear, well-founded, infinite, past bounded split-frames with maximal intervals. Such structures can be generated from linear, discrete, infinite, lower-bounded flows of time, that is, flows of time isomorphic to $(\mathbb{N}, <)$, where $<$ is the usual ordering of the natural numbers.

For a fixed $n \geq 1$, let $\mathrm{INT}_n(\mathbb{N})$ be the set of all and only the intervals on $(\mathbb{N}, <)$ that satisfy the following condition: for every $0 \leq i \leq n$, if $x = 2^i k$ with $k \in \mathbb{N}$, then $\langle x, x + 2^i \rangle \in \mathrm{INT}_n(\mathbb{N})$. $\mathrm{INT}_n(\mathbb{N})$ is a split-domain in which the length of the intervals is bounded by 2^n and intervals with the same length are pairwise disjoint. The length of an interval $\langle x, y \rangle$ is $\mathrm{len}(\langle x, y \rangle) = y - x$. In this section, we consider the class $\mathcal{C}$ of the interval structures isomorphic to $(\mathrm{INT}_n(\mathbb{N}), \sqsubset, \prec)$, for some $n \geq 1$. The idea is to map split-interpretations based on split-frames in $\mathcal{C}$ on 2-refinable $(n + 1)$-layered structures in order to transfer decidability results for granular structures to SL.

Given a first-order formula φ we denote by $\varphi\{x/t\}$ the substitution of the free occurrences of the variable x with the term t. Given an assignment σ mapping variables to elements of the domain, we denote by $\sigma[x_1/d_1, \ldots, x_n/d_n]$ the assignment which differs from σ, if at all, only because it assigns $d_1, \ldots, d_n$ to $x_1, \ldots, x_n$, respectively.

We now provide a translation of SL-formulae into $\mathrm{MFO}[<_1, <_2, \downarrow_0, \downarrow_1]$ (cf. Section 2.2). Let $Q \in AP$ be a proposition letter and φ and ψ be SL-formulae. The translation τ is defined by the following inductive clauses:

- $\tau(Q) = q(x)$, where $Q \in AP$ and q is a unary predicate symbol;
- $\tau(\neg\varphi) = \neg(\tau(\varphi))$;
- $\tau(\varphi \wedge \psi) = \tau(\varphi) \wedge \tau(\psi)$;
- $\tau(\langle \mathsf{D} \rangle \varphi) = \exists y \, (x <_2 y \wedge \tau(\varphi)\{x/y\})$;
- $\tau(\langle \bar{\mathsf{D}} \rangle \varphi) = \exists y \, (y <_2 x \wedge \tau(\varphi)\{x/y\})$;
- $\tau(\langle \mathsf{P} \rangle \varphi) = \exists y \, ((y <_1 x \wedge \tau(\varphi)\{x/y\}) \vee \exists z \, (\downarrow_0(z) \leq_2 y \wedge \downarrow_1(z) \leq_2 x \wedge \tau(\varphi)\{x/y\}))$;
- $\tau(\langle \bar{\mathsf{P}} \rangle \varphi) = \exists y \, ((x <_1 y \wedge \tau(\varphi)\{x/y\}) \vee \exists z \, (\downarrow_0(z) \leq_2 x \wedge \downarrow_1(z) \leq_2 y \wedge \tau(\varphi)\{x/y\}))$;
- $\tau(\varphi \, \mathsf{C} \, \psi) = \exists y \exists z (\downarrow_0(x) = y \wedge \downarrow_1(x) = z \wedge \tau(\varphi)\{x/y\} \wedge \tau(\psi)\{x/z\})$;
- $\tau(\varphi \, \mathsf{T} \, \psi) = \exists y \exists z (\downarrow_0(z) = x \wedge \downarrow_1(z) = y \wedge \tau(\varphi)\{x/y\} \wedge \tau(\psi)\{x/z\})$;
- $\tau(\varphi \, \mathsf{D} \, \psi) = \exists y \exists z (\downarrow_0(z) = y \wedge \downarrow_1(z) = x \wedge \tau(\varphi)\{x/y\} \wedge \tau(\psi)\{x/z\})$.

Referring to Figure 1, every point in a layered structure can be determined by a pair of coordinates d_l, where l is the l-th domain and d is the distance from the origin of that domain, also called the *displacement* of the point in the domain. It is possible to show that the function $\delta \colon \mathrm{INT}_n(\mathbb{N}) \to \bigcup_{i=0}^{n} T^i$ such that, for every $\langle a, b \rangle \in \mathrm{INT}_n(\mathbb{N})$, $\delta(\langle a, b \rangle) = d_l$, where $d = a/\mathrm{len}(\langle a, b \rangle)$ and $l = n - \log_2 \mathrm{len}(\langle a, b \rangle)$, is an effective bijection. Using δ, we can establish a correspondence between models in SL and models in $\mathrm{MFO}[<_1, <_2, \downarrow_0, \downarrow_1]$.

Definition 6. *Let $M = (\mathrm{INT}_n(\mathbb{N}), \sqsubset, \prec, V)$ be a split-interpretation and let $(S, \mathcal{I})$ be a 2-refinable $(n+1)$-LS S for $\mathrm{MFO}[<_1, <_2, \downarrow_0, \downarrow_1]$-formulae paired with an interpretation $\mathcal{I}$ of predicate symbols. We say that $(S, \mathcal{I})$ corresponds to M if the following properties are satisfied:*

1. *the domain $\bigcup_{i=0}^{n} T^i$ is the mapping through δ of $\mathrm{INT}_n(\mathbb{N})$;*
2. *for every propositional letter Q, the interpretation $\mathcal{I}(\tau(Q))$ of the predicate $\tau(Q)$ is $\delta(V(Q))$, where, given a set I of intervals, $\delta(I) = \{\delta(i) \mid i \in I\}$.*

The previous correspondence is the key for proving decidability. The proof of the following result proceeds by induction on the complexity of the formulae.

Theorem 1. *Let M be a split-interpretation based on a split-frame in $\mathcal{C}$, i an interval of M and φ an SL-formula. Then $M, i \Vdash \varphi$ if and only if $(S, \mathcal{I}), \sigma[x/\delta(i)] \models \tau(\varphi)$, where $(S, \mathcal{I})$ is a 2-refinable $(n + 1)$-LS that corresponds to M.*

Corollary 1. *The satisfiability problem in SL with respect to $\mathcal{C}$ is decidable.*

Discrete Frames and UULSs. The previously considered class of split-frames can be easily extended by relaxing the contraint of the existence of maximal intervals. It turns out that, in this case, we must look at UULSs as a granular counterpart for such a class of frames.

Formally, let us consider the set $\text{INT}_\infty(\mathbb{N})$ of all and only the intervals over $(\mathbb{N}, <)$ such that for every $i \geq 0$, if $x = 2^i k$, with $k \in \mathbb{N}$, then $\langle x, x + 2^i \rangle \in \text{INT}_\infty(\mathbb{N})$. $\text{INT}_\infty(\mathbb{N})$ can be seen as the split-domain obtained as the union, for every n, of the split-domains $\text{INT}_n(\mathbb{N})$. We are interested in the class $\mathcal{C}_\infty$ of the split-frames isomorphic to $(\text{INT}_\infty(\mathbb{N}), \sqsubset, \prec)$. A bijective function $\delta : \text{INT}_\infty(\mathbb{N}) \to \bigcup_{i \geq 0} T^i$ can be defined, for $\langle a, b \rangle \in \text{INT}_\infty(\mathbb{N})$, by $\delta(\langle a, b \rangle) = (a/\text{len}(\langle a, b \rangle))_{\log_2 \text{len}(\langle a, b \rangle)}$. In this definition of δ, we take into account the fact that the layers in UULSs are counted from the tree leaves.

The correspondence between split-interpretations and layered structures of Definition 6 can be immediately adapted to UULSs. The translation of SL-formulae in $\text{MFO}[<_2, \downarrow_0, \downarrow_1]$-formulae (cf. Section 2.2) can be given as in the previous case, with the exception of the cases relative to $\langle P \rangle$ and $\langle \bar{P} \rangle$ which change as follows:

- $\tau(\langle P \rangle \varphi) = \exists y \exists z \, (\downarrow_0(z) \leq_2 y \wedge \downarrow_1(z) \leq_2 x \wedge \tau(\varphi)\{x/y\});$
- $\tau(\langle \bar{P} \rangle \varphi) = \exists y \exists z \, (\downarrow_0(z) \leq_2 x \wedge \downarrow_1(z) \leq_2 y \wedge \tau(\varphi)\{x/y\}).$

A result analogous to Theorem 1 holds.

Theorem 2. *Let M be a split-interpretation based on a split-frame in $\mathcal{C}_\infty$, i an interval of M and φ an SL-formula. Then we have $M, i \Vdash \varphi$ if and only if $(S, \mathcal{I}), \sigma[x/\delta(i)] \models \tau(\varphi)$, where $(S, \mathcal{I})$ is a 2-refinable UULS that corresponds to M.*

Corollary 2. *The satisfiability problem for SL with respect to $\mathcal{C}_\infty$ is decidable.*

Dense Frames and DULSs. Consider now the class of linear, dense, past bounded and future unbounded split-frames with maximal intervals. When a structure is dense, intervals can be divided *ad infinitum*. Then, DULSs are a natural granular counterpart for dense split-frames.

Adequate interval structures are obtained from such flows of time as $(\mathbb{Q}^+, <)$ and $(\mathbb{R}^+, <)$ with the usual ordering. Let $\text{INT}(\mathbb{Q}^+)$ be the split-domain recursively built as follows:

- for every integer $n \geq 0$, $\langle n, n + 1 \rangle \in \text{INT}(\mathbb{Q}^+)$;
- if $\langle x, y \rangle \in \text{INT}(\mathbb{Q}^+)$, then $\langle x, (x + y)/2 \rangle, \langle (x + y)/2, y \rangle \in \text{INT}(\mathbb{Q}^+)$.

We consider the class $\mathcal{D}$ of the split-frames isomorphic to $(\text{INT}(\mathbb{Q}^+), \sqsubset, \prec)$. A bijection $\delta \colon \text{INT}(\mathbb{Q}^+) \to \bigcup_{i \geq 0} T^i$ between split-frames in $\mathcal{D}$ and DULSs is the following: for every $\langle a, b \rangle \in \text{INT}(\mathbb{Q}^+)$ let $\delta(\langle a, b \rangle) = (a/\text{len}(\langle a, b \rangle))_{-\log_2 \text{len}(\langle a,b \rangle)}$.

Once again, the notion of correspondence between a split-interpretation and a DULS provided with a suitable interpretation of predicate symbols is straight-forward from Definition 6. Moreover, the translation of SL-formulae is the same as in the case of n-LSs. We can therefore state the following result.

Theorem 3. *Let M be a split-interpretation based on a split-frame in $\mathcal{D}$, i an interval of M and φ an SL-formula. Then $M, i \Vdash \varphi$ if and only if $(S, \mathcal{I}), \sigma[x/\delta(i)] \models \tau(\varphi)$, where $(S, \mathcal{I})$ is a 2-refinable DULS that corresponds to M.*

Corollary 3. *The satisfiability problem for SL with respect to $\mathcal{D}$ is decidable.*

It is not hard to see that the given translations can be accomplished, by reusing variables, using at most three variables and that every such formula contains exactly one free variable, which intuitively marks the current interval. Moreover, such a translation actually maps SL into particular restrictions of the previous theories, namely, the *guarded fragment* [2] GF_3 of $\text{MFO}[<_1, <_2, \downarrow_0, \downarrow_1]$ for n-LSs and DULSs (of $\text{MFO}[<_2, \downarrow_0, \downarrow_1]$ for UULSs) with three variables and predicates at most ternary. Since it is possible to show that also every GF_3-formula has an equivalent translation into SL, the following result holds[3]:

Theorem 4. *SL is expressively complete with respect to GF_3 restricted to formulae with one free variable.*

5   On Decidable Extensions of SL

SL can be extended with other interval operators. We now list a few and give their translation into $\text{MFO}[(<_1), <_2, \downarrow_0, \downarrow_1]$. We remark that these translations, given the results for time granularity, imply the decidability of the extended logic (which can be proved as we did for basic SL). Besides, the following formulae are not GF_3-formulae: we conjecture that they are not equivalent to any GF_3-formula and that the logics obtained by adding these operators are non-conservative (decidability-preserving) extensions of SL.

Given a split-interpretation M and an interval i, we define the semantics of the *beginning subinterval* and *ending subinterval* operators $\langle B \rangle$ and $\langle E \rangle$, and of the *consecutive*, or *meeting interval*, operator $\langle A \rangle$ (leaving to the reader the dual definitions) as follows:

- $M, i \Vdash \langle B \rangle \varphi$ iff for some j we have j starts i and $M, j \Vdash \varphi$;
- $M, i \Vdash \langle E \rangle \varphi$ iff for some j we have j ends i and $M, j \Vdash \varphi$;
- $M, i \Vdash \langle A \rangle \varphi$ iff for some j we have i meets j and $M, j \Vdash \varphi$.

---

[3] Such a result can be easily generalized to formulae with *at most* one free variable. From the modal point of view, sentences are always evaluated to either true or false.

We use the following abbreviations:

$$y \text{ starts } x \equiv x <_2 y \wedge \neg \exists z \, (x <_2 z \wedge \exists w \, (\downarrow_0(w) \leq_2 z \wedge \downarrow_1(w) \leq_2 y));$$
$$y \text{ ends } x \equiv x <_2 y \wedge \neg \exists z \, (x <_2 z \wedge \exists w \, (\downarrow_0(w) \leq_2 y \wedge \downarrow_1(w) \leq_2 z));$$
$$\text{maximal}(x) \equiv \neg \exists y \, y <_2 x.$$

The previous operators can be translated as follows:

$$\tau(\langle B \rangle \, \varphi) = \exists y \, (y \text{ starts } x \wedge \tau(\varphi\{x/y\})); \quad \tau(\langle E \rangle \, \varphi) = \exists y \, (y \text{ ends } x \wedge \tau(\varphi\{x/y\}));$$
$$\tau(\langle A \rangle \, \varphi) = \exists y \exists v \exists w \exists z \, (\downarrow_0(z) = v \wedge \downarrow_1(z) = w \wedge (x \text{ ends } v \vee x = v) \wedge$$
$$(y \text{ starts } w \vee y = w) \wedge \tau(\varphi\{x/y\})) \vee \exists y \exists t \exists u \, (\text{maximal}(t) \wedge$$
$$\wedge \, \text{maximal}(u) \wedge t <_1 u \wedge \neg \exists z \, (t <_1 z <_1 u) \wedge (x \text{ ends } t \vee x = t) \wedge$$
$$\wedge \, (y \text{ starts } u \vee y = u) \wedge \tau(\varphi\{x/y\})).$$

To exemplify the usefulness of these extensions of SL we borrow from [6] a couple of examples in the domain of qualitative physics and automatic planning, respectively. The first is the sentence "if you open the tap, then, unless someone punctures the canteen, the canteen will eventually be filled". This statement can be written pretty in the same way as in HS:

$$\text{open-tap} \rightarrow \langle A \rangle \, (\neg \, \langle D \rangle \, \text{punctures} \rightarrow \langle E \rangle \, [E] \, \text{filled}). \tag{3}$$

There are some differences with respect to the original formulation of (3) in HS. In particular, we intend (3) to be interpreted on (interval structures corresponding to) DULSs, so we do not take into account intervals' endpoints (which could be identified with atomic intervals), as Halpern and Shoham do. In this context, even the shortest occurring events, such as filled or open-tap, have some duration. However, being able to refine every interval, such a duration can be as small as one likes.

The second example is the following statement: "if the robot executes the charge-battery routine, then, at the beginning of the following execution of the navigate routine, its batteries will be fully charged". We say that a proposition is *solid* if no two distinct overlapping intervals ever satisfy it. Since we do not have partially overlapping intervals, this definition reduces to the formula $\text{solid}(\varphi) \equiv \varphi \rightarrow \neg \langle D \rangle \, \varphi$. The "next time that" statement can be written

$$[\![\text{NTT}]\!](\varphi, \psi) \equiv [A] \, ((\neg \varphi \wedge [D] \, \neg \varphi \rightarrow [A] (\varphi \rightarrow \langle B \rangle \, [B] \, \psi)) \vee (\varphi \wedge \langle B \rangle \, [B] \, \psi)), \tag{4}$$

where φ is a solid proposition. The robot statement becomes

$$\text{charge-battery} \rightarrow [\![\text{NTT}]\!](\text{navigate}, \text{battery-full}). \tag{5}$$

6 Concluding Remarks

In this paper, we have proposed an approach to the decidability of interval temporal logics based on a specialization of their semantic structures and a connection with theories of time granularity. As a by-product, we provided granular structures, which are intrinsecally interval-based (they talk about days, hours, seconds, which are time periods), with suitable standard interval operators. Notice that, unlike most of the existing approaches, we made no restricting hypotheses on the valuation of the formulae. We are currently investigating the possibility of reducing the satisfiability of some class of formulae over the induced interval structures (cf. Section 2.1) to the satisfiability over split-frames. Of course, this cannot be the case for C, D, and T: however, the unary modalities seem not to have the same severe restrictions. This work can be extended in several directions. First, one can try to deal with general split-frames as well as to augment the domain, e.g. by including partially overlapping intervals. Such attempts would allow one to properly determine the boundaries beyond which undecidability is attained. Second, more powerful operators can be added to capture full first-order and second-order decidable theories for time granularity. Finally, it would be useful to devise a specific decision procedure for SL.

References

1. J. F. Allen. Maintaining Knowledge about Temporal Intervals. *Communications of the ACM*, 26:832–843, 1983.
2. P. Blackburn, M. de Rijke, and Y. Venema. *Modal Logic*. Cambridge University Press, 2001.
3. H. Bowman and S. J. Thompson. A tableaux method for interval temporal logic with projection. *Lecture Notes in Artificial Intelligence*, 1397:108–123, 1998.
4. Z. Chaochen and M. R. Hansen. An Adequate First Order Interval Logic. *Lecture Notes in Computer Science*, 1536:584–608, 1998.
5. J. Y. Halpern, Z. Manna, and B. Moszkowski. A Hardware Semantics Based on Temporal Intervals. *Lecture Notes in Computer Science*, 154:278–291, 1983.
6. J. Y. Halpern and Y. Shoham. A Propositional Modal Logic of Time Intervals. *Journal of the ACM*, 38(4):935–962, 1991.
7. A. Montanari, A. Peron, and A. Policriti. Decidable theories of ω-layered metric temporal structures. *Logic Journal of the IGPL*, 7(1):79–102, 1999.
8. A. Montanari and A. Policriti. Decidability results for metric and layered temporal logics. *Notre Dame Journal of Formal Logic*, 37:260–282, 1996.
9. A. Montanari, G. Sciavicco, and N. Vitacolonna. Decidability of Interval Temporal Logics over Split-Frames via Granularity. Research Report 01/02, Department of Mathematics and Computer Science, University of Udine, February 2002.
10. A. Montanari. *Metric and Layered Temporal Logic for Time Granularity*. PhD thesis, ILLC, University of Amsterdam, 1996.
11. B. C. Moszkowski. *Reasoning about digital circuits*. PhD thesis, Stanford University, June 1983.
12. J. van Benthem. *The Logic of Time*. Kluwer Academic Publisher, 2nd ed., 1991.
13. Y. Venema. A Modal Logic for Chopping Intervals. *Journal of Logic and Computation*, 1(4):453–476, 1991.

Uncertainty and Partial Non-uniform Assumptions in Parametric Deductive Databases

Yann Loyer and Umberto Straccia

Istituto di Elaborazione della Informazione -C.N.R.
Via G. Moruzzi,1 I-56124 Pisa (PI) Italy

Abstract. Different many-valued logic programming frameworks have been proposed to manage uncertain information in deductive databases and logic programming. A feature of these frameworks is that they rely on a predefined assumption or hypothesis, i.e. an interpretation that assigns the same default truth value to all the atoms of a program, e.g. in the open world assumption, by default all atoms have unknown truth value. In this paper we extend these frameworks along three directions: (i) we will introduce non-monotonic modes of negation; (ii) the default truth values of atoms need not necessarily to be all equal each other; and (iii) a hypothesis can be a partial interpretation. We will show that our approach extends the usual ones: if we restrict our attention to classical logic programs and consider total uniform hypotheses, then our semantics reduces to the usual semantics of logic programs. In particular, under the everything false assumption, our semantics captures and extends the well-founded semantics to these frameworks.

1 Introduction

An important issue to be addressed in applications of logic programming is the management of uncertainty whenever the information to be represented is of imperfect nature (which happens quite often). The problem of uncertainty management in logic programs has attracted the attention of many researchers and numerous frameworks have been proposed [1,2,3,6,8,9,10,11,13,14,15,16,17]. Each of them addresses the management of different kind of uncertainty: (i) probability theory [6,10,13,14,15]; (ii) fuzzy set theory [1,16,17]; (iii) multi-valued logic [8,9,11]; and (iv) possibilistic logic [3]. Apart from the different notion of uncertainty they rely on, these frameworks differ in the way in which uncertainty is associated with the facts and rules of a program. With respect to this latter point, these frameworks can be classified into *annotation based* (AB) and *implication based* (IB), which we briefly summarize below. In the AB approach, a rule is of the form $A : f(\beta_1, \ldots, \beta_n) \leftarrow B_1 : \beta_1, \ldots, B_n : \beta_n$, which asserts "the certainty of atom A is at least (or is in) $f(\beta_1, \ldots, \beta_n)$, whenever the certainty of atom B_i is at least (or is in) β_i, $1 \leq i \leq n$". Here f is an n-ary computable function and β_i is either a constant or a variable ranging over an appropriate certainty domain. Examples of AB frameworks include [8,9,14,15]. In the IB approach, a rule is of the form $A \xleftarrow{\alpha} B_1, \ldots, B_n$, which says that the certainty associated with the implication $B_1 \wedge \ldots \wedge B_n \rightarrow A$ is α. Computationally, given an assignment v of certainties to the B_is, the certainty of A is computed

S. Flesca et al. (Eds.): JELIA 2002, LNAI 2424, pp. 271–282, 2002.
© Springer-Verlag Berlin Heidelberg 2002

by taking the "conjunction" of the certainties $v(B_i)$ and then somehow "propagating" it to the rule head. The truth values are taken from a certainty lattice. Examples of the IB frameworks include [10,11,17] (see [11] for a more detailed comparison between the two approaches). We recall the following facts [11]: (*i*) while the way implication is treated in the AB approach is closer to classical logic, the way rules are fired in the IB approach has a definite intuitive appeal and (*ii*) the AB approach is strictly more expressive than the IB. The down side is that query processing in the AB approach is more complicated, *e.g.* the fixpoint operator is not continuous in general, while it is in the IB approaches. From the above points, it is believed that the IB approach is easier to use and is more amenable for efficient implementation. Nonetheless both approaches stress important limitations for real-world applications, which we will address in this paper: (*i*) they do not address any mode of *non-monotonic reasoning* (in particular, no negation operation is defined). The need of non-monotonic formalisms for real-world applications is commonly accepted: our knowledge about the world is almost always *incomplete* and, thus, we are forced to reason in the *absence of complete information*. As a result we often have to revise our conclusions, when new information becomes available; (*ii*) they rely on predefined *uniform assumptions*, *i.e.* they assign the same default truth value to all the atoms. Widely used and well known examples of uniform assumptions are the *Open World Assumption* (OWA), which corresponds to the assumption that every atom whose truth can not be inferred from the program has *unknown* truth value, and the *Closed World Assumption* (CWA), which corresponds to the assumption that every such atom's truth value is *false*. While only uniform assumptions are used, the need of non-uniform assumptions has already been highlighted in the domains of (a) logic-based information retrieval [6], and (b) information integration [12], as shown in the following example.

Example 1 (A motivating example). Consider a legal case where a judge has to decide whether to charge a person named Ted accused of murder. To do so, the judge first collects facts from two different sources: the public prosecutor and the person's lawyer. The judge then combines the collected facts using a set of rules in order to reach a decision. For the sake of our example, let us suppose that the judge has collected a set of facts $F = \{\texttt{witness(John)}, \texttt{friends(John, Ted)}\}$ that he combines using a set of rules R as follows[1]:

$$
R = \left\{
\begin{array}{ll}
\texttt{suspect(X)} & \leftarrow \texttt{motive(X)} \\
\texttt{suspect(X)} & \leftarrow \texttt{witness(X)} \\
\texttt{innocent(X)} & \leftarrow \texttt{alibi(X, Y)} \wedge \neg\texttt{friends(X, Y)} \\
\texttt{innocent(X)} & \leftarrow \texttt{presumption\_of\_innocence(X)} \wedge \neg\texttt{suspect(X)} \\
\texttt{friends(X, Y)} & \leftarrow \texttt{friends(Y, X)} \\
\texttt{friends(X, Y)} & \leftarrow \texttt{friends(X, Z)} \wedge \texttt{friends(Z, Y)} \\
\texttt{charge(X)} & \leftarrow \texttt{suspect(X)} \\
\texttt{charge(X)} & \leftarrow \neg\texttt{innocent(X)}
\end{array}
\right\}
$$

The two first rules of R describe how the prosecutor works: in order to support the claim that a person X is a suspect, the prosecutor tries to provide a motive (first rule) or a witness against X (second rule). The third and fourth rules of R describe how the lawyer works: in order to support the claim that X is innocent,

---

[1] For ease of presentation we leave uncertainties out. For instance, there might well be some uncertainty in the facts and rules, as we will see later on.

the lawyer tries to provide an alibi for X by a person who is not a friend of X (third rule), or to use the presumption of innocence if the person is not suspect (fourth rule), *i.e.* the defendant is *assumed* innocent until proved guilty. Finally, the last two rules of R are the judge's "decision making rules".

Now, what should the value of charge(Ted) be? Ted should be charged if he has been proved effectively suspect or not innocent. We can easily remark that uniform hypotheses, as the CWA and the OWA, do not fit with our expectation. According to the CWA, then the judge will infer that Ted is not innocent and must be charged. According to the OWA, then the atoms suspect(Ted), innocent(Ted) and charged(Ted) are unknown and the judge cannot take a decision (that semantics is often considered as too weak). Another uniform hypothesis is to assign to all atoms the default value true, but under such an assumption, the judge will infer that Ted is suspect and must be charged.

An intuitively appealing *non-uniform assumption* in this situation is to assume by default that the atoms motive(Ted), witness(Ted) and suspect(Ted) are false, that the atom presumption_of_innocence(Ted) is true and that the others are unknown. With such a hypothesis, the judge could infer that Ted is innocent, not suspect and should not be charged. □

We believe that we should not be limited to consider logic program without negation under uniform assumptions only, but be able to associate to any logic program a semantics based on any given hypothesis, which represents our default or assumed knowledge. To this end, we will extend the *parametric* IB framework [11], a unifying umbrella for IB frameworks, along three directions: (i) we will introduce negation into the programs, *i.e.* we will extend the IB frameworks with the non-monotonic mode of negation and extend to that framework the usual semantics of logic programs with negation; (ii) we will consider assumptions that do not necessarily assign the same default truth values to all the atoms; and (iii) we will not only consider total assumptions but also partial assumptions, *i.e.* we will not require that every atom has a default truth value (an atom's truth value may be still unknown). We will show that our approach extends the usual ones: restricting our attention to logic programs and considering total uniform hypotheses, then our semantics reduces to the usual semantics of logic programs. In particular, under the *everywhere false assumption* (i) for programs without negation we obtain the semantics presented in [11]; and (ii) for Datalog programs with negation we obtain the *Well Founded Semantics* (WFS) [18]. On the other hand, under the *almost everywhere empty hypothesis* our semantics includes the *Kripke-Kleene semantics* of Fitting [4].

In the next section we introduce the syntax of our logical language, we define the notion of satisfiability and present fixpoint operators, through which in Section 3 the intended semantics of our logic programs is specified. Section 4 compares our semantics with others, while Section 5 concludes.

2   Syntax and Semantics: Preliminaries

We recall the syntactical aspects of the parametric IB framework presented in [11] and extend it with negation. Let $\mathcal{L}$ be an arbitrary first order language that contains infinitely many variable symbols, finitely many constants, and predicate symbols, but no function symbols. While $\mathcal{L}$ does not contain function symbols, it contains symbols for families of *propagation* $(\mathcal{F}_p)$, *conjunction* $(\mathcal{F}_c)$ and *disjunction* functions $(\mathcal{F}_d)$, called *combination functions*.

Let $\langle \mathcal{T}, \preceq, \otimes, \oplus \rangle$ be a certainty lattice (a complete lattice) and $\mathcal{B}(\mathcal{T})$ the set of finite multisets over $\mathcal{T}$. With $\bot$ and $\top$ we denote the least and greatest element in $\mathcal{T}$, respectively. A *propagation function* is a mapping from $\mathcal{T} \times \mathcal{T}$ to $\mathcal{T}$ and a *conjunction* or *disjunction* function is a mapping from $\mathcal{B}(\mathcal{T})$ to $\mathcal{T}$. Each kind of function must verify some of the following properties:

1. monotonicity w.r.t. (with respect to) each one of its arguments;
2. continuity w.r.t. each one of its arguments;
3. bounded-above: $f(\alpha_1, \alpha_2) \preceq \alpha_i$, for $i = 1, 2, \forall \alpha_1, \alpha_2 \in \mathcal{T}$;
4. bounded-below: $f(\alpha_1, \alpha_2) \succeq \alpha_i$, for $i = 1, 2, \forall \alpha_1, \alpha_2 \in \mathcal{T}$;
5. commutativity: $f(\alpha_1, \alpha_2) = f(\alpha_2, \alpha_1), \forall \alpha_1, \alpha_2 \in \mathcal{T}$;
6. associativity: $f(\alpha_1, f(\alpha_2, \alpha_3)) = f(f(\alpha_1, \alpha_2), \alpha_3), \forall \alpha_1, \alpha_2, \alpha_3 \in \mathcal{T}$;
7. $f(\{\alpha\}) = \alpha, \forall \alpha \in \mathcal{T}$;
8. $f(\emptyset) = \bot$;
9. $f(\emptyset) = \top$;
10. $f(\alpha, \top) = \alpha, \forall \alpha \in \mathcal{T}$.

We require that [11]: (i) any conjunction function in $\mathcal{F}_c$ satisfies properties 1, 2, 3, 5, 6, 7, 9 and 10; (ii) any propagation function in $\mathcal{F}_p$ satisfies properties 1, 2, 3 and 10; and (iii) any disjunction function in $\mathcal{F}_d$ satisfies properties 1, 2, 4, 5, 6, 7 and 8. We also assume that there is a *negation function* $\neg: \mathcal{T} \to \mathcal{T}$ that is anti-monotone w.r.t. $\preceq$ and satisfies $\neg\neg\alpha = \alpha, \forall \alpha \in \mathcal{T}$ and $\neg\bot = \top$.

Definition 1 (Normal parametric program). *A normal parametric program P (np-program) is a tuple $\langle \mathcal{T}, \mathcal{R}, \mathcal{C}, \mathcal{P}, \mathcal{D} \rangle$, defined as follows:*

1. *$\mathcal{T}$ is a set of truth values partially ordered by $\preceq$. We assume that $\langle \mathcal{T}, \preceq, \otimes, \oplus \rangle$ is a complete lattice, where $\otimes$ is the meet operator and $\oplus$ the join operator;*
2. *$\mathcal{R}$ is a finite set of normal parametric rules r (np-rules), each of which is a statement of the form $r : A \xleftarrow{\alpha_r} B_1, ..., B_n, \neg C_1, ..., \neg C_m$, where A is an atomic formula and $B_1, ..., B_n, C_1, ..., C_m$ are atomic formulas or values in $\mathcal{T}$ and $\alpha_r \in \mathcal{T} \setminus \{\bot\}$ is the certainty of the rule;*
3. *$\mathcal{C}$ maps each np-rule to a conjunction function in $\mathcal{F}_c$;*
4. *$\mathcal{P}$ maps each np-rule to a propagation function in $\mathcal{F}_p$;*
5. *$\mathcal{D}$ maps each predicate symbol in P to a disjunction function in $\mathcal{F}_d$.* ∎

For ease of presentation, we write $r : A \xleftarrow{\alpha_r} B_1, ..., B_n, \neg C_1, ..., \neg C_m; \langle f_d, f_p, f_c \rangle$ to represent a np-rule in which $f_d \in \mathcal{F}_d$ is the disjunction function associated with the predicate symbol A and, $f_c \in \mathcal{F}_c$ and $f_p \in \mathcal{F}_p$ are respectively the conjunction and propagation functions associated with r. The intention is that the conjunction function (*e.g.* $\otimes$) determines the truth value of the conjunction of $B_1, ..., B_n, \neg C_1, ..., \neg C_m$, the propagation function (*e.g.* $\otimes$) determines how to "propagate" the truth value resulting from the evaluation of the body to the head, by taking into account the certainty α_r associated to the rule r, while the disjunction function (*e.g.* $\oplus$) dictates how to combine the certainties in case an atom is head of several rules. Note that np-programs without negation are parametric programs (*p-programs*) as defined in [11]. We further define the *Herbrand* *base* $\mathcal{HB}_P$ of a np-program P as the set of all instantiated atoms corresponding to atoms appearing in P and define P^* to be the *Herbrand instantiation of P*, i.e. the set of all ground instantiations of the rules in P. A classical logic program is a np-program such that $\otimes$ is the unique conjunction and propagation function, $\oplus$ is the unique disjunction function and $\alpha_r = \top$, for all rules $r \in P$. Such a program will be denoted in the classical way. If not stated otherwise, with P we will always denote an np-program.

Example 2. Consider the complete lattice $\langle \mathcal{T}, \preceq, \otimes, \oplus \rangle$, where $\mathcal{T}$ is $[0,1]$, $\forall$, $a, b \in [0,1]$, $a \preceq b$ iff $a \le b$, $a \otimes b = \min(a,b)$, and $a \oplus b = \max(a,b)$. Consider $f_d(\alpha,\beta) = \alpha + \beta - \alpha \cdot \beta$, $f_c(\alpha,\beta) = \alpha \cdot \beta$, $f_p = f_c$ and $\neg(\alpha) = 1 - \alpha$. Then the following is a np-program P:

$$P = \left\{ \begin{array}{ll} \texttt{suspect(X)} & \overset{0.6}{\leftarrow} \texttt{motive(X)} \ \langle f_d, \otimes, \otimes \rangle \\ \texttt{suspect(X)} & \overset{0.8}{\leftarrow} \texttt{witness(X)} \ \langle f_d, \otimes, \otimes \rangle \\ \texttt{innocent(X)} & \overset{1}{\leftarrow} \texttt{alibi(X,Y)} \wedge \neg\texttt{friends(X,Y)} \ \langle f_d, f_p, \otimes \rangle \\ \texttt{innocent(X)} & \overset{1}{\leftarrow} \texttt{presumption\_of\_innocence(X)} \wedge \neg\texttt{suspect(X)} \ \langle f_d, f_p, \otimes \rangle \\ \texttt{friends(X,Y)} & \overset{1}{\leftarrow} \texttt{friends(Y,X)} \ \langle \oplus, f_p, \otimes \rangle \\ \texttt{friends(X,Y)} & \overset{0.7}{\leftarrow} \texttt{friends(X,Z)} \wedge \texttt{friends(Z,Y)} \ \langle \oplus, f_p, f_c \rangle \\ \texttt{charge(X)} & \overset{1}{\leftarrow} \texttt{suspect(X)} \ \langle \oplus, f_p, \otimes \rangle \\ \texttt{charge(X)} & \overset{1}{\leftarrow} \neg\texttt{innocent(X)} \ \langle \oplus, f_p, \otimes \rangle \\ \texttt{witness(John)} & \overset{1}{\leftarrow} 1 \ \langle \oplus, f_p, \otimes \rangle \\ \texttt{motive(Jim)} & \overset{1}{\leftarrow} 0.8 \ \langle \oplus, f_p, \otimes \rangle \\ \texttt{alibi(Jim,John)} & \overset{1}{\leftarrow} 1 \ \langle \oplus, f_p, \otimes \rangle \\ \texttt{friends(John,Ted)} & \overset{1}{\leftarrow} 0.8 \ \langle \oplus, f_p, \otimes \rangle \\ \texttt{friends(Jim,Ted)} & \overset{1}{\leftarrow} 0.6 \ \langle \oplus, f_p, \otimes \rangle \end{array} \right\}$$

Note that *e.g.* for predicate $\texttt{suspect}$, the disjunction function f_d is associated, as if there are different ways to infer that someone is suspect, then we would like to increase our suspicion and not just to choose the maximal value. □

An interpretation of a np-program P is a function that assigns to all atoms of the Herbrand base of P a value in $\mathcal{T}$. We denote $\mathcal{V}_P(\mathcal{T})$ the set of all interpretations of P. Of course, an important issue is to determine which is the semantics of a np-program. In the usual approach, the semantics of a program P is determined by selecting a particular interpretation of P in the set of models of P. In logic programs without negation, as well as in the parametric IB framework, that chosen model is usually the least model of P w.r.t. $\preceq$. Introducing negation in classical logic programs, and in particular in our parametric IB framework, has as consequence that some np-programs do not have a unique minimal model.

Example 3. Consider $\mathcal{T} = [0,1]$, $f_c(\alpha,\beta) = \min(\alpha,\beta)$, $f_d(\alpha,\beta) = \max(\alpha,\beta)$, $f_p(\alpha,\beta) = \alpha \cdot \beta$ and the usual negation function. Consider the program $P = \{A \overset{1}{\leftarrow} \neg B; \langle f_d, f_p, f_c \rangle, B \overset{1}{\leftarrow} \neg A; \langle f_d, f_p, f_c \rangle, A \overset{1}{\leftarrow} 0.2; \langle f_d, f_p, f_c \rangle, B \overset{1}{\leftarrow} 0.3; \langle f_d, f_p, f_c \rangle\}$. This program will have an infinite number of models I_x^y, where $0.2 \le x \le 1, 0.3 \le y \le 1, y \ge 1 - x$, $I_x^y(A) = x$ and $I_x^y(B) = y$. There are also an infinite number of minimal models. These models I_x^y are such that $y = 1 - x$. □

A usual way to deal with such situations in classical logic consists in considering partial interpretations *i.e.* interpretations that assign values only to some atoms of $\mathcal{HB}_P$ and are not defined for the other atoms. A *partial interpretation* I of P is a partial function from $\mathcal{HB}_P$ to $\mathcal{T}$. A partial interpretation I can also be seen as the set $\{A : I(A) \mid A \in \mathcal{HB}_P \text{ and } I(A) \text{ defined}\}$. Partial interpretations will be used as functions or as sets following the context. Furthermore, in the following, given a np-program P, (i) we denote with r_A a rule $(r : A \xleftarrow{\alpha_r} B_1, ..., B_n,$ $\neg C_1, ..., \neg C_m; \langle f_d, f_p, f_c \rangle) \in P^*$, whose head is A; (ii) given an interpretation I such that each premise in the body of r_A is defined under I, with $I(r_A)$ we denote the evaluation of the body of r_A w.r.t. I, *i.e.* $I(r_A) = f_p(\alpha_r, f_c(\{I(B_1),$ $..., I(B_n), \neg I(C_1), ..., \neg I(C_m)\}))$; and (iii) $I(r_A)$ is undefined in case some premise in the body is undefined in I, except for the case where there is an i such that $I(B_i) = \bot$ or $I(C_i) = \top$. In that case, we define $I(r_A) = \bot$.

Definition 2 (Satisfaction of a np-program). *A partial interpretation I satisfies (is a model of) P, denoted $\models_I P$, iff $\forall A \in \mathcal{HB}_P$:*

1. *if there is a rule $r_A \in P^*$ such that $I(r_A) = \top$, then $I(A) = \top$;*
2. *if for all rules $r_A \in P^*$, $I(r_A)$ is defined, then $I(A) \succeq f_d(X)$, where $X = \{I(r_A) : r_A \in P^*\}$. f_d is the disjunction function associated with $\pi(A)$, the predicate symbol of A.* ∎

Example 4. In Example 3, the interpretations I_x^y are all models of P. The interpretation I undefined on A and B is a model of P as well. □

Restricting our attention to positive programs only, the definition of satisfiability of np-programs reduces to that of satisfiability of p-programs defined in [11], where the interpretation I is not partial but total, *i.e.* defined for all atoms in $\mathcal{HB}(P)$. Note that for total interpretations, case 1 is a consequence of case 2.

From now on, for ease of presentation and without loss of generality, by "programs" we mean "instantiated" programs. We extend the ordering on $\mathcal{T}$ to the space of interpretations $\mathcal{V}_P(\mathcal{T})$. Let I_1 and I_2 be in $\mathcal{V}_P(\mathcal{T})$, then $I_1 \preceq I_2$ if and only if $I_1(A) \preceq I_2(A)$ for all ground atoms A. Under this ordering $\mathcal{V}_P(\mathcal{T})$ becomes a complete lattice, and we have $(I_1 \otimes I_2)(A) = I_1(A) \otimes I_2(A)$, and similarly for the other operators. The actions of functions can be extended from atoms to formulae as follows: $I(f_c(X, Y)) = f_c(I(X), I(Y))$, and similarly for the other functions. Finally, for all α in $\mathcal{T}$ and for all I in $\mathcal{V}_P(\mathcal{T})$, $I(\alpha) = \alpha$.

We now define a new operator T_P^H inspired by [5,12]. That operator is parameterized by an interpretation H on $\{\bot, \top\}$. That interpretation represents our default knowledge and we will call it a *hypothesis* to stretch the fact that it represents default knowledge and not "sure knowledge". Such a hypothesis asserts that some atoms are assumed $\bot$ (false) and some others are assumed to be $\top$ (true). In the context of logic programming with uncertainty, a more general approach would consist in considering any interpretation over $\mathcal{T}$ as a possible assumption. Nevertheless, the need of non-uniform assumptions like those of the type defined in this paper, *i.e.* by default the truth value of an atom maybe *true*, *false* or *unknown*, where already considered of interest by the literature [6,12]. We are aware that this is a limitation and that allowing a hypothesis being any interpretation would give us the most complete approach. But yet unresolved computational difficulties prevent us to consider the generalised case.

The operator T_P^H infers new information from two interpretations: the first one is used to evaluate the positive literals, while the second one is used to evaluate the negative literals of the bodies of rules in P.

Definition 3 (Parameterized immediate consequence operator). *Let P and H be any np-program and a hypothesis, respectively. The immediate consequence operator T_P^H is a mapping from $\mathcal{V}_P(\mathcal{T}) \times \mathcal{V}_P(\mathcal{T})$ to $\mathcal{V}_P(\mathcal{T})$, defined as follows: for every pair (I, J) of interpretations in $\mathcal{V}_P(\mathcal{T})$, for every atom A, if there is no rule in P with A as its head, then $T_P^H(I, J)(A) = H(A)$, else $T_P^H(I, J)(A) = f_d(X)$, where f_d is the disjunction function associated with $\pi(A)$, the predicate symbol of A, and $X = \{f_p(\alpha_r, f_c(\{I(B_1), \dots, I(B_n), \neg J(C_1), \dots, \neg J(C_m)\})) : (r : A \xleftarrow{\alpha_r} B_1, \dots, B_n, \neg C_1, \dots, \neg C_m; \langle f_d, f_p, f_c \rangle) \in P\}$.* ∎

Note that in case negation is absent and H assigns the value $\perp$ to all the atoms, then T_P^H reduces to the immediate consequence operator defined in [11].

Proposition 1. *T_P^H is monotonic in its first argument, and anti-monotonic in its second argument w.r.t. $\preceq$.* ∎

Using Proposition 1 and the Knaster-Tarsky theorem, we can define an operator S_P^H, likewise [7] and derived from T_P^H, that takes an interpretation J as input, first evaluates the negative literals of the program w.r.t. J, and then returns the model of the resulting "positive" np-program obtained by iterations of T_P^H beginning with H. But, in order to deal with non-uniform hypotheses, we need first to define the notion of stratification w.r.t. positive cycles.

Definition 4 (Extended positive cycle). *A positive cycle of P is a set of rules $\{r_{A_1}, \dots, r_{A_n}\}$ of P such that for $1 \leq i \leq n$, A_i (resp. A_n) appears positively in the body of $r_{A_{i+1}}$ (resp. r_{A_1}). An extended positive cycle is a positive cycle C extended with the rules in P whose head is the head of one of the rules of C.* ∎

Definition 5 (Stratification w.r.t. extended positive cycles). *A stratification w.r.t. extended positive cycles of a np-program P is a sequence of np-programs $P_1, \dots, P_n$ such that for the mapping σ from rules of P to $[1...n]$,*

1. *$P_1, \dots, P_n$ is a partition of P and every rule r is in $P_{\sigma(r)}$;*
2. *for any r_1 and r_2 in P, where the head of r_2 appears in the body of r_1 and there is no extended positive cycle of P containing r_1, $\sigma(r_1) = \sigma(r_2)$ holds;*
3. *for any r_1 and r_2 in P appearing in the same extended positive cycle, $\sigma(r_1) = \sigma(r_2)$ holds;*
4. *if r_1 and r_2 in P are such that the head of r_2 appears in the body of r_1 and there is an extended positive cycle of P containing r_1 but no extended positive cycle of P containing both r_1 and r_2, then $\sigma(r_2) < \sigma(r_1)$ holds.* ∎

Note that every np-program has a stratification w.r.t. extended positive cycles.

Proposition 2. *Given a np-program P with a stratification $P_1 = P$ w.r.t. extended positive cycles, an interpretation J be over $\mathcal{T}$ and a partial hypothesis H over $\{\perp, \top\}$ such that for all extended positive cycles $\{r_{A_1}, \dots, r_{A_k}\}$ of P, $H(A_1) = \dots = H(A_k)$ holds. Then the sequence defined by $a_0 = H$ and $a_{n+1} = T_P^H(a_n, J)$ converges.* ∎

Definition 6 (The parameterized alternating operator S_P^H). *Consider P with stratification w.r.t. the extended positive cycles $P_1, ..., P_n$ and let J be an interpretation over $\mathcal{T}$. Let H be an interpretation over $\{\bot, \top\}$ such that for all extended positive cycles $\{r_{A_1}, ..., r_{A_k}\}$ of P, $H(A_1) = ... = H(A_k)$ holds. Then $S_P^H(J)$ is the limit of the following sequence: (i) a_1 is the iterated fixpoint of the function $\lambda x.T_{P_1}^H(x, J)$ obtained when beginning the computation with H; (ii) a_i is the iterated fixpoint of the function $\lambda x.T_{P_1 \cup ... \cup P_i}^H(x, J)$ obtained when beginning the computation with a_{i-1}.* ∎

Intuitively, during the computation of $S_P^H(J)$, we fix the value of the negative premises in P with their values in J. Then we consider the "positive program" and evaluate that program stratum by stratum. After the evaluation of a stratum, we know that the knowledge obtained cannot be modified by what we will infer by activating the rules of the next strata. While a program may have more than one stratification w.r.t. extended positive cycles, the result of the computation does not depend on the stratification used for the computation. Note that the notion of stratification and the condition on H that we have introduced are indispensable for the convergence of the computation.

Example 5. Let $H = \{A : \top, B : \bot, C : \bot, D : \bot\}$ be a hypothesis and let $P = \{A \leftarrow \bot, B \leftarrow \bot, C \leftarrow A, D \leftarrow B, C \leftarrow D, D \leftarrow C\}$. If we compute the sequence $I_0 = H$, $I_i = T_P^H(I_{i-1}, J)$ then we have $I_1 = \{A : \bot, B : \bot, C : \top, D : \bot\}$, $I_2 = \{A : \bot, B : \bot, C : \bot, D : \top\}$, $I_3 = \{A : \bot, B : \bot, C : \top, D : \bot\}, ...$ This computation does not terminate. If we consider the definition of S_P^H, then we have a stratification of P with two strata: the first one contains the two first rules of P and the second one the four last rules of P. The computation terminates, and we have $I_1 = I_2 = \{A : \bot, B : \bot, C : \bot, D : \bot\}$. □

Example 6. Let $P = \{A \leftarrow B, B \leftarrow A\}$ and $H = \{A : \top, B : \bot\}$. The condition on H is not satisfied, *i.e.* $H(A) \neq H(B)$, and the computation does not terminate. □

3   Semantics under Non-uniform Assumptions

In this section we will determine what model, among all the models, is the intended model of a np-program w.r.t. a given hypothesis. For the rest of the paper, if not stated otherwise, *any hypothesis is supposed to assign the same default value to the atoms that are heads of rules of a same extended positive cycle*. From Proposition 1, we derive the following property of S_P^H.

Proposition 3. *Given P and a total non-uniform hypothesis H, S_P^H is anti-monotone w.r.t. $\preceq$ and, thus $S_P^H \circ S_P^H$ is monotone.* ∎

There is a well-know property, which derives from the Knaster-Tarski theorem and deals with anti-monotone functions on complete lattices:

Proposition 4 ([19]). *For a anti-monotone function f on a complete lattice $\mathcal{T}$, there are two extreme oscillation points of f, μ and ν in $\mathcal{T}$, such that: (i) μ and ν are the least and greatest fixpoint of the composition $f \circ f$; (ii) f oscillates between μ and ν, i.e. $f(\mu) = \nu$ and $f(\nu) = \mu$; (iii) if x and y are also elements of $\mathcal{T}$ between which f oscillates then x and y lie between μ and ν.* ∎

Under the ordering $\preceq$, S_P^H is anti-monotone and $\mathcal{V}_P(\mathcal{T})$ is a complete lattice, so S_P^H has two extreme oscillation points under this ordering. Let $I_\perp$ be the interpretation that assigns the value $\perp$ to all atoms of $\mathcal{HB}(P)$, i.e. the minimal element of $\mathcal{V}_P(\mathcal{T})$ w.r.t. $\preceq$, while let $I_\top$ be the interpretation that assigns the value $\top$ to all atoms of $\mathcal{HB}(P)$, i.e. the maximal element of $\mathcal{V}_P(\mathcal{T})$ w.r.t. $\preceq$.

Proposition 5. *Let P and H be any np-program and a total non-uniform hypothesis, respectively. S_P^H has two extreme oscillation points, $S_\perp^H = (S_P^H \circ S_P^H)^\infty(I_\perp)$ and $S_\top^H = (S_P^H \circ S_P^H)^\infty(I_\top)$, with $S_\perp^H \preceq S_\top^H$* [2]. ∎

Similarly to van Gelder's alternating fixpoint approach [7], $S_\perp^H$ and $S_\top^H$ are respectively a under-estimation and an over-estimation of P, but w.r.t. any hypothesis H. As the meaning of P we propose to consider as defined only the atoms whose values coincide in both limit interpretations. The truth value of atoms, whose truth value oscillates the "unknown" value is assigned.

Proposition 6. *Let P and H be any np-program and a total non-uniform hypothesis, respectively. Then $\models_{S_\perp^H \cap S_\top^H} P$.* ∎

The interpretation $S_\perp^H \cap S_\top^H$ is a model of P, and will be the intended meaning or semantics of P w.r.t. the assumption H.

Definition 7 (Compromise semantics). *The compromise semantics of np-program P w.r.t. a total non-uniform assumption H is defined by $M^H(P) = S_\perp^H \cap S_\top^H$.* ∎

Example 7. Let P be the np-program of Example 2 and $I_\perp$, then we have[3] $M^{I_\perp}(P) \supset \{$s(John):0.8, s(Jim):0.6, s(Ted):0, i(John):0, i(Jim):0.664, i(Ted):0, c(John):1, c(Jim):0.6, c(Ted):1$\}$. Now let H be the following hypothesis $H = \{$m(X):0, w(x):0, s(X):0, p(X):1, a(X,Y):0, f(X,Y):0, i(X):1, c(X):0$\}$. Then we have $M^H(P) \supset \{$s(John):0.8, s(Jim):0.6, s(Ted):0, i(John):0.2, i(Jim):0.7984, i(Ted):1, c(John):0.8, c(Jim):0.6, c(Ted):0$\}$. □

Finally, let us briefly show the difficulties introduced in case generalised hypotheses are allowed, as anticipated previously.

Example 8. Given the np-program $P = \{A \leftarrow B, C; B \leftarrow A; B \leftarrow D\}$ and the hypothesis H such that $H(A) = 0.3, H(B) = 0.3, H(C) = 0.5, H(D) = 0.5$. As disjunction and conjunction functions, we will consider the functions $f_d(x, y) = \min\{1, x+y\}$ and $f_c(x, y) = \max\{0, x+y-1\}$, which are also known as the Łukasiewicz disjunction and conjunction, respectively. Consider any interpretation J for negative literals. Now, it can be verified that the iterated fixpoint a_1 of the function $\lambda x.T_P^H(x, J)$ obtained when beginning the computation with H, as specified in Definition 6, does not exist. Indeed, the iteration oscillates between the two interpretations $I = \{A: 0, B: 0.8, C: 0.5, D: 0.5\}$ and $I' = \{A: 0.3, B: 0.5, C: 0.5, D: 0.5\}$. Therefore, the limit of $S_P^H(J)$ is undefined and, thus, the compromise semantics of P is undefined as well. □

---

[2] For ease, we omit the P in $S_\perp^H$ and $S_\top^H$.

[3] In the following, for ease of presentation, we will denote each predicate symbol of P by its first letter. Moreover, in the different semantics of P, we will indicate only the values of atoms associated to the symbols of predicates **suspect**, **innocent** and **charge**.

Until know we dealt with total non-uniform assumptions. Let us now address the case where assumptions may be partial. A possible idea to deal with such a situation is to introduce a new logical value u and define a new lattice $\mathcal{T}' = \mathcal{T} \cup \{u\}$. That value represents an unknown or undefined value that means that u is used to replace a value in $\mathcal{T}$ that is currently not known. We would like to extend conjunction and disjunction functions in the following way: (i) $f_c(u, x) =$ if $x \neq \bot$ then u else $\bot$; and (ii) $f_d(u, x) =$ if $x \neq \top$ then u else $\top$. We need also to extend the order $\preceq$ in $\mathcal{T}$ to $\mathcal{T}'$. We know that for all $x \in \mathcal{T}'$, $\bot \preceq x \preceq \top$. But, from the first constraint it follows that $u \preceq x$ for all $x \neq \bot$ and, similarly, from the second one it follows that $x \preceq u$ for all $x \neq \top$. But then, there is a solution only if $\mathcal{T} = \{\bot, \top\}$. We follow another way: a partial hypothesis H on $\{\bot, \top\}$ can be seen as the intersection between two total interpretations $\underline{H}$ and $\overline{H}$, where $\underline{H}$ is as H except that $\bot$ is assumed for the unknown atoms, while $\overline{H}$ is as H except that $\top$ is assumed for the unknown atoms. Note that $\underline{H} \cap \overline{H} = H$. In order to assign a semantics to a np-program w.r.t. such a partial interpretation, we propose to consider the intersection or consensus between the two semantics.

Proposition 7. *Let P be any np-program and let H be a partial non-uniform hypothesis. It follows that* $\models_{M\underline{H}(P) \cap M\overline{H}(P)} P$. ∎

Definition 8 (Consensus semantics w.r.t. H). *Let P be any np-program and let H be a partial non-uniform hypothesis. The* consensus semantics *of P w.r.t. H, $\mathcal{C}^H(P)$, is defined by $\mathcal{C}^H(P) = M^{\underline{H}}(P) \cap M^{\overline{H}}(P)$[4].* ∎

Example 9. Given P of Example 2 and H as suggested in the introduction, *i.e.* $H = \{$m(X):0, w(x):0, s(X):0, p(X):1$\}$, it follows that $\mathcal{C}^H(P) \supset \{$s(John) : 0.8, s(Jim):0.6, s(Ted):0, i(Ted):1, c(John):0.8, c(Jim):0.6, c(Ted):0$\}$. □

4   Comparisons with Usual Semantics

One obvious question would be whether hypothesis maybe simulated by just adding the facts to the program and compute the semantics according to classical approach. This is not true as the following example shows.

Example 10. Let $P = \{A \leftarrow B; B \leftarrow A; D \leftarrow C; C \leftarrow D\}$ and consider the assumption H such that $H(A) = \bot$, and $H(B) = \bot$. The consensus semantics is $\{A : \bot, B : \bot\}$. Now, suppose that we add $A \leftarrow \bot$ and $B \leftarrow \bot$ to P. Then we can consider two cases, whether we are using the OWA or the CWA. In the former case, the classical semantics of the program will be $\emptyset$, while in the latter example the classical semantics of the program will be $\{A : \bot, B : \bot, C : \bot; D : \bot\}$, which are both different from the consensus semantics. □

Our semantics extends the Lakshmanan and Shiri's semantics [11] of parametric programs to normal parametric programs. This is due to the fact that the machinery developed in order to deal with negation has no effect on positive programs, thus for the everywhere false hypothesis $I_\bot$, we have

---

[4] Note that any compromise semantics is also a consensus semantics.

Proposition 8. *If P is a np-program without negation then the compromise semantics $M^{I_\perp}(P)$ of P (or equivalently the consensus semantics $C^{I_\perp}(P)$) w.r.t. the hypothesis $I_\perp$ coincides with the Lakshmanan and Shiri's semantics of P.* ∎

Now, we compare our semantics with the well-founded semantics [18].

Proposition 9. *Let P be a Datalog program with negation. The compromise semantics $M^{I_\perp}(P)$ of P (or equivalently the consensus semantics $C^{I_\perp}(P)$) w.r.t. the hypothesis $I_\perp$ coincides with the well-founded semantics of P.* ∎

Our approach extends the well-founded semantics to the IB framework as well.

Example 11. Consider Example 2 and hypothesis $I_\perp$. Given the Datalog program with negation P' replacing in P all the truth values by 1, $f_d = \oplus$ and $f_c = \otimes$, $C^{I_\perp}(P') \supset \{\texttt{s(John)}:1, \texttt{s(Jim)}:1, \texttt{s(Ted)}:0, \texttt{i(John)}:0, \texttt{i(Jim)}:0, \texttt{i(Ted)}:0, \texttt{c(John)}:1, \texttt{c(Jim)}:1, \texttt{c(Ted)}:1\}$ follows. □

Finally, we can compare the semantics with the usual semantics and in particular with the Kripke-Kleene semantics [4]. Let us define the *almost everywhere empty hypothesis* H_P w.r.t. P as follows: $H(A) = \perp$ if A is not the head of any rule, else $H(A)$ is undefined.

Proposition 10. *Let P be a Datalog program with negation and H_P the almost everywhere empty hypothesis w.r.t. P. Let $WFS(P)$ be the well-founded semantics of P and $KK(P)$ be the Kripke-Kleene semantics of P. Then $KK(P) \subseteq C^{H_P}(P) \subseteq WFS(P)$ holds.* ∎

The consensus semantics $C^{H_P}(P)$ of P represents more knowledge than the Kripke-Kleene semantics of P, but less than the well-founded semantics of P. This results shows the well-known fact that the Kripke-Kleene semantics of P is weaker than the well-founded semantics of P.

Example 12. For $P = \{B \leftarrow A, B \leftarrow \neg A, A \leftarrow A\}$, $KK(P) = \emptyset \subset C^{H_P}(P) = \{B:\top\} \subset WFS(P) = \{A:\perp, B:\top\}$ holds. □

5   Conclusion

We have presented a framework for reasoning about uncertainty and negation in deductive databases and logic programming. Our framework uses parameterized semantics of implication-based logic programming with negation under non-uniform assumptions for the missing information. We have also seen that when we restrict our framework to uniform assumptions only, our approach captures and extends the semantics of conventional logic programs. Obviously, having considered a restricted, still useful, form of hypothesis, puts the generalisation to arbitrary hypothesis to be our primary topic for future work.

References

1. True H. Cao. Annotated fuzzy logic programs. *Fuzzy Sets and Systems*, 113(2):277–298, 2000.
2. Alex Dekhtyar and V.S. Subrahmanian. Hybrid probabilistic programs. *Journal of Logic Programming*, 43(3):187–250, 2000.
3. Didier Dubois, Jérome Lang, and Henri Prade. Towards possibilistic logic programming. In *Proc. of the 8th Int. Conf. on Logic Programming (ICLP-91)*, pages 581–595. The MIT Press, 1991.
4. Melvin Fitting. A Kripke-Kleene semantics for logic programs. *Journal of Logic Programming*, 2(4):295–312, 1985.
5. Melvin Fitting. The family of stable models. *Journal of Logic Programming*, 17(2/3 & 4):197–225, 1993.
6. Norbert Fuhr. Probabilistic datalog: Implementing logical information retrieval for advanced applications. *Journal of the American Society for Information Science*, 51(2):95–110, 2000.
7. Allen Van Gelder. The alternating fixpoint of logic programs with negation. In *Proc. of the 8th ACM SIGACT SIGMOD Sym. on Principles of Database Systems (PODS-89)*, pages 1–10, 1989.
8. M. Kifer and Ai Li. On the semantics of rule-based expert systems with uncertainty. In *Proc. of the Int. Conf. on Database Theory (ICDT-88)*, number 326 in Lecture Notes in Computer Science, pages 102–117. Springer-Verlag, 1988.
9. Michael Kifer and V.S. Subrahmanian. Theory of generalized annotaded logic programming and its applications. *Journal of Logic Programming*, 12:335–367, 1992.
10. Laks V.S. Lakshmanan and Nematollaah Shiri. Probabilistic deductive databases. In *Int'l Logic Programming Symposium*, pages 254–268, 1994.
11. Laks V.S. Lakshmanan and Nematollaah Shiri. A parametric approach to deductive databases with uncertainty. *IEEE Transactions on Knowledge and Data Engineering*, 13(4):554–570, 2001.
12. Y. Loyer, N Spyratos, and D. Stamate. Integration of information in four-valued logics under non-uniform assumptions. In *Proceedings of the 30th IEEE International Symposium on Multi-Valued Logics (ISMVL 2000)*, pages 185–191, Portland, Oregon, 2000. IEEE Press.
13. Thomas Lukasiewicz. Probabilistic logic programming. In *Proc. of the 13th European Conf. on Artificial Intelligence (ECAI-98)*, pages 388–392, Brighton (England), August 1998.
14. Raymond Ng and V.S. Subrahmanian. Stable model semantics for probabilistic deductive databases. In Zbigniew W. Ras and Maria Zemenkova, editors, *Proc. of the 6th Int. Sym. on Methodologies for Intelligent Systems (ISMIS-91)*, number 542 in Lecture Notes in Artificial Intelligence, pages 163–171. Springer-Verlag, 1991.
15. Raymond Ng and V.S. Subrahmanian. Probabilistic logic programming. *Information and Computation*, 101(2):150–201, 1993.
16. Ehud Y. Shapiro. Logic programs with uncertainties: A tool for implementing rule-based systems. In *Proc. of the 8th Int. Joint Conf. on Artificial Intelligence (IJCAI-83)*, pages 529–532, 1983.
17. M.H. van Emden. Quantitative deduction and its fixpoint theory. *Journal of Philosophical Logic*, (1):37–53, 1986.
18. Allen Van Gelder, Kenneth A. Ross, and John S. Schlimpf. The well-founded semantics for general logic programs. *Journal of the ACM*, 38(3):620–650, January 1991.
19. S. Yablo. Truth and reflection. *Journal of Philosophical Logic*, 14:297–349, 1985.

A Qualitative Reasoning
with Nuanced Information

Mazen El-Sayed and Daniel Pacholczyk

University of Angers, 2 Boulevard Lavoisier, 49045 ANGERS Cedex 01, France
{elsayed,pacho}@univ-angers.fr

Abstract. This paper presents a new model for handling *nuanced information* expressed in an affirmative form like "x is m_α A". In this model, *nuanced information* are represented in a qualitative way within a symbolic context. For that purpose, vague terms and linguistic modifiers that operate on them are defined. The model presented is based on a symbolic M-valued predicate logic and provides a new deduction rule generalizing the Modus Ponens rule.

Keywords: Knowledge representation and reasoning, Imprecision, Vagueness, Multiset theory, Many-valued logic.

1 Introduction

In this paper, we present a model dealing with *nuanced information* expressed in an affirmative form as they may appear in knowledge bases including, rules like "if the tomato is red then it's ripe" and facts like, "the tomato is very red". The model has been conceived in such a way that the user can deal with statements expressed in natural language, that is to say, referring to a *graduation scale* containing a finite number of *nuances*. These *nuanced statements*, like *"Jo is rather tall"* or *"Jo is really very young"*, can be represented more formally under the form "x is m_α A" where m_α and A are labels denoting respectively a nuance and a vague term. The management of this type of knowledge consists both on the representation of this knowledge and their exploitation. There are mainly two formalisms for handling with nuanced information.

The first one refers to *fuzzy logic* introduced by Zadeh in [12,13] and which is used when the imprecise information is evaluated in a *numerical way*. In this formalism, each vague term, like "red" and "young", is represented by a fuzzy set. This last is defined by a *membership function* that characterizes the gradual membership to the fuzzy set and indicates some semantic properties of the term like *precision, imprecision and fuzziness*. The nuances m_α are defined as *fuzzy modifiers* [3,4,11] that operate on fuzzy sets by modifying some of their semantic properties. The second formalism refers to a symbolic many-valued logic [9,11] which is used when the imprecise information is evaluated in a *symbolic way*. This logic is the logical counterpart of *multiset theory* introduced by De Glas in [9]. This theory can be seen as an axiomatic approach of fuzzy sets theory and in which, the nuances m_α represent *linguistic membership degrees* of this

S. Flesca et al. (Eds.): JELIA 2002, LNAI 2424, pp. 283–295, 2002.

theory. Agreeing on this idea, Pacholczyk [11] considers nevertheless that some nuances of natural language can not be interpreted as membership degrees and must be instead defined such as *linguistic modifiers*. The modifiers have not been studied within a multiset context. The introduction of linguistic modifiers in this context constitutes a departure idea of our work. As we noticed previously, the modifiers operate on the term by modifying some of their semantic properties. Within a multiset context, there are not concepts used to represent the semantic properties of a term. So, before defining linguistic modifiers we have to propose a new representation model based on multiset theory and in which we can describe concretely a vague term by defining their semantic properties. This will be our first contribution in this paper. The new model generalizes the results of fuzzy sets theory, namely when the domains are not necessarily numerical scales. Our basic idea is to associate to each vague term a new *symbolic* concept called *"rule"*. This symbolic concept is equivalent to the membership function within a fuzzy context.

In other words, its geometry (1) modelizes the gradual membership to the multiset representing the term, and (2) indicates some semantic properties for the term like *precision, imprecision and fuzziness*.

Then, based on this new concept we can define the *linguistic modifiers* within a multiset context.

Our second contribution in this paper is to propose a deduction rule dealing with nuanced information. For that purpose, we propose a deduction rule generalizing the *Modus Ponens* rule in a many-valued logic proposed by Pacholczyk [11]. Note that the first version of this rule has been proposed in a fuzzy context by Zadeh [13] and has been studied later by various authors [1,3,5,10]:

Rule	: if "X is A" then "Y is B"
Fact	: "X is A'"
Conclusion	: "Y is B'"

Where X and Y are fuzzy variables and A, B, A' and B' are fuzzy concepts.

This paper is organized as follows. In section 2, we present briefly the basic concepts of the M-valued logic which forms the backbone of our work. Section 3 introduces our new approach for the symbolic representation of vague terms. In section 4, we define new linguistic modifiers in a purely symbolic way. In section 5, we propose a new *Generalized Modus Ponens* rule.

2   M-Valued Predicate Logic

Consider the statement "the tomato is v_α red" where v_α is a nuance of natural language. Zadeh [13] uses a fuzzy modifier for representing, from the fuzzy set "red", the fuzzy set "v_α red". So, "x is v_α A" is interpreted by Zadeh as "x is $(v_\alpha$ A)" and regarded as many-valued statement. De Glas [9,11] proposed another interpretation in which "x is v_α A" means "x (is v_α) A", and then regarded as boolean statement. According to De Glas, the term v_α linguistically expresses the degree to which the object x satisfies the term A. Within a multiset context, to a vague term A and a nuance v_α are associated respectively a multiset $\mathbb{A}$ and a symbolic degree τ_α. So, the statement "x is v_α A" means that x belongs to multiset $\mathbb{A}$ with a degree τ_α [1]. The M-valued predicate logic [11] forms the logical counterpart of the multiset theory. In this logic, the qualitative values v_α and τ_α are associated by the relation: "x is v_α A" $\Leftrightarrow$ "x is v_α A" is true $\Leftrightarrow$ "x is A" is τ_α−true.

2.1   Algebraic Structures

This logic supposes that the degrees of truth are symbolic degrees which form an ordered set $\mathcal{L}_M = \{\tau_\alpha, \alpha \in [1, M]\}$. This set is provided with the relation of a total order: $\tau_\alpha \leq \tau_\beta \Leftrightarrow \alpha \leq \beta$, and whose smallest element is τ_1 and the largest element is τ_M. We can then define in $\mathcal{L}_M$ two operators $\wedge$ and $\vee$ and a decreasing involution $\sim$ as follows: $\tau_\alpha \vee \tau_\beta = \tau_{max(\alpha,\beta)}, \tau_\alpha \wedge \tau_\beta = \tau_{min(\alpha,\beta)}$ and $\sim \tau_\alpha = \tau_{M+1-\alpha}$. One obtains then a chain $\{\mathcal{L}_M, \vee, \wedge, \leq\}$ having the structure of De Morgan lattice [11]. On this set, an implication $\rightarrow$ and a T-norm T can be defined respectively as follows: $\tau_\alpha \rightarrow \tau_\beta = \tau_{min(\beta-\alpha+M,M)}$ and $T(\tau_\alpha, \tau_\beta) = \tau_{max(\beta+\alpha-M,1)}$.

Example 1. For example, by choosing M=9, we can introduce: $\mathcal{L}_9=\{not\ at\ all, little, enough, fairly, moderately, quite, almost, nearly, completely\}$.

In [11], Pacholczyk noticed that some nuances like *"very"* and *"really"*, can not be interpreted as truth degrees and they must be defined such as linguistic modifiers. In fact, "m_α A" represent new multiset result from the multiset A. In section 4, we will define these modifiers in the multiset theory. They generalize some fuzzy modifiers [3,4,13] within a purely symbolic context. A fuzzy modifier operates on fuzzy sets by modifying their membership functions. In the following section, we propose a symbolic model for vague terms while inspiring by the representation method within a fuzzy context. More precisely, we associate to each multiset a symbolic concept which has the same role as the membership function associated to a fuzzy set.

3   Symbolic Representation of Vague Terms

Let us suppose that our knowledge base is characterized by a finite number of concepts C_i. A set of terms P_{ik} is associated with each concept C_i, whose respective domains is denoted as X_i. The terms P_{ik} are said to be the *basic terms* connected with the concept C_i. As an example, basic terms such as *"small"*, *"moderate"* and *"tall"* are associated with the particular concept *"size"*. A finite set of *linguistic modifiers* m_α allows to define *nuanced term*, denoted as "$m_\alpha P_{ik}$". Linguists distinguish [6] three signed terms: a negative term like "small", a positive term like "tall" and a neutral term like "moderate". This distinction is

---

[1] In the multiset theory, $x \in_\alpha A \Leftrightarrow$ x belongs to multiset $\mathbb{A}$ with a τ_α degree. It corresponds to $\mu_{\mathbb{A}}(x) = \tau_\alpha$ within a fuzzy context [12].

important since we define the linguistic modifiers. We suppose that the set of basic terms covers the domain X_i and that each one of these terms is signed. Given that each term P_{ik} is represented by a multiset denoted as P_{ik}, we can propose the following axiom:

Axiom 1. *For each concept C_i, defined on a domain X_i, is associated a family of multisets, denoted as $\mathbb{C}_i = \{P_{i1}, ..., P_{iN}\}$, which covers the domain X_i. In other words, $\forall x \in X_i, \exists\ P_{ik} \in \mathbb{C}_i, \exists \alpha > 1 \Rightarrow x \in_\alpha P_{ik}$.*

3.1 Representation with *"rules"*

In the following, we propose a symbolic representation to modelize the vague terms which define a "concept". We suppose that a domain of a vague term, denoted by X, is not necessarily a numerical scale. It can for example be "set of men", "set of animals", etc. This domain is simulated by a *"rule"* (cf. Fig. 1) representing an arbitrary set of objects. Thus, the set {small, moderate, tall} can be represented as follows:

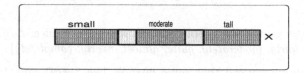

Fig. 1. Representation with *"rule"* of a domain X

The basic idea is to associate to each multiset a concept which represents a symbolic equivalent to the membership function in the fuzzy sets theory. In our work, we focus only on to vague terms which can be represented by a membership L-R function. The new concept, called "rule", has a geometry similar to a membership L-R function and its role is to illustrate the membership graduality to the multiset. In order to define the geometry of this "rule", we use concepts similar to those defined within a fuzzy context like the core, the support and the fuzzy part of a fuzzy set [13]. The core represents the typical elements of the term, the support contains the elements satisfying at least a little the term, and the fuzzy part represents the atypical elements satisfying partially the term. For example, for the term "tall", the core of the associated multiset represents the perfectly tall men, its support represents the men qualified in the class of tall people, and its fuzzy part represents the more or less tall men.

Definition 1. *The core of a multiset P, denoted as Core(P), is defined by:* $Core(P) = \{x \in X \mid x \in_M P\}$.

Definition 2. *The fuzzy part of a multiset P, denoted as F(P), is defined by:* $F(P) = \{x \in X \mid x \in_\alpha P\ and\ \alpha \in [2, M-1]\}$.

Definition 3. *The support of a multiset P, denoted as Sp(P), is defined by:*
$Sp(P) = \{x \in X \mid x \in_\alpha P \text{ and } \tau_\alpha > \tau_1\}$.

We associate for each multiset a "rule" that contains the elements of its support (cf. Fig. 2). Since for any multiset P_i, $Sp(P_i) = Core(P_i) \cup F(P_i)$ and by supposing that the fuzzy part is the union of two disjoined subsets, we can say that the "rule" associated to a multiset is the union of three disjoined subsets: *the left fuzzy part, the right fuzzy part* and *the core*. For a multiset P_i, they are denoted respectively by L_i, R_i and C_i. In order to define formally the concept of directions (left and right) between subsets, we introduce a relation of strict order whose role is to order classical subsets in the universe X.

Definition 4. *Let A and B be two disjoined subsets of X. A is said to be on the left compared to B, denoted as $A \prec B$, if and only if, by traversing the "rule" X of left on the right, one meets A before meeting B.*

We use the relation which has been just introduced to define the fuzzy parts L_i and R_i. We want to say by the left fuzzy part of a multiset the subset of $F(P_i)$ located on the left of the core of this multiset. This part is maximal in the meaning of it contains all elements of $F(P_i)$ which are on the left of C_i. In other words, it represents the largest subset of $F(P_i)$ located on the left of C_i. In the same way, we can define the right fuzzy part of P_i as the largest subset of $F(P_i)$ located on the right of C_i. We can thus define them formally as follows.

Definition 5. *Let L_i be a subset of $F(P_i)$. Then, L_i is called left fuzzy part of P_i if and only if: $\forall A$, $A \subset F(P_i)$, if $A \prec C_i$ then $A \subset L_i$.*

Definition 6. *Let R_i be a subset of $F(P_i)$. Then, R_i is called right fuzzy part of P_i if and only if: $\forall A$, $A \subset F(P_i)$, if $C_i \prec A$ then $A \subset R_i$.*

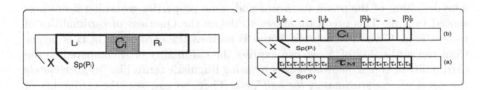

Fig. 2. Parts of a *"rule"*   Fig. 3. Graduality in a *"rule"*

We recall that each fuzzy part contains the elements belonging to P_i with degrees varying from τ_2 to τ_{M-1}. We thus suppose that each fuzzy part L_i and R_i is the union of M-2 subsets which partition it and of which each one gathers the elements belonging to P_i with the same degree (cf. Fig. 3). These subsets are defined in the following way:

Definition 7. *The set of the elements of L_i belonging to P_i with a τ_α degree, denoted as $[L_i]_\alpha$, is defined as follows: $[L_i]_\alpha = \{x \in L_i \mid x \in_\alpha P_i\}$.*

Definition 8. *The set of the elements of R_i belonging to P_i with a τ_α degree, denoted as $[R_i]_\alpha$, is defined as follows: $[R_i]_\alpha = \{x \in R_i \mid x \in_\alpha P_i\}$.*

In order to keep a similarity with the fuzzy sets of type L-R, we choose to place, in a "rule" associated to a multiset, the subsets $[L_i]_\alpha$ and $[R_i]_\alpha$ so that the larger α is, the closer the $[L_i]_\alpha$ sets and $[R_i]_\alpha$ are to the core C_i (cf. Fig. 3). That can be interpreted as follows: the elements of the core of a term represent the typical elements of this term, and the more one object moves away from the core, the less it satisfies the term. Finally, we can propose the definition of a multiset represented by a "rule".

Definition 9. *A multiset P_i is defined by the triplet (L_i, C_i, R_i), denoted as $P_i = (L_i, C_i, R_i)$, such that:*

- *$\{L_i, C_i, R_i\}$ is totally ordered by the relation $\prec$ and partitions $Sp(P_i)$,*
- *$\{[L_i]_2, ..., [L_i]_{M-1}\}$ is totally ordered by the relation $\prec$ and partitions L_i,*
- *$\{[R_i]_{M-1}, ..., [R_i]_2\}$ is totally ordered by the relation $\prec$ and partitions R_i.*

One supposes that the "rules" associated to multisets have the same geometry but the position of each "rule" and the sizes (or the cardinalities) of its parts depend on the semantics of the term to which it is associated. In the paragraph 3.3, we introduce symbolic parameters to represent these "rules". These parameters are symbolic values using essentially the notion of symbolic cardinality of a subset. This notion is introduced briefly in the next paragraph.

3.2   Symbolic Quotient of Cardinalities

To model the notion of the cardinality of an ordinary subset, we use a binary predicate called *Rcard* and defined on boolean formulas of the logic language. The definition of the predicate *Rcard* and some properties governing it are presented in [7,8]. This predicate allows to define the Quotient of cardinalities of two subsets. Given two subsets A and B such as the cardinality of B is bigger than the cardinality of A, we can express the cardinality of A compared to the cardinality of B in a qualitative way by using linguistic terms like *"approximately the quarter"*, *"approximately the half"*, etc. Then, we can say "the cardinality of A is *"approximately the half"* among that of B". These terms constitute a set of M symbolic degrees of Quotient of cardinalities: $\mathcal{Q}_M = \{Q_\alpha, \alpha \in [1, M]\}$. More generally, we can say "the cardinality of A is Q_α among that of B" which will be denoted as A $\trianglelefteq_\alpha$ B.

Example 2. For M=9, we can introduce the following set: $\mathcal{Q}_9 = \{$*nothing at all, less of the quarter, approximately the quarter, approximately the third, approximately the half, approximately the two thirds, approximately the three quarters, near to equal, equal*$\}$.

3.3 Symbolic Parameters Defining a Multiset

Within a fuzzy context, a fuzzy set is characterized by a numerical parameters set. Within a symbolic context, we want to define a multiset by a symbolic parameters set. These parameters are given by experts which describe the "rule" in a qualitative way. We distinguish two types of parameters: parameters describing the sign of the term and the internal geometry of the "rule". The description of the internal geometry concerns (1) the relative sizes of the fuzzy parts and the core compared to the "rule", and (2) the relative size of each one of the $[L_i]_\alpha$ (respectively $[R_i]_\alpha$) subsets compared to L_i (respectively R_i). The second type of parameters relates to the size of the "rule" and its position in the domain. The position of a *"rule"* is given compared to another, known as multiset or "rule" of reference. For example, for the concept "size of men" described by the basic terms {small, moderate, tall} and presented in Fig. 1, we can say that *"moderate"* is on the right compared to *"small"* and *"tall"* on the right compared to *"moderate"*. Equivalently, we can say that *"moderate"* is on the left compared to *"tall"* and *"small"* on the left compared to *"moderate"*. Even, the "rules" representing two terms near one to the other, overlap. Thus, to locate a "rule" representing a multiset P_i, we introduce two parameters that indicate: (1) the position of this "rule" compared to a "rule" representing a multiset of reference P_r and (2) to what degree these "rules" overlap (cf. Fig. 4).

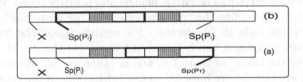

Fig. 4. Relative position for a *"rule"*

Then, we can introduce the following parameters to represent a multiset:

- $Q_{l_i} \in Q_M$: indicates the relative size of the left fuzzy part compared to the "rule". In other words, we have: $L_i \trianglelefteq_{l_i} Sp(P_i)$.
- $Q_{r_i} \in Q_M$: indicates the relative size of the right fuzzy part compared to the "rule" i.e. $R_i \trianglelefteq_{r_i} Sp(P_i)$.
- $Q_{c_i} \in Q_M$: indicates the relative size of the core compared to the "rule". In other words, we have: $C_i \trianglelefteq_{c_i} Sp(P_i)$.
- $\{Q_{\delta_\alpha}\}_{\alpha \in [2..M-1]}$: each Q_{δ_α} degree indicates the relative size of $[L_i]_\alpha$ compared to L_i. In other words, we have: $[L_i]_\alpha \trianglelefteq_{\delta_\alpha} L_i$.
- $\{Q_{\lambda_\alpha}\}_{\alpha \in [2..M-1]}$: each Q_{λ_α} degree indicates the relative size of $[R_i]_\alpha$ compared to R_i. In other words, we have: $[R_i]_\alpha \trianglelefteq_{\lambda_\alpha} R_i$.
- $Q_{\epsilon_i} \in Q_M$: indicates the relative size of the *"rule"* compared to the domain X. In other words, we have: $Sp(P_i) \trianglelefteq_{\epsilon_i} X$. This parameter determines the precision of the term. More this degree is bigger, more the term is imprecise.

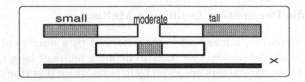

Fig. 5. Terms associated with the concept of *size of men*

- $\sigma_i \in \{-1, 0, +1\}$: indicates the sign of P_i. $\sigma_i = -1$ if P_i is negative, $\sigma_i = 0$ if P_i is neutral and $\sigma_i = +1$ if P_i is positive.
- $s_i \in \{\text{"}l\text{"}, \text{"}r\text{"}\}$: indicates the position of P_i compared to P_r. $s_i = \text{"}l\text{"}$ if P_i is on the left compared to P_r and $s_i = \text{"}r\text{"}$ if P_i on the right compared to P_r.
- $Q_{\rho_i} \in \mathcal{Q}_M$: indicates the relative size of the intersection between the "rules" representing respectively P_i and P_r i.e. $Sp(P_i \cap P_r) \trianglelefteq_{\rho_i} Sp(P_r)$.

Finally, we will represent a multiset P_i by:

$$P_i = \{< P_r, Q_{\rho_i}, s_i, Q_{\epsilon_i} >, < \sigma_i, Q_{l_i}, Q_{c_i}, Q_{r_i}, \{Q_{\delta_\alpha}\}_{\alpha \in [2..M-1]}, \{Q_{\lambda_\alpha}\}_{\alpha \in [2..M-1]} >\}.$$

Example 3. We consider the "size of men" concept which is described by the three following basic terms: $\mathbb{C} = \{P_i | i \in [1..3]\} = \{\text{small, moderate, tall}\}$ which are considered respectively as negative, neutral and positive terms. We can show, as an example, how to define the "rule" representing the term "tall". Its position is defined as on the right to "moderate". The relative size of the "rule" and the sizes of the parts forming it can be given as follows: (1) the size of the "rule" is "approximately the third" of that of X, and in other words, "approximately the third" of men are tall. So, we have $Q_{\epsilon_i} = Q_4$. (2) the size of the core is "approximately the quarter" of that of the "rule", and in other words, "approximately the quarter" of tall men are perfectly tall. Thus, we have $Q_{c_i} = Q_3$. In the same way, we can define the other parameters as $Q_{l_i} = Q_4$ and $Q_{r_i} = Q_4$ which mean respectively that the size of the left (resp. right) fuzzy part is "approximately the third" of that of the "rule". By choosing $\{Q_{\delta_\alpha}\}_\alpha = \{Q_{\lambda_\alpha}\}_\alpha = \{Q_3, Q_2, Q_2, Q_2, Q_2, Q_2, Q_2\}$, we can define the basic terms in the following way:

- *small:* $P_1 = \{< P_1, Q_M, \text{"}r\text{"}, Q_4 >, < -1, Q_1, Q_6, Q_4, \{Q_{\delta_\alpha}\}_\alpha, \{Q_{\lambda_\alpha}\}_\alpha >\}.$
- *moderate:* $P_2 = \{< P_1, Q_4, \text{"}r\text{"}, Q_4 >, < 0, Q_4, Q_3, Q_4, \{Q_{\delta_\alpha}\}_\alpha, \{Q_{\lambda_\alpha}\}_\alpha >\}.$
- *tall:* $P_3 = \{< P_2, Q_4, \text{"}r\text{"}, Q_4 >, < +1, Q_4, Q_6, Q_1, \{Q_{\delta_\alpha}\}_\alpha, \{Q_{\lambda_\alpha}\}_\alpha >\}.$

4   Linguistic Modifiers

We have noted previously that some nuances can not be interpreted as symbolic degrees and they must be defined as *linguistic modifiers* [3,11]. These modifiers provide new vague terms starting from a vague basic term. Thus, from a particular term *"tall"* one obtains new vague terms like *"very tall"* and *"really tall"*.

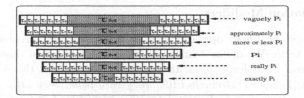

Fig. 6. Precision modifiers

In this section, we define linguistic modifiers in a completely symbolic way and we are interested in some modifiers known as precision modifiers and translation modifiers. We define these modifiers within a symbolic context in which one uses the *"rules"* representation of vague terms.

4.1   Precision Modifiers

The *precision modifiers* make it possible to increase or decrease the precision of the basic term. We distinguish two types of precision modifiers: contraction modifiers and dilation modifiers. A contraction (resp. dilation) modifier m produces nuanced term mP_i more (resp. less) precise than the basic term P_i. In other words, the "rule" associated to mP_i is smaller (resp. bigger) than that associated to P_i. We define these modifiers in a way that the contraction modifiers contract simultaneously the core and the support of a multiset P_i, and the dilation modifiers dilate them. The amplitude of the modification (contraction or dilation) for a precision modifier m is given by a new parameter denoted as τ_γ. The higher τ_γ, the more important the modification is. We give now two definitions for these types of modifiers.

Definition 10. *Let P_i be a multiset. m is said to be a τ_γ-contraction modifier if, and only if it is defined in the following way:*

1. *if $P_i = (L_i, C_i, R_i)$ then $mP_i = (L_i', C_i', R_i')$ such as $R_i' \trianglelefteq_M L_i$ and $R_i' \trianglelefteq_M R_i$*
2. *$\forall x, x \in_\alpha P_i$ with $\tau_\alpha < \tau_M \Rightarrow x \in_\beta mP_i$ such as $\beta = max(1, \alpha - \gamma + 1)$*

Definition 11. *Let P_i be a multiset. m is said to be a τ_γ-dilation modifier if, and only if it is defined in the following way:*

1. *if $P_i = (L_i, C_i, R_i)$ then $mP_i = (L_i', C_i', R_i')$ such as $L_i' \trianglelefteq_M L_i$ et $R_i' \trianglelefteq_M R_i$*
2. *$\forall x, x \in_\alpha P_i$ with $\tau_\alpha > \tau_1 \Rightarrow x \in_\beta mP_i$ such as $\beta = min(M, \gamma + \alpha - 1)$*

In this paper, we use $\mathbb{M}_6 = \{m_k | k \in [1..6]\} = \{exactly, really, \emptyset, more\ or\ less, approximately, vaguely\}$ which is totally ordered by $j \leq k \Leftrightarrow m_j \leq m_k$ (Fig. 6). $\mathbb{M}_6$ contains a modifier by default, denoted as $\emptyset$, which keeps unchanged the basic term. The modifiers situated after $\emptyset$ are *dilation modifiers* and those preceding it are *contraction modifiers*.

4.2 Translation Modifiers

The *translation modifiers* operate both a translation and precision variation on the basic term. We define translation modifiers similar to those defined by Desmontils and Pacholczyk [4] within a fuzzy context. In this work, we use $\mathbb{T}_9 = \{t_k | k \in [1..9]\} = \{$*extremely little, very very little, very little, rather little, $\emptyset$, rather, very, very very, extremely*$\}$ totally ordered by $k \leq l \iff t_k \leq t_l$ (Fig. 7 and 8). $\mathbb{T}_9$ contains a particular modifier, denoted as $\emptyset$, which keeps unchanged the multiset P_i to which it operates. The modifiers preceding $\emptyset$ produce dilations as well as translations on the right if P_i is negative and translations on the left if P_i is positive. The modifiers following $\emptyset$ produce contractions as well as translations on the right if P_i is positive and translations on the left if P_i is negative. The translation amplitudes, the contraction or dilation amplitudes are calculated in such a way that the multisets $t_k P_i$ cover the universe X.

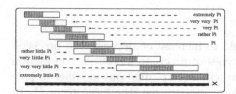 

Fig. 7. Translation modifiers(P_i is negative)

Fig. 8. Translation modifiers(P_i is positive)

Within a fuzzy context, a modifier operates on the membership function associated to a fuzzy set and modifies the numerical parameters defining it. In a similar way, we define translation modifiers which operate on multisets by modifying their symbolic parameters. So, we can define them as follows:

Definition 12. *Let P_i be a multiset such as $P_i = \{< P_r, Q_{\rho_i}, s_i, Q_{\epsilon_i} >< \sigma_i, Q_{l_i}, Q_{c_i}, Q_{r_i} >\}$. The nuanced multiset $t_k P_i$ is defined in the following way:*

- $t_k P_i = P_i = \{< P_r, Q_{\rho_i}, s_i, Q_{\epsilon_i} >< \sigma_i, Q_{l_i}, Q_{c_i}, Q_{r_i} >\}$ *if $\sigma_i = 0$ or k=5*
- $t_k P_i = \{< t_{k+1} P_i, Q_{\rho_k}, s'_i, Q_{\epsilon'_i} >< \sigma'_i, Q_{l_i}, Q_{c_i}, Q_{r_i} >\}$ *if $1 \leq k < 5$*
- $t_k P_i = \{< t_{k-1} P_i, Q_{\rho_k}, s'_i, Q_{\epsilon'_i} >< \sigma'_i, Q_{l_i}, Q_{c_i}, Q_{r_i} >\}$ *if $5 < k \leq 9$, with:*

1. σ'_i=-1 if $\{\sigma_i = -1$ and $k > 5\}$ or $\{\sigma_i = +1$ and $k < 5\}$ and $\sigma'_i = +1$ otherwise,

2. $s'_i=$ "r" if $\{\sigma_i = -1$ and $k > 5\}$ or $\{\sigma_i = -1$ and $k < 5\}$ and $s'_i=$ "l" otherwise,

3. $Q_{\epsilon'_i} \leq Q_{\epsilon_i}$ if $k > 5$ and $Q_{\epsilon'_i} \geq Q_{\epsilon_i}$ otherwise.

Let us notice that the parameters Q_{ρ_k} and $Q_{\epsilon'_i}$ are defined in such a way that the "rules", associated to multisets $\{t_k P_i\}_{1 \leq k \leq 9}$, cover the universe X.

5   Exploitation of Vague Knowledge

In this section, we treat the problem of knowledge exploitation. In particular, we are interested to propose a generalization of the Modus Ponens rule within a many-valued context [11]. In the M-valued logic on which we work, a generalization of Modus Ponens rule has one of the following forms:

F1- If we know that $\{If$ *"x is A" then "y is B" is* τ_β-*true and "x is A'" is* τ_ϵ-*true$\}$ and that $\{A'$ is more or less near to A$\}$, what can we conclude for "y is B", in other words, to what degree "y is B" is true?

F2- If we know that $\{If$ *"x is A" then "y is B" is* τ_β-*true and "x is A'" is* τ_ϵ-*true$\}$ and that $\{A'$ is more or less near to A$\}$, can we find a B' such as $\{B'$ is more or less near to B$\}$ and to what degree "y is B'" is true?

These two forms of the *Generalized Modus Ponens* rule have been studied firstly by Pacholczyk in [11] and later by El-Sayed in [7,8]. In Pacholczyk's versions, the concept of nearness binding multisets A and A' is modelled by a similarity relation which is defined as follows:

Definition 13. *A is said to be* τ_α-*similar to B, denoted as* $A \approx_\alpha B$, *if and only if:* $\forall x | x \in_\gamma A$ *and* $x \in_\beta B \Rightarrow min\{\tau_\gamma \to \tau_\beta, \tau_\beta \to \tau_\gamma\} \geq \tau_\alpha$.

This relation generalizes the equivalence relation in a many-valued context as the similarity relation of Zadeh [13] has been in a fuzzy context. It is (1) reflexive: $A \approx_M A$, (2) symmetrical: $A \approx_\alpha B \leftrightarrow B \approx_\alpha A$, and (3) weakly transitive: $\{A \approx_\alpha B, B \approx_\beta C\} \Rightarrow A \approx_\gamma C$ with $\tau_\gamma \geq T(\tau_\alpha, \tau_\beta)$ where T is a T-norm.

   In this paper, we only study the first form (F1) of the *Generalized Modus Ponens* rule. By using the similarity relation to modelize the nearness binding between multisets, the inference rule can be interpreted as: $\{more\ the\ rule\ and\ the\ fact\ are\ true\}$ and $\{more\ A'\ and\ A\ are\ similar\}$, *more the conclusion is true*. In particular, when A' is more precise than A ($A' \subset A$) but they are very weakly similar, any conclusion can be deduced or the conclusion deduced isn't as precise as one can expect. This is due to the fact that the similarity relation isn't able alone to modelize in a satisfactory way the nearness between A' and A. For that, we add to the similarity relation a new relation called *nearness relation* and which has as role to define the nearness of A' to A when $A' \subset A$. In other words, it indicates the degree to which A' is included in A.

Definition 14. *Let* $A \subset B$. *A is said to be* τ_α-*near to B, denoted as* $A \sqsubset_\alpha B$, *if and only if:* $\forall x \in F(B)$, $x \in_\gamma A$ *and* $x \in_\beta B \Rightarrow \tau_\alpha \to \tau_\beta \leq \tau_\gamma$.

Proposition 1. *The nearness relation satisfies the following properties:*

1. Reflexivity: $A \sqsubset_M A$

2. Weak transitivity: $A \sqsubset_\alpha B$ *and* $B \sqsubset_\beta C \Rightarrow A \sqsubset_\gamma C$ *with* $\tau_\gamma \leq min(\tau_\alpha, \tau_\beta)$.

We can notice that the properties satisfied by the nearness relation are similar to those satisfied by the resemblance relation proposed by Bouchon-Meunier and Valverde [2] within a fuzzy context. Finally, by using similarity and nearness relations, we can propose our *Generalized Modus Ponens* rule.

Proposition 2. *Let A and A', B and B' be predicates associated respectively with the concepts C_i and C_e. Given the following assumptions:*

1. it is τ_β-true that if "x is A" then "y is B"

2. "x is A'" is τ_ϵ-true with $A' \approx_\alpha A$.

> *Then, we conclude : "y is B" is τ_δ-true with $\tau_\delta = T(\tau_\beta, T(\tau_\alpha, \tau_\epsilon))$.*
> *If the predicate A' is, in plus, such as $A' \sqsubset_{\alpha'} A$,*
> *then, we conclude: "y is B" is τ_δ-true with $\tau_\delta = T(\tau_\beta, \tau_{\alpha'} \longrightarrow \tau_\epsilon)$.*

Example 4. Given that "really red" $\approx_8$ "red" and "really red" $\sqsubset_8$ "red", from the following rule and fact:
- it is true that if *"the tomato is red"* then *"it is ripe"*
- *"the tomato is really red"* is quite-true,

we can deduce: *"the tomato is ripe"* is almost-true. With the Pacholczyk's inference rule one obtains: *"the tomato is ripe"* is fairly-true. Given that almost-true > fairly-true, we can remark clearly that, when the term in the fact (A') is more precise than the term in the antecedent of the rule (A), our new result is more strong and more precise than that obtained with the Pacholczyk's inference rule. For the other cases, the two results are identical.

6   Conclusion

In this paper, we have proposed a model dealing with the nuanced information. In this model, we defined a term by symbolic parameters provided by the expert in a qualitative way. With this representation, we can represent the abstract terms of the natural language which are unusable within a fuzzy context. Based on this representation method, we defined some linguistic modifiers in a purely symbolic way. Lastly, we presented a new *Generalized Modus Ponens* rule. With this rule, we obtain completely satisfactory results. Note that other deduction rules are presented in [7,8] and deal with a more general scheme of multiconditional approximate reasoning. Finally, we plan to generalize our model of reasoning in order to reason on gradual rules like *"the more the tomato is red, the more it is ripe"*.

References

1. J. F. Baldwin. A new approach to approximate reasoning using fuzzy logic. *Fuzzy sets and systems*, 2:309 – 325, 1979.
2. B. Bouchon-Meunier and L. Valverde. A ressemblance approach to analogical reasoning function. *Lecture notes in computer sciences*, 1188:266–272, 1997.
3. B. Bouchon-Meunier and J. Yao. Linguistic modifiers and imprecise categories. *Int. J. of intelligent systems*, 7:25–36, 1992.
4. E. Desmontils and D. Pacholczyk. Towards a linguistic processing of properties in declarative modelling. *Int. J. of CADCAM and Comp. Graphics*, 12:351–371, 1997.

5. D. Dubois and H. Prade. Fuzzy sets in approximate reasoning, part 1 : Inference with possibility distributions. *Fuzzy sets and systems*, 40:143–202, 1991.
6. O. Ducrot and J-M. Schaeffer. Nouveau dictionnaire encyclopédique des sciences du langage. *Editions du Seuil*, 1995.
7. M. El-Sayed. Une approche logico-symbolique des connaissances nuancees via des modificateurs linguistiques. *Proc. RJCIA'00, France, 113-126*, 2000.
8. M. El-Sayed. *Une approche logico-symbolique des connaissances nuancees via des modificateurs linguistiques*. PhD thesis, University of Angers, 2001.
9. M. De glas. Knowladge representation in fuzzy setting. Technical Report 48, LAFORIA, 1989.
10. L. D. Lascio, A. Gisolfi, and U. C. Garcia. Linguistic hedges and the generalized modus ponens. *Int. Journal of intelligent systems*, 14:981–993, 1999.
11. D. Pacholczyk. *Contribution au traitement logico-symbolique de la connaissance*. PhD thesis, University of Paris VI, 1992.
12. L. A. Zadeh. Fuzzy sets. *Information and control*, 8:338–353, 1965.
13. L. A. Zadeh. A theory of approximate reasoning. *Int. J. Hayes, D. Michie and L. I. Mikulich (eds); Machine Intelligence*, 9:149–194, 1979.

Dependent and Independent Variables
in Propositional Satisfiability

Enrico Giunchiglia, Marco Maratea, and Armando Tacchella

DIST, Università di Genova
Viale Causa 13 – 16145 Genova, Italy
{enrico,marco,tac}@mrg.dist.unige.it

Abstract. Propositional reasoning (SAT) is central in many applications of Computer Science. Several decision procedures for SAT have been proposed, along with optimizations and heuristics to speed them up. Currently, the most effective implementations are based on the Davis, Logemann, Loveland method. In this method, the input formula is represented as a set of clauses, and the space of truth assignments is searched by iteratively assigning a literal until all the clauses are satisfied, or a clause is violated and backtracking occurs. Once a new literal is assigned, pruning techniques (e.g., unit propagation) are used to cut the search space by inferring truth values for other variables.

In this paper, we investigate the "independent variable selection (IVS) heuristic", i.e., given a formula on the set of variables N, the selection is restricted to a – possibly small – subset S which is sufficient to determine a truth value for all the variables in N. During the search phase, scoring and selection of the literal to assign next are restricted to S, and the truth values for the remaining variables are determined by the pruning techniques of the solver. We discuss the possible advantages and disadvantages of the IVS heuristic. Our experimental analysis shows that obtaining either positive or negative results strictly depends on the type of problems considered, on the underlying scoring and selection technique, and also on the backtracking scheme.

1 Introduction and Motivations

Propositional reasoning (SAT) is central in many applications of Computer Science. Several decision procedures for SAT have been proposed, along with optimizations and heuristics to speed them up. Currently, the most effective implementations are based on the Davis, Logemann, Loveland method (DLL) [Davis et al., 1962]. In this method, the input formula is represented as a set of clauses, and the space of truth assignments is searched by iteratively assigning a literal until all the clauses are satisfied, or a clause is violated and backtracking occurs. Once a new literal is assigned, pruning techniques (e.g., unit propagation) are used to cut the search space by inferring truth values for other variables. Needless to say, a crucial component in every SAT solver is the heuristic used to score the literals and select the next one to assign. Every year, new heuristics

S. Flesca et al. (Eds.): JELIA 2002, LNAI 2424, pp. 296–307, 2002.

are proposed and evaluated, each one tuned for a particular set of problems (see, e.g., [Li and Anbulagan, 1997,Copty *et al.*, 2001,Dubois and Dequen, 2001]).

In this paper, we investigate the "independent variable selection (IVS) heuristic", i.e., given an input formula on the set of variables N, the selection is restricted to a – possibly small – subset S which is sufficient to determine a truth value for all the variables in N. During the search phase, scoring and selection of the literal to assign next are restricted to S, and the truth values for the remaining variables are determined by the pruning techniques of the solver. The completeness of the solver is maintained because all the variables are assigned once those in S are. Moreover, the worst-case size of the search space goes down from $2^{|N|}$ to $2^{|S|}$. IVS has been proposed and used several times in combination with different scoring and selection techniques. The results have been mixed, but most of the times big benefits have been reported. In particular, in [Crawford and Baker, 1994] the IVS heuristic has been first proposed and applied to scheduling problems: no benefits are reported on these instances; in [Giunchiglia *et al.*, 1998] IVS has been applied to planning problems generated with MEDIC [Ernst *et al.*, 1997]: improvements reach 4 orders of magnitude; in [Shtrichman, 2000] and [Copty *et al.*, 2001] IVS is experimented in the context of formal verification: the authors report significant improvements on most instances. On the implementation side, the SAT solvers SIM [Giunchiglia *et al.*, 2001] and SIMO [Copty *et al.*, 2001] both incorporate the IVS heuristic along with a variety of underlying scoring and selection techniques.

We discuss the possible advantages and disadvantages of using the IVS heuristic. Our conclusion is that it is difficult to predict whether IVS will improve performances or not. Our experimental analysis shows that obtaining either positive or negative results strictly depends on the type of problems considered, on the underlying scoring and selection techniques, and also on the backtracking scheme.

The paper is structured as follows. In Section 2 we review the DLL method (Section 2.1), the concept of variable dependency (Section 2.2), and we discuss the impact that one may expect from the IVS heuristic (Section 2.3). In Section 3 we briefly describe the instances (Section 3.1) as well as the scoring and selection techniques that we experimented with (Section 3.2), and we give a detailed presentation as well as an overall summary of the results obtained (Section 3.3). We end the paper in Section 4 with some final remarks.

2 SAT, DLL and Variable Dependency

Propositional satisfiability is the task of deciding whether a given propositional formula is satisfiable or not. Most procedures do not deal with arbitrary formulas, but only with formulas in conjunctive normal form (CNF). A CNF formula is represented as a set of set of literals. A set of literals $\{l_1, \ldots, l_n\}$ $(n \geq 0)$ stands for the clause $(l_1 \lor \ldots \lor l_n)$, and a set of clauses $\{c_1, \ldots, c_m\}$ $(m \geq 0)$ stands for the CNF formula $(c_1 \land \ldots \land c_m)$. Different methods can be used to determine a satisfying assignment, i.e., a consistent set of literals entailing the set of clauses. Our work focuses on DLL, one of the most popular solving methods. In the

LOOK-AHEAD(Γ, U)   DLL-SOLVE(Γ, U)
 1 **while** a unit clause $\{l\}$ is in Γ **do**   1 **if** $f = \emptyset$ **then return** T
 2   $U \leftarrow U \cup \{l\}$ 2 **if** $\emptyset \in f$ **then return** F
 3   **for** each clause $c \in \Gamma$ **do**   3 LOOK-AHEAD(Γ, U)
 4   **if** $l \in c$ **then**   4 $l \leftarrow$ CHOOSE-LITERAL(Γ)
 5       $\Gamma \leftarrow \Gamma \setminus \{c\}$ 5 **return** DLL-SOLVE($\Gamma \cup \{l\}$, U) **or**
 6   **else if** $\bar{l} \in c$ **then**   DLL-SOLVE($\Gamma \cup \{\bar{l}\}$, U)
 7       $\Gamma \leftarrow (\Gamma \setminus \{c\}) \cup \{c \setminus \bar{l}\}$

Fig. 1. The DLL method.

following, we use $l, l_1, \ldots$ to denote literals; $c, c_1, \ldots$ to denote clauses; $|l|$ to denote the variable in l; $\neg l$ to denote $\neg|l|$ if $l = |l|$, and $|l|$ otherwise.

2.1 DLL

The function DLL-SOLVE in Figure 1 is the pseudo-code of the DLL method. The parameters of DLL-SOLVE are a set of clauses Γ, and an assignment U. Initially, Γ is the set of clauses corresponding to the input formula, and U is the empty set. DLL-SOLVE returns "T" exactly when Γ is satisfiable, and "F" otherwise.

Most implementations of the DLL method differ in the scoring and selection techniques used by CHOOSE-LITERAL, and in the kind of simplifications performed by LOOK-AHEAD. In particular, the LOOK-AHEAD procedure in Figure 1, simplifies the set of clauses by detecting and propagating unit clauses only. This technique is also known as *Boolean constraint propagation* (BCP). Another popular simplification technique is *monotone literal fixing* (MLF): For each literal l, if $\neg l$ does not belong to any clause in Γ, then we can add $\{l\}$ to the set of clauses. The addition of MLF preserves the correctness and completeness of the method.

Another difference among DLL implementations is the backtracking scheme. The function DLL-SOLVE in Figure 1 implements *chronological backtracking*. According to this scheme, once an empty clause is found, the search resumes from the latest literal selected by CHOOSE-LITERAL. In DLL-SOLVE this is accomplished by a disjunction of two recursive calls (line 5). Most modern implementations of DLL (see, e.g., [Giunchiglia *et al.*, 2001]) feature much more advanced backtracking schemes, the most popular being backjumping and learning. *Backjumping* enables DLL to backtrack and skip over literals that are not responsible for the generation of an empty clause; *Learning* augments the input formula with clauses inferred during the backtrack phase. For a detailed description of these schemes see, e.g., [Giunchiglia *et al.*, 2001]. Here it is enough to say that backjumping and learning have had a substantial impact in practice and are implemented in most state-of-the-art DLL solvers.

2.2 Variable Dependency

The idea behind variable dependency in DLL is simple. A variable x is *dependent* on a set of independent variables $x_1, \ldots, x_n$ if for any assignment to $x_1, \ldots, x_n$

the value of x becomes determined by LOOK-AHEAD. Thus, the notion of variable dependency is defined with respect to a given set of variables and a specific LOOK-AHEAD procedure. For example, in the formula:

$$\{\{\neg l \vee l_1 \vee \ldots l_n\}, \{\neg l_1 \vee l\}, \ldots, \{\neg l_n \vee l\}\}$$

where $l, l_1, \ldots, l_n$ are distinct literals, we can say that $|l|$ depends on $|l_1|, \ldots, |l_n|$ if LOOK-AHEAD enforces BCP, and each $|l_i|$ depends on $|l|$ if LOOK-AHEAD enforces MLF. Our working hypotheses for the remainder of the paper are that LOOK-AHEAD is limited to BCP as in Figure 1, and that the set of independent variables is known a priori in all the problems that we consider.

2.3   DLL and Variable Dependency

If S is a set of independent variables, it is rather easy to modify CHOOSE-LITERAL to enforce IVS, i.e., to restrict scoring and selection to S. Now the question is: what can we expect by using IVS? For one thing, the unrestricted CHOOSE-LITERAL can simulate the restricted one, but the converse is not true. If the input formula φ is satisfiable, this is not necessarily a problem: they are both allowed to pick a set of literals satisfying φ. On the other hand, if the input formula is unsatisfiable, we may witness a substantial degradation of DLL performances when using the IVS heuristic. For example, let φ be an unsatisfiable formula on the set of variables S. Assume that refuting φ with DLL requires a search tree of exponential size (the existence of such formulas is discussed, e.g., in [Urquhart, 1995]). Now let ψ be the following formula on the set of variables $N = S \cup \{a, b, c\}$:

$$(\varphi \leftrightarrow a) \wedge (a \leftrightarrow b) \wedge (a \leftrightarrow c) \wedge (b \leftrightarrow \neg c).$$

Clearly, ψ itself is unsatisfiable and the variables a, b, c are dependent on the set of variables S. If we try to have DLL refute ψ by enabling the IVS heuristic, then we are bound to explore a search tree of exponential size. At the end of each branch we determine a truth value for a, and then backtrack occurs because of an inconsistency found by running LOOK-AHEAD. On the other hand, it is sufficient for an unrestricted CHOOSE-LITERAL to pick any of the variables in the set $\{a, b, c\}$ in order to quickly refute ψ.

Notwithstanding the above considerations that may suggest to abandon the idea of restricting CHOOSE-LITERAL, in practice it is easy to see how exponential improvements can be obtained with the IVS heuristic. For example, given a formula φ on a set S of variables, we can construct a superformula ψ of φ that introduces denumerately many new variables, all depending on S. If we introduce exponentially many new such variables and try to solve ψ, the first call to an unrestricted CHOOSE-LITERAL is enough to cause a substantial worsening with respect to a restricted one.

Table 1. Statistics on the ratio $|S|/|N|$.

Statistic	DES	Parity	BMC	Pretolani	Planning
Min	0.01	0.01	0.05	0.35	0.67
Q_1	0.01	0.02	0.10	0.34	0.68
Q_2	0.03	0.03	0.18	0.37	0.70
Q_3	0.06	0.05	0.24	0.37	0.71
Max	0.18	0.13	0.40	0.46	0.74

3   Experimental Results

3.1   Test Set

The test set used to evaluate the IVS heuristic consists of 157 CNF formulas, 102 satisfiable and 55 unsatisfiable, yielding an overall 64% chance of a satisfiable instance. Some of these instances are also known to be challenging for currently available SAT solvers, but selecting hard instances was not our focus. In assembling the test set, we privileged problems that have already been used to compare SAT solvers; we tried to maximize the number of different problem classes, and the number of problems in each class. Our choice was constrained by the availability of instances for which we are able to determine a set of independent variables. In particular, we choosed:

- 32 Data Encryption Standard (DES) problems, see [Massacci and Marraro, 2000, Li, 2000];
- the "famous" 30 parity problems, see, e.g., [Selman *et al.*, 1997];
- 34 instances of bounded model checking (BMC), see [Biere *et al.*, 1999, Li, 2000];
- 24 Pretolani problems, see, e.g., [Li, 2000].
- 37 planning problems generated by BlackBox [Kautz and Selman, 1998];

For the sake of our analysis, the most representative parameter is the $|S|/|N|$ ratio, i.e., the fraction of the set of total variables N which is also in the set S of independent variables.

Table 1 gives an idea of how the ratio $|S|/|N|$ is distributed among the instances in each of the above problem classes. We remind that the $p\%$-percentile is the value x such that $p\%$ of the observed data is smaller than x. In Table 1: Q_1 denotes the 25%-percentile, Q_2 the 50%-percentile, and Q_3 the 75%-percentile of the observed ratios; "Min" and "Max" denote, respectively, the minimum and the maximum of the observed ratios. This set of statistics is known as the "five-number summary" and is most useful for comparing distributions [Moore and McCabe, 1993]. From Table 1 we can see that the parameter $|S|/|N|$ is distributed quite differently across the problem classes considered. For instance, while $|S|/|N|$ is almost normally distributed around 0.18 from a minimum of 0.05 to a maximum of 0.40 in BMC problems, in DES and Parity instances the distribution is biased towards small values of $|S|/|N|$ since the 75% of the data is smaller than 0.06 for DES and 0.05 for Parity problems, but the maximum ratio is 0.18 for DES and 0.13 for Parity problems.

3.2   DLL Implementation

As we mentioned in Section 1, the SAT solver SIM supports the IVS heuristic. Moreover, SIM comes with different implementations of CHOOSE-LITERAL that can be selected from the command line. Using compile-time options, it is also possible to augment SIM with backjumping and learning. Therefore, SIM provided the ideal test bench for our purposes. In our experiments, we run SIM with 5 different implementations of CHOOSE-LITERAL, with and without backjumping and learning. For each version of CHOOSE-LITERAL we run the default implementation as well as the one with the IVS heuristic, for a total of 20 different configurations tested. Unless explicitly mentioned, the version of SIM used to produce the data is the one with chronological backtracking. The implementations of CHOOSE-LITERAL that we evaluated are:

- MOMS (M), introduced in [Pretolani, 1993], which prefers variables that occur frequently in the shortest clauses;
- Jeroslow-Wang (JW), see [Jeroslow and Wang, 1990], where the occurrences of variables in short clauses are exponentially better than those in long clauses;
- Böhm (B), discussed in [Buro and Buning, 1992], which considers occurrences in clauses of any length and, in case of ties, prefers variables occurring frequently in short clauses;
- SATZ (S), as explained in [Li and Anbulagan, 1997], which features a complex scoring mechanism based on BCP and a modified version of JW;
- Unitie0 (U0), introduced by [Copty et al., 2001] under the name "Unit", which prefers variables producing the highest simplification with BCP.

In all the cases above, using the IVS heuristic amounts to restricting the scoring and selection process to the variables in S. To distinguish between the unrestricted CHOOSE-LITERAL and the one with the IVS heuristic, we use "*" as a suffix for the latter. For instance, "M*" means MOMS scoring with IVS enabled.

3.3   Effects of the IVS Heuristic

Tables 2 to 6 report the results of our experimental analysis using the instances and the configurations of SIM described in the previous subsections. The ordering of the tables is in accordance with the value of Q_2 for each problem class, from the lowest (DES instances) to the highest (Planning instances). Indeed, considering the discussion in Section 2.3, we expected that using the IVS heuristic would produce greater benefits for problems with small values of $|S|/|N|$.

Each line in the tables reports the following data:

- the configuration of SIM, e.g., "M" and "M*" for MOMS;
- the cumulative sum $C(t)$ of the problems solved by the configuration within time t, for $t = \{1, 2, 4, \ldots, T_f\}$; T_f is 1200 seconds;
- the root mean square (RMS) of $C(t)$ calculated as:

$$\mathrm{RMS}[C(t)] = \sqrt{\frac{\sum_{s=1}^{T_f/T} C(sT)^2}{T_f/T}}$$

Table 2. Data Encryption Standard, 32 problems, all satisfiable.

Heur	RMS	1	2	4	8	16	32	64	128	256	512	T_f
M	15.81	3	3	5	6	10	13	14	16	16	16	16
M*	15.90	3	4	5	9	12	14	15	16	16	16	16
B	15.83	3	4	5	6	9	13	15	16	16	16	16
B*	15.91	4	5	5	8	12	15	16	16	16	16	16
JW	15.66	2	2	3	4	4	8	13	15	16	16	16
JW*	15.83	2	2	4	4	7	13	14	16	16	16	16
S	16.23	16	16	16	16	16	16	16	16	16	16	17
S*	16.22	16	16	16	16	16	16	16	16	16	16	17
U0	23.66	16	18	21	22	22	22	22	22	23	24	24
U0*	16.00	16	16	16	16	16	16	16	16	16	16	16

where T is a sampling constant that divides the range $[0; T_f]$ into intervals of equal length; in our calculations $T = 12$.

The value $\mathrm{RMS}[C(t)]$ summarizes the performances of a given configuration, and enables the comparison among different configurations. Intuitively, it represents the weighted distance of $C(t)$ from the "worst possible configuration" $C_0(t) = 0$, i.e., the configuration which cannot solve any problem within T_f. The use of $\mathrm{RMS}[C(t)]$ privileges the configurations that converge quickly and solve many problems. $\mathrm{RMS}[C(t)]$ is going to be small for configurations that either converge slowly or saturate at a small number of problems. This captures precisely our intuition of a "bad" behavior of a configuration on a problem class[1].

In Table 2 the data about DES problems is reported. Notice that none of the configurations is able to solve all the problems in the class. Looking at the statistics for $|S|/|N|$ in Table 1, we see small ratios for these instances, always less than 0.18. Nevertheless, introducing the IVS heuristic does not help in speeding up the convergence of any configuration, modulo some minor improvements on MOMS, Böhm and Jeroslow-Wang. The null impact on SATZ, is contrasted by a sharp worsening of the Unitie0 heuristic: "U0*" solves 1/3 less problems than the unrestricted "U0" configuration.

In Table 3 we report the data about Parity problems. As for the DES class, none of the configurations is able to solve all the problems in the class. This is to be expected, since these problems have been shown to be very challenging for the current state-of-the-art SAT solver. On the other hand, the statistics for the $|S|/|N|$ ratio in Table 1 tell us that the percentage of independent variables is quite small (13% at most). Indeed, introducing the IVS heuristic helps a little in speeding up the convergence of some configurations, namely MOMS, Böhm, Unitie0, but it has a negative impact on Jeroslow-Wang and a null impact on SATZ configurations. Moreover, the IVS heuristic does not help in solving more problems (see the T_f column). Parity problems are thus a clear example of how

---

[1] All the experiments run on a network of identical workstations equipped with PentiumIII 600Mhz, 128MB of RAM, and Linux Suse ver. 6.2. SIM is compiled with gcc 2.95.2; time is measured in CPU seconds.

Table 3. Parity, 30 problems, all satisfiable.

Heur	RMS	1	2	4	8	16	32	64	128	256	512	T_f
M	19.99	10	10	12	17	19	20	20	20	20	20	20
M*	20.00	12	13	15	19	20	20	20	20	20	20	20
B	19.99	11	13	13	16	20	20	20	20	20	20	20
B*	20.00	12	15	20	20	20	20	20	20	20	20	20
JW	19.99	13	16	19	20	20	20	20	20	20	20	20
JW*	20.00	10	13	15	17	18	20	20	20	20	20	20
S	19.99	12	15	16	18	20	20	20	20	20	20	20
S*	19.99	12	15	16	18	20	20	20	20	20	20	20
U0	19.63	11	11	12	12	14	16	18	19	19	20	20
U0*	20.00	14	17	19	20	20	20	20	20	20	20	20

Table 4. Bounded Model Checking, 34 problems, all unsatisfiable.

Heur	RMS	1	2	4	8	16	32	64	128	256	512	T_f
M	26.11	9	11	12	13	16	16	18	19	21	26	30
M*	29.71	11	12	15	16	18	19	20	24	26	32	32
B	25.70	8	10	12	13	16	16	18	19	21	26	30
B*	29.67	11	12	14	16	18	19	20	24	26	32	32
JW	17.10	9	9	10	11	13	13	14	15	17	17	18
JW*	28.58	11	14	16	17	18	20	21	23	25	28	32
S	21.22	10	12	12	14	14	16	17	17	20	21	24
S*	21.20	10	12	12	14	14	16	17	17	20	21	24
U0	17.95	9	9	10	12	12	13	14	15	17	18	20
U0*	21.96	11	12	13	13	14	16	18	18	20	22	25

the IVS heuristic can be successful for some configurations and unsuccessful for others.

In Table 4 the data about BMC problems is reported. In this problem class (see Table 1) the median $|S|/|N|$ ratio is 0.18, and it is higher than the maximum ratio observed on DES and Parity problems. Nevertheless, with the only exception of SATZ scoring, introducing the IVS heuristic helps in solving more problems (see the T_f column), and also in speeding up convergence (see the RMS column). The data is in accordance with the good results reported on similar problems in the literature (see, e.g., [Shtrichman, 2000] and [Copty et al., 2001]).

Table 5 reports about Pretolani instances. On this class we see again some improvement brought by the IVS heuristic. The distribution of $|S|/|N|$ is concentrated in the interval $[0.35; 0.46]$ with a median of 0.37. Notwithstanding the fairly big number of variables left to examine, in at least one configuration, namely Böhm, introducing the IVS heuristic enables to solve more problems within T_f. In some configurations, namely MOMS, Jeroslow-Wang and Unitie0, the convergence of the configurations featuring IVS is quicker than their unrestricted counterparts. On the other hand, SATZ performances worsen with the introduction of IVS. Indeed, SATZ with IVS does not examine all the variables

Table 5. Pretolani, 24 problems, 12 satisfiable, 12 unsatisfiable.

Heur	RMS	1	2	4	8	16	32	64	128	256	512	T_f
M	8.68	4	5	5	5	7	7	8	8	8	9	9
M*	8.76	6	8	8	8	8	8	8	8	8	9	9
B	8.65	3	3	3	3	4	5	6	6	6	6	6
B*	14.75	11	12	12	12	12	12	12	12	12	12	12
JW	14.45	11	13	14	14	14	14	14	14	14	14	15
JW*	14.55	13	14	14	14	14	14	14	14	14	14	15
S	12.55	8	10	10	11	11	11	11	11	12	13	13
S*	9.15	7	7	7	8	8	8	8	8	9	9	10
U0	14.22	10	11	13	14	14	14	14	14	14	14	15
U0*	14.66	12	13	14	14	14	14	14	14	14	15	15

Table 6. Planning (BlackBox), 37 problems, 28 satisfiable, 9 unsatisfiable.

Heur	RMS	1	2	4	8	16	32	64	128	256	512	T_f
M	5.63	0	2	3	4	4	5	5	5	5	5	7
M*	7.80	0	2	5	5	5	6	6	6	6	7	9
B	2.04	0	0	0	0	0	0	2	2	2	2	3
B*	2.33	0	0	0	0	0	0	2	2	2	2	3
JW	0.97	0	0	0	0	0	0	0	1	1	1	1
JW*	0.97	0	0	0	0	0	0	0	1	1	1	1
S	27.99	10	11	13	17	19	20	21	24	27	28	31
S*	27.99	10	11	13	17	19	20	21	24	27	28	31
U0	27.79	7	10	10	19	22	23	24	25	26	28	30
U0*	26.92	5	11	16	20	21	21	22	22	24	27	30

and this amounts to a loss of accuracy in the selection of the next variable. Such loss is not compensated by the speed gain obtained by examining an approximate 40% of the variables only.

We conclude our report with the data about Planning problems in Table 6. From the table we can immediately grasp the inadequacy of non-BCP based heuristics on this problem class. MOMS, Böhm and Jeroslow-Wang fail to be really competitive, and the improvements introduced by the IVS heuristic are quite marginal, with the only exception of MOMS. SATZ and Unitie0 configurations are much more performant, but again the IVS heuristic is not able to really improve them in any sense.

In Table 7 we summarize the results of our experiments in a compact way, with the following notation. Each line corresponds to a configuration, and the comparison is between the unrestricted version and the one featuring the IVS heuristic. There are two blocks of results in the table. The upper block summarizes the results obtained using SIM with chronological backtracking, while the data in the lower block is obtained using SIM augmented with backjumping and learning. Each column corresponds to a problem class. To compute the data in the Table, we use the RMS values for each configuration. Given $C(t)$

Table 7. Evaluation of the IVS heuristic.

Heur	DES	Parity	BMC	Pretolani	Planning
M	+	+	+ +	+	+
B	+	+	+ +	+ + +	+
JW	+	+	+ + +	+	=
S	−	=	−	− −	=
U0	− − −	+	+ +	+	−
M	+	+	+	− −	+
B	+	+	+	−	+
JW	+	−	++	− −	+
S	−	=	−	−	=
U0	−	+	++	−	+

and $R = \text{RMS}[C(t)]$ for an unrestricted configuration, we denote with $C^*(t)$ and $R^* = \text{RMS}[C^*(t)]$ the corresponding parameters for the same configuration with the IVS heuristic. With these definitions in mind, a "+"(resp., "−") in Table 7 means that $R^* > R$ (resp. $R^* < R$), and a "=" means that $R^* = R$. To quantify how much the RMS changes going from $C(t)$ to $C^*(t)$, let P be the total number of problems in the class and r be the ratio

$$r = \frac{|R^* - R|}{P}$$

In Table 7, given $\odot \in \{+, -\}$, a single "$\odot$" means that $r \leq 0.1$, a "$\odot\odot$" means that $0.1 < r \leq 0.2$, and a "$\odot\odot\odot$" means that $r > 0.2$. For instance, the "+ +" corresponding to BMC and U0 in Table 7 means that U0* is 10% to 20% better than U0. The upper block of Table 7 evidentiates that both the problem class and the underlying scoring technique determine the behavior of IVS heuristic, and the lower block of Table 7 evidentiates that also the backtracking scheme should be included among the factors that make up for IVS effectiveness.

Overall, on the basis of the results in Table 7, we can conclude that whether IVS improves performances or not strictly depends on the type of problems considered, on the underlying scoring and selection technique, and also on the backtracking scheme. Still, according to the data in Table 7, IVS introduces some benefits on average: in the Table there are 40 "+", and 19 "−".

4 Conclusions

In this paper, we have investigated the "independent variable selection (IVS) heuristic". We have discussed the possible advantages and disadvantages of using IVS that one may expect a priori, and we concluded that determining whether the heuristic will improve the performances or not is far from being obvious. The experimental analysis that we presented confirms this intuition. We showed that obtaining either positive or negative results strictly depends on the type of problems considered, on the underlying scoring and selection techniques, and on the backtracking scheme. Nevertheless, the potential of the heuristic weighted against its simplicity is fairly big, and this suggests that, whenever possible, IVS should be included in the experimental assessment of SAT instances.

References

Biere *et al.*, 1999. A. Biere, A. Cimatti, E. Clarke, and Y. Zhu. Symbolic model checking without BDDs. In *Proceedings of the Fifth International Conference on Tools and Algorithms for the Construction and Analysis of Systems (TACAS '99)*, 1999.

Buro and Buning, 1992. M. Buro and H. Buning. Report on a SAT competition. Technical Report 110, University of Paderborn, Germany, November 1992.

Cimatti *et al.*, 2002a. A. Cimatti, E. Clarke, E. Giunchiglia, F. Giunchiglia, M. Pistore, M. Roveri, R. Sebastiani, and A. Tacchella. NuSMV 2: An opensource tool for symbolic model checking. In *Proc. CAV*, 2002. To appear.

Cimatti *et al.*, 2002b. A. Cimatti, E. Giunchiglia, M. Pistore, M. Roveri, R. Sebastiani, and A. Tacchella. Integrating BDD-based and SAT-based symbolic model checking. In A. Armando, editor, *Proceedings of the 4rd International Workshop on Frontiers of Combining Systems (FroCoS 2002)*, volume 2309 of *Lecture Notes in Computer Science*, pages 49–56. Springer-Verlag, 2002.

Copty *et al.*, 2001. Fady Copty, Limor Fix, Enrico Giunchiglia, Gila Kamhi, Armando Tacchella, and Moshe Vardi. Benefits of bounded model checking at an industrial setting. In *Proc. 13th International Computer Aided Verification Conference (CAV)*, 2001.

Crawford and Baker, 1994. James M. Crawford and Andrew B. Baker. Experimental results on the application of satisfiability algorithms to scheduling problems. In *Proceedings of the Twelfth National Conference on Artificial Intelligence (AAAI-94)*, volume 2, pages 1092–1097, Seattle, Washington, USA, August 1994. AAAI Press/MIT Press.

Davis *et al.*, 1962. M. Davis, G. Logemann, and D. Loveland. A machine program for theorem proving. *Journal of the ACM*, 5(7), 1962.

Dubois and Dequen, 2001. Olivier Dubois and Gilles Dequen. A backbone-search heuristic for efficient solving of hard 3-SAT formulae. In Bernhard Nebel, editor, *Proceedings of the seventeenth International Conference on Artificial Intelligence (IJCAI-01)*, pages 248–253, San Francisco, CA, August 4–10 2001. Morgan Kaufmann Publishers, Inc.

Ernst *et al.*, 1997. Michael Ernst, Todd Millstein, and Daniel Weld. Automatic SAT-compilation of planning problems. In *Proc. IJCAI-97*, 1997.

Giunchiglia and Sebastiani, 1999. E. Giunchiglia and R. Sebastiani. Applying the Davis-Putnam procedure to non-clausal formulas. In Evelina Lamma and Paola Mello, editors, *Proceedings of AI*IA'99: Advances in Artificial Intelligence, LNAI 2175*, pages 84–94. Springer Verlag, 1999.

Giunchiglia *et al.*, 1998. E. Giunchiglia, A. Massarotto, and R. Sebastiani. Act, and the rest will follow: Exploiting determinism in planning as satisfiability. In *Proc. AAAI*, 1998.

Giunchiglia *et al.*, 2001. Enrico Giunchiglia, Marco Maratea, Armando Tacchella, and Davide Zambonin. Evaluating search heuristics and optimization techniques in propositional satisfiability. In *Proc. of the International Joint Conference on Automated Reasoning (IJCAR'2001), LNAI 2083*, 2001.

Jeroslow and Wang, 1990. Robert G. Jeroslow and Jinchang Wang. Solving propositional satisfiability problems. *Annals of Mathematics and Artificial Intelligence*, 1:167–187, 1990.

Kautz and Selman, 1998. Henry Kautz and Bart Selman. BLACKBOX: A new approach to the application of theorem proving to problem solving. In *Working notes of the Workshop on Planning as Combinatorial Search, held in conjunction with AIPS-98*, 1998.

Li and Anbulagan, 1997. Chu Min Li and Anbulagan. Heuristics based on unit propagation for satisfiability problems. In *Proceedings of the 15th International Joint Conference on Artificial Intelligence (IJCAI-97)*, pages 366–371, San Francisco, August 23–29 1997. Morgan Kaufmann Publishers.

Li, 2000. Chu Min Li. Integrating equivalence reasoning into Davis-Putnam procedure. In *Proc. AAAI*, 2000.

Massacci and Marraro, 2000. Massacci and Marraro. Logical cryptanalysis as a SAT problem. *JAR: Journal of Automated Reasoning*, 24, 2000.

Moore and McCabe, 1993. D. S. Moore and G. P. McCabe. *Introduction to the Practice of Statistics*. W. H. Freeman and Co., 1993.

Pretolani, 1993. Daniele Pretolani. *Satisfiability and Hypergraphs*. PhD thesis, Università di Pisa, 1993.

Selman et al., 1997. Bart Selman, Henry Kautz, and David McAllester. Ten challenges in propositional reasoning and search. In *Proc. IJCAI-97*, pages 50–54, 1997.

Shtrichman, 2000. O. Shtrichman. Tuning SAT checkers for bounded model-checking. In *Proc. 12th International Computer Aided Verification Conference (CAV)*, 2000.

Urquhart, 1995. Alasdair Urquhart. The complexity of propositional proofs. *The Bulletin of Symbolic Logic*, 1(4):425–467, December 1995.

A DPLL-Based Calculus
for Ground Satisfiability Modulo Theories

Cesare Tinelli

Department of Computer Science, University of Iowa, USA
tinelli@cs.uiowa.edu

Abstract. We describe and discuss DPLL($\mathcal{T}$), a parametric calculus for proving the satisfiability of ground formulas in a logical theory $\mathcal{T}$. The calculus tightly integrates a decision procedure for the satisfiability in $\mathcal{T}$ of sets of literals into a sequent calculus based on the well-known method by Davis, Putman, Logemann and Loveland for proving the satisfiability of propositional formulas. For being based on the DPLL method, DPLL($\mathcal{T}$) can incorporate a number of very effective search heuristics developed by the SAT community for that method. Hence, it can be used as the formal basis for novel and efficient implementations of satisfiability checkers for theories with decidable ground consequences.

1 Introduction

Proving the satisfiability of ground formulas in a given first-order theory is an important research problem with applications in many areas of computer science and artificial intelligence, such as software/hardware verification, compiler optimization, constraint-based planning, scheduling, and so on. Since this problem is decidable for many theories of interest, a lot of research effort has gone into trying to devise efficient decision procedures for such theories. Typically, the effort has concentrated on the simpler problem of devising procedures that decide the satisfiability in a theory $\mathcal{T}$ of just conjunctions of ground literals over some signature Σ. ¿From a theoretical point of view, this is enough to decide the satisfiability in $\mathcal{T}$ of arbitrary ground formulas over Σ. One simply needs to convert the formula into disjunctive normal form and then invoke the decision procedure on each disjunct until a satisfiable disjunct is found. In practice, however, this approach is extremely inefficient because of the exponential explosion caused by the conversion into DNF. Existing checkers for ground satisfiability modulo theories (e.g. SVC [3], STeP [5], Simplify [14]) have relied instead on alternative ways to deal with the Boolean structure of a formula. In most cases, the approach followed was modeled more or less closely on the what is often called the DPLL method, a method collectively due to Davis, Putnam, Logemann and Loveland [7,6].

In the last years, there has been much renewed interest in the DPLL method in the propositional satisfiability (SAT) community. The method is now the basis for the great majority of current state-of-the art SAT solvers. Several improvements and variations on it have been developed which have lead to spectacular

S. Flesca et al. (Eds.): JELIA 2002, LNAI 2424, pp. 308–319, 2002.
© Springer-Verlag Berlin Heidelberg 2002

increases in the performance of SAT solvers. Such successes have pushed several researchers interested in satisfiability modulo theories to find ways to harness the power of modern DPLL-based solvers by coupling them with decision procedures. Possibly the first work along these lines is that described in [1]. Very recent, independent research on the same idea is reported in [2,4,8]. Very briefly, the idea common to all these works is the following: given a set of ground clauses to be checked for satisfiability in some theory $\mathcal{T}$, use an off-the-shelf solver to obtain a propositional model of the set; then pass the model (as a set of literals) to a decision procedure for $\mathcal{T}$ and check its consistency with $\mathcal{T}$ before succeeding. Oversimplifying a bit, the major difference among these works is the degree of "laziness" with which the decision procedure is invoked. Some invoke the procedure after a complete propositional model has been found, others invoke it incrementally, as the model is being built, in order to minimize backtracking on wrong choices.

The approaches in [1,2,4,8] are all described procedurally. In this paper, we propose instead a general declarative framework, given as a sequent calculus, for extending the DPLL method with decision procedures. While the calculus is general enough that it can model (with minor changes) each of the approaches above, it also allows a much tighter integration of decision procedures into the DPLL method. This sort of integration is analogous to that achieved in constraint logic programming (CLP) [11] between SLD-resolution and constraint solving. As in CLP, in our calculus the decision procedure for the given theory can be used to *drive* the search toward a solution, as opposed to validate a (partial) solution after it has been found. In principle, this leads to a more efficient search than with the other approaches, while still benefitting from the various optimizations developed for the DPLL method.

We say "in principle" for two reasons. The first is of course that there always a risk that the speed-up obtained by a more focused search is actually offset by the cost of frequently calling the decision procedure. Only experimental work and fine tuning can make sure that that is not the case. The second reason is that, contrary to what seems to be a common belief, the optimization strategies used in DPLL-based SAT solvers do not immediately lift to satisfiability modulo theories[1]. Our current research is aimed at establishing which heuristics do lift and how, and how effective they are in practice. For that we find it more useful to work with a declarative description of the DPLL method which separates control and optimization issues (including the calls to the decision procedure) from the essence of the method. The control aspects of the DPLL method and of modern DPLL-based systems can be conveniently modeled as search strategies for our calculus, instead of being more of less hidden in the details of the various implementations. This paper provides an initianl, incomplete account of our theoretical work in this direction.

To simplify the exposition, we start in Section 2 with a description of the basic DPLL method in terms of a simple sequent calculus. Given the simplicity

---

[1] This is a concern not only for our approach but also for the ones mentioned above, even more so given that they use existing SAT solvers more or less as they are.

of the original method, this results in a clean calculus that is easy to reason about and extend. Then, in Section 3 we show how to extend the calculus with decision procedures to obtain a sound, complete and terminating calculus for deciding the satisfiability of ground formulas in certain logical theories. Finally, in Section 4 we discuss the lifting to the extended calculus of some of the general optimization strategies developed for the DPLL method. For space constraints, we must omit the proofs of the results given here. All proofs, together with a more detailed discussion of the issues and the results presented in this paper and some initial experimental results, can be found in [15].

1.1 Formal Preliminaries

We assume that the reader is familiar with basic theorem proving concepts and terminology. Some specific notions and notation we use are defined below.

We will consider propositional logic as a special case of first-order logic, one in which all atomic formulas consist of predicates of zero arity. We call an atomic formula—whether propositional or first-order—an *atom*. A *(ground) literal* is an atom or a negated atom (with no variables). We denote the complement of a literal l by $\bar{l}$. A *ground clause* (henceforth, a clause, as we consider *only* ground clauses here) is a disjunction of zero or more ground literals. We denote by $l \vee C$ a clause D such that l is a literal of D and C is the (possibly empty) clause obtained by removing one occurrence of l from D. If Φ is a clause set, $Ats(\Phi)$ is the set of all atoms occurring in the clauses of Φ.

A sentence is a closed first-order formula. Let Φ be a set of sentences. A first-order structure $\mathcal{A}$ *satisfies* Φ or *is a model of* Φ if every sentence of Φ is true in $\mathcal{A}$; otherwise, $\mathcal{A}$ *falsifies* Φ. The set Φ is *satisfiable* if it has a model, and is *unsatisfiable* otherwise. A *theory* is a satisfiable set of sentences. The set Φ is *(un)satisfiable in* a theory $\mathcal{T}$ if there is a (no) model of $\mathcal{T}$ that satisfies Φ; equivalently, if $\mathcal{T} \cup \Phi$ is (un)satisfiable. If ψ is a sentence, Φ *entails* ψ *in* $\mathcal{T}$, written $\Phi \models_{\mathcal{T}} \psi$, if every model of $\mathcal{T}$ that satisfies Φ satisfies ψ as well.

2   A Sequent Calculus for the DPLL Method

The DPLL method can be used to decide the satisfiability of propositional formulas in conjunctive normal form, or, more precisely but equivalently, the satisfiability of finite sets of propositional clauses. The three essential operations of the DPLL method are unit resolution with backward subsumption, unit subsumption, and recursive reduction to smaller problems. The method can be roughly described as follows[2].

Given an input clause set Φ, apply *unit propagation* (aka *Boolean constraint propagation*) to it, that is, close Φ under unit resolution with backward subsumption, and eliminate in the process (a) all non-unit clauses subsumed by a unit clause in the set and (b) all unit clauses whose (only) atom occurs only once in

---

[2] See the original papers [7,6], among others, for a more complete description.

(subsume) $\dfrac{\Lambda \vdash \Phi,\, l \vee C}{\Lambda \vdash \Phi}$ if $l \in \Lambda$		**(resolve)** $\dfrac{\Lambda \vdash \Phi,\, l \vee C}{\Lambda \vdash \Phi,\, C}$ if $\bar{l} \in \Lambda$	
(assert) $\dfrac{\Lambda \;\vdash \Phi,\, l}{\Lambda, l \vdash \Phi,\, l}$ if $l \notin \Lambda$ and $\bar{l} \notin \Lambda$		**(empty)** $\dfrac{\Lambda \vdash \Phi,\, \Box}{\Lambda \vdash \Box}$ if $\Phi \neq \emptyset$	
(split) $\dfrac{\Lambda \;\vdash\; \Phi}{\Lambda, p \vdash \Phi \quad \Lambda, \neg p \vdash \Phi}$ if $p \in Ats(\Phi)$, $p \notin \Lambda$ and $\neg p \notin \Lambda$			

Fig. 1. The rules of the DPLL calculus

the set. If the closure Φ^* of Φ contains the empty clause, then fail. If Φ^* is the empty set, then succeed. Otherwise, choose an arbitrary literal l from Φ^* and check recursively, and separately, the satisfiability of $\Phi^* \cup \{l\}$ and of $\Phi^* \cup \{\bar{l}\}$, succeeding if and only if one of the two subsets is satisfiable.

The essence of this method can be captured by a sequent calculus, whose rules are described in Figure 1. The calculus manipulates sequents of the form $\Lambda \vdash \Phi$, where Λ, the *context* of the sequent, is a finite multiset of ground literals and Φ is a finite multiset of ground clauses[3]. The intended use of the calculus is to derive a sequent of the form $\Lambda \vdash \emptyset$ from an initial sequent $\emptyset \vdash \Phi_0$, where Φ_0 is a clause set to be checked for satisfiability. If that is possible, then Φ_0 is satisfiable; otherwise, Φ_0 is unsatisfiable. Informally, the purpose of the context Λ is to store incrementally a set of *asserted literals*, i.e., a set of literals in Φ_0 that must or can be true for Φ_0 to be satisfiable. When $\Lambda \vdash \emptyset$ is derivable from $\emptyset \vdash \Phi_0$, the context Λ is indeed a witness of Φ_0's satisfiability as it describes a (Herbrand) model of Φ_0: one that satisfies an atom p in Φ_0 iff p occurs positively in Λ.

The context is grown by the **assert** and the **split** rules. The **assert** rule models the fact that every literal occurring as a unit clause in the the current clause set must be satisfied for the whole clause set to be satisfied. The **split** rule corresponds to the decomposition in smaller subproblems of the DPLL method. This rule is the only *don't-know* non-deterministic rule of the calculus. Its intended use is to guess the truth value of an *undetermined* atom p in the clause set of the current sequent $\Lambda \vdash \Phi$, where by undetermined we mean not already asserted either positively or negatively in the context Λ. The guess allows the continuation of the derivation with either the sequent $\Lambda, p \vdash \Phi$ or with the sequent $\Lambda, \neg p \vdash \Phi$. The other two main operations of the DPLL method, unit resolution with backward subsumption and unit subsumption, are modeled respectively by the **resolve** and the **subsume** rule. The **resolve** rule removes from a clause all literals whose complement has been asserted (which corresponds to generating the simplified clause by unit resolution and then discarding the old clause by backward subsumption). The **subsume** rule removes all clauses that contain an asserted literal (because all of these clauses will be satisfied in any model in

---

[3] As customary, we write $\Lambda, l \vdash \Phi, C$, say, to denote the sequent $\Lambda \cup \{l\} \vdash \Phi \cup \{C\}$.

which the asserted literal is true). The **empty** rule is in the calculus just for convenience and could be removed with no loss of completeness. It models the fact that a derivation can be terminated as soon as the empty clause ($\square$) is derived. Note that the **assert** rule as well could be removed without loss of completeness since it is really an optimization of the **split** rule. This optimization is crucial for practical purposes, if not theoretical ones. It is well known that in the DPLL method, unit propagation—achieved in our calculus through the combined use of **assert**, **subsume** and **resolve**—is possibly the single most important factor in the speed of DPLL-based systems [9,13].

As it is the DPLL calculus is not strong enough for producing practical SAT solvers because, if implemented naively, it basically enumerates all possible Herbrand interpretations of the initial set of clauses. In retrospect, all implementations of the DPLL method can be seen as procedures for exploring systematically, but efficiently, the search space generated by this calculus. Modern implementations follow a number of optimization strategies in the way they perform unit propagation and interleave it with the guessing of undetermined literals. These strategies can be modeled at a more abstract level as derivation strategies for the DPLL calculus. The optimizations found in modern DPLL-based systems go well beyond the choice of the next derivation rule to apply. But these optimizations too can be modeled as (additional) search strategies for the calculus. For instance, a heuristics that chooses the next atom on which to split the search can be modeled in the calculus by adding a selection function to the **split** rule. Similarly, the way and the extent to which unit resolution is applied to any one clause can be modeled with the addition of a proper clause/literal selection function to the **resolve** rule. Finally, modern systems also have sophisticated ways of pruning the search space by intelligent backjumping (to previous decision points created by the **split** rule), and by learning *lemmas* from failed derivations (see later). All these techniques can be recast as search heuristics for the DPLL calculus. Perhaps more importantly, especially for the extension of the calculus described later, their correctness can be proved formally using established proof techniques from the automated deduction research.

In the following, we will give a sense of how various optimizations can be described in terms of the calculus. We will do that, however, not for DPLL itself but for a strictly more powerful extension of it that encapsulates decision procedures for certain first-order theories.

3   The DPLL($\mathcal{T}$) Calculus

In this section we describe the DPLL($\mathcal{T}$) calculus, an extension of the calculus in the previous section obtained by replacing propositional satisfiability with ground satisfiability with respect to a first-order *background theory* $\mathcal{T}$. The calculus, which is parametric in the background theory $\mathcal{T}$, can be used to verify the satisfiability in $\mathcal{T}$ of ground CNF formulas.

The extended calculus works again with ground sequents of the form $\Lambda \vdash \Phi$, where the literals in Λ and the clauses in Φ are now over some fixed signature Σ.

$$\textbf{(subsume)} \quad \frac{\Lambda \vdash \Phi, l \vee C}{\Lambda \vdash \Phi} \quad \text{if } \Lambda \models_{\mathcal{T}} l \qquad\qquad \textbf{(resolve)} \quad \frac{\Lambda \vdash \Phi, l \vee C}{\Lambda \vdash \Phi, C} \quad \text{if } \Lambda \models_{\mathcal{T}} \bar{l}$$

$$\textbf{(assert)} \quad \frac{\Lambda \ \vdash \Phi, l}{\Lambda, l \vdash \Phi, l} \quad \text{if } \begin{array}{l} \Lambda \not\models_{\mathcal{T}} l \text{ and} \\ \Lambda \not\models_{\mathcal{T}} \bar{l} \end{array} \qquad\qquad \textbf{(empty)} \quad \frac{\Lambda \vdash \Phi, \square}{\Lambda \vdash \square} \quad \text{if } \Phi \neq \emptyset$$

$$\textbf{(split)} \quad \frac{\Lambda \ \vdash \ \Phi}{\Lambda, p \ \vdash \ \Phi \quad \Lambda, \neg p \ \vdash \ \Phi} \quad \text{if } p \in \mathit{Ats}(\Phi) \text{ and } \Lambda \not\models_{\mathcal{T}} p \text{ and } \Lambda \not\models_{\mathcal{T}} \neg p$$

Fig. 2. The rules of the DPLL($\mathcal{T}$) calculus

Its rules, given in Figure 2, are *exactly* the same as in the DPLL calculus. The only difference lies in their side conditions. Whereas in DPLL these conditions involve membership of certain literals in the context Λ of the rule's premise, in DPLL($\mathcal{T}$) they involve entailment by Λ in $\mathcal{T}$. We point out that, in general, the tests in the side conditions of DPLL($\mathcal{T}$)'s rules may not be computable for a given theory $\mathcal{T}$ and signature Σ, which means that DPLL($\mathcal{T}$) does not always yield a decision procedure. For decidability purposes it is necessary, and sufficient, to assume that the satisfiability in $\mathcal{T}$ of finite sets of ground Σ-literals is decidable.

The DPLL($\mathcal{T}$) calculus includes the DPLL calculus as one of its instances: the one in which $\mathcal{T}$ is empty and Σ is a set of propositional variables. To see that, it is enough to notice that in that instance the side conditions of the corresponding rules of DPLL and DPLL($\mathcal{T}$) become equivalent.

For the rest of the paper, $\mathcal{T}$ will be a fixed background theory in which the satisfiability of finite sets of ground Σ-literals is decidable. We will implicitly assume the availability of a corresponding decision procedure for $\mathcal{T}$. We will say that a sequent $\Lambda \vdash \Phi$ is *satisfiable in* $\mathcal{T}$ iff the set $\Lambda \cup \Phi$ is satisfiable in $\mathcal{T}$.

We describe the salient properties of the DPLL($\mathcal{T}$) calculus in the following. For that, we need an appropriate notion of derivation and proof. As in other sequent calculi, derivations in DPLL($\mathcal{T}$) involve the construction of derivation trees.

Definition 1. *A* derivation tree *(in DPLL($\mathcal{T}$)) is a labeled tree each of whose nodes is labeled by a sequent and such that, for each non-leaf node N, the sequents labeling its successor(s) node(s) can be obtained by applying a rule of DPLL($\mathcal{T}$) to the sequent labeling N.*

Definition 2. *A* branch *in a derivation tree is (a)* successful *if its leaf is labeled by a sequent of the form $\Lambda \vdash \emptyset$, (b)* failed *if its leaf is labeled by a sequent of the form $\Lambda \vdash \square$, and (c)* incomplete *otherwise.*

We say that a derivation tree is a *derivation tree of $\Lambda \vdash \Phi$* iff its root is labeled by $\Lambda \vdash \Phi$; we say that it is a *proof tree of $\Lambda \vdash \Phi$* iff the tree has either a successful branch or only failed branches. In the latter case, we call it a *refutation tree*. Derivation trees in DPLL($\mathcal{T}$) satisfy the following invariant.

Lemma 3. *Let N, N' be two nodes in a derivation tree with respective labels $\Lambda \vdash \Phi$, $\Lambda' \vdash \Phi'$. Whenever N' is a descendant of N the following holds:*

1. *$\Lambda' \cup \Phi' \models_{\mathcal{T}} \Lambda \cup \Phi$;*
2. *Λ' is satisfiable in $\mathcal{T}$ iff Λ is satisfiable in $\mathcal{T}$.*

The DPLL($\mathcal{T}$) calculus is easily proven terminating, in the sense that every sequent $\Lambda \vdash \Phi$ has a (finite) proof tree in DPLL($\mathcal{T}$). Using termination and Lemma 3, we prove in [15] that it is also sound and complete.

Proposition 4 (Soundness and Completeness). *A clause set Φ is unsatisfiable in $\mathcal{T}$ iff the sequent $\emptyset \vdash \Phi$ has a refutation tree in DPLL($\mathcal{T}$).*

We also prove that DPLL($\mathcal{T}$) is confluent in the following sense.

Proposition 5 (Confluence). *If Φ is unsatisfiable in $\mathcal{T}$, then every proof tree of $\emptyset \vdash \Phi$ in DPLL($\mathcal{T}$) is a refutation tree.*

Let us say that a derivation strategy for DPLL($\mathcal{T}$) is *fair* iff it produces a proof tree from every initial sequent $\emptyset \vdash \Phi_0$. Proposition 5 entails that any fair derivation strategy in DPLL($\mathcal{T}$) is complete.

As in the DPLL calculus, the final context of a successful branch in a derivation tree in DPLL($\mathcal{T}$) of a sequent $\emptyset \vdash \Phi_0$ describes a "partial model" of Φ_0. More precisely, and more generally, we have the following.

Proposition 6. *Let $\Lambda_0 \vdash \Phi_0$ be a sequent such that Λ_0 is satisfiable in $\mathcal{T}$ and $\Lambda_0 \vdash \Phi_0$ has a derivation tree in DPLL($\mathcal{T}$) with a successful branch $\Lambda_0 \vdash \Phi_0, \ldots, \Lambda_n \vdash \emptyset$. Let*

$$\Lambda := \{p \mid p \in Ats(\Phi_0) \ and \ \Lambda_n \models_{\mathcal{T}} p\} \cup \{\neg p \mid p \in Ats(\Phi_0) \ and \ \Lambda_n \models_{\mathcal{T}} \neg p\}$$

Then, (i) Λ is satisfiable in $\mathcal{T}$ and (ii) $\Lambda \models_{\mathcal{T}} \Phi_0$, i.e., every model of $\mathcal{T}$ that satisfies Λ is also a model of Φ_0.

We call Λ above a *partial model* of Φ_0 because in general it may contain only a subset of the atoms in Φ_0. When this is the case, nothing can be said without further computation about the truth value of the atoms in $Ats(\Phi_0) \setminus Ats(\Lambda)$. In particular, and contrarily to the DPLL calculus, one cannot always take the atoms not in Λ to be false. To do that more assumptions on the theory $\mathcal{T}$ are needed. As we show in [15], a sufficient assumption is that the background theory $\mathcal{T}$ is *convex* (see Definition 7 in the next section).

4   Strategies for DPLL($\mathcal{T}$)

In spite of the simplicity of the DPLL method and its extension with decision procedures, one should be careful in assuming that the very same optimization that work for DPLL in the propositional case also work in the modulo theories case. Some optimizations simply become incorrect in the general case[4]; some others, although still correct, may lose their competitiveness with respect to other techniques. A survey of which of the optimization strategies used in current DPLL-based system remain correct or effective when applied to the DPLL($\mathcal{T}$) calculus is beyond the scope of this paper. In this section, we provide just a sample of them, concentrating on the changes they need to remain correct.

Literal Selection. The choice of the literal to which to apply the **split** rule is a critical one in DPLL-based systems. The SAT literature provides ample experimental evidence that on many problem classes a change in the literal selection strategy can improve (or degrade) performance by orders of magnitude.

Now, not all literal selection strategies from the SAT literature lift immediately to DPLL($\mathcal{T}$). In general, the reason is that some of these strategies are based on specific properties of propositional logic. An example would be, in terms of our calculi, the property that a literal's truth value gets determined only after it or its complement has been added to the current context. This property holds in DPLL but not in DPLL($\mathcal{T}$) typically[5]. This means that strategies based on the number of (positive/negative) occurrences of a literal in the current clause set are not necessarily as effective as in the propositional case. When there is a background theory, this number is a much less accurate measure of the impact a literal can have in unit propagation: in extreme cases, a literal may occur only once but entail in the theory all the other literals in the set.

In the following we discuss a general strategy, specializable in a number of ways, that is just as effective in the general case as in the propositional one. The strategy is interesting also because its correctness for DPLL($\mathcal{T}$) is not immediate. As a matter of fact, the strategy is incorrect unless the theory $\mathcal{T}$ is *convex*.

Definition 7. *A theory $\mathcal{T}$ is* convex *iff for every set Λ of literals and every finite non-empty set P of positive literals, $\Lambda \models_{\mathcal{T}} \bigvee_{p \in P} p$ iff $\Lambda \models_{\mathcal{T}} p$ for some $p \in P$.*

By well known results about Horn logic (see, e.g. [10]), one can show that the class of convex theories (properly) includes all Horn theories.

The general strategy we propose is motivated by the following result.

Proposition 8. *Let Λ be a set of ground literals satisfiable in a convex theory $\mathcal{T}$, and let Φ be a set of non-positive ground clauses. If $\Lambda \not\models_{\mathcal{T}} p$ for all $p \in Ats(\Phi)$, then $\Lambda \cup \Phi$ is satisfiable in $\mathcal{T}$.*

Proposition 8 entails that for any fair derivation strategy in DPLL($\mathcal{T}$) with $\mathcal{T}$ convex, one can restrict the application of the **split** rule to literals that occur in positive clauses in the current set. In fact, suppose a branch in the derivation tree of some initial sequent $\emptyset \vdash \Phi_0$ contains a sequent $\Lambda \vdash \Phi$ with no positive clauses and such that no atom p is entailed by Λ in $\mathcal{T}$. By Lemma 3, Λ is clearly

---

[4]   This is also recognized in [4], which discusses as an example the incompleteness of the "pure literal" rule in the modulo theories case.

[5]   Consider, for instance, the derivation trees in DPLL($\mathcal{T}$) of the sequent $\emptyset \vdash \{p(a), \neg q(a) \vee r(b)\}$ where $\mathcal{T} := \{\forall x\, p(x) \Rightarrow q(x)\}$.

satisfiable in $\mathcal{T}$, which implies by Proposition 8 that $\Lambda \cup \Phi$ is also satisfiable in $\mathcal{T}$. But then, by Lemma 3 again, $\emptyset \vdash \Phi_0$ is satisfiable in $\mathcal{T}$. In practice this means that one can stop a derivation of $\emptyset \vdash \Phi_0$ above as soon as a sequent like $\Lambda \vdash \Phi$ is generated. This optimization applies with no loss of completeness to any literal selection strategy for the DPLL calculus—and is in fact applied, for instance, in the DPLL-based system described in [12]. In terms of the result above this is justified by the fact that the empty theory is trivially convex. But the optimization is not correct for arbitrary theories[6].

Another consequence of the previous result concerns clauses with *undetermined* literals, that is, literals l in a sequent $\Lambda \vdash \Phi$, such that neither $\Lambda \models_{\mathcal{T}} l$ nor $\Lambda \models_{\mathcal{T}} \bar{l}$. As long as a clause C has one undetermined negative literal $\neg p$ in the current sequent of a derivation, it is not necessary to apply the **resolve** rule to the other literals of C. Delaying the application of **resolve** to C until $\neg p$ becomes determined (if ever) causes no loss of completeness. In the worst case one ends up with a sequent $\Lambda \vdash \Phi$ all of whose clauses have an undetermined negative literal. But then, as one can easily show by an application of Proposition 8, the sequent is guaranteed to be satisfiable in $\mathcal{T}$. In practice, one may want to try to further simplify a clause like C above anyway because that may lead to more unit propagation. See [15] for a more detailed discussion on this.

Lemma Generation. Modern SAT solvers exhibit a primitive but highly effective form of learning. When their sequence of split choices leads them to the generation of the empty clause, they perform some kind of conflict analysis on the failure and then generate a clause that records, in a sense, the decisive wrong choices. This clause is then used to avoid repeating those wrong choices later in the search. This sort of process can applied to the DPLL($\mathcal{T}$) calculus as well. Its logical underpinning is provided by the following result.

Proposition 9. *Let* **B** *be a branch in a derivation tree of the sequent* $\emptyset \vdash \Phi_0$ *and let* $\Lambda_m \vdash \Phi_m$ *be the sequent labeling* **B**'s *leaf. If* **B** *is failed, then there is a subset* S *of* Λ_m *such that* $\Phi_0 \models_{\mathcal{T}} \bigvee_{l \in S} \bar{l}$.

The proposition implies that from the literals asserted along a failed branch of a derivation tree it is possible to generate a clause that is a logical consequence in $\mathcal{T}$ of the initial clause set—hence the name *lemma*. One can use a lemma to refine the search for a successful derivation in implementations of the calculus by adding it to the current clause set as soon as it is discovered. Since the lemma is a consequence (in $\mathcal{T}$) of the initial clause set, its addition preserves the satisfiability of the set. However, as in the case of DPLL solvers, together with a proper derivation strategy, the lemma's presence makes sure that certain portions of the search space leading to unsuccessful derivations are never explored.

We prove in [15] a stronger result of which the above proposition is an immediate corollary. This result shows that for any given failed branch **B**, the set S in Proposition 9, often called the *conflict set* in the SAT literature, can be

---

[6] Consider for instance the non-convex theory $\mathcal{T} := \{p \vee q\}$ and the $\mathcal{T}$-unsatisfiable input set $\{\neg p \vee \neg q, p \vee \neg q, \neg p \vee q\}$.

always chosen so that it includes none of the literals asserted by the **assert** rule—we call such a set a *split conflict set induced by* **B**. Intuitively, the reason for this possibility is that the contribution of such literals to a failed branch can be always traced back to literals asserted previously by the **split** rule. This property is well-known in the SAT world and is exploited in all systems with lemma learning. These systems use techniques aimed not only at finding conflict sets like S above, but also at minimizing their size. The idea is that the smaller the conflict set, the less assertions it takes for the corresponding lemma to drive the search away from dead ends in the search space. The challenge in the DPLL($\mathcal{T}$) case is again that current conflict set discovery and minimization techniques are based on specific properties of propositional logic, and so they do not immediately lift to DPLL($\mathcal{T}$). Now, there is a general, if naive, algorithm for producing minimal conflict sets from a failed branch in DPLL($\mathcal{T}$): once a branch $\emptyset_0 \vdash \Phi_0, \ldots, \Lambda_n \vdash \square$ is generated by a system implementing the calculus,

1. collect in a set Ψ the clause in Φ_0 that has reduced to $\square$ in the last sequent, plus all the clauses of Φ_0 that became unit at some point in the branch;
2. where S_n is the set of literals in Λ_n asserted by the **split** rule, consider every subset S of S_n and run the system recursively on $S \vdash \Psi$;
3. return any minimal S among the above for which the system fails.

Considering all possible subsets of S_n above to discover and select conflict sets is clearly impractical because its worst-case time complexity is exponential in the size of S_n. We describe in [15] a greedy algorithm whose complexity is instead quadratic. The down-side of this algorithm is that it returns only one minimal conflict set per failed branch. Furthermore, although minimal, the returned set may not be optimal, in the sense of having the smallest cardinality among all minimal conflict sets induced by the branch. However, our initial experimental evidence seems to indicate that this is not a problem in practice because failed branches rarely generate more than one minimal conflict set.

Pruning. Additional optimizations in SAT solvers involve explicit pruning strategies, as opposed or in addition to the implicit pruning caused by lemmas. In systems that traverse the search space in a depth-first manner—basically all the DPLL-based systems we know of—this is often achieved as some form of non-chronological backtracking (aka, intelligent backjumping) that skips entire areas of the search space. In the context of DPLL($\mathcal{T}$), a simple and complete heuristic for non-chronological backtracking is suggested by the following result.

Proposition 10. *Let* **T** *be a derivation tree containing a node* N *with label* $\Lambda \vdash \Phi$ *and successors* N_1 *and* N_2 *with respective labels* $\Lambda, l \vdash \Phi$ *and* $\Lambda, \bar{l} \vdash \Phi$. *Suppose all branches of the subtree of* **T** *rooted at* N_1 *are failed. Let* Φ_f *be the set of clauses in* Φ *that reduce to the empty clause in one of those failed branches. If* $\Lambda, \bar{l} \vdash \Phi_f$ *is unsatisfiable in* $\mathcal{T}$ *then* $\Lambda, \bar{l} \vdash \Phi$ *is also unsatisfiable in* $\mathcal{T}$.

Operationally, this result should be interpreted as follows. If one has verified that the branches of one of the two subtrees of a "split node" $\Lambda \vdash \Phi$ are all failed, one can sometimes avoid exploring the other subtree altogether by doing the following. First build the set Φ_f defined in the proposition and then verify separately the unsatisfiability of Φ_f under the context $\Lambda \cup \{\bar{l}\}$ (by exploring the derivation tree of $\Lambda, \bar{l} \vdash \Phi_f$). If $\Lambda, \bar{l} \vdash \Phi_f$ is unsatisfiable in $\mathcal{T}$, do not bother exploring the subtree rooted at $\Lambda, \bar{l} \vdash \Phi$ because all of its branches are guaranteed to be failed. If the derivation tree of $\Lambda, \bar{l} \vdash \Phi_f$ has a successful branch, nothing can be said in general on the satisfiability of $\Lambda, \bar{l} \vdash \Phi$, therefore do explore the subtree rooted at $\Lambda, \bar{l} \vdash \Phi$.

In [15], we describe and prove complete a smarter, but also more expensive, pruning strategy that can be used in conjunction with lemma generation. To decide whether to prune or not, the strategy performs an analysis of the split conflict sets induced by each failed branch passing through a node like N in the proposition above. The analysis of the lemmas and the correctness of the strategy depend on the following general result.

Proposition 11. *Let* $\mathbf{T}$ *be a derivation tree containing a node N with label $\Lambda \vdash \Phi$ and successors N_1 and N_2 with respective labels $\Lambda, l \vdash \Phi$ and $\Lambda, \bar{l} \vdash \Phi$. Suppose that all branches $\mathbf{B}_1, \ldots, \mathbf{B}_n$ of $\mathbf{T}$ that end in the subtree of $\mathbf{T}$ rooted at N_1 are failed. For $j \in \{1, \ldots, n\}$, let S_j be a split conflict set induced by branch $\mathbf{B}_i$. If l does not occur in any of the S_j's, then $\Lambda \vdash \Phi$ is unsatisfiable in $\mathcal{T}$.*

5   Conclusion

We have presented DPLL($\mathcal{T}$), a calculus based on the DPLL method that can be used to prove the satisfiability of ground formulas in theories with decidable ground consequences. The main attractiveness of this calculus is that it can incorporate, with proper changes, various types of optimization developed by the SAT community for the DPLL method. The calculus represents at least in principle an improvement over other approaches with the same goal because it allows a tighter integration of theory-specific satisfiability procedures into a DPLL-based engine. In fact, and differently from other approaches, in DPLL($\mathcal{T}$) the decision procedure is used for driving the engine's search at each derivation step, instead of just checking the viability of a possible solution after it has been computed by the engine.

An additional contribution of the work presented here is that it frames the problem of integrating decision procedures into the DPLL method in a declarative setting. The essence of the integration is captured by a simple calculus, DPLL($\mathcal{T}$), that abstracts away control aspects and optimization issues. These aspects can then be better described as search strategies for the calculus. We believe that such an approach makes it easier to describe, compare, and prove correct present and future optimizations and variants of the method.

We are currently working on an implementation of a DPLL($\mathcal{T}$)-based system with the goal of verifying experimentally the extent of the calculus' strengths in practical applications.

References

1. Alessandro Armando, Claudio Castellini, and Enrico Giunchiglia. SAT-based procedures for temporal reasoning. In S. Biundo and M. Fox, editors, *Proceedings of the 5th European Conference on Planning (Durham, UK)*, volume 1809 of *Lecture Notes in Computer Science*, pages 97–108. Springer, 2000.
2. Gilles Audemard, Piergiorgio Bertoli, Alessandro Cimatti, Artur Kornilowicz, and Roberto Sebastiani. A SAT-based approach for solving formulas over boolean and linear mathematical propositions. In Reiner Hähnle, editor, *Proceedings of the 18th International Conference on Automated Deduction*, Lecture Notes in Artificial Intelligence. Springer, 2002. (to appear).
3. Clark W. Barrett, David L. Dill, and Jeremy R. Levitt. Validity checking for combinations of theories with equality. In M. K. Srivas and A. Camilleri, editors, *Proceedings of the First International Conference on Formal Methods in Computer-Aided Design (Palo Alto, CA)*, volume 1166 of *Lecture Notes in Computer Science*, pages 187–201. Springer, 1996.
4. Clark W. Barrett, David L. Dill, and Aaron Stump. Checking satisfiability of first-order formulas by incremental translation to SAT. In J. C. Godskesen, editor, *Proceedings of the International Conference on Computer-Aided Verification*, Lecture Notes in Computer Science, 2002. (to appear).
5. Nikolaj S. Bjørner, Mark. E. Stickel, and Tomás E. Uribe. A practical integration of first-order reasoning and decision procedures. In W. McCune, editor, *Proceedings of the 14th International Conference on Automated Deduction, CADE-14 (Townsville, Australia)*, volume 1249 of *Lecture Notes in Artificial Intelligence*, pages 101–115, 1997.
6. Martin Davis, George Logemann, and Donald Loveland. A machine program for theorem proving. *Communications of the ACM*, 5(7):394–397, July 1962.
7. Martin Davis and Hilary Putnam. A computing procedure for quantification theory. *Journal of the ACM*, 7(3):201–215, July 1960.
8. Leonardo de Moura and Harald Rueß. Lemmas on demand for satisfiability solvers. Presented at the Fifth International Symposium on the Theory and Applications of Satisfiability Testing (SAT'02), Cincinnati, USA, May 2002.
9. Jon W. Freeman. *Improvements to Propositional Satisfiability Search Algorithms*. PhD thesis, Departement of computer and Information science, University of Pennsylvania, Philadelphia, 1995.
10. Wilfrid Hodges. Logical features of Horn clauses. In D.M. Gabbay, C.J. Hogger, and J.A. Robinson, editors, *Handbook of Logic in Artificial Intelligence and Logic Programming*, volume 1, pages 449–503. Oxford University Press, 1993.
11. Joxan Jaffar and Michael Maher. Constraint Logic Programming: A Survey. *Journal of Logic Programming*, 19/20:503–581, 1994.
12. Shie-Jue Lee and David A. Plaisted. Eliminating duplication with the hyper-linking strategy. *Journal of Automated Reasoning*, 9(1):25–42, August 1992.
13. Matthew W. Moskewicz, Conor F. Madigan, Ying Zhao, Lintao Zhang, and Sharad Malik. Chaff: Engineering an Efficient SAT Solver. In *Proceedings of the 38th Design Automation Conference (DAC'01)*, June 2001.
14. Greg Nelson and Dave Detlefs. *The Simplify user's manual*. Compaq Systems Research Center. (http://research.compaq.com/SRC/esc/Simplify.html).
15. Cesare Tinelli. A DPLL-based calculus for ground satisfiability modulo theories. Technical report, Department of Computer Science, University of Iowa, 2002.

Paraconsistent Reasoning via Quantified Boolean Formulas, I: Axiomatising Signed Systems[*]

Philippe Besnard[1], Torsten Schaub[1], Hans Tompits[2], and Stefan Woltran[2]

[1] Institut für Informatik, Universität Potsdam
Postfach 90 03 27, D–14439 Potsdam, Germany
{besnard,torsten}@cs.uni-potsdam.de

[2] Institut für Informationssysteme 184/3, Technische Universität Wien
Favoritenstraße 9–11, A–1040 Vienna, Austria
{tompits,stefan}@kr.tuwien.ac.at

Abstract. Signed systems were introduced as a general, syntax-independent framework for paraconsistent reasoning, that is, non-trivialised reasoning from inconsistent information. In this paper, we show how the family of corresponding paraconsistent consequence relations can be axiomatised by means of quantified Boolean formulas. This approach has several benefits. First, it furnishes an axiomatic specification of paraconsistent reasoning within the framework of signed systems. Second, this axiomatisation allows us to identify upper bounds for the complexity of the different signed consequence relations. We strengthen these upper bounds by providing strict complexity results for the considered reasoning tasks. Finally, we obtain an implementation of different forms of paraconsistent reasoning by appeal to the existing system QUIP.

1 Introduction

In view of today's rapidly growing amount and distribution of information, it is inevitable to encounter inconsistent information. This is why methods for reasoning from inconsistent data are becoming increasingly important. Unfortunately, there is no consensus on which information should be derivable in the presence of a contradiction. Nonetheless, there is a broad class of consistency-based approaches that reconstitute information from inconsistent data by appeal to the notion of consistency. Our overall goal is to provide a uniform basis for these approaches that makes them more transparent and easier to compare. To this end, we take advantage of the framework of quantified Boolean formulas (QBFs). To be more precise, we concentrate here on axiomatising the class of so-called *signed systems* [2] for paraconsistent reasoning; a second paper will deal with maximal-consistent sets and related approaches (cf. [4,5]).

Our general methodology offers several benefits: First, we obtain uniform axiomatisations of rather different approaches. Second, once such an axiomatisation is available, existing QBF solvers can be used for implementation in a uniform setting. The availability of efficient QBF solvers, like the systems described in [3,10,9], makes such a rapid prototyping approach practically applicable. Third, these axiomatisations provide

---

[*] The work was partially supported by the Austrian Science Foundation under grant P15068.

S. Flesca et al. (Eds.): JELIA 2002, LNAI 2424, pp. 320–331, 2002.
© Springer-Verlag Berlin Heidelberg 2002

a direct access to the complexity of the original approach. Finally, we remark that this approach allows us, in some sense, to express paraconsistent reasoning in (higher order) classical propositional logic and so to harness classical reasoning mechanisms from (a conservative extension of) propositional logic,

Our elaboration of paraconsistent reasoning is part of an encompassing research program, analysing a large spectrum of reasoning mechanisms in Artificial Intelligence, among them nonmonotonic reasoning [7], (nonmonotonic) modal logics [8], logic programming [13], abductive reasoning [15], and belief revision [6].

In order to keep our paper self-contained, we must carefully introduce the respective techniques. Given the current space limitations, we have thus decided to reduce the motivation and rather concentrate on a thorough formal elaboration. This brings us to the following outline: Section 2 lays down the formal foundations of our work, introducing QBFs and Default Logic. Section 3 is devoted to signed systems as introduced in [2]. Apart from reviewing the basic framework, we provide new unifying characterisations that pave the way for the respective encodings in QBFs, which are the subject of Section 4. That section comprises thus our major contribution: a family of basic QBF axiomatisations that can be assembled in different ways in order to accommodate the variety of paraconsistent inference relations within the framework of signed systems. We further elaborate upon these axiomatisations in Section 5 for analysing the complexity of the respective reasoning tasks. Finally, our axiomatisations are also of great practical value since they allow for a direct implementation in terms of existing QBF-solvers. Such an implementation is described in Section 6, by appeal to the system QUIP [7,13,8].

2   Foundations

We deal with propositional languages and use the logical symbols $\top$, $\bot$, $\neg$, $\vee$, $\wedge$, $\rightarrow$, and $\equiv$ to construct formulas in the standard way. We write $\mathcal{L}_\Sigma$ to denote a language over an alphabet Σ of *propositional variables* or *atoms*. Formulas are denoted by Greek lower-case letters (possibly with subscripts). Finite sets $T = \{\phi_1, \ldots, \phi_n\}$ of formulas are usually identified with the conjunction $\bigwedge_{i=1}^{n} \phi_i$ of its elements. The set of all atoms occurring in a formula ϕ is denoted by $var(\phi)$. Similarly, for a set S of formulas, $var(S) = \bigcup_{\phi \in S} var(\phi)$. The classical derivability operator, $\vdash$, is defined in the usual way. The *deductive closure* of a set $S \subseteq \mathcal{L}_\Sigma$ of formulas is given by $Cn_\Sigma(S) = \{\phi \in \mathcal{L}_\Sigma \mid S \vdash \phi\}$. We say that S is *deductively closed* iff $S = Cn_\Sigma(S)$. Furthermore, S is *consistent* iff $\bot \notin Cn_\Sigma(S)$. If the language is clear from the context, we usually drop the index "Σ" from $Cn_\Sigma(\cdot)$ and simply write $Cn(\cdot)$ for the deductive closure operator. An occurrence of a formula φ is *positive* (resp., *negative*) in a formula ψ iff the number of implicit or explicit negation signs preceding φ in ψ is even (resp., odd).

Given an alphabet Σ, we define a disjoint alphabet $\Sigma^\pm$ as $\Sigma^\pm = \{p^+, p^- \mid p \in \Sigma\}$. For $\alpha \in \mathcal{L}_\Sigma$, we define $\alpha^\pm$ as the formula obtained from α by replacing each negative occurrence of p by $\neg p^-$ and by replacing each positive occurrence of p by p^+, for each propositional variable p in Σ. For example $(p \wedge (p \rightarrow q))^\pm = p^+ \wedge (\neg p^- \rightarrow q^+)$. This is defined analogously for sets of formulas. Observe that for any set $T \subseteq \mathcal{L}_\Sigma$, $T^\pm$ is consistent, even if T is inconsistent.

Quantified Boolean Formulas. Quantified Boolean formulas (QBFs) generalise ordinary propositional formulas by the admission of quantifications over propositional variables (QBFs are denoted by Greek upper-case letters). Informally, a QBF of form $\forall p \, \exists q \, \Phi$ means that for all truth assignments of p there is a truth assignment of q such that Φ is true. The precise semantical meaning of QBFs is defined as follows.

First, some ancillary notation. An occurrence of a propositional variable p in a QBF Φ is *free* iff it does not appear in the scope of a quantifier Qp ($Q \in \{\forall, \exists\}$), otherwise the occurrence of p is *bound*. If Φ contains no free variable occurrences, then Φ is *closed*, otherwise Φ is *open*. Furthermore, we write $\Phi[p_1/\phi_1, \ldots, p_n/\phi_n]$ to denote the result of uniformly substituting each free occurrence of a variable p_i in Φ by a formula ϕ_i, for $1 \leq i \leq n$.

By an *interpretation*, M, we understand a set of atoms. Informally, an atom p is true under M iff $p \in M$. In general, the truth value, $\nu_M(\Phi)$, of a QBF Φ under an interpretation M is recursively defined as follows:

1. if $\Phi = \top$, then $\nu_M(\Phi) = 1$;
2. if $\Phi = p$ is an atom, then $\nu_M(\Phi) = 1$ if $p \in M$, and $\nu_M(\Phi) = 0$ otherwise;
3. if $\Phi = \neg\Psi$, then $\nu_M(\Phi) = 1 - \nu_M(\Psi)$;
4. if $\Phi = (\Phi_1 \wedge \Phi_2)$, then $\nu_M(\Phi) = min(\{\nu_M(\Phi_1), \nu_M(\Phi_2)\})$;
5. if $\Phi = \forall p \Psi$, then $\nu_M(\Phi) = \nu_M(\Psi[p/\top] \wedge \Psi[p/\bot])$;
6. if $\Phi = \exists p \Psi$, then $\nu_M(\Phi) = \nu_M(\Psi[p/\top] \vee \Psi[p/\bot])$.

The truth conditions for $\bot, \vee, \rightarrow$, and $\equiv$ follow from the above in the usual way. We say that Φ is *true under* M iff $\nu_M(\Phi) = 1$, otherwise Φ is *false under* M. If $\nu_M(\Phi) = 1$, then M is a *model* of Φ. If Φ has some model, then Φ is said to be *satisfiable*. If Φ is true under any interpretation, then Φ is *valid*. As usual, we write $\models \Phi$ to express that Φ is valid. Observe that a closed QBF is either valid or unsatisfiable, because closed QBFs are either true under each interpretation or false under each interpretation. Hence, for closed QBFs, there is no need to refer to particular interpretations. Two sets of QBFs (or ordinary formulas) are *logically equivalent* iff they possess the same models.

In the sequel, we use the following abbreviations in the context of QBFs: For a set $P = \{p_1, \ldots, p_n\}$ of propositional variables and a quantifier $Q \in \{\forall, \exists\}$, we let $QP\Phi$ stand for the formula $Qp_1 Qp_2 \cdots Qp_n \Phi$. Furthermore, for indexed sets $S = \{\phi_1, \ldots, \phi_n\}$ and $T = \{\psi_1, \ldots, \psi_n\}$ of formulas, $S \leq T$ abbreviates $\bigwedge_{i=1}^{n}(\phi_i \rightarrow \psi_i)$. The following result is needed in the sequel:

Proposition 1. *Let $S = \{\phi_1, \ldots, \phi_n\}$ and T be finite sets of formulas, let $P = var(S \cup T)$, and let $G = \{g_1, \ldots, g_n\}$ be a set of new variables. Furthermore, for any $S' \subseteq S$, define the interpretation $M_{S'} \subseteq G$ such that $\phi_i \in S'$ iff $g_i \in M_{S'}$, for $1 \leq i \leq n$. Then,*

1. *$T \cup S'$ is consistent iff $M_{S'}$ is a model of the QBF $\mathcal{C}[T, S] = \exists P (T \wedge (G \leq S))$.*
2. *S' is a maximal subset of S consistent with T iff $M_{S'}$ is a model of the QBF $\mathcal{C}[T, S] \wedge \bigwedge_{i=1}^{n}(\neg g_i \rightarrow \neg \mathcal{C}[T \cup \{\phi_i\}, S \setminus \{\phi_i\}])$.*

Default Logic. The primary technical means for dealing with "signed theories" is *default logic* [14], whose central concepts are *default rules* along with their induced *extensions* of an initial set of premises. A default rule (or *default* for short) $\frac{\alpha \colon \beta}{\gamma}$ has two types of antecedents: a *prerequisite* α which is established if α is derivable and a *justification* β which is established if β is consistent. If both conditions hold, the *consequent* γ is concluded by default. For convenience, we denote the prerequisite of a default δ by $p(\delta)$, its justification by $j(\delta)$, and its consequent by $c(\delta)$. Accordingly, for a set of defaults D, we define $p(D) = \{p(\delta) \mid \delta \in D\}, j(D) = \{j(\delta) \mid \delta \in D\}$, and $c(D) = \{c(\delta) \mid \delta \in D\}$.

A *default theory* is a pair (D, W) where D is a set of default rules and W a set of formulas. A set E of formulas is an *extension* of (D, W) iff $E = \bigcup_{n \in \omega} E_n$, where $E_1 = W$ and, for $n \geq 1$, $E_{n+1} = Cn(E_n) \cup \{\gamma \mid \frac{\alpha : \beta}{\gamma} \in D, \alpha \in E_n, \neg\beta \notin E\}$.

3   Signed Systems

The basic idea of signed systems is to transform an inconsistent theory into a consistent one by renaming propositional variables and then to extend the resulting signed theory by equivalences using default logic.

Starting with a possibly inconsistent finite theory $W \subseteq \mathcal{L}_\Sigma$, we consider the default theory obtained from $W^\pm$ and a set of default rules $D_\Sigma = \{\delta_p \mid p \in \Sigma\}$ defined in the following way. For each propositional letter p in Σ, we define

$$\delta_p = \frac{: p^+ \equiv \neg p^-}{(p \equiv p^+) \wedge (\neg p \equiv p^-)}. \tag{1}$$

Using this definition, we define the first family of paraconsistent consequence relations:

Definition 1. *Let W be a finite set of formulas in $\mathcal{L}_\Sigma$ and let φ be a formula in $\mathcal{L}_\Sigma$. Let Ext be the set of all extensions of $(D_\Sigma, W^\pm)$. For each set of formulas $S \subseteq \mathcal{L}_{\Sigma \cup \Sigma^\pm}$, let $\Pi_S = \{c(\delta_p) \mid p \in \Sigma, \neg j(\delta_p) \notin S\}$. Then, we define*

$$W \vdash_c \varphi \text{ iff } \varphi \in \bigcup_{E \in \text{Ext}} Cn(W^\pm \cup \Pi_E) \qquad \text{(credulous unsigned}^1 \text{ consequence)}$$
$$W \vdash_s \varphi \text{ iff } \varphi \in \bigcap_{E \in \text{Ext}} Cn(W^\pm \cup \Pi_E) \qquad \text{(skeptical unsigned consequence)}$$
$$W \vdash_p \varphi \text{ iff } \varphi \in Cn(W^\pm \cup \bigcap_{E \in \text{Ext}} \Pi_E) \qquad \text{(prudent unsigned consequence)}$$

For illustration, consider the inconsistent theory $W = \{p, q, \neg p \vee \neg q\}$. For obtaining the above paraconsistent consequence relations, W is turned into the default theory^2 $(D_\Sigma, W^\pm) = (\{\delta_p, \delta_q\}, \{p^+, q^+, p^- \vee q^-\})$. We obtain two extensions, viz. $Cn(W^\pm \cup \{c(\delta_p)\})$ and $Cn(W^\pm \cup \{c(\delta_q)\})$. The following relations show how the different consequence relations behave: $W \vdash_c p$, $W \nvdash_s p$, $W \nvdash_p p$, but, for instance, $W \vdash_c p \vee q$, $W \vdash_s p \vee q$, $W \nvdash_p p \vee q$.

For a complement, the following "signed" counterparts are defined.

Definition 2. *Given the prerequisites of Definition 1, we define*

$$W \vdash_c^\pm \varphi \text{ iff } \varphi^\pm \in \bigcup_{E \in \text{Ext}} Cn(W^\pm \cup \Pi_E) \qquad \text{(credulous signed consequence)}$$
$$W \vdash_s^\pm \varphi \text{ iff } \varphi^\pm \in \bigcap_{E \in \text{Ext}} Cn(W^\pm \cup \Pi_E) \qquad \text{(skeptical signed consequence)}$$
$$W \vdash_p^\pm \varphi \text{ iff } \varphi^\pm \in Cn(W^\pm \cup \bigcap_{E \in \text{Ext}} \Pi_E) \qquad \text{(prudent signed consequence)}$$

---

[1] The term "unsigned" indicates that only unsigned formulas are taken into account.

[2] For simplicity, we omitted all δ_x for $x \in \Sigma \setminus \{p, q\}$.

As shown in [2], these relations compare to each other in the following way.

Theorem 1. *Let C_i be the operator corresponding to $C_i(W) = \{\varphi \mid W \vdash_i \varphi\}$ where i ranges over $\{p, s, c\}$, and similarly for $C_i^{\pm}$. Then, we have*

1. $C_i(W) \subseteq C_i^{\pm}(W)$;
2. $C_p(W) \subseteq C_s(W) \subseteq C_c(W)$ and $C_p^{\pm}(W) \subseteq C_s^{\pm}(W) \subseteq C_c^{\pm}(W)$.

That is, signed derivability gives more conclusions than unsigned derivability and within each series of consequence relations the strength of the relation is increasing.

Moreover, they enjoy the following logical properties:

Theorem 2. *Let C_i be the operator corresponding to $C_i(W) = \{\varphi \mid W \vdash_i \varphi\}$ where i ranges over $\{p, s, c\}$, and similarly for $C_i^{\pm}$. Then, we have*

3. $W \subseteq C_i^{\pm}(W)$;
4. $C_p(W) = Cn(C_p(W))$ and $C_s(W) = Cn(C_s(W))$;
5. $C_i^{\pm}(W) = C_i^{\pm}(C_i^{\pm}(W))$;
6. $Cn(W) \neq \mathcal{L}_\Sigma$ only if $Cn(W) = C_i(W) = C_i^{\pm}(W)$;
7. $C_i(W) \neq \mathcal{L}_\Sigma$ and $C_i^{\pm}(W) \neq \mathcal{L}_\Sigma$;
8. $W \subseteq W'$ does not imply $C_i(W) \subseteq C_i(W')$, and $W \subseteq W'$ does not imply $C_i^{\pm}(W) \subseteq C_i^{\pm}(W')$.

The last item simply says that all of our consequence relations are nonmonotonic. For instance, we have $C_i(\{A, A \to B\}) = C_i^{\pm}(\{A, A \to B\}) = Cn(\{A, B\})$, while neither $C_i(\{A, \neg A, A \to B\})$ nor $C_i^{\pm}(\{A, \neg A, A \to B\})$ contains B.

Refinements. The previous relations embody a somewhat global approach in restoring semantic links between positive and negative literals. In fact, the application of a rule δ_p re-establishes the semantic link between all occurrences of proposition p and its negation $\neg p$ at once. A more fine-grained approach is to establish the connections between complementary occurrences of an atom individually.

Formally, for a given W and an index set I assigning different indices to all occurrences of all atoms in W, define

$$\delta_p^{i,j} = \frac{: (p \equiv p_i^+) \wedge (\neg p \equiv p_j^-)}{(p \equiv p_i^+) \wedge (\neg p \equiv p_j^-)} \tag{2}$$

for all $p \in \Sigma$ and all $i, j \in I$, provided that i and j refer to complementary occurrences of p in W, otherwise set $\delta_p^{i,j} = \delta_p$. Denote by D_Σ^1 this set of defaults and by $W_I^{\pm}$ the result of replacing each $p^+ \in W^{\pm}$ (resp., $p^- \in W^{\pm}$) by p_i^+ (resp., p_i^-) where i is the index assigned to the corresponding occurrence, provided that there are complementary occurrences of p in W.

Finally, abandoning the restoration of semantical links and foremost restoring original (unsigned) literals leads to the most adventurous approach to signed inferences. Consider the following set of defaults, defined for all $p \in \Sigma$ and $i, j \in I$,

$$\delta_p^{i+} = \frac{: (p \equiv p_i^+)}{(p \equiv p_i^+)} \qquad \delta_p^{j-} = \frac{: (\neg p \equiv p_j^-)}{(\neg p \equiv p_j^-)} \tag{3}$$

for all positive and negative occurrences of p, respectively. As above, we use these defaults provided that there are complementary occurrences of p in W, otherwise use δ_p. A set of defaults of form (3) with respect to W is denoted by D_Σ^2.

Thus, further consequence relations are defined when $(D_\Sigma, W^\pm)$ in Definition 1 is replaced by $(D_\Sigma^1, W_I^\pm)$ or by $(D_\Sigma^2, W_I^\pm)$. Similar results to Theorem 1 and 2 can be shown for these families of consequence relations.

In the following, we identify all introduced default theories as follows. Given a finite set $W \subseteq \mathcal{L}_\Sigma$, the class $\mathsf{DT}(W)$ contains (D_Σ, W), as well as $(D_\Sigma^1, W_I^\pm)$ and $(D_\Sigma^2, W_I^\pm)$ for any index set I. Furthermore, $\mathsf{DT} = \bigcup_{W \subseteq \mathcal{L}_\Sigma} \mathsf{DT}(W)$ denotes the class of all possible default theories under consideration.

Whenever a problem instance may give rise to several solutions, it is useful to provide a preference criterion for selecting a subset of preferred solutions. This is accomplished in [2] by means of a *ranking function* $\varrho : \Sigma \to \mathbb{N}$ on the alphabet Σ for inducing a hierarchy on the default rules in D_Σ:

Definition 3. *Let* $\varrho : \Sigma \to \mathbb{N}$ *be some ranking function on alphabet* Σ, *and* $(D, V) \in \mathsf{DT}$. *We define the hierarchy of* D *with respect to* ϱ *as the partition* $\langle D_n \rangle_{n \in \omega}$ *of* D *such that for each* $\delta \in D$ *with* δ *of form* $\delta_p, \delta_p^{i,j}, \delta_p^{i+}, \delta_p^{i-}$, *for* $p \in \Sigma$ *and* $i, j \in I$, $\delta \in D_n$ *iff* $\varrho(p) = n$ *holds.*

Strictly speaking, $\langle D_n \rangle_{n \in \omega}$ is not always a genuine partition, since D_n may be the empty set for some values of n.

Definition 4. *Let* W *be a finite set of formulas in* $\mathcal{L}_\Sigma$, $(D, V) \in \mathsf{DT}(W)$, *and* E *a set of formulas. Let* $\langle D_n \rangle_{n \in \omega}$ *be the hierarchy of* D *with respect to some ranking function* ϱ.

Then, $E = \bigcup_{n \in \omega} E_n$ *is a* hierarchic extension *of* (D, V) *relative to* ϱ *if* $E_1 = V$ *and* E_{n+1} *is an extension of* (D_n, E_n) *for all* $n \geq 1$.

Let $\langle D_n \rangle_{n \in \omega}$ be the hierarchy of D with respect to some ranking function ϱ, and let Ext_h be the set of all hierarchic extensions of a default theory $(D, V) \in \mathsf{DT}$ in Definition 1. Then, we immediately get corresponding consequence relations $\vdash_{ch}, \vdash_{sh}$, and $\vdash_{ph}$. Furthermore, applying hierarchic extensions on default theories (D_Σ, W) in accordance to Definition 2 yields new relations $\vdash_{ch}^\pm, \vdash_{sh}^\pm$, and $\vdash_{ph}^\pm$.

In concluding this section, let us briefly recapitulate all paraconsistent consequence relations introduced so far. As a basic classification, we have credulous, skeptical and prudent consequence. For each of these relations, we defined unsigned operators, which are invokable on three different classes of default theories (viz. on $(D_\Sigma, W^\pm)$, $(D_\Sigma^1, W_I^\pm)$, and $(D_\Sigma^2, W_I^\pm)$), either on ordinary extensions ($\vdash_i$) or on hierarchic extensions ($\vdash_{ih}$), and, on the other hand, signed operators also relying on ordinary extensions ($\vdash_i^\pm$) or hierarchic extensions ($\vdash_{ih}^\pm$) of the default theory $(D_\Sigma, W^\pm)$. This gives in total 18 unsigned and 6 signed paraconsistent consequence relations, which shall all be considered in the following two sections.

4 Reductions

In this section, we show how the above introduced consequence relations can be mapped into quantified Boolean formulas in polynomial time.

Recall the set $DT(W)$ for finite $W \subseteq \mathcal{L}_\Sigma$. In what follows, we use finite default theories $DT^*(W) = \{(D_W, V) \mid (D, V) \in DT(W)\}$ where $D_W = \{\delta \in D \mid var(\delta) \cap var(W) \neq \emptyset\}$. Hence, D_W contains each default from D having an unsigned atom which also occurs in W.

We first show the adequacy of these default theories, and afterwards we develop our QBF-reductions based on these finite default theories.

Lemma 1. *Let $W \subseteq \mathcal{L}_\Sigma$ be a finite set of formulas and $(D, V) \in DT(W)$ a default theory. Moreover, let $C \subseteq D$ and $C_W = \{\delta \in C \mid var(\delta) \cap var(W) \neq \emptyset\}$. Then,*

1. *$Cn(V \cup c(C_W)) \cap \mathcal{L}_\Sigma = Cn(V \cup c(C)) \cap \mathcal{L}_\Sigma$; and*
2. *for each $\varphi^\pm \in \mathcal{L}_{\Sigma^\pm}$, $\varphi^\pm \in Cn(V \cup c(C))$ iff $\varphi^\pm \in Cn(V \cup c(C_W) \cup c(D_\varphi))$ where $D_\varphi = \{\delta_p \mid p \in var(\varphi) \setminus var(W)\}$.*

Both results show that having computed a (possibly hierarchic) extension, one has a finite set of generating defaults sufficient for deciding whether a paraconsistent consequence relation holds. The following result shows that these sets are also sufficient to compute the underlying extensions themselves.

Theorem 3. *Let W, (D, V), C, and C_W be as in Lemma 1, and let $D_W = \{\delta \in D \mid var(\delta) \cap var(W) \neq \emptyset\}$.*

Then, there is a one-to-one correspondence between the extensions of (D, V) and the extensions of (D_W, V). In particular, $Cn(V \cup c(C))$ is an extension of (D, V) iff $Cn(V \cup c(C_W))$ is an extension of (D_W, V). Similar relations hold for hierarchic extensions as well.

The next result gives a uniform characterisation for all default theories under consideration. It follows from the fact that, for each δ_p, the consequent $(p \equiv p^+) \wedge (\neg p \equiv p^-)$ is actually equivalent to $(p^+ \equiv \neg p^-) \wedge (p \equiv p^+)$, and, furthermore, that defaults of form (2) and (3) share the property that their justifications and consequents are identical. Hence, given W and I as usual, it holds that $c(\delta) \models j(\delta)$, for each $\delta \in D$, with $(D, V) \in DT^*(W)$.

Theorem 4. *Let $W \subseteq \mathcal{L}_\Sigma$ be a finite set of formulas, let $(D, V) \in DT^*(W)$ be a default theory, and let $C \subseteq D$.*

Then, $Cn(V \cup c(C))$ is an extension of (D, V) iff $j(C)$ is a maximal subset of $j(D)$ consistent with V.

Note that the subsequent QBF reductions, obtained on the basis of the above result, represent a more compact axiomatics than the encodings given in [7] for arbitrary default theories.

We derive an analogous characterisation for hierarchic extensions. In fact, each hierarchic extension is also an extension (but not vice versa) [2]. Thus, we can characterise hierarchic extensions of a default theory (D, V) as ordinary extensions, viz. by $Cn(W \cup c(C))$ with $C \subseteq D$ suitably chosen. The following result generalises Theorem 4 with respect to a given partition on the defaults. In particular, if $\langle D_n \rangle_{n \in \omega} = \langle D \rangle$, Theorem 5 corresponds to Theorem 4.

Theorem 5. *Let W, (D, V), and C be given as in Theorem 4.*

Then, $Cn(V \cup c(C))$ is a hierarchic extension of (D, V) with respect to partition $\langle D_n \rangle_{n \in \omega}$ on D iff for each $i \in \omega$, $j(D_i \cap C)$ is a maximal subset of $j(D_i)$ consistent with $V \cup \bigcup_{j < i} c(D_j \cap C)$.

Finally, in order to relate extensions of default theories to paraconsistent consequence operators, we note the following straightforward observations.

Let Π_S be as in Definition 1. Then, for each extension E of $(D, V) \in \mathsf{DT}(W)$, there exists a $C \subseteq D$ such that $c(C) = \Pi_E$. However, since we have to check whether a given formula is contained in some $Cn(V \cup \Pi_E)$, by Lemma 1 it is obviously sufficient to consider just the generating defaults of an extension of the corresponding restricted default theory from $\mathsf{DT}^*(W)$. In view of Theorems 4 and 5, this immediately implies that all paraconsistent consequence relations introduced so far can be characterised by maximal subsets of the consequences $c(D)$ of the corresponding default theory $(D, V) \in \mathsf{DT}^*(W)$. More specifically, credulous and skeptical paraconsistent consequence reduces to checking whether a given formula is contained in at least one or respectively all such maximal subsets. Additionally, prudent consequence enjoys the following property.

Lemma 2. *Let $W \subseteq \mathcal{L}_\Sigma$ be a finite set of formulas, and $(D, V) \in \mathsf{DT}^*(W)$.*

Then, for each $\varphi \in \mathcal{L}_\Sigma$, we have that $W \not\vdash_p \varphi$ (resp., $W \not\vdash_{ph} \varphi$) iff there exists a set $C \subseteq D$ such that $\varphi \notin Cn(V \cup c(C))$ and, for each $\delta \in D \setminus C$, there is some extension (resp., hierarchic extension) E of (D, V) such that $c(\delta) \notin E$. An analogous result holds for relations $\vdash_p^{\pm}$ and $\vdash_{ph}^{\pm}$.

Main Construction. We start with some basic QBF-modules. To this end, recall the schema $\mathcal{C}[\cdot, \cdot]$ from Proposition 1.

Definition 5. *Let $W \subseteq \mathcal{L}_\Sigma$ be a finite set of formulas and $\varphi \in \mathcal{L}_\Sigma$. For each finite default theory $T = (D, V) \in \mathsf{DT}^*(W)$, let $D = \{\delta_1, \ldots, \delta_n\}$, and define*

$$\mathcal{E}[T] = \mathcal{C}[V, j(D)] \wedge \bigwedge_{i=1}^{n} \left(\neg g_i \rightarrow \neg \mathcal{C}[V \cup \{j(\delta_i)\}, j(D \setminus \{\delta_i\})] \right);$$

$$\mathcal{D}[T, \varphi] = \forall P \left(V \wedge (G \leq c(D)) \rightarrow \varphi \right),$$

where P denotes the set of atoms occurring in T or φ, and $G = \{g_i \mid \delta_i \in D\}$ is an indexed set of globally new variables corresponding to D.

Lemma 3. *Let W, $T = (D, V)$, and G be as in Definition 5. Furthermore, for any set $C \subseteq D$, define the interpretation $M_C \subseteq G$ such that $g_i \in M_C$ iff $\delta_i \in C$, for $1 \leq i \leq n$.*

Then, the following relations hold:

1. *$Cn(V \cup c(C))$ is an extension of T iff $\mathcal{E}[T]$ is true under M_C; and*
2. *$\varphi \in Cn(V \cup c(C))$ iff $\mathcal{D}[T, \varphi]$ is true under M_C, for any formula φ in $\mathcal{L}_\Sigma$.*

Observe that the correctness of Condition 1 follows directly from Proposition 1(2), since we have that $\mathcal{E}[T]$ is true under M_C iff $j(C)$ is a maximal subset of $j(D)$ consistent with V, and, in view of Theorem 4, the latter holds iff $Cn(V \cup c(C))$ is an extension of T. Moreover, Condition 2 is reducible to Proposition 1(1). Combining these two QBF-modules, we obtain encodings for the basic inference tasks as follows:

Theorem 6. *Let $W \subseteq \mathcal{L}_\Sigma$ be a finite set of formulas, $T = (D, V)$ a default theory from $\mathsf{DT}^*(W)$ with $D = \{\delta_1, \ldots, \delta_n\}$, φ a formula in $\mathcal{L}_\Sigma$, and $G = \{g_1, \ldots, g_n\}$ the indexed set of variables occurring in $\mathcal{E}[T]$ and $\mathcal{D}[T, \varphi]$.*

Then, paraconsistent credulous and skeptical consequence relations can be axiomatised by means of QBFs as follows:

1. *$W \vdash_c \varphi$ iff $\models \exists G(\mathcal{E}[T] \wedge \mathcal{D}[T, \varphi])$; and*
2. *$W \vdash_s \varphi$ iff $\models \neg \exists G(\mathcal{E}[T] \wedge \neg \mathcal{D}[T, \varphi])$.*

Moreover, for prudent consequence, let $G' = \{g_i' \mid g_i \in G\}$ be an additional set of globally new variables and $\Psi = \bigwedge_{i=1}^n (\neg g_i' \rightarrow \exists G(\mathcal{E}[T] \wedge \neg \mathcal{D}[T, c(\delta_i)]))$. Then,

3. *$W \vdash_p \varphi$ iff $\models \neg \exists G'(\neg \mathcal{D}_{G \leftarrow G'}[T, \varphi] \wedge \Psi)$,*

where $\mathcal{D}_{G \leftarrow G'}[T, \varphi]$ denotes the QBF obtained from $\mathcal{D}[T, \varphi]$ by replacing each occurrence of an atom $g \in G$ in $\mathcal{D}[T, \varphi]$ by g'.

In what follows, we discuss the remaining consequence relations under consideration. We start with signed consequence. Here, we just have to adopt the calls to $\mathcal{D}[(D, V), \varphi]$ with respect to Lemma 2, by adding those defaults δ_p to $W^\pm$ such that $p \in var(\varphi) \setminus var(W)$. Observe that in the following theorem this addition is *not* necessary for the module Ψ. Furthermore, recall that signed consequence is applied only to default theories $(D_\Sigma, W^\pm)$.

Theorem 7. *Let $W \subseteq \mathcal{L}_\Sigma$ be a finite set of formulas and φ a formula in $\mathcal{L}_\Sigma$. Moreover, let $D_W = \{\delta_p \mid p \in var(W)\}$ and $D_\varphi = \{\delta_p \mid p \in var(\varphi) \setminus var(W)\}$, with the corresponding default theories $T = (D_W, W^\pm)$ and $T' = (D_W, W^\pm \cup c(D_\varphi))$, and let G, G', and Ψ be as in Theorem 6.*

Then, paraconsistent signed consequence relations can be axiomatised by means of QBFs as follows:

1. *$W \vdash_c^\pm \varphi$ iff $\models \exists G(\mathcal{E}[T] \wedge \mathcal{D}[T', \varphi^\pm])$;*
2. *$W \vdash_s^\pm \varphi$ iff $\models \neg \exists G(\mathcal{E}[T] \wedge \neg \mathcal{D}[T', \varphi^\pm])$; and*
3. *$W \vdash_p^\pm \varphi$ iff $\models \neg \exists G'(\Psi \wedge \neg \mathcal{D}_{G \leftarrow G'}[T', \varphi^\pm])$,*

where, as above, $\mathcal{D}_{G \leftarrow G'}[\cdot, \cdot]$ replaces each g by g'.

It remains to consider the consequence relations based on hierarchical extensions. To this end, we exploit the characterisation of Theorem 5.

Definition 6. *Let $W \subseteq \mathcal{L}_\Sigma$ be a finite set of formulas, $T = (D, V)$ a default theory from $\mathsf{DT}^*(W)$ with $D = \{\delta_1, \ldots, \delta_n\}$, and $P = \langle D_n \rangle_{n \in \omega}$ a partition on D. We define*

$$\mathcal{E}_h[T, P] = \bigwedge_{i \in \omega} \left(\mathcal{E}[(V \wedge \bigwedge_{\delta_j \in D_1 \cup \ldots \cup D_{i-1}} (g_j \rightarrow c(\delta_j)), D_i)] \right),$$

where $G = \{g_i \mid \delta_i \in D\}$ is the same indexed set of globally new variables corresponding to D as above appearing in each $\mathcal{E}[\cdot]$.

Lemma 4. *Let W, (D, V), G, and P be as in Definition 6. Furthermore, for any set $C \subseteq D$, define the interpretation $M_C \subseteq G$ such that $g_i \in M_C$ iff $\delta_i \in C$, for $1 \leq i \leq n$.*

Then, $Cn(V \cup c(C))$ is a hierarchic extension of T with respect to P iff $\mathcal{E}_h[T, P]$ is true under M_C.

Theorem 8. *Paraconsistent consequence relations $\vdash_{ch}, \vdash^{\pm}_{ch}, \vdash_{sh}, \vdash^{\pm}_{sh}, \vdash_{ph},$ and $\vdash^{\pm}_{ph}$ are expressible in the same manner as in Theorems 6 and 7 by replacing $\mathcal{E}[T]$ with $\mathcal{E}_h[T, P]$.*

5   Complexity Issues

In the sequel, we derive complexity results for deciding paraconsistent consequence in all variants discussed previously. We show that all considered tasks are located at the second level of the polynomial hierarchy. This is in some sense not surprising, because the current approach relies on deciding whether a given formula is contained in an extension of a suitably constructed default theory. This problem was shown to be Σ^P_2-complete by Gottlob [11], even if normal default theories are considered. However, this completeness result is not directly applicable here because of the specialised default theories in the present setting. Furthermore, for dealing with hierarchic extensions, it turns out that the complexity remains at the second level of the polynomial hierarchy as well. This result is interesting, since the definition of hierarchic extensions is somewhat more elaborate than standard extensions. In any case, this observation mirrors in some sense complexity results derived for cumulative default logic (cf. [12]).

In the same way as the satisfiability problem of classical propositional logic is the "prototypical" problem of NP, i.e., being an NP-complete problem, the satisfiability problem of QBFs in *prenex form* possessing k quantifier alternations is the "prototypical" problem of the k-th level of the polynomial hierarchy, as expressed by the following well-known result:

Proposition 2 ([16]). *Given a propositional formula ϕ whose atoms are partitioned into $i \geq 1$ sets $P_1, \ldots, P_i$, deciding whether $\exists P_1 \forall P_2 \ldots Q_i P_i \phi$ is true is Σ^P_i-complete, where $Q_i = \exists$ if i is odd and $Q_i = \forall$ if i is even, Dually, deciding whether $\forall P_1 \exists P_2 \ldots Q'_i P_i \phi$ is true is Π^P_i-complete, where $Q'_i = \forall$ if i is odd and $Q_i = \exists$ if i is even.*

Given the above characterisations, we can estimate upper complexity bounds for the reasoning problems discussed in Section 3 simply by inspecting the quantifier order of the respective QBF encodings. This can be argued as follows. First of all, by applying quantifier transformation rules similar to ones in first-order logic, each of the above QBF encodings can be transformed in polynomial time into a QBF in prenex form having exactly one quantifier alternation. Then, by invoking Proposition 2 and observing that completeness of a decision problem D for a complexity class C implies membership of D in C, the quantifier order of the resultant QBFs determines in which class of the polynomial hierarchy the corresponding reasoning task belongs to.

Table 1. Complexity results for all paraconsistent consequence relations.

	$T_0 = (D_\Sigma, W^\pm)$	$T_1 = (D_\Sigma^1, W_I^\pm)$	$T_2 = (D_\Sigma^2, W_I^\pm)$
$\vdash_c$	Σ_2^P	Σ_2^P	Σ_2^P
$\vdash_s$	Π_2^P	Π_2^P	Π_2^P
$\vdash_p$	Π_2^P	in Π_2^P	in Π_2^P
$\vdash_c^\pm$	Σ_2^P	-	-
$\vdash_s^\pm$	Π_2^P	-	-
$\vdash_p^\pm$	in Π_2^P	-	-
$\vdash_{ch}$	Σ_2^P	Σ_2^P	Σ_2^P
$\vdash_{sh}$	Π_2^P	Π_2^P	Π_2^P
$\vdash_{ph}$	Π_2^P	in Π_2^P	in Π_2^P
$\vdash_{ch}^\pm$	Σ_2^P	-	-
$\vdash_{sh}^\pm$	Π_2^P	-	-
$\vdash_{ph}^\pm$	in Π_2^P	-	-

Applying this method to our considered tasks, we obtain that credulous paraconsistent reasoning lies in Σ_2^P, whilst skeptical and prudent paraconsistent reasoning are in Π_2^P. Furthermore, note that the QBFs expressing paraconsistent reasoning using the concept of hierarchical extensions share exactly the same quantifier structures as those using ordinary extensions.

Concerning lower complexity bounds, it turns out that most of the above given estimations are *strict*, i.e., the considered decision problems are hard for the respective complexity classes. The results are summarised in Table 1. There, all entries denote completeness results, except where a membership relation is explicitly stated. The following theorem summarises these relations:

Theorem 9. *The complexity results in Table 1 hold both for ordinary as well as for hierarchical extensions of* T_i ($i = 0, 1, 2$) *as underlying inference principle.*

Some of these complexity results have already been shown elsewhere. As pointed out in [2], prudent consequence, $W \vdash_p \varphi$, on the basis of the default theory $(D_\Sigma, W^\pm)$ captures the notion of *free-consequences* as introduced in [1]. This formalism was shown to be Π_2^P-complete in [4].

Finally, [5] considers the complexity of a number of different paraconsistent reasoning principles, among them the completeness results for $\vdash_s$ and $\vdash_s^\pm$. Moreover, that paper extends the intractability results to some restricted subclasses as well.

6   Discussion

We have shown how paraconsistent inference problems within the framework of signed systems can be axiomatised by means of quantified Boolean formulas. This approach has several benefits: First, the given axiomatics provides us with further insight about how paraconsistent reasoning works within the framework of signed systems. Second, this axiomatisation allows us to furnish upper bounds for precise complexity results, going beyond those presented in [5]. Last but not least, we obtain a straightforward implementation technique of paraconsistent reasoning in signed systems by appeal to existing QBF solvers.

For implementing our approach, we rely on the existing system QUIP [7,13,8]. The general architecture of QUIP consists of three parts, namely a filter program, a QBF-evaluator, and an interpreter. The input filter translates the given problem description (in our case, a signed system and a specified reasoning task) into the corresponding quantified Boolean formula, which is then sent to the QBF-evaluator. For attaining a high degree of flexibility, QUIP is supplied with interfaces to utilise most of the currently available QBF-solvers. Depending on the capabilities of the employed QBF-evaluator, the interpreter provides an explanation in terms of the underlying problem instance. This task relies on a protocol mapping of internal variables of the generated QBF into concepts of the problem description.

References

1. S. Benferhat, D. Dubois, and H. Prade. Argumentative Inference in Uncertain and Inconsistent Knowledge Bases. In *Proc. UAI-93*, pages 411–419, 1993.
2. P. Besnard and T. Schaub. Signed Systems for Paraconsistent Reasoning. *Journal of Automated Reasoning*, 20:191–213, 1998.
3. M. Cadoli, A. Giovanardi, and M. Schaerf. An Algorithm to Evaluate Quantified Boolean Formulae. In *Proc. AAAI-98*, pages 262–267. AAAI Press, 1998.
4. C. Cayrol, M. Lagasquie-Schiex, and T. Schiex. Nonmonotonic Reasoning: From Complexity to Algorithms. *Ann. of Mathematics and Artificial Intelligence*, 22(3–4):207–236, 1998.
5. S. Coste-Marquis and P. Marquis. Complexity Results for Paraconsistent Inference Relations. In *Proc. KR-02*, pages 61–72, 2002.
6. J. Delgrande, T. Schaub, H. Tompits, and S. Woltran. On Computing Solutions to Belief Change Scenarios. In *Proc. ECSQARU-01*, pages 510–521. Springer Verlag, 2001.
7. U. Egly, T. Eiter, H. Tompits, and S. Woltran. Solving Advanced Reasoning Tasks Using Quantified Boolean Formulas. In *Proc. AAAI-00*, pages 417–422. AAAI Press, 2000.
8. T. Eiter, V. Klotz, H. Tompits, and S. Woltran. Modal Nonmonotonic Logics Revisited: Efficient Encodings for the Basic Reasoning Tasks. In *Proc. TABLEAUX-02*, 2002. To appear.
9. R. Feldmann, B. Monien, and S. Schamberger. A Distributed Algorithm to Evaluate Quantified Boolean Formula. In *Proc. AAAI-00*, pages 285–290. AAAI Press, 2000.
10. E. Giunchiglia, M. Narizzano, and A. Tacchella. QuBE: A System for Deciding Quantified Boolean Formulas Satisfiability. In *Proc. IJCAR-01*, pages 364–369. Springer Verlag, 2001.
11. G. Gottlob. Complexity Results for Nonmonotonic Logics. *Journal of Logic and Computation*, 2(3):397–425, 1992.
12. G. Gottlob and Z. Mingyi. Cumulative Default Logic: Finite Characterization, Algorithms, and Complexity. *Artificial Intelligence*, 69(1–2):329–345, 1994.
13. D. Pearce, H. Tompits, and S. Woltran. Encodings for Equilibrium Logic and Logic Programs with Nested Expressions. In *Proc. EPIA-01*, pages 306–320. Springer Verlag, 2001.
14. R. Reiter. A Logic for Default Reasoning. *Artificial Intelligence*, 13(1–2):81–132, 1980.
15. H. Tompits. Expressing Default Abduction Problems as Quantified Boolean Formulas. In *AI Communications*, 2002. To appear.
16. C. Wrathall. Complete Sets and the Polynomial-Time Hierarchy. *Theoretical Computer Science*, 3(1):23–33, 1976.

Three-Valued Logics for Inconsistency Handling

Sébastien Konieczny[1] and Pierre Marquis[2]

[1] IRIT/CNRS - Université Paul Sabatier
118 route de Narbonne
31062 Toulouse - France
konieczny@irit.fr
[2] CRIL/CNRS - Université d'Artois
SP 16 - rue de l'Université
62300 Lens - France
marquis@cril.univ-artois.fr

Abstract. While three-valued paraconsistent logic is a valuable framework for reasoning under inconsistency, the corresponding basic inference relation is too cautious and fails in discriminating in a fine-grained way the set of expected consequences of belief bases. To address both issues, we point out more refined inference relations. We analyze them from the logical and computational points of view and we compare them with respect to their relative cautiousness.

1 Introduction

Inconsistency appears very often in actual, large sized belief bases used by intelligent systems such as autonomous robots or infobots. As a consequence, autonomous belief based agents have to handle inconsistency some way, to prevent inference from trivializing. Indeed, paraconsistency is acknowledged for a while as an important feature of common-sense reasoning, strongly connected to several central AI issues, like reasoning with exceptions and counterfactuals, and helpful for many applications (for instance, model-based diagnosis).

In the following, the focus is laid on *three-valued paraconsistent logic*. The additional third value (called middle element) intuitively means "both true and false" and allows to still reasoning meaningfully with variables that are not embedded directly in a contradiction.

Several inference relations can be defined in three-valued paraconsistent logic. For any of them, trivialization is avoided by weakening the classical entailment relation. Compared with other approaches to inconsistency handling, like belief merging or those based on the selection of preferred consistent subbases where trivialization is avoided by weakening the belief base (while keeping classical entailment as the inference mechanism), the three-valued logic approach is helpful in the situation where a single source of inconsistent information must be treated. The basic inference relation from three-valued paraconsistent logic has the advantage to benefit from a simple semantics, where each connective is

S. Flesca et al. (Eds.): JELIA 2002, LNAI 2424, pp. 332–344, 2002.

truth functional. Furthermore, the corresponding decision problem is only coNP-complete in the general case [8], while tractable fragments (for which classical entailment is intractable, like the CNF one) exist [6].

However, the basic inference relation from three-valued paraconsistent logic suffers from important drawbacks. One of them (shared by many paraconsistent inference relations) is the fact that inference is too cautious. In particular, it does not coincide with classical entailment in the case where the belief base is classically consistent. Another important drawback is that consequences of the underlying belief base with different epistemic status are not discriminated. Indeed, when some piece of information is derived from a belief base, we cannot state whether:

- It is *necessary*, which means that its negation cannot be the case.
- It is *plausible*, which means that its negation is not a consequence (intuitively, there is no reason to question the piece of information, even if it cannot be completely discarded that it could be false).
- It is *possible*, which means that its negation also is a consequence (there are some arguments in favor of the piece of information, and other arguments against it).

Such a myopia can be really problematic, especially because the set of all consequences of a paraconsistent relation based on three-valued logic can be classically inconsistent. Thus, in some situations, missing the consequences of the belief base that are only possible can be a good point. A still more cautious agent would even prefer to focus only on the necessary consequences of its beliefs since it forms a classically consistent set.

This paper contributes to fill the gap. Inference relations are pointed out, for which the separation between different epistemic status of consequences is handled. Following Priest [21] and others (e.g. [2]), cautiousness is avoided by focusing on preferential refinements of the basic inference relation. Typically, a principle of *inconsistency minimization* is at work: roughly, the worlds that are as close as possible to classical interpretations are preferred. While minimization is understood with respect to set inclusion in Priest's LP_m logic, other minimization schemes can be taken into account, especially those for which some variables are more important than others [18].

Then three mechanisms are suggested to refine both the basic and the preferential inference relations of three-valued logic. The first one is based on a principle of *argumentation*: α is derivable from the belief base Σ if α is a consequence of Σ but its negation is not. This way, possible consequences are avoided. The second one relies on a principle of *uncertainty minimization*: only those α that are evaluated to true (and not the middle value) in every model of Σ are kept. Thus, only the necessary consequences of Σ are kept. The third one can be viewed as a generalization of the second one, α is a consequence of Σ if for every interpretation ω, $\omega(\alpha)$ is "at least as true" and "at most as false" as $\omega(\Sigma)$ (which means that uncertainty about α decreased).

Our contribution is a systematic investigation of these inference relations along two fundamental dimensions:

- The *logical* dimension. We check each inference relation against the three-valued counterpart of system P (for preferential), a normative set of postulates that interesting valuable inference relations should satisfy [13,15].
- The *computational* dimension. We identify the computational complexity of the decision problem corresponding to our inference relations.

We also compare all the inference relations that are considered with respect to cautiousness. This additional dimension is orthogonal to the two other ones since an inference relation can satisfy high standards for both the logical and the computational dimensions without being interesting if it is very cautious. The results from our analysis constitute a base line from which an inference relation offering the best compromise with respect to what is expected (cautiousness, myopia, logical properties, complexity) can be elected.

The rest of this paper is organized as follows. In Section 2, both the syntax and the semantics of the three-valued logic we are concerned with are presented; the corresponding (basic) inference relation is defined. In Section 3, more refined inference relations are described, and analyzed both from their logical side and from their computational side; they are also compared with respect to cautiousness. In Section 4 we study some special cases of preferential inference relations of interest. As a conclusion, we briefly discuss in Section 5 the results of the paper and we give some hints about future work.

2   A Three-Valued Paraconsistent Logic

In the following, we consider a three-valued paraconsistent logic. Let's take some space to explain the meaning of the third truth value. We do not embrace here the paradigm of many-valued logics where additional truth values are "in between" true and false. We stay in the classical paradigm where the truth value of a formula is true or false. In fact, even with two truth values, there are more than two epistemic attitudes about a formula (see [10]), there are four distinct ones depending on whether or not we can prove truth or falsity of the formula from the base:

{} We cannot prove the truth nor the falsity of the formula. This is typically the case when there is not enough information in the belief base to conclude.

{0} We can prove the falsity of the formula (but not its truth), so the formula is "false" in the usual meaning.

{1} We can prove the truth of the formula (but not its falsity), so the formula is "true" in the usual meaning.

{0,1} We can prove both the truth and the falsity of the formula, i.e. the formula is "contradictory" in the usual meaning.

The problem is that in classical logic if a formula is contradictory, then it pollutes all the belief base (*"ex falso quodlibet sequitur"*). We want to avoid this contagion, and so we will use a logic in which a truth value "both" denotes that a formula can be proved at the same time "true" and "false" in the belief base. This will allow to highlight contradictory formulas, but still reasoning "reasonably" about the other formulas. Thus the third truth value "⊤" we will use has to be understood as some encoding of the epistemic attitude {0,1}, and not as a truth value like "0" and "1".

2.1 Syntactical Aspects

Several presentations of the logic are possible, depending on the chosen set of connectives. We focus on one that is functionally complete [2], contrariwise to several presentations based on more restricted fragments, like those reported in [9], [20], [11] or [16].

Definition 1 (language). $\mathcal{L}^*$ *is the propositional language over a finite set $\mathcal{L}$ of propositional symbols, generated from the constant symbols true, false and both, the unary connective $\neg$ and the binary connectives $\vee$, $\wedge$, and $\supset$.*

We will write propositional symbols a, b, ... and formulas will be denoted by lower case Greek letters α, β, ... A belief base, that will be denoted by an upper case Greek letter such as Σ, is a finite set of formulas (conjunctively interpreted).

Clearly enough, the fragment of $\mathcal{L}^*$ built up from $\neg$, $\vee$, $\wedge$ coincides with a standard language for classical propositional logic. It is referred to as $\{\neg, \wedge, \vee\}$ *fragment*. A proper subset of this fragment is composed by the *CNF formulas*, i.e. the (finite) conjunctions of clauses, where a clause is a (finite) disjunction of literals (the symbols from $\mathcal{L}$, possibly negated).

2.2 Semantical Aspects

Definition 2 (interpretation). *An interpretation ω over $\mathcal{L}$ is a total function from $\mathcal{L}$ to the set of truth values $\{0, 1, \top\}$. The set of all interpretations over $\mathcal{L}$ is noted $\mathcal{W}$.*

Whatever the interpretation ω from $\mathcal{W}$, we have $\omega(true) = 1$, $\omega(false) = 0$ and $\omega(both) = \top$. All the connectives are truth functional ones and the semantics of a formula α from $\mathcal{L}^*$ in an interpretation is defined in the obvious compositional way given the following truth tables (Table 1).

When working with more than two truth values, one has to set the set of designated values, i.e. the set of values that a formula can take to be considered as satisfied. Since we want to define a paraconsistent logic, we choose $\mathcal{D} = \{1, \top\}$: intuitively, a formula is satisfied if it is "at least true" (but it can also be false!).

We are now ready to define notions of models and of consequences:

Definition 3 (model, consequence).

- ω *is a model of Σ, denoted $\omega \models \Sigma$, iff for all $\alpha \in \Sigma$, $\omega(\alpha) \in \mathcal{D}$. $mod(\Sigma)$ denotes the set of models of Σ.*
- α *is a consequence of Σ, noted $\Sigma \models \alpha$, iff every model of Σ is a model of α.*
- Σ *is consistent iff it has at least one model ($mod(\Sigma) \neq \emptyset$).*

It is easy to see that many additional connectives can be defined as syntactic sugars in the three-valued logic we focus on. For instance:

Table 1. Truth tables.

α	β	$\neg\alpha$	$\alpha \wedge \beta$	$\alpha \vee \beta$	$\alpha \supset \beta$
0	0	1	0	0	1
0	1	1	0	1	1
0	⊤	1	0	⊤	1
1	0	0	0	1	0
1	1	0	1	1	1
1	⊤	0	⊤	1	⊤
⊤	0	⊤	0	⊤	0
⊤	1	⊤	⊤	1	1
⊤	⊤	⊤	⊤	⊤	⊤

- $\alpha \leftrightarrow \beta =_{def} (\alpha \supset \beta) \wedge (\beta \supset \alpha)$. $\leftrightarrow$ is an equivalence operator. $\alpha \leftrightarrow \beta$ is evaluated to a designated truth value iff both α and β are evaluated to a designated truth value, or none of them is (or, equivalently, α and β have the same set of models).
- $\Box\alpha =_{def} (\neg\alpha) \supset false$. $\Box\alpha$ is evaluated to 1 when α is evaluated to 1, otherwise $\Box\alpha$ is evaluated to 0. Thus, $\Box$ is a necessity operator.
- $\Diamond\alpha =_{def} \neg\Box\neg\alpha$. $\Diamond$ is the (dual) possibility operator.
- $\odot\alpha = (\Box\alpha) \vee (\Box\neg\alpha)$. $\odot\alpha$ is evaluated to 1 when α is evaluated classically (to 1 or 0), otherwise $\odot\alpha$ is evaluated to 0.

One can observe that the implication connective $\supset$ does not coincide with usual material implication $\Rightarrow$[1]. This does not change anything when truth values 0 and 1 are considered, only, so the $\supset$ connective can be considered as one of the possible generalizations of the implication connective of classical logic. It is the "right" generalization of classical implication, because $\supset$ is the internal implication connective [3] for the defined inference relation in the sense that a deduction (meta)theorem holds for it: $\Sigma \wedge \alpha \models \beta$ iff $\Sigma \models \alpha \supset \beta$.

An interesting feature of the inference relation $\models$ is that inconsistency cannot occur in the $\{\neg, \wedge, \vee\}$ fragment (this is not the case when the full language is considered since, for instance, $false$ and $\Box(a \wedge \neg a)$ are inconsistent formulas). Indeed, every formula from the $\{\neg, \wedge, \vee\}$ fragment has at least one model [6].

As evoked in the introduction, $\models$ has several other interesting properties. From the computational side, deciding it is "only" coNP-complete in the general case [8], and is even in P in the CNF fragment [16,6]. From the logical side, it satisfies all the (three-valued counterparts of) postulates from system P and is even monotonic.

But the price to be paid is a very weak inference relation. Especially, it is well-known that disjunctive syllogism is not satisfied: $a \wedge (\neg a \vee b) \not\models b$. Subsequently, the set of consequences from a classically consistent belief base does not necessarily coincide with its classical deductive closure (we will see how to circumvent this).

Furthermore, $\models$ does not make any distinction between consequences with different epistemic status. For example, consider the following belief base:

---

[1] $\alpha \Rightarrow \beta =_{def} (\neg\alpha) \vee \beta$.

$$\Sigma = \{(\Box a) \wedge b \wedge c \wedge \neg c\}.$$

From the belief base Σ, both a, b and c can be derived, whereas they have quite different status. a for example is *necessary*, since in each model of Σ, a is necessarily true. b is *plausible*, since we have some evidence about its truth but no evidence at all about its falsity. c is only *possible*, since we have contradictory pieces of evidence about it.

3   A Study of Refined Consequence Relations

3.1   Refining Basic Inference

In order to avoid both weak and myopic inference relations, four mechanisms can be exploited:

- taking advantage of some preferential information to focus on a subset of the set of models of the belief base.
- considering only argumentative consequences of the belief bases.
- selecting those consequences of the belief base that are necessarily true.
- selecting as consequences of the belief base formulas that are so to speak "more true" than the belief base.

Formally, the four principles above give rise to the following inference relations. Let $\leq$ be any binary relation on $\mathcal{W}$; $min(mod(\Sigma), \leq)$ denotes the set $\{\omega \in mod(\Sigma) \mid \not\exists \omega' \in mod(\Sigma) \ \omega' \leq \omega \text{ and } \omega \not\leq \omega'\}$.

Definition 4 (refined inference relations).

- *Let $\leq$ be a standard binary relation on $\mathcal{W}^2$:*
- $\Sigma \models^{\leq} \alpha$ *iff* $\forall \omega \in min(mod(\Sigma), \leq)$, $\omega \models \alpha$.
- $\Sigma \models_{arg} \alpha$ *iff* $\Sigma \models \alpha$ *and* $\Sigma \not\models \neg\alpha$.
- $\Sigma \models_1 \alpha$ *iff* $\forall \omega \in mod(\Sigma)$, $\omega(\alpha) = 1$.
- $\Sigma \models_t \alpha$ *iff* $\forall \omega \in \mathcal{W}$, $\omega(\Sigma) \leq_t \omega(\alpha)$, *where the truth ordering $\leq_t$ is given by the reflexive-transitive closure of $0 <_t \top <_t 1$.*

Combining the first mechanism with any of the three other ones results in some additional inference relations:

Definition 5 (refined inference relations). *Let $\leq$ be a standard binary relation on $\mathcal{W}$:*

- $\Sigma \models^{\leq}_{arg} \alpha$ *iff* $\Sigma \models^{\leq} \alpha$ *and* $\Sigma \not\models^{\leq} \neg\alpha$.
- $\Sigma \models^{\leq}_1 \alpha$ *iff* $\forall \omega \in min(mod(\Sigma), \leq)$, $\omega(\alpha) = 1$.
- $\Sigma \models^{\leq}_t \alpha$ *iff* $\forall \omega \in min(mod(\Sigma), \leq)$, $\omega(\Sigma) \leq_t \omega(\alpha)$.

---

[2] We will call *standard* any binary relation on $\mathcal{W}$ whose definition is independent from the belief base Σ under consideration.

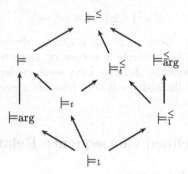

Fig. 1. Cautiousness (assuming Σ consistent).

3.2 Cautiousness

Assuming that the belief base is consistent[3], we have derived the following results:

Theorem 1. *The inclusions between inference relations reported in Figure 1 hold.*

Figure 1 gives a Hasse diagram of inclusion in the set of our inference relations. An arrow $X \to Y$ means that relation X is strictly more cautious than Y, i.e. $X \subsetneq Y$. Arrows that would stem from transitivity of inclusion are omitted.

As comments to these cautiousness results one can note that, unsurprisingly, the preferential inference relations usually contain their original counterparts, except that $\models_{arg}$ is not contained in $\models_{\overline{arg}}^{\leq}$. The fact that all the inference relations are contained in $\models$ or $\models^{\leq}$ is not surprising since they aim at separating consequences with different epistemic status: $\models_{arg}$, $\models_1$, $\models_t$ are less cautious than $\models$. Similarly, the relations $\models_{\overline{arg}}^{\leq}$, $\models_{\overline{1}}^{\leq}$ and $\models_{\overline{t}}^{\leq}$ are less cautious than $\models^{\leq}$. The strong principle of uncertainty minimization (focusing on truth value 1) is more demanding than both the weak one (based on the $\leq_t$ pre-order) and argumentation ($\models_1$ is included in $\models_t$ and in $\models_{arg}$) and this is still the case when some preference information is taken into account ($\models_{\overline{1}}^{\leq}$ is included in $\models_{\overline{t}}^{\leq}$ and $\models_{\overline{arg}}^{\leq}$).

3.3 Logical Properties

Following seminal works in non-monotonic logic [12,17,13,15], a set of normative properties that a non-monotonic inference relation should satisfy has been given in [13]. This set of properties is called system P (for Preferential).

---

[3] Without this assumption, many of the inference relations trivialize, either because they coincide with the total relation $\mathcal{L}^* \times \mathcal{L}^*$ or with the empty one (argumentative relations). The only change with respect to cautiousness is that $\models_1$ (resp. $\models_{\overline{1}}^{\leq}$) is no longer included in $\models_{arg}$ (resp. $\models_{\overline{arg}}^{\leq}$).

Table 2. Logical Properties of the Inference Relations.

	Ref	LLE	RW	Or	Cut	CM	Mon
$\models$	✓	✓	✓	✓	✓	✓	✓
$\models^{\leq}$	✓	✓	✓	✓	✓	✓	
$\models_{arg}$		✓		✓	✓	✓	
$\models_1$		✓		✓	✓	✓	✓
$\models^{\leq}_{arg}$		✓		✓	✓	✓	
$\models^{\leq}_1$		✓		✓	✓	✓	
$\models_t$	✓			✓	✓	✓	✓
$\models^{\leq}_t$	✓			✓	✓	✓	

Definition 6 (system P). *An inference relation $\vdash\!\!\sim$ is preferential if it satisfies the following properties (system P):*

(Ref) $\alpha\vdash\!\!\sim\alpha$		*Reflexivity*
(LLE) *If $\models \alpha \leftrightarrow \beta$ and $\alpha\vdash\!\!\sim\gamma$, then $\beta\vdash\!\!\sim\gamma$*		*Left Logical Equivalence*
(RW) *If $\models \beta \supset \gamma$ and $\alpha\vdash\!\!\sim\beta$, then $\alpha\vdash\!\!\sim\gamma$*		*Right Weakening*
(Or) *If $\alpha\vdash\!\!\sim\gamma$ and $\beta\vdash\!\!\sim\gamma$, then $\alpha \vee \beta\vdash\!\!\sim\gamma$*		*Or*
(Cut) *If $\alpha \wedge \beta\vdash\!\!\sim\gamma$ and $\alpha\vdash\!\!\sim\beta$, then $\alpha\vdash\!\!\sim\gamma$*		*Cut*
(CM) *If $\alpha\vdash\!\!\sim\beta$ and $\alpha\vdash\!\!\sim\gamma$, then $\alpha \wedge \beta\vdash\!\!\sim\gamma$*		*Cautious Monotony*

Those properties have been stated in the framework of classical logic, but as we work here in a three-valued setting, we have to consider that $\models$ denotes the three-valued inference relation, as given in Definition 3. In the same vein, we refer to the "classical" three-valued implication connective $\supset$, and the equivalence connective $\leftrightarrow$ in the properties above. Following Arieli and Avron [2], we call the relations satisfying those properties three-valued preferential relations.

We will say that a relation is monotonic if it satisfies the following:

(Mon) If $\alpha\vdash\!\!\sim\gamma$, then $\alpha \wedge \beta\vdash\!\!\sim\gamma$ Monotony

Theorem 2. *The logical properties of P satisfied by the inference relations considered in the paper are as given in Table 2.*

One can note that $\models^{\leq}$ inference relations, that are the less cautious ones, satisfy all properties of system P, and that all the preferential inference relations have the same logical properties as their original counterpart (except monotony of course). (Or),(Cut), (CM) are always satisfied. We can also observe that, unsurprisingly, (RW) is lost for all relations aiming at discriminating consequences obtained by $\models$ and $\models^{\leq}$.

3.4 Computational Complexity

We assume the reader familiar with some basic notions of complexity, especially the complexity classes coNP and Π_2^p of the polynomial hierarchy PH and the class BH_2 of the Boolean hierarchy (see [19] for a survey).

We have derived the following results:

Table 3. Complexity Results.

Inference	Complexity of its decision problem
$\models$	coNP-complete
$\models_1$	coNP-complete
$\models_t$	coNP-complete
$\models$arg	BH_2-complete
$\models^{\leq}$	in Π_2^p
$\models_{\overline{\text{arg}}}^{\leq}$	in Δ_3^p
$\models_1^{\leq}$	in Π_2^p
$\models_t^{\leq}$	in Π_2^p

Theorem 3. *The complexity results reported in Table 3 hold (where it is assumed that $\leq$ can be tested in (deterministic) polynomial time).*

In the light of these results, the following observations can be done. First, all the inference relations considered in this paper are intractable, the complexity varying from the first level to the second level of the polynomial hierarchy. Second, focusing on the necessary consequences does not imply a complexity shift ($\models_1$ is just as complex as $\models$, and $\models_1^{\leq}$ is just as complex as $\models^{\leq}$). As it is the case in other frameworks [7], the corresponding argumentative versions of inference relations are mildly harder. Finally, as expected, preferring some models may definitely lead to more complex inference (under the standard assumptions of complexity theory). Especially, when $\leq$ is the preference pre-ordering proposed by Priest (preferring interpretations that are as classical as possible with respect to set inclusion), the decision problems associated to $\models^{\leq}$ and $\models_1^{\leq}$ are complete for Π_2^p, and this is still the case when the belief base Σ is from the CNF fragment and the query is an atom. Intuitively, when Priest's preference relation is considered, two independent sources of complexity must be dealt with: the first one lies in the number of preferred models and the second one in the difficulty to check whether a model is preferred. The decision problem associated to $\models_{\overline{\text{arg}}}^{\leq}$ is both Σ_2^p-hard and Π_2^p-hard, showing that it is not in $\Sigma_2^p \cup \Pi_2^p$, unless the polynomial hierarchy collapses.

4   Preference Based Inference Relations

In the previous section, for the inference relations $\models^{\leq}$, $\models_{\overline{\text{arg}}}^{\leq}$ and $\models_1^{\leq}$ we consider a binary relation $\leq$ with no special property. But one can expect this relation to express some kinds of preferences and thus to have some specific properties. A first intuitive need is to work with a pre-order for example, since preference relations are often transitive ones.

In this section we will investigate more deeply and compare four particular relations. Two of them prefer the most defined interpretations, i.e. the interpretations with a maximum of classical truth values. The first one takes the maximum for set inclusion (it was defined by Priest in [21]), the second one for

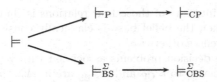

Fig. 2. Cautiousness.

cardinality. The last two relations give preference to interpretations that satisfy the more formulas in the belief base (w.r.t. set inclusion and cardinality). They are inspired by an inference relation defined by Besnard and Schaub [5]. Before defining formally those relations, we first need the following definitions:

Definition 7 (inconsistent set, satisfaction set).

- *The inconsistent set of an interpretation ω is*
  $\omega! = \{a \in \mathcal{L} \mid \omega(a) = \top\}$.
- *The satisfaction set of an interpretation ω given a belief base Σ is*
  $\mathcal{S}_\Sigma(\omega) = \{\alpha \in \Sigma \mid \omega(\alpha) = 1\}$.

Definition 8 (preferential inference relations). *Let ω and ω' be two inter-pretations from $\mathcal{W}$. $\leq_P$, $\leq_{CP}$, $\leq_{BS}^\Sigma$ and $\leq_{CBS}^\Sigma$ are defined by:*

- $\omega \leq_P \omega'$ *iff* $\omega! \subseteq \omega'!$
- $\omega \leq_{CP} \omega'$ *iff* $card(\omega!) \leq card(\omega'!)$
- $\omega \leq_{BS}^\Sigma \omega'$ *iff* $\mathcal{S}_\Sigma(\omega) \supseteq \mathcal{S}_\Sigma(\omega')$
- $\omega \leq_{CBS}^\Sigma \omega'$ *iff* $card(\mathcal{S}_\Sigma(\omega)) \geq card(\mathcal{S}_\Sigma(\omega'))$

The corresponding preferential inference relations $\models_P$, $\models_{CP}$, $\models_{BS}^\Sigma$, $\models_{CBS}^\Sigma$ are those obtained using respective pre-orders $\leq_P$, $\leq_{CP}$, $\leq_{BS}^\Sigma$, $\leq_{CBS}^\Sigma$ for the definition of the preferential relation $\models^\leq$.

Note that $\leq_{BS}^\Sigma$ and $\leq_{CBS}^\Sigma$ are non-standard binary relations since they depend on a belief base Σ. The logical properties have been studied for standard binary relations. Non-standard binary relations give operators that do not satisfy all properties ((LLE) is often missing).

Theorem 4. *The inclusions between inference relations reported in figure 2 hold.*

As the pre-orders $\leq_P$ and $\leq_{CP}$ are standard pre-orders, from Theorem 2 we get that the two inference relations $\models_P$ and $\models_{CP}$ are three-valued preferential relations (they satisfy all the logical properties).

Theorem 5. *$\models_P$ and $\models_{CP}$ satisfy (Ref), (LLE), (RW), (Or), (Cut) and (CM). $\models_{BS}^\Sigma$ and $\models_{CBS}^\Sigma$ satisfy (Ref), (RW), (Or), (Cut) and (CM)[4].*

---

[4] Note that those two preference relations are based on sets of formulas, so one has to consider a generalization of the logical properties to sets of formulas (see e.g. [2]).

One of the main interests of those four relations is that they coincide with classical inference when the belief base is classically consistent, and that they give meaningful inferences otherwise.

Finally, while the decision problems associated with $\models_P$ and $\models_{BS}^{\Sigma}$ are Π_2^p-complete, those associated to $\models_{CP}$ and $\models_{CBS}^{\Sigma}$ are in Δ_2^p, "only".

5   Conclusion

In this paper, we have investigated several three-valued inference relations for paraconsistent reasoning, both from the logical and the computational point of view. We have highlighted the fact that the basic three-valued inference relation can be refined with respect to the status of derived facts.

In the light of the results obtained, it appears that no relation is better than all the other ones with respect to both criteria. On the one hand, discriminating consequences does not imply a major complexity shift but leads to lose some valuable expected properties. On the other hand, avoiding too cautious relations can be achieved while keeping many interesting logical properties but typically leads to an increase in complexity. The choice of a good compromise depends mainly on what is expected in priority (avoiding cautiousness or myopia).

An interesting family of three-valued inference relations are those based on the selection of preferred models based on cardinality. Indeed, those relations have good logical properties, they also coincide with classical inference when the belief base is classically consistent (provided that a suitable preference relation has been chosen), and to give meaningful conclusions when the belief base is classically inconsistent. Furthermore, their decision problem remains at the first level of the polynomial hierarchy.

When working with more than two truth values a question that may arise is how many truth values are needed. In [2], Arieli and Avron showed that four-valued logics play a central role in billatice-based multi-valued logics, showing that more than four values are not necessary (the other logics can be characterized by a four-valued one). In such four-valued logics (e.g. [22,1]), based on Belnap's seminal work [4], the fourth value $\bot$ means "not known", i.e. it denotes the epistemic attitude where we can prove neither the truth nor the falsity of the formula (see Section 2). Even if this truth value adds expressivity to the language and is useful to express ignorance (when one wants to be able to express the fact that an agent is agnostic about a formula), it does not help much as far as paraconsistency is concerned.

A future work concerns the design of three-valued inference relations as "blackbox" tools for paraconsistent reasoning in the classical framework. The idea is, from a classical two-valued belief base (possibly inconsistent), to derive facts with a three-valued logic (allowing to rule out the ex falso quodlibet), and finally to come back to the classical framework by translating three-valued models into two-valued ones. Several means can be envisioned for the last step, in particular one can use a generalization of the forgetting operator [14] to three-valued logics.

Acknowledgements

The authors want to thank two anonymous referees for their careful reading. The second author has been partly supported by the IUT de Lens, the Université d'Artois, the Région Nord/Pas-de-Calais under the TACT-TIC project, and by the European Community FEDER Program.

References

1. O. Arieli and A. Avron. Four-valued diagnoses for stratified knowledge-bases. In *Proceedings of CSL'96*, LNCS 1258, pages 1–17, 1997.
2. O. Arieli and A. Avron. The value of four values. *Artificial Intelligence*, 102:97–141, 1998.
3. A. Avron. Simple consequence relations. *Information and Computation*, 92:105–139, 1991.
4. N.D. Belnap. *A useful four-valued logic*, pages 7–37. Modern Uses of Multiple-Valued Logic. Reidel, 1977.
5. Ph. Besnard and T. Schaub. Circumscribing inconsistency. In *Proceedings of IJCAI'97*, pages 150–155, 1997.
6. M. Cadoli and M. Schaerf. On the complexity of entailment in propositional multivalued logics. *Annals of Mathematics and Artificial Intelligence*, 18:29–50, 1996.
7. C. Cayrol and M.-C. Lagasquie-Schiex. Non-monotonic syntax-based entailment: a classification of consequence relations. In *Proceedings of ECSQARU'95*, LNAI 946, pages 107–114, 1995.
8. S. Coste-Marquis and P. Marquis. Complexity results for paraconsistent inference relations. In *Proceedings of KR'02*, pages 61–72, 2002.
9. I.M.L. D'Ottaviano and N.C.A. da Costa. Sur un problème de Jaśkowski. In *Comptes Rendus de l'Académie des Sciences de Paris*, volume 270, pages 1349–1353. 1970.
10. D. Dubois and H. Prade. Possibility theory, probability theory and multiple-valued logics : A clarification. *Annals of Mathematics and Artificial Intelligence*, 32:35–66, 2001.
11. A.M. Frisch. Inference without chaining. In *Proceedings of IJCAI'87*, pages 515–519, 1987.
12. D. M. Gabbay. Theoretical foundations for nonmonotonic reasoning in experts systems. In K. Apt, editor, *Logic and Models of Concurrent Systems*. Springer Verlag, 1985.
13. S. Kraus, D. Lehmann, and M. Magidor. Nonmonotonic reasoning, preferential models and cumulative logics. *Artificial Intelligence*, 44:167–207, 1990.
14. J. Lang and P. Marquis. Resolving inconsistencies by variable forgetting. In *Proceedings of KR'02*, pages 239–250, 2002.
15. D. Lehmann and M. Magidor. What does a conditional knowledge base entail? *Artificial Intelligence*, 55:1–60, 1992.
16. H.J. Levesque. A knowledge-level account of abduction (preliminary version). In *Proceedings of IJCAI'89*, pages 1061–1067, 1989.
17. D. Makinson. *Handbook of Logic in Artificial Intelligence and Logic Programming*, volume III, chapter General Pattern in nonmonotonic reasoning, pages 35–110. Clarendon Press, Oxford, 1994.

18. P. Marquis and N. Porquet. Resource-bounded inference from inconsistent belief bases. In *Proceedings of IJCAI'01*, pages 103–108, 2001.
19. Ch. H. Papadimitriou. *Computational Complexity*. Addison-Wesley, 1994.
20. G. Priest. Reasoning about truth. *Artificial Intelligence*, 39:231–244, 1989.
21. G. Priest. Minimally inconsistent LP. *Studia Logica*, 50:321–331, 1991.
22. E. Sandewall. A functional approach to non-monotonic logic. In *Proceedings of IJCAI'85*, pages 100–106, 1985.

Paraconsistent Logic Programs*

João Alcântara, Carlos Viegas Damásio, and Luís Moniz Pereira

Centro de Inteligência Artificial (CENTRIA)
Departamento de Informática, Universidade Nova de Lisboa
2829-516 Caparica, Portugal.

Abstract. We propose a framework which extends Antitonic Logic Programs [2] to an arbitrary complete bilattice of truth-values, where belief and doubt are explicitly represented. Based on Fitting's ideas, this framework allows a precise definition of important operators found in logic programming such as explicit negation and the default negation. In particular, it leads to a natural integration of explicit negation with the default negation through the coherence principle [19]. According to this principle, the explicit negation entails the default negation. We then define Coherent Answer Sets, and the Paraconsistent Well-founded Model semantics, generalizing paraconsistent semantics for logic programs (for instance, $WFSX_p$ [4]). Our framework is an extension of important classes of Antitonic Logic Programs, and is general enough to capture Probabilistic Deductive Databases, Possibilistic Logic Programming, Hybrid Probabilistic Logic Programs, and Fuzzy Logic Programming. Thus, we have a powerful mathematical formalism for dealing with default reasoning, paraconsistency, and uncertainty.

1 Introduction

Several frameworks for manipulating uncertainty, incompleteness, and inconsistency have been proposed in the form of extensions to classical logic programming and deductive databases. Usually, the authors characterize their programs with a model theoretical semantics, where a minimum model is guaranteed to exist, and a corresponding monotonic fixpoint operator too.

The underlying uncertainty formalism in the proposed frameworks includes probability theory [14,17], fuzzy set theory [20,22], many-valued logic [7,8,12], possibilistic logic [6]. Furthermore, different ways of dealing with uncertainty may be required for one given application [15]. All these formalisms are monotonic, and none of them allow negation.

Following an algebraic approach to both the language and the semantics of logic programs, Damásio and Pereira define in [3] a rather general framework of Monotonic Logic Programs, where the rules are constituted by arbitrary monotonic body functions and by propositional symbols in the head. These programs extend definite logic programming, i.e. those without non-monotonic or default

---

* João Alcântara is a PhD student supported by CAPES - Brasília, Brazil. The authors also thank the TARDE and FLUX projects, sponsored by MCT - Portugal.

S. Flesca et al. (Eds.): JELIA 2002, LNAI 2424, pp. 345–356, 2002.

negation, to arbitrary complete lattices of truth-values with an appropriate notion of implication. It is also shown that they are general enough to capture several distinct logic programming semantics such as the uncertainty formalisms referred above. In [2], the same authors generalize the framework to allow for rules with arbitrary antitonic bodies over general complete lattices, of which normal programs are a special case, and show that all the standard logic programming theoretical results carry over to such Antitonic Logic Programs, and define for them Stable and Well-founded Model semantics alike.

Notwithstanding, a specific treatment for explicit negation forms in Antitonic Logic Programs is not provided. In the present work we extend the framework for these programs to an arbitrary complete bilattice of truth-values, where both belief and doubt are explicitly represented. We dub the resultant framework Paraconsistent Logic Programs. In its presentation, we are motivated by Fitting's bilattices [8], and by Lakshmanan and Sadri's work on probabilistic deductive databases [14]. Fitting's bilattices support an elegant framework for logic programming involving belief and doubt. In particular, they lead to a precise definition of explicit negation operators. We further use these results to properly characterize default negation and to ensure obedience to the coherence principle, which states negation entails default negation, i.e., anything that is explicitly false must be default false as well. On the other hand, in [14], the authors argue about the convenience of explicitly representing both belief and doubt when dealing with incomplete knowledge, where different evidence may contradict one another.

Besides satisfying the coherence principle, a semantics for Paraconsistent Logic Programs must deal with both contradiction and uncertain information. In order to define a semantics with these requirements, we generalize the paraconsistent well-founded semantics for extended logic programs, ($WFSX_p$) [4]. As we do not impose any specific characterization for explicit negation, we can introduce in our framework any negation operator supported by Fitting's bilattice. In the sequel, we also present a semantics based on Coherent Answer Sets. An illustrative example is exhibited, where our framework is used to encode a rather complex decision table.

2   Bilattices

Aiming at the characterization of uncertainty, several varieties of fixed point semantics for logic programming have been proposed. In common, they require a suitable machinery to ensure the existence of fixed points of the operator associated with a program. It is claimed by Fitting in [8] that the notion of bilattice, as presented by Ginsberg [11], can be applied to most of kinds of fixed point semantics and provides an account of the intended partial ordering, for each of the truth functional connectives, and the interactions between them. Following Fitting's ideas, we recall below how to construct a bilattice:

Definition 1 (Bilattice construction). *Given two complete lattices $\langle C, \leq_1 \rangle$ and $\langle D, \leq_2 \rangle$ the structure $\mathcal{B}(C, D) = \langle C \times D, \leq_k, \leq_t \rangle$ is a bilattice, where the* *knowledge ordering is defined as* $\langle c_1, d_1 \rangle \leq_k \langle c_2, d_2 \rangle$ *if* $c_1 \leq_1 c_2$ *and* $d_1 \leq_2 d_2$, *and the truth ordering as* $\langle c_1, d_1 \rangle \leq_t \langle c_2, d_2 \rangle$ *if* $c_1 \leq_1 c_2$ *and* $d_2 \leq_2 d_1$. *To each ordering are associated the following join* $(\oplus)$ *and meet* $(\otimes)$ *operations:*

$$\langle c_1, d_1 \rangle \otimes_k \langle c_2, d_2 \rangle = \langle c_1 \sqcap_1 c_2, d_1 \sqcap_2 d_2 \rangle \quad \langle c_1, d_1 \rangle \otimes_t \langle c_2, d_2 \rangle = \langle c_1 \sqcap_1 c_2, d_1 \sqcup_2 d_2 \rangle$$
$$\langle c_1, d_1 \rangle \oplus_k \langle c_2, d_2 \rangle = \langle c_1 \sqcup_1 c_2, d_1 \sqcup_2 d_2 \rangle \quad \langle c_1, d_1 \rangle \oplus_t \langle c_2, d_2 \rangle = \langle c_1 \sqcup_1 c_2, d_1 \sqcap_2 d_2 \rangle$$

The intuition here is that C provides the evidence for (and D evidence against or doubt) believing in the truth of a statement. If $\langle c_1, d_1 \rangle \leq_k \langle c_2, d_2 \rangle$, then situation 2 has more information than 1, i.e. knowledge is increased, both in truth and in falsity. If $\langle c_1, d_1 \rangle \leq_t \langle c_2, d_2 \rangle$, then we have more reasons to believe in situation 2 than in 1, because the reasons for believing the statement either increased or the reasons against it are weaker, i.e. $\langle c_2, d_2 \rangle$ is truer than $\langle c_1, d_1 \rangle$.

Observe that negation is not granted by this construction. In order to introduce it, Ginsberg [11] requires that the negation mesh well with the orderings and satisfy the double negation property:

Definition 2 (Negation). *A bilattice* $\mathcal{B}(C, D)$ *has a negation operation if there is a mapping* $\neg : C \times D \to C \times D$ *such that*

1) $a \leq_k b \Rightarrow \neg a \leq_k \neg b$;   *2)* $a \leq_t b \Rightarrow \neg b \leq_t \neg a$;   *3)* $\neg \neg a = a$.

Fitting [8] introduced one more basic operator on bilattices: conflation.

Definition 3 (Conflation). *A bilattice* $\mathcal{B}(C, D)$ *enjoys a conflation operation if there is a mapping* $- : C \times D \to C \times D$ *such that*

1) $a \leq_k b \Rightarrow -b \leq_k -a$;   *2)* $a \leq_t b \Rightarrow -a \leq_t -b$;   *3)* $- - a = a$.

Hence, negation should reverse the degree of truth, but preserve that of knowledge. Conflation is similar, but with the roles of $\leq_k$ and $\leq_t$ exchanged. Moreover, if $\neg \neg a = a$ (resp. $- - a = a$) is not verified, the negation (resp. conflation) operator is said to be weak.

In [8], Fitting further states that after applying the conflation operator, we are moving to "default" evidence. This means that given $L \in C \times D$, where $\mathcal{B}(C, D)$ is a bilattice with the conflation operator, in $-L$ we are to count as "for" whatever did not count as "against" before, and "against" what did not count as "for". Thus, $-\neg L$ resembles *not* L, where *not* is the default negation operator found in many logic programming formalisms.

Definition 4 (Default Negation). *Let* $\mathcal{B}(C, D)$ *a bilattice. Consider* $\neg$ *and* $-$ *respectively a negation and a conflation operator on* $\mathcal{B}(C, D)$. *We define* $not : C \times D \to C \times D$ *as the default negation operator where* $not\ L = -\neg L$.

The default operator plays a central role in our framework. In Section 3, following ideas expressed in [19], we will relate it with the explicit negation operator through the *coherence principle*.

3   Paraconsistent Logic Programs

In the framework of Monotonic Logic Programs [3], the rules are constituted by arbitrary isotonic[1] body functions and by propositional symbols in the head. In [2], Damásio and Pereira extend the syntax of Monotonic Logic Programs allowing for rules with antitonic bodies (Antitonic Logic Programs), of which normal logic programs are a special case. The authors also show that all the standard logic programming theoretical results carry over to such Antitonic Logic Programs through both Stable and Well-founded semantics alike. Because of their arbitrary monotonic and antitonic operators over a complete lattice, these programs pave the way to combine and integrate into a single framework several forms of reasoning, e.g., fuzzy, probabilistic, uncertain, and paraconsistent ones.

Many works (e.g. [10,13,24,19]) have argued about the convenience of introducing into logic programming a way to distinguish what can be shown to be false from what is false by default because it cannot be proven true. So called Extended Logic Programs add explicit negation to normal programs. In [19], it is claimed that explicit negation should entail default negation. This is the *coherence principle*. Unfortunately antitonic logic programs are not suitable to characterize this principle as we can see below.

Following another path, Lakshmanan and Sadri [14] proposed a framework for modeling uncertainty, where both belief and doubt are explicitly incorporated. Motivated by these results, we shall extend the syntax of antitonic logic programs to an arbitrary complete bilattice of truth-values. Then we employ the characterization of the default negation operator presented in the section 2 to impose coherence on it.

When defining paraconsistent logic programs, we adopt an algebraic characterization of both the language and interpretations of operators. This is a very general and powerful framework, allowing for a simple relation between the syntax and its semantics. We start its presentation by introducing the syntax of paraconsistent logic programs:

Definition 5 (ℬ-algebras). *Consider the complete bilattice $\mathcal{B}(C,C)$ with negation ($\neg$) and conflation ($-$) operators, where C is a given complete lattice. We define the ℬ-algebra $\mathfrak{P}$ associated to $\mathcal{B}(C,C)$ as an algebra whose carrier set is $C \times C$, and whose operators must include at least $\neg, -$, the operator $\otimes_k$ of $\mathcal{B}(C,C)$, and constants corresponding to the elements $\langle c, d \rangle$ in $C \times C$.*

Having defined the alphabet, we can present the corresponding algebra of expressions, frow which we select the subalgebra of well-formed formulae:

Definition 6 (Formulae). *Let $\mathfrak{P}$ be the ℬ-algebra associated with a complete bilattice. We define the alphabet $A_{\Pi,\Delta}$ as the disjoint union $\Pi \cup \Delta \cup S$, where Π is a countably infinite set of propositional symbols, Δ is the set of operators found in $\mathfrak{P}$, and S is the set of auxiliary symbols "(", ")", and ",". Furthermore,*

---

[1] A function is isotonic (antitonic) iff the value of the function increases (decreases) when we increase any argument while the remaining arguments are kept fixed.

consider the algebra $\mathfrak{E}$ of expressions corresponding to the alphabet $A_{\Pi,\Delta}$. As usual, we define the well-formed formulae (in short formulae) generated by Δ over Π as the elements of the carrier set of the least subalgebra of $\mathfrak{E}$ containing Π. We name such subalgebra of $FORM_{\mathfrak{P}}(\Pi)$.

Given the definitions above, Paraconsistent Logic Programs are defined as

Definition 7 (Paraconsistent Logic Programs). *Let $\mathfrak{P}$ be the $\mathcal{B}$-algebra associated with a complete bilattice $\mathcal{B}(C,C)$, Π a set of propositional symbols, and $FORM_{\mathfrak{P}}(\Pi)$ the corresponding algebra of freely generated formulae. A paraconsistent logic program P is a set of rules of the form $A \leftarrow \Psi$ such that:*

1. *The body formula Ψ is any formula of $FORM_{\mathfrak{P}}(\Pi)$;*
2. *The head A of the rule is a propositional symbol of Π;*
3. *Let $A_1, \ldots, A_m, B_1, \ldots, B_n$ $(m, n \geq 0)$ be a sequence with all occurrences of propositional symbols in Ψ. If $A \leftarrow \Psi$ belongs to P, then Ψ corresponds to a function having $A_1, \ldots, A_m, B_1, \ldots, B_n$ as arguments and which is isotonic (antitonic) with relation to $A_1, \ldots, A_m$ (resp. $B_1, \ldots, B_n$). Sometimes we will denote a rule $A \leftarrow \Psi$ of P by $A \leftarrow \Psi[A_1, \ldots, A_m \mid B_1, \ldots, B_n]$.*

We assume, in the rest of this work, a $\mathcal{B}$-algebra $\mathfrak{P}$ associated to a complete bilattice $\mathcal{B}(C,C)$. We will add the subscript $\mathfrak{P}$ to the "symbols" of the operators to denote they are defined in $\mathfrak{P}$. However, when that may not cause any confusion, we will deliberately omit this subscript from the operators. We also assume the set with the constants corresponding to the elements in $C \times C$ is implicit in the $\mathcal{B}$-algebra and we will do any reference to it in the examples. Consider still that a set Π of propositional symbols and the corresponding algebra $FORM_{\mathfrak{P}}(\Pi)$ are given.

We refer to P as monotonic logic program if for each rule $A \leftarrow \Psi$ in P, the body formula Ψ corresponds to a isotonic function, i.e. rules are of the kind $A \leftarrow \Psi[A_1, \ldots, A_m \mid]$. We refer to P as antitonic logic program if each rule is either of the kind $A \leftarrow \Psi[A_1, \ldots, A_m \mid]$ or $A \leftarrow \Psi[\mid B_1, \ldots, B_n]$. Mark the body formula Ψ can be isotonic with relation to some occurrences of a propositional symbol A and antitonic with relation to other occurrences of the same propositional symbol A.

We proceed by exhibiting the semantics for paraconsistent logic programs. As usual, an interpretation is simply an assignment of truth-value to each propositional symbol in the language.

Definition 8 (Interpretation). *An interpretation is a mapping $I : \Pi \to C \times C$. The interpretation extends uniquely to a valuation $\hat{I} : FORM_{\mathfrak{P}}(\Pi) \to C \times C$. The set of all interpretations of the formulas with respect to the algebra $\mathfrak{P}$ is denoted by $\mathcal{I}_{\mathfrak{P}}$.*

The unique homomorphic extension theorem guarantees that for every interpretation of propositional symbols there is an unique associated valuation function. The ordering $\leq_k$ on the truth-values in $\mathfrak{P}$ is extended to the set of interpretations as follows:

Definition 9 (Lattice of Interpretations). *Consider $\mathcal{I}_{\mathfrak{P}}$ the set of all interpretations with respect to algebra $\mathfrak{P}$, and two interpretations $I_1, I_2 \in \mathcal{I}_{\mathfrak{P}}$. Then, $\langle \mathcal{I}_{\mathfrak{P}}, \sqsubseteq \rangle$ is a complete lattice where $I_1 \sqsubseteq I_2$ iff $\forall_{p \in \Pi} I_1(p) \leq_k I_2(p)$. The least interpretation $\triangle$ maps every propositional symbol to the least element under $\leq_k$ of $C \times C$, and the greatest interpretation $\triangledown$ maps every propositional symbol to the top element under $\leq_k$ of the complete bilattice of truth-values $C \times C$.*

Extending the results of van Emden and Kowalski [21] to the general theoretical setting of algebras, we define below the immediate consequences operator:

Definition 10. *Let P be a monotonic logic program. Define the immediate consequences operator $T_P^{\mathfrak{P}} : \mathcal{I}_{\mathfrak{P}} \to \mathcal{I}_{\mathfrak{P}}$, mapping interpretations to interpretations:*

$$T_P^{\mathfrak{P}}(I)(A) = lub_k \left\{ \hat{I}(\Psi) \text{ such that } A \leftarrow \Psi \in P \right\},$$

where A is a propositional symbol.

The use of the knowledge ordering is fundamental. Assume that we state that a proposition, say a, is both true and false via the rules $a \leftarrow \langle \top, \bot \rangle$ and $a \leftarrow \langle \bot, \top \rangle$. Using the truth-ordering, we would obtain in the least model that a is true, whilst under knowledge ordering a is mapped to $\langle \top, \top \rangle$. For capturing default negation, a new notion of interpretation is also required:

Definition 11 (Partial Interpretations). *A partial interpretation is a pair of interpretations $\langle I^t, I^{tu} \rangle$. The set of all partial interpretations is $\mathcal{I}_{\mathfrak{P}}^p$.*

The I^t component contains what is "true" in the interpretation, while I^{tu} contains what is "non-false", i.e. true or undefined. It is important to mark that consistency of interpretations (i.e. $I^t \sqsubseteq I^{tu}$) is not imposed and, consequently, paraconsistency is allowed, i.e. something may be "true and false" (by being not "true or undefined"). Following the general construction of a bilattice, two orderings among partial interpretations can be defined:

Definition 12 (Standard and Fitting Ordering). *Let I_1 and I_2 be two partial interpretations. The standard and Fitting orderings among partial interpretations are defined by: $I_1 \sqsubseteq_s I_2$ iff $I_1^t \sqsubseteq I_2^t$ and $I_1^{tu} \sqsubseteq I_2^{tu}$ (Standard); $I_1 \sqsubseteq_f I_2$ iff $I_1^t \sqsubseteq I_2^t$ and $I_2^{tu} \sqsubseteq I_1^{tu}$ (Fitting). The set of partial interpretations ordered by $\sqsubseteq_s$ or $\sqsubseteq_f$ is a complete lattice. The bottom and top elements of these lattices are $\perp_s = \langle \triangle, \triangle \rangle$ (all is false), $\top_s = \langle \triangledown, \triangledown \rangle$ (all is true), $\perp_f = \langle \triangle, \triangledown \rangle$ (all is undefined) and $\top_f = \langle \triangledown, \triangle \rangle$ (all is true and false).*

Given a partial interpretation, the models of a paraconsistent logic program are defined as per below:

Definition 13 (Models). *Let P be a paraconsistent logic program and $I = \langle I^t, I^{tu} \rangle$ a partial interpretation[2]. Consider a formula $\Psi[A_1, \ldots A_m \mid B_1, \ldots, B_n]$ in $FORM_{\mathfrak{P}}(\Pi)$. We define $\hat{I}(\Psi) = \Psi_{\mathfrak{P}}[I^t(A_1), \ldots I^t(A_m) \mid I^{tu}(B_1), \ldots, I^{tu}(B_n)]$. The partial interpretation I satisfies a rule $A \leftarrow \Psi$ of P iff $\hat{I}(\Psi) \leq_k \hat{I}(A)$. We say that I is a model of P iff I satisfies all rules of P.*

---

[2] This extends the notion of interpretation to the case of partial interpretations.

The next definition is based on the usual way of defining well-founded and stable model semantics for normal logic programs. It is a Gelfond-Lifschitz like division operator [9] which transforms Paraconsistent Logic Programs into Monotonic ones, for which we know how to compute the corresponding least models through the immediate consequences operator.

Definition 14 (Program Division). *Consider a paraconsistent logic program P and an interpretation I. The division of P by I is the monotonic logic program:*
$$\frac{P}{I} = \left\{ A \leftarrow \Psi[A_1, \dots, A_m \mid I(B_1), \dots I(B_n)] \right.$$
$$\left. such\ that\ A \leftarrow \Psi[A_1, \dots, A_m \mid B_1, \dots B_n] \in P \right\}$$

The program division $\frac{P}{I}$ evaluates according to I all occurrences of antitonic propositional symbols in P. Then the least model of the resulting program can be determined by resorting to a Γ operator:

Definition 15 (Gamma operator). *Let P be a paraconsistent logic program and J an interpretation. Define $\Gamma_P^{\Psi}(J) = \mathrm{lfp}\ T_{\frac{P}{J}}^{\Psi} = T_{\frac{P}{J}}^{\Psi}\!\uparrow^{\lambda}$, for some ordinal λ.*

Notwithstanding, according to [19], negation and default negation are not unrelated: the coherence principle ensures that the former entails the latter. From an epistemic viewpoint, coherence can be seen as an instance of the necessitation principle, which states that if something is known then it is believed. Therefore, one must have $A \leq_k not\ \neg A$ (coherence principle). In order to enforce coherence, we will resort to the semi-normal program, which is a generalization of the approach taken in the definition of the paraconsistent well-founded semantics with explicit negation $WFSX_p$ [4]:

Definition 16 (Semi-normal program). *Let P be a paraconsistent logic program. The semi-normal version of P, denoted P_s, is the paraconsistent logic program obtained from P replacing every $A \leftarrow \Psi$ belonging to P by $A \leftarrow \Psi \otimes_k -A$.*

Notice that as Antitonic Logic Programs do not support semi-normal programs, they can not characterize adequately the coherence principle. In [4], an alternating fixpoint definition of $WFSX_p$ is provided, relying on the application of two anti-monotonic operators, $\Gamma_P \Gamma_{P_s}$. Before generalizing this result to our framework we need to guarantee the following theorem:

Theorem 1. *Consider the paraconsistent logic program P. Let I_1 and I_2 be two interpretations such that $I_1 \leq I_2$. Then $\Gamma_P^{\Psi} \Gamma_{P_s}^{\Psi}(I_1) \leq \Gamma_P^{\Psi} \Gamma_{P_s}^{\Psi}(I_2)$.*

Thus we can define the paraconsistent well-founded semantics:

Definition 17 (Paraconsistent Well-founded Semantics). *Consider a paraconsistent logic program P and a partial interpretation $M = \langle M^t, M^{tu} \rangle$. M is a partial paraconsistent model for P iff $M^t = \Gamma_P^{\Psi}(\Gamma_{P_s}^{\Psi}(M^t))$ and $M^{tu} = \Gamma_{P_s}^{\Psi}(M^t)$.*

The least partial paraconsistent model under the Fitting ordering is defined as the paraconsistent well-founded model $WFM_p(P)$, and can be obtained by iterating $\Gamma_P^{\Psi} \Gamma_{P_s}^{\Psi}$ from $\triangle$. Then, given that I_α is the least fixpoint of $\Gamma_P^{\Psi} \Gamma_{P_s}^{\Psi}$, we shall have $WFM_p(P) = \left\langle \Gamma_P^{\Psi}(\Gamma_{P_s}^{\Psi}(I_\alpha)), \Gamma_{P_s}^{\Psi}(I_\alpha) \right\rangle$.

Letting $\Omega_P^{\mathfrak{P}}(J) = \left\langle \Gamma_P^{\mathfrak{P}}(J^{tu}), \Gamma_{P_s}^{\mathfrak{P}}(J^t) \right\rangle$, the paraconsistent partial stable models of the program P are the fixpoints of $\Omega_P^{\mathfrak{P}}$. Since $\Omega_P^{\mathfrak{P}}$ is monotonic with respect to $\sqsubseteq_f$, the least fixpoint under Fitting ordering (the paraconsistent well-founded model) is guaranteed to exist. Now we define the coherent answer sets:

Definition 18 (Coherent Answer Sets). *Let P be a paraconsistent logic program. A coherent answer set is a partial paraconsistent model of the form* $\langle M, M \rangle$.

As usual, coherent answer sets are not guaranteed to exist. However, as for paraconsistent well-founded models, coherent answer sets do comply with the coherence principle, i.e., for every propositional symbol A and partial paraconsistent model M, $\hat{M}(\neg A) \sqsubseteq \hat{M}(-\neg A)$.

4   Example

Paraconsistent Logic Programs have a large range of applications. We will use the following example adapted from [18] to encode a decision table based on rough relations. Such relations are determined from *Rough Sets* (cf. [18]), introduced to deal with imprecise information. In [16], a logic programming language, *Rough Datalog*, is defined, making possible to describe systems of rough relations and to reason about them. On some points, Rough Datalog resembles our framework. However, Paraconsistent Logic Programs appear to be more generic.

The symptoms *fever*, *cough*, *headache*, and *muscle-pain* are used to decide whether a patient has a flu. The diagnosis is performed according to the decision table[3] in Table 1:

Table 1. Decision table for flu

fever	cough	headache	muscle-pain	flu
no	no	no	no	no (in 99% of the cases)
yes	no	no	no	no (in 80% of the cases)
yes	yes	no	no	no (in 30% of the cases)
yes	yes	no	no	yes (in 60% of the cases)
yes	yes	yes	yes	yes (in 75% of the cases)

Mark that in the 3rd and 4th lines of table 1 we have contradictory conclusions for the same set of symptoms, and that in 10% of the cases the physician remains undecided.

We resort to the bilattice $\mathcal{B}([0,1],[0,1])$ to encode the above decision table. We also assume an $\mathcal{B}$-algebra $\mathfrak{P}$, whose carrier set is $[0,1] \times [0,1]$. The $\mathcal{B}$-algebra $\mathfrak{P}$ has the operators $\neg(\langle \alpha, \beta \rangle) = \langle \beta, \alpha \rangle$, $-(\langle \alpha, \beta \rangle) = \langle 1 - \beta, 1 - \alpha \rangle$, and $\otimes_k(\langle \alpha, \beta \rangle, \langle \gamma, \delta \rangle) = \langle min(\alpha, \gamma), min(\beta, \delta) \rangle$. The first case can be represented by

$$flu \leftarrow \neg \left(\langle 0.99, 0.0 \rangle \otimes_k \neg fever \otimes_k \neg cough \otimes_k \neg headache \otimes_k \neg muscle\_pain \right)$$

which reduces to[4]

---

[3] The figures are fictitious.
[4] From [8], we have $\neg(A \otimes_k B) = (\neg A \otimes_k \neg B)$.

$$flu \leftarrow \langle 0.0, 0.99 \rangle \otimes_k fever \otimes_k cough \otimes_k headache \otimes_k muscle\_pain \quad (1)$$

Similarly, the second diagnosis case can be implemented via the following rule:

$$flu \leftarrow \langle 0.0, 0.80 \rangle \otimes_k \neg fever \otimes_k cough \otimes_k headache \otimes_k muscle\_pain$$

The translation of the last case is immediate:

$$flu \leftarrow \langle 0.75, 0.0 \rangle \otimes_k fever \otimes_k cough \otimes_k headache \otimes_k muscle\_pain \quad (2)$$

The reader surely will notice that the body of rule (2) is almost identical to that of rule (1), with the exception of the confidence degrees in the rules. These two rules can be combined into a single one:

$$flu \leftarrow \langle 0.75, 0.99 \rangle \otimes_k fever \otimes_k cough \otimes_k headache \otimes_k muscle\_pain \quad (3)$$

Thus, the above rule expresses both positive and negative evidence for diagnosing a flu:

- if a patient has fever, cough, headache, and muscle-pain, then flu is a correct diagnosis in 75% of the cases.
- if a patient **doesn't** have fever, **doesn't** cough, **doesn't** have neither headache nor muscle-pain, then he **doesn't** have flu in 99% of the situations.

So, the positive evidence for the consequent is only concluded when all the propositions in the body of the rule have positive evidence for them. Symmetrically, the negative evidence for the conclusion is only gotten when all propositions in the body have negative evidence.

For the remaining situation (fever,cough,not headache, and not muscle_pain) two distinct rules are required for concluding both that the patient might have or not have a flu:

$$flu \leftarrow \langle 0.0, 0.3 \rangle \otimes_k \neg fever \otimes_k \neg cough \otimes_k headache \otimes_k muscle\_pain$$

$$flu \leftarrow \langle 0.60, 0.0 \rangle \otimes_k fever \otimes_k cough \otimes_k \neg headache \otimes_k \neg muscle\_pain$$

Assume now that antibiotics are prescribed when flu is not concluded. We will compare two possible translations of this statement, represented by either of the following rules: $antibiotics \leftarrow \neg flu$ or $antibiotics \leftarrow -\neg flu$.

The former allows us to conclude that antibiotics should be prescribed when there is explicit negative evidence for flu. With the latter rule, antibiotics are recommended when there is no evidence[5] for flu. The rules for diagnosing flu are

$$flu \leftarrow \langle 0.0, 0.80 \rangle \otimes_k \neg fever \otimes_k cough \otimes_k headache \otimes_k muscle\_pain$$
$$flu \leftarrow \langle 0.75, 0.99 \rangle \otimes_k fever \otimes_k cough \otimes_k headache \otimes_k muscle\_pain$$
$$flu \leftarrow \langle 0.0, 0.3 \rangle \otimes_k \neg fever \otimes_k \neg cough \otimes_k headache \otimes_k muscle\_pain$$
$$flu \leftarrow \langle 0.60, 0.0 \rangle \otimes_k fever \otimes_k cough \otimes_k \neg headache \otimes_k \neg muscle\_pain$$

[5] This is not the same has having negative evidence!

We now illustrate the behaviour of paraconsistent well-founded semantics in several situations. Table 2 contains six different models of the above program. The first line of every model corresponds to the T component of the model, while the second line represents the TU component of the same model. The five leftmost columns represent the interpretation, and the two rightmost columns the confidence degrees of explicit and of default negations.

Table 2. Models for the flu program

fever	cough	headache	muscle-pain	flu	$\neg$flu	$-\neg$flu
$\langle 0,1 \rangle$	$\langle 0,1 \rangle$	$\langle 0,1 \rangle$	$\langle 0,1 \rangle$	$\langle 0,0.99 \rangle$	$\langle 0.99,0 \rangle$	$\langle 1,0.01 \rangle$
$\langle 0,1 \rangle$	$\langle 0,1 \rangle$	$\langle 0,1 \rangle$	$\langle 0,1 \rangle$	$\langle 0,0.99 \rangle$	$\langle 0.99,0 \rangle$	$\langle 1,0.01 \rangle$
$\langle 1,0 \rangle$	$\langle 0,1 \rangle$	$\langle 0,1 \rangle$	$\langle 0,1 \rangle$	$\langle 0,0.8 \rangle$	$\langle 0.8,0 \rangle$	$\langle 1,0.2 \rangle$
$\langle 1,0 \rangle$	$\langle 0,1 \rangle$	$\langle 0,1 \rangle$	$\langle 0,1 \rangle$	$\langle 0,0.8 \rangle$	$\langle 0.8,0 \rangle$	$\langle 1,0.2 \rangle$
$\langle 1,0 \rangle$	$\langle 1,0 \rangle$	$\langle 0,1 \rangle$	$\langle 0,1 \rangle$	$\langle 0.6,0.3 \rangle$	$\langle 0.3,0.6 \rangle$	$\langle 0.4,0.7 \rangle$
$\langle 1,0 \rangle$	$\langle 1,0 \rangle$	$\langle 0,1 \rangle$	$\langle 0,1 \rangle$	$\langle 0.6,0.3 \rangle$	$\langle 0.3,0.6 \rangle$	$\langle 0.4,0.7 \rangle$
$\langle 1,0 \rangle$	$\langle 1,0 \rangle$	$\langle 1,0 \rangle$	$\langle 1,0 \rangle$	$\langle 0.75,0 \rangle$	$\langle 0,0.75 \rangle$	$\langle 0.25,1 \rangle$
$\langle 1,0 \rangle$	$\langle 1,0 \rangle$	$\langle 1,0 \rangle$	$\langle 1,0 \rangle$	$\langle 0.75,0 \rangle$	$\langle 0,0.75 \rangle$	$\langle 0.25,1 \rangle$
$\langle 0.4,0.6 \rangle$	$\langle 0.7,0.3 \rangle$	$\langle 0.1,0.9 \rangle$	$\langle 0.2,0.7 \rangle$	$\langle 0.4,0.3 \rangle$	$\langle 0.3,0.4 \rangle$	$\langle 0.6,0.7 \rangle$
$\langle 0.4,0.6 \rangle$	$\langle 0.7,0.3 \rangle$	$\langle 0.1,0.9 \rangle$	$\langle 0.2,0.7 \rangle$	$\langle 0.4,0.3 \rangle$	$\langle 0.3,0.4 \rangle$	$\langle 0.6,0.7 \rangle$
$\langle 0.4,0.6 \rangle$	$\langle 0.7,0.3 \rangle$	$\langle 0.7,0.9 \rangle$	$\langle 0.2,0.7 \rangle$	$\langle 0.4,0.3 \rangle$	$\langle 0.3,0.4 \rangle$	$\langle 0.7,0.7 \rangle$
$\langle 0.4,0.6 \rangle$	$\langle 0.7,0.3 \rangle$	$\langle 0.1,0.3 \rangle$	$\langle 0.2,0.7 \rangle$	$\langle 0.3,0.3 \rangle$	$\langle 0.3,0.3 \rangle$	$\langle 0.6,0.7 \rangle$

The first model in Table 2 is obtained by adding the following set of facts (the confidence degrees are extracted from the T component of the model) to the previous rules :

$$fever \leftarrow \langle 0,1 \rangle \quad cough \leftarrow \langle 0,1 \rangle \quad headache \leftarrow \langle 0,1 \rangle \quad muscle\_pain \leftarrow \langle 0,1 \rangle$$

The first four models correspond to the 4 cases about diagnosing flu. Notice the column for flu is in accordance with the evidence expressed in Table 1.

The distinctive effect of the rules $antibiotics \leftarrow \neg flu$ and $antibiotics \leftarrow -\neg flu$ can be observed from the columns for $\neg flu$ and $-\neg flu$. By the coherence principle, it is always the case that for every model $\hat{M}(\neg flu) \leq_k \hat{M}(-\neg flu)$ as the reader can check in the T-lines of the models. For instance, in the second model we derive $\neg flu$ with degree of evidence $\langle 0.8,0 \rangle$ and $-\neg flu$ with evidence $\langle 1,0.2 \rangle$, and as expected $\langle 0.8,0 \rangle \leq_k \langle 1,0.2 \rangle$. Since flu has value $\langle 0,0.8 \rangle$, and $-\neg flu$ has value $\langle 1,0.2 \rangle$, antibiotics should be prescribed according to rule $antibiotics \leftarrow -\neg flu$ as there is no positive evidence for having a flu. The situation where flu is diagnosed appears in the fourth model, and so antibiotics are not prescribed.

In the fifth model the physician is not certain regarding all symptoms. The interesting aspect of this case, is that the degree of evidence for flu is obtained by combining the degrees of evidence of several rules. Finally, the last model illustrates how paraconsistency is handled by our semantics. The fact *headache* ← $\langle 0.7, 0.9 \rangle$ is inconsistent in Fitting's sense (and thus also inconsistent in the WFM_p). Since *flu* is true with degree $\langle 0.4, 0.3 \rangle$ and true or undefined with degree $\langle 0.3, 0.3 \rangle$ then *flu* is inconsistent in the well-founded model of the program. All other models are coherent answer sets.

5 Conclusion

We have defined Paraconsistent Logic Programs, which are a generalization of Antitonic Logic Programs [2]. An important merit of this work is the introduction into a general framework, of an appropriate kind, of the concepts that cope with explicit negation and default negation. It is certified that default negation complies with the coherence principle. Program rules have bodies corresponding to compositions of arbitrary monotonic and antitonic operators over a complete bilattice in the sense of Fitting [8], and provide an elegant way to present belief and doubt. In order to define its semantics we resort to a program division in the spirit of [9], which transforms paraconsistent logic programs into monotonic logic programs. Then we can similarly apply an immediate consequences operator. A minimum paraconsistent well-founded model is guaranteed to exist.

In [1], we provide a translation of Extended Logic Programs under $WFSX_p$ [4] into Paraconsistent Logic Programs. Other settings are easily embeddable into our framework, such as Probabilistic Logic Programs [14], Possibilistic Logic Programming [6], Hybrid Probabilistic Logic Programs [5], and Fuzzy Logic Programs [23]. On the one hand, the merit of these translations is in their allowing to deal with negation, paraconsistency, and non-monotonic reasoning within the uncertain formalisms above. On the other hand, we can now study the behaviour of $WFSX_p$, and of the most important paraconsistent semantics for Extended Logic Programs when uncertain reasoning is introduced into them.

As future work, we will generalize our structure to consider rules with more complex heads, where we can have, for instance, disjunctions of atoms. An interesting point of research is the study of the various types of negation in our framework, specially if we allow for weak negation operators as well. This offers the opportunity for studying how the coherence principle functions in such cases. The definition of derivation procedures is also envisaged.

References

1. J. Alcântara, C. V. Damásio, and L. M. Pereira. Paraconsistent logic programs. Workshop on Paraconsistent Logic (WoPaLo), 2002.
2. C. V. Damásio and L. M. Pereira. Antitonic logic programs. In T. Eiter and M. Truszczynski, editors, *Procs. of the 6th Int. Conf. on Logic Programming and Nonmonotonic Reasoning (LPNMR'01)*, LNCS/LNAI, pages 748–759. Springer, 2001.
3. C. V. Damásio and L. M. Pereira. Monotonic and residuated logic programs. In S. Benferhat and P. Besnard, editors, *6th European Conf. on Symbolic and Quantitative Approaches to Reasoning with Uncertainty (ECSQARU'01)*, LNCS/LNAI. Springer, 2001.

4. C. V. Damásio. *Paraconsistent Extended Logic Programming with Constraints.* PhD thesis, Universidade Nova de Lisboa, 1996.
5. A. Dekhtyar and V. S. Subrahmanian. Hybrid probabilistic programs. *Journal of Logic Programming*, 43(3):197–250, 2000.
6. D. Dubois, J. Lang, and H. Prade. Towards possibilistic logic programming. In *Proc. of ICLP'91*, pages 581–598. MIT Press, 1991.
7. M. Fitting. Logic programming on a topological bilattice. *Fundamentae Mathematicae*, XI:209–218, 1988.
8. M. Fitting. Bilattices and the semantics of logic programming. *The Journal of Logic Programming*, 11:91–116, 1991.
9. M. Gelfond and V. Lifschitz. The stable model semantics for logic programming. In R. Kowalski and K. A. Bowen, editors, *5th International Conference on Logic Programming*, pages 1070–1080. MIT Press, 1988.
10. M. Gelfond and V. Lifschitz. Logic programs with classical negation. In Warren and Szeredi, editors, *7th International Conference on Logic Programming*, pages 579–597. MIT Press, 1990.
11. M. Ginsberg. Multivalued logics: A uniform approach to reasoning in artificial intelligence. *Computational Intelligence*, 4:265–316, 1988.
12. M. Kifer and V. S. Subrahmanian. Theory of generalized annotated logic programming and its applications. *The Journal of Logic Programming*, 12(1, 2, 3 & 4):335–367, 1992.
13. R. Kowalski and F. Sadri. Logic programs with exceptions. In Warren and Szeredi, editors, *7th International Conference on Logic Programming*. MIT Press, 1990.
14. L. Lakshmanan and F. Sadri. On a theory of probabilistic deductive databases. *Theory and Practice of Logic Programming*, 1(1):5–42, 2001.
15. L. Lakshmanan and N. Shiri. A parametric approach to deductive databases with uncertainty. *Knowledge and Data Engineering*, 13(4):554–570, 2001.
16. J. Maluszynski and A. Vitória. Towards rough datalog: embedding rough sets in prolog. In A. Skowron Accepted in: S. K. Pal, L. Polkowski, editor, *Rough-Neuro Computing*, AI Series. Springer-Verlag, 2002.
17. R. Ng and V. S. Subrahmanian. Probabilistic logic programming. *INFCTRL: Information and Computation (formerly Information and Control)*, 101, 1992.
18. Z. Pawlak. *Rough Sets. Theoretical aspects of reasoning about data.* Kluwer Academic Publishers, Dordrecht, 1991.
19. L. M. Pereira and J. J. Alferes. Well-founded semantics for logic programs with explicit negation. In B. Neumann, editor, *European Conference on Artificial Intelligence*, pages 102–106, Wien-Austria, 1992. John Wiley & Sons.
20. E. Shapiro. Logic programs with uncertainties: A tool for implementing expert systems. In *Proc. IJCAI'83*, pages 529–532. William Kauffmann, 1983.
21. M. van Emden and R. Kowalski. The semantics of predicate logic as a programming language. *Journal of ACM*, 4(23):733–742, 1976.
22. M. van Emden. Quantitative deduction and its fixpoint theory. *Journal of Logic Programming*, 3(1):37–53, 1986.
23. P. Vojtás and L. Paulík. Soundness and completeness of non-classical extended SLD-resolution. In *Proc. of the Ws. on Extensions of Logic Programming (ELP'96)*, LNCS 1050, pages 289–301. Springer-Verlag, 1996.
24. G. Wagner. A database needs two kinds of negation. In B. Thalheim, J. Demetrovics, and H-D. Gerhardt, editors, *Mathematical Foundations of Database Systems*, pages 357–371. LNCS 495, Springer-Verlag, 1991.

Interpolation Properties of Action Logic: Lazy-Formalization to the Frame Problem

Dongmo Zhang[1] and Norman Foo[2]

[1] School of Computing and Information Technology
University of Western Sydney, Australia
dongmo@cit.uws.edu.au
[2] School of Computer Science and Engineering
The University of New South Wales, Australia
norman@cse.unsw.edu.au

Abstract. This paper makes a contribution to the meta-theory of reasoning about action. We present two interpolation properties of action logic. We show that the frame axioms which are required for answering a query involve only the objects which are relevant to the query and action description. Moreover, if the action description is expressed by normal form, the required frame axioms depend on only the query itself. Therefore the frame problem may be mitigated by localizing descriptions and postponing the listing of frame axioms till a query occurs. This offers a pragmatic solution to the frame problem. This solution does not rest on any meta-hypotheses most existing solutions to the frame problem rely on.

1 Introduction

The theory of action and change has been a focus of AI for over twenty years. Most fundamental problems in this area, such as the frame problem, ramification problem, and qualification problem, have been widely investigated with varying degrees of success. The time has come to analyze, compare and systematize these formalisms and solutions in order to obtain a more complete and solid theory of action. This paper makes a contribution to the meta-theory in order to fill the gap between action logic and meta-hypotheses which most exiting solutions to the frame problem rely on.

As a central issue in reasoning about action, the frame problem arises upon the assumption that the specification of a system (and its underlying reasoning mechanism) should be strong enough to answer any query by direct inference. With the assumption, a dilemma appears inevitable. On the one hand, most actions have only local effects. So, if one has to explicitly mention all the things that are unaffected, the list (frame axioms) will usually be unmanageably large; On the other hand, if soundness and completeness are desired for the reasoning system, not a single frame axiom can be omitted. Many solutions to the problem have been proposed. These can be grouped into two categories: *monotonic* and *nonmonotonic*.

Monotonic approaches seek automatic procedures to generate frame axioms from effect axioms based on some meta-hypothesis, such as *Explanation Closure Assumption* or *Causal Completeness Assumption*[17][20][18].

Nonmonotonic approaches attempt to introduce new inference mechanisms based on meta-hypothesis such as the *common sense law of inertia* or *minimization*, to capture defaults about the effects of actions implied by frame axioms [7][1][21] [5].

S. Flesca et al. (Eds.): JELIA 2002, LNAI 2424, pp. 357–368, 2002.

It has been pointed out by several authors that all these meta-hypotheses are essentially equivalent despite the difference in their appearance [11] [12] [13] [4]. Because of their reliance on meta-hypothesis, these theories are apt to overcommit. For instance, when the effect of an action on a fluent is unknown, most formalisms of action would assume, indeed assert, that there is no effect at all but not flag such an assumption. Another price for accommodating such kind of meta-hypotheses is that the associated action logics become more complicated and may lose the completeness of logical inference. This paper aims to introduce an approach to the frame problem which releases the underlying action logic from meta-hypotheses while preserves the soundness and completeness of the logic. To see the possibility, let us consider a simple example.

The following figure shows a circuit in which only switch 1 is connected to the circuit. There are also some other switches and lights in the environment.

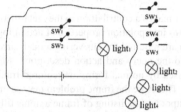

We describe this circuit from two points of view: engineering and AI:

1. Engineering description:

"Turning on Switch 1 causes the light to be on, turning it off causes the light to be off. The action with Switch 2 does not change the state of the light."

2. AI description:

"Turning on Switch 1 causes the light to be on, turning it off causes the light to be off. Any other action does not affect the state of the light."

Both descriptions seem to work, but the second sentence in the second description sounds a bit unnatural and arbitrary. It expresses *the common sense law of inertia* or *causal completeness assumption*. With this statement, we can answer "No!" confidently when asked "Does the cough of an ET cause the light to be off?". But while most engineers would regard the seriousness of such questions sceptically, they may not simply answer "No". Instead, they may regard it as a hint that an expected or hitherto unknown influence may exist, and therefore answer, "Possibly."

Then why do engineers not worry about the frame problem? The reasons might be the following. On one hand, for an engineering system, the possible future queries about the system can generally be foreseen. Therefore engineers can localize their language so that it involves only relevant components yet is sufficient for specifying the system and expressing possible future queries. On the other hand, they believe that answering a query in the local language might only require local frame axioms. Therefore the number of frame axioms will mainly depend on the size of the local language.

In this example, if all the possible queries are only concerned with sw_1, sw_2 and $light_1$, the frame axioms required for answering these queries can be restricted to the actions and fluents which are only relevant to these elements. Even though the other switches and lights in the environment are concerned, the size of the frame axioms is still manageable. In this sense, the full-blown frame problem can be avoided. However, this localization approach relies again on another meta-hypothesis: *local queries requires only local frame axioms*. More precisely, let Σ and φ be a set of effect axioms of actions in a system and a query about the system respectively, expressed in an action language $\mathcal{L}$. Suppose that Δ_φ is the set of frame axioms which is required for answering the query. That is,

$$\Sigma \cup \Delta_\varphi \models_{AL} \varphi \ (\text{or} \ \neg\varphi)$$

where $\models_{AL}$ is the entailment of underlying action logic. Then the assumption we made is that all the frame axioms (Δ_φ) required for the inference are expressible in the sublanguage of $\mathcal{L}$ which only involves symbols in Σ and φ. This reminds us the Craig Interpolation Theorem of classical first-order logic, which says that if $\varphi \models \psi$, then there exists a sentence θ such that $\varphi \models \theta$, $\theta \models \psi$ and all the symbols which occur in θ occur in φ and ψ (see [3]). In fact, if the frame axioms can be any formula and $\models_{AL}$ has the similar interpolation property, the assumption mentioned above will be implied by the interpolation theorem.

In this paper we present two interpolation properties of action logic to verify the assumption. Since local queries require only local frame axioms and a query generally involves only few objects, the frame axioms required in a reasoning can be reduced to a reasonable size. Therefore we can simply avoid the frame problem by postponing the listing of the frame axioms until they are needed. We call this approach *lazy-formalization*, which is similar to the technique of *lazy-evaluation* or *by-need* in automated reasoning and programming. A significant difference between our solution and the others is that our solution does not rely on any meta-hypothesis except the logic itself. It becomes a property of the associated action logic. The hard part is how to verify this property. To this end, we need:

1. A formal framework for expressing and reasoning about actions and their effects, enhanced with interpolation property.

2. A normalized expression of frame axioms in order that we can easily generate frame axioms when needed.

3. A suitable inference mechanism for lazy-listing of frame axioms.

There are several formalisms for reasoning about actions. To our knowledge, none of them has been proved to have the interpolation property[1]. However, we shall use the extended propositional dynamic logic ($EPDL$), introduced by Zhang and Foo in [22], as the action description language and reasoning framework to take advantage of its sound and complete axiomatization and facilities for reasoning about action effects.

We remark that there have been several results about the the interpolation property of modal logic and dynamic logic but these results are not exactly what we want because a frame axiom may not be an arbitrary formula[14][15] [16].

2 Extended Propositional Dynamic Logic (EPDL)

In this section, we briefly summarize some basic facts of EPDL(see [22] for more details).

The language of $EPDL$ consists of a set **Flu** of fluent symbols and a set $\mathbf{Act}_P$ of primitive action symbols. There are two types of formulas: *propositional formula*

---

[1] Some action logics are first-order or have some fragment which is first-order. This does not mean that such a logic has the interpolation property.

$\varphi \in \mathbf{Fma_P}$, which does not include modal operators, and *ordinary formula* $A \in \mathbf{Fma}$. The syntax of an action $\alpha \in \mathbf{Act}$ is as same as programs in PDL.

The BNF rules of the language are as follows:

$\varphi ::= f \mid \neg\varphi \mid \varphi_1 \to \varphi_2$

$A ::= f \mid \neg A \mid A_1 \to A_2 \mid [\alpha]A \mid [\varphi]A$

$\alpha ::= a \mid \alpha_1; \alpha_2 \mid \alpha_1 \cup \alpha_2 \mid \alpha^* \mid A?$

where $f \in \mathbf{Flu}$ and $a \in \mathbf{Act_P}$.

$[\gamma]A$ reads as "γ (always) causes A", where γ can be an action or a propositional formula. For instance, $[Shoot]\neg alive$ represent the causal relation "Shooting at a turkey kills the turkey"(See Example 1). $[\neg alive]\neg walking$ means "The death of the turkey causes it to be disable to walk". The dual operator $\langle\alpha\rangle$ of $[\alpha]$, defined as usual, reads as "α is executable and possibly causes A to be true". Specially, $\langle\alpha\rangle\top$ represents α is executable.

The axiomatic system of $EPDL$ consists of the following axiom schemes and inference rules:

(1). Axiom schemes:

• all tautologies of the propositional calculus.
• all axioms for compound programs (see [8]).
• EK axiom: $[\gamma](A \to B) \to ([\gamma]A \to [\gamma]B)$
• CW axiom: $[\varphi]A \to [\varphi?]A$

(2). Inference rules:

• MP: From A and $A \to B$, infer B.
• EN: From A, infer $[\gamma]A$.
• LE: From $\varphi_1 \leftrightarrow \varphi_2$, infer $[\varphi_2]A \leftrightarrow [\varphi_1]A$.

where $\varphi, \varphi_1, \varphi_2 \in \mathbf{Fma_P}$, $A \in \mathbf{Fma}$, $\alpha \in \mathbf{Act}$ and $\gamma \in \mathbf{Fma_P} \cup \mathbf{Act}$.

A formula A is a theorem of $EPDL$, denoted by $\vdash A$, if it can derived from the axiom system.

An *action description* of a dynamic system is a finite set of $EPDL$ formulas, which specifies the effects of actions in the system.

Let Σ be an action description. A formula A is a Σ-*theorem*, written by $\vdash^\Sigma A$, if it belongs to the least set of formulas which contains all the theorems of $EPDL$ and all the elements of Σ, and is closed under MP and EN.

If Γ is a set of formulas, then A is Σ-*provable* from Γ, written by $\Gamma \vdash^\Sigma A$, if there exists $A_1, \cdots, A_n \in \Gamma$ such that $\vdash^\Sigma (A_1 \wedge \cdots \wedge A_n) \to A$.

An action description Σ is *uniformly consistent* if $\not\vdash^\Sigma \bot$. Γ is Σ-*consistent* if $\Gamma \not\vdash^\Sigma \bot$.

Intuitively, $\Gamma \vdash^\Sigma A$ means A can be derived from the premises Γ by the axioms of $EPDL$, action axioms in Σ and inference rules of $EPDL$.

Example 1 Consider the Yale Shooting Problem ([9]), which states that we have a turkey that gets killed if it is shot by a loaded gun. This problem can be described by the following action description:

$$\Sigma = \left\{ \begin{array}{l} \neg loaded \to [Load]loaded \\ loaded \to [Shoot]\neg alive \\ loaded \to [Shoot]\neg loaded \\ \langle Load \rangle\top, \langle Wait \rangle\top, \langle Shoot \rangle\top \end{array} \right\}$$

The first three sentences state the effects of action *Load* and *Shoot* on fluent *loaded* and *alive* (effect axioms). The last three represent the executability of actions (qualification axioms). Then we can have the following assertion:

$\{\neg loaded\} \vdash^{\Sigma} [Load; Shoot] \neg alive.$

A standard model M of $EPDL$ is a Σ-model if for any $B \in \Sigma$, $M \models B$. It has been proved that A is Σ-provable if and only if it is valid in all Σ-models. An action description Σ is uniformly consistent if and only if there exists a Σ-model.

3 Lazy-Formalization

To model a dynamic system, effect axioms (which specify what is affected by actions) are generally listed in the action description unless effects of some actions are unknown. Often this is easy because most actions affect only few relevant facts. However listing all the frame axioms is tedious. They are much more numerous than effect axioms. In Example 1, only effect axioms were listed. There are nine frame axioms, such as $alive \rightarrow [Load] alive, loaded \rightarrow [Wait] loaded$ and etc., were not added. Without these axioms, the action description is not complete. We cannot even establish the intuitive assertion $\{\neg loaded, alive\} \vdash^{\Sigma} [Load] alive$.

In this section, we introduce a formal approach for reasoning about effects of actions with the frame axioms which are not included in action descriptions.

3.1 Supplementary Frame Axioms

We call a formula in the form $\varphi \wedge L \rightarrow [a] L$ a *frame axiom*, where φ is a propositional formula, a a primitive action and L is a literal. φ and L are called the *pre-condition* and the *body* of the axiom, respectively.

Definition 1 Let Γ be Σ-consistent. For a given formula A, if a set Δ of frame axioms satisfies that Γ is $\Sigma \cup \Delta$-consistent and $\Gamma \vdash^{\Sigma \cup \Delta} A$, then A is called to be Σ-*provable from Γ with* Δ, denoted by $\Gamma \vdash^{\Sigma}_{\Delta} A$. The elements of Δ are called *supplementary axioms* [2].

Roughly speaking, $\Gamma \vdash^{\Sigma}_{\Delta} A$ means that A can be derived from Γ under the action description Σ with the additional assumption Δ of frame axioms.

We generally call "$\Gamma \vdash^{\Sigma} A$" a *query*. If $\Gamma \vdash^{\Sigma}_{\Delta} A$, then Δ is called the frame axioms involved in the query.

Consider Example 1 again. We can prove that $\{\neg loaded\} \vdash^{\Sigma}_{\Delta} [Load; Wait; Shoot] \neg alive$, where $\Delta = \{loaded \rightarrow [Wait] loaded\}$.

3.2 Localization of Supplementary Frame Axioms

We now investigate how lazy-formalization can be used to reason about effects of actions without an explicitly provided complete set of frame axioms. *Given an action description Σ of a system and a certain query "$\Gamma \vdash^{\Sigma} A$" about the system, which frame axioms would be really needed to answer the query?* Do they only depend on Σ, Γ and A, or even only depend on the query itself. Let us initially check the first possibility, which seems more intuitive. To make this more precise, we make the following:

Conjecture 1 *If $\Gamma \vdash^{\Sigma}_{\Delta} A$, then there exists a set Δ' of frame axioms such that*

1. $\Gamma \vdash^{\Sigma}_{\Delta'} A$,
2. $\Delta \vdash \Delta'$ and
3. *every non-logical symbol which occurs in Δ' occurs in $\Sigma \cup \Gamma \cup \{A\}$.*

----
[2] Note that some frame axioms could have been included in Σ.

This means that in order to answer the query "$\Gamma \vdash^\Sigma A$", the supplementary axioms really needed are the ones which are relevant to Σ, Γ and A.

We easily associate the conjecture with the Craig Interpolation Theorem (Criag IT) of first order logic([3]). Informally, we can transform $\Gamma \vdash^\Sigma_\Delta A$ into the inference relation:

$$\Gamma \cup \{[\text{any}]B : B \in \Sigma\} \cup \{[\text{any}]B : B \in \Delta\} \vdash A \tag{1}$$

Then we move all the formulas in Γ and $\{[\text{any}]B : B \in \Sigma\}$ from the left hand side to the right hand side of the inference relation. The resulting expression will have the following form:

$$F_1(\Delta) \vdash F_2(\Gamma, \Sigma, A).$$

If $EPDL$ has Craig IT-like property, there exists an interpolant formula F such that $F_1(\Delta) \vdash F$, $F \vdash F_2(\Gamma, \Sigma, A)$ and all the non-logical symbols which occur in F occur in $F_1(\Delta)$ and $F_2(\Gamma, \Sigma, A)$. Granted that it has, we still can not affirm the conjecture because we can't guarantee that the formula F can be transformed into a set of frame axioms as it is required in the conjecture. In the other words, the conjecture requires a special form of interpolant, *an interpolant of frame axioms*. The following lemmas manifest partial feature of such an interpolant.

Lemma 1 *Let Γ be finite[3]. If $\Gamma \vdash^\Sigma_\Delta A$, then there exists a subset Δ' of Δ such that $\Gamma \vdash^\Sigma_{\Delta'} A$ and the body of each frame axiom in Δ' occurs in $\Sigma \cup \Gamma \cup \{A\}$.*

Lemma 2 *Let Γ be finite. If $\Gamma \vdash^\Sigma_\Delta A$, then there exists a subset Δ' of Δ such that $\Gamma \vdash^\Sigma_{\Delta'} A$ and the action symbol in each frame axiom in Δ' occurs in $\Sigma \cup \Gamma \cup \{A\}$.*

The results show that we can delete from Δ all the frame axioms in which either their bodies or action symbols do not occur in $\Sigma \cup \Gamma \cup \{A\}$. Now we might try deleting or substituting all the symbols contained in the pre-conditions of the frame axioms but which do not occur in $\Sigma \cup \Gamma \cup \{A\}$. Unfortunately, this is not always feasible:

Example 2 Let $\Sigma = \{\langle a \rangle \top\}$. We can verify that

$$\{f_1, f_2, [a](\neg f_1 \vee \neg f_2)\} \vdash^\Sigma_\Delta ([a]f_1 \vee [a]f_2) \tag{2}$$

where $\Delta = \{f_3 \wedge f_1 \rightarrow [a]f_1, \neg f_3 \wedge f_2 \rightarrow [a]f_2\}$. However, there is no set Δ' of frame axioms which satisfies the conditions in Conjecture 1.□

It is easy to see that the supplementary axiom we really need to answer the query (2) is $(f_1 \rightarrow [a]f_1) \vee (f_2 \rightarrow [a]f_2)$. We call such a disjunction of frame axioms *disjunctive frame axiom*. The example shows that disjunctive frame axioms can be introduced by using "alien" fluent symbols (f_3).

Conjecture 1 is therefore false. However, Example 2 is actually an illustration of the worst case. The following interpolation theorem declare that if we admit disjunctive frame axioms as supplementary axiom, the interpolant stated by Conjecture 1 exists.

Let Δ be a set of frame axiom. We call the set $\{B_1 \vee \ldots \vee B_n : B_1, \ldots, B_n \in \Delta\}$ the *disjunctive extension* of Δ.

Theorem 1 *Let Γ be finite. If $\Gamma \vdash^\Sigma_\Delta A$, then there exists a set Δ' of frame axioms such that*

---

[3] The finitary restriction is required by the local completeness of EPDL

1. $\Gamma \vdash_{\Psi}^{\Sigma} A$, where Ψ is the disjunctive extension of Δ',
2. $\Delta \vdash \Delta'$, and
3. every non-logical symbol in Δ' occurs in $\Sigma \cup \Gamma \cup \{A\}$.

Conversely, if $\Gamma \vdash_{\Psi}^{\Sigma} A$, Ψ *is a set of disjunctive frame axioms, then there exists a set* Δ *of frame axioms such that* $\Gamma \vdash_{\Delta}^{\Sigma} A$.

We have obtained the soundness of lazy-formalization approach to the frame problem at the price of allowing the use of disjunctive frame axioms. We can also keep the original form of Conjecture 1 by prohibiting any potential use of disjunctive frame axioms at the price of the loss of reasoning about nondeterministic effects of actions; Pednault's Completeness Assumption and Reiter's Causal Completeness Assumption(see [17][20] are examples of such a restriction. For instance, in the Reiter's approach ([20]), the successor state axioms of Example 2 are

$$f_1 \leftrightarrow [a]f_1, \ f_2 \leftrightarrow [a]f_2.$$

The query (1) then become illegal because the premises are inconsistent with the action theory. In other words, Reiter's approach does not allow non-deterministic use of frame axioms.

4 Lazy-Formalization with Normal Action Descriptions

Theorem 1 shows that the lazy-formalization approach to the frame problem is reliable, and feasible if local effects are "small". Therefore, if we believe that we shall never have a query such as "Does a cough of an ET causes the light to be off?", we will never need to include the frame axiom: "A cough of an ET does not cause the light to be off" in our inference even if ET is a formal object in our language. The frame axioms involve the elements other than sw_1 and $light$ are also not required if they are not involved in any queries.

One might think that this solution is still unsatisfactory because we can only reduce the frame axioms to the language of $\Sigma \cup \Gamma \cup \{A\}$ rather than a query itself. If Σ is the specification of a huge system, it could involve a quite large set of symbols. Additionally, the frame axioms generated by the monotonic approach to the frame problem are generally expressible by the language of Σ (the set of effect axioms). So their frame axioms are at worst the same in size as that which lazy-formalization generates. What then is the advantage of lazy-formalization? The following section shows that lazy-formalization could do much better than the monotonic approach does. The reason is that most monotonic solutions exploit some syntactic restrictions, and with the same restrictions lazy-formalization can dramatically reduce the size of frame axioms further.

4.1 Normal Action Descriptions

In [23], a normalized form of action description was introduced to discuss consistency of action descriptions. An action description Σ is *normal* if each formula in Σ is in the form:

$$\varphi \rightarrow [a]L, \ \varphi \rightarrow \langle a \rangle \top,$$

called an *action law*, where $\varphi \in \mathbf{Fma}_P$, $a \in \mathbf{Act}_P$ and L is a fluent literal[4].

---

[4] To serve the purpose of the paper, we only consider deterministic action laws.

For any fluent f and any primitive action a, if we merge the action laws about f and a in the same form together, there will be at most three action laws about f and a in Σ as follows:

$\varphi_0 \to \langle a \rangle \top$, $\varphi_1 \to [a]f$, $\varphi_2 \to [a]\neg f$

We then call a normal action description Σ *safe* if for any a and f, the related action laws in Σ satisfy $\vdash \neg\varphi_0 \vee \neg\varphi_1 \vee \neg\varphi_2$. [5]

It is easy to see that the condition of safety is introduced to guarantee the consistency of action description.

Proposition 1 *[23] Let Σ be normal and safe, Γ be a set of propositional formulas. Γ is Σ-consistent if and only if Γ is consistent.*

This proposition make the Σ-consistency checking easier, and Definition 1 more accessible.

We remark that the normal form is quite expressive. Most normal forms in other action theories can be transformed into normal form (propositional case only). For instance, action descriptions in the *propositional* situation calculus language (i.e., there are no sorts *object* and function symbols in the language [20]) can be translated into normal form If we extend the normal form to allow an expression of causal laws and non-deterministic action laws [23], most components of action languages [5] can also be expressed by normal form.

The next interpolation theorem further reduces the search space for supplementary frame axioms.

Theorem 2 *Let Σ be normal and Γ be finite. If $\Gamma \vdash^{\Sigma}_{\Delta} A$ and $\Sigma \cup \Delta$ is safe, then there exists a subset Δ' of Δ such that $\Gamma \vdash^{\Sigma}_{\Delta'} A$ and each action symbol in Δ' occurs in $\Gamma \cup \{A\}$.*

The theorem shows that under the restriction of normality, the required frame axioms depend on only the query itself. This significantly reduced the number of frame axioms. For instance, to answer the query:

$\{\neg loaded, alive\} \vdash^{\Sigma} [Wait; Shoot]alive$,

we only need to consider the frame axioms about action $Wait$ and $Shoot$ (6 out of 9).

5   Discussion and Conclusion

We introduced an inference mechanism, called *lazy-formalization*, for reasoning with incomplete action descriptions by postponing the listing of frame axioms until they are needed for answering a query. As a contribution to the meta-theory of reasoning about action, we presented two interpolation properties of action logic, based on dynamic logic, to show that the lazy formalization can mitigate and even avoid the frame problem in the following sense:

1. The frame axioms required for answering a query are the ones in which the non-logical symbols are in the action description and the query, provided we are allowed to use disjunctive frame axioms.
2. If the action description is written in normal form and is safe, the frame axioms can be further reduced to the ones in which the action symbols are in the query.

---

[5] If there is no a relative form of the action law, say $\varphi_1 \to [a]f$, we assume $\varphi_1 \leftrightarrow \bot$.

As we have mentioned in the introduction, all the existing solutions to the frame problem rest on some meta-hypotheses. The first result releases the lazy-formalization approach from meta level assumption. Since most such kind of meta-hypotheses are essentially equivalent[4] and express a similar idea: effect of actions should be minimalised and action description should be localized, this result may be used in other formalisms of action to fill the gap between underlying logics and meta-hypotheses.

The second result provides a computational perspective to the lazy-formalization approach. If we express an action description in normal form as most formalisms of action do[4], the process for generating frame axioms is in linear time with respect to the size of effect axioms, which is exactly the same as Reiter's procedure. However, the inference for answering the query is normally in exponential time. Therefore, even a minor reduction of inputs would gain a significant improvement in computation. Therefore lazy-formalization can be viewed as a refinement of Reiter's solution from computational point of view.

We remark that although the results in the work are based on the propositional dynamic logic, the approach of lazy-formalization to the frame problem is applicable to other formalisms of action because the persistence of fluents is independent to its representation.

Appendix: Proofs of Theorems

Proof of Lemma 1: We shall remove from Δ the frame axiom which body does not occur in $\Sigma \cup \Gamma \cup \{A\}$ one by one.

Firstly we assume that we have only one supplementary frame axiom. Let $\Gamma \vdash_{\Delta}^{\Sigma} A$ and $\Delta = \{\varphi \wedge L \rightarrow [a]L\}$, in which the fluent symbol, say f_0, of L does not occur in $\Sigma \cup \Gamma \cup \{A\}$. We prove that $\Gamma \vdash^{\Sigma} A$.

By completeness of EPDL, $\Gamma \not\vdash^{\Sigma} A$ implies $\Gamma \not\models^{\Sigma} A$, that is, there exists a Σ-model $M = (W, \mathcal{R}, V)$ of language $\mathcal{L}\backslash\{f_0\}$ such that $M \models \Gamma$ but $M \not\models A$. We construct a model $M' = (W', \mathcal{R}', V')$ of language $\mathcal{L}$ as follows:

$W' = \{0, 1\} \times W$

For any $\alpha \in \mathbf{Act_P}$, $((i, u), (j, v)) \in R'_\alpha$ iff $i = j$ and $(u, v) \in R_\alpha$;

For any $\varphi \in \mathbf{Fmap_P}$, $((i, u), (j, v)) \in R'_\varphi$ iff $i = j$ and $(u, v) \in R_\varphi$;

For any $f \in \mathbf{Flu}$, if $f \neq f_0$, $V(f) = \{(0, w) : w \in V(f)\} \cup \{(1, w) : w \in V(f)\}$; otherwise, $V(f) = \{0\} \times W$, that is, $V(f_0) = \{0\} \times W$.

Then we can make the following claims:

Claim 1: For any $B \in \mathbf{Fma}$, if B does not contain f_0, then $M' \models_{(i,w)} B$ if and only if $M \models_w B$

Claim 2: $M' \models \Gamma$ and $M' \not\models A$

Claim 3: M' is still a Σ-model.

Claim 4: M' is a $\Sigma \cup \Delta$-model.

The claim 1 can be easily verified by induction on the structure of formulas. The claim 2 and 3 is followed by the claim 1. For the last one, suppose that $M' \models_{(i,u)} \varphi \wedge L$. Then for any $(j, v) \in W'$ such that $((i, u), (j, v)) \in R'_a$, we have $i = j$ according to the construction of model M'. Hence $M' \models_{(j,v)} L$ no matter whether L is f_0 or $\neg f_0$. Therefore $M' \models \Delta$.

According to the soundness of Σ-provability, $\Gamma \not\vdash^{\Sigma \cup \Delta} A$, which contradicts $\Gamma \vdash_{\Delta}^{\Sigma} A$. Thus $\Gamma \vdash^{\Sigma} A$.

By following this step, we can remove all the supplementary frame axioms which bodies do not occur in $\Sigma \cup \Gamma \cup \{A\}$ one by one. $\square$

Proof of Lemma 2: Without lost of generality, we suppose that Δ only contains one frame axiom $\varphi \wedge L \rightarrow [a]L$, where a does not occur in $\Sigma \cup \Gamma \cup \{A\}$. We prove that $\Gamma \vdash_\Delta^\Sigma A$ implies $\Gamma \vdash^\Sigma A$.

Suppose that $\Gamma \vdash_\Delta^\Sigma A$, we prove $\Gamma \vdash^\Sigma A$ by contraposition. So assume that $\Gamma \not\vdash^\Sigma A$. Then there exists a Σ-model $M = (W, \mathcal{R}, V)$ of the language $\mathcal{L} \backslash \{a\}$ such that $M \models \Gamma$ but $M \not\models A$. We extend M to a model $M' = (W, \mathcal{R}, V)$ of language $\mathcal{L}$ as follows:

$W' = W$ and $V' = V$

$\mathcal{R}'$ is as same as R except for the accessibility relation R'_a for action a and each R'_α for the compound action α involving a. We define R'_a in the following and the others can be done by standard model conditions.

For any $u', v' \in W'$, $(u', v') \in R_a$ iff $u' = v'$ and $M \models_u \varphi$. Obviously $M' \models \Delta$. Hence we have that M' is a $\Sigma \cup \Delta$-model, $M' \models \Gamma$ and $M' \not\models A$, which contradicts $\Gamma \vdash_\Delta^\Sigma A$. $\square$

Proof of Theorem 1

According to the lemma 1 and 2, we can delete from Δ all the frame axioms in which either their bodies or action symbols do not occur in $\Sigma \cup \Gamma \cup \{A\}$. So we just need to consider the fluent symbols which occur in the pre-conditions of frame axioms in Δ but not in $\Sigma \cup \Gamma \cup \{A\}$.

For convenience, we write a frame axiom $\varphi \wedge L \rightarrow [a]L$ in the form $\varphi \rightarrow \gamma$, where $\gamma = \neg L \vee [a]L$. Then all the elements of Δ can be listed uniformly as follows:

$\varphi_1 \rightarrow \gamma_1, \cdots, \varphi_n \rightarrow \gamma_n$

Suppose that f_0 is a fluent symbol which occurs in Δ but does not occur in $\Sigma \cup \Gamma \cup \{A\}$. According to the above assumption, f_0 can only occur in some pre-conditions φ_i. For each such a pre-condition φ_i, let ψ'_i be the result of everywhere replacing occurrences of f_0 in φ_i by $\top$, and ψ''_i by $\bot$.

Let $\psi = \bigwedge_{i=1}^{n} (\neg \psi'_i \vee \gamma_i) \vee \bigwedge_{i=1}^{n} (\neg \psi''_i \vee \gamma_i)$

We prove that $\Gamma \vdash_\Delta^\Sigma A$ implies $\Gamma \vdash^{\Sigma \cup \{\psi\}} A$. Firstly, it is not hard to verify the following facts:

Fact 1: $\varphi_i \vdash\!\dashv (f_0 \wedge \psi'_i) \vee (\neg f_0 \wedge \psi''_i)$.

Fact 2: $\Delta \vdash \psi$.

Fact 3: $\Sigma \cup \{\psi\}$ is uniformly consistent.

Suppose that $\Gamma \vdash^{\Sigma \cup \{\psi\}} A$ is not true. Then there must be a $\Sigma \cup \{\psi\}$-model $M = (W, \mathcal{R}, V)$ such that $M \models \Gamma$ but for some $w_0 \in W$, $M \models_{w_0} \neg A$. Now we transform M into a $\Sigma \cup \Delta$-model $M' = (W, \mathcal{R}, V')$ by changing valuation of fluent f_0 as follows: for any $w \in W$,

1. if $M \models_w \bigwedge_{i=1}^{n} (\neg \psi'_i \vee \gamma_i)$, then let $w \in V'(f_0)$; otherwise $w \notin V'(f_0)$. In this case,

$M \models_w \bigwedge_{i=1}^{n} (\neg \psi''_i \vee \gamma_i)$ because $M \models_w \psi$.

2. $V'(f) = V(f)$ if $f \neq f_0$.

Then we prove M' is a $\Sigma \cup \Delta$-model. In fact, M' is a Σ-model and for any $w \in W$, if $w \in V'(f_0)$, that is, $M' \models_w \bigwedge_{i=1}^{n} (\neg \psi'_i \vee \gamma_i)$, then $M' \models_w (\neg f_0 \vee \bigwedge_{i=1}^{n} (\neg \psi'_i \vee \gamma_i)) \wedge (f_0 \vee \bigwedge_{i=1}^{n} (\neg \psi''_i \vee \gamma_i))$. It follows $M' \models_w \bigwedge_{i=1}^{n} (\varphi_i \rightarrow \gamma_i)$; If $w \notin V'(f_0)$, $M' \models_w \bigwedge_{i=1}^{n} (\neg \psi''_i \vee \gamma_i)$, so $M' \models_w \bigwedge_{i=1}^{n} (\varphi_i \rightarrow \gamma_i)$. That means $M' \models_w \Delta$. Therefore M' is a $\Sigma \cup \Delta$-model. Since f_0 does not occur in $\Gamma \cup \{A\}$, $M' \models \Gamma$ and $M' \models_w \neg A$. Thus $\Gamma \not\models^{\Sigma \cup \Delta} A$, which contradicts $\Gamma \vdash_\Delta^\Sigma A$. Therefore $\Gamma \vdash_\Delta^\Sigma A$ implies $\Gamma \vdash^{\Sigma \cup \{\psi\}} A$.

In this way, we can remove all the fluent symbols which occur in Δ but do not occur in $\Sigma \cup \Gamma \cup \{A\}$, and obtain a set Ψ of formulas such that $\Gamma \vdash_{\Delta}^{\Sigma} A$ implies $\Gamma \vdash^{\Sigma \cup \Psi} A$. Obviously, Ψ can be expressed by a set of disjunctive frame axioms.

For the reverse, assume that Ψ is a set of formulas, each of which has the form

$$\bigwedge_{i=1}^{m} (\neg \psi_i' \vee \gamma_i) \vee \bigwedge_{j=1}^{n} (\neg \psi_j'' \vee \gamma_j) \tag{3}$$

where ψ_i' and ψ_i'' are any propositional formulas, γ_i has the form of $\neg L \vee [a]L$, and all the fluent and action symbols occur in them occur in $\Sigma \cup \Gamma \cup \{A\}$. We need to prove that if $\Gamma \vdash^{\Sigma \cup \Psi} A$, then there exists is a set Δ of frame axioms such that $\Gamma \vdash_{\Delta}^{\Sigma} A$.

To construct such a Δ, we start from an empty set. For each formula in the form of equation (3) in Ψ, we introduce a new fluent symbols f, and add the following "axioms" into Δ :

$f \wedge \psi_i' \rightarrow \gamma_i, \neg f \wedge \psi_j'' \rightarrow \gamma_j, (i = 1, \cdots, m \text{ and } j = 1, \cdots, n)$

Now we prove that if Γ is $\Sigma \cup \Psi$-consistent, then $\Gamma \vdash^{\Sigma \cup \Psi} A$ implies $\Gamma \vdash_{\Delta}^{\Sigma} A$.

To this end, we prove that Γ is $\Sigma \cup \Delta$-consistent. Since Γ is $\Sigma \cup \Psi$-consistent, there exists a $\Sigma \cup \Psi$-model $M = (W, \mathcal{R}, V)$ such that for some $w_0 \in W$, $M \models_{w_0} \Gamma$. Construct a model $M' = (W', \mathcal{R}', V')$ of the language with the new introduced fluent symbols. Let $W' = W$ and $\mathcal{R}' = \mathcal{R}$. V' is different from V only in the valuation of new fluent symbols:

For any $w \in W$, $w \in V'(f)$ iff $M' \models_w \bigwedge_{i=1}^{m} (\neg \psi_i' \vee \gamma_i)$

Thus, for each $f \wedge \psi_i' \rightarrow \gamma_i \in \Delta$, if $M' \models_w \neg f$, then $M' \models_w f \wedge \psi_i' \rightarrow \gamma_i$; if $M' \models_w f$, then $M' \models_w \bigwedge_{i=1}^{m} (\neg \psi_i' \vee \gamma_i)$, so $M' \models_w \neg \psi_i' \vee \gamma_i$. This means $M' \models_w f \wedge \psi_i' \rightarrow \gamma_i$.

For each $\neg f \wedge \psi_j'' \rightarrow \gamma_j \in \Delta$, if $M' \models_w f$, then $M' \models_w \neg f \wedge \psi_j'' \rightarrow \gamma_j$. If $M' \models_w \neg f$, then by $M \models_w \bigwedge_{i=1}^{m} (\neg \psi_i' \vee \gamma_i) \vee \bigwedge_{j=1}^{n} (\neg \psi_j'' \vee \gamma_j)$, we have that $M' \models_w \bigwedge_{j=1}^{n} (\neg \psi_j'' \vee \gamma_j)$, so $M' \models_w \neg \psi_j'' \vee \gamma_j$. That is $M' \models_w \neg f \wedge \psi_j'' \rightarrow \gamma_j$. It's easy to see that M' is a Σ-model and $M' \models_w \Gamma$. Therefore we have proved that M' is a $\Sigma \cup \Delta$-model and Γ is $\Sigma \cup \Delta$-consistent. Because $\Delta \vdash \Psi$, $\Gamma \vdash^{\Sigma \cup \Psi} A$ implies $\Gamma \vdash_{\Delta}^{\Sigma} A$. □

Proof of Theorem 2

Without loss of generality, we suppose that Δ only contains the supplementary axioms on a primitive action symbol a which does not in $\Gamma \cup \{A\}$. We prove that $\Gamma \vdash_{\Delta}^{\Sigma} A$ implies $\Gamma \vdash^{\Sigma} A$.

Assume that $\Gamma \not\vdash^{\Sigma} A$. Then there exists a canonical model $M^C = (W^C, \mathcal{R}^C, V^C)$ of Σ such that

$W^C = \{w^C : w^C \text{ is a maximal } \Sigma\text{-consistent set of formulas}\}$

and $M^C \models \Gamma$ but $M^C \not\models A$. Let $M^\Gamma = (W^\Gamma, \mathcal{R}^\Gamma, V^\Gamma)$ be the $FL(\Sigma \cup \Delta \cup \Gamma \cup \{A\})$-filtration of M^C. It is easy to see that M^Γ is a Σ-model, $M^\Gamma \models \Gamma$ and $M^\Gamma \not\models A$. Now we transform M^Γ into a $\Sigma \cup \Delta$-model if it is not. Assume that $\Sigma \cup \Delta$ contains the following causal laws about a :

$\varphi_0 \rightarrow \langle a \rangle \top, \varphi_1 \rightarrow [a]L_1, \cdots, \varphi_m \rightarrow [a]L_m$

Let $M = (W, \mathcal{R}, V)$ be a model which is as same as M^Γ except for the accessibility relation R_a for a and relative accessibility relations for compound actions involving a. We define R_a as follows: for any $w, w' \in W$, $(w, w') \in R_a$ iff

1. $M \models_w \varphi_0$;
2. for each $i (1 \leq i \leq m)$, if $M \models_w \varphi_i$, then $M \models_{w'} L_i$;

It is easy to see that $M \models \Gamma$ and $M \not\models A$. It is not hard to prove that M is a $\Sigma \cup \Delta$-model. Therefore $\Gamma \not\vdash^{\Sigma \cup \Delta} A$, which contradicts $\vdash_{\Delta}^{\Sigma} A$. We conclude that $\vdash_{\Delta}^{\Sigma} A$ implies $\vdash^{\Sigma} A$. □

References

1. A. Baker, Nonmonotonic reasoning in the framework of situation calculus, *Artificial Intelligence*, 49:5-23, 1991.
2. M. A. Castilho, O. Gasquet and A. Herzig, Formalizing action and change in modal logic I: the frame problem, *J. of Logic and Computations,* 701-735(9), 1999.
3. C.C. Chang and H. J. Keisler, *Model Theory*, North Holland, 1973.
4. N. Foo, D. Zhang, Y. Zhang, S. Chopra and B. Vo, Encoding solutions of the frame problem in dynamic logic. T. Eiter, W. Faber, and M. Truszczynski eds., *Logic Programming and Nonmonotonic Reasoning (LPNMR'01)*, LNAI 2173, Springer, 240-253.
5. M. Gelfond and V. Lifschitz, Action languages, *Electronic Transactions on AI*, 16(3), 1998.
6. G. De Giacomo and M. Lenzerini, PDL-based framework for reasoning about actions, In M. Gori and G. Soda (Eds.), *Topics in Artificial Intelligence*, LNAI 992, Springer, 1995, 103-114.
7. M. L. Ginsberg and D. E. Smith, Reasoning about action I: a possible worlds approach, *Artificial Intelligence*, 35(1988), 165-195.
8. R. Goldblatt, *Logics of Time and Computation,* Center for the Study of Language and Information Lecture Notes 7, Stanford Univ. Press, 1987.
9. S. Hanks and D. McDermott, Nonmonotonic logic and temporal projection, *Artificial Intelligence,* 33(3): 379-412, 1987.
10. V. Lifschitz, Frames in the space of situations, *Artificial Intelligence,* 46:365-376,1990.
11. F. Lin and Y. Shoham, Provably correct theories of action, *AAAI-91*, 349-354, 1991.
12. G. Kartha, Soundness and completeness theorems for three formalization of action, *IJCAI-93*, 724-729, 1993.
13. G. Kartha: On the range of applicability of Baker's approach to the frame problem. *AAAI-96* ,664-669, 1996.
14. L. Maksimova, Amalgamation and interpolation in normal modal logics, *Studia Logica,* L(3/4), 457-471, 1991.
15. J. X. Madarász, The Craig interpolation theorem in multi-modal logics, *Bulletin of the Section of Logic,* 3(24), 147-151, 1995.
16. M. Marx, Interpolation in Modal Logic, *LNCS 1548*, 154–163, 1999.
17. E. Pednault, ADL: Exploring the middle ground between STRIPS and the situation calculus, *KR'89,* 1989, 324-332.
18. F. Pirri and R. Reiter, Some contributions to the metatheory of the situation calculus.*J.ACM,* 3(46),325-361, 1999.
19. H. Prendinger, and G. Schurz, Reasoning about action and change: A dynamic logic approach, *J. of Logic, Language, and Information,* 5:209-245,1996.
20. R. Reiter, The frame problem in the situation calculus: a simple solution (sometimes) and a completeness result for goal regression, In V. Lifschitz editor, *Artificial Intelligence and Mathematical Theory of Computation*, Academic Press, 359-380, 1991.
21. M. Shanahan, Solving the frame problem: a mathematical investigation of the common sense law of inertia, *The MIT Press*, 1997.
22. D. Zhang and N. Foo, EPDL: a logic for causal reasoning, *IJCAI-01,* 131-136, 2001.
23. D. Zhang and S. Chopra, Consistency of action descriptions, in: *Proceedings of the 4th Workshop on Nonmonotonic Reasoning, Action, and Change (NRAC'01)*, 78-85, 2001.

Reasoning about Actions in Prioritized Default Theory

Tran Cao Son and Enrico Pontelli

Department of Computer Science
New Mexico State University
{tson,epontell}@cs.nmsu.edu

Abstract. This paper shows how action theory in the language $\mathcal{B}$ can be naturally encoded using prioritized default theory. We also show how prioritized default theory can be extended to express preferences between *rules* and *formulae*. This extension provides a natural framework to introduce *preferences over trajectories* in $\mathcal{B}$. We illustrate how these preferences can be expressed and how they can be represented within extended prioritized default theory. We also discuss how this framework can be implemented in terms of answer set programming.

1 Introduction

Research in reasoning about action and change (RAC) has been concentrated on developing formalisms for representing and reasoning about actions and their effects. In general, an action theory is a set of propositions written in a specialized language such as situation calculus [12], event calculus [7], STRIPS [2], action description language [15,4] etc. that was developed for representing and reasoning about actions and their effects. The semantics of an action theory is then defined by an entailment relation that determines what will be true after an action sequence is executed from a given state.

For several years, the frame problem [12], the ramification problem [6], and the qualification problem [11] have been at the center of RAC's research. In short, the frame problem is the problem of describing, in a concise way, the non-effects of actions, i.e., to express what *does not change* after an action is executed. The ramification problem is concerned with the representation of static domain constraints or indirect effects of actions. The qualification problem, on the other hand, is concerned with actions that may not be executable in a certain situation. To date, solutions to these problems have been discussed in several RAC's approaches.

In this paper we show that prioritized default theory [5] provides a natural framework for representing and reasoning about actions and their effects. We show that by viewing dynamic and static causal laws as rules and the inertial law as defaults, action theories—in this work we concentrate on the language $\mathcal{B}$ [4]— can be translated into semantically equivalent prioritized default theories. The novelty of this work is a methodology of translating action theories into prioritized default theory. Furthermore, we propose an extension of prioritized default theory in which preferences between rules and formulae can be enforced in the process of proving consequences. The advantage of this new formalism is that it provides a convenient way to incorporate different forms of *preferences* in the process of representing and reasoning about trajectories (or plans in deterministic action theories). Conventional logic-based approaches to reasoning about

S. Flesca et al. (Eds.): JELIA 2002, LNAI 2424, pp. 369–381, 2002.
© Springer-Verlag Berlin Heidelberg 2002

actions provide the ability to derive trajectories leading to states satisfying a predefined goal. Nevertheless, in many situations, it is desirable to find one, among several possible trajectories, that satisfies certain constraints. Thus, we would like to allow the action language to include a description of users' preferences in how to accomplish the goal. In this work we explore alternative forms of preferences at the level of the action language: *(1)* preferences between actions; *(2)* preferences between final states; *(3)* general preferences between trajectories. These preferences could be viewed as *soft constraints* on a trajectory or a plan, that may or may not be satisfied depending on the particular situation. We illustrate how these different forms of preferences can be represented and handled in the context of prioritized default theories. As a consequences, prioritized default theory and its implementation in logic programming automatically provide an effective methodology to derive preferred trajectories.

2   Background

2.1   The Action Language $\mathcal{B}$

In this section, we present the basic terminology associated to the language $\mathcal{B}$ [4]. The alphabet of $\mathcal{B}$ consists of two nonempty, disjoint sets, **F** and **A**, of *fluent names* and *action names*, respectively. A *fluent literal* is a fluent name possibly preceded by $\neg$. A *domain description* (or *domain*) is a set of propositions of the forms

$$a \quad \textbf{causes} \quad f \textbf{ if } p_1, \ldots, p_n \tag{1}$$

$$f \quad \textbf{if} \quad p_1, \ldots, p_m \tag{2}$$

$$a \textbf{ executable\_if } p_1, \ldots, p_n \tag{3}$$

where a is an action name and f and p_i's are fluent literals. They are called *dynamic*, *static laws*, and *executability condition* respectively. The dynamic law (1) represents the effect of action a on fluent f while the causal law (2) states that the fluent f will be true in any state in which $p_1, \ldots, p_m$ are true. The proposition (3) represents the conditions under which the action a can be executed. Axioms in $\mathcal{B}$ are propositions of the form

$$\textbf{initially } f \tag{4}$$

where f is a fluent literal. This axiom states that the fluent literal f is true in the initial state. Finally, a query in $\mathcal{B}$ is of the form

$$\varphi \textbf{ after } \alpha \tag{5}$$

where φ is a fluent formula and α is a sequence of actions. Intuitively, the query asks whether the fluent formula φ is true in all the states resulting from the execution of the action sequence α from the current state. An *action theory* is a pair (D, Γ), where D is a collection of propositions of the type (1)–(3), called a *domain description*, while Γ is a collection of propositions of type (4), called a *initial state*. The next example illustrates the use of the language $\mathcal{B}$ in describing a simple dynamic domain.

Example 1. Consider the problem of describing the functioning of a briefcase [20]; the briefcase is provided with two clasps, and it will not open unless both clasps are unfastened. The domain description makes use of the fluents

| open | *briefcase is open* |
| fastened(X) | *clasp X is fastened* |

We provide a single domain action to change the status of the clasp:

unfastened(X) **causes** ¬fastened(X)

Finally, a static causal law is used to propagate the effect of unfastening both clasps:

open **if** ¬fastened($clasp_1$), ¬fastened($clasp_2$)

A domain description given in $\mathcal{B}$ defines a transition function (Φ) from actions and states to a set of states. Intuitively, given an action a and a state s, the function Φ defines the set of states $\Phi(a, s)$ that may be reached after executing the action a in state s. If $\Phi(a, s)$ is an empty set it means that a is not executable in s.

Let D be a domain description in $\mathcal{B}$. An *interpretation* I of the fluents in D is a maximal consistent set of fluent literals from **F**. A fluent f is said to be true (resp. false) in I iff $f \in I$ (resp. ¬$f \in I$). The truth value of a fluent formula in I is defined recursively over the propositional connectives in the usual way. For example, $f \wedge q$ is true in I iff f is true in I and q is true in I. We say that a formula φ holds in I (or I satisfies φ), denoted by $I \models \varphi$, if φ is true in I.

Let u be a consistent set of fluent literals and K a set of static causal laws. We say that u is closed under K if for every static causal laws " **if** ($\{p_1, \ldots, p_n\}, f$)" in K, if $\{p_1, \ldots, p_n\} \subseteq u$ then so does f. By $Cl_K(u)$ we denote the least consistent set of literals from D that contains u and is also closed under K. A *state* of D is an interpretation of the fluents in **F** that is closed under the set of static causal laws belonging to D. An action a is *executable* in a state s if there exists a proposition

$$a \textbf{ executable\_if } f_1, \ldots, f_n$$

in D such that $s \models f_1 \wedge \ldots \wedge f_n$. If "$a$ **executable_if true**" belongs to D, then a is executable in every state of D. The *immediate effect of an action* a in state s is the set

$$E(a, s) = \{f \mid D \text{ contains a dynamical law "} a \textbf{ causes } f \textbf{ if } f_1, \ldots, f_n \text{"}$$
$$\text{and } s \models f_i \text{ for } i = 1, \ldots, n\}.$$

For a domain description D, $\Phi(a, s)$, the set of states that may be reached by executing a in s, is defined as follows: if a is executable in s, then

$$\Phi(a, s) = \{s' \mid s' \text{ is a state and } s' = Cl_{D_C}(E(a, s) \cup (s \cap s'))\}$$

where D_C is the set of static causal laws in D; if a is not executable in s, then $\Phi(a, s) = \emptyset$. Every domain description D in $\mathcal{B}$ has a unique transition function Φ, and we say Φ is the transition function of D.

For a domain D with transition Φ, a sequence $s_0 a_1 s_1 \ldots a_n s_n$ where s_i's are states and a_i's are actions is called a *trajectory* in D if $s_{i+1} \in \Phi(s_i, a_{i+1})$ for $i \in \{0, \ldots, n-1\}$. A trajectory $s_0 a_1 s_1 \ldots a_n s_n$ is a trajectory of a fluent formula Δ if $s_n \models \Delta$.

A domain description D is *consistent* iff for every action a and state s, if a is executable in s, then $\Phi(a, s) \neq \emptyset$. An action theory (D, Γ) is consistent if D is consistent and $s_0 = \{f \mid$ " **initially** f" $\in \Gamma\}$ is a state of D. An action theory (D, Γ) is *complete* if, for each fluent f, we have that either " **initially** f" or " **initially** ¬f" belongs to Γ.

s_0 will be called the initial state of (D, Γ). Finally, for an action theory (D, Γ) whose initial state s_0 and an action sequence $\alpha = a_1, \ldots, a_n$, we say that the query φ **after** α is entailed by (D, Γ), denoted by $(D, \Gamma) \models \varphi$ **after** α if for every possible trajectory $s_0 a_1 s_1 \ldots a_n s_n$, φ holds in s_n.

In what follows, we will consider only consistent and complete action theories. We will also omit the description of the set of action names and the set of fluent names.

Example 2. Let D_b be the domain description in Example 1 and Γ be the initial state contains the three propositions

initially ¬open,
initially ¬fastened($clasp_1$), and
initially ¬fastened($clasp_2$).

The initial state s_0 in this action theory is

$$\{\neg\text{open}, \neg\text{fastened}(clasp_1), \neg\text{fastened}(clasp_2)\}.$$

The action unfastened($clasp_1$) is executable in s_0. We can easily check that

$$\text{if } s \in \Phi(\text{unfastened}(clasp_1), s_0) \text{ then } s \models \neg\text{fastened}(clasp_1).$$

This implies that $(D_b, \Gamma) \models \neg\text{fastened}(clasp_1)$ **after** unfastened($clasp_1$). If we consider also the action unfastened($clasp_2$) then we can obtain

$$\text{if } s_1 \in \Phi(\text{unfastened}(clasp_2), s_2) \text{ and } s_2 \in \Phi(\text{unfastened}(clasp_1), s_0)$$
$$\text{then } s_1 \models \text{open}.$$

Hence, $(D_b, \Gamma) \models \text{open}$ **after** unfastened($clasp_1$), unfastened($clasp_2$).

2.2 Prioritized Default Theory

Prioritized default theory has been discussed in [5]. In this paper we decided to rely on prioritized default theory because of two major reasons. First of all, its syntax is simple and intuitive. Furthermore, the semantics of prioritized default theory is defined in terms of logic programs and answer set semantics [3]. Not only this avoids the creation of an ad-hoc semantics, but this also allows us to reuse existing inference systems developed for answer set semantics (e.g., **smodels** and **dlv**) to compute the entailment relation of prioritized default theory. In this paper we begin with the theory proposed by Gelfond and Son in [5]. We then extend it to allow new type of preferences such as those between rules or formulas to be encoded.

A prioritized default theory comprises of facts, defaults, rules, and preferences between defaults. Rules and defaults are used to derive new conclusions. Nevertheless, the use of rules and defaults is different. A rule is used to derive a conclusion whenever all its premises are satisfied. On the other hand, a default can be used to derive a conclusion as long as such conclusion does not introduce inconsistencies into the theory—even if all its premises are satisfied. Formally, a default theory over a multi-sorted logic language $\mathcal{L}$ (or a *domain*) is a set of literals of the form

$$rule(r, l_0, [l_1, \ldots, l_m]); \tag{6}$$
$$default(d, l_0, [l_1, \ldots, l_m]); \tag{7}$$
$$prefer(d_1, d_2); \tag{8}$$

where r is a rule name, d, d_1, d_2 are default names, $l_0, \ldots, l_n$ are literals of the language $\mathcal{L}$, and $[\ ]$ is the list operator. For a rule r, let $body(r)$ denote the list $[l_1, \ldots, l_n]$ and let $head(r)$ denote the literal l_0. Similar notation will be used for defaults. We assume that default names and rule names are two disjoint sets. The semantics of a default theory T is defined by the answer set semantics of a logic program, consisting of T and the following set of independent axioms:

- **Rules for Inference:**

$$holds(L) \leftarrow rule(R, L, Body), hold(Body). \tag{9}$$
$$holds(L) \leftarrow default(D, L, Body), hold(Body), \tag{10}$$
$$\qquad not\ defeated(D), not\ holds(\neg L).$$
$$hold([\ ]) \leftarrow \tag{11}$$
$$hold([H|T]) \leftarrow holds(H), hold(T). \tag{12}$$

- **Rules for Defeating Defaults:**

$$defeated(D) \leftarrow default(D, L, Body), \tag{13}$$
$$\qquad holds(\neg L).$$
$$defeated(D) \leftarrow default(D, L, Body), \tag{14}$$
$$\qquad default(D_1, L_1, Body_1),$$
$$\qquad prefer(D_1, D),$$
$$\qquad hold(Body_1),$$
$$\qquad not\ defeated(D_1).$$

This collection of axioms is different from the original one presented in [5]:

1. we do not distinguish between *holds* and *holds_by_default*, since our goal is to use prioritized default theories in reasoning about actions; in this context it is not interesting to know whether a fluent is made true by an action or by inertia[1].
2. in rule (14) we do not require D and $D1$ to be conflicting defaults.

3   Action Theories as Prioritized Default Theories

We will show now how each action theory can be represented by a prioritized default theory, whose semantics coincides with the action theory's entailment relation. The language to represent an action theory (D, Γ) in prioritized default theories consists of

---

[1] There are other approaches in reasoning about actions that do emphasize this point, but we are not interested in this distinction at this point in time.

- atoms of the form $f(T)$ (f is true at the time moment T),
- atoms of the form $possible(a, T)$ (a is executable at the time moment T),
- atoms of the form $occ(A, T)$ (action A occurs at the time moment T),
- rule names of the form $dynamic(f, a, T)$,
- rule names of the form $causal(f, T)$,
- rule names of the form $executable(a, T)$,
- default names of the form $inertial(f, T)$,

where f is a fluent literal, a is an action, and T is an integer representing units of time along a history. The translation of an action theory (D, Γ) into a prioritized theory $\Pi(D, \Gamma)$ is as follows[2]:

- For each dynamic law "a **causes** f **if** $p_1, \ldots, p_n$" in D, $\Pi(D, \Gamma)$ contains the rules

$$rule(dynamic(f, a, T), f(T+1), [p_1(T), \ldots, p_n(T), possible(a, T)])$$
$$\leftarrow occ(a, T) \quad (15)$$

- For each executability condition "a **executable_if** $q_1, \ldots, q_m$", $\Pi(D, \Gamma)$ contains

$$rule(executable(a, T), possible(a, T), [q_1(T), \ldots, q_m(T)]) \quad (16)$$

- For each static causal law "f **if** $p_1, \ldots, p_m$", $\Pi(D, \Gamma)$ contains the set of rules

$$rule(causal(f, T), f(T), [p_1(T), \ldots, p_n(T)]) \quad (17)$$

- The inertial axiom is represented by the set of defaults

$$default(inertial(f, a, T), f(T+1), [f(T)]) \quad (18)$$

where f is a fluent literal, a is an action, and T is a sequence of actions.

- Finally, for each axiom " **initially** f" in Γ, $\Pi(D, \Gamma)$ contains the fact

$$holds(f(0)). \quad (19)$$

For each action theory (D, Γ), let $\Pi^k(D, \Gamma)$ be the logic program consisting of *(i)* The set of independent rules (9)-(14); *(ii)* The set of rules (15)-(18) in which T ranges between 0 and n, and *(iii)* The set of facts of the form (19). In the next two theorems, we prove the correctness of $\Pi^k(D, \Gamma)$. That is, we prove that the semantics provided by the prioritized default theory coincides with the action theory semantics. Let M be an answer set of $\Pi^k(D, \Gamma)$. Let $s_i(M) = \{f \mid holds(f(i)) \in M\}$. We begin with the soundness of $\Pi^k(D, \Gamma)$.

Theorem 1. *Let (D, Γ) be a complete and consistent action theory. Then, for every sequence of actions $a_1, \ldots, a_k$ such that there exists a trajectory $s_0 a_1 s_1 \ldots a_k s_k$,*

- *for every answer set M of*
$$\Pi^k(D, \Gamma) \cup \{occ(a_i, i-1) \mid i = 1, \ldots, k\},$$
$s_{i+1}(M) \in \Phi(a, s_i(M))$ for every i, $0 \leq i \leq k - 1$;

- *for every trajectory $s_0 a_1 s_1' \ldots a_k s_k'$ there exists an answer set M of*
$$\Pi^k(D, \Gamma) \cup \{occ(a_i, i-1) \mid i = 1, \ldots, k\},$$
such that $s_i(M) = s_i'$ for every i, $1 \leq i \leq k$.

---

[2] In all of the rules and defaults, T is an integer representing time units.

4   Computing the Entailment Relation $\models$

The program $\Pi(D, \Gamma)$ can be implemented using **smodels** [14]. To make this possible, we need to introduce a collection of predicates to overcome the limitations of the input language; in particular, **smodels** does not support the list operator and requires finite domains and domain predicates to perform grounding.

Let us call the **smodels** program $SM(D, \Gamma)$. It is similar to the implementations of answer set planning proposed in the literature [8,18]. It makes use of a time variable representing time instants along a trajectory. In all rules described below, we denote the time variable with T. The program $SM(D, \Gamma)$ makes use of the following predicates[3]:

- for each action a and for each fluent f we introduce the facts $action(a)$ and $fluent(f)$.
- each rule of the form

$$rule(dynamic(f, a, T), f(T+1), [p_1(T), \dots, p_n(T), possible(a, T)])$$
$$\leftarrow occ(a, T).$$

is encoded as the **smodels** rule

$$rule(dynamic(f, a, T), true(f, T+1), precondition\_set(a, T))$$
$$\leftarrow occ(a, T). \quad (20)$$

where the predicate $true(f, T)$ represents the truth value of the fluent literal f at time T (if $holds(true(f, T))$ is true, then f is true at time T). The predicate $precondition\_set(a, T)$ is defined by the following rules:

$$in(true(p_1, T), precondition\_set(a, T)).$$
$$\dots$$
$$in(true(p_n, T), precondition\_set(a, T)).$$
$$in(true(possible(a, T)), precondition\_set(a, T)).$$

Similar encoding is used for the rules of the form (16)-(18).

- The two rules (11)-(12) are replaced by the rules

$$set(nil) \leftarrow \qquad\qquad (21)$$
$$not\_holds\_set(S) \leftarrow set(S), in(F, S), not\ holds(F). \qquad (22)$$
$$holds\_set(S) \leftarrow set(S), not\ not\_holds\_set(S). \qquad (23)$$

These rules state when a set (the body of a rule or a default is true). The first rule defined the constant nil representing the empty set.

- The predicate $name$ is used to define the names of rules and defaults, e.g., $name(dynamic(a, f, T))$ is introduced for the dynamic law "a **causes** f **if** $p_1, \dots, p_n$."

---

[3] **smodels** codes for some examples and the domain independent rules can be found at www.cs.nmsu.edu/~tson/preferences.

- The predicate $contrary$, defined by the rule $contrary(true(L, T), true(\neg L, T))$, is introduced to derive the negation of a literal in the prioritized default theory language. This is used to facilitate the application of defaults and rules, i.e., to implement the rules (10), (13), and (14).

Let (D, Γ) be a complete and consistent action theory, and let $\alpha = a_1, \dots, a_n$ be a sequence of actions. With $SM^n(D, \Gamma)$ we denote the above **smodels**-rules for (D, Γ) in which the time variable ranges from 0 to n. With $SM^\alpha(D, \Gamma)$ we denote the program containing $SM^{|\alpha|}(D, \Gamma)$ and the set of action occurrences $\{occ(a_1, 0), \dots, occ(a_n, n - 1)\}$. Following the result from [10,18] we can show that $SM^\alpha(D, \Gamma)$ and $\Pi^\alpha(D, \Gamma)$ have "equivalent" answer sets—each answer set of $SM^\alpha(D, \Gamma)$ can be converted into an answer set of $\Pi^\alpha(D, \Gamma)$ and vice versa.

5   Finding a Trajectory Using $SM^n(D, \Gamma)$

The discussion in the previous section shows that $SM^n(D, \Gamma)$ can be used to compute the entailment relation of (D, Γ). In this section, we discuss the use of $SM^n(D, \Gamma)$ in finding a trajectory $s_0 a_1 \dots a_n s_n$ that satisfies the following properties:

1. $s_n \models \varphi$ for some given fluent formula φ—this means that the trajectory is a possible plan to accomplish the goal φ;
2. the trajectory $s_0 a_1 \dots a_n s_n$ satisfies some soft constraints that are expressed as preferences between actions, between fluent formula, or between the trajectories.

5.1   Finding A Trajectory for φ

Let (D, Γ) be an action theory and φ be a conjunction of fluent literals $f_1 \wedge \dots \wedge f_k$ [4]. We are interested in finding a trajectory $s_0 a_0 \dots a_n s_n$ for φ. As it is customary in answer set planning, we add to $SM^n(D, \Gamma)$ the set of rules to generate action occurrences and to represent the goal. This set of rules consists of:

$$goal(T) \leftarrow time(T), holds(true(f_1, T)), \tag{24}$$

$$\dots,$$

$$holds(true(f_k, T)).$$

$$\leftarrow not\ goal(length). \tag{25}$$

$$1\{occ(A, T) : action(A)\}1 \leftarrow time(T), T < length. \tag{26}$$

Let $SM^{Plan,n}(D, \Gamma, \varphi)$ be the program consisting of the rules of $SM^n(D, \Gamma)$ and the set of rules (24)-(26), in which time variable takes values from 0 to n. It is easy to see that the following holds:

1. If $s_0 a_1 \dots a_n s_n$ is a trajectory for φ then $SM^{Plan,n}(D, \Gamma, \varphi)$ has an answer set S [5] such that
   (a) $occ(a_i, i - 1) \in S$ for every integer i, $1 \leq i \leq n$, and
   (b) $s_i = \{f \mid holds(true(f, i)) \in S\}$.

---

[4]   Fluent formula can be dealt with as in [18].
[5]   Observe that S is actually a stable model.

2. If $SM^{Plan,n}(D, \Gamma, \varphi)$ has an answer set S such that
   (a) $occ(a_i, i - 1) \in S$ for every integer i, $1 \le i \le n$, and
   (b) $s_i = \{f \mid holds(true(f, i)) \in S\}$
   then $s_0 a_1 \ldots a_n s_n$ is a trajectory for φ.

5.2 Finding a Preferred A Trajectory

A trajectory for a fluent formula φ is a possible plan to achieve φ. In many situations, it is desirable to find one, among several possible trajectories, that satisfies certain constraints. For example, *riding a bus* and *taxi* are two alternatives to go to the airport. An agent might choose to take the bus because he does not like taxi drivers. But he is willing to take the taxi if the bus does not run. Here, the agent has a preference between the actions he can execute and he would like to choose the trajectory that suits him best. We will call this a preference between trajectories and discuss how we can generate trajectories satisfying an agent's preferences using $SM^{Plan,n}(D, \Gamma, \varphi)$. In the process, we extend the prioritized default theory for representing the preferences between rules and literals. We will discuss preferences between actions, formulas, and trajectories.

Preferences Between Rules. To say that we do not prefer a rule r means that we do not want to use r. It does not necessarily mean that r cannot be applied, but it means that if r can be replaced, then we should do so. For this reason, we use literals of the form

$$block(r, [l_1, \ldots, l_m]); \tag{27}$$

to describe conditions under which a rule r should not be used. In particular, literals of this type can be used to represent preferences between the rules. For example, if we want to express the fact that if two rules r_1, r_2 have the same consequence and we prefer to use r_2 instead of r_1, then we can write $block(r_1, body(r_2))$.

To implement the new type of rules in prioritized default theory, we replace rule (9) by the following rule:

$$holds(L) \leftarrow rule(R, L, Body), hold(Body), not\ blocked(R). \tag{28}$$

and add the next rule to $\Pi(D, \Gamma)$:

$$blocked(R) \leftarrow block(R, Body), hold(Body). \tag{29}$$

This is used to block the application of the rule R. Observe that blocking a rule is different than defeating a default; a rule can be blocked only at the explicit will of the domain specifier, while a default can be defeated if its application introduces inconsistencies.

We now show that this modification allows us to deal with preferences between actions. We assume that we have an irreflexive partial order between actions, $prefer(a, b)$, to represent the preferences between actions. Intuitively, this means that action a is preferred to action b and we would like to consider all the trajectories containing a in the place of b before considering those containing b. More precisely:

Definition 1 (Preferred Trajectory). *A trajectory* $\alpha = s_0 a_1 s_1 \ldots, a_n s_n$ *is said to be preferred to a trajectory* $\beta = s_0 b_1 s_1' \ldots, b_n s_n'$ *with respect to a set of preferences* P, *denoted by* $\alpha \prec_P \beta$, *if*

1. *there exists an integer i, $1 \le i \le n$, such that $prefer(a_i, b_i) \in P$, and*
2. *for every integer j, $1 \le j < i$, $prefer(b_j, a_j) \notin P$.*

Definition 2 (Most Preferred Trajectory). *A trajectory $\alpha = a_1, \ldots, a_n$ is said to be a* most preferred *trajectory with respect to a set of preferences P if there exists no trajectory β such that $\beta \prec_P \alpha$.*

Remark 1. $\prec_P$ is an antisymmetric, transitive, and irreflexive relation.

Let us now encode the preferences between actions as rules of $SM^{Plan,n}(D, \Gamma)$. For simplicity, instead of translating the set of preferences between actions into literals of the form (27) we will encode it directly into logic programming. For each $prefer(a, b)$, and for each dynamic causal law "a **causes** g **if** $p_1, \ldots, p''_m$", we define a rule

$$block(dynamic(F, b, T), [true(p_1, T), \ldots, true(p_m, T), possible(a, T)])$$
$$\leftarrow goal(length). \qquad (30)$$

Intuitively, this rule says that if (at the time moment T) it is possible to execute the action a and the goal is achievable, then action b should not be executed. Let (D, Γ) be an action theory and P be a set of preferences on actions in D. Let $SM^{Pref,n}(D, \Gamma, \varphi)$ be the program consisting of (1) the program $SM^{Plan,n}(D, \Gamma, \varphi)$, and (2) the set of rules (30) with the time variable ranging between 0 and n. It is easy to see that, when $prefer(a, b)$ is present and both actions are executable and lead to the goal, then a will be used first. However, the rules of the form (30) do not warrant completeness, i.e., it does not guarantee that a trajectory is found if the problem has a solution[6].

On the other hand, if we use the **smodels** construct **maximize**, the most preferred trajectory can always be found, by adding the following optimal rule to the program $SM^{Pref,n}(D, \Gamma, \varphi)$: for each $prefer(a, b)$ and for each time point t

$$\mathbf{maximize}[occ(a, t) = 1, occ(b, t) = 0].$$

In our future work, we plan to investigate whether a sound and complete implementation in the prioritized default theory can be realized.

Preferences between Formula. The second type of preferences that we consider is between formulae. Unlike preferences between rules, this type of preference is often a soft constraint or a secondary goal that an agent has in mind when selecting a trajectory for his goal. Consider for example our agent in the previous section. He might prefer to take the bus because it is cheap ($save\_money$). Here, the primary goal of the agent is to be at the airport and his soft constraint is to save money. The trivial choice would be to take the bus. Taking a taxi would be used as the last resource. This type of preference can be added to a prioritized default theory by introducing preferences of the form

$$\varphi_1 \prec \varphi_2. \qquad (31)$$

Again, we assume that $\prec$ is an irreflexive partial order. Thus, for a finite set of preferences of the form (31), there exists a finite number of maximal length sequences of formulas

---

[6] For instance, when two actions a and b are possible, and a is preferred to b but does not lead to the final goal, then the program may fail to produce a trajectory.

$\varphi_1 \prec \ldots \prec \varphi_p$. To implement (31), for each maximal sequence $\varphi_1 \prec \ldots \prec \varphi_p$, we add the optimal rule [13]

$$\mathbf{maximize}[\varphi_1 = 0, \ldots, \varphi_p = p] \tag{32}$$

to $SM^{Plan,n}(D, \Gamma)$. We are assuming that the computation of the answer sets maximizes each rule of type (32). Observe that the current implementation of **smodels** does not guarantee this behavior[7]. If we want to use the current version of **smodels**, then we need to additionally require that the preference relation $\prec$ is total order.

General Preferences Between Trajectories. In general, an agent can have several preferences on a trajectory. For example, he might prefer to use an action a over an action b, he might also prefer that whenever he has to execute an action c then d should be the next action, etc. It has been discussed in [1] that many preferences or constraint of this type can be conveniently expressed as a temporal logic formula. Since the truth value of a temporal logic formula can be easily checked given a trajectory, this feature can be added to our framework by

- adding rules for checking the truth value of temporal logic formulae, that associate each temporal logic formula, say φ, to a new boolean variable φ^T, whose truth value in the final state corresponds to the satisfiability of φ w.r.t. the chosen trajectory (as illustrated in [18]),
- adding an optimal rule

$$\mathbf{maximize}[\varphi^T = 1, not \ \varphi^T = 0]$$

to the program $SM^{Plan,n}(D, \Gamma)$, that allows us to find trajectories satisfying φ before considering those not satisfying it.

6   Conclusions

In this paper we present a formalism for reasoning about actions in the context of prioritized default theory. In this process, we provide an encoding of an action theory in prioritized default theory, whose answer set semantics coincides with the entailment relation of the action theory. In addition, prioritized default theory are very expressive and can be used to model dynamic domains that cannot be expressed using, e.g., the language $\mathcal{B}$; for example

- domains with non-inertial fluents (e.g., a spring-loaded door is open immediately after the push action is performed, but it will automatically revert to close at the next moment of time).
- domains with exogenous actions (e.g., a domain where a driver agent stops at the traffic light, and expects the light to change color; i.e., the driver agent expects the change color action to occur (exogenously)).

Our focus in this work is on using prioritized default theory to encode different forms of preferences between trajectories. In the process, we extend prioritized default theory to allow preferences between rules and formulae. We show how these features can be easily implemented in answer set programming. We also employ these new features to

---

[7] Currently **smodels** maximizes only the last optimal rule in the program.

directly express three different types of preferences between trajectories, i.e., preferences between actions, between final states, and general preferences between trajectories.

The preliminary experiments performed have provided encouraging results, and work is in progress to establish the full range of capabilities of this approach. In particular, we intend to use the proposed framework in the design of bioinformatics applications—i.e., software agents in charge of mapping high-level biological process descriptions into a predefined collection of software services [16]—and in the development of Web accessibility agents for visually impaired individuals [17].

Several other approaches to dealing with preferences between logic programming rules have been proposed[8]. In our future work we plan to investigate the use of these methods in representing and reasoning with preferences among actions.

Acknowledgments

The authors wish to thank M. Gelfond and the anonymous referees for the comments on various drafts of this work. Research has been supported by NSF grants EIA-0130887, CCR-9875279, HRD-9906130, and EIA-9810732 and by a grant from NASA.

References

1. F. Bacchus and F. Kabanza. Using temporal logics to express search control knowledge for planning. *Artificial Intelligence*, 116(1,2):123–191, 2000.
2. R. Fikes and N. Nilson. STRIPS: A new approach to the application of theorem proving to problem solving. *Artificial Intelligence*, 2(3–4):189–208, 1971.
3. M. Gelfond and V. Lifschitz. The Stable Model Semantics for Logic Programs. In *ILPS*, MIT Press, 1988.
4. M. Gelfond and V. Lifschitz. Action languages. *ETAI*, 3(6), 1998.
5. M. Gelfond and T.C. Son. Prioritized default theory. In *Selected Papers from the Workshop on Logic Programming and Knowledge Representation*, pages 164–223. Springer, 1998.
6. M. Ginsberg and D. Smith. Reasoning about actions I. *Artificial Intelligence*, 35, 1988.
7. R. Kowalski and M. Sergot. A logic-based calculus of events. *NGC*, 4:67–95, 1986.
8. V. Lifschitz. Answer set planning. In *Int. Conf. Logic Programming*, pages 23–37, 1999.
9. V. Lifschitz and H. Turner. Splitting a logic program. In Pascal Van Hentenryck, editor, *Proceedings of the Eleventh International Conf. on Logic Programming*, pages 23–38, 1994.
10. V. Lifschitz and H. Turner. Representing transition systems by logic programs. In *Proceedings Int. Conf. on Logic Programming and Nonmonotonic Reasoning*, pages 92–106, 1999.
11. J. McCarthy. Epistemological problems of artificial intelligence. In *Proceedings Int. Joint Conference on Artificial Intelligence*, pages 1038–1044. 1977.
12. J. McCarthy and P. Hayes. Some philosophical problems from the standpoint of artificial intelligence. In *Machine Intelligence*, volume 4, pages 463–502. 1969.
13. I. Niemelä. Logic programming with stable model semantics as a constraint programming paradigm. *Annals of Mathematics and Artificial Intelligence*, 25(3,4):241–273, 1999.
14. I. Niemelä and P. Simons. Smodels - an implementation of the stable model and well-founded semantics for normal logic programs. In *Procs. LPNMR*, pages 420–429, 1997.

---

[8] References to these proposals are omitted due to lack of space.

15. E. Pednault. ADL and the state-transition model of actions. *Journal of Logic and Computation*, 4(5):467–513, October 1994.
16. E. Pontelli, G. Gupta, D. Ranjan, and B. Milligan. A Domain Specific Language for Solving Philogenetic Inference Problems. TR-CS-001/2002, New Mexico State University, 2002.
17. E. Pontelli and T. Son. Navigating HTML Tables: Planning, Reasoning, and Agents. In *Int. Conference on Assistive Technologies*. ACM Press, 2002.
18. T.C. Son, C. Baral, and S. McIlraith. Domain dependent knowledge in planning - an answer set planning approach. In *Procs. LPNMR*, pages 226–239, Vienna, 2001.
19. T.C. Son and E. Pontelli. Reasoning About Actions in Prioritized Default Theory. TR-CS-002/002, New Mexico State U., 2002.
20. H. Turner. Representing actions in logic programs and default theories. *Journal of Logic Programming*, 31(1-3):245–298, May 1997.

Towards a Conditional Logic
of Actions and Causation

Laura Giordano[1] and Camilla Schwind[2]

[1] Dipartimento di Informatica - Università del Piemonte Orientale
laura@di.unito.it
[2] CNRS, Luminy
schwind@lim.univ-mrs.fr

Abstract. In this paper we present a new approach to reason about actions and causation which is based on a conditional logic. The conditional implication is interpreted as causal implication. This makes it possible to formalize in a uniform way causal dependencies between actions and their immediate and indirect effects. Also, it provides a natural formalization of concurrent actions and causal dependencies between actions. An abductive semantics is adopted for dealing with the frame problem.

1 Introduction

Causality plays a prominent role in the context of reasoning about actions, as the ramification effects of actions can be regarded as causal dependencies. Many approaches for reasoning about actions have been proposed which allow causal dependencies to be captured [5,14,16,22,1]. Schwind [19] has studied how causal inferences have been integrated and used in action theories by analyzing four formalisms, which are approaches to action and causality, and comparing them with respect to criteria she established for causality. Namely, the article analyses Lin's approach [13,14], McCain and Turner's causal theory for action and change [16,23], Thielscher's theory of ramification and causation [22], and Giordano, Martelli and Schwind's dynamic causal action logic [6]. More recently, Zhang and Foo [24,2,3] propose to extend propositional dynamic logic, where actions are modalities, by introducing modalities which are propositions. Sentence "ϕ causes ψ" is represented by the formula $[\phi]\psi$, where $[\phi]$ is a new modality. Note that this representation corresponds to a conditional logic approach, since EPDL formula $[\phi]\psi$ is interpreted as conditional formula $\phi > \psi$. Zhang and Foo's approach has the merit of providing a clean representation of causation as well as a uniform representation of direct and indirect effects of actions. But the notion of causality as defined in EPDL is too strong since it entails material implication. This property, $[\phi]\psi \rightarrow (\phi \rightarrow \psi)$, comes from a crucial axiom introduced for actions in EPDL, and is motivated by the fact that when "ϕ causes ψ" then the state constraint $\phi \rightarrow \psi$ must also hold. While we agree with this argument, we may object that the status of causal laws (and consequently of material implications) in [24] is not that of domain constraints. Instead, causal laws are

S. Flesca et al. (Eds.): JELIA 2002, LNAI 2424, pp. 382–393, 2002.

regarded as domain axioms, which gives the corresponding material implications also the status of domain axioms, so that they can be used for inference in all possible states, together with their contrapositive forms, which may lead to unintended conclusions. Though EPDL preserves the directionality of causation (from $[\phi]\psi$ we cannot conclude that $[\neg\psi]\neg\phi$), the fact that causation entails material implication (from $[\phi]\psi$ we can derive $\phi \to \psi$ and thus $\neg\psi \to \neg\phi$) anyhow leads to unwanted conclusions when reasoning about the effects of actions. As another difference with our proposal, in EPDL, syntactically, actions are not formulas. This makes it impossible to combine assertions about actions with assertions about causality: it is not possible to express for example that action a and fact B cause the effect C and concurrent actions cannot be defined.

We propose to represent causality by a binary logical operator. Our causality operator has the properties of causality relations as discussed in [19]. It is non-monotonic and does not entail material implication which makes it weaker than the one proposed in [24]. Traditionally, considering a conditional as a causal implication has frequently attracted the attention of researchers in conditional logic and in AI ([10,12,18]. It allows to model both causal laws and action laws: the causal law "ϕ causes ψ" is represented by the conditional formula $\phi > \psi$ and the action law "action a causes proposition ψ" is represented by the conditional formula $do(a) > \psi$, where $do(a)$ is a special atomic proposition associated with each action a. This uniform representation of the causal relationship between actions and their results as well as between facts and their effects gives us a great flexibility for handling both concepts in an simple way when representing actions. For example, in this setting, concurrent execution of actions is naturally modelled by conjunctions of the form $do(a_1) \wedge \ldots \wedge do(a_n)$ in the antecedents of conditionals. It is also very natural to express dependency (and independency) relations between actions and actions, actions and propositions, etc.

2   The Causal Action Logic AC

The language, $\mathcal{L}_>$, of our action logic is that of propositional logic augmented with a conditional operator $>$. The set of propositional variables in $\mathcal{L}_>$, Var, includes the set $\{do(a) : a \in \Delta_0\}$, where Δ_0 is a set of *elementary actions* including the "empty" action ϵ. Formulas are defined as usual and the modalities $\square$ and $\Diamond$ are defined by $\square A \equiv (\neg A > \bot)$ and $\Diamond A \equiv \neg\square\neg A$. Intuitively, $\square A$ means that A necessarily holds (always holds), while $\Diamond A$ means that A is possible. If A is an action proposition $do(a)$, $\Diamond do(a)$ means that a is executable. The following is an axiom system for logic AC.

Definition 1 (AC). *The conditional logic AC is the smallest logic containing the following axioms and deduction rules:*

(CLASS) All classical propositional axioms and inference rules
(CV) $(\neg(A > \neg C) \wedge (A > B)) \to (A \wedge C) > B$
(CA) $(A > C) \wedge (B > C) \to ((A \vee B) > C)$
(CE) $(do(a) > B) \wedge (do(a) > (B > C)) \to (do(a) > C)$, where $a \in \Delta_0$

(MOD) $\Box A \rightarrow (B > A)$

(UNIV) $\Box A \rightarrow \Box\Box A$ $\Diamond A \rightarrow \Box\Diamond A$ $\Box A \rightarrow A$

(RCEA) if $\vdash A \leftrightarrow B$*, then* $\vdash (A > C) \equiv (B > C)$

(RCK) if $\vdash A_1 \wedge \ldots \wedge A_n \rightarrow B$*, then* $\vdash (C > A_1) \wedge \ldots \wedge (C > A_n) \rightarrow (C > B)$.

Note that all axioms and inference rules are standard in conditional logics and, in particular, they belong to the axiomatization of Lewis's logic VCU (see [11]). However, we have excluded several of the standard axioms of conditional logics such as (ID), (MP) and (CS) since they model unwanted properties of causality. Reflexivity axiom (ID) $A > A$ is excluded since a proposition (or an action) should not cause itself. Axiom (MP) $(A > B) \rightarrow (A \rightarrow B)$ should not hold for causal implication: we do not want to be able to infer the material implication from a causal rule, as the former would give undesired properties to the latter[1]. (CS) $A \wedge B \rightarrow (A > B)$ should not be a property of causal implication: A and B could both hold conjunctively without A being a cause of B.

Axiom (CE) allows action laws and causal laws to interact, it provides the chain effects between causal laws and action laws. (CE) says that the causal consequences of action effects are in turn action effects: if executing action a (in a state S) causes B in the next state S' $(do(a) > B)$, and the causal law $B > C$ holds in S', then executing action a (in S) causes C to hold in S'. (CE) weakens (MP) as it is clear form the following formulation of (CE) $(do(a) > (B > C)) \rightarrow ((do(a) > B) \rightarrow (do(a) > C))$, which can be obtained from (MP) by (RCK). (CE) has similarities with the property of transitivity (TRANS) $(do(a) > B) \wedge (B > C) \rightarrow (do(a) > C)$ [2], which however requires that the causal law $B > C$ holds in the state S in which the action is executed. As we will see in our action theory causal laws do not necessarily hold in all possible states, as they may have preconditions which make them hold in some states only[3].

(MOD)and (UNIV) define a necessity operator and give it S5-properties. They allow to deduce $\Box A \rightarrow (do(a_1) > \ldots > (do(a_n) > A) \ldots)$ for any finite sequence of actions $a_1, \ldots a_n$ $(n \geq 0)$ including the empty sequence and meaning that a formula A which is true in every state is also true after the occurrence of any finite sequence of actions. So, the subsequent occurrence of actions structures a world and its subsequent states according to time, although time is not represented explicitly in our formalism.

---

[1]   Adding axiom (MP) to the logic above would allow $A > \neg B$ to be inferred from $A > \neg C$ and $B > C$. This is clearly unintended, as it makes a contrapositive use of causal rule $B > C$. A similar problem arises in EPDL: if $[A]\neg C$ and $[B]C$ are causal laws in Σ then $\vdash^\Sigma [A]\neg B$. Another unintended effect of (MP) is outlined in section 3.2 when discussing Example 1.

[2] For standard conditional logic with reflexivity, adding TRANS would collapse the conditional to material implication. But this is not the case for our causal action logic AC, since reflexivity $A > A$ is not an axiom.

[3] As an example of causal law with precondition consider the following one: $\Box(at(y,r) \rightarrow (at(z,r) > at(y, next(r))))$ taken from [5] below, which says that if block y is at r then moving block z to position r causes y to move to a next position.

Entailment $\vdash$ is defined as usual and given a set of formulas E, the deductive closure of E is denoted by $Th(E)$. AC is characterized semantically in terms of selection function models.

Definition 2. *An AC-structure M is a triplet $\langle W, f, [[\ ]] \rangle$, where W is a non-empty set, whose elements are called possible worlds, f, called the selection function, is a function of type $\mathcal{L}_> \times W \to 2^W$, $[[\ ]]$, called the evaluation function, is a function of type $\mathcal{L}_> \to 2^W$ that assigns a subset of W, $[[A]]$ to each formula A. The following conditions have to be fulfilled by $[[\ ]]$: (1) $[[A \wedge B]] = [[A]] \cap [[B]]$; (2) $[[\neg A]] = W - [[A]]$ [4]; (3) $[[A > B]] = \{w : f(A, w) \subseteq [[B]]\}$*

We assume that the selection function f satisfies the following properties which correspond to the axioms of our logic AC:

(S-RCEA) if $[[A]] = [[B]]$ then $f(A, w) = f(B, w)$
(S-CV) if $f(A, w) \cap [[C]] \neq \emptyset$ then $f(A \wedge C, w) \subseteq f(A, w)$
(S-CA) $f(A \vee B, w) \subseteq f(A, w) \cup f(B, w)$
(S-CE) if $f(do(a), w) \subseteq [[B]]$ then $f(do(a), w) \subseteq f(B, f(do(a), w))$
(S-MOD) if $f(B, w) \cap [[A]] \neq \emptyset$ then $f(A, w) \neq \emptyset$
(S-UNIV) if $[[A]] \neq \emptyset$, there is a formula B such that $f(B, w) \cap [[A]] \neq \emptyset$

where $a \in \Delta_0$ and $f(B, f(do(a), w))$ represents the set of worlds $\{z \in f(B, x) : x \in f(do(a), w)\}$.

We say that a formula A is true in a AC-structure $M = \langle W, f, [[\ ]] \rangle$ if $[[A]] = W$. We say that a formula α is AC-valid ($\models A$)if it is true in every AC-structure. Given a AC-structure M, a set of formulas S and a formula A, $S \models_M A$ means that for all $w \in M$ if $w \in [[B]]$ for all $B \in S$, then $w \in [[A]]$.

The above axiom system is sound and complete with respect to the semantics.

Theorem 1. $\models A$ *iff* $\vdash A$

The completeness proof is shown by the canonical model construction [20]. Moreover, the axiomatization is consistent and the logic is decidable. Since the logic AC is weaker than VCU, each VCU-structure is an AC-structure, which shows that the logic AC is "non-trivial" in some sense.

3 Action Theories

3.1 Domain Descriptions

We use atomic propositions $f, f_1, f_2, \ldots \in Var$ for *fluent names*. A *fluent literal*, denoted by l , is a fluent name f or its negation $\neg f$. Given a fluent literal l, such that $l = f$ or $l = \neg f$, we define $|l| = f$. Moreover, we will denote by $\mathcal{F}$ the set of all fluent names, by Lit the set of all fluent literals, and by small greek letters α, β, ... any formula not containing conditional formulas.

---

[4] Using the standard boolean equivalences, we obtain $[[A \vee B]] = [[A]] \cup [[B]]$, $[[A \to B]] = (W - [[A]]) \cup [[B]]$, $[[\top]] = W$, $[[\bot]] = \emptyset$.

We define a *domain description* as a tuple $(\Pi, Frame_0, Obs)$. Π is a set of laws and constrains as follows: *Action laws* have the form: $\Box(\pi \rightarrow (do(a) > \rho))$, for an action a with precondition π and effect ρ: executing action a in a state where π holds causes ρ to hold in the resulting state. For action laws with no precondition, i. e. $\pi = true$, we just obtain $\Box(do(a) > \rho)$. *Causal laws* have the form: $\Box(\pi \rightarrow (\alpha > \beta))$, meaning that "if π holds, then α causes β". *Precondition laws* have the form: $\Box(\pi \equiv \neg(do(a) > \bot))$, meaning that "action a is executable iff π holds". According to the definition of $\Diamond$, this is equivalent to $\Box(\pi \equiv \Diamond do(a))$. *Domain constraints* include formulas of the form: $\Box\alpha$, (meaning that "α always holds"). *Causal independency constraints* have the form: $\Box(\neg(A > \neg B))$, meaning that A does not cause $\neg B$ (that is, B might be true in a possible situation caused by A). In particular, when the above constraints concern action execution, we have $\Box\neg(do(a) > \neg do(b))$, meaning that the execution of action a does not prevent action b from being executed (does not interfere with its execution). Note that as a consequence of this constraint we have, by (CV), that $(do(a) > C) \rightarrow (do(a) \wedge do(b) > C)$, namely, the effects of action a are also effects of the concurrent execution of a and b, as a does not interfere with b. Moreover, from $(do(a) > \bot) \rightarrow (do(a) \wedge do(b) > \bot)$, we have that if a is not executable it cannot be executed concurrently with b.

$Frame_0$ is a set of pairs $(f, do(a))$, where $f \in \mathcal{F}$ is a fluent and $a \in \Delta_0$ is an elementary action, meaning that f is a *frame fluent* for action a, that is, f is a fluent to which persistency applies when a is executed. Fluents which are non-frame with respect to a do not persist and may change in a nondeterministic way when a occurs. The set $Frame_0$ defines a sort of *independence* relationship between elementary actions and fluents. It is closely related to dependency (and influence) relations that have been used and studied by several authors including Thielscher [22], Giunchiglia and Lifschitz [7], and Castilho, Gasquet and Herzig [9]. We use $Frame_0$ for defining persistency rules of the form $A_1 > \ldots > A_n > (l \rightarrow (do(a) > l))$ for every literal l, such that $(|l|, a) \in Frame_0$. These persistency rules behave like *defaults*: they belong to an "action extension" whenever no inconsistency arises. The $Frame_0$-relationship is extended to concurrent actions. Let us denote by $Frame$ the extension of $Frame_0$ to concurrent actions. (i) $Frame_0 \subset Frame$; (ii) If $(f, do(a_1)), \ldots, (f, do(a_n)) \in Frame$ then $(f, do(a_1) \wedge \ldots \wedge do(a_n)) \in Frame$.

Obs is a set of observations about the value of fluents in different *states* which we identify with action sequences. Though our language does not provide an explicit representation of time, as we abandon (MP), time can be embedded in the operator $>$. Given the properties of $>$ we assume a delay between happening of an action and occurrence of its effects, while we do not assume any delay between causes and their effects in causal laws. Observations are formulas of the form: $A_1 > \ldots > A_j > \alpha$ (where each A_i is a possibly concurrent action formula of the form $do(a_1) \wedge \ldots \wedge do(a_n)$), meaning that α holds after the concurrent execution of the actions in A_1, then those in A_2, $\ldots$, then those of in A_n. So, every action execution leads from one state to a new state. In particular, we assume an *initial state* characterized by the occurrence of the empty action ϵ. If

Obs contains observations α about fluents in the initial state this is written as $do(\epsilon) > \alpha$ [5]. Sometimes, when we do not want to consider observations, we will then use the notion of *domain frame*, which is a pair $(\Pi, Frame_0)$.

Let us consider the following example from [24], which formalizes an electrical circuit with two serial switches.

Example 1. There is a circuit with two switches and a lamp. If both switches are on, the lamp is alight. One of the switches being off causes the lamp not to be alight. There are two actions of toggling each of the switches. The domain description is the following (for $i = 1, 2$):

Π: $\Box(\neg sw_i \to (do(tg_i) > sw_i))$ $\Box(sw_i \to (do(tg_i) > \neg sw_i))$
   $\Box(sw_1 \land sw_2 > light)$ $\Box(\neg sw_1 \lor \neg sw_2 > \neg light)$
   $\Box(\neg(do(tg_1) > \neg do(tg_2)))$ $\Box(\neg(do(tg_2) > \neg do(tg_1)))$
Obs: $do(\epsilon) > (\neg sw_1 \land \neg sw_2 \land \neg light)$
$Frame_0$ $= \{(f, a) : a \in \Delta_0, f \in \mathcal{F}\}$.

The first two rules in Π describe the immediate effects of the action of toggling a switch. The third and forth rule are causal laws which describe the dependencies of the light on the status of the switches. The last two laws are constraints saying that the two actions tg_1 and tg_2 do not interfere. All fluents are supposed to be persistent and the actions tg_1 and tg_2 are independent. As we will see, from the above domain description we can derive $do(tg_1) > \neg light$, $do(tg_1) > do(tg_2) > light$ and $do(tg_1) \land do(tg_2) > (sw_1 \land sw_2 \land light)$ (as actions $do(tg_1)$ and $do(tg_i)$ are independent). Observe that we could have avoided introducing $\neg light$ in the initial state, as it can be derived, for instance, from $\neg sw_1$: from $do(\epsilon) > \neg sw_1$ and the forth action law we can derive $do(\epsilon) > \neg light$ by (CE).

Axiom (CA) makes it possible to deduce consequences of actions even when it is not deterministically known which action occurs.

Example 2. If the temperature is low, then going to swim causes you to get a cold. If you if you have no umbrella, then raining causes you to get cold. We have the following domain description:

Π: $\Box(cold \to (do(swim) > get\_cold))$
       $\Box(no\_umbrella \to (do(rain) > get\_cold))$
Obs: $do(\epsilon) > (cold \land no\_umbrella)$
$Frame_0 = \{(f, a) : a \in \Delta_0, f \in \mathcal{F}\}$

From this theory, we can derive $do(swim) \lor do(rain) > get\_cold$.

Example 3. There is a bowl of soup. Assuming that initially the soup is not spilled, it is expected that, whenever Mary tries to lift the bowl with one hand, she spills the soup. When she uses both hands, she does not spill the soup.

---

[5] In the following, when identifying a state with an action sequence $A_1, \ldots, A_j$, we will implicitly assume that $A_1 = do(\epsilon)$. Also, in a conditional formula $A_1 > \ldots > A_j > \alpha$, we will assume that $A_1 = do(\epsilon)$.

$$\Box(do(lift\_l) > up\_left) \qquad \Box(do(lift\_r) > up\_right)$$
$$\Box(up\_left \wedge \neg up\_right > spilled) \qquad \Box(\neg up\_left \wedge up\_right > spilled)$$
$$\Box(\neg(do(lift\_l) > \neg do(lift\_r))) \qquad \Box(\neg(do(lift\_r) > \neg do(lift\_l)))$$

Obs: $do(\epsilon) > (\neg up\_left \wedge \neg up\_right \wedge \neg spilled)$

$Frame_0 = \{(f,a) : a \in \Delta_0, f \in \mathcal{F}\}.$

As actions $lift\_l$ and $lift\_r$ are independent, the action $lift\_l$ has always the effect of lifting the left hand side of the bowl, also when it is executed in parallel to $lift\_r$. On the one hand, we get $(do(lift\_l) > (up\_left \wedge spilled))$, by first action law and the third (causal) law, by assuming persistency of $\neg up\_right$. On the other hand, we get $(do(lift\_l) \wedge do(lift\_r)) > (up\_left \wedge up\_right \wedge \neg spilled)$, when the two actions are executed concurrently, $spilled$ is not caused, so that $\neg spilled$ persists from the initial state.

The following example is inspired by one discussed by Halpern and Pearl in [8]. Suppose that heavy rain occurred in April causing wet forests in May and electrical storms in May and June. The lightning in May did not cause forest fires since the forests were still wet. But the lightning in June did since the forest dried in the meantime. Pearl and Halpern argue that the April rain caused that the fire did not occur in May and occurred in June instead. We think rather that the April rain prevents the fire from occurring in may which is expressed by the precondition of the action law[6].

Example 4. i is ranging over months, such that $i + 1$ is the month following i.

$\Pi{:}\Box(do(rain_i) > wet\_forest_{i+1})$
$\quad \Box(do(rain_i) > (do(lightning_{i+1}) \wedge do(lightning_{i+2})))$
$\quad \Box(wet\_forest_i \rightarrow (do(lightning_i) > \neg forest\_fire_i))$
$\quad \Box(\neg wet\_forest_i \rightarrow (do(lightning_i) > forest\_fire_i))$
$\quad \Box(do(sun_i) > \neg wet\_forest_{i+1})$
$\quad \Box(\neg(do(sun_i) > \neg do(rain_j))) \quad \Box(\neg(do(rain_j) > \neg do(sun_i)))$ (for $i \neq j$)

Obs: {}

$Frame_0 = \{(f,a) : a \in \Delta_0, f \in \mathcal{F}\}.$

The second action law allows to say that rain in April causes electrical storms in May and June. ¿From the first two action laws we derive $do(rain_{April}) > (wet\_forest_{May} \wedge do(lightning_{May}) \wedge do(lightning_{June}))$. Then by (CE), from the third action law (for $i = May$) we get $do(rain_{April}) > \neg forest\_fire_{May}$. Moreover, it hods that $\Box(do(sun_{May}) > \neg wet\_forest_{June})$ (fifth action law) and, as actions $do(rain_{April})$ and $do(sun_{May})$ are independent, we can derive $do(rain_{April}) \wedge do(sun_{May}) > (\neg wet\_forest_{June} \wedge do(lightning_{June}))$. Then, by (CE), from the forth action law (for $i = June$), we conclude: $do(rain_{April}) \wedge do(sun_{May}) > forest\_fire_{June}$. Hence, we have that $do(rain_{April}) \wedge do(sun_{May}) > \neg forest\_fire_{May} \wedge forest\_fire_{June}$.

---

[6] It has to be noticed that the focus of our work is different from that in [8]. Our work aims at incorporating causality in action theories. Instead, the focus of Halpern and Pearl's work is concerned with extracting the *actual causality* relation from a background knowledge, including a causal model (describing causal influence among fluents) and a specific scenario.

3.2   Extensions for a Domain Description

In order to address the frame problem, we introduce a set of persistency laws, which can be assumed in each extension. Persistency laws are essentially frame axioms. They are used, in addition to the formulas in Π, to determine the next state when an action is performed. As a difference with the formulas in Π, persistency laws are *defeasible*. They are regarded as assumptions to be maximized. Changes in the world are minimized by maximizing these assumptions. Moreover, persistency laws have to be assumed if this does not lead to inconsistencies.

Let $A_1, \ldots, A_n$ be (possibly) concurrent actions of the form $do(a_1) \wedge \ldots \wedge do(a_m)$ (for $m = 1$ we have an atomic action). We introduce a set of *persistency laws* of the form $A_1 > \ldots > A_n > (l \rightarrow (A > l))$ for every sequence of (concurrent) actions $A_1, \ldots, A_n$ and for every fluent literal l which is a frame fluent with respect to the (concurrent) action A (according to the definition of *Frame* in the last subsection), that is, for every fluent literal l which is frame for *every elementary action* in A. The persistency law says, that, "if l holds in the state obtained by executing the sequence of actions $A_1, \ldots, A_n$, then l persists after executing action A in that state"[7].

Our notion of extension will require to introduce two different kinds of assumptions. The first kind of assumptions, as we have seen, are persistency assumptions. Given a set $Frame$ of frame fluents, the set of persistency assumptions $WP_{A_1,\ldots,A_n}$ is defined as follows: $WP_{A_1,\ldots,A_n} = \{A_1 > \ldots > A_{n-1} > (l \rightarrow (A_n > l)))\ :\ (|l|, A) \in Frame\}$. Note that the set of persistency assumptions has been defined relative to a sequence of (concurrent) actions, that is, a state. A second kind of assumptions is needed to deal with non frame fluents. If a fluent f is not persistent with respect to a concurrent action A then, in the state obtained after executing A, the value of f might be either true or false. Hence, we introduce assumptions which allow to assume, in any state, the value true or false for each nonframe fluent f, as well as assumptions for all fluents in the initial state. Given a set $Frame$ of frame fluents, we define the set of assumptions $Ass_{A_1,\ldots,A_n}$ (relative to a sequence $A_1, \ldots, A_n$) as follows: $Ass_{A_1,\ldots,A_n} = \{A_1 > \ldots > A_n > l\ :\ (|l|, A_n) \notin Frame\} \cup \{do(\epsilon) > l\ :\ l \in Lit\}$ We represent a generic assumption in this set by $A_1 > \ldots > A_n > l$, which includes assumptions on the initial state (for $n = 0$).

We can now define our notion of extension, for domain frames and for domain descriptions. An extension E of a domain frame is obtained by augmenting Π by as many as possible persistency laws, such that E is consistent. We define an extension *relative to a state*, which can be identified by the sequence of actions $A_1, \ldots, A_n$ leading to that state.

Definition 3. *An extension of a domain frame* $D = (\Pi, Frame_0)$ *relative to the action sequence* $A_1, \ldots, A_n$ *is a set* $E = Th(\Pi \cup WP' \cup F)$, *such that* $WP' \subseteq WP_{A_1,\ldots,A_n}$, $F \subseteq Ass_{A_1,\ldots,A_n}$ *and*

---

[7] Notice that introducing persistency laws of the form $\Box(l \rightarrow (A > l))$ wouldn't be enough to deal with the persistency of literals at each different state.

a) *if* $A_1 > \ldots > A_{n-1} > (l \to (A_n > l)) \in WP_{A_1,\ldots,A_n}$ *then:*

$A_1 > \ldots > A_{n-1} > (l \to (A_n > l)) \in WP' \iff A_1 > \ldots > A_n > \neg l \notin E$

b) *if* $A_1 > \ldots > A_n > l \in Ass_{A_1,\ldots,A_n}$ *then*

$A_1 > \ldots > A_n > l \in F \iff A_1 > \ldots > A_n > \neg l \notin E.$

The $\Rightarrow$-part of condition a) is a consistency condition, which guarantees that a persistency axiom $A_1 > \ldots > A_{n-1} > (l \to (A_n > l))$ cannot be assumed in WP' if $\neg l$ can be deduced as an immediate or indirect effect of the action A_n. We say that the formula $A_1 > \ldots > A_n > \neg l$ blocks the persistency axiom. The $\Leftarrow$-part of condition a) is a maximality condition which forces the persistency axiom to be assumed in WP', if the formula $A_1 > \ldots > A_n > \neg l$ is not proved. Condition b) forces each state of an extension to be complete: for all finite sequences of actions $A_1, \ldots, A_n$ each non persistent fluent must be assumed to be true or false in the state obtained after executing them. In particular, since the sequence of actions may be empty, the initial state has to be complete in a given extension E. This is essential for dealing with domain descriptions in which the initial state is incompletely specified and with postdiction. The conditions above have a clear similarity with the applicability conditions for a default rule in an extension. We refer to [5] for a detailed description of the relationship between a similar notion of extension and default extensions.

Definition 4. *E is an* extension *for a domain description* $(\Pi, Frame_0, Obs)$ *relative to the action sequence* $A_1, \ldots, A_n$ *if it is an extension for the domain frame* $(\Pi, Frame_0)$ *relative to the action sequence* $A_1, \ldots, A_n$ *and* $E \vdash Obs.$

Notice that first we have defined extensions of a domain frame $(\Pi, Frame_0)$; then we have used the observations in Obs to filter out those extensions which do not satisfy them. As a difference with [4,5] an extension only describes a single course of actions, and assumptions are localized to that sequence of actions. In this way, we deal with concurrent actions without the need of introducing two different modalities for actions, which in [4] are called open and closed modalities and they are introduced to avoid that the (AND) law $(do(a) > C \to do(a) \land do(b) > C)$ is applied to the non-monotonic consequences of actions, derived by means of the persistency assumptions. In our present approach, we can derive $do(a) \land do(b) > C$ from $do(a) > C$ using the axiom (CV) provided a and b are independent. Independency is formulated in the action language by $\neg(do(a) > \neg do(b)) \land \neg(do(b) > \neg do(a)).$

Let us consider again Example 1. Relative to the action sequence $\{do(\epsilon)\}$, $\{do(tg_1)\}$, $\{do(tg_2)\}$ we get one extension E containing the frame laws (a) $do(\epsilon) > (\neg light \to (do(tg_1) > \neg light))$, (b) $do(\epsilon) > (\neg sw_2 \to (do(tg_1) > \neg sw_2))$, (c) $do(\epsilon) > (do(tg_1) > (sw_1 \to (do(tg_2) > sw_1)))$, in which the following sentences hold: (1) $do(\epsilon) > (do(tg_1) > \neg light)$, (2) $do(\epsilon) > (do(tg_1) > (do(tg_2) > light))$, (3) $do(\epsilon) > (do(tg_1) \land do(tg_2) > light)$, (4) $do(\epsilon) > (do(tg_1) > ((do(tg_1) \land do(tg_2)) > \neg light))$.

An extension E relative to $A_1, \ldots, A_n$ determines an initial state and a transition function among the states obtained by executing actions $A_1, \ldots, A_n$. In particular, the *state* reachable through an action sequence $A_1, \ldots, A_j$ $(0 \le j \le n)$

in E can be defined as : $S^E_{A_1,\ldots,A_j} = \{l : E \vdash A_1 > \ldots > A_j > l\}$, where S^E_ε represents the initial state. Due to condition (b) of definition 3, we can prove that each state $S^E_{A_1;\ldots;A_j}$ is *complete*: for each fluent f, it contains either f or $\neg f$. Moreover, it can be shown that the state obtained after execution of the sequence of actions $A_1, \ldots, A_n$, is only determined by the assumptions made from the initial state up to that state.

Referring to Example 1, the extension E above relative to the action sequence $\{do(\epsilon)\}, \{do(tg_1)\}, \{do(tg_2)\}$ determines the states: $S^E_\varepsilon = \{\neg sw_1, \neg sw_2, \neg light\}$, $S^E_{\{do(\epsilon)\},\{do(tg_1)\}} = \{sw_1, \neg sw_2, \neg light\}$, $S^E_{\{do(\epsilon)\},\{do(tg_1)\},\{do(tg_2)\}} = \{sw_1, sw_2, light\}$. Observe that for the domain description in Example 1 we do not obtain the unexpected extension in which $do(tg_1) > (do(tg_2) > (\neg sw_1 \wedge sw_2 \wedge \neg light)$ holds: we do not want to accept that toggling sw_2 in the state $\{sw_1, \neg sw_2, \neg light\}$ mysteriously changes the position of sw_1 and lets $\neg light$ persist. To avoid this extension it is essential that causal rules are directional (see [1,15,13,22]). Indeed, the causal rules in Π are different from the constraint $\Box((sw_1 \wedge sw_2) \to light)$ and, in particular, they do not entail the formula $sw_2 \wedge \neg light \to \neg sw_1$. As observed in [13] and [22], though this formula must be clearly true in any state, it should not be applied for making causal inferences. In our formalism, contra-position of causal implication is ruled out by the fact that the conditional $>$ is not reflexive: from $\Box(\alpha > \beta)$ and $\Box\neg\beta$ we cannot conclude $\Box\neg\alpha$. On the other hand, it is easy to see that, in any state of any extension, if $\alpha > \beta$ holds, and α holds, β also holds.

Our solution to the frame problem is an abductive solution and is different from the solution proposed for EPDL in [3]. There persistency laws of the form $l \to [a]l$ are added explicitly at every state. In EPDL, persistency laws are not global to an extension but they have to be added state by state, according to which action is expected. In our theory, the frame problem is solved globally by minimizing changes modulo causation. As a further difference, in [3] unexpected solutions can be obtained by adding persistency laws as above to the domain description. As observed by Zhang and Foo (see [3], Example 4.1) in the circuit example above the state $S_1 = \{sw_1, \neg sw_2, \neg light\}$ has two possible next states under action $toggle_2$, namely $S'_2 = \{sw_1, sw_2, light\}$ and $S''_2 = \{\neg sw_1, sw_2, \neg light\}$. The second one is unexpected.

This behaviour is a side effect of (MP), which holds for EPDL and allows the material implication to be derived form the causal implication. To overcome this problem, Zhang and Foo propose an alternative approach to define the next-state function which makes use of a fixpoint property in the style of McCain and Turner's fixpiont property [15]. Their definition employs the causal operator for determining whether the indirect effects of the action are caused by its immediate effects together with the unchanged part of the state, according to the causal laws. It has to be observed, that this definition of the next state function does not require any integrated use of causal laws and action laws in the theory. In fact, "if the direct effects of an action have been given, $EPDL^-$ [that is, the logic obtained from EPDL when the set of action symbols is empty] is enough to determine how effects of actions are propagated by causal laws" [3]. On the contrary, our solution to the frame problem in the conditional logic CA relies on an integrated use of action laws and causal laws to derive conclusion about actions effects.

A domain description may have no extension or extensions with inconsistent states: the cocnurrent execution of two actions declared as being independent may nevertheless produce an inconsistent state.

Example 5. Consider a swinging door and two actions *push_in* and *push_out* the first one opening the door by pushing from out-side to open it and the second by pushing it in the opposite direction. We get the following formalization:

Π:$\square(do(push\_in) > open\_in)$ $\square(do(push\_out) > open\_out)$
    $\square(open\_in > \neg open\_out)$ $\square(open\_out > \neg open\_in)$
    $\square(\neg(do(push\_in) > \neg do(push\_out)))$ $\square(\neg(do(push\_out) > \neg do(push\_in)))$
$Frame_0 = \{(f, a) : a \in \Delta_0, f \in \mathcal{F}\}.$

We have assumed that the two actions are independent. But when trying to perform them at the same moment, an inconsistent state is obtained, because there is a conflict between the effects of the two actions. All the extensions of the theory contain the formulas: (1) $do(push\_in) > open\_in$,   (2) $do(push\_out) > open\_out$, (3) $do(push\_in) \wedge do(push\_out) > \bot$. We argue that the outcome of an inconsistent state (or the absence of the resulting state) may hint at some implicit qualification which are missing, or it may suggests that the two actions are actually dependent. In this example, if actions $do(push\_in)$ and $do(push\_out)$, were declared to be dependent, we would not derive the inconsistency (3). Actually, we would not derive the effects $open\_in$ and $open\_out$ for the concurrent action $do(push\_in) \wedge do(push\_out)$.

4   Conclusion

We have presented a new logical approach to actions and causality which uses a single implication > for causal consequence. Action execution and causal implication are represented uniformly. This makes it possible to integrate reasoning about mutual action dependence or independence into the language of the logic itself. This possibility distinguishes our approach from many other approaches, for example [9], who formulate dependencies outside the logic. Our action language can handle (co-operating, independent and conflicting) concurrent actions in a natural way without adding extra formal devices, and we believe that the language can be naturally extended to handle other boolean expressions concerning action performance.

There are several issues which have to be addressed. First an evaluation of the complexity of this causal logic is required. In particular, an interesting issue is determining if the formalism can be made tractable under suitable syntactic restrictions (as, for instance, restricting to clausal form and to propositional antecedents). Another issue to be tackled is developing extensive comparisons with the many accounts of causality which have been provided in the context of AI (and, in particular, in the area of reasoning about actions and change), as well as in the context of philosophical logic. Finally, it would be worth exploring a spectrum of different notions of causality, which can be obtained by changing some of the postulates (as it has been done, for instance, in [24] for DLTL).

References

1. G. Brewka and J. Hertzberg, 'How to do things with worlds: on formalizing actions and plans', *Journal of Logic and Computation*, **3**(5), (1993).
2. N. Foo, D. Zhang, Y. Zhang, S. Chopra, and B. Vo. Encoding solutions of the frame problem in dynamic logic, *Proc. LPNMR'01*, LNAI 2173, pp. 240–253, 2001.
3. N. Foo and D. Zhang. Dealing with the ramification Problem in extended Propositional Dynamic logic. *Advances in Modal Logic*, volume 3 of *CSLI*, 2000.
4. L. Giordano, A. Martelli, and C. Schwind. Dealing with concurrent actions in modal action logic, in P*roc.ECAI'98*, pp. 537–541, Wiley & Sons, Ltd, (1998).
5. L. Giordano, A. Martelli and C. Schwind. Ramification and Causality in a Modal Action Logic. *Journal of Logic and Computation*, vol. 10 No. 5, pp. 625-662, 2000.
6. L. Giordano, A. Martelli and C. Schwind. Reasoning about actions in dynamic linear time temporal logic, *Journal of the IGPL*, Vol. 9, No. 2, pp. 289-303, 2001.
7. E. Giunchiglia and V. Lifschitz, 'Dependent fluents', in *Proc. IJCAI'95*, pp. 1964–1969, Montreal, Canada, 1995. Morgan Kaufmann.
8. J. Halpern and J. Pearl. Causes and Explanations: A structural model Approach – Part I: Causes. *Proc. of the 7th Conference on Uncertainty in Artificial Intelligence*, San Francisco, CA: Morgan Kaufmann, 194–202, 2001.
9. A. Herzig, M. A. Castilho, O. Gasquet. Formalizing action and change in modal logic i: the frame problem. *J. of Logic and Computation*, **9**(5), 701–735, (1999).
10. F. Jackson, 'A causal theory of counterfactuals', *Australian Journal of Philosophy*, **55**(1), 3–21, (1977).
11. D. Lewis, 'Counterfactuals', *Blackwell*, (1973).
12. D. Lewis, 'Causation', *Journal of Philosophy*, **70**, 556–567, (1973).
13. F. Lin, 'Embracing causality in specifying the indirect effects of actions', In *Proc. IJCAI'95* pp. 1985–1991, Montreal, Canada, 1995. Morgan Kaufmann.
14. F. Lin, 'Embracing causality in specifying the indeterminate effects of actions', in *Proc. AAAI-96*, pp. 1985–1991. AAAI Press / The MIT Press, (August 1996).
15. N. McCain and H. Turner. A causal theory of ramifications and qualifications, in *Proc. IJCAI'95*, pp. 1978–1984, Montreal, Canada, 1995. Morgan Kaufmann.
16. N. McCain and H. Turner. Causal theories of action and change, in *Proc. AAAI-97*, pp. 460–465. AAAI Press / The MIT Press, (July 1997).
17. D. Nute, *Topics in Conditional Logic*, Reidel, Dordrecht, 1984.
18. J. Pearl, "Causality: Models, Reasoning and Inference", 2000, Cambridge U.P.
19. C. Schwind, 'Causality in action theories', *Electronic Articles in Computer and Information Science*, **3**(A), 27–50, (1999).
20. K. Segerberg, 'Notes on conditional logic', *Studia Logica*, **48**, 157–168, (1989).
21. J. R. Shoenfield. Mathematical Logic, Addison-Wesley, (1967).
22. M. Thielscher. Ramification and causality, *Artificial Intelligence*, **89**, 317–364, 1997.
23. H. Turner. A logic of universal causation, *Artificial Intelligence*, **113**, 87–123, 1999.
24. D. Zhang and N. Foo. EPDL: A logic for causal reasoning, in *Proc. AAAI-2001* pp. 131–136, Seattle, USA, (2001). Morgan Kaufmann.

Axiomatising Nash-Consistent Coalition Logic

Helle Hvid Hansen[1] and Marc Pauly[2]

[1] Universiteit van Amsterdam, Netherlands
hhhansen@science.uva.nl
[2] University of Liverpool, United Kingdom
pauly@csc.liv.ac.uk

Abstract. We add a rule for Nash-consistency to Coalition Logic, a modal logic for reasoning about the abilities and rights of groups in multi-agent systems. Rights of agents (constitutions) can be formalised using Coalition Logic, and the additional inference rule of Nash-consistency will guarantee that any multi-agent system implementing these rights will be stable, i.e., for any preferences the agents might have, there will be rights they can exercise such that no individual deviation will be profitable. We apply this logic to obtain a formal analysis of Gibbard's paradox, and we provide meta-theoretic results, in particular a complete axiomatisation.

1 Introduction

Cooperation and coalition formation are issues of central concern in the study of multi-agent systems. The complexity of studying multi-agent systems derives from the difficulty of having to model, e.g., how the abilities and rights of different (groups of) agents interact. While there has been much recent interest in the artificial intelligence community in coalition formation and cooperation [11], there have only been few attempts to capture these notions within a logical formalism [8,7,2]. In this latter line of research, coalitional ability is formalised in a modal logic which contains expressions of the form $[C]\varphi$ which express that a group of agents C has the ability to bring about a state which satisfies φ. Here, ability is interpreted as having a joint strategy in a strategic game played by the agents. Past research has focused on the analysis and implementation of *constitutions*: does a given system of interaction guarantee the agents particular rights? Or given a set of rights, is there a system of interaction which implements these rights? The system of rights is specified as a set of formulas of a logical language, and analysis and implementation problems then will amount to questions of model checking and satisfiability checking.

In the present paper, we extend this approach to incorporate preferences besides rights. For even if a particular procedure can guarantee all agents their respective rights, the outcome of the procedure may not be their most preferred. An agent might observe, for instance, that he can obtain a more preferred outcome by exercising a different right. This in turn will change the outcome of the procedure, possibly provoking another agent to change his strategy, etc..

S. Flesca et al. (Eds.): JELIA 2002, LNAI 2424, pp. 394–406, 2002.

Since such behaviour demonstrates a lack of stability, we will in general want to exclude procedures where such a scenario can occur. To this end, we will extend Coalition Logic [8] to Nash-consistent systems of interaction, those which have a Nash-equilibrium no matter what preferences the players have. For Nash-consistent procedures, no agent will want to change his strategy since his choice of strategy is optimal given the strategies chosen by the other agents.

Gibbard's paradox, a concrete example of an implementation problem and the role of Nash-consistency, will be discussed in section 4. We begin by defining the notions needed to obtain a semantics for Nash-consistent Coalition Logic in section 2. The logical language of Coalition Logic is introduced in section 3, where we also provide a complete axiomatisation and some other meta-theoretic results.

2   Nash-Consistent Mechanisms

In this section we formally define strategic games and game forms (mechanisms) as is standard in game theory [6]. We then proceed to link game forms to effectivity functions [5,4,1,9] in order to characterise the effectivity functions which correspond to Nash-consistent mechanisms (theorem 2). This result is a small adaptation of a result first obtained in [10] to the class of playable effectivity functions (definition 1).

2.1   Games and Mechanisms

Let N be a finite nonempty set of agents or players, and let S be a nonempty set of states of the world or alternatives. Agents can prefer one state of the world to another, and we shall model this preference by a complete and transitive relation $\succeq_i \subseteq S \times S$ for each agent $i \in N$. As usual, we define $s \succ_i t$ iff $s \succeq_i t$ and $t \not\succeq_i s$. We let $Prf(S)$ be the set of preference profiles over S, i.e., the set of all $\succeq_N = (\succeq_i)_{i \in N}$ such that each $\succeq_i$ is a preference relation on S. Finally, $L(s, \succeq_i) = \{t \in S | s \succeq_i t\}$ is the lower contour set of s under $\succeq_i$, i.e., all the states not strictly preferred to s by agent i.

A *mechanism* or *strategic game form* $G = (N, \{\Sigma_i | i \in N\}, o, S)$ consists of a set of agents N, a nonempty set of strategies or actions Σ_i for every player $i \in N$, a set of states S and an outcome function $o : \Pi_{i \in N} \Sigma_i \to S$ which associates with every tuple of strategies of the players (strategy profile) an outcome state in S. For notational convenience, let $\sigma_C = (\sigma_i)_{i \in C}$ denote the strategy tuple for coalition $C \subseteq N$ which consists of player i choosing strategy $\sigma_i \in \Sigma_i$. Then given two strategy tuples σ_C and $\sigma_{\overline{C}}$ (where $\overline{C} = N \backslash C$), $o(\sigma_C, \sigma_{\overline{C}})$ denotes the outcome state associated with the strategy profile induced by σ_C and $\sigma_{\overline{C}}$.

Given a mechanism $G = (N, \{\Sigma_i | i \in N\}, o, S)$ and a preference profile $\succeq_N$ we obtain a *strategic game* $G^{\succeq_N}$. A strategy profile σ_N is a *Nash-equilibrium* iff

$$\forall i \in N \; \forall \tau_i : o(\sigma_i, \sigma_{-i}) \succeq_i o(\tau_i, \sigma_{-i}),$$

where σ_{-i} abbreviates $\sigma_{N \backslash \{i\}}$, i.e., $o(\sigma_N) = o(\sigma_i, \sigma_{-i})$. A mechanism G is called *Nash-consistent* iff for every $\succeq_N$ the strategic game $G^{\succeq_N}$ has a Nash-equilibrium.

2.2   Effectivity Functions

Let $\mathcal{P}(A)$ denote the powerset of a set A. An *effectivity function* is any function $E : \mathcal{P}(N) \to \mathcal{P}(\mathcal{P}(S))$ which is outcome-monotonic: $\forall C \subseteq N, X \subseteq Y \subseteq S$: $X \in E(C) \Rightarrow Y \in E(C)$. The function E associates to every group of players the sets of outcomes for which the group is effective. In case the group is a singleton, we write $E(i)$ for $E(\{i\})$. Different kinds of effectivity can be linked to strategic games, depending on what precise interpretation one has in mind. Given a mechanism $G = (N, \{\Sigma_i | i \in N\}, o, S)$ a coalition $C \subseteq N$ will be *α-effective* for a set $X \subseteq S$ iff the coalition has a joint strategy which will result in an outcome in X no matter what strategies the other players choose. More formally, its *α-effectivity function* $E_G^\alpha : \mathcal{P}(N) \to \mathcal{P}(\mathcal{P}(S))$ is defined as follows:

$$X \in E_G^\alpha(C) \text{ iff } \exists \sigma_C \forall \sigma_{\overline{C}} \ o(\sigma_C, \sigma_{\overline{C}}) \in X.$$

We say that a mechanism G *represents* an effectivity function $E : \mathcal{P}(N) \to \mathcal{P}(\mathcal{P}(S))$ iff $E = E_G^\alpha$. G is a *Nash-consistent representation* of E iff G represents E and is Nash-consistent.

While the preceding discussion shows that every mechanism can be linked to an effectivity function, not every effectivity function will be the α-effectivity function of some mechanism. The properties required to obtain a precise characterisation result are the following, which we place in a separate definition due to their importance.

Definition 1. *An effectivity function* $E : \mathcal{P}(N) \to \mathcal{P}(\mathcal{P}(S))$ *is* playable *if it satisfies the following four conditions:*

1. $\forall C \subseteq N : \emptyset \notin E(C)$.
2. $\forall C \subseteq N : S \in E(C)$.
3. *E is N-maximal: for all X, if $\overline{X} \notin E(\emptyset)$ then $X \in E(N)$.*
4. *E is* superadditive: *for all X_1, X_2, C_1, C_2 such that $C_1 \cap C_2 = \emptyset$, $X_1 \in E(C_1)$ and $X_2 \in E(C_2)$ imply that $X_1 \cap X_2 \in E(C_1 \cup C_2)$.*

The following lemma states that playable effectivity functions guarantee that opposing coalitions cannot force contradictory outcomes. The result follows easily from playability conditions *1* and *4*.

Lemma 1. *Every playable effectivity function* $E : \mathcal{P}(N) \to \mathcal{P}(\mathcal{P}(S))$ *is regular, i.e., for all $X \subseteq S$ and $C \subseteq N$, $X \in E(C)$ implies $\overline{X} \notin E(\overline{C})$.*

We define the *polar* $E^* : \mathcal{P}(N) \to \mathcal{P}(\mathcal{P}(S))$ of an effectivity function E as

$$E^*(C) = \{X \subseteq S | \forall X' \in E(\overline{C}) : X \cap X' \neq \emptyset\}.$$

Note that by monotonicity, $X \in E^*(C)$ iff $\overline{X} \notin E(\overline{C})$. For playable effectivity functions, we can think of the polar of E as a kind of maximally consistent completion of E: we give all coalitions as much power as possible, i.e., without contradicting the powers of anyone else.

When given an effectivity function together with a preference profile, we would like to obtain a prediction regarding the outcomes which are likely to result. A natural solution concept to apply is the core which singles out all outcomes s for which there is no coalition which is effective for a set of outcomes all of which are preferred to s by that coalition. Formally, given an effectivity function $E : \mathcal{P}(N) \to \mathcal{P}(\mathcal{P}(S))$ and a preference profile $\succeq_N$, we call a state s *dominated* if there is a set of states X and a coalition $C \subseteq N$ such that $X \in E(C)$ and for all $i \in C$ and all $x \in X$, $x \succ_i s$. The *core* of E under $\succeq_N$, denoted as $C(E, \succeq_N)$, is the set of undominated states. An effectivity function E is *stable* if for all preference profiles $\succeq_N$, $C(E, \succeq_N) \neq \emptyset$. These notions are well-known in cooperative game theory [6], but they are usually defined for coalitional games with transferrable payoffs rather than the more general effectivity functions.

2.3 Characterisation Results

The first main result characterises the effectivity functions which have a Nash-consistent representation in terms of lower contour sets. It extends the proof of the following result from [8].

Proposition 1. *An effectivity function E has a representation if and only if E is playable.*

Theorem 1. *An effectivity function $E : \mathcal{P}(N) \to \mathcal{P}(\mathcal{P}(S))$ has a Nash-consistent representation if and only if E is playable and in addition satisfies the following condition:*

$$\forall \succeq_N \in Prf(S) \ \exists s \in S \ \forall i \in N : \ L(s, \succeq_i) \in E(N \setminus \{i\}). \tag{1}$$

The following lemma links Nash-consistency to stability, making use of the auxiliary notions of polarity and residuation. Using the polar of E, we define the *residual* $\hat{E} : \mathcal{P}(N) \to \mathcal{P}(\mathcal{P}(S))$ as follows:

$$\hat{E}(C) = \begin{cases} \emptyset & \text{if } C = \emptyset \\ E^*(i) & \text{if } C = \{i\} \\ \{S\} & \text{if } |C| > 1 \end{cases}$$

Since Nash-equilibria are only concerned with individual deviation, the intuition is that $\hat{E}$ captures the maximal power which can be attributed to individuals, or more precisely, what individuals cannot be prevented from achieving.

Lemma 2. *An effectivity function E has a Nash-consistent representation if and only if E is playable and $\hat{E}$ is stable.*

Lemma 3. *Given a playable effectivity function $E : \mathcal{P}(N) \to \mathcal{P}(\mathcal{P}(S))$ over finite S, $\hat{E}$ is stable if and only if*

$$\forall (X_i)_{i \in N} : \ \forall i \in N (X_i \in E^*(i)) \text{ implies } \bigcap_{i \in N} X_i \neq \emptyset. \tag{2}$$

As a direct consequence of lemmas 2 and 3 we obtain our main characterisation result:

Theorem 2. *For finite S, an effectivity function $E : \mathcal{P}(N) \to \mathcal{P}(\mathcal{P}(S))$ has a Nash-consistent representation if and only if E is playable and satisfies condition (2).*

Remark 1. Condition (2) is equivalent to the following:

$$\forall (X_i)_{i \in N} : \bigcup_{i \in N} X_i = S \text{ implies } \exists i \in N : X_i \in E(N \setminus \{i\}) \tag{3}$$

Also note that one direction of theorem 2 is not restricted to finite models: if E has a Nash-consistent representation then it is playable and satisfies condition (2). This is due to the fact that only the sufficiency part of lemma 3 uses the assumption that the domain is finite.

3 Nash-Consistent Coalition Logic

In this section, we first recall the syntax and semantics of Coalition Logic [8] and define the extension, CLNC_N, of the smallest coalition logic, CL_N, with the NC inference rule which captures condition (3). Since our characterisation of Nash-consistency is for finite models, we need to build a finite model to prove completeness. To this end we define a filtration (definition 3) of coalition models, and we show soundness and weak completeness of CLNC_N with respect to Nash-consistent coalition models (theorem 4) by proving that the filtration of the canonical CLNC_N-model satisfies condition (3). The strong finite model property of CL_N and CLNC_N follows as an easy corollary (corollary 1).

3.1 Syntax, Semantics and Axiomatics

For a finite nonempty set of players $N = \{1, \ldots, n\}$ and a (countable) set of proposition letters Φ_0, we define the syntax of Coalition Logic over the language $\mathcal{L} = \mathcal{L}(N, \Phi_0)$ as follows: $\varphi \in \mathcal{L}$ can have the following syntactic form:

$$\varphi := \bot \mid p \mid \neg \varphi \mid \varphi \vee \varphi \mid [C]\varphi \qquad \text{where } p \in \Phi_0, C \subseteq N.$$

$\top, \wedge, \to$ and $\leftrightarrow$ are defined as the usual abbreviations.

A set of formulas Λ over $\mathcal{L}$ is a *coalition logic for N*, if Λ contains all propositional tautologies, is closed under Modus Ponens (MP) and Monotonicity (RM):

$$\frac{\varphi \quad \varphi \to \psi}{\psi} \text{ MP} \qquad\qquad \frac{\varphi \to \psi}{[C]\varphi \to [C]\psi} \text{ RM}$$

and contains all instances of the following axiom schemas:

$(\bot)$ $\neg[C]\bot$
$(\top)$ $[C]\top$
(N) $\neg[\emptyset]\neg\varphi \to [N]\varphi$
(S) $([C_1]\varphi \wedge [C_2]\psi) \to [C_1 \cup C_2](\varphi \wedge \psi))$
     where $C_1 \cap C_2 = \emptyset$.

Let CL_N denote the smallest coalition logic for N and define CLNC_N as CL_N together with the following inference rule:

$$\frac{\bigvee_{i \in N} \varphi_i}{\bigvee_{i \in N} [N \setminus \{i\}] \varphi_i} \text{ NC}$$

Similarly to the Coalition Logic axioms, the NC rule is a straightforward translation of condition (3) into $\mathcal{L}$. The NC rule was first proposed in [7].

A *coalition model* for the language $\mathcal{L}$ is a triple $\mathcal{M} = (S, E, V)$, where S is a nonempty set of states, $V : \Phi_0 \to \mathcal{P}(S)$ is a valuation and

$$E : S \to (\mathcal{P}(N) \to \mathcal{P}(\mathcal{P}(S)))$$

is the playable effectivity structure of $\mathcal{M}$. That is, for all $s \in S$, $E(s)$ is a playable effectivity function. We will use the notation $sE_C X$ for $X \in E(s)(C)$ and when $sE_C X$ is not the case, we will write $\neg sE_C X$. Furthermore, we will denote the length of a formula φ with $|\varphi|$, and the cardinality of a set A with $card(A)$.

Truth in a coalition model $\mathcal{M} = (S, E, V)$ at a state $s \in S$, is defined as follows:

$$\mathcal{M}, s \nvDash \bot$$
$$\mathcal{M}, s \vDash p \quad \text{iff } p \in \Phi_0 \text{ and } s \in V(p)$$
$$\mathcal{M}, s \vDash \neg\varphi \quad \text{iff } \mathcal{M}, s \nvDash \varphi$$
$$\mathcal{M}, s \vDash \varphi \vee \psi \text{ iff } \mathcal{M}, s \vDash \varphi \text{ or } \mathcal{M}, s \vDash \psi$$
$$\mathcal{M}, s \vDash [C]\varphi \quad \text{iff } sE_C \varphi^{\mathcal{M}}$$

where $\varphi^{\mathcal{M}} = \{s \in S \mid \mathcal{M}, s \vDash \varphi\}$. Due to the characterisation of proposition 1, we can associate a mechanism $G(s)$ with each state $s \in S$ in a coalition model $\mathcal{M}$, which implies that $[C]\varphi$ holds at a state s iff the coalition C is effective for $\varphi^{\mathcal{M}}$ in $G(s)$. The notion of Nash-consistency can also be lifted to coalition models: a *coalition model $\mathcal{M}$ is Nash-consistent* if for all $s \in S$, $G(s)$ is Nash-consistent.

We will use the following standard terminology and definitions: if φ is a formula and $\mathcal{M}$ is a model with S as its set of states, then φ is *valid in* $\mathcal{M}$ (denoted by $\mathcal{M} \vDash \varphi$) iff $\varphi^{\mathcal{M}} = S$, and φ is *valid in a class of models* K (denoted by $\vDash_{\mathsf{K}} \varphi$) iff for all $\mathcal{M} \in \mathsf{K} : \mathcal{M} \vDash \varphi$. The set of formulas that are valid in a class of models K will be denoted by Λ_{K}. If Σ is a set of formulas, then $\mathcal{M}, s \vDash \Sigma$ denotes that all $\sigma \in \Sigma$ are true at s in $\mathcal{M}$, and $\Sigma \vDash_{\mathsf{K}} \varphi$ denotes that φ is a local logical consequence of Σ in K, i.e. for all $\mathcal{M} \in \mathsf{K}$ and all $s \in S$, if $\mathcal{M}, s \vDash \Sigma$ then $\mathcal{M}, s \vDash \varphi$. If Λ is a coalition logic, we will write $\vdash_{\Lambda} \varphi$ if φ is a theorem of Λ (i.e. $\varphi \in \Lambda$). For a set of formulas Σ, $\Sigma \vdash_{\Lambda} \varphi$ denotes that φ is deducible from Σ in Λ, i.e. $\vdash_{\Lambda} \varphi$ or there are $\sigma_1, \ldots, \sigma_n \in \Sigma$ such that $\vdash_{\Lambda} (\sigma_1 \wedge \ldots \wedge \sigma_n) \to \varphi$. If $\Sigma \vdash_{\Lambda} \varphi$ is not the case, we write $\Sigma \nvdash_{\Lambda} \varphi$. A set of formulas Σ is Λ-consistent if $\Sigma \nvdash_{\Lambda} \bot$, and Λ-inconsistent otherwise. A formula φ is Λ-consistent if $\{\varphi\}$ is Λ-consistent, otherwise φ is Λ-inconsistent.

A logic Λ is *strongly complete* with respect to a class of models K if for all $\Sigma \cup \{\varphi\} \subseteq \mathcal{L}$, $\Sigma \vDash_{\mathsf{K}} \varphi$ implies $\Sigma \vdash_{\Lambda} \varphi$; Λ is *weakly complete* with respect to K if for all $\varphi \in \mathcal{L}$, $\vDash_{\mathsf{K}} \varphi$ implies $\vdash_{\Lambda} \varphi$, and Λ is *sound* with respect to K if for all $\varphi \in \mathcal{L}$, $\vdash_{\Lambda} \varphi$ implies $\vDash_{\mathsf{K}} \varphi$. Note that another way of stating that Λ is sound and weakly complete with respect to K, is to write $\Lambda = \Lambda_{\mathsf{K}}$. If K is a class of finite coalition models (i.e. for all $\mathcal{M} \in \mathsf{K}$, $\mathcal{M}$ has a finite universe S), then a coalition logic Λ has the *finite model property with respect to* K, if $\Lambda = \Lambda_{\mathsf{K}}$, and Λ has the *strong finite model property with respect to* K, if $\Lambda = \Lambda_{\mathsf{K}}$ and there is a computable function $f(n)$ such that every Λ-consistent formula φ is satisfiable in a model in K containing at most $f(|\varphi|)$ states. Λ has the *(strong) finite model property* if there is a class K of finite coalition models such that Λ has the (strong) finite model property with respect to K.

Completeness of coalition logics can be obtained via canonical model constructions. If Λ is a coalition logic and Γ is a Λ-consistent set of formulas, we can extend Γ to a maximally Λ-consistent set using the standard argument of Lindenbaum's Lemma for which the usual properties hold: $\forall \varphi, \psi \in \mathcal{L}$: (1) $\varphi \in \Gamma$ or $\neg \varphi \in \Gamma$, (2) $\varphi \vee \psi \in \Gamma$ iff $\varphi \in \Gamma$ or $\psi \in \Gamma$, and (3) if $\Gamma \vdash_\Lambda \varphi$ then $\varphi \in \Gamma$. We define the *canonical Λ-model* $\mathcal{C}^\Lambda = (S^\Lambda, E^\Lambda, V^\Lambda)$ as follows:

$$
\begin{aligned}
S^\Lambda &= \text{all maximally } \Lambda\text{-consistent sets,} \\
s E_C^\Lambda X \quad &\text{iff} \quad \begin{cases} \exists \widehat{\varphi} \subseteq X : [C]\varphi \in s & \text{for } C \neq N, \\ \forall \widehat{\varphi} \subseteq \overline{X} : [\emptyset]\varphi \notin s & \text{for } C = N, \end{cases} \\
s &\in V^\Lambda(p) \quad \text{iff} \quad p \in s,
\end{aligned}
$$

where $\widehat{\varphi} = \{s \in S^\Lambda \mid \varphi \in s\}$. It can be checked that E^Λ is well-defined and playable, hence $\mathcal{C}^\Lambda$ is indeed a coalition model. See [8] for details. From [8] we also have the following results:

Lemma 4 (Truth Lemma). *If* $\mathcal{C}^\Lambda = (S^\Lambda, E^\Lambda, V^\Lambda)$ *is the canonical Λ-model for a coalition logic Λ, then for all $s \in S^\Lambda$ and $\varphi \in \mathcal{L}$:*

$$
\mathcal{C}^\Lambda, s \vDash \varphi \quad \text{iff} \quad \varphi \in s.
$$

Theorem 3. CL_N *is sound and strongly complete with respect to the class of all coalition models.*

3.2   Filtration of Coalition Models

Let $\mathcal{M} = (S, E, V)$ be a coalition model and Σ a subformula closed set of formulas over $\mathcal{L}$. Then $\equiv_\Sigma$ is the equivalence relation induced by Σ on S which is defined as follows for all $s, t \in S$:

$$
s \equiv_\Sigma t \quad \text{iff} \quad \forall \varphi \in \Sigma : \mathcal{M}, s \vDash \varphi \Leftrightarrow \mathcal{M}, t \vDash \varphi.
$$

Let $S_\Sigma = \{ |s| \mid s \in S \}$ be the set of equivalence classes induced by Σ on S. For $Y \subseteq S$, denote by $|Y|$ the set $\{ |s| \mid s \in Y \}$, and for $X \subseteq S_\Sigma$ let $\langle X \rangle$ be the set $\{ s \in S \mid |s| \in X \}$. Then we have the following identities which will be used without further reference:

$$
\begin{aligned}
\langle |\varphi^\mathcal{M}| \rangle &= \varphi^\mathcal{M} & \text{for } \varphi \in \Sigma, \\
|\langle X \rangle| &= X & \text{for } X \subseteq S_\Sigma, \\
\langle X \cap Y \rangle &= \langle X \rangle \cap \langle Y \rangle & \text{for } X, Y \subseteq S_\Sigma, \\
\overline{|\varphi^\mathcal{M}|} &= |(\neg\varphi)^\mathcal{M}| & \text{for } \varphi \in \Sigma, \\
\langle \overline{X} \rangle &= \overline{\langle X \rangle} & \text{for } X \subseteq S_\Sigma.
\end{aligned}
$$

Definition 2. *Let $\mathcal{M} = (S, E, V)$ be a coalition model and Σ a subformula closed set of formulas over $\mathcal{L}$. Then a coalition model $\mathcal{M}_\Sigma^f = (S^f, E^f, V^f)$ is a filtration of $\mathcal{M}$ through Σ if*

> *(i) $S^f = S_\Sigma$,*
> *(ii) $\forall C \subseteq N \; \forall \varphi \in \Sigma : s E_C \varphi^\mathcal{M} \Rightarrow |s| E_C^f |\varphi^\mathcal{M}|$,*
> *(iii) $\forall C \subseteq N : \; If \; |s| E_C^f X \; then \; \forall \varphi \in \Sigma : \dagger X \dagger \subseteq \varphi^\mathcal{M} \Rightarrow s E_C \varphi^\mathcal{M}$,*
> *(iv) $V^f(p) = |V(p)| \quad for \; all \; proposition \; letters \; p \in \Sigma$.*

The conditions (ii) and (iii) are designed such that we can prove the following lemma.

Lemma 5 (Filtration Lemma). *If $\mathcal{M}_\Sigma^f = (S^f, E^f, V^f)$ is a filtration of $\mathcal{M}$ through Σ, then for all formulas $\varphi \in \Sigma$ and all $s \in S$ we have:*

$$\mathcal{M}, s \vDash \varphi \quad iff \quad \mathcal{M}_\Sigma^f, |s| \vDash \varphi.$$

In other words, for all $\varphi \in \Sigma : |\varphi^\mathcal{M}| = \varphi^{\mathcal{M}_\Sigma^f}$.

We can now define the announced filtration, which will provide the finite model needed in the completeness proof. Let δ be a formula in the language $\mathcal{L}$, then $sfor(\delta)$ denotes the set of subformulas of δ. Define $\Sigma(\delta)$ as the boolean closure of $sfor(\delta)$, i.e. $sfor(\delta) \subseteq \Sigma(\delta)$ and $\forall \varphi, \psi \in \Sigma(\delta) : \neg\varphi, \varphi \vee \psi \in \Sigma(\delta)$. $\Sigma(\delta)$ is clearly subformula closed and since $sfor(\delta)$ is finite, $\Sigma(\delta)$ is finite up to logical equivalence, which is sufficient to yield a finite model when filtrating through $\Sigma(\delta)$. In fact, $card(sfor(\delta)) \leq |\delta|$, the length of δ, hence a filtration through $\Sigma(\delta)$ has at most $2^{2^{|\delta|}}$ states.

Definition 3. *Let $\mathcal{M} = (S, E, V)$ be a coalition model and δ any formula in $\mathcal{L}$. Then we define $\mathcal{F}_\delta^\mathcal{M} := (S^\mathcal{F}, E^\mathcal{F}, V^\mathcal{F})$ where*

> *(1) $S^\mathcal{F} = S_{\Sigma(\delta)}$,*
> *(2) $|s| E_C^\mathcal{F} X \; iff \; \begin{cases} \exists \varphi \in \Sigma(\delta) : \varphi^\mathcal{M} \subseteq \dagger X \dagger \; and \; s E_C \varphi^\mathcal{M} \; for \; C \neq N, \\ not \; |s| E_\emptyset^\mathcal{F} X \qquad\qquad\qquad\qquad for \; C = N, \end{cases}$*
> *(3) $V^\mathcal{F}(p) = |V(p)| \quad for \; all \; proposition \; letters \; p \in \Sigma(\delta)$.*

Note that for $C \neq N$, $E_C^\mathcal{F}$ is the smallest filtration of E_C, i.e. we have only added the X to $E_C^\mathcal{F}(|s|)$ which are necessary to satisfy definition 2 (ii). However, $E_N^\mathcal{F}$ is the largest filtration of E_N, which can easily be seen by N-maximality and regularity of E. It is straightforward to show that $\mathcal{F}_\delta^\mathcal{M}$ is indeed a filtration.

Proposition 2. *If $\mathcal{M} = (S, E, V)$ is a coalition model and $\delta \in \mathcal{L}$, then $\mathcal{F}_\delta^\mathcal{M} = (S^\mathcal{F}, E^\mathcal{F}, V^\mathcal{F})$ is a filtration of $\mathcal{M}$ through $\Sigma(\delta)$.*

3.3 Soundness and Weak Completeness of CLNC$_N$

In order to prove that CLNC$_N$ is weakly complete with respect to Nash-consistent coalition models, we first observe that all subsets of $S^\mathcal{F}$ are definable by a formula in $\Sigma(\delta)$.

Lemma 6 (Definability). *Let $\mathcal{M} = (S, E, V)$ be a coalition model and $\mathcal{F}_\delta^{\mathcal{M}} = (S^{\mathcal{F}}, E^{\mathcal{F}}, V^{\mathcal{F}})$ as defined in definition 3, then for each $X \subseteq S^{\mathcal{F}}$, there is a formula $\Psi_X \in \Sigma(\delta)$ such that for all $s \in S$:*

$$s \in \Psi_X^{\mathcal{M}} \text{ iff } |s| \in X$$

As a consequence, $|\Psi_X^{\mathcal{M}}| = X$ and $\Psi_X^{\mathcal{M}} = \dagger X \dagger$.

With the definability lemma, we can prove the following preservation result:

Proposition 3. *If $\mathcal{M} = (S, E, V)$ is a coalition model satisfying condition (3) and $\delta \in \mathcal{L}$, then $\mathcal{F}_\delta^{\mathcal{M}} = (S^{\mathcal{F}}, E^{\mathcal{F}}, V^{\mathcal{F}})$ also satisfies condition (3).*

Finally, we are ready to prove our main result of this section:

Theorem 4. *CLNC$_N$ is sound and weakly complete with respect to the class* NC *of Nash-consistent coalition models.*

Proof. The soundness of the playability axioms of CLNC$_N$ with respect to NC is clear. To see that the NC rule is also sound with respect to NC, let $\mathcal{M} = (S, E, V) \in$ NC and assume that $\mathcal{M} \vDash \bigvee_{i \in N} \psi_i$. This means that $\bigcup_{i \in N} \psi_i^{\mathcal{M}} = S$. As $\mathcal{M}$ satisfies condition (3) by theorem 2 and remark 1, it follows that for all $s \in S$ there is an $i \in N$ such that $sE_{[N \setminus \{i\}]} \psi_i^{\mathcal{M}}$, hence $\mathcal{M} \vDash \bigvee_{i \in N}[N \setminus \{i\}] \psi_i$.

To show weak completeness, suppose δ is a CLNC$_N$-consistent formula. Again by the characterisation of theorem 2 and remark 1, it suffices to show that δ is satisfiable on a finite coalition model which satisfies condition (3). As δ is CLNC$_N$-consistent, it can be extended to a maximally CLNC$_N$-consistent set s. Let $\mathcal{C} = (S, E, V)$ be the CLNC$_N$-canonical model, then we have from the truth lemma 4 that $\mathcal{C}, s \vDash \delta$. Taking the filtration $\mathcal{F}_\delta^{\mathcal{C}} = (S^{\mathcal{F}}, E^{\mathcal{F}}, V^{\mathcal{F}})$ of $\mathcal{C}$ through $\Sigma(\delta)$ we obtain a finite coalition model by proposition 2, which, by the filtration lemma 5, satisfies δ at state $|s| \in S_{\mathcal{F}}$, so by the characterisation of theorem 2 and remark 1, it only remains to show that $\mathcal{F}_\delta^{\mathcal{C}}$ satisfies condition (3).

Assume that $B_i \subseteq S^{\mathcal{F}}$, $i \in N$, and $\bigcup_{i \in N} B_i = S^{\mathcal{F}}$. By the definability lemma 6 and and the filtration lemma there are $\psi_1, \ldots, \psi_n \in \Sigma(\delta)$ such that $\psi_i^{\mathcal{F}_\delta^{\mathcal{C}}} = |\psi_i^{\mathcal{C}}| = B_i$, hence from the assumption $\mathcal{F}_\delta^{\mathcal{C}} \vDash \bigvee_{i \in N} \psi_i$. Note, since $\Sigma(\delta)$ is closed under boolean connectives, $\bigvee_{i \in N} \psi_i \in \Sigma(\delta)$, so from the filtration lemma it follows that for all $s \in S$, $\mathcal{C}, s \vDash \bigvee_{i \in N} \psi_i$ and from the truth lemma and properties of maximally CLNC$_N$-consistent sets, $\bigvee_{i \in N} \psi_i \in$ CLNC$_N$. Applying the NC rule we obtain $\bigvee_{i \in N}[N \setminus \{i\}] \psi_i \in$ CLNC$_N$ which, again by properties of maximally CLNC$_N$-consistent sets and the truth lemma, implies that for all $s \in S$ there is an $i \in N$ such that $\mathcal{C}, s \vDash [N \setminus \{i\}] \psi_i$, i.e. $sE_{N \setminus \{i\}} \psi_i^{\mathcal{C}}$. As $\mathcal{F}_\delta^{\mathcal{C}}$ is a filtration, it satisfies (ii) of definition 2, hence $|s|E_{N \setminus \{i\}}^{\mathcal{F}} |\psi_i^{\mathcal{C}}|$, and since $|\psi_i^{\mathcal{C}}| = B_i$ and s was arbitrary in S, we have shown that for all $|s| \in S^{\mathcal{F}}$, there is an $i \in N$ such that $|s|E_{N \setminus \{i\}}^{\mathcal{F}} B_i$. □

Remark 2. An easy inspection of the above proof of theorem 4 shows that CLNC$_N$ is also sound and weakly complete with respect to the class **FNC** of *finite* Nash-consistent coalition models: soundness of the NC rule follows from theorem 2 and remark 1, the characterisation of FNC in terms of condition (3), and the weak completeness result of theorem 4 is, in fact, proved by showing the stronger result of weak completeness of CLNC_N with respect to FNC. Hence we have $\text{CLNC}_N = \Lambda_{NC} = \Lambda_{FNC}$.

3.4   Strong Finite Model Property

The completeness results for CL_N and CLNC_N together with the properties of the filtration of definition 3 allow us to show the strong finite model property for both of these coalition logics.

Corollary 1. *CL_N and $CLNC_N$ both have the strong finite model property.*

The question arises whether we can improve on the double-exponential bound given by the filtration. In particular, is it possible to filtrate through a $\Sigma(\delta)$ which has size linear in $|\delta|$? This would provide a single-exponential bound. For CLNC_N, there seems to be no improvement possible on the size of $\Sigma(\delta)$, since we need each subset of the filtrated model to be definable by a formula in $\Sigma(\delta)$. But it turns out that the bound for CL_N can indeed be improved, if we allow $card(\Sigma(\delta))$ to be expressed in terms of the number of agents, as well as $|\delta|$. Applying an alternative of definition 3 in which

$$|s|E^{\mathcal{F}}_C X \text{ iff } \begin{cases} \exists [C]\varphi \in \Sigma_{\mathcal{F}} : \varphi^{\mathcal{M}} \subseteq \{X\} \text{ and } sE_C\varphi^{\mathcal{M}} \text{ for } C \neq N \\ \text{not } |s|E^{\mathcal{F}}_{\emptyset} X \qquad\qquad\qquad\qquad\qquad\qquad \text{ for } C = N, \end{cases}$$

and adjusting definition 2 accordingly, it can be shown that the filtrated model has at most a number of states of the order $2^{|\delta|} \cdot 2^{2^n}$, where n is the number of agents. This bound is achieved by observing that for CL_N we do not need $\Sigma(\delta)$ to be closed under boolean operations, but we do need $\Sigma(\delta)$ to contain $[C]\top$ for all $C \subsetneq N$.

If n is much smaller than $|\delta|$, the improvement is clearly substantial. However, if we do not allow n to be part of the expression of $card(\Sigma(\delta))$, then the best upper bound we can give on n is $|\delta| - 1$, consider $\delta = [1][2]\ldots[n]p$, in which case we are back at the double-exponential bound.

For CLNC_N, the alternative filtration definition will not work, since we are unable to prove that $\mathcal{F}^C_\delta$ satisfies condition (3) with this definition. The problem is that we need a formula $[N\backslash\{i\}]\psi_i \in \Sigma(\delta)$, where ψ_i is the formula provided by the definability lemma and the NC rule, to show that $|s|E^{\mathcal{F}}_{N\backslash\{i\}}|\psi^C_i|$ in the very last step of the proof of theorem 4. The definability lemma ensures that ψ_i is in $\Sigma(\delta)$, but it is certainly not clear that $[N\backslash\{i\}]\psi_i$ should also be in $\Sigma(\delta)$. The only way to ensure this, would be to close $\Sigma(\delta)$ under $[C]$-formulas, but since we can make infinitely many different sequences of $[C]$'s, we would no longer have a logically finite set, and hence no finite filtration.

4   Applications

As a simple illustration of the decentralisation of a constitution, consider the following example which is essentially Gibbard's paradox [3]: Abelard and Eloise each have a white and a blue shirt, and they have to decide which shirt to wear.

Each person has the right to determine the colour of his/her own shirt. Using Coalition Logic, we can model this situation by letting $N = \{a, e\}$ and using two atomic proposition p_a and p_e, where p_a should be read as "Abelard wears white" and p_e as "Eloise wears white". The rights of Abelard and Eloise can then be captured by the following formula ρ^+ of Coalition Logic:

$$[a]p_a \wedge [a]\neg p_a \wedge [e]p_e \wedge [e]\neg p_e$$

Furthermore, we assume that these are the only rights which we want to give to them, formalised by formula ρ^-:

$$\bigwedge_{i \in \{a,e\}} \neg[i]((p_a \wedge p_e) \vee (\neg p_a \wedge \neg p_e)) \wedge \bigwedge_{i \in \{a,e\}} \neg[i]((p_a \wedge \neg p_e) \vee (\neg p_a \wedge p_e))$$

To ask whether this constitution can be decentralised or implemented by a mechanism means checking whether $\rho = \rho^+ \wedge \rho^-$ is satisfiable by a coalition model. The following coalition model $\mathcal{M} = (S, E, V)$ with $S = \{s_0, (w, w), (w, b), (b, w), (b, b)\}$ satisfies ρ at state s_0: $V(p_a) = \{(w, w), (w, b)\}$, $V(p_e) = \{(w, w), (b, w)\}$, and $E(s_0)$ is the α-effectivity function associated with the following strategic game:

	w	b
w	(w, w)	(w, b)
b	(b, w)	(b, b)

For states other than s_0, E can be defined arbitrarily. At state s_0, each player can choose which shirt to wear, and the resulting state reflects Abelard's choice in the first component and Eloise's choice in the second.

As it turns out, however, this game form is not Nash-consistent. Consider the situation where Abelard is primarily conformist, preferring to wear the same colour as Eloise, and besides that he prefers white to blue. Eloise on the other hand has the same colour preference, but she primarily is a non-conformist, wanting to avoid the same colour. The following game captures these preferences:

	w	b
w	$(4, 2)$	$(2, 3)$
b	$(1, 4)$	$(3, 1)$

As can easily be checked, the game has no Nash equilibrium. Intuitively, the mechanism is not stable under the given preferences. If Abelard and Eloise both wear white, Eloise will want to change to wearing blue, which will in turn induce Abelard to wear blue as well, which will lead to Eloise wearing white again, etc., precisely the kind of instability mentioned earlier. In fact, there is no stable mechanism guaranteeing each individual to choose their own shirt, i.e., it can be shown that the constitution given has no Nash-consistent representation [10]. Using Coalition Logic, this impossibility of a Nash-consistent representation can be formally deduced, for one can show that in a system $\Lambda \supseteq \textbf{CLNC}$, ρ is inconsistent: since

$$((p_a \wedge p_e) \vee (\neg p_a \wedge \neg p_e)) \vee ((p_a \wedge \neg p_e) \vee (\neg p_a \wedge p_e))$$

is a propositional tautology, we can use the NC inference rule to derive

$$[a]((p_a \wedge p_e) \vee (\neg p_a \wedge \neg p_e)) \vee [e]((p_a \wedge \neg p_e) \vee (\neg p_a \wedge p_e))$$

which contradicts ρ^-.

To sum up, we have seen a very simple example of how a system of rights, represented by an effectivity function, can be decentralised in a strategic game form. Formalising the rights as coalition logic formulas, this decentralisation problem can be turned into a satisfiability problem, and this approach can be extended to cover Nash-consistent decentralisation. The logical reformulation of constitutional decentralisation has the advantage that it can easily handle partial specifications of rights. In the example of the two shirts, we have assumed that the players' rights were completely specified. This forced us to add a conjunct ρ^- which specified what the players were unable to bring about. In order to avoid such an additional conjunct, we would have to make use of some kind of non-monotonic reasoning mechanism which would allow us to conclude that the rights specified are *all* the rights the players are supposed to have. On the other hand, we may also treat ρ^+ as a partial specification, where we want to ensure that the players have the rights specified in ρ^+ but do not care about whether players also obtain additional rights. Checking satisfiability of ρ^+ thus corresponds to decentralising a partially defined effectivity function, a problem which does not seem to have received much attention in the social choice theory literature.

5 Conclusions

As we have shown in the previous section, Nash-consistency can play a role in the formalisation of strategic stability in multi-agent systems. To our knowledge, this paper presents the first attempt to express the notion of Nash-consistency in a formal logical system.

Based on adaptations of the characterisation results of Nash-consistent effectivity functions in [10] to the setting of Coalition Logic [8], we have extended the minimal coalition logic, $\mathrm{CL_N}$, with a new inference rule (NC), and the obtained coalition logic, $\mathrm{CLNC_N}$, is proved to be sound and weakly complete with respect to Nash-consistent coalition models. The main tool used in the completeness proof is a filtration of coalition models, which in turn provides the strong finite model property for $\mathrm{CL_N}$ and $\mathrm{CLNC_N}$.

The principal result of this paper is the axiomatisation of Nash-consistency purely in modal terms, i.e. without introducing preferences into the language. This is, partially, a consequence of the characterisation in [10] of Nash-consistency in terms of the effectivity function alone. But it is noteworthy, that the NC rule yields soundness and (weak) completeness with respect to arbitrary Nash-consistent coalition models, since the rule is a translation of the characterising condition (3) of Nash-consistency for effectivity functions over finite domains. The condition for Nash-consistency of arbitrary effectivity functions is a generalisation of (2) where $E^*(i)$ is replaced by $I(E^*(i))$, the closure of $E^*(i)$ under descending chains (Lemma 3.5 of [10]). This is a condition which is not (immediately) translatable into the language of Coalition Logic.

The main open problems are whether a strong completeness result can also be obtained for $CLNC_N$, whether we can improve the double-exponential bound given by the filtration, and which implications this has for the complexity of the satisfiability problem.

References

1. J. Abdou and H. Keiding. *Effe ctivity F unctions in Soial Choice.* Kluwer, 1991.
2. R. Alur, T. Henzinger, and O. Kupferman. Alternating-time temporal logic. In *Compositionality: The Significant Difference*, LNCS 1536, pages 23–60. Springer, 1998.
3. A. Gibbard. A pareto-consistent libertarian claim. *Journal of Economic Theory,* 7(4):388–410, 1974.
4. H. Moulin. *The Strategy of So cial Choie.* North-Holland, 1983.
5. H. Moulin and B. Peleg. Cores of effectivity functions and implementation theory. *Journal of Mathematical Economics,* 10(1):115–145, 1982.
6. M. Osborne and A. Rubinstein. *A Course in Game Theory.* MIT Press, 1994.
7. M. Pauly . *L ogic for So cial Softwæ:* PhD thesis, University of Amsterdam, 2001.
8. M. P auly . A modal logic for coalitional power in games. *Journal of L ogic and Computation,* 12(1):149–166, 2002.
9. B. Peleg. Effectivity functions, game forms, games and rights. *Social Choice and Welfare,* 15:67–80, 1998.
10. B. Peleg, H. Peters, and T. Storcken. Nash consistent represen tation of constitutions: A reaction to the Gibbard paradox. *Mathematical Social Sciences,* 43:267–287, 2002.
11. T. Sandholm. Distributed rational decision making. In G. Weiss, editor, *Multiagent Systems: A Modern Intr oductioto Distribute d Artificial Intelligence*, pages 201–258. MIT Press, 1999.

Representing Possibilities in Relation to Constraints and Agents

Richard J. Wallace

Cork Constraint Computation Center
University College Cork, Cork, Ireland
r.wallace@4c.ucc.ie

Abstract. In this paper we describe a framework for overcoming agent ignorance within a setting for collaborative problem solving. As a result of privacy concerns, agents may not reveal information that could be of use in problem solving. In this case, under certain assumptions agents can still reason about this information in terms of the possibilities that are consistent with what they know. This is done using constraint-based reasoning in a framework consisting of an ordinary CSP, which is only partly known, and a system of "shadow CSPs" that represent various forms of possibilistic knowledge. This paper proposes some properties of good structure for this system and shows that a reasonable set of deductions used during the solving process preserves these properties. Extensions to the basic framework and relations to other work are also discussed.

1 Introduction

Multi-agent systems offer new opportunities for information sharing and problem solving. At the same time, the emergence of such systems raises new issues, among them the issue of privacy, which arises whenever independent agents need to share information in order to solve a problem of mutual interest. Heretofore, most multi-agent systems have operated on the assumption that agents will be open about communicating information that they have and that might be relevant to solving a problem [5]. However, this may not always be the case in such settings; agents may want to maintain their privacy as much as possible while still engaging in collaborative problem solving [2]. Agents may, therefore, need to make decisions as to how much information they will reveal and how this will affect the efficiency of problem solving.

Because of privacy concerns, agents may often need to operate under conditions of partial ignorance. In such cases, even though critical information may not be known, agents may be able to reason in terms of sets of possibilities, such as the set of possible values for a known variable. The purpose of this paper is to describe a system for inferring information about possibilities (and actualities) during the course of problem solving and to demonstrate its soundness.

A critical component of this system is constraint-based reasoning. Constraint satisfaction is a proven technology that has been successfully extended to distributed artificial intelligence problems [7]. The present work differs from earlier work in this field in that we are studying an independent agent paradigm where agents communicate with each other to solve a problem of mutual interest rather than solving parts of a single problem.

S. Flesca et al. (Eds.): JELIA 2002, LNAI 2424, pp. 407–418, 2002.

In fact, in the present system each agent has its own problem, but the solutions must all be mutually consistent. Because this system is based on a combination of ideas from constraint satisfaction and standard modal logic, it supports consistency reasoning under conditions of partial ignorance.

We have tested the efficacy of our methods in a simplified situation, This is a type of meeting-scheduling problem, where agents have pre-existing schedules, but need to add a new meeting that all of them can attend. Elsewhere, we show that the present approach can in fact improve problem solving efficiency, and can also ameliorate the privacy/efficiency tradeoff [6]. We have also shown that at the same time this form of reasoning affords new opportunities for agents to 'invade' each other's privacy, which raises new issues in this domain. As a result, these new developments may serve to put the problem of privacy into high relief.

The next section describes the basic situation we have used to study the problem of privacy in collaborative problem solving and gives an overview of how our agents operate. Section 3 describes how possibilities are represented within a constraint satisfaction framework, and establishes some requirements for the well-formedness of the basic information structures. Section 4 states the deduction rules and shows that they support the requirements laid out in Section 3. Section 5 describes a further extension of the system, in which certain possibilities are associated with events that gave rise to them. Section 6 considers the system in relation to previous discussions of agent epistemology and to other 'non-standard' CSP formulations. Section 7 gives conclusions.

2   A Motivating Example

2.1   The Basic Problem

Our thinking in this area was inspired by an experimental case study, which was based on an agent scheduling problem. In this problem there are k agents, each with its own calendar, which consists of appointments in different cities at different times of the week. The task is to find a meeting time that all agents have free and which they can attend given their existing schedules and constraints on travel time.

For purposes of analysis, we added some simplifications. We assume a fixed set of cities where meetings can be held: London, Paris, Rome, Moscow and Tbilisi. We also restrict meeting times to be an hour in length and to start on the hour between 9 AM to 6 PM, inclusive, on any day of one week.

The basic constraints are the times (in hours) required for travel between meetings in different cities, indicated in Fig. 1. Travel times within one region (Western Europe or the former Eastern Bloc) are shown beside arcs connecting cities; the arc between the two ellipses represents travel time between a city in one region and any city in the other.

2.2   Agents and Constraint Satisfaction

This problem can be represented as a binary constraint satisfaction problem (CSP). Loosely, this is the problem of assigning *values* to *variables* such that all of the *constraints* in the problem are satisfied. Each assignment is a member of a set of values associated

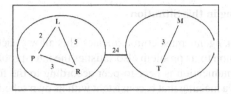

Fig. 1. Time constraint graph for a meeting scheduling problem. Cities are London, Paris, Rome, Moscow and Tbilisi. Further details in text.

with a particular variable, called the *domain* of that variable. Constraints are relations based on Cartesian products of the domains of values associated with the variables in the constraint. Binary CSPs are often (partly) represented as graphs, where nodes represent variables and arcs represent the constraints between variables.

More formally, a constraint satisfaction problem can be defined as a tuple, $P = \{V, D, C\}$. V is a set of variables, $\{v_i\}$. D is a set of domains, $\{d_i | d_i$ is associated with variable $v_i\}$, where each d_i is defined in turn as a set, $\{x_{ik} | x_{ik}$ is a value that can be assigned to v_i, with $1 \leq k \leq |domain(v_i)|\}$. C is a set of constraints, $\{c_{ij} | c_{ij}$ a constraint between v_i and $v_j\}$, where each constraint c_{ij} defines a set of pairs of values that are allowed by the constraint. That is, $c_{ij} = \{(x_{im}, x_{jn}) | x_{im} \in domain(v_i), x_{jn} \in domain(v_j),$ and (x_{im}, x_{jn}) is allowed by the constraint$\}$. We will also consider the *scope* of a constraint, or the projection of V on the variables of c_{ij}, denoting it C_{ij}, where $C_{ij} = \{v_k | k = i \ or \ k = j\}$. A *solution* to the problem P is a set of values $S = \{x_{1a_1}, x_{2a_2}, ..., x_{|V|a_{|V|}}\}$ s.t. $\forall c_{ij} \in C, (x_{ia_i}, x_{ja_j}) \in c_{ij}$.

An important part of constraint programming, i.e. the solving of constraint satisfaction problems, has been the development of algorithms that establish a degree of local consistency among the domains of the problem. Consistency is defined in general as a guarantee that for any $k - 1$ assignments and any unassigned variable, one can assign a value to this variable so as to satisfy any constraints among these k variables. A simple but important example is called *arc consistency*, where $k = 2$. A CSP is arc consistent if the variables are pairwise consistent, so that an assignment to variable v_i is consistent with at least one value in each of the other variables that are in the scope of a constraint involving v_i.

In the present situation, each agent's own meeting scheduling problem can be viewed as a CSP involving 70 variables, one for each time slot. Each variable has a domain of five values, one for each city. The problem for each agent is to add a city-value to one of the empty slots such that its constraints are satisfied. Note that at the beginning of the task each agent already has a solution to a personal meeting scheduling problem in the form of a (preexisting) schedule. This schedule forms an important part of the task-problem, which involves a further assignment to another one of its variables. This can be thought of as adjusting a global constraint that specifies that k slots must be assigned a city as a value, to the requirement that $k + 1$ slots must have this property. In addition, there is a new 'inter-problem' constraint that this assignment be the same for all agents, i.e. that it involves the same variable and value.

2.3   Problem Solving in this Situation

To solve this problem, agents must communicate. This allows each agent to determine whether a (new) solution to its problem also satisfies the inter-problem constraint. Here, we assume that communication is peer-to-peer according to the following protocol. A single agent proposes a meeting that is consistent with its own schedule to the other $n-1$ agents. Each of the latter then replies to the first agent indicating whether it accepts or rejects the proposal. There may be a single agent that takes the role of the proposer or this role may shift so that each agent proposes a meeting in turn ("round robin protocol"); but this difference is not important for the present discussion. Communication continues until a time and place are found that is acceptable to all agents. This protocol has the advantage that all agents can keep track of how the task is going. Variant protocols such as answering a proposal with a counter-proposal are not considered here, but can easily be accomodated in the present framework.

This problem could be solved without further elaboration by simple bookkeeping. Since each proposal is broadcast to all other agents, each agent can keep track of the previous proposals, so that with a finite number of variables and values, the procedure will terminate, either with a solution or with the agents having established that no solution exists. However, we have found that the efficiency of this process can be considerably enhanced if agents store information about other agents that can be deduced from the communications and use arc consistency processing to reduce the number of proposals that need to be considered in each round.

The means of storing and using such information will be described informally in the rest of this section, before proceeding to a more careful description. The information that an agent has about another agent will be referred to as the *view* that the first agent has of the second. In this view there are different kinds of information, that may include actual meetings and times that are open ("open slots"). Provided they have some general information about the situation, here, the set of possible meeting-sites and times as well as constraints on travel times, agents can also consider each other's schedules in terms of acceptable possibilities for these values even if they don't know what the other schedules actually are.

Deductions are made on the basis of the communications. From proposals and acceptances, the agent that receives the message can deduce that the other agent has an (actual) open slot. It can also deduce that certain meetings that might have been in the other agent's schedule are, in fact, not possible; otherwise, given the travel constraints, the agent could not have proposed (accepted) a given meeting in that slot. From a rejection a simple reduction in the set of possibilities can be made that refers to the meeting just proposed. In addition, the agent receiving this message can also deduce a disjunctive set of possible causes for this rejection. Finally, if even a small number of actual meetings are communicated, then many more possibilities can be excluded.

These deductions can then be used either to narrow down the set of acceptable meetings that an agent can propose, or to suggest which proposals are more likely to be effective. Most importantly, agents can avoid making proposals that they have deduced are impossible for at least one agent. In some cases (cf. Section 5), they can also reduce a set of possibilities until, under the usual closed-world assumptions associated with CSPs, an actual value can be deduced.

3   Representing Possibilistic Information within a CSP Framework

Our approach to carrying out the deductions just described involves combining CSP ideas with basic concepts from modal logic. In addition to gathering actual information about other agents' schedules, in particular their open times, agents keep track of possibilities in regard to meetings of other agents. This information is maintained in CSP-like representations, where time-slots are again taken as variables. In one of these CSPs, domain values represent meetings that another agent might have, which we term "possible-has-meeting" values, in another the values represent meetings that that agent might be able to attend ("possible-can-meet" values), and in the third the values represent meetings that are possible causes for any rejections made by the other agent ("possible-cause" values). At the beginning of a session, when an agent knows nothing about another agent's schedule, all values for possible-has-meeting's and possible-can-meet's must be considered, since any value is possible. So both of these CSPs have five values per time-slot, i.e. five possible-has-meeting values, or five possible-can-meet values. At the same time, the domains of possible-cause values are all empty.

'Possibilistic' domain values can be given straightforward interpretations in CSP terms. Possible-has-meeting and possible-cause values represent possible existing assignments to variables; possible-can-meet values represent possibilities for future assignments. These values can be considered as 'possibilistic' because they only exist in relation to values in some associated, actual CSP. In keeping with ordinary intuitions about possibilities, the same possible-has-meeting and possible-can-meet value can be present in the corresponding domains of their respective possibilistic CSPs, i.e. the two are independent.

To indicate the close semantic relation between these CSPs, which represent possible values, and the actual CSP of an agent, we call the former "shadow CSPs". Appropriately, shadow CSPs cannot be said to exist on their own, as can ordinary CSPs. Moreover, they do not have solutions in the ordinary sense. And in the present case, there are no real binary constraints. However, they are composed of variables, each with a domain of values, some of which can be deleted, as shown below. In fact, they can be described as a tuple $P = \{V, D, C\}$, just as ordinary CSPs, although in this case C only includes unary constraints, i.e. constraints on domain inclusion.

The above account suggests that values in shadow CSPs can be considered as ordinary CSP values to which the possibility operator $\diamond$ is attached; for this reason, they will be termed "modal values".

As already indicated, in this situation we have two basic kinds of shadow CSPs, related to existing and future assignments. In addition, there are some other requirements that we can derive from consideration of the given problem. The most important is that the set inclusion relation should hold between the corresponding domains of an actual CSP and any related shadow CSP, where "corresponding" means being associated with the same variable. In addition, the same relation must hold between corresponding domains of shadow CSPs related to the same actual CSP, here between domains of possible-cause values and corresponding domains of possible-has-meeting values. Generalizing from this, we will require that:

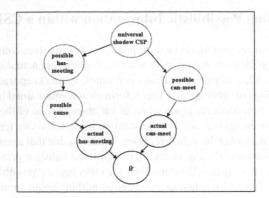

Fig. 2. Structure of shadow CSP system for the meeting-scheduling problem. Shadow CSPs are shown as dashed circles. Arrows represent the realization relation holding between the domains of super- and subordinate CSPs.

1. The entire set of shadow CSPs plus the representation of the actual CSP has a supremum, which we can call the "universal" (shadow) CSP and an infimum which may be the null set (cf. Fig. 2).
2. For this entire set, the set inclusion relations are reflexive and transitive.
3. These relations have an additional property of good-structure in that if a domain of shadow CSP X is a subset of the corresponding domain of shadow CSP Y, then another domain of X will be a subset of the corresponding domain of Y.

The first two requirements, of course, insure that there is a partial order on each set of corresponding domains under the set inclusion relation. Requirement three gives a transitive, reflexive relation for the set composed of the entire shadow CSPs. It should also be noted that these requirements do not preclude the presence of redundant values within a set of shadow CSPs; there is no notion of partitioning here, and as later arguments will show this is not, in general, desireable.

In general, the set inclusion relation can be interpreted as a requirement that the domains of a 'subordinate' CSP must be valid "realizations" of the corresponding domains of all of its superordinates. For example, in the present problem a domain in the CSP that represents possible-causes must be a proper realization of the corresponding domain of possible-has-meeting's. As another example, consider a problem where, instead of simply communicating rejections, agents specify the type of rejection by saying "rejection-meeting" or "rejection-conflict", by which they mean that they cannot accept a proposal either because they have a meeting at that time or the proposal conflicts with an existing meeting. This situation could be represented by two possible-cause CSPs, both of which are proper realizations of possible-has-meetings, but neither of which is necessarily a realization of the other. (A possible-cause-meeting value might have been ascertained that is not among the possible-cause-conflicts that have been deduced, and vice versa.)

The relation between corresponding elements in an actual CSP and any of its super-ordinate shadow CSPs is equivalent to the theorem,

$$x \implies \Diamond x.$$

This means that in this case the set inclusion requirement is derivable as a theorem assuming that the theses of a standard modal logic hold within this system. This raises the question of the relation between a shadow CSP system and the systems of modal logic. In particular, what is the relation between the present representation and the well-known possible-worlds semantics [3]? With respect to a single domain of size D, clearly there are 2^D possible worlds (PWs) associated with its values. In a shadow system, successively more inclusive shadow CSPs represent collections of values from successively more PWs, all of which (in contrast to a PW) are treated as possibilities directly. Hence, the subset relation holding among corresponding domains in the shadow CSP system is not equivalent to any accessibility relation in a PW system. It is, therefore, unclear whether any theses of standard modal logic are excluded. In practice, it has not been found necessary to go outside the system S1.

4 Making Deductions in the Present Framework

4.1 Allowable Inferences

If "modal values" as described above fall within the bounds of a standard modal logic, then the inferences that we can make must also follow the rules of this system. Since our real concern here is actual CSP values (i.e. the actual meetings of another agent), this puts considerable limitations on our ability to carry out inferences in the usual constraint-based manner. In particular, we would like to be able to carry out something like the normal arc consistency processing by which we delete values that cannot be part of any solutions, based on the fact that they are not supported by either the original domain or the current assignment to an adjacent variable.

For example, in an ordinary CSP, given a constraint between two variables that prevents values x and y from appearing together in a solution, from the presence of x we can infer $\neg y$. (This is an instance of arc consistency processing, as described above.) But, while from $\Diamond x$ we could infer $\Diamond \neg y$ on this basis [3], we cannot then infer $\neg \Diamond y$ and from that $\neg y$. More importantly, under the ordinary rules of our logic if we discover that a value x is impossible, we cannot make a deduction based on the implication, $\neg x \implies \neg \Diamond x$. Among other unpleasant consequences, this would violate the Law of Transposition, unless we wanted to assume that x is equivalent to $\Diamond x$.

However, we can make a deduction like this if we adopt a closed world assumption. This is, in fact, what one ordinarily does when representing problems as CSPs, where the domains in question are considered closed worlds. In this case, $\neg x$, entails $\Box \neg x$. But,

$$\Box \neg x \equiv \neg \Diamond \neg \neg x \equiv \neg \Diamond x$$

Under this assumption, therefore, an agent can make deductions from whatever 'hard' information it can glean during the scheduling session in order to 'refine' domains in the shadow CSPs.

For instance, when another agent makes or accepts a proposal, since we are assuming honest communications, the recipient of this information knows that the other agent has no meeting in that slot. Therefore, up to five possible-has-meeting values can be deleted, since under closed world assumptions $\neg x$ entails $\neg \Diamond x$. Moreover, in this case if x implies

$\neg y$, then x also entails $\neg\Diamond y$; hence, arc consistency based on the original constraint graph can be used to delete possible-has-meeting values for other variables (i.e. other cities in nearby time slots).

In addition, for possible has-meetings, it is possible to make inferences back to actual values. This follows because $\neg\Diamond x$ implies $\neg x$. Moreover, if for all cities, x, associated with a single time-slot, we have inferred $\neg\Diamond x$, then we can infer that the agent has no meeting at that time, i.e. it has an open slot.

The closed world assumption also allows us to infer from a rejection that one possible-can-meet value is invalid. However, if an actual meeting is given as a reason, it is possible to remove up to four possible-has-meeting and five possible-can-meet values from its time slot, and to delete other possible-can-meet values based on the known constraints between hard values.

Using arc consistency reasoning, we can also make inferences from rejections to possible-cause values. From a simple rejection, within the framework of the actual CSP, we can infer a disjunction of values that might have been responsible for this rejection. Then, from the rule that x implies $\Diamond x$, a set of valid possible-cause values can be inferred. In addition, since the shadow CSP representing possible causes is subordinate to that representing possible has-meeting's, any possible cause values without values in the corresponding domain of the superordinate shadow CSP can be deleted.

4.2   Rules for Deduction

We can summarize the valid inferences relating actual and shadow information by a set of rules. Theses rules state the conditions for adding or deleting values in the CSP or shadow CSPs. In all of this it is essential to keep in mind that these rules refer to a view that represents another agent a_k. To avoid clutter, instead of writing (a_k, x_i) for a value x_i in the view for a_k, we simply write (x_i).

These rules fall into two classes, that can be referred to as epistemic and communication rules. In these rules, a term like x_i refers to value x in the domain of variable i, i.e. to a specific meeting. The predicates, "can" and "has" without the possibility operator refer to domain values in an actual CSP; when they are preceded by the operator they refer to the appropriate shadow CSP. In addition, the predicate "cause", which is always preceded by the possibility operator refers to another shadow CSP. In addition, we use the predicates, "reject", "accept", "propose", and "meeting" to refer to the four kinds of communication we are considering in the present version of a meeting-scheduling problem. (The last predicate represents the case where an agent explicitly communicates a meeting that it has.) Finally, the sign $\hookrightarrow$ is used to designate entailment, while $\Longrightarrow$ denotes material implication.

The epistemic rules are:

Rule E1. $\forall x_i \, \text{can}(x_i) \hookrightarrow \bigwedge_{x_i' \in d_i} \neg\Diamond\text{has}(x_i')$

Rule E2. $\forall x_i \, \text{can}(x_i) \hookrightarrow \bigwedge_{j \in C_{ij}, (x_i, x_j) \notin c_{ij}} \neg\Diamond\text{has}(x_j)$

Rule E3. $\forall x_i \, \neg\text{can}(x_i) \hookrightarrow \neg\Diamond\text{can}(x_i)$

Rule E4. $\forall x_i \, \text{has}(x_i) \Longrightarrow \bigwedge_{j \in C_{ij}, (x_i, x_j) \notin c_{ij}} \neg\text{has}(x_j)$

Rule E5. $\forall x_i \text{ has}(x_i) \implies \bigwedge_{j \in C_{ij}, (x_i, x_j) \notin c_{ij}} \neg\text{can}(x_j)$

Rule E6. $\forall x_i \text{ has}(x_i) \hookrightarrow \bigwedge_{x_i' \in d_i, x_i' \neq x_i} \neg\Diamond\text{has}(x_i')$

Rule E7. $\forall x_i \text{ has}(x_i) \hookrightarrow \bigwedge_{x_i' \in d_i} \neg\Diamond\text{can}(x_i')$

Rule E8. $\forall x_i \neg\text{has}(x_i) \hookrightarrow \neg\Diamond\text{has}(x_i)$

Rule E9. $\forall x_i \neg\text{can}(x_i) \hookrightarrow \bigvee_{j \in C_{ij}, (x_i, x_j) \notin c_{ij}} \Diamond\text{cause}(x_j)$

Rule E10. $\forall x_i \neg\Diamond\text{has}(x_i) \hookrightarrow \neg\Diamond\text{cause}(x_i)$

Rule E11. $\forall x_i \neg\Diamond\text{has}(x_i) \implies \neg\text{has}(x_i)$

Rules E4 and E5 follow from the consistency relations within the actual CSP; they are expressions of arc consistency pruning. Rule E11 is a thesis of S1. Rules E1-E3 and E6-E10 express inferences from values of the actual CSP to values in shadow CSPs. They can be derived from theses in S1, consistency assumptions of CSPs, and/or the closed world assumption in a straightforward fashion. In addition, the following useful rules can be derived from Rules E4 and E8 and from E5 and E3, respectively:

Rule E12. $\forall x_i \text{ has}(x_i) \hookrightarrow \bigwedge_{j \in C_{ij}, (x_i, x_j) \notin c_{ij}} \neg\Diamond\text{has}(x_j)$

Rule E13. $\forall x_i \text{ has}(x_i) \hookrightarrow \bigwedge_{j \in C_{ij}, (x_i, x_j) \notin c_{ij}} \neg\Diamond\text{can}(x_j)$

The communication rules are:

Rule C1. $\forall x_i \text{ accept}(x_i) \hookrightarrow \text{can}(x_i)$

Rule C2. $\forall x_i \text{ propose}(x_i) \hookrightarrow \text{can}(x_i)$

Rule C3. $\forall x_i \text{ reject}(x_i) \hookrightarrow \neg\Diamond\text{can}(x_i)$

Rule C4. $\forall x_i \text{ meeting}(x_i) \hookrightarrow \text{has}(x_i)$

The rules for the actual addition or deletion of values are also straightforward:

1. If $\text{has}(x_i)$ is a consequent of a rule, then if it is negated, x_i can be deleted from the actual CSP if it exists, and if it is not negated, x_i can be added to this CSP.
2. If a modal value is a consequent, then if it is negated, it can be deleted from the appropriate shadow CSP if it exists; if it is not negated, it can be added.

The next step is to show that our deductive rules insure that the system of shadow CSPs is well-structured, in the sense that at any point in the solving process (i.e. after any set of inferences based on these rules), the system has the properties described in Section 3.

At this point we introduce the notion of system state; this is simply the sets of domain values in the full shadow system at any step in the solving process. In the initial state, all domains of the universal shadow CSP as well as possible-has-meeting and possible-can-meet CSPs have all possible values, while the domains of the possible-cause shadow CSP and the actual CSPs are empty. Thereafter, the only changes are the deletion of values from the possible-has-meeting and possible-can-meet shadows or addition of values to the possible-cause shadow and the actual CSPs.

First we derive two lemmas before we present the basic theorem of good structure.

Lemma 1. If the meeting-scheduling problem is solved using the epistemic and communication rules listed above, then it cannot reach a state where there is a value in the actual has-meeting CSP without a corresponding value in the possible-has-meeting shadow CSP.

Proof: A value is added to the actual CSP only if a meeting is communicated (Rule C4). If the corresponding shadow value had been discarded due to epistemic rule E12, this would violate the assumption that agent k's schedule is arc consistent. If the corresponding $\Diamond$has value were discarded due to epistemic rule E1 or E6, this would reflect an assignment violation. If it were discarded due to rule E2, this would mean that a proposal or acceptance had been made that contradicts the meeting that was communicated. □

Lemma 2. If the meeting-scheduling problem is solved using the epistemic and communication rules listed above, then it cannot reach a state where there is a value in the actual can-meet CSP without a corresponding value in the possible-can-meet shadow CSP.

Proof: If the shadow value corresponding to an actual can-meet value were discarded via rules E7 or E13, this would mean that there was an existing meeting that was in conflict with the actual can-meet value. If it were discarded due to communication rule C3, this would also mean that there was a meeting in conflict with the actual value. □

As a preliminary to the main theorem on good structure, it is worth noting the crux of the proposition is that, since we are only discarding values from the possible-has-meeting and possible-can-meet shadow CSPs, we must never reach a state where their domains are not supersets of the corresponding domains in the actual CSP. On the other hand, since we add values to the possible-cause shadow CSP, then states can be allowed where there is an actual value without a corresponding possible-cause value; what cannot be allowed is a state where there is an actual value for which the corresponding possible-cause value has been ruled out.

Theorem 1. If the meeting-scheduling problem is solved using the epistemic and communication rules listed above, then the shadow CSP system can never reach a state in which the property of good structure is no longer realizable, i.e. it is not longer possible to achieve by appropriate additions and deletions to the actual and shadow CSPs.

Proof: There are three ways in which the properties of good-structure could be violated:

1. There is an actual value with no corresponding value in a superordinate shadow CSP.
2. There is a shadow CSP value without a corresponding value in the universal shadow CSP.
3. There is a possible-cause value with no corresponding possible-has-meeting value.

The second case can never happen by virtue of the definition of the universal shadow CSP and the fact that no values are ever deleted from it. The third case is prevented by epistemic Rule E10. The first case could happen in either of two ways: (i) we deduce an actual value for which there is no corresponding modal value in some shadow CSP, (ii) we deduce that some modal value is impossible, but there is a corresponding actual value. These cases are ruled out for the possible-has-meeting and possible-can-meet shadow CSPs by Lemmas 1 and 2. The only way a violation could occur with respect to the possible-cause shadow CSP is if an actual has-meeting value is added for which the corresponding possible-cause value is (in some state) deleted. But the latter can only occur (via Rule E10) if the corresponding value is discarded from the possible-has-meeting shadow CSP. But this would violate Lemma 1. □

5 Grounding Possible-Cause Values

In our implementation, we have found that the effectiveness of possible-cause's could be greatly enhanced (and further deductions could be realized) if each set of possible-cause's associated with a rejection is maintained separately. This yields two advantages: (i) as possible-cause values are discarded, in accordance with Rule E10, instances occur where the set is reduced to a singleton; in these cases, we can infer an actual meeting and then make further inferences from that, (ii) after the sets have been appreciably reduced, they support very effective heuristics in which proposals that conflict with known possible-causes's are put off temporarily in favor of those that don't.

In terms of the shadow CSP system, this separation of possible-cause's amounts to maintaining a set of shadow CSPs. In this case, however, each CSP represents a subgraph of the original network consisting of domains of variables that have constraints with the variable associated with a rejection. (Note that we cannot consider these as having all the domains of the actual CSP where some of the domains are degenerate, because this would violate the property of good structure for the system.) There will, of course, often be a high degree of redundancy among the values of these shadow CSPs, but as indicated earlier, this is perfectly acceptable. is perfectly acceptable.

Theorem 2 With this elaboration, the system of shadow CSPs still cannot enter a state where it can no longer achieve a state in conformance with the property of good structure.
Proof The same arguments apply as in the proof of Theorem 1, since the elaboration is simply a redistribution of the same values.

6 Relations to Other Work

Work on modeling agents has considered models that incorporate ideas from modal logic. However, as far as I know these models have only been concerned with representing agent behavior in general, so as to demonstrate consistency between beliefs and goals and similar issues [4]. In fact, there seems to have been little work done on agent views that corresponds to the present research.

In the CSP field, there has been a fair amount of work on "non-standard" CSPs; almost all of this has been concerned with "soft constraints", i.e. constraints or constraint problems whose satisfaction is graded rather than all-or-none. These problems are modeled by associating constraints or constraint tuples with numerical values, together with rules for comparing values and combining them [1]. Some of this work, which is concerned with preferences or relative importance among values or constraints, is outside the concerns of the present work. In other cases, the concern is to represent uncertainty, either in terms of probabilities or fuzzy measures. In general, this approach appears to be orthogonal with the present representation.

7   Conclusions

This work introduces a new formalism for dealing with the problem of information that is not directly available, when this is pertinent to collective problem solving. In the present paper, we have described the basic framework and identified properties that support valid deductions about such information. This system employs concepts from constraint satisfaction and modal logic in order to reason about information that cannot be known directly but which belongs to a well-defined universe of values. We have also described a set of deductions that support the properties of good structure in this system.

Based on our initial experience with a system based on these principles, the present framework appears to allow improved efficiency of problem solving in a situation where this would be not otherwise be possible.

References

1. S. Bistarelli, H. Fargier, U. Montanari, F. Rossi, T. Schiex, and G. Verfaillie. Semiring-based csps and valued csps: Basic properties and comparison. In M. Jampel, E. Freuder, and M. Maher, editors, *Over-Constrained Systems*, volume 1106, pages 111–150. Springer, Berlin, 1996.
2. L. Garrido and K. Sycara. Multi-agent meeting scheduling: Preliminary experimental results. In *Proc., Second International Conference on Multi-Agent Systems, ICMAS-96*, Menlo Park, CA, 1996. AAAI Press.
3. G. E. Hughes and M. J. Cresswell. *An Introduction to Modal Logic*. Routledge, London and New York, 1968.
4. A. S. Rao and M. P. Georgeff. Modeling rational agents with a bdi-architecture. In *Proc. Second International Conference on Principles of Knowledge Representation and Reasoning, KR'91*, pages 473–484, San Mateo, CA, 1991. Morgan Kaufmann.
5. S. Sen, T. Haynes, and N. Arora. Satisfying user preferences while negotiating meetings. *Internat. J. Human-Computer Stud.*, 47:407–427, 1997.
6. R. J. Wallace, E. C. Freuder, and M. Minca. Consistency reasoning and privacy/efficiency relations in multi-agent systems. In *submitted for publication*, 2002.
7. M. Yokoo. *Distributed Constraint Satisfaction. Foundations of Cooperation in Multi-agent Systems*. Springer, Berlin, 1998.

An Abductive Logic Programming Architecture for Negotiating Agents

Fariba Sadri[1], Francesca Toni[1], and Paolo Torroni[2]

[1] Department of Computing, Imperial College
180 Queens Gate, SW7 London, UK
{fs,ft}@doc.ic.ac.uk
[2] DEIS, Università di Bologna
Viale Risorgimento 2, 40136 Bologna, Italy
ptorroni@deis.unibo.it

Abstract. In this paper, we present a framework for agent negotiation based on abductive logic programming. The framework is based on an existing architecture for logic-based agents, and extends it by accommodating dialogues for negotiation. As an application of negotiating agents, we propose a resource-exchanging problem. The innovative contribution of this work is in the definition of an operational model, including an agent cycle and dialogue cycle, and in the results that apply in the general case of abductive agents and in the specific case of a class of agent systems.

1 Introduction

In multi-agents systems, agents may need to interact in order to exchange resources, when the resources they own are not enough to achieve their goals prior to exchange. If each agent has global visibility of the other agents' resources and intentions, a "global" plan can be generated by a single individual. However, a global plan cannot be possibly generated if there is no such visibility or if the design of the system is based on agent autonomy. Also, the autonomous agent behaviour and the consequent dynamic evolution of the system could make any such plan obsolete before completion. In there comes negotiation.

The focus of this work is the knowledge and the reasoning that is required to build negotiation dialogues between agents, in order to exchange resources that help achieve the agents' objectives. We express such knowledge in a declarative way, as logic programs and integrity constraints, as in abductive logic programming [1], with the dialogue moves treated as abducibles/hypotheses, and dialogue/negotiation policies treated as integrity constraints.

We propose an operational model, based on the abductive reasoning mechanism and on an agent cycle, and show that it can be used to generate (negotiation) dialogues. The framework extends an agent architecture initially proposed in [2], to enable dialogue generation. The agent architecture in [2] relies upon executing the IFF abductive proof-procedure defined in [3] as the reasoning engine

S. Flesca et al. (Eds.): JELIA 2002, LNAI 2424, pp. 419–431, 2002.

of the agent. We identify the inadequacy of the IFF procedure for our domain of application, and adopt the procedure in [4] instead. This paper represents in many respects a progress from previous related work [5,6]. It provides a better formalization of the framework for negotiation, by defining an agent cycle that accommodates dialogues as a result of the agent reasoning. This improvement is necessary to prove some strong results about the general negotiation framework. The paper also defines two classes of agents (N-agents and N^+-agents), that implement the behaviour of self-interested resource-bounded agents and that are provably able to solve a resource reallocation problem.

The paper is organized as follows: in Section 2 we review and revise the dialogue framework of [6,5], in Section 3 we augment this framework with new concepts to characterise the state of negotiating agents and specify a concrete variety of negotiating agents, referred to as self-interested agents, in Section 4 we define the abductive framework, abductive agents and concrete instances of abductive agents referred to as N-agents and N^+-agents, and in Section 5 we present the formal results. Section 6 concludes.

2   Background: Knowledge and Dialogues for Negotiation

Agents negotiate using a shared language, consisting of possible utterances, or *dialogue moves*, defined as follows[1]:

Definition 1. A *dialogue move* (between X and Y) is an instance of a schema $tell(X, Y, \textbf{Subject}, D, T)$, where X is the *utterer* and Y is the *receiver* of the dialogue move, $X \neq Y$, D is the *identifier* of the dialogue to which the move belongs, and T is the *time* when the move is uttered. **Subject** is the *content* of the move, expressed in some given *content language*.

Note that the identifier of a dialogue uniquely determines the dialogue that includes the dialogue move. Note also that this component of a dialogue move is new and was not present in the definition in [5].

A concrete example of a dialogue move is $tell(a, b, \textbf{request}(\textbf{give}(nail)), d, 1)$, where **Subject** is **request**(**give**(*nail*)). Intuitively, this utterance expresses a's request to b at time 1 for a nail, in the course of a dialogue identified by d.

Definition 2. A *language for negotiation* $\mathcal{L}$ is a (possibly infinite) set of (possibly non ground) dialogue moves. For a given $\mathcal{L}$, we define two (possibly infinite) subsets of moves, $\mathcal{I}(\mathcal{L})$, $\mathcal{F}(\mathcal{L}) \subseteq \mathcal{L}$, called respectively *initial* moves and *final* moves. Each final move is either *successful* or *unsuccessful*.

A simple example of language for negotiation is ($\mathcal{N}$ stands for *negotiation*):
$$\mathcal{L}_\mathcal{N} = \{ \ tell(X, Y, \textbf{request}(\textbf{give}(Resource)), D, T),$$
$$tell(X, Y, \textbf{accept}(\textbf{request}(\textbf{give}(Resource))), D, T)$$
$$tell(X, Y, \textbf{refuse}(\textbf{request}(\textbf{give}(Resource))), D, T) \ \}$$
The initial and final moves are:
$$\mathcal{I}(\mathcal{L}_\mathcal{N}) = \{tell(X, Y, \textbf{request}(\textbf{give}(Resource)), D, T)\}$$
$$\mathcal{F}(\mathcal{L}_\mathcal{N}) = \{ \ [succ. \ moves:] \ tell(X, Y, \textbf{accept}(\textbf{request}(\textbf{give}(Resource))), D, T)$$
$$[unsucc. \ moves:] \ tell(X, Y, \textbf{refuse}(\textbf{request}(\textbf{give}(Resource))), D, T)\}$$

---

[1] Terms starting with capital/lower-case letters stand for variables/ground terms, resp.

In this example all moves are either initial or final, although this is not always the case (see [6]). We sometimes represent a dialogue move in abbreviated form as $p(D, T)$ or simply as p, if the discussion is independent of the missing parameters.

Definition 3. An *agent system* consists of: a language for negotiation $\mathcal{L}$; and a finite set A, with at least two elements, where each $X \in A$ is a ground term, representing the name of an agent, and each agent is equipped at each time T with a *knowledge base* $\mathcal{K}_{X,T}$.

In the sequel, we will sometimes drop X and/or T, if clear from the context.

We assume that the knowledge base of each agent is represented in some logic-based language equipped with a notion of entailment $\vdash$. For simplicity, we assume that agents share the logic-based language and $\vdash$ (but not the knowledge bases necessarily). In Section 4, we will adopt abductive logic programming [1] as the logic-based language used to model the knowledge base of agents.

The knowledge base $\mathcal{K}_{X,T}$ of agent X at time T consists of *(1) domain-dependent beliefs* about the world, such as the information about the agent system, e.g., $agents(\{a, b, c\})$; *(2) domain-independent beliefs*, used to regulate the negotiation dialogues, e.g. see $IC.1 - IC.3$ later in this section, and to represent changes in the agent's own state, such as its ownership of resources, e.g. see $D.1 - D.4$ later in this section; *(3)* information about the *resources* the agent owns before the dialogues start, e.g., $have(picture, 0)$, with 0 the initial time; *(4)* the agent's *goal*, e.g., $goal(hung(picture))$; *(5)* the agent's *intention*, represented as $plan(P, Req)$, i.e., the *plan* P that the agent intends to carry out in order to achieve its goal, associated with the set of resources Req that are required to carry it out, e.g., $plan(\langle hit(nail), hang(picture)\rangle, \{picture, nail, hammer\})$; and finally, *(6)* the past (time-stamped) *utterances*, e.g. $tell(a, b, \mathbf{request}(\mathbf{give}(nail)), d, 1)$, $tell(b, a, \mathbf{accept}(\mathbf{request}(\mathbf{give}(nail))), d, 3)$.

It is worth noting that the goal and the intention are not time-stamped. In fact, we assume that plans in intentions are given initially and do not change. The only part of $\mathcal{K}_{X,T}$ that changes over time is the the set of past utterances *(6)*, as this part grows monotonically during the course of dialogues.

The following definitions of *have* and *need* for agent $a \in A$ (similarly for the other agents in A) may be part of the domain-independent beliefs *(2)* in $\mathcal{K}_a$:

$(D.1)$ $have(R, T) \leftarrow have(R, 0) \;\wedge 0 < T \wedge \neg[gave\_away(R, T1), 0 < T1 \leq T]$
      $have(R, T) \leftarrow obtained(R, T1) \;\wedge T1 < T$
                  $\wedge \;\neg[gave\_away(R, T2), T1 < T2 \leq T]$
$(D.2)$ $obtained(R, T) \leftarrow tell(X, a, accept(request(give(R))), D, T)$
$(D.3)$ $gave\_away(R, T) \leftarrow tell(a, X, accept(request(give(R))), D, T)$
$(D.4)$ $need(R, T) \leftarrow have(R, T) \;\wedge plan(P, Req) \wedge R \in Req$

Note that we assume that resources are considered not to be owned if they have been "promised" to another agent, i.e., as a consequence of the acceptance of another agent's request, even if the actual delivery has not yet been carried out. Indeed, here we are not concerned with the execution of a plan, and we assume that agents will obtain the resources they have been promised by the time the plan needs to be executed.

For a given agent $X \in A$, where A is an agent system equipped with a language for negotiation $\mathcal{L}$, we define the sets $\mathcal{L}_X^{in}$, of all dialogue move schemata of which X is the receiver, and $\mathcal{L}_X^{out}$, of all dialogue move schemata of which X is the utterer. Then, negotiation policies can be specified by sets of dialogue constraints, defined as follows:

Definition 4. Given an agent system A, equipped with a language for negotiation $\mathcal{L}$, and an agent $X \in A$, a *dialogue constraint* for X is a (possibly non-ground) if-then rule $p(D,T) \wedge C \Rightarrow [\exists\, T'(\hat{p}(D,T') \wedge T < T')]$, where

- $p(D,T) \in \mathcal{L}_X^{in}$ and $\hat{p}(D,T') \in \mathcal{L}_X^{out}$,
- the utterer of $p(D,T)$ is the receiver of $\hat{p}(D,T')$, and the receiver of $p(D,T)$ is the utterer of $\hat{p}(D,T')$,
- C is a conjunction of literals in the language of the knowledge base of X [2],
- any variables not explicitly quantified are implicitly universally quantified over the constraint.

The move $p(D,T)$ is referred to as the *trigger*, $\hat{p}(D,T')$ as the *next move* and C as the *condition* of the dialogue constraint.

Intuitively, the dialogue constraints of an agent X express X's negotiation policies. The intuitive meaning of a dialogue constraint $p(D,T) \wedge C \Rightarrow [\exists\, T'(\hat{p}(D,T') \wedge T < T')]$ of agent X is as follows: if at time T in a dialogue D some other agent Y utters $p(D,T) = tell(Y,X,Subject,D,T)$, then the corresponding instance of the dialogue constraint *is triggered* and, if the condition C is entailed by $\mathcal{K}_{X,T'}$, then the constraint *fires* and X will utter $\hat{p}(D,T') = tell(X,Y,Subject',D,T')$, at a later time T' that is available for utterances. The instantiation of T' is left to the agent cycle, and can be performed as explained in section 4.

A negotiation policy can be seen as a set of properties that must be satisfied at all times, by enforcing (uttering) the conclusion of the constraints that represent them, whenever they fire. In this sense, constraints behave like active rules in databases and integrity constraints in abductive logic programming. In Section 4, we will adopt the negotiation policy $\mathcal{N}$ consisting of the following three dialogue constraints (a is the name of the agent which has $\mathcal{N}$ in its knowledge base), which are part of the domain-independent beliefs *(2)* in $\mathcal{K}_a$:

$(IC.1)\;\; tell(X,a,\mathbf{request}(\mathbf{give}(R))), D,T) \wedge\; have(R,T)\; \wedge\; \neg need(R,T)$
$\qquad\qquad \Rightarrow \exists\, T'(tell(a,X,\mathbf{accept}(\mathbf{request}(\mathbf{give}(R)))), D,T')\; \wedge T < T')$
$(IC.2)\;\; tell(X,a,\mathbf{request}(\mathbf{give}(R))), D,T) \wedge\; have(R,T)\; \wedge\; need(R,T)$
$\qquad\qquad \Rightarrow \exists\, T'(tell(a,X,\mathbf{refuse}(\mathbf{request}(\mathbf{give}(R)))), D,T')\; \wedge T < T')$
$(IC.3)\;\; tell(X,a,\mathbf{request}(\mathbf{give}(R))), D,T) \wedge\; \neg have(R,T)$
$\qquad\qquad \Rightarrow \exists\, T'(tell(a,X,\mathbf{refuse}(\mathbf{request}(\mathbf{give}(R)))), D,T')\; \wedge T < T')$

Definition 5. Given an agent system A equipped with $\mathcal{L}$, a *dialogue* between two agents X and Y in A is a set of ground dialogue moves in $\mathcal{L}$, $\{p_0, p_1, p_2, \ldots\}$, such that, for a given set of time lapses $0 \le t_0 < t_1 < t_2 < \ldots$:

---

[2] Note that C in general might depend on several time points, possibly but not necessarily including T; thus, we do not indicate explicitly any time variable for C.

1. $\forall\, i \geq 0$, p_i is uttered at time t_i;
2. $\forall\, i \geq 0$, if p_i is uttered by agent X (viz. Y), then p_{i+1} (if any) is uttered by agent Y (viz. X);
3. $\forall\, i > 0$, p_i can be uttered by agent $U \in \{X, Y\}$ only if there exists a (grounded) dialogue constraint $p_{i-1} \wedge C \Rightarrow [p_i \wedge t_{i-1} < t_i] \in \mathcal{K}_U$ such that $\mathcal{K}_{U,t_i} \wedge p_{i-1} \vdash C$;
4. there is an identifier D such that, $\forall\, i \geq 0$, the dialogue identifier of p_i is D;
5. $\forall t$, $t_{i-1} < t < t_i$, $\forall i > 0$ s.t. p_i and p_{i-1} belong to the dialogue, there exist no utterances with either X or Y being either the receiver or the utterer.

A dialogue $\{p_0, p_1, \ldots p_m\}$, $m \geq 0$, is *terminated* if p_m is a ground final move, namely p_m is a ground instance of an utterance in $\mathcal{F}(\mathcal{L})$.

By condition 1, a dialogue is in fact a *sequence* of moves. By condition 2, agents alternate utterances in a dialogue. By condition 3, dialogues are generated by the dialogue constraints, together with the given knowledge base to determine whether the constraints fire. In condition 3, t represents the time at which the incoming utterance is recorded by the receiving agent. By condition 4, the dialogue moves of a dialogue share the same dialogue identifier. By condition 5, dialogues are *atomic* and *interleaved*, where by *atomicity* we mean that each agent is involved in at most one dialogue at each time and by *interleaving* we mean that dialogue moves must alternate between the two agents within the dialogue. Conditions 4 and 5 are new and were not present in the definition of dialogues in [5]. The purpose of these new conditions is to avoid having to deal with multiple negotiation dialogues involving the same agent at the same time. To accommodate such concurrent dialogues we need to extend our set of subjects in the dialogue moves and to provide some form of concurrency control mechanisms, both of which are beyond the scope of this paper.

In Section 4 we propose a concrete agent framework that can produce dialogues, according to the above definition. In this paper we are interested in dialogues starting with the request of a resource R, defined as follows.

Definition 6. Given an agent system A equipped with $\mathcal{L}$, a *request dialogue* with respect to a resource R of an agent $X \in A$ is a dialogue $\{p_0, p_1, p_2, \ldots\}$ between X and some other agent $Y \in A$ such that, for some $T \geq 0$,

- $p_0 = tell(X, Y, request(give(R)), D, T)$, and
- $\mathcal{K}_{X,T} \vdash plan(P, Req) \wedge R \in Req \wedge \neg have(R, T)$.

In the sequel, unless otherwise stated, by *dialogue* we mean *request dialogue*.

In order to obtain all the resources missing in a plan, a single dialogue might not be enough, in general, and a *sequence of dialogues* might be needed for an agent to obtain all the required resources. In order to produce sequences of dialogues, agents may run a *dialogue cycle*, having the following properties $\mathcal{P}$:

1. no agent is asked twice for the same resource within the dialogue sequence;
2. if a resource is not obtained from one agent, then it is asked from some other agent, if any;
3. if a resource is not obtained after asking all agents, then the agent dialogue cycle terminates with failure.

The idea behind 3 is that the agent will not carry on asking for the other resources, since, at least one resource in the current intention cannot be obtained, the plan in the intention will not be executable. After the cycle, if successful in obtaining all the resources, the agent can execute the plan in its intention. One dialogue cycle with these properties is defined in [5]. In Section 4 we give a concrete implementation of an agent dialogue cycle with these properties.

Within our dialogue framework we can specify properties of the knowledge of agents and, as we will see in Section 4, of the behaviours of agents.

The following definitions give two useful properties of the knowledge of agents (KB stands for "knowledge base") paving the way towards building agents producing one and only one move in response to any non-final move of other agents.

Definition 7. An agent KB $\mathcal{K}_X$ is *deterministic* iff for each incoming dialogue move $p(D, T)$ which is a ground instance of a schema in $\mathcal{L}_X^{in}$, there exists at most one dialogue constraint in $\mathcal{K}_X$ which is triggered by $p(D, T)$ and which fires.

Definition 8. An agent KB $\mathcal{K}_X$ is *exhaustive* iff for each dialogue move $p(D, T)$ which is a ground instance of a schema in $\mathcal{L}_X^{in} \setminus \mathcal{F}(\mathcal{L})$, there exists at least one dialogue constraint that is triggered by $p(D, T)$ and which fires.

3   Specification of Agents' States

We can characterise the state of the agents in terms of their need and ownership of resources. To this end, let us consider an agent X with an intention $\mathcal{I}_X$. Let $\mathcal{R}(\mathcal{I}_X)$ be the set of resources required to carry out the plan in $\mathcal{I}_X$ (namely, if $\mathcal{I}_X = plan(P, Req)$, then $\mathcal{R}(\mathcal{I}_X) = Req$). Also, let $\mathcal{R}_{X,T}$ be the set of resources X owns at time T. Then, for any resource R, we define the following predicates **a**, **m**, **n**, **i**, standing for *available*, *missing*, *needed*, and *indifferent*, respectively:

- **a**(R, T): X has R and does not need it ($R \in \mathcal{R}_{X,T} \land R \notin \mathcal{R}(\mathcal{I}_X)$)
- **m**(R, T): X does not have R but needs it ($R \notin \mathcal{R}_{X,T} \land R \in \mathcal{R}(\mathcal{I}_X)$)
- **n**(R, T): X does have R and does need it ($R \in \mathcal{R}_{X,T} \land R \in \mathcal{R}(\mathcal{I}_X)$)
- **i**(R, T): X does not have R and does not need it ($R \notin \mathcal{R}_{X,T} \land R \notin \mathcal{R}(\mathcal{I}_X)$)

Assuming a formal definition of "have" and "need" in $\mathcal{K}_{X,T}$, e.g. $D.1 - D.4$ in section 2, the above **a**, **m**, **n**, **i** can be formally defined as follows:

- $\mathcal{K}_{X,T} \vdash \mathbf{a}(R, T)$ *iff* $\mathcal{K}_{X,T} \vdash have(R, T) \land \mathcal{K}_{X,T} \vdash \neg need(R, T)$
- $\mathcal{K}_{X,T} \vdash \mathbf{m}(R, T)$ *iff* $\mathcal{K}_{X,T} \vdash \neg have(R, T) \land \mathcal{K}_{X,T} \vdash plan(P, Req) \land R \in Req$
- $\mathcal{K}_{X,T} \vdash \mathbf{n}(R, T)$ *iff* $\mathcal{K}_{X,T} \vdash need(R, T) \land \mathcal{K}_{X,T} \vdash have(R, T)$
- $\mathcal{K}_{X,T} \vdash \mathbf{i}(R, T)$ *iff* $\mathcal{K}_{X,T} \vdash \neg have(R, T) \land \mathcal{K}_{X,T} \vdash \neg need(R, T)$

In the sequel, unless otherwise specified, we will not assume any specific definition of "have" and "need", but we will assume that, for any agent X, time T and resource R, either $\mathcal{K}_{X,T} \vdash have(R, T)$ or $\mathcal{K}_{X,T} \vdash \neg have(R, T)$ and either $\mathcal{K}_{X,T} \vdash need(R, T)$ or $\mathcal{K}_{X,T} \vdash \neg need(R, T)$.

State transitions, as a result of dialogues, can be characterised in terms of **a**, **m**, **n**, **i**.

In general, after a terminated request dialogue D between X and Y, initiated by X with respect to a resource R and an intention $\mathcal{I}_X$, X might have been successful or not in obtaining the resource R from Y: Let us suppose that D

started at time T and terminated at time $T1$, and let $T' > T1$. If D is successful, the knowledge bases of X and Y change as follows:

$\mathcal{K}_{X,T} \vdash \mathbf{m}(R,T)$ and $\mathcal{K}_{X,T'} \vdash \mathbf{n}(R,T')$

$\mathcal{K}_{Y,T} \vdash \mathbf{a}(R,T)$ and $\mathcal{K}_{Y,T'} \vdash \mathbf{i}(R,T')$.

If D has been unsuccessful, then neither agents' knowledge about resources changes, and X might decide to engage in a new dialogue to obtain R from a different agent.

While dialogues can be characterised by the initial and final states of the knowledge of the participants, negotiation policies can be characterised by the possible dialogues (with consequent changes in states) that they generate:

Definition 9. An agent X is called *self-interested* if, for all request dialogues D, with respect to a resource R, between agents X and Y starting at time T and terminating at time $T1$, and for any time T' such that $T < T1 < T'$:

- if $\mathcal{K}_{X,T} \vdash \mathbf{a}(R,T)$ then either $\mathcal{K}_{X,T'} \vdash \mathbf{a}(R,T')$ or $\mathcal{K}_{X,T'} \vdash \mathbf{i}(R,T')$;
- if $\mathcal{K}_{X,T} \vdash \mathbf{m}(R,T)$ then either $\mathcal{K}_{X,T'} \vdash \mathbf{m}(R,T')$ or $\mathcal{K}_{X,T'} \vdash \mathbf{n}(R,T')$;
- if $\mathcal{K}_{X,T} \vdash \mathbf{n}(R,T)$ then $\mathcal{K}_{X,T'} \vdash \mathbf{n}(R,T')$;
- if $\mathcal{K}_{X,T} \vdash \mathbf{i}(R,T)$ then either $\mathcal{K}_{X,T'} \vdash \mathbf{i}(R,T')$ or $\mathcal{K}_{X,T'} \vdash \mathbf{a}(R,T')$;
- for all $\hat{R} \in \mathcal{R}(\mathcal{I}_X)$, $\hat{R} \neq R$, then
  if $\mathcal{K}_{X,T} \vdash \mathbf{a}(\hat{R},T)$ then either $\mathcal{K}_{X,T'} \vdash \mathbf{a}(\hat{R},T')$ or $\mathcal{K}_{X,T'} \vdash \mathbf{i}(\hat{R},T')$,
  if $\mathcal{K}_{X,T} \vdash \mathbf{m}(\hat{R},T)$ then either $\mathcal{K}_{X,T'} \vdash \mathbf{m}(\hat{R},T')$ or $\mathcal{K}_{X,T'} \vdash \mathbf{n}(\hat{R},T')$,
  if $\mathcal{K}_{X,T} \vdash \mathbf{n}(\hat{R},T)$ then $\mathcal{K}_{X,T'} \vdash \mathbf{n}(\hat{R},T')$;
  if $\mathcal{K}_{X,T} \vdash \mathbf{i}(\hat{R},T)$ then either $\mathcal{K}_{X,T'} \vdash \mathbf{i}(\hat{R},T')$ or $\mathcal{K}_{X,T'} \vdash \mathbf{a}(\hat{R},T')$.

Note that the main characteristic of self-interested agents is that they never give away resources they need.

4   An Operational Model for the Agent Reasoning and Dialogue Cycle

We give an operational model of the negotiation framework, consisting of an abductive logic program [1] for $\mathcal{K}$, an abductive proof-procedure for agent reasoning, and an agent cycle for interleaving reasoning with observing and acting.

An abductive logic program is a triple $\langle T, Ab, IC \rangle$, where T is a *logic program*, namely a set of if-rules of the form $H \leftarrow C$, where H is an atom and C is a conjunction of literals, and every variable is universally quantified from the outside; IC is a set of *integrity constraints*, namely if-then-rules of the form $C \Rightarrow H$, where C is a conjunction of literals and H is an atom, and every variable is universally quantified from the outside; Ab is a set of ground atoms, whose predicates, that we call "abducibles", occur in T or IC, but not in the head H of any if-rule. The knowledge $\mathcal{K}$ of an agent can be represented as an abductive logic program as follows. Ground dialogue moves are represented as abducibles. Dialogue constraints are represented as integrity constraints[3].

---

[3] Note that dialogue constraints do not conform to the syntax of integrity constraints, but they can be written so that they do. A dialogue constraint $p(D,T) \wedge C \Rightarrow [\exists T'(\hat{p}(D,T') \wedge T < T')]$ can be rewritten as $p(D,T) \wedge C \Rightarrow q(D,T)$ together with an if-rule $q(D,T) \leftarrow \hat{p}(D,T') \wedge T < T'$ in the logic program component of the abductive logic program representing $\mathcal{K}$.

To cycle at time T,

   (*i*) [observe] **observe any input** at time T, and put it in *input*;
      (*i*.1) [filter observations] if *input* = $\emptyset$, then go to (*iv*);
      (*i*.2) [filter observations] if *ongoing*=D, $D \neq nil$ and either $\nexists\, p \in$ input such that $p = tell(X, a, Subject, D, T)$ or not *waiting*, then go to (*iv*);
   (*ii*) [record input] if *ongoing*=D then **record an input** $b \in$ *input* such that $b = tell(X, a, Subject, D, T)$; otherwise, if *ongoing*=*nil* (reply to a new dialogue D'): **record an input** $p \in$ *input* (say, $p = tell(X, a, Subject, D', T)$), and set *ongoing*=$D'$ to true;
      (*ii*.1) [update dialogue status] if p is a final move then set *ongoing*=*nil*, otherwise set *waiting* to false;
   (*iii*) [think] **resume ST** by propagating the inputs, if any;
   (*iv*) [think] **continue applying ST**, for a total of r units of time;
      (*iv*.1) [filter actions] if there does not exist an atomic action which can be executed at time $T' = T + r$, or if *waiting*, then go to step (*vii*);
      (*iv*.2) [filter actions] if *ongoing*=D and $D \neq nil$ and there does not exist an atomic action $tell(a, X, Subject, D, T)$ which can be executed at time $T' = T + r$, then go to step (*vii*);
   (*v*) [select action] if *ongoing*=D and $D \neq nil$ then **select an atomic action** $tell(a, X, Subject, D, T'')$ that is an abducible computed by ST which can be executed at time $T' = T + r$ and instantiate T'' to T'; otherwise, if *ongoing*=*nil* (start a new dialogue D'): **select an atomic action** $tell(a, X, Subject, D', T'')$ that is an abducible computed by ST which can be executed at time $T' = T + r$, instantiate T'' to T' and set *ongoing*=D';
      (*v*.1) [update dialogue status] if the selected action is a final move then set *ongoing*=*nil*, otherwise set *waiting* to true;
   (*vi*) [act] **execute the selected action** at time T' and record the result;
   (*vii*) [cycle] **cycle** at time $T' + 1$.

Fig. 1. Extended agent cycle for an agent a

The rest of the knowledge $\mathcal{K}$ of agents is split between the logic program and the integrity constraints.

We use the proof-procedure of [4], henceforth called ST, which is a modification of the IFF proof-procedure [3]. The IFF procedure forms the reasoning engine of the agents of the architecture of [2] that we adopt and modify, as we will explain later. IFF and ST share inference rules that allow *backward reasoning* with the logic programs and *forward reasoning*, modus ponens-like, with the integrity constraints. IFF proved inadequate for the purpose of producing dialogues as defined in section 2, in that it fails to produce the triggering and firing (production/active rule) behaviour of dialogue constraints that we describe in Section 2. This is due to the definition of *negation rewriting* in [3], that replaces an if-then-rule $[\neg A \Rightarrow B]$ with the disjunction $A \vee B$. To illustrate the problem, consider a dialogue (integrity) constraint $requested\_resource \wedge have\_resource \Rightarrow accept\_request$, where $have\_resource$ is defined as $have\_initially \wedge \neg gave\_away$.

Given *requested_resource* and *have_initially*, the constraint would be rewritten by IFF as *gave_away* ∨ *accept_request*. The second disjunct could be selected, and the request accepted, even in the case the resource has already been given away.

ST modifies IFF in the handling of negation in if-then-rules. The modification involves replacing an if-then-rule ¬A ⇒ B with the disjunction [*provable*(A)] ∨ [(A ⇒ *false*) ∧ B], which results in achieving a "negation as failure" behaviour for the negations in if-then-rules, more appropriate for the production/active rule behaviour required. For a detailed description of ST see [4].

In the architecture of [2], each agent, henceforth referred to as KS-agent, is an abductive logic program. The abducibles are *actions* to be executed as well as *observations* to be performed. In our case, actions are dialogue moves uttered by the agent, and observations are dialogue moves uttered by other agents. The behaviour of KS-agents is regulated by an observe-think-act cycle. The cycle starts at time T by observing and recording any observations from the environment. Then, the proof procedure is applied for r units of time. The amount of resources r available in the "think" phase is predefined. Forward reasoning is applied first, in order to allow for an appropriate reaction to the observations. Then, an action is selected and executed, in the "act" phase, taking care of recording the result.

We modify the agent cycle of [2] to enforce atomicity and interleaving of dialogues, as discusses in Section 1. The modified cycle for an agent a is in Figure 1. This is a modification of the original KS agent cycle in that filtering/updating steps are added, according to the state of the dialogue, for what concerns both the recording of an incoming dialogue move and the possible uttering of an outgoing move. It is worth noticing that such modifications are independent of the thinking part of the agent, namely the application of the proof-procedure. Also, in our cycle we make the simplifying assumption that time is only consumed by the application of the proof procedure, and not by the decisions about whether or not to process observations and whether or not to execute an action.

In order to enforce the properties of atomicity and interleaving, we use the following data structures:

- an input buffer, *input*, that contains all the observed predicates (namely the incoming dialogue moves) that have not yet been recorded by the agent;
- a flag *ongoing*, that either contains the identifier of the ongoing dialogue, or the constant *nil*, i.e., a new identifier that is not any dialogue identifier. Initially, *ongoing* is set to *nil*;
- a flag *waiting/0*, initially false, that is true if the agent is expecting a dialogue move from another agent within an ongoing dialogue.

Note that a move p with dialogue identifier D, observed during step i of the cycle is recorded (in step ii) only if the agent is not already involved in another dialogue, or if there is an ongoing dialogue D and p is a move of D. Also, the agent can utter a move p only if there is no ongoing dialogue (p is the first utterance of a new dialogue), or there is an ongoing dialogue D, and p is part of it.

In order for agents to generate sequences of dialogues with the properties $\mathcal{P}$ given in Section 2, the dialogue cycle of the agents may be specified by the following abductive logic program:

$$
\begin{aligned}
&\textbf{(D.5)} \quad get\_all(M) \leftarrow M = \emptyset \\
&\phantom{\textbf{(D.5)}} \quad get\_all(M) \leftarrow R \in M \wedge get(R) \wedge R' = M \setminus \{R\} \wedge get\_all(R') \\
&\textbf{(D.6)} \quad get(R) \leftarrow agents(A) \wedge ask\_agents(A, R) \\
&\textbf{(D.7)} \quad ask\_agents(A, R) \leftarrow X \in A \wedge tell(a, X, request(give(R)), d(a, X, R, T), T) \\
&\phantom{\textbf{(D.7)} \quad ask\_agents(A, R) \leftarrow} \wedge A' = A \setminus \{X\} \wedge process(X, A', R, d(a, X, R, T), T) \\
&\textbf{(D.8)} \quad process(X, A, R, D, T) \leftarrow tell(X, a, accept(request(give(R))), D, T') \\
&\phantom{\textbf{(D.8)}} \quad process(X, A, R, D, T) \leftarrow tell(X, a, refuse(request(give(R))), D, T') \wedge \\
&\phantom{\textbf{(D.8)} \quad process} ask\_agents(A, R) \\
&\textbf{(D.9)} \quad to\_be\_asked(M) \leftarrow plan(\_, Req) \wedge missing(Req, \emptyset, M) \\
&\textbf{(D.10)} \quad missing(Set, Acc, Out) \leftarrow Set = \emptyset \wedge Out = Acc \\
&\phantom{\textbf{(D.10)}} \quad missing(R \cup Set, Acc, Out) \leftarrow have(R, 0) \wedge missing(Set, Acc, Out) \\
&\phantom{\textbf{(D.10)}} \quad missing(R \cup Set, Acc, Out) \leftarrow \neg have(R, 0) \wedge missing(Set, Acc \cup \{R\}, Out) \\
&\textbf{(D.11)} \quad X \in Y \leftarrow Y = [X|X'] \\
&\\
&\textbf{(IC.4)} \quad to\_be\_asked(M) \Rightarrow get\_all(M) \\
&\textbf{(IC.5)} \quad ask\_for(A, R) \wedge A = \emptyset \Rightarrow \bot
\end{aligned}
$$

The two integrity constraints are used to start the negotiation process (IC.4) from the missing resources of the agent's plan, and to determine failure (IC.5) once the agent has failed to get a specific resource after asking all the agents in the system (but itself). Note that definition D.7 performs the allocation of a unique dialogue identifier to a newly started dialogue. This identifier is a function(d) of the agent starting the dialogue, the receiver of the request, the requested resource and the time of the utterance. Note also that definition D.11 assumes a list-like implementation of sets.

5   Formal Results

We define the following agent types and give some formal results.

Definition 10. An abductive agent X is exhaustive and deterministic if X produces one and only one ground move, in response to any non-final move of other agents of which X is the receiver.

Definition 11. An *abductive agent* is an agent whose *knowledge base* $\mathcal{K}$ is an abductive logic program, with, in particular, the dialogue moves in the negotiation language $\mathcal{L}$ of the agent represented as abducibles in the abductive logic program, the dialogue constraints in $\mathcal{K}$ represented as integrity constraints in the abductive logic program, equipped with the *ST abductive proof-procedure* as its reasoning engine with the entailment $\mathcal{K}$ is equipped with provided by provability in ST, and with the *extended agent cycle*.

An $\mathcal{N}$-*agent* is a particular instance of an abductive agent whose logic program consists of definitions D.1-D.4, appropriate definition for **a, m, n, i**, and integrity constraints IC.1-IC.3.

An $\mathcal{N}^+$-*agent* is an $\mathcal{N}$-agent whose knowledge is extended by the dialogue cycle given by D.5-D.11 and IC.4-IC.5.

Theorem 1 If X is an $\mathcal{N}$-agent, then $\mathcal{K}_X$ is exhaustive and deterministic.

Theorem 2 $\mathcal{N}$-agents are self-interested agents.

Theorem 3 If X is an abductive agent and $\mathcal{K}_X$ is exhaustive and deterministic then X is exhaustive and deterministic.

Corollary 1. $\mathcal{N}$-agents are exhaustive and deterministic.

Theorem 4 $\mathcal{N}^+$-agents are self-interested agents.

Theorem 5 If X is an $\mathcal{N}^+$-agent, then $\mathcal{K}_X$ is exhaustive and deterministic.

Corollary 2. $\mathcal{N}^+$-agents are exhaustive and deterministic.   We prove that the framework described in Section 4 is capable of generating dialogues, provided that the agents in the system are exhaustive and deterministic with respect to the negotiation language. In fact, if an agent X is exhaustive and deterministic, then X will produce *exactly one* reply to a (non final) move made by the other agent. If both agents involved in a dialogue are exhaustive and deterministic, then exactly one agent is guaranteed to produce only one dialogue move, after a dialogue is initiated by either agent, until a final move is made, thus producing a dialogue that conforms to the definition given in Section 1.

Theorem 6 (*production of dialogues*) Let X and Y be two agents sharing a language $\mathcal{L}$ for negotiation. Suppose X and Y are both deterministic and exhaustive. Let $S = \{p_1, p_2, \ldots, p_n\}$ be the sequence of all utterances between X and Y (i.e., for each p_i the utterer is either X or Y and the receiver is either X or Y) such that the p_i all share the same identifier D. Then S is a dialogue according to Definition 5.

6   Conclusions

We have presented a framework for agent dialogue and negotiation based on abductive reasoning. In order to provide an operational model for the framework, we introduced a modified version of the agent cycle of [2], with respect to the proof-procedure introduced in [4], rather than the IFF that [2] chooses to adopt. Our model is able to produce sequences of negotiation dialogues that conform to the given definition.

Following other related work on agent dialogue, we defined dialogue in a two-agents setting. It is possible to extend it to accommodate multi-part negotiation schemes, e.g. by means of auction-like interaction patterns, but this goes beyond the scope of this paper. Some work done in this direction is that of [7]. Among the current approaches to negotiation via dialogue, our work is to the best of our knowledge the only one that is based on abductive logic programming. An approach to agent communication and negotiation that makes use of abduction is proposed in [8], where the authors use deduction to derive information from a received message, and abduction to obtain proposals in reply to requests. In our framework, abduction is used not only to formulate replies to requests, but it is the main form of agent reasoning. This allows us to prove Theorem 6.

Kraus et al. [9], Amgoud et al. [10] and Parsons et al. [11] are some of the argumentation-based approaches proposed to agent negotiation. In general, such approaches, focused on argumentation and persuasion, lead to different results from ours, being somewhat more descriptive, and not aiming to determine specific properties of the policy regulations.

The innovative contribution of our work is in the definition of the operational model, including the proposed agent cycle and dialogue cycle, and in the results that apply in the general case of abductive agents and in the specific case of $\mathcal{N}$-systems. We consider this to be an important achievement, because it provides a high-level specification of a system that is directly implementable, and that guarantees certain properties to hold. On the other hand, since we prose a complete approach to a complex problem such as resource reallocation, a weak point of this work could be its scalability, if we want to apply it to the case, for instance, of agents that can can dynamically modify their plans. To cope with huge search spaces, we believe that we could profitably build on the formal results of our work and apply incomplete search methods like those based on metaheuristics. Some work has already been done towards the combination of the two approaches [12]. In the future, we aim at extending our framework to cope with exchange of uncountable resources, or of resources that may have a different "meaning" for autonomous reasoning agents, such as information.

Acknowledgements

We would like to thank Bob Kowalski for his interest in this work and for helpful discussions and suggestions about the dialogue cycle, and the anonymous referees for their helpful comments. This work has been supported by the EU funded project IST-2001-32530, Societies Of ComputeeS (SOCS), and by the Marco Polo research grant (University of Bologna).

References

1. Kakas, A.C., Kowalski, R.A., Toni, F.: The role of abduction in logic programming. Handbook of Logic in AI and Logic Programming **5** (1998) 235–324
2. Kowalski, R.A., Sadri, F.: From logic programming to multi-agent systems. Annals of Mathematics and AI (1999)
3. Fung, T.H., Kowalski, R.A.: The IFF proof procedure for abductive logic programming. Journal of Logic Programming (1997)
4. Sadri, F., Toni, F.: Abduction with negation as failure for active and reactive rules. In Proc. AI*IA'99. LNAI 1792, Springer-Verlag (2000) 49–60
5. Sadri, F., Toni, F., Torroni, P.: Dialogues for negotiation: agent varieties and dialogue sequences. In: Intelligent Agents VIII. LNAI 2333, Springer-Verlag (2002)
6. Sadri, F., Toni, F., Torroni, P.: Logic agents, dialogues and negotiation: an abductive approach. In: Proc. AISB'01 Convention, York, UK. (2001)
7. Torroni, P., Toni, F.: Extending a logic based one-to-one negotiation framework to one-to-many negotiation. In: ESAW II. LNAI 2203, Springer-Verlag (2001)

8. Hindriks, K., de Boer, F., van der Hoek, W., Meyer, J.: Semantics of communicating agents based on deduction and abduction. In: Proc. CABS. (1999)
9. Kraus, S., Sycara, K., Evenchik, A.: Reaching agreements through argumentation; a logical model and implementation. Artificial Intelligence **104** (1998) 1–69
10. Amgoud, L., Parsons, S., Maudet, N.: Arguments, dialogue and negotiation. In: Proc. 14th ECAI, Berlin, Germany, IOS Press (2000)
11. Parsons, S., Sierra, C., Jennings, N.R.: Agents that reason and negotiate by arguing. Journal of Logic and Computation **8** (1998) 261–292
12. Roli, A., Torroni, P.: Logics, local search and resource allocation (short paper). In: Proc. STAIRS, Lyon, France. (2002)

Preferred Answer Sets for Ordered Logic Programs

Davy Van Nieuwenborgh* and Dirk Vermeir

Dept. of Computer Science
Vrije Universiteit Brussel, VUB
{dvnieuwe,dvermeir}@vub.ac.be

Abstract. We extend answer set semantics to deal with inconsistent programs (containing classical negation), by finding a "best" answer set. Within the context of inconsistent programs, it is natural to have a partial order on rules, representing a preference for satisfying certain rules, possibly at the cost of violating less important ones. We show that such a rule order induces a natural order on extended answer sets, the minimal elements of which we call preferred answer sets. We characterize the expressiveness of the resulting semantics and show that it can simulate negation as failure as well as disjunction. We illustrate an application of the approach by considering database repairs, where minimal repairs are shown to correspond to preferred answer sets.

1 Introduction

The intuition behind the stable model semantics, and, more generally, behind answer set semantics for (extended) logic programs is both intuitive and elegant. Given a program P and a candidate answer set M, one computes a reduct program P_M of a simpler type for which a semantics $P_M^\star$ is known. The reduct P_M is obtained from P by taking into account the consequences of accepting the proposed truth values of the literals in M. The candidate set M is then an answer set just when $P_M^\star = M$, i.e. M is "self-supporting".

In this paper, we apply this reduction technique to deal with inconsistent programs, e.g. programs with (only) classical negation (denoted as $\neg$) where the immediate consequence operator would yield inconsistent interpretations. For example, computing the least fixpoint of the program $\{a \leftarrow, b \leftarrow, \neg a \leftarrow b\}$, where negative literals $\neg a$ are considered as fresh atoms, yields the inconsistent $\{a, b, \neg a\}$. To prevent this, we will allow for a rule to be defeated by an opposing rule w.r.t. an interpretation. In the example, $\{a, b\}$ will be accepted because the rule $\neg a \leftarrow b$ is defeated by the rule $a \leftarrow$. The definition of answer set remains the same (see, e.g., [7]), but the reduct is restricted to rules that are not defeated. We show that the semantics thus obtained can be simulated by an extended logic program $E(P)$ that is trivially constructed from the original program P.

The above technique can be generalized to ordered programs where a partial order, representing preference or specificity, is defined on the rules of a program. E.g. one may prefer certain "constraint" rules to be satisfied, possibly at the expense of defeating

---

* Supported by the FWO

S. Flesca et al. (Eds.): JELIA 2002, LNAI 2424, pp. 432–443, 2002.
© Springer-Verlag Berlin Heidelberg 2002

less important "optional" or "default" rules. We show that such a preference structure on the rules induces a natural partial order on the reducts of the program, and hence on its candidate answer sets. Minimal elements in this induced partial order are called preferred answer sets.

The resulting semantics for ordered programs has applications in several areas. E.g. we show that the minimal repairs of a database D [1] w.r.t. a set of constraints C correspond with the preferred answer sets of an ordered program $P(D, C)$ that can be trivially constructed out of D and C.

The remainder of this paper is organized as follows: Section 2 extends the usual answer set semantics to cover also inconsistent programs. In Section 3, we introduce ordered programs where rules are partially ordered according to preference. It is shown that the rule-order induces a partial order on extended answer sets. The minimal elements in the latter order are called preferred answer sets. We characterize the expressiveness of the resulting semantics and show that it can simulate negation as failure as well as disjunction. Section 4 proposes an algorithm to compute such preferred answer sets and shows that the complexity of deciding whether there exists a proper preferred answer set containing a given atom is Σ_2^P-complete. Section 5 illustrates the use of preferred answer set semantics in solving database repair problems. We believe that our approach may have further natural applications, e.g. in diagnostic systems [8,2] where the order can be used to differentiate between the normal and fault models of the system. Due to space restrictions, all proofs and a full account of relationships with other approaches had to be omitted.

2 Extended Answer Sets for Simple Programs

In this section, we consider simple programs, e.g. logic programs with only classical negation (and no disjunction in the head of a rule).

We use the following basic definitions and notation. A *literal* is an *atom* a or a negated atom $\neg a$. For a set of literals X we use $\neg X$ to denote $\{\neg p \mid p \in X\}$ where $\neg(\neg a) \equiv a$. Also, X^+ denotes the positive part of X, i.e. $X^+ = \{a \in X \mid a \text{ is an atom}\}$. The *Herbrand base* of X, denoted $\mathcal{B}_X$, contains all atoms appearing in X, i.e. $\mathcal{B}_X = (X \cup \neg X)^+$. A set I of literals is *consistent* if $I \cap \neg I = \emptyset$.

The following definitions (see, e.g. [7]) will also be useful. A *disjunctive logic program* (DLP) is a countable set of rules of the form $\alpha \leftarrow \beta, not(\gamma)$ where α and $\alpha \cup \beta \cup \gamma$ are nonempty finite sets of literals (we use *not* to denote negation as failure, $not(\gamma)$ is an abbreviation for $\{not(c) \mid c \in \gamma\}$). If α is always a singleton, we drop the "disjunctive" qualification. If, for all rules, all literals in $\alpha \cup \beta \cup \gamma$ are atoms, the program is called *seminegative* and if, furthermore, $\gamma = \emptyset$, the program is said to be *positive*. An *interpretation* for a DLP is any consistent set of literals (for seminegative programs, we can restrict to a set of atoms).

For a DLP P without negation as failure ($\gamma = \emptyset$), an *answer set* is a minimal interpretation I that is *closed* under the rules of P (i.e. for a rule $\alpha \leftarrow \beta$, $\alpha \cap I \neq \emptyset$ whenever $\beta \subseteq I$). For a DLP P containing negation as failure and an interpretation I, the Gelfond-Lifschitz transformation [4] yields the *reduct* program P^I that consists of those rules $\alpha \leftarrow \beta$ where $\alpha \leftarrow \beta, not(\gamma)$ is in P and $\gamma \cap I = \emptyset$ (note that all rules in P^I

are free from negation as failure). An interpretation I is then an *answer set* of P iff I is an answer set of the reduct P^I.

Simple logic programs are logic programs without negation as failure.

Definition 1. *A **simple logic program** (SLP) is a countable set P of **rules** of the form $a \leftarrow \alpha$ where $\{a\} \cup \alpha$ is a finite set of literals[1].*

*The **Herbrand base** B_P of P contains all atoms appearing in P. An **interpretation** I of P is any consistent subset of $B_P \cup \neg B_P$. An interpretation I is **total** if $B_P \subseteq I \cup \neg I$.*

*A rule $r = a \leftarrow \alpha$ is **satisfied** by I, denoted $I \models r$, if $\{a\} \subseteq I$ whenever $\alpha \subseteq I$, i.e. if r is **applicable** $(\alpha \subseteq I)$ then it must be **applied** $(\alpha \cup \{a\} \subseteq I)$. The rule r is **defeated** w.r.t. I iff there exists an applied **competing rule** $\neg a \leftarrow \alpha'$ in P, such a rule is said to defeat r.*

Thus, a rule $r = a \leftarrow \alpha$ cannot be left unsatisfied unless one accepts the opposite conclusion $\neg a$ which is motivated by a competing applied rule $\neg a \leftarrow \alpha'$ that *defeats* r.

Example 1. Consider the SLP P_1 containing the rules $\neg a \leftarrow$, $\neg b \leftarrow$, $a \leftarrow \neg b$, and $b \leftarrow \neg a$. For the interpretation $I = \{\neg a, b\}$ we have that I satisfies all rules in P_1 but one: $\neg a \leftarrow$ and $b \leftarrow \neg a$ are applied while $a \leftarrow \neg b$ is not applicable. The unsatisfied rule $\neg b \leftarrow$ is defeated by $b \leftarrow \neg a$.

For a set of rules R, we use $R^\star$ to denote the unique minimal[10] model of the positive logic program consisting of the rules in R where negative literals $\neg a$ are considered as fresh atoms. This operator is monotonic, i.e. if $R \subseteq Q$ then $R^\star \subseteq Q^\star$.

For the program of Example 1, we have that $P_1^\star = \{\neg a, \neg b, a, b\}$ is inconsistent. The following definition allows us to not apply certain rules, when computing a consistent interpretation for programs such as P_1.

Definition 2. *The reduct $P_I \subseteq P$ of P w.r.t. I contains just the rules satisfied by I, i.e. $P_I = \{r \in P \mid I \models r\}$. An interpretation I is **founded** if $P_I^\star = I$.*

*A founded interpretation I is an **extended answer set** of P if all rules in P are satisfied or defeated.*

Thus, extended answer set semantics deals with inconsistency in a simple yet intuitive way: when faced with contradictory applicable rules, just select one for application and ignore (defeat) the other. In the absence of extra information (e.g. regarding a preference for satisfying certain rules at the expense of others), this seems a reasonable strategy for extracting a consistent semantics from inconsistent programs.

Using the above definition, it is easy to verify that the program P_1 from Example 1 has three extended answer sets, namely $M_1 = \{\neg a, b\}$, $M_2 = \{a, \neg b\}$ and $M_3 = \{\neg a, \neg b\}$. Note that $P_{1 M_1} = P_1 \setminus \{\neg b \leftarrow\}$ while $P_{1 M_2} = P_1 \setminus \{\neg a \leftarrow\}$, and $P_{1 M_3} = P_1 \setminus \{a \leftarrow \neg b, b \leftarrow \neg a\}$, i.e. $\neg b \leftarrow$ is defeated w.r.t. M_1, $\neg a \leftarrow$ is defeated w.r.t. M_2 and both $a \leftarrow \neg b$ and $b \leftarrow \neg a$ are defeated w.r.t. M_3.

The definition of extended answer set is rather similar to the definition of answer sets for (non-disjunctive) programs without negation as failure; the only non-technical difference being that, for extended answer sets, a rule may be left unsatisfied if it is defeated by a competing (i.e. a rule with opposite head) rule. This is confirmed by the following theorem.

---

[1] As usual, we assume that programs have already been grounded.

Theorem 1. *Let P be a simple logic program and let M be an answer set of P Then M is the unique extended answer set of P.*

While allowing for P_M, with M an extended answer set, to be a strict subset of P, Definition 2 still maximizes the set of satisfied rules w.r.t. an extended answer set.

Theorem 2. *Let P be a simple logic program and let M be an extended answer set for P. Then P_M is maximal among the reducts of founded interpretations of P.*

The reverse of Theorem 2 does not hold in general, as can be seen from the following example.

Example 2. Consider the program P_2 containing the following rules.

$$\neg a \leftarrow$$
$$b \leftarrow$$
$$\neg b \leftarrow \neg a$$

The interpretation $N = \{b\}$ is founded with $P_{2N} = \{b \leftarrow, \neg b \leftarrow \neg a\}$ which is obviously maximal since $P_2^\star$ is inconsistent. Still, N is not an extended answer set because $\neg a \leftarrow$ is not defeated.

However, for total interpretations, founded interpretations with maximal reducts are extended answer sets.

Theorem 3. *Let P be a simple logic program and let M be a total founded interpretation such that P_M is maximal among the reducts of founded interpretations of P. Then M is an extended answer set.*

The computation of extended answer sets reduces to the computation of answer sets for seminegative non-disjunctive logic programs, using the following transformation, which is similar to the one used in [5] for logic programs with exceptions.

Definition 3. *Let P be a SLP. The **extended version** $E(P)$ of P is the (non-disjunctive) logic program obtained from P by replacing each rule $a \leftarrow \alpha$ by its extended version $a \leftarrow \alpha, not(\neg a)$.*

Note that the above definition captures our intuition about defeat: one can ignore an applicable rule $a \leftarrow \alpha$ if it is defeated by evidence for the contrary $\neg a$, thus making $not(\neg a)$ false and the rule $a \leftarrow \alpha, not(\neg a)$ not applicable.

Theorem 4. *Let P be an SLP. The extended answer sets of P coincide with the answer sets of $E(P)$.*

Let P be a simple program. Consider the function $\delta_P : 2^{\mathcal{B}_P} \to 2^{\mathcal{B}_P}$ where $\delta_P(I) = \{a \notin I \mid \neg a \notin I \wedge (a \leftarrow \alpha) \in P \wedge \alpha \subseteq I\}$. Clearly, any sequence $I_0 = \emptyset, I_1, \ldots$ where, for $i \geq 0$, $I_{i+1} = I_i \cup \{a\}$ for some $a \in \delta_P(I_i)$ if $\delta_P(I_i) \neq \emptyset$, and $I_{i+1} = I_i$ otherwise, is monotonically increasing and thus reaches a fixpoint $I_\star$ which is easily seen to be an extended answer set. Hence the extended answer set semantics is universal.

Theorem 5. *Each simple logic program has extended answer sets.*

3   Ordered Programs and Preferred Answer Sets

When constructing extended answer sets for simple logic programs, one can defeat any rule for which there is an applied competing rule. In many cases, however, there is a clear preference among rules in the sense that one would rather defeat less preferred rules in order to keep the more preferred ones satisfied.

As an example, reconsider the program P_1 from Example 1 and assume that we prefer not to defeat the rules with positive conclusion ($\{a \leftarrow \neg b,\ b \leftarrow \neg a\}$). Semantically, this should result in the rejection of $M_3 = \{\neg a, \neg b\}$ in favor of either $M_1 = \{\neg a, b\}$ or $M_2 = \{a, \neg b\}$ because the latter two sets are consistent with our preferences.

In ordered programs, such preferences are represented by a partial order on the rules of the program.

Definition 4. *An **ordered logic program** (OLP) is a pair $\langle R, < \rangle$ where R is a a simple program and $<$ is a well-founded strict[2] partial order on the rules in R[3]. For subsets R_1 and R_2 of R we define $R_1 \sqsubseteq R_2$ iff $\forall r_2 \in R_2 \setminus R_1 \cdot \exists r_1 \in R_1 \setminus R_2 \cdot r_1 < r_2$. We write $R_1 \sqsubset R_2$ just when $R_1 \sqsubseteq R_2$ and $R_1 \neq R_2$.*

In the examples we will often represent the order implicitly using the format

$$\frac{\begin{array}{c} \cdots \\ \hline R_2 \\ \hline R_1 \end{array}}{R_0}$$

where each R_i, $i \geq 0$, represents a set of rules, indicating that all rules below a line are more preferred than any of the rules above the line, i.e. $\forall i \geq 0 \cdot \forall r_i \in R_i \cdot \forall r_{i+1} \in R_{i+1} \cdot r_i < r_{i+1}$ or $\forall i \geq 0 \cdot R_i < R_{i+1}$ for short.

Intuitively, $r_1 < r_2$ indicates that r_1 is more preferred than r_2 while the definition of $\sqsubset$ shows how this preference carries over to reducts: a reduct R_1 is preferred over a reduct R_2 if every rule r_2 which is in R_2 but not in R_1 is "countered" by a stronger rule $r_1 < r_2$ from R_1 which is not in R_2. Note that, unlike other approaches, e.g. [6], we do not require that r_1 is applied and neither does r_1 need to be a competitor of r_2, as illustrated in the following example.

Example 3. Consider $P_4 = \langle R, < \rangle$, were R is shown below and the interpretations $M_1 = \{study, pass\}$, $M_2 = \{\neg study, pass\}$, $M_3 = \{\neg study, \neg pass\}$, and $M_4 = \{study, \neg pass\}$. The program indicates a preference for not studying, a strong desire to pass[4] and an equally strong (and uncomfortable) suspicion that not studying leads to failure.

---

[2] A strict partial order $<$ on a set X is a binary relation on X that is antisymmetric, anti-reflexive and transitive. The relation $<$ is well-founded if every nonempty subset of X has a $<$-minimal element.

[3] Strictly speaking, we should allow R to be a multiset or, equivalently, have labeled rules, so that the same rule can appear in several positions in the order. For the sake of simplicity of notation, we will ignore this issue in the present paper: all results also hold for the general multiset case.

[4] Note that the rule $pass \leftarrow \neg pass$ can only be satisfied by an interpretation containing $pass$, *without* providing a justification for it.

$$r_4 : pass \leftarrow study$$
$$r_3 : study \leftarrow$$
$$\overline{r_2 : \neg study \leftarrow}$$
$$r_1 : \neg pass \leftarrow \neg study$$
$$r_0 : pass \leftarrow \neg pass$$

It is easily verified that $R_{M_1} \sqsubseteq R_{M_2}$, $R_{M_1} \sqsubseteq R_{M_3}$, $R_{M_1} \sqsubseteq R_{M_4}$ (vacuously) and $R_{M_3} \sqsubseteq R_{M_4}$. Here, e.g. $R_{M_1} = \{r_0, r_1, r_3, r_4\} \sqsubseteq R_{M_2} = \{r_0, r_2, r_4\}$ because $r_2 \in R_{M_2} \setminus R_{M_1}$ is countered by $r_1 \in R_{M_1} \setminus R_{M_2}$ which is neither applied nor a competitor of r_2.

The following theorem implies that the relation $\sqsubseteq$ is a partial order on reducts.

Theorem 6. *Let $<$ be a well-founded strict partial order on a set X. The binary relation $\sqsubseteq$ on 2^X defined by $X_1 \sqsubseteq X_2$ iff $\forall x_2 \in X_2 \setminus X_1 \cdot \exists x_1 \in X_1 \setminus X_2 \cdot x_1 < x_2$ is a partial order.*

Preferred answer sets for ordered programs correspond to minimal reducts in the $\sqsubseteq$-partial order that is induced by the rule preference order.

Definition 5. *Let $P = \langle R, < \rangle$ be an ordered logic program. A **preferred answer set** for P is any extended answer set M of R such that R_M is minimal w.r.t $\sqsubseteq$ among the reducts of all extended answer sets of R. An extended answer set is **proper** if it satisfies all minimal (according to $<$) rules in R.*

Proper extended answer sets respect the strongest (minimal) rules of the program. The following theorem confirms that taking the minimal (according to the $\sqsubseteq$ order on the corresponding reducts) elements among the proper extended answer sets is equivalent to selecting the proper elements among the preferred answer sets.

Theorem 7. *Let P be an ordered program. The set of minimal proper extended answer sets of P coincides with the set of proper preferred answer sets of P.*

In Example 3, $M_1 = \{pass, study\}$ is the only proper preferred answer set.

Example 4. Consider the ordered program $\langle P_1, < \rangle$ where P_1 is as in Example 1 and $<$ is as shown below.

$$\neg a \leftarrow$$
$$\neg b \leftarrow$$
$$\overline{a \leftarrow \neg b}$$
$$b \leftarrow \neg a$$

The reducts of the extended answer sets of P_1 are $P_{1 M_1} = P_1 \setminus \{\neg b \leftarrow\}$, $P_{1 M_2} = P_1 \setminus \{\neg a \leftarrow\}$, and $P_{1 M_3} = P_1 \setminus \{a \leftarrow \neg b, b \leftarrow \neg a\}$ which are ordered by $P_{1 M_1} \sqsubseteq P_{1 M_3}$ and $P_{1 M_2} \sqsubseteq P_{1 M_3}$. Thus $\langle P_1, < \rangle$ has two (proper) preferred answer sets: $M_1 = \{\neg a, b\}$ and $M_2 = \{a, \neg b\}$.

Note that, in the above example, the preferred answer sets correspond to the stable models (answer sets) of the logic program $\{a \leftarrow not(b), b \leftarrow not(a)\}$, i.e. the stronger rules of $\langle P_1, < \rangle$ where negation as failure (*not*) replaces classical negation ($\neg$). In fact, the ordering of P_1, which makes the rules $\neg a \leftarrow$ and $\neg b \leftarrow$ less preferred, causes $\neg$ to behave as negation as failure, under the preferred answer set semantics.

In general, we can easily simulate negation as failure using classical negation and a trivial ordering.

Theorem 8. *Let P be an (non-disjunctive) seminegative logic program. The ordered version of P, denoted $N(P)$ is defined by $N(P) = \langle P' \cup P_\neg, < \rangle$ with $P_\neg = \{\neg a \leftarrow | a \in \mathcal{B}_P\}$ and P' is obtained from P by replacing each negated literal $not(p)$ by $\neg p$. The order is defined by $P' < P_\neg$ (note that $P' \cap P_\neg = \emptyset$). Then M is a stable model of P iff $M \cup \neg(\mathcal{B}_P \setminus M)$ is a proper preferred answer set of $N(P)$.*

Interestingly, preference can also simulate disjunction.

Definition 6. *Let P be a positive disjunctive logic program. The ordered version of P, denoted $D(P)$, is defined by $D(P) = \langle P_+ \cup P_- \cup P_p, < \rangle$ where $P_+ = \{a \leftarrow | a \in \mathcal{B}_P\}$, $P_- = \{\neg a \leftarrow | a \in \mathcal{B}_P\}$, $P_p = \{a \leftarrow \beta \cup \neg(\alpha \setminus \{a\}) | (\alpha \leftarrow \beta) \in P \wedge a \in \alpha\}$, and $P_p < P_- < P_+$.*

Intuitively, the rules from $P_+ \cup P_-$ guess a total interpretation I of P while the rules in P_p ensure that I^+ is a model of P. Minimality is assured by the fact that negations are preferred.

Example 5. Consider the disjunctive program $P_5 = \{a \vee b \leftarrow, a \leftarrow b, b \leftarrow a\}$. This program illustrates that the shifted version[5] of a disjunctive program need not have the same models, see e.g.[11]. The program $D(P_5)$ is represented below.

$$
\begin{array}{cc}
a \leftarrow & b \leftarrow \\
\hline
\neg a \leftarrow & \neg b \leftarrow \\
\hline
b \leftarrow \neg a & a \leftarrow \neg b \\
a \leftarrow b & b \leftarrow a
\end{array}
$$

$D(P_5)$ has a single proper preferred answer set $\{a, b\}$ which is also the unique minimal model of P_5. Note that both $\neg a \leftarrow$ and $\neg b \leftarrow$ are defeated because minimization is overridden by satisfaction of more preferred non-disjunctive rules.

Theorem 9. *Let P be a positive disjunctive logic program. M is a minimal model of P iff $M' = M \cup \neg(\mathcal{B}_P \setminus M)$ is a proper preferred answer set of $D(P)$.*

In view of Theorem 8 and Theorem 9, it is natural to try to simulate programs that combine negation as failure and disjunction.

Definition 7. *Let P be a seminegative disjunctive logic program. The ordered version of P, denoted $D_n(P)$, is defined by $D_n(P) = \langle P_c \cup P_- \cup P_p, < \rangle$ where $P_c = \{a \leftarrow \beta' | (\alpha \leftarrow \beta) \in P \wedge a \in \alpha\}$, $P_- = \{\neg a \leftarrow | a \in \mathcal{B}_P\}$, $P_p = \{a \leftarrow \beta' \cup \neg(\alpha \setminus \{a\}) | (\alpha \leftarrow \beta) \in P \wedge a \in \alpha\}$, and $P_p < P_- < P_c$. Here, β' is obtained from β by replacing all occurrences of $not(a) \in \beta$ by $\neg a \in \beta'$.*

---

[5] The shifted version of a disjunctive program is a seminegative program where each disjunctive rule $\alpha \leftarrow \beta$ is replaced by the set of rules containing $a \leftarrow \beta \cup not((\alpha \setminus \{a\}))$ for each $a \in \alpha$.

Intuitively, the rules in P_c apply disjunctive rules by choosing a literal from the head of the original rule; rules in P_p ensure that any proper answer set is a model and the preference $P_- < P_c$ supports minimization.

Theorem 10. *Let P be a seminegative disjunctive logic program. If M is an answer set of P then $M \cup \neg(\mathcal{B}_P \setminus M)$ is a proper preferred answer set of $D_n(P)$.*

Unfortunately, $D_n(P)$ may have too many proper preferred answer sets, as illustrated by the following example.

Example 6. Consider the seminegative disjunctive program $P_6 = \{a \vee b \leftarrow, b \leftarrow a, a \leftarrow not(a)\}$. This program does not have an answer set. Indeed, any answer set M would need to contain a and thus, by the rule $b \leftarrow a$, also b, thus $M = \{a, b\}$. But the reduct $P_6^M = \{a \vee b \leftarrow, b \leftarrow a\}$ has only one minimal answer set $\{b\} \neq M$.

However, $\{a, b\}$ is the unique minimal preferred answer set of $D_n(P_6)$ which is shown below.

$$\frac{a \leftarrow \qquad b \leftarrow}{\dfrac{\neg a \leftarrow \qquad \neg b \leftarrow}{\begin{array}{cc} b \leftarrow a & a \leftarrow \neg a \\ a \leftarrow \neg b & b \leftarrow \neg a \end{array}}}$$

In fact, the preferred answer sets semantics of $D_n(P)$ corresponds to the possible model semantics of [9].

Theorem 11. *Let P be a seminegative DLP. An interpretation M is a proper preferred answer set of $D_n(P)$ iff M^+ is a minimal possible model of P.*

In the next section, we'll see that, nevertheless, the expressiveness of the preferred answer set semantics of OLP is similar to that of seminegative disjunctive programs.

4 Computing Preferred Answer Sets

In this section, we only consider finite programs (corresponding to datalog-like rules).

In the algorithm below, we use *extended literals*, i.e. literals of one of the forms a, $\neg a$, $not(a)$ or $not(\neg a)$. A set of extended literals is consistent if for any ordinary literal l in I, neither $\neg l$ nor $not(l)$ appear in I. A set of extended literals I can be *normalized* by removing $not(l)$ whenever $\neg l$ is in I. We use $\phi(I)$ to denote the normalized version of I and $\psi(I)$ to denote $I \setminus \{not(l) \mid l \in (\mathcal{B}_P \cup \neg \mathcal{B}_P)\}$.

The *not*-forms are needed in the procedure because, for an interpretation I, a rule $a \leftarrow \alpha$ may be satisfied without being applied or blocked, e.g. when α contains literals that are neither true nor false in I, i.e. $\mathcal{B}_\alpha \setminus \mathcal{B}_I \neq \emptyset$.

The following auxiliary procedure returns a, possibly empty, set of extensions of I that *decide* a given rule r, where $\dot{a} \leftarrow \alpha$ is decided by I if either $a \in I$, in which case the rule is certainly satisfied (and possibly applied), or $\exists b \in \alpha \cdot I \cap \{\neg b, not(b)\} \neq \emptyset$, i.e. the rule is not applicable.

```
set<set<extended literal>>
extend(set<extended literal> I, rule r ≡ a ← α){
if (a ∈ I) /* i.e. a ∈ ψ(I) */
    return {I};
if (∃b ∈ α · I ∩ {¬b, not(b)} ≠ ∅) /* r ''blocked'' */
    return {I};
if (α ⊆ I) /* r applicable */
    if (I ∩ {¬a, not(a)} = ∅) /* apply r */
        return {I ∪ {a}};
    else /* r cannot be applied */
        return ∅;
/* r could become applied or not applicable */
result = {I ∪ α ∪ {a}} ; /* r will be applied */
for each (b ∈ α\I)
    result = result ∪{I ∪ {not(b)}} ; /* r will not be applicable */
return result;
}
```

Hence, when extending I to satisfy a rule r, one may demand that a certain literal l will not occur in the answer set by adding $not(l)$ to I. If, later on, $\neg l$ is added as well, normalization will remove $not(l)$.

The following algorithm can be used to compute preferred answer sets.

```
bool
aset(set<extended literal> I, set<rule> P, out set<literal> M){
R = {r ∈ P | ψ(I) ⊭ r}
if (R = ∅)
    if (P* = ψ(I))
        M ← ψ(I) /* ψ(I) is a preferred answer set of P */
        return true;
    else
        return false;
/* R ≠ ∅ */
choose minimal r ∈ R
for each J ∈ extend(I,r){ /* J is a minimal
        consistent extension of I that decides r */
    if aset(φ(J),P,M)
        return true;
}
/* ∀J ⊃ I · ψ(J) ⊭ r, r will be defeated */
return aset(I, P\{r}, M)
}
```

It is straightforward to show that the aset procedure satisfies the following proposition.

Theorem 12. *For P an OLP, I a set of extended literals such that $\psi(I)$ is founded, $aset(I, P, M)$ returns* **true** *iff there exists an extension $M \supseteq I$ such that $\psi(M)$ is a preferred answer set of P.*

From Theorem 12, it follows that $aset(\emptyset, P, M)$ will compute a preferred answer set M of P.

Of course, the above algorithm can be improved in many ways: e.g. the test whether $P^\star = \psi(I)$ can be performed incrementally by keeping two sets of (extended) literals: one for literals that already have a motivation and one for literals that still must be confirmed using a proper rule application. Also, rule satisfaction may look ahead to only consider feasible extensions (that may be supported by weaker rules).

The following results shed some light on the complexity of the preferred answer set semantics.

It is straightforward to show that checking whether M is not a (proper) preferred answer set of an OLP P is in NP. Finding a (proper) preferred answer set M can then be performed by an NP algorithm that guesses M and uses an NP oracle to verify that it is not the case that M is not a (proper) preferred answer set. Hence the following theorem.

Theorem 13. *The problem of deciding whether, given an arbitrary ordered program P and a literal a, whether a occurs in any proper preferred answer set of P is in Σ_2^P.*

To show that the problem of Theorem 13 is Σ_2^P-hard, we use a reduction of the known Σ_2^P-hard problem of deciding whether a quantified boolean formula $\phi = \exists x_1, \ldots, x_n \cdot \forall y_1, \ldots, y_m \cdot F$ is valid, where we may assume that $F = \vee_{c \in C} c$ with each c a conjunction of literals over $X \cup Y$ with $X = \{x_1, \ldots, x_n\}$ and $Y = \{y_1, \ldots, y_m\}$ $(n, m > 0)$. The construction is inspired by a similar result in [3] for disjunctive logic programs.

The program P corresponding to ϕ is shown below where we have introduced new atoms w, u, $Y' = \{y' \mid y \in Y\}$ and for each $c \in C$, c' is obtained by replacing each occurrence of $y \in Y$ with the corresponding $y' \in Y'$.

$$\frac{\frac{\{\neg b \leftarrow \ b \leftarrow \ \mid b \in Y \cup Y'\} \cup \{\neg w \leftarrow\}}{\{w \leftarrow c \mid c \in C\} \cup \{\neg u \leftarrow c' \mid c \in C\}}}{\{u \leftarrow \neg u\} \cup \{\neg a \leftarrow \ a \leftarrow \ \mid a \in X\}}$$
$$w \leftarrow \neg w$$

It can then be shown that $\neg u \in M$ for some proper preferred answer set M iff ϕ is valid. Intuitively, if one succeeds in falsifying ϕ for some assignment to Y', $\neg u$ will not be in M and M will satisfy $u \leftarrow \neg u$, making it preferred over answer sets corresponding to other assignments of Y'.

Theorem 14. *The problem of deciding whether, given an arbitrary ordered program P and a literal a, whether a occurs in any proper preferred answer set of P is Σ_2^P-hard.*

Corollary 1. *The problem of deciding whether, given an arbitrary ordered program P and a literal a, whether a occurs in any proper preferred answer set of P is Σ_2^P-complete.*

5   Repairing Databases Using Ordered Programs

We review some definitions from [1], using a simplified notation.

Definition 8. *A **database** is a consistent set of literals. A **constraint** is a set A of literals, to be interpreted as a disjunction, $c = \vee_{a \in A} a$. The Herbrand base $\mathcal{B}_C$ of a set of* constraints C is defined by $\mathcal{B}_C = \cup_{c \in C} \mathcal{B}_c$. A database D is **consistent** with a set of constraints C, where $\mathcal{B}_C \subseteq \mathcal{B}_D$, just when $D \models \wedge_{c \in C} c$, i.e. D is a classical model of C. A set of constraints C is consistent iff there exists a database D such that D is consistent with C.

Definition 9. Let D and D' be databases with $\mathcal{B}_D = \mathcal{B}_{D'}$. We use $\Delta_D(D')$ to denote the difference $D' \backslash D$. A database D induces a partial order relation[6] $\leq_D$ defined by

$$D_1 \leq_D D_2 \text{ iff } \Delta_D(D_1) \subseteq \Delta_D(D_2)$$

Intuitively, $\Delta_D(D')$ contains the update operations that must be performed on D to obtain D'. A negative literal $\neg a$ in $\Delta_D(D')$ means that the fact a must be removed from D while $a \in \Delta_D(D')$ suggests adding a to D.

The $\leq_D$ relation represents the closeness to D: $D_1 \leq_D D_2$ means that D_1 is a better approximation of D than D_2 (note that $D \leq_D D$).

Definition 10. Let D be a database and let C be a set of constraints with $\mathcal{B}_C \subseteq \mathcal{B}_D$. A database D' is a C-**repair** of D iff $D' \models C$ and D' is minimal in the $\leq_D$ partial order; i.e. $D'' \leq_D D'$ implies that $D'' = D'$.

This definition differs from the one in [1] where $\leq_D$ was defined based on the symmetric difference $\Delta(D, D') = (D^+ \backslash D'^+) \cup (D'^+ \backslash D^+)$ rather than our $\Delta_D(D')$. However, it is straightforward to show that both definitions lead to the same $\leq_D$, i.e. $\Delta_D(D_1) \subseteq \Delta_D(D_2)$ iff $\Delta(D, D_1) \subseteq \Delta(D, D_2)$ and thus Definition 10 is equivalent to the one in [1].

Next we provide a construction that maps a database D and a set of constraints C to an ordered logic program $P(D, C)$ which, as shall be shown further on, has the C-repairs of D as answer sets. Using ordered logic instead of logic programs with exceptions [5] greatly simplifies (w.r.t. [1]) constructing repairs: we can dispense with the shadow versions of each predicate and we do not need disjunction. Moreover, our approach handles constraints of arbitrary size, while [1] is limited to constraints containing up to two literals.

Definition 11. Let D be a database and let C be a consistent set of constraints with $\mathcal{B}_C \subseteq \mathcal{B}_D$. The **ordered version** of D w.r.t. C, denoted $P(D, C)$, is shown below.

$$
\begin{array}{ll}
\{\neg a \leftarrow \mid a \in D\} & (n) \\
\hline
\{a \leftarrow \mid a \in D\} & (d) \\
\hline
\{a \leftarrow \neg(A \backslash \{a\} \mid \vee_{a \in A} a \in C\} & (c)
\end{array}
$$

Intuitively, the c-rules enforce the constraints (they are also the strongest rules according to the partial order). The d-rules simply input the database as "default" facts while the n-rules will be used to provide a justification for literals needed to satisfy certain c-rules, thus defeating d-rules that would cause constraints to be violated.

Theorem 15. Let D be a database and let C be a consistent set of constraints with $\mathcal{B}_C \subseteq \mathcal{B}_D$. A database R is a repair of D w.r.t. C iff R is a proper preferred answer set of $P(D, C)$.

---

[6] The proof that $\leq_D$ is a partial order is straightforward.

Example 7. Consider the propositional version of the example from [1] where the database $D = \{p, q, r\}$ and the set of constraints $C = \{\neg p \vee q, \neg p \vee \neg q, \neg q \vee r, \neg q \vee \neg r, \neg r \vee p, \neg r \vee \neg p, \}$. The program $P(D, C)$ is shown below.

$\neg p \leftarrow$	$\neg q \leftarrow$	$\neg r \leftarrow$
$p \leftarrow$	$q \leftarrow$	$r \leftarrow$
$\neg p \leftarrow \neg q$	$q \leftarrow p$	$\neg p \leftarrow q$
$\neg q \leftarrow p$	$\neg q \leftarrow \neg r$	$r \leftarrow p$
$\neg r \leftarrow q$	$\neg q \leftarrow r$	$p \leftarrow r$
$\neg r \leftarrow \neg p$	$\neg p \leftarrow r$	$\neg r \leftarrow p$

It is easily verified that $R = \{\neg p, \neg q, \neg r\}$ is the only repair of D w.r.t. C and the only proper preferred answer set of $P(D, C)$.

References

1. Marcelo Arenas, Leopoldo Bertossi, and Jan Chomicki. Specifying and querying database repairs using logic programs with exceptions. In *Proceedings of the 4th International Conference on Flexible Query Answering Systems*, pages 27–41, Warsaw, Octobre 2000. Springer-Verlag.
2. Thomas Eiter, Georg Gottlob, and Nicola Leone. Abduction from logic programs: Semantics and complexity. *Theoretical Computer Science*, 189(1-2):129–177, 1997.
3. T. Eiter and G. Gottlob. Complexity results for disjunctive logic programming and application to nonmonotnic logics. In *Proceedings of the 1983 International Logic Programming Symposium*, pages 266–279, Vancouver, October 1993. MIT Press.
4. Michael Gelfond and Vladimir Lifschitz. The stable model semantics for logic programming. In Robert A. Kowalski and Kenneth A. Bowen, editors, *Logic Programming, Proceedings of the Fifth International Conference and Symposium*, pages 1070–1080, Seattle, Washington, August 1988. The MIT Press.
5. Robert A. Kowalski and Fariba Sadri. Logic programs with exceptions. In David H. D. Warren and Peter Szeredi, editors, *Proceedings of the Seventh International Conference on Logic Programming*, pages 598–613, Jerusalem, 1990. The MIT Press.
6. Els Laenens and Dirk Vermeir. Assumption-free semantics for ordered logic programs: On the relationship between well-founded and stable partial models. *Journal of Logic and Computation*, 2(2):133–172, 1992.
7. Vladimir Lifschitz. Answer set programming and plan generation. *Journal of Artificial Intelligence*, to appear.
8. Raymond Reiter. A theory of diagnosis from first principles. *Artificial Intelligence*, 32(1):57–95, 1987.
9. Chiaki Sakama and Katsumi Inoue. An alternative approach to the semantics of disjunctive logic programs and deductive databases. *Journal of Automated Reasoning*, 13(1):145–172, 1994.
10. M.H. van Emden and R. Kowalski. The semantics of predicate logic as a programming language. *Journal of the Association for Computing Machinery*, 23(4):733–742, 1976.
11. M. De Vos and D. Vermeir. Semantic forcing in disjunctive logic programs. *Computational Intelligence*, 17(4):651–684, 2001.

Implementing Ordered Disjunction
Using Answer Set Solvers for Normal Programs

Gerhard Brewka[1], Ilkka Niemelä[2], and Tommi Syrjänen[2]

[1] Universität Leipzig, Institut für Informatik
Augustusplatz 10-11, 04109 Leipzig, Germany
brewka@informatik.uni-leipzig.de
[2] Helsinki University of Technology, Dept. of Computer Science and Engineering
Lab. for Theoretical Computer Science
P.O.Box 5400 FIN-02015 HUT, Finland
{Ilkka.Niemela,Tommi.Syrjanen}@hut.fi

Abstract. Logic programs with ordered disjunction (*LPOD*s) add a new connective to logic programming. This connective allows us to represent alternative, ranked options for problem solutions in the heads of rules: $A \times B$ intuitively means: if possible A, but if A is not possible, then at least B. The semantics of logic programs with ordered disjunction is based on a preference relation on answer sets. In this paper we show how *LPOD*s can be implemented using answer set solvers for normal programs. The implementation is based on a generator which produces candidate answer sets and a tester which checks whether a given candidate is maximally preferred and produces a better candidate if it is not. We also discuss the complexity of reasoning tasks based on *LPOD*s.

1   Introduction

In [1] a propositional logic called Qualitative Choice Logic (*QCL*) is introduced. The logic contains a new connective $\times$ representing ordered disjunction. Intuitively, $A \times B$ stands for: if possible A, but if A is impossible then (at least) B. In [2] it is shown how ordered disjunction can be added to logic programs with two kinds of negation under answer set semantics. The resulting logic programs with ordered disjunction (*LPOD*s for short) allow us to combine default knowledge with knowledge about preferences in a simple and elegant way.

In this paper we show how *LPOD*s can be implemented using answer set solvers (ASP solvers) for normal (non-disjunctive) programs. This means that when implementing *LPOD*s it is possible to directly exploit constantly improving performance of ASP solvers for standard logic programs such as *Smodels* and *dlv*. The implementation is based on two normal logic programs, a generator which produces candidate answer sets and a tester which checks whether a given candidate is maximally preferred. The tester produces a better answer set if the candidate is not preferred. Iteration thus leads to a maximally preferred answer set. We also discuss the complexity of reasoning tasks based on *LPOD*s.

We will restrict our discussion in this paper to propositional programs. However, as usual in answer set programming, we admit rule schemata containing

S. Flesca et al. (Eds.): JELIA 2002, LNAI 2424, pp. 444–456, 2002.
© Springer-Verlag Berlin Heidelberg 2002

variables bearing in mind that these schemata are just convenient representations for the set of their ground instances.

We have constructed a prototype implementation for *LPOD*s based on *Smodels*, an efficient ASP solver developed at Helsinki University of Technology. The generator and tester programs use special rule types of the *Smodels* system, but they can be modified to work with any ASP solver. The prototype implementation is available at `http://www.tcs.hut.fi/Software/smodels/priority`.

The rest of the paper is organized as follows. In the next section we recall the basic notions underlying syntax and semantics of *LPOD*s. For a more detailed discussion the reader is referred to [2]. Section 3 discusses several alternative preference relations on answer sets which can be obtained based on the satisfaction degrees of rules. Section 4 presents our *Smodels* based implementation. Section 5 gives complexity results. Section 6 gives a short discussion on applying preferences on the problem of configuration management. Section 7 concludes.

2   Logic Programs with Ordered Disjunction

Logic programming with ordered disjunction is an extension of logic programming with two kinds of negation (default and strong negation) [4]. The new connective × representing ordered disjunction is allowed to appear in the head of rules only. A (propositional) *LPOD* thus consists of rules of the form

$$C_1 \times \cdots \times C_n \leftarrow A_1, \ldots, A_m, \text{not } B_1, \ldots, \text{not } B_k$$

where the C_i, A_j and B_l are ground literals.

The intuitive reading of the rule head is: if possible C_1, if C_1 is not possible, then C_2, ..., if all of $C_1, \ldots, C_{n-1}$ are not possible, then C_n. The literals C_i are called choices of the rule. Extended logic programs are a special case where $n = 1$ for all rules. We omit $\leftarrow$ whenever $m = 0$ and $k = 0$. Moreover, rules of the form $\leftarrow body$ (constraints) are used as abbreviations for $p \leftarrow \text{not } p, body$ for some p not appearing in the rest of the program. The effect is that no answer sets containing *body* exist. We use the notations $At(P)$ and $Lit(P)$ to denote the sets of atoms and literals occurring in a *LPOD* P.

As discussed in [2] answer sets of *LPOD*s cannot be inclusion minimal because this would in certain cases exclude answer sets from consideration which, intuitively, satisfy the rules best. The definition of answer sets for *LPOD*s is therefore based on the notion of a split program. This notion was first used in [7] for disjunctive logic programs. A split program consists of single head rules obtained from the original program by picking one of the available alternatives. Our definition of split programs for *LPOD*s differs in two respects from Sakama and Inoue's to comply with the intuitive reading of ordered disjunction:

1. we require that a split program contains exactly one of the alternatives provided in the original program by a single rule,
2. our single head rules are slightly more complicated to guarantee that a choice is only made if a better choice isn't already derived through some other rule.

The precise definition is as follows:

Definition 1. *Let* $r = C_1 \times \cdots \times C_n \leftarrow body$ *be a rule. For* $k \leq n$ *we define the* k*th option of* r *as*

$$r^k = C_k \leftarrow body, not\ C_1, \ldots, not\ C_{k-1}.$$

Definition 2. *Let* P *be an LPOD. Then* P' *is a split program of* P *if it is obtained from* P *by replacing each rule in* P *by one of its options.*

Here is a simple example. Let P consist of the rules

$$A \times B \leftarrow not\ C$$
$$B \times C \leftarrow not\ D \tag{1}$$

We obtain 4 split programs

$$A \leftarrow not\ C \qquad\qquad A \leftarrow not\ C$$
$$B \leftarrow not\ D \qquad\qquad C \leftarrow not\ D, not\ B$$

$$B \leftarrow not\ C, not\ A \qquad B \leftarrow not\ C, not\ A$$
$$B \leftarrow not\ D \qquad\qquad C \leftarrow not\ D, not\ B$$

Split programs do not contain ordered disjunction. We thus can define:

Definition 3. *Let* P *be an LPOD. A set of literals* A *is an answer set of* P *if it is a consistent answer set of a split program* P' *of* P.

We exclude inconsistent answer sets from consideration since they do not represent possible problem solutions. In the example above we obtain 3 answer sets: $\{A, B\}, \{C\}, \{B\}$. Note that one of the answer sets is a proper subset of another answer set. On the other hand, none of the rules in the original *LPOD* sanctions more than one literal in any of the answer sets, as intended.

Not all of the answer sets satisfy our most intended options. Clearly, $\{A, B\}$ gives us the best options for both rules, whereas $\{C\}$ gives only the second best option for the latter and $\{B\}$ the second best option for the former rule. We therefore introduce the notion of a preferred answer set in the next section.

3   Preferred Answer Sets

To distinguish between more and less intended answer sets we introduce the degree of satisfaction of a rule in an answer set:

Definition 4. *Let* S *be an answer set of an LPOD* P. *Then* S *satisfies the rule*

$$C_1 \times \ldots \times C_n \leftarrow A_1, \ldots, A_m, not\ B_1, \ldots, not\ B_k$$

– to degree 1 if $A_j \notin S$, *for some* j, *or* $B_i \in S$, *for some* i,

$-$ *to degree j ($1 \leq j \leq n$) if all $A_j \in S$, no $B_i \in S$, and $j = min\{r \mid C_r \in S\}$.*

The degrees can be viewed as penalties: the higher the degree the less satisfied we are. If the body of a rule is not satisfied, then there is no reason to be dissatisfied and the best degree 1 is obtained. We denote the degree of r in S by $deg_S(r)$.

The satisfaction degrees of the rules of a program P are the basis for defining a preference relation on the answer sets of P. There are many different ways of inducing such a preference relation. We will discuss three of them in this paper.

The first preference criterion is based on the cardinality of the sets of rules satisfied to a particular degree. For a set of literals S, let $S^i(P) = \{r \in P \mid deg_S(r) = i\}$. Now cardinality based preference can be defined as follows:

Definition 5. *Let S_1 and S_2 be answer sets of an LPOD P. Then S_1 is cardinality-preferred to S_2 ($S_1 >_c S_2$) iff there is i such that $|S_1^i(P)| > |S_2^i(P)|$, and for all $j < i$, $|S_1^j(P)| = |S_2^j(P)|$.*

In certain applications counting does not provide the best way of defining preferences among answer sets. We therefore propose a second, inclusion based criterion. This is the criterion originally used in [2]:

Definition 6. *Let S_1 and S_2 be answer sets of an LPOD P. The answer set S_1 is inclusion-preferred to S_2 ($S_1 >_i S_2$) iff there is k such that $S_2^k(P) \subset S_1^k(P)$, and for all $j < k$, $S_1^j(P) = S_2^j(P)$.*

Although inclusion-preference is more cautious than cardinality-preference it is sometimes not cautious enough; in some cases adding unattainable preferences changes the set of preferred answer sets. Consider the following decision over possible desserts:

$$r_1 : \textit{ice-cream} \times \textit{cake}$$
$$r_2 : \textit{coffee} \times \textit{tea} \tag{2}$$
$$r_3 : \leftarrow \textit{coffee}, \textit{ice-cream}$$

Now there are two preferred answer sets, $\{ice\text{-}cream, tea\}$ and $\{coffee, cake\}$. Neither of them dominates the other because they both satisfy one rule to the first degree and one rule to the second degree. Now replace r_1 by

$$r_1' : \textit{cookie} \times \textit{ice-cream} \times \textit{cake}$$

and add the fact $\neg cookie$ to the program. Then, $\{coffee, cake, \neg cookie\}$ is the only preferred answer set. By adding an unsatisfiable preference to cookies, we inadvertently made the second preference more important than the first. To avoid effects of this kind one can use the following Pareto criterion[1]:

Definition 7. *Let S_1 and S_2 be answer sets of an LPOD P. Then S_1 is Pareto-preferred to S_2 ($S_1 >_p S_2$) iff there is $r \in P$ such that $deg_{S_1}(r) < deg_{S_2}(r)$, and for no $r' \in P$ $deg_{S_1}(r') > deg_{S_2}(r')$.*

[1] The Pareto-criterion was suggested to us by Harri Haanpää.

The proof of the following proposition is straightforward:

Proposition 1. *Let S_1 and S_2 be answer sets of an LPOD P. Then $S_1 >_p S_2$ implies $S_1 >_i S_2$ and $S_1 >_i S_2$ implies $S_1 >_c S_2$.*

Definition 8. *A set of literals S is a k-preferred (where $k \in \{c, i, p\}$) answer set of an LPOD P iff S is an answer set of P and there is no answer set S' of P such that $S' >_k S$.*

Given a particular preference criterion k, we say a literal l is a conclusion of an *LPOD* P iff l is contained in all k-preferred answer sets of P. In many applications, for instance in design and configuration, each preferred answer set represents a solution that satisfies the preferences best.

Sometimes we may want to express that one preference is more important than another. Consider again the dessert program (2) in its original form. Assume that we would rather have ice-cream than coffee. Now we would like have a mechanism that could express the differences in preference importance. A convenient way is to express these meta-preferences by defining a relation $\succ$ on rules. In our case we could simply say $r_1 \succ r_2$. It is not difficult to take these rule preferences into account. Let us illustrate this using Pareto preference:

Definition 9. *Let S_1 and S_2 be answer sets of an LPOD P, $\succ$ a preference relation on the rules of P. S_1 is Pareto-preferred to S_2 ($S_1 >_p S_2$) iff*

1. *there is $r \in P$ such that $deg_{S_1}(r) < deg_{S_2}(r)$, and*
2. *for each $r' \in P$: $deg_{S_1}(r') > deg_{S_2}(r')$ implies there is r'' such that $r'' \succ r'$ and $deg_{S_1}(r'') < deg_{S_2}(r')$.*

In principle, it is possible to represent preferences among rules within the programs and thus to make them context dependent. However, since the rule preference information then is part of the generated answer sets one has to be careful not to loose anti-symmetry. For instance, if we have

$$r_1 : a \times \neg a \qquad r_2 \succ r_1 \leftarrow a$$
$$r_2 : \neg a \times a \qquad r_1 \succ r_2 \leftarrow \neg a$$

then, from the perspective of each of the two answer sets, the other answer set is preferred. As long as different answer sets do not disagree about preferences among rules, one is on the safe side. We will not pursue this issue further here.

4   Implementation

We can compute preferred answer sets of an *LPOD* P using standard answer set implementations and two programs. A similar approach is used in [5] to compute stable models of disjunctive programs using *Smodels*. The two programs are:

- A *generator* $G(P)$ whose stable models correspond to the answer sets of P; and

– A *tester* $T(P, M)$ for checking whether a given answer set M of P is preferred.

The two programs are run in an interleaved fashion. First, the generator constructs an answer set M of P. Next, the tester tries to find an answer set M' that is strictly better than M. If there is no such M', we know that M is a preferred answer set. Otherwise, we use $G(P)$ to construct the next candidate. When we want to find only one preferred answer set we can save some effort by taking M' directly as the new answer set candidate.

The basic idea of $G(P)$ is to encode all possible split programs of P into one program by adding an explicit choice over the options of each ordered disjunction. We encode the choice using new atoms of the form $c(r, k)$ to denote that we are using the kth option of rule r.

To make model comparison easier we also add another set of new atoms, $s(r, k)$ to denote that the rule r is satisfied to the degree k. These atoms are not strictly necessary but they make the programs more readable.

Definition 10. *Let P be an LPOD and $r = C_1 \times \cdots \times C_n \leftarrow body$ be a rule in P. Then the translation $G(r, k)$ of the kth option of r is defined as follows:*

$$G(r, k) = \{C_k \leftarrow c(r, k), \text{not } C_1, \ldots, \text{not } C_{k-1}, body; \tag{3}$$
$$\leftarrow C_k, \text{not } c(r, k), \text{not } C_1, \ldots, \text{not } C_{k-1}, body\} \tag{4}$$

The satisfaction translation $S(r)$ is:

$$S(r) = \{s(r, 1) \leftarrow \text{not } c(r, 1), \ldots, \text{not } c(r, n)\} \cup \tag{5}$$
$$\{s(r, i) \leftarrow c(r, i) \mid 1 \leq i \leq n\} \tag{6}$$

The translation $G(r)$ is:

$$G(r) = \{1 \{c(r, 1), \ldots, c(r, n)\} 1 \leftarrow body\} \cup \bigcup\{G(r, k) \mid k \leq n\} \cup S(r) \tag{7}$$

The generator $G(P)$ is defined as follows:

$$G(P) = \bigcup\{G(r) \mid r \in P\} \tag{8}$$

The definition of $G(P)$ is rather straightforward, but a few points may need explaining. First, the rule $1 \{c(r, 1), \ldots, c(r, n)\} 1 \leftarrow body$ states that if $body$ is true, then exactly one of the atoms $c(r, k)$ is true. Its formal semantics is defined in [6] but it can also be seen as a shorthand for n pairs of rules of the form:

$$c(r, k) \leftarrow \text{not } \neg c(r, k), body$$
$$\neg c(r, k) \leftarrow \text{not } c(r, k)$$

and $n^2 - n$ constraints $\leftarrow c(r, i), c(r, j), i \neq j$.

Also, the reason for having two rules in $G(r, k)$ may not be clear, since (3) already ensures that only correct answer sets of the split program P' will be generated. Now consider the situation where some C_j, $j < k$, is a consequence of a different part of the program. Then without (4) we could have an answer set where $c(r, k)$ is true, but C_k is not because C_j blocks (3). In other words, we would have chosen to satisfy r to the degree k, but it actually would be satisfied to the degree j. The rule (4) prevents this unintuitive behavior by always forcing us to choose the lowest possible degree.

Example 1. The program (1) is translated to:

$$1 \; \{c(1, 1), c(1, 2)\} \; 1 \leftarrow \text{not } C \qquad\qquad A \leftarrow c(1, 1), \text{not } C$$
$$1 \; \{c(2, 1), c(2, 2)\} \; 1 \leftarrow \text{not } D \qquad\qquad B \leftarrow c(2, 1), \text{not } D$$
$$\leftarrow \text{not } c(1, 1), A, \text{not } C \qquad\qquad B \leftarrow c(1, 2), \text{not } A, \text{not } C$$
$$\leftarrow \text{not } c(1, 2), B, \text{not } A, \text{not } C \qquad C \leftarrow c(2, 2), \text{not } B, \text{not } D$$
$$\leftarrow \text{not } c(2, 1), B, \text{not } D \qquad\qquad s(1, 1) \leftarrow \text{not } c(1, 1), \text{not } c(1, 2)$$
$$\leftarrow \text{not } c(2, 2), C, \text{not } B, \text{not } D \qquad s(2, 1) \leftarrow \text{not } c(2, 1), \text{not } c(2, 2)$$
$$s(1, 1) \leftarrow c(1, 1) \quad s(1, 2) \leftarrow c(1, 2) \qquad s(2, 1) \leftarrow c(2, 1) \quad s(2, 2) \leftarrow c(2, 2)$$

It has three answer sets: $\{A, B, c(1, 1), c(2, 1), s(1, 1), s(2, 1)\}$, $\{B, c(1, 2), c(2, 1), s(1, 2), s(2, 1)\}$, and $\{C, c(2, 2), s(1, 1), s(2, 2)\}$. Note that in the last case there is no atom $c(1, k)$ since the body of the first rule is not satisfied.

Proposition 2. *Let P be an LPOD. Then M is an answer set of $G(P)$ if and only if $M \cap Lit(P)$ is an answer set of P.*

Proof. Let M be an answer set of P. Now, for each rule $r = C_1 \times \cdots \times C_n \leftarrow body$ define $p(M, r) = \{c(r, k), s(r, k) \mid body \text{ is satisfied in } M, C_k \in M, \text{ and } \forall i < k : C_i \notin M\} \cup \{s(r, 1) \mid r \in P \text{ and } body \text{ is unsatisfied in } M\}$. Let $M' = M \cup \bigcup_{r \in P} p(M, r)$. By definition of $p(M, r)$, M' satisfies all rules (3)–(6). Finally, (7) is satisfied since exactly one atom $c(r, k)$ was added to M' for each rule r that had its body true. It follows that M' is an answer set of $G(P)$. Now, suppose that M' is an answer set of $G(P)$. Then for each atom $C \in M = M' \cap Lit(P)$, there exists a rule of the form (3) where C is the head and some atom $c(r, k) \in M'$ occurs positively in the body. We define $P' = \{r^k \mid c(r, k) \in M'\} \cup \{r^1 \mid \neg \exists k : c(r, k) \in M'\}$. We see that P' is a split program of P that generates M as its answer set so M is an answer set of P.

Since we have three different optimality criteria, we need three different tester programs. They all consist of a common core $C(P, M)$ augmented by case-specific rules T_c, T_i, or T_p. Since we want the tester to find an answer set M' that is strictly better than a given M, we define two new atoms, namely *better* and *worse* with the intuition that *better* (*worse*) is true when M' is in some aspect better (worse) than M. If both are true, then the answer sets are incomparable.

Definition 11. *Let P be an LPOD. Then the core tester $C(P, M)$ is defined as follows:*

$$C(P, M) = G(P) \cup \{o(r, k) \mid s(r, k) \in M\} \cup \{rule(r) \leftarrow \mid r \in P\}$$
$$\cup \{degree(d) \leftarrow \mid \exists r \in P \text{ such that } r \text{ has at least } d \text{ options}\}$$
$$\cup \{\leftarrow \text{not } better; \leftarrow worse\}$$

$$better \leftarrow s(R, I), o(R, J), I < J, rule(R), degree(I), degree(J)$$
$$worse \leftarrow s(R, J), o(R, I), I < J, rule(R), degree(I), degree(J)$$

Fig. 1. The Pareto-preference tester T_p

$$better(D_1) \leftarrow s(R, D_1), o(R, D_2), D_1 < D_2, rule(R), degree(D_1), degree(D_2)$$
$$worse(D_1) \leftarrow s(R, D_2), o(R, D_1), D_1 < D_2, rule(R), degree(D_1), degree(D_2)$$
$$better \leftarrow \{worse(D_2) : degree(D_2) \wedge D_2 \leq D_1\} \, 0, better(D_1), degree(D_1)$$
$$worse \leftarrow \{better(D_2) : degree(D_2) \wedge D_2 \leq D_1\} \, 0, worse(D_1), degree(D_1)$$

Fig. 2. The inclusion preference tester T_i

$$s\text{-}card(K, N) \leftarrow N \, \{s(R, N) : rule(R)\} \, N, degree(K)$$
$$o\text{-}card(K, N) \leftarrow N \, \{o(R, N) : rule(R)\} \, N, degree(K)$$
$$better(D) \leftarrow s\text{-}card(D, N_1), o\text{-}card(D, N_2), N_1 > N_2, degree(D)$$
$$worse(D) \leftarrow s\text{-}card(D, N_1), o\text{-}card(D, N_2), N_1 < N_2, degree(D)$$
$$better \leftarrow better(D), degree(D)$$
$$worse \leftarrow \{better(D_2) : degree(D_2) \wedge D_2 < D_1\} \, 0, worse(D_1), degree(D_1)$$

Fig. 3. The cardinality preference tester T_c

The k-preference tester $(k \in \{c, i, p\})$ $T_k(P, M)$ *is defined as follows:*

$$T_k(P, M) = C(P, M) \cup T_k$$

The case-specific parts of the three different testers are shown in Figures 1–3. The atoms $o(r, k)$ are used to store the degrees of satisfaction in the original answer set M so that $o(r, k)$ is added as a fact to $T(P, M)$ whenever $s(r, k) \in M$.

The p-preference tester T_p (Fig. 1) is by far the simplest. It states that M' is better if there exists some rule that has a lower degree of satisfaction in M' than in M, and worse if some rule has a higher degree. The i-preference tester T_i (Fig. 2) considers each different degree of satisfaction separately. Now M' is preferred over M if there exists some degree k that M' satisfies better and for all degrees $k' \leq k$ M' is not worse than M. The c-preference tester T_c (Fig. 3) is quite similar to T_i but we add new atoms $s\text{-}card(k, n)$ and $o\text{-}card(k, n)$ to encode the cardinalities of the sets S^k, and make the comparisons based on them.

Proposition 3. *Let P be an LPOD and M be an answer set of G(P). Then M' is an answer set of $T_k(P, M)$ $(k \in \{c, i, p\})$ iff $M' \cap Lit(P)$ is an answer set of P which is k-preferred to $M \cap Lit(P)$.*

$$better(R) \leftarrow s(R, I), o(R, J), I < J, rule(R), degree(I), degree(J)$$
$$worse \leftarrow s(R, J), o(R, I), \text{not } excused(R), I < J, rule(R), degree(I), degree(J)$$
$$excused(R_1) \leftarrow R_2 \succ R_1, better(R_2), rule(R_1), rule(R_2)$$
$$better \leftarrow better(R), rule(R)$$

Fig. 4. A meta-preference tester

Proof. (For p-preference) First, suppose that $T_p(P, M)$ has an answer set M'. Then $better \in M'$ and $worse \notin M'$. We see that $better$ is true exactly when $\exists r : deg_{M'}(r) < deg_M(r)$. Since $worse \notin M'$, we know that $\neg \exists r : deg_{M'}(r) > deg_M(r)$ so $M' \cap Lit(P) >_p M$. Conversely, if there exists $M' >_p M$, then M' is generated by the $G(P)$ part of $T(P, M)$ so $M' \cup \bigcup_{r \in P} p(M', r) \cup \{better\}$ is an answer set of $T_p(P, M)$. The cases for c- and i-preference are analogous.

The following corollary is immediate from Proposition 3:

Corollary 1. *Let P be an LPOD and M be an answer set of $G(P)$. Then M is k-preferred $(k \in \{c, i, p\})$ iff $T_k(P, M)$ does not have any answer set.*

We can handle meta-preferences by modifying the rules of the *worse* atom. We define a new predicate $excused(r)$ to denote that some more important rule r', $r' \succ r$, is satisfied to a lower degree in M' than it was in M so we allow r to be satisfied to a higher degree. Figure 4 shows how the p-preference tester has to be modified to take the meta-information into account. The i-preference tester can be altered in a similar fashion. However, adding meta-preferences to the c-preference tester is more complex and we do not discuss it here.

5   Complexity

In the previous section we defined two extended logic programs that can be interleaved to compute k-preferred answer sets. Would it be possible to compute them using a single disjunction-free program? Unfortunately, this is impossible in the general case unless the polynomial hierarchy collapses; credulous reasoning on *LPOD*s is $\Sigma_2^{\mathbf{P}}$-complete for $\{i, p\}$-preferences. The c-preference is slightly easier computationally and it stays in $\Delta_2^{\mathbf{P}}$. Whether it is $\Delta_2^{\mathbf{P}}$-complete or not is still an open question. In this section we prove these complexity results.

We start by noting that since the three different $>_k$ relations are all anti-symmetric and well-founded, an *LPOD* P has at least one k-preferred answer set if it has any answer sets at all.

Theorem 1. *Let P be an LPOD. Then deciding whether P has a k-preferred $(k \in \{c, i, p\})$ answer set is **NP**-complete.*

Theorem 2. *Let P be an LPOD and M an answer set of P. Then deciding whether M is k-preferred $(k \in \{c, i, p\})$ is **coNP**-complete.*

Proof. Inclusion: If M is not a k-preferred answer set of P, then there exists an answer set M' such that $M' >_k M$. Since we can find M' with one query to an NP-oracle, showing that M is preferred is in **coNP**.

Hardness: Given a 3-SAT-instance S, we can construct an *LPOD* P with the property that $M = \{\neg sat, d\}$ is a k-preferred answer set exactly when S is unsatisfiable. This translation $t(S)$ is as follows:

$$t(S) = \{sat \times \neg sat; d \leftarrow \text{not } \neg d; \neg d \leftarrow \text{not } d; \neg sat \leftarrow d; sat \leftarrow \text{not } \neg sat\}$$

$$\cup \{\neg sat \leftarrow \text{not } A_1, \text{not } A_2, \text{not } A_3 \mid A_1 \vee A_2 \vee A_3 \in S\}$$

$$\cup \{a \leftarrow \text{not } \neg a, \neg d; \neg a \leftarrow \text{not } a, \neg d \mid a \in At(S)\}$$

Theorem 3. *Given an LPOD P and a literal $l \in Lit(P)$, deciding whether there exists a $\{i, p\}$-preferred answer set M such that $l \in M$ is Σ_2^P-complete.*

Proof. Inclusion: We can first guess M such that $l \in M$ and verify that M is an answer set. Then by Theorem 2 we can use an **NP**-oracle to verify that M is $\{i, p\}$-preferred.

Hardness: Given a 3-SAT-instance S and a literal l, it is Σ_2^P-hard to decide whether l is true in a minimal model of S [3]. We construct a *LPOD* $t(S)$ such that l is true in a $\{i, p\}$-preferred answer set of $t(S)$ iff l is true in a minimal model of S.

$$t(S) = \{\leftarrow \bar{A}_1, \bar{A}_2, \bar{A}_3 \mid A_1 \vee A_2 \vee A_3 \in S\} \tag{9}$$

$$\cup \{\neg a \times a \mid a \in At(S)\} \tag{10}$$

Now M is a preferred answer set of $t(S)$ iff it is a minimal model of S. We can see this by noting that the rules of the form (10) generate all possible truth valuations for atoms of S and all rules (9) are satisfied whenever all clauses are.

Suppose that M is a minimal model of S and that there exists an answer set M' such that $M' >_{i,p} M$. By (10) this implies that there exists an atom a such that $a \in M$ and $a \notin M'$, and there does not exist an atom b such that $b \in M'$ and $b \notin M$. Thus, $M' \subset M$. However, this is a contradiction since M' is also a model of S and we assumed that M is minimal.

Next, suppose that M is a $\{i, p\}$-preferred answer set of $t(S)$. This implies that there is no answer set M' such that $\exists a \in At(S) : a \in M \wedge a \notin M'$. Thus, there is no $M' \subset M$ and M is a minimal model of S.

Theorem 4. *Given an LPOD P and a literal $l \in Lit(P)$, deciding whether there exists a c-preferred answer set M such that $l \in M$ is in Δ_2^P.*

Proof. Each answer set M of P induces a tuple $(|M^1|, \ldots, |M^d|)$ where $|M^k|$ denotes the number of rules satisfied to the degree k by M. We can see from Definition 5 that each c-preferred answer set induces the same tuple, $(c^1, \ldots, c^d)$. We can find the correct value of c^1 using $O(\log r)$ adaptive **NP**-oracle queries where r is the number of rules in P. We add to P rules to force $|M^1|$ to be within given upper and lower bounds (u, l) and then perform a binary search to narrow the bounds. The bound rules may be expressed using the notation of Fig. 3 as follows:

$$\leftarrow s\text{-}card(1, N), N < l, degree(N)$$
$$\leftarrow s\text{-}card(1, N), N > u, degree(N)$$

After establishing c^i, we proceed to establish c^{i+1}. Since both r and d are linear with respect to the size n of P, we can find out all c^i using $O(n \log n)$ **NP**-queries. Finally, we add $\leftarrow$ not l and issue one more query to see whether l is true in a c-preferred answer set.

6   An Application: Configuration Management

To illustrate *LPODs* we want to briefly discuss an application in configuration management. Answer set programming techniques seem to be suitable for modeling many different configuration domains [8,6]. During a configuration process we have often more than one alternative way to satisfy a requirement. For example, a workstation may have more than one possible email client.

We now consider two examples that show how *LPODs* can be used to model several kinds of different preference criteria in Linux configuration domain. First, there are usually several available versions for any given software package. In most cases we want to install the latest version, but sometimes we have to use an older one. We can handle these preferences by defining a new atom for each different version and then demanding that at least one version should be selected if the component is installed. For example, the following rule defines that there are three versions of emacs available:

$$emacs\text{-}21.1 \times emacs\text{-}20.7.2 \times emacs\text{-}19.34 \leftarrow emacs$$

Second, a component may have also different variants. For example, most programming libraries come in two versions: a normal version containing only files that are necessary to run programs that are linked against the library, and a developer version with header or class files that allow a developer to create new applications. Now, a common user would prefer to have the normal variant while a programmer would prefer the developer version. We may model these preferences in the following way:

$$libc6 \times libc6\text{-}dev \leftarrow need\text{-}libc6, \text{not } c\text{-}developer$$
$$libc6\text{-}dev \times libc6 \leftarrow need\text{-}libc6, c\text{-}developer \ .$$

There are also many other possible preference criteria in the configuration domain. It is not at all clear how they should be combined into one comprehensive preference structure, and further work into this direction is needed.

7   Conclusion

In this paper we show how *LPODs* can be implemented using ASP solvers for non-disjunctive programs with a two-step approach. We first create a disjunction-free generator program that has the same answer sets as P, and use the ASP solver to find a candidate answer set S. Next we use a disjunction-free tester program to check whether S is preferred or not. Since the tester is based on a declarative representation of the preference criterion it is easy to switch between different notions of preference, or to define new ones.

Further contributions of this paper are a Pareto-style preference criterion which, to the best of our knowledge, has not been used in prioritized non-monotonic reasoning before, a combination of ordered disjunctions with preferences among rules, and several complexity results. For a discussion of related approaches to logic programming with context dependent priorities see [2].

In future work we want to study more general qualitative decision making problems. In such settings it is not always sufficient to consider the most preferred answer sets only since this amounts to an extremely optimistic view about how the world will behave (this view is sometimes called wishful thinking). As is well-known in decision theory, for realistic models of decision making it is necessary to clearly distinguish what is under the control of the agent (and thus may constitute the agent's decision) from what is not.

In answer set programming this can be done by distinguishing a subset of the literals as decision literals. *LPODs* can be used to describe possible actions or decisions and their consequences, states of the world and desired outcomes. Based on the preference ordering on answer sets an ordering on possible decisions can be defined based on some decision strategy. We plan to work this out in more detail in a separate paper.

Acknowledgements

We would like to thank Tomi Janhunen for helpful comments. The second and third author thank Academy of Finland (project 53695) and HeCSE for financial support.

References

1. G. Brewka, S. Benferhat, and D. Le Berre. Qualitative choice logic. In *Proc. Principles of Knowledge Representation and Reasoning, KR-02*, pages 158–169. Morgan Kaufmann, 2002.
2. G. Brewka. Logic programming with ordered disjunction. In *Proc. 18th National Conference on Artificial Intelligence, AAAI-2002*. Morgan Kaufmann, 2002.
3. T. Eiter and G. Gottlob. Propositional circumscription and extended closed-world reasoning are Π_2^P-complete. *Theoretical Computer Science*, 114:231–245, 1993.
4. M. Gelfond and V. Lifschitz. Classical negation in logic programs and disjunctive databases. *New Generation Computing*, 9:365–385, 1991.
5. Tomi Janhunen, Ilkka Niemelä, Patrik Simons, and Jia-Huai You. Unfolding partiality and disjunctions in stable model semantics. In *Principles of Knowledge Representation and Reasoning: Proceedings of the 7th International Conference*, pages 411–419. Morgan Kaufmann Publishers, April 2000.
6. Ilkka Niemelä and Patrik Simons. Extending the Smodels system with cardinality and weight constraints. In Jack Minker, editor, *Logic-Based Artificial Intelligence*, pages 491–521. Kluwer Academic Publishers, 2000.
7. C. Sakama and K. Inoue. An alternative approach to the semantics of disjunctive logic programs and deductive databases. *Journal of Automated Reasoning*, 13:145–172, 1994.

An Infinite-Valued Semantics
for Logic Programs with Negation[*]

Panos Rondogiannis[1] and William W. Wadge[2]

[1] Department of Informatics & Telecommunications
University of Athens
Panepistimiopolis, 157 84 Athens, Greece
prondo@di.uoa.gr

[2] Department of Computer Science
University of Victoria
PO Box 3055, STN CSC, Victoria, BC, Canada V8W 3P6
wwadge@csr.uvic.ca

Abstract. We give a purely model-theoretic (denotational) characterization of the semantics of logic programs with negation allowed in clause bodies. In our semantics (the first of its kind) the meaning of a program is, as in the classical case, the unique *minimum* model in a program-independent ordering. We use an expanded truth domain that has an uncountable linearly ordered set of truth values between *False* (the minimum element) and *True* (the maximum), with a *Zero* element in the middle. The truth values below *Zero* are ordered like the countable ordinals. The values above *Zero* have exactly the reverse order. Negation is interpreted as reflection about *Zero* followed by a step towards *Zero*; the only truth value that remains unaffected by negation is *Zero*. We show that every program has a unique minimum model M_P, and that this model can be constructed with a T_P iteration which proceeds through the countable ordinals. Furthermore, collapsing the true and false values of the infinite-valued model M_P to (the classical) *True* and *False*, gives a three-valued model identical to the well-founded one.

1 The Problem of Negation

One of the paradoxes of logic programming is that such a small fragment of formal logic serves as such a powerful programming language. This contrast has led to many attempts to make the language more powerful by extending the fragment, but these attempts generally backfire. The extended languages can be implemented, and are in a sense more powerful; but these extensions usually disrupt the relationship between the meaning of programs *as programs* and the meaning *as logic*. In these cases the implementation of the program-as-program can no longer be considered as computing a distinguished model of the program-as-logic. Even worse, the result of running the program may not correspond to any model at all.

---

[*] This work has been partially supported by the University of Athens under the project "Extensions of the Logic Programming Paradigm".

S. Flesca et al. (Eds.): JELIA 2002, LNAI 2424, pp. 456–468, 2002.

The problem is illustrated by the many attempts to extend logic programming with negation (of atoms in the clause bodies). The generally accepted computational interpretation of negated atoms is negation-as-failure. Intuitively, a goal $\neg A$ succeeds iff the subcomputation which attempts to establish A terminates and fails. For example, given the program

$$p \leftarrow$$
$$r \leftarrow \neg p$$
$$s \leftarrow \neg q$$

the query $\leftarrow r$ fails because p succeeds, while $\leftarrow s$ succeeds because q fails.

If we assemble the results of these queries, we see that the negation-as-failure computational rule assigns the value *True* to p and s and the value *False* to q and r. These values do constitute a model of the program-as-logic, but not the only one. One can easily see that there exist five other models of the program, four of which can be ruled out as non-minimal; the remaining model however (in which r and s are *False* and p and q are *True*) is also minimal and can not be immediately ruled out. The problem is that the program, considered as logic, does not give us any grounds (any model-theoretic grounds) for distinguishing between the "right" model according to the implementation and its companion minimal model (which is computationally "wrong"). To make the point more forcefully, consider the program which results by changing the last clause in the program to $q \leftarrow \neg s$. The "wrong" model of the original program is the "right" model of the changed program and vice versa. But the new clause is *logically equivalent* to the old clause, so that the two programs are also logically equivalent. They have the same *model theory* (set of models), but not the same computational meaning. Obviously, the computational meaning does not have a purely model theoretic specification.

A construction that produces a single model is the so-called *stratified semantics* [2,10], which uses a mixture of syntactic and model-theoretic concepts. This semantics fails for programs in which some variables are defined (directly or indirectly) in terms of their own negations. For such programs we need an extra intermediate (neutral) truth value for certain of the negatively recursively defined variables. This approach yields the "well-founded" model [15].

There is a general feeling (which we share) that the well-founded model is the right one. There still remains however a question about its legitimacy, mainly because the well-founded model is in fact one of the *minimal* models of the program and not a *minimum* one. In other words, there is nothing that distinguishes it *as a model*. This leads to the situation described above: two programs may have exactly the same set of models but a different well-founded model. Our goal is to remove the last doubts surrounding the well-founded model by providing a purely model theoretic semantics (the *infinite-valued semantics*) which is compatible with the well-founded model, but in which every program with negation has a unique *minimum* model. Consequently, the advantage of the proposed semantics with respect to the existing approaches to negation is that whenever two programs have the same set of infinite-valued models then they have the same minimum model.

Informally, we extend the domain of truth values and use these extra values to distinguish between ordinary negation and negation-as-failure, which we see as being strictly weaker. For example, in the program cited earlier, both p and s receive the value *True*. We would argue, however, that in some sense p is "truer" than s. Namely, p is true because there is a rule which says so, whereas s is true only because we are never obliged to make q true. In a sense, s is true only by default. Our truth domain adds a "default" truth value T_1 just below the "real" truth T_0, and (by symmetry) a weaker false value F_1 just above ("not as false as") the real false F_0. We can then understand negation-as-failure as combining ordinary negation with a weakening. Thus $\neg F_0 = T_1$ and $\neg T_0 = F_1$. Since negations can effectively be iterated, our domain requires a whole sequence $\ldots, T_3, T_2, T_1$ of weaker and weaker truth values below T_0 but above the neutral value 0; and a mirror image sequence $F_1, F_2, F_3 \ldots$ above F_0 and below 0. In fact, to capture the well-founded model in full generality, we need a T_α and a F_α for every countable ordinal α.

We show that, over this extended domain, every logic program with negation has a unique *minimum* model; and that in this model, if we collapse all the T_α and F_α to T_0 and F_0 respectively, we get the three-valued well-founded model. For our example program, the minimum model is $\{(p, T_0), (q, F_0), (r, F_1), (s, T_1)\}$. This collapses to $\{(p, True), (q, False), (r, False), (s, True)\}$. It is important to note that changing the last clause as described above changes the minimum model to $\{(p, T_0), (q, T_1), (r, F_1), (s, F_0)\}$. This is not a paradox any more, since the two programs do not have the same set of infinite-valued models.

2   Infinite Valued Models

In this section we define infinite-valued interpretations and infinite-valued models of programs. In the following discussion we assume familiarity with the basic notions of logic programming [7]. We consider the class of normal logic programs:

Definition 1. *A normal program clause is a clause whose body is a conjunction of literals. A normal logic program is a finite set of normal program clauses.*

We follow a common practice in the area of negation, which dictates that instead of studying (finite) logic programs it is more convenient to study their (possibly infinite) *ground instantiations* [4]:

Definition 2. *If P is a normal logic program, its associated ground instantiation P^* is constructed as follows: first, put in P^* all ground instances of members of P; second, if a clause $A \leftarrow$ with empty body occurs in P^*, replace it with $A \leftarrow$ true; finally, if the ground atom A is not the head of any member of P^*, add $A \leftarrow$ false.*

The program P^* is in essence a (generally infinite) propositional program. In the rest of this paper, we will assume that all programs under consideration (unless otherwise stated) are of this form.

The basic idea behind the proposed approach is that in order to obtain a *minimum* model semantics for logic programs with negation, it is necessary to consider a very refined multiple valued logic which is based on an infinite set of truth values, ordered as follows:

$$F_0 < F_1 < \cdots < F_\omega < \cdots < F_\alpha < \cdots < 0$$
$$< \cdots < T_\alpha < \cdots < T_\omega < \cdots < T_1 < T_0$$

Intuitively, F_0 and T_0 are the classical *False* and *True* values and 0 is the *undefined* value. The values below 0 are ordered like the countable ordinals. The values above 0 have exactly the reverse order. The intuition behind the new values that have been introduced is that they express different levels of truthfulness and falsity. In the following we denote by V the set consisting of the above truth values. A notion that will prove useful in the sequel is that of the *order* of a given truth value:

Definition 3. *The* order *of a truth value is defined as follows:* $order(T_\alpha) = \alpha$, $order(F_\alpha) = \alpha$ *and* $order(0) = +\infty$.

The notion of "Herbrand interpretation of a program" can now be generalized:

Definition 4. *An (infinite-valued) interpretation I of a program P is a function from the Herbrand Base B_P of P to V.*

In the rest of the paper, the term "interpretation" will always mean an infinite-valued one (unless otherwise stated). As a special case of interpretation, we will use $\emptyset$ to denote the interpretation that assigns the F_0 value to all atoms of a program.

In order to define the notion of *model* of a given program, we need to extend the notion of interpretation to apply to literals, to conjunctions of literals and to the two constants `true` and `false` (notice that for the purposes of this paper it is not actually needed to extend I to more general formulas):

Definition 5. *Let I be an interpretation of a given program P. Then, I can be extended as follows:*

— *For every negative atom $\neg p$ appearing in P:*

$$I(\neg p) = \begin{cases} T_{\alpha+1} & \text{if } I(p) = F_\alpha \\ F_{\alpha+1} & \text{if } I(p) = T_\alpha \\ 0 & \text{if } I(p) = 0 \end{cases}$$

— *For every conjunction of literals $l_1, \ldots, l_n$ appearing as the body of a clause in P:*

$$I(l_1, \ldots, l_n) = min\{I(l_1), \ldots, I(l_n)\}$$

Moreover, $I(\texttt{true}) = T_0$ and $I(\texttt{false}) = F_0$.

The notion of satisfiability of a clause can now be defined:

Definition 6. *Let P be a program and I an interpretation of P. Then, I satisfies a clause $p \leftarrow l_1, \ldots, l_n$ of P if $I(p) \geq I(l_1, \ldots, l_n)$. Moreover, I is a model of P if I satisfies all clauses of P.*

Given an interpretation of a program, we adopt a specific notation for the set of predicate symbols of the program that are assigned a specific truth value:

Definition 7. *Let P be a program, I an interpretation of P and $v \in V$. Then the set of predicate symbols of P that have truth value v is denoted by $I \parallel v$ and defined as: $I \parallel v = \{p \in B_P \mid I(p) = v\}$.*

The following relations will prove useful in the rest of the paper:

Definition 8. *Let I and J be interpretations of a given program P and α be a countable ordinal. We write $I =_\alpha J$, if for all $\beta \leq \alpha$, $I \parallel T_\beta = J \parallel T_\beta$ and $I \parallel F_\beta = J \parallel F_\beta$.*

Definition 9. *Let I and J be interpretations of a given program P and α be a countable ordinal. We write $I \sqsubset_\alpha J$, if for all $\beta < \alpha$, $I =_\beta J$ and either $I \parallel T_\alpha \subset J \parallel T_\alpha$ and $I \parallel F_\alpha \supseteq J \parallel F_\alpha$, or $I \parallel T_\alpha \subseteq J \parallel T_\alpha$ and $I \parallel F_\alpha \supset J \parallel F_\alpha$. We write $I \sqsubseteq_\alpha J$ if $I =_\alpha J$ or $I \sqsubset_\alpha J$.*

Definition 10. *Let I and J be interpretations of a given program P. We write $I \sqsubset_\infty J$, if there exists a countable ordinal α such that $I \sqsubset_\alpha J$. We write $I \sqsubseteq_\infty J$ if either $I = J$ or $I \sqsubset_\infty J$.*

It is easy to see that the relation $\sqsubseteq_\infty$ is a partial order (ie. it is reflexive, transitive and antisymmetric). On the other hand, the relation $\sqsubseteq_\alpha$ is a preorder (ie. reflexive and transitive). The relation $\sqsubseteq_\infty$ will be used in the coming sections in order to define a *minimum* model semantics for logic programs with negation.

Example 1. Consider the program P:

$$p \leftarrow \neg q$$
$$q \leftarrow \texttt{false}$$

It can easily be seen that the interpretation $M_P = \{(p, T_1), (q, F_0)\}$ is the least one (with respect to $\sqsubseteq_\infty$) among all infinite-valued models of P.

We can now define a notion of monotonicity that will be the main tool in defining the infinite-valued semantics of logic programs:

Definition 11. *Let P be a program and let α be a countable ordinal. A function Φ from the set of interpretations of P to the set of interpretations of P is called α-monotonic, iff for all interpretations I and J of P, $I \sqsubseteq_\alpha J \Rightarrow \Phi(I) \sqsubseteq_\alpha \Phi(J)$.*

Based on the notions defined above, we can now define and examine the properties of an immediate consequence operator for logic programs with negation.

3   The Immediate Consequence Operator

In this section we demonstrate that one can easily define a T_P operator for logic programs with negation, based on the notions developed in the last section. As it will be demonstrated, T_P is α-monotonic, a property that allows us to prove that it has a least fixpoint. The procedure required for getting this least fixpoint is more subtle than that for classical logic programs, and will be described shortly.

Definition 12. *Let P be a program and let I be an interpretation of P. The operator T_P is defined as follows*[1]:

$$T_P(I)(p) = lub\{I(l1,\ldots,l_n) \mid p \leftarrow l_1,\ldots,l_n \in P\}$$

T_P is called the immediate consequence operator *for P.*

One can easily see that any subset of the set V of truth values has a *lub*, and therefore the immediate consequence operator is well-defined. One basic property of T_P that will be used in the rest of the paper, is that it is α-monotonic:

Lemma 1. *The immediate consequence operator T_P is α-monotonic, for all countable ordinals α.*

Proof. The proof is by transfinite induction on α. Assume the lemma holds for all $\beta < \alpha$. We demonstrate that it also holds for α. More specifically, let I, J be two interpretations of P such that $I \sqsubseteq_\alpha J$. We demonstrate that $T_P(I) \sqsubseteq_\alpha T_P(J)$.

It is easy to see that for all $\beta < \alpha$, it is $T_P(I) =_\beta T_P(J)$. It remains therefore to show that $T_P(I) \parallel T_\alpha \subseteq T_P(J) \parallel T_\alpha$ and that $T_P(I) \parallel F_\alpha \supseteq T_P(J) \parallel T_\alpha$. We show the former part (the latter part concerning the F_α values can be established in a similar way). Assume that for some predicate p in P we have $T_P(I)(p) = T_\alpha$. We need to show that $T_P(J)(p) = T_\alpha$. We start by first demonstrating that $T_P(J)(p) \leq T_\alpha$ and subsequently we establish the stronger result. Assume that $T_P(J)(p) > T_\alpha$. Then, there exists a clause $p \leftarrow q_1,\ldots,q_n, \neg w_1,\ldots,\neg w_m$ in P whose evaluation under J results to a value that is $> T_\alpha$. This means that for all q_i, $1 \leq i \leq n$, $J(q_i) > T_\alpha$, and for all w_i, $1 \leq i \leq m$, $J(\neg w_i) > T_\alpha$. This implies that $J(w_i) < F_\alpha$. But I and J agree on all values that are $> T_\alpha$ or $< F_\alpha$. Therefore, $T_P(I)(p) > T_\alpha$. This is a contradiction and therefore $T_P(J)(p) \leq T_\alpha$.

Consider now the fact that $T_P(I)(p) = T_\alpha$. This easily implies that there exists a rule of the form $p \leftarrow q_1,\ldots,q_n, \neg w_1,\ldots,\neg w_m$ in P whose body evaluates under I to the value T_α. Then, either there exists a q_r, $1 \leq r \leq n$ such that $I(q_r) = T_\alpha$, or there exists a w_r, $1 \leq r \leq m$ such that $I(\neg w_r) = T_\alpha$. This means that for all q_i, $1 \leq i \leq n$, it is $I(q_i) \geq T_\alpha$ and for all w_i, $1 \leq i \leq m$, it is $I(\neg w_i) \geq T_\alpha$, which implies that $I(w_i) < F_\alpha$. But $I \sqsubseteq_\alpha J$ and also I and J agree on all values that are either $< F_\alpha$ or $> T_\alpha$. Therefore, the evaluation of the above rule under the interpretation J also results to the value T_α.   □

---

[1] The notation $T_P(I)(p)$ is possibly more familiar to people having some experience with functional programming: $T_P(I)(p)$ is the value assigned to p by the interpretation $T_P(I)$.

It is natural to wonder whether T_P is monotonic with respect to the relation $\sqsubseteq_\infty$. This is not the case, as the following example illustrates:

Example 2. Consider the program:

$$p \leftarrow \neg q$$
$$s \leftarrow p$$
$$t \leftarrow \neg s$$
$$t \leftarrow u$$
$$u \leftarrow t$$
$$q \leftarrow \texttt{false}$$

Consider the following interpretations: $I = \{(p, T_1), (q, F_0), (s, F_0), (t, T_1), (u, F_0)\}$ and $J = \{(p, T_1), (q, F_0), (s, F_1), (t, F_1), (u, F_1)\}$. Obviously, $I \sqsubseteq_\infty J$ because $I \sqsubseteq_0 J$. However, we have $T_P(I) = \{(p, T_1), (q, F_0), (s, T_1), (t, T_1), (u, T_1)\}$ and $T_P(J) = \{(p, T_1), (q, F_0), (s, T_1), (t, T_2), (u, F_1)\}$. Clearly, $T_P(I) \not\sqsubseteq_\infty T_P(J)$.

The fact that T_P is not monotonic under $\sqsubseteq_\infty$ suggests that if we want to find the minimum (with respect to $\sqsubseteq_\infty$) fixpoint of T_P, we should not rely on approximations based on the relation $\sqsubseteq_\infty$. The way that this minimum fixpoint can be constructed, is described in the following section.

4   Construction of the Minimum Model M_P

The construction of the minimum model M_P of a given program P can informally be described as follows. As a first approximation to M_P, we start with the interpretation that assigns to every atom the value F_0 (namely with $\emptyset$). We start iterating T_P on $\emptyset$ until both the set of atoms that have a F_0 value and the set of atoms having a T_0 value, stabilize. We keep all these atoms whose values have stabilized and reset the values of all remaining atoms to the next false value (namely F_1). The procedure is repeated until the F_1 and T_1 values stabilize, and we reset the remaining atoms to a value equal to F_2, and so on. Since the Herbrand Base of P is countable, there exists a countable ordinal δ for which this process will not produce any new atoms having F_δ or T_δ values. At this point we stop the iterations and reset all remaining atoms to the value 0. The above process is illustrated by the following example:

Example 3. Consider the program:

$$p \leftarrow \neg q$$
$$q \leftarrow \neg r$$
$$s \leftarrow p$$
$$s \leftarrow \neg s$$
$$r \leftarrow \texttt{false}$$

We start from the interpretation $I = \{(p, F_0), (q, F_0), (r, F_0), (s, F_0)\}$. Iterating T_P twice, we get the interpretation $\{(p, F_2), (q, T_1), (r, F_0), (s, T_1)\}$ in which the order 0 values have stabilized. We reset the values of all other atoms to F_1 getting the interpretation $\{(p, F_1), (q, F_1), (r, F_0), (s, F_1)\}$. We iterate T_P two more times and we get the interpretation $\{(p, F_2), (q, T_1), (r, F_0), (s, T_2)\}$ in which the order 1 values have converged. We reset all remaining values to F_2 getting the interpretation $\{(p, F_2), (q, T_1), (r, F_0), (s, F_2)\}$. After two more iterations of T_P we get $\{(p, F_2), (q, T_1), (r, F_0), (s, F_4)\}$ in which the order 2 values have stabilized. We reset the value of s to F_3 and iterate one more time getting the interpretation $\{(p, F_2), (q, T_1), (r, F_0), (s, T_4)\}$. The fact that we do not get any order 3 value implies that we have reached the end of the iterations. The final model results by setting the value of s to 0, getting the interpretation $M_P = \{(p, F_2), (q, T_1), (r, F_0), (s, 0)\}$.

The above notions are formalized by the definitions that follow.

Definition 13. *Let P be a program and let I be an interpretation of P. Then, we define:*

$$T_{P,\alpha}^\omega(I)(p) = \begin{cases} I(p) & \text{if } order(I(p)) < \alpha \\ T_\alpha & \text{if } p \in \bigcup_{n<\omega}(T_P^n(I) \parallel T_\alpha) \\ F_\alpha & \text{if } p \in \bigcap_{n<\omega}(T_P^n(I) \parallel F_\alpha) \\ F_{\alpha+1} & \text{otherwise} \end{cases}$$

Definition 14. *Let P be a program, I an interpretation of P and let β be a countable ordinal. Then the subset of I of order β is defined as: $I \natural \beta = \{(p, v) \in I \mid order(v) = \beta\}$.*

We now define a sequence of interpretations of a given program P (which can be thought of as better and better approximations to the minimum model of P):

Definition 15. *Let P be a program and let:*

$$\begin{aligned} M_0 &= T_{P,0}^\omega(\emptyset) \\ M_\alpha &= T_{P,\alpha}^\omega(M_{\alpha-1}) && \text{for successor ordinal } \alpha \\ M_\alpha &= T_{P,\alpha}^\omega(\textstyle\bigsqcup_{\beta<\alpha} M_\beta) && \text{for limit ordinal } \alpha \end{aligned}$$

where:

$$(\bigsqcup_{\beta<\alpha} M_\beta)(p) = \begin{cases} (\bigcup_{\beta<\alpha}(M_\beta \natural \beta))(p) & \text{if this is defined} \\ F_\alpha & \text{otherwise} \end{cases}$$

The $M_0, M_1, \ldots, M_\alpha, \ldots$ are called the approximations to the minimum model of P.

Theorem 1. *For all countable ordinals α, $T_P(M_\alpha) =_\alpha M_\alpha$.*

Proof. (Outline) The proof is by transfinite induction on α. The basis case ($\alpha = 0$) is easy to establish. We outline the induction step for the case where α is a successor ordinal (a similar proof applies in the case where α is a limit ordinal). It is easy to see that: $M_{\alpha-1} \sqsubseteq_\alpha T_P(M_{\alpha-1}) \sqsubseteq_\alpha \cdots \sqsubseteq_\alpha T_P^n(M_{\alpha-1}) \sqsubseteq_\alpha \cdots$ (the proof is by an inner induction on n using the α-monotonicity of T_P). By the definition of M_α, it follows that for all $n < \omega$, $T_P^n(M_{\alpha-1}) \sqsubseteq_\alpha M_\alpha$. Moreover, it can be shown that $M_\alpha \sqsubseteq_\alpha J$ for every interpretation J that is an upper bound (with respect to $\sqsubseteq_\alpha$) of the chain $\{T_P^n(M_{\alpha-1})\}_{n<\omega}$. Using the above facts, one can demonstrate that $T_P(M_\alpha) \sqsubseteq_\alpha M_\alpha$ and $M_\alpha \sqsubseteq_\alpha T_P(M_\alpha)$ which implies that $T_P(M_\alpha) =_\alpha M_\alpha$ (we omit the details).   □

We can now formally define the interpretation M_P of a given program P (which as will be demonstrated in the next section, is the minimum model of P with respect to $\sqsubseteq_\infty$). Since B_P is countable, there exists the smallest countable ordinal δ such that $M_\delta \parallel T_\delta = \emptyset$ and $M_\delta \parallel F_\delta = \emptyset$. The ordinal δ is called the *depth* of P [2]. We can then define M_P as:

$$M_P(p) = \begin{cases} M_\delta(p) & \text{if } order(M_\delta(p)) < \delta \\ 0 & \text{otherwise} \end{cases}$$

As it will be shown shortly, M_P is the least fixpoint of T_P, the minimum model of P, and when it is restricted to three-valued logic it coincides with the well-founded model [15].

5   Properties of M_P

In this section we demonstrate that the interpretation M_P is a model of P. Moreover, we show that M_P is in fact the *minimum* model of P under $\sqsubseteq_\infty$.

Theorem 2. *The interpretation M_P of a program P is a fixpoint of T_P.*

Proof. By the definition of M_P, for all countable ordinals α it is $M_P =_\alpha M_\alpha$. Then, for all α, $T_P(M_P) =_\alpha T_P(M_\alpha) =_\alpha M_\alpha =_\alpha M_P$. Therefore, M_P is a fixpoint of T_P.   □

Theorem 3. *The interpretation M_P of a program P is a model of P.*

Proof. Let $p \leftarrow B$ be a clause in P. It suffices to show that $M_P(p) \geq M_P(B)$. We have:

$$\begin{aligned} M_P(p) &= T_P(M_P)(p) && \text{(because M_P is a fixpoint of T_P)} \\ &= lub\{M_P(B_C) \mid (p \leftarrow B_C) \in P\} && \text{(Definition of T_P)} \\ &\geq M_P(B) && \text{(Property of lub)} \end{aligned}$$

Therefore, M_P is a model of P.   □

Theorem 4. *The infinite-valued model M_P is the least (with respect to $\sqsubseteq_\infty$) among all models of P.*

---

[2] The term "depth" was first proposed by T. Przymusinski in [11].

Proof. (Outline) Let N be another model of P. It suffices to show that for all countable ordinals α, if for all $\beta < \alpha$ it is $M_P \parallel T_\beta = N \parallel T_\beta$ and $M_P \parallel F_\beta = N \parallel F_\beta$ then $M_P \parallel T_\alpha \subseteq N \parallel T_\alpha$ and $M_P \parallel F_\alpha \supseteq N \parallel F_\alpha$. This can be established by a straightforward (but lengthy) transfinite induction on α.   □

Corollary 1. *The infinite-valued model M_P is the least (with respect to $\sqsubseteq_\infty$) among all the fixpoints of T_P.*

Proof. It can easily be seen that every fixpoint of T_P is a model of P. The result follows immediately since M_P is the least model of P.   □

Finally, the following theorem provides the connection between the infinite-valued semantics and the existing semantic approaches to negation:

Theorem 5. *Let N_P be the interpretation that results from M_P by collapsing all true values to True and all false values to False. Then, N_P is the well-founded model of P.*

Proof. (Outline) We consider the definition of the well-founded model given by T. Przymusinski in [11]. This construction uses three-valued interpretations but proceeds in a similar way as the construction of the infinite-valued model. More specifically, the approximations of the well-founded model are defined in [11] as:

$$M_0 = \langle T_\emptyset, F_\emptyset \rangle$$
$$M_\alpha = M_{\alpha-1} \cup \langle T_{M_{\alpha-1}}, F_{M_{\alpha-1}} \rangle \qquad \text{for successor ordinal } \alpha$$
$$M_\alpha = (\textstyle\bigcup_{\beta<\alpha} M_\beta) \cup \langle T_{\bigcup_{\beta<\alpha} M_\beta}, F_{\bigcup_{\beta<\alpha} M_\beta} \rangle \text{ for limit ordinal } \alpha$$

For a detailed explanation of the above notation, see [11]; the definition for the case of limit ordinals is slightly different than the one given in [11], but leads to exactly the same model (obtained in a smaller number of steps). One can show by a transfinite induction on α that the above construction introduces at each step exactly the same true and false atoms as the infinite-valued approach.   □

6   Related Work

The research area of negation in logic programming is very broad and many different approaches have been proposed (comprehensive surveys include [1,9,4]). In this section we give a brief overview of some of the most generally accepted results and discuss how they relate to the infinite-valued approach.

The *stratified semantics* [2] is one of the first widely-accepted approaches to negation. Informally speaking, a program is stratified if it does not contain cyclic dependencies of predicates through negation. Every stratified logic program has a unique *perfect* model. An extension of the notion of stratification is *local stratification* [10]; in a locally stratified program, predicates may depend negatively on themselves as long as no cycles are formed when the rules of the program are instantiated. Again, every locally stratified program has a unique perfect

model [10]. Stratification is a syntactically determinable condition; local stratification is generally undecidable [3] (but for certain classes of logic programs it is
decidable and can lead to interesting and practical forms of negation [16,12,8]).
As it will be further discussed below, both the stratified and the locally stratified
semantics are compatible with the infinite-valued approach.

The *stable model semantics* was defined in [5] through the use of the so-called
stability transformation. A given program may have zero, one or many stable
models. This fact introduces a kind of uncertainty regarding the conclusions that
can be inferred from a given program [1]. The *well-founded semantics* [15] con-
fronts this situation by creating a single three-valued model (instead of possibly
more than one two-valued stable models). Many different constructive definitions of the well-founded model have been proposed; two of the most well-known
ones are the *alternating fixpoint* [13,14] and the *iterated least fixed point* [11]. As
shown in the previous section, when we collapse the infinite-valued model to a
three-valued one, we get exactly the well-founded model. It is well-known that
the well-founded model of a locally stratified program coincides with its unique
perfect model [15]; therefore, when we collapse the infinite-valued model of a
locally stratified program, we get its unique perfect model as a result.

7   Discussion: Infinitesimal Truth Values

In this section we demonstrate (at an informal level) that the proposed approach
to the semantics of negation is closely related to the idea of *infinitesimals* used
in Nonstandard Analysis. Actually, our truth domain can be understood as the
result of extending the classical truth domain by adding a neutral zero and a
whole series of *infinitesimal truth values* arbitrarily close to, but not equal to,
the zero value.

Infinitesimals can be understood as values that are smaller than any "normal" real number but still nonzero. In general, each infinitesimal of order $n + 1$
is considered to be infinitely smaller than any infinitesimal of order n. It should
be clear now how we can place our nonstandard logic in this context. We consider negation-as-failure as ordinary negation followed by "multiplication" by an
infinitesimal ϵ. T_1 and F_1 can be understood as the first order infinitesimals ϵT
and ϵF, T_2 and F_2 as the second order infinitesimals $\epsilon^2 T$ and $\epsilon^2 F$, and so on.

Our approach differs from the "classical" infinitesimals in that we include
infinitesimals of transfinite orders. Even in this respect, however, we are not
pioneers. John Conway, in his famous book *On Numbers and Games*, constructs a
field **No** extending the reals that has infinitesimals of order α for *every* ordinal α -
not just, as our truth domain, for every countable ordinal. Lakoff and Nunez give
a similar (less formal) construction of what they call the *granular numbers* [6].
It seems, however, that we are the first to propose infinitesimal truth values.

But why are the truth values we introduced really infinitesimals? There is
one vital analogy with the classical theory of infinitesimals that emerges when
we study the nonstandard ordering between models introduced. Consider the
problem of comparing two hyperreals each of which is the sum of infinitesimals

extensions thereof. Namely, one wants to know under what conditions update rules can be ignored or permanently deleted, or how the transformed program may be compacted without loss of information for a class of queries. Related to this is the topic of making the most of tabling techniques to avoid repeated recomputations via the inertial rule.

The applications motivation of this technical work stems from some important application areas: e-commerce rule updating and preferring, including the updating of preferences; abductive reasoning with updatable preferences on the abducibles; updatable preferring among actions in planning; dynamically reconfigurable web-sites which adapt to updatable user profiles; reasoning under nonmonotonic uncertainty, where a solution must be sought and preferred among changing options.

Future work, apart from exploring some of the above mentioned application areas (e.g., the web-site one in project FLUX), will involve theoretical and technical solutions towards combining preferences and updates within the purview of well-founded semantics, namely by preferring among its partial stable models.

References

1. J. J. Alferes, P. Dell'Acqua, and L. M. Pereira. A compilation of updates plus preferences. Technical report, LiTH-ITN-R-2002-7, Dept. of Science and Technology, Linköping University, Sweden, 2002. Available at: http://www.itn.liu.se/english/research/.
2. J. J. Alferes, J. A. Leite, L. M. Pereira, H. Przymusinska, and T. C. Przymusinski. Dynamic updates of non-monotonic knowledge bases. *The J. of Logic Programming*, 45(1-3):43–70, 2000.
3. J. J. Alferes and L. M. Pereira. Updates plus preferences. In M. O. Aciego, I. P. de Guzman, G. Brewka, and L. M. Pereira (eds.) *Logics in AI, Procs. JELIA'00*, LNAI 1919, pp. 345–360, Berlin, 2000. Springer.
4. J. J. Alferes and L. M. Pereira. Logic Programming Updating - a guided approach - Essays in honour of Robert Kowalski. In A. Kakas and F. Sadri (eds.) *Computational Logic: From Logic Programming into the Future*. Springer, 2002. To appear. Available at: http://centria.di.fct.unl.pt/~lmp/.
5. G. Brewka. Well-founded semantics for extended logic programs with dynamic preferences. *Journal of Artificial Intelligence Research*, 4, 1996.
6. G. Brewka and T. Eiter. Preferred answer sets for extended logic programs. *Artificial Intelligence*, 109, 1999.
7. G. Brewka and T. Eiter. Preferred answer sets for extended logic programs. *Artificial Intelligence*, 109:297–356, 1999.
8. B. Cui and T. Swift. Preference logic grammars: Fixed-point semantics and application to data standardization. *Artificial Intelligence*, 2002. To appear.
9. J. Delgrande, T. Schaub, and H. Tompits. A compilation of Brewka and Eiter's approach to prioritization. In M. O. Aciego, I. P. de Guzman, G. Brewka, and L. M. Pereira (eds.), *Logics in AI, Procs. JELIA'00*, LNAI 1919, pp. 376–390, 2000.
10. M. Gelfond and V. Lifschitz. The stable model semantics for logic programming. In R. A. Kowalski and K. Bowen (eds.) *Proceedings of the Fifth International Conference on Logic Programming*, pp. 1070–1080, 1988. The MIT Press.
11. B. Grosof. Courteous logic programs: Prioritized conflict handling for rules. Research Report RC 20836, IBM, 1997.
12. K. Inoue and C. Sakama. Negation as failure in the head. *Journal of Logic Programming*, 35:39–78, 1998.
13. V. Lifschitz and T. Woo. Answer sets in general non-monotonic reasoning (preliminary report). In B. Nebel, C. Rich, and W. Swartout (eds.) *KR'92*. Morgan-Kaufmann, 1992.
14. H. Prakken. *Logical Tools for Modelling Legal Argument: A Study of Defeasible Reasoning in Law*, volume 32 of *Law and Philosophy Library*. Kluwer academic publishers, 1997.

More on noMoRe

Thomas Linke, Christian Anger, and Kathrin Konczak

Universität Potsdam, Institut für Informatik
{linke,canger,konczak}@cs.uni-potsdam.de

Abstract. This paper focuses on the efficient computation of answer sets for normal logic programs. It concentrates on a recently proposed rule-based method (implemented in the noMoRe system) for computing answer sets. We show how noMoRe and its underlying method can be improved tremendously by extending the computation of deterministic consequences. With these changes noMoRe is able to deal with more challenging problem classes.

1 Introduction

Answer set programming (ASP) is a programming paradigm, which allows for solving problems in a compact and highly declarative way. The basic idea is to specify a given problem in a declarative language, e.g. normal logic programs[1], such that the different answer sets given by answer sets semantics [8] correspond to the different solutions of the initial problem [10]. As an example, consider the independent set problem, which is to determine if there exists a maximal (wrt set inclusion) independent subset of nodes for a given graph. A subset $S \subseteq V$ of nodes of a graph $G = (V, E)$ is called *independent* if there are no edges between nodes in S. Let

$$P = \left\{ \begin{array}{ll} in(a) \leftarrow not\ in(d), not\ in(b) & in(b) \leftarrow not\ in(a), not\ in(c) \\ in(c) \leftarrow not\ in(b), not\ in(d) & in(d) \leftarrow not\ in(c), not\ in(a) \end{array} \right\} \quad (1)$$

be a logic program and let us call the rules r_a, r_b, r_c and r_d, respectively. Then program (1) encodes the independent set problem for graph $G = (\{a, b, c, d\}, \{(a, b), (b, c), (c, d), (d, a)\})$. Program (1) has two answer sets $X_1 = \{in(a), in(c)\}$ and $X_2 = \{in(b), in(d)\}$ corresponding to the two independent sets of graph G.

Currently there exist a number of interesting applications of answer set programming (e.g. [3,13,14]) as well as reasonably efficient implementations (e.g. smodels [15] and dlv [5]). Since computation of answer sets is NP-complete for normal logic programs (and Σ_2^P-complete for disjunctive logic programs), most algorithms contain a non-deterministic part (making choices) and a part computing deterministic consequences (for these choices). In contrast to [7], where different heuristics are investigated in order to make "good" choices, we improve the deterministic consequences of the recently proposed rule-based noMoRe system [1] in this paper. For all ASP systems mentioned so far, non-deterministic choices and deterministic consequences determine the behavior of the resulting algorithm.

---

[1] The language of normal logic programs is not the only one suitable for ASP. Others are disjunctive logic programs, propositional logic or DATALOG with constraints [4].

S. Flesca et al. (Eds.): JELIA 2002, LNAI 2424, pp. 468–480, 2002.
© Springer-Verlag Berlin Heidelberg 2002

In [11] we proposed a graph theoretical approach for computing answer sets for normal logic programs with at most one positive body atom. A special program transformation was introduced in order to be able to deal with multiple positive body atoms. The drawback was a lack of efficiency. One of the contributions of this paper is the extension of the underlying theory and its implementation in order to deal directly with multiple positive body atoms. Furthermore, we redefine propagation of so-called a-colorings as introduced in [11] such that we are able to include *backward propagation*. In addition, we introduce a technique called *jumping* to ensure complete backward propagation and give experimental results showing the impact of the presented concepts.

2   Background

We deal with normal logic programs which contain the symbol *not* used for *negation as failure*. A *normal logic program* is a set of rules of the form $p \leftarrow q_1, \ldots, q_n, not\ s_1, \ldots, not\ s_k$ where p, q_i $(0 \leq i \leq n)$ and s_j $(0 \leq j \leq k)$ are propositional atoms. A rule is a *fact* if $n = k = 0$, it is called *basic* if $k = 0$ and *quasi-fact* if $n = 0$. For a rule r like above we define $head(r) = p$ and $body(r) = \{q_1, \ldots, q_n, not\ s_1, \ldots, not\ s_k\}$. Furthermore, let $body^+(r) = \{q_1, \ldots, q_n\}$ denote the set of positive body atoms and $body^-(r) = \{s_1, \ldots, s_k\}$ the set of negative body atoms. Definitions of the head, the body, the positive and negative body of a rule are generalized to sets of rules in the usual way. We denote the set of all facts of a program P by $Facts(P)$ and the set of all atoms of P by $Atoms(P)$.

Let r be a rule. Then r^+ denotes the rule $head(r) \leftarrow body^+(r)$, obtained from r by deleting all negative body atoms in the body of r. For a logic program P let $P^+ = \{r^+ \mid r \in P\}$. A set of atoms X is *closed under* a basic program P iff for any $r \in P$, $head(r) \in X$ whenever $body(r) \subseteq X$. The smallest set of atoms which is closed under a basic program P is denoted by $\mathrm{Cn}(P)$. The *reduct*, P^X, of a program P *relative to* a set X of atoms is defined by $P^X = \{r^+ \mid r \in P \text{ and } body^-(r) \cap X = \emptyset\}$. We say that a set X of atoms is an *answer set* of a program P iff $\mathrm{Cn}(P^X) = X$.

A set of rules P is *grounded* iff there exists an enumeration $\langle r_i \rangle_{i \in I}$ of P such that for all $i \in I$ we have that $body^+(r_i) \subseteq head(\{r_1, \ldots, r_{i-1}\})$. Observe that there exists a unique maximal (wrt set inclusion) grounded set $P' \subseteq P$ for each program P. For a set of rules P and a set of atoms X we define the set of generating rules of P wrt X as $GR(P, X) = \{r \in P \mid body^+(r) \subseteq X, body^-(r) \cap X = \emptyset\}$. Then X is an answer set of P iff we have $X = \mathrm{Cn}(GR(P, X)^+)$. This characterizes answer sets in terms of generating rules. Observe, that in general $GR(P, X)^+ \neq P^X$ (take $P = \{a \leftarrow, b \leftarrow c\}$ and $X = \{a\}$).

We need some graph-theoretical terminology . A *directed graph* (or *digraph*) G is a pair $G = (V, A)$ such that V is a finite, non-empty set (vertices) and $A \subseteq V \times V$ is a set (arcs). For a digraph $G = (V, A)$ and a vertex $v \in V$, we define the set of all *predecessors* of v as $\mathrm{Pred}(v) = \{u \mid (u, v) \in A\}$. Analogously, the set of all *successors* of v is defined as $\mathrm{Succ}(v) = \{u \mid (v, u) \in A\}$. Let $G = (V, A)$ and $G' = (V', A')$ be digraphs. Then G' is a *subgraph* of G if $V' \subseteq V$ and $A' \subseteq A$. G' is an *induced subgraph* of G if G' is a subgraph of G s.t. for each $v, v' \in V'$ we have that $(v, v') \in A'$ iff $(v, v') \in A$.

In order to represent more information in a directed graph, we need a special kind of arc labeling. $G = (V, A^0 \cup A^1)$ is a directed graph whose arcs $A^0 \cup A^1$ are labeled zero (A^0) and one (A^1). We call arcs in A^0 and A^1 *0-arcs* and *1-arcs*, respectively. For G we distinguish 0-predecessors (0-successors) from 1-predecessors (1-successors) denoted by $\mathrm{Pred0}(v)$ $(\mathrm{Succ0}(v))$ and $\mathrm{Pred1}(v)$ $(\mathrm{Succ1}(v))$ for $v \in V$, respectively.

Block Graphs for Normal Logic Programs. Next we summarize the central definitions of block graphs for logic programs and a-colorings of block graphs (cf. [11,12]).

Definition 1 *Let P be a logic program and let P' be the maximal grounded subset of P. The* block graph $\Gamma_P = (V_P, A_P^0 \cup A_P^1)$ *of P is a directed graph with vertices $V_P = P'$ and two different kinds of arcs defined as follows*

$$A_P^0 = \{(r', r) \mid r', r \in P' \text{ and } head(r') \in body^+(r)\}$$
$$A_P^1 = \{(r', r) \mid r', r \in P' \text{ and } head(r') \in body^-(r)\}.$$

This definition captures the conditions under which a rule r' blocks another rule r (i.e. $(r', r) \in A^1$). We introduce a 1-arc (r', r) in Γ_P if $r' = (q \leftarrow \ldots)$ and $r = (\ldots \leftarrow \ldots, not\ q, \ldots)$. We also gather all groundedness information in Γ_P, because we only introduce a 0-arc (r', r) (between rules $r' = (q \leftarrow \ldots)$ and $r = (\ldots \leftarrow q, \ldots)$) if r and r' are in the maximal grounded subset of P.[2] Figure 1 shows the block graph of program (1). Since the nodes of Γ_P are the rules of logic program P, operations $head(r)$, $body^+(r)$ and $body^-(r)$ (for $r \in P$) are also operations on the nodes of Γ_P.

In order to define so-called *application colorings* or *a-colorings* for block graphs we need the following definition.

Definition 2 *Let P be a logic program and let $\Gamma_P = (V_P, A_P^0 \cup A_P^1)$ be the corresponding block graph. Furthermore, let $r \in P$ and let $G_r = (V_r, A_r)$ be a graph. Then G_r is a* grounded 0-graph *for r in Γ_P iff the following conditions hold:*

1. *G_r is an acyclic subgraph of Γ_P s.t. $A_r \subseteq A_P^0$*
2. *$r \notin V_r$ and $body^+(r) \subseteq head(V_r)$*
3. *for each node $r' \in V_r$ and for each $q' \in body^+(r')$ there exists a node $r'' \in V_r$ s.t. $q' = head(r'')$ and $(r'', r') \in A_r$.*

Observe, that the nodes of a grounded 0-graph are grounded according to definition. Furthermore, the different grounded 0-graphs for rule r in Γ_P correspond to the different classical "proofs" for $head(r)$ in P^+, ignoring the default negations of all rules.

Definition 3 *Let P be a logic program, let $\mathcal{C} : P \rightarrow \{\ominus, \oplus\}$ be a total mapping[3]. We call r* grounded wrt Γ_P and $\mathcal{C}$ *iff there exists a grounded 0-graph $G_r = (V_r, A_r)$ for r in Γ_P s.t. $\mathcal{C}(V_r) = \oplus$. A rule r is called* blocked wrt Γ_P and $\mathcal{C}$ *if there exists $r' \in Pred1(r)$ s.t. $\mathcal{C}(r') = \oplus$.*

Now we are ready to define a-colorings.

Definition 4 *Let P be a logic program, let Γ_P be the corresponding block graph and let $\mathcal{C} : P \rightarrow \{\ominus, \oplus\}$ be a total mapping. Then $\mathcal{C}$ is an* a-coloring *of Γ_P iff the following condition holds for each $r \in P$*

---

[2] Observe, that for program $P = \{p \leftarrow q, q \leftarrow p\}$ the maximal grounded subset of rules is empty and therefore Γ_P contains no 0-arcs.

[3] A mapping $\mathcal{C} : P \rightarrow C$ is called *total* iff for each node $r \in P$ there exists some $\mathcal{C}(r) \in C$. Oppositely, mapping $\mathcal{C}$ is called partial if there are some $r \in P$ for which $\mathcal{C}(r)$ is undefined.

AP $C(r) = \oplus$ *iff r is grounded and r is not blocked wrt Γ_P and C.*

Let C be an a-coloring of some block graph Γ_P. Rules are then intuitively applied wrt some answer set of P iff they are colored $\oplus$, that is, condition **AP** captures the intuition of applying a rule wrt to some answer set. Similarly, the negation of condition **AP** (r is **not** grounded **or** r is blocked) captures the intuition when a rule is not applicable.

The main result in [11] states that Program P has an answer set X iff Γ_P has an a-coloring C s.t. $GR(P, X) = \{r \in P \mid C(r) = \oplus\}$. This result constitutes a rule-based method to compute answer sets by computing a-colorings. In Figure 1 we have depicted the two a-colorings of the block graph of program (1) left and right from '/', respectively.

Observe, that there are programs for which the corresponding block graph has no a-

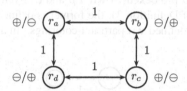

Fig. 1. Block graph and a-colorings of program (1).

coloring and thus no answer set. Let r_p be rule $p \leftarrow not\ p$. Then the 1-loop (r_p, r_p) is the only arc of the block graph of program $P = \{r_p\}$. By Definition 4 there is no a-coloring of Γ_P. If we color r_p with $\oplus$ we get a direct contradiction to **AP**, since then r_p is blocked. On the other hand, if we color r_p with $\ominus$ then r_p is trivially grounded and not blocked.

3 Propagation

In the **nonmonotonic reasoning** system noMoRe [1] the approach described in the last section is implemented. Let us assume that each program is grounded. In order to describe the deterministic part of the implementation and its improvements, we need some central properties of nodes. All those properties are defined wrt partial a-colorings. We call a partial mapping $C : P \rightarrow \{\ominus, \oplus\}$ a *partial a-coloring of Γ_P* if C is an a-coloring of the induced subgraph of Γ_P with nodes $Dom(C)^4$.

Definition 5 *Let P be a logic program and let C be a partial a-coloring of Γ_P. For each node $r \in P$ we define the following properties wrt Γ_P and C:*

1. *p-grounded(r) iff $\forall q \in body^+(r) : \exists r' \in Pred0(r) : q = head(r')$ and $C(r') = \oplus$*
2. *p-notgrounded(r) iff $\exists q \in body^+(r) : \forall r' \in Pred0(r) : q \neq head(r')$ or $C(r') = \ominus$*
3. *p-blocked(r) iff $\exists r' \in Pred1(r) : C(r') = \oplus$*
4. *p-notblocked(r) iff $\forall r' \in Pred1(r) : C(r') = \ominus$.*

Notice the difference between total and partial a-colorings. For example, if p-notgrounded(r) holds for r wrt some total a-coloring C then p-grounded(r) is the

---

4 $Dom(C)$ denotes the domain of mapping C.

negation of p-notgrounded(r). This does not hold for partial a-coloring C, since there may be nodes for which C is undefined. For this reason, we have to define both p-grounded (p-blocked) and p-notgrounded (p-notblocked), respectively, because they cannot be defined through each other wrt partial a-colorings. However, we have the following result for total a-colorings:

Theorem 1 *Let P be a logic program and let C be a total a-coloring of Γ_P. Then a node $r \in P$ is grounded wrt Γ_P and C iff p-grounded(r) holds wrt Γ_P and C. Furthermore, r is blocked wrt Γ_P and C iff p-blocked(r) holds wrt Γ_P and C.*

Clearly, to be grounded (wrt Γ_P and C for node r) is a global concept wrt Γ_P whereas p-grounded(r) is defined locally wrt Γ_P and C. Furthermore, observe the difference between r is blocked and p-blocked(r) wrt Γ_P and C. Even if the definitions of both concepts are the same (cf Definition 3), the former is defined wrt to total a-colorings, whereas the latter one is defined wrt partial a-colorings. In a situation like in Figure 2

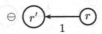

Fig. 2. Some block graph with partial a-coloring.

we do not have p-blocked(r') and we do not have p-notblocked(r') wrt the depicted partial a-coloring. But we always have either that r is blocked or not blocked wrt total a-colorings.

Definition 6 *Let C be a partial a-coloring of Γ_P and let U be the set of uncolored nodes wrt C. Then each node $r \in U$ can be colored $\oplus$ by propagation of C iff we have p-grounded(r) and p-notblocked(r) wrt Γ_P and C. Node r can be colored $\ominus$ by propagation of C iff we have p-notgrounded(r) or p-blocked(r) wrt Γ_P and C.*

Notice, that propagation of partial a-colorings to uncolored nodes is global wrt Γ_P, since in order to propagate C as much as possible we have to check all nodes in U which in general are distributed over Γ_P. According to Definitions 5 and 6 nodes colored by propagation always have colored predecessors. Therefore we obtain a more procedural way to propagate partial a-colorings by *localized* propagation conditions.

Definition 7 *Let P be a logic program, let Γ_P be the corresponding block graph and let C be a partial a-coloring of Γ_P. We define an extended mapping C^e of C s.t. for each $r \in Dom(C)$ we have $C^e(r) = C(r)$ and for each $r, r' \in P$ the following conditions hold wrt Γ_P and C^e:*

(A) *if $r \in Succ1(r')$ and $C^e(r') = \oplus$ then $C^e(r) = \ominus$*

(B) *if $r \in Succ1(r')$ and $C^e(r') = \ominus$ and p-notblocked(r) and p-grounded(r) then $C^e(r) = \oplus$*

(C) *if $r \in Succ0(r')$ and $C^e(r') = \oplus$ and p-notblocked(r) and p-grounded(r) then $C^e(r) = \oplus$*

(D) *if $r \in Succ0(r')$ and $C^e(r') = \ominus$ and p-notgrounded(r) then $C^e(r) = \ominus$.*

of different orders, ie. the problem of determining whether or not $A < B$, where $A = a_0 + a_1 * \epsilon + a_2 * \epsilon^2 + a_3 * \epsilon^3 + \cdots$ and $B = b_0 + b_1 * \epsilon + b_2 * \epsilon^2 + b_3 * \epsilon^3 + \cdots$ (with the a_i and b_i standard reals). We first compare a_0 and b_0. If $a_0 < b_0$ then we immediately conclude that $A < B$ without examining any other coefficients. Similarly, if $a_0 > b_0$ then $A > B$. It is only in the case that $a_0 = b_0$ that the values a_1 and b_1 play a role. If they are unequal, A and B are ordered as a_1 and b_1. Only if a_1 and b_1 are *also* equal do we examine a_2 and b_2, and so on.

To see the analogy, let I and J be two of our nonstandard models and consider the problem of determining whether or not $I \sqsubseteq_\infty J$. It is not hard to see that the formal definition given above can be characterized (somewhat informally) as follows. First, let I_0 be the finite partial model which consists of the *standard* part of I - the subset $I \parallel T_0 \cup I \parallel F_0$ of I obtained by restricting I to those variables to which I assigns standard truth values. Next, I_1 is the result of restricting I to variables assigned order 1 infinitesimal values (T_1 and F_1), and then replacing T_1 and F_1 by T_0 and F_0 (so that I_1 is also a standard interpretation). The higher "coefficients" $I_2, I_3, \ldots$ are defined in the same way. Then (stretching notation) $I = I_0 + I_1 * \epsilon + I_2 * \epsilon^2 + \cdots$ and likewise $J = J_0 + J_1 * \epsilon + J_2 * \epsilon^2 + \cdots$. Then to compare I and J we first compare the standard interpretations I_0 and J_0 using the standard relation. If $I_0 \sqsubseteq_0 J_0$, then $I \sqsubseteq_\infty J$. But if $I_0 = J_0$, then we must compare I_1 and J_1, and if they are also equal, I_2 and J_2, and so on. The analogy is actually very close, and reflects the fact that higher order truth values are negligible (equivalent to 0) compared to lower order truth values. We have good reason, then, to characterize them as infinitesimals.

References

1. K. Apt and R. Bol. Logic Programming and Negation: A Survey. *Journal of Logic Programming*, 19,20:9–71, 1994.
2. K.R. Apt, H.A. Blair, and A. Walker. Towards a Theory of Declarative Knowledge. In J. Minker, editor, *Foundations of Deductive Databases and Logic Programming*, pages 89–148. Morgan Kaufmann, Los Altos, CA, 1988.
3. P. Cholak and H.A. Blair. The Complexity of Local Stratification. *Fundamenta Informaticae*, 21(4):333–344, 1994.
4. M. Fitting. Fixpoint Semantics for Logic Programming: A Survey. *Theoretical Computer Science*. (to appear).
5. M. Gelfond and V. Lifschitz. The Stable Model Semantics for Logic Programming. In *Proceedings of the Fifth Logic Programming Symposium*, pages 1070–1080. MIT Press, 1988.
6. G. Lakoff and R. Nunez. *Where Mathematics comes from*. Basic Books, 2000.
7. J. Lloyd. *Foundations of Logic Programming*. Springer-Verlag, 1987.
8. C. Nomikos, P. Rondogiannis, and M. Gergatsoulis. A Stratification Test for Temporal Logic Programs. In *Proceedings of the 3rd Panhellenic Logic Symposium*, July 17-21 2001. Crete, Greece.
9. H. Przymusinska and T. Przymusinski. Semantic Issues in Deductive Databases and Logic Programs. In R. Banerji, editor, *Formal Techniques in Artificial Intelligence*, pages 321–367. North Holland, 1990.

both possibilities fail **color**$_P$ returns false. Therefore, we say that node r is used as a
choice point. Beeing a choice point is not a property of a node, because choice points
are dynamic wrt each solution. Observe, that all different a-colorings are obtained via
backtracking over choice points in **color**$_P$.

Notice, that procedure **propagate**$_P$ works locally according to conditions (A) to (D)
of Definition 7 and colors are propagated only in arc direction (if possible). The color
of a node is propagated immediately after getting colored, because the test whether the
node was colored correctly is done during propagation. That is, **color**$_P$ fails only during
propagation.

4 Backward Propagation

Partial a-colorings can also be propagated in opposite arc direction which improves our
algorithm. Clearly, as for propagation in arc direction, we have four backward propagation cases. However, there is a problem with defining localized conditions for backward
propagation (as in Definition 7).   Assume that Figure 4 depicts a part of some block

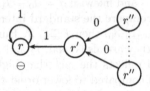

Fig. 4. Part of some block graph with partial a-coloring.

graph together with some partial a-coloring. On the one hand, we know that r' has to be
colored $\oplus$ (provided that there are no other predecessors of r), because this is the only
way to block r. If r is not blocked the depicted partial a-coloring cannot be extended
to a total one. On the other hand, we cannot color r' with $\oplus$, because we do not have
p-grounded(r') (see Definition 6). Therefore we need so-called *transitory a-colorings* .

Definition 8 *Let P be some logic program. We call a partial mapping $C : P \to$
$\{\ominus, \oplus, +\}$ a transitory a-coloring of Γ_P iff C is an a-coloring of the induced subgraph
of Γ_P with nodes $C_\ominus \cup C_\oplus$.*

A transitory a-coloring is a partial a-coloring where some nodes may be uncolored or
colored with +. Color + is used instead of $\oplus$ to color node r' in situations like in
Figure 4, where p-grounded(r') does not hold, yet. In order to transform some transitory
a-coloring (during the execution of **color**$_P$) into a total a-coloring, color + is replaced
by color $\oplus$, if possible. This is achieved by propagation. Whenever a node is colored,
this color is propagated to all its neighbors immediately, no matter whether these already
have been colored or not. In case a node already colored + ($\oplus$) has to be colored $\ominus$ via
propagation, propagation fails due to contradiction. When a node already colored + has
to be colored $\oplus$ via propagation, color + is simply replaced by $\oplus$. That is, either every
color + will become $\oplus$, or **color**$_P$ fails. We need the following properties wrt transitory
a-colorings:

Definition 9 *Let P be a logic program, let C be a transitory a-coloring of Γ_P and let $r \in P$ be some node. Then* groundable(r) *holds wrt Γ_P and C iff $\forall q \in body^+(r) : \exists r' \in Pred0(r)$ with $q = head(r')$ s.t. $C(r') = \oplus$ or r' is uncolored.*

Here groundable(r) means that either r is grounded or that there is some uncolored 0-predecessor, which can possibly be colored $\oplus$ when C is further extended. For each $r \in P$ and $q \in body^+(r)$ we define $S_q \subseteq Pred0(r)$ as $S_q = \{r' \mid r' \in Pred0(r)$ and $q = head(r')\}$. Furthermore, for a set of rules $S \subseteq P$ we define p-grounded(S) wrt Γ_P and transitory a-coloring C iff there is some $r \in S$ s.t. $C(r) = \oplus$. Now we are ready to define the four localized backward propagation cases.

Definition 10 *Let P be a logic program, let Γ_P be the corresponding block graph and let C be a transitory a-coloring of Γ_P. We define an extended mapping $C^e : P \to \{\ominus, \oplus, +\}$ of C s.t. for each $r \in Dom(C)$ we have $C^e(r) = C(r)$ and conditions (A) to (D) of Definition 7 as well as the following conditions hold for all $r, r' \in P$ wrt Γ_P and C^e:*

(bA) *if $C^e(r') = \oplus$ and $r \in Pred1(r')$ then $C^e(r) = \ominus$*

(bB) *if $C^e(r') = \ominus$ and p-grounded(r') and $r \in Pred1(r')$ s.t. $\forall r'' \in Pred1(r') : (C^e(r'') = \ominus$ iff $r'' \neq r)$ then $C^e(r) = +$*

(bC) *if $C^e(r') = \oplus$ and there is some $q \in body^+(r')$ s.t. $q = head(r)$ for some $r \in S_q$ and groundable(r) and for each $r'' \in S_q : (C^e(r'') = \ominus$ iff $r'' \neq r)$ then $C^e(r) = +$*

(bD) *if $C^e(r') = \ominus$ and p-notblocked(r') and there is some $q \in body^+(r')$ with $q = head(r)$ for some $r \in S_q$ s.t. for each $q' \in body^+(r')$: (p-grounded($S_{q'}$) iff $S_{q'} \neq S_q$) then $C^e(r) = \ominus$.*

Intuitively, these cases ensure that an already $\oplus$-colored node is grounded (bC) and not blocked (bA) while an already $\ominus$-colored node is blocked (bB) or not grounded (bD). So in a sense, the purpose of these cases is to justify the color of a node. Observe, that cases (bB) and (bC) use color $+$ instead of $\oplus$ (see Definition 8). We have the following result corresponding to Theorem 2:

Theorem 3 *Let P be a logic program and let C and $C^e : P \to \{\ominus, \oplus, +\}$ be partial mappings. Then we have: If C is a transitory a-coloring of Γ_P and C^e is an extension of C as in Definition 10 then $C_\ominus \subseteq C^e_\ominus$, $C_\oplus \subseteq C^e_\oplus$ and C^e is a transitory a-coloring of Γ_P.*

Let us show how **color**$_P$ computes the a-colorings of the block graph of program (1) (see Figure 1). At the beginning we cannot propagate anything, because there is no fact and no 1-loop. We take r_a as a choice. First, we try to color r_a with $\oplus$ by calling **color**$_P(U, N, C)$ with $U = P \setminus \{r_a\}$, $N = \{r_a\}$ and $C = (\emptyset, \{r_a\})$. Now, **propagate**$_P(N, C)$ is executed. By propagating $C(r_a) = \oplus$ with case (A) we get $C(r_b) = \ominus$ and $C(r_d) = \ominus$. Recursively, through case (B) $C(r_c) = \oplus$ is propagated. This gives $C = (\{r_b, r_d\}, \{r_a, r_c\})$. Since U becomes the empty set, **choose**$_P$ fails and C is the first output. So far we did not need backward propagation.

Now, we color r_a with $\ominus$ through calling **color**$_P(U, N, C)$ with U and N as above and $C = (\emptyset, \{r_a\})$. Since no (backward) propagation is possible we have to compute the next choice. For **choose**$_P$ all three uncolored nodes are possible choices. Assume $C(r_b) = \oplus$ as next choice. Through propagation case (A) we get $C(r_c) = \ominus$. This color of r_c has to be propagated by executing **propagate**$_P(\{r_c\}, (\{r_a, r_c\}, \{r_b\}))$. By using propagation case (B) we obtain $C(r_d) = \oplus$. Recursively, propagation of $\oplus$ for r_d gives no contradiction and $C = (\{r_a, r_c\}, \{r_b, r_d\})$ is the second a-coloring. By assuming $C(r_b) = \ominus$, that is, $C = (\{r_a, r_b\}, \emptyset)$, r_c is colored with $\oplus$ through backward propagation case (bB). By propagation of this color with case (A) node r_d is colored with $\ominus$. By applying case (B) to the color of r_d we obtain that r_a has to be colored with $\oplus$, because it is not blocked, but this is a contradiction to $C(p_a) = \ominus$. Thus, there is no further solution and we have found the two solutions with two choices. Observe that the usage of (bB) saves one additional choice, since without backward propagation the partial coloring $C = (\{r_a, r_b\}, \emptyset)$ could not have been extended any more and another choice would have been necessary. Thus backward propagation reduces the number of necessary choices.

5   Jumping

A further improvement of backward propagation is the so-called *jumping*. Backward propagation according to (bB), (bC) and (bD) requires certain conditions to be fulfilled, which may not be known when a node is colored. For (bA) this is not the case, because in (bA) there is no further condition. Take the following program P and its corresponding block graph Γ_P (see Figure 5):

$$P = \begin{cases} a \leftarrow not\ a, not\ b, not\ d \\ b \leftarrow not\ c \qquad\qquad d \leftarrow not\ e \\ c \leftarrow not\ b \qquad\qquad e \leftarrow not\ d \end{cases} \tag{2}$$

We know that $C(\{r_a\}) = \ominus$, otherwise there would not be an answer set at all. Since

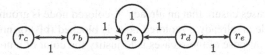

Fig. 5. Block graph of program (2).

r_a is trivially grounded, it has to be blocked. This can be achieved by coloring r_b or r_d with $\oplus$, though one is sufficient. We do not know yet, *which* of the two should be colored $\oplus$. Later on, when e.g. r_b has been used as a choice and is colored $\ominus$, this is achieved via jumping. That is, case (bB) is used again for node r_a and thus r_d is colored $\oplus$. Finally, with (A) node r_e is colored $\ominus$. In this way jumping helps to avoid unnecessary choices, because without jumping we would need another choice to color nodes r_d and r_e. Therefore backward propagation would not be complete without jumping. In general, whenever a $\ominus$ is propagated along a 1-arc to an already $\ominus$-colored node, we check backward propagation case (bB) for this node again. Similarly, we check (bC) and (bD) again for $\oplus$-colored and $\ominus$-colored 0-successors of already colored and propagated nodes, respectively.

As an example, Figure 6 shows the implementation of procedure **jumpB**$_P$, which jumps to an already colored node in order to check backward propagation (bB) again. Procedures **jumpC**$_P$ and **jumpD**$_P$ are implemented analogously. By using procedure **propagate**$_P$ (in Figure 3) as defined in Figure 6 we obtain an algorithm for computing a-colorings including backward propagation and jumping. The four procedures

procedure **propagate**$_P$(N : list, $\mathcal{C}$: part. mapping)
  var r' : node;
    <u>while</u> $N \neq \emptyset$ do
      select r' from N;
      <u>if</u> ($r' \in \mathcal{C}_\oplus$) <u>then</u>
(A)   <u>if</u> **propA**$_P$(r', $\mathcal{C}$) fails <u>then</u> fail;
(C)   <u>if</u> **propC**$_P$(r', $\mathcal{C}$) fails <u>then</u> fail;
(bA)   <u>if</u> **backpropA**$_P$(r', $\mathcal{C}$) fails <u>then</u> fail;
(bC)   <u>if</u> **backpropC**$_P$(r', $\mathcal{C}$) fails <u>then</u> fail;
       <u>if</u> **jumpC**$_P$(r', $\mathcal{C}$) fails <u>then</u> fail;
      <u>else</u>
(B)   <u>if</u> **propB**$_P$(r', $\mathcal{C}$) fails <u>then</u> fail;
(D)   <u>if</u> **propD**$_P$(r', $\mathcal{C}$) fails <u>then</u> fail;
(bB)   <u>if</u> **backpropB**$_P$(r', $\mathcal{C}$) fails <u>then</u> fail;
(bD)   <u>if</u> **backpropD**$_P$(r', $\mathcal{C}$) fails <u>then</u> fail;
       <u>if</u> **jumpB**$_P$(r', $\mathcal{C}$) fails <u>then</u> fail;
       <u>if</u> **jumpD**$_P$(r', $\mathcal{C}$) fails <u>then</u> fail;

procedure **jumpB**$_P$(r' : node; $\mathcal{C}$: partial mapping;
  var S : set of nodes;
    S := Succ1(r')
    <u>while</u> $S \neq \emptyset$ do
      select r' from S;
      <u>if</u> $\mathcal{C}(r') = \ominus$ <u>then</u> **backpropB**$_P$(r', $\mathcal{C}$);

Fig. 6. Extended propagation procedures including backward propagation and jumping.

backpropA$_P$, **backpropB**$_P$, **backpropC**$_P$, and **backpropD**$_P$ are the implementations of conditions (bA), (bB), (bC) and (bD), respectively. Procedures **propA**$_P$, **propB**$_P$, **propC**$_P$, and **propD**$_P$ are the implementations of conditions (A), (B), (C) and (D), respectively.

6 Results

For a partial mapping $\mathcal{C} : P \rightarrow \{\ominus, \oplus, +\}$ we define the set of *induced answer sets* $A_\mathcal{C}$ as $A_\mathcal{C} = \{X \mid X$ is answer set of $P, \mathcal{C}_\oplus \subseteq GR(P, X)$ and $\mathcal{C}_\ominus \cap GR(P, X) = \emptyset\}$. If $\mathcal{C}$ is undefined for all nodes then $A_\mathcal{C}$ contains all answer sets of P. If $\mathcal{C}$ is a total mapping s.t. no node is colored with $+$ then $A_\mathcal{C}$ contains exactly one answer set of P (if $\mathcal{C}$ is an a-coloring). With this notation we formulate the following result:

Theorem 4 *Let P be a logic program, let $\mathcal{C}$ and $\mathcal{C}'$: $P \rightarrow \{\ominus, \oplus, +\}$ be partial mappings. Then for each $r \in (\mathcal{C}_\ominus \cup \mathcal{C}_\oplus \cup \mathcal{C}_+)$ we have if* **propagate**$_P$($\{r\}$, $\mathcal{C}$) *succeeds and $\mathcal{C}'$ is the partial mapping after its execution then $A_\mathcal{C} = A_{\mathcal{C}'}$.*

This theorem states that **propagate**$_P$ neither discards nor introduces answer sets induced by a partial mapping $\mathcal{C}$. Hence, only nodes used as choices lead to different answer sets. Finally, let C_P be the set of all solutions of **color**$_P$. We obtain correctness and completeness of **color**$_P$.

Theorem 5 *Let P be a logic program, let Γ_P be its block graph, let $\mathcal{C} : P \to \{\ominus, \oplus\}$ be a mapping and let $\mathcal{C}_P$ the set of all solutions of $\textbf{color}_P$ for program P. Then $\mathcal{C}$ is an a-coloring of Γ_P iff $\mathcal{C} \in \mathcal{C}_P$.*

7   Experiments

As benchmarks, we used some instances of NP-complete problems proposed in [2], namely, the independent set problem for circle graphs[5], the problem of finding Hamiltonian cycles in complete graphs and the problem of finding classical graph colorings. Furthermore we have tested some planning problems taken from [6] and the n-queens problem. In Table 1 we have counted the number of choices instead of measuring time, since the number of choices (theoretically) indicates how good an algorithm deals with a non-deterministic problem[6]. That is, for very large examples an algorithm using less choices will be faster than one using more choices (provided that the implementations of the deterministic parts of both algorithms need polynomial time). Therefore counting choices gives rather theoretical than practical results on the behavior of noMoRe. For smodels results with and without lookahead (results in parentheses) are shown[7].

Table 1. Number of choices (all solutions) for different problems.

	noMoRe			smodels	
backprop	no	yes	yes	with	(without)
jumping	no	no	yes	lookahead	
ham_k_7	14335	14335	2945	4814	(34077)
ham_k_8	82200	82200	24240	688595	(86364)
ind_cir_20	539	317	276*	276	(276)
ind_cir_30	9266	5264	4609*	4609	(4609)
p1_step4	-	464	176	7	(69)
p2_step6	-	13654	3779	75	(3700)
col4x4	27680	27680	7811	7811	(102226)
col5x5	-	-	580985	580985	(2.3 Mil)
queens4	84	84	5	1	(11)
queens5	326	326	13	9	(34)

* minimal number of choices, since at least $(n - 1)$ choices are needed for n solutions.

The influence of backward propagation and jumping on the number of choices is plain to see. There are also some problems where we did not obtain a solution after more than 12 hours without backward propagation. Table 1 impressively shows that noMoRe with backward propagation and jumping is now (theoretically) comparable with smodels

---

[5] A so-called circle graph Cir_n has n nodes $\{v_1, \cdots, v_n\}$ and arcs $A = \{(v_i, v_{i+1}) \mid 1 \leq i < n\} \cup \{(v_n, v_1)\}$.

[6] For time measurements for these examples see [1].

[7] Whereas smodels and noMoRe make exactly one choice at each choice point in the search space, dlv makes several choices at the same point of the search space. Therefore there are no results for dlv in Table 1.

on several problem classes; especially if we disable the lookahead of smodels[8]. The difference between smodels and noMoRe for planning examples and the n-queens problems seems to come from different heuristics for making choices. We have just started to investigate the influence of more elaborated heuristics. The noMoRe system including test cases is available at http://www.cs.uni-potsdam.de/~linke/nomore.

8   Conclusion

We have generalized and advanced an approach to compute answer sets for normal logic programs which was introduced in [11]. Now we are able to deal directly with logic programs with multiple positive body literals. We have shown that by introducing backward propagation together with jumping the rule-based algorithm implemented in noMoRe has been greatly improved. A related method of backward propagation wrt answer set semantics for normal logic programs was proposed in [9]. However, a lot of the obtained improvement is due to the concept of a third color +. There seems to be a close relation between noMoRe's color + and dlv's must-be-true truth value [6], though this has to be studied more thoroughly, because noMoRe is rule-based and dlv (as well as smodels) is literal-based. Through the conducted experiments the impact of the improvements is shown. NoMoRe is now comparable to smodels on many different problem classes in terms of the number of choices. This improvement was obtained by improving the deterministic consequences of noMoRe. However, there are still some interesting open questions. The main one is whether rule-based computation of answer sets is different from atom-based (literal-based) or not. During our experiments we have detected programs (with a high rule per atom ratio) for which atom-based computations are more suitable and other programs (with a low rule per atom ratio) for which rule-based computation performs better. Currently, we have no general answer to this question and a general comparison between atom-based and rules-based methods for logic programs will be necessary.

Acknowledgements

This work author was partially supported by the German Science Foundation (DFG) under grant FOR 375/1-1, TP C.

References

1. C. Anger, K. Konczak, and T. Linke. NoMoRe: Non-Monotonic Reasoning with Logic Programs. In I. Ianni and S. Flesca, editors, *Eighth European Workshop on Logics in Artificial Intelligence (JELIA'02)*, vol. 2424 of *LNCS*. Springer, 2002.
2. P. Cholewiński, V. Marek, A. Mikitiuk, and M. Truszczyński. Experimenting with nonmonotonic reasoning. In *Proc. of the International Conference on Logic Programming*, p. 267–281. MIT Press, 1995.
3. Y. Dimopoulos, B. Nebel, and J. Koehler. Encoding planning problems in non-monotonic logic programs. Proc. of the 4th European Conference on Planing, p. 169–181, Toulouse, France, 1997. Springer Verlag.

---

[8] Observe, that currently noMoRe has no lookahead.

4. D. East and M. Truszczyński. dcs: An implementation of datalog with constraints. In *Proc. of the AAAI*. MIT Press, 2000.

5. T. Eiter, N. Leone, C. Mateis, G. Pfeifer, and F. Scarcello. A deductive system for nonmonotonic reasoning. In J. Dix, U. Furbach, and A. Nerode, editors, *Proc. of the LPNMR*, vol. 1265 of *LNAI*, p. 363–374. Springer Verlag, 1997.

6. W. Faber, N. Leone, and G. Pfeifer. Pushing goal derivation in dlp computations. In M. Gelfond, N. Leone, and G. Pfeifer, editors, *LPNMR*, vol. 1730 of *LNAI*, p. 177–191, El Paso, Texas, USA, 1999. Springer Verlag.

7. W. Faber, N. Leone, and G. Pfeifer. Experimenting with heuristics for answer set programming. In B. Nebel, editor, *Proc. of the IJCAI*, p. 635–640. Morgan Kaufmann Publishers, 2001.

8. M. Gelfond and V. Lifschitz. Classical negation in logic programs and deductive databases. *New Generation Computing*, 9:365–385, 1991.

9. N. Iwayama and K. Satoh. Computing abduction by using TMS with top-down expectation. *Journal of Logic Programming*, 44:179–206, 2000.

10. V. Lifschitz. Answer set planning. In *Proc. of the 1999 International Conference on Logic Programming*, p. 23–37. MIT Press, 1999.

11. T. Linke. Graph theoretical characterization and computation of answer sets. In B. Nebel, editor, *Proc. of the IJCAI*, p. 641–645. Morgan Kaufmann Publishers, 2001.

12. T. Linke. Rule-based computation of answer sets. 2002. submitted.

13. X. Liu, C. Ramakrishnan, and S.A. Smolka. Fully local and efficient evaluation of alternating fixed points. Proc. of the 4th Int. Conf. on Tools and Algorithms for the Construction Analysis of Systems, p. 5–19, Lisbon, Portugal, 1998. Springer Verlag.

14. I. Niemelä. Logic programming with stable model semantics as a constraint programming paradigm. *Annals of Mathematics and Artificial Intelligence*, 25(3,4):241–273, 1999.

15. I. Niemelä and P. Simons. Smodels: An implementation of the stable model and well-founded semantics for normal logic programs. In J. Dix, U. Furbach, and A. Nerode, editors, *Proc. of the LPNMR*, p. 420–429. Springer, 1997.

Answer Set Programming
by Ant Colony Optimization

Pascal Nicolas, Frédéric Saubion, and Igor Stéphan

LERIA – University of Angers
2, bd Lavoisier – F-49045 Angers cedex 01 – France
{pascal.nicolas,frederic.saubion,igor.stephan}@univ-angers.fr

Abstract. Answer Set Programming is a very convenient framework to represent various problems issued from Artificial Intelligence (non-monotonic reasoning, planning, diagnosis...). Furthermore, it can be used to neatly encode combinatorial problems. In all cases, the solutions are obtained as sets of literals: the Answer Sets.

Ant Colony Optimization is a general metaheuristics that has been already successfully used to solve hard combinatorial problems (traveling salesman problem, graph coloring, quadratic assignment...). It is based on the collective behavior of artificial ants exploring a graph and exchanging pieces of information by means of pheromone traces.

The purpose of this work is to show how Ant Colony Optimization can be used to compute an answer set of a logic program.

1   Introduction

Since few years Answer Set Programming (ASP) is recognized as a very convenient framework to represent various problems issued from Artificial Intelligence (non-monotonic reasoning, planning, diagnosis...). Furthermore, it can be used to neatly encode combinatorial problems (graph coloring, SAT problems...). Knowledge representation with the help of a logic program can be done in various syntactic and semantic ways (see [1]). One can firstly mention Stable Model semantics [8] for Normal Logic Programs augmented by Negation as Failure (NLPNF). Then, Answer Set [9] semantics has been proposed for Extended Logic Programs (ELP) which extend NLPNF by allowing positive and negative literals in the rules. Answer Set semantics is also used for Extended Disjunctive Logic Programs (EDLP) [9] which extend ELP by allowing a disjunction in the head of the rules.

Deciding the existence of a stable model is $NP-complete$ [12]. This is the same for the existence of an answer set of an ELP since an ELP can be encoded into an NLPNF even in linear time. In case of an EDLP, the complexity grows up to $\Sigma_2^p - complete$ [7]. These preliminary considerations have led us to firstly deal with stable model semantics for NLPNF since it covers a large class of problems while staying at a reasonable level of complexity. Previous works have ended in some operational systems. For instance, DLV [6] and Smodels [16] are able to solve non-trivial problems with thousands of rules. All these systems are based

S. Flesca et al. (Eds.): JELIA 2002, LNAI 2424, pp. 481–492, 2002.

on complete methods and use different heuristics in order to prune the search space as much as possible.

Few researches have already investigated alternative non-complete approaches in the domain of Answer Set Programming. [10] uses local search techniques being inspired by works on SAT problems. [17] transforms the computation of an answer set into a graph coloring problem, solved by a genetic algorithm. [14,15] use genetic algorithms and Ant Colony Optimization (ACO) [5,4] to compute an extension of a Default Theory [18].

The purpose of our present work is to show how ACO can be used to propose a specific system for ASP in order to be able to exploit the peculiarities of logic programs and therefore to compute a stable model of a logic program. This approach is based on the collective behavior of artificial ants exploring a graph and exchanging pieces of information by means of pheromone traces.

2   Stable Model Semantics for Logic Programming

In this work, a *Logic Program* Π is a finite set of rules of the form :
$$c \leftarrow a_1, \ \ldots, \ a_n, \ not \ b_1, \ \ldots, \ not \ b_m \quad n \geq 0, m \geq 0$$
where $a_1, \ \ldots, \ a_n, \ b_1, \ \ldots, \ b_m$ and c are atoms. For such a rule r we denote[1]:

$$body^+(r) = \{a_1, \ \ldots, \ a_n\} \ body^-(r) = \{b_1, \ \ldots, \ b_m\}$$
$$head(r) = c \qquad\qquad r^+ = head(r) \leftarrow body^+(r)$$

Definition 1. *The* reduct Π^A *of a program* Π *wrt. a set of atoms* A *is the program* $\Pi^A = \{r^+ \mid r \in \Pi \ and \ body^-(r) \cap A = \emptyset\}$

Therefore, the resulting program Π^A contains no negation. So, it has a unique minimal Herbrand model that can be obtained by computing its deductive closure $Cl(\Pi^A)$ and the Stable Model semantics [8] of a program Π is defined as follows.

Definition 2. *Let* Π *be a logic program and* S *a set of atoms.* S *is a stable model of* Π *if and only if* $S = Cl(\Pi^S)$.

Contrary to numerous works, we do not deal with a stable model in terms of set of atoms but in terms of *applied* rules as it is the case in [11] from which we adopt some notions.

 − A rule r is *blocked* by an atom set A if $body^-(r) \cap A \neq \emptyset$.
 − A rule r *blocks* a rule r' if $head(r) \in body^-(r')$.
 − A rule which blocks itself as $x \leftarrow \ldots, not \ x, \ldots$ is called a *forbidden rule*.
 − A rule r is *applicable* in an atom set A if $body^+(r) \subseteq A$.
 − Two rules r and r' are compatible if r does not block r', r' does not block r, $body^+(r) \cap body^-(r') = \emptyset$ and $body^+(r') \cap body^-(r) = \emptyset$.

---

[1] Such notations are extended to rule set when their first letter is capitalized.

```
procedure ACO
begin
    Set parameters
    Initialize pheromone trails
    repeat
        construct some candidate solutions
        Update pheromone trails
    until a solution is found or maximum number of iterations reached
end
```

Fig. 1. Ant Colony Optimization algorithm

- A rule set R is *grounded* if there exists an enumeration $\langle r_1, \ldots, r_n \rangle$ of R such that $\forall i \in \{1, \ldots, n\}, r_i$ is applicable in the set $Head(\{r_1, \ldots, r_{i-1}\})$.
- Let Π be a logic program and A an atom set. The set of *Generating Rules* of Π wrt. A is $R(\Pi, A) = \{r \in \Pi | r$ is applicable in A and not blocked by $A\}$.

Computing a stable model of a logic program Π is equivalent to find a particular subset of rules $P \subseteq \Pi$ as we show in the next result.

Lemma 1. *Let $P \subseteq \Pi$ be a subset of a logic program Π. $Head(P)$ is a stable model of Π iff P is grounded and $P = GR(\Pi, Head(P))$.*

The main goal of our search method is to find a set of rules P satisfying lemma 1. Such a set of rules P is called the *Generator* of the stable model $Head(P)$ and all its rules are said to be *applied*. It is easy to check that all rules in a Generator P are pairwise compatible. Firstly, the previous lemma entails that a rule can not block another rule in the same Generator. Secondly, if $r = b \leftarrow a, \ldots$ is a rule in P, it means that $a \in Head(P)$ and then any rule like $r' = c \leftarrow \ldots, not\ a, \ldots$ cannot belong to P. This characteristic is similar to the notion developed in [13] about compatibility between default rules.

3   Ant Colony Optimization for Stable Models

3.1   Ant Colony Optimization Principles

Ant Colony Optimization (ACO) [5,4] has been inspired by the observation of the collective behavior of ants when they are seeking food. Every ant puts a little bit of pheromone all along its walk and directs itself by choosing its way taking into account the amount of pheromone left by previous ants on each possible path. Since the pheromone evaporates, these probabilistic choices evolve continuously. This collective behavior, based on a kind of shared memory (pheromone on paths), can be used for the resolution of any optimization problem or constraint satisfaction problem which can be encoded as the search of an optimal path in a graph. Following [19] we can resume the general ACO algorithm as in the figure 1.

3.2   Problem Representation

We describe here our original design of an Ant Colony Optimization algorithm for stable model search.

Definition 3. *We associate to a logic program Π the graph $G(\Pi) = (r \in \Pi \cup \{in, out\}, A)$ where each rule becomes a vertex and in and out are two particular vertices added to the rule set. The arc set A is defined by :*

$$A = \{(in, r), \forall r \in \Pi \mid body^+(r) = \emptyset\}$$
$$\cup \{(r, r') \in \Pi^2 \mid r \neq r', r \text{ and } r' \text{ are compatible}\}$$
$$\cup \{(r, out), \forall r \in \Pi\}$$
$$\cup \{(in, out)\}$$
$$\setminus \{(r, r'), (r', r), \forall r, r' \in \Pi \mid r \text{ is a forbidden rule }\}$$

In addition, each arc $(i, j) \in A$ is weighted by an artificial pheromone $\tau_{i,j}$ which is a positive real number.

Example 1. The logic program :
$$\Pi = \begin{cases} a \leftarrow not\ f & b \leftarrow not\ c & c \leftarrow a & f \leftarrow b \\ d \leftarrow a,\ not\ b & d \leftarrow not\ d & e \leftarrow d, not\ f \end{cases}$$
is represented by the following graph (:- stands for $\leftarrow$) :

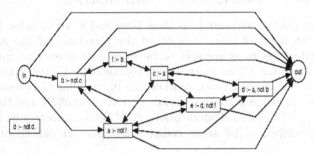

In the sequel, we identify vertices of the graph (different from *in* and *out*) and rules of the logic program and we indifferently use P as a path in the graph (ie a sequence of vertices) or as a set of rules.

An *admissible path* is a cycle free path P from *in* to *out* in the graph $G(\Pi)$. It induces a *Candidate Generator* by implicitly discarding *in* and *out*. Thus, the goal of Ant Colony Optimization is to find an admissible path P such that it is a true Generator of a stable model $Head(P)$. For instance, in example 1, the path $P = \langle in, \quad a \leftarrow not\ f, \quad d \leftarrow a,\ not\ b, \quad c \leftarrow a, \quad e \leftarrow d, not\ f, \quad out \rangle$ leads to a true Generator of the stable model $Head(P) = \{a, c, d, e\}$.

The definition 3 in which we try to build the graph $G(\Pi)$ with the smallest arc set possible is justified by the following remarks :

- Since we seek a grounded set of rules, all paths have to begin (just after *in*) by a rule that is applicable in $\emptyset$.

- Only compatible rules may belong to the same Generator (see end of section 2) so it is useless to put an arc between two rules which are not compatible.
- *out* has to be the last vertex of every path.
- The empty set may be a stable model so we need the arc (in, out).
- Since no Generator can contain a forbidden rule we isolate every rule of the form $x \leftarrow \dots, not\ x, \dots$. By this way no path can contain such rules.

During the initialization stage, the pheromone on every arc of the graph is initialized to 1 in order to give equal chances to all paths. During the process this pheromone globally evaporates on all arcs and it increases on arcs that are on good paths in order to concentrate a great number of ants on the most promising parts of the graph.

3.3   The Ant's Travel

In order to reduce the search space to explore, an ant is not allowed to build any admissible path, since some of them can obviously not lead to a solution[2]. We limit its choices to the set defined below.

Definition 4. *Let an ant be on the last vertex $v = last(P)$ of a partial path $P = \langle in, \dots, v \rangle$ that it is currently building; it can only choose the next vertex in the set :*

$$Next(P) = \left\{ r \in \Pi \left| \begin{array}{l} (last(P), r) \text{ is an arc of } G(\Pi) \\ r \text{ is applicable in } Head(P) \\ \forall r' \in P, r \text{ and } r' \text{ are compatible} \end{array} \right. \right\}$$

Furthermore, as it is usual in the design of an Ant System we introduce a local evaluation function η to weight every possible next vertex. The idea is to give the higher values to the vertices which seem to be the better ones to continue the construction of the Candidate Generator.

Definition 5. *Let $P = \langle in, \dots \rangle$ be a path in the graph $G(\Pi)$ and $r \in Next(P)$ a possible rule to choose to continue the path.*

$$\eta(P, r) = \begin{cases} 1/10 & \text{if } head(r) \in Head(P) \\ 1/10 & \text{if } \exists r' \in \Pi \mid r' \text{ is forbidden, not blocked} \\ & \text{by } P \text{ and applicable in } P \cup \{head(r)\} \\ k \times 10 & \text{with } k = card(\{r' \in \Pi \mid r' \text{ is forbidden,} \\ & \text{applicable in } P, \text{ not blocked by } P \text{ and} \\ & \text{blocked by } r\}) \text{if this set is non empty} \\ 1 & \text{otherwise} \end{cases}$$

The global idea of the heuristic η is based on the fact that a necessary (but not sufficient) condition for a set of atoms to be a true Generator is that it blocks every applicable forbidden rule. This aim is achieved by the four cases of η detailed below.

---

[2] We recall that ants build only cycle free paths but we do not detail how it is done since this is well known.

- If the head of a rule is already in the partial Candidate Generator then it seems not really informative to add the same atom again. Furthermore its negative body would still reduce the possible choices of the next rules.
- If the head of a rule makes applicable a forbidden rule, we have to avoid to choose it. Indeed, if Π contains a rule like $r = b \leftarrow a, not\ b, \ldots$ applying a rule like $a \leftarrow \ldots$ forces to add in the future a rule which will block r. Otherwise, the resulting set is obviously not a true Generator.
- As a supplement of the previous case, we favor a rule if it can block some applicable forbidden rules.
- We give a medium value to all of the other rules.

This local function combined with the recorded pheromone on the graph leads to the definition of the attractivity of a vertex r for an ant staying on the last vertex of a partial path $P = \langle in, \ldots \rangle$.

Definition 6. *Let $G(\Pi)$ be a graph for a logic program Π and $P = \langle in, \ldots, r_i \rangle$ a partial path. We define the attractivity of each vertex $r_j \in Next(P)$ by*

$$A(P, r_j) = \frac{\tau_{i,j} \times \eta(P, r_j)}{\sum_{r_k \in Next(P)} \tau_{i,k} \times \eta(P, r_k)}$$

On each vertex r_i (the last one of its current path) during its travel from in to out, an ant chooses the next vertex by a random choice between all possible next vertices r_j. This choice is biased by the attractivity in such a way that every vertex r_j has a probablity to be chosen equal to $A(P, r_j)$. By definition of the set $Next(P)$ the only paths that can be explored correspond to rule sets that are grounded. If at any time during the process the set $Next(P)$ becomes empty then the ant goes directly to out and the journey is finished. This is the only way for an ant to reach out. Let us remark that the definition of set $Next(P)$ ensures that a final path $P = \langle in, \ldots, out \rangle$ is maximal in the sense that there exists no rule $r \in \Pi \setminus P$ such that r is applicable in $Head(P)$ and r is not blocked by $Head(P)$ except if r is forbidden or if it blocks at least one rule in P. Last, when an ant has chosen its next vertex r, the partial path becomes $P = \langle in, \ldots, r \rangle$. If a non-forbidden rule r' satisfying

$$\begin{cases} r' \text{ is applicable in } Head(P) \\ head(r') \notin Body^-(P) \\ body^-(r') \subseteq Body^-(P) \end{cases}$$

appears, then the ant goes directly on r' because if a Generator $S \supseteq P$ exists then S must contain r'. This deterministic inference is applied as long as possible.

3.4   Path Evaluation

Definition 7. *Let P be a Candidate Generator for a logic program Π. Its evaluation is defined by :*

$$eval(P) = card\left(\left\{ r \in \Pi \setminus P \;\middle|\; \begin{array}{l} r \text{ is applicable in } Head(P) \\ and \text{ not blocked by } Head(P) \end{array} \right\}\right)$$

By using lemma 1 it is obvious to check that $eval(P) = 0 \iff Head(P)$ is a stable model of Π. So the goal of the ants is to minimize the value of $eval(P)$ over the set of possible paths from in to out in $G(\Pi)$ in order to find a path with a null evaluation.

At this point we can informally state that we have a problem of complexity still in class NP, since there is an exponential number of possible paths P, but checking if $eval(P) = 0$ can be done in a polynomial time.

3.5   Pheromone Updating

The goal of pheromone updating is to concentrate ants on the paths that minimize the value of $eval$ and this can be done in many various ways. Here we choose an elitist and ranking strategy [2] to update the pheromone trails. So, if the colony contains N ants then we obtain a set S of $N' \leq N$ different paths. If no path has a null evaluation (otherwise a solution is reached) then, we can order S as a sequence of subsets from the better to the worst paths.

$$S = S_{v_1} \cup \ldots \cup S_{v_n}, \forall i > 0, \begin{cases} \forall s \in S_{v_i}, \ eval(s) = v_i \\ v_i < v_{i+1} \end{cases}$$

If we have fixed to enforce the K better paths of S then we determine the least value $k, 1 \leq k \leq n$ such that $\sum_{i=1}^{k} card(S_{v_i}) \geq K$. Given a global reinforcement coefficient $\Delta, 0 < \Delta < 1$, then all paths in S_{v_1} are reinforced by Δ, those in S_{v_2} by Δ^2, ..., those in $S_{v_{k-1}}$ by Δ^{k-1} and, at last, $K - \sum_{i=1}^{k-1} card(S_{v_i})$ paths, randomly chosen in S_{v_k}, are reinforced by Δ^k. The reinforcement of a path $P = \langle in, r_1, \ldots, r_p, out \rangle$ by a value Δ^k does not consist simply in updating the pheromone on arcs $(in, r_1), (r_1, r_2), \ldots, (r_p, out)$. In fact, for a graph $G(\Pi) = (\Pi \cup \{in, out\}, A)$ all arcs $(r_i, r_j) \in (P \times P) \cap A$ are reinforced by Δ^k, that is :

$$\tau_{i,j} \leftarrow \begin{cases} \tau_{i,j} + \Delta^k \text{ if } (r_i, r_j) \in S_{v_k} \text{ and } \tau_{i,j} < 10 \\ \tau_{i,j} \text{ otherwise} \end{cases}$$

Therefore, it enables us to record in the pheromone the fact that all the vertices in P seem "to get well together". Then, an ant of the next colony, standing on a vertex $r \in P$ will be more incited to choose any rule $r' \in P$ even if (r, r') was not exactly an arc of P. Obviously, this will be possible only if the groundedness condition is respected (this is always checked by the function $Next$). Furthermore, we force the pheromone to stay lesser than 10 in order to let a chance to every arc to be chosen by an ant.

Finally, the evaporation process acts on every arc (r_i, r_j) by :

$$\tau_{i,j} \leftarrow \tau_{i,j} \times 0.99 \text{ if } \tau_{i,j} > 0.1$$

If the pheromone is already lesser than 0.1, we leave it unchanged in order to keep a minimal chance to every arc to be chosen by an ant. On the other side, we force the pheromone trail to stay lesser than 10. It has been shown [19] that this bounding of the pheromone improves the performances of ant systems.

To conclude this section, we give in figure 2 the whole general algorithm which includes the different components described above.

Input :
    $G(\Pi)$ the graph representing the logic program
    $MaxIt$ the maximum number of iterations (colonies)
    NbA the number of ants in the colony
    NbR the number of paths to be reinforced
    Δ the reinforcement coefficient
Begin
    Sol:-false
    i:-1
    Repeat // launch one colony
        For j:-1 to NbA Do
            according to the attractivity of every vertex the ant j
            builds a stochastic admissible path P_j in G
            If $eval(P_j) = 0$ Then Sol:-P_j EndIf
        EndFor
        increase pheromone on the NbR better paths
        let the pheromone evaporate on every arc of the graph
        i:-$i + 1$
    Until $(Sol \neq false)$ or $(i > MaxIt)$
    return Sol
End

Fig. 2. Ant Colony Optimization algorithm

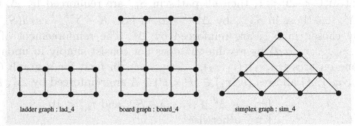

ladder graph : lad_4   board graph : board_4   simplex graph : sim_4

Fig. 3. Graphs for experimental studies

4 Experimental Validation

We have implemented this whole algorithm in a system called ASACO (Answer
Set by ACO) using the java language (jdk1.2.2) and we report here some
experiments aiming at tuning some parameters monitoring the system : the
number of ants in a colony, the number of paths that are reinforced and the rate
of this reinforcement. In order to have scalable and understandable examples,
we have studied two kinds of problems on graphs : the Hamilton cycle problem
and the 3-coloring problem. We used the three kinds of graphs (ladder, board
and simplex) presented in figure 3. Both problems have been generated and
encoded in a logic program by means of system *TheoryBase* [3] and we refer to
the different problems by the following conventions : ham_lad_N is an hamiltonian
cycle problem on a ladder graph with $2N$ vertices, ham_sim_N is an hamiltonian

Table 1. Influence of ant colony size

	ham_sim_5 (203 rules)			
NbA	NbR = 5, Δ = 0.5		NbR = 10, Δ = 0.9	
	%suc	NbIt	%suc	NbIt
50	36	21	36	13
100	73	17	70	14
150	96	13	86	9
200	100	11	96	9
300	100	9	100	7
400	100	6	100	4
(MaxIt = 1) 5000	20	-	-	-

cycle problem on a simplex graph with N vertices on each side and col_board_N is a 3-coloring problem on a board graph with N^2 vertices. For each test we performed, we ran 30 times our system with exactly the same parameters in order to have a good approximation of its average behavior. In all subsequent tables, results are averages over these 30 runs and we use the following notations :

- NbA is the number of ants in a colony.
- $MaxIt$ is the maximum number of iterations (ie : the maximum number of ant colonies that are launched).
- NbR is the percentage of paths or the absolute number of paths (it is mentioned in each case) that are reinforced after each iteration of an ant colony.
- Δ is the basic rate of reinforcement ($\Delta, \Delta^2, \Delta^3, \ldots$ are used).
- $\%suc$ is the ratio of the number of runs which find a stable model over the number of all runs.
- $NbIt$ is the number of iterations (or colonies) needed to find a solution when the method succeeds.

Each problem has at least one stable model and our system stops after having found one or after $MaxIt$ iterations. Then, we can use the different rates of success $\%suc$ to compare the efficiency of the different choices of values for the parameters.

In table 1, we report the influence of the ant colony size. We can see that it is necessary to use a large enough ant colony if we want to be sure to solve the problem in less than $MaxIt$ iterations (here $MaxIt = 30$). The best performances are obtained when we reinforce 10 paths with a basic rate $\Delta = 0.9$ since in this case about 1600 ants (4 colonies of 400 ants) are used to find a stable model in the best case. While at least 2400 ants (6 colonies of 400 ants) are used when only 5 paths are reinforced with a basic rate $\Delta = 0.5$. So, whatever the updating of pheromone is, a minimal size of the colony is required. For the last line of table 1 we launch 5000 ants at one time and we stop just after one iteration. So, this is a pure stochastic search and the results are very poor : 20 % of success after 5000 tries. So, the general heuristics of Ant Colony Optimization is efficient since, with a good choice of parameters, we obtain 100% of success with less than 2000 tries.

Table 2. Influence of pheromone reinforcement.

ham_lad_10 (134 rules) $NbA = 100$					
NbR	$\Delta = 0.1$		$\Delta = 0.5$		$\Delta = 0.9$
	%suc NbIt		%suc NbIt		%suc NbIt
0%	50	11	-	-	-	-
5%	63	12	43	12	50	10
10%	80	9	70	8	76	9
20%	50	9	70	13	86	9
col_board_7 (399 rules) $NbA = 20$					
NbR	$\Delta = 0.1$		$\Delta = 0.5$		$\Delta = 0.9$
	%suc NbIt		%suc NbIt		%suc NbIt
0%	13	7	-	-	-	-
5%	13	14	63	19	76	14
10%	20	17	56	17	80	15

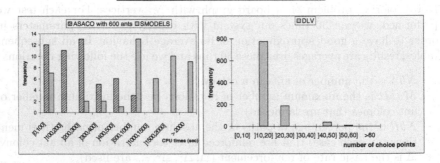

Fig. 4. Comparative results for ham_sim_6

In table 2 we report the influence of the pheromone updating on the performance of our system. When $NbR = 0\%$, Δ has no influence. This explains why there is only one result on these lines. In these cases, the method acts as a pure stochastic search and the percentage of success is again very low. On the other hand, the performances increase with the coefficient of reinforcement and the best results are obtained when at least 10% of the paths are updated. So, once again, this is an argument to demonstrate the efficiency of Ant Colony Optimization. We have made some comparative studies of ASACO versus Smodels [16] and DLV [6]. For these both systems we performed many tests on the same problem by shuffling the input file for each test since we remarked that the performances of these systems may depend on the order of the rules. In figure 4 we detail the distributions of CPU times for Smodels and ASACO for ham_sim_6 to illustrate that we are able to obtain interesting results on a problem which is very difficult to solve for one of the best available systems. Even if DLV has very good performances, we can see on the last picture of figure 4 that there exist some configurations of the input file for which the number of explored choice points highly increases.

5   Conclusion

In this paper, we have designed an Ant Colony Optimization based algorithm to compute a stable model by trying to determine which rules in the logic program have to be applied together. By lack of time we have not realized a complete set of experiments in order to tune all the parameters that control our system. Nevertheless, the implementation provides performances promising enough to incite us to continue in this way in order to improve the pheromone updating influence and its combination with the local evaluation. Furthermore, we have also developed another implementation in which a step of local search improves some paths built by the ants, and future directions of work are the parallelization of the system.

References

1. Gerhard Brewka and Jürgen Dix. Knowledge Representation with Logic Programs. In J. Dix, L. Pereira, and T. Przymusinski, editors, *Logic Programming and Knowledge Representation*, volume 1471 of *LNAI*, pages 1–55. Springer Verlag, 1998.
2. B. Bullnheimer, R. Hartl, and C. Strauss. A new rank based version of the ant system — a computational study. *Central European Journal of Operations Research*, 7(1):25–38, 1999.
3. P. Cholewiński, V. Marek, A. Mikitiuk, and M. Truszczyński. Computing with default logic. *Artificial Intelligence*, 112:105–146, 1999.
4. D. Corne, M. Dorigo, and F. Glover. *New Ideas in Optimization*. Mac Graw Hill, 1999.
5. M. Dorigo, E. Bonabeau, and G. Theraulaz. Ant algorithms and stimergy. *Future Generation Computer Systems*, 16:851–871, 2000.
6. T. Eiter, W. Faber, N. Leone, and G. Pfeifer. Declarative problem solving using the dlv system. In J Minker, editor, *Logic Based AI*, pages 79–103. Kluwer Academic Publishers, 2000.
7. T. Eiter and G. Gottlob. Complexity results for disjunctive logic programming and application to nonmonotonic logics. In D. Miller, editor, *ILP Symposium*, pages 266–278. MIT Press, 1993.
8. M. Gelfond and V. Lifschitz. The stable model semantics for logic programming. In Robert A. Kowalski and Kenneth Bowen, editors, *Proceedings of the International Conference on Logic Programming*, pages 1070–1080. The MIT Press, 1988.
9. M. Gelfond and V. Lifschitz. Classical negation in logic programs and deductive databases. *New Generation Computing*, 1991.
10. N. Leone, S. Perri, and P. Rullo. Local search techniques for disjunctive logic programs. In E. Lamma and P. Mello, editors, *AI*IA'99: Advances in Artificial Intelligence*, number 1792 in LNAI, pages 107–118. Springer, 2000.
11. Th. Linke. Graph theoretical characterization and computation of answer sets. In B. Nebel, editor, *Proceedings of the IJCAI*, pages 641–645. Morgan Kaufmann Publishers, 2001.
12. W. Marek and M. Truszczyński. Autoepistemic logic. *Journal of the ACM*, 38(3):588–619, 1991.
13. R. Mercer, L. Forget, and V. Risch. Comparing a pair-wise compatibility heuristic and relaxed stratification: Some preliminary results. In S. Benferhat and P. Besnard, editors, *Proceedings of ECSQARU*, volume 2143 of *LNCS*, pages 580–591. Springer Verlag, 2001.

14. P. Nicolas, F. Saubion, and I. Stéphan. GADEL : a genetic algorithm to compute default logic extensions. In *Proceedings of the European Conference on Artificial Intelligence*, pages 484–488, 2000.

15. P. Nicolas, F. Saubion, and I. Stéphan. New generation systems for non-monotonic reasoning. In T. Eiter, M. Truszczynski, and W. Faber, editors, *International Conference on Logic Programming and NonMonotonic Reasoning*, LNCS, pages 309–321, 2001.

16. I. Niemelä, P. Simons, and T. Syrjanen. Smodels: a system for answer set programming. In *Proceedings of the 8th International Workshop on Non-Monotonic Reasoning*, Breckenridge, Colorado, USA, 2000.

17. A. Provetti and L. Tari. Answer sets computation by genetic algorithms. In *Genetic and Evolutionary Computation Conference*, pages 303–308, 2000.

18. R. Reiter. A logic for default reasoning. *Artificial Intelligence*, 13(1-2):81–132, 1980.

19. T. Stützle and Holger H. Hoos. Max-min ant system. *Future Generation Computer systems*, 16(8):889–914, 2000.

Testing the Equivalence of Logic Programs under Stable Model Semantics[*]

Tomi Janhunen and Emilia Oikarinen

Helsinki University of Technology
Department of Computer Science and Engineering
Laboratory for Theoretical Computer Science
P.O. Box 5400, FIN-02015 HUT, Finland
{Tomi.Janhunen,Emilia.Oikarinen}@hut.fi

Abstract. Solving a problem in the answer set programming approach means constructing a logic program so that the answer sets of the program correspond to the solutions to the problem. Typically, a programmer develops a series of improved formulations for a particular problem. Consequently, the programmer is confronted by another problem, namely ensuring that subsequent formulations are equivalent, i.e., give rise to the same answer sets. To ease answer set programming, we propose a methodology for testing the equivalence of logic programs. The basic idea is to translate the logic programs P and Q under consideration into a single logic program R whose answer sets (if such exist) yield counter-examples to the equivalence of P and Q. The translation function presented in the paper has been implemented as a translator program LPEQ that enables the equivalence testing of logic programs using the SMODELS system. Experiments performed with LPEQ and SMODELS suggest that establishing the equivalence of logic programs in this way is in certain cases much faster than explicit cross-checking of answer sets.

1 Introduction

Answer set programming (ASP) has recently been promoted as a self-standing logic programming paradigm [8,9]. Indeed, the paradigm is receiving increasing attention and numerous applications have emerged since efficient implementations such as DLV [4] and SMODELS [12] became available in the late nineties. It is interesting to note that the current applications of ASP are already quite diverse ranging, e.g., from wire routing to a decision support system of the space shuttle (c.f. the topics of the 2001 AAAI Spring Symposium on ASP).

ASP is a very appealing approach because of its declarative nature, but it shares some problems with conventional approaches regarding the development of programs. Although logic programs lend themselves to concise encodings of the problems being solved, such encodings are by no means unique. Typically, a

---

[*] The research reported in this paper is affiliated with the project "Applications of Rule-Based Constraint Programming" (#53695) funded by the Academy of Finland.

S. Flesca et al. (Eds.): JELIA 2002, LNAI 2424, pp. 493–504, 2002.

programmer ends up with a series of improved programs for a particular problem, e.g., when optimizing the execution time and space. In this setting, there is a need to ensure that subsequent programs that differ in performance yield the same output. In case of ASP, this means establishing that given two logic programs P and Q give rise to the same answer sets, i.e., P and Q are semantically equivalent. This is the weaker notion of equivalence addressed by Lifschitz et al. [5]. In addition, they introduce a stronger notion of equivalence: P and Q are *strongly equivalent* if P and Q yield same answer sets in all possible contexts (i.e., as parts of any other programs). The strong equivalence can be characterized as equivalence in the logic of *here-and-there* (HT). As later shown by Pearce et al. [13], satisfiability in HT is reducible to propositional satisfiability (SAT), which implies that existing SAT solvers can be used for testing the strong equivalence of logic programs. Quite recently, Lin [6] reduces strong equivalence directly to propositional entailment without using HT as an intermediate logic. Unfortunately, these theoretical results lack an experimental evaluation to verify that the transformations are computationally feasible in practice.

The aim of this paper is to characterize the equivalence of logic programs directly in logic programming terms so that existing ASP implementations can be used for computations. For now we have developed a translation that captures the weak equivalence of logic programs supported by the SMODELS system as follows: the translation of P and Q has an answer set if and only if P has an answer set that is not an answer set of Q. This enables the search of counterexamples to the equivalence of P and Q using the translation and SMODELS.

The rest of the paper is organized as follows. Section 2 reminds the reader about the various kinds of rules supported by the current SMODELS system. It is then explained in Section 3 how the semantics of the rules is encompassed by stable models proposed by Gelfond and Lifschitz [2]. In Section 4, the translation for the equivalence testing of logic programs is presented. The correctness of the translation is also addressed. Results from experiments performed with an implementation (a translator called LPEQ) and SMODELS are reported in Section 5. The results indicate that in certain cases equivalence testing with LPEQ is one or two orders of magnitude faster than naive cross-checking of stable models. Finally, we end the paper with a brief conclusion in Section 6.

2   The SMODELS Language

Definition 1 lists the forms of rules supported by the current SMODELS system [14]. Besides *basic rules* (1) of conventional logic programs, there are also other rules available: *constraint rules* (2), *choice rules* (3), and *weight rules* (4).

Definition 1. *Rules are expressions of the forms*

$$h \leftarrow a_1, \ldots, a_n, \sim b_1, \ldots, \sim b_m \qquad (1)$$

$$h \leftarrow k \ \{a_1, \ldots, a_n, \sim b_1, \ldots, \sim b_m\} \qquad (2)$$

$$\{h_1, \ldots, h_l\} \leftarrow a_1, \ldots, a_n, \sim b_1, \ldots, \sim b_m \qquad (3)$$

$$h \leftarrow w \leq \{a_1 = w_1, \ldots, a_n = w_n, \sim b_1 = w_{n+1}, \ldots, \sim b_m = w_{n+m}\} \qquad (4)$$

where $n \geq 0$, $m \geq 0$, *and* $l > 0$, *and where* h, $a_1, \ldots, a_n$, $b_1, \ldots, b_m$, *and* $h_1, \ldots, h_l$ *are atoms and* k, $w_1, \ldots, w_{n+m}$, *as well as* w, *are natural numbers.*

The symbol $\sim$ in Definition 1 denotes *default negation* or *negation as failure* to prove [1]. We define *default literals* in the standard way as atoms a or their negations $\sim a$. The exact model-theoretic semantics of rules is deferred to Section 3, but – informally speaking – the rules can be used for inference as follows. The head h of a basic rule can be inferred if the atoms $a_1, \ldots, a_n$ are inferable and the atoms $b_1, \ldots, b_m$ are *not* inferable. The head h of a constraint rule can be inferred if the number of inferable atoms among $a_1, \ldots, a_n$ plus the number of non-inferable atoms among $b_1, \ldots, b_m$ is at least k. Note that a constraint rule becomes equivalent to a basic rule if $k = n + m$. A choice rule is similar to a basic rule except that any subset (even the empty set) of the set of head atoms $\{h_1, \ldots, h_l\}$ can be inferred instead of a single atom h. A weight rule involves summing as follows: the weight w_i of a_i (w_i of $\sim b_i$) is one of the summands if and only if a_i is inferable (b_i is not inferable). The head h can be inferred if such a sum of weights is at least w. A weight rule reduces to a constraint rule when $w_1 = 1, \ldots, w_{n+m} = 1$, and $w = k$. Note that default literals may be assigned different weights in different weight rules, i.e., weights are local.

The four types of rules defined above are already well-suited for a variety of knowledge representation and reasoning tasks in a number of domains. Example 1 demonstrates the use of rules in a practical setting. The reader is referred to [9,10,11] for more examples and for more general rules that can be captured by the rules supported by the SMODELS system using suitable transformations.

Example 1. Consider describing coffee orders by the following rules[1]. An order is acceptable if and only if the atom acceptable can be inferred using the rules.

{coffee, tea, biscuit, cake, cognac}. {cream, sugar} ← coffee. cognac ← coffee.
{milk, lemon, sugar} ← tea. coagulation ← milk, lemon.
satisfied ← 1 {biscuit, cake, cognac}.
bankrupt ← 6 ≤ {coffee = 1, tea = 1, biscuit = 1, cake = 2, cognac = 4}.
acceptable ← satisfied, ∼bankrupt, ∼coagulation.

A *logic program* P is a finite set of rules of the forms (1)–(4). We write $\mathrm{Hb}(P)$ for the Herbrand base of P, i.e., the set of atoms that appear in P. In addition to the four types of rules described above, logic programs supported by the SMODELS system may contain additional control information, namely *compute statements* and *maximize/minimize statements*. The exact syntax of this control information is not important for our purposes, and for this reason these aspects of SMODELS programs are addressed in later sections of this paper.

3   Stable Model Semantics

The semantics of *normal logic programs* (i.e., logic programs that consist solely of basic rules) is determined by *stable models* proposed by Gelfond and Lifschitz [2].

---

[1] Rules are separated with full stops and the symbol "←" is dropped from a basic rule (1) or a choice rule (3) if the *body* of the rule is empty ($n = 0$ and $m = 0$).

The idea is to reduce a normal logic program P with respect to a model candidate M by pre-interpreting negative literals that appear in the rules. The resulting program P_M – also known as the Gelfond-Lifschitz *reduct* of P – is *positive*, i.e., free of default negation. A positive program P has a well-established semantics determined by the *least model* of P [7]. The least model semantics extends for normal logic programs in a straightforward way: a model $M \subseteq \mathrm{Hb}(P)$ is stable if and only if M is the least model of P_M. Stable models need not be unique: a normal logic program P may possess several stable models or no stable model at all. However, this is not considered as a problem in answer set programming, since the aim is to capture solutions to the problem at hand with the stable models of a program constructed for the problem.

Simons [14] shows how the principles behind stable models can be used for defining the semantics of other rules presented in Section 2. However, the reduced program is not explicitly present in the semantical definitions given by Simons. This is why we resort to an alternative definition (see Definition 3 below). The forthcoming definition can be understood as a special case of that given by Niemelä and Simons [10] for more general classes of rules. In contrast to their definitions that involve deductive closures of rules, our intention is to formulate the stable model semantics purely in model-theoretic terms.

Given a logic program P, an *interpretation* is a subset of $\mathrm{Hb}(P)$ defining which atoms a are considered to be *true* ($a \in I$) and which *false* ($a \notin I$). Given an interpretation $I \subseteq \mathrm{Hb}(P)$, an atom $a \in \mathrm{Hb}(P)$ is *true/satisfied* in I (denoted by $I \models a$) $\iff a \in I$. Negative literals $\sim a$ are given a classical interpretation at this point: $I \models \sim a \iff I \not\models a$ ($\iff a \notin I$). The satisfaction relation $I \models r$ is defined for the rules r under consideration as follows.

Definition 2. *Given an interpretation $I \subseteq \mathrm{Hb}(P)$ for a logic program P,*

- *a basic rule (1) is satisfied in I*
  $\iff I \models a_1, \ldots, I \models a_n$ *and* $I \models \sim b_1, \ldots, I \models \sim b_m$ *imply* $I \models h$,
- *a constraint rule (2) is satisfied in I*
  $\iff k \leq |\{a_i \mid I \models a_i\} \cup \{\sim b_j \mid I \models \sim b_j\}|$ *implies* $I \models h$,
- *a choice rule (3) is always satisfied in I, and*
- *a weight rule (4) is satisfied in I*
  $\iff I \models h$ *is implied by* $w \leq \sum_{I \models a_i} w_i + \sum_{I \models \sim b_j} w_{n+j}$.

An interpretation I is a *model* of a logic program P (denoted by $I \models P$) if and only if $I \models r$ for every $r \in P$. However, stable models are not arbitrary models of logic programs. As hinted in the beginning of this section, the stable model semantics involves a reduction of logic programs which is based on a pre-interpretation of negative literals. The following definition gives the Gelfond-Lifschitz reduction for the four rule types. Note that in addition to valuating negative literals in the bodies of rules, the head atoms $h \in \{h_1, \ldots, h_l\}$ of choice rules (3) are subject to a special treatment: an essential prerequisite for including $h \leftarrow a_1, \ldots, a_n$ in the reduct P_M is that $M \models h$, i.e., $h \in M$. This is the way in which the choice regarding h takes place technically.

Definition 3. *For a logic program P and $M \subseteq \mathrm{Hb}(P)$, the reduct P_M contains*

- *a basic rule $h \leftarrow a_1, \ldots, a_n$ $\iff$ there is a basic rule (1) in P such that $M \models \sim b_1$, $\ldots$, $M \models \sim b_m$, or there is a choice rule (3) in P such that $h \in \{h_1, \ldots, h_l\}$, $M \models h$, and $M \models \sim b_1$, $\ldots$, $M \models \sim b_m$.*
- *a constraint rule $h \leftarrow k' \{a_1, \ldots, a_n\}$ $\iff$ there is a constraint rule (2) in P and $k' = \max(0, k - |\{\sim b_i \mid M \models \sim b_i\}|)$,*
- *a weight rule $h \leftarrow w' \leq \{a_1 = w_1, \ldots, a_n = w_n\}$ $\iff$ there is a weight rule (4) in P and $w' = \max(0, w - \sum_{M \models \sim b_j} w_{n+j})$.*

It is clear by Definition 3 that the reduct P_M is free of default negation and it contains only basic rules, constraint rules and weight rules. Thus we call a logic program P *positive* if each rule $r \in P$ is of the forms (1), (2) and (4) restricted to the case $m = 0$. The least model semantics can be generalized for this particular class of programs as follows. A model $M \models P$ is *minimal* (with respect to subset inclusion) if and only if there is no $M' \subset M$ such that $M' \models P$. Within the class of positive programs under consideration, every program P is guaranteed to have a unique minimal model $\mathrm{LM}(P)$ which is the *least model* of P. Moreover, the intersection $I = \bigcap \{M \subseteq \mathrm{Hb}(P) \mid M \models P\}$ is also a model of P and $I = \mathrm{LM}(P)$.

Now the semantics of a logic program P with default negation can be defined very concisely: M is a stable model of P if and only if $M = \mathrm{LM}(P_M)$. Note that a positive program P has a unique stable model $\mathrm{LM}(P)$, as $P_M = P$ holds always. It is also worth noting that $M = \mathrm{LM}(P_M)$ implies $M \models P$ in the sense of Definition 2. However, the converse does not hold in general, i.e., $M \models P$ need not imply $M = \mathrm{LM}(P_M)$. E.g., interpretations $M_1 = \{a\}$ and $M_2 = \{a, b\}$ are models of $P = \{a \leftarrow 1 \{\sim a, \sim b\}\}$, but only the former model is a stable one.

Example 2. Recall the set of rules P given in Example 1. According to SMODELS there are 33 acceptable orders, i.e., stable models of P containing acceptable. One of them is $M_7 = \{\mathsf{acceptable}, \mathsf{satisfied}, \mathsf{lemon}, \mathsf{tea}, \mathsf{biscuit}\}$. The reader may compute P_{M_7} using Definition 3 and verify that $M_7 = \mathrm{LM}(P_{M_7})$ is the case.

4   Translation for Equivalence Testing

Lifschitz et al. [5] address two major notions of equivalence for logic programs. The first one arises naturally from the stable model semantics. Logic programs P and Q are *equivalent* (denoted by $P \equiv Q$) if and only if P and Q have exactly the same stable models. The second notion is definable in terms of the first: P and Q are *strongly equivalent* (denoted by $P \equiv_s Q$) if and only if $P \cup R \equiv Q \cup R$ for all logic programs R. Here R can be understood as an arbitrary context in which P and Q could be placed. This is how strongly equivalent logic programs are semantics preserving substitutes of each other and the relation $\equiv_s$ can be understood as a congruence relation among logic programs. It is easy to see that $P \equiv_s Q$ implies $P \equiv Q$ but not vice versa: $\equiv_s$ relates fewer programs than $\equiv$.

In this paper, we concentrate on developing an implementation for the relation $\equiv$ and leave $\equiv_s$ as future work. Roughly speaking, our idea is to translate

given logic programs P and Q into a single logic program $\mathrm{EQT}(P,Q)$ which has
a stable model if and only if P has a stable model M which is *not* a stable model
of Q. This is how our aim is to use the translation for finding a counter-example
for the relationship $P \equiv Q$. However, in order to support the compute statements of SMODELS programs mentioned in Section 2, we have to cover a slightly
more general setting. Using a compute statement, a programmer can specify additional constraints on the stable models of P to be computed. This is achieved
by declaring a set of default literals L which is construed as follows. An interpretation I is *compatible* with L if and only if (i) $a \in I$ for each $a \in L$ and (ii) $a \notin I$
for each $\sim a \in L$. Given a logic program P and a set of default literals L based on
$\mathrm{Hb}(P)$, a *constrained (logic) program* $P[L]$ is understood to have a stable model
M if and only if M is a stable model of P and M is compatible with L. Note that
compute statements can be avoided (if necessary) by adding extra rules to the
program. Given a new atom $f \notin \mathrm{Hb}(P)$, the stable models of $P[L]$ are captured
by $P' = P \cup \{f \leftarrow a, \sim f \mid \sim a \in L\} \cup \{f \leftarrow \sim a, \sim f \mid a \in L\}$. Nevertheless, we
have to take compute statements into account in order to cover arbitrary SMOD-
ELS programs. For instance, a typical *headless* rule $\leftarrow a, \sim b$, which is supported
by the front-end LPARSE, is passed to SMODELS as a rule $f \leftarrow a, \sim b$ accompanied
by a compute statement which requires compatibility with $\{\sim f\}$.

We are now ready to formulate a translation $\mathrm{EQT}(P,Q,L)$ involving two
constrained programs $P[K]$ and $Q[L]$ satisfying $\mathrm{Hb}(P) = \mathrm{Hb}(Q)$ [2]. Note that K
plays no role in $\mathrm{EQT}(P,Q,L)$, but the stable models of $\mathrm{EQT}(P,Q,L)[K]$ will be
of our interest later on. We introduce a new atom $a^\star$ for each $a \in \mathrm{Hb}(Q)$. Such
atoms are additional (renamed) copies of atoms that are needed to compute
$\mathrm{LM}(Q_M)$ given a stable model M of $P[K]$. We write $A^\star = \{a^\star \mid a \in A\}$ for any
set of atoms A and $P^\star$ denotes a *positive* program P whose atom occurrences a
have been systematically replaced by the respective new atoms $a^\star$.

Definition 4. *Let P be a logic program P and $Q[L]$ a constrained program such
that $\mathrm{Hb}(P) = \mathrm{Hb}(Q)$. Let c, d, and e be new atoms not appearing in P nor Q.
The translation $\mathrm{EQT}(P,Q,L)$ contains the following rules:*

1. *all rules of P without modifications,*
2. *a rule $h^\star \leftarrow a_1^\star, \ldots, a_n^\star, \sim b_1, \ldots, \sim b_m$ for each basic rule (1) in Q,*
3. *a rule $h^\star \leftarrow k \{a_1^\star, \ldots, a_n^\star, \sim b_1, \ldots, \sim b_m\}$ for each constraint rule (2) in Q,*
4. *a rule $h_i^\star \leftarrow a_1^\star, \ldots, a_n^\star, h_i, \sim b_1, \ldots, \sim b_m$ for each choice rule (3) in Q and
   head atom $h_i \in \{h_1, \ldots, h_l\}$,*
5. *a rule $h^\star \leftarrow w \leq \{a_1^\star = w_1, \ldots, a_n^\star = w_n, \sim b_1 = w_{n+1}, \ldots, \sim b_m = w_{n+m}\}$ for
   each weight rule (4) in Q,*
6. *a rule $c \leftarrow \sim a$ for each $a \in L$ and a rule $c \leftarrow a$ for each $\sim a \in L$,*
7. *rules $d \leftarrow a, \sim a^\star$ and $d \leftarrow a^\star, \sim a$ for each $a \in \mathrm{Hb}(P) = \mathrm{Hb}(Q)$,*
8. *rules $e \leftarrow c$ and $e \leftarrow d$.*

Note that $\mathrm{Hb}(\mathrm{EQT}(P,Q,L))$ equals to $\mathrm{Hb}(P) \cup \mathrm{Hb}(Q)^\star \cup \{c,d,e\}$. Moreover,
the translation is close to being linear. The fourth item in Definition 4 makes

---

[2] Note that this restriction is not significant, as it is possible to extend any logic
   program P with useless rules $a \leftarrow a$ without affecting the stable models of P

an exception in this respect, but linearity can be achieved by introducing a new atom b_r for each choice rule r. Then the rules in the fourth item can be replaced by $h_i^\star \leftarrow h_i, b_r$ ($h_i \in \{h_1, \ldots, h_l\}$) and $b_r \leftarrow a_1^\star, \ldots, a_n^\star, \sim b_1, \ldots, \sim b_m$. However, we use the current definition to simplify the correctness proof.

The rules in the translation $\mathrm{EQT}(P, Q, L)$ serve the following purposes. The program P is included as such, since the goal is to compute a stable model M for $P[K]$. The remaining rules provide means to check that M is not a stable model of $Q[L]$. Rules from the second item to the fifth capture $\mathrm{LM}(Q_M)$ but expressed in $\mathrm{Hb}(Q)^\star$ rather than $\mathrm{Hb}(Q)$. The rules in the sixth item check if M is not compatible with L. The rules in the seventh item check if M and $\mathrm{LM}(Q_M)$ differ. The last two rules summarize the reasons for M **not** being a stable model of $Q[L]$. The correctness of the translation $\mathrm{EQT}(P, Q, L)$ is addressed next.

Lemma 1. *Let P be a logic program and $Q[L]$ a constrained program such that $\mathrm{Hb}(P) = \mathrm{Hb}(Q)$ and I an interpretation for the translation $\mathrm{EQT}(P, Q, L)$. Define $J_1 = I \cap \mathrm{Hb}(P)$ and $J_2 = \{a \in \mathrm{Hb}(Q) \mid a^\star \in I\}$ so that $J_2^\star = I \cap \mathrm{Hb}(Q)^\star$. The reduct $\mathrm{EQT}(P, Q, L)_I$ consists of the following rules:*

- *the rules of P_{J_1} as such,*
- *a rule $h^\star \leftarrow a_1^\star, \ldots, a_n^\star$*
  $\iff$ there is a basic rule (1) in Q such that $J_1 \models \sim b_1, \ldots, J_1 \models \sim b_m$,
- *for each constraint rule (2) in Q, a rule $h^\star \leftarrow k' \{a_1^\star, \ldots, a_n^\star\}$ with $k' = \max(0, k - |\{\sim b_j \mid J_1 \models \sim b_j\}|)$,*
- *a rule $h_i^\star \leftarrow a_1^\star, \ldots, a_n^\star, h_i$*
  $\iff$ there is a choice rule (3) in Q such that $J_1 \models \sim b_1, \ldots, J_1 \models \sim b_m$,
- *for each weight rule (4) in Q, a rule $h^\star \leftarrow w' \leq \{a_1^\star = w_1, \ldots, a_n^\star = w_n\}$ with $w' = \max(0, w - \sum_{J_1 \models \sim b_j} w_{n+j})$,*
- *the rule $c \leftarrow \iff$ there is $a \in L$ such that $a \notin J_1$,*
- *a rule $c \leftarrow a$ for each $\sim a \in L$,*
- *a rule $d \leftarrow a \iff$ there is $a \in \mathrm{Hb}(Q)$ such that $a \notin J_2$,*
- *a rule $d \leftarrow a^\star \iff$ there is $a \in \mathrm{Hb}(P)$ such that $a \notin J_1$, and*
- *the rules $e \leftarrow c$ and $e \leftarrow d$.*

Lemma 1 can be easily verified by inspecting the definition of $\mathrm{EQT}(P, Q, L)$ (Definition 4), the definitions of J_1 and J_2 and the generalization of Gelfond-Lifschitz reduct for the various rule types (Definition 3). Proposition 1 (see below) lists the essential properties of $\mathrm{LM}(\mathrm{EQT}(P, Q, L)_I)$, which are sufficient to establish the main result of this paper given as Theorem 1 (proofs are omitted due to space restrictions). As a corollary of Theorem 1, we obtain a new method for testing whether the equivalence $P[K] \equiv Q[L]$ holds or not.

Proposition 1. *Assume the same setting and definitions as in Lemma 1.*

(i) The intersection $\mathrm{LM}(\mathrm{EQT}(P, Q, L)_I) \cap \mathrm{Hb}(P) = \mathrm{LM}(P_{J_1})$.

(ii) If $J_1 = \mathrm{LM}(P_{J_1})$, then $\mathrm{LM}(\mathrm{EQT}(P, Q, L)_I) \cap \mathrm{Hb}(Q)^\star = \mathrm{LM}(Q_{J_1})^\star$.

(iii) If $J_1 = \mathrm{LM}(P_{J_1})$ and $J_2 = \mathrm{LM}(Q_{J_1})$, then $A = \mathrm{LM}(\mathrm{EQT}(P, Q, L)_I) \cap \{c, d, e\}$ satisfies (1) $c \in A \iff J_1$ is not compatible with L, (2) $d \in A \iff J_1 \neq J_2$, and (3) $e \in A \iff c \in A$ or $d \in A$.

Theorem 1. *For any constrained programs $P[K]$ and $Q[L]$ satisfying* $\mathrm{Hb}(P) =$ $\mathrm{Hb}(Q)$, *the constrained translation* $\mathrm{EQT}(P, Q, L)[K \cup \{e\}]$ *has a stable model* $\Longleftrightarrow P[K]$ *has a stable model M which is not a stable model of $Q[L]$.*

Corollary 1. *For any constrained logic programs $P[K]$ and $Q[L]$ with* $\mathrm{Hb}(P) =$ $\mathrm{Hb}(Q)$, $P[K] \equiv Q[L] \Longleftrightarrow$ *the constrained translations* $\mathrm{EQT}(P, Q, L)[K \cup \{e\}]$ *and* $\mathrm{EQT}(Q, P, K)[L \cup \{e\}]$ *have no stable models.*

5 Experiments

The translation function EQT presented in Section 4 has been implemented in the C programming language under the Linux operating system. The translator – which we have named as LPEQ – takes two logic programs as its input and produces the translation as its output. The program assumes the internal format of SMODELS which enables using the front-end LPARSE of SMODELS in conjunction with LPEQ. Moreover, the translation is printed in a textual form upon request. The current implementation of LPEQ is available in the World Wide Web (http://www.tcs.hut.fi/Software/lpeq/) for testing purposes. Some examples related with our experiments are also provided. It is yet important to note that LPEQ checks that the *visible* Herbrand bases of the programs being compared are exactly the same (a visible atom has a name in the symbol table of the program). However, the front-end LPARSE may produce some *invisible* atoms that are not taken into account in this comparison. To support programs produced by LPARSE, such atoms keep their roles in the respective programs.

To assess the feasibility of LPEQ in practice we ran various tests with different test cases. The running times of the LPEQ approach were compared with those of a fictitious approach: in the NAIVE approach, one (i) generates a stable model M of P, (ii) tests whether M is a stable model of Q, (iii) stops if not, and otherwise continues from step (i) until all stable models of P get enumerated. It is obvious that a similar testing has to be carried out in the other direction to establish $P \equiv Q$ (in analogy to Corollary 1). There is still room for optimization in both approaches. If one finds a counter-example in one direction, then $P \not\equiv Q$ is known to hold and there is no need to do testing in the other direction except if one wishes to perform a thorough analysis. However, we decided not to follow this optimization principle, because running times turned out to scale differently depending on the direction. Thus we counted running times in both directions.

In both approaches, the SMODELS system (version 2.26) was responsible for the computation of stable models. In the LPEQ approach, the total running time (in one direction) is the running time needed by SMODELS for trying to compute *one* stable model of the translation produced by LPEQ. The actual translation time is not taken into account, as it is negligible. In the NAIVE approach, we tried to exclude possible overhead due to implementing the NAIVE approach as a shell script. Thus the total running time (in one direction) consists solely of the running time of SMODELS for finding the necessary (but not necessarily all) stable models of P plus the individual running times of SMODELS for testing that the stable models found are also stable models of Q. These tests were realized

Table 1. Results for two equivalent logic programs (n-queens).

n	stable models	t_{ave} (s) LPEQ	t_{ave} (s) NAIVE	t_{ave} NAIVE/ t_{ave} LPEQ	choices LPEQ	choices NAIVE	$|EQT(Q_n, Q'_n)|+$ $|EQT(Q_n, Q'_n)|$	$|Q_n|+$ $|Q'_n|$
1	1	0.000	0.024	-	0	0	49	13
2	0	0.015	0.008	0.533	0	0	194	68
3	0	0.017	0.013	0.780	0	0	521	205
4	2	0.025	0.057	2.280	0	2	1110	464
5	10	0.124	0.285	2.298	4	18	2041	885
6	4	0.392	0.276	0.705	14	16	3394	1508
7	40	1.439	2.404	1.671	44	84	5249	2373
8	92	5.415	8.117	1.499	158	245	7686	3520
9	352	24.455	41.501	1.697	598	962	10785	4989
10	724	118.848	132.319	1.113	2525	3036	14626	6820
11	2680	647.307	672.410	1.039	12144	13792	19289	9053
12	14200	3808.970	4364.230	1.146	59759	69329	24854	11728

in practice by adding M as a compute statement to Q. All the tests were run under the Linux 2.2.13/4 operating system on 450MHz Pentium III computers.

The first experiment was based on the program Q_n formulated by Niemelä [9, p. 260] to solve the n-queens problem. The second program Q'_n is a variant of Q_n where the choice between placing or not placing a queen in a particular cell is equivalently formulated using choice rules and constraint rules rather than basic rules. We tested the equivalence of these two programs using both the LPEQ and the NAIVE approach. The number n of queens was varied from 1 to 12 and the equivalence test was repeated 10 times for each number of queens to eliminate any inaccuracies caused by the system clock. The results of this experiment are shown in Table 1. In case of two equivalent well-structured logic programs the performance of the LPEQ approach is somewhat better than that of NAIVE approach. Also the number of *choice points* (i.e., the number of choices made by SMODELS while searching for stable models) is slightly smaller in the LPEQ approach than in the NAIVE approach. This is a further indication that verifying the equivalence of logic programs is easier using the LPEQ approach.

We also performed some tests with random logic programs. We generated logic programs that solve an instance of a random 3-sat problem with a constant clauses to variables ratio $c/v = 4$. Such instances are typically satisfiable, but so close to the *phase transition point* (approximately 4.3) that finding models is already demanding for satisfiability solvers. To simulate a sloppy programmer making mistakes, we dropped one random rule from each program. Then we tested the equivalence of the modified program and the original program to see if making a mistake affects the stable models of the program or not. As a consequence, the tested pairs of programs included both equivalent and nonequivalent cases. In our first experiment with random 3-sat programs, we varied the number of variables v from 10 to 50 with steps of 5. For each number of variables we repeated the test 100 times – generating each time a new random instance. The average running times of both approaches are plotted in Figure 1. The LPEQ

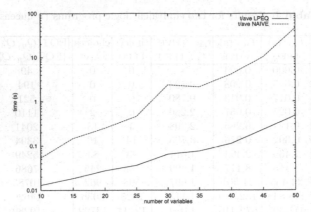

Fig. 1. The equivalence testing with random 3-sat instances with the ratio $c/v = 4$.

approach turned out to be significantly faster than the NAIVE one. Moreover, the difference in running times increases as the sizes of the programs grow.

In our second experiment with random 3-sat instances we generated the programs as in the previous experiment, but we kept the number of variables constant, $v = 40$, and varied the ratio c/v from 3.75 to 4.75 with steps of 0.125. For each value of the ratio c/v, we repeated the test 100 times generating each time a new random instance. The motivation behind this experiment was to see how the LPEQ approach performs compared to the NAIVE one as the programs change from almost always satisfiable (many stable models) to almost always unsatisfiable (no stable models). With lower values of c/v the LPEQ approach was significantly better than the NAIVE one, as in the previous experiment. As the ratio increased the performance of the NAIVE approach gradually improved, but still the LPEQ approach performed slightly better.

Finally, we combined structured logic programs with randomness. We used two graph problems and the respective formulations by Niemelä [9, p. 262], namely n-coloring of a graph with n colors, and finding a Hamiltonian circuit for a graph. Using the Stanford GraphBase library, we generated random planar graphs with v vertices where v ranged from 10 to 17. Using the front-end LPARSE, the logic programs for 4-coloring and Hamiltonian circuit were instantiated for the generated graphs. As in the preceding experiments with random 3-sat programs, the second program for equivalence testing was obtained by dropping one random rule from the one instantiated by LPARSE. The tests were repeated 100 times for each value of v using a new random planar graph each time. The average running times for both experiments are presented in Figure 2. In both experiments the LPEQ approach was significantly better than the NAIVE approach, though running times differed more in case of 4-coloring random planar graphs.

6   Conclusion

In this paper, we proposed a translation-based approach for testing the equivalence of logic programs under the stable model semantics. The current translation

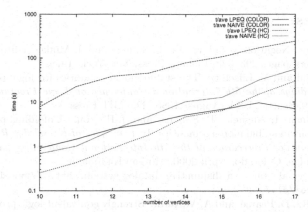

Fig. 2. Results for 4-coloring random planar graphs and finding Hamiltonian circuits.

and the implementation LPEQ cover the types of rules supported by the SMOD-ELS system. Since the internal format of SMODELS is used, more general forms of rules implemented in the front-end LPARSE are also covered. The experiments carried out in Section 5 suggest that the translation-based approach can be useful in practice. In many cases, the number of choice points and time needed for computations is less than in a naive cross-checking approach. To the best of our understanding, this is because the translation provides an explicit specification of a counter-example for $P \equiv Q$ that guides the search performed by SMODELS. This is not possible in the NAIVE approach where the stable models of P and Q are of interest. However, if the programs being compared are likely to have few stable models or no stable models at all, we expect that the NAIVE approach becomes superior to ours (c.f. Table 1). Recall that P is included in the translation $EQT(P, Q, L)[K]$ which has no stable models if $P[K]$ has no stable models.

There are further issues to be addressed. (i) The current translation and implementation do not support minimize/maximize statements (and global weights of default literals) that are available in SMODELS. (ii) Other notions of equivalence – such as the stronger notion of equivalence proposed by Lifschitz et al. [5] – should be covered by devising suitable translations. (iii) At the moment, we rely on the fact that $\mathrm{Hb}(P) = \mathrm{Hb}(Q)$ holds for the programs P and Q under comparison (except that any invisible atoms introduced by LPARSE are ignored). One possibility to cover programs not satisfying $\mathrm{Hb}(P) = \mathrm{Hb}(Q)$ is to extend P and Q to programs P' and Q' (respectively) by adding useless rules not affecting stable models so that $\mathrm{Hb}(P') = \mathrm{Hb}(Q')$. (iv) The case of disjunctive logic programs is also interesting, as efficient implementations are available: DLV [4] and GNT [3]. The latter uses SMODELS for actual computations in analogy to the translation-based approach followed by this paper. We expect that a translation similar to the one presented in this paper can be developed for disjunctive programs as well. (v) Even more general classes of logic programs – such as *nested* programs [5] – are worth addressing once implementations become available.

References

1. K.L. Clark. Negation as failure. In H. Gallaire and J. Minker, editors, *Logic and Data Bases*, pages 293–322. Plenum Press, New York, 1978.
2. M. Gelfond and V. Lifschitz. The stable model semantics for logic programming. In *Proceedings of the 5th International Conference on Logic Programming*, pages 1070–1080, Seattle, USA, August 1988. The MIT Press.
3. T. Janhunen, I. Niemelä, P. Simons, and J.-H. You. Unfolding partiality and disjunctions in stable model semantics. In *Principles of Knowledge Representation and Reasoning: Proceedings of the 7th International Conference*, pages 411–419, Breckenridge, Colorado, April 2000. Morgan Kaufmann.
4. N. Leone et al. DLV – a disjunctive datalog system. http://www.dbai.tuwien.ac.at/proj/dlv/.
5. V. Lifschitz, D. Pearce, and A. Valverde. Strongly equivalent logic programs. *ACM Transactions on Computational Logic*, 2:526–541, 2001.
6. F. Lin. Reducing strong equivalence of logic programs to entailment in classical propositional logic. In *Principles of Knowledge Representation and Reasoning: Proceedings of the 8th International Conference*, pages 170–176, Tolouse, France, April 2002. Morgan Kaufmann.
7. J.W. Lloyd. *Foundations of Logic Programming*. Springer-Verlag, Berlin, 1987.
8. W. Marek and M. Truszczyński. Stable models and an alternative logic programming paradigm. In *The Logic Programming Paradigm: a 25-Year Perspective*, pages 375–398. Springer-Verlag, 1999.
9. I. Niemelä. Logic programs with stable model semantics as a constraint programming paradigm. *Annals of Mathematics and Artificial Intelligence*, 25(3,4):241–273, 1999.
10. I. Niemelä and P. Simons. Extending the Smodels system with cardinality and weight constraints. In Jack Minker, editor, *Logic-Based Artificial Intelligence*, chapter 21, pages 491–521. Kluwer Academic Publishers, 2000.
11. I. Niemelä, P. Simons, and T. Soininen. Stable model semantics of weight constraint rules. In *Proceedings of the 5th International Conference on LP & NMR*, pages 317–331, El Paso, Texas, USA, December 1999. Springer-Verlag. LNAI 1730.
12. I. Niemelä, P. Simons, and T. Syrjänen. Smodels: a system for answer set programming. In *Proceedings of the 8th International Workshop on Non-Monotonic Reasoning (cs.AI/0003073)*, Breckenridge, Colorado, USA, April 2000. cs.AI/0003033.
13. D. Pearce, H. Tompits, and S. Woltran. Encodings for equilibirium logic and logic programs with nested expressions. In P. Brazdil and A. Jorge, editors, *Proceedings of the 10th Portuguese Conference on Artificial Intelligence*, pages 306–320, Porto, Portugal, December 2001. Springer Verlag. LNAI 2258.
14. P. Simons. Extending the stable model semantics with more expressive rules. In *Proceedings of the 5th International Conference on LP & NMR*, pages 305–316, El Paso, Texas, USA, December 1999. Springer-Verlag. LNAI 1730.

Argumentative Reasoning with ABEL

Rolf Haenni

Computer Science Department, University of California, Los Angeles, CA 90095
rolf.haenni@gmx.net
http://haenni.shorturl.com

Abstract. Most formal approaches to argumentative reasoning under uncertainty focus on the analysis of qualitative aspects. An exception is the framework of probabilistic argumentation systems. Its philosophy is to include both qualitative and quantitative aspects through a simple way of combining logic and probability theory. Probabilities are used to weigh arguments for and against particular hypotheses. ABEL is a language that allows to describe probabilistic argumentation systems and corresponding queries about hypotheses. It then returns arguments and counter-arguments with corresponding numerical weights.

1 Introduction

In the last couple of years, *argumentation* has gained growing recognition as a new and promising research direction in artificial intelligence. As a consequence of this increasing interest, different authors have investigated argumentation and its application in various domains. By looking at today's literature on this subject, one realizes that argumentation is understood in fairly different ways. The common feature of most approaches is their restriction to particular types of logic. As a consequence, they are all limited in the way they combine arguments for and against a particular hypothesis.

The approach we present in this paper is known as *probabilistic argumentation systems* (PAS) [8]. The idea of the PAS framework goes back to the concept of *assumption-based truth maintenance systems* (ATMS) [5]. It is also closely related to *abduction* [4,9]. The idea is to understand argumentation as a deductive tool that helps to judge *hypotheses*, that is open questions about the unknown or future world, in the light of the given uncertain and partial knowledge. From a qualitative point of view, the problem is to derive *arguments* in favor and *counter-arguments* against the hypothesis of interest. Every argument is a defeasible proof built on uncertain *assumptions*. In other words, arguments are chains of true or false assumptions that make the hypothesis true. Efficient algorithms are obtained by focusing the search on the most relevant arguments [6,7]. In a second step, a quantitative judgement of the situation is obtained by considering the probabilities that the arguments are valid. The credibility of a hypothesis can then be measured by the probabilities that it is supported or defeated by at least one argument. Conflicts are handled through conditioning. The resulting *degrees of support* and *possibility* correspond to *belief* and *plausibility*,

S. Flesca et al. (Eds.): JELIA 2002, LNAI 2424, pp. 505–508, 2002.
© Springer-Verlag Berlin Heidelberg 2002

respectively, in the Dempster-Shafer theory of evidence [11,12,10]. Although a qualitative judgement may be valuable in many ways, a quantitative judgement is often more useful and helps to decide whether a hypothesis can be accepted, rejected, or whether the available knowledge does not permit to decide.

A system called ABEL [2,3] is an example of implementing probabilistic argumentation systems (check out `http://www2-iiuf.unifr.ch/tcs/ABEL`). It includes an appropriate modeling and query language, as well as corresponding inference mechanisms. Problems from a broad spectrum of application domains show that the ABEL system is very general and powerful [1]. It has an open architecture that permits the later inclusion of further or more advanced deduction techniques. The aim of this paper is to provide a short introduction to ABEL. Our hope is to increase the recognition of PAS as a legitimate formal model and ABEL as powerful tool for reasoning under uncertainty.

2   Probabilistic Argumentation Systems

The basic ingredients for probabilistic argumentation systems (PAS) are *propositional logic* and *probability theory*. More formally, we require two disjoint sets $P = \{p_1, \ldots, p_n\}$ and $A = \{a_1, \ldots, a_m\}$ of propositional symbols. The elements of P are called *propositions* and the elements of A *assumptions*. With $\mathcal{L}_{A \cup P}$ we denote the corresponding propositional language that consist of elements of $A \cup P$ only. Furthermore, we require a propositional sentence $\xi \in \mathcal{L}_{A \cup P}$ that expresses the qualitative part of the given knowledge. The formula ξ is called *knowledge base*. Finally, a set $\Pi = \{p(a_i) : a_i \in A\}$ of independent probabilities is required to expresses the quantitative knowledge. Note how the connection between propositional logic and probability theory is established through the assumptions. A quadruple (P, A, Π, ξ) is called *probabilistic argumentation system* (PAS). The knowledge base ξ is usually assumed to be satisfiable. Note that ξ is often given as a conjunction $\xi = \xi_1 \wedge \cdots \wedge \xi_r$ of sentences $\xi_i \in \mathcal{L}_{A \cup P}$. In such a case, it is useful to consider the corresponding set $\Sigma = \{\xi_1, \ldots, \xi_r\}$ and to call Σ knowledge base.

Example 1. Let $P = \{X, Y, Z\}$ and $A = \{a_1, a_2, a_3, a_4, a_5\}$ be the sets of propositions and assumptions, respectively. Furthermore, suppose that

$$\Pi = \{p(a_1) = 0.2,\ p(a_2) = 0.4,\ p(a_3) = 0.8,\ p(a_4) = 0.3,\ p(a_5) = 0.3\}$$

are the probabilities of the assumptions and

$$\xi = (a_1 \rightarrow X) \wedge ((a_2 \vee \neg a_3) \rightarrow Y) \wedge ((X \wedge Y) \rightarrow Z) \wedge (\neg a_4 \rightarrow Z)$$
$$\wedge ((a_5 \wedge Y) \rightarrow \neg Z)$$

the given knowledge base. This forms a probabilistic argumentation system (P, A, Π, ξ). Note that the knowledge base ξ is a conjunction that can be represented more easily as a set of five individual formulas:

$$\Sigma = \{a_1 \rightarrow X,\ (a_2 \vee \neg a_3) \rightarrow Y,\ (X \wedge Y) \rightarrow Z,\ \neg a_4 \rightarrow Z,\ (a_5 \wedge Y) \rightarrow \neg Z\}.$$

The question now is how to use a PAS for the purpose of analyzing and answering queries about *hypotheses*. A hypothesis h is usually expressed by simple a expression that includes symbols of $A \cup P$. To be most general, we consider arbitrary propositional formulas $h \in \mathcal{L}_{A \cup P}$. The approach we promote is to construct arguments and counter-arguments based on the set of assumptions A and to weigh them with the aid of the given probabilities Π. For corresponding formal definitions and descriptions of appropriate inference techniques we refer to the literature [8,6,7].

3 ABEL

Working with ABEL typically involves two sequential steps. First, the given information is *modeled* using the command **tell**. It is used to define the two sets A and P, the probabilities Π, and the knowledge base ξ. Second, queries about the knowledge base are expressed using the command **ask**. An ABEL model usually starts with the declaration of the sets P, A, and Π. The distinction between the elements of P and A is made by using two distinct commands **var** and **ass**. Look below how it's done for the example introduced in the previous section. Assumptions with different probabilities must be defined on different lines. The keyword **binary** means that only two values are allowed (*true* and *false*). Note that ABEL also supports variables with more than two values [2,3,1]. The knowledge base ξ is then described using a LISP-like prefixed language. If ξ is given as a set of statements Σ, then every individual statement is written on a separate line. Again, consider the example of the previous section and look how it's done.

```
(tell                        (tell
  (var X Y Z binary)           (-> a1 X)
  (ass a1 binary 0.2)          (-> (or a2 (not a3)) Y)
  (ass a2 binary 0.4)          (-> (and X Y) Z)
  (ass a3 binary 0.8)          (-> (not a4) Z)
  (ass a4 a5 binary 0.3))      (-> (and a5 Y) (not Z)))
```

Note that the statements can also be distributed among different **tell**-commands. Furthermore, it is also possible to mix variable declarations and statements about the knowledge base. The only rule is that every variable must be declared before it is first used. ABEL supports different types of queries. In the context of argumentative reasoning, the most important commands are **sp** (support), **dsp** (degree of support), and **dps** (degree of possibility). Suppose Z is the hypothesis of interest in Example 1. Observe how **sp** can be used to compute arguments and counter-arguments for Z.

```
? (ask (sp Z))                 ? (ask (sp (not Z)))
  53.3% : (NOT A4) (NOT A5)      56.3% : A2 A4 A5 (NOT A1)
  24.0% : A1 A2 (NOT A5)         43.7% : A4 A5 (NOT A1) (NOT A3)
  18.7% : A1 (NOT A3) (NOT A5)
   4.0% : A3 (NOT A2) (NOT A4)
```

In this simple case, we have four arguments and two counter-arguments. The first argument for Z is $\neg a_4 \wedge \neg a_5$. Note that $\neg a_4$ alone is not an argument for

Z (because $\neg a_4$ together with a_5 produces a conflict). To get a quantitative evaluation of the hypothesis, we can compute corresponding degrees of support and possibility.

```
? (ask (dsp Z))        ? (ask (dps Z))
  0.695                  0.958
```

The above numerical results tell us that the hypothesis Z is supported by a relatively high degree. At the same time, there are only few reasons against Z which leads to a degree of possibility close to 1.

References

1. B. Anrig, R. Bissig, R. Haenni, J. Kohlas, and N. Lehmann. Probabilistic argumentation systems: Introduction to assumption-based modeling with ABEL. Technical Report 99-1, Institute of Informatics, University of Fribourg, 1999.
2. B. Anrig, R. Haenni, J. Kohlas, and N. Lehmann. Assumption-based modeling using ABEL. In D. Gabbay, R. Kruse, A. Nonnengart, and H. J. Ohlbach, editors, *First Internat. Joint Conf. on Qualitative and Quantitative Practical Reasoning; ECSQARU-FAPR'97*. Lecture Notes in Artif. Intell., Springer, 1997.
3. B. Anrig, R. Haenni, and N. Lehmann. ABEL – a new language for assumption-based evidential reasoning under uncertainty. Technical Report 97-01, University of Fribourg, Institute of Informatics, 1997.
4. D. Berzati, R. Haenni, and J. Kohlas. Probabilistic argumentation systems and abduction. In C. Baral and M. Truszczynski, editors, *Proc. of the 8th Internat. Workshop on Non-Monotonic Reasoning, Breckenridge Colorado*, 2000.
5. J. de Kleer. An assumption-based TMS. *Artificial Intelligence*, 28:127–162, 1986.
6. R. Haenni. Cost-bounded argumentation. *International Journal of Approximate Reasoning* 26(2):101–127, 2001.
7. R. Haenni. A query-driven anytime algorithm for argumentative and abductive reasoning. In D. Bustard, W. Liu, and R. Sterrit, editors, *Soft-Ware 2002, 1st International Conference on Computing in an Imperfect World, Belfast*, pages 114–127. Lecture Notes in Computer Science 2311, Springer, 2002.
8. R. Haenni, J. Kohlas, and N. Lehmann. Probabilistic argumentation systems. In J. Kohlas and S. Moral, editors, *Handbook of Defeasible Reasoning and Uncertainty Management Systems, Volume 5: Algorithms for Uncertainty and Defeasible Reasoning* Kluwer, Dordrecht, 2000.
9. D. Poole. Probabilistic Horn abduction and Bayesian networks. *Artificial Intelligence*, 64:81–129, 1993.
10. N. Lehmann R. Haenni. Probabilistic argumentation systems: a new perspective on dempster-shafer theory. *International Journal of Intelligent Systems, Special Issue on Dempster-Shafer Theory of Evidence*, 2002. accepted for publication.
11. G. Shafer. *The Mathematical Theory of Evidence*. Princeton University Press, 1976.
12. Ph. Smets and R. Kennes. The transferable belief model. *Artificial Intelligence*, 66:191–234, 1994.

COBA: A Consistency-Based Belief Revision System

James P. Delgrande[1], Aaron Hunter[1], and Torsten Schaub[2],*

[1] School of Computing Science, Simon Fraser University
Burnaby, B.C., Canada V5A 1S6
{jim,amhunter}@cs.sfu.ca
[2] Institut für Informatik, Universität Potsdam
Postfach 60 15 53, D–14415 Potsdam, Germany
torsten@cs.uni-potsdam.de

Abstract. Although the theory of belief revision has been studied extensively, there has not been a great deal of emphasis put on the implementation of belief revision systems. In a recent paper, two of the authors presented a new consistency-based approach to belief revision, and it was argued that the approach was well suited for implementation [3,2]. In order to test this claim, we implemented the system as a simple java applet. In this paper, we will present a partial sketch of the approach to revision, and we will walk through the simple algorithm used to implement it. Although the system could still be improved in terms of efficiency, we found that the approach to belief revision under consideration was, in fact, well suited for implementation.

1 Introduction

Given a knowledge base K and a sentence α for revision, the basic problem of belief revision is to determine what sentences should be in the revised knowledge base. Intuitively, we want the revised knowledge base to contain α along with as much of K as consistently possible.

In this paper, we discuss COBA, a prototype implementation of a specific approach to consistency-based belief revision. In section 2, we briefly outline the approach. In section 3, we look at some of the implementation details. We conclude with some possible improvements that could be made to streamline the system.

2 The Approach

The approach implemented by COBA is described in [3]. We briefly outline the approach here. Throughout the following discussion, we let K denote a knowledge base and we let α denote a sentence for revision. The new knowledge base obtained by revising K by α will be denoted by $K \dotplus \alpha$. The belief change paradigm presented in [3] can also be used for contraction and belief update [4]. We focus here solely on belief revision.

The first step in the revision is to create a new knowledge base K' that is obtained from K by replacing each occurrence of an atomic sentence p by a new atomic sentence

---

* Affiliated with the School of Computing Science at Simon Fraser University, Burnaby, Canada.

S. Flesca et al. (Eds.): JELIA 2002, LNAI 2424, pp. 509–512, 2002.

p'. Clearly, if K and α are both consistent, then $K' \cup \{\alpha\}$ will be consistent as well. We now draw a correspondence between the language of K' and the language of α by adding $p \equiv p'$ wherever consistently possible. Let EQ denote a maximal set of sentences of the form $p \equiv p'$ such that $K' \cup \{\alpha\} \cup EQ$ is consistent. Clearly every model of $K' \cup \{\alpha\} \cup EQ$ will be a model of α in the original language. Hence, if we can re-express $K' \cup \{\alpha\} \cup EQ$ in the original language, then we have a candidate for a revised knowledge base. Each maximal set EQ generates one such candidate revision. We call such candidates *choice* revisions, because they depend on how the set EQ is chosen. If we want $K \dotplus \alpha$ to represent a skeptical revision, then we simply take the intersection of all possible choice revisions.

The preceding approach does not rely on the syntactic representation of the knowledge base or the sentence for revision. Moreover, it satisfies most of the AGM postulates [1] and it is suitable for iterated belief revision. For a detailed discussion of the properties of this revision operator, we refer the reader to [3,2].

In the preceding discussion, we mentioned that we need to re-express $K' \cup \{\alpha\} \cup EQ$ in the original language of K and α. More precisely, for each set EQ, we need to find a sentence in the original language $\mathcal{L}$ that has the same models as $Cn(K' \cup \{\alpha\} \cup EQ) \cap \mathcal{L}$. Finding such a sentence is surprisingly straightforward. Since EQ is a maximal set of equivalences such that $K' \cup \{\alpha\} \cup EQ$ remains consistent, we can simply perform the following substitutions:

- for $p \equiv p' \in EQ$, substitute p uniformly for p' in K'
- for $p \equiv p' \notin EQ$, substitute $\neg p$ uniformly for p' in K'

After performing these substitutions, the sentence $K' \wedge \alpha$ will be in the language $\mathcal{L}$, and its deductive closure will be equivalent to the choice revision determined by the set EQ. Hence, by taking the disjunction of all such sentences, we will get a sentence that is equivalent to the general revision, $K \dotplus \alpha$ [3].

3   Implementation Details

COBA is implemented in java. The program was originally implemented as a stand-alone application, and then an applet interface was designed that is suitable for testing any belief revision software. The interface allows the user to enter sentences to the knowledge base or the revision list through a text box; then they can simply click a button to perform the revision. The revised knowledge base appears in a preview window. If the user wants to keep the revised knowledge base, they click a button to confirm the revision. In this manner, iterated revision can be carried out very easily. Currently, the consistency-based approach described above is the only revision system that has been plugged into the generic interface.

The algorithms employed by COBA are straightforward, and they could be improved in terms of speed. The current implementation is a simple proof-of-concept to illustrate the ease with which our approach may be implemented. The main procedure is called *getRevisedKB* and it takes two arguments, the first of which is a sentence K representing the knowledge base, while the second is a sentence α for revision. We outline the basic algorithm and then explain important subroutines in the discussion below.

Algorithm *getRevisedKB* (K, α)
1. *CommonAtoms* := $\{p \mid p$ is an atom in K and $\alpha\}$
2. K' := *primeAtoms(CommonAtoms, K)*
3. *Equivs* := $\{p \equiv p' \mid p \in CommonAtoms \}$
4. *MaxEquivs* := $\emptyset$
5. **for each** $e \subseteq$ *Equivs*, **do:**
    if $e \cup \{K' \wedge \alpha\} \nvdash \bot$ **then** *MaxEquivs* := *MaxEquivs* $\cup \{e\}$
6. **for each** $m \in$ *MaxEquivs*, **do:**
    if m is not maximal, **then** *MaxEquivs* := *MaxEquivs* $\setminus m$
7. *Sent* := $\bot$
8. **for each** $M \in$ *MaxEquivs*:
    Sent := *Sent* $\vee$ *SubNeg*(K', M)
9. *Sent* := *Sent* $\wedge \alpha$
10. **Return**(*Simplify(Sent)*)

There are three subroutines in the preceding algorithm that require explanation. First of all, *primeAtoms* simply takes a set of atomic sentence letters S and a sentence β as arguments, and returns a new sentence which is just like β except that every occurrence of a sentence letter p from S is replaced with p'. Second, *SubNeg* is a subroutine that takes two arguments, the first of which is a sentence K and the second is a set of equivalences M of the form $p \equiv p'$. The output of *SubNeg* is determined through the following replacement scheme. For each atom of the form p' in K:

1. If $p \equiv p' \in M$, then replace p' by p.
2. If $p \equiv p' \notin M$, then replace p' by $\neg p$.

The last subroutine is *Simplify*. In COBA, the simplification can take several different forms. For example, the user may choose to have the results given in Conjunctive Normal Form(CNF). In this case, a standard algorithm for converting sentences to CNF is applied before the result is shown on screen. The simplification algorithm is straightforward, and it attempts to remove redundant literals from the display whenever possible. We should mention that this simplification step is entirely superficial. Internally, sentences are represented as objects that are composed of different sentence objects through the operations of conjunction, disjunction and negation. The sentence object is able to return a label for itself in several different formats.

The interface for COBA is intended to provide a simple framework for testing any belief revision system. However, for this project, we did not employ any formal testing methodology. Different knowledge bases and sentences for revision were simply tested in an ad hoc manner. The system was found to be functional, but speed becomes a problem with sentences involving more than a handful of literals.

4 Performance

As mentioned above, speed becomes an issue for COBA if the input sentences are too large. However, for small examples the system works very effectively. It was easy to implement the revision algorithm in a modular fashion, so that different components can be updated individually without modifying the entire system. Although the algorithm does not depend on the syntactic representation of sentences, it operates through simple search-and-replace routines on atomic subformulas. This kind of operation is very easy to implement quickly and efficiently.

Performance could be improved by adding an efficient SAT checker for consistency checks. As the system is set up now, consistency checks are essentially done through exhaustive search on truth tables. Performance could also be improved by changing the way in which maximally consistent sets are found. Steps 5 and 6 in the algorithm can trivially be modified so that sets of candidate literals are generated in order of size, from larger sets to smaller. However there is also significant room here to heuristically prune the search over candidate sets. Finally, the system could be improved by adding more simplification heuristics for the resulting formula.

5   Conclusion

In [3], the authors claim that their approach to belief revision is well-suited to implementation. In order to test this claim, we built a naïve implementation of the approach as a java applet with a simple user interface. The approach was, in fact, straightforward to implement, and it lends itself to a modular design that is easy to develop in stages.

In the preceding section, we identified several areas in which COBA could be improved. We would like to stress at this point that the system was intended to simply illustrate how easily the given belief revision system could be implemented. From this perspective, COBA has been successful, despite the obvious improvements that could be made in terms of the performance.

The prototype implementation can be accessed from

```
http://www.cs.sfu.ca/research/groups/CL/Software.html .
```

References

1. C.E. Alchourrón, P. Gärdenfors, and D. Makinson. On the logic of theory change: Partial meet contraction and revision functions. *Journal of Symbolic Logic*, 50(2):510–530, 1985.
2. J. Delgrande and T. Schaub. A consistency-based paradigm for belief change. 2001. (submitted).
3. J.P. Delgrande and T. Schaub. A consistency-based model for belief change: Preliminary report. In *Proceedings of the AAAI National Conference on Artificial Intelligence*, pages 392–398, Austin, TX, 2000.
4. H. Katsuno and A. Mendelzon. On the difference between updating a knowledge base and revising it. In P. Gärdenfors, editor, *Belief Revision*, pages 183–203. Cambridge University Press, 1992.

Constraint Lingo: A Program for Solving Logic Puzzles and Other Tabular Constraint Problems

Raphael Finkel, Victor W. Marek, and Mirosław Truszczyński

Department of Computer Science
University of Kentucky
Lexington, KY 40506-0046, USA

1 Introduction

Constraint Lingo is a high-level language for specifying and solving tabular constraint problems [FMT01]. We show the syntax of this language through examples. Our software translates Constraint Lingo programs into a variety of back-end logic formalisms, including *smodels* [NS00], *dlv* [ELM+98], *ECLiPSe* [WNS97] and *aspps* [ET01]. The associated logic engine then generates a set of answers, each of which our software converts to a human-readable table.

2 Tabular Constraint-Satisfaction Problems

Informally, a tabular constraint-satisfaction problem (tCSP) is one that has a specified number of rows and columns. The values in the table are subject to constraints, both implicit and explicit.

Logic puzzles are good examples of tCSPs, as are some graph problems. For example, we present a simplified version of the "French Phrases, Italian Soda" puzzle (or French puzzle, for short)[1]:

> Claude and five others (three women: Jeanne, Kate, and Liana, and two men: Martin and Robert) sat at a circular table. Each person described a trip to a different place. Each person sipped a different soda. Match each person with his or her seat (numbered one through six [circularly]) and determine the soda that each drank, as well as the place that each plans to visit.
>
> 1. The person who is planning a trip to Quebec, who drank either blueberry or lemon soda, didn't sit in seat number one.
> 2. Robert, who didn't sit next to Kate, sat directly across from the person who drank peach soda.
> 3. The three men are the person who is going to Haiti, the one in seat number three, and Claude's brother.
> 4. The three people who sat in even-numbered seats are Kate, Claude, and a person who didn't drink lemon soda, in some order.

A solution has five columns, representing **name**, **gender**, **position**, **soda** and **country** (each with its associated domain). Each row represents a particular

---

[1] Copyright 1999, Dell Magazines; quoted by permission. We present only four of the nine clues.

S. Flesca et al. (Eds.): JELIA 2002, LNAI 2424, pp. 513–516, 2002.
© Springer-Verlag Berlin Heidelberg 2002

combination, that is, a person of some gender sitting in some position, drinking some soda, and planning to visit some country. The implicit constraints include the legitimate values for each column (Haiti is a value that may occur only in the country column) and that all columns but gender are key: all the legitimate values are used exactly once. This solution satisfies all nine clues of the French puzzle:

name	gender	position	soda	country
claude	man	6	tangelo	haiti
jeanne	woman	1	grapefruit	ivory
kate	woman	4	kiwi	tahiti
liana	woman	5	peach	belgium
martin	man	3	lemon	quebec
robert	man	2	blueberry	martinique

3   Representation in Constraint Lingo

We encode the implicit constraints of the French puzzle by the following Constraint Lingo code.

```
CLASS person: claude jeanne kate liana martin robert
PARTITION gender: men women
CLASS position: 1 .. 6 circular
CLASS soda: blueberry lemon peach tangelo kiwi grapefruit
CLASS visits: quebec tahiti haiti martinique belgium ivory
```

These lines declare the names of the five columns, specify the values that may appear in those columns, and indicate whether the columns are key (by the indicator CLASS). They also indicate that the position column has numeric values to be treated with modular arithmetic.

We encode the explicit constraints involved in the statement of the problem and the four clues by the following Constraint Lingo code.

```
# from the statement of the problem
AGREE men: martin robert
AGREE women: jeanne kate liana

# clue 1
CONFLICT quebec 1
REQUIRED quebec blueberry OR quebec lemon

# clue 2
OFFSET !+-1 position: robert kate
OFFSET +-3 position: robert peach

# clue 3
VAR brother
CONFLICT brother claude
AGREE men: haiti 3 brother
CONFLICT haiti 3 brother
```

```
    # clue 4
VAR unlemon
MATCH 2 4 6, kate claude unlemon
CONFLICT unlemon lemon
```

Comments start with **#** and continue to the end of the line. Clue 1, which says that the person going to Quebec is not sitting in seat 1, becomes a single CONFLICT constraint. Both `quebec` and 1 are values in the table; the CONFLICT constraint indicates these values must be in distinct rows. A REQUIRED constraint indicates that two values appear in the same row. The OFFSET constraints in Clue 2 say that Robert and Kate are not in adjacent positions (circularly) and that Robert and the row identified with Peach are 3 positions apart (circularly). Other encodings require a touch of cleverness. Clue 3 talks about Claude's brother. We encode this person's row by a variable `brother` constrained to refer to a man other than Claude. The complex English statements of the French puzzle reduce to a small set of short, clear, constraints.

4   Applying Constraint Lingo to Graph Problems

Despite a restricted repertoire of operators aimed initially at solving logic problems, Constraint Lingo is sufficient to model such important combinatorial problems as independent sets, graph coloring, and finding Hamiltonian cycles.

An *independent set* in a graph is a set of v vertices no two of which share an edge. The independent-set problem is to find an independent set with at least k vertices. We represent the problem in the following Constraint Lingo program, setting $v = 100$ and $k = 30$, with edges (2, 5) and (54, 97), for concreteness. There are two attributes: a class `vertex`, to represent vertices of the graph (line 1 below) and a partition `status`, to indicate the membership of each vertex in an independent set (line 2). We employ USED to constrain the independent set to have at least k elements (line 3). The REQUIRED constraints in lines 4 and 5 enforce the independent-set constraint.

```
1  CLASS vertex: 1..100 # v = 100
2  PARTITION status: in out
3  USED 30 <= in # k = 30
4  REQUIRED 2 out OR 5 out # edge (2,5): at least one vertex is out
5  REQUIRED 54 out OR 97 out # edge (54,97): at least one vertex is out
```

5   Translation of Constraint Lingo into a Logic Formalism

We use Perl scripts to translate Constraint Lingo into logic **formalisms** such as *smodels* [NS00], *dlv* [ELM+98], *ECLiPSe* [WNS97] and *aspps* [ET01] by means of a **strategy**. The **standard strategy** introduces a cross-class predicate for every pair of columns. The **best-class** strategy chooses a special column and introduces cross-class predicates between it and the other columns. The **row-number** strategy numbers the rows and introduces equality and inequality constraints on row numbers. We have programmed many but not all combinations of formalism and strategy. No logic formalism is uniformly best, although *aspps* is generally fastest for the standard strategy. No strategy is uniformly best, but the best-class strategy is often fastest, especially when the best class is picked by a good heuristic.

The time taken by the translation and post-processing of the logic-engine output is negligible. Most of the 80 puzzles we have programmed are solved in well under a second by any combination of logic engine and translation strategy. We can generate graph-based problems requiring arbitrarily large computation time.

6   Demonstration

Our demonstration will display several puzzles and graph problems. We will examine the logic-formalism code generated by our translator for various formalism-strategy pairs, particularly {standard, *smodels*}, {best-class, *smodels*}, and {row-number, *ECLiPSe*}. All the software we use is publicly available, including our translators; we need only a Unix laptop loaded with our software to demonstrate our work. Our translation software and a set of puzzles can be found at http://www.cs.uky.edu/ai/cl.html.

References

ELM⁺98.   T. Eiter, N. Leone, C. Mateis, G. Pfeifer, and F. Scarcello. A KR system dlv: Progress report, comparisons and benchmarks. In *Proceeding of the Sixth International Conference on Knowledge Representation and Reasoning (KR '98)*, pages 406–417. Morgan Kaufmann, 1998.

ET01.   D. East and M. Truszczyński. Propositional satisfiability in answer-set programming. In *Proceedings of Joint German/Austrian Conference on Artificial Intelligence, KI'2001*, volume 2174, pages 138–153. Lecture Notes in Artificial Intelligence, Springer Verlag, 2001.

FMT01.   R. Finkel, V. Marek, and M. Truszczyński. Tabular constraint-satisfaction problems and answer-set programming. *AAAI-2001 Spring Symposium Series, Workshop on Answer Set Programming*, 2001.

NS00.   I. Niemelä and P. Simons. Extending the smodels system with cardinality and weight constraints. In J. Minker, editor, *Logic-Based Artificial Intelligence*, pages 491–521. Kluwer Academic Publishers, 2000.

WNS97.   M. Wallace, S. Novello, and J. Schimpf. ECLiPSe: A platform for constraint logic programming, 1997. http://www.icparc.ic.ac.uk/eclipse/reports/eclipse.ps.gz.

$\mathcal{LDL}$–$\mathcal{M}_{ine}$: Integrating Data Mining with Intelligent Query Answering

Fosca Giannotti[1] and Giuseppe Manco[2]

[1] CNUCE - CNR
Via Alfieri 1 - I56010 Ghezzano (PI)
Fosca.Giannotti@cnuce.cnr.it
[2] ISI - CNR
Via Bucci 41c - I87036 Rende (CS)
manco@isi.cs.cnr.it

Current applications of data mining techniques highlight the need for flexible knowledge discovery systems, capable of supporting the user in specifying and refining mining objectives, combining multiple strategies, and defining the quality of the extracted knowledge. A key issue is the definition of *Knowledge Discovery Support Environment*, i.e., a query system capable of obtaining, maintaining, representing and using high level knowledge in a unified framework. This comprises representation and manipulation of domain knowledge, extraction and manipulation of new knowledge and their combination.

In such a context, in [2,3] we envisaged an integrated architecture of data mining, further developed and experimented in [5] and resulting in the $\mathcal{LDL}$–$\mathcal{M}_{ine}$ environment. The basic philosophy of the environment is to integrate both inductive and deductive capabilities in a unified framework. A $\mathcal{LDL}$–$\mathcal{M}_{ine}$ program is composed of three main parts: source knowledge, modeled by facts; background knowledge, modeled by deductive clauses; and induced knowledge, modeled by inductive clauses. Inductive clauses provide a suitable interface to data mining algorithms: they define predicates that represent mining patterns, but can be used as deductive predicates and facts. This allows to amalgamate induction and deduction, and to model both interactive and iterative features of a data mining process.

Figure 1 shows the main features of the system. $\mathcal{LDL}$–$\mathcal{M}_{ine}$ is built on top of the $\mathcal{LDL}$++ system [8]. Indeed, the system exploits most of the functionalities of the $\mathcal{LDL}$++ system, such as Application programming interface, deductive engine, and access to external databases. In addition, $\mathcal{LDL}$–$\mathcal{M}_{ine}$ implements an inductive engine that allows, by means of inductive clauses, interaction between mining algorithms and deductive components. In its current stage, the inductive engine implements three main data mining schemes, namely association rules mining [1], Bayesian Classification [7], and (both supervised and unsupervised) discretization of continuous attributes [6]. Each scheme corresponds to a specific inductive clause. In the following we show by examples how the notion of inductive clause is formalized within the $\mathcal{LDL}$–$\mathcal{M}_{ine}$ system, and some specific inductive clauses currently implemented.

S. Flesca et al. (Eds.): JELIA 2002, LNAI 2424, pp. 517–520, 2002.
© Springer-Verlag Berlin Heidelberg 2002

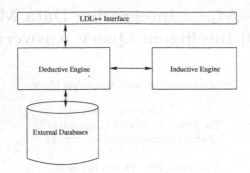

Fig. 1. Architecture of the $\mathcal{LDL}$–$\mathcal{M}_{ine}$ system.

Mining Aggregates

The main feature that $\mathcal{LDL}$–$\mathcal{M}_{ine}$ shares from the $\mathcal{LDL}$++ system is capability of specifying and efficiently computing aggregates. More generally, the datalog++ logic-based database language [8], which provides a theoretical basis for the $\mathcal{LDL}$–$\mathcal{M}_{ine}$ environment, provides a general framework for dealing with user-defined aggregates. For example, the following rule

$$\mathtt{ans}(\mathtt{count}\langle C\rangle) \leftarrow \mathtt{transaction}(D, C, I, P, Q).$$

specifies the computation of the count aggregate over the instantiations of the variable C resulting from the instances of the *Transaction* relation defined in fig. 2. We exploit such a capability for specifying [2,3] (and computing [5]) mining aggregates, and define an *inductive rule* defining a generic **ans** predicate as a rule of the form

$$\mathtt{ans}(\alpha, Aggr\langle\beta\rangle) \leftarrow rule\ body$$

where *Aggr* is a mining aggregate, and the meta-variables α and β represent terms obtained from the tuples resulting from the evaluation of *rule body*.

In the current implementation, the $\mathcal{LDL}$–$\mathcal{M}_{ine}$ system implements three mining aggregates:

- the **patterns** aggregate, for specifying frequent patterns discovery [1];
- the **nbayes** aggregate, for specifying Bayesian Classification [7];
- the **discr** aggregate, for accomplishing discretization tasks [6].

Example 1. Let us consider the relation **transaction** with extension shown in fig. 2. In order to compute association rules from transactions grouped by customer and by date, we need to *i*) group the transaction, and to *ii*) specify the mining aggregate:

$$\mathtt{trans}(D, C, \langle I\rangle) \leftarrow \mathtt{transaction}(D, C, I, P, Q).$$

$$\mathtt{rules}(SP, CF, \mathtt{patterns}\langle(SP, CF, IS)\rangle) \leftarrow \mathtt{trans}(D, C, IS).$$

Customer	Name	Address	Age	Income	Profitable
	Ron	pisa	adult	high	yes
	Jeff	rome	young	low	no
	Sam	pisa	adult	high	yes
	Tim	florence	young	low	yes
	Phil	pisa	old	high	yes
	Nat	rome	young	low	no

Transaction	Date	Customer	Item	Price	Qty
	11-2-97	Ron	beer	10	10
	12-2-97	Ron	chips	3	20
	21-2-97	Ron	chips	5	2
	15-2-97	Ron	wine	20	2
	14-2-97	Jeff	wine	15	3
	14-2-97	Sam	beer	10	10
	15-2-97	Sam	chips	3	8
	13-2-97	Tim	beer	4	3
	15-2-97	Tim	chips	4	3
	18-2-97	Tim	nachos	4	3
	...				

Fig. 2. Sample Customers database.

The `patterns` aggregate in the above clauses specifies the computation of association rules, from the transactions resulting by the instantiation of the variable IS, satisfying the support and confidence constraints resulting from the instantiation of the variables S and C. A sample session is given below:

```
ldl++(4)> query rules(20.0,80.0,R)
Querying : rules(20.0,80.0,R) ...
        (20, 80, rule({chips, wine}, {beer}, 3, 100))
        (20, 80, rule({beer}, {chips}, 5, 83))

The number of records is 2.
```

□

Example 2. Let us consider the *Customer* relation of fig. 2 specifying distinguishing features of each customer. We can specify the construction of a classifier model by means of the following aggregate rule, exploiting the `nbayes` aggregate:

```
classifier(nbayes⟨(addr(D), age(A), income(I), C)⟩) ← customer(N, D, A, I, C).
```

Here, each feature has a tag attached, that specifies the attribute to which the current value is associated. For example, the predicate `customer(ron, pisa, adult, high, yes)` specifies the feature vector `addr(pisa)`, `age(adult)` and `income(high)`. We can query the above rule in order to obtain the model associated to the given instance:

```
ldl++(5)> query classifier(C)
Querying : classifier(C) ...
            (bayes(addr(pisa), yes, 3, 4, 6))
            (bayes(age(adult), yes, 2, 4, 6))
            (bayes(income(high), yes, 3, 4, 6))
            (bayes(addr(rome), no, 2, 2, 6))
            (bayes(age(young), yes, 1, 4, 6))
            (bayes(age(young), no, 2, 2, 6))
            (bayes(income(low), yes, 1, 4, 6))
            (bayes(income(low), no, 2, 2, 6))
            (bayes(addr(florence), yes, 1, 4, 6))
            (bayes(age(old), yes, 1, 4, 6))

The number of records is 10.
```

The exploitation of the above model in further inductive clauses allows the computation of the posterior class probabilities, and consequently of a predictor predicate classify:

classify$(N, D, A, I, \text{argmax}\langle(C, P)\rangle) \leftarrow$ posterior_class_prob(D, A, I, C, P).

posterior_class_prob$(D, A, I, C, P) \leftarrow$ classifier(bayes(addr(D)), C, Cd, CC, N)),
classifier(bayes(age(A)), C, Ca, CC, N)),
classifier(bayes(income(I)), C, Ci, CC, N)),
$P = (CC/N) \times (Cd/CC) \times (Ca/CC) \times (Ci/CC)$.

Such a predicate, in fact, allows to classify unseen cases by selecting the class exhibiting the highest posterior probability. For example, by considering the case with features name(john), addr(pisa), age(adult), income(high), we obtain:

```
ldl++(6)> query classify(john,pisa,adult,high,C)
Querying : classify(john,pisa,adult,high,C) ...
         (luigi, pisa, adult, high, yes)

The number of records is 1.
```

□

The current $\mathcal{LDL}$–$\mathcal{M}_{ine}$ prototype was developed with the aim of providing a set of mining schemes likely to be profitably combined, in order to build complex knowledge discovery schemes. Such peculiarities were demonstrated useful in significant application domains, such as Market-Basket analysis and Fraud Detection [4]. We plan to further extend such schemes, e.g., with clustering and decision-tree algorithms, in order to allow the adoption of the system in domains like, for example, Web Content and Usage Mining.

References

1. R. Agrawal, T. Imielinski, and A. Swami. Mining Association Rules between Sets of Items in Large Databases. In *Procs. SIGMOD93 Conf.*, pages 207–216, 1993.
2. F. Giannotti and G. Manco. Querying Inductive Databases via Logic-Based User-Defined Aggregates. In *Procs. PKDD99 Conf.*, LNAI 1704, pages 125–135, 1999.
3. F. Giannotti and G. Manco. Making Knowledge Extraction and Reasoning Closer. In *Procs.PAKDD2000 Conf.*, LNCS 1805, 2000.
4. F. Giannotti, G. Manco, D. Pedreschi, and F. Turini. Experiences with a Knowledge Discovery Support Environment. In *Procs. ACM SIGMOD DMKD Workshop*, 1999.
5. F. Giannotti, G. Manco, and F. Turini. Specifying Mining Algorithms with Iterative User-Defined Aggregates: A Case Study. In *Procs PKDD2001 Conf.*, LNAI 2168, pages 128–139, 2001.
6. R. Kerber. ChiMerge: Discretization of Numeric Attributes. In *Proc. AAAI92 Conf.*, pages 123–127. 1992.
7. J. Mitchell. *Machine Learning*. McGraw-Hill, 1997.
8. C. Zaniolo, N. Arni, and K. Ong. Negation and Aggregates in Recursive Rules: The $\mathcal{LDL}$++ Approach. In *Procs. DOOD93 Conf.*, LNCS 760, 1993.

NoMoRe: Non-monotonic Reasoning with Logic Programs

Christian Anger, Kathrin Konczak, and Thomas Linke

Universität Potsdam, Institut für Informatik
{canger,konczak,linke}@cs.uni-potsdam.de

1 Introduction

The **non-monotonic reasoning** system noMoRe [2] implements answer set semantics for normal logic programs. It realizes a novel, rule-based paradigm to compute answer sets by computing non-standard graph colorings of the *block graph* associated with a given logic program (see [8,9,6] for details). These non-standard graph colorings are called *a-colorings* or *application-colorings* since they reflect the set of generating rules (applied rules) for an answer set. Hence noMoRe is rule-based and not atom-based like most of the other known systems. In the recent release of noMoRe we have added *backward propagation* of partial a-colorings and a technique called *jumping* in order to ensure full (backward) propagation [6]. Both techniques improve the search space pruning of noMoRe. Furthermore, we have extended the syntax by integrity, weight and cardinality constraints [11,5][1].

The noMoRe-system is implemented in the programming language Prolog; it has been developed under the ECLiPSe Constraint Logic Programming System [1] and it was also successfully tested with SWI-Prolog [12]. The system is available at http://www.cs.uni-potsdam.de/~linke/nomore. In order to use the system, ECLiPSe-or SWI-Prolog is needed [1,12][2].

2 Theoretical Background

The current release of the noMoRe system implements nonmonotonic reasoning with normal logic programs under answer set semantics [4]. We consider rules r of the form $p \leftarrow q_1, \ldots, q_n, not\ s_1, \ldots, not\ s_k$ where p, q_i ($0 \leq i \leq n$) and s_j ($0 \leq j \leq k$) are atoms, $head(r) = p$, $body^+(r) = \{q_1, \ldots, q_n\}$, $body^-(r) = \{s_1, \ldots, s_k\}$ and $body(r) = body^+(r) \cup body^-(r)$.

The block graph of program P is a directed graph on the rules of P:

---

[1] Observe, that we use a transformation for weight and cardinality constraints into normal logic programs, which is exponential in the worst case. That is, so far we did not consider efficiency issues when dealing with these constraints.

[2] Both Prolog systems are freely available for scientific use.

S. Flesca et al. (Eds.): JELIA 2002, LNAI 2424, pp. 521–524, 2002.

Definition 1. *([8]) Let P be a logic program and let $P' \subseteq P$ be maximal grounded[3]. The block graph $\Gamma_P = (V_P, A_P^0 \cup A_P^1)$ of P is a directed graph with vertices $V_P = P'$ and two different kinds of arcs*

$$A_P^0 = \{(r', r) \mid r', r \in P' \text{ and } head(r') \in body^+(r)\}$$
$$A_P^1 = \{(r', r) \mid r', r \in P' \text{ and } head(r') \in body^-(r)\}.$$

Since groundedness (by definition) ignores negative bodies, there exists a unique maximal grounded set $P' \subseteq P$ for each program P, that is, Γ_P is well-defined. Definition 1 captures the conditions under which a rule r' blocks another rule r (i.e. $(r', r) \in A_P^1$). We also gather all groundedness information in Γ_P, due to the restriction to rules in the maximal grounded part of P. This is essential because a block relation between two rules r' and r becomes effective only if r' is groundable through other rules. Therefore Γ_P captures all information necessary for computing the answer sets of program P.

Answer sets are characterized as special non-standard graph colorings of block graphs. Let P be a logic program and let Γ_P be the corresponding block graph. For $r \in P$ let $G_r = (V_r, A_r)$ be a directed graph. Then G_r is a *grounded 0-graph for r in Γ_P* iff the following conditions hold: 1. G_r is an acyclic subgraph of Γ_P s.t. $A_r \subseteq A_P^0$, 2. $r \notin V_r$ and $body^+(r) \subseteq head(V_r)$ and 3. for each node $r' \in V_r$ and for each $q' \in body^+(r')$ there exists a node $r'' \in V_r$ s.t. $q' = head(r'')$ and $(r'', r') \in A_r$. The different grounded 0-graphs for rule r in Γ_P correspond to the different classical "proofs" for $head(r)$ in P^+, ignoring the default negations of all rules. Now let $\mathcal{C} : P \mapsto \{\ominus, \oplus\}$ be a total mapping[4]. We call r *grounded wrt* Γ_P *and* $\mathcal{C}$ iff there exist a grounded 0-graph $G_r = (V_r, A_r)$ for r in Γ_P s.t. $\mathcal{C}(V_r) = \oplus$. r is called *blocked wrt* Γ_P *and* $\mathcal{C}$ if there exists some $r' \in \text{Pred1}(r)$ s.t. $\mathcal{C}(r') = \oplus$. Now we are ready to define a-colorings.

Definition 2. *Let P be a logic program, let Γ_P be the corresponding block graph and let $\mathcal{C} : P \mapsto \{\ominus, \oplus\}$ be a total mapping. Then $\mathcal{C}$ is an a-coloring of Γ_P iff the following condition holds for each $r \in P$*

AP $\mathcal{C}(r) = \oplus$ *iff r is grounded wrt Γ_P and $\mathcal{C}$ and r is not blocked wrt Γ_P and $\mathcal{C}$.*

Observe, that there are programs (e.g. $P = \{p \leftarrow not\ p\}$) s.t. no a-coloring exists for Γ_P. Intuitively, each node of the block graph (corresponding to some rule) is colored with one of two colors, representing application ($\oplus$) or non-application ($\ominus$) of the corresponding rule. In [8] we show that there is a one-to-one correspondence between a-colorings and answer sets. That is, the set of all $\oplus$-colored rules wrt some a-coloring are the generating rules for some answer set of the corresponding program.

3   Description of the System

NoMoRe uses a compilation technique to compute answer sets of a logic program P in three steps (see Figure 1). At first, the block graph Γ_P is computed. Secondly, Γ_P is

---

[3] A set of rules S is *grounded* iff there exists an enumeration $\langle r_i \rangle_{i \in I}$ of S such that for all $i \in I$ we have that $body^+(r_i) \subseteq head(\{r_1, \cdots, r_{i-1}\})$. A maximal grounded set P' is a grounded set that is maximal wrt set inclusion. We generalize the definition of the head of a rule to sets of rules in the usual way.

[4] A mapping $\mathcal{C} : P \mapsto C$ is called *total* iff for each node $r \in P$ there exists some $\mathcal{C}(r) \in C$. Oppositely, mapping $\mathcal{C}$ is called partial if there are some $r \in P$ for which $\mathcal{C}(r)$ is undefined.

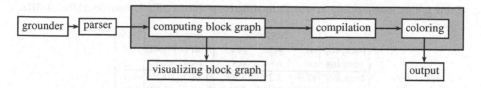

Fig. 1. The architecture of noMoRe.

compiled into Prolog code in order to obtain an efficient coloring procedure. Users may choose between two different kinds of compilation, one which is fast but which gives a lot of compiled code and another one which is a little bit slower but which produces less compiled code than the other. The second way of compiling has to be used with large logic programs, depending on the memory management of the underlying Prolog system. The compiled Prolog code (together with the example-independent code) is then used to actually compute the answer sets. To read logic programs we use a parser (eventually after running a grounder, e.g. lparse or dlv) and there is a separate part for interpretation of a-colorings into answer sets. Additionally, noMoRe comes with an interface to the graph drawing tool DaVinci [10] for visualization of block graphs. This allows for a structural analysis of programs.

The noMoRe system is used for purposes of research on the underlying paradigm. But even in this early state, usability for anybody familiar with the logic programming paradigm is given. The syntax accepted by noMoRe is Prolog-like, like that of dlv and smodels. For example, a rule $a \leftarrow b, not\ c$ is represented through a:-b, not c. Furthermore, noMoRe is able to deal with integrity constraints as well as weight and cardinality constraints, which are some of the most interesting syntactical features of smodels [11,5].

All discussed features (e.g. backward propagation, jumping, daVinci output and some experimental features) can be controlled by corresponding flags (see the noMoRe manual [7]).

4 Evaluating the System

As benchmarks, we used some instances of NP-complete problems proposed in [3], namely, the independent set problem for circle graphs[5], the problem of finding Hamiltonian cycles in complete graphs and the problem of finding classical graph colorings. Furthermore we have tested some instances of the n-queens problem. In Table 1 we have time measurements for noMoRe, smodels and dlv (from left to right)[6].

For Hamiltonian and n-queens problems we clearly see an improvement when using backward propagation and jumping. For independent set and coloring problems noMoRe becomes slower, but uses less choices than without backward propagation and jumping (see [6]). For coloring problems a similar behavior can be observed for the smodels system.

---

[5] A so-called circle graph Cir_n has n nodes $\{v_1, \cdots, v_n\}$ and arcs $A = \{(v_i, v_{i+1}) \mid 1 \leq i < n\} \cup \{(v_n, v_1)\}$.

[6] For number of choices for these examples see [6]

Table 1. Time measurements in seconds for different problems (all solutions) on AMD 1.4 GHz.

	noMoRe			smodels		dlv
backprop	no	yes	yes	with	(without)	
jumping	no	no	yes	lookahead		
ham_k_7	17.6	3.25	3.92	0.38	(0.16)	0.1
ham_k_8	328.86	35.86	44.23	7.69	(3.57)	0.71
ind_cir_40	5.84	7.18	7.24	1.31	(0.77)	1.97
ind_cir_50	106.15	127.45	128.99	23.87	(16.81)	40.62
col4x4	1.92	2.51	1.96	0.1	(0.27)	0.36
col5x5	179.38	223.42	180.35	11.54	(41.17)	24.79
queens7	0.73	0.84	0.5	0.08	(0.03)	0.05
queens8	3.82	4.3	1.86	0.32	(0.09)	0.12

References

1. A. Aggoun, D. Chan, P. Dufresne, et al. Eclipse user manual release 5.0, 2000.
2. C. Anger, K. Konczak, and T. Linke. NoMoRe: A system for non-monotonic reasoning under answer set semantics. In W. Faber T. Eiter and M. Truszczyński, editors, *Proceedings of the 6th International Conference on Logic Programming and Nonmonotonic Reasoning (LPNMR'01)*, pages 406–410. Springer, 2001.
3. P. Cholewiński, V. Marek, A. Mikitiuk, and M. Truszczyński. Experimenting with nonmonotonic reasoning. In *Proceedings of the International Conference on Logic Programming*, pages 267–281. MIT Press, 1995.
4. M. Gelfond and V. Lifschitz. Classical negation in logic programs and deductive databases. *New Generation Computing*, 9:365–385, 1991.
5. P. Simons I. Niemel and T. Soininen. Stable model semantics of weight constraint rules. In M. Gelfond, N. Leone, and G. Pfeifer, editors, *Proceedings of the 5th International Conference on Logic Programming and Nonmonotonic Reasoning (LPNMR'99)*, volume 1730 of *Lecture Notes in Artificial Intelligence*, pages 177–191, El Paso, Texas, USA, 1999. Springer Verlag.
6. T. Linke, C. Anger, and K. Konczak. More on nomore. In G. Ianni and S. Flesca, editors, *Eighth European Workshop on Logics in Artificial Intelligence (JELIA'02)*, volume 2424 of *Lecture Notes in Artificial Intelligence*. Springer Verlag, 2002.
7. T. Linke, K. Konzcak, and C. Anger, 2000–2002.
8. T. Linke. Graph theoretical characterization and computation of answer sets. In B. Nebel, editor, *Proceedings of the International Joint Conference on Artificial Intelligence*, pages 641–645. Morgan Kaufmann Publishers, 2001.
9. T. Linke. Rule-based computation of answer sets, 2002. submitted.
10. M.Werner. davinci v2.1.x online documentation, 1998.
11. P. Simons. Extending the stable model semantics with more expressive rules. In M. Gelfond, N. Leone, and G. Pfeifer, editors, *Proceedings of the 5th International Conference on Logic Programming and Nonmonotonic Reasoning (LPNMR'99)*, volume 1730 of *Lecture Notes in Artificial Intelligence*, pages 177–191, El Paso, Texas, USA, 1999. Springer Verlag.
12. J. Wielemaker. Swi-prolog 3.4.3 reference manual, 1990–2000.

Process Miner – A Tool for Mining Process Schemes from Event-Based Data

Guido Schimm

Oldenburger Forschungs- und Entwicklungsinstitut
für Informatik-Werkzeuge und -Systeme (OFFIS)
schimm@offis.de

Abstract. Today, process schemes are required for a lot of purposes. Extracting process schemes from event-based data is an alternative to creating them manually. Process Miner is a research prototype that can extract process schemes from event-based data. Its extracting procedure is a multistage data mining that uses a special process model. This paper outlines the main features of the tool and gives an insight into the theoretical background. Also, it describes shortly its implementation and outlines its experimental evaluation.

1 Introduction

Execution of processes is often driven by schemes. Most business processes, for example, are executed by many people together with various computer systems and possibly other tools. Here, a process schema acts as a template for process execution. It explicates a specific set of tasks, their order of execution, decision points branching to alternative executing paths, and the rules that are applied to make such decisions. In order to recognize, manage or control processes the respective schemes are needed. For example, a companies knowledge management saves and propagates process based knowledge in form of process schemes, advisory systems are based on process schemes, and workflow systems need process schemes in order to control business processes automatically.

The implicated need of process schemes requires schema development in any form. In the case that schema development is performed manually, it was realized that it is often difficult, time consuming, error prone, and expensive. An alternative to this is to generate schemes automatically. One kind of generating process schemes is extracting process schemes from event traces of properly executed processes.

Process miner is a tool that implements a complete mining procedure that extracts process schemes from event-based data. The mined schemes are complete and minimal: Complete in the sense that all recorded processes are covered by the extracted schema, minimal in the sense that only recorded processes are covered. Additionally, decision rules needed to decide between alternative paths of execution are extracted by the tool's mining procedure, too.

S. Flesca et al. (Eds.): JELIA 2002, LNAI 2424, pp. 525–528, 2002.
© Springer-Verlag Berlin Heidelberg 2002

2   Process Miner's Major Features

The main feature of Process Miner is the process mining procedure. Mining process schemes is based on a large amount of appropriate data. Therefore, the tool expects data to be stored in a database. The user starts the procedure from a menu entry of the tool's graphical user interface. At first, Process Miner connects to a database and shows a dialog that contains a list of all process data that are in the database. The user selects the process data that should be used as input for the mining procedure. The procedure can be controlled through parameter settings. The parameters determine which mining steps should be performed, some adjustable thresholds and the levels of detail for writing the logs. After the user confirms the settings the mining procedure starts. Process Miner automatically performs the procedure as a sequence of several steps. While the mining procedure runs, the user gets a detailed log of all mining steps. The last step represents the extracted schema in a separate editor window.

Beside the mining procedure implementation Process Miner has some other noteworthy features. One of them is the schema editor. It provides two different views of a process schema at the same time. One view represents a schema as diagram, the other view shows a schema in form of a tree. Both views can be scrolled and zoomed independently. Browsing through a schema and analyzing it is very comfortable, in the case that, for example, the tree view represents an overview and the diagram view is used to show details of the schema.

The user can also edit schemes. For this purpose the editor provides functions like *add, delete, copy, paste, clone, move* etc. that can be applied to schema elements in both views. For example, the user can cut off parts of a mined schema and then build sub schemes or integrate them in other schemes. Also the user can model complete schemes from scratch. All schemes can be exported to other tools in form of text files in XML-format.

Another useful feature of Process Miner is its simulation component. It allows simulating processes from a particular schema in a specific context. Such a simulation context consists of a set of feature-value pairs. According to the current values alternative paths of execution inside a schema are selected by the simulation component. Altering the context of a simulation leads to different process executions. Contexts can be created by the user with an editor. Alternatively, contexts can be created automatically by Process Miner, too. During a simulation all events of starting or stopping tasks and the context states are stored into a database.

3   Implementation

Process Miner is a research prototype that is considered to be a starting point of application-specific versions. The software is designed in an object-oriented manner and implemented with Java 1.3. The current version comes in form of a single jar archive. It consists of approximately 200 classes spread over nine packages.

Process Miner is multithreaded, i.e. that all tasks are performed in separate program threads. This is important for the execution of long running mining procedures. While such a procedure is executed the user can continue his interaction with the tool.

Process Miner comes with a customizable graphical user interface. The interface is build up in form of a multi-document interface, i.e. it consists of a desktop frame that contains and manages as many other frames as needed. The included frames are of different types. There are schema and context editor frames as well as frames for managing master data and customizing the tool. Additionally, there is a single log frame that provides commands like a simple text editor. The user interacts with the tool via a main menu, object specific pop up menus and different dialog windows. Process Miner connects to databases via JDBC-ODBC. It can store and exchange schemes as serialized objects or in XML format.

4   Theoretical Background

Process Miner's main purpose is to extract process schemes from event-based data. This extraction can be considered a special kind of knowledge discovery from databases (KDD) [FPSS96,HK01]. The most specific parts of Process Miner's kind of KDD are the process model and the data mining step called process mining. Both parts were developed at the OFFIS institute of the University of Oldenburg.

The process model is a generic linear process model [Sch00]. This model defines schemes in form of nested blocks. There are two main types of blocks: Operands and operators. The tasks of a process and sub processes are operands. They are nested in operators, which build up the control flow of a particular process. The most important operators are the sequence, the parallel, and the alternative. Furthermore, the process model has an algebra. The algebra's axioms cover distributivity, associativity, and commutativity. They are the basis of a term rewriting system. This system can be used in order to transform schemes, for example, into normal forms. A normal form defines a special structure of operators.

Process mining is a multistage procedure that is based on the above process model. It can be divided into six different steps performed in sequential order.

At the first step, the procedure reads event-based data that belongs to a certain process and builds a trace for each process instance from this data. A trace is a data structure that contains all events of a process instance in alternating start and end groups that are in correct chronological order. After building the traces, they are condensed on the basis of their sequence of start and end events. Each group constitutes a path in the process schema.

At the second step, a time-forward algorithm constructs a process schema from the trace groups that is in the disjunctive normal form (DNF). A process schema in DNF starts with an alternative block and enumerates inside this block all possible paths of execution as blocks that are built up without any alternative block.

The next step deals with relations between tasks that result from the random order of performing tasks without a real precedence relation between them. These pseudo precedence relations are identified and then removed from the schema.

Because the process schema was built in DNF, it is necessary to split the schema's initial alternative and to move the partial alternatives as near as possible to the point in time where a decision can't be retarded any longer. This is done by a transformation step. It merges blocks what also leads to a more compact schema.

It follows a decision-mining step that is based on decision tree induction [HK01,Qui98]. In this step an induction is performed for each decision point of the schema. The decision trees are transformed into rules and then the rules are attached to the particular alternative operators. The last step displays the extracted schema.

5   Experimental Evaluation

Up to now, the evaluation of Process Miner was based on simulated data. The tool let the user edit process schemes. These schemes can be applied for a simulation of a set of processes by Process Miner's simulation component. While it simulates processes, events of starting and ending tasks are generated and written into a database. Simulation can be parameterized and running in different contexts, so that a large amount of process variants can be generated. After simulating a process schema, a new schema can be mined from the database. If the mining procedure works accurately, the extracted schema is equal to the schema from which the data was generated.

The evaluation of Process Miner based on real world data is just in progress. First projects are in two different fields of application. One is the mining of workflow descriptions from audit logs for a workflow management system. The other should mine process schemes from production data for analytical purposes. In both cases Process Miner is supplemented by one routine that reads the special input and another routine that exports the extracted schemes in a special target format.

References

FPSS96.   U. Fayyad, G. Piatetsky-Shapiro, and P. Smyth. From data mining to knowledge discovery in databases. *AI Magazine*, 1996.

HK01.   J. Han and M. Kamber. *Data Mining – Concepts and Techniques*. Academic Press, 2001.

Qui98.   J. R. Quinland. *C4.5 – Programs for Machine Learning*. Morgan Kaufmann, 1998.

Sch00.   G. Schimm.   Generic linear business process modeling.   In S. W. Liddle, H. C. Mayr, and B. Thalheim, editors, *Proceedings of ER 2000, International Workshop on Conceptual Modeling Approaches for E-Business (eCOMO2000)*, volume 1921 of *Lecture Notes in Computer Science*, Salt Lake City, 2000. Springer.

SMILES: A Multi-purpose Learning System*

V. Estruch, C. Ferri, J. Hernández, and M.J. Ramírez

DSIC, UPV, Camino de Vera s/n, 46020 Valencia, Spain
{vestruch,cferri,jorallo,mramirez}@dsic.upv.es

Abstract. A machine learning system is useful for extracting models from data that can be used for many applications such as data analysis, decision support or data mining. SMILES is a machine learning system that integrates many different features from other machine learning techniques and paradigms, and more importantly, it presents several innovations in almost all of these features, such as ensemble methods, cost-sensitive learning, and the generation of a comprehensible model from an ensemble. This paper contains a short description of the main features of the system as well as some experimental results.

Keywords: Decision tree learning, machine learning, data mining, cost-sensitive learning, comprehensibility, ensemble methods.

1 Introduction

SMILES (Stunning Multi-purpose Integrated LEarning System) is a machine learning system that contains features from some of the most recent directions in machine learning. In particular, it extends classical decision tree learners in many ways (new splitting criteria, non-greedy search, new partitions, extraction of several and different solutions, combination of solutions), and it can be configured to minimise misclassification costs.

In this paper we focus on the three main contributions of SMILES. First, we present the structure used in the system: a decision multi-tree. This kind of structure allows the generation of a set of hypotheses taking into consideration limited computational capabilities. We also combine the hypotheses in order to improve the overall accuracy, defining a new ensemble method. Secondly, we show an interesting capability of the system: the generation of a single representative solution from an ensemble of solutions. Finally, we introduce other features of the system on cost-sensitive learning.

2 The Structure of the SMILES System

The construction of decision trees is performed in two different steps: first, the whole decision tree is constructed by using a splitting criterion that selects the best split; secondly, unuseful parts of the tree are removed (*pruning*). Thus, a decision tree is built in a eager way, which allows a quick construction of a model. However, bad models may be produced because the alternatives that

---

* This work has been partially supported by CICYT under grant TIC2001-2705-C03-01 and by Generalitat Valenciana under grant GV00-092-14.

S. Flesca et al. (Eds.): JELIA 2002, LNAI 2424, pp. 529–532, 2002.

are not selected by the splitting criterion are immediately rejected. The main algorithm of SMILES is based on a new structure in which the rejected splits are not removed, but stored as *suspended* nodes. The further exploration of these nodes after the first solution has been built allows the extraction of new models from this structure. Since each new model is obtained by continuing the construction of the multi-tree, these models share their common parts. For this reason, a decision multi-tree can also be seen as an AND/OR tree [4], if one consider the alternative nodes as OR-nodes, and the nodes generated by an exploited OR-node as AND-nodes. Because each new solution is built following the construction of a complete tree, our method differs from other approaches such as *boosting* or *bagging* [6], which induce a new decision tree for each solution. The result is a multi-tree rather than a forest, with the advantage that a multi-tree shares the common parts and the forest does not. We perform a greedy search for each solution, but once the first solution is found the following ones can be obtained taking into account a limited computation time (the time and memory which are required to produce the next n solutions increases in a sublinear way). For more details on the structure, we refer to [5].

The number of trees (OR-nodes) to be explored and how to select them determines the resulting multi-tree. With all these opened branches we can do two things: select one solution or combine a set of solutions. For the former, we have implemented several selection criteria to specify which of all the possible solutions must be selected (*Occam, coverage best,...*). For the latter, one way to use the multiplicity in the multi-tree is to combine the results of different branches. SMILES implements several criteria to combine a set of solutions given in the multi-tree (*shared ensemble*) [1].

3   Selecting an Archetype from a Shared Ensemble

A combined hypothesis is usually a voting of many hypotheses and, as a result, the comprehensibility of the single solution is lost. For this reason, SMILES is also able to select one single solution (we call it the *archetype* of the ensemble [3]) that is semantically close to the combined hypothesis. This is done without the use of an extra validation dataset but the use of an invented random dataset.

The use of an archetype hypothesis is a way to obtain similar results to other methods such as *boosting* or *bagging*, but maintaining the comprehensibility of a declarative model.

4   Cost-Sensitive Learning and ROC Analysis Features

Accuracy (or error), i.e., percentage of instances that are correctly classified (respectively incorrectly classified) has traditionally been used as a measure of the quality of classifiers. However, in most situations, not every misclassification has the same consequences. SMILES contains different methods for cost-sensitive learning: assignment of classes based on costs, cost-sensitive splitting criteria,...

The usefulness of cost-sensitive learning does not only apply when the misclassification costs or class distributions are known a priori. If they are not known, one or many classifiers can be generated in order to behave well in the

Table 1. Accuracy comparison between ensemble methods.

#	Bagging			Boosting			Multi-tree		
	10	100	300	10	100	300	10	100	300
balance-scale	82.24	82.76	82.87	78.72	76.00	75.60	77.89	83.02	85.50
cars	93.89	94.36	94.29	95.92	97.07	97.15	89.34	90.90	91.53
dermatology	96.40	97.19	97.30	96.62	96.51	96.65	91.43	94.00	95.71
ecoli	83.90	85.15	85.56	83.66	84.29	84.20	78.58	80.09	79.64
house-votes	95.40	95.73	95.77	95.19	95.24	95.42	94.56	95.93	96.21
iris	94.20	94.27	94.53	94.20	94.53	94.53	94.27	94.47	94.47
monks1	99.95	100.00	100.00	99.46	99.46	99.46	96.45	99.89	100.00
monks2	65.52	67.51	67.94	76.67	82.17	83.40	75.33	77.15	79.37
monks3	98.76	98.88	98.88	97.96	97.92	97.92	97.84	97.62	97.65
new-thyroid	94.33	94.66	94.81	94.98	95.31	95.22	93.43	92.57	92.71
post-operative	63.11	64.89	64.78	59.67	59.00	59.00	63.00	67.00	67.75
soybean-small	97.75	97.95	97.95	97.95	97.95	97.95	96.00	94.75	95.75
tae	60.10	61.11	61.05	64.81	64.81	64.81	65.00	65.13	65.40
tic-tac	83.06	84.05	83.91	82.11	82.62	82.55	79.23	82.68	83.72
wine	94.90	95.90	96.35	95.90	96.85	96.57	93.29	92.53	91.94
GeoMean	85.77	86.59	87.03	86.61	86.99	86.70	84.91	86.49	87.16

widest range of circumstances or contexts. The Receiver Operating Characteristic (ROC) analysis provides tools to select a set of classifiers that would behave optimally and reject some other useless classifiers. In particular, **SMILES** is the first system which incorporates measures based on the area under the ROC curve to generate and select models which behave well in the presence of variable cost contexts or class distribution changes [2].

5 Experiments

In this section we present an experimental evaluation of the **SMILES** system. Here, we only present results of the combined hypothesis of our ensemble method w.r.t. other well-known methods. A deeper experimental evaluation of other features can be found in [1,2,3].

Table 1 presents a comparison of accuracy between our method (*multi-tree*), *boosting* and *bagging*, depending on the number of iterations. We have employed the **Weka**[1] implementation of these two ensemble methods. For all the experiments we have used *GainRatio* as splitting criterion, and we have chosen a simple random method for populating the multi-tree and a fusion strategy based on selecting the branch that gives a maximum cardinality for the majority class. The datasets have been extracted from the UCI repository[2]. The experiments were performed with a Pentium III-800Mhz with 180MB of memory running linux 2.4.2. Since there are many sources of randomness, we have performed the experiments by averaging 10 results of a 10-fold cross-validation (1500 runs in total). The results present the mean accuracy for each dataset, and finally the geometric mean of all the datasets. Although initially our method obtains lower results with a few iterations, with a higher number of iterations it surpasses the other systems.

Nevertheless, the major advantage of the method is appreciated by looking at the consumption of resources. Figure 1 shows the average training time de-

---

[1] http://www.cs.waikato.ac.nz/~ml/weka/
[2] http://www.ics.uci.edu/~mlearn/MLSummary.html

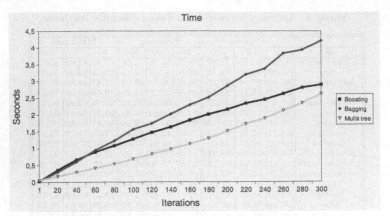

Fig. 1. Time comparison between ensemble methods.

pending on the number of iterations (1-300) for the three methods. Note that the time increase of *Bagging* is linear, as expected. *Boosting* behaves better with high values because the algorithm implemented in Weka trickily stops the learning if it does not detect a significant increasing of accuracy. Finally, SMILES presents a sub-linear increase of required time due to the sharing of common components of the multi-tree structure.

6   Conclusions

Summing up, the SMILES system surpasses other ensemble learning methods in terms of accuracy and resource requirements by the use of shared ensembles. It also allows a wide range of applications in data mining, especially when cost-information can hazardously vary at application time or whenever a comprehensible model is required with high accuracy. These comprehensible models can be embodied into other kinds of AI systems: expert systems, knowledge-based systems and decision-support systems.

References

1. V. Estruch, C. Ferri, J. Hernández, and M.J. Ramírez. Shared Ensembles using Multi-trees. In *the 8th Ib. Conf. on A. I., Iberamia'02*. (Submitted), 2002.
2. C. Ferri, P. Flach, and J. Hernández. Learning Decision Trees using the Area Under the ROC Curve. In *Int. Conf. on Machine Learning, ICML'02*. (To appear), 2002.
3. C. Ferri, J. Hernández, and M.J. Ramírez. From Ensemble Methods to Comprehensible Models. In *the 5th Int. Conf. on Discovery Science*. (Submitted), 2002.
4. C. Ferri, J. Hernández, and M.J. Ramírez. Induction of Decision Multi-trees using Levin Search. In *Int. Conf. on Computational Science, ICCS'02*, volume 2329 of *LNCS*, pages 166–175, 2002.
5. C. Ferri, J. Hernández, and M.J. Ramírez. SMILES System, a multi-purpose learning system. http://www.dsic.upv.es/~flip/smiles/, 2002.
6. J. R. Quinlan. Bagging, Boosting, and C4.5. In *Proc. of the 13th Nat. Conf. on A.I. and the Eighth Innovative Applications of A.I. Conf.*, pages 725–730. AAAI Press / MIT Press, 1996.

The *aspps* System

Deborah East[1] and Mirosław Truszczyński[2]

[1] Department of Computer Science, Southwest Texas State University
San Marcos TX 78666, USA
[2] Department of Computer Science, University of Kentucky
Lexington KY 40506-0046, USA

1 Introduction

The *aspps* system is an answer-set programming system based on the extended logic of propositional schemata [2], which allows variables but not function symbols in the language. We denote this logic PS^+. A theory in the logic PS^+ is a pair (D, P), where D is a set of ground atoms (only constant symbols as arguments) representing an *instance of a problem* (input data), and P is a set of PS^+-clauses representing a *program* (an abstraction of a problem). The meaning of a PS^+-theory $T = (D, P)$ is given by a *family* of PS^+-models [2].

The *aspps* program and an associated module *psgrnd* allow one to compute models of PS^+ theories. First, a theory is grounded using the program *psgrnd*. The theory obtained in this way is an input to the *aspps* solver, which computes models of the ground theory and, hence, of the original theory, as well.

The language of logic PS^+ accepted by *psgrnd* includes special constructs, such as those to model cardinality constraints on sets. The theories produced by *psgrnd* maintain the structure of these constructs. The *aspps* solver is based on the Davis-Putnam algorithm for satisfiability checking. There is however a major difference. The solver accepts and takes advantage of special constructs in the ground theories to improve search.

Both *psgrnd* and *aspps*, examples of PS^+-programs and the corresponding performance results are available at http://www.cs.uky.edu/ai/aspps/.

In this document we update an earlier note describing our system [1]. We present the syntax of PS^+-programs that is accepted by *psgrnd*. We also provide instructions for executing *psgrnd* and *aspps* and discuss some of the available options. For theoretical underpinnings of *aspps*, we refer the reader to [2].

2 PS^+-Theories

The language of PS^+ contains variable, constant and predicate symbols but not function symbols. Predicates in a PS^+ theory are classified as *data* and *program* predicates. Ground atoms built of data predicates represent a problem instance. They form the component D (data) of a theory (D, P). The program P consists of clauses built of atoms involving both data and program predicates. Clauses are written as implications and explicit negation of atoms is not allowed (the

S. Flesca et al. (Eds.): JELIA 2002, LNAI 2424, pp. 533–536, 2002.
© Springer-Verlag Berlin Heidelberg 2002

implication symbol is omitted if a clause has an empty conjunction of atoms as the antecedent). The program is written to capture all the relevant constraints specifying the problem to be solved.

The key difference between the logic PS^+ and the logic of propositional schemata is in the definition of a model. Following the intuition that computation must not modify the data set, a set of ground atoms M is a model of a PS^+ theory (D, P) if M is a propositional model of the grounding of (D, P) and if it coincides with D on the part of the Herbrand Universe given by data predicates.

Data for an instance is given in one or more data files. The following set of atoms is an example of a data file for an instance of graph coloring.

$vtx(1)$. $\quad vtx(2)$. $\quad vtx(3)$. $\quad vtx(4)$.
$edge(1, 4)$.
$edge(1, 2)$.
$edge(3, 2)$.
$clr(r)$.
$clr(g)$.
$clr(b)$.

The rule file (only one rule file is allowed) includes a preamble, where program predicates are defined and variables declared. The preamble in the program file restricts the way program predicates are grounded. The following lines form an example of the preamble for a graph-coloring program.

pred $color(vtx, clr)$.
var vtx X, Y.
var clr K, C.

The program predicate $color$ is a binary predicate. Its first argument must be a constant from the extension of the data predicate vtx, as defined in the data file. Its second argument must be a constant from the extension of the data predicate clr. Only unary data predicates can be used to define *types* of arguments of program predicates. Binary data predicates can also be used in the predicate definitions to restrict their extensions. An example (not related to graph coloring) is:

pred $hc(vtx, vtx) : edge$.

This statement restricts the extension of the program predicate hc to a subset of the extension of the data predicate $edge$. The preamble also declares types of variable symbols used in the program. Variables are declared by means of unary data predicates (examples are given above). The declaration of variables allows for more efficient grounding and further error checking.

The preamble is followed by clauses describing constraints of the problem. An example of a program for graph coloring follows.

Clause 1. $color(X, r) | color(X, g) | color(X, b)$.
Clause 2. $color(X, K), color(X, C) \to K == C$.
Clause 3. $color(X, K), color(Y, K), edge(X, Y) \to$.

Clause 1 ensures that each vertex is assigned at least one color. Clause 2 enforces that at most one color is assigned to each vertex. The last clause prohibits assigning the same color to vertices connected by an edge.

In some cases, the consequent of a clause must be a disjunction of a set of atoms that depends on a particular data instance. To build such disjunctions, we introduced in the language of the logic PS^+ the notion of an *e-atom*. An example of an e-atom (in the context of our graph-coloring setting) is $color(X, \_)$. It stands for the disjunction of all atoms of the form $color(X, c)$, where c is a constant from the extension of the data predicate clr. The use of the special construct for existential atoms (e-atoms) allows us to rewrite Clause 1 as "$color(X, \_)$.". Our current version of logic PS^+ allows also for more complex variants of e-atoms.

Another powerful modeling concept in the language of logic PS^+ is that of a cardinality atom. An example of a cardinality atom is $k\{color(X, \_)\}m$. We interpret the expression within the braces as a specification of the *set* of all ground atoms of the form $color(X, c)$, where c is a constant from the extension of the data predicate clr. The meaning of the atom $k\{color(X, \_)\}m$ is: at least k and no more than m atoms of the form $color(X, c)$ are true.

Using the concept of a cardinality atom, we can replace Clause 1 and 2 with a single clause "$1\{color(X, \_)\}1$.". We preserve the structure of cardinality atoms in ground theories and take advantage of the structure in the solver.

In addition to the program and data predicates, the *aspps* implementation includes *predefined* predicates and function symbols such as the equality operator $==$, arithmetic comparators $<=$, $>=$, $<$ and $>$, and arithmetic operations $+$, $-$, $*$, $/$, $abs()$ (absolute value), $mod(N, b)$, $max(X, Y)$ and $min(X, Y)$. We assign to these symbols their standard interpretation. We emphasize that the domains are restricted only to those constants that appear in a theory.

3   Grounding PS^+-Theories

The grounding of logic PS^+ programs is performed by the module *psgrnd*. When grounding, we first evaluate all expressions built of predefined operators. We then form ground instantiations of all program clauses. Next, we evaluate and simplify away all atoms built of predefined predicates. We also simplify away all atoms built of data predicates (as they are fully determined by the data part). Therefore, the ground PS^+-theory contains only ground atoms built of program predicates.

The required input to execute *psgrnd* is a single program file, one or more data files and optional constants. If no errors are found while reading the files and during grounding, an output file is constructed. The output file is a machine readable file. Included in the output file is a mapping from the program predicates to machine readable form for each predicate. A list of all ground atoms built of program predicates that were determined during grounding is also given. The name of the output file is a catenation of the constants and file names with the extension **.aspps**.

psgrnd -r rfile -d dfile1 dfile2 ... [-c c1=v1 c2=v2 ...]

Required arguments

-r **rfile** is the file describing the problem. There must be exactly one program file.

-d **datafilelist** is a list of one or more files containing data that will be used to instantiate the theory.

Optional arguments

-c **name=value** This option allows the use of constants in both the data and rule files. When **name** is found while reading input files it is replaced by **value**; **value** can be any string that is valid for the data type. If **name** is to be used in a range specification, then **value** must be an integer.

4 Solving PS^+-Theories

The solver *aspps* is used to compute models of the ground PS^+-theory produced by *psgrnd*. The solver takes advantage of the special constructs by allowing search to branch based on the status of cardinality atoms. This possibility often significantly reduces the size of the search space. In addition, the heuristics for selecting atoms on which to branch are guided by the structure of the original problem, preserved by the grounding process.

The name of the file containing the theory is input on the command line. After executing the *aspps* program, a file named aspps.stat is created or appended with statistics concerning this execution of *aspps*.

aspps -f filename [-A] [-P] [-C [x]] [-L [x]] [-S name]

Required arguments

-f **filename** is the name of the file containing a theory produced by *psgrnd*.

Optional arguments

-A Prints atoms that are true in the computed model in readable form.

-P Prints the input theory and then exits.

-C [x] Counts the number of solutions. This information is recorded in the statistics file. If **x** is specified it must be a positive integer; *aspps* stops after finding **x** solutions or exhausting the whole search space, whichever comes first.

-S **name** Shows positive atoms with predicate **name**.

References

1. D. East and M. Truszczyński. *aspps* — an implementation of answer-set programming with propositional schemata. In *Proceedings of Logic Programming and Nonmonotonic Reasoning Conference, LPNMR 2001*, LNAI 2173, pages 402–405, Springer Verlag, 2001.
2. D. East and M. Truszczyński. Propositional satisfiability in answer-set programming. In *Proceedings of Joint German/Austrian Conference on Artificial Intelligence, KI'2001*, LNAI 2174, pages 138–153, Springer Verlag, 2001.

The DLV System*

Nicola Leone[1], Gerald Pfeifer[2], Wolfgang Faber[2], Francesco Calimeri[1],
Tina Dell'Armi[1], Thomas Eiter[2], Georg Gottlob[2], Giovambattista Ianni[1],
Giuseppe Ielpa[1], Christoph Koch[2], Simona Perri[1], and Axel Polleres[2]

[1] Department of Mathematics, University of Calabria
87030 Rende (CS), Italy
{leone,calimeri,dellarmi,ianni,ielpa,perri}@mat.unical.it
[2] Institut für Informationssysteme, TU Wien
A-1040 Wien, Austria
{pfeifer,gottlob,koch}@dbai.tuwien.ac.at
{faber,eiter,axel}@kr.tuwien.ac.at

1 Introduction

The development of the DLV system has started as a research project financed by
FWF (the Austrian Science Funds) in 1996, and has evolved into an international
collaboration over the years. Currently, the University of Calabria and TU Wien
participate in the project, supported by a scientific-technological collaboration
between Italy and Austria. At the time of writing, the latest version of the system
has been released on April 12, 2002.

The system is based on disjunctive logic programming without function symbols under the consistent answer set semantics [5], has the following important
features:

Advanced knowledge modeling capabilities DLV provides support for declarative problem solving in several respects:

- High expressiveness in a formally precise sense (Σ_2^P), so any such problem can be uniformly solved by a fixed program over varying input.
- Declarative problem solving following a "Guess&Check" paradigm where
  a solution to a problem is guessed by one part of a program and then
  verified through another part of the program.
- A number of front-ends for dealing with specific AI applications.

Solid Implementation Much effort has been spent on sophisticated algorithms
and techniques for improving the performance, including

- deductive database optimization techniques, and
- non-monotonic reasoning optimization techniques.

Database Interfaces The DLV system provides an experimental interface to a
relational database management system (Oracle) and, by means of a special

---

* This work was supported by FWF (Austrian Science Funds) under the projects
Z29-INF and P14781, by MURST under project COFIN-2000 "From Data to Information (D2I)," and by the European Commission under project IST-2002-33570.

S. Flesca et al. (Eds.): JELIA 2002, LNAI 2424, pp. 537–540, 2002.

query tool, also to an object-oriented database management system (Objectivity), which is useful for the integration of specific problem solvers developed in DLV into more complex systems. An ODBC interface is currently being developed.

For up-to-date information on the system and a full manual please refer to the URL http://www.dlvsystem.com, where you can also download binaries of the current release and various examples.

2   Languages

2.1   Kernel Language

The kernel language of DLV is disjunctive datalog extended with strong negation and weak constraints under the consistent answer set semantics [5].

Let $a_1, \cdots, a_n, b_1, \cdots, b_m$ be classical literals (atoms possibly preceded by the classical negation symbol "$-$") and $n \geq 0$, $m \geq k \geq 0$. A *(disjunctive) rule r* is a formula

$$a_1 \text{ v } \cdots \text{ v } a_n :- b_1, \cdots, b_k, \text{ not } b_{k+1}, \cdots, \text{ not } b_m.$$

A *strong constraint* is a rule with empty head ($n = 0$). A *weak constraint* is

$$:\sim b_1, \cdots, b_k, \text{ not } b_{k+1}, \cdots, \text{ not } b_m. [Weight : Level]$$

where both Weight and Level are positive integers. A *(disjunctive) program* $\mathcal{P}$ is a finite set of rules and constraints.

The semantics of these programs is provided in [1] as an extension of the classical answer set semantics given in [5].

2.2   Front-Ends

In addition to its kernel language, DLV provides a number of application frontends that show the suitability of our formalism for solving various problems from the areas of Artificial Intelligence, Knowledge Representation and (Deductive) Databases. In particular, currently front-ends for model-based diagnosis [2], SQL3, logic programming with inheritance, and knowledge based planning are available.

3   System Architecture

The architecture of DLV is illustrated in Figure 1. The general flow in this picture is top-down. The principal User Interface is command-line oriented, but also a Graphical User Interface (GUI) for the core systems and most front-ends is available. Subsequently, front-end transformations might be performed. Input data can be supplied by regular files, and also by Oracle or Objectivity databases. The DLV kernel (the shaded part in the figure) then produces answer sets one at a

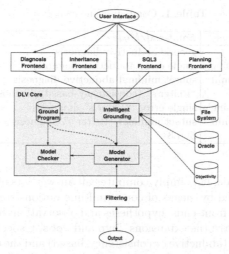

Fig. 1. The System Architecture of DLV

time, and each time an answer set is found, "Filtering" is invoked, which performs post-processing (dependent on the active front-ends) and controls continuation or abortion of the computation.

The DLV kernel consists of three major components: The "Intelligent Grounding," "Model Generator," and "Model Checker" modules share a principal data structure, the "Ground Program". It is created by the Intelligent Grounding using differential (and other advanced) database techniques together with suitable data structures, and used by the Model Generator and the Model Checker. The Ground Program is guaranteed to have exactly the same answer sets as the original program. For some syntactically restricted classes of programs (e.g. stratified programs), the Intelligent Grounding module already computes the corresponding answer sets.

For harder problems, most of the computation is performed by the Model Generator and the Model Checker. Roughly, the former produces some "candidate" answer sets (models) [3,4], the stability and minimality of which are subsequently verified by the latter.

The Model Checker (MC) verifies whether the model at hand is an answer set. This task is very hard in general, because checking the stability of a model is known to be co-NP-complete. However, MC exploits the fact that minimal model checking — the hardest part — can be efficiently performed for the relevant class of *head-cycle-free* (HCF) programs.

4 Usage

While DLV also comes with a graphical user interface (GUI), the computational engine and its front-ends are implemented as a command-line tool, controlled by command-line options; it reads input from text files whose names are provided on the command-line, and any output is written to the standard output.

Table 1. Command-line switches

Option	Front-end/Mode
-FD	generic abductive diagnosis
-FDsingle	single error abductive diagnosis
-FDmin	subset minimal abductive diagnosis
-FR	"Reiter's" (consistency-based) diagnosis
-FRsingle	single error "Reiter's" diagnosis
-FRmin	subset minimal "Reiter's" diagnosis
-FS	SQL3

In its default mode, DLV simply computes all answer sets of its input; specific front-ends are invoked by means of command-line options starting with "-F".

For the diagnosis front-ends, hypotheses and observations have to be stored in files whose names carry the extensions .hyp and .obs, respectively. The type of diagnostic reasoning (abductive or consistency-based) and the desired minimality criterion (none, single error, subset minimality) is selected by specifying one of the options depicted in Table 1.

The SQL front-end is selected by means of the -FS command-line option. Input files whose names end with .sql are processed with an SQL parser.

5 Current Work

Our current activities concentrate on three issues: Language extensions, efficiency enhancements, and interoperability.

Concerning language extensions, we are working on aggregates and function symbols in the kernel system, but also on further front-ends, such as qualitative diagnosis. Regarding efficiency, we work on a generalization of magic set techniques, and we are investigating alternative heuristics. Finally, in order to support better integration of DLV in large systems, we work on providing an API to DLV and on an ODBC interface to relational databases.

References

1. F. Buccafurri, N. Leone, and P. Rullo. Enhancing disjunctive datalog by constraints. *IEEE TKDE*, 12(5), September/October 2000.
2. T. Eiter, W. Faber, N. Leone, and G. Pfeifer. The Diagnosis Frontend of the dlv System. *AI Communications*, 12(1–2):99–111, 1999.
3. W. Faber, N. Leone, and G. Pfeifer. Pushing Goal Derivation in DLP Computations. *LPNMR'99*, pp. 177–191.
4. W. Faber, N. Leone, and G. Pfeifer. Experimenting with Heuristics for Answer Set Programming. In *IJCAI 2001*, pp. 635–640, Seattle, WA, USA, August 2001. Morgan Kaufmann Publishers.
5. M. Gelfond and V. Lifschitz. Classical Negation in Logic Programs and Disjunctive Databases. *New Generation Computing*, 9:365–385, 1991.

The DLV$^{\mathcal{K}}$ Planning System: Progress Report*

Thomas Eiter[1], Wolfgang Faber[1],
Nicola Leone[2], Gerald Pfeifer[1], and Axel Polleres[1]

[1] Institut für Informationssysteme, TU Wien, A-1040 Wien, Austria
{eiter,faber,axel}@kr.tuwien.ac.at
pfeifer@dbai.tuwien.ac.at
[2] Department of Mathematics, University of Calabria, 87030 Rende, Italy
leone@unical.it

1 Introduction

The knowledge based planning system DLV$^{\mathcal{K}}$ implements answer set planning on top of the DLV system [1]. It is developed at TU Wien and supports the declarative language $\mathcal{K}$ [2,3] and its extension $\mathcal{K}^c$ [5]. The language $\mathcal{K}$ is syntactically similar to the action language $\mathcal{C}$ [7], but semantically closer to answer set programming (by including default negation, for example). $\mathcal{K}$ and $\mathcal{K}^c$ offer the following distinguishing features:

- *Handling of incomplete knowledge:* for a fluent f, neither f nor its opposite $\neg f$ need to be known in any state.
- *Nondeterministic effects:* actions may have multiple possible outcomes.
- *Optimistic and secure (conformant) planning:* construction of a "credulous" plan or a "sceptical" plan, which works in all cases.
- *Parallel actions:* More than one action may be executed simultaneously.
- *Optimal cost planning:* In $\mathcal{K}^c$, one can assign an arbitrary cost function to each action, where the total costs of the plan are minimized.

An operational prototype of DLV$^{\mathcal{K}}$ is available at

<URL:http://www.dlvsystem.com/K/>.

We report here briefly the architecture and new features of the system which we have accomplished in the last year.

2 System Architecture

The architecture of DLV$^{\mathcal{K}}$ is outlined in Figure 1. The input of the system consists of domain descriptions (DLV$^{\mathcal{K}}$ files) and optional static background knowledge specified by a disjunctive logic program having a unique answer set. Input is read from an arbitrary number of files, converted to an internal representation and stored in a common database.

* This work was supported by FWF (Austrian Science Funds) under the projects P14781 and Z29-INF.

S. Flesca et al. (Eds.): JELIA 2002, LNAI 2424, pp. 541–544, 2002.

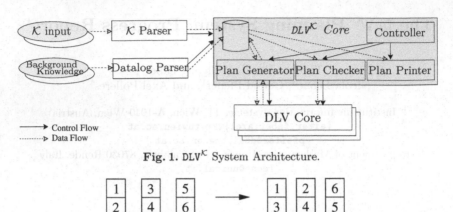

Fig. 1. DLV$^{\mathcal{K}}$ System Architecture.

Fig. 2. A blocks world example.

The actual DLV$^{\mathcal{K}}$ front-end consists of four main modules: The *Controller* manages the other three modules; it performs user interactions (where appropriate), and controls the execution of the entire front-end. The Controller first invokes the *Plan Generator*, which translates the planning problem at hand into a suitable program in the core language of DLV (disjunctive logic programming under the answer set semantics). The Controller then invokes the DLV kernel to solve the corresponding problem. The resulting answer sets (if any exist) are fed back to the Controller, which extracts the solutions to the original problem from these answer sets and transforms them back to the original planning domain.

If the user specified that secure/conformant planning should be performed, the Controller then invokes the *Plan Checker*. Similarly to the Plan Generator, the Checker uses the original problem description and, in addition, the optimistic plan computed by the Generator to generate a disjunctive logic program which verifies whether this plan is in fact also secure.

The *Plan Printer*, finally, translates the solutions found by the Generator (and optionally verified by the Checker) back into user output and prints it.

Details about the transformations mentioned above can be found in [4].

3   DLV$^{\mathcal{K}}$ Example: Blocks World

We assume that the reader is familiar with action languages and the notion of actions, fluents, goals, and plans; see e.g. [6], for a background, and [3,5] for the detailed syntax and semantics of our language $\mathcal{K}^c$.

To give a flavor of DLV$^{\mathcal{K}}$, we show the encoding of a planning problem in the well-known blocks world. The problem is turning the configuration of blocks on the left hand side of Figure 2 into the one on the right hand side. The static background knowledge of our blocks world is the following logic program:

```
block(1). block(2). block(3). block(4). block(5). block(6).
location(table).  location(B) :- block(B).
```

Referring to Figure 2, we want to turn the initial configuration of blocks into the goal state in three steps, concurrent moves allowed.

The $\mathcal{K}$ domain description uses an action `move` and the fluents `on` and `blocked`. In this simple example, we assume that in the initial state the locations of all blocks are known. The domain is described by the following DLV$^\mathcal{K}$ program:

```
fluents:    on(B,L) requires block(B), location(L).
            blocked(B) requires block(B).
actions:    move(B,L) requires block(B), location(L) costs 1.
always:     executable move(B,L) if B <> L.
            nonexecutable move(B,L) if blocked(B).
            nonexecutable move(B,L) if blocked(L).
            nonexecutable move(B,L) if move(B1,L), B <> B1, block(L).
            nonexecutable move(B,L) if move(B,L1), L <> L1.
            nonexecutable move(B,B1) if move(B1,L).
            caused on(B,L) after move(B,L).
            caused -on(B,L) after move(B,L1), on(B,L), L <> L1.
            inertial on(B,L).
            caused blocked(B) if on(_,B).
initially: on(1,2). on(2,table). on(3,4). on(4,table). on(5,6). on(6.table)
goal:      on(1,3), on(3,table), on(2,4), on(4,table), on(6,5), on(5,table)
           ? (3)
```

Actions may have assigned costs, which should be minimized. In our case, each `move` has cost 1, resulting in plans, where a minimum number of moves is executed to achieve the plan.

The rules following the declarations of actions and fluents describe the transitions and constraints on the initial states of the domain. Finally, the `goal:` section defines the goal to be reached and the plan length.

4 Usage of the System

Assume that the above background knowledge and planning program are given in files `blocks.bk` and `blocks.plan`, respectively. The execution of the command:

```
$ dlv -FP blocks.bk blocks.plan -n=1
```

computes the following result:

```
PLAN: move(3,table), move(5,table); move(1,3), move(6,5); move(2,4)
COST: 5
```

where parallel actions are separated by "," and plan steps are separated by ";".

The command-line option `-n=1` tells DLV to compute only one plan. Option `-FP` is used to invoke the planning front-end in DLV. Alternatively, one can use the options `-FPopt` and `-FPsec`, which explicitly enforce optimistic and secure planning, respectively. For planning problems with a unique initial state and a deterministic domain, these two options do not make a difference, as optimistic and secure plans coincide in this case. But for problems with multiple initial states or nondeterministic effects, the latter computes only secure (conformant) plans. With -FP the user can interactively decide whether to check plan security.

Checking plan security is Π_P^2-complete in general, but we have identified subclasses where "cheaper" checks can be applied (for details, see [3,4]). By means of the command-line options -check=1 and -check=2 a particular method to check plan security can be chosen, where 1 is the default. Check 1 is applicable to programs which are false-committed (defined in [4]). This condition is e.g. guaranteed for the class of $\mathcal{K}$ domains which are stratified, when viewed as a logic program. Check 2 is applicable for domains where the existence of a legal transition (i.e., executability of some action leading to a consistent successor state) is always guaranteed. In [5] we have shown that using these two checks we can solve relevant conformant planning problems. More general secure checks are on the agenda. As mentioned above, the DLV$^{\mathcal{K}}$ system has been recently extended by the possibility to assign costs to actions, in order to generate cost optimal plans [5]. Apart from optimal plans the system can also compute "cost bound" plans, i.e., all plans which do not exceed a certain cost limit, by means of the command line option -costbound=N. In our example, by -costbound=6 we could also compute plans involving 6 moves.

Performance and experimental results are reported in [4]. However, the results there do not include optimal planning. For example, we performed some promising experiments for parallel blocksworld under action costs. Using the encoding above, the instances P1–P4 from [4] can be solved in less than one second.

References

1. T. Eiter, W. Faber, N. Leone, and G. Pfeifer. Declarative Problem-Solving Using the DLV System. In: *Logic-Based Artificial Intelligence*, pp. 79–103. Kluwer, 2000.
2. T. Eiter, W. Faber, N. Leone, G. Pfeifer, and A. Polleres. Planning under incomplete knowledge. *CL2000*, pp. 807–821, London, UK, July 2000. Springer Verlag.
3. T. Eiter, W. Faber, N. Leone, G. Pfeifer, and A. Polleres. A Logic Programming Approach to Knowledge-State Planning: Semantics and Complexity. Technical Report INFSYS RR-1843-01-11, TU Wien, December 2001.
4. T. Eiter, W. Faber, N. Leone, G. Pfeifer, and A. Polleres. A Logic Programming Approach to Knowledge-State Planning, II: the DLV$^{\mathcal{K}}$ System. Technical Report INFSYS RR-1843-01-12, TU Wien, December 2001.
5. T. Eiter, W. Faber, N. Leone, G. Pfeifer, and A. Polleres. Answer set planning under action costs. Unpublished manuscript, available from the authors.
6. M. Gelfond and V. Lifschitz. Action languages. *Electronic Transactions on Artificial Intelligence*, 2(3-4):193–210, 1998.
7. E. Giunchiglia and V. Lifschitz. An Action Language Based on Causal Explanation: Preliminary Report. In *AAAI '98*, pp. 623–630, 1998.

Z-log: Applying System-Z

Michael Minock and Hansi Kraus

The University of Umeå, Sweden
{mjm,c97hks}@cs.umu.se

Abstract. We present Z-log – a practical system that employs the system-Z [13] semantics. Z-log incurs polynomial cost for compilation and entailment in the horn and q-horn [2] cases. Z-log's complexity is intractable in the unrestricted case – but intractable in the number of defaults that cause the violation of the q-horn property.
We present here initial performance results over two alternative rules-bases. The results indicate that Z-log currently scales to problems on the order of 1000's of propositional rules when the rules are in q-Horn form. We shall be applying Z-log in cognitive disease diagnosis.

1 Introduction

Efforts have revolved around extending KLM [9] equivalent semantics to more practical *adventurous* semantics [13][5][6][3][10]. Although these semantics exhibit many desirable features of common sense, in general they have rather high computational cost. For example, in the general case, entailment in system-Z [8] requires $O(log(n))$ satisfiability tests, once $O(n^2)$ satisfiability tests are issued to compile a knowledge base of n-defaults. And system-Z is the computationally least expensive semantics of the aforementioned and the only one that is tractable in the horn and q-horn cases [4]. The q-horn [2] case represents the combination of disguised horn clauses[1] and 2-SAT problems. Q-horn form thus extends common horn form, allowing for limited use of disjunction in the antecedents of rules.

During compilation system-Z builds a unique ranked partition of the rule-base. The kappa value of a propositional formula (ϕ) is the highest rank at which the formula and the rules at such a rank and higher are inconsistent. The kappa value indicates the degree of surprise associated with ϕ - that is $P(\phi) < \epsilon^{\kappa(\phi)}$. This κ function is the basis of the system-Z entailment semantics [13] [8].

Although there have been prototype implementations of system-Z [7][3], and an exact counterpart to system-Z using possibility measures [1], Z-log represents the most advanced direct system-Z implementation to date. For example DRS [3] is a semantically based system, calculating an actual rank for all possible worlds. As such it is only applicable to systems of approximately 16 propositions and 20 defaults. To be fair the intention of DRS was to explore the virtues of Maximum Entropy with variable strength rules, not to build a practical system-Z 'system'.

---

[1] That is CNFs where propositions may be renamed to reduce the number of positive literals to at most 1 per clause.

S. Flesca et al. (Eds.): JELIA 2002, LNAI 2424, pp. 545–548, 2002.

2   Z-log

We are calling our implementation of the system-Z^2 Z-log. See [12] for an in-depth discussion of Z-log's optimization techniques and its (optional) extended semantics $\hat{Z}$. The key point is that the system is tractable in q-horn cases. Moreover the degree of intractability of the system depends on the number of rules that cause the violation of the q-horn property. Thus when the number of such non-q-horn rules is bounded, we may consider their cost constant and may consider problems that contain larger numbers of 'friendly' q-horn form rules.

Z-log is run by providing a definition file (.def) in which strong and default propositional rules are specified and a query file (.qry) where facts are asserted (or retracted) and a stream of entailment and κ queries are processed. The following is the definition file catAndMouse.def [3].

```
/* We may (optionally) declare propositions before we use them with '+'. */
+cheese chedder tasty dirty .  // Features of the cheese,
+starving seekCheese.  // the mouse,
+catAtHome catInKitchen catInDen, catInLivingRoom catInBedroom.// the cat
+night. // and the world.

/* The defaults: prolog style, order unimportant */
cheese := chedder. // A hard rule.
tasty :- cheese. // A default.
!tasty :- cheese & dirty.
tasty :- cheese & dirty & starving.

!catInKitchen := catInDen.
!catInLivingRoom := catInDen.
!catInLivingRoom := catInKitchen.
!catInBedroom := true. // false is also a built-in proposition.

catInKitchen | catInLivingRoom | catInDen :- catAtHome.
catInDen :- night.
seekCheese :- !catInKitchen & cheese.
seekCheese :- starving & cheese.
!seekCheese :- catInKitchen.
```

The following is a query file that corresponds to a fact context and a stream of queries over the definition file sylvester.qry.

```
chedder.
!catInLivingRoom.
?tasty.  // TRUE.
?catInKitchen. // UNDECIDED.
?!catInBedRoom. // TRUE.
?seekCheese. // UNDECIDED.
night.
?catInKitchen. // FALSE.
?seekCheese. // TRUE.
dirty.
?tasty. // FALSE.
starving.
?tasty. // TRUE.
```

---

[2] Our implementation also supports $\hat{Z}$. $\hat{Z}$ enables the inheritance of stable properties to exceptional subclasses.

[3] Note the PROLOG like syntax. The default $\neg a \wedge b \rightarrow c$ is written c :- !a & b. The hard rule $a \Rightarrow b \vee c$ is written b | c := a. Comments are as in C.

```
/* Kappa value queries */
#cheese & !tasty. // is 1.
#night & !catInDen. // is 1 under Z, 2 under Z-hat.
```

At the command line one types:

```
java Zlog -Z^ catAndMouse.def sylvester.qry
```

This sends to standard output the results from compiling `catAndMouse.def` and then processing all the queries in `sylvester.qry` under $\hat{Z}$ semantics. Note that a `catAndMouse.par` file is written to disk so Z-log does not need to recompute the partition over multiple program invocations.

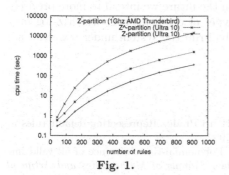 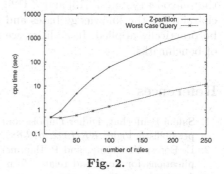

Fig. 1.   **Fig. 2.**

2.1 Performance

Figure 1 shows the costs for partition construction in a simplified, non-deterministic version of Wumpus world. It is non-deterministic in that forward actions may or may not be performed, and simplified in that the world is an array of black and white tiles. Although this is, no doubt, a toy problem, such a spatial-temporal reasoning problem generates many hundreds of propositional rules for even small array sizes. The CPU times for entailment queries over this Wumpus world example uniformly take less than 10 seconds.

Figure 2 shows an example generating the worst case partition depth for system Z. In this example the rule $p_1 \rightarrow q$ is followed by $p_1 \wedge p_2 \rightarrow \neg q$ which is followed by $p_1 \wedge p_2 \wedge p_3 \rightarrow q$, and so forth. The query is, given p_1, does q follow?

3 Medical Decision Support – Cognitive Disorder Diagnosis

We believe that Z-log may be of utility within a medical decision support tool. *Medical decision support systems* give advice to medical personal. Such advice is relative to a patient's complex and often incomplete medical record. Published clinical guidelines serve as a knowledge source from which to author initial defaults and hard constraints. The knowledge-base is then refined by medical personnel to capture unwritten knowledge of the domain.

We are currently building a Z-log knowledge-base devoted to the problem of computing cognitive disorder diagnosis. Our knowledge was obtained from clinical guidelines and discussions with physicians [11]. Currently we have a system with approximately 100 hard rules and 30 defaults. The advice that the system generates seems sound. Soon we shall solicit feedback from medical personal.

4   Conclusion

We have described the first implementation of Z-log: a q-horn tractable system that encodes system-Z [13] and $\hat{Z}$ [12]. In the future we intend to more precisely characterize the knowledge bases and types of problems over which Z-log may be practically applied. In addition we shall run the system under a wider class of benchmarks.

References

1. Salem Benferhat, Didier Dubois, and Henri Prade. Representing default rules in possibilistic logic. *KR 1992: 673-684*, 1992.
2. E. Boros, Y. Crama, and P. Hammer. Polynomial-time inference of all valid implications for horn and related formulae. *Annals of Mathematics and Artificial Intelligence*, 1:21–32, 1990.
3. R. Bourne and S. Parsons. Maximum entropy and variable strength defaults, 1999.
4. Thomas Eiter and Thomas Lukasiewicz. Complexity results for default reasoning from conditional knowledge bases. In *KR2000: Principles of Knowledge Representation and Reasoning*, pages 62–73, San Francisco, 2000. Morgan Kaufmann.
5. H. Gefner. Default reasoning: causal and conditional theories, 1992.
6. Moisés Goldszmidt, Paul Morris, and Judea Pearl. A maximum entropy approach to nonmonotonic reasoning. In *Proceedings of the Eighth National Conference on Artificial Intelligence*, Menlo Park, CA, 1990. AAAI Press.
7. M. Goldszmidt. *Qualitative Probabilities: A Normative Framework for Commonsense Reasoning*. PhD thesis, University of California, California, 1992.
8. Goldszmidt and Judea Pearl. Qualitative probabilities for default reasoning, belief revision, and causal modeling. *Artificial Intelligence*, 84(1-2):57–112, 1996.
9. S. Kraus, D. Lehmann, and M. Magidor. Preferential models and cumulative logics. *Artificial Intelligence, 44:167–207.*, 1990.
10. Daniel J. Lehmann. Another perspective on default reasoning. *Annals of Mathematics and Artificial Intelligence*, 15(1):61–82, 1995.
11. Helena Lindgren. Decision support systems and diagnosing cognitive disorders. Master's thesis, University of Umeå, Sweden, 2000.
12. Michael Minock and Hansi Kraus. Z-log: A system-z (and $\hat{Z}$) 'system'. Technical Report 02.05, The Univeristy of Umea, Umea, Sweden, May 2002.
13. J. Pearl. A natural ordering of defaults with tractable applications to default reasoning. *Proceedings of the 3rd Conference on Theoretical Aspects of Reasoning about Knowledge, pages 121–135.*, 1990.

Hypergraph Transversal Computation and Related Problems in Logic and AI

Thomas Eiter and Georg Gottlob

Institut für Informationssysteme, Technische Universität Wien
Favoritenstraße 9–11, A-1040 Wien, Austria
eiter@kr.tuwien.ac.at, gottlob@dbai.tuwien.ac.at

Abstract. Generating minimal transversals of a hypergraph is an important problem which has many applications in Computer Science. In the present paper, we address this problem and its decisional variant, i.e., the recognition of the transversal hypergraph for another hypergraph. We survey some results on problems which are known to be related to computing the transversal hypergraph, where we focus on problems in propositional Logic and AI. Some of the results have been established already some time ago, and were announced but their derivation was not widely disseminated. We then address recent developments on the computational complexity of computing resp. recognizing the transversal hypergraph. The precise complexity of these problems is not known to date, and is in fact open for more than 20 years now.

1 Introduction

A *hypergraph* $\mathcal{H} = (V, E)$ consists of a finite collection E of sets over a finite set V. The elements of E are called *hyperedges*, or simply *edges*. A *transversal* (or *hitting set*) of $\mathcal{H}$ is a set $T \subseteq V$ that meets every edge of E. A transversal is *minimal*, if it does not contain any other transversal as a subset. The set $\mathcal{T}$ of all minimal transversals of $\mathcal{H} = (V, E)$, constitutes together with V also a hypergraph $Tr(\mathcal{H}) = (V, \mathcal{T})$, which is called the *transversal hypergraph* of $\mathcal{H}$.

The famous Transversal Hypergraph Problem (TRANS-HYP) is then as follows:

Problem: HYPERGRAPH TRANSVERSAL (TRANS-HYP)
Instance: Two hypergraphs $\mathcal{G} = (V, E)$ and $\mathcal{H} = (V, F)$ on a finite set V.
Question: Does $\mathcal{G} = Tr(\mathcal{H})$ hold ?

Rephrased as a computation problem rather, the statement is as follows:

Problem: TRANSVERSAL ENUMERATION (TRANS-ENUM)
Instance: A hypergraph $\mathcal{H} = (V, E)$ on a finite set V.
Output: The edges of the transversal hypergraph $Tr(\mathcal{H})$.

From the point of computability in polynomial time, the decisional and the computational variant of the transversal hypergraph problem are in fact equivalent: It is known that, for any class $\mathcal{C}$ of hypergraphs, TRANS-ENUM is solvable in *polynomial total time* (or *output-polynomial time*), i.e., in time polynomial in

S. Flesca et al. (Eds.): JELIA 2002, LNAI 2424, pp. 549–564, 2002.
© Springer-Verlag Berlin Heidelberg 2002

the combined size of $\mathcal{H}$ and $Tr(\mathcal{H})$, if and only if TRANS-HYP is in the class P for all pairs $(\mathcal{H}, \mathcal{G})$ such that $\mathcal{H} \in \mathcal{C}$ [3].

The problems TRANS-HYP and TRANS-ENUM have a large number of applications in many areas of Computer Science, including Distributed Systems, Databases, Boolean Circuits and Artificial Intelligence. There, they have important applications in Diagnosis, Machine Learning, Data Mining, and Explanation Finding, see e.g. [11,13,24,28,32,33,36] and the references therein.

Let us call a decision problem Π TRANS-HYP-*hard*, if problem TRANS-HYP can be reduced to it by a standard polynomial time transformation. Furthermore, Π is TRANS-HYP-*complete*, if Π is TRANS-HYP-hard and, moreover, Π can be polynomially transformed into TRANS-HYP; that is, Π and TRANS-HYP are equivalent modulo polynomial time transformations. We use analogous terminology of TRANS-ENUM-*hardness* and TRANS-ENUM-*completeness* for computations problems, i.e., problems with output. Here, Π reduces to Π', if there a polynomial functions f, g s.t. for any input I of Π, $f(I)$ is an input of Π', and if O is the output for $f(I)$, then $g(O)$ is the output of I, cf. [40]; we also request that O has size polynomial in the size of the output for I (if not, trivial reductions may exist).

The rest of this paper is organized as follows. In the next two sections, we illustrate some of the applications of TRANS-HYP and TRANS-ENUM in Logic and in Artificial Intelligence. Some of the results have been established already some time ago [10,11], and were announced in [11] but remained yet unpublished. After that, Section 4 is dedicated to a review of recent developments on complexity of TRANS-HYP, and a new result is contributed (Theorem 11). The final Section 5 presents some open issues.

We close this section with some terminology. For any decision problem Π, we denote by co-Π the complementary problem, which has yes- and no-instances exchanged. A hypergraph $\mathcal{H} = (V, E)$ is *simple* (or *Sperner, clutter-free*), if no edge e of $\mathcal{H}$ strictly contains any other edge e' of $\mathcal{H}$, i.e., $\forall e, e' \ in E : e \subseteq e \Rightarrow e = e'$. We denote by $\min(\mathcal{H})$ the hypergraph on V whose edges are the ones of $\mathcal{H}$ which are minimal with respect to set inclusion, i.e., $\min(\mathcal{H}) = (V, \{e \in E \mid \forall e' \in \mathcal{E} \, e' \not\subset e\})$. We refer to $\overline{\mathcal{H}} = (V, \{V \setminus e \mid e \in E\})$ as the *complemented hypergraph of* $\mathcal{H}$. If $\mathcal{H} = \overline{\mathcal{H}}$, then $\mathcal{H}$ is called *self-complemented*.

2   Applications in Logic

2.1   Satisfiability Checking

The satisfiability problem of propositional formulas, in particular of sets of clauses, has special importance in complexity theory. There is a strong interconnection between satisfiability of a set of clauses and 2-colorability of hypergraphs, and these problems are decidable by similar resolution methods, cf. [34].

Recall that the satisfiability problem (SAT) is to decide whether a set of propositional clauses $\mathcal{C} = \{C_1, \ldots, C_m\}$, where each C_i is a set of literals, on atoms $X = \{x_1, \ldots, x_n\}$ is satisfied by some truth assignment to X. Its restriction MSAT, where every clause of C must be either positive or negative, i.e., must not contain any negative or positive literal, respectively, is still NP-hard.

In what follows, let us denote $Y^\neg = \{\neg y \mid y \in Y\}$ for any set of atoms Y, and for any instance C of MSAT on atoms X, let $C^+(C)$ and $C^-(C)$ denote the hypergraphs of the families of atom sets in the positive and the negative clauses of C, respectively, i.e., $C^+(C) = (X, C)$ and $C^-(C) = (X, \{Y \subseteq X \mid Y^\neg \in C\})$. If C is clear, we simply write C^+ and C^- for $C^+(C)$ and $C^-(C)$, respectively.

Example 1. Let $X = \{x_1, \ldots, x_4\}$, and $C = \{\{x_1\}, \{x_2, x_4\}, \{\neg x_2, \neg x_4\}, \{\neg x_3\}\}$. Then $C^+ = (X, \{\{x_1\}, \{x_2, x_4\}\})$ and $C^- = (X, \{\{x_2, x_4\}, \{x_3\}\})$.

The following lemma, which can be found in various forms in the literature, links satisfiability to hypergraph transversals. Let, for hypergraphs $\mathcal{H} = (V, E)$ and $\mathcal{H}' = (V, E')$, denote $\mathcal{H} \succeq \mathcal{H}'$ that every edge of $\mathcal{H}$ contains some edge of $\mathcal{H}'$, i.e., $\forall e \in E \; \exists e' \in E' : e' \subseteq e$ holds.

Lemma 1. *An instance C of MSAT is unsatisfiable iff $Tr(C^+) \succeq C^-$.*

Proof. We may identify every truth value assignment ϕ to X with the set $X_\phi \subseteq X$ of atoms which are assigned the value true. Let $\mathcal{X}_\phi^+$ denote the set of all truth assignments that satisfy the positive clauses in C. Clearly, every $\tau \in \mathcal{X}_\phi^+$ must be a transversal of C^+, i.e. $(X, \mathcal{X}_\phi^+) \succeq Tr(C^+)$ holds. Now assume $Tr(C^+) \succeq C^-$ is true. Since $\succeq$ is transitive, $(X, \mathcal{X}_\phi^+) \succeq C^-$ holds and each $\tau \in \mathcal{X}_\phi^+$ assigns all literals in some negative clause of C false, hence C is unsatisfiable. Conversely, if C^- is unsatisfiable, then $(X, \mathcal{X}_\phi^+) \succeq C^-$ holds. Since for each $\tau \in Tr(C^+)$, clearly $\tau \in \mathcal{X}_\phi^+$, we have $Tr(C^+) \succeq (X, \mathcal{X}_\phi^+)$ and thus $Tr(C^+) \succeq C^-$. $\square$

The first subcase of MSAT which we consider is made up of instances with the property that every pair of a positive clause and a negative clause resolves, i.e. there is an atoms which occurs unnegated in the positive and negated in the negative clause. This subcase of MSAT, which we refer to turns out to be computationally equivalent to TRANS-HYP.

More formally, a set of clauses C (on atoms X) is an instance of INTERSECT-ING MSAT (IMSAT), if C is an instance of MSAT and, moreover, C satisfies $\forall e \in C^+ \forall e' \in C^- : e \cap e' \neq \emptyset$.

We have the following characterization of satisfiable IMSAT clause sets.

Theorem 1. *An instance C of IMSAT is satisfiable iff $Tr(\min(C^+)) = \min(C^-)$.*

Proof. Since C is an IMSAT instance, $\min(C^-) \succeq Tr(\min(C^+))$ holds. Furthermore, as easily checked, $\succeq$ is a partial order on simple hypergraphs, i.e., for any simple hypergraphs $\mathcal{G}$ and $\mathcal{H}$, $\mathcal{H} \succeq \mathcal{G}$ and $\mathcal{G} \succeq \mathcal{H}$ is equivalent to $\mathcal{H} = \mathcal{G}$. Thus, $Tr(\min(C^+)) = \min(C^-)$ is equivalent to $Tr(\min(C^+)) \succeq \min(C^-)$. By Lemma 1, C is satisfiable iff $Tr(C^+) \not\succeq C^-$, which is equivalent to $Tr(\min(C^+)) \not\succeq \min(C^-)$. Hence, the result follows. $\square$

Corollary 1. *Problem co-IMSAT is TRANS-HYP-complete.*

Proof. By Theorem 1, unsatisfiability testing for any IMSAT instance C is clearly polynomial transformable into TRANS-HYP. Conversely, any instance of co-TRANS-HYP is also easily transformable into an equivalent instance of co-IMSAT by Theorem 1.   □

We remark that for the more general class of SAT instances where *every* pair of (distinct) clauses resolves, SAT is decidable in polynomial time. This follows from the observation of D.A. Plaisted (1991, personal communication) that such a clause set $C = \{C_1, \ldots, C_m\}$ is satisfiable if and only if $\sum_{i=1}^{m} 2^{-|C_i|} \neq 1$, provided that no clause is subsumed by some other clause and that no variable occurs both negated and unnegated in the same clause. (Note that since all numbers $|C_i|$ are given in *unary* notation, computing this sum is easy.)

In comparison to this subclass of SAT, the intersection restriction on the clause sets in IMSAT is weaker in a sense, since positive and negative clauses, respectively, are not interrelated among each other, and hence the whole clause set "splits" into two groups. However, imposing the intersection condition also on the positive and negative clauses makes IMSAT no easier.

Let SYMMETRIC IMSAT (SIMSAT) be the restriction of IMSAT to instances C where the negative clauses are precisely all clauses C^- such that $C^- = \{\neg u : u \in C^+\}$ for some positive clause $C^+ \in C$. (By this restriction, nonempty positive clauses of C are mutually intersecting.)

Corollary 2. *Problem co-SIMSAT is TRANS-HYP-complete.*

Proof. By Corollary 1, any SIMSAT instance C can be polynomially transformed into a TRANS-HYP instance $(\mathcal{H}, \mathcal{G})$ such that C is unsatisfiable iff $(\mathcal{H}, \mathcal{G})$ is a yes-instance of TRANS-HYP. On the other hand, as shown in [11], instances $(\mathcal{H}, \mathcal{G})$ of TRANS-HYP such that $\mathcal{H} = \mathcal{G}$ are TRANS-HYP-hard. We may, without loss of generality, assume in addition that $\mathcal{H} = (V, E)$ is simple, that $e \cap e' \neq \emptyset$, for all $e, e' \in E$, and that $|E| > 0$. By Theorem 1, the clause set $C = E \cup \{e^- \mid e \in E\}$ on atoms V is satisfiable iff $\mathcal{H} \neq Tr(\mathcal{H})$; since C is efficiently constructible from $\mathcal{H}$, the result follows.   □

Yet other subcases of SAT can be found whose unsatisfiability is equivalent to TRANS-HYP; one are MSAT instances where the positive clauses are a collection of partitions of the variable set X, i.e. if $X' \subseteq X$ appears, then also $X - X'$ appears, such that no positive clause subsumes any other, and the negative clauses are the clauses which result if, for each clause C_i, a positive atom from $X \setminus C_i$ is added to C_i in all ways, and then all atoms are negated.

There is an interesting observation regarding the clause sizes of the instances. Problem MSAT remains NP-complete even if each clause contains at most three literals (M3SAT, [20]); if an instance C of M3SAT is also an instance of IM3SAT, however, deciding satisfiability is polynomial: We may select any positive clause C_1 and negative clause C_2 from C, and for every of the at most $2^5 = 32$ truth value assignments to the literals in $C_1 \cup C_2$, the clause set is reducible to an instance of 2SAT, since each such assignment leaves in every clause at most two literals unassigned; 2SAT is well-known polynomial [20].

By Theorem 1 and results in [11], polynomiality of satisfiability testing generalizes from IM3SAT to IMkSAT, the restriction of IMSAT in which the clause size is bounded by a constant k, and even more general, also to the subclass where the size of either only the positive clauses or the negative clauses is bounded by k. Note that for $k > 3$, checking whether C is satisfiable for the at most 2^{k-1} many truth assignments to a positive clause C_1 and a negative clause C_2 is not promising for an efficient procedure, since the reduced clause sets are not evidently contained in a tractable subclass of SAT.

2.2   Dualization

There is a well-known and close connection of TRANS-ENUM to the well-known dualization problem of Boolean Functions:

> *Problem:* DUALIZATION
> *Instance:* A CNF φ of a Boolean function $f = f(x_1, \ldots, x_n)$
> *Output:* A prime CNF ψ of its dual f^d, i.e., the function which has value 1 in input vector $b = (b_1, \ldots, b_n)$ iff f has value 0 on the input vector $\bar{b} = (b_1 \oplus 1, \ldots, b_n \oplus 1)$.

Recall that a CNF φ is prime, if it consists of prime clauses, i.e., no literal may be removed from any clause γ of φ without violating logical equivalence.

Special algorithms for the dualization problem can be tracked down at least to the 60's of the past century, cf. [2]. It is not hard to see that this problem is intractable; in fact, its decisional variant:

> *Problem:* DUAL
> *Instance:* CNFs φ and ψ of Boolean functions f and g, respectively.
> *Output:* Do φ and ψ represent a pair (f, g) of dual Boolean functions?

is co-NP-complete, where hardness holds even if ψ is asserted to be a prime CNF of g. In case of monotone Boolean functions, the dualization problem is equivalent to determining the transversal hypergraph. Let MONOTONE DUALIZATION be the subcase of DUALIZATION where f is a monotone Boolean function, and similarly MONOTONE DUAL the subcase of DUAL where f is a monotone Boolean function. (Notice that in general, deciding whether a given CNF represents a monotone function is intractable, and thus strictly speaking these cases are promise problems [29], since valid input instances are not recognized in polynomial time. Under suitable syntactic restrictions, such as that the CNFs for f are negation-free, this can be ensured.)

The following result summarizes well-known results that are part of the folklore.

Theorem 2. MONOTONE DUALIZATION *is* TRANS-ENUM-*complete, and* MONOTONE DUAL *is* TRANS-HYP-*complete.*

Proof. Let φ be a CNF expression for a monotone Boolean function f on variables $X = \{x_1, \ldots, x_n\}$. Then, the CNF φ' which results from φ by removing all negative literals from φ is logically equivalent to φ. Indeed, clearly φ' logically implies φ. On the other hand, each clause γ in φ must be subsumed by same prime implicate γ^* of f. As well known, a Boolean function f is monotone iff every prime implicate of f is positive, i.e., contains no negative literal. Thus, γ is replaced in φ' by some clause γ' such that $\gamma^* \subseteq \gamma'$; hence, φ logically implies φ'. The clauses of the (unique) prime CNF ψ of the dual function $g = f^d$ are then given by the edges of $Tr(\mathcal{C}^+(C))$, where $\mathcal{C}^+(C)$ is the hypergraph associated with the set C of clauses in φ'.

Thus, MONOTONE DUALIZATION and reduces in polynomial time to TRANS-ENUM. Similarly, MONOTONE DUAL reduces in polynomial time to TRANS-HYP, since f^d is monotone if f is monotone, and if a CNF ψ representing a monotone Boolean function g is $\neg$-free, then the unique prime CNF of g is described by the edges of $\min(\mathcal{C}^+)$. On the other hand, by the correspondence $\mathcal{C}^+(C)$ between a monotone clause set C and a hypergraph, TRANS-ENUM and TRANS-HYP trivially reduce to MONOTONE DUALIZATION and MONOTONE DUAL, respectively, in polynomial time.   □

3   Applications in Artificial Intelligence

3.1   Theory Revision

Dealing with *knowledge in flux*, i.e. with knowledge bases that are subject to change in the light of new information, is an important problem of artificial intelligence. The subject has been studied in the database research community as well (e.g., [16,45]) and has also attracted attention of philosophers of reasoning (e.g., [1,19]). A number of different change approaches have been proposed (see [45,39] for overviews); many of them adhere to the principle of *Minimal Change*, according to which the body of knowledge should change as little as possible if new information is incorporated.

A well-known knowledge change approach is the Set-Of-Theories approach, a formula-based change method first defined in [16] in the context of databases and considered for AI applications e.g. in [22,38]. This method works as follows. Assume that the sentence p must be incorporated into the knowledge base T, which is a finite set of sentences. If T is consistent with p, then p is simply added to T; otherwise, $\neg p$ is provable from T. In this case, a set R of sentences is removed from T such that $\neg p$ is no longer provable from $T - R$, and then p is added; by the principle of Minimal Change, this set R is selected as small as possible under set inclusion.

Observe that R must pick a sentence from every subset $T' \subseteq T$ of sentences from which $\neg p$ is provable. Denote the collection of all such subsets $T' \subseteq T$ by $\mathcal{P}(T; \neg p)$. Thus, R must be a transversal of the hypergraph $(T, \mathcal{P}(T; \neg p))$; since R is selected as small as possible, R must even be minimal.

In general, R will not be unique; the result of the update, $\mathcal{U}(T; p)$, is thus defined as the set of all KBs obtained by removing some possible R and adding p. The possible R's constitute, as easily seen, the edges of $Tr(T, \mathcal{P}(T; \neg P))$.

Formally, let $T = \{f_1, \ldots, f_n\}$ be a finite set of satisfiable sentences and let p be a satisfiable sentence in a suitable logic. Then, define

$$\mathcal{P}(T; \neg p) = \{T' \subseteq T \mid T' \models \neg p\},$$
$$\mathcal{W}(T; p) = \{T - R \mid Tr(T, \mathcal{P}(T; \neg p)) = (T, E), R \in E\},$$
$$\mathcal{U}(T; p) = \{W \cup \{p\} \mid W \in \mathcal{W}(T; p)\}.$$

$\mathcal{W}(T; p)$ denotes the "possible worlds" [22], which are with respect to set inclusion maximal subsets of T in which the sentence p may be true. It is easily verified that $\mathcal{W}(T; p)$ is the collection of all *maximal independent sets* of the hypergraph $\mathcal{P}(T; \neg p) = (T, E)$, i.e., the maximal sets (under set inclusion) $W \subseteq T$ such that $S \not\subseteq W$ for every $S \in E$, and that $\mathcal{W}(T; p) = \{T' \subseteq T \mid T' \not\models \neg p \wedge \forall U : T' \subset U \subseteq T \Rightarrow U \models \neg p\}$. A sentence f is implied by $\mathcal{U}(T; p)$ (denoted $\mathcal{U}(T; p) \models f$), if $T' \models f$ for each T' from $\mathcal{U}(T; p)$, i.e., if f follows from the logical disjunction of the knowledge bases in $\mathcal{U}(T; p)$.

Example 2. Let $T = \{x_1, x_2, x_1 \wedge x_2 \Rightarrow x_3\}$ and $p = \neg x_3$ in propositional logic, where x_1, x_2, x_3 are propositional atoms. Then

$$\mathcal{P}(T; \neg p) = \{\{x_1, x_2, x_1 \wedge x_2 \Rightarrow x_3\}\},$$
$$Tr(T, \mathcal{P}(T; \neg p)) = \{\{x_1\}, \{x_2\}, \{x_1 \wedge x_2 \Rightarrow x_3\}\},$$
$$\mathcal{W}(T; p) = \{\{x_2, x_1 \wedge x_2 \Rightarrow x_3\}, \{x_1, x_1 \wedge x_2 \Rightarrow x_3\}, \{x_1, x_2\}\},$$
$$\mathcal{U}(T; p) = \{\{x_2, x_1 \wedge x_2 \Rightarrow x_3, \neg x_3\}, \{x_1, x_1 \wedge x_2 \Rightarrow x_3, \neg x_3\}, \{x_1, x_2, \neg x_3\}\}.$$

We have $\mathcal{U}(T; p) \models x_1 \vee x_2$, but neither $\mathcal{U}(T; p) \models x_1$ nor $\mathcal{U}(T; p) \models x_2$.

Procedures to compute $\mathcal{U}(T; p)$ are described in [22,23]. They basically proceed in two steps: In the first step, the set $\mathcal{MP}(T; \neg p)$ of all minimal proofs of $\neg p$ from T, i.e. $(T, \mathcal{MP}(T; \neg p)) = \min(T, \mathcal{P}(T; \neg p)))$, is computed by a theorem prover. Then, $\mathcal{U}(T; p)$ is computed from $\mathcal{MP}(T; \neg p)$ collecting all sets $S = (T \cup \{p\}) - R$, where R is a transversal of $\mathcal{MP}(T; \neg p)$, such that S is maximal under set inclusion; [22] suggests to compute $\mathcal{U}(T; p)$ incrementally, i.e. "world by world". The essential task in step 2 of this method is to determine $\mathcal{W}(T; p)$. Consider the following decision problem:

Problem: ADDITIONAL WORLD
Instance: A finite satisfiable set T of first-order sentences, a satsifiable first-order sentence p, the collection $\mathcal{MP}(T; \neg p)$, and a collection $\mathcal{W} \subseteq \mathcal{W}(T; p)$.
Question: Does there exist $T' \in \mathcal{W}(T; p) - \mathcal{W}$?

If this problem is intractable, then no output-polynomial algorithm to compute the possible worlds $\mathcal{W}(T; p)$ from $\mathcal{MP}(T; \neg p)$ is likely to exist. We note the following result, which appears in [10]:

Theorem 3. *Problem co-*ADDITIONAL WORLD *is* TRANS-HYP-*complete*.

Proof. It is easily seen that $\mathcal{W}(T; p)$ are the edges of $\overline{Tr(T, \mathcal{MP}(T; \neg p))}$. Since $\mathcal{W} \subseteq \mathcal{W}(T; p)$, this problem is thus easily reduced in polynomial time transformable to the complement of TRANS-HYP. On the other hand, let $(\mathcal{H}; \mathcal{G})$ be a

TRANS-HYP instance, such that $\mathcal{H}$ and $\mathcal{G}$ are simple, $\mathcal{H} \subseteq Tr(\mathcal{G})$, and $\mathcal{G} = (V, E)$ has no empty edge.

Take V as propositional atoms, and denote by $f(e_i)$ the formula $\neg v_1 \vee \cdots \vee \neg v_k$, where $e_i = \{v_1, \ldots, v_k\}$ and $E = \{e_1, \ldots, e_m\}$, for $1 \leq i \leq m$. Then, define $T = V$ and $p = f(e_1) \wedge \cdots \wedge f(e_m)$. It is immediately verified that T as well as p is satisfiable and that $\mathcal{MP}(T; \neg p) = E$. Therefore, $\mathcal{W}(T; p) = \overline{Tr(T, \mathcal{MP}(T; \neg p))} = \overline{Tr(\mathcal{G})}$. Since $\mathcal{H} \subseteq Tr(\mathcal{G})$, we have that $\overline{\mathcal{H}} \subseteq \overline{Tr(\mathcal{G})} = \mathcal{W}(T; p)$. Therefore, $\mathcal{H} = Tr(\mathcal{G})$ holds iff there exists no additional world for p, i.e. $\mathcal{W}(T; p) = \overline{\mathcal{H}}$. Hence, co-ADDITIONAL WORLD is TRANS-HYP-hard. □

Note that [24] showed (independently) TRANS-ENUM-hardness of computing $\mathcal{U}(T; p)$ from T and p if all formulas in T and p are Horn; this result is implicit in the proof above.

By results in [11], computing $\mathcal{W}(T; p)$ from $\mathcal{MP}(T; \neg p)$ is polynomial in the input size if $\neg p$ has few minimal proofs from T, and is output-polynomial if the minimal proofs for $\neg p$ only refer to at most constantly many sentences of T.

3.2   Machine Learning and Data Mining

Im machine learning, the hypergraph transversal problem is related to problems in learning Boolean functions. In a simple model, an adversary fixes a Boolean function $f : \{0, 1\}^n \to \{0, 1\}$, which models a concept in the world. The learner should find out f, or an approximation of it, given access to an oracle which discloses partial information about f. In particular, a *membership query oracle* $MQ(f)$ allows the learner to ask the value of f at a given vector $b \in \{0, 1\}^n$. The hypothesis on f produced by the learner is a Boolean formula, which is typically a CNF or a DNF expression.

The following result is due to [28]. Let, for any monotone Boolean function f, denote $CNF(f)$ and $DNF(f)$ its unique prime CNF and prime DNF, respectively.

Theorem 4. *If* TRANS-ENUM *can be solved in output-polynomial time, then there exists a learning algorithm for monotone Boolean functions f with membership queries, which produces both a CNF and a DNF representation of the function. The number of membership queries is bounded by $|CNF(f)| \cdot (|DNF(f)| = n^2)$ and the running time of the algorithm is polynomial in n, $|CNF(f)|$, and $|DNF(f)|$.*

There is also a relation to hypergraph transversals in the other direction, which has also been pointed out in [28].

Theorem 5. *If there is a learning algorithm for monotone Boolean functions f with membership queries, which produces both a DNF representation of the function and whose running time and number of queries to $MQ(f)$ are bounded by a function $T(n + |DNF(f)| + |CNF(f)|)$, then* TRANS-ENUM *can be solved in time $T(n + |DNF(f)| + |CNF(f)|)$.*

Thus, if $T()$ is a polynomial, then TRANS-ENUM can be solved in output-polynomial time. Note that as shown in [43], for almost all monotone Boolean functions a polynomial $T()$ exists if n tends to infinity.

These results are closely related to results on generating frequent sets in data mining. Given a $0/1$ $m \times n$ matrix A and an integral threshold t, associate with each subset $C \subseteq \{1, \ldots, n\}$ of column indices the subset $R(C)$ of all rows $r \in \{1, \ldots, m\}$ in A such that $A(r, j) = 1$ for every $j \in C$. Then C is called *frequent*, if $|R(C)| \geq t$, and C is called *infrequent*, if $|R(C)| < t$. Let us denote by $F_t(A)$ and $\hat{F}_t(A)$ the sets of all frequent and infrequent column sets C in A, respectively.

The generation of frequent and infrequent sets in A is a key problem in knowledge discovery and data mining, which occurs in mining association rules, correlations, and other tasks. Of particular interest are the maximal frequent sets $M_t \subseteq F_t$ and the minimal infrequent sets $I_t \subseteq \hat{F}_t$, since they mark the boundary of frequent sets (both maximal and minimal under set inclusion). The following result has been recently proved in [6].

Theorem 6. *The problem of computing, given a $0/1$ matrix A and a threshold t, the sets M_t and I_t is TRANS-ENUM-complete.*

A related but different task in data mining is dependency inference. Here the problem is, given a (not necessarily $0/1$) $m \times n$ matrix A, to find the dependencies $C_{i_1} C_{i_2} \cdots C_{i_k} \to C_{i_0}$ which hold on A (denoted $A \models C_{i_1} C_{i_2} \cdots C_{i_k} \to C_{i_0}$), i.e., for each pair of rows $r, r' \in \{1, \ldots, m\}$, either $A(r, i_j) \neq A(r', i_j)$ for some $j \in \{1, \ldots, k\}$ or $A(r, i_0) = A(r', i_0)$. Such implications are known as *functional dependencies* (FDs) in databases. The set $Dep(A) = \{f \mid A \models f\}$ of all dependencies which hold on A, is usually represented by a subset $C \subseteq Dep(A)$, called a *cover*, such that $\{f \mid C \models f\} = Dep(A)$, where $C \models f$ is logical implication. Consider thus the following problem:

> *Problem:* FD-RELATION EQUIVALENCE (FD-EQ)
> *Instance:* A $m \times n$ matrix A, a set D of dependencies.
> *Question:* Is D a cover for $Dep(A)$?

This problem, as shown in [27], is TRANS-HYP-hard; however, it is not known whether FD-EQ is reducible to TRANS-HYP in polynomial time; as shown in the extended version of [11], this is possible if D is in *MAK*-form, i.e., $D = \{X \to C_{i_0} \in Dep(A) \mid X = C_{i_1} \cdots C_{i_k}, \text{ and } X \setminus C_{i_j} \to C_{i_0} \notin Dep(A), \text{ for all } j \in \{1, \ldots, k\}\}$. (Informally, X is a minimal key or prime implicant for attribute C_{i_0}.)

Theorem 7. *Problem* FD-EQ *for instances (A, D) where D is in MAK-form is* TRANS-HYP-*complete.*

Some polynomial cases of FD-EQ are given in [27]. As shown in [33], FD-EQ is related to similar problems involving charcteristic models and Horn CNFs. For these and further results about problems in data mining equivalent to TRANS-ENUM and TRANS-HYP, see [33].

3.3   Model-Based Diagnosis

Different from the heuristic approach, model-based diagnosis [41,8] takes a logical description of the technical system and the behavior of its components as a basis for diagnosing faults by means of consistency. Since model-based diagnosis offers several advantages, much efforts were spent on it in the last 15 years.

Briefly, a *system* is a pair $(SD, COMP)$, where SD, the *system description*, is a set of sentences from an underlying decidable fragment of first-order logic (e.g., propositional logic) and $COMP$ is a set of constants which model the system *components*. SD is used together with a set OBS of sentences, which are particular *observations* on the system behavior, to diagnose faults. For that, SD makes use of a distinguished predicate $AB(c)$ which reads "component c operates in abnormal mode". Now a *diagnosis* for $(SD, COMP, OBS)$ is a minimal (under inclusion) set $\Delta \subseteq COMP$ of components such that

$$T = SD \cup OBS \cup \{AB(c) \mid c \in \Delta\} \cup \{\neg AB(c) \mid c \in COMP \setminus \Delta\}$$

is satisfiable.If there is no fault, $\Delta = \emptyset$ must be a diagnosis, otherwise the system description SD is not sound.

In [41] a characterization of diagnoses in terms of so called conflict sets is given. A *conflict set* is a set $C \subseteq COMP$ such that $SD \cup OBS \cup \{\neg AB(c) \mid c \in C\}$ is unsatisfiable; C is minimal, if no proper subset of C is a conflict set. In terms of hypergraphs, the fundamental theorem on conflict sets and diagnoses in [41] is as follows. Let $CS(DP)$ denote the collection of all all minimal conflict sets of $DP = (SD, COMP, OBS)$.

Theorem 8. $\Delta \subseteq COMP$ *is a diagnosis for* $DP = (SD, COMP, OBS)$ *iff* $\Delta \in Tr(COMP, CS(DP))$.

Therefore, we obtain the following result for computing all dignoses.

Corollary 3. *The problem of computing, given* $CS(DP)$ *of s diagosis problem* $DP = (SD, COMP, OBS)$, *all diagnoses of* DP *is* TRANS-ENUM-*complete*.

Proof. By Theorem 8, it remains to show TRANS-ENUM-hardness. Let $\mathcal{H} = (V, E)$ be simple and define $DP = (SD, COMP, OBS)$ by $SD = \{AB(v_1) \vee \cdots \vee AB(v_k) \vee a \mid \{v_1, \ldots, v_k\} \in E\}$, $OBS = \{\neg a\}$, and $COMP = V \cup \{a\}$, where a is a fresh symbol. As easily checked, $CS(DP) = \mathcal{H}$, and thus the edges of $Tr(\mathcal{H})$ are given by the diagnoses of DP.   □

We remark that modulo the costs of satisfiability checking, a diagnosis for $DP = (SD, COMP, OBS)$ can be found in polynomial time: Set $C = COMP$, and test if C is a superset of some diagnosis. Subsequently remove any component c from C such that $C - \{c\}$ is also superset of a diagnosis. Repeating this elimination step until no longer possible, the procedure stops with C as a diagnosis. However, given a set D of diagnoses for DP, deciding whether there is another diagnosis not in D was proved NP-complete in [18] for propositional Horn theories, where consistency checking is polynomial.

3.4 Horn Envelope

Recall that a logical theory Σ is *Horn*, if it is a set of Horn clauses, i.e., disjunctions $l_1 \vee \cdots \vee l_m$ of literals l_i such that at most one of them is positive. Semantically, Horn theories are characterized by the property that their set of models, $mod(\Sigma)$, is closed under intersection, i.e., $M, M' \in mod(\Sigma)$ implies $M \cap M' \in mod(\Sigma)$; here, $M \cap M'$ is the model M'' which results by atomwise logical conjunction of M and M', i.e., $M'' \models a$ iff $M \models a$ and $M' \models a$, for every atom a.

Any theory Σ has a unique *Horn envelope*, which is the strongest (w.r.t. implication) Horn theory Σ' such that $\Sigma \models \Sigma'$. The Horn envelope might be represented by different Horn theories, but there is a unique representation, which we denote by $HEnv(\Sigma)$, which consists of all prime clauses of Σ'. The following result was established in [33], where the TRANS-ENUM hardness part was proved in [32].

Theorem 9. *The problem of computing, given the models $mod(\Sigma)$ of a propositional theory Σ, the Horn envelope $HEnv(\Sigma)$ is TRANS-ENUM-complete.*

3.5 Abductive Explanations

Abduction is a fundamental mode of reasoning, which has been recognized as an important principle of common-sense reasoning which is in particular used for finding explanations. Given a Horn theory Σ, called the background theory, a formula q (called query), and a set of literals $A \subseteq Lit$, an *explanation of q w.r.t. A* is a minimal set of literals E over A such that (i) $\Sigma \cup E \models q$, and (ii) $\Sigma \cup E$ is satisfiable.

As shown by Kautz *et al.* [31], it is possible to generate an explanation for a query q that is an atom, w.r.t. a given set $A = S \cup \{\neg p \mid p \in S\}$ of literals over a given subset S of the atoms, in polynomial time, if Σ is semantically represented by the set of its characteristic models, $char(\Sigma)$; under syntax-based representation, the problem is intractable [42]. A model m of Σ is *characteristic*, if $m \notin Cl_\wedge(mod(\Sigma) \setminus \{v\})$, where $Cl_\wedge(S)$ denotes for any set of models S its closure under intersection, i.e., the least set of models $S' \supseteq s$ such that $M, M' \in S'$ implies $M \cap M' \in S'$.

The polynomial abduction algorithm in [31] implicitly involves the computation of a minimal transversal of a hypergraph, which is the bulk of the computation effort. This result has been extended in [13] to the following result.

Theorem 10. *Given the characteristic set $char(\Sigma)$ of a Horn theory Σ, a query literal q, and a subset A of all literals, computing the set of all explanations for q from Σ w.r.t. A is TRANS-ENUM-complete.*

Thus, the generation of explanations and of the transversal hypergraph are intimately related in the model-based representation framework.

4   Recent Developments on Complexity of the Problems

4.1   Structural Complexity

Let us first turn to issues of *structural* complexity. In a landmark paper, Fredman and Khachiyan [17] proved that TRANS-HYP can be solved in time $n^{o(\log n)}$, and thus in quasi-polynomial time. This shows that the problem is most likely not co-NP-complete, since no co-NP-complete problem is known which is solvable in quasi-polynomial time; if any such problem exists, then all problems in NP and co-NP can be solved in quasi-polynomial time.

A natural question is whether TRANS-HYP lies in some lower complexity class based on other resources than just runtime. In a recent paper [12], it was shown that the complement of this problem is solvable in polynomial time with *limited nondeterminism*, i.e, by a nondeterministic polynomial-time algorithm that makes only a poly-logarithmic number of guesses in the size of the input. For a survey on complexity classes with limited nondeterminism, and for several references see [25]. More precisely, [12] shows that non-duality of a pair $\mathcal{G}, \mathcal{H}$) can be proved in polynomial time with $O(\chi(n) \cdot \log n)$ suitably guessed bits, where $\chi(n)$ is given by $\chi(n)^{\chi(n)} = n$; note that $\chi(n) = o(\log n)$.

This result is surprising, because most researchers dealing with the complexity of the transversal hypergraph thought so far that these problems are completely unrelated to limited nondeterminism.

4.2   Tractable Cases

A large number of tractable cases of TRANS-HYP and TRANS-ENUM are known in the literature, e.g. [7,5,4,9,11,14,12,21,35,37], and references therein.

Examples of tractable classes are instances $(\mathcal{H}, \mathcal{G})$ where $\mathcal{H}$ has the edge sizes bounded by a constant, or where $\mathcal{H}$ is *acyclic*. Various "degrees" of hypergraph acyclicity have been defined in the literature [15]. The most general notion of hypergraph acyclicity (applying to the largest class of hypergraphs) is α-acyclicity; less general notions are (in descending order of generality) β-, γ-, and Berge-acyclicity (see [15]). In [11], it was shown that Hypergraph transversal instances with β-acyclic $\mathcal{H}$ are tractable. In [12], this tractability result has been recently improved to instances where $\mathcal{H}$ is α-acyclic and simple. This result is a corollary to a more general tractability result for hypergraphs whose *degeneracy* is bounded by a constant; simple, α-acyclic hypergraphs have degeneracy 1.

Furthermore, [12] shows that instances $(\mathcal{H}, \mathcal{G})$ of TRANS-HYP where the vertex-hyperedge incidence graphs of $\mathcal{H}$ (or of $\mathcal{G}$) have *bounded treewidth* are solvable in polynomial time. Note that this class of hypergraphs does not generalize α-acyclic hypergraphs. In [26] a concept of *hypertree width* of a hypergraph was defined, which generalizes α-acyclicity properly, as follows[1].

A *hypertree for a hypergraph* $\mathcal{H} = (V, E)$ is a triple $\langle T, \chi, \lambda \rangle$ where T is a rooted tree (N, A) and $\chi : N \to 2^V$ and $\lambda :\to 2^E$ are labeling functions which

---

[1] Actually, this notion was defined for conjunctive queries rather than hypergraphs, but is obvious from the natural correspondence between queries and hypergraphs.

associate with each node $n \in T$ a set of vertices $\chi(n) \subseteq V$ and a set of edges $\lambda(n) \subseteq E$. For any subtree $T' = (N', A')$ of T, we denote $\chi(T') = \bigcup_{n \in N'} \chi(n)$.

Definition 1. *A hypertree* $\langle T, \chi, \lambda \rangle$ *for a hypergraph* $\mathcal{H} = (V, E)$ *is a hypertree decomposition of* $\mathcal{H}$, *if it satisfies the following conditions:*

1. *for each* $e \in E$, *there exists some* $n \in N$ *such that* $e \subseteq \chi(n)$, *i.e., each edge of* E *is covered by some vertex label of* T;
2. *for each vertex* $v \in V$, *the set* $\{n \in N \mid v \in \lambda(n)\}$ *induces a connected subtree in* T;
3. *for each node* $n \in N$, $\chi(n) \subseteq \bigcup \lambda(n)$ *holds, i.e., each vertex in the vertex label occurs in some edge of the edge label; and*
4. *for each node* $n \in N$, $\bigcup \lambda(n) \cap \chi(T_n) \subseteq \chi(n)$, *where* T_n *denotes the subtree of* T *rooted at* n; *that is, each vertex* v *that occurs in some edge of the edge label and in the vertex label of* n *or some node below, must already occur in the vertex label of* n.

The width *of hypertree decomposition* $\langle T, \chi, \lambda \rangle$ *is given by* $\max_{n \in N} |\lambda(n)|$, *i.e., the largest size of some edge label.*

Then, the *hypertree width* of a hypergraph $\mathcal{H}$ is the minimum width over all hypertree decompositions for $\mathcal{H}$.

A (nonempty) hypergraph is α-acyclic, if and only if its hypertree width is equal to one. It was shown that several NP-hard decision problems whose underlying structure can be described by a hypergraph become tractable if its hypertree width is bounded by a constant. In particular, this turned out to be the case for answering Boolean conjunctive queries and for finite-domain constraint satisfaction problems. However, as the following result shows, even a bound on the hypertree-with as low as two does not imply the tractability of TRANS-HYP (unless P=NP). Denote by HT_k the subcase of TRANS-HYP where the hypertree width of $\mathcal{H}$ in instances $(\mathcal{H}, \mathcal{G})$ is bounded by k.

Theorem 11. HT_2 *for instances* $(\mathcal{H}, \mathcal{G})$ *where* $\mathcal{H}$ *is simple is TRANS-HYP-hard.*

Proof. It obviously suffices to logspace-reduce a TRANS-HYP instance $(\mathcal{H}, \mathcal{G})$ to an instance $(\mathcal{H}^*, \mathcal{G}^*)$ of HT_2, where $\mathcal{H} = (V, E)$ is simple and $|E| > 1$. We define $\mathcal{H}^* = (V^*, E^*)$ as follows. Let $V^* = V \cup \{a, b\}$, where a and b are new distinct vertices, and let E^* consist of the following edges:

- $e_{ab} := \{a, b\}$,
- $e_{aV} := \{a\} \cup V$,
- $e_b := e \cup \{b\}$, for each $e \in E$.

It is not hard to see that $\mathcal{H}^*$ is simple and has hypertree width bounded by 2. In fact, a hypertree decomposition of width 2 is given by the hypertree decomposition $\langle T, \chi, \lambda \rangle$ where the root of T groups together the two edges e_{ab} and e_{aV}, and where each edge e_b is appended as a singleton child to the root. Moreover, all variables at each node n of the decomposition are "relevant", i.e., in terms of [26], $\chi(n) = \bigcup \lambda(n)$. On the other hand, there is no hypertree decomposition $\langle T, \chi, \lambda \rangle$ for $\mathcal{H}$ which has width 1.

Now observe that the minimal transversals of $\mathcal{H}^*$ are the following subsets of V^*: $\{a, b\}$, $\{a\} \cup \tau$, where $\tau \in Tr(\mathcal{H})$, and $\{b, x\}$, where $x \in V$.

Let $\mathcal{G}^* = (V^*, F^*)$ where F^* consists of the edges $\{a, b\}$, $\{a\} \cup \tau$, where $\tau \in \mathcal{G}$, and $\{b, x\}$, where $x \in V$. It is clear that $Tr(\mathcal{H}) = \mathcal{G}$ iff $Tr(\mathcal{H}^*) = \mathcal{G}^*$. Moreover, the reduction is clearly feasible in polynomial time (in fact, even in logspace).

Note that this reduction can also be used to transform TRANS-ENUM to the subcase of HT$_2$ instances in polynomial time. $\square$

Thus, different from hypergraph degeneracy, bounded hypertree-width alone is not a criterion which lets us establish tractability of TRANS-HYP.

5   Conclusion

Computing some or all minimal transversals of hypergraph is an important problem, which has applications to many areas of computer science, and in particular to logic and AI. While many algorithms or solving this problem exist, cf. e.g. [30,10,12], unfortunately the complexity of this problem is not fully understood today, and it is open whether the problem is tractable (in the sense of permitting output-polynomial algorithms [30]) or not. Recent progress on the status of this problem, and in particular solvability by limited nondeterminism, suggests however that this problem is more likely to be expected tractable than intractable.

Several open issues remain for further work. One is whether the amount of nondeterminism for solving TRANS-HYP and TRANS-ENUM can be further significantly decreased, e.g., to $O(\log \log v \cdot \log v)$ many bits. Another issue is, of course, to find new tractable cases; an interesting question is whether the tractability result for TRANS-HYP where either $\mathcal{G}$ or $\mathcal{H}$ has edge size bounded by a constant can be generalized to a non-constant bound, in particular to bound $O(\log n)$. Finally, it remains to formally assess that known algorithms for solving TRANS-HYP (see, e.g., [10]) are non-polynomial; only most recently, it was shown that a simple, well-known algorithm which uses additional information is not polynomial [44].

Acknowledgments

This work was supported by the Austrian Science Fund (FWF) Project Z29-INF.

References

1. C. Alchourrón, P. Gärdenfors, and D. Makinson. On the logic of theory change: Partial meet contraction and revision functions. *J. Symb. Logic*, 50:510–530, 1985.
2. C. Benzaken. Algorithme de dualisation d'une fonction booléenne. *Revue Francaise de Traitement de l'Information – Chiffres*, 9(2):119–128, 1966.

3. C. Bioch and T. Ibaraki. Complexity of identification and dualization of positive Boolean functions. *Information and Computation*, 123:50–63, 1995.
4. E. Boros, K. Elbassioni, V. Gurvich, and L. Khachiyan. An efficient incremental algorithm for generating all maximal independent sets in hypergraphs of bounded dimension. *Parallel Processing Letters*, 10(4):253–266, 2000.
5. E. Boros, V. Gurvich, and P. L. Hammer. Dual subimplicants of positive Boolean functions. *Optimization Methods and Software*, 10:147–156, 1998.
6. E. Boros, V. Gurvich, L. Khachiyan, and K. Makino. On the complexity of generating maximal frequent and minimal infrequent sets. In *Proc. STACS-02*, LNCS 2285, pp. 133–141, 2002.
7. E. Boros, P. Hammer, T. Ibaraki, and K. Kawakami. Polynomial time recognition of 2-monotonic positive Boolean functions given by an oracle. *SIAM J. Comput.*, 26(1):93–109, 1997.
8. J. de Kleer and B. C. Williams. Diagnosing multiple faults. *Artificial Intelligence*, 32:97–130, 1987.
9. C. Domingo, N. Mishra, and L. Pitt. Efficient read-restricted monotone CNF/DNF dualization by learning with membership queries. *Machine Learning*, 37:89–110, 1999.
10. T. Eiter. *On Transversal Hypergraph Computation and Deciding Hypergraph Saturation*. PhD thesis, Institut für Informationssysteme, TU Wien, Austria, 1991.
11. T. Eiter and G. Gottlob. Identifying the minimal transversals of a hypergraph and related problems. *SIAM Journal on Computing*, 24(6):1278–1304, 1995.
12. T. Eiter, G. Gottlob, and K. Makino. New results on monotone dualization and generating hypergraph transversals. In *Proc. ACM STOC-2002*, pp. 14–22, 2002. Full paper Tech. Rep. INFSYS RR-1843-02-05, TU Wien. Available as *Computer Science Repository Report (CoRR) nr. cs.DS/0204009* via URL: http://arxiv.org/abs/cs/0204009.
13. T. Eiter and K. Makino. On computing all abductive explanations. In *Proc. 18th National Conference on Artificial Intelligence (AAAI '02)*. AAAI Press, 2002.
14. T. Eiter, K. Makino, and T. Ibaraki. Decision lists and related Boolean functions. *Theoretical Computer Science*, 270(1-2):493–524, 2002.
15. R. Fagin. Degrees of acyclicity for hypergraphs and relational database schemes. *Journal of the ACM*, 30:514–550, 1983.
16. R. Fagin, J. D. Ullman, and M. Y. Vardi. On the semantics of updates in databases. In *Proc. PODS-83*, pp. 352–365, 1983.
17. M. Fredman and L. Khachiyan. On the complexity of dualization of monotone disjunctive normal forms. *Journal of Algorithms*, 21:618–628, 1996.
18. G. Friedrich, G. Gottlob, and W. Nejdl. Physical negation instead of fault models. In *Proc. AAAI-91*, July 1990.
19. P. Gärdenfors. *Knowledge in Flux*. Bradford Books, MIT Press, 1988.
20. M. Garey and D. S. Johnson. *Computers and Intractability – A Guide to the Theory of NP-Completeness*. W. H. Freeman, New York, 1979.
21. D. Gaur and R. Krishnamurti. Self-duality of bounded monotone Boolean functions and related problems. In *Proc. 11th International Conference on Algorithmic Learning Theory (ALT)*, LNCS 1968, pp. 209–223. Springer, 2000.
22. M. L. Ginsberg. Counterfactuals. *Artificial Intelligence*, 30:35–79, 1986.
23. M. L. Ginsberg and D. E. Smith. Reasoning about action I: A possible worlds approach. *Artificial Intelligence*, 35:165–195, 1988.
24. G. Gogic, C. Papadimitriou, and M. Sideri. Incremental recompilation of knowledge. *J. Artificial Intelligence Research*, 8:23–37, 1998.

25. J. Goldsmith, M. Levy, and M. Mundhenk. Limited nondeterminism. *SIGACT News*, 27(2):20–29, 1978.
26. G. Gottlob, N. Leone, and F. Scarcello. Hypertree decompositions and tractable queries. In *Proc. 18th ACM Symp. on Principles of Database Systems (PODS-99)*, pp. 21–32, 1999. Full paper to appear in *Journal of Computer and System Sciences*.
27. G. Gottlob and L. Libkin. Investigations on Armstrong relations, dependency inference, and excluded functional dependencies. *Acta Cybernetica*, 9(4):385–402, 1990.
28. D. Gunopulos, R. Khardon, H. Mannila, and H. Toivonen. Data mining, hypergraph transversals, and machine learning. In *Proc. 16th ACM Symp. on Principles of Database Systems (PODS-97)*, pp. 209–216, 1997.
29. D. S. Johnson. A Catalog of Complexity Classes. In J. van Leeuwen, ed., *Handbook of Theoretical Computer Science*, A, chapter 2. Elsevier, 1990.
30. D. S. Johnson, M. Yannakakis, and C. H. Papadimitriou. On generating all maximal independent sets. *Information Processing Letters*, 27:119–123, 1988.
31. H. Kautz, M. Kearns, and B. Selman. Reasoning with characteristic models. In *Proc. AAAI-93*, pp. 34–39, 1993.
32. D. Kavvadias, C. Papadimitriou, and M. Sideri. On Horn envelopes and hypergraph transversals. In W. Ng, editor, *Proc. 4th International Symposium on Algorithms and Computation (ISAAC-93)*, LNCS 762, pp. 399–405, 1993.
33. R. Khardon. Translating between Horn representations and their characteristic models. *J. Artificial Intelligence Research*, 3:349–372, 1995.
34. N. Linial and M. Tarsi. Deciding hypergraph 2-colorability by H-resolution. *Theoretical Computer Science*, 38:343–347, 1985.
35. K. Makino and T. Ibaraki. A fast and simple algorithm for identifying 2-monotonic positive Boolean functions. *Journal of Algorithms*, 26:291–302, 1998.
36. H. Mannila and K.-J. Räihä. Design by Example: An application of Armstrong relations. *Journal of Computer and System Sciences*, 22(2):126–141, 1986.
37. N. Mishra and L. Pitt. Generating all maximal independent sets of bounded-degree hypergraphs. In *Proc. Tenth Annual Conference on Computational Learning Theory (COLT-97)*, pp. 211–217, 1997.
38. B. Nebel. A knowledge level analysis of belief revision. In *Proc. 1st Intl. Conf. on Principles of Knowledge Representation and Reasoning (KR-89)*, pp. 301–311, 1989.
39. B. Nebel. How Hard is it to Revise a Belief Base ? In D. Gabbay and Ph.Smets, eds, *Handbook on Defeasible Reasoning and Uncertainty Management Systems*, volume III: Belief Change, pp. 77–145. Kluwer Academic, 1998.
40. C. H. Papadimitriou. *Computational Complexity*. Addison-Wesley, 1994.
41. R. Reiter. A theory of diagnosis from first principles. *Artificial Intelligence*, 32:57–95, 1987.
42. B. Selman and H. J. Levesque. Abductive and default reasoning: A computational core. In *Proc. AAAI-90*, pp. 343–348, 1990.
43. I. Shmulevich, A. Korshunov, and J. Astola. Almost all monotone boolean functions are polynomially learnable using membership queries. *Information Processing Letters*, 79:211–213, 2001.
44. K. Takata. On the sequential method for listing minimal hitting sets. In *Proc. Workshop on Discrete Mathematics and Data Mining, 2nd SIAM International Conference on Data Mining, April 11-13, Arlington, Virginia, USA*, 2002.
45. M. Winslett. *Updating Logical Databases*. Cambridge University Press, 1990.

Alternation

Moshe Y. Vardi*

Rice University, Department of Computer Science, Houston, TX 77005-1892, USA

Abstract. Alternation was introduced in the late 1970s as a complexity-theoretic construct, capturing the computational aspect of games. Since then it has also been shown that alternation can be viewed as a powerful high level algorithmic construct, which is particularly suitable for automated reasoning. In this talk I will explain how to turn alternation from a complexity-theoretic construct to an algorithmic construct and demonstrate its applicability in the context of modal and temporal reasoning. A particular emphasis will be put on the use of alternating automata as an algorithmic tool.

References

1. O. Kupferman, M.Y. Vardi, and P. Wolper. An automata-theoretic approach to branching-time model checking. *Journal of the ACM*, 47(2):312–360, March 2000.
2. C. Stirling. Games and modal μ-calculus. In *Proc. 13th Symp. on Theoretical Aspects of Computer Science*, volume 1055 of *Lecture Notes in Computer Science*, pages 298–312. Springer-Verlag, 1996.
3. M.Y. Vardi. On the complexity of epistemic reasoning. In *Proc. 4th IEEE Symp. on Logic in Computer Science*, pages 243–252, Asilomar, June 1989.
4. M.Y. Vardi. Alternating automata – unifying truth and validity checking for temporal logics. In W. McCune, editor, *Proc. 14th International Conference on Automated Deduction*, volume 1249 of *Lecture Notes in Artificial Intelligence*, pages 191–206. Springer-Verlag, Berlin, july 1997.
5. T. Wilke. Alternating tree automata, parity games, and modal μ-calculus. *Bull. Soc. Math. Belg.*, 8(2), May 2001.

* Supported in part by NSF grants CCR-9988322, IIS-9908435, IIS-9978135, and EIA-0086264, by BSF grant 9800096, and by a grant from the Intel Corporation. URL: http://www.cs.rice.edu/~vardi.

S. Flesca et al. (Eds.): JELIA 2002, LNAI 2424, p. 565, 2002.

The USA-Advisor:
A Case Study in Answer Set Programming

Michael Gelfond

Department of Computer Science
Texas Tech University
Lubbock, TX 79409, USA
mgelfond@cs.ttu.edu

Abstract. Answer set programming [8] is a new declarative programming paradigm suitable for solving a large range of problems related to knowledge representation and search. The paradigm is rooted in recent developments in several areas of artificial intelligence. Answer set programming starts by encoding relevant domain knowledge as a (possibly disjunctive) logic program, Π. The connectives of this program are normally understood in accordance with the answer set (stable model) semantics [4, 5]. The language's ability to express defaults, i.e. statements of the form "normally, objects of class C have property P", coupled with its natural treatment of recursion, and other useful features, often leads to a comparatively concise and clear representation of knowledge. Insights on the nature of causality and its relationship with the answer sets of logic programs [6, 7, 10] allows description of the effects of actions which solves the frame, ramification, and qualification problems, which for a long time have caused difficulties in modeling knowledge about dynamic domains.

In the second stage of the programming process, a programming task is reduced to finding the answer sets of a logic program $\Pi \cup R$ where R is normally a simple and short program corresponding to this task. The answer sets are found with the help of programming systems [9, 2, 3] implementing various answer set finding algorithms.

During the last few years the answer set programming paradigm seems to have crossed the boundaries of artificial intelligence and has started to attract people in various areas of computer science.

In this talk I will briefly describe the basic idea of the approach and outline its use for the development of the USA-Advisor decision support system for the Space Shuttle. The largest part of this work was done by my former and current students Monica Nogueira, Marcello Balduccini, and Dr. Richard Watson, in close cooperation with Dr. Matt Barry from the USA Advanced Technology Development Group [1]. Our goals in creating the USA-Advisor were two-fold. From a scientific standpoint we wanted to test if the rapidly developing answer set programming methodologies, algorithms, and systems could be successfully applied to the creation of medium size, knowledge intensive applications. From the standpoint of engineering, the goal was to design a system to help flight

S. Flesca et al. (Eds.): JELIA 2002, LNAI 2424, pp. 566–567, 2002.

controllers plan for correct operation of the shuttle in situations where multiple failures have occurred. Even though the engineering part of the project is not yet fully completed it is clear that the approach proved to be successful. In this talk I'll share some lessons and observations learned from this work.

References

1. M. Balduccini, M. Barry, M. Gelfond, M. Nogueira, and R. Watson An A-Prolog decision support system for the Space Shuttle. *Lecture Notes in Computer Science - Proceedings of Practical Aspects of Declarative Languages'01*, (2001), 1990:169–183
2. S. Citrigno, T. Eiter, W. Faber, G. Gottlob, C. Koch, N. Leone, C. Mateis, G. Pfeifer and F. Scarcello. The dlv system: Model generator and application frontends. In *Proceedings of the 12th Workshop on Logic Programming*, 128–137, 1997.
3. P. Cholewinski, W. Marek and M. Truszczyński. Default Reasoning System DeReS. In *International Conference on Principles of Knowledge Representation and Reasoning*, 518-528. Morgan Kauffman, 1996.
4. M. Gelfond and V. Lifschitz. The Stable Model Semantics for Logic Programs. In *Proceedings of the 5th International Conference on Logic Programming*, 1070-1080, 1988.
5. M. Gelfond and V. Lifschitz. Classical Negation in Logic Programs and Disjunctive Databases. *New Generation Computing*, 9(3/4):365-386, 1991.
6. M. Gelfond and V. Lifschitz. Representing Actions and Change by Logic Programs. *Journal of Logic Programming*, 17:301–323, 1993.
7. N. McCain and H. Turner. Causal theories of action and change. In *14th National Conference of Artificial Intelligence (AAAI'97)*, 460–465, 1997.
8. W. Marek, and M. Truszczyński. Stable models and an alternative logic programming paradigm. In *The Logic Programming Paradigm: a 25-Year Perspective*, 375–398, Spring-Verlag. 1999.
9. I. Niemelä, and P. Simons. Smodels - an implementation of the stable model and well-founded semantics for normal logic programs. In *Proceedings of the 4th International Conference on Logic Programming and Non-Monotonic Reasoning*, 420–429, 1997.
10. H. Turner. Representing actions in logic programs and default theories: A situation calculus approach. *Journal of Logic Programming*, Vol. 31, No. 1-3, 245-298, 1997.

Author Index

Lecture Notes in Artificial Intelligence (LNAI)

Lecture Notes in Computer Science